The British Boxing Board of Control

BOXING

YEARBOOK

2006

Edited and compiled by
Barry J. Hugman

Queen Anne Press

First published in Great Britain in 2005 by
Queen Anne Press
a division of Lennard Associates Ltd
Mackerye End, Harpenden
Hertfordshire, AL5 5DR

A CIP catalogue record for this book
is available from the British Library

ISBN 1 85291 666 4

Typeset and designed by
Typecast (Artwork & Design)
Labrador Way, Northfield Lane
Watergore, South Petherton
Somerset, TA13 5LH

Printed and bound in Great Britain by
Biddles Ltd

Front cover
Ricky Hatton (right) and Kostya Tszyu in their IBF light welterweight
title fight at the MEN Arena, Manchester in June 2005
(John Gichigi/Getty Images)

Back cover:
Clinton Woods (right) and Rico Hoye in their IBF light heavyweight
title fight at the Magna Centre, Rotherham in March 2005
(Les Clark)

Contents

TARA BOXING PROMOTIONS & MANAGEMENT

Doughty⬚s Gym, Princess Road, Shaw , Oldham OL2 7AZ
Tel/Fax: 01706-845753 (Office)
Tel: 01706-846763 (Gym)

Trainer/Manager: JACK DOUGHTY
Trainers: EAMON VICKERS, RA Y ASHTON, ANDY JESSIMAN
Matchmaker: RICHARD POXON - M.C. MICHAEL PASS

BOXERS

Shinny Bayaar - Flyweight
Gary Ford - Bantamweight
Choi Tseveenpurev - British Masters Featherweight Champion
Charles Shepherd - Former British, Commonwealth & IBO
World Super-Featherweight Champion
Gary Hadwin - Light-Middleweight
Wayne Shepherd - Light-Middleweight
Gary Dixon - Super-Middleweight
Darren Stubbs - Super-Middleweight

Acknowledgements

For the past 22 years this has been a considerable team effort, with many of the original members still participating, and I would like to take time out and thank all those who have helped to establish the *British Boxing Yearbook* as the 'Wisden' of British boxing.

As in previous years, I am indebted to the BBBoC's General Secretary, Simon Block, along with Lynne Conway, Helen Oakley and Donna Streeter, for their continued help and support in placing information at my disposal and being of assistance when required. Simon's assistant, Robert Smith, who is also the Southern Area Secretary and a former pro fighter of note, was again extremely helpful, as was Glynn Thomas, the new Welsh and Western Area Secretary who now works out of the Board's Cardiff office. I wish the departing Dai Corp every happiness in his retirement.

On a business front, I would like to thank the BBBoC for their support and Bernard Hart, the Managing Director of the Lonsdale International Sporting Club, for his efforts in organising the annual British Boxing Board of Control Awards Luncheon where the book will be launched. The Awards Luncheon has been an ongoing function since 1984, when it was established by myself and the Board to coincide with the launch of the first *Yearbook* and Bernard, ably backed up by Kymberley and Chas Taylor, makes sure the standard remains top class. At the same time, I would like to thank all of those who advertised within these pages for their support.

Ron Olver has been with the *Yearbook* from day one. Once again, despite it being another difficult year and suffering continued ill-health, Ron has produced the Directory of Ex-Boxers' Associations. A former Assistant Editor of both *Boxing News* and *Boxing World*, he is also well known as the British correspondent of the *Ring*; the author of *The Professionals*; for producing the boxing section within *Encyclopedia Britannica*; his work on *Boxing*, Foyles' library service; and as the former co-editor of the *Boxing News Annual*. His honorary work, which included being the Chairman of the BBBoC Charity Grants' Committee; the Vice-President of many ex-boxers' associations; the Public Relations Officer of the London Ex-Boxers' Association; membership of the Commonwealth Boxing Council as New Zealand's representative; and the International Hall of Fame has, in recent years, seen him honoured by the Boxing Writers' Club, the BBBoC, and the Commonwealth Boxing Council. He has been further honoured by the Boxing Writers' Club, who have made him an Honorary Life Member. It was due to Ron's promptings that the ex-boxers' associations came into being as we now know them, and he will always be remembered by the *Boxing News'* readership as the man responsible for the 'Old Timers' page, now in its 38th year.

Members of the *Yearbook* 'team' who wrote articles for this year's edition and who have recently been published, or are in the process of publishing their own books, are: John Jarrett (is currently researching a biography to be titled '*Ray Arcel and all the Great Champions he Trained*'); Bob Lonkhurst (having published '*Fen Tiger: The Success of Dave 'Boy' Green*', which was his fourth biography in seven years, he took time out to catch up with his life. However, he is now thinking seriously of producing a book on Eric Boon as a natural follow up to the Green story); Ralph Oates (having completed '*The Heavyweight Boxing Quizbook*', which is still out on sale, Ralph is now working on two prospective books, one titled '*Aspects of Heavyweight Boxing*' and the other being the '*Muhammad Ali Quizbook*'); Tony Gee (is preparing a book on the history of bare-knuckle fighting in Scotland as a follow-up to '*Up To Scratch*'); Melanie Lloyd (is currently working on '*Sweet Fighting Man – Volume 11*'); Tracey Pollard (continues to work on a book about the life and times of Brian London, the former British heavyweight champion); Keith Robinson (is looking to publish an in-depth work on Bob Fitzsimmons); Patrick Myler (has recently released '*Ring of Hate: The Brown Bomber and Hitler's Hero*') and Brian Donald (is putting the finishing touches to '*Scottish Ring Greats*').

Yet again, Wynford Jones, the Class 'A' referee, came to my rescue when travelling to the Board's offices on a regular basis in order to collate vital data required for this publication, and also produced an article titled: 'Peerless' Jim Driscoll: A Legend. Other members of the *Yearbook* 'team' are Bob Yalen, who has covered boxing with ABC across the world and looks after the World Title Bouts' section; Harold Alderman, an unsung hero who has spent over 40 years researching the early days of boxing through to modern times, has extended the Early Gloved Championship Boxing section to all weights above 170lbs. He was helped in the typing department by Janet and Patsy, relatives of Charlie Allum, the English welterweight champion between 1903 and 1904; Chris Kempson, who produces Highlights from the Amateur Season, is our man in the world of amateur boxing; Eric Armit, the Chairman of the Commonwealth Boxing Council and a leading authority on boxers' records throughout the world, is responsible for the A-Z of Current World Champions; and Derek O'Dell, a former amateur boxer and Chairman of Croydon EBA, produces the Obituaries' section.

Regarding photographs, as in previous years the great majority were produced by Les Clark (Les also writes the Boxing Quiz with a Few Below the Belt within these pages), who has possibly the largest library of both action and poses from British rings. If anyone requires a copy of a photo that has appeared in the *Yearbook* credited to Les, or requires a list, he can be reached at 352 Trelawney Avenue, Langley, Berks SL3 7TS. Other photos were supplied by my good friend Philip Sharkey, and Paul Speak. More help came in the shape of Larry Braysher, a well-known collector, who supplied several photos for the Obituaries' section and the Chatteris Champions, Johnny Hill and Young Ahearn articles.

Also, additional input came from Neil Blackburn (who yet again provided information to make the Obituaries' section as complete as possible); Mrs Enza Jacoponi, the Secretary of the European Boxing Union (EBU Championship data covering the past 12 months); Simon Block (Commonwealth and British Championship data); Patrick Myler (Irish amateur boxing); Malcolm Collins (Welsh amateur boxing); Moira, John McKay and Brian Donald (Scottish amateur boxing); Peter Foley, Dave Cockell, Saphire Lee, Jenny Peake, Dave Norman and Mary from the National Association of Clubs for Young People (English amateur boxing); and Glynn Thomas, John Jarrett, Brian McAllister, Ken Morton, Les Potts, and Robert Smith (Area title data). Although the research on world title bouts since gloves continues to wind down, I would again like to praise the efforts of men such as Tracy Callis and Luckett Davis, who are always available to help track down old-time fighters' records from abroad, and I must mention John Sheppard, of BoxRec.Com, who kindly delivered the current British-based boxers' records in order for me to start my audit. Finally, my thanks go to Jean Bastin, who continued to produce a high standard of typesetting and design, and my wife, Jennifer, who looks after the proof reading.

SecondsOut.com

"the only serious contender"

Introduction

by Barry J. Hugman

It gives me great pleasure to welcome you to the 22nd edition of the *British Boxing Yearbook*. The format hasn't changed too much over the years, certainly not since the 1993 edition, as myself and the team continue to monitor and update the current goings on, while also continuing to research the past and pass on our findings.

Beginning with the modern era, once again we have decided to stay with the way we produce Current British Based-Boxers: Complete Records. The decision to have one alphabet, instead of separating champions, being taken on the grounds that because there are so many champions these days – British, Commonwealth, European, IBF, WBA, WBC, WBO, and more recently WBU, IBO, WBF, etc, etc, and a whole host of Inter-Continental and International titles – it would cause confusion rather than what was really intended. If you wish to quickly locate whether or not a boxer fought during the past season (1 July 2004 to 30 June 2005) then the Boxers' Record Index at the back of the *Yearbook* is the place to look. Also, as in the very first edition, we chart the promotions in Britain throughout the season, thus enabling one to refer to the exact venue within a boxer's record.

Regarding our records, if a fighter is counted out standing up we have continued to show it as a stoppage rather than that of a kayo or technical kayo, as in fights where the referee dispenses with the count. Thus fights are recorded as count outs (the count being tolled with the fighter still on the canvas), retirements (where a fighter is retired on his stool or by his corner during a contest) and referee stopped contest. Of course, other types of decisions would take in draws, no contests, and no decisions. In these days of health and safety fears, more and more boxers are being counted out either standing up or when initially floored, especially when a referee feels that the man on the receiving end is unable to defend himself adequately or requires immediate medical attention. One of the reasons that we have yet to discriminate between cut-eye stoppages and other types of endings, is because a fighter who is stopped because of cuts is often on his way to a defeat in the first place. Thus, if you want to get a true reflection on the fight it is probably better to consult the trade paper, Boxing News, rather than rely on a referee's decision to tell you all you want to know; the recorded result merely being a guide.

Continuing the trend, there are always new articles to match the old favourites. Regular features such as Home and Away with British Boxers (John Jarrett), World Title Bouts During the Season (Bob Yalen), A-Z of Current World Champions (Eric Armit), Highlights from the Amateur Season (Chris Kempson), Directory of Ex-Boxers' Associations (Ron Olver), Obituaries (Derek O'Dell) and two regular quizzes (Ralph Oates and Les Clark), etc, being supported this year with interesting articles such as Chatteris Champions (Bob Lonkhurst); Colin Lynes: The Best Is Yet To Come (Ralph Oates); Muhammad Ali: Was He Really The Greatest? (Patrick Myler); Au Revoir Mike Tyson (Melanie Lloyd); 'Peerless'

Jim Driscoll: A Legend (Wynford Jones); Ken's Lads: Tales from a Professional Boxing Gym (Tracey Pollard); From Stage-fighting Fame to the Gallows at Tyburn: James Field – Pugilist and Criminal (Tony Gee); Johnny Hill: Scotland's First World Champion (Brian Donald) and Who Was Young Ahearn? (Keith R. Robinson).

Elsewhere, hopefully, you will find all you want to know about British Area, English, Celtic, British, Commonwealth, European and world title bouts that took place in 2004-2005, along with the amateur championships that were held in England, Scotland, Wales and Ireland, as well as being able to access details on champions from the past, both amateur and professional.

Historically, what was started several years ago under the heading of Early Gloved Championship Boxing, has now been extended from 170lbs and above in this edition. Much of this work was due to Harold Alderman painstakingly piecing together results for the pre-Lonsdale Belt and named-weight division period. There are still many who believe as gospel much of what was reported down the ages by 'respected' men such as Nat Fleischer, the owner of *The Ring Magazine* and the *Ring Record Book*, and then copied by numerous historians who failed to grasp what the sport was really like before the First World War. We have now completed the exercise with this edition and will need to review how we show champions prior to 1909 in future editions.

Basically, boxing prior to the period in question was a shambles, following bare fists with an assortment of driving gloves, knuckle gloves, and two-ounce gloves, etc, until it arrived at what we recognise today. There were no commissions, newspapermen becoming all-powerful by naming their own champions at all kinds of weights, and in much of America the sport was illegal, no-decision contests rescuing it from being abolished. If you thought today was dire, then boxing prior to that period was almost impossible in all divisions bar the heavyweights. Because travel was difficult and news travelled slowly, fighters were able to move from town to town proclaiming themselves to be the best and 'ringers' constantly prevailed. With today's research being aided by access to early newspapers, and the use of computers, it is becoming clear that men like Fleischer 'took' the best fighters of the day and then 'fitted' them into the named-weight divisions we now know so well. If that is still as clear as mud, then turn to the pages in question.

Abbreviations and Definitions used in the record sections of the Yearbook:
PTS (Points), CO (Count Out), RSC (Referee Stopped Contest), RTD (Retired), DIS (Disqualification), NC (No Contest), ND (No Decision).

British Boxing Board of Control Ltd: Structure

(Members of the Commonwealth Boxing Council and European Boxing Union)

PRESIDENT	Lord Brooks of Tremorfa DL
CHAIRMAN	Charles Giles
VICE CHAIRMAN	John Handelaar
GENERAL SECRETARY	Simon Block
ADMINISTRATIVE STEWARDS	Baroness Golding* Sir Geoffrey Inkin OBE Nicky Piper John Rees QC Dave Roden Andrew Vanzie* Billy Walker*
REPRESENTATIVE STEWARDS	Tony Behan* Geoff Boulter Bernard Connolly Ken Honniball Alec Kirby* Kevin Leafe* Phil Lundgren Ron Pavett* Fred Potter John Ratnage* Brian Renney Derry Treanor* John Williamson
STEWARDS OF APPEAL*	Robin Simpson QC His Honour Brian Capstick QC Geoffrey Finn William Tudor John Robert Kidby Prof. Andrew Lees Timothy Langdale QC John Mathew QC Colin Ross-Munroe QC Peter Richards FRCS Nicholas Valios QC
HONORARY STEWARDS*	Frank Butler OBE Sir Henry Cooper OBE, KSG Capt. Robert Graham BEM Mary Peters DBE Leonard Read QPM Dr Oswald Ross Bill Sheeran
HONORARY MEDICAL CONSULTANT*	Dr Roger C. Evans FRCP
HONARARY PARLIAMENTARY CONSULTANT*	Jimmy Wray MP
LEGAL CONSULTANT	Michael Boyce DL
HEAD OFFICE	The Old Library Trinity Street Cardiff CF10 1BH Tel: 02920 367000 Fax: 02920 367019 E-mail: sblock@bbbofc.com Website: www.bbbofc.com

* Not directors of the company

AREA COUNCILS - AREA SECRETARIES

AREA NO 1 (SCOTLAND)
Brian McAllister
11 Woodside Crescent, Glasgow G3 7UL
Telephone 0141 3320392. Fax 0141 3312029
E-Mail bmacallister@mcallisters-ca.com

AREA NO 2 (NORTHERN IRELAND)
John Campbell
8 Mount Eden Park, Belfast, Northern Ireland BT9 6RA
Telephone 02890 683310. Fax 02890 683310
Mobile 07715 044061

AREA NO 3 (WALES)
Glynn Thomas
The Old Library, Trinity Street, Cardiff CF10 1BH
Telephone 02920 367000
Fax 02920 367019

AREA NO 4 (NORTHERN)
(Northumberland, Cumbria, Durham, Cleveland, Tyne and Wear, North Yorkshire [north of a line drawn from Whitby to Northallerton to Richmond, including these towns].)
John Jarrett
5 Beechwood Avenue, Gosforth, Newcastle upon Tyne NE3 5DH
Telephone/Fax 01912 856556
E-Mail john.jarrett5@btopenworld.com

AREA NO 5 (CENTRAL)
(North Yorkshire [with the exception of the part included in the Northern Area - see above], Lancashire, West and South Yorkshire, Greater Manchester, Merseyside and Cheshire, Isle of Man, North Humberside.)
Richard Jones
1 Churchfields, Croft, Warrington, Cheshire WA3 7JR
Telephone/Fax 01925 768132
E-Mail r.m.jones@mmu.ac.uk

AREA NO 6 (SOUTHERN)
(Bedfordshire, Berkshire, Buckinghamshire, Cambridgeshire, Channel Islands, Isle of Wight, Essex, Hampshire, Kent, Hertfordshire, Greater London, Norfolk, Suffolk, Oxfordshire, East and West Sussex.)
Robert W. Smith
The Old Library, Trinity Street, Cardiff CF10 1BH
Telephone 02920 367000. Fax: 02920 367019
E-Mail rsmith@bbbofc.com

AREA NO 7 (WESTERN)
(Cornwall, Devon, Somerset, Dorset, Wiltshire, Avon, Gloucestershire.)
Glynn Thomas
The Old Library, Trinity Street, Cardiff CF10 1BH
Telephone 02920 367000
Fax 02920 367019

AREA NO 8 (MIDLANDS)
(Derbyshire, Nottinghamshire, Lincolnshire, Salop, Staffordshire, Herefordshire and Worcestershire, Warwickshire, West Midlands, Leicestershire, South Humberside, Northamptonshire.)
Les Potts
1 Sunnyside Villas, Gnosall, Staffordshire
Telephone 01785 823641. Mobile 07973 533835
E-Mail lezpotts@hotmail.com

Foreword

by Simon Block *(General Secretary, British Boxing Board of Control)*

All in all, I think, a very good year with much reason for optimism about the future.

Ricky Hatton's success in defeating the great Kostya Tszyu must not only rank as one of the great British victories of the year but also of all time, comparable to Turpin v Robinson, Stracey v Napoles, Honeyghan v Curry, Benn v McClellan and maybe some of Ken Buchanan's victories abroad. Let us not overlook, however, the achievement of Clinton Woods, who at the fourth time of asking finally captured the IBF world light-heavyweight championship with a superb display over a boxer who came here with a reputation as a dangerman.

I am always pleased when domestic titles (British, Commonwealth and European) produce great matches and we have had quite a number of these over the last 12 months, including Graham Earl v Kevin Bennett at lightweight, Jamie Moore v Michael Jones at light-middleweight and Martin Power v Dale Robinson at bantamweight. The championship contests involving Alex Arthur v Craig Docherty and Nicky Cook v Dazzo Williams I thought might well rank among the best contests of the year, but in the event both Alex Arthur and Nicky Cook proved to be overwhelming winners.

It is good to see ITV back in the sport and many of the great contests of the '90s took place on that channel, although I am disappointed that the BBC do not appear to be showing much interest in live British professional boxing at this time. SKY have made a fantastic contribution to the sport over the last ten years and I am glad to see they are continuing their coverage of British Boxing, albeit at a slightly reduced rate than has applied in the past. The interest of some of the other channels like Sentanta and Bravo also suggests that the future of the televised sport remains bright.

As from the 1st September 2005 there will be judges and a non-scoring referee for all British and Commonwealth championships and this, of course, is a dramatic change. There has been varied opinion, particularly over the last four or five years in the press and among fans about the desirability of continuing important contests with just one scoring referee in charge, and there are persuasive arguments both for and against. This will bring Great Britain into line with every other major boxing country in the world and all the sanctioning organisations, including those of which we remain a member. For the foreseeable future, however, all other contests including English, Celtic and Area titles will continue to be handled by a sole-scoring referee and I am sure some of our struggling promoters will be grateful for that.

What a wealth of young talent we have got coming into the sport and this is always a good sign for the future health of the game. Kevin Mitchell continues to improve and impress and, of course, Amir Khan will be the one that everyone will be watching out for. Young John Murray impressed greatly in his American debut in August and his excellent six-round win over the experienced Johnny Walker on the Lacy v Reid undercard at the St Petersburg Times Forum in Tampa, Florida, was undoubtedly the best contest on the undercard. I hear a lot of good things about young Kell Brook and Young Muttley and we still await a step up in class from the oldest prospect currently in the business, Audley Harrison, who has retained his British Boxing Board of Control licence despite basing his career in America at this time.

Although Ricky Hatton had his career-defining contest this year, which is something that still evades Joe Calzaghe, at the time of writing it is expected that the Welshman's showdown against Jeff Lacy will take place in November of this year. As General Secretary of the Board I am not allowed to have favourites among boxers, but I cannot help holding Johnny Nelson in high regard, both as an athlete and as a person. He has been inactive, but is expected to defend his WBO cruiserweight title against Vicenzo Cantatore before the year end and I for one would very much welcome a re-match with that old warrior, Carl Thompson, who still holds the IBO title.

On a particularly sad note for both me and boxing I learned of the passing of my friend and former Administrative Steward, Bob Graham, as I was preparing this foreword. Bob was a much loved figure around the world, where he represented the Board on so many occasions at major championship contests and boxing conventions, and also in the north-east of England, where he was one of our key people for over four decades or more. He had been ill for a long while but, nevertheless, the news causes me great sadness (As we are currently at the printers, a proper obituary for Bob will appear in next year's edition).

I use the Yearbook extensively throughout the year as a reference point and I am always impressed by the diligence of the editor, Barry Hugman, and his team of helpers for compiling the information contained herein. Thanks once again to them and Lennard Queen Anne Press for making this possible.

PROFESSIONAL BOXING PROMOTERS' ASSOCIATION

PRESENTS

THE BRITISH MASTERS CHAMPIONS

UNDER BBB OF C RULES

HEAVY:	CARL BAKER
CRUISER:	CARL WRIGHT
LIGHT-HEAVY:	STEVEN SPARTACUS
SUPER-MIDDLE:	SIMEON COVER
MIDDLE:	LEE BLUNDELL
LIGHT-MIDDLE:	TAZ JONES
WELTER:	NATHAN WARD
LIGHT-WELTER:	BARRY MORRISON
LIGHTWEIGHT:	ALAN TEMPLE
SUPER-FEATHER:	ANDREW FERRANS
FEATHER:	CHOI TSEVEENPUREV
SUPER-BANTAM:	CHRIS EDWARDS
BANTAM:	VACANT
FLYWEIGHT:	DELROY SPENCER

THE ONLY ALLCOMERS TITLE OPERATING IN BRITISH BOXING. OUR CHAMPIONS HAVE TO DEFEND WHEN A VALID CHALLENGE IS MADE WITH MORE THAN 30 DAYS NOTICE. TO CHALLENGE FOR OUR TITLE, PROMOTERS SHOULD APPLY TO:

THE PBPA	TEL: 020 7592 0102
P O BOX 25188	FAX: 020 7592 0087
LONDON	EMAIL: bdbaker@tinyworld.co.uk
SW1V 3WL	

CHAIRMAN: Bruce Baker
GENERAL SECRETARY: Greg Steene
DIRECTORS: B. Baker, G. Steene, J. Gill, J. Evans

MEMBERSHIP IS BY INVITATION. INTERESTED PROMOTERS PLEASE APPLY

British Boxing Board of Control Awards

The Awards, inaugurated in 1984 in the form of statuettes of boxers, and designed by Morton T. Colver, are supplied by Len Fowler Trophies of Holborn. Len was an early post-war light-heavyweight favourite. As in 2004, the Awards Ceremony, which has reverted back to a luncheon format, is due to be held this coming Autumn in London and will again be co-hosted by the Lonsdale International Sporting Club's Bernard Hart.

British Boxer of the Year: The outstanding British Boxer at any weight. 1984: Barrry McGuigan. 1985: Barry McGuigan. 1986: Dennis Andries. 1987: Lloyd Honeyghan. 1988: Lloyd Honeyghan. 1989: Dennis Andries. 1990: Dennis Andries. 1991: Dave McAuley. 1992: Colin McMillan. 1993: Lennox Lewis. 1994: Steve Robinson. 1995: Nigel Benn. 1996: Prince Naseem Hamed. 1997: Robin Reid. 1998: Carl Thompson. 1999: Billy Schwer. 2000: Glenn Catley. 2001: Joe Calzaghe. 2002: Lennox Lewis. 2003: Ricky Hatton. 2004: Scott Harrison.

British Contest of the Year: Although a fight that took place in Europe won the 1984 Award, since that date, the Award, presented to both participants, has applied to the best all-action contest featuring a British boxer in a British ring. 1984: Jimmy Cable v Said Skouma. 1985: Barry McGuigan v Eusebio Pedroza. 1986: Mark Kaylor v Errol Christie. 1987: Dave McAuley v Fidel Bassa. 1988: Tom Collins v Mark Kaylor. 1989: Michael Watson v Nigel Benn. 1990: Orlando Canizales v Billy Hardy. 1991: Chris Eubank v Nigel Benn. 1992: Dennis Andries v Jeff Harding. 1993: Andy Till v Wally Swift Jnr. 1994: Steve Robinson v Paul Hodkinson. 1995: Steve Collins v Chris Eubank. 1996: P. J. Gallagher v Charles Shepherd. 1997: Spencer Oliver v Patrick Mullings. 1998: Carl Thompson v Chris Eubank. 1999: Shea Neary v Naas Scheepers. 2000: Simon Ramoni v Patrick Mullings. 2001: Colin Dunne v Billy Schwer. 2002: Ezra Sellers v Carl Thompson. 2003: David Barnes v Jimmy Vincent. 2004: Michael Gomez v Alex Arthur.

Overseas Boxer of the Year: For the best performance by an overseas boxer in a British ring. 1984: Buster Drayton. 1985: Don Curry. 1986: Azumah Nelson. 1987: Maurice Blocker. 1988: Fidel Bassa. 1989: Brian Mitchell. 1990: Mike McCallum. 1991: Donovan Boucher. 1992: Jeff Harding. 1993: Crisanto Espana. 1994: Juan Molina. 1995: Mike McCallum. 1996: Jacob Matlala. 1997: Ronald Wright. 1998: Tim Austin. 1999: Vitali Klitschko. 2000: Keith Holmes. 2001: Harry Simon. 2002: Jacob Matlala. 2003: Manuel Medina. 2004: In-Jin Chi.

Special Award: Covers a wide spectrum, and is an appreciation for services to boxing. 1984: Doctor Adrian Whiteson. 1985: Harry Gibbs. 1986: Ray Clarke. 1987: Hon. Colin Moynihan. 1988: Tom Powell. 1989: Winston Burnett. 1990: Frank Bruno. 1991: Muhammad Ali. 1992: Doctor Oswald Ross. 1993: Phil Martin. 1994: Ron Olver. 1995: Gary Davidson. 1996: Reg Gutteridge and Harry Carpenter. 1997: Miguel Matthews and Pete Buckley. 1998: Mickey Duff and Tommy Miller. 1999: Jim Evans and Jack Lindsey. 2000: Henry Cooper. 2001: John Morris and Leonard 'Nipper' Read. 2002: Roy Francis and Richie Woodhall. 2003: Michael Watson. 2004: Dennie Mancini and Bob Paget.

Sportsmanship Award: This Award recognises boxers who set a fine example, both in-and-out of the ring. 1986: Frank Bruno. 1987: Terry Marsh. 1988: Pat Cowdell. 1989: Horace Notice. 1990: Rocky Kelly. 1991: Wally Swift Jnr. 1992: Duke McKenzie. 1993: Nicky Piper. 1994: Francis Ampofo. 1995: Paul Wesley. 1996: Frank Bruno. 1997: Lennox Lewis. 1998: Johnny Williams. 1999: Brian Coleman. 2000: Michael Ayers and Wayne Rigby. 2001: Billy Schwer. 2002: Mickey Cantwell. 2003: Francis Ampofo. 2004: Dale Robinson and Jason Booth.

Scott Harrison was the worthy recipient of the 2004 'Fighter of the Year' award presented to him by His Honour Alan Simpson, the then Chairman of the BBBoC
Les Clark

The 'Contest of the Year' award went to Michael Gomez (pictured here) and Alex Arthur, who was stopped inside five rounds of furious action in Edinburgh on 25 October 2003

Les Clark

Colin Lynes: The Best Is Yet To Come

by Ralph Oates

I think we would all agree that boxing is often viewed with a cynical eye by many critics who, in truth, do not really understand the sport. Mention the word boxing and immediately they associate those involved in the game to be violent people often to be feared. This is of course nonsense and often far from the truth. Over the years the game has turned out a long list of fighters who have been held in high esteem by the public at large, often going out of their way to help a vast assortment of charities. Men like former British, European and Commonwealth heavyweight champion, Sir Henry Cooper, former world heavyweight kings, Lennox Lewis and Frank Bruno, plus a host of other former world champions such as Charlie Magri (fly), John Conteh (light-heavy), John H. Stracey (welter) and Jim Watt (light). The role of honour is long and proud and even active champions do their bit to help out any just cause when and if they can.

Yet boxers, like all sportsmen, are constantly under the microscope and one wrong move outside of the ring and those who are against the sport come down like a ton of bricks in condemnation. All the good which had previously been done is soon forgotten. However, it can be said that more often than not fighters do act in a responsible way when out of the ring, which in turn serves a knockout blow to those who are so keen to downgrade the sport.

Colin seen at home with his wife Kelly and daughter Cortney

One such fighter who is an excellent ambassador for boxing in and out of the ring is the present IBO light-welterweight champion, Colin Lynes, from Essex. Here is a man who has his feet firmly on the ground. Colin loves the sport and is a fine example for all that is good in boxing. The local paper in the Hornchurch area constantly reports the good deeds of Lynes, who is often opening fetes of one description or another and has truly helped to boost the image of boxing. Colin is a keen family man who fully appreciates what he has both in life and sport. He also knows that you never stop learning and is quick to correct any mistakes he may have made during a respective bout. Winning the IBO title was not easy for Colin, who had to work hard and make sacrifices to get to his present level, and he knows that he must keep defending his crown successfully in order to get himself into a position where he can be involved in lucrative unification championship fights in the near future. Boxing is a demanding sport and all the hard work to get to the top can be undone in just a moment by one punch. The way up can be long, the way down can be quick. A fact that Colin is all too aware of and one which keeps him sharp and very much on his toes. On behalf of the Yearbook I carried out the following interview with Colin.

(Ralph Oates) In which year were you born?
(Colin Lynes) 1977.
(RO) Where were you born?
(CL) At the Royal London Hospital in Whitechapel.
(RO) How old were you when you first started to box?
(CL) I was ten years of age, but I was in the gym for about four months and had my first contest when I was 11.
(RO) Have any other members of your family ever boxed?
(CL) Yes my younger brother Vincent and older brother Danny both boxed in the amateurs and went on to win junior national titles.
(RO) Do they box now?
(CL) No, I am the only one now keeping the Lynes flag flying in the sport.
(RO) What made you take up boxing?
(CL) Well, I went to the John Bosco summer camp in Hornchurch some years ago, where the basic moves of boxing were shown and I really got interested in the sport from this time on. Then, when I returned home, I was really disappointed to discover that my football club had folded. I know it was not exactly the end of the world, but it was a blow, since I really loved football. Because I wanted to do something I went down to the gym at the Hornchurch & Elm Park ABC and hence it started from there after someone gave me a skipping rope.
(RO) So you started your boxing at the Hornchurch & Elm Park ABC and stayed with them throughout your amateur career?

(CL) Yes I did and it was a great club, it really was and, may I say, still is.

(RO) Who were your trainers at the club?

(CL) Pete Thatcher and Tony Martin were both first class and I cannot give them enough praise. Tony is still at the club but, sadly, Pete has now passed away, but his son Chris is there, also in a trainers capacity. I would also like to give a word of praise to two other trainers, father and son team, Billy and Jimmy Bush. They both work hard and deserve a great deal of credit for all the time and effort they put in. Tony, Jimmy and Billy are always present at my professional shows cheering me on and giving every encouragement.

(RO) Approximately how many amateur bouts did you have?

(CL) I believe it was 72.

(RO) Can you remember how many you actually won?

(CL) Yes I can – 62.

(RO) Do you still attend any amateur shows?

(CL) Yes I do whenever time allows. Hornchurch & Elm Park ABC in particular. It's always nice to show support, where I started out. The boys always see me as a role model and this is something which I am aware of and indeed proud of.

(RO) In which stance do you box?

(CL) Orthodox.

(RO) Many people do not like fighting southpaws. How do you feel about meeting them in combat?

(CL) I don't mind fighting them and have no problem with the style whatsoever. I know the southpaw stance can be a nightmare to some, but certainly not to me.

(RO) You had quite a successful amateur career?

(CL) I would say yes. I feel very proud of my achievements, which included winning two national junior titles a national senior title and the London ABAs. I was also selected to represent England.

(RO) Do you ever come across a fighter in the amateur ranks who you always had difficulty with?

(CL) There was a certain fighter, who always seemed very mature for his age. I found him very difficult and very strong. In fact I fought him three times, losing the first two bouts but winning our third encounter. I understand that I was the first man to defeat him and that gave me a great deal of satisfaction.

(RO) You claimed your first pro title after winning a bout for the vacant IBO Inter-Continental light-welterweight on 7 December 2002 when you stopped American Richard Kiley in nine rounds. This must have been an exciting moment for you?

(CL) Yes, winning your first pro title gives you a great feeling. I know the Inter-Continental championship is not exactly the world crown, but it is still a step up and a step in the right direction.

(RO) Losing the title in your first defence to Samuel Malinga on 8 March 2003, along with your undefeatedf record in your 22nd bout must have been a real disappointment to you?

(CL) Disappointment is not the word. Malinga was a good fighter, a very good operator, but I really felt prior to the contest that I could beat him. I don't like to make excuses, but at the end of the day I lost and I take nothing away from Malinga. However, I was working full time, employed as a printer at a newspaper plant, so I wasn't able to really train as well as I would have liked to due to the 12-hour shifts which I had to work and obviously the eye injury didn't help.

(RO) Who would you say was your most difficult opponent in the professional ranks to date?

(CL) Well, clearly Samuel Malinga who gave me my first defeat in the professionals, followed closely by Pablo Sarmiento from whom I took the IBO world light-welterweight title from on 8 May 2004. He was a good fighter, a very good champion who was more experienced than me, and really knew his way around the ring. I have to say I found it hard going, having to work and think all the time with this man, but I kept one step ahead of him and went 12 rounds for the first time in my paid career. I felt I had learned a great deal from this bout, leaving the ring that night a better fighter for the experience, and would like to say that I have nothing but respect for Sarmiento.

(RO) You must have been pleased to have made a first successful defence of your title on 13 February 2005?

(CL) It's always good to get the first defence out of the way. My challenger, Juaquin Gallardo of America, was tricky, but I felt I had the answers to the problems he set. Once again it was a good solid 12 rounds, which can only be for the good in terms of ring education and experience. However, I could have done without the low blows which I had to endure during the bout.

(RO) On 18 May 2002 you stopped Kevin Bennett. Do you consider this a good win in view of the fact that he later went on to claim the Commonwealth lightweight title?

(CL) I would say that any win is good, but I understand what you mean. Yes, my victory over Kevin is one I value, since this was a real test for me in the professional ranks and a good 50-50 bout. In fact, I would say this contest was the one which really decided if I was to progress any further. I duly stopped Bennett in four rounds on the undercard of the Prince Naseem Hamed v Manuel Calvo vacant IBO featherweight title bout at Millwall. Kevin of course went on to stop the former WBU and WBF lightweight king, Colin Dunne, in two rounds and after that outpointed Michael Muya over 12 rounds to win the Commonwealth lightweight title. Let's also not forget that on 1 May 2004 he also challenged Jason Cook for the IBO lightweight crown and gave a good account of himself before losing a 12-round points decision. Yes, the win over Kevin was a good one.

(RO) Who is your present trainer?

(CL) Paul Cook. He is a great trainer and also the father of Nicky Cook, who at the time of this interview is the British, European and Commonwealth featherweight champion.

(RO) Who is your promoter?

(CL) Barry Hearn, who I would like to thank for giving me ever opportunity.

(RO) What made you decide to join the professional ranks?

(CL) I always knew that one day I would fight professional, but what really pushed me to punch for pay was the computer scoring. It may well suit some fighters but not me. I lost a couple of decisions which I really felt I had won and it seems that the system favours those who score and then move away for the rest of the round, which is not a good thing. Such tactics fail to provide entertainment for those who watch.

(RO) Do you believe that boxing instils discipline and respect into those who participate in the sport?

(CL) Yes in general I believe it does. You might get the odd individual who goes off the rails, but then boxers are human beings at the end of the day and like anyone else can make mistakes. However, mostly the sport gives those who put on the gloves a sense of respect for themselves and others.

(RO) So far what would you say was your proudest moment?

(CL) Hearing the words "and the new IBO world light-welterweight champion" announced, after I had defeated Sarmiento for the title. It was a night I will never forget.

(RO) How do you feel before the start of a contest?

(CL) I always feel edgy with a degree of tension. However, that's a good thing since it keeps you both alert and focused for the contest.

(RO) Is there any particular reason why you did not take the traditional route towards the world title by winning the British, Commonwealth and then European titles first?

(CL) I would have liked to have won British, Commonwealth and European titles, but you cannot turn down a championship opportunity when it comes along. The chance came for me to challenge for the IBO crown first and I took it and I am glad to say it paid off.

(RO) How do you feel about female involvement in the sport? The two leading women fighters in this country being of course Jane Couch and Cathy Brown.

(CL) I would not like to see my wife or daughter box, however, if women want to fight it's their choice and you have to respect that fact. It is a changing world and we all have to accept these kind of situations. Jane and Cathy seem to be doing well and they clearly love and respect the sport, so good luck to them. I wish them every success in their respective careers.

(RO) Who is your favourite old time fighter?

(CL) Muhammad Ali. The man was special and really brought a great deal to boxing. Ali really was a true great.

(RO) How do you feel about title fights being held over the duration of 12 rounds rather than 15?

(CL) Well I know some of the older fans felt that going 15 rounds was a mark of a true champion and were not too happy when the rounds were reduced, but to be quite honest from my pint of view I think that 12 rounds really are quite sufficient for any fighter to have to travel. Let's not forget some years ago title fights were held over 20 and 25 rounds. No doubt some of the fans then were not happy when they were reduced.

(RO) How do you feel boxers today compare with past boxers with regard to both their skill and technique?

(CL) I feel that today's boxers do stand up very well when compared to past boxers with regard to skill and technique. Present day training methods are vastly improved and this, in turn, helps to improve the technique and skill. However, I would add that many of the fighters of the bygone age were probably tougher than today's boxers when you consider the conditions and the hard times in which many of them had to live. Hard times create hard fighters.

(RO) Who is your favourite modern-day boxer?

(CL) Well I have two and both were rivals of each other. I refer to Nigel Benn and Chris Eubank, who were, in my view, great fighters who gave British boxing a boost during their careers. Nigel, who won the IBO world middleweight title and the WBC super-middleweight crown, was pure excitement. I liked his aggressive style, he really came to fight he took no prisoners. Eubank had a style of his own full of confidence, but boy could he deliver when he had to. Chris could box really clever and really knew how to work the fans. It's an often used expression, but Chris really could talk the talk and walk the walk. Eubank, like Benn, held a world championship in two weight divisions, having been the world WBO title holder at middleweight and super-middleweight. The domestic game would be the richer if we had a few more boxers like Chris and Nigel around today.

(RO) Which is your favourite weight division, apart from the one you box in?

(CL) Any of the lighter weight divisions, since they appear to produce more action and excitement.

(RO) Who in your opinion is the best world heavyweight champion in the history of the sport?

(CL) I have no doubt in my mind it's Muhammad Ali. This man was pure magic, he really was fantastic. He gave the game a tonic when it needed it the most.

Colin (right) on his way to winning the IBO light-welterweight title from Pablo Sarmiento in May 2004

Les Clark

(RO) Which is your favourite world heavyweight title fight?

(CL) Over the years there have been some really great fights. However, I have two favourites. The 'Rumble in the Jungle' on 30 October 1974 when Muhammad Ali, against all the odds, regained the world heavyweight title against the undefeated and feared champion, George Foreman, knocking him out in round eight. If there was ever any doubt about Ali's greatness, then he truly confirmed it that night in Zaire. My second choice is the bout which took place on 1 October 1975 namely 'The Thriller in Manila', in which once again that man Muhammad Ali retained his title against Joe Frazier, who retired in round 14. Both fighters gave their very all in this bout. It really took a great deal out of Ali and Frazier and I know it's always clever to be wise after the event but perhaps Muhammad should have quit after this fight. He really had done it all, there being nothing left to prove, and his place in boxing history was well and truly secured.

(RO) How do you feel about the fighters who continue to box on, even when middle aged?

(CL) I see no problem with this just as long as the respective fighter is able to pass the required medical examinations and they are not taking excessive punishment in their fights.

(RO) What changes, if any, would you like to see made in the sport?

(CL) I have always wanted to see the introduction of judges in British and Commonwealth title fights, so I was very pleased to learn recently that three judges will officiate at British and Commonwealth title fights in the near future.

(RO) Out of all the boxers in recent years, who would you say was an excellent role model for the sport?

(CL) I would have to say former world heavyweight champion, Lennox Lewis. The man was a class act. He always acted impeccably inside and outside of the ring, bringing credit to the championship, and was a fine example for boxing.

(RO) What annoys you most in boxing?

(CL) What really annoys me most is the lack of recognition given to the sport by the media. In many cases it is difficult to find the results of various bouts which have taken place the night before in most newspapers. This is not fair for the game or the fans who follow it. I have often seen the most obscure sport given a great deal of page space, with boxing given just a few lines, if any at all.

(RO) How do you feel about the vast number of world governing bodies in the sport at the moment?

(CL) To be frank I have a split view about this. I know that a number of fans feel that so many governing bodies are bad for the sport, since it causes confusion and cheapens the term world champion. However, if we did have just one title holder in each weight division how many times a year would he be able to defend his crown? once, twice, three times maybe. That could mean that a more than worthy contender might have to wait a good few years to get his shot at the title and when or if his chance came he could be past his peak. Look at the past and see how many worthy

fighters were not given their chance. At least today many good fighters are getting a chance at a championship of one kind or another. So in that respect I think it's a good thing that we do have various governing bodies. However, on saying that I don't think we need to see any more world governing bodies on the scene.

(RO) How do you feel about there being so many weight divisions in the sport today?

(CL) I am quite happy about it. I know some critics will say in many cases there's only a few pounds difference between the divisions, but let me tell you that very often that so-called few pounds can be difficult to move. I am all for the variouis weight divisions.

(RO) I understand that at the start of your pro career you had difficulty balancing your boxing with your job as a printer?

(CL) Yes I did. I was working 12-hour shifts up to the Sarmiento bout, which did not help me with my training. It really did prove difficult. Shift work and training hard burns you out and affects your home life.

(RO) Now you box full time do you see a difference?

(CL) Most certainly. I am able to train without any problems and I am really starting to feel the benefit of this.

(RO) How many hours a day do you train?

(CL) About four to five hours a day, depending if I have a fight coming up. I have a rest on Saturday then I go for a gentle run on Sunday.

(RO) You did have plans at one time, I understand, to emigrate to Australia, have you now changed your mind?

(CL) I did intend to emigrate to Australia. It was all set up, but at the moment I am holding fire due to various circumstances.

(RO) If the opportunity came for you to box in America would you do so?

(CL) I would if the chance presented itself and the respective purse made it worth my while.

(RO) What would you say to those who would like to ban boxing?

(CL) To understand the sport more and perhaps it would change their mind. Boxing has helped many people over the years, it's kept them out of trouble and given them a direction in life. True, there are dangers in the sport, but then there's much more risk and danger in other sports. I won't name them since I feel they are obvious to everyone. Also, if boxing was banned it would go underground and the implications of that would be truly horrendous.

(RO) There have been a number of films made about boxing over the years, do you have a favourite?

(CL) For my money it's got to be 'Raging Bull'. This film based on the life story of the former world middleweight champion, Jake LaMotta. LaMotta was quite a character, a hard man living in hard and difficult times. The production was first class, with Robert DeNiro really throwing himself into the role. This movie really was and I have to say it, since it suits the sport, a knockout.

(RO) What was the best advice you have been given when boxing?

(CL) Keep your hands up and your chin down. To be

serious I was once told if you fail to prepare then prepare to fail. That was sound advice.

(RO) Looking at the domestic scene at the moment, who do you tip for the very top?

(CL) I may sound a little biased, since he is a good friend of mine, but Nicky Cook. I spar a great deal with Nicky and each time it is tough. He appears to get better and better and really is a class act. Nicky put on a good performance in knocking out the holder, Dazzo Williams, in two rounds to take the British crown. Dazzo, let's not make any mistake, was a good boxer and for Nicky to take him out like that speaks volumes for him. Over the years Britain's produced a number of boxers at featherweight who have won the world title and I think it's only a matter of time before Nicky adds his name to that illustrious list by winning a world crown. I really do think he's that good.

(RO) I understand you switched on the Hornchurch Christmas lights last year (December 2004)?

(CL) Yes this was quite an honour. I was asked, due to my achievements in the ring and for the work which I do for the community.

(RO) How long have you been married?

(CL) I have been married to Kelly for seven years now.

(RO) Does Kelly like you boxing?

(CL) Kelly certainly supports me and has done so since my amateur days – she always gives me encouragement. However, Kelly doesn't actually like it when I am in the ring fighting and I am sure most boxers spouses are the same.

(RO) Do you have children?

(CL) Yes, a daughter named Cortney aged eight, who often likes to train with me.

(RO) What do your parents think about your boxing career to date?

(CL) My parents, Sheila and David, are very proud of my boxing achievements so far and, like my wife Kelly, they really give me every encouragement.

(RO) As you are self managed, do you find this difficult having to concentrate on the business side as well as your boxing?

(CL) Not really, since Kelly is a great help here. I always say that Mrs Lynes looks after my corner and I am sure Barry Hearn would agree with that statement.

(RO) Do you discuss boxing a great deal at home?

(CL) I would say a fair bit since boxing is a great part of my life and, indeed, Kelly's. We even have a miniature Dachshund called Oscar, who was named after Oscar de la Hoya. That name was Kelly's and Cortney's idea and shows you how much we are truly into boxing. However, we sometimes do turn off, especially when Arsenal are playing on the box.

(RO) Do you have a hobby?

(CL) I used to go fishing. I really enjoyed that because it's so quiet and peaceful, but these days, with one thing or another, I don't get the time, or is it that I don't catch any fish. However, I will go back to it again one day when time allows.

(RO) What advice would you give to anyone embarking on a career in boxing?

(CL) Think long and hard about your decision. Consider the demands the sport will make on your body and the endless hours of training you must do if you want to succeed. If you have the mental strength, which is vital, and the support of your family, then go for it. I have been lucky for I have the support of my wife Kelly, plus my parents. This is all a great booster to me and helps me when times are hard. Make no mistake, family support puts you a round up even before you throw the first punch.

(RO) On 21 February 2005 at the Upminster Golf Club you were presented with the Havering Sports Council's Presidents Award. What was this for exactly?

(CL) I was given the award for outstanding achievements in sport. Once again I felt very proud of winning this award, for it also brought boxing into the spotlight.

(RO) Looking back at your boxing career to date, would you do anything different if you had your time over?

(CL) Well, I think I would sign from the off with a promoter who had a great deal of input with television. Since I feel that TV exposure is vital to a fighter's career.

(RO) When you retire from boxing will you stay with the sport, perhaps in the capacity of a trainer?

(CL) At this stage of my life I don't really know. It is something I would love to do, although it might be selfish of me to spend more time away from home when I finally hang up the gloves. I don't think that I would be prepared to put in all kinds of hours and although I love boxing, I also love my home life. So all I can say is I will have to wait and see if it suits my mode of life when the time comes.

(RO) What ambitions do you now have with regards your immediate boxing future?

(CL) I want to meet a higher calibre of opponent in the near future and I would like to avenge my only defeat to date by meeting Samuel Malinga in the ring again. This is a bout I really want.

It is clear that Colin is a man who is good for British boxing and is doing a great PR job for the sport wherever he goes. The IBO light-welterweight champion still strives to get better and improve his skills to be able to maintain his present position. Colin even gave up his job to be able to concentrate on his training and some might say that in this day and age that was quite a gamble. Not to Colin, who is fully dedicated to the sport he loves. The man from Essex is also fortunate to have the full backing of his wife Kelly and his parents. Any boxer, indeed any sportsman, will tell you, when you have this kind of support you have a head start since it gives you peace of mind and the incentive to concentrate fully on the task ahead. The light-welterweight division is a very hard and competitive one and Colin will have to overcome some very tough rivals in the months to come. Talking to Colin one gets the impression that the best is yet to come and he is more than ready to go up against the very best at the poundage. In fact he more than welcomes the challenge. When that moment comes, win or lose, the opposition will know that Colin Lynes was a true champion in every sense of the word.

On behalf of the Yearbook I wish Colin, his wife Kelly, and daughter Cortney, the very best for the future.

Au Revoir Mike Tyson

by Melanie Lloyd

"Having watched him come from where he was to what he is, I can say honestly I have a very deep affection for him. I do. He's my boy. He's with me." **(Cus D'Amato – 1908 to 1985)**

The date was 22 November 1986 and the boxing drug infiltrated my system for the very first time as Mike Tyson won his first world heavyweight title, against Trevor Berbick. It was the first boxing match I ever really watched and that night I felt the force and it changed my life forever. This was the beginning of my love affair with boxing. Therefore, I felt it fitting this year to mark Mike Tyson's retirement with a fond farewell. I don't know how he will manage financially now, but please God, let him still be in retirement when this article goes to print, and forever afterwards.

Various letters printed in the Boxing News in July 2005 summed up the general feeling towards this once great fighter. For so spectacular was his talent in his early years that his fans still love him, and many of us choose to think of him with warmth and love rather than dwell on his tragic and painful decline. So to those who stopped believing in him a long time ago, please forgive my nostalgic viewpoint and feel free to call me a blatant sentimentalist if you want to, but I intend to focus on the good times and the excitement and the thrill that Mike Tyson brought to our hearts, even if only for a relatively short time.

So we will lay the foundation stones to this story of hope with the Brownsville ghetto in Brooklyn where, on the 30th June 1966, a star was born onto those desperate streets. His name was Michael Gerard Tyson. His mother was on welfare and he was known in the neighbourhood as 'Dirty Mike'. He played in abandoned and derelict buildings and in his world, violence and robbery were ways of survival. Talking candidly about where he came from, he once declared: "Me and your world are so vastly different, you could never understand"

By the age of 12, Mike had clocked up several convictions for theft and violence and he was detained in Spofford Juvenile Centre in the Bronx. He was subsequently adjudicated a juvenile delinquent and sent to the tough Tryon Youth Campus. It was here that Tyson met an ex-boxer, Bobby Stewart, and these two did a deal that would take Mike's life in a totally different direction. When Mike was 12 years old he weighed 190 lbs and, initially, Stewart was wary of the young tearaway in his charge. He squared up to Mike in a macho way and Mike explained that he wanted to be a fighter, to which Stewart replied: "You haven't got the balls to be a fighter!" But in return for Stewart's help, Mike agreed to completely revise his behaviour and he kept his side of the bargain. As his reward, Stewart took Mike to meet Cus D'Amato in the old man's Catskills' home. Cus, christened Constantine, had guided the likes of Floyd Patterson and Jose Torres to world title glory. He once said: "What I do is discover and uncover," and on meeting this lost boy, Cus had no doubt in his mind that he would one day become the heavyweight champion of the world.

Cus D'Amato took Mike into his home and he and his partner of 40 years, Camille Ewald, became Mike's adoptive parents. Cus oversaw Mike's training at the Catskill Boxing Club, above the local police station, having assigned Teddy Atlas as his amateur trainer, and they developed a happy working relationship. Video footage of a young Mike Tyson growing up is always a joy to watch. In those days, the sheer ferocity of his shadowboxing skills could excite more than some world title fights. The speed of those fists as he threw arrays of hooks and jabs, and that spectacular upper body movement, always sets me on fire. The vision of this impressionable young man travelling to the 1982 Junior Olympics in Colorado to win the heavyweight gold medal is one that will remain with many of us eternally. And the naked vulnerability of his tears of insecurity before he went in to win the final will always melt my heart. Teddy Atlas reasoned that maybe, God had given Mike such a strong body that he would have to become strong in other ways on his own. Mike and Atlas' relationship broke down with an argument over a girl and Cus displayed his unconditional love for Mike by letting Teddy go.

Mike's knowledge of his contemporaries, past and present, is phenomenal. His very first idol was Jack Dempsey. He once said: "I'm crazy about him because of his ferocious intensity. There's no one like him. No one like him." And when I watch some of the early Tyson tapes I am spookily reminded of the 'Manassa Mauler', with that two-handed, relentless hooking style.

Mike turned professional at the age of 18 and was co-managed by Bill Cayton and Jim Jacobs. Along with Cus, Jim Jacobs became a strong and positive influence in Mike's life. For the record, Jacobs was a prominent athlete himself in his day, and was the 1956 world handball champion. The other prominent man on the team in those days was unreserved trainer, Kevin Rooney. The philosophy of the team was to keep Mike busy at all times, never giving him time to get into any trouble. Jacobs once said: "He fights everybody like they stole something from him". And so the scene was set for future greatness and everything seemed so hopeful. Leading up to his first world title fight, Mike had 27 straight wins and had knocked out 25 of those opponents. Cus taught him what he called 'elusive aggression' and as his style developed the boxing world became ignited by the spark that would go on to become the blaze. It really looked like this new young sensation was going to become a legend, a word that is used far too easily in this day and age.

But on the 4th November 1985, Mike suffered a knockout blow that was more brutal than any fist could ever deliver. Cus D'Amato died of pneumonia. Shortly before

Cus' untimely death he declared on film: "I often say to him, 'You know, I owe you a lot,' and he doesn't know what I mean. But I'm going to tell him now what I mean. If he weren't here I probably wouldn't be alive today. I will stay alive and I will watch him become a success. That's the motivation I have to keep me alive and keep me going." There is now a street in New York named E14th Street and Cus D'Amato Way.

Mike continued his ruthless and rapid climb up the ladder and in Britain, ITV started showing his fights. Each

Mike Tyson seen in his prime

Peter Goldfield

knockout was as devastating as the last. Before his clinical two-round destruction of Alphonso Ratliff (the fight before Trevor Berbick), our own Reg Gutteridge summed up Mike's style with these words. "He just strolled into the ring there, Tyson, a real old gladiator. No socks, no robe, no fuss, he didn't even acknowledge the crowd. Just get down to business is all he wants to do". After that fight, Jim Watt declared: "I'm really impressed by him. The fact is that he's not as easy to hit as I first thought the first couple of times I saw him box. As he moves in his hands are high. His head moves all the time. He can knock out with either hand. He's probably the only complete fighter in the heavyweight division we have in the world today".

A year after the death of Cus, Mike won his first world title, the one that got me hooked (pardon the pun!). His demolition of Trevor Berbick came in the second round when Mike knocked the Canadian down three times, with the same punch! It was that famous left hook. But the joy of this 20-year-old man, who was now the youngest ever heavyweight champion of the world, was heavily weighed down with the sorrow. His old friend was no longer at his side and he missed him desperately. At the time he declared:

"Now that all this is happening, and he put in all the effort and all the time, and all the misery and heartbreak, and he's not around to enjoy it". The naked bewilderment in Mike's face said it all.

But life had to go on and along with being heavyweight champion of the world came all the status and notoriety that went with it. Mike was not happy or comfortable trapped in the media glare, but on his own terms he became a man of the people. He remained approachable and was always happy to stop and shake hands with the man, and woman, in the street. He was an inspiration to the children of the world's ghettos and he tried his best to use his fame and popularity to help those who moved him. Despite the series of sad events that led to his boxing decline, he has always retained that philanthropic side to his nature. For example, the Finchley Amateur Boxing Club make an annual trip to Las Vegas to box against the local lads. Finchley stalwart, Jim Oliver, told me that they met Mike back in the early years at the gym where Jim's son, Danny, trained as a professional with Cornelius Boza-Edwards. When Mike learned of these amateur shows he readily agreed to turn up and present the trophies, and this is a commitment which he

Mike in a happy mood among the young amateurs of Finchley ABC in Las Vegas   Chris Calvert

has always upheld (For the record, Finchley ABC was where our very own Barry Hugman used to box - a fair old while ago!). And, most poignantly, Mike paid thousands of dollars for Camille Ewald's care home during the final years of her life. Camille lived to be 96 and perhaps the love that Tyson showed her right up to the end contributed to her longevity.

Mike went on to unify the world heavyweight title against Tony Tucker and early in 1988, shortly after his fourth-round knockout of Larry Holmes, he married Robin Givens. And then in March that year, Mike received another shocking body blow. Jim Jacobs, probably the only person alive who Mike looked to for guidance and direction, died of cancer. By this stage, the notorious promoter, Don King had firmly established himself in Mike's life and the rest, as they say, is history. There have been so many millions of words written about the madness that followed that I feel no inclination to put down too many more of them.

The shock of the Buster Douglas defeat in Tokyo, a place where Tyson was hero-worshiped, was one of the biggest boxing upsets of all time. The fallen champion on his hands and knees, desperately pawing the canvas to retrieve his gumshield, paints such a sad picture. And the lunacy of that facial tattoo that he had done just before the Brian Nielsen fight gave us all a shock. We all hoped it was Mike's little joke on the media, possibly a henna creation. But as time went on, we realized it was the real thing. And it seems unbelievable that a man who once earned a quarter of a million dollars a second, in his fight with Michael Spinks, can now be a bankrupt. But, on the other hand, the life of Michael Gerald Tyson has been full of paradoxes.

For me, the saddest image of all was that of Mike in handcuffs after he was convicted for the rape of Desiree Washington. As he was being driven away he showed the cuffs to the photographers who were frantically flashing their cameras through the car window. The look of resignation on this face said that maybe, aside from those golden years under the protective wing of Cus D'Amato, he had always known that this would be his destiny, and that by this point he was past caring anyway. Whatever happened in that hotel room that night, there are only two people who will ever really know for sure. Mike was sentenced to spend six years in a jail called the Indiana Youth Centre. I used to have a lovely print of him on my wall and I kept it up there throughout his sentence. Many friends who visited my flat would ask me why I had a picture of a psychopathic rapist on my wall. I was always defiant and declared that it was my flat and my wall and if I wanted that picture up there, it would remain so. But on the 28th June 1997, when Mike bit both of Evander Holyfield's ears in their re-match, I watched the horror unfold with friends at their home and we couldn't believe what we were seeing. At 6 o'clock the following Sunday morning I arrived home and took the picture down.

Some of the toughest fighters I have ever known have been the possessors of the most disarming sense of ambivalence, that special ability to be so hard and so sweet at the same time, and to me Mike Tyson has been the epitome of this. Since the beginning of organised fighting, the audience has always been drawn to the bad boys, and Mike Tyson is a classic case – a tortured soul who lost control. Despite the fiasco that his career eventually became, he was still the biggest draw. He had more charisma in his little finger than all the other champions put together. His loves and losses have been scrutinised and twisted and spread naked under the harsh glare of the spotlight and sometimes, when he's all on his own and he thinks about everyone he has known and everywhere he has been and everything that he has done and everything that happened to him along the way, he must find it hard to contain it all inside. I am well aware that the majority of boxers have come from the ghettos, the council estates, the gypsy sites, and all the other places that form the tough side of this world. Many would ask then, what singles out Mike Tyson for my kid glove treatment? But we should never forget that he gave us all something so very special. He planted the seed of hope in our hearts and, for a little while, we were watching the unfolding talent of one of the greatest boxers of all time. Many boxing fans in this country went off the boil after the decline of Muhammad Ali, and Mike Tyson single handedly influenced a staunch British boxing revival.

After I watched Danny Williams knock Mike out in July 2004, I prayed I would never see him in the ring again. I have not even seen the Kevin McBride fight and I never want to. I remember in the mid-'90s, there were some exotic photographs published in many of the tabloids of Mike wrestling with his new pet, a white tiger. I was talking about it on the phone to my father and he said: "Mel, I don't think that boy is going to live to see old age". My father is not often wrong, but in this case I pray that he is way off the mark.

The English translation of au revoir is 'goodbye for the present' and, hopefully, when we see Mike Tyson again it will not be in a boxing ring. With a bit of luck the next time we see Mike Tyson he will no longer be fighting, either inside or outside the ring, because he deserves to find some peace now.

God Bless you, champ. There will never be another Mike Tyson.

Ken's Lads: Tales from a Professional Boxing Gym

by Tracey Pollard

Of course, if they could have known what would happen they would never have been so cocky in the first place. They were team-handed so they felt no fear and as they passed the guy in his fancy new Ford Capri (it's the '70s by the way) they gave it a kick. Then the guy jumps out and he's not in the least bit intimidated but it's okay, he's just one man, one rather mean looking man. Here's what they don't know: he's a professional boxer and he's just pulled up outside the gym. They can't see the gym because it's in the basement of a building on this central Manchester street but somebody has seen them and alerted everybody inside. Suddenly boxers, some in boxing gloves and even headguards and gumshields, pour into the street as if from the very bowels of the earth. Now, there's a pitch battle under way in the middle of this busy street. People stop to watch, traffic is disrupted. One of the battlers looks round in amazement and shouts, "Where are all these boxers coming from?" The end result is fairly predictable, after all, these are boxers.

Later a couple of police officers enter the gym. They had watched the whole thing from the comfort of their van. They hadn't felt any need to intervene because they had a fair idea what was going to happen. They seemed to find it all very amusing. It was unavoidable really. The guy with the new car was welterweight, Mickey Flynn, not known for his infinite patience and the cocky gang were from nearby Salford, a large area of which makes an even higher weekly body count. It was never going to end in a handshake and it left some people unable to see the funny side.

There are similar professional boxing gyms all across the country with a wealth of great stories to tell, some funny, some sad. Some produce great champions, many produce good contenders and 'could'a beens'. Most have their share of characters and it makes for a fascinating boxing tapestry. This gym was woven from all of the above or, rather, this stable, because it was relocated on more than one occasion. The aforementioned incident took place outside a gym on Whitworth Street in Manchester, which was home to a very successful stable of boxers trained by Ken Daniels. The name of the gym cannot be repeated for reasons of copyright or some such but it has a lot in common with a certain boxing Earl. The gym was also shared with Ken's fellow Manchester trainers, Stan Skinkiss and Pop Edwards, and their fighters, many of them managed by Pop's son, Jack. The disadvantage, or, possibly, advantage of these rather unusual basement premises was that they were also home to a strip club. So, bizarrely, at one end of the corridor men danced around a ring in a state of undress while, at the other end, women danced around a pole in an even worse state. It's hard to believe that the owners of the nightclub, Jack Dillon and his son Arthur, thought this combination could work. Then again, perhaps it made very good business sense.

It's uncertain whether the doormen (a boxing gym with doormen!) were there to throw people in or out. One of said doormen was a big chap, a very, very big chap called 'Crazy Horse". If he had another name only a select few could have known it, probable his mother and the vicar at the christening, unless they were responsible for the new name. The lads and his friends who were on first name terms with him called him 'Crazy', presumably to everyone else he was 'Mr Horse'. Anyway, we digress, but I promise you it's all true. Funnily enough to digress further, when Mr Horse left and went to work at another nightclub nearby called 'Mr Smith's' – honest, it was a well-known Manchester club – one of the boxers, Terry Armstrong, went to see him. He found him painting murals of cartoon figures on the walls of the club (strictly at the owner's request). It's an incongruous image which still has Terry shaking his head as if he had stepped into a twilight zone.

Still, the boxers managed to soldier on under these arduous working conditions and the stable thrived. When Stan Skinkiss retired from training boxers he asked Ken Daniels to take over. Ken had great respect for Stan as a trainer and he was pleased to accept. The late Tommy Miller, the manager and matchmaker who became known as 'Mr Boxing', asked Ken to train his fighters too. Tommy

Ken Daniels in his fighting days

23

was a great boxing character from Halifax in Yorkshire. He had boxed in the days when a shower was a bucket of cold water and boxing gyms were often housed in real stables. When you've trained alongside horses, you're unlikely to object to training alongside strippers and, strangely enough, there were never that many objections from the younger boxers either. Tommy was a successful boxer who fought as 'The Blond Bantam' and was unbeaten in his first 39 fights. He had around 200 fights, added to countless contests on the boxing booths, which he described to me not long before he died in 2005. "I worked the booths from 1934 until 1947 as a boxer, then took over from the boss as barker, MC and referee, plus engaging the fighters. I could honestly say I could have had around 1,000 fights as a booth fighter. In a lot of fairs we could have three or four fights per night and, if it was running in the afternoon and then 'till midnight, you could have as many as ten fights. I was a bantam and featherweight for years and the challengers always picked on the small booth boxers". He was granted his manager's licence in 1946 and became a matchmaker in '47. In the '70s he managed more fighters than any other manager in Britain and they were mostly trained by Ken Daniels. The two had first met when Ken was boxing out of a gym in his home town, Ashton-Under-Lyne, seven miles out of Manchester. Ken's stablemate was a young welterweight from London called Harry Warner, who was managed by Tommy. Harry was later a familiar figure for many years in his role as a top referee and would often find himself back in the ring with Tommy and Ken in their respective roles as ref, manager and trainer. Harry died six months before Tommy.

During the '70s and early '80s, Ken would train countless Central Area champions, quite possibly more than any other trainer ever has. Many had the talent to go on to further titles and some of them did. Others missed out because of verdicts that didn't go their way in the ring or even verdicts that weren't in their favour out of the ring (if you know what I mean). One of the latter kind had an unintentional helping hand in that respect when he got into a spot of bother. Many trainers and managers find themselves putting in a good word for their fighters when they fall foul of the law. Nat Basso, who felt that, as a well-known manager and matchmaker and Chairman of the Central Area Council he commanded sufficient respect to sway a judge. He offered to provide a character reference for the boxer who was implicated and stressed his potential as a talented boxer. "Your honour", he said earnestly, "this young man has the best right hand in the business". His friends from the gym looked incredulous and groaned in dismay. The judge was not swayed. In fact, he was singularly unimpressed. Bang went the gavel, 12 months. The boxer was surprisingly ungrateful, he had been looking at a possible six months until the judge heard how good he was with his fists. Nat was totally oblivious and Ken did his best to dissuade him from his attempts to chat with the lad after he got out.

Ken had established a very healthy stable of fighters who nearly all did well, a considerable number of them becoming Central Area champions. These included, Peter Freeman, Mickey Flynn, Phil Martin, Alex Pernaski, Prince Rodney, Gordon Kirk, Gerry McBride, Robbie Robinson, Dave Owens, Robbie Davies, Francis Hands, Eddie Smith,

The late Tommy Miller (right) in the early 1950s with Harry Warner (next to him) and the rest of the boys

Brian Roche, Mike Whalley, Carlton Lyons, Jimmy Bunclarke and Lee Hartshorn. He also trained many other excellent fighters like Blaine Longsden, Richard Scarth, Wayne Barker and Billy Aherne. Ken tells the amazing story of one of Billy Aherne's fights. Between rounds, Nat Basso pointed out to Ken that one side of the ring was collapsing. Unbelievably, he told Ken to try and get Billy to keep the fight on the other side of the ring, not out of concern for his safety but to avoid the fight having to be stopped! Ken's lads often topped the bill and many had their own large crowd of loyal supporters, but on one occasion he was feeling sorry for Billy as the hall was half empty. To make things worse, the fire alarm went off in the middle of the fight and the hall had to be completely evacuated. Finally the all-clear was given and everybody was allowed back in for the fight. When Ken looked around he realised that the hall was now full! More fans had been waiting outside and twice as many poured in after the 'false alarm'.

Dave Ward was another great fighter and Ken described him at the time as being very strong indeed and said that he could easily have taken him to a title fight. He was part of a large family from Middleton in Manchester and some of his brothers also boxed. Unfortunately, Dave's powerful punching got him into trouble outside the ring, but at this time he was better known for his boxing prowess and was one of the most accurate punchers in the gym. It didn't require any great insight to recognise this. Ken had his own infallible gauge, his chin, which must have been the best in boxing. So many of his fighters would miss the pads and catch Ken instead that it's a wonder he's still so pretty. "Not Dave though", he remembers: "Dave was a lovely, accurate puncher". One time, Ken was caught by heavyweight, Peter Freeman, and the side of his face swelled up like a pudding but, just as in his own boxing days, he was never knocked out. Another young fighter tried to model himself on Muhammad Ali. "He was so busy studying his footwork in the mirror that he missed the pads and hit me", says Ken. That teenager won most of his fights, but his real success came much later when he followed in Ken's footsteps as a trainer. His greatest achievement has been in guiding Ricky Hatton to his recent victory over Kostya Tszyu. Billy Graham has gone from trying to emulate world champions to creating them but he's still a big Ali fan. Fellow Manchester trainer, Bob Shannon, trained alongside Billy as an amateur. He has a team photo from the old B.D.S. club but Billy isn't on it. Instead, he points out a little square shape on the wall. "Billy never turned up for the photos, but that's his picture of Ali that he pinned on the wall behind the punchbag". You can't argue with his choice of inspiration.

Another graduate of the B.D.S. joined Billy at Ken's gym and also went on to train champions of his own. Ken remembers the day a shy young lad came to the gym and asked Ken to train him. He recognised him immediately as Phil Adelagan who had only lost about 15 of 127 fights as an amateur. Phil was ready to turn professional and wanted Ken to be his trainer. He would fight under the name of Phil Martin and was very successful, winning the Central Area title and going on to fight for the British light-heavyweight championship. Unfortunately, he lost that fight against Tim

Wood on a controversial decision and Ken wasn't the only person who felt that Phil had been robbed of the verdict. Phil would go on to greater things though as a trainer himself with his renowned gym, The Champ's Camp, in Moss Side. For Phil's story see the 2004 Yearbook.

Ken not only had a good chin, he also discovered that he had retained a knockout punch. One night he was alone in the gym tidying up after the lads had gone when a drunk staggered in from the street. The drunk was loud and aggressive and built like the back of a largish barn. He grabbed Ken, who had boxed at bantamweight, and threw him across the room. Ken knew he was in big trouble and as he got to his feet he desperately put everything he had behind one big punch which sent the 'barn' crashing to the floor. He was out cold. "If I could only have found a punch like that when I was boxing I would have been a world champion", he laments, "but my arms were black and blue for days where he'd picked me up to throw me". With the assistance of Big John, one of the bouncers, the drunk was carried back upstairs and left on the street. John was very impressed. He'd had trouble with the same drunk on another occasion and had cracked him over the head with a baseball bat with no effect! It wasn't a unique occurrence. On another occasion a man came into the gym demanding to spar, insisting that he had the ability to take on any boxer. This is not an uncommon occurrence in boxing gyms and it usually comes to nothing, but this time Ken had extra cause for concern. The boxer he was gloving up at the time was permanently on a very short fuse. Some fighters can make a trainer feel more like a handler trying to control a dangerous animal. The two had been alone in the gym on this Sunday afternoon and Ken repeatedly told the man that there was nobody to spar with him but he kept insisting. "What about him?", he demanded, pointing at the heavyweight with Ken. He was obviously full of himself (or full of something), but he had no idea what he was letting himself in for. Quietly, the boxer picked up a pair of gloves and gave them to Ken, "Put them on for him", he said.

The heavyweight was Paul Sykes. Paul was a boxer with great potential but, more often than not, his temper got the better of him. It's no exaggeration to say that he was a dangerous man, particularly outside the ring. Tommy Miller had been so keen to sign up Paul Sykes that when he saw him on the beach at Blackpool where he was working as a lifeguard, he actually waded into the sea after him in his socks and shoes to get his attention! It was worth it. Paul was highly rated by Joe Frazier, who he had sparred with, and he would later fight for the British heavyweight title. His boxing career was seriously hampered by the fact that he spent most of his life in prison and it didn't help that he had a Tyson-esque approach to his fights. In 1978 he fought Neil Malpass twice for the Central Area title that Malpass had won from Peter Freeman. Before the start of the first fight he spotted Malpass going into the Gents and told Ken and Tommy that he was going in after him to soften him up a bit first. "No, no, no!" they shouted and managed to talk him out of it. During the fight he was actually doing well, although it was not a clean fight, and Harry Warner had to issue repeated warnings. Malpass, not unreasonably, seemed to object to the butting in particular but Paul was still ahead until he blatantly butted Malpass in the seventh round and Harry bravely disqualified him. Paul never did win the Area title. Malpass successfully defended it in a return with Sykes which resulted in a draw and was himself disqualified in his next defence against Terry Mintus. He then regained the title in a return with Mintus.

In his next fight, which was in his home town of Wakefield, Paul fought Dave Wilson, stopping him in the third round. Wilson was treated for 15 minutes in the ring before being rushed to hospital where he spent one month recovering from a cerebral blood clot. Ken and his wife, June, visited Wilson in hospital and were relieved to hear from the ward sister that he was recovered. "It's time to send him home", she complained, "He's chasing my nurses all over the ward". Because he had spent nine of the last 14 years behind bars, Paul had been denied a licence by the BBBoC several times, consequently, at the age of 32 this was only his sixth professional fight. At first he had been delighted with his victory but later, as he sat beside the American's hospital bed, he wept openly. The following year Paul fought John L. Gardner for the British title. Gardner boxed in a calm and controlled manner, the antithesis of Paul's style, and, for the most part, it proved effective, effective enough to cause the referee to call a halt in the sixth round when Paul apparently turned his back on Gardner and quit. The shame of that result haunted him for years and, at the age of 44, after one of his long spells in prison, he contacted Gardner and asked if they could fight again in a private contest. "I never heard from Gardner and I'm forced to live with it for ever", he told journalist, Colin Hart. Pity little Paul Dykes, the boxer who entered the ring one time to find himself facing a towering heavyweight opponent who was expecting to fight Paul Sykes!

Mickey Flynn (the man with the new Capri) won the Central Area welterweight title in 1972 with a sixth-round stoppage over Amos Talbot. He successfully defended it the following year with another stoppage, this time in the second round against Tommy Joyce. Mickey then retained it in a draw against Alan Tottoh. It was a fight that Ken thought he should win if he hadn't been fighting with a serious handicap. Throughout the fight at the King's Hall, Belle Vue, in Manchester, Ken was becoming increasingly irritated by Mickey's fringe! Mickey's fashionably long hair meant that he had to keep pushing his fringe out of his eyes as he fought. This was infuriating Ken and the next time Mickey returned to his corner Ken was waiting with his scissors. He quickly snipped the fringe off before Mickey could react, to the amusement of the crowd who all cheered. This enraged Mickey who returned to the fight with a fresh surge of aggression. The fight resulted in a draw but, if he'd had a short back and sides, who knows?

Looking back at the first edition of this wonderful tome in 1985, it contains the record of world light-middleweight champion, Maurice Hope. It lists Hope's non-championship wins by stoppage, KO and on points, 20 in all, and just one defeat – to Mickey. In fact, Mickey was one of only two men to beat Hope before he won his world title, the other being Bunny Sterling, who had already won the British (undefeated), Commonwealth and European middleweight titles at the time. Hope would only be beaten four times in all. Mickey fought many top boxers, including British champions, Larry Paul and Henry Rhiney. He twice went the distance with Rhiney, who was also the European champion, resulting in one draw and one loss. When Mickey lost their third meeting by TKO in 1977 he decided to call it a day. He was perhaps one of Ken's 'could'a beens', fighters who distinguished themselves during their careers but didn't make it to the top for whatever reason. Another was light-heavyweight, Alek Penarski, whose final fight was also a loss by TKO to a future British champion, Herbie Hide (mind you, he only received the 'phone call offering him the fight the night before). Like Mickey, Alek also gave some good boxers good fights along the way.

Nowadays, heavier boxers are a rare and valuable species, but back in the good old days, before they were hunted to extinction or God knows what, Ken seemed to have an abundance of big chaps. Among his light-heavies, Phil Martin had defeated Pat Thompson to take the Central Area light-heavyweight title. Thompson later won it with a points win over Terry Armstrong (trained by Pop Edwards and managed by Jack), but lost it on points to Penarski. Alek lost it the same way to Francis Hands, also trained by Ken. Like Mickey Flynn, Alek would also face his share of British champions. Six years before that final loss to Hide, he scored a victory on points against future champ, Tom Collins. Earlier, he suffered a points defeat after a tough ten rounds with Dennis Andries, before Andries won the title. He lost the fight by just half a point after a point was deducted for use of the head in the second round. He also avenged the controversial verdict against his stablemate, Phil Martin, by defeating Tim Wood the year after Wood lost the title that he had won in the fight with Phil.

Ken was often called upon to work in the corner for other top fighters, but one of his more unusual jobs was to train TV detective, Taggert! Actor, Mark McManus, who later played 'Taggert' was to play Benny Lynch, the world flyweight champion, in a TV documentary. Ken was called in to give him tips for the fight scenes. Afterwards, Ken offered him a lift to the TV studios but, ironically, when they got outside he found that his car had been stolen. A journalist gave McManus a lift and Ken was left to walk to the nearest police station. Where's Morse when you need him?

Ken even found himself in the corner with fighters he had never met before. He arrived at Liverpool Stadium one night and Tommy said, "You're looking after five fighters tonight, Ken". He then informed him that he'd be working alone as the other members of his corner team were stranded in foggy Yorkshire! Ken usually worked with Tommy's sons, Tom and Charlie. It was a disastrous night. The leg broke on Ken's stool and he crashed over and smashed his jar of Vaseline. He then had to borrow some from other trainers because his was full of broken glass! "I didn't have a single winner that night", he groans.

The stable was constantly changing as fighters joined from Liverpool or were brought from Huddersfield and Bolton by Tommy Miller. Others left when they relocated to different parts of the country or signed with new managers. The stable itself was also forced to relocate from Whitworth Street due to what could certainly be described as unforseen circumstances. Jack and Arthur Dillon decided that the gym could be making money in the hours when it was not in use so they decided to turn it into a bar – a gay bar. Now, Tommy was definitely 'old school', a broad-speaking Yorkshireman, who looked like the stereotype of a boxing manager in his pork-pie hat and braces. He could turn a blind eye to the strippers (and, by all accounts, this was the best way to view most of them), but this new turn of events was just too much. His gym was re-christened, 'Mandy's Bar', redecorated and strung with fairy lights (I kid you not) and the gay gentlemen danced in the ring when the boxers left. "Nay", said poor Tommy, "I can't have this. They keep coming in early and looking at my lads". There really isn't a P.C. way of telling this story. So, it was decided that the lads had to be rescued. Terry Armstrong's friend, Barry Germain, offered the use of the building at the rear of his house on Taunton Road in Ashton-Under-Lyne. Tommy and Ken thought it would be ideal. Amazingly, Ken was about to return to Taunton Road where, just two blocks away, he had boxed as a 16-year-old amateur and then as a professional at Len Steele's gym many years earlier. In fact, Len attended the official opening of Ken's new gym by Nat Basso, along with sports writer, Graham Houston, and cricketer, Peter Lever.

Najib Daho was a talented young fighter trained by Ken, who became Manchester's first British boxing champion in 25 years when he won the super-featherweight title in 1986 with a first-round stoppage over Pat Cowdell. One of the first people to congratulate Ken on that night was Phil Martin, now a trainer himself with fighters on the same bill. Ken thought a lot of Najib, an immensely likeable lad, born in Morocco and known as the 'Casbah Kid'. His career had not gotten off to a good start before he joined Ken, but the two of them made a winning team and became very close. Najib was managed by Jack Trickett and was a true Manchester warrior, involved in some real tough battles. It's surprising really that he would become that one fighter for Ken that a trainer can sometimes come across, the one that they will develop a special bond with. Surprising, because Ken's biggest problem was usually finding him! "I've turned up at his house to collect him for training and he has walked up behind me, just arriving home from a night in the clubs", says Ken. Jack said he should have been called 'The Disco Kid', but Najib managed to juggle being a chef by day and spending time in the clubs at night and still manage to win titles. According to Jack, "He had good reflexes and he was a decent hitter and he could hit you with either hand. He also had a very, very good jab. The only thing with him of course, was he used to lose his temper and go ragged or he would go on the missing list and come back and have no co-ordination".

Najib won the Central Area lightweight title in 1979 and when he also won the super-featherweight title six years later he earned a shot at the British super-featherweight title. His opponent was Birmingham's Pat Cowdell and at this time a Birmingham opponent did not guarantee a win.

Although he was not known for knockouts, with only seven in 48 fights, Najib had Cowdell down three times in the first round and was on him again as soon as the second round started. Cowdell had no chance to recover as the crowd invaded the ring immediately when the ref stepped between the two fighters. The chaos that followed nearly prevented Najib from receiving his title. Six months later he challenged Australia's Barry Michael for the IBF world super-featherweight title. They had fought seven years earlier with Najib winning on points. Since then, Michael had fought in 21 title fights and nobody doubted that this would be a tough contest. It was. Jack was in the corner with Ken and the late Ernie Fossey. "Najib had little else going for him after about the fifth round", he recalls. "After the ninth round he came back looking a bit of a mess and Ernie said, "Come on, Najib, listen to the crowd, the crowd's with you", and Najib looked up and said, "I wish I was with the crowd". That stands out in my mind. He was that cool in the corner. The fight went the full 15 rounds and was very bloody, like so many of Najib's battles, but this time Michael was the victor.

Najib also lost his next fight when he challenged for the European super-featherweight title. He hadn't learnt his lesson yet according to Jack. "After winning the British title he got a lot of adulation, everyone wanting to buy him champagne. He thought this was lovely, better than boxing and it is, let's face it. He thought he just had to turn up and win, he didn't need all this preparation". That said, Najib was ahead on points by the fifth when he suddenly pulled away from Jean-Marc Renaud, obviously in pain. A tooth had come loose and stuck in his lower gum and he had no option but to retire. Shortly after he fought a return with Cowdell. He couldn't just turn up to win this time. After nine hard-fought rounds the referee stopped the fight and he lost his title. The same thing happened in the same round one year later when he lost an eliminator with Pat Doherty. But the two would meet again seven months later when Najib challenged Doherty for the Commonwealth lightweight title. The 11 gruelling rounds were described as a bloodbath, a typically tough Najib war, which earned him the title. He successfully defended the title against John Kalbhenn but lost it to Carl Crook. Both were tough distance fights and another one followed for the vacant Commonwealth lightweight title, which he also lost. When he failed to regain his Commonwealth lightweight title in 1991 in his 60th fight, a return with Crook, that became his final ten rounds of boxing. When he announced his retirement he received a standing ovation that lasted for ten minutes.

Outside of the ring it would be easy to underestimate the strength of a super-featherweight, particularly in Najib's case with his boyish good looks and cheerful smile. The car thief who tried to make off with Najib's Ford XR3 probably got quite a shock. Someone had stolen the car radio earlier and throughout the night Najib kept jumping up to check on the car. Suddenly he spotted the thief and dashed downstairs, telling his wife to phone the police. The thief was already in the car and Najib told him the police were on the way, but he managed to start the engine. Quick as a flash, Najib, 5'5" and 9st 9lbs, punched him through the window and dragged him out of the car. The thief stabbed him in the thigh with a screwdriver. "There was blood and teeth flying everywhere. I gave it to him good", he later told the press. "People round here don't know who I am. They just see this little black man going in and out of the house. But this guy will know in future". Which is a good job because when the police arrived and took charge, the thief ran off. "I'd had two training sessions that day", laughed Najib, "so this made it three. My manager will be well pleased". It wasn't the first time thugs had come unstuck at the hands of the little champ. Early in his career, Najib had rushed to the aid of a man who was being attacked by two muggers. It was a set up and suddenly the three of them turned on Najib and demanded he hand over his watch. The incident was reported in the newspapers. "They were really big blokes", said 19-year-old Najib, "so I got in first and knocked them all out. It was the easiest fight I've ever had".

Najib had been honoured by the King of Morocco when he won the British title and it was during a holiday there that he was killed in a car accident in August 1993, aged 34. He was one of 18 children and left two children of his own. Ken was always told that there was some controversy surrounding Najib's death, but there was no doubt that the likeable and charming young boxer was widely mourned. A tribute video was later made with Jim Watt and Reg Gutteridge, who said that Najib was one of the most exciting fighters you're likely to see.

Sadly, Phil Martin also died young, at the height of his success as a trainer. Paul Sykes proved himself to be surprisingly intelligent for such a violent man (a menacing combination) and it was during his time behind bars that he obtained an Open University degree in physical sciences and also turned to writing. He wrote articles, one of which appeared in the *Sunday Times* magazine and his autobiographical book, *Sweet Agony* won the Arthur Koestler Award for Literature. A television documentary was also made about his life. At that time he had spent 21 of the last 26 years in prison. He is now said to be living rough on the streets of Wakefield after spending many more years in prison for serious crimes. At one time he had been running a boys' club in Wakefield, where the activities included a variety of sports. Boxing was deliberately not included because, as Paul the Paradox explained, "I hate to see young lads beating hell out of each other"! And if you're wondering what happened to the idiot who walked into the gym and demanded to spar with him all those years ago, well, he's probably feeling better by now. Paul Dykes, incidentally, is also now involved in training boxers as are Wayne Barker and Alek Penarski. Amazingly, Wayne and Alek decided to make a comeback in 2001, fighting each other! The contest between the two of them, both in their late 40s, received a great deal of attention in the press, but was repeatedly postponed and eventually cancelled. Dave Ward now has his own successful security firm and his services have even been called upon to help prevent vandalism at a local church! He recognises that his reputation is usually enough to deter troublemakers, as he told a Manchester newspaper, "My reputation does

somewhat precede me. Perhaps, as a result of my experience, I can show young, disenfranchised people in and around Middleton there is a better way. Perhaps even guiding them away from the inevitable route of courts and prison".

Tommy Miller was still actively involved in boxing right up to his death, aged 88, and was the longest serving licence holder in the country. He travelled the country with his son, Tom, who continued in his role of ringwhip. Sadly, as this was being written his other son, Charlie, died from cancer. Tommy's son-in-law, Colin Roberts, is still regularly at ringside acting as time-keeper. Jack Edwards, while still an active member of the Manchester Ex-Boxers Association, recently retired as their chairman. Stan Skinkiss became a prominent local councillor but, sadly, has lost both of his legs over the past year as a result of his diabetes. Eventually it became necessary to find a more central location for Ken's fighters, many of them travelling regularly from Liverpool. The final home of Ken's stable was Selwyn Demmy's gym in the Newton Heath district of Manchester, where they remained for several years. Ken continued to train boxers, travelling all over the world with them. He had just been asked to join Jack Doughty at Tara Boxing Club when ill health forced him to retire. Ken is regarded as one of boxing's most experienced and knowledgeable trainers and is respected by many of today's trainers including, Bob Shannon, who is happy to admit to trying to pick Ken's brain when he opened his own gym. One of Najib's brothers used to lend a helping hand at Bob's gym. Ken is a regular guest at Billy Graham's Phoenix gym, where he is part of three generations of trainers, past, present and future – himself, Billy and Ricky Hatton, who already knows where his future lies.

Billy Graham, once an aspiring fighter, now a leading trainer
Harry Goodwin

Chatteris Champions

by Bob Lonkhurst

A sleepy market town in Cambridgeshire, Chatteris is not renowned for producing a string of quality boxers. Yet two of the most exciting British fighters were developed in this Fenland region better known for agriculture. Although they boxed at different weights some 40 years apart, Eric Boon and Dave 'Boy' Green had many similarities.

Both were mean, aggressive, big-punching young men who thrilled the crowds. Consequently, both were able to sell out the major arenas in London some 90 miles from their roots. They did their roadwork across the bleak Fenland lanes in all weathers and hardened themselves pounding an anvil at a local blacksmith's forge.

Despite being only a lightweight, Boon was described as having the shoulders of a middleweight. Green, a welterweight, also had massive shoulders developed humping 28lb bags of carrots on to lorries six days a week at a Fenland farm. Each day, he and his workmates loaded up to 80 tons.

During the late 1930s when Boon was at his peak, posters advertising his fights were displayed in the windows of shops, pubs and houses. Huge banners were strung across the streets of Chatteris, and special trains laid on to convey his army of fans to London where his big fights took place.

Green generated the same degree of excitement during the 1970's. His fans travelled to the capital by coach, car and train and on fight nights it was claimed that the town was half empty. The Fen people were a revelation, dressing up in farm attire and costumes, blowing horns and bugles, and packing Wembley and the Royal Albert Hall whenever he fought.

The two Chatteris fighters got to know each other when Dave was an amateur. Boon quickly warmed to his style and took a close but unobtrusive interest in his career as a professional. He frequently watched him in the gym, gave words of encouragement before and after fights, and generally became his inspiration.

They attended local charity events together, and in private conversation often compared their careers and discussed the advantages and disadvantages of the times in which they fought. They were frequently interviewed by the media and each always paid tribute to the other. "What I like about Dave Green is his will to win", Boon told a *Cambridgeshire Times* reporter. "The fight game is not just a sideline with him, it's his whole life".

"Eric Boon gave me my enthusiasm for the job when I first started boxing," Green told the *Chatteris Advertiser* after Boon's death in 1981. "He was the person I set out to try and emulate. He was there for my first pro fight and was there when I won the British title. He gave me plenty of inspiration and I'll never forget that".

Born at Chatteris on 28 December 1919, Boon started boxing at the age of 11. He was coached at the local club by Arthur Binder, a legend in the town who had been an amateur boxer during the First World War. Eric developed

rapidly, winning a host of trophies as a junior. Less than a month after his 15th birthday, he had his first paid fight stopping his opponent in six rounds at Peterborough.

An interested spectator that night was London referee, Jack Hart, who recommended the youngster to Jack Solomons, then promoting weekly Sunday afternoon shows at the Devonshire Club, a converted church at Hackney, Solomons agreed to put Boon on his show on 10 March 1935, but when details appeared in their local newspaper, Eric's parents forbade him from travelling to London.

Ignoring their wishes, the youngster got up early on the Sunday morning and left Chatteris on his bicycle intent on riding all the way to London. He would never have got there on time but for a friendly lorry driver who lifted him and his cycle on top of the load of cabbages and drove him to the east end.

Although Boon was only awarded a draw against local boxer, Young Higgins, Solomons had seen enough to know that he could become a crowd-pleaser. He put him on again a month later and then at regular intervals over the next three years, during which time he engaged in 36 bouts, winning 31. He usually won so impressively that fans

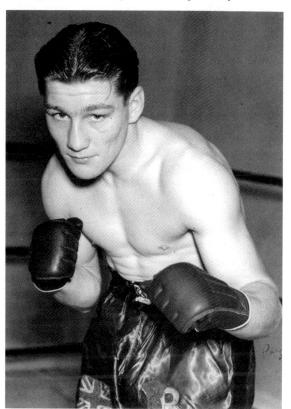

Eric Boon

eventually went home disappointed if he did not score a knockout. Initially as 'Boy' Boon and then Roy Boon, the Chatteris youngster also boxed at venues across East Anglia. The money he earned enabled him to give up his bicycle and travel by train.

During the early part of his pro career, Boon was managed by Arthur Binder, but once he became established, Solomons persuaded his father to allow him to take over his management and move to London. Boon's ability to look after himself ensured that he fought regularly. Under Solomons guidance he had 20 contests in 1936, 28 the following year and 18 in 1938. Many of his victories were by clean knockout, such was his incredible punching power.

By May 1938, Solomons knew his young charge was verging on championship class. Taking a massive gamble he manoeuvred him into a ten-round contest against reigning British lightweight champion, Jimmy Walsh. The bout topped the bill on the first ever professional boxing show to be staged at Chatteris.

Although local people knew all about Eric's success from the newspapers, few had seen him fight. Shrewdly promoted in conjunction with the annual county show, a crowd of more than 6,000 assembled at the town football ground amid pouring rain. By fight time, however, the weather improved, and Boon put on a magnificent display to narrowly outpoint his vastly experienced opponent.

Three months later, Boon thrilled another huge crowd at an open air show at Engineer Fields, Chatteris, by smashing experienced Belgian champion, Raymond Renard, to defeat in just 30 seconds of the opening round. The Belgian, who had campaigned in continental rings for eight years and never been knocked out, was blasted to the floor by three vicious hooks. His right eye swollen and discoloured, he struggled to his feet at the count of nine, but was barely conscious. As Boon strode forward to finish the job, he had just enough strength to raise his left glove in token of surrender.

Solomons kept his man busy and after five more victories secured him a fight against Dave Crowley for the British lightweight title on Sydney Hulls promotion at Harringay Arena on 15 December 1938. A fast, versatile and scientific boxer, Crowley had taken the title from Jimmy Walsh six months earlier. Like Eric he had been boxing since he was a boy. His only downfall was that he lacked the

Boon (right) throws a right hand at Danahar in the latter stages of their memorable 1939 contest

Chatteris man's greatest asset – a really destructive punch. A professional since 1928, Dave had built a long and impressive record. He was nine years older than Boon, who by the day of the fight would still be 13 days short of his 19th birthday.

Predictably, Boon's attacks were vicious and relentless, but his success rate poor. Never before had he met a man possessing the defensive skills of Crowley. For the first ten rounds the champion made him look like a raw novice, jabbing at will with a piston-like straight left, clipping him firmly with an accurate right cross, and tying him up at close quarters. Boon was not given room to unload his powerful swings with any degree of accuracy and many of his big shots just hit thin air. Eric sustained damage to his left eye as early as the opening round. By the tenth it was completely closed from the champion's constant jabbing and a purple egg-sized lump protruded beneath it. The Chatteris youngster, however, was unperturbed. He kept forcing the fight because he knew no other way and in round 11 his persistence finally paid off. A terrific right uppercut crashed into Crowley's solar plexus, sending him to his knees. He complained bitterly that the blow was low, but referee, Mr C. B. Thomas, ignored him and took up the count. With great courage, Dave was up at seven and fought back doggedly to thwart Boon's efforts to finish the job. The champion appeared to regain control in the 12th, cleverly avoiding Boon's lunging attacks. With only one eye functioning the challenger missed wildly, but was still strong and willing. Well behind on points, he went straight on the attack in the 13th and although Crowley initially held him at bay, the sheer brute force of Boon was decisive. Two left hooks wobbled the champion and a well-timed right swing to the jaw sent him crashing to the floor. Bravely rising at 'nine', Dave made the mistake of trying to fight it out with Boon. In doing so he left his chin exposed and, despite having only one good eye, the Chatteris man crashed home a left and right that sent Crowley heavily to the floor and almost out of the ring. The count out was a formality.

News was immediately flashed to Chatteris, where a stream of green rockets shot into the sky in celebration. Eric Boon had become the town's first ever British champion and the locals celebrated in style. The following day he was taken around the town on a horse and cart proudly displaying the Lonsdale Belt above his head.

Two months later, Boon made the first defence of his title against Arthur Danahar from Bethnal Green. The epic contest is still remembered as being one of the greatest ever to take place in a British ring. It was so well chronicled that subsequent generations of enthusiasts were able to capture its intensity.

Danahar came from a big east-end boxing family. Just a few months older than Boon, he had climaxed a brilliant amateur career by winning the ABA lightweight championship in 1937. He then turned professional under sponsorship from the National Sporting Club and became a real favourite on club promotions. Unlike Boon, however, he lacked experience in the pro ring, having taken part in only 14 contests, and not gone beyond eight rounds.

Somewhat surprisingly, it was originally planned for the two young lightweights to clash at a private function some weeks before Boon fought Crowley. A well-meaning sportsman signed them to fight at a plush hotel in the west end of London with selected guests paying 100 guineas each for the privilege of being there. Public opinion, however, quickly scuppered those plans and soon after Boon became champion, the promoter, Sydney Hulls, moved quickly to stage the bout at Harringay on 23 February 1939. The response was massive and the huge venue sold out three weeks in advance.

Although the fans expected a tremendous scrap, nobody could have anticipated the sheer ferocity and intensity displayed by each man. Boon attacked from the opening bell just as he did against Crowley, only to be out-boxed as Danahar countered effectively. The champion, however, was content to take a few to land his own heavier punches. Consequently, by round four his left eye was badly swollen. Danahar dominated the first seven rounds, but in the eighth Boon stepped up a gear and when he unleashed his full battery of punches it was all downhill for the challenger. Bleeding badly from the nose and his left eye completely closed Boon twice smashed the Bethnal Green man to the floor for counts of nine. Eric was on the floor in the ninth and, during the tenth, Danahar boxed carefully, held on tightly and generally frustrated the champion's efforts to apply the finish. Despite his left eye being in a terrible state, Boon got on top again in round 11, flooring Danahar just before the bell. Arthur was down again for nine in the 12th and three times in round 13, all from vicious rights to the head. Boon went all out for the finish at the start of the 14th and a right hook smashed the challenger to the canvas. Again he bravely rose at nine, but as Boon moved forward referee, Barrington Dalby, stepped in. Whilst Danahar showed courage way beyond the call of duty, Boon confirmed that he was a true champion, displaying incredible physical strength and stamina, power in both hands, speed, plus amazing spirit and guts.

History was made at Harringay that night. Apart from the fight repeatedly being described as "the lightweight contest of the century", it became the first for general

Eric Boon congratulates Green on beating Derek Simpson at Cambridge on 12 February 1975

viewing by a British television audience. Cameras relayed the action into three London News Theatres owned by the Gaumont – British Corporation and played to full houses. Boon received a purse of £2,765, plus £450 from television, which was a record for a British lightweight champion.

With two notches already on the Lonsdale Belt, Boon was anxious to make it his own property as soon as possible, especially with Dave Crowley emerging from eliminators as the official challenger. The contest was difficult to stage because of the war, but after a series of postponements it eventually took place at Harringay on the afternoon of 12 December 1939. Even so, the authorities limited the attendance to 3,000 and insisted on a matinee because of the danger of air raids.

Although Crowley more than held his own for several rounds, Boon's big punches always looked to be the deciding factor. It was therefore somewhat disappointing when the end came after he appeared to hurl Dave to the floor in round seven. The challenger looked to be in agony as he was counted out and it was later revealed that he had torn his achilles tendon.

Although Boon had made the Lonsdale Belt his own property in the space of 11 months and 24 days, disappointment awaited. As he stood in the centre of the ring expecting a presentation, a Board of Control official reminded him that all valuable trophies had been recalled at the outbreak of war and deposited in bank strong-rooms. It was two months before he received his trophy.

Dave 'Boy' Green

Despite still not having reached his 20th birthday, the effects of his stirring battles began to show on Boon. He was clearly past his peak, and throughout the war years took part in just 13 contests, losing six. His reign as champion ended at Cardiff on 12 August 1944 when Ronnie James knocked him out in ten rounds.

Although he carried on fighting intermittently until 1952, he lost as many as he had won. In May 1946, Arthur Danahar stopped him in six rounds in an eliminator for the British welterweight title and, in December the following year, Ernie Roderick outpointed him in a title challenge.

In fairness to Boon, he never lost his punch and the contests he won were inside the distance. Sadly, he went on too long, losing his last seven contests, all inside schedule in rings in Canada, America and Australia. Nevertheless, his record of 93 victories from 122 contests, with 63 stoppages, was extremely credible for a country lad who first fought for pay at the age of 15.

In many respects Dave 'Boy' Green was more fortunate than Boon, thanks mainly to the guidance of his astute manager Andy Smith. As soon as the sparkle had gone, Smith pulled him out of the sport and ensured that he never went back. Dave was never allowed to become a trial-horse for up and coming youngsters and as a result has reaped the rewards.

Born at Chatteris on 2 June 1953, his father being a farmer, as a schoolboy Green looked to have a promising future as a footballer, captaining Cambridgeshire County Schools team at the age of 11. He was also a good cross-country runner, winning county championships in consecutive years when aged 13 and 14, and representing Cambridgeshire in the All-England championships.

Dave had no interest in boxing until 1967 when a school pal asked him to accompany him to the local amateur club where Eric Boon learned his trade over 30 years earlier.

Initially Dave was trained by Arthur Binder, but as he developed was taken over by Jim Moore, a former Army physical training instructor. They formed a close relationship and Dave learned well. He was a model pupil because he possessed an in-built desire to be the best at everything he did. As with football and athletics he put everything into his training. There were many evenings when he was still working long after all the other lads had gone home.

Although a major championship eluded him, Green had a successful amateur career between 1967 and 1974, in which he won 74 of 105 contests with 33 stoppages. The fans loved his all-action style, and throughout East Anglia comparisons were frequently made between him and Boon.

Even at a young age Dave feared nobody and as a senior amateur he faced most of the leading men at his weight. He beat Kirkland Laing three times, England international Peter Turrell twice, Paul Fitzgerald, Mickey Spencer, Andy Braidwood, Albert Hillman and a host of others. His style was well suited to the professional ranks and it came as no surprise when he moved over following defeat by Terry Waller in the 1974 ABA semi-finals.

Much of Green's professional career has been

documented in a previous article: *Andy Smith – An Appreciation* (Boxing Yearbook 2005). To avoid repetition, reference will therefore only be made to aspects not contained in that article.

Affectionately known as the 'Fen Tiger', Green lived up to all expectations as a professional, winning most of his early fights inside the distance. When he was matched with Joey Singleton for the British light-welterweight title on 1 June 1976, Chatteris became gripped in fight fever.

His success united the small farming community as he became the talk of the pubs, cafes and on the buses. 'Fen Tiger' T-shirts rolled off the production lines on a local industrial estate and were worn by many people in the town during the build-up to the fight. The George Hotel in the High Street, where Freddie Mills once trained for a world title fight, became the central meeting place for fans. Elderly folk who remembered Mills, Boon and other national fighting heroes, were revitalised.

"Boon used to put 'em to sleep", one old character told a local newspaper reporter, "Greeny does the same". "The thing about Boon was he knew how to take a punch", remarked another. "Green's the same – he's a good boy".

Eric Boon was among the army of fanatical Fenland supporters who travelled to London to witness the biggest test of their idol's career. "It brings it all back", he told the *Chatteris Advertiser*. "There is a tremendous feeling of excitement in the air. I think David will wear Singleton down and stop him". The old champion's prediction was spot on because Green's strength and aggression forced the champion to retire after six rounds. Boon was one of the first to congratulate him. "You were great", he told Dave, "simply great".

The following day local councillors were quick to show their appreciation by organising a civic reception and victory parade in Dave's honour. At 12 noon, together with wife Kay and manager Andy Smith, he boarded a dray drawn by two Suffolk Punch horses and was taken around the crowded streets of his home town. The scenes were reminiscent of those following Boon's defeat of Dave Crowley 38 years earlier.

Six months later more than 200 excited Fenland fans gathered at the Palace, Chatteris to celebrate Green's victory over Frenchman, Jean Baptiste Piedvache, to secure the European light-welterweight championship. Presentations were made to him on behalf of Fenland District Council, Chatteris Parish Council and his own newly formed supporters club which organised the event. Earlier that day, Isle of Ely MP, Clement Freud, put forward a motion asking that parliament recognised Dave's success.

Next up was John H.Stracey. It was a natural show-down, and a fight the fans had relished for over a year. When terms were agreed for it to take place at Wembley on 29 March 1977, comparisons were made with the Boon-Danahar classic 38 years earlier. It was Chatteris against Bethnal Green all over again and the prospects were mouth watering.

On paper, Green faced a more formidable opponent, because Stracey, a former world champion, had the experience of 50 professional contests, winning 45. He had boxed at the highest level and was Dave's greatest test to date. Critics were divided as to the likely outcome. Wembley was sold out weeks ahead of the fight, which more than lived up to it's billing. It was one of the most exciting seen in a British ring for more than a decade, containing raw drama, hard punching and unrestrained, uncompromising action from start to finish.

Green made an explosive start, but as he went for an early finish, forgot the niceties of the game. Twice he was warned by the referee, Harry Gibbs, for low blows and also sternly reprimanded for careless use of the head. There was some needle after he received a further warning towards the end of round two and they had to be pulled apart at the bell.

The pace of the fight was incredible, with Green the aggressor and Stracey punching back well, despite being under intense pressure. In the fourth the crowd were on their feet screaming with excitement. When Dave's head again crashed into Stracey's face, referee Gibbs grabbed him by the hair and marched him to the far side of the ring. "Do that again son and you're out", he growled.

By round six, Stracey's left eye had narrowed to a mere slit, but there were signs that Green was tiring. There was a real turnaround in the seventh as Dave's punches became wilder and were not so effective. Using all his experience, John put together his own powerful combinations and got back into the fight. Two-fisted attacks hurt Green, who was beaten to the punch throughout rounds eight and nine.

It was then, however, that the Chatteris man's incredible strength took over. Propelled by a burning desire for victory, he dug deep to deny Stracey at a time when he appeared to be taking over. It was anyone's fight as they came out for the tenth, but Green's determination soon changed all that. Big punches crashed against John's head and, unable to see out of his left eye, he was a defenceless, half-blind target. All the fight had been knocked out of him and when he stopped punching back Mr Gibbs mercifully called a halt.

Victory elevated Dave into a world welterweight championship fight with Carlos Palomino, who had taken the title from Stracey. Again, Wembley was completely sold out, with Green personally disposing of £35,000 worth of tickets. He was a massive draw, having sold £20,000 worth for the Stracey fight and £13,000 worth when he fought Piedvache.

Palomino was a class act, but in Green he faced a capable and determined challenger. Each round was bitterly contested with fortunes swaying one way then the other. It quickly developed into a real world championship encounter, as Green attacked viciously and the champion countered with fast accurate combinations. The crowd roared with excitement every time Dave exploded his big punches and put Carlos under pressure. His best round was the seventh when he smashed punch after punch to Palomino's head. The champion was cut over his left eye in the eighth, but when he hit back Green looked to be in trouble. Palomino also sustained a cut on the right eye lid early in the ninth, but remained calm and hit back with great accuracy as Green put on the pressure.

The fight was very much in the balance, but Wembley

erupted when Green landed the best shot of the fight in the tenth. A massive overarm right caught the champion flush on the chin and forced him to the ropes. He was badly hurt, and Dave looked on the verge of a dramatic victory. Palomino, however, was a great champion. He pulled himself together, hit back fiercely and forced Green to give ground. After a terrible clash of heads, the challenger reeled away, his left eye almost closed. Although Green was still willing as they began round 11, he was severely handicapped. Asserting his class, Palomino cut loose, and as Dave retreated a perfect left hook crashed against his chin. His head thudded against the canvas as he fell, and was out cold as Jim Brimmell completed the count.

It was no consolation for Dave that he had produced one of the greatest ever world title challenges by a British boxer. He was convinced that had it not been for the sickening clash of heads closing his eye in round ten, he would have gone on to win.

Chatteris again honoured their hero and the following day he was the guest at a civic reception organised by the Parish Council. Hundreds of people waited to greet him. Despite losing to Palomino, he let nobody down.

The Palomino fight was undoubtedly the peak of Green's career and whilst he continued fighting for a further four years, he never reached the same heights. He was still good enough, however, to beat top American, Andy 'Hawk' Price, and take the European welterweight title from Henry Rhiney in five rounds. When he lost that title to Jorgen Hansen, the big pay days appeared to have gone and he was therefore somewhat fortunate that his connections secured him a lucrative fight with Sugar Ray Leonard for the world welterweight title in the USA in March 1980.

It has been well documented that Leonard knocked Green out in four rounds with one of the best punches thrown in his entire career, but that clash sparked what is still a close friendship. When Sugar Ray travelled to England on a filming trip in 1982, he visited Dave at his Chatteris home and they lunched at a local pub. In return, Green travelled to America for many of Sugar Ray's big fights and was always given the red-carpet treatment. In October 2004, Dave and wife Kay celebrated their 30th wedding anniversary as guests of Leonard at his home in California. The American superstar also provided the foreword for Green's recently published biography – Fen Tiger.

Dave quit the ring in 1981 and moved into business. Encouraged and supported by his manager, Andy Smith, he became very successful. For many years he has also made massive contributions to charity, supporting events throughout the United Kingdom, usually at his own expense.

A role-model for sport and a tireless worker for charity, Dave and his family were recently invited to a garden party at Buckingham Palace in recognition of his good works. Surely, it will not be too long before he picks up an award in the New Year or Queens Birthday Honours!

Although life has been good to him, Dave never fails to remind people of those who helped him along the way. Referring to his manager, Andy Smith, he frequently remarks: "If it hadn't been for Mr Smith there would have been no Dave Green the boxer, nor would I have been successful in business". He is equally quick to remark that his inspiration for boxing was Eric Boon.

Chatteris may not be a town familiar to a large percentage of the country's population, but it can take pride from the fact that it produced two of Britain's most exciting boxing champions.

Green (right) seen in his epic fight against the former world welterweight champion, John H. Stracey

Muhammad Ali: Was He Really The Greatest?

by Patrick Myler

When Muhammad Ali first made his audacious 'I am The Greatest' statement, people reacted with varying degrees of amusement, outrage and scepticism. Most waited for someone to come along and stuff a sock (or an eight-ounce glove) into that ever-open mouth. They were kept waiting. As victim after victim fell before his flashing fists, the sceptics were forced to admit that there just might be some merit in his boast. "I am the astronaut of boxing," he proclaimed to all who would listen. "Joe Louis and Jack Dempsey were just jet pilots. I'm in a world of my own."

Now that Ali's career is confined to history, it is legitimate to ask the pertinent question: how justified was he in proclaiming that he was superior to all the greats of the past? Was his skill enough to overcome murderous punchers like Joe Louis and Jack Dempsey? Could he have mastered brilliant technicians like Gene Tunney and Jack Johnson? And that's only the heavyweights! How well did he match up to legends of the lighter divisions like Henry Armstrong, Willie Pep, and the two Sugar Rays, Leonard and Robinson? Well, in fairness to Ali, he did admit that Robinson was greater than he was, so let's confine our study to the heavyweights.

One of the main problems in trying to assess where Ali ranks among the immortals is piercing the massive aura that surrounds the man. If criteria such as fame, personal magnetism and historical impact are to be given priority, then Muhammad leads the rest of the pack by a thousand miles. No other fighter transcended his sport to the extent that he did. There's hardly a person in any corner of the globe who hasn't heard of Muhammad Ali. As the man himself once said: "Will they ever have another fighter who writes poems, predicts rounds, beats everybody, makes people laugh, makes people cry, and is as tall and extra pretty as me?" Point taken, but it's his fistic ability that most concerns us here. Was Ali really that great? Could he have conquered any other fighter in history who stood in the ring with him? Ultimately, was he more bluff than substance?

In the early days of his professional career, after first coming to public attention by picking up gold in the 1960 Olympics, Cassius Clay, as he was then, relied on fast footwork, lightning reflexes and rapid, accurate punching to run up an impressive winning streak. Critics noted his lack of real power, his tendency to keep his hands low, and a cockiness that would surely prove his downfall when he came up against a big puncher.

That prediction looked about to come true when, in his 11th fight, he was clowning around and sticking out his chin when supposedly overmatched Sonny Banks caught him with a long left in the second round. Clay hit the deck for the first time. "On the way down, his eyes were closed," said trainer Angelo Dundee, "but when his butt hit the canvas, he woke up." Cassius was more shocked than hurt. He got up and began to dance around Banks. Fully back on top, he waited until the fourth round to force a stoppage and fulfil his prediction. "I told you," he reminded reporters. "The man fell in four."

Eight fights later, it was Britain's Henry Cooper who found the route to that exposed chin with one of his potent left hooks in the fourth round. Clay went down with his back against the ropes. On rising, he looked dazed, and was lucky that the bell rang to end the round. Claims that Angelo Dundee took advantage of the interval to rip open a small tear in his man's glove and gain extra time were exaggerated. Cassius was fully recovered by the start of the fifth. His stinging punches worsened a cut by the side of Cooper's eye, forcing the referee to come to the rescue of the blood-smeared Briton. Years later, Clay admitted: "He hit me so hard it jarred my kinfolk in Africa."

If the knockdowns suffered against Cooper and Banks seemed to expose his vulnerability to a hard punch, time would prove that Cassius had anything but a chin of 'Clay'. Only one other opponent, Joe Frazier, would knock him off his feet in a 61 fight career spanning 21 years. That's if you discount the time Chuck Wepner was credited with flooring him, although the film footage revealed he was standing on Ali's foot when he hit him on the chest.

Even with a 19-0 record going into his challenge to Sonny Liston for the world heavyweight title on 25 February 1964, few pundits predicted he would stand up for long against the fearsome champion. Liston had felled Floyd Patterson in one round to win the title and completed the demolition with another quick knockout in the return. Clay, if he got on his bicycle and back-pedalled furiously, might survive for a few rounds, ran the perceived wisdom, but inevitably Liston would catch up sooner or later. Instead, Clay tamed 'the Big Ugly Bear' with his dazzling ringcraft and ripping punches, leading the totally demoralised Liston to quit on his stool after six rounds.

"I shook up the world. I am the greatest. I'm king of the world," Clay screamed to the 8,295 in attendance at the Convention Hall in Miami and the millions of shocked TV observers around the world. Liston, blaming a damaged shoulder for his defeat, got his chance to regain the title a year later and was counted out in the first round after taking a seemingly innocuous right to the head. By then, Cassius Clay had embraced the Muslim faith and changed his name to Muhammad Ali.

In eight further title defences, he showed how much he had developed into a superb all-rounder. Floyd Patterson, Henry Cooper, in a rematch, Brian London, Karl Mildenberger and Zora Folley were all sent packing inside the scheduled course. Many consider his three-round destruction of Cleveland Williams the most impressive performance of his career. Even his sternest critics were forced to admit they might have been wrong to doubt his ability. "That night he was the most devastating fighter who ever lived," said broadcaster Howard Cosell.

Sure, George Chuvalo and Ernie Terrell took him the

distance, but Chuvalo was one of the toughest men who ever pulled on a boxing glove, and he let Terrell survive because he wanted to torture him for refusing to call him by his Muslim name. "What's my name?" Ali kept repeating as he stung the outclassed challenger with hard punches. Along with his cruel taunting of Joe Frazier at a later date, his unforgivable behaviour in the Terrell fight revealed the worst side of Muhammad's character.

There is no doubt whatsoever that Ali's three and a half years exile from the ring, when he was stripped of his title and banned after refusing to be inducted into the US army to serve in Vietnam, slowed down his movement and forced him to change his style. The 1970s Ali could still move gracefully, but he couldn't keep dancing for 15 rounds as before, and learned to stand his ground more. That meant he got hit more. Oscar Bonavena shook him to his heels with a big left hook in the ninth round, leading Ali to confess afterwards: "I was numb all over." It was Ali, however, who landed the decisive punches, dropping the tough Argentinian three times before the referee stopped the fight in the 15th round. The tired, but effusive, victor announced: "I've done what Joe Frazier couldn't do. I've knocked out Oscar Bonavena. Now I want Joe Frazier."

He got his wish in March 1971. In many ways, although he was to suffer the first defeat of his career against the reigning world heavyweight champion, it was a career defining fight for Ali. Forced to meet the relentless Frazier head-on, he proved his immense courage and punch resistance in a thrilling encounter that saw both men endure severe punishment. The fight was still in the balance in the 15th round when a venomous left hook caught Ali square on the chin and sent him crashing on his back for the third count of his career. Anyone else would have stayed down, but Muhammad scrambled shakily to his feet and fought back well in the remaining minutes of the fight. The verdict for Frazier was unanimous. 'The Greatest' had been humbled, but he won almost as much praise for losing as he ever did in winning.

Ali was again forced to dig deep into his well of courage when he suffered a broken jaw in the second round against Ken Norton. Angelo Dundee wanted him to pull out, but he insisted: "No, I can beat this sucker. He won't touch my jaw." Remarkably, he fought on for the ten rounds distance, losing a narrow decision. Throughout his career, to his everlasting credit, Ali never ducked a worthy opponent. He knew that Norton, a body beautiful with skills and a strong punch, had the style to always give him trouble. Yet he faced Norton twice more, winning both, even if the decisions in both bouts were close enough for argument.

Most people agree that Ali reached the pinnacle of his remarkable career when he regained the world heavyweight title by knocking out George Foreman in Zaire on 30 October 1974. It wasn't just that he scored an upset win over a much-feared ogre, it was the way he did it that astounded everyone. If he was to have any chance, the experts predicted, he would have to be the old, dancing Ali, scoring points from a distance and never letting himself get lured into a slugging match with such an explosive hitter.

Muhammad Ali (right) went 2-1 up against Joe Frazier following 'The Thrilla in Manila'

Muhammad turned those theories completely upside down. Basically, his plan was to lie against the ropes and let the champion hit him. Eventually, he figured, Foreman would get tired of punching at a target that refused to wilt, and he would be so exhausted that he would be unable to withstand Ali's counter attack. What seemed like a suicidal policy worked out to perfection. Archie Moore, who was in Foreman's corner, remembered: "Everything we'd planned was designed to get Ali on the ropes, where George could hit him. But once George got him there and Ali stayed there, George didn't know what to do."

The encounter that has gone down in history as 'The Rumble in the Jungle' ended sensationally in the eighth round, when Ali sprang from the ropes and landed a succession of punches, culminating in a right to the head, to send the champion spinning to the canvas to be counted out. What makes the result even more remarkable is that Ali, not the hardest punching heavyweight in history, was the only fighter to stop Foreman in a career spanning almost three decades.

If the Foreman victory was the best performance of Ali's career, the best fight was undoubtedly the last in the trilogy with Joe Frazier. Both men were past their best when they clashed on 1 October 1975, but that made no difference. It lived up to, even exceeded, promoter Don King's pre-fight hype for 'The Thrilla in Manila'. These two well-matched rivals waged savage war, with no quarter sought or given, and absorbed such punishment that it almost certainly left permanent marks on both men's health. "Man, I hit him with punches that would bring cities down," Frazier said afterwards. As Ali trudged back to his stool at the end of the 14th round, he wasn't sure he could fight another round. "It was the closest thing to death that I could feel," he later admitted. If Ali felt bad, Frazier was worse. The referee had to guide him back to his corner, where trainer Eddie Futch told him: "Sit down, son, it's over. But no one will ever forget what you did here today."

The rest of Ali's career was anti-climatic. He looked dreadful against Jimmy Young and Alfredo Evangelista, who both took him the full 15 rounds, and needed a good last round to scrape home against Ken Norton. He lost the title to Leon Spinks, an eight-fight novice, regained it in a return, then was stopped for the first and only time in his career by Larry Holmes. That should have been it, but he wanted to go out a winner. It didn't happen. Clearly not well, he should never have fought Trevor Berbick, who took a convincing points decision over the 39-year-old ex-champion on 11 December 1981. Ali announced his retirement the following day. "I won't miss fighting: fighting will miss me," he declared. How right he was.

So, having summarised Ali's career, it's time to examine the case for his claim to be 'The Greatest'. One of the main difficulties in comparing great fighters of different eras is deciding the time of the mythical showdowns. If we pluck a name out of history and put him up against someone today, the old-timer would be handicapped without the benefits of modern, highly developed training methods, scientifically approved diets, and general improvement in all-round condition. On the other hand, would the fighters of today

have the stamina, endurance and patience to go 20 or more rounds like the ringmen of yore?

In assessing Ali, too, we have to remember that he was a different fighter in the two separate phases of his career, before and after his enforced three and a half years absence from the ring in the late 1960s. The younger, faster Muhammad would have left early heavyweight champions like John L. Sullivan and James J. Jeffries, idols in their day, struggling to land a decent punch as he effortlessly picked them off from a distance. Gentleman Jim Corbett was a master boxer, with more tricks than a conjuror, but he wasn't as fast or as durable as Ali. Could you see Muhammad, who absorbed vicious body punches from powerful hitters like Foreman and Frazier, succumbing to the solar plexus shot from Bob Fitzsimmons, a middleweight, that cost Corbett his heavyweight crown?

Jack Johnson, a defensive master with knockout power in both hands, might have posed Ali plenty of problems, blocking many of his long-range punches and tying him up if he got close. But Muhammad, while finding it difficult to catch his wily rival, would not have allowed himself to be lured into traps. The likely outcome would be a clear points win for Ali after a deadly dull match. Jack Dempsey, one of the most destructive hitters of all time, would have tried to bully Ali to the ropes before unleashing his deadly combinations. But the 'Manassa Mauler' couldn't put away Tom Gibbons, a clever boxer not in Ali's class, inside 15 rounds, and he was twice outsmarted by Gene Tunney,

'The Greatest' in playful pose Harry Goodwin

albeit when he was past his prime. Tunney, a much under-rated heavyweight king, might have stood a better chance than most of disproving 'The Greatest' theory. Gene was a master technician, nippy on his feet, with a solid chin and a harder punch than he is generally credited with. Tunney vs Ali would have been a real battle of wits, with Muhammad probably having the edge.

Perhaps the only heavyweight champion who might have exposed the Ali myth was Joe Louis. Rated by *The Ring* as the hardest puncher in history, Louis also had probably the best left jab of any heavyweight, and he could box. He knew how to be patient, work for openings and when to cut loose. Few opponents managed to survive his bombs. Not only was he a murderous puncher, his blows were delivered with astonishing accuracy. He never wasted a shot. "Joe Louis could drive his fists through a knothole and never touch the sides," said writer Paul Gallico. Louis, however, wasn't the fastest mover on his feet and he would have been torn apart in frustration trying to pin an effective punch on the young Ali. Against the later Ali, it might have been a different story. It's hard to see Muhammad getting away with his 'rope-a-dope' tactics against someone as precise and powerful a hitter as 'the Brown Bomber'. His great chin would certainly have been put to the utmost test in what would have been a intriguing match-up.

Rocky Marciano, with his bobbing and weaving style and his ability to knock anyone out with a single shot, would have done some damage if Ali let him get close. But 'The Rock', five inches shorter and with a reach of only 68 inches, compared to Ali's 82, would have needed spring-heeled shoes to get within range. Besides, with his tendency to cut, Marciano would probably have been sliced up by Ali's rangy punches before the referee came to his rescue.

Of the heavyweight champions of more recent vintage, Mike Tyson's chances could not be ruled out in a mythical match with Ali. The young Tyson, who blasted away opponent after opponent on the way to becoming the youngest world heavyweight champion in history, bears comparison with the best in the division. He could match anyone for power and he was no wild slugger. He cleverly weaved his way in close to unleash his weapons of destruction. Many of his rivals were so fearful of what was to come that they were beaten before they climbed between the ropes. In time, Tyson's mental demons served to damage his fearsome reputation. He would grow frustrated if he failed to dispose of his opponents quickly, and often resorted to despicable fouling in a bid to get the job done. That lack of control, and an apparent inability to dig down deep when the going got rough, are the black marks that cast doubt on Iron Mike's greatness.

Bigger men like Lennox Lewis and Vitali Klitschko would have made it hard for Ali to outscore them from a distance, but Muhammad would not have feared their power and had a much more complete arsenal than either man. He would have found a way to beat them.

In the final analysis, it's hard to dispute Ali's right to the loftiest position on the heavyweight podium. Once he was ridiculed as a pompous upstart, tagged 'the Louisville Lip' and 'Gaseous Cassius'. As his true talent began to show, tolerance gradually turned to admiration. Today, most people seem prepared to accept that he was what he always claimed to be – 'The Greatest'.

Ring of Hate: the Brown Bomber and Hitler's Hero

By Patrick Myler

In his latest book, which reached No. 1 in the UK sports best sellers, Patrick Myler recalls the excitement and the poisoned political atmosphere that engulfed the famous fight between Joe Louis and Max Schmeling for the world heavyweight title in 1938. With the world heading inexorably towards war, both fighters were handed the banners of their countries' contrasting ideologies. Louis was told by President Roosevelt on a visit to the White House: "Joe, we need muscles like yours to beat Germany." Schmeling was portrayed by Adolf Hitler as the prime example of Aryan superiority over the black man. The fight lasted just two minutes, Louis leaving his opponent helpless before his onslaught. The book tells the remarkable story of two decent men drawn together by their chosen profession and divided by the demands of warring nations. Ultimately, they put the legacy of hate behind them to form a lifelong friendship.

"Myler's literary muscle brings together the careers and lives of Louis and Schmeling into a vivid and absorbing portrait" – Brian Doogan, *The Ring*.

"Thoroughly researched, as solid and as accurate as Louis's famous left jab" – Nick Pitt, *Sunday Times*.

"Well written in the fluid Myler style, it should appeal to both pugilist-specialist-readers and general readers whose interest in the subject may have been awakened by Herr Max's recent passing. Highly recommended" – John Exshaw, *Boxing Monthly*.

"Myler's remarkable book is peopled with athletes, gangsters, film stars and politicians. It's an astonishing story expertly told" – Eamon Carr, *Evening Herald* (Dublin).

"Many books have been written about Louis and Schmeling, but I consider this the best story about these greats. Any serious collector should own a copy" – Ron Jackson, (South Africa).

Ring of Hate (hardback, 256 pages) is published by Mainstream at £15.99.

Johnny Hill: Scotland's First World Champion

by Brian Donald

No Scottish world champion has been treated more shabbily than Edinburgh-born Johnny Hill, particularly by Scotland's current crop of newspaper boxing writers, who stubbornly peddle the inconsistent nonsense that Benny Lynch was Scotland's first world champion and Scotland has only had eight world champions, comments made by almost every Scottish newspaper and television text service company, after Cambuslang's 'world' – ie: WBO only, version, champion, Scott Harrison, beat Argentina's Julio Pablo Chacon – in great style – in October 2002. Even the BBC got in on the act two years or so ago, by trotting out famous Scottish actor, the late Russell Hunter, who, as boxing historians go, was a very good actor – to prolong this absurd fiction about Lynch being Scotland's first ever world champion, in a documentary shown on Scottish television.

Now, as I know and work with, almost all of Scotland's current crop of boxing writers, I know that there is no malice in this stubborn refusal to face facts– the truth is they don't know all the facts. Neither have these gentlemen thought the matter through thoroughly, or they would see clearly, just how untenable it is to ignore Edinburgh-born Johnny Hill as Scotland's first world boxing champion.

The problems surrounding recognition started when Nat Fleischer's influential Ring Record Book, published between 1942 and 1987, omitted Hill from the world flyweight champions' section until its final edition, under the editorship of Herb Goldman, which listed him as being recognised in Britain. Although Hill beat California's 'world' champion, 'Newsboy' Brown, in August 1928 to win a fight billed in Britain as being for the world title it was unclear whether Hill was recognised by the Californian Boxing Commission. What is clear, however, is that the Californian Boxing Commission didn't set up another tournament following Brown's defeat. Hill was also listed as a world flyweight champion by the British Boxing Yearbook when it was first published in 1985 and although his name was deleted for a while, further research has since established that most of a fragmented Britain recognised Hill as a world champion in 1928, despite the newly formed BBBoC not allowing world title billing to be attached to Hill's two 1929 defences of the British title against Ernie Jarvis.

The flyweight championship mess had come about after Fidel LaBarba retired and California (where LaBarba was based), the NYSAC (representing New York and two or three like-minded States) and the NBA (representing the rest of America) set up tournaments to find a world champion. At the time of Hill v Brown, Izzy Schwartz was recognised by the NYSAC and Frankie Genaro by the NBA/IBU. Following Hill's victory and the NYSAC's disenchantment with Schwartz (who had defended his title outside New York and had lost a non-title contest against Emile Pladner on 1 December 1928), Charles Harvey, the chairman of the NYSAC, wrote a letter to Johnny Hill's father and ring mentor, David Hill, on headed New York State Athletic Commission paper, stating that his ruling body would recognise Johnny Hill as champion as long as he agreed to take part in a tournament against American claimants like Schwartz and Genaro in the near future. Although Schwartz was eventually stripped by the NYSAC at the end of August 1929, because Hill was already booked to meet Genaro for the NBA/IBU title he was not seen as a participant by that body. Tragically, Hill would die on the eve of his ring battle against Genaro on 27 September 1929. This letter was buried, unseen, in Johnny Hill's posthumous papers and, in fairness, none of Scotland's current crop of newspaper boxing writers have ever seen it, as I have, courtesy of Hill's sole surviving brother, Alf, who still lives in the Fife village of Strathmiglo.

Johnny Hill, as shown in the 'Famous Boxers' Series'

Bearing this in mind it is fair to say that Hill had a far wider recognition than that granted to Paul Weir and Pat Clinton, both WBO champions who were also not recognised universally as 'world' champions. Yet, the contemporary Scottish, peddlers of the 'Scotland has had only eight world boxing champions' nonsense always resort to the rather pathetic excuse of 'But Hill wasn't universally recognised.' This conveniently ignores, that in its entire history, Scotland has only had three universally recognised world boxing champions – Glasgow flyweight Jackie Paterson and Edinburgh lightweight Ken Buchanan (after 1971) and Benny Lynch (but only after 1937, in the USA – two years after he beat Manchester's Jackie Brown).

There is also no doubt that Britain's leading, post-Second World War boxing promoter, Jack Solomons, clearly knew Scottish boxing history better than today's crop of Scottish newspaper boxing writers. When Solomons promoted Walter McGowan and Salvatore Burruni for the WBC title in London in 1966, he had a montage of Scotland's world champions on the programme cover– and first boxer on the cover? – Johnny Hill.

But, the use by the 'Johnny Hill wasn't Scotland's first world champion lobby' of non-universal title recognition, as their main criteria for ignoring the Edinburgh-born boxer's claim, exposes them to charges of hypocrisy. Why? – because in December 1991, I contacted New York-based Steve Farhood, then Editor of *Ring* magazine. Responding to a question I put to him, by transatlantic telephone, about Pat Clinton, of Croy, being recognised, as a 'world champion', by his magazine and American boxing pundits, Farhood replied: "We don't recognise the WBO, so we won't recognise Clinton's proposed battle in Glasgow (for the WBO flyweight title which he won in 1992) whatever the outcome, as a world title fight". So, by the same token, neither of Ayrshire's Paul Weir's WBO titles were recognised in the USA as 'world' titles by American Farhood's criteria.

Yet, the Scottish boxing press, were, all falling over themselves to include, Weir and Pat Clinton, among their fictitious figure of 'Scotland has had only eight world champions' after Scott Harrison's WBO title win, in October 2002.

Furthermore, search any issue of *Ring* magazine between 1988 and 1995 – when Clinton and Weir were at their peaks as 'world' champions – and what do we find?

Clinton not only never appeared higher than ninth in *Ring's* top ten world ratings of boxers, but was also initially listed as coming from America! Clinton's bogus American status, conferred by *Ring* magazine, only changed when I pointed this out to his manager, Tommy Gilmour, who subsequently contacted the magazine, who, in turn, rectified Clinton's nationality, but not his world rating status.

Equally, Paul Weir was never listed, or rated, in *Ring,* or any other American boxing magazine! as a 'world' title holder, during his reign as Scotland's first double 'world champion'!

Compare that with Johnny Hill's unequivocal recognition on 12 December 1928 from the NYSAC! So the question must be put to the 'Hill-wasn't-a-world-champion' faction. And the question is:- Given that, equality of treatment is basic to the moral and legal concept of natural justice. Given, Hill enjoyed far greater recognition worldwide than Weir or Clinton, who were included in the eight world champion listings published in October 2002 by the anti-Hill lobby in their respective newspapers, what valid criteria is there for denying that Johnny Hill was Scotland's first world champion? – I submit, none whatsoever.

Furthermore, I challenge any Scottish or British boxing writer, to provide one – just one– valid criteria, particularly on the issue of non-recognition, for denying Johnny Hill his rightful place as Scotland's first world champion, that does not apply with equal force to every Scottish world champion since boxing began – apart from Jackie Paterson.

Finally, as I know both Pat Clinton and Paul Weir well, and have always admired their ring abilities, I have no problem recognising them as bona fide 'world' champions, but if they were, so too, was Johnny Hill, who had a far greater degree of recognition in America, during his lifetime than either Weir and Clinton ever had.

Nobody in America ever, wrongly, called – for two years – Johnny Hill a US boxer; nor was he ever buried at number 15 in the US world ratings while holding his 'world' title. Even Nat Fleisher's World Ratings for 1928 had Hill at number two behind Emile Pladner.

Even-handed treatment, even to persons now dead, like Hill, is the first principle of natural justice.

Johnny Hill was Scotland's first world champion – bar none!

* * * * *

Johnny Hill was born on 14 December 1905, at No 5 Brunswick Road, just off that broad Edinburgh boulevard that sweeps from London Road, to the Kirkgate in Leith, known as Leith Walk. Number 5 Brunswick Road, was then, in 1905, and remains, a substantial Victorian tenement, a million miles removed from the dismal Gorbals tenement slum, inhabited in childhood, by that other great Scottish flyweight, Benny Lynch.

But then, Johnny Hill's father, David Hill was no John Lynch, father of Benny. Where Lynch senior was an alcoholic and child neglecter, David Hill was a sober, industrious, stonemason, who had not only boxed for Edinburgh's long-vanished Netherbow boxing club with some distinction, but was a frugal, teetotaller and an excellent, prosperous, sought-after craftsman. Facts that allowed Hill senior to bring up his brood, including Johnny, in a style and comfort beyond that normally enjoyed by early 20th century working-class craftsmen. A daily, childhood, life style that the early Benny Lynch would have regarded with envy.

Again, Brunswick Road is not only a few hundred yards from the Sparta boxing club gym in McDonald Road where another Scottish ring great, Ken Buchanan, first threw a ring punch, but at its southern end also lies, just off Easter Road, Bothwell Street.

In 1920, having taken Johnny Hill, aged 12, to the Melbourne amateur boxing club, situated in Edinburgh's St James Square, David Hill also introduced his son to two brothers from Bothwell Street and their uncle. The uncle was featherweight boxer, James 'Tancy' Lee, Scotland's first outright Lonsdale Belt winner. The Bothwell Street boys were Lee's boxing nephews, George and James McKenzie. The elder McKenzie, George, had a brilliant amateur career, which included winning Olympic bronze at Antwerp in 1920, and he would often spar with young Johnny Hill, as would his younger brother, James McKenzie. It was watching the young novice swap ring leather with future 1924 Paris Olympics flyweight silver medallist, James McKenzie, that alerted both 'Tancy' Lee and David Hill, that Johnny had the makings of an outstanding talent.

Nevertheless, it was when he finally followed the McKenzies, from the Melbourne club, to the Leith Victoria, that the ring greatness of Johnny Hill, while evident in his Melbourne club days, really began to flower. One who remembered Hill well was Leith Vics clubmate and future world-class referee, Eugene Henderson. "I was the same age as Hill – and sparred with him many times, worked out moves with him, in the Leith Victoria gym, I liked him immensely, he was quiet but with a devilish sense of humour – more importantly he looked frail – like Welsh ring great, Jimmy Wilde, but like Wilde, he could punch hard – very hurtfully, against boxers in the club of his own weight, but he was a beautiful boxer, with a great left jab and he could hook and uppercut like a master".

So it proved, as Johnny cut a swathe through the amateurs. On winning his first Scottish senior flyweight title, in February 1925, (while still a Melbourne club boxer) by beating Glasgow's Western District champion, Willie Barr, one newspaper commented: "…Young Hill was quite simply, the most polished boxer on view…".

Even greater things were to follow during the following year of 1926. On Saturday, 20 February 1926, in Edinburgh's Claremont Street TA Drill Hall, Johnny Hill won the Eastern District title by first outscoring Edinburgh ABC's Jimmy Smith, the local press observing: "…Hill was faster with the heavier punch…". Next, he knocked out Willie Gibb of Armadale, with a pulverising left hook that caused the press to observe: "…there is little clue to Hill's ferocious hitting power in his slight, boyish physique…". After disposing of Fife's Pat Healey in the final, the scene was set for Johnny Hill to defend his Scottish flyweight crown on 26 March 1926 and win the Scottish bantamweight title as well!

Fighting at the Hippodrome, Glasgow, the *Leith Observer* newspaper reported: "Johnny Hill won all four bouts to retain the Scottish flyweight title and was never really extended". In his first title defence bout – against Kilmarnock's George Skilling – the Ayrshire man had no answer for Johnny's big punching, the towel being thrown in during the first round. Three subsequent wins against western Scottish rivals, Pat Devine, Jackie Ferguson and Dan Docherty, in the final, on points, clinched the title once again. Then it was on to the Scottish bantamweight

championships held at Edinburgh's Claremont Street Drill Hall, on Saturday 10 April 1926… The *Leith Observer* reported: "In the semi-final between Hill and Alex Morrison of Dennistoun, the boxing of Hill was a feature of the evening …in the final, Hill met clubmate, George Shaw. Hill did all that was expected of him. He forced the fight from beginning to end.…". This was the same George Shaw, who would, 30 years later, play a key role, as Sparta coach, in the rise of the young Ken Buchanan.

George loved to tell we 1962 vintage Sparta members about his 1920s scrap with Johnny Hill. The Shaw verdict: "Johnny Hill was a great boxer, who could hurt you with both hands".

Shortly following the Shaw win, Johnny Hill went south to contest the British ABA flyweight title, in London's Albert Hall, in April 1926. His opponent, a previous winner in 1924 and 1925, was Ernie Warwick. Warwick was far too good a boxer to be simply bowled over, but he nevertheless received a boxing lesson. To the extent that not only did Johnny win the ABA title, but also the ringside judges' cup for the best ring stylist. Yet, there was no surprise in any of this given, what Johnny Hill, told the *Topical Times* magazine, in 1927: "The man who takes up boxing as a job must be as serious about it as any other job he chooses to do for a living…". And according to Johnny's youngest brother, Alf Hill, who still lives in Strathmiglo today, his brother lived by this strict code, as he told me: "Johnny never smoked, drank or did anything that would interfere with progressing his boxing career – besides my father's word was law to him in boxing matters". And, it was David Hill who set out the strategy, once the decision to go pro' was reached in August 1926.

* * * * *

Johnny Hill's decision to turn professional was as sensational as his impact on Britain's paid flyweight boxers. Johnny's shrewd dad had received tempting offers from the Edinburgh promoter, Nat Dresner, then Scotland's number one boxing impresario, but 'Tancy' Lee advised both father and son, that they should follow his example. Especially, if they wanted to emulate Lee's feat of winning a Lonsdale Belt, and fight in London, and try to impress the Czar of British boxing, 'Peggy' Bettinson, boss of the *National Sporting Club*, which ruled British boxing. A decision made easy by the fact that David and Johnny Hill had both been working for three months, as stonemasons in the English capital.

So, when a chance arose to have his first paid scrap as a substitute at London's famous *Premierland Arena*, against Stepney's Billy Huntly, not only did the future Leith ring great accept, but a London newspaper informed its readers: "Hill made short work of Huntly, whom he stopped in five rounds…". Even more sensational – for all the wrong reasons – was Hill's second paid bout – with Stepney's Mark Lesnick, again in London, on 17 October 1926. As anyone knows who recalls the hash that the American former world heavyweight champion, Jersey Joe Walcott, made of the second Ali v Liston fight in 1965, in Lewiston,

Johnny Hill on the eve of his contest against 'Newsboy' Brown

Maine, with confusion reigning supreme everywhere in and outside the ropes, former world champions are not always as good at officiating. So it proved, when the former world welterweight champion, Ted 'Kid' Lewis, declared Johnny's tussle with Stepney's Mark Lesnick a 'No Contest' – after 15 rounds! Reports show that Lewis was increasingly frustrated by Lesnick's persistent holding, as Hill hurt him with body and head punches, whenever the pair were at distance, in the ring. Yet, ex-champion Lewis, should have disqualified Lesnick, not penalised Hill.

Still, what followed this disappointment was a whirlwind campaign. Between 2 November and 29 November 1926, Johnny Hill fought five back-to-back bouts. Two 15 and two 12-round scraps – in London. Arthur Cunningham of Camden Town was kayoed in the seventh round in Johnny's first appearance at the NSC in Covent Garden, while Birmingham's Billy James drew, again over 15 rounds. It was Hill's second appearance at 'Peggy' Bettinson's NSC, but even some papers' claims that Hill was fortunate, did not stop him being quickly invited back to box. Particularly, as he had impressed referee of a thousand fights, Eugene Corri, who wrote in a London newspaper: "The more I see of Johnny Hill, the more I am certain that he will become a pugilist of high degree…". And a trawl through the contemporary London press shows Corri's views were well founded. For example, the London based *Star*, headlined Johnny's win over Sheffield's Frank Maurier, on 16 November 1926, with: "Great Display by ex-Amateur Flyweight Champion, adding… "In the fourth round Hill brought up his heavy artillery and reduced Maurier (who had given top British contender, Alf Barber, a hard fight just before his clash with Johnny) to impotence…".

But one of his most significant wins in this period was his win before the future King Edward VIII, later Duke of Windsor, on 29 November 1926, at the NSC, when Hill stopped the Londoner, Young Brown. A win captured on a photograph which shows Johnny's Dad, David, sitting beside the then Prince of Wales, as Johnny impressively showed he had bottle as well as a knockout punch, having had to climb off the canvas in round three, before stopping Brown, who couldn't answer the bell for the 12th round. A win hailed by the top British 'paper *The Sporting Life*, who headlined: "Johnny Hill Scores Great Victory", while the *Daily Herald* proclaimed: "Astonishing Display by Johnnie Hill". Commented Johnny's surviving brother, Alf: "The Prince of Wales was a huge fan of my brother, making a point of visiting him in his dressing room in the NSC".

1927 was as equally sensational. A January points victory over one 'Tiny' Smith in London, where Hill was now the toast of the English capital, was followed by a thrilling knockout of Frenchman, 'Young' Denain, with the London *Star* trumpeting: "Hurricane Flyweight Fight" – All over in six rounds – Young Scot Gains Applause For Great Display".

Hill's next bout, against the Londoner, Phil Lolosky, on 16 February, was notable for two reasons. The manner in which he won it and the fact that his Dad, David, announced, in public, that henceforth, Johnny should be billed as Johnny Hill of Strathmiglo, rather than Leith, in deference to their adopted Fife home.

Of his 16 February Lolosky win in the 15th round, the *Daily Herald* reported: "The Scot showed rare accuracy with his right, paving the way with his smart left hand and had Lolosky troubled as early as the third round". It was in this period too, that Johnny fought his only pro' ring battle in his Edinburgh birthplace, knocking out Belfast rival, Jim Hanna, in round 11 at the capital's Waverely Market venue. This was a win that propelled Johnny into a British flyweight title clash, in a record nine months. His opponent for the title vacated by Glasgow's 'Elky' Clark – due to eye injury – was Alf Barber of Brighton, a tough, swarming, bodypuncher. The magazine *Boxing and Racing* declared: "In the end it was all Hill, Barber being battered into a dummy". Not surprisingly the bout was stopped in the 14th round and Scotland had her third flyweight Lonsdale Belt winner since 'Tancy' Lee, in 1915.

By March 1928, the European title was won by beating, at the NSC, (for a second time) the Frenchman, Emile 'Spider' Pladner, over 15 rounds, despite being decked in the ninth round by a vicious left hook. The *Daily Telegraph* for 20 March 1928, commented on Johnny's win: "Hill wastes few blows… he is such a master of distance, both in attack and defence… and his footwork is the footwork of a champion….".

Now, the stage was set for Johnny Hill to win, in just 23 months, world, British and European flyweight titles, a record that still stands today (among Scots, only Paul Weir, who won a light-flyweight WBO title after six pro' bouts, has won a world title with fewer fights than Johnny Hill). Thus a world flyweight title clash with California's 'Newsboy' Brown, at Clapton Orient Football ground on 29 August 1928 would attract a then record crowd for an outdoor world title bout in Britain, in the pre-television age, of 50,000 spectators! Incidentally, Brown, who was of Russian-Jewish origin, had a real name that was very Scottish – Dave Montrose! The London based *Sunday Pictorial* had absolutely no doubts that Hill v 'Newsboy' Brown was for the world flyweight title reporting: "This is stated to be for a world title…I see no reason why it should not be billed as such…neither Izzy Schwartz or anyone else in America holds it". Similarly, Britain's then number one all-sports paper, the London-based *Sporting Life*, of Thursday, 30 August 1928, hailed Johnny Hill's 15-round points win over American 'Newsboy' Brown before a British record crowd of 50,000 thus: "Britain Regains A World Title", while the London *Daily Chronicle* proclaimed: "Johnny Hill World Champion!" *The Sporting Life* added: "There began the greatest flyweight contest seen in this country since the war, culminating in a British victory and the return to this country of the world flyweight championship which Jimmy Wilde lost to Pancho Villa…in New York five years ago…". *The Scotsman* of 30 August 1928 hailed Hill's coronation as Caledonia's first world champion thus: "Johnny Hill gave a superb display of boxing…Hill won because he was slightly the quicker…and because 'Newsboy' Brown's tactics were ruined by his inability to avoid Hill's straight left…". *The Scotsman*, however, used the words 'reputed' about Hill's status as world champion, although they cannot be condemned for that.

Yet, nobody could then have foreseen that just 12 months later, at the age of just 23, Scotland's first ever world champion would be dead, the victim in a pre-antibiotics age of a blood clot in the lung.

* * * * *

After the euphoria of August 1929, Johnny Hill's career acquired a certain air of anti-climax about it. On 7 February 1929, with his world and European titles not at stake, Paris proved no more lucky for Hill than it had proved for his British flyweight title predecessor and fellow Leither, 'Tancy' Lee, as Emile Pladner, whom Johnny had previously twice outpointed, knocked him out in six rounds before 20,000 fans at the Velo D'Hiver, in the French capital. Johnny Hill's reason for his defeat by Pladner was in suffering seasickness due to a rough Channel crossing.

In action again, he returned to his winning ways, in back-to-back, British title defences, against the tough, swarthy, English challenger, Ernie Jarvis of Millwall, a brawler in the American style. The first Jarvis bout was won over 15 rounds at the Royal Albert Hall, London, but their second title clash was anti-climatic on two counts. Held at Glasgow's Carntyne Dog Racing Stadium, where Scottish ring great Tommy Milligan had ended his illustrious career, the crowd of just 6,000, was only a fragment of the 32,000 who had watched Milligan bow out shortly before. Again, it was halted when Jarvis was disqualified controversially in the tenth round by London referee, Eugene Corri, Jarvis allegedly hitting Hill low, which saw the Scot ending up on the canvas.

Enter Jeff Dickson, late of Natchez, Mississippi, USA, then one of Europe's leading promoters, both in Paris and London, with an offer for Johnny Hill to defend his version of the world crown against the American holder of the NBA/IBU version, Frankie Genaro. Genaro, the Olympic flyweight champion at Antwerp in 1920, was the unluckiest world title contender in boxing history. Scheduled to meet Pancho Villa, the Filipino conqueror of Welshman, Jimmy Wilde, in 1925, Genaro saw the Filipino die, just prior to their meeting, from blood poisoning. Now another shock awaited Genaro. Although beaten by 'Newsboy' Brown on points two years before, the American, having beaten France's Emile Pladner shortly before, was recognised by the NBA and Europe as world flyweight champion. When the former 1920 Olympic champion arrived by cross-channel ferry from Paris, he was met at Folkstone by the promoter, Jeff Dickson, who told Genaro that, once again, incredibly, a defending champion had died on him!

According to Johnny's surviving brother Alf: "Johnny caught a chill training. His condition deteriorated and a blood clot in the lung killed him. We were all shocked but I recall the funeral well, especially the memory of Frankie Genaro coming up to Strathmiglo. He was smartly dressed

like a character in a James Cagney gangster movie, with his girlfriend, but he was a really nice guy". Also up from London, was future world light-heavyweight champion, Freddie Mills's manager Ted Broadribb, who represented the promoter, Jeff Dickson (Dickson would himself die tragically. His US Air Force B-17 bomber would be shot down over France in 1943). Added Alf Hill: "Genaro was heartbroken, and acted as a pallbearer. It was strange, he should have fought my brother, yet Frankie ended up attending his funeral".

So died Johnny Hill. Ironically, despite avoiding the alcoholic excesses of Benny Lynch and living a spartan life of self-discipline totally at odds with Lynch's boozy lifestyle, he died aged exactly ten years younger than Lynch was when the Glasgow ring great perished, aged 33, in 1946. But his claims to Caledonian ring greatness have been ignored and downgraded long enough. No other Scottish flyweight champion has won versions of world, British and European crowns in just 23 months as Johnny Hill did. Neither Lynch, or Paterson, or McGowan, ever won European flyweight titles, as Hill did. None of them lost only one bout as Hill did, although Hill's career was the shortest. Although Irvine's Paul Weir, among Scottish world champions, had an identical 18 total career bouts as Hill did, Weir lost five contests compared to Hill's single loss.

Ted Broadribb (left), Jeff Dickson's right-hand man, is seen here with Frankie Genaro and his wife prior to attending Johnny Hill's funeral

'Peerless' Jim Driscoll: A Legend

by Wynford Jones

Jim Driscoll was born in Cardiff on 15 December, 1881, the son of Irish immigrants. His parents came from Cork and the family settled in Ellen Street in the Newtown area of the city. This was the heart of the long-established Irish community where Jim would become such a popular figure. He would spend the whole of his life here and eventually bought the 'Duke of Edinburgh' pub which became a focal point for soldiers injured during the war. His father, a railwayman, was tragically killed in the nearby goods yard when Jim was only a few months old, and to make ends meet, his doting mother had to take work unloading potatoes in the docks, also selling fish around the streets of the city. It is bitterly ironic that her children appeared so well cared for that her parish relief payment was reduced thus compounding their problems.

As a boy Jim worked on the Western Mail newspaper, where he learned to box with his workmates who used to tie wastepaper around their hands as no gloves were available. He later became involved in the boxing booths, notably Jack Scarott's where he started at the age of 14. As a booth fighter he had several hundred contests and just like so many of his contemporaries this was where he learned his craft. There is a story of a booth contest in 1908, which tells of an encounter with a man called Ben Barrow. A round passed in which Barrow threw a hundred punches but Driscoll was not hit once, neither did he throw a single punch as he kept his hands at his sides for the full three minutes.

In a career of approximately 70 contests, Jim lost only three times. He was beaten by Harry Mansfield in Cardiff, a defeat which was subsequently avenged, and he was disqualified against Freddie Walsh in Cardiff on 20 December, 1910. His third defeat came in his final contest when he was an old man in sporting terms and already suffering from tuberculosis.

During the first few years of his career Driscoll boxed in places such as Aberdare, Pontypridd, Cardiff and Bristol and it was only after beating Jack Roberts in February, 1906 that he began to appear regularly at the National Sporting Club in London's Covent Garden, where he became a great favourite. He became British featherweight champion by beating Joe Bowker on points over 15 rounds at the NSC on 28 May, 1906 but relinquished the title. Jim had been due to face Johnny Summers, but following the withdrawal of the latter Bowker was substituted. He met Bowker again at the beginning of Derby Week on 1 June 1907 and regained the title when knocking his rival out in the seventh round. The artist, W. Howard Robinson, produced a painting of their encounter with the crowd scene featuring the faces of distinguished club members. The painting hangs in the board room of the British Boxing Board of Control in Cardiff and is a wonderful reminder of a bygone era.

In February 1908, Jim won the Empire title when he beat Charlie Griffin at the NSC and later that year set sail for America where he met the likes of Matty Baldwin, Grover Hayes and Leach Cross, boxing in places such as New York, Boston and Philadelphia. He put together a string of impressive performances in what were no-decision contests because of the legal situation in these states regarding boxing.

Within days of boxing the hard-hitting Leach Cross over ten rounds, he faced Abe Attell on 19 February, 1909 over ten rounds at the National Athletic Club in New York. Although the match was made at 125lbs in order to protect Attell's version of the 122lbs world title, American boxing experts generally acknowledged that Attell's reign as world champion was at an end. Tad Dorgan commented: "He didn't knock the American out, but he had such a lead that there was no question as to which was the better man". The Police Gazette account ran: "Jim Driscoll gave Abe Attell an artistic trouncing, and it was generally agreed that Attell won no more than two of the ten rounds, while one was even, but in spite of an agreement that the title should go with the newspaper decision, Attell chose to forget this following the contest. His performance against Attell drew comment from other important sources. He earned the description 'Peerless' from none other than Bat Masterson, the former Marshall of Dodge City – turned sports columnist – who was so impressed by his skills, while Nat Fleischer, the founder of the Ring magazine, believed that Driscoll had easily outpointed Attell and that he was the best featherweight in the world. It is interesting to note that Fleischer lists Driscoll in second place in his list of all-time greats in the featherweight division, with Abe Attell taking third place and Terry McGovern taking the number one spot.

Following the contest Driscoll returned home having promised the sisters of Nazareth House in Cardiff that he would assist with one of their fund-raising events. He had agreed to be back by 1 March, St David's Day to box an exhibition at their fair and he kept his word. The event was a huge success and the sum of £6,000 was raised. This would be significant by present day standards, but the fact that the year was 1909 puts the figure almost beyond belief. Jim was a devout Catholic and cared deeply for the children of Nazareth House, but by returning home he missed out on a return contest with Attell and an opportunity to challenge for the world title. He returned to America in 1910 for a rematch with Attell but sadly, the contest did not materialise.

He was clearly a man of principle and cared deeply for the people of his community. Stories of his generosity abound and he used much of his ring earnings to ease the abject poverty of those around him. There are stories of him providing shoes for young children and of returning to the local butcher-shop several times to provide poultry for the poor at Christmas time.

The year 1909 saw the introduction of the National Sporting Club Challenge Belt, later to become known as the

This famous picture shows three Welshmen with their Lonsdale Belts. From left to right, Driscoll, Tom Thomas and Freddie Welsh

Lonsdale Belt. Freddie Welsh was the first winner in the lightweight division, with Tom Thomas being the first winner at middleweight. In 1910, Jim Driscoll became the first winner in the featherweight division when he stopped Seaman Arthur Hayes in the sixth round on 14 February. This was undoubtedly a golden era for Welsh boxing and a series of photographs showing Driscoll, Thomas and Welsh wearing their respective belts is proof of this.

The contest with Hayes was generally regarded as a mismatch and with Driscoll now aged 29, a match with Owen Moran would have been much more attractive. Hayes was a favourite at the Club, but there were calls for the contest to be stopped in the fourth round and when he went down in the sixth round the referee stopped the contest.

Two months after the Hayes fight, Jim was back at the NSC to face Spike Robson. Driscoll was the consummate stylist and from a tactical point of view Robson needed to take the initiative early on. This was the obvious tactic and Driscoll's eyes began to mark up and there were times when he was visibly shaken. The beginning of the fifth round saw an amazing incident when Robson raced across the ring towards Driscoll and, as the latter side-stepped, Robson gashed his shaven head on Driscoll's chair. This injury gradually took its toll and by the last round Driscoll was in complete control, sending Robson almost through the ropes with a straight right, before flooring him again with another right and bringing the eventful contest to an end.

At the end of the year Jim was matched with Freddie Welsh at the Cardiff Skating Rink. They were good friends and often went to the races together, but it seems that the hype preceding this contest may have soured their relationship somewhat. The spoiling tactics of Welsh annoyed Driscoll, who was finally disqualified for a head-butt in the tenth round of what had been a bad tempered affair. From a financial point of view, Driscoll emerged as the winner, taking £1,500, compared with the £1,000 received by Welsh. This story is borne out by Kitty Flynn, Jim's great niece, who claims that the deal was put in place so that the loser would not lose face.

In January, 1911, Jim Driscoll returned to the NSC for his rematch with Spike Robson. This time, he stopped Robson in the 11th round and thereby took outright possession of the National Sporting Club Challenge Belt. This remains with the family and is taken around to various boxing and charity functions by Mike Flynn, husband of Kitty, who was formerly the landlady of the Royal Oak in Cardiff's Broadway, a virtual shrine in memory of Driscoll. Mike often says that the old boy (Jim) would be pleased to know that the belt is still raising money for good causes.

During 1911, Driscoll was matched with Owen Moran in what was an eagerly awaited clash. Moran was a fighter of the highest quality, but had not managed to win a contest with the Lonsdale Belt at stake. He obviously felt there was more money to be made by boxing in America, where he engaged in two contests with Abe Attell and also boxed Ad Wolgast, an opponent of Freddie Welsh. The contest between Driscoll and Moran had been set for Birmingham, but on the eve of the contest the boxers were hauled before the local magistrates and were both bound over to keep the peace. This meant that the contest could not go ahead and it would be 18 months before they would face each other across the ring. During the early years of the century boxing had struggled for acceptability in the eyes of the law, but as time passed it became less likely that the police would intervene, while Lord Lonsdale and the National Sporting Club were clearly instrumental in overcoming the legal hurdles which faced the sport.

On 3 June, 1912, Jim was matched with Jean Poesy. The Frenchman was a national champion and with Driscoll as British champion, the contest was announced as being for the European title. Driscoll established his superiority from the outset and it soon became clear that Poesy's only chance was to win by knockout, but although he attempted to work on the inside Driscoll was always in control. The Frenchman picked up the pace in the tenth and 11th rounds and a fierce attack in the 12th brought a right from Driscoll which floored Poesy. Seconds later, Driscoll's right landed again and Poesy was counted out.

His long-awaited clash with Owen Moran was set for 27 January, 1913 and, as expected, the NSC was packed, especially since Driscoll had indicated that this would be his final bout. The cheapest tickets were priced at three guineas and by fight-time the club was packed. Obviously Jim wanted to end his career on a high note and looked in good shape, while Moran, on the other hand, looked very confident and was clearly in peak condition. It turned into an absorbing tactical battle, with Driscoll clearly in charge by the half-way stage, before the second half of the contest saw Moran's strength and fitness begin to tell. During the 17th round, Jim was driven around the ring and over the final three rounds he weakened dramatically, so much so

Driscoll stands supreme in Bute Terrace, Cardiff

Wynford Jones

47

that he was almost floored on two occasions. It was only his dogged determination which kept him on his feet and at the final bell, honours were shared.

The year 1914 saw the outbreak of war and along with other eminent sportsmen Driscoll served in the Army, together with Johnny Basham and Jimmy Wilde. When the war ended Jim was short of money and was forced to return to the ring. In March, 1919 he beat Pedlar Palmer at Hoxton Baths in what was a sad spectacle. Palmer had held the British bantamweight championship between 1895 and 1900 and was a big favourite at the National Sporting Club, but those days were now little more than a distant memory. In May, Jim drew with Francis Rossi on points over 20 rounds at the Mountain Ash Pavilion, a cavernous hall, which was also the venue for the contest between Freddie Welsh and Henri Piet for the European lightweight championship in August, 1909. In 1935, it would also host the contest between Tommy Farr and Eddie Phillips for the British light-heavyweight championship.

When Jim was matched with the Frenchman, Charles Ledoux, at the NSC on 20 October, 1919 he was almost 38 years old, while Ledoux, who was handled by Francois Descamps, the manager of Georges Carpentier, was aged 27. Descamps was a shrewd matchmaker and the French camp rejected the initial offer of a 15-round contest and pushed for 20 rounds. The truth of the matter was, that in spite of appearances, Driscoll was already a sick man, but for 14 rounds he gave Ledoux a boxing lesson. However, the visitors had deliberately pushed for a longer contest knowing that Driscoll would have the superior boxing skills, but also believing that, ultimately, youth would prevail. The early rounds were summed up by 'Peggy' Bettinson of the NSC, when he wrote: "It was Driscoll all the time. We often talk and write about the straight left, but we rarely see it as it was introduced and employed by Driscoll on this night. It was wonderful to behold". As the rounds passed, Driscoll did most of the scoring, but he was also beginning to show signs of age. He even floored his younger opponent in the 14th round, but Ledoux rallied in the 15th to have Driscoll in big trouble as the bell sounded to end the round. As they came out for the 16th, Jim was felled by a blow to the heart and the towel was thrown in. Ledoux had prevailed, though he was the first to acknowledge Driscoll's greatness. The contest also left a lasting impression on Bettinson who stated of Driscoll: "He showed us that which we had almost forgotten – that boxing is a wondrous and exacting science." Within a few minutes of the conclusion of the contest, members of the NSC had raised almost £2,000 for Driscoll, but within five years this phenomenal boxing artist with the shoulder-level straight left, right hand drawn back and ghost-like movement in the ring was dead.

On the day of his funeral it is said that over 100,000 people lined the streets of Cardiff as the cortege made its way to Cathays Cemetery. The service took place at St Paul's Church in Tyndall Street and floral tributes arrived from around the world, with both Jim's regiment and the children of Nazareth House figuring prominently in the procession.

Cardiff had never witnessed anything like this before and it is an indication that Jim Driscoll had become something more than a champion boxer. For decades, there had been hostility towards the Irish in Cardiff, partly because Irish workers were prepared to undercut the rates of pay being received by Welsh workers. It led to the Non-Conformist community in Wales holding a deep distrust of Catholicism, but Jim Driscoll seems to have succeeded in bringing the whole community together in a way which few people can ever achieve. The modern day equivalent of this must surely be the way in which Barry McGuigan succeeded in uniting Catholics and Protestants in Ireland during a remarkable career which saw him become featherweight champion of the world during the 1980s, a time when sectarian violence seemed to dominate our newspapers and television screens.

Jim Driscoll understood poverty and clearly did everything in his power to improve the conditions endured by those around him. His charitable deeds and his accomplishments in the boxing ring ultimately touched the lives of so many people. His grave stone was provided by the sisters of Nazareth House, who never forgot Jim's generosity, and his picture still hangs in one of the communal areas there. In recent years a statue in his memory has been placed at the top of Bute Terrace, near where he once lived, thus ensuring that one of Welsh boxing's true greats will always remain very much in our thoughts.

The final resting place in Cathays Cemetery, Cardiff

Wynford Jones

Who Was Young Ahearn?

by K R Robinson

In the early years of the 20th century, Britain's role as Europe's premier boxing nation was challenged by France in the form of one slim, elegant fighter who ruled the roost above 11 stone – Georges Carpentier. However, for a couple of months before the outbreak of World War One, a now forgotten Lancashire-born middleweight was boosted as the saviour of Britain's fistic honour.

Jacob Woodward first saw the light of day at Preston, on 18 December 1892. The Woodwards were of a nomadic bent and young Jake lived in Preston, Bolton, Wigan and Liverpool with a spell in Nottinghamshire, before the family set off for America when he was aged 13. Jake's uncles had been active in the professional ring and Jake followed suit in June 1909, fighting his first recorded bout against Kid Julian at Syracuse, but losing on points over six rounds.

Once in his stride, adopting the name of Young Ahearn, he made regular appearances in New York rings to build up an impressive tally with newspaper verdicts over solid performers such as 'Hop' Harry Stone, Charlie Griffin, Dave Deshler and Grover Hayes. Young Jake was developing into a brilliant boxer with dazzling footwork, which earned him the sobriquet of the 'Brooklyn Dancing Master'. After more than 50 bouts he was matched with Packey McFarland, the crack Chicago lightweight. A veteran of over 70 fights with but one defeat, McFarland toyed with the youngster for eight rounds before dispatching him with a right over the heart.

After a month's rest Jake came back to compile another string of newspaper wins over such as Frank Loughrey, his brother Young Loughrey, Kid Graves, Kid Alberts and Soldier Bartfield, a run marred only by a ten round draw with Ray Temple in New Orleans. This good form saw him paired with the consummate ring mechanic, Jack Britton, on his home ground of Brooklyn.

The importance of this bout was not lost on Jake, who may have over trained when weighing-in light at 136³/₄ lbs, a pull of 1³/₄ lbs over Jack. Easily outboxed by Ahearn in the early rounds, Britton dug deep and powered in to work the body, almost sweeping the 'Dancing Master' out of the ring in the seventh round when Jake was badly staggered by rights to the chin and bundled to the canvas. Jake showed his mettle by battling back to outjab Jack in the closing seconds and then fighting on even terms till the final bell. The *New York Times* commented that: "for speed and cleverness Ahearn was easily Britton's master". The newspaper verdict a draw. So impressed was Jack's manager 'Dumb' Dan Morgan that he took over Jake's management and Ahearn quickly slotted back into his winning ways on the east coast circuit.

Fellow Brooklynite, Al McCoy, or Al Rudolph to give him his straight name, was a tough, free-swinging, aggressive welterweight who was unbeaten after more than 70 fights. He and Jake were matched over ten rounds at St Nicholas Rink, New York on 14 May 1913. What appeared on paper to be a good boxer v slugger fight didn't gel – Jake was a far better boxer than Al was a slugger. Ahearn had Al's number and outboxed him with ease, avoiding his swings, nullifying his aggression and taking the newspaper verdict.

Neither the world's welterweights nor middleweights had an undisputed champion. Foremost amongst the claimants for both titles was Mike Gibbons, the 'St Paul Phantom'. Mike was skilful and elusive, sharp punching and tough. He had moved from Minnesota to east-coast rings in late 1911 and had built up an admirable reputation, facing such as Willie Lewis, Jeff Smith, Londoner Sid Burns and Eddie McGoorty.

Gibbons and Ahearn were matched over ten rounds at Madison Square Garden on 13 June 1913, sharing top billing with Mike's brother Tom, against Jack Denning.

Young Ahearn in fighting pose

Weighing-in at 149lbs, Mike had almost 5lbs on Jake, who held his own in the first couple of rounds, and raised a mouse under Mike's left eye. Mike was content to jab and move till he staggered his opponent midway through the third with a right uppercut to the jaw. A similar blow had the same effect in the fourth and a third knocked Ahearn cold before the round ended. Referee Billy Joh dispensed with the count.

Jake was at a crossroads. He stood head and shoulders above any but the top class – McFarland, Britton and Gibbons, men now considered all-time greats – but seemed to lack the power and durability required to go all the way. After wins over Soldier Bartfield, Bert Fagan and Paddy Sullivan, he relocated to Paris where he came under the management of Dan McKetrick. Dan was a leading player in French boxing, managing Willie Lewis and Joe Jeannette, who were Parisian favourites. After years as cannon fodder for British and American imports, the French had developed some pretty useful fighters of their own. Carpentier, Charles Ledoux and Eugene Criqui were world class and most French champions were now a match for their British counterparts.

Ahearn's initial continental engagement was with the Swiss welterweight, Albert Badoud, over 20 rounds at the Salle Wagram. Badoud had a reputation as a resilient never-say-die competitor with stopping power. This was Jake's first long distance bout and he kept Badoud on the end of his left for round after round. Going into the 18th, Albert appeared to be weakening under withering fire from the Brooklyn dancer, but suddenly unleashed a left swing to the stomach to put Ahearn on the canvas. Rising hurt at the count of nine, Jake took another left to the body and was counted out.

Four weeks later, Ahearn was back in the ring at the Wonderland Francais to face the French welterweight champion, Henri Piet, who was knocked out in seven.

Jake's first bout on English soil was at Liverpool Stadium on 11 December 1913, against Private Johnny Basham of the Royal Welsh Fusiliers over 15 rounds. Well matched for speed and skill, the advantage was first with one and then the other. Basham scored the only knockdown in the first, then concentrated on his opponent's body, while Ahearn showed consistent skill and determination both inside and at long range. Johnny nicked the last two rounds and the verdict, which could have gone either way.

Jake returned to Preston to visit relatives and found himself challenged by local hooligans – or so the *Mirror of Life* tells. Young Woodward faced eight of Preston's best, bare fisted and hobnail booted, on a vacant lot. After dispatching the leader with a few well-placed punches and a kick or two Jake was acknowledged as local champion and peace was restored.

Ahearn now divided his time between Preston and Paris. Gunner Budgen and the 'Fighting Scot', Johnny Mathieson, were beaten at home. In gay Parie, Marcel Thomas was outpointed over 15 rounds and the French lightweight champ, Georges Papin, suffered the same fate. Jake's best win in Europe so far came with his stoppage of Adrien Hogan in 11 rounds. Coming off a 17-round stoppage win

over Pat O'Keefe, Hogan was arguably the best middleweight in France. Carpentier was European champion, having won that title in February 1912, the light-heavy title in February 1913 and the heavies title the following June. Georges had not made 160lbs since October 1912 and claims were made on Young Ahearn's behalf.

Pat O'Keefe was the reigning British middleweight champion and holder of the Lonsdale Belt. A wily old evergreen, Pat was a great favourite at the National Sporting Club and had only begun his second tenure as champion on beating Harry Reeve at the Club on 23 February 1914. He was now matched to defend against the former champion, Jim Sullivan, on 25 May. Having made it known that he would like to contest the title, but never having appeared in London let alone at the Club, Jake was the wild card in the middleweight pack.

The current Club 'pet' was one Private Braddock of the Royal Marines. Charlie Braddock was the archetypal middleweight slugger. He'd cut a swath through the Army and Navy list and his appearances at the Club had been sensational, though the last had resulted in a loss by disqualification to Marcel Moreau. A match between Braddock and Ahearn was a perfect support to the battle of the veterans and was soon arranged. The *Mirror of Life* was sold on Jake.

> "What Ahearn did to Braddock was a caution, the gallant ex-marine, as game and persevering a fighter as ever took the ring, finding Ahearn a 'Will o' the Wisp'. His speed, his science, his coolness, his ducking and hitting startled and electrified the spectators and were too much for the Chatham man, who was all at sea".

Jake's performance was a revelation, especially when compared with the 20 round battle of tactics to decide the British championship won by O'Keefe. Braddock had his only chance early in the ninth when he landed a hard hook to Ahearn's chin. Jake clinched, and having gotten back into the fight by shooting left jabs to the Marine's face, drew Braddock on to a short right uppercut which lifted him from the floor and laid him face down for the count.

Four days after his triumph at the Club, Jake was back in Preston to outpoint Harry Duncan over 15 rounds. He was on a run of seven wins, three inside, since the tight loss to Basham, and a match against O'Keefe for the title seemed a certainty for the Club in the new season. Meanwhile, he could flit between London, Paris and Preston, keeping fit and swelling his bank balance. Whether due to Parisian cuisine or Lancashire hotpot Jake was struggling to make welterweight. At five feet eight and a half inches tall, and still only 22, he seemed destined to be at least a light-heavy if not a heavyweight. For any fighter weighing over 11 stone the dream match was with Carpentier, who currently had his hands full with a challenge for the 'White Heavyweight Championship' against Gunboat Smith of America, booked for Olympia on 16 July.

Dan McKetrick was a very experienced mentor who knew the value of publicity. On 6 June a letter appeared in the *Mirror of Life* above Dan's signature thanking the press and the NSC for their praise of Young Ahearn. Comparing

Jake favourably with Stanley Ketchel, Dan announced that he had been offered a match with Billy Murray for the vacant world middleweight title. Just in passing, Dan flung out challenges to Dick Smith for the British light-heavyweight title and the winner of the upcoming bout between heavyweights, Bombardier Billy Wells and Colin Bell.

Jake next took to the Premierland ring in east London on 15 June to face Algate's Sid Burns. Though recently returned from a tour of Australia, which had concluded with wins over Arthur Evernden and Sid Stagg, Burns was not match fit and was knocked out with a straight left in the second.

* * * * *

Horatio Bottomley was an MP and the editor of *John Bull* – a popularist weekly rag. He was also a swindler and a con-man, who would eventually be convicted of fraud in 1922. Bottomley, who had his fingers on the pulse of public opinion, announced in *John Bull* on 27 June under the headline **A BRITISH BOXER AT LAST!** that the 'all British' Young Ahearn, henceforth to be known as 'John Bull's Boy', was to be matched with Carpentier for the white heavyweight championship on 3 August. Should Georges lose to Gunboat Smith the bout would go ahead with his International Boxing Union world light-heavy-weight title at stake. Horatio would finance the match, making available £10,000 for the purse and expenses, with the boxers sharing a minimum of £6,000.

Wealthy aristocrats and sportsmen had long been involved in the prize-ring as backers and businessmen often adopted the role of promoter with varying success. And the wholesome image projected by Carpentier and Bombardier Billy Wells would gain them lucrative advertising work in the popular press. However, Bottomley's scheme of adopting Ahearn for *John Bull*, extolling Jake's skills and character in his journal and providing risk capital for the promotion must rank as one of the earliest examples of sporting sponsorship, certainly in the British Isles. Horatio's reputation was not untarnished at that point so he used the age old ploy of surrounding himself with men of unimpeachable character. C.B. Cochran, then England's premier promoter who was staging the Carpentier v Smith bout, was appointed to manage the enterprise on a percentage of the gate and Eugene Corri, the respectable stockbroker and referee of the same fight, was named as stakeholder and third man.

Jake relaxed by spending some days walking in Kent before setting up his training camp at the King and Queen Hotel in Brighton. He was joined by sparring partners, Kid Black and Zulu Kid (Mike Flamier), who had sparred Gunboat Smith. A steady stream of boxing personalities, including Freddie Welsh and Jimmy Britt, were attracted to 'London by the sea' to view the new white hope. Veteran boxing scribe A.G. 'Smiler' Hales of the *Daily Sketch* donned the mitts to put Jake through his paces. 'Smiler' declared himself convinced that 'John Bull's Boy' would prove to be Carpentier's master.

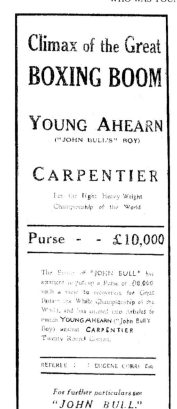

The Gunboat was contracted to be available to take Carpentier's place should the American win and Georges withdraw from the great match. But they need not have worried, Carpentier, always to be a lucky fighter in English rings, won on a disqualification in six rounds.

The match against Ahearn seemed a certain crowd puller. Georges was the perfect gentleman, a courageous and skilled boxer who was always surrounded by controversy and reporters. A year younger than Jake, he was a veteran of the ring, fighting from the age of 13, and had fought in every division from fly to heavy. Carpentier had beaten British champions such as Jack Goldswain, Arthur Evernden, Young Joseph, Jim Sullivan, Bombardier Billy Wells and Pat O'Keefe, though failing against American hard men Dixie Kid, Frank Klaus and Billy Papke.

Ahearn was getting good publicity. The *Mirror of Life* serialised his lifestory and he impressed reporters with his detailed analysis of the contest and his confident, if modest, belief in his own abilities. Bottomley cranked up his ballyhoo machine, with articles on Ahearn among the few with photographs in *John Bull*. Interviews with boxing insiders lauded Jake and his wonderful skills. Not only would 'our boy' beat Carpentier, he would eventually bring the undisputed heavyweight title back home to England by defeating the black champion, Jack Johnson.

The fight was set for Monday 17 August at the Shepherd's Bush Stadium, prices from one shilling to ten guineas. The stadium, capacity 25,000, had never previously been sold out. Cochran was putting together a first-class bill, featuring the tiny Welsh sensation, unbeaten Jimmy Wilde against Young Joe Symonds of Plymouth – his toughest test to date. The First World War had broken out on 4 August and Bottomley, true to his popularist creed, declared that the promotion would be in aid of the War Distress Fund.

Suddenly, the whole promotion was cast into turmoil when Carpentier quit training and returned home to France to volunteer. Strangely, Bottomley hosted a farewell luncheon at the Hotel Metropole for the departing fighter, who expressed his hope that the match would not be long delayed. Jake shook Georges' hand as he boarded the train.

Since his defeat by Carpentier, Gunboat Smith had kept in training and now had a chance to move back into contention. Cochran and Bottomley approached Smith's manager, Jim Buckley, and an agreement was reached for the American to take Carpentier's place on the same financial terms. *John Bull* featured Smith and the story of his career – particularly his recent 12-round points win over the great Sam Langford.

On Thursday 13 August, Ahearn finished his heavy training. He kept loose on Friday and went sea-bathing on Saturday, but by the next morning was diagnosed as suffering from a chill or an attack of acute muscular rheumatism. His physician, Dr Sharlow, insisted that he could not fight and the contest was postponed. Promotion manager Cochran sent out sandwich-boardmen to walk the major London thoroughfares announcing the postponement,

telegrams were sent to Preston to prevent the departure of Jake's fans, press agencies were alerted and advertisements were placed in Monday's newspapers.

Buckley and McKetrick met with Bottomley and Cochran to discuss the situation. Buckley agreed for the bout to be re-scheduled for Monday 24 and Bottomley gave a cheque for £100 to cover Smith's extra expenses. Informed of the agreement by his manager, Gunboat Smith started packing, while voicing his doubts that Ahearn would be ready to fight. Though confronted by Cochran and offered a £500 forfeit against the non-appearance of his opponent, the Gunboat was adamant. He sailed for America with Buckley, the £100, without paying his own forfeit and leaving Bottomley £5,000 out of pocket.

Why had Smith gone? asked *John Bull*. No satisfactory answer was forthcoming, but rumours abounded. Carpentier was the crowd puller, whatever the skills and accomplishments of Smith or Ahearn. Cochran had queried the viability of the promotion even with Carpentier and perhaps without the star of the show Bottomley himself engineered the cancellation. Cochran received £400 when the show was cancelled. It is not recorded if Jake received a similar consideration.

Now fit and raring to go, Ahearn needed a title. Bottomley and McKetrick put their heads together and determined to push Jake forward for a bout against Pat O'Keefe for the middleweight championship and Lonsdale Belt. Dick Smith, the light-heavyweight beltholder, and Bandsman Dick Rice were also prime targets. Meantime, Jake took to the music hall stage with a short tour in the north, starting at Stockport then on to Wakefield and Middlesbrough, in company with his sparring partners, George Marchant and Harry Smith.

However, all thoughts of big fights soon faded from view. The NSC was rumored to be closing it's doors until the New Year. Pat O'Keefe had become Rifleman O'Keefe, attached to the 1st Surrey Rifles; Dick Smith, Bandsman Rice, Bombardier Wells and indeed every fighter of note, was joining up.

On 19 September Young Jake Ahearn, with his wife and father-in-law, accompanied by Mr and Mrs Dan McKetrick, boarded the 'Philadelphia' at Liverpool and sailed for New York.

While Jake had been away his old opponent, Al McCoy, had laid claim to the world's middleweight title with a smashing 45-second knockout win over George Chip. Chip had claimed the title by way of a pair of wins over Frank Klaus, who in turn had outclassed Carpentier in Paris. Poor Al never gained the support of even his hometown fans, being dubbed the 'Cheese Champ' and regularly hooted and catcalled when in the ring. Jake was convinced that the title was his for the taking, but wins in Europe meant little in New York and it was the loss to Mike Gibbons that loomed large in the ordinary fan's memory.

On 31 October, Ahearn outclassed Freddie Wicks and forced him to retire after six rounds in New York, Jake's first bout in the States for 12 months. Next in line were tough and skilful Leo Houck and hard-punching Buck Crouse, both outpointed in Philadelphia over six rounds by newspaper decision. Ringsiders noted that, as a middleweight, Jake was more aggressive and harder punching.

Jack Dillon of Indiana, the 'Giant Killer', was a leading contender and title claimant for both the middleweight and light-heavyweight championships. Dillon was a very dangerous man, particularly if out-weighed by a couple of stone or three – he just loved to beat up the big guys. Ahearn was matched with Jack for Philadelphia on 1 January 1915. The *Philadelphia Inquirer's* headlines summed up the match with the heading:

"AHEARN'S CLEVERNESS SMOTHERS DILLON:
Englishman Gives Wonderful Exhibition of His
Ability to Sidestep and Duck.
Jack Lands Smash to Face in Fifth That Nearly
Ended Bout at the Olympic"

Those ringsiders who appreciated scientific boxing had Jake as the winner while those who relished aggression and big punching called it for Jack. The newspaper consensus was a draw in a match made at 165lbs ringside, with Dillon weighing 164 and Ahearn 156. Dillon's middleweight claims faded with this match, but Ahearn's claims to middleweight recognition were strengthened and tenuous claims were directed at the light heavyweight title.

In a contest billed for the 160lbs title, Jake eliminated the aging Willie Lewis with a two round kayo in Havana, Cuba, before going back to Philadelphia where he outclassed a leading contender, Jimmy Clabby, over six rounds. The *Philadelphia Inquirer* waxed lyrical over Jake:

"Young Ahearn [is] as good as any middleweight in the world. He beat Clabby up more in six rounds than Mike Gibbons had been able to do in ten. …he accomplished it with such ridiculous ease, he is now being called a second Kid McCoy [Norman Selby]. There was that same icy, expressionless face, showing no emotion in even the most terrific exchanges; no blows wasted; that cruel sneer of contempt …and above all, the extreme confidence in his own ability".

Panama Joe Gans was then beaten over ten rounds at home in Brooklyn. All these matches were defenses of his title claim. Jake then twice gave away a stone to Leo Houck at Brooklyn and Albany and took ten-round newspaper verdicts in both.

Jake's ambitions to fight heavyweights were satisfied when he faced Boer Rodel over ten rounds at Brighton Beach, New York on 24 July 1915. He won handily enough but didn't have the firepower to worry the South African, who lacked the speed and skills to nail a man he outweighed by 23lbs.

Ahearn's form as a middleweight since his return from Europe had been a revelation and he was rated a clear contender for McCoy's championship. Al, a tough and awkward southpaw, had a dangerous left swing, as George Chip had discovered, but it was so wild and inaccurate that

few succumbed. In this era of the no-decision bout, since succeeding Chip as champion McCoy had risked his title on 16 occasions with seven wins, seven losses and two draws. Until knocked out by an opponent weighing within the 158lbs US limit, Al was safe.

Ahearn gained his chance when matched with the champion over ten rounds at Ebbet's Field, Brooklyn on 9 September 1915. Jake was reported to be recently recovered from a serious illness and scarcely in condition for the challenge. If further incentive was required, Jake had received an offer from Australia to face Les Darcy should he win. The weights were announced as Young Ahearn 154lbs, McCoy 157$\frac{1}{2}$lbs, meaning the title was on the line. Ahearn boxed with caution, but great skill, winning each of the first seven rounds by a margin. McCoy's southpaw stance proved no problem for Jake, who slotted in fast and accurate left jabs to the head, followed by jolting right crosses. The 'Dancing Master' opened up in the last three rounds pouring on the punishment, battering the champion with punches to the head, opening a cut over his right eye and staggering him with rights. Jake slugged it out with the tiring champion through the ninth and tenth, ignoring Al's punches, hitting him hard and fast and inflicting more facial damage. Try as he might Jake couldn't find the punch to bring McCoy to the canvas and the half-blinded titleholder survived to the final bell. Ahearn won the newspaper decision and the headlines.

Without a knockout victory, the trip to Australia was off and Jake had to content himself with a defense of his title claim against old sparring partner Zulu Kid. At New York on 16 October the Kid lasted the distance to lose the newspaper vote.

Four more ten round bouts in New York, including a defense of his title claim against Kid Wagner on 25 November led to a return with McCoy on New Year's day 1916, again on homeground in Brooklyn. The champ had risked his title, losing to Silent Martin and getting draws with Soldier Bartfield and Zulu Kid, all by newspaper verdicts, since their last meeting. If anything, Jake's win was more emphatic than his previous victory. In a change of tactics he targeted Al's body and punished the champion unmercifully, despite McCoy's attempts to clinch and spoil. Outpaced and outpunched throughout, the champ would have been humiliated but for his indomitable courage and determination. In the eighth round, McCoy landed a hard left swing to Ahearn's body only for his tormentor to up his pace and slug it out to the end.

If Al McCoy was the champion by succession, Mike Gibbons was probably the best middleweight then active. Mike's win over Ahearn in 1913 had been overwhelming and, even had Jake beaten McCoy decisively, with that loss on his record he could never claim to be champ. However, a knockout win over Gibbons might give Jake sufficient public support to successfully adopt the mantle of champion.

The return fight had been arranged for 10 December, prior to the McCoy bout, but was postponed when Mike claimed a cold. Jake and Mike had met on 8 December to agree a referee and after shaking hands with Gibbons Jake remarked to Dan McKetrick, in Mike's hearing: "Gibbons is a bundle of nerves. I wouldn't be surprised if he flunked out of the fight". A couple of hours later Gibbons told the promoter that he was ill. McKetrick's remark that Mike had 'cold feet' was widely circulated.

Re-scheduled for 18 January, the pair met in Mike's hometown at the St Paul Auditorium before the largest crowd ever till then gathered together for a boxing match in the State of Minnesota. Billed as being for the middleweight championships of England and America, both men weighed well inside the 158lbs limit.

The bout started at a trot with each man landing fast but light punches at long range, feinting and shifting and not punching in the clinches. If anything, Mike appeared the faster and more confident but nobody was getting hurt. Half way through the first round the pair were sparring in a neutral corner when Mike feinted with his left and then sent in a terrific short right which landed flush on Jake's jaw. Ahearn fell backwards to the canvas, tried to rise at three, then lapsed into unconsciousness as the referee tolled the ten count. Helped to his corner by Mike and the referee it was many minutes before Jake came to. Mike Gibbons was not a fighter who strived for knockouts. He would just as well display his skills and send his fans home satisfied in the knowledge that they's seen just about the cutest slugger there ever was.

Jake didn't have to wait long for a chance to re-establish his position when he was matched with George Chip over six rounds at Brooklyn's Broadway Sporting Club on 22 February. Chip had had a fair measure of support as champion before his upset loss to McCoy and apart from McCoy only the top flight had beaten him – Crouse, Dillon, Jeff Smith, Houck and Clabby. Though tough and aggressive, George was not considered the world's greatest puncher.

For two rounds Chip pressed ahead with a hooking attack mostly aimed at Jake's chin. Ahearn's defensive skills were to the fore as he used fast left jabs and right swings to keep George at bay and 'tie' him up when he came close. Chip's heavier punching spelled danger, but he was wild and Jake was boxing at his best. Round three followed the same pattern till a heavy left swing from George caught Jake on the jaw and floored him as he backed on to the ropes. Rising at the count of nine, Ahearn easily avoided Chip's awkward follow up and soon regained his rhythm with George being made to miss at the bell.

Round four proved to be the last. Chip had Jake trapped on the ropes but was being frustrated by Ahearn's effective defense. George wrenched his left fist free and scythed in a hook to the body which landed hard in Jake's groin. Referee John Hauckop leapt in, parted the men and called on the doctor to examine Jake and pass judgement, whereupon Ahearn was declared to have been incapacitated and made the popular winner. Though by all accounts the decision was correct, Jake gained little credit.

After a routine ten rounder against Zulu Kid, Jake again faced Al McCoy in the fourth and final bout of their series. Since their last encounter Al had risked his title on three occasions, including a ten-round newspaper loss to Chip. Meeting at Brooklyn on 9 May, Jake once again outclassed his opponent. Ahearn doubled up a right to the stomach with another to the jaw in the fourth to stagger McCoy, but although he rained rights and lefts on the champion's chin he was unable to land a finisher. Had he done so the title would not have changed hands as both were overweight. In four meetings with McCoy, Jake had lost hardly a round but never gained an official victory.

On 23 August, Jake fought Jack Blackburn at Philadelphia on what was a six round no-decision bout. Jack had fought Joe Gans, Sam Langford, Joe Grim, 'Philadelphia' Jack O'Brien and half a dozen other legends before serving time for manslaughter and this was only his fourth bout in nine years. The *Philadelphia Inquirer* wasted few words on the contest:

> "Jack Blackburn, of this city, handed Young Ahearn of England a beating in the windup at the Special Show... last night. Young Ahearn did not have a round to him".

After another workout against the Zulu Kid, Ahearn renewed acquaintance with Blackburn over ten rounds at the Harlem Sporting Club on 8 September. For seven rounds it was reported that the skills displayed by both men were barely third rate. However, Jake showed some of his real ability in the final three rounds, while Jack engaged in spoiling tactics and the crowd made it clear it's displeasure. Jake was the newspaper winner, while 'Chappie' Blackburn would later gain boxing immortality as the trainer and mentor to Joe Louis.

Sadly, Jake was now on the slide. He was still winning his fair share of fights, but against the top flight his lack of punch resistance was letting him down. Back-to-back knockout defeats against Harry Greb and Jeff Smith spelt the end of Jake as a contender.

On 2 April 1917 at Pittsburgh, Greb knocked him out in a round with a short, chopping right to the jaw, while Jake was off balance due to a slip. To add insult to injury, Horatio Bottomley announced shortly after that Young Ahearn was no longer 'John Bull's Boy' due to his refusal to return to England and join the fight against the Kaiser.

Globetrotting Jeff Smith turned the trick in five rounds at New Orleans on 23 April. Jake outpointed Jeff for four rounds then, coming out of a clinch, Smith slipped a left hook under his elbow and into his short ribs. Counted out, Ahearn suffered agonies for 20 minutes while doctors worked on him.

Jake continued boxing for another four years without ever regaining championship form. Contemporary reports suggest that 'Young' Ahearn at his best was an outstanding boxer who was both brave and confident. Although he was blessed with shrewd management and had chances to prove himself against the top contenders, he twice failed to win the championship from the tough, but limited, Al McCoy. Judged by the form he displayed in Europe, but tempered by his lack of experience over the 20 rounds championship distance, he might have relieved Pat O'Keefe of his middleweight championship, but victory over Carpentier would doubtless have been beyond him.

From Stage-fighting Fame to the Gallows at Tyburn: James Field - Pugilist and Criminal

by Tony Gee

Today his name is mostly only known to specialist art historians (for reasons explained later in this article), but in the Broughtonian era of the prize-ring James Field earned both fistic fame and criminal notoriety before his life ended prematurely, in 1751, on the gallows. A strong indication that, in some quarters at least, it was thought that the latter reputation was an inevitable consequence of the former can be seen from the following derogatory comment relating to pugilists, which appeared in the *London Daily Advertiser* less than two years after Field had been put to death at Tyburn:

> It is a Thing known to every body, that when these Fellows have fought all the GREAT MEN in that Way, they have nothing to do, after they have spent what Money they got, as they are soon out of Date, but, like FIELD, to plunder his Majesty's Subjects, and then put their Country to the Trouble and Expence [sic] of hanging them, except by some lucky Accident they go off a quicker Way.

(Previously, shortly before Field was hanged, the *Penny London Post; or, the Morning Advertiser*'s seemingly tongue-in-cheek suggestion of a memorial match for the doomed pugilist had included a statement that Broughton's Amphitheatre – usually advertised to have been "in [London's] Oxford-Road" – had the "Reputation of being a Nursery for Tyburn", a place strongly associated with public executions.)

Since newspapers of the period had a tendency to refer to combatants in connection with their current or former occupations, it is logical to assume that a linking of 'Sailor' with Field's name during his fighting career indicated that he had spent some time at sea. It can be said that from the time he came to notice on the London fistic scene (although an infrequent protagonist compared with various other well-known men competing in bareknuckle stage contests then being promoted regularly and legally in amphitheatres and booths), Field met some of the best fighters of his day. (Jack Broughton, the age's predominant pugilistic figure, was the most obvious exception.) However, as I pointed out in my book on the London prize-ring, *Up to Scratch*, which contained much new information on a notable opponent of Field, Benjamin Boswell, the former has been even more inexplicably ignored by ring historians than the latter. The renowned 19th century chronicler of the sport Pierce Egan, for instance, wrote a mere paragraph on Boswell but included only one oblique reference to Field in what is usually recognised as his definitive work on the subject.

Field's first major pugilistic battle in the metropolis seems to have occurred against Boswell on 15 November 1743 at the "Great Booth at Tottenham-Court". This event also appears to have been his stage-fighting debut. Nevertheless, Field's advertised brag that he would "give the Gentlemen who shall honour us with their Presence an agreeable Satisfaction" was not found to be wanting, the underdog beating his noted adversary in a contest described by the *Daily Advertiser* as "one of the sharpest that has been for a considerable time". Since Boswell had previously registered at least one victory over George Taylor (then considered second only to Broughton), this was an impressive success by Field against a fighter known for his "Jaw-breaking Talent". Incidentally, at a later date he claimed to have beaten Boswell in "two Engagements".

The two most renowned opponents of Field were Taylor and Broughton's future conqueror, Jack Slack. An encounter with the former, again at the Great Booth, was Field's reward for (as boasted in a notice for the event) "lately beating the noted Mr. Boswell, without any Difficulty". The *Daily Advertiser*, briefly mentioning the forthcoming occasion, to take place on Wednesday, 7 December, made reference to both the general consensus of opinion that the confrontation would be an extremely hard fought one and the considerable amount of money having been wagered on the result. However, that publication does not appear to have subsequently reported the fight. This is hardly surprising since, as explained in *Up to Scratch* and my article on Slack in *The British Boxing Board of Control Yearbook 1999*, whilst advertisements for stage contests regularly appeared in newspapers, accounts of such affairs were infrequent. Some idea of the outcome, though, can nevertheless be ascertained from a mention three days afterwards in the *Daily Advertiser* when it informed its readers that another match had been arranged, to occur on the 20th of the same month at Broughton's Amphitheatre, between Field and Taylor, "who fought last Wednesday a terrible Battle for twenty Minutes". (Incidentally, the newspaper stated that the forthcoming set-to was to be for £100 – five times the amount mentioned in the advertisement for their previous engagement.) Thereafter, a notice for the event on the 20th included Field's claim that, although recently defeated by Taylor, it had been "with great Difficulty". Their second encounter obviously also ended in a victory for Taylor, since when a third was advertised, to take place on 13 March of the next year at the Great Booth, both losses (albeit each said to have lasted 18 minutes) were blamed by Field on "not [being] used to the Stage".

Slack had also suffered defeat at the hands of Taylor on at least two occasions before he fought Field at Broughton's Amphitheatre on 9 February 1749. In one of their contests Taylor had sustained a burst blood vessel during a "very doubtful and bloody" confrontation before managing to prevail over Slack, in front of what the *Penny London Post* described as a "great Concourse of People of Fashion". The Field v Slack set-to was another match which obviously would have had an appeal to a select audience, for it was advertised that "By particular Desire, the Matted Gallery will be kept for Persons of Distinction". Those from the upper echelons of society who chose to witness the spectacle would not have been disappointed since the "very long battle", the *Gentleman's Magazine, and Historical Chronicle* noted, consisted of "sheer boxing" in which there was a complete absence of "hugging" or "standing still". Although Field was eventually forced to succumb, he would no doubt have emerged from the encounter with his reputation enhanced from having so keenly contested with an adversary of Slack's calibre. (As shown in both my *Yearbook* article on Slack and my more recent one on the pugilist for the *Oxford Dictionary of National Biography*, the victor was considerably more experienced and competitive at the top level prior to his conquest of Broughton than has been generally recognised.) It seems as though Field and Slack faced one another at other times besides the above mentioned. They were certainly scheduled to fight on additional occasions in the two years before that of 1750, when Slack's career reached its zenith and Field's downfall commenced.

The range of Field's criminal activities appears to have been quite extensive, Justice Fielding having granted several warrants against him for "Robberies on the Highway, Burglaries, Rescues, and other Crimes". (According to the historian G M Trevelyan, the "novelist Henry Fielding and his remarkable half-brother Sir John, who was blind from birth, were the best magistrates London had in the [18th] century". The period in question points to the Justice being, in this case, the former.) The arrest which led to Field's appearance on the gallows occurred at an alehouse in London's Drury Lane on 6 December 1750, and was widely reported. The *London Evening-Post* and the *Penny London Post*, for instance, both contained almost the same full details of his capture and then a similar corrected and more comprehensive account one week later. Comparing the original and amended versions, it is disappointing to note that Field's apparently valiant resistance with his fists (as befitted a pugilist of his standing), related in the former, was described quite differently, and less heroically, in the latter. Initially, he was stated to have "exercised his old Trade of bruising" and knocked down two soldiers, before others came to their assistance. However, it was later said that, when soldiers closed with Field after he drew a pistol, he broke the finger of one and struck another in the eye with the weapon, and was then overpowered.

The following day Field was committed to Newgate Prison (although it should be noted that the occasional newspaper, when taking the information from others at a slightly later time, neglected to change the date accordingly). On 8 December the *Daily Advertiser* reported that Field's trial would take place "This Day", but on the 10th the publication stated that it had been prevented and would now "certainly come on this Morning". In fact, Field was not tried until the next Sessions began at the Old Bailey Sessions House on 16 January 1751, when he was condemned to death for having robbed one David Woodman of a pair of spectacles, a tobacco box, a handkerchief, and 13 shillings, near Moorfields. This was despite having previously impeached 28 members of the gang to which he

had belonged, as reported shortly after his arrest. (Several of his accomplices, incidentally, were captured at Hockley in the Hole, a place long associated with public diversions including fistic contests.) Field was one of 13 criminals who received a death sentence at the Sessions. Richard Adams, the Recorder of the City of London, made his "Report of the Malefactors under Sentence of Death in Newgate" to his "Majesty in Council" on 5 February, when Field was amongst ten men "ordered for Execution" on the 11th. He was duly hanged on that day, having been taken from the prison to Tyburn with his legs chained together since there were fears that his fellow pugilists might attempt to rescue him. Two boys were apparently apprehended for picking pockets at the scene (the considerable crowds at these extremely popular 'entertainments' providing potentially lucrative spoils); it is reasonable to assume that they would have been back at Tyburn as main participants on a future execution day.

Press coverage, such as that mentioned above, of Field's passage to the gallows was not merely confined to the metropolis. Provincial newspapers also considered it of sufficient interest to warrant subsequent reporting (under news from London). A full analysis would prove rather tedious, but some extant examples include the *Bath Journal*; *Derby Mercury*; *Gloucester Journal*; *Ipswich Journal*; *Kentish Post, or Canterbury News-Letter*; *Leedes Mercury* [sic]; *Newcastle Journal*; *Western Flying-Post; or, Sherborne and Yeovil Mercury*; and the *Worcester Journal*. Of these, one third contained five items relating to Field, beginning with his December 1750 arrest (which included his being committed to Newgate) and ending with his February 1751 hanging. Although less than half of the remainder detailed the former, all but one covered the latter (**Fig 1**).

	a	b	c	d	e
Bath Journal	-	✓	✓	✓	✓
Derby Mercury	✓	✓	✓	✓	✓
Gloucester Journal	-	-	✓	✓	✓
Ipswich Journal	✓	✓	✓	✓	✓
Kentish Post	✓	✓	✓	✓	✓
Leedes Mercury	-	✓	-	✓	✓
Newcastle Journal	✓	✓	-	-	-
Western Flying-Post	-	-	-	✓	✓
Worcester Journal	✓	-	✓	✓	✓
		*	*		

a. Arrested, etc; b. Impeached Gang Members; c. Sentenced to Death; d. Ordered for Execution; e. Hanged.

1. *Table analysing the coverage in some provincial newspapers of James Field's criminal downfall.*

As was usual when a well-known person was hanged, Field's purported life story found its way into print. A pamphlet sold for 3d, *The Bruiser knock'd down: or, Jemmy on his Back*, was publicised as being first available on 6 February. It was obviously an immediate commercial success as by the actual day of Field's execution a second edition had been published. Advertisements in the *Penny London Post* for both editions contained an apt comment attributed to Field, namely "They have knock'd me down; – this is the hardest Cross-Buttock I ever had in my Life".

Unfortunately, though, no known copies of the pamphlet now appear to exist. However, another one, albeit relating to all the ten men hanged on the 11th (namely the Ordinary of Newgate's account), has survived, and can be seen at The Honourable Society of King's Inns Library, Dublin, and Guildhall Library, Corporation of London. Priced at 6d, this was advertised as going on sale on 14 February, and including "some Memoirs of the remarkable Life of James Field", although more attention was given to the "very extraordinary Life of Mr. Parsons" (executed for returning from transportation).

Such popular publications were not especially known for their reliability. Certainly the claim in the account by John Taylor, the Newgate Prison Ordinary (or chaplain), that Field participated in many contests was not reflected in contemporary newspaper notices and, even allowing for the possibility that not all his fights were publicised in that manner, the earlier observation regarding his comparative lack of pugilistic activity remains a valid one. Likewise, the statement that "in his bruising Capacity here in *England*, (so much in Vogue now-a-Days, and followed by all Ranks) we don't find there is much to be said to his Praise" seems rather harsh, bearing in mind, for instance, the complimentary comments made in the press relating to Field's battles with Boswell, Taylor, and Slack. However, assertions such as that Field was a native of Dublin and had been to sea (particularly the latter given, as previously observed, the 'Sailor' references linked to his name) were far more likely to have had a basis in truth. Also, a mention of an advertisement that "he [Field] published soon after he was apprehended, [in which] he never would own a Fact [of guilt], lest he should destroy that Innocence he then pretended to", was in all probability a notice that appeared in the *Daily Advertiser* (although it did not deny his criminal activities but merely disputed the circumstances relating to his arrest and his impeaching gang members).

As mentioned at the beginning of the article, it is mostly specialist art historians who are likely to be familiar with Field's name. This is because it appeared twice in William Hogarth's series of four prints on the subject of cruelty of 1751, certainly evidence of Field's notoriety given that Sheila O'Connell, Assistant Keeper of the Department of Prints and Drawings, British Museum, has likened low-priced prints to today's tabloid newspapers. (The series, as she observed, was "one of a number of works of the period that Hogarth aimed at a wider audience than was usual for him". When advertised, it was stated that he had published them "in the cheapest Manner possible".)

In the street scene depicted in the 'Second Stage of Cruelty', a sign on the wall, above one for cock-fighting, clearly advertised a contest between Field and Taylor at Broughton's Amphitheatre. Although foremost Hogarthian expert Ronald Paulson has professed to being unaware of whether the two men ever fought, as shown above they definitely did on more than one occasion. There is, of course, no way of telling categorically if Hogarth actually knew this, but given the extensive knowledge reflected in his work (including an apparent interest in pugilism), it is almost certain that he did.

The last print in the series, 'The Reward of Cruelty' **(Fig 2)**, contained the name "James Field" above one of two skeletons hanging in the background of a scene depicting

2. *William Hogarth's 1751 print 'The Reward of Cruelty', with Field's name topically appearing above the skeleton on the left in the background of the depicted dissection scene.*

the dissection of the body of a criminal following execution. (When referring to the skeleton, a 1768 publication, *Hogarth Moralized*, said to be sold at the house of the artist's widow, described Field as "the noted bruiser", a "notorious" fellow whose death occurred at the end of a rope.) Interestingly, the early state of the print held by the British Museum (and featured in a major 250th anniversary exhibition, 'London 1753') shows that Hogarth originally intended the skeleton to have been that of 'Gentleman Harry', Henry Sim(m)s. Described by the *London Evening-Post* as a "notorious Offender" when capitally convicted for highway robbery in February 1747, Simms was hanged in the June; both that newspaper and the *General Evening Post* observed that before he left Newgate he removed and gave away his footwear "to avoid a Reflection often thrown upon him, that he was born to die in his Shoes". The skeleton opposite (in both the early state and the published one) was a representation of the body of James Maclaine (other spellings included Macleane, as used by Hogarth). Maclaine, who stated at his trial that he was the son of a clergyman, was the gentleman highwayman, hanged in October 1750, whose victims included the writer Horace Walpole.

Although the date given on both the early and published states of 'The Reward of Cruelty' was 1 February 1751, it can be seen from various newspaper advertisements that the series was not available until well into the month – in fact, the 21st. (This is evident from notices in, for instance, the *London Evening-Post*, the *General Advertiser*, and the *Daily Advertiser*, although a tendency in advertisements for 'this day' to be stated for the date of publication after the actual event can be confusing. Incidentally, the same pattern was perceived with those relating to the earlier mentioned pamphlets, a reasonable assumption being that it was primarily to save on the cost of new typesetting.) The later date of 21 February would have allowed Hogarth more than enough time to be sure that Field was neither reprieved nor rescued (or even conceivably resuscitated after hanging) before he made what Ronald Paulson considered must have been a "last-minute change to catch the popular reaction".

Hogarth, however, could well have taken artistic licence with 'The Reward of Cruelty' by his naming of both the skeletons on display in the dissection scene. Certainly, with regard to Maclaine, if newspapers such as the *General Advertiser* and the *Penny London Post* were correct, it appears that he was buried at Uxbridge. Field, too, may have avoided the unwelcome fate of succumbing to the surgeon after execution, for the inference in the *London Evening-Post* and the *Country Journal or the Craftsman*, for example, was that he was taken away from Tyburn to be interred. (According to Simon Chaplin, Curator of the Museums of the Royal College of Surgeons of England, there is no record of Field's body being dissected at the Company of Surgeons, although this does not preclude the possibility of it having taken place elsewhere.) Given, though, as observed by Sheila O'Connell, that Hogarth's "interest would have been in naming well-known criminals in order to attract an audience, rather than in recording history", any artistic licence is understandable.

To conclude, a brief comment about the end of the period in which Field was pugilistically active. Although it has been said that the Broughtonian era finished with Broughton's defeat by Jack Slack in 1750, the closure of his amphitheatre did not in fact follow the contest as is usually stated, it remaining in existence for over three years afterwards. By August 1754, however, the *Gentleman's Magazine* was lamenting the "cruelty of that law, which has shut up our amphitheatres"; the circumstances under which Field had acquired his fistic fame would never be repeated. The next time regular pugilistic promotions would take place in established sporting venues without threat from the law, bouts would be governed by regulations less rudimentary than Broughton's Rules and, of course, fists would be encased by padded gloves.

The author would like to thank Sheila O'Connell for her kind help in the preparation of this article and, together with Elizabeth Einberg of the Paul Mellon Centre for Studies in British Art, for proofreading same.

UP TO SCRATCH
Bareknuckle Fighting and Heroes of the Prize-ring
by Tony Gee

An acclaimed anecdotal history of the London prize-ring containing a wealth of material never previously appearing in book form and extensively researched from contemporary sources.

'Fascinating subject matter and meticulous research make *Up to Scratch* a lively and educational read'.
The Ring

Published by QUEEN ANNE PRESS, Windmill Cottage, Mackerye End, Harpenden, Herts., AL5 5DR. TEL: 01582 715866.   E-mail: stephenson@lennardqap.co.uk. Price £12.99.

If you are interested in Tony Gee's next book, on bareknuckle fighting in Scotland (again primarily researched from contemporary sources), contact the publisher, as above, to receive prior information regarding availability.

DISCLAIMER

The Bare Knuckle Record Book has been published in Poland by Jan Skotnicki fraudulently using my name as author. This book was not compiled by me and I completely disassociate myself from it. I wish to place on record that apart from providing minor help to Bill Matthews, who assisted Skotnicki, I had nothing whatsoever to do with this publication, and the only part of my work it contains is information taken, ignoring my express wishes, from my book *Up to Scratch* (and an earlier article that I wrote for the *Yearbook*).

Although Skotnicki had previously used my name in conjunction with others and also spuriously claimed that records were corrected by Bill Matthews and myself, I did not think (in retrospect unwisely) that either matter was worth contesting. However, a book of records purporting to have been compiled by me, which contains numerous inaccuracies and perpetuates many of the prize-ring myths and half-truths that I have always worked so hard to dispel, cannot be allowed to appear unchallenged under my name.

Tony Gee

Home and Away with British Boxers, 2004-2005

by John Jarrett

JULY

This month had a lovely start and an explosive ending, with not much in between. But it was summer, after all. In Cardiff, the Board of Control celebrated its 75th anniversary with a dinner at City Hall and you couldn't walk two paces without bumping into a former British champion. Over 300 had been tracked down and invited and if they didn't all respond it was their loss. I was lucky enough to be at the 50th and I made this one as well. So what if I miss the Centenary bash?

One man who missed this one was Brixton heavyweight, Danny Williams, training in New York City for his fight with Mike Tyson, scheduled for Louisville, Kentucky. It was the chance of a lifetime for Danny, a former British and Commonwealth champion, who hadn't been setting any fires of late. He had crashed against Sinan Samil Sam when challenging for the European championship and blown his British and Commonwealth titles against former victim, Michael Sprott. With a couple of knockover jobs since to take his pro log to 31-3 (26 inside), Williams was offered the fight against Tyson in Ali's hometown. On paper it looked a helluva long shot for the likeable Londoner. Tyson, even at 38, was still a power

to reckon with, especially in the early rounds. That power had taken Mike to 44 knockouts of one sort or another in 50 winning fights and most reckoned it would still be enough to see Danny off.

But Mr Williams was up for this one, hammered into fine condition by Jim McDonnell, and when Tyson roared from his corner for round one, Danny was ready. He took some good shots and was still there at the bell. Mike still had some stuff left and he took rounds two and three. In round four, however, Danny leapt into action with a shocking all-out assault that suddenly wrecked Tyson and dropped him by the ropes. It was all over, Danny Williams from old London Town was the new face of heavyweight boxing. After the fight, Evander Holyfield said he thought for three rounds that Mike looked the best he had in years. But in the fourth round, Danny Williams looked the best he ever had been since putting on gloves, and it couldn't have happened to a nicer fellow.

It wasn't so good the next day for Julius Francis, who had won and lost to Williams in British and Commonwealth title bouts. Julius went to Stuttgart, in Germany, as a late sub to box the unbeaten Ukranian prospect, Aleksander Dimitrenko. Francis hauled his 19st

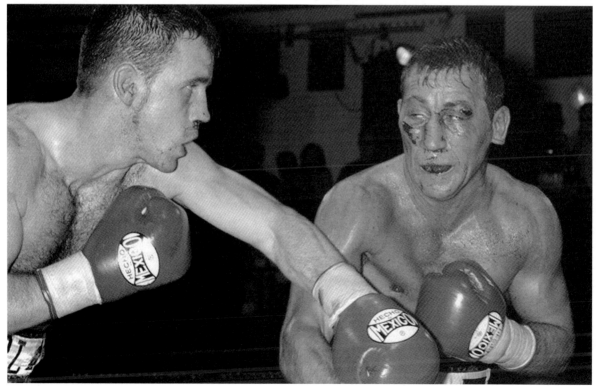

In a rematch, Graham Earl (left) yet again stopped Steve Murray, this time in the sixth round of a British lightweight title bout

Les Clark

4lbs frame around for eight rounds as this 'Aleksander the Great' took his record to 15-0 with a unanimous decision. "I had only one day sparring, no more," said Julius as he came out of the ring.

Sticking with the heavies, Wayne Llewelyn lost his big chance when forced to pull out of a fight with former world champ, Hasim Rahman, in Rochester, New York, due to a virus. Big John McDermott, with an English title bout against Mark Krence on his dance card, didn't impress in his second comeback fight although he got the knockout over Armenian import, Suren Kalachyan, who went down and out in round seven at York Hall. And, happy to be out of it all, Lennox Lewis became a father when his partner, Violet Chang, presented him with a son.

Big puncher Enzo Maccarinelli was taken the full 12 rounds by the Belgian challenger, Ismail Abdoul, before keeping his WBU cruiserweight title in Newport. The 23-year-old Swansea man had won 17 of 18 bouts, with 13 inside, and was making the fourth defence of his title. Enzo beat the visitor easily enough, but maybe it was too soon to talk about Johnny Nelson and his WBO championship.

On a steamy night at York Hall, the British lightweight champion, Graham Earl, retained his title with a sixth-round cuts stoppage over Harlow's Steve Murray. The challenger improved on their first bout, when he was beaten inside two rounds, and was giving Earl a stiff argument until the blood ran, first from the right cheek in round three, then from the left eyebrow in the fourth. The eye injury worsened and it was stopped in the sixth round of a heroic battle.

Boxing has to be one of the most international sports out there. At Coventry, the British Masters featherweight champion, Choi Tseveenpurev, a Mongolian based in Oldham, retained his title when his challenger, Harry Ramogoadi, a South African based in Rugby, pulled out after six rounds claiming stomach cramps.

Check-weighed two weeks ahead of his proposed interim WBO super-featherweight fight against Californian Mike Anchondo in Dallas, Gavin Rees failed to meet the Board's requirement and his match was vetoed. This was bad news for the former Commonwealth lightweight champion, Michael Muya, as the undefeated Welshman worked out his frustration on the lanky Kenyan when they met at Newport. Gavin took his record to 21-0 with 13 inside, needing only two rounds to stop Muya.

Coventry southpaw, Andy Halder, racked up his hat trick over Wolverhampton's Conroy McIntosh, this time over ten rounds, to claim the vacant Midlands Area middleweight title and take his pro log to 11-2. "I'm a champion and I love it," cried the delighted winner when it was over.

Over two years since his last fight, Prince Naseem Hamed was still being tempted with big money to pull on the gloves again. This month there was an offer of $250,000 to meet the unbeaten Hungarian super-featherweight, Janos Nagy.

AUGUST
The Hull cruiserweight, Tony Booth, is not used to being idle. In a 14-year professional career, Tony has crammed 130 bouts on to his resume against some of the best in the business and had managed to win 44 of them, drawn eight, and lost 78. However, when you run an eye over his record, names like Eddie Smulders, Maurice Core, James Cook, Ralf Rocchigiani, Montell Griffin, Neil Simpson, Crawford Ashley, Omar Sheika, Michael Sprott and Enzo Maccarinelli leap off the page.

Faced with a blank domestic calendar this month, Tony threw his kit into a bag and headed for Nigeria to fight Bash Ali in Lagos. The local man's WBF title would be on the line, but what clinched it for Tony was the £8,000 purse, especially when he received six grand before leaving home. This could be the right time to meet the champion; after all, he was 48 years old, while our Tony was a mere boy of 34! Keeping Tony company and looking after stuff outside the ring was manager Eugene Maloney's head honcho, James Russell. "The Africans fell in love with Tony," said Russell. "They were calling him Tony Boot!" Still, Tony could have done without slipping in a ditch and hurting his leg before the fight. "In the second he had Ali all over the place, Ali was gone," said James. "But by the fourth his leg was playing him up and he couldn't get out of the way of the punches and it was stopped."

In between juggling his options of boxing Jason Booth for his IBO super-flyweight title or chasing Brahim Asloum for his European flyweight title, Belfast's Damaen Kelly had daughter, Reise, his and Margaret's third, christened at the Holy Trinity Catholic Church in the city with his old pal, Brian Magee, standing in as godfather.

Although there was no boxing, the bells were still ringing for Clinton Woods and ex-champ, Glenn McCrory, but they were wedding bells. Sheffield's Woods, the former undefeated British, European, WBC International and Commonwealth light-heavyweight champion and former Commonwealth super-middleweight champ, tied the knot with long-time partner, Natalia. With that match signed and sealed, Clinton was looking for a fight with Joe Calzaghe. North-east hero, McCrory, the former IBF, British and Commonwealth cruiserweight champion, inked the contract with his American partner, Miranda, with Jim Watt, Billy Hardy and Audley Harrison looking on. Hardy absolutely refused to wear the bridesmaid's dress!

The name on everyone's lips this month was that of Amir Khan, a 17-year-old boy from Bolton, who, believe it or not, was Britain's only boxer at the Olympic Games in Athens. Give the kid his due, he carried the burden all the way through to the lightweight final where he had the misfortune to encounter Cuba's world champ, Mario Kindelan. It was a fight too far for the lad from Lancashire and he came second, but the silver medal he brought home would surely prove to be pure gold. Frank Warren was already throwing money at the kid, whose professional future is something to look forward to.

If the rest of the world can do it, why can't we? The British Boxing Board of Control announced that from 1 September they would be introducing Celtic titles to involve boxers from Scotland, Northern Ireland, and Wales.

SEPTEMBER

The fight game is all about style and substance. The great ones have both. In a lot of fights you have one against the other, style in one corner and substance in the other. Take that fight between Carl Thompson and David Haye at Wembley. You couldn't accuse Thompson of being stylish, but he has substance coming out of his ears. That's why he was still topping the bill at 40, still a champion. That's why he won this fight.

David Haye, a World Amateur Championship runner-up, 17 years younger than the old guy across the ring, unbeaten in ten fights, all via the short route, brought the style. He did well for the best part of two rounds, landing his big shots on the veteran, but when the smoke cleared Thompson was still standing. As David himself admitted after being stopped in five rounds: "He took my best shots, and I didn't take his." Former world champ, Lloyd Honeyghan, said bluntly: "It was such a bad fight for him. He's ruined now. He'll never fulfil his potential after this." Lloyd was right; it was a bad fight for him. Too much, too soon and whether or not he fulfils his potential remains to be seen.

Another guy on the card to learn a lesson the hard way was Chesterfield heavyweight, Mark Krence, with one defeat in 21 fights and already matched with John McDermott for the English title. Mark was two stones heavier than his opponent, Konstantin Prizyuk, a Ukranian with only four wins in 13 fights, and was comfortably ahead going into the sixth and final round. That's when the bomb landed as a right and left hook saw Krence hit the deck. Up at five, he was still out of it and it was stopped. It's never over till the fat lady sings, and this dame packs a punch!

Like his old rival, Carl Thompson, Johnny Nelson has been around the block a few times and at 37 shows no sign of flagging. The Sheffield man, who took his WBO cruiserweight title off Thompson way back in 1999 and was defending his crown for the 12th time, was in top form against Rudiger May in Essen. The tall German was a friend and sometime sparring partner of Nelson, but there was no love lost once the bell sent them on their way. Johnny is a big lad, but the German had height and reach advantages and he took the first two rounds. But the champion took charge in round three and ended it in the seventh, the referee calling it off as May fell for the second time in the round. Then they were old pals again!

Believe it or not, we have three 'world' cruiserweight champions in this tight little island, Thompson (IBO), Nelson (WBO) and Enzo Maccarinelli (WBU), and they were all in action this month. Enzo can punch with the best of them and he dismantled Danish challenger, Jesper Kristiansen, inside three rounds at Newport to retain his title for the fifth time. Recording his 20th win (14 inside) against one defeat, the Welshman punched with bad intentions and ate up this Danish pastry, decking him in round two and finishing him in the third with a crippling left hook to the body. Heading for the showers, Enzo was calling out Nelson. No hurry, he's only 24.

One minute Howard Eastman was topping the bill at Nottingham Arena with a defence of his European middleweight title against the Spanish strong man, Jorge Sendra, next thing you know Sendra couldn't pass the physical and, Eastman was fighting Jerry Elliott, a German-based Nigerian. However, top of the bill was what it had been all along for most fans, Carl Froch defending his Commonwealth super-middle-weight title against Derby's Damon Hague, with the vacant British championship thrown into the pot as a sweetener. Local hero Froch stormed into his man with a blistering attack and Hague was soon on the deck from a right to the temple. When he got back in the fight, Froch sent him crashing again with a right, left hook. The bell ending round one rang, but the referee, Mickey Vann, took up the count as per the rules. Damon made it up at four, but Vann waved it off at three minutes and ten seconds of round one. Carl Froch was British and Commonwealth champion and still undefeated in 14 fights, 11 early, and the future looks brighter than orange for the Nottingham boxer. Eastman won his fight, dropping Elliott in the final round to seal the decision. Jorge Sendra was unable to have an MRI scan as required by the Board's regulations because of metal fragments in his neck. It is a bullet actually, souvenir of a car-jacking incident in South Africa. You get all sorts in this business!

I was ringside at a riot in Gateshead when Sunderland-based Scot Ryan Kerr defended his Northern Area super-middleweight title against Carlisle's Gary Dixon. Kerr was on top when dropping Dixon twice in round seven for the finish. It was actually the start, as Carlisle fans erupted and had themselves a brawl that ended only when police reinforcements arrived. Spoiled a good night, and a good fight.

Determined to carry on boxing despite a thrashing by Scott Harrison when challenging for the WBO featherweight title some 18 months earlier, Wayne McCullough was too good for the likes of Nebraska's Mike Juarez who was down and out inside two rounds of their contest in Temecula, California.

One of the few promoters operating without television, Chris Sanigar gave Scott Dann hometown advantage for his crack at the British middleweight title vacated by Howard Eastman. In the first ever British title bout in Plymouth, Scott did his part by hammering Steven Bendall to summary defeat in six rounds of an all-southpaw battle. It was Scott's 20th win, with 14 inside and two defeats. He has the punch that matters.

It was red hot inside York Hall and for Margate battler, Takaloo, it got even hotter inside the ring as he swapped punches with Wayne Alexander for the vacant WBU light-middleweight title. For the best part of two rounds, Takaloo fought the perfect fight. Then, like a bolt from the blue, Wayne threw probably the best left hook he has ever thrown and there was Takaloo flat on his back, out to the world. Alexander had trained ten weeks in Northern Ireland with John Breen. The fight lasted less than ten minutes! That's the fight business for you. Former British and Commonwealth heavyweight champion, Michael Sprott, finished work early, dumping Robert Sulgan of the Czech Republic on the floor for a 52-second stoppage. And while

Kevin Mitchell is a fine talent, the Dagenham lightweight was lucky to escape disqualification against a guy he was beating up easily enough, a hapless Hungarian named Arpad Toth. Mitchell was ruthless, okay, but he was rough when he didn't have to be, hitting the visitor when he was down and shoving him. If you are that good Kevin, and you appear to be a genuine comer, you don't need the other stuff.

At York Hall, Chas 'The Bomb' Symonds added the vacant British Masters welter-weight title to his Southern Area belt with a ten rounds decision over Welsh tough guy, Keith Jones, but the Croydon man had to fight all the way against a man who is never easy.

Don't let the pink gear fool you; Dublin's Jim Rock can fight. Back in action in his hometown, Jim hammered out a decision over late sub Matt Galer from Burton-on-Trent. Southpaw Matt was at work in the afternoon when he got the call from his manager, John Ashton, and he got to Dublin virtually in time to enter the ring.

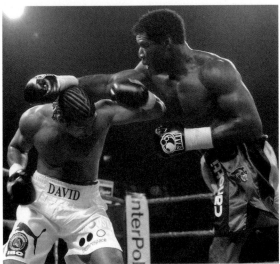

Challenging for the IBO cruiserweight title, the younger David Haye (left) came unstuck against the 40-year-old champion, Carl Thompson   Les Clark

OCTOBER

Finally Ricky Hatton looked like moving out of the WBU rut he had been stuck in since claiming that title when knocking out Canada's Tony Pep in March 2001. Making his 14th defence in his own backyard, Manchester's huge MEN Arena, the local favourite also won a final eliminator for the IBF championship held by Kostya Tszyu when he blew away American Mike Stewart inside five rounds. Frank Warren had Vivian Harris almost hooked and landed for a defence of his WBA title on this show before things fell apart. Money was the problem, but most likely the Guyanese didn't really fancy the stuff that Hatton dishes out and Warren had to look elsewhere. He came up with Stewart, who lost a fight to fellow-American, Sharmba Mitchell, in Manchester the night Hatton stopped

the Dane, Dennis Holbaek Pedersen. Mitchell gave Stewart a beating that night and Ricky Hatton gave him a beating this night, dropping the American twice in the opening round and finishing the job in round five with a brutal left hook. Undefeated now in 37 pro fights (27 stoppages) Ricky Hatton was as ready as he will ever be. Bring on the Champion!

Joe Calzaghe was in the same boat as Hatton, making multiple defences of his WBO super-middleweight title while his name was linked with men like Roy Jones, Glengoffe Johnson, Sven Otke, and Bernard Hopkins, but only on paper. In reality, Joe had to fight guys like Kabary Salem, a household name only in his own household. The 32-year-old Welsh southpaw celebrated seven years as WBO champion as he made his 15th defence against Salem in Edinburgh, winning a unanimous decision over the Egyptian, who fights out of Brooklyn, New York City, in a messy, sometimes dirty fight. Calzaghe dropped his man in the final round after suffering the indignity of being floored himself in the fourth. Joe took his record to 38-0 (30 inside), but it was a bad day at the office.

Mismatch! That summed up the WBO featherweight title contest between the champion, Scott Harrison, and his inept challenger, Samuel Kebede, from Ethiopia on a Sky Sports-Frank Warren promotion at Renfrew's Braehead Arena. Inside 59 seconds of round one, the visitor was floored twice and on his way to the showers. This was billed and sold as a world championship fight, yet Kebede had as much chance of beating Harrison as I did. The WBO, to their shame, had ranked the man from Ethiopia number FIVE in their world ratings. Although he was undefeated in 24 contests, Kebede had beaten nobody of any consequence and was in no way a worthy opponent for Scott Harrison. The Scottish fans were the losers this night; they paid good money for this farce. Trouble is, some of them won't come back.

There was one decent fight on the bill. Scottish lightweight champion, Martin Watson, outboxed and outpunched the former British light-welter champ, Mark Winters, over ten good rounds to take the new Celtic championship. The loser was from Antrim.

Sheffield light-heavyweight, Clinton Woods, kept his name in the frame for another crack at the IBF title when he stopped a tough Aussie, Jason DeLisle, in the 12th and final round in his hometown. The fight was an official eliminator and victory put the Yorkshireman in the number two spot to old rival Glengoffe Johnson, the IBF champion. Yet he was on the deck in the first minute of the fight, courtesy of a quick right hand from the Aussie. Clinton paid him back in round seven when a heavy right hook to the head sent DeLisle sprawling for the mandatory eight count. Woods had his man in bother in the 11th and turned it on in the last to force a stoppage halfway through the round. Now he was looking for Johnson again, after drawing with, then losing a decision to the man who would knock out Roy Jones.

At Brentwood, Dagenham's Nicky Cook retained his European featherweight title and his unbeaten record (now 24-0) with a comprehensive points win over a teak-tough

Frenchman, Johnny Begue, who soaked up punches like a heavy bag in the gym. Cook's knuckles were swollen from beating on this chunk of granite from across the Channel.

On the Ricky Hatton bill at Manchester, Michael Gomez came through another tough one to force a sixth-round retirement against the Russian, Leva Kirakosyan. Gomez took the early rounds, but it almost went pear-shaped in the fifth when the visitor landed a series of heavy rights and Gomez was cut on the right eye. However, he was able to fight his way back through the sixth and when Kirakosyan's right eye closed up he turned it in at the bell. Gomez retained his WBU super-featherweight title in his second reign as champion, although the fights are getting harder.

Unbeaten Chorley welterweight, Michael Jennings, took the English title off the former British champion, Chris Saunders, when the Barnsley southpaw was pulled out after five rounds with a bad cut over his right eye. Michael was on the deck in round one but it was the only success Saunders would have as Jennings took his record to 24-0.

Another former champion came to the end of the line when Gary Thornhill bowed out after being stopped in nine rounds by the English featherweight champion, Stephen Foster, who retained his belt. The 36-year-old Liverpool man was a former undefeated British champion and was also unbeaten as WBO Inter-Continental and Central Area champion at super-feather. He gave Foster a run for his money before coming apart in round eight when a left hook shook him and another dropped him. He survived into the ninth, but was floored twice by heavy shots and was all in when the referee waved it off. Before he left the ring, Gary took the mike to announce "...this is my last fight."

NOVEMBER

Junior Witter continued on his winning ways at the Wembley Conference Centre where he retained his European light-welterweight title against a hapless Pole named Krzysztof Bienias. The visitor was cut over the right eyebrow by a long left and when the injury worsened in round two the referee did the Pole a favour and stopped the fight. Witter was never extended in taking his 30th win in 33 fights (30-1-2) and it was his 15th inside victory since losing a world title shot against Zab Judah four years ago. Junior still yearns for a fight with Ricky Hatton, as do many fans, but that one is fading into the background with every passing minute. "I'm number one for the WBO and IBF," said Hatton, when the fight was mentioned again: "Why would I want to box him?" If Junior wants to add a world title to his British, Commonwealth, and European belts, he may have to look beyond Mr Ricky Hatton.

Francis Barrett was the European Union light-welterweight champion and he came through a tough defence against Alan Bosworth on the Wembley bill. It was never pretty, with Bosworth suffering his by-now obligatory broken nose and Barrett on the deck in the first, finishing with cuts on both eyes, before coming out with the decision.

Best fight on the Wembley card saw Peter Haymer take the English light-heavyweight title off Steve Spartacus in a terrific ten rounder. Spartacus, the Warrior, got off to a good lead only for Haymer to come on in the homestretch and win by a nose.

A sellout crowd at York Hall was disappointed in the Matt Skelton-Keith Long British and Commonwealth heavyweight championship, having to wait until the penultimate round to see some action. The champion nailed Long with a right uppercut and down he went. Keith beat the count, but Skelton knew what he had to do and Long was shipping heavy blows when it was stopped at the 2.45 mark of the round. Matt has won all 15 fights, 14 inside, but he's 37 and the clock is ticking.

Lee Meager looked a good winner in his fight with the English lightweight champion, Danny Hunt, but at the final bell the referee, Mark Green, had it for Hunt, winner and still champion! Most of the York Hall crowd were stunned by the verdict, seeing the Salford man as the new champion. But Danny survived a punishing ninth round and came home with his title still intact. Win some, lose some.

A former British heavyweight contender, Dave Garside, is keeping Hartlepool on the boxing map as manager/promoter of local star, Michael Hunter. Running without television, Dave staged a double championship bill that brought the fans in and whetted their appetites for the future. Hunter defended his British super-bantamweight title against gutsy challenger, Marc Callaghan, the referee saving the Barking man as the towel fluttered in from his corner. Hunter was always going well as he removed the only blemish on his pro log, Callaghan having forced a draw with Michael in a previous six-rounder.

Hunter's stablemate in Neil Fannan's gym is Kevin Bennett, Commonwealth light-weight champion, and he made it a double as he turned back the gritty challenge of Dean Phillips with a comprehensive decision. As with Callaghan, Phillips lacked the firepower to make the difference against a strong champion.

Another Welshman, Jason Cook, crossed the border to defend his IBO lightweight title in Hereford against Argentina's Aldo Rios, a former Ricky Hatton victim. Rios was not considered a dangerous puncher, but in the third round he decked the champion with rights to the head then poured on the leather forcing the referee to stop it. Although he denied it, weight-making was thought to have been Cook's trouble.

On the same bill, the local favourite, Dazzo Williams, retained his British featherweight title over John Simpson with a 115-114 vote from referee Phil Edwards that did not sit well with the punters. Even Dazzo's supporters thought their man lucky to hang on to his crown against the young Scot. Dazzo started well, fell away, then put in a storming finish. But many thought it wasn't enough. There were no doubts concerning Scott Gammer's two-rounds stoppage of the veteran Pole, Roman Bugaj, as the Welsh heavyweight took his record to 11-0-1, a heavy knockdown in round two bringing the referee's intervention.

British welterweight champion, David Barnes, made it 16-0 (9) but, more importantly, secured permanent possession of the Lonsdale Belt as he stopped his challenger, James Hare, in six rounds at Halifax. The Manchester southpaw floored his man in the fourth round and closed the show in round six, winner and still champion!

It was a bad night for the British light-middleweight champion, Jamie Moore, as he lost his title to Michael Jones on a third-round disqualification at Altrincham. Moore had knocked out Michael's gumshield, and, when Dave Parris called "stop boxing" so that the mouthpiece could be replaced, Moore landed a solid left hook to the chin that dropped Jones. Parris called a time out, but when it was obvious that Jones could or would not carry on, the champion was ruled out.

Belfast southpaw, Brian Magee, bounced back from a loss to Robin Reid to stop Neil Linford inside seven rounds. The former IBO super-middleweight champion was on top all the way and almost finished his man in round six. In the seventh, Linford was taken to the corner for an inspection of his damaged left eye and his cornerman, Ronnie Davies, indicated his man had taken enough. Magee moved to 23-1 and could be a champ again.

Stockwell's former IBO light-middleweight champion and undefeated Commonwealth and WBF champion, Richard Williams, came back with a third-round stoppage of Hungarian, Szabolcs Rimovszky. At 33, Williams could still be a force.

Matt Skelton (right), defending the British and Commonwealth heavyweight belts, eventually got to Keith Long in the 11th round   Les Clark

DECEMBER

There's a line in an old show tune that goes something like this: "It's not how you start, it's how you finish!" In his challenge to WBC heavyweight champion, Vitali Klitschko, in Las Vegas, Danny Williams made a disastrous start and things just got worse. Unfortunately, by round eight Danny was finished after the dream had become a nightmare. The shock knockout of Mike Tyson that earned Williams this shot was put in its true perspective by this brutal beating at the thudding fists of

the huge Ukrainian. Williams was never in with a shout against this 6'7" giant champion, who reminds you of Ivan Drago of Rocky fame. He has been called robotic, stiff-as-a-board, and lacking in the game's finer points. So Vitali isn't a Billy Conn, or a big Willie Pep, but what he is, is effective, efficient and he gets the job done. Check the stats. In 37 pro fights, the big fellow has won 35, 34 inside schedule. In hindsight, it was quite literally too big a task for the gutsy Londoner. Williams, perhaps unwisely, entered the ring weighing a career-heaviest 19st 4lbs, almost two stones more than the champion and it was weight he could have done without. Danny needed to move around the big guy, not stand in front of him. Klitschko found him easy to hit from the first bell and by the end of the round Danny was bleeding from a cut on his right eye and had barely escaped a knockout, just beating the ten count. From there it just went downhill until the 86-second mark of round eight when the referee, Jay Nady, rescued him. "The brutality of the beating showed on Williams' face," wrote Tim Smith in the New York Daily News. "His right eye was swollen completely shut and he was bleeding profusely from a cut above the right eye. Klitschko barely had a scratch on him." "He was a little more awkward than I anticipated," said Danny afterwards, "and very clever. I thought I could beat him, but I couldn't handle his style."

The American, Ray Oliveira, had a similar train of thought running through his befuddled brain before almost ten rounds of aggravation at the hammering fists of Ricky Hatton at London's ExCel Arena ended with him being counted out as he knelt in a corner, glove pressed to his left ear which was obviously giving him pain. A burst eardrum was later confirmed. Oliveira was 47-9-2 coming in and was the only man to have beaten Vivian Harris, the WBA champion at the weight, and had never been stopped. Defending his WBU light-welterweight championship for the 15th time, Hatton was relentless, dropping the American in rounds one and ten and giving him a rough time in between. Still unbeaten after 38 fights, Hatton sent out a message to Kostya Tszyu.

Jason Booth gave Damaen Kelly a nice belt for Christmas; his IBO super-flyweight championship belt. Actually Jason had planned on taking his belt back home to Nottingham after their fight at Huddersfield Sports Centre, but the three judges all agreed that the 31-year-old Irishman had done enough to win the fight, even if he looked like the loser! Mind you, Mr Booth also looked rather the worse for wear at the end. It had been that kind of fight, two gritty little battlers giving their all in a gruelling 12-round contest. Kelly's old cut-eye bugbear plagued him again and he finished with both eyes bloodied, while Jason was banged up around the eyes, if not so bloody. He fought like a champion to keep his crown in his second defence, but Kelly brought the touch of class to edge the decision and become a champion once again. Damaen had been British, Commonwealth, European and IBO champion at flyweight, only coming a cropper when challenging Columbia's IBF champ, Irene Pacheco, in his own backyard. Beating Booth was his third win since as he showed he still had something in the tank.

Edinburgh stylist Alex Arthur looked to be over his traumatic defeat by Michael Gomez some 14 months beforehand as he coasted to a one-sided decision over Argentine super-featherweight champion, Nazareno Ruiz, at the Meadowbank Sports Centre in his hometown. In his third fight since Gomez dented his unbeaten record, and with the Manchester man sitting ringside, Arthur gave Ruiz a boxing lesson to take his pro log to 19-1, 16 inside, and pick up the IBF Inter-Continental belt, which Alex knows is no substitute for the Lonsdale Belt Gomez took off him. That's the one he wants back!

On the same card, Willie Limond easily retained his European Union super-featherweight title with a decision over the Spanish champion, Alberto (Tito) Lopez. Glasgow's Limond had lost only to Arthur in a 25-fight career and would relish another crack at his fellow Scot, but Arthur probably has other fish to fry.

Sheffield's Hillsborough Leisure Centre staged an interesting card with heavyweight hopeful, Roman Greenberg, testing himself against the former champion, Julius Francis. The Finchley-based Israeli had no bother taking his first ten-rounder, but his performance lacked fire and he seemed happy just to go the distance, as was his veteran opponent. The fireworks came in the tenth and final round of the fight between the English light-heavyweight champion, Peter Haymer, and Mark Brookes. In this, their third meeting, Brookes looked to be getting on top after nine excellent rounds, but in the last session Haymer sent Mark reeling with a left hook, right cross.

Peter went for the finish only for the referee, John Keane, to tumble to the canvas and when they resumed battle Brookes was again in trouble, slumping from a savage right uppercut to bring Mr Keane's intervention. Worse was to come. Brookes collapsed at home and was later operated on for a blood clot. Fortunately for the Swinton man he recovered within a few days and boxing breathed again.

Damaen Kelly (left) just about edged out Jason Booth to land the IBO super-flyweight title, held by the latter since September 2003   Les Clark

JANUARY

If at first you don't succeed, try, try again. Since 1999, the Columbian featherweight, Victor Polo, has been trying

to win a world title. Any one! Challenging IBF champion, Manuel Medina, Polo was beaten on a split technical decision in the ninth round when Medina suffered a cut eye in a clash of heads. It went to the cards with the champion taking a split vote. Polo bounced back to tackle the WBA titleholder, Derrick Gainer, in his Florida backyard, only to lose another split decision after a tough fight. Switch to London, 2002, and here is Victor fighting Argentina's Julio Pablo Chacon for the WBO title. Another rugged 12 rounds and guess what? Chacon retains on a split decision! Who was it said third time lucky? Try fourth time lucky.

The Columbian southpaw hooked up with Scott Harrison in the WBO champion's Braehead backyard and after the final bell many sound judges, including one of the official ones, England's John Coyle, had Polo pegged as the winner. Judge Melvina Lathan didn't think Victor had lost it either, but then again she didn't think he had won it, voting a draw. Harrison received the other fellow's vote and the draw meant that he had retained his title. He finished a fight he would be happy to forget with the left side of his face swollen and bloody, the eye hammered shut, while the only damage suffered by Victor Polo was the black eye handed him by Fate. For five rounds the fight was evenly balanced, but Polo came on strong from the sixth and Harrison was in bother by round 11 as the South American outboxed and outpunched him. Three minutes from glory! But the champion fought back and at the final bell still had his title. But only just! The decision was yet another kick in the teeth for the 34-year-old Columbian after fifteen years in the business. Add the name of Victor Polo to the list of Boxing's Nearly Men.

On the Braehead bill, British welterweight champion, David Barnes, worked some of the kinks out in a comfortable ten-rounds decision over Juho Tolppola of Finland. The Manchester southpaw improved his pro log to 17-0 and looks as good as he fights.

A guy looking for a crack at Barnes is Scotland's Kevin Anderson, who won the inaugural Celtic welterweight championship with a fourth-round cuts stoppage of Ireland's Glenn McClarnon at Glasgow's St Andrew's Sporting Club. It was shaping up as a cracking contest when the blood came, from McClarnon's left eyebrow. Goodnight!

He's young at 24, he's big at 6'4" and he's dangerous. In winning 20 of 21 pro fights, his big hammering fists sent his opponent off to an early shower 15 times. As the WBU cruiserweight champion, he has knocked back six challengers in his 18 months reign. If you haven't heard of him, you will! Enzo Maccarinelli. The American veteran, Rich LaMontagne, wasn't too sure what he was up against when he arrived in Wales to fight Enzo at the Bridgend Recreation Centre. It didn't take long for him to get the message as he was hammered from pillar to post, floored in rounds one and two, and ready for the cleaners when the referee called a humane halt in the fourth round. It was Enzo's most impressive showing to date and must have given WBO champion, Johnny Nelson, pause for thought in his ringside seat. One day they will meet...

In a supporting bout, an unfortunate clash of heads

ended the unbeaten nine-fight run of former Commonwealth Games gold medal winner, Jamie Arthur, leaving London-based Pakistani, Haider Ali, the winner and the Welshman considering plastic surgery for the cut over his left eye. Promising Pontypool welterweight Tony Doherty kept on the winning trail with a second round stoppage of France's Emmanuel Fleury, taking his record to 13 wins, seven inside.

Bermondsey cruiserweight, David Haye, started on the comeback trail at the Fountain Leisure Centre in Brentford with a scheduled six-threes against the old pro, Garry Delaney. The former amateur star had crashed in his last fight against another veteran, Carl Thompson, in a fight too far, so an easier job was called for. The 34-year-old Delaney had seen better days in his 41 fight-career and he never troubled Haye, pulling out after three rounds with a damaged right eye. Garry had been dropped by a whistling right hand seconds before the round ended. Haye moved to 12-1, all wins inside the distance. Take your time, son.

Overseas action saw wins for big boys, Wayne Llewelyn and Roman Greenberg. The South London southpaw was in Berlin to fight Robert Sulgan at the Box-Tempel, but instead found himself facing an old opponent in Vladislav Druso. Llewelyn had beaten the Czech via a six rounds decision two years previously, but didn't hang about this time, it was all over at 1.40 of round one.

Greenberg, from Russia via Israel and London, won his fight in New York, but failed to set the place alight. Matched with Marcus McGee, a 33-year-old from Tuscaloosa, Alabama, with a 12-5 pro log, Roman fought like he was in with one of the Klitschkos and the crowd at the Manhattan Center Arena booed the lack of action. McGee looked as though he would rather be back home in Alabama and the referee dismissed him in round four after he had been falling all over the ring, mainly from slips. Taking his pro record to 18 victories, 13 inside, Roman Greenberg needs stiffer opposition than this Tuscaloosa tumbler if he is to make his mark among the big boys.

FEBRUARY

It was billed as 'The Executioner versus The Battersea Bomber', but you knew the middleweight title fight between champion Bernard Hopkins and Howard Eastman was never going to be Zale v Graziano. But it promised a keen contest between two men who used brain rather than brawn, even though they had won 66 of their 85 victories inside the distance. The power was always there, but to be used economically when the time was right. For Howard Eastman maybe the time will never be right for him to breach the final frontier, the middleweight championship of the world. In 41 pro fights, the Londoner has lost only once – when challenging William Joppy for the WBA version of

Putting the Carl Thompson defeat behind him, David Haye (left) forced West Ham's Garry Delaney to retire at the end of the third round of their cruiserweight contest at Brentford

Les Clark

the title in 2001. Howard even dropped the American in the final round, but he had waited too long and lost by majority decision.

This time, against Hopkins in Los Angeles, Eastman again let caution flavour his recipe for success and his goose was cooked by the master chef from the bleak streets of Philadelphia. The undisputed world champion outboxed and outpunched Eastman to win his 20th title defence and, at the age of 40, looks like ruling the division until he retires, which he has promised to do before his next birthday, January 2006.

On the same card, Junior Witter showed Eastman how to do it when he punched out a solid decision over the Australian tough guy, Lovemore Ndou, to retain his Common-wealth light-welterweight title, scoring two heavy knockdowns in rounds three and four to give his career a tremendous boost in the place where it matters most. The Halifax southpaw took his record to 31-1-2 and Witter's promoter Mick Hennessy was over the moon, saying: "Oscar De La Hoya's going to make Junior the superstar he wants to be."

Wayne McCullough is a fighter down to his toenails. Even when they said he couldn't fight anymore after discovering a cyst on his brain scan, he fought the authorities and was eventually cleared. They let him back in the ring again, but he took a hammering from Scott Harrison and this night in Leemore, California, he came up short again when trying to take the WBC super-bantamweight title from Mexico's Oscar Larios. It was a hard, tough fight, especially for McCullough, and once again there were calls for this Belfast battler to hang up his gloves. The signs were that Wayne wasn't listening, but where does he go from here, at 34 after 13 years in the ring?

Another fighter giving concern for his welfare was Manchester's Michael Gomez as he was hammered loose from his WBU super-featherweight belt in six painful rounds by slick Argentinian, Javier Alvarez, at the MEN Arena. Gomez the warrior had talked tough at the weigh-in, but when it mattered Alvarez let his fists do the talking and their message was loud and clear. But will Michael Gomez, will Wayne McCullough, heed the warnings that have been hammered into them. Probably not.

If in doubt, knock 'em out! That was the credo followed by Stephen Foster into his contest with Livinson Ruiz of Columbia for the vacant World Boxing Union featherweight belt. Going into the tenth round, the Salford fighter was ahead, but it wasn't a formality. Better make sure. A left hook smacked the Columbian on the chin and he crashed flat on his back. Count to ten, give him the belt. Foster won fight number 18 and is one to watch.

Matt Skelton is all about heavyweight boxing. He's big, strong, heavy at 18stone odd, comes to fight not fiddle about. So he's 38, but that's not old these days, not for a heavyweight anyway. Coming from martial arts to boxing, the Bedford banger won the British and Commonwealth titles and at Wembley he roughed up Fabio Moli of the Argentine in six rounds to win the WBU title and stay unbeaten in 16 fights.

Opportunity knocked for Coatbridge's Ricky Burns when he was matched over eight rounds with British lightweight champion, Graham Earl, who was killing time until a unification match with the Commonwealth champion, Kevin Bennett, could be arranged. At the Wembley ringside, Bennett wasn't impressed by the champion. Neither was Ricky Burns who boxed calmly to take the decision and have the fans checking their programme notes on the young Scot. Ricky Burns, 21, now 10-0. Watch this lad.

Welsh farmer Alan Jones was a sacrificial lamb fed to the rampaging British middleweight champion, Scott Dann, before his hometown fans who jammed the Pavilions in Plymouth to see their hero put a second notch on the Lonsdale Belt. The champion, a knockout puncher with 14 stoppages in 20 winning fights (2 defeats), crushed Jones in three rounds and was never troubled by a challenger in over his head. Alan went in with a woefully inadequate 9-0-1 record and didn't figure to bother a strong, powerful champion. He didn't!

Colin Lynes retained his IBO light-welterweight title at Brentwood with a close majority decision over America's Jauquin Gallardo, taking his pro log to 26-1. Gallardo staged a grand finish and there were some in the Leisure Centre who thought he had done enough to take the title. It was not to be.

Runcorn's super-middleweight contender and former champion, Robin Reid, failed to sparkle in a six-rounder with the rugged French-Algerian, Ramdane Serdjane, winning the decision but little else. It was Reid's first fight in eight months.

Portsmouth favourite Tony Oakey was another fighter coming back, having been out for a year on a drugs ban, and he struggled to beat the Birmingham Armenian, Varuzhan Davtyan, at the Mountbatten Centre. Davtyan had Oakey in all kinds of trouble before pulling out after five rounds, claiming a damaged right hand.

The young Scot, Ricky Burns (left), caused a major surprise when he outscored the British lightweight champion, Graham Earl, over eight rounds at Wembley   Les Clark

MARCH

It all came good for Clinton Woods as he stopped America's Rico Hoye inside five rounds at Rotherham's Magna Centre to win the vacant IBF light-heavyweight title, referee Ian John-Lewis calling a halt with the man from Detroit taking stick on the ropes with nothing coming back. It was a well-deserved triumph for the Sheffield man after coming up short in three previous attempts, against Roy Jones (6 rds) and Glengoffe Johnson (draw, then points loss). Jones was still the top man when he beat Clinton and Johnson went on to flatten Jones and beat Antonio Tarver to lead the world at light-heavy. In their wisdom, the IBF stripped Johnson of their title for taking the unification fight with Tarver, thus opening the door for Woods to have another shot at making his dream come true. In the other corner was Rico Hoye, a guy with a criminal record (ten years in the slammer for a gangland killing) and an unbeaten fight record of 18 wins, with 14 finishing early, 13 inside three rounds. The guy could punch! Yet when push came to shove, Clinton Woods outpunched the Detroit slugger after outboxing him and Hoye couldn't stay with him. He didn't go down but in round five he looked like he might fall as Woods poured it on and the American was rescued by the referee. "It's very satisfying," said his new trainer, Richard Poxon: "nobody thought he'd do it. But on that display there's not a fighter in the world to worry about." "People said I wasn't world class," said Clinton. "They're not saying it now." Indeed they aren't!

Bermondsey cruiserweight, David Haye, showed he was over the Carl Thompson defeat with a two rounds blitz of quality Australian, Glen Kelly, on the Rotherham bill. Haye didn't put a punch wrong, dropping Kelly in round one with a powerful right to the head and ending matters in the second with another whistling right.

When they refurbished the Borough Hall in Hartlepool recently I hope they strengthened the roof, because if they didn't this venerable old venue won't take

Improving every time out, Nigel Wright (left) added the English light-welter crown to his CV with a seventh-round kayo win over Dean Hickman

Les Clark

many more Michael Hunter fights without suffering serious structural damage. The girders rattled ominously as Hunter's rabid fans roared him to victory yet again as he retained his British super-bantamweight title, stopping Sean Hughes of Pontefract in round six to put a third notch on the Lonsdale Belt. Southpaw Hughes just couldn't hold off the rampaging champion. Hunter builds his momentum from round one and by the sixth round he rolled over poor Sean. Dropped to the canvas by a furious barrage, Hughes beat the count but he couldn't beat the champion. Michael turned it on again and the referee did the right thing.

On the Hartlepool bill, Hunter's stablemate, the Commonwealth lightweight champion, Kevin Bennett, hit too hard and too often for the Gateshead light-middle, Danny Moir, stopping his man in three rounds of a catchweights contest.

Another north-east fighter making his way is light-welterweight Nigel Wright, a southpaw from Crook in County Durham. Yet to fight on his home patch after 13 fights (1 defeat) Wright was in Doncaster to lift the vacant English title with a fine victory over undefeated Dean Hickman, who was knocked out in the seventh round. It was a mature performance from Wright who looks headed for bigger things.

Matthew Barney was in a tough one. He was fighting Thomas Ulrich for his European light-heavyweight title, a man with height and reach advantages who had stopped 19 of his 27 victims, while losing only to Glengoffe Johnson, who would go on to become world champion. And did I mention the fight was in Germany? Yes, I know the old cliché, knock them out to get a draw, but Barney was not a puncher. Although the British super-middleweight and WBU light-heavy champion had a 21-4-1 record, he only had six wins inside. Matthew went to Riesa in Germany looking to be a champion again. Forget the money that had already been spent on training expenses for the fight which had been postponed so often the Southampton boxer didn't believe it was actually on until he stood in the ring waiting for the opening bell. The bell rang and Barney boxed the big fellow's ears off and after 12 rounds the champion's right eye was shuttered tight and black and blue. But he was still the champion!

Eamonn Magee is the Miracle Man of Belfast. Twelve months after being left lying in the street following a vicious beating by men with baseball bats, Magee was back in the ring, boxing when they said he wouldn't walk again! Left leg broken, left knee fractured, a lung punctured, blood clots. Yet he lived, he walked, and this night in the King's Hall, he fought in the ring again and won. Although the Danish welterweight, Alan Vester, was not considered a threat to Magee's WBU title, a three-round stoppage win for the latter supporting this train of thought, this was not about a boxing contest. It was about a much bigger fight, and the big man who won it.

Sheffield's Dean Walker was in Hungary, at a place called Tapulca, fighting Hungarian hotshot Jozsef Nagy for his IBF Inter-Continental middleweight belt. Nagy had won all nine fights inside the distance and he was too much for Walker, who was pulled out by Glyn Rhodes in the eighth round.

One punch! That's all it takes to render the referee's points score academic. At the Equinox Nightclub in Leicester Square, Jamie Hearn was beating Simeon Cover in their contest for the vacant British Masters super-middleweight title Cover had been stripped of. Going into the seventh round Hearn looked in control, headed for victory, when it happened. A right uppercut sent him crashing and it was all over! Knockout!

APRIL

The fight was for all the marbles. Lonsdale Belt, British and Commonwealth super-featherweight championships, and bragging rights in Scotland. That was the scenario at Edinburgh's Meadowbank Sports Centre when the hometown favourite, Alex Arthur, met Glasgow's Craig Docherty, 12 rounds or less. It proved to be less as Arthur retained his British title and claimed Docherty's Commonwealth bauble with a knockout in round nine. Craig boxed well for three rounds but from the fourth, Arthur moved up a gear and the Glaswegian couldn't stay with him. His nose was broken and he was swallowing blood the rest of the way until round nine when a whistling left hook sunk into his pain-wracked body and he crumpled to the canvas for the countout. Delighted at winning the Lonsdale Belt outright, Arthur took his record to 20-1. He hits hard for his weight, as witness his 17 wins inside the distance, and was looking forward to challenging Boris Sinitsin for his European title.

In supporting contests, the Coatbridge super-featherweight, Ricky Burns, followed up his victory over British lightweight champion, Graham Earl, with an easy six-round verdict over Buster Dennis...Big John McDermott, a loser to Mark Krence last time out when going for the English heavyweight title, dumped Alvin (Slick) Miller twice for a first-round stoppage. Mac had dusted off Miller in 62 seconds in his debut, this time it took him two minutes, 33 seconds.

Hull veteran Tony Booth was on the road again, stopping off in Copenhagen this time for a bout with local favourite, Johnny Jensen. Tony didn't expect to win and he didn't, but he gave the lad six rounds work and earned his pay...Garry Delaney was in Austria to test the unbeaten Russian heavyweight, Valery Chechenev. The Londoner gave two stones to the big fellow, who chalked up his eighth straight win.

Hooray for Hollywood! It wasn't Las Vegas or the Garden in New York, but a little nightclub just off Hollywood Boulevard in Los Angeles where Nottingham's British and Commonwealth super-middleweight champion, Carl Froch, made his American debut against Henry Porras, a tough guy from Costa Rica with a respectable 30-4-1 pro log, even if he was 34 years old. Carl was ring rusty after eight months out, but he still punched too fast and too hard for Porras, who soaked it up until it was stopped in round eight. Froch was pleased to get the win, his 15th, 12 inside, but knocked up the knuckles on his right hand. Carl's promoter, Mick Hennessy, has linked up with Oscar De La

Hoya's Golden Boy Promotions and Carl had finished off his training in De La Hoya's private gym.

I had seen Ali Nuumbembe give a consummate beating to Darlington's undefeated Franny Jones, so was not surprised when he forced a draw with another unbeaten fighter, the British welterweight champion, David Barnes, a few weeks later at the Barnsley Metrodome. A Namibian based in Glossop, Ali is a well-rounded fighter and will beat more than beat him. He thought he had won this one, but then so did Barnes, but the Manchester boy appeared to take the African lightly and he paid the price.

Former British light-middleweight champion, Ryan Rhodes, bounced back after a year out and still had enough left to take a six rounds decision from Peter Jackson, despite the Lonsdale Belt winner tripping and hurting his right ankle. Referee Howard Foster gave him time to recover, and, at 28, Rhodes, who twice challenged for the WBO title, can still make some noise.

Another on the comeback trail was Jon Thaxton. The Norwich lightweight climbed off the deck to stop Christophe De Busillet in the fourth round of their contest for the vacant WBF championship. It was Jon's third win since resuming after a career-threatening car crash. Still only 30, Mr Thaxton could be around for a while.

Ross Minter had a lot to live up to. His father, Alan, had been undisputed middle-weight champion of the world and a tough act to follow. So the pressure was on as Ross went for the Southern Area welterweight title at Southwark against the champion, Chas Symonds, at 22 four years the younger. They had similar records, 12-1-1 for Minter, while Chas was unbeaten in 12. After three rounds, Symonds moved to 12-1 as Ross cut him down with a ruthless display of punching that destroyed the cocky kid from Croydon. Down in the second, Chas was sent crashing twice in the third and it was all over.

British middleweight champion, Scott Dann, eased to a third notch on his Lonsdale Belt with another stunning knockout as his Coventry challenger, Andy Halder, was sent crashing for the full count at 2.45 of the opening round. While the hometown boy delighted the Plymouth crowd, his opponent, like first challenger Alan Jones, left something to be desired. Scott Dann is a strong, powerful puncher and this was his 16th inside victory from 22 winning bouts, with two defeats. His next defence would give him the Lonsdale Belt for keeps, but it must be a mandatory and, hopefully, against someone who can stand up for a few rounds.

Horsham super-middleweight, Alan Gilbert, was always struggling against South Africa's Ruben Groenewald at the Equinox Nightclub in Leicester Square, where the vacant WBF Inter-Continental title was on the line. Alan almost made it to the final bell, almost. Ruben, based in Ramsgate, found the punches that mattered and it was ended 68 seconds into round ten. In a supporting bout, Julius Francis used his 19st 7lbs bulk and his experience to hold off West Ham's Mickey Steeds for eight rounds. The former champion put in a spirited finish, but Mickey maintained his points lead to the bell, taking his record to five wins against a thrilling loss to Scott Gammer.

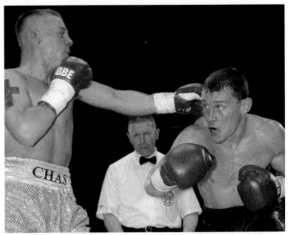

Chas Symonds (left) was unable to halt the progress of Ross Minter, the son of the former world middleweight champion, and surrendered his Southern Area welterweight title inside three rounds　　Les Clark

MAY

As Joe Calzaghe headed off to Germany to defend his WBO super-middleweight title against former victim, Mario Veit, he was still seeking that career-defining fight all champions need to feed their ego. There was talk of a unification contest with IBF titleholder, Jeff Lacy, but Joe wanted more. "I don't know whether Lacy is the fight I've been after," he said. "I don't think Jeff Lacy is a great fighter." First things first, however. Herr Veit was waiting in Brunswick at the Volkswagen-halle eager to show that his first round flop against the Welshman in their first meeting in April 2001 was a one-off. Mario had won all 15 fights since then and Calzaghe was still the only man to beat him in 46 professional fights. The German had even been recognised as the interim champion when he beat Kabary Salem, after Calzaghe had intimated he would move to light-heavyweight. Joe didn't move up and Salem made him look bad in a stinker in his last fight. It was time to shine. Mario Veit didn't fall inside two minutes this time, it was round five before Calzaghe sent him crashing. Joe didn't have time to finish the job, he had to wait for round six to drop his man again. Veit got up and his corner were ready to surrender but the referee, Geno Rodriguez, waved them away only to call it off a few seconds later. Joe Calzaghe had retained his title for the 16th time in seven years and was still unbeaten since he was an amateur some 15 years ago. But Joe was now 33. "I'm still hungry," he said. "I still have the desire for that big fight."

Scott Gammer was another Welshman looking for a big fight. The man from Pembroke Dock got a foot on the ladder when he hammered the English heavyweight champion, Mark Krence, to bloody defeat inside eight rounds of their British title eliminator at Sheffield. At 28, Gammer was unbeaten in 13 fights, one draw, and is one to watch.

The crowd at the Elephant & Castle Leisure Centre in

South London were looking forward to a good fight, and they got one. Camden's undefeated (16-0) Martin Power was in with Huddersfield's Dale Robinson for the vacant British bantamweight title. The Yorkshireman, a former Commonwealth flyweight champion, had just one loss in 18 fights. As amateurs, Robinson had stopped Power and he figured he could do it again. "He's pretty much the same fighter now," he said. Dale got a shock as Martin stuck with him all the way to come out with the decision and claim the title. By the halfway mark, Robinson looked on his way to victory, his experience and body punching a decisive factor. Martin, however, finished like a train and the referee, Paul Thomas, saw him a winner. There was a controversial incident in round two when Power's head opened a gash over Dale's left eye. Television replays showed it was a blatant butt and, fortunately for Power, he got away with it. And fortunately for Robinson the blood flowed to the side of his eye, allowing him to get through the fight. But it didn't help his cause in a tight one. He'd love a return.

That grand old warrior Alan Bosworth, at 37 and after a 17-15-2 pro log, reached journey's end at Spennymoor Leisure Centre in County Durham, where the local hero, Nigel Wright, retained his English light-welterweight title to send his fans into raptures and make a statement. On this night he was the (W)right man for the job. The hard man from Northampton gave it his all, as usual, but southpaw Nigel, having his first fight at home (he's from nearby Crook) in 15 fights (1 defeat) came through a few sticky patches to box and punch his way to a fine victory. Beating a man who had shared a ring with Junior Witter, Eamonn Magee, Shea Neary, Colin Dunne, Jan Bergman and Wayne Rigby, was a fine achievement for the former amateur star who should be in the mix when Witter vacates as is expected.

In the chief supporting bout, the British super-bantamweight champion, Michael Hunter, stayed unbeaten as he overpowered a tough little Frenchman in Kamel Guerfi inside six rounds to take his record to 22-0-1. Hunter is looking for a fight with Esham Pickering, the European champion at the weight. The Newark man was in action at Bradford where he took a points decision over Noel Wilders in an eight-round warm-up for a title defence against Spain's Miguel Mallon. The Castleford southpaw was a former IBO, European, and British bantamweight champion, but at 30 had seen better days and Pickering was a good winner.

On the same Bradford show, local star Junior Witter was presented with the Lonsdale Belt to take home and stick in his trophy cupboard. Southpaw Witter had defeated Alan Bosworth for the vacant British light-welterweight title in March 2002 and had been unable to win the Belt outright in the three years since as no one was deemed good enough to fight him for it. So the Board decided to award the coveted Lonsdale trophy to the champion, as they had done with flyweights Charlie Magri and Walter McGowan, both of whom had only been able to get one notch on their Belts.

In Dublin's fair city, where the girls are so pretty, the boxers aren't bad either. Local hotshot Bernard Dunne sent his fans home happy from the National Stadium after racking up his 16th straight victory with a decision over Yuri Voronin, but it was almost a disaster. Almost. In the tenth and final round, the Ukrainian featherweight champion slammed a right to the back of Dunne's head and suddenly the favourite was on Queer Street, reeling across the ring and tumbling to the canvas twice, before he was able to regroup and get back into the fight. Voronin chased frantically in an effort to finish it, but Bernard's boxing brain pulled him through the fog and when the mist cleared the bell rang and Dunne had won another fight, only his second on home turf after coming back from the States with a 14-0 record. Another Barry McGuigan?

JUNE

After 38 consecutive victories, Ricky Hatton finally got the fight he wanted against world's number one light-welterweight, Kostya Tszyu, right in his own backyard, the huge MEN Arena in Manchester, and with a capacity 22,000 crowd cheering him on, Ricky Hatton delivered the goods. After 11 gruelling rounds, Tszyu was pulled out of the fight by trainer Johnny Lewis and the roar from the fans woke up the rest of the city. It was three o'clock in the morning! In the cold light of day, the win can be put into perspective. The Russian-born Aussie was 35-years-old, had been plagued by injury and inactivity, while Hatton was 26, undefeated and hungry for what Tszyu had enjoyed for the best part of ten years. He was meeting the veteran at the right time and, certainly, in the right place. Tickets for the fight, scheduled to start at 2.00am, sold out within two hours. Incredible! Promoter Frank Warren said they could have sold out the place three times over. So to the fight. Hatton was unstoppable, climbing all over Tszyu from the opening bell; jabs, hooks, right hands, strong-arm stuff, and Kostya was unable to stem the tide as Ricky rolled over him. The Russian did his best stuff in the middle rounds, but Hatton sucked it up and when he went for the finish line, Tszyu was not able to stay with him. Battered and bruised, he couldn't face the final three minutes and Ricky Hatton was the new world champion. He beat the man!

David Barnes could not share the success of his fellow Mancunian in the chief supporting bout. The British welterweight champion was trying to add the Commonwealth title to his collection, but the titleholder, Joshua Okine, had other ideas, dominating the fight, dropping Barnes in the fifth and forcing the referee's intervention in the final round. David had won 17 fights before being held to a draw by Ali Nuumbembe, and now the man from Ghana had destroyed him.

Frank Warren's fistic extravaganza had kicked off the night before with another local favourite in Michael Brodie reaching for the big one again. It was Brodie's fourth crack at a world title after being robbed against Willie Jorrin (WBC), boxing a stirling draw with In-Jin Chi (WBC) and suffering a crushing defeat in a rematch with the strong Korean. Now Michael was going in with Scott Harrison for his WBO featherweight title. Harrison had been barred from the pubs in Glasgow for unsocial behaviour and the same thing could happen in Manchester after what he did to Brodie. The local man had boxed most of his career at super-bantamweight, winning British, Commonwealth, and European titles, while Harrison is a big, solid featherweight. Brodie gave him a fight, but when the chips were down the champ's strength and power were too much. He rocked Brodie as the third ended and finished him in round four with a crippling body shot, his fifth defence in his second reign. While he was hoping Warren could get him a super fight, Michael Brodie hung up his gloves after an honourable 35-3-1 pro log.

On a sweltering night at the refurbished York Hall, it was even hotter inside the ring where Commonwealth lightweight champion, Kevin Bennett, was on his way to a unification victory over British titleholder, Graham Earl. Outboxing and outpunching his man, Hartlepool's Bennett dropped Earl heavily in the sixth. But Graham got up and staged a remarkable comeback and suddenly Bennett started to unravel. By round nine Earl was on top and Kevin was reeling all over the ring, out on his feet. It was stopped and Graham Earl was British and Commonwealth champion.

At the Goresbrook Leisure Centre in Dagenham, the hometown favourite, Nicky Cook, defended his European and Commonwealth featherweight titles against British champion, Dazzo Williams, picking up all the marbles with a stunning second-round knockout and taking his record to 25-0. Next!

Overseas action this month saw Esham Pickering retain his European super-bantam-weight title with a tenth-round stoppage over the unbeaten (26-0) Spaniard, Miguel Mallon, at Alcobendes, near Madrid. The local got into the fight after four rounds and had his fans roaring, but he was in over his head and Pickering took him apart in the tenth, a right dropping Miguel. He beat the count, but his legs weren't listening to his head and it was stopped.

Out in California, the former Olympic champ, Audley Harrison, kick-started his stuttering pro career with a seventh-round stoppage of Robert Davis, his first outing in a year for various reasons. The big southpaw was impressive in the seventh round, but up till then was his usual cautious self. Harrison is pushing 34 and it's time he got out of second gear before his engine burns out.

Audley would have given his eye teeth for the opportunity that Ireland's Kevin McBride seized with both hands, upsetting the odds with a career-ending defeat of former champ, Mike Tyson, in Washington, DC. Slumped on the canvas after six rounds, Mike got up, sat on his stool, and his amazing rocket-ride to fame and fortune fizzled out at the age of 38. In hindsight, I don't think Harrison would have taken the fight anyway.

Up-and-coming heavyweight, Roman Greenberg, the London-based Israeli, was in Las Vegas to knock over moderate Josh Gutcher inside four rounds, moving his unbeaten record to 19-0, 14 via the short route, and was booked for Monte Carlo next. Roman is seeing the world but it's time he was meeting somebody with a pulse.

Chatham southpaw, John Armour, was back in the ring after two years out and it was two years too late for the former WBU bantam champion and undefeated European and Commonwealth titleholder as he was beaten over six rounds by former French champ, Tuncay Kaya.

Facts and Figures, 2004-2005

There were 577 (594 in 2003-2004) British-based boxers who were active between 1 July 2004 and 30 June 2005, spread over 177 (183 in 2003-2004) promotions held in Britain, not including the Republic of Ireland, during the same period. Those who were either already holding licenses or had been re-licensed amounted to 442, while there were 121 (112 in 2003-2004) new professionals. There were also nine men who started their careers elsewhere and five women.

Unbeaten During Season (Minimum Qualification: 6 Contests)

7: Martin Concepcion, Tony Doherty. 6: Ryan Barrett, Ricky Burns, Dean Cockburn, John Fewkes, Matthew Hall, Lee Haskins, Kevin Mitchell, Anthony Small.

Longest Unbeaten Sequence (Minimum Qualification: 10 Contests)

39: Joe Calzaghe, Ricky Hatton. 28: Thomas McDonagh (2 draws). 26: Michael Jennings. 25: Nicky Cook. 23: Michael Hunter (1 draw). 22: Gavin Rees. 20: Johnny Nelson (1 draw). 19: Roman Greenberg. 18: Steve Foster, Audley Harrison, Enzo Maccarinelli. 17: Martin Power. 16: Young Muttley, Matt Skelton, Junior Witter, Gary Woolcombe. 15: Carl Froch, Ajose Olusegun, Nadeem Sidique, Dave Stewart. 14: Kevin Anderson, Tony Doherty, Scott Gammer (1 draw), Kevin Mitchell, Paul Smith. 13: Danny Hunt, Danny Smith (1 draw), Isaac Ward (2 draws), Gary Young. 12: Ricky Burns, Lee Haskins, Ryan Kerr, Derry Matthews, Erik Teymour, Carl Wright (1 draw). 11: Martin Concepcion, Matthew Hatton (1 draw), Andy Morris, John Murray. 10: Stefy Bull, Lenny Daws, Craig Dickson (1 draw), Peter Haymer (1 draw), Mark Hobson, Barry Morrison.

Most Wins During Season (Minimum Qualification: 6 Contests)

8: Gary Woolcombe. 7: Kell Brook, Martin Concepcion, Tony Doherty. 6: Ryan Barrett, Ricky Burns, Dean Cockburn, John Fewkes, Matthew Hall, Lee Haskins, Kevin Mitchell, Anthony Small.

Most Contests During Season (Minimum Qualification: 10 Contests)

25: Ernie Smith. 22: Pete Buckley. 16: Daniel Thorpe. 15: Howard Clarke. 14: Geraint Harvey. 13: Jason Nesbitt. 11: Peter Dunn. 10: Brian Coleman, Simeon Cover, Hastings Rasani.

Most Contests During Career (Minimum Qualification: 50 Contests)

249: Pete Buckley. 172: Brian Coleman. 136: Tony Booth. 107: Keith Jones. 103: Paul Bonson, Karl Taylor. 99: Ernie

Smith. 97: Arv Mittoo. 94: Anthony Hanna. 92: Howard Clarke. 89: Leigh Wicks. 87: Ojay Abrahams. 85: Michael Pinnock. 76: Dave Hinds. 68: Lee Williamson. 67: David Kirk. 66: Carl Allen. 59: Daniel Thorpe. 58: Johnny Nelson, Jason Nesbitt. 56: Jason Collins, Chris Woollas. 54: Peter Dunn, Richard Inquieti.

Stop Press: Results for July/August 2005 (British-based fighters' results only)

Ibis Hotel, Fulham, London – 1 July (Promoter: John Merton Promotions)
Ovill McKenzie w pts 6 Hastings Rasani, Gareth Lawrence w pts 6 Michael Banbula, Gareth Couch w pts 4 Silence Saheed, Oscar Milkitas w pts 6 Arv Mittoo.

Dundalk, Ireland – 2 July
Martin Lindsay w rsc 2 Henry Janes, Michael Kelly w pts 4 Daniel Thorpe.

The Leisure Centre, Altrincham – 8 July (Promoter: Matchroom)
Jamie Moore w rsc 6 Michael Jones (British L.Middleweight Title), John Murray w pts 8 Mounir Guebbas, Ali Nuumembe w rsc 2 Dmitry Yanushevich, Neil Dawson w rsc 4 Tony Moran, Gyorgy Hidvegi w pts 4 Michael Pinnock, John Marshall w rsc 3 Zoltan Surman, Johnny Rocco w pts 4 Joe Mitchell.

The Arena, Nottingham – 9 July (Promoter: Hennessy Sports)
Carl Froch w pts 12 Matthew Barney (British & Commonwealth S.Middleweight Titles), Junior Witter w pts 12 Andreas Kotelnik (European L.Welterweight Title), Lee Meager w pts 10 Martin Watson, David Walker w pts 4 Howard Clarke, Lenny Daws w pts 6 Ivor Bonavic, Billy Corcoran w pts 6 Steve Gethin, Kell Brook w rsc 2 Jonathan Whiteman, John O'Donnell w rtd 3 Ben Hudson, Darren Barker w pts 6 Ernie Smith.

Whitchurch Leisure Centre, Bristol – 9 July (Promoter: Bristol Boxing Academy)
Dean Francis w pts 6 Paul Bonson, Carl Johanneson w rsc 3 Daniel Thorpe, Chris Long w pts 6 Kristian Laight, Paddy Ryan w rsc 6 Shane White, John Smith w pts 6 Gary Thompson, Liam Stinchcombe w pts 6 Mark Phillips, Danny Gwilym w rsc 3 Arv Mittoo, Luke Simpkin w rsc 3 Henry Smith

The Arena, Bolton – 16 July (Promoter: Sports Network)
Matt Skelton w rtd 7 Mark Krence (British Heavyweight Title), Michael Jennings w co 1 Jimmy Vincent (British Welterweight Title), Steve Foster w rtd 5 Jim Betts, Ryan Rhodes w rsc 2 Alan Gilbert, Tony Doherty nc 2 Ernie Smith, Ivor Bonavic w rsc 2 Martin Concepcion, Amir Khan w rsc 1 David Bailey, Derry Matthews w rsc 3 Dai Davies, Craig Watson w pts 4 Billy Smith.

Prince Regent Hotel, Chigwell – 16 July (Promoter: Tony Burns Promotions)
Dave Stewart w pts 8 Antony Mezaache, Darren Barker w pts 6 Dean Walker, Daniel Cadman w pts 6 Danny Thornton.

Nuremburg, Germany – 16 July
Vitaly Tsypko w pts 12 Brian Magee (European S.Middleweight Title), Arthur Abraham w pts 12 Howard Eastman (WBA Inter-Continental Middleweight Title).

Monte Carlo – 20 July
Roman Greenberg w pts 8 Mamadou Sacko, Anthony Small w rsc 1 David Lefranc.

Lemoore, California, USA – 21 July
Jessica Rakoczy w rsc 6 Jane Couch.

Meadowbank Arena, Edinburgh – 23 July (Sports Network)
Alex Arthur w pts 12 Boris Sinitsin (European S.Featherweight Title). Colin McNeil w pts 10 Taz Jones (Celtic L.Middleweight Title), Takaloo w pts 8 Delroy Mellis, Lee McAllister w pts 4 Billy Smith, Ricky Burns w pts 4 Alan Temple, Harry Ramogoadi w rsc 5 Jamie Arthur, Craig Lynch w pts 4 Robert Burton, Nathan Cleverly w pts 4 Ernie Smith.

The Eqinox, Leicester Square, London – 24 July (Promoter: Joe Pyle/Jonathan Feld)
Micky Steeds w pts 6 Garry Delaney, Terry Dixon w pts 4 Mal Rice, Toks Owoh w pts 4 Paul Bonson, Coleman Barrett w pts 4 Tony Booth, Jamal Morrison w pts 4 Casey Brooke, Judex Memea w pts 4 Beki Moyo, Garry Buckland w rsc 2 Danny Gwilym, Michael Grant w pts 4 David Kehoe.

The Octagon, Sheffield – 24 July (Promoter: Dennis Hobson/Evans-Waterman Promotions)
John Fewkes w pts 6 Karl Taylor, Geard Ajetovic w pts 6 Conroy McIntosh, Femi Fehintola w pts 6 Jason Nesbitt, Terry Adams w pts 6 Gavin Smith, Scott Lawton w pts 6 Pete Buckley, Dwayne Hill w rsc 3 Gary Coombes, Stuart Brookes w pts 6 Tony Randell, Lee Edwards w pts 6 Lee Williamson, Nick Smedley w pts 6 Lance Verallo, Craig Bromley w pts 4 Neil Read.

Atlantic City, New Jersey, USA – 4 August
Matthew Macklin w rsc 3 Leo Laudat.

St Petersburg, Florida, USA – 7 August
Jeff Lacy w rsc 7 Robin Reid (IBF S.Middleweight Title), John Murray w pts 6 Johnny Walker.

Rimini, Italy – 7 August
Stefiana Bianchini w pts 10 Cathy Brown (WBC Women's Flyweight Title), Brunet Zamora w pts 6 Peter McDonagh, Leonard Bundu w pts 6 Brett James.

74

Diary of British Boxing Tournaments, 2004-2005

Tournaments are listed by date, town, venue and promoter and cover the period 1 July 2004 – 30 June 2005

Code: SC = Sporting Club

Date	Town	Venue	Promoters
03.07.04	Newport	The Sports Centre	Sports Network
03.07.04	Blackpool	Winter Gardens	Ellis
03.07.04	Bristol	Dolman Exhibition Hall	A Force Promotions/Chris Sanigar
08.07.04	The Strand	Savoy Hotel	Evans-Waterman Promotions
08.07.04	Birmingham	Aston Villa Leisure Centre	Bradley
10.07.04	Coventry	Sky Blue Connexion	Shakespeare Promotions
30.07.04	Bethnal Green	York Hall	Sports Network
03.09.04	Newport	The Sports Centre	Sports Network
03.09.04	Doncaster	The Dome	Rushton
10.09.04	Wembley	The Arena	Hobson/Evans-Waterman Promotions
10.09.04	Liverpool	Everton Park Sports Centre	Lee Maloney
10.09.04	Bethnal Green	York Hall	Sports Network
12.09.04	Shrewsbury	Liquid Nightclub	Bradley
17.09.04	Plymouth	The Pavilions	Chris Sanigar
17.09.04	Sheffield	Don Valley Stadium	Hobson
18.09.04	Newark	Grove Leisure Centre	Scriven
20.09.04	Glasgow	Holiday Inn Hotel	St Andrew's SC
20.09.04	Cleethorpes	Winter Gardens	Dalton
23.09.04	Gateshead	Federation Brewery Lancastrian Suite	Conroy
24.09.04	Nottingham	The Arena	Hennessy Sports
24.09.04	Bethnal Green	York Hall	Maloney Promotions
24.09.04	Millwall	Britannia Hotel	Merton
26.09.04	Stoke	King's Hall	Dykes
27.09.04	Cleethorpes	Winter Gardens	Frater
30.09.04	Hull	Willerby Manor	Pollard
30.09.04	Glasgow	Hilton Hotel	Evans-Waterman Promotions
01.10.04	Manchester	MEN Arena	Sports Network
01.10.04	Bristol	Dolman Exhibition Hall	Chris Sanigar
05.10.04	Dudley	The Town Hall	Bradley
08.10.04	Brentwood	The International Centre	Matchroom/Harding
08.10.04	Glasgow	Marriott Hotel	Morrison
09.10.04	Norwich	The Sports Village	Featherby/Ingle
11.10.04	Birmingham	Holiday Inn	Cowdell
11.10.04	Glasgow	Holiday Inn Hotel	St Andrew's SC
15.10.04	Glasgow	Kelvin Hall	Matchroom/Tommy Gilmour
16.10.04	Dagenham	Goresbrook Leisure Centre	Roe
22.10.04	Edinburgh	Royal Highland Showground	Sports Network
22.10.04	Mansfield	The Leisure Centre	Scriven
23.10.04	Wakefield	Light Waves Leisure Centre	Hobson
24.10.04	Sheffield	Octagon Centre	Hobson
28.10.04	Sunderland	Marriott Hotel	Conroy
28.10.04	Belfast	Ulster Hall	Callahan & Breen Promotions/Sports Network
29.10.04	Renfrew	Braehead Arena	Sports Network
29.10.04	Doncaster	The Dome	Rushton
29.10.04	Worksop	Van Dyke's Hotel	Ingle
31.10.04	Shaw	Tara Leisure Centre	Doughty
04.11.04	Piccadilly	Café Royal	Helliet
05.11.04	Hereford	The Leisure Centre	Matchroom
06.11.04	Coventry	Leofric Hotel	Shakespeare Promotions

09.11.04	Leeds	Elland Road Conference & Exhibition Centre	Spratt
12.11.04	Halifax	Northbridge Leisure Centre	Sports Network
12.11.04	Wembley	The Conference Centre	Hennessy Sports
12.11.04	Belfast	Shorts Recreational Club	Maloney Promotions
15.11.04	Glasgow	Holiday Inn Hotel	St Andrew's SC
18.11.04	Shrewsbury	Albrighton Hotel	Bradley
18.11.04	Blackpool	Central Workingmens' Club	Veitch
19.11.04	Hartlepool	Borough Hall	Garside
19.11.04	Bethnal Green	York Hall	Sports Network
20.11.04	Coventry	Leofric Hall	Coventry SC
21.11.04	Bracknell	The Leisure Centre	Evans-Waterman Promotions
24.11.04	Mayfair	Hilton Hotel	Evans-Waterman Promotions
25.11.04	Birmingham	Aston Villa Leisure Centre	Bradley
26.11.04	Bethnal Green	York Hall	Maloney Promotions
26.11.04	Hull	KC Banqueting Rooms	Hull & District SC
26.11.04	Altrincham	The Leisure Centre	Matchroom
02.12.04	Crystal Palace	National Sports Centre	Williams
02.12.04	Bristol	Thistle Hotel	Couch
03.12.04	Edinburgh	Meadowbank Sports Centre	Sports Network
03.12.04	Bristol	Dolman Exhibition Hall	Chris Sanigar
06.12.04	Leicester	Ramada Jarvis Hotel	Griffin/Shakespeare Promotions
06.12.04	Leeds	Queen's Hotel	Walker
06.12.04	Bradford	Hilton Hotel	Celebanski
08.12.04	Longford	Thistle Hotel	Ingle/Carman
09.12.04	Sunderland	Marriott Hotel	Conroy
09.12.04	Stockport	Acton Court Hotel	Dixon
10.12.04	Sheffield	Hillsborough Leisure Centre	Hobson/Evans-Waterman Promotions
10.12.04	Mansfield	The Leisure Centre	Scriven
11.12.04	Canning Town	ExCel Arena	Sports Network
12.12.04	Glasgow	Marriott Hotel	Morrison
13.12.04	Cleethorpes	Winter Gardens	Dalton
13.12.04	Birmingham	Burlington Hotel	Cowdell
15.12.04	Sheffield	Silver Blades Ice Rink	Coldwell
16.12.04	Cleethorpes	Winter Gardens	Frater
17.12.04	Huddersfield	The Sports Centre	Matchroom
17.12.04	Liverpool	Everton Park Sports Centre	Lee Maloney
17.12.04	Coventry	The Sports Centre	Shakespeare Promotions
19.12.04	Bolton	Reebok Stadium	Wood
19.12.04	Bethnal Green	York Hall	Roe
21.01.05	Brentford	Fountain Leisure Centre	Hobson/Evans-Waterman Promotions
21.01.05	Bridgend	The Recreation Centre	Sports Network
27.01.05	Piccadilly	Café Royal	Helliet
28.01.05	Renfrew	Braehead Arena	Sports Network
31.01.05	Glasgow	Holiday Inn Hotel	St Andrew's SC
04.02.05	Plymouth	The Pavilions	Jamie Sanigar
04.02.05	Doncaster	The Dome	Rushton
06.02.05	Southampton	The Guildhall	Bishop
11.02.05	Manchester	MEN Arena	Sports Network
12.02.05	Portsmouth	Mountbatten Centre	Maloney Promotions
13.02.05	Brentwood	The International Centre	Matchroom/Harding
13.02.05	Bradford	The Town & Country Club	Ingle
17.02.05	Dudley	The Town Hall	Bradley
18.02.05	Brighton	Metropole Hotel	Pyle
20.02.05	Sheffield	Octagon Centre	Coldwell
20.02.05	Bristol	Thistle Hotel	Couch

21.02.05	Peterborough	Moat House Hotel	Pauly
21.02.05	Birmingham	Burlington Hotel	Cowdell
21.02.05	Glasgow	Holiday Inn Hotel	St Andrew's SC
24.02.05	Sunderland	Marriott Hotel	Conroy
25.02.05	Wembley	The Conference Centre	Sports Network
25.02.05	Irvine	Volunteer Rooms	Tommy Gilmour
26.02.05	Burton	Meadowside Leisure Centre	Bradley
04.03.05	Rotherham	Magna Centre	Hobson/Evans-Waterman Promotions
04.03.05	Hartlepool	Borough Hall	Garside
05.03.05	Southwark	Elephant & Castle Leisure Centre	Maloney Promotions
05.03.05	Dagenham	Goresbrook Leisure Centre	Roe
06.03.05	Mansfield	The Leisure Centre	Scriven
06.03.05	Shaw	Tara Leisure Centre	Doughty
11.03.05	Doncaster	The Dome	Sports Network
18.03.05	Belfast	King's Hall	Sports Network
21.03.05	Glasgow	Holiday Inn Hotel	St Andrew's SC
23.03.05	Leicester Square	Equinox Nightclub	Baker/Evans-Waterman Promotions/Roe
26.03.05	Hackney	The Empire	Williams
01.04.05	Glasgow	Marriott Hotel	Morrison
07.04.05	Birmingham	Aston Villa Leisure Centre	Bradley
08.04.05	Bristol	Dolman Exhibition Hall	Chris Sanigar
08.04.05	Edinburgh	Meadowbank Sports Centre	Sports Network
09.04.05	Norwich	The Sports Village	Featherby
10.04.05	Brentwood	The International Centre	TBS Promotions
15.04.05	Shrewsbury	Albrighton Hotel	Bradley
18.04.05	Bradford	Hilton Hotel	Garber
21.04.05	Dudley	The Town Hall	Bradley
22.04.05	Barnsley	The Metrodome	Sports Network/Coldwell
24.04.05	Derby	Heritage Hotel	Ashton
24.04.05	Leicester Square	Equinox Nightclub	Pyle
24.04.05	Askern	Miners' Welfare Club	Scriven
25.04.05	Glasgow	Holiday Inn Hotel	St Andrew's SC
25.04.05	Cleethorpes	Winter Gardens	Frater
26.04.05	Leeds	Elland Road Conference & Exhibition Centre	Spratt
28.04.05	Clydach	Manor Park Country House	Boyce
29.04.05	Southwark	Elephant & Castle Leisure Centre	Maloney Promotions/Sports Network
29.04.05	Plymouth	The Pavilions	Chris Sanigar
30.04.05	Coventry	Leofric Hotel	Coventry SC
30.04.05	Wigan	Robin Park Sports Centre	Dixon
30.04.05	Dagenham	Goresbrook Leisure Centre	Roe
08.05.05	Sheffield	Grosvenor House Hotel	Rhodes
08.05.05	Bradford	The Town & Country Club	Ingle
12.05.05	Sunderland	Marriott Hotel	Conroy
13.05.05	Liverpool	Everton Park Sports Centre	Lee Maloney
14.05.05	Aberdeen	Beach Ballroom	Ingle
15.05.05	Sheffield	Octogon Centre	Hobson
16.05.05	Birmingham	Holiday Inn	Cowdell
20.05.05	Glasgow	Thistle Hotel	Morrison
20.05.05	Southwark	Elephant & Castle Leisure Centre	Maloney Promotions/Sports Network
20.05.05	Doncaster	The Dome	Rushton
23.05.05	Cleethorpes	Winter Gardens	Dalton
26.05.05	Piccadilly	Café Royal	Helliet
27.05.05	Spennymoor	The Leisure Centre	Sports Network/Robinson
27.05.05	Motherwell	The Concert Hall	Chris Gilmour
01.06.05	Leeds	Queen's Hotel	Walker

02.06.05	Yarm	Tall Trees Hotel	Garside
02.06.05	Peterborough	Moat House Hotel	Pauly
03.06.05	Hull	KC Banqueting Rooms	Hull & District SC
03.06.05	Manchester	MEN Arena	Sports Network
04.06.05	Manchester	MEN Arena	Sports Network
06.06.05	Glasgow	Holiday Inn Hotel	St Andrew's SC
11.06.05	Kirkcaldy	The Ice Centre	Tommy Gilmour
12.06.05	Leicester Square	Equinonox Nightclub	Pyle/Feld
16.06.05	Dagenham	Goresbrook Leisure Centre	Matchroom
16.06.05	Mayfair	Millenium Hotel	Evans-Waterman Promotions
17.06.05	Glasgow	Kelvin Hall	Sports Network/Morrison
18.06.05	Coventry	The Skydrome	Shakespeare Promotions
18.06.05	Barnsley	The Metrodome	Konkrete Promotions
19.06.05	Bethnal Green	York Hall	Maloney Promotions
20.06.05	Longford	Thistle Hotel	Carman
25.06.05	Melton Mowbray	The Cattle Market	Shakespeare Promotions
25.06.05	Wakefield	Light Waves Leisure Centre	Rhodes
26.06.05	Southampton	The Guildhall	Bishop

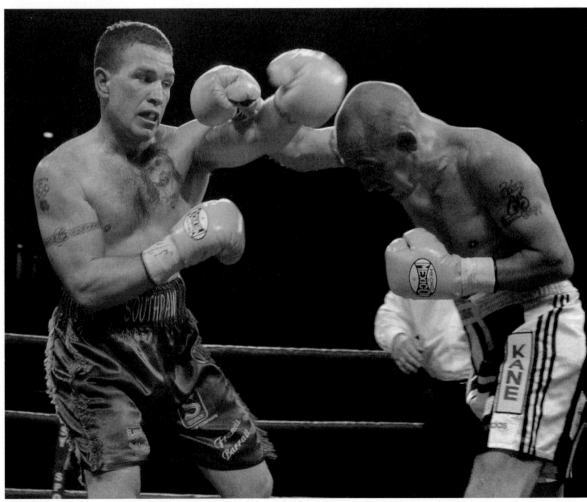

Making a successful defence of his European Union light-welterweight title, Francis Barrett (left) eventually overcame the tough Alan Bosworth at the Wembley Conference Centre on 12 November　　　　Les Clark

Active British-Based Boxers: Career Records

Shows the complete record for all British-based boxers who have been active between 1 July 2004 and 30 June 2005. Names in brackets are real names, where they differ from ring names, and the first place name given is the boxer's domicile. Boxers are either shown as being self-managed or with a named manager, the information being supplied by the BBBoC shortly before going to press. Also included are foreign-born fighters who made their pro debuts in Britain, along with others like Shinny Bayaar (Mongolia), Varuzhan Davtyan (Armenia), Ruben Groenewald (South Africa), Oscar Milkitas (Lithuania), Hastings Rasani (Zimbabwe), Harry Ramogoadi (South Africa), Paulie Silva (Portugal), Jed Syger (Turkey) and Choi Tseveenpurev (Mongolia), who, although starting their careers elsewhere, now hold BBBoC licenses.

Ojay Abrahams

Watford. *Born* Lambeth, 17 December, 1964
S.Middleweight. Former British Masters Middleweight Champion. Ht. 5'8½"
Manager Self

21.09.91	Gordon Webster W RSC 3 Tottenham
26.10.91	Mick Reid W RSC 5 Brentwood
26.11.91	John Corcoran W PTS 6 Bethnal Green
21.01.92	Dave Andrews DREW 6 Norwich
31.03.92	Marty Duke W RSC 2 Norwich
19.05.92	Michael Smyth L PTS 6 Cardiff
16.06.92	Ricky Mabbett W PTS 6 Dagenham
13.10.92	Vince Rose L RSC 3 Mayfair
30.01.93	Vince Rose DREW 6 Brentwood
19.05.93	Ricky Mabbett L RSC 4 Leicester
18.09.93	Ricky Mabbett L PTS 6 Leicester
09.12.93	Nick Appiah W PTS 6 Watford
24.01.94	Errol McDonald W RSC 2 Glasgow
09.02.94	Vince Rose W PTS 6 Brentwood
23.05.94	Spencer McCracken L PTS 6 Walsall
11.06.94	Darren Dyer W RSC 1 Bethnal Green
29.09.94	Gary Logan L PTS 10 Bethnal Green
	(Southern Area Welterweight Title Challenge)
13.12.94	Geoff McCreesh L PTS 6 Potters Bar
11.02.95	Gary Murray L PTS 8 Hamanskraal, South Africa
17.07.95	Andreas Panayi L PTS 8 Mayfair
02.10.95	Larbi Mohammed L RTD 5 Mayfair
08.12.95	Jason Beard W CO 2 Bethnal Green
09.04.96	Kevin Thompson W RSC 3 Stevenage
07.05.96	Harry Dhami L RSC 5 Mayfair
	(Vacant Southern Area Welterweight Title)
12.11.96	Spencer McCracken L PTS 8 Dudley
22.04.97	Paul King W RSC 4 Bethnal Green
29.05.97	Paul Ryan L RSC 3 Mayfair
30.06.97	Ahmet Dottuev L RSC 4 Bethnal Green
08.11.97	Anthony McFadden L PTS 8 Southwark
24.03.98	Leigh Wicks W PTS 6 Bethnal Green
28.04.98	Jim Webb W RSC 2 Belfast
10.09.98	Delroy Leslie L PTS 10 Acton
	(Vacant Southern Area L. Middleweight Title)
19.12.98	Michael Jones L PTS 6 Liverpool
23.01.99	Wayne Alexander L DIS 1 Cheshunt
	(Vacant Southern Area L. Middleweight Title)
01.05.99	Wayne Alexander L RSC 3 Crystal Palace
26.06.99	Geoff McCreesh L PTS 8 Millwall
05.10.99	Hussain Osman L PTS 4 Bloomsbury
23.10.99	Paul Samuels L PTS 8 Telford
18.01.00	Howard Eastman L RSC 2 Mansfield
23.03.00	Pedro Thompson DREW 6 Bloomsbury
08.04.00	Anthony Farnell L PTS 8 Bethnal Green
16.05.00	Ryan Rhodes L PTS 6 Warrington
23.05.00	Alexandru Andrei L PTS 6 Paris, France
04.07.00	Lester Jacobs L PTS 4 Tooting
21.09.00	Harry Butler W PTS 6 Bloomsbury
07.10.00	Kofi Jantuah L RTD 3 Doncaster
25.11.00	Donovan Smillie W RSC 2 Manchester
16.12.00	Marlon Hayes L RTD 6 Sheffield
15.01.01	Gordon Behan DREW 6 Manchester
24.02.01	Ruben Groenewald L PTS 6 Bethnal Green
22.04.01	Harry Butler W PTS 6 Streatham
17.05.01	Lee Murtagh W RSC 2 Leeds
	(Vacant British Masters L. Middleweight Title)
21.06.01	Charden Ansoula L PTS 4 Earls Court
28.07.01	Gary Logan L RSC 4 Wembley
10.12.01	Jimmy Vincent L PTS 10 Birmingham
	(British Masters L. Middleweight Title Challenge)
28.01.02	Ian Cooper W PTS 6 Barnsley
16.03.02	John Humphrey L PTS 10 Bethnal Green
	(Vacant Southern Area L.Middleweight Title)
13.04.02	Mihaly Kotai L PTS 6 Liverpool
20.04.02	Freeman Barr L PTS 8 Cardiff
10.05.02	Carl Froch L RSC 1 Bethnal Green
15.06.02	Sam Soliman L PTS 4 Tottenham
17.08.02	Wayne Elcock L PTS 4 Cardiff
17.09.02	David Starie L RSC 4 Bethnal Green
25.10.02	Gilbert Eastman L PTS 4 Bethnal Green
12.12.02	Allan Gray L PTS 10 Leicester Square
	(Southern Area Middleweight Title Challenge. Vacant WBF International Middleweight Title)
05.03.03	David Walker L PTS 6 Bethnal Green
19.04.03	Geard Ajetovic L PTS 4 Liverpool
12.05.03	Jason Collins L PTS 10 Birmingham
	(Vacant British Masters S.Middleweight Title)
05.07.03	Allan Foster L PTS 4 Brentwood
18.09.03	Steve Roache W CO 2 Mayfair
18.10.03	Michael Jones L PTS 6 Manchester
22.11.03	Jason McKay L PTS 4 Belfast
01.12.03	Omar Gumati L PTS 6 Leeds
10.02.04	Daniel Teasdale L PTS 6 Barnsley
23.02.04	Matt Galer L PTS 4 Nottingham
08.03.04	Hamed Jamali L PTS 8 Birmingham
02.04.04	Scott Dann L RSC 6 Plymouth
06.05.04	Daniel Teasdale L PTS 4 Barnsley
13.05.04	Conroy McIntosh L RSC 2 Bethnal Green
12.06.04	Matthew Macklin L PTS 4 Manchester
10.09.04	Paul Smith L PTS 4 Liverpool
29.10.04	Tom Cannon L PTS 4 Renfrew
12.11.04	Matthew Hall L RSC 1 Halifax
27.01.05	Eder Kurti L PTS 6 Piccadilly
27.05.05	Paul Buchanan L PTS 6 Spennymoor
04.06.05	Ricardo Samms L PTS 4 Manchester
18.06.05	Jon Ibbotson L PTS 4 Barnsley

Career: 87 contests, won 20, drew 4, lost 63.

Terry Adams

Birmingham. *Born* Birmingham, 1 November, 1978
L.Middleweight. Ht. 5'8"
Manager T. Nerwal

19.02.04	Neil Addis W CO 2 Dudley
15.04.04	Geraint Harvey W PTS 6 Dudley
08.07.04	Geraint Harvey W RSC 6 Birmingham
15.10.04	Jamie Coyle L RSC 5 Glasgow
13.02.05	Michael Lomax L RSC 1 Brentwood
07.04.05	Keith Jones W PTS 6 Birmingham

Career: 6 contests, won 4, lost 2.

Terry Adams   Les Clark

Neil Addis

Ferndale. *Born* Church Village, 7 July, 1980
Middleweight. Ht. 5'11"
Manager D. Davies

15.11.03	Richard Mazurek L PTS 6 Coventry
22.11.03	Ciaran Healy L RSC 2 Belfast
10.02.04	Dean Walker L PTS 6 Barnsley

19.02.04	Tony Adams L CO 2 Dudley
27.03.04	Scott Forsyth L RSC 3 Edinburgh
03.07.04	Darren McDermott L PTS 4 Newport
24.09.04	Jake Guntert L PTS 6 Bethnal Green
08.10.04	Michael Rennie L RSC 2 Brentwood

Career: 8 contests, lost 8.

Neil Addis   Les Clark

Geard Ajetovic

Liverpool. *Born* Beocin, Yugoslavia, 28
February, 1981
Middleweight. Ht. 5'8½"
Manager D. Hobson

19.04.03	Ojay Abrahams W PTS 4 Liverpool
17.05.03	Jason Samuels W PTS 4 Liverpool
26.09.03	Gary Beardsley W RSC 3 Reading
07.11.03	Joel Ani W RTD 1 Sheffield
06.02.04	Tomas da Silva W RSC 4 Sheffield
12.05.04	Dmitry Donetskiy W PTS 6 Reading
10.12.04	Conroy McIntosh W PTS 6 Sheffield
21.01.05	Dmitry Yanushevich W RSC 4 Brentford

Career: 8 contests, won 8.

Henry Akinwande

Dulwich. *Born* London, 12 October, 1965
Heavyweight. Former Undefeated WBN,
IBF Inter-Continental & WBC FeCarBox
Heavyweight Champion. Former
Undefeated WBO, European &
Commonwealth Heavyweight Champion.
Ht. 6'7"
Manager Self

04.10.89	Carlton Headley W CO 1 Kensington
08.11.89	Dennis Bailey W RSC 2 Wembley
06.12.89	Paul Neilson W RSC 1 Wembley
10.01.90	John Fairbairn W RSC 1 Kensington
14.03.90	Warren Thompson W PTS 6 Kensington
09.05.90	Mike Robinson W CO 1 Wembley
10.10.90	Tracy Thomas W PTS 6 Kensington
12.12.90	Francois Yrius W RSC 1 Kensington
06.03.91	J. B. Williamson W RSC 2 Wembley
06.06.91	Ramon Voorn W PTS 8 Barking
28.06.91	Marshall Tillman W PTS 8 Nice, France
09.10.91	Gypsy John Fury W CO 3 Manchester *(Elim. British Heavyweight Title)*
06.12.91	Tim Bullock W CO 3 Dussledorf, Germany

28.02.92	Young Joe Louis W RSC 3 Issy les Moulineaux, France
26.03.92	Tucker Richards W RSC 2 Telford
10.04.92	Lumbala Tshimba W PTS 8 Carquefou, France
05.06.92	Kimmuel Odum W DIS 6 Marseille, France
18.07.92	Steve Garber W RTD 2 Manchester
19.12.92	Axel Schulz DREW 12 Berlin, Germany *(Vacant European Heavyweight Title)*
18.03.93	Jimmy Thunder W PTS 12 Lewisham *(Vacant Commonwealth Heavyweight Title)*
01.05.93	Axel Schulz W PTS 12 Berlin, Germany *(Vacant European Heavyweight Title)*
06.11.93	Frankie Swindell W PTS 10 Sun City, South Africa
01.12.93	Biagio Chianese W RSC 4 Kensington *(European Heavyweight Title Defence)*
05.04.94	Johnny Nelson W PTS 10 Bethnal Green
23.07.94	Mario Schiesser W CO 7 Berlin, Germany *(European Heavyweight Title Defence)*
08.04.95	Calvin Jones W CO 2 Las Vegas, Nevada, USA
22.07.95	Stanley Wright W RSC 2 Millwall
16.12.95	Tony Tucker W PTS 10 Philadelphia, Pennsylvania, USA
27.01.96	Brian Sergeant W RSC 1 Phoenix, Arizona, USA
23.03.96	Gerard Jones W DIS 7 Miami, Florida, USA
29.06.96	Jeremy Williams W CO 3 Indio, California, USA *(Vacant WBO Heavyweight Title)*
09.11.96	Alexander Zolkin W RSC 10 Las Vegas, Nevada, USA *(WBO Heavyweight Title Defence)*
11.01.97	Scott Welch W PTS 12 Nashville, Tennessee, USA *(WBO Heavyweight Title Defence)*
12.07.97	Lennox Lewis L DIS 5 Stateline, Nevada, USA *(WBC Heavyweight Title Challenge)*
13.12.97	Orlin Norris W PTS 12 Pompano Beach, Florida, USA *(Final Elim. WBA Heavyweight Title)*
06.03.99	Reynaldo Minus W RSC 2 St Paul, Minnesota, USA
15.05.99	Najeed Shaheed W RSC 9 Miami, Florida, USA
22.02.00	Chris Serengo W RSC 1 Capetown, South Africa
25.05.00	Russull Chasteen W CO 5 Tunica, Mississippi, USA
08.12.00	Ken Craven W CO 1 Tallahassee, Florida, USA *(Vacant WBC FeCarBox Heavyweight Title)*
17.03.01	Peter McNeeley W CO 2 Tallahassee, Florida, USA
16.06.01	Maurice Harris W CO 1 Cincinnati, USA
17.11.01	Oliver McCall L CO 10 Las Vegas, Nevada, USA
08.03.02	Curt Paige W RSC 1 Kissimmee, Florida, USA
29.10.02	Sam Ubokane W RSC 7 Capetown, South Africa
10.12.02	Roman Sukhoterin W PTS 12 Constanta, Romania

	(WBN Inter-Continental Heavyweight Title Challenge)
31.05.03	Timo Hoffmann W PTS 12 Frankfurt, Germany *(IBF Inter-Continental Heavyweight Title Challenge)*
10.04.04	Anton Nel W RSC 10 Carabas, Nigeria *(IBF Inter-Continental Heavyweight Title Defence)*
14.05.05	Alex Vasiliev W PTS 8 Bayreuth, Germany

Career: 49 contests, won 46, drew 1, lost 2.

Wayne Alexander

Croydon. *Born* Tooting, 17 July, 1973
WBU L.Middleweight Champion. Former
Undefeated British & European
L.Middleweight Champion. Former
Undefeated Southern Area L.Middleweight
Champion. Ht. 5'8³/₄"
Manager F. Warren

10.11.95	Andrew Jervis W RTD 3 Derby
13.02.96	Paul Murray W PTS 4 Bethnal Green
11.05.96	Jim Webb W RSC 2 Bethnal Green
13.07.96	John Janes W RSC 3 Bethnal Green
05.06.97	Prince Kasi Kaihau W CO 4 Bristol
29.11.97	John Janes W RSC 1 Norwich
21.03.98	Darren Covill W RSC 2 Bethnal Green
09.05.98	Pedro Carragher W CO 2 Sheffield
14.07.98	Lindon Scarlett W RSC 5 Reading
05.12.98	Jimmy Vincent W RSC 3 Bristol
23.01.99	Ojay Abrahams W DIS 1 Cheshunt *(Vacant Southern Area L. Middleweight Title)*
01.05.99	Ojay Abrahams W RSC 3 Crystal Palace
07.08.99	George Richards W RSC 2 Dagenham
19.02.00	Paul Samuels W RSC 3 Dagenham *(Vacant British L. Middleweight Title)*
12.08.00	Paul Denton W RSC 1 Wembley
10.02.01	Harry Simon L RSC 5 Widnes *(WBO L. Middleweight Title Challenge)*
28.07.01	Viktor Fesetchko W PTS 8 Wembley
17.11.01	Joe Townsley W RSC 2 Glasgow *(British L. Middleweight Title Defence)*
19.01.02	Paolo Pizzamiglio W RSC 3 Bethnal Green *(Vacant European L. Middleweight Title)*
18.01.03	Viktor Fesetchko W PTS 6 Preston
06.12.03	Delroy Mellis L RSC 8 Cardiff
07.02.04	Howard Clarke W RSC 2 Bethnal Green
10.09.04	Takaloo W RSC 2 Bethnal Green *(Vacant WBU L. Middleweight Title)*
11.12.04	Delroy Mellis W PTS 10 Canning Town
04.06.05	Christian Bladt W CO 5 Manchester

Career: 25 contests, won 23, lost 2.

Amir Ali

Sheffield. *Born* Sheffield, 10 January, 1985
L. Welterweight. Ht. 5'10"
Manager D. Coldwell

23.11.03	Jason Nesbitt W PTS 6 Rotherham
06.05.04	Pete Buckley W PTS 4 Barnsley
08.06.04	Nigel Senior W PTS 6 Sheffield
20.09.04	Rocky Flanagan W PTS 4 Glasgow
15.12.04	Paul Holborn W PTS 6 Sheffield

Career: 5 contests, won 5.

Haider Ali

Shadwell. *Born* Quetta, Pakistan, 12 November, 1979
S. Featherweight. Ht. 5'8½"
Manager F. Warren

24.05.03	Buster Dennis W PTS 4 Bethnal Green
17.07.03	Jason Nesbitt W PTS 4 Dagenham
29.11.03	Jus Wallie W PTS 4 Renfrew
22.05.04	Steve Bell L PTS 6 Widnes
21.01.05	Jamie Arthur W RSC 3 Bridgend
17.06.05	Ricky Burns L PTS 8 Glasgow

Career: 6 contests, won 4, lost 2.

Carl Allen

Wolverhampton. *Born* Wolverhampton, 20 November, 1969
Lightweight. Former Undefeated Midlands Area S. Bantamweight Champion.
Ht. 5'7¼"
Manager Self

26.11.95	Gary Jenkinson W PTS 6 Birmingham
29.11.95	Jason Squire L PTS 6 Solihull
17.01.96	Andy Robinson L PTS 6 Solihull
13.02.96	Ervine Blake W RSC 5 Wolverhampton
21.02.96	Ady Benton L PTS 6 Batley
29.02.96	Chris Jickells W PTS 6 Scunthorpe
27.03.96	Jason Squire DREW 6 Whitwick
26.04.96	Paul Griffin L RSC 3 Cardiff
30.05.96	Roger Brotherhood W RSC 5 Lincoln
26.09.96	Matthew Harris W PTS 10 Walsall
	(*Midlands Area S. Bantamweight Title Challenge*)
07.10.96	Emmanuel Clottey L RTD 3 Lewisham
21.11.96	Miguel Matthews W PTS 8 Solihull
30.11.96	Floyd Havard L RTD 3 Tylorstown
29.01.97	Pete Buckley W PTS 8 Stoke
11.02.97	David Morris DREW 8 Wolverhampton
28.02.97	Ian McLeod L RTD 3 Kilmarnock
21.05.97	David Burke L PTS 4 Liverpool
30.06.97	Duke McKenzie L PTS 8 Bethnal Green
12.09.97	Brian Carr L PTS 8 Glasgow
04.10.97	Sergei Devakov L PTS 6 Muswell Hill
03.12.97	Chris Lyons W PTS 8 Stoke
21.05.98	Roy Rutherford L PTS 6 Solihull
09.06.98	Scott Harrison L RSC 6 Hull
30.11.98	Gary Hibbert L PTS 4 Manchester
09.12.98	Chris Jickells W RSC 3 Stoke
04.02.99	Mat Zegan L PTS 4 Lewisham
17.03.99	Craig Spacie W PTS 8 Stoke
08.05.99	Phillip Ndou L RSC 2 Bethnal Green
14.06.99	Pete Buckley W PTS 6 Birmingham
22.06.99	David Lowry L PTS 4 Ipswich
11.10.99	Lee Williamson L PTS 6 Birmingham
19.10.99	Tontcho Tontchev L CO 2 Bethnal Green
20.12.99	Nicky Cook L CO 3 Bethnal Green
08.02.00	Lee Williamson W PTS 8 Wolverhampton
29.02.00	Bradley Pryce L PTS 4 Widnes
28.03.00	Lee Williamson W PTS 8 Wolverhampton
16.05.00	Bradley Pryce L RSC 3 Warrington
24.06.00	Michael Gomez L CO 2 Glasgow
10.10.00	Steve Hanley W PTS 8 Brierley Hill
05.02.01	Lee Meager DREW 6 Hull
12.03.01	Pete Buckley W PTS 6 Birmingham
27.03.01	Pete Buckley W PTS 8 Brierley Hill
15.09.01	Esham Pickering L PTS 6 Derby
17.11.01	Steve Conway L PTS 8 Dewsbury
08.12.01	Esham Pickering L PTS 8 Chesterfield
07.02.02	Mark Bowen L PTS 6 Stoke
20.04.02	Esham Pickering L PTS 6 Derby
21.07.02	Eddie Nevins L PTS 4 Salford
07.09.02	Colin Toohey DREW 6 Liverpool
26.10.02	Dazzo Williams W RSC 2 Maesteg
02.12.02	Esham Pickering L PTS 6 Leicester
28.01.03	Lee Meager L PTS 8 Nottingham
09.05.03	Jeff Thomas DREW 6 Doncaster
08.11.03	Baz Carey W RSC 2 Coventry
28.11.03	Carl Greaves L PTS 4 Derby
28.02.04	Michael Kelly L PTS 4 Bridgend
03.04.04	Andy Morris L PTS 4 Manchester
16.04.04	Dave Stewart L PTS 6 Bradford
17.06.04	Scott Lawton L PTS 10 Sheffield
	(*Vacant Midlands Area Lightweight Title*)
03.09.04	Gavin Rees L PTS 6 Newport
22.10.04	Craig Johnson L PTS 6 Mansfield
12.11.04	Billy Corcoran L RSC 5 Wembley
13.12.04	Jonathan Thaxton L RSC 1 Birmingham
05.03.05	Ryan Barrett L PTS 4 Dagenham
15.05.05	Scott Lawton L PTS 6 Sheffield
18.06.05	Joe McCluskey L PTS 6 Coventry

Career: 66 contests, won 18, drew 5, lost 43.

Peter Allen   Les Clark

Peter Allen

Birkenhead. *Born* Birkenhead, 13 August, 1978
Lightweight. Ht. 5'5"
Manager Self

30.04.98	Sean Grant L PTS 6 Pentre Halkyn
21.06.98	Garry Burrell W PTS 6 Liverpool
20.09.98	Simon Chambers L PTS 6 Sheffield
16.11.98	Stevie Kane W PTS 6 Glasgow
07.12.98	Simon Chambers L PTS 6 Bradford
28.02.99	Amjid Mahmood L PTS 6 Shaw
12.03.99	Marc Callaghan L PTS 4 Bethnal Green
15.09.99	Steve Brook L PTS 6 Harrogate
07.10.99	Nicky Wilders L PTS 6 Sunderland
18.10.99	Mark Hudson L PTS 6 Bradford
15.11.99	Craig Docherty L RSC 1 Glasgow
09.12.01	Jeff Thomas L PTS 6 Blackpool
01.03.02	Andrew Ferrans L PTS 8 Irvine
15.03.02	Ricky Burns L PTS 6 Glasgow
17.04.02	Andrew Smith W PTS 6 Stoke
24.06.02	Tasawar Khan L PTS 6 Bradford
14.09.02	Carl Greaves L PTS 6 Newark
08.10.02	Andrew Ferrans L PTS 8 Glasgow
21.10.02	Tony McPake L PTS 6 Glasgow
17.11.02	Choi Tsveenpurev L RSC 4 Shaw
16.02.03	Darryn Walton L PTS 6 Salford
31.05.03	Mally McIver L PTS 6 Barnsley
29.08.03	Steve Mullin L PTS 6 Liverpool
25.04.04	Craig Johnson L PTS 6 Nottingham
08.05.04	Michael Graydon L PTS 6 Bristol
30.05.04	Willie Valentine W PTS 4 Dublin
10.09.04	Steve Mullin L PTS 4 Liverpool
05.11.04	Damian Owen L RSC 1 Hereford
04.03.05	Isaac Ward DREW 6 Hartlepool
10.04.05	Lloyd Otte L PTS 6 Brentwood
30.04.05	Eddie Nevins W PTS 6 Wigan

Career: 31 contests, won 5, drew 1, lost 25.

Leigh Alliss

Stroud. *Born* Stroud, 11 September, 1975
Western Area L. Heavyweight Champion.
Ht. 5'9½"
Manager C. Sanigar

06.03.03	Ovill McKenzie L PTS 4 Bristol
12.05.03	Mark Phillips W PTS 6 Southampton
13.06.03	Egbui Ikeagbu W PTS 6 Bristol
09.10.03	Mark Phillips W PTS 4 Bristol
05.12.03	Dale Nixon W RSC 2 Bristol
13.02.04	Hastings Rasani W PTS 6 Bristol
08.05.04	Michael Pinnock W PTS 4 Bristol
03.07.04	Karl Wheeler W PTS 4 Bristol
01.10.04	Shane White W RSC 2 Bristol
	(*Vacant Western Area L.Heavyweight Title*)
03.12.04	Valery Odin L RSC 5 Bristol
29.04.05	Varuzhan Davtyan W PTS 4 Plymouth

Career: 11 contests, won 9, lost 2.

Leigh Alliss   Les Clark

81

Adnan Amar

Nottingham. *Born* Nottingham, 17
February, 1983
Welterweight. Ht. 5'9"
Manager M. Shinfield

11.06.01	Steve Hanley W PTS 4 Nottingham
13.11.01	Duncan Armstrong W PTS 6 Leeds
21.10.02	Jason Gonzales W PTS 6 Cleethorpes
23.02.03	Arv Mittoo W PTS 6 Shrewsbury
16.03.03	Gareth Wiltshaw W PTS 6 Nottingham
16.04.03	Dave Cotterill W PTS 4 Nottingham
28.04.03	Ernie Smith W PTS 6 Cleethorpes
12.05.03	Pedro Thompson W RSC 4 Birmingham
08.06.03	David Kirk W PTS 6 Nottingham
06.09.03	Chris Duggan W PTS 4 Aberdeen
23.02.04	Wayne Shepherd W RSC 5 Nottingham
10.05.04	Ernie Smith W PTS 6 Birmingham
04.06.04	Dean Hickman L RSC 8 Dudley
	(Vacant Midlands Area L.Welterweight Title)
29.10.04	Daniel Thorpe W PTS 4 Worksop
25.06.05	Ernie Smith W PTS 6 Melton Mowbray

Career: 15 contests, won 14, lost 1.

(Lee) Eddie Anderson

Fareham. *Born* Reading, 10 August, 1972
Lightweight. Ht. 5'7"
Manager W. Fuller

29.04.05	Lee Cook L RSC 2 Southwark

Career: 1 contest, lost 1.

(Terry) Junior Anderson

Southampton. *Born* Leeds, 23 May, 1974
Lightweight. Ht. 5'8"
Manager M. Roe

17.03.03	Neil Read L CO 2 Southampton
21.02.04	John Alldis L CO 1 Brighton
01.05.04	John Mackay L CO 2 Gravesend
01.10.04	Lee Haskins L CO 3 Bristol
16.06.05	Jed Syger L CO 2 Mayfair

Career: 5 contests, lost 5.

Junior Anderson   Les Clark

Kevin Anderson

Buckhaven. *Born* Kirkcaldy, 26 April, 1980
Celtic Welterweight Champion. Ht. 5'8"
Manager T. Gilmour

12.04.03	Paul McIlwaine W RSC 2 Bethnal Green
19.04.03	Piotr Bartnicki W RSC 2 Liverpool
17.05.03	Georges Dujardin W RSC 1 Liverpool
05.07.03	Mohamed Bourhis W CO 2 Brentwood
06.09.03	Sergei Starkov W PTS 6 Huddersfield
01.11.03	Alban Mothie W PTS 8 Glasgow
14.02.04	Andrei Napolskikh W PTS 8 Nottingham
13.03.04	Lance Hall W RSC 1 Huddersfield
22.04.04	Dmitri Yanushevich W RSC 2 Glasgow
27.05.04	Danny Moir W RSC 1 Huddersfield
15.10.04	Stephane Benito W RSC 6 Glasgow
26.11.04	Tagir Rzaev W PTS 6 Altrincham
31.01.05	Glenn McClarnon W RSC 4 Glasgow
	(Vacant Celtic Welterweight Title)
11.06.05	Vladimir Borovski W PTS 10 Kirkcaldy

Career: 14 contests, won 14.

Rod Anderton

Nottingham. *Born* Nottingham, 17 August, 1978
L.Heavyweight. Ht. 5'11"
Manager M. Shinfield

22.04.05	Michael Pinnock W PTS 6 Barnsley
18.06.05	Nicki Taylor W RSC 4 Barnsley

Career: 2 contests, won 2.

Csaba Andras

Langport. *Born* Hungary, 9 September, 1979
Cruiserweight. Ht. 6'0"
Manager T. Woodward

25.02.05	Billy McClung L PTS 6 Irvine
12.06.05	Coleman Barrett L RSC 1 Leicester Square

Career: 2 contests, lost 2.

Csaba Andras   Les Clark

John Anthony

Doncaster. *Born* Doncaster, 16 October, 1974
Cruiserweight. Ht. 5'11"
Manager D. Coldwell

22.04.05	Gary Thompson W PTS 4 Barnsley
18.06.05	Lee Mountford W RSC 5 Barnsley

Career: 2 contests, won 2.

John Armour

Chatham. *Born* Chatham, 26 October, 1968
S.Bantamweight. Former WBU
Bantamweight Champion. Former
Undefeated European & Commonwealth
Bantamweight Champion. Ht. 5'4¾"
Manager T. Toole

24.09.90	Lupe Castro W PTS 6 Lewisham
31.10.90	Juan Camero W RSC 4 Crystal Palace
21.01.91	Elijro Mejia W RSC 1 Crystal Palace
30.09.91	Pat Maher W CO 1 Kensington
29.10.91	Pete Buckley W PTS 6 Kensington
14.12.91	Gary Hickman W RSC 6 Bexleyheath
25.03.92	Miguel Matthews W PTS 6 Dagenham
30.04.92	Ndabe Dube W RSC 12 Kensington
	(Vacant Commonwealth Bantamweight Title)
17.10.92	Mauricio Bernal W PTS 8 Wembley
03.12.92	Albert Musankabala W RSC 5 Lewisham
	(Commonwealth Bantamweight Title Defence)
28.01.93	Ricky Romero W CO 1 Southwark
10.02.93	Morgan Mpande W PTS 12 Lewisham
	(Commonwealth Bantamweight Title Defence)
09.06.93	Boualem Belkif W PTS 10 Lewisham
01.12.93	Karl Morling W CO 3 Kensington
14.01.94	Rufus Adebayo W RSC 7 Bethnal Green
	(Commonwealth Bantamweight Title Defence)
23.09.94	Shaun Anderson W RSC 11 Bethnal Green
	(Commonwealth Bantamweight Title Defence)
14.02.95	Tsitsi Sokutu W RSC 7 Bethnal Green
	(Commonwealth Bantamweight Title Defence)
19.04.95	Antonio Picardi W RSC 8 Bethnal Green
	(Vacant European Bantamweight Title)
19.05.95	Matthew Harris W RSC 3 Southwark
29.11.95	Redha Abbas W CO 5 Bethnal Green
	(European Bantamweight Title Defence)
17.12.96	Lyndon Kershaw W RSC 8 Bethnal Green
29.01.97	Petrica Paraschiv W PTS 12 Bethnal Green
	(Vacant Interim WBC International Bantamweight Title)
20.05.97	Anatoly Kvitko W RSC 8 Gillingham
28.11.97	Ervine Blake W PTS 10 Bethnal Green
12.12.98	Carlos Navarro L RSC 4 Southwark
	(WBU S. Bantamweight Title Challenge)
19.06.99	Mohamed Ouzid W RSC 5 Dublin
25.07.00	Alexander Tiranov W PTS 8 Southwark
09.12.00	Francis Ampofo W PTS 12 Southwark
	(Vacant WBU Bantamweight Title)
01.12.01	Ian Turner W PTS 8 Bethnal Green
11.05.02	Francis Ampofo W PTS 12 Dagenham
	(WBU Bantamweight Title Defence)
21.09.02	Francis Ampofo W PTS 12 Brentwood
	(WBU Bantamweight Title Defence)
05.07.03	Nathan Sting L RTD 11 Brentwood
	(WBU Bantamweight Title Defence)
16.06.05	Tuncay Kaya L PTS 6 Dagenham

Career: 33 contests, won 30, lost 3.

(Shaun) Lee Armstrong

Huddersfield. *Born* Hartlepool, 18 October, 1972
L.Middleweight. Former Undefeated Central Area L.Middleweight Champion. Former Undefeated Central Area S.Featherweight Champion. Ht. 5'8"
Manager C. Aston

26.04.96	Daryl McKenzie W RSC 4 Glasgow	
10.05.96	Charlie Rumbol W PTS 6 Wembley	
23.05.96	Ian Richardson W PTS 6 Queensferry	
04.10.96	Michael Gibbons L RSC 3 Wakefield	
18.11.96	Garry Burrell W PTS 6 Glasgow	
20.02.97	Carl Greaves W RSC 4 Mansfield	
10.04.97	Chris Lyons W PTS 6 Sheffield	
28.04.97	Hugh Collins W RTD 5 Glasgow	
26.06.97	Garry Burrell W PTS 6 Sheffield	
06.10.97	Roger Sampson L PTS 6 Bradford	
13.11.97	Graeme Williams W PTS 6 Bradford	
30.11.97	Gary Jenkinson W PTS 6 Shaw	
06.02.98	Nigel Leake W PTS 6 Wakefield	
05.04.98	John T. Kelly W PTS 4 Shaw	
21.05.98	Pete Buckley W PTS 6 Bradford	
14.06.98	Pete Buckley W PTS 6 Shaw	
23.10.98	Nigel Leake W RSC 3 Wakefield	

(Vacant Central Area S. Featherweight Title)

11.12.98	Ian McLeod L RSC 8 Prestwick	

(IBO Inter-Continental S. Featherweight Title Challenge)

21.02.99	Bobby Lyndon W RSC 5 Bradford	
03.04.99	John T. Kelly L PTS 6 Carlisle	
25.04.99	Chris Lyons W PTS 8 Leeds	
02.10.99	Jamie McKeever DREW 6 Cardiff	
14.11.99	Keith Jones W PTS 6 Bradford	
11.12.99	Jason Dee L RSC 4 Merthyr	
21.02.00	Gary Flear W PTS 8 Glasgow	
27.03.00	Sebastian Hart L CO 4 Barnsley	
24.09.00	Dave Travers W PTS 6 Shaw	
23.10.00	Craig Docherty DREW 8 Glasgow	
10.12.01	Arv Mittoo W PTS 6 Bradford	
27.04.02	Keith Jones W PTS 6 Huddersfield	
09.05.02	Richard Inquieti L RSC 5 Sunderland	
22.02.03	Gavin Wake W PTS 10 Huddersfield	

(Vacant Central Area L. Middleweight Title)

17.11.03	Harry Dhami L PTS 6 Glasgow	
01.10.04	Matthew Hatton L PTS 8 Manchester	
09.12.04	Ali Nuumbembe L PTS 6 Stockport	
11.03.05	Jason Rushton L PTS 10 Doncaster	

(Vacant Central Area L.Middleweight Title)

Career: 36 contests, won 23, drew 2, lost 11.

Alex Arthur

Edinburgh. *Born* Edinburgh, 26 June, 1978
British & Commonwealth S.Featherweight Champion. Former UndefeatedWBO Inter-Continental, WBA Inter-Continental & IBF Inter-Continental S.Featherweight Champion. Former British S.Featherweight Champion. Ht. 5'9"
Manager F. Warren

25.11.00	Richmond Asante W RSC 1 Manchester	
10.02.01	Eddie Nevins W RSC 1 Widnes	
26.03.01	Woody Greenaway W RTD 2 Wembley	
28.04.01	Dafydd Carlin W PTS 4 Cardiff	
21.07.01	Rakhim Mingaleev W PTS 4 Sheffield	
15.09.01	Dimitri Gorodetsky W RSC 1 Manchester	
27.10.01	Alexei Slyautchin W RSC 1 Manchester	
17.11.01	Laszlo Bognar W RSC 3 Glasgow	
19.01.02	Vladimir Borov W RSC 2 Bethnal Green	
11.03.02	Dariusz Snarski W RSC 10 Glasgow	

(Vacant IBF Inter-Continental S.Featherweight Title)

08.06.02	Nikolai Eremeev W RTD 5 Renfrew	

(Vacant WBO Inter-Continental S.Featherweight Title)

17.08.02	Pavel Potipko W CO 1 Cardiff	
19.10.02	Steve Conway W CO 4 Renfrew	

(Vacant British S. Featherweight Title)

14.12.02	Carl Greaves W RSC 6 Newcastle	

(British S.Featherweight Title Defence)

22.03.03	Patrick Malinga W RSC 6 Renfrew	

(Vacant WBA Inter-Continental S.Featherweight Title)

12.07.03	Willie Limond W RSC 8 Renfrew	

(British S.Featherweight Title Defence)

25.10.03	Michael Gomez L RSC 5 Edinburgh	

(British S.Featherweight Title Defence)

27.03.04	Michael Kizza W CO 1 Edinburgh	

(Vacant IBF Inter-Continental S.Featherweight Title)

22.10.04	Eric Odumasi W RSC 6 Edinburgh	

(IBF Inter-Continental S.Featherweight Title Defence)

03.12.04	Nazareno Ruiz W PTS 12 Edinburgh	

(IBF Inter-Continental S.Featherweight Title Defence)

08.04.05	Craig Docherty W CO 9 Edinburgh	

(Vacant British S.Featherweight Title. Commonwealth S.Featherweight Title Challenge)

Career: 21 contests, won 20, lost 1.

Jamie Arthur

Cwmbran. *Born* Aberdeen, 17 December, 1979
S. Featherweight. Ht. 5'9"
Manager F. Warren/F. Maloney

22.03.03	Daniel Thorpe W PTS 4 Renfrew	
28.06.03	James Gorman W PTS 4 Cardiff	
13.09.03	Dave Hinds W RTD 1 Newport	
11.10.03	Dafydd Carlin W RSC 4 Portsmouth	
15.11.03	Andrei Mircea W RSC 3 Bayreuth, Germany	
06.12.03	Jus Wallie W PTS 6 Cardiff	
27.03.04	Karl Taylor W PTS 6 Edinburgh	
03.07.04	Frederic Bonifai W PTS 6 Newport	
03.09.04	Buster Dennis W PTS 6 Newport	
21.01.05	Haider Ali L RSC 3 Bridgend	

Career: 10 contests, won 9, lost 1.

Andiano Aubrey

Nottingham. *Born* Glasgow, 6 June, 1981
Middleweight. Ht. 5'9"
Manager M. Scriven

22.10.04	Cafu Santos L PTS 6 Mansfield	

Career: 1 contest, lost 1.

Alex Arthur   Les Clark

David Bailey

Pimlico. *Born* London, 23 August, 1980
S. Featherweight. Ht. 5'6"
Manager Self

07.05.04 Dean Ward W PTS 6 Bethnal Green
25.06.04 Mickey Coveney L PTS 4 Bethnal Green
18.09.04 Craig Johnson W PTS 6 Newark
27.09.04 Rendall Munroe L PTS 6 Cleethorpes
21.01.05 David Pereira L PTS 6 Brentford
05.03.05 Mickey Bowden L PTS 6 Southwark
20.05.05 Warren Dunkley W PTS 4 Southwark
Career: 7 contests, won 3, lost 4.

Colin Bain

Glasgow. *Born* Hawick, 10 August, 1978
Lightweight. Ht. 5'8"
Manager K. Morrison

14.03.03 Dafydd Carlin W PTS 6 Glasgow
16.05.03 Martin Hardcastle W PTS 6 Glasgow
12.07.03 Gareth Wiltshaw W PTS 4 Renfrew
25.10.03 Dave Hinds W PTS 4 Edinburgh
27.03.04 Dave Hinds W PTS 4 Edinburgh
23.04.04 Pete Buckley W PTS 6 Glasgow
19.06.04 Henry Jones W PTS 4 Renfrew
29.10.04 Pete Buckley W PTS 4 Renfrew
12.12.04 Ricky Burns L PTS 6 Glasgow
Career: 9 contests, won 8, lost 1.

Carl Baker   Les Clark

Carl Baker

Sheffield. *Born* Sheffield, 3 January, 1982
British Masters Heavyweight Champion.
Ht. 6'4"
Manager B. Ingle

06.09.03 Dave Clarke W RSC 1 Aberdeen
15.09.03 Billy Wilson W RSC 2 Leeds
28.11.03 Slick Miller W CO 1 Hull
03.04.04 Paul King L PTS 6 Sheffield
17.09.04 Scott Gammer L PTS 4 Plymouth

04.03.05 Paul King W RSC 2 Rotherham
26.04.05 Luke Simpkin L RSC 4 Leeds
25.06.05 Scott Lansdowne W RSC 8 Melton Mowbray
(Vacant British Masters Heavyweight Title)
Career: 8 contests, won 5, lost 3.

Vince Baldassara

Clydebank. *Born* Clydebank, 6 November, 1978
L. Middleweight. Ht. 5'11"
Manager B. Winter

14.03.03 George Telfer L PTS 4 Glasgow
28.02.04 Rob MacDonald W PTS 6 Manchester
08.10.04 Barrie Lee DREW 6 Glasgow
09.12.04 Eddie Haley W PTS 6 Sunderland
21.02.05 Cafu Santos W CO 2 Glasgow
08.04.05 Barrie Lee L PTS 4 Edinburgh
25.04.05 Ciaran Healy W RSC 4 Glasgow
20.05.05 Mark Wall W PTS 6 Glasgow
17.06.05 Jak Hibbert W RSC 1 Glasgow
Career: 9 contests, won 6, drew 1, lost 2.

(Mikhail) Michael Banbula

Staines. *Born* Poland, 26 December, 1980
S.Middleweight. Ht. 5'11½"
Manager G. Carman

30.04.05 Gareth Lawrence L PTS 6 Dagenham
14.05.05 Tommy Tolan L PTS 4 Dublin
02.06.05 Cello Renda DREW 6 Peterborough
Career: 3 contests, drew 1, lost 2.

Ted Bami (Minsende)

Brixton. *Born* Zaire, 2 March, 1978
L.Welterweight. Former WBF
L.Welterweight Champion. Ht. 5'7"
Manager B. Hearn

26.09.98 Des Sowden W RSC 1 Southwark
11.02.99 Gary Reid W RSC 2 Dudley
10.03.00 David Kehoe W PTS 4 Bethnal Green
08.09.00 Jacek Bielski L RSC 4 Hammersmith
29.03.01 Keith Jones W PTS 4 Hammersmith
05.05.01 Francis Barrett W PTS 6 Edmonton
31.07.01 Lance Crosby W PTS 6 Bethnal Green
19.03.02 Michael Smyth W CO 4 Slough
23.06.02 Keith Jones W RSC 4 Southwark
17.08.02 Bradley Pryce W RSC 6 Cardiff
26.10.02 Adam Zadworny W PTS 4 Maesteg
07.12.02 Sergei Starkov W PTS 4 Brentwood
08.03.03 Andrei Devyataykin W RSC 1 Bethnal Green
12.04.03 Laszlo Herczeg W RSC 9 Bethnal Green
(Vacant WBF L.Welterweight Title)
26.07.03 Samuel Malinga L RSC 3 Plymouth
(WBF L.Welterweight Title Defence)
09.10.03 Zoltan Surman W RSC 3 Bristol
31.01.04 Jozsef Matolcsi W PTS 6 Bethnal Green
08.05.04 Viktor Baranov W RSC 2 Dagenham
08.10.04 Rafal Jackiewicz W PTS 8 Brentwood
13.02.05 Ricardo Daniel Silva W CO 2 Brentwood
Career: 20 contests, won 18, lost 2.

Darren Barker

Barnet. *Born* Harrow, 19 May, 1982
Middleweight. Ht. 5'11¾"
Manager T. Sims

24.09.04 Howard Clarke W PTS 6 Nottingham
12.11.04 David White W RSC 2 Wembley
26.03.05 Leigh Wicks W RTD 4 Hackney
10.04.05 Andrei Sherel W RSC 3 Brentwood
Career: 4 contests, won 4.

David Barnes (Smith)

Manchester. *Born* Manchester, 16 January, 1981
Welterweight. Former Undefeated British
Welterweight Champion. Ht. 5'8½"
Manager F. Warren

07.07.01 Trevor Smith W RSC 2 Manchester
15.09.01 Karl Taylor W PTS 4 Manchester
27.10.01 Mark Sawyers W RSC 2 Manchester
15.12.01 James Paisley W RTD 2 Wembley
09.02.02 David Kirk W RTD 1 Manchester
04.05.02 David Baptiste W CO 3 Bethnal Green
01.06.02 Dimitri Protkunas W RSC 1 Manchester
28.09.02 Sergei Starkov W PTS 6 Manchester
12.10.02 Rusian Ashirov W PTS 6 Bethnal Green
14.12.02 Rozalin Nasibulin W RSC 3 Newcastle
18.01.03 Brice Faradji W PTS 6 Preston
05.04.03 Viktor Fesetchko W PTS 8 Manchester
17.07.03 Jimmy Vincent W PTS 12 Dagenham
(Vacant British Welterweight Title)
13.12.03 Kevin McIntyre W RTD 8 Manchester
(British Welterweight Title Defence)
03.04.04 Glenn McClarnon W PTS 12 Manchester
(British Welterweight Title Defence)
12.11.04 James Hare W RSC 6 Halifax
(British Welterweight Title Defence)
28.01.05 Juho Tolppola W PTS 10 Renfrew
22.04.05 Ali Nuumbembe DREW 12 Barnsley
(Vacant WBO Inter-Continental Welterweight Title)
04.06.05 Joshua Okine L RSC 12 Manchester
(Commonwealth Welterweight Title Challenge)
Career: 19 contests, won 17, drew 1, lost 1.

David Barnes   Les Clark

Matthew Barney

Southampton. *Born* Fareham, 25 June, 1974
L.Heavyweight. Former Undefeated WBU
L.Heavyweight Champion. Former
Undefeated British, IBO Inter-Continental,
Southern Area & British Masters
S.Middleweight Champion. Ht. 5'10¾"
Manager Self

04.06.98	Adam Cale W PTS 6 Barking	
23.07.98	Adam Cale W PTS 6 Barking	
02.10.98	Dennis Doyley W PTS 4 Cheshunt	
22.10.98	Kevin Burton W PTS 6 Barking	
07.12.98	Freddie Yemofio W PTS 4 Acton	
17.03.99	Simon Andrews W RTD 4 Kensington	
09.05.99	Gareth Hogg W PTS 4 Bracknell	
20.05.99	Bobby Banghar W RSC 5 Kensington	
	(British Masters S. Middleweight Final)	
05.06.99	Paul Bowen DREW 10 Cardiff	
	(Southern Area S. Middleweight Title Challenge)	
20.08.99	Adam Cale W PTS 4 Bloomsbury	
05.10.99	Delroy Leslie L PTS 10 Bloomsbury	
	(Vacant Southern Area Middleweight Title)	
15.04.00	Mark Dawson W PTS 6 Bethnal Green	
06.05.00	Jason Hart W PTS 10 Southwark	
	(Vacant Southern Area S. Middleweight Title)	
30.09.00	Neil Linford L PTS 10 Peterborough	
	(Elim. British S. Middleweight Title)	
02.02.01	Darren Covill W PTS 6 Portsmouth	
16.03.01	Matt Mowatt W RSC 1 Portsmouth	
	(British Masters S. Middleweight Title Defence)	
14.07.01	Robert Milewics W PTS 8 Wembley	
20.10.01	Jon Penn W RSC 4 Portsmouth	
26.01.02	Hussain Osman L RTD 9 Dagenham	
	(Vacant IBO Inter-Continental S.Middleweight Title. Southern Area S.Middleweight Title Defence)	
08.04.02	Hussain Osman W PTS 12 Southampton	
	(IBO Inter-Continental & Southern Area S. Middleweight Title Challenges)	
22.09.02	Paul Owen W CO 7 Southwark	
	(Vacant British Masters S.Middleweight Title)	
20.10.02	Chris Nembhard W PTS 10 Southwark	
	(Southern Area S. Middleweight Title Defence)	
29.03.03	Dean Francis W PTS 12 Wembley	
	(Vacant British S.Middleweight Title)	
01.08.03	Charles Adamu L PTS 12 Bethnal Green	
	(Vacant Commonwealth S.Middleweight Title)	
11.10.03	Tony Oakey W PTS 12 Portsmouth	
	(WBU L.Heavyweight Title Challenge)	
10.09.04	Simeon Cover W PTS 4 Wembley	
26.03.05	Thomas Ulrich L PTS 12 Riesa, Germany	
	(European L.Heavyweight Title Challenge)	

Career: 27 contests, won 21, drew 1, lost 5.

Matthew Barr

Walton. *Born* Kingston, 22 May, 1977
Middleweight. Ht. 5'11"
Manager Self

02.12.97	Keith Palmer L RSC 3 Windsor	

23.02.98	Martin Cavey W RSC 1 Windsor	
14.05.98	Gerard Lawrence L RSC 1 Acton	
29.10.98	Sonny Thind W RSC 2 Bayswater	
20.05.99	Paul Knights L RSC 1 Barking	
31.10.99	Allan Gray W PTS 4 Raynes Park	
25.02.00	John Humphrey W RSC 1 Newmarket	
06.05.00	Ernie Smith W PTS 4 Southwark	
22.10.00	Ernie Smith W PTS 4 Streatham	
23.11.00	Harry Butler W PTS 4 Bayswater	
23.11.01	John Humphrey L RSC 2 Bethnal Green	
13.09.02	Brian Knudsen W PTS 6 Randers, Denmark	
29.03.03	Lee Hodgson W RSC 1 Wembley	
29.10.03	Jimi Hendricks W RSC 4 Leicester Square	
27.11.03	Leigh Wicks W PTS 4 Longford	
21.01.05	Gareth Lawrence W RSC 2 Brentford	

Career: 16 contests, won 12, lost 4.

Coleman Barrett

Wembley. *Born* Galway, 10 November, 1982
Cruiserweight. Ht. 6'1"
Manager R. McCracken

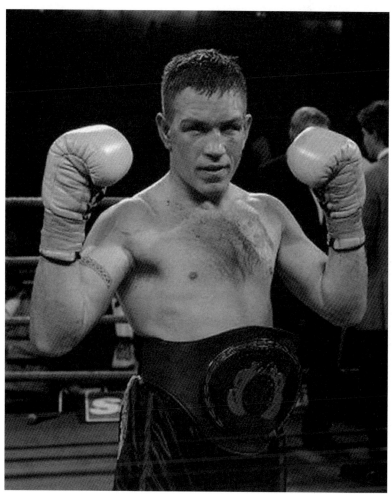

Francis Barrett   Les Clark

11.12.03	Marcus Lee W PTS 4 Bethnal Green	
12.03.04	Dave Clarke W PTS 6 Nottingham	
02.06.04	Terry Morrill W PTS 4 Nottingham	
05.03.05	Valery Semishkur W PTS 6 Durres, Albania	
12.06.05	Csaba Andras W RSC 1 Leicester Square	

Career: 5 contests, won 5.

Francis Barrett

Wembley. *Born* Galway, 7 February, 1977
European Union & Southern Area
L.Welterweight Champion. Ht. 5'7"
Manager Self

12.08.00	Mohamed Helel W PTS 4 Wembley	
23.09.00	Trevor Smith W RSC 1 Bethnal Green	
21.10.00	Keith Jones W PTS 4 Wembley	
24.02.01	David White W PTS 4 Bethnal Green	
10.03.01	Karl Taylor W RSC 3 Bethnal Green	
26.03.01	Tony Montana W PTS 4 Wembley	
05.05.01	Ted Bami L PTS 6 Edmonton	
22.09.01	Gary Reid W PTS 4 Bethnal Green	
19.01.02	Dafydd Carlin W PTS 4 Bethnal Green	
25.05.02	David Kirk W PTS 6 Portsmouth	
25.10.02	Darren Covill W PTS 4 Bethnal Green	

21.12.02 Keith Jones W PTS 6 Dagenham
05.03.03 Jon Honney W PTS 10 Bethnal Green
(Vacant Southern Area L.Welterweight Title)
27.05.03 Silence Saheed L RSC 1 Dagenham
04.10.03 David Kirk W PTS 6 Muswell Hill
11.12.03 Oscar Hall W PTS 10 Bethnal Green
02.06.04 Gavin Down W PTS 10 Nottingham
(Vacant European Union L.Welterweight Title)
12.11.04 Alan Bosworth W PTS 10 Wembley
(European Union L.Welterweight Title Defence)
19.02.05 Oscar Milkitas W PTS 6 Dublin
12.06.05 Ivor Bonavic L RSC 2 Leicester Square
Career: 20 contests, won 17, lost 3.

Ryan Barrett

Thamesmead. *Born* London, 27 December, 1982
Lightweight. Ht. 5'10"
Manager M. Roe

13.06.02 Gareth Wiltshaw W PTS 4 Leicester Square
06.09.02 Jason Gonzales W PTS 4 Bethnal Green
12.12.02 Martin Turner W RSC 1 Leicester Square
08.03.03 David Vaughan DREW 4 Bethnal Green
04.10.03 Dafydd Carlin L PTS 4 Belfast
01.05.04 Marty Kayes W RSC 2 Gravesend
19.06.04 Kristian Laight W PTS 4 Muswell Hill
16.10.04 Daniel Thorpe W PTS 4 Dagenham
19.12.04 James Paisley W DIS 5 Bethnal Green
21.01.05 Peter McDonagh W PTS 8 Brentford
05.03.05 Carl Allen W PTS 4 Dagenham
23.03.05 Pete Buckley W PTS 6 Leicester Square
20.06.05 Anthony Christopher W RSC 1 Longford
Career: 13 contests, won 11, drew 1, lost 1.

(Alex) Sandy Bartlett

Inverness. *Born* Dingwall, 20 April, 1976
S. Bantamweight. Ht. 5'7"
Manager T. Gilmour

15.03.04 Marty Kayes W PTS 6 Glasgow
19.04.04 Abdul Mougharbel L PTS 6 Glasgow
11.10.04 Abdul Mougharbel W PTS 6 Glasgow
05.11.04 Ricky Owen L RSC 2 Hereford
Career: 4 contests, won 2, lost 2.

(Shinebayer) Shinny Bayaar (Sukhbaatar)

Carlisle. *Born* Mongolia, 27 August, 1977
Flyweight. Ht. 5'0"
Manager J. Doughty

30.07.99 Saohin Sorthanikul L RSC 4 Bangkok, Thailand
25.02.00 Yura Dima DREW 10 Erdene, Mongolia
28.06.00 Manny Melchor L PTS 12 Manila, Philippines
(WBC International M.Flyweight Title Challenge)
10.10.01 Damien Dunnion L PTS 8 Stoke
09.12.01 Delroy Spencer W PTS 4 Shaw
17.11.02 Anthony Hanna W PTS 6 Shaw
20.03.03 Sunkanmi Ogunbiyi L PTS 4 Queensway

08.06.03 Darren Cleary W RSC 2 Shaw
19.10.03 Delroy Spencer W PTS 6 Shaw
21.02.04 Reidar Walstad W RSC 1 Cardiff
31.10.04 Delroy Spencer W PTS 6 Shaw
11.12.04 Martin Power L PTS 10 Canning Town
Career: 12 contests, won 6, drew 1, lost 5.

Lee Beavis

Northolt. *Born* Isleworth, 9 April, 1982
Lightweight. Ht. 5'8"
Manager F. Warren/F. Maloney

11.10.03 James Gorman W PTS 4 Portsmouth
06.11.03 Daniel Thorpe W PTS 4 Dagenham
01.04.04 James Gorman W RTD 2 Bethnal Green
24.04.04 Anthony Hanna W PTS 4 Reading
13.05.04 Pete Buckley W PTS 4 Bethnal Green
30.07.04 Jason Nesbitt W PTS 4 Bethnal Green
19.11.04 Henry Janes W PTS 4 Bethnal Green
11.12.04 Chris McDonagh W RSC 6 Canning Town
25.02.05 Jon Honney W PTS 6 Wembley
Career: 9 contests, won 9.

Jimmy Beech

Walsall. *Born* Walsall, 19 January, 1979
Lightweight. Ht. 5'7"
Manager Self

23.06.99 Ike Halls W RTD 2 West Bromwich
03.09.99 Tom Wood W PTS 6 West Bromwich
07.04.00 Willie Limond L RSC 2 Glasgow
28.01.01 Lenny Hodgkins W PTS 6 Wolverhampton
16.11.01 Pete Buckley W PTS 6 West Bromwich
23.11.01 Henry Castle L PTS 4 Bethnal Green
07.02.02 Dave Cotterill W PTS 6 Stoke
25.02.02 Mickey Bowden W PTS 4 Slough
09.03.02 Tony Mulholland L PTS 6 Manchester
05.05.02 James Rooney W RSC 5 Hartlepool
25.05.02 Henry Castle L PTS 4 Portsmouth
07.09.02 Ricky Eccleston W RSC 3 Liverpool
28.09.02 Michael Gomez L RSC 4 Manchester
14.12.02 Gavin Rees L PTS 4 Newcastle
22.03.03 Willie Limond L CO 4 Renfrew
28.04.03 Tony McPake L PTS 6 Nottingham
27.05.03 Billy Corcoran W PTS 6 Dagenham
26.09.03 Jimmy Beech L RTD 2 Reading
14.11.03 Scott Lawton L RSC 5 Bethnal Green
24.01.04 Steve Murray L RSC 4 Wembley
28.01.05 Martin Watson L PTS 4 Renfrew
26.02.05 Scott Haywood L PTS 6 Burton
11.03.05 Stefy Bull L PTS 4 Doncaster
08.05.05 Carl Johanneson L CO 2 Bradford
Career: 24 contests, won 9, lost 15.

Andy Bell (Langley)

Nottingham. *Born* Doncaster, 16 July, 1985
Featherweight. Ht. 5'8"
Manager M. Scriven

22.10.04 Steve Gethin W RSC 5 Mansfield
10.12.04 Dean Ward W PTS 6 Mansfield
06.03.05 Abdul Mougharbel W PTS 4 Mansfield
24.04.05 Wayne Bloy L PTS 4 Askern
Career: 4 contests, won 3, lost 1.

Steve Bell

Manchester. *Born* Manchester, 11 June, 1975
S. Featherweight. Ht. 5'10"
Manager F. Warren

08.05.03 Jus Wallie DREW 4 Widnes
27.09.03 Jaz Virdee W RSC 1 Manchester
13.12.03 Fred Janes W PTS 4 Manchester
03.04.04 Pete Buckley W PTS 4 Manchester
22.05.04 Haider Ali W PTS 6 Widnes
01.10.04 Daniel Thorpe W PTS 6 Manchester
11.02.05 Henry Janes W RTD 3 Manchester
03.06.05 Buster Dennis DREW 6 Manchester
Career: 8 contests, won 6, drew 2.

Steve Bell   Paul Speak

Steven Bendall

Coventry. *Born* Coventry, 1 December, 1973
Middleweight. Former Undefeated IBO Inter-Continental & WBU Inter-Continental Middleweight Champion. Ht. 6'0"
Manager Self

15.05.97 Dennis Doyley W RSC 2 Reading
13.09.97 Gary Reyniers W PTS 4 Millwall
27.02.99 Israel Khumalo W PTS 4 Oldham
02.07.99 Darren Covill W RTD 3 Bristol
24.09.99 Sean Pritchard W PTS 6 Merthyr
03.12.99 Ian Toby W PTS 6 Peterborough
07.04.00 Des Sowden W RSC 3 Bristol
02.06.00 Simon Andrews W RSC 5 Ashford
08.09.00 Jason Barker W PTS 6 Bristol
03.11.00 Eddie Haley W RSC 1 Ebbw Vale
01.12.00 Peter Mitchell W PTS 8 Peterborough
22.08.01 Bert Bado W RSC 1 Hammanskraal, South Africa
29.09.01 Alan Gilbert W RTD 3 Southwark
08.12.01 Jason Collins W PTS 12 Dagenham
(Vacant WBU Inter-Continental Middleweight Title)
02.03.02 Ahmet Dottouev W RTD 4 Brakpan, South Africa
(WBU Inter-Continental Middleweight Title Defence)
26.04.02 Viktor Fesetchko W RSC 10 Coventry
(Vacant IBO Inter-Continental Middleweight Title)
13.07.02 Phillip Bystrikov W RSC 5 Coventry
06.09.02 Tomas da Silva W RSC 8 Bethnal Green
24.01.03 Lee Blundell W RSC 2 Sheffield
(IBO Inter-Continental Middleweight Title Defence)

26.04.03	Mike Algoet W PTS 12 Brentford	

    (IBO Inter-Continental Middleweight
    Title Defence)
14.11.03 Kreshnik Qato W PTS 8 Bethnal Green
17.09.04 Scott Dann L RSC 6 Plymouth
    (Vacant British Middleweight Title)
18.06.05 Ismael Kerzazi W PTS 8 Coventry
Career: 23 contests, won 22, lost 1.

Kevin Bennett

Hartlepool. *Born* Birmingham, 15 August, 1975
Lightweight. Former Commonwealth Lightweight Champion. Ht. 5'7"
Manager M. Marsden

01.12.99 Karim Bouali W PTS 4 Yarm
28.03.00 Les Frost W RSC 2 Hartlepool
25.06.00 Steve Hanley W PTS 6 Wakefield
23.07.00 Gary Reid W RSC 4 Hartlepool
28.10.00 Gary Harrison W RTD 2 Coventry
27.11.00 Keith Jones W PTS 4 Birmingham
23.01.01 Tommy Peacock W RSC 5 Crawley
03.03.01 Iain Eldridge W PTS 6 Wembley
08.05.01 Keith Jones W PTS 6 Barnsley
04.06.01 Gary Ryder L RSC 6 Hartlepool
20.10.01 Paul Denton W PTS 4 Portsmouth
03.11.01 Mark Ramsey W PTS 6 Glasgow
26.01.02 Glenn McClarnon L PTS 8 Dagenham
18.05.02 Colin Lynes L RSC 4 Millwall
21.03.03 Keith Jones W PTS 4 West Bromwich
21.06.03 Zoltan Surman W RSC 4 Manchester
05.07.03 Colin Dunne W RSC 2 Brentwood
08.11.03 Michael Muya W PTS 12 Bridgend
    (Commonwealth Lightweight Title
    Challenge)
01.05.04 Jason Cook L PTS 12 Bridgend
    (IBO Lightweight Title Challenge)
19.11.04 Dean Phillips W PTS 12 Hartlepool
    (Commonwealth Lightweight Title
    Defence)
04.03.05 Danny Moir W RSC 3 Hartlepool
19.06.05 Graham Earl L RSC 9 Bethnal Green
    (Commonwealth Lightweight Title
    Defence. British Lightweight Title
    Challenge)
Career: 22 contests, won 17, lost 5.

Billy Bessey   Les Clark

Billy Bessey

Portsmouth. *Born* Portsmouth, 8 January 1974
Heavyweight. Ht. 6'1"
Manager J. Bishop

01.10.00 Paul Fiske W PTS 6 Hartlepool
26.02.01 Mark Hobson L PTS 4 Nottingham
06.05.01 Luke Simpkin W PTS 6 Hartlepool
04.06.01 Gary Williams W PTS 4 Hartlepool
21.11.04 Ebrima Secka W PTS 6 Bracknell
06.02.05 Paul King L PTS 6 Southampton
18.03.05 Martin Rogan L PTS 4 Belfast
Career: 7 contests, won 4, lost 3.

Jim Betts

Scunthorpe. *Born* Tickhill, 6 October, 1977
Featherweight. Former Undefeated British Masters Flyweight Champion. Ht. 5'6¹/₂"
Manager Self

26.03.98 Des Gargano W PTS 6 Scunthorpe
13.05.98 David Jeffrey W RSC 3 Scunthorpe
05.06.98 Chris Price W PTS 6 Hull
11.09.98 Marty Chestnut W PTS 6 Newark
16.10.98 Marty Chestnut W PTS 6 Salford
28.11.98 Ola Dali W PTS 4 Sheffield
17.05.99 Dave Travers W RTD 4 Cleethorpes
17.07.99 Ross Cassidy W RSC 1 Doncaster
27.09.99 Graham McGrath W PTS 6 Cleethorpes
19.02.00 Chris Price W PTS 6 Newark
19.06.00 Chris Price W PTS 4 Burton
30.08.00 David Coldwell W RSC 2 Scunthorpe
    (Vacant British Masters Flyweight
    Title. Elim. British Flyweight Title)
26.02.01 Chris Emanuele L PTS 6 Nottingham
08.05.01 Sean Grant W RSC 3 Barnsley
11.06.01 Daniel Ring W PTS 6 Nottingham
15.09.01 Nicky Booth L RSC 7 Nottingham
    (British & Commonwealth
    Bantamweight Title Challenges)
18.03.02 Ian Turner W RTD 4 Crawley
18.05.02 Gareth Payne W PTS 6 Millwall
27.07.02 Colin Moffett W PTS 6 Nottingham
27.04.04 Jason Nesbitt W PTS 6 Leeds
19.12.04 Rocky Dean L PTS 8 Bethnal Green
19.02.05 Bernard Dunne L CO 5 Dublin
30.04.05 Mickey Coveney L CO 4 Dagenham
Career: 23 contests, won 18, lost 5.

Paul Billington

Warrington. *Born* Billinge, 1 March, 1972
Cruiserweight. Ht. 5'10"
Manager J. Gill

14.09.02 Michael Monaghan L RSC 4 Newark
29.05.03 Karl Wheeler L PTS 6 Sunderland
21.09.03 Shane White DREW 6 Bristol
12.10.03 Danny Grainger L PTS 6 Sheffield
01.12.03 Mark Flatt W RSC 2 Bradford
21.12.03 Shane White L RSC 2 Bristol
22.04.04 Steve McGuire L RTD 3 Glasgow
08.07.04 Jonjo Finnegan L PTS 6 Birmingham
15.12.04 Jon Ibbotson L PTS 4 Sheffield
Career: 9 contests, won 1, drew 1, lost 7.

Chris Black

Coatbridge. *Born* Bellshill, 19 November, 1979
L. Middleweight. Ht. 5'7¹/₂"
Manager A. Morrison/R. Bannan

22.10.04 Brian Coleman W PTS 4 Edinburgh
12.12.04 Jak Hibbert W RSC 2 Glasgow
28.01.05 Geraint Harvey W PTS 4 Renfrew
01.04.05 Tony Randell W PTS 6 Glasgow
17.06.05 Ciaran Healy DREW 4 Glasgow
Career: 5 contests, won 4, drew 1.

Wayne Bloy

Grimsby. *Born* Grimsby, 30 November, 1982
S.Bantamweight. Ht. 5'5"
Manager S. Fleet

14.06.04 Neil Read DREW 6 Cleethorpes
20.09.04 Gary Ford W PTS 6 Cleethorpes
24.04.05 Andy Bell W PTS 4 Askern
23.05.05 Neil Marston W PTS 6 Cleethorpes
Career: 4 contests, won 3, drew 1.

Lee Blundell

Wigan. *Born* Wigan, 11 August, 1971
British Masters Middleweight Champion. Former Undefeated WBF Inter-Continental Middleweight Champion. Former Undefeated Central Area L. Middleweight Champion. Ht. 6'2"
Manager L. Veitch/J. Gill

25.04.94 Robert Harper W RSC 2 Bury
20.05.94 Freddie Yemofio W RSC 6 Acton
08.09.94 Gordon Blair DREW 6 Glasgow
07.12.94 Kesem Clayton W RTD 2 Stoke
18.02.95 Glenn Catley L RSC 6 Shepton Mallet
11.12.95 Martin Jolley W PTS 6 Morecambe
16.03.97 Martin Jolley W PTS 6 Shaw
08.05.97 Paul Jones L RSC 4 Mansfield
19.09.99 Dean Ashton W RSC 4 Shaw
28.10.99 Jason Collins DREW 6 Burnley
06.12.99 Danny Thornton W PTS 6 Bradford
05.03.00 Ian Toby W RTD 3 Shaw
21.05.00 Phil Epton W RSC 2 Shaw
30.11.00 Danny Thornton W RSC 8 Blackpool
    (Vacant Central Area L.Middleweight
    Title)
08.03.01 Paul Wesley W RSC 3 Blackpool
03.04.01 Spencer Fearon W PTS 6 Bethnal Green
26.07.01 Harry Butler W RSC 4 Blackpool
15.09.01 Anthony Farnell L RSC 2 Manchester
    (Vacant WBO Inter-Continental
    L.Middleweight Title)
09.12.01 Neil Bonner W RSC 3 Blackpool
16.03.02 Ryan Rhodes W RSC 3 Bethnal Green
    (Vacant WBF Inter-Continental
    Middleweight Title)
03.08.02 Alan Gilbert W RSC 6 Blackpool
    (WBF Inter-Continental Middleweight
    Title Defence)
26.10.02 Darren McInulty W RSC 1 Wigan
    (WBF Inter-Continental Middleweight
    Title Defence)
24.01.03 Steven Bendall L RSC 2 Sheffield
    (IBO Inter-Continental Middleweight
    Title Challenge)
19.12.04 Michael Pinnock W PTS 6 Bolton
06.03.05 Howard Clarke W PTS 6 Shaw
30.04.05 Simeon Cover W PTS 10 Wigan
    (Vacant British Masters Middleweight
    Title)
13.05.05 Michael Pinnock W PTS 4 Liverpool
Career: 27 contests, won 21, drew 2, lost 4.

(Aivaras) Ivor Bonavic (Urbonavicius)

Canning Town. *Born* Jonava, Russia, 22 April, 1982
Welterweight. Ht. 5'8"
Manager Self

12.03.04 Chris Long L PTS 6 Millwall
08.05.04 Arek Malek L PTS 4 Dagenham
05.06.04 Gary Woolcombe L PTS 4 Bethnal Green
08.07.04 Robert Lloyd-Taylor L PTS 4 The Strand
30.09.04 Neil Jarmolinski DREW 4 Glasgow
08.10.04 Arek Malek W PTS 4 Brentwood
15.10.04 George McIlroy DREW 4 Glasgow
22.10.04 Colin McNeil L PTS 4 Edinburgh
29.10.04 George Telfer L PTS 4 Renfrew
24.11.04 Rocky Muscus W PTS 4 Mayfair
21.01.05 Robert Lloyd-Taylor L CO 2 Brentford
12.06.05 Francis Barrett W RSC 2 Leicester Square

Career: 12 contests, won 3, drew 2, lost 7.

Paul Bonson

Featherstone. *Born* Castleford, 18 October, 1971
Cruiserweight. Former Central Area L. Heavyweight Champion. Ht. 5'10"
Manager M. Marsden

04.10.96 Michael Pinnock W PTS 6 Wakefield
14.11.96 Michael Pinnock DREW 6 Sheffield
22.12.96 Pele Lawrence DREW 6 Salford
20.04.97 Shamus Casey W PTS 6 Leeds
26.06.97 Andy Manning L PTS 6 Sheffield
19.09.97 Mike Gormley W PTS 6 Salford
03.10.97 Rudi Marcussen L PTS 4 Copenhagen, Denmark
03.12.97 Alex Mason DREW 6 Stoke
14.12.97 Willie Quinn L RSC 4 Glasgow
15.01.98 Alex Mason L PTS 6 Solihull
13.02.98 Peter Mason L PTS 4 Seaham
23.02.98 Martin McDonough W PTS 6 Windsor
07.03.98 Michael Bowen L PTS 6 Reading
14.03.98 Alain Simon L PTS 6 Pont St Maxence, France
08.04.98 Tim Brown DREW 4 Liverpool
21.05.98 Mark Hobson L PTS 6 Bradford
21.06.98 Kenny Rainford L PTS 6 Liverpool
01.09.98 Roberto Dominguez L PTS 8 Vigo, Spain
23.10.98 Rob Galloway W PTS 6 Wakefield
16.11.98 Chris P. Bacon L PTS 8 Glasgow
11.12.98 Robert Zlotkowski L PTS 4 Prestwick
20.12.98 Glenn Williams L PTS 6 Salford
24.04.99 Kenny Gayle DREW 4 Peterborough
29.05.99 Dave Johnson L PTS 6 South Shields
19.06.99 Sebastiaan Rothmann L PTS 8 Dublin
12.07.99 Jim Twite L PTS 4 Coventry
07.08.99 Juan Perez Nelongo L PTS 8 Arona, Tenerife
11.09.99 Mark Hobson L PTS 4 Sheffield
02.10.99 Enzo Maccarinelli L PTS 4 Cardiff
16.10.99 Robert Zlotkowski L PTS 6 Bethnal Green
27.10.99 Peter McCormack W PTS 6 Birmingham
04.12.99 Glenn Williams W PTS 4 Manchester
11.12.99 Chris Davies L PTS 4 Merthyr
05.02.00 Paul Maskell L PTS 4 Bethnal Green
11.03.00 Tony Dodson L PTS 4 Kensington
26.03.00 Wayne Buck L PTS 8 Nottingham
29.04.00 Cathal O'Grady L PTS 4 Wembley
13.05.00 Mark Hobson L PTS 4 Barnsley
25.06.00 Andy Manning W PTS 10 Wakefield
(*Vacant Central L. Heavyweight Title*)
08.09.00 Robert Milewicz L PTS 4 Hammersmith

21.10.00 Jon Penn L PTS 6 Sheffield
12.11.00 Glenn Williams L PTS 10 Manchester
(*Central Area L.Heavyweight Title Defence*)
24.11.00 Alex Mason L PTS 6 Darlington
09.12.00 Mark Baker L PTS 6 Southwark
23.01.01 Calvin Stonestreet W PTS 4 Crawley
03.02.01 Tony Dodson L PTS 4 Manchester
18.02.01 Butch Lesley L PTS 6 Southwark
13.03.01 Konstantin Schvets L PTS 6 Plymouth
07.04.01 Rob Hayes-Scott L PTS 4 Wembley
26.04.01 Mike White L PTS 6 Gateshead
17.05.01 Clint Johnson W PTS 6 Leeds
24.05.01 Sven Hamer L PTS 4 Kensington
04.06.01 Joe Gillon DREW 6 Glasgow
11.06.01 Darren Chubbs L PTS 4 Nottingham
21.06.01 Michael Pinnock W PTS 6 Sheffield
27.07.01 Clinton Woods L PTS 6 Sheffield
09.09.01 Eamonn Glennon W PTS 6 Hartlepool
28.09.01 Elvis Michailenko L PTS 6 Millwall
13.11.01 Tony Moran L PTS 6 Leeds
23.11.01 Elvis Michailenko L PTS 6 Bethnal Green
06.12.01 Shaun Bowes W RSC 5 Sunderland
16.12.01 Tommy Eastwood L PTS 4 Southwark
26.01.02 Dominic Negus L PTS 4 Bethnal Green
10.02.02 Butch Lesley L PTS 4 Southwark
25.02.02 Roman Greenberg L PTS 6 Slough
15.03.02 Michael Thompson L PTS 6 Spennymoor
22.03.02 Mark Smallwood L PTS 6 Coventry
19.04.02 Michael Thompson L PTS 6 Darlington
11.05.02 Mark Brookes L PTS 4 Chesterfield
15.06.02 Peter Haymer L PTS 4 Tottenham
23.06.02 Scott Lansdowne W PTS 4 Southwark
13.07.02 Jason Brewster W PTS 6 Wolverhampton
27.07.02 Albert Sosnowski L PTS 4 Nottingham
08.09.02 Varuzhan Davtyan L PTS 4 Wolverhampton
22.09.02 Neil Linford L PTS 6 Southwark
29.09.02 Tony Dowling L PTS 6 Shrewsbury
12.10.02 Andrew Lowe L PTS 4 Bethnal Green
25.10.02 Carl Froch L PTS 6 Bethnal Green
30.11.02 Robert Norton L PTS 6 Coventry
14.12.02 Nathan King W PTS 4 Newcastle
18.01.03 Enzo Maccarinelli L PTS 4 Preston
08.02.03 Steven Spartacus L PTS 6 Norwich
05.03.03 Marcus Lee W PTS 4 Bethnal Green
18.03.03 Mark Krence L PTS 4 Reading
28.03.03 Eric Teymour L PTS 6 Millwall
19.04.03 Tony Moran L PTS 4 Liverpool
12.05.03 Colin Kenna L PTS 6 Southampton
10.06.03 Lee Swaby L PTS 4 Sheffield
26.09.03 Garry Delaney L PTS 6 Reading
06.10.03 Pinky Burton L PTS 6 Barnsley
07.11.03 Carl Thompson L PTS 6 Sheffield
14.11.03 Tony Booth L PTS 6 Hull
01.12.03 David Ingleby W PTS 6 Leeds
20.02.04 Colin Kenna L PTS 6 Southampton
13.03.04 Neil Dawson L PTS 4 Huddersfield
16.04.04 John Keeton L PTS 4 Bradford
01.05.04 Carl Wright L PTS 6 Coventry
26.11.04 Tony Booth L PTS 6 Hull
06.12.04 Robert Norton L CO 6 Leicester
(*Vacant British Masters Cruiserweight Title*)
06.02.05 Ovill McKenzie L PTS 4 Southampton
30.04.05 Tony Moran L PTS 6 Wigan
14.05.05 John Keeton L PTS 4 Aberdeen
18.06.05 Neil Simpson L PTS 6 Coventry

Career: 103 contests, won 19, drew 6, lost 78.

Jason Booth

Nottingham. *Born* Nottingham, 7 November, 1977
Flyweight. Former IBO S.Flyweight Champion. Former Undefeated British Flyweight Champion. Former Undefeated Commonwealth Flyweight Champion. Ht. 5'4"
Manager M. Shinfield

13.06.96 Darren Noble W RSC 3 Sheffield
24.10.96 Marty Chestnut W PTS 6 Lincoln
27.11.96 Jason Thomas W PTS 4 Swansea
18.01.97 David Coldwell W PTS 4 Swadlincote
07.03.97 Pete Buckley W PTS 6 Northampton
20.03.97 Danny Lawson W RSC 3 Newark
10.05.97 Anthony Hanna W PTS 6 Nottingham
19.05.97 Chris Lyons W PTS 6 Cleethorpes
31.10.97 Mark Reynolds W PTS 6 Ilkeston
31.01.98 Anthony Hanna W PTS 6 Edmonton
20.03.98 Louis Veitch W CO 2 Ilkeston
(*Elim. British Flyweight Title*)
09.06.98 Dimitar Alipiev W RSC 2 Hull
17.10.98 Graham McGrath W RSC 4 Manchester
07.12.98 Louis Veitch W RSC 5 Cleethorpes
08.05.99 David Guerault L PTS 12 Grande Synthe, France
(*European Flyweight Title Challenge*)
12.07.99 Mark Reynolds W RSC 3 Coventry
16.10.99 Keith Knox W RSC 10 Belfast
(*British & Commonwealth Flyweight Title Challenges*)
22.01.00 Abie Mnisi W PTS 12 Birmingham
(*Commonwealth Flyweight Title Defence*)
01.07.00 John Barnes W PTS 6 Manchester
13.11.00 Ian Napa W PTS 12 Bethnal Green
(*British & Commonwealth Flyweight Title Defences*)
26.02.01 Nokuthula Tshabangu W CO 2 Nottingham
(*Commonwealth Flyweight Title Defence*)
30.06.01 Alexander Mahmutov L PTS 12 Madrid, Spain
(*European Flyweight Title Challenge*)
23.02.02 Jason Thomas W PTS 6 Nottingham
01.06.02 Mimoun Chent L TD 8 Le Havre, France
(*Vacant European Flyweight Title*)
16.11.02 Kakhar Sabitov W RSC 6 Nottingham
28.04.03 Lindi Memani W PTS 8 Nottingham
20.09.03 Lunga Ntontela W PTS 12 Nottingham
(*IBO S.Flyweight Title Challenge*)
13.03.04 Dale Robinson W PTS 12 Huddersfield
(*IBO S.Flyweight Title Defence*)
17.12.04 Damaen Kelly L PTS 12 Huddersfield
(*IBO S.Flyweight Title Defence*)

Career: 29 contests, won 25, lost 4.

Tony Booth

Hull. *Born* Hull, 30 January, 1970
Heavyweight. Former Undefeated British Masters L. Heavyweight Champion. Former Undefeated British Central Area Cruiserweight Champion. Ht. 5'11¾"
Manager B. Ingle

08.03.90 Paul Lynch L PTS 6 Watford
11.04.90 Mick Duncan W PTS 6 Dewsbury
26.04.90 Colin Manners W PTS 6 Halifax

16.05.90	Tommy Warde W PTS 6 Hull
05.06.90	Gary Dyson W PTS 6 Liverpool
05.09.90	Shaun McCrory L PTS 6 Stoke
08.10.90	Bullit Andrews W RSC 3 Cleethorpes
23.01.91	Darron Griffiths DREW 6 Stoke
06.02.91	Shaun McCrory L PTS 6 Liverpool
06.03.91	Billy Brough L PTS 6 Glasgow
18.03.91	Billy Brough W PTS 6 Glasgow
28.03.91	Neville Brown L PTS 6 Alfreton
17.05.91	Glenn Campbell L RSC 2 Bury
	(Central Area S. Middleweight Title Challenge)
25.07.91	Paul Murray W PTS 6 Dudley
01.08.91	Nick Manners DREW 8 Dewsbury
11.09.91	Jim Peters L PTS 8 Hammersmith
28.10.91	Eddie Smulders L RSC 6 Arnhem, Holland
09.12.91	Steve Lewsam L PTS 8 Cleethorpes
30.01.92	Serg Fame W PTS 6 Southampton
12.02.92	Tenko Ernie W RSC 4 Wembley
05.03.92	John Beckles W RSC 6 Battersea
26.03.92	Dave Owens W PTS 6 Hull
08.04.92	Michael Gale L PTS 8 Leeds
13.05.92	Phil Soundy W PTS 6 Kensington
02.06.92	Eddie Smulders L RSC 1 Rotterdam, Holland
18.07.92	Maurice Core L PTS 6 Manchester
07.09.92	James Cook L PTS 8 Bethnal Green
30.10.92	Roy Richie DREW 6 Istrees, France
18.11.92	Tony Wilson DREW 8 Solihull
25.12.92	Francis Wanyama L PTS 6 Izegem, Belgium
09.02.93	Tony Wilson W PTS 8 Wolverhampton
01.05.93	Ralf Rocchigiani DREW 8 Berlin, Germany
03.06.93	Victor Cordoba L PTS 8 Marseille, France
23.06.93	Tony Behan W PTS 6 Gorleston
01.07.93	Michael Gale L PTS 8 York
17.09.93	Ole Klemetsen L PTS 8 Copenhagen, Denmark
07.10.93	Denzil Browne DREW 8 York
02.11.93	James Cook L PTS 8 Southwark
12.11.93	Carlos Christie W PTS 6 Hull
28.01.94	Francis Wanyama L RSC 2 Waregem, Belgium
	(Vacant Commonwealth Cruiserweight Title)
26.03.94	Torsten May L PTS 6 Dortmund, Germany
21.07.94	Mark Prince L RSC 3 Battersea
24.09.94	Johnny Held L PTS 8 Rotterdam, Holland
07.10.94	Dirk Wallyn L PTS 6 Waregem, Belgium
27.10.94	Dean Francis L CO 1 Bayswater
23.01.95	Jan Lefeber L PTS 8 Rotterdam, Holland
07.03.95	John Foreman L PTS 6 Edgbaston
27.04.95	Art Stacey W PTS 10 Hull
	(Vacant Central Area Cruiserweight Title)
04.06.95	Montell Griffin L RSC 2 Bethnal Green
06.07.95	Nigel Rafferty W RSC 7 Hull
22.07.95	Mark Prince L RSC 2 Millwall
06.09.95	Leif Keiski L PTS 8 Helsinki, Finland
25.09.95	Neil Simpson W PTS 8 Cleethorpes
06.10.95	Don Diego Poeder L RSC 2 Waregem, Belgium
11.11.95	Bruce Scott L RSC 3 Halifax
16.12.95	John Marceta L RSC 2 Cardiff
20.01.96	Johnny Nelson L RSC 2 Mansfield
15.03.96	Slick Miller W PTS 6 Hull

27.03.96	Neil Simpson L PTS 6 Whitwick
17.05.96	Mark Richardson W RSC 2 Hull
13.07.96	Bruce Scott L PTS 8 Bethnal Green
03.09.96	Paul Douglas L PTS 4 Belfast
14.09.96	Kelly Oliver L RSC 2 Sheffield
06.11.96	Martin Jolley W PTS 4 Hull
22.11.96	Slick Miller W RSC 5 Hull
11.12.96	Crawford Ashley L RSC 1 Southwark
18.01.97	Kelly Oliver L RSC 4 Swadlincote
27.02.97	Kevin Morton L PTS 6 Hull
25.03.97	Nigel Rafferty DREW 8 Wolverhampton
04.04.97	John Wilson L PTS 6 Glasgow
16.04.97	Robert Norton L RSC 4 Bethnal Green
15.05.97	Phill Day W PTS 4 Reading
11.09.97	Steve Bristow L PTS 4 Widnes
22.09.97	Martin Langtry W PTS 6 Cleethorpes
04.10.97	Bruce Scott W PTS 8 Muswell Hill
28.11.97	Martin Jolley W PTS 6 Hull
15.12.97	Nigel Rafferty W PTS 6 Cleethorpes
06.03.98	Peter Mason W RSC 3 Hull
09.06.98	Crawford Ashley L RSC 6 Hull
	(British L. Heavyweight Title Challenge. Vacant Commonwealth L. Heavyweight Title)
18.07.98	Omar Sheika W PTS 8 Sheffield
26.09.98	Toks Owoh L PTS 6 Norwich
29.10.98	Nigel Rafferty W PTS 8 Bayswater
14.12.98	Sven Hamer W PTS 6 Cleethorpes
05.01.99	Ali Saidi W RSC 4 Epernay, France
17.05.99	Darren Ashton W PTS 6 Cleethorpes
12.07.99	Neil Simpson L PTS 10 Coventry
	(Elim. British L. Heavyweight Title)
27.09.99	Adam Cale W PTS 6 Cleethorpes
16.10.99	Cathal O'Grady L CO 4 Belfast
18.01.00	Michael Sprott L PTS 6 Mansfield
12.02.00	Thomas Hansvoll L PTS 6 Sheffield
29.02.00	John Keeton L RSC 2 Widnes
09.04.00	Greg Scott-Briggs W PTS 10 Alfreton
	(Vacant British Masters L. Heavyweight Title)
15.05.00	Michael Pinnock L PTS 6 Cleethorpes
19.06.00	Toks Owoh L RSC 3 Burton
08.09.00	Dominic Negus W PTS 6 Bristol
30.09.00	Robert Norton L RSC 3 Peterborough
31.10.00	Firat Aslan L RSC 2 Hammersmith
11.12.00	Mark Krence L PTS 6 Sheffield
05.02.01	Denzil Browne L RSC 5 Hull
	(Vacant Central Area Cruiserweight Title)
01.04.01	Kenny Gayle DREW 4 Southwark
10.04.01	Mark Baker L PTS 4 Wembley
16.06.01	Butch Lesley L RSC 3 Dagenham
09.09.01	Tommy Eastwood L PTS 4 Southwark
22.09.01	Peter Haymer L PTS 4 Bethnal Green
15.10.01	Colin Kenna L PTS 6 Southampton
01.11.01	Terry Morrill W RSC 7 Hull
24.11.01	Matt Legg L PTS 4 Bethnal Green
16.12.01	Blue Stevens L PTS 4 Southwark
19.01.02	John McDermott L RSC 1 Bethnal Green
20.04.02	Enzo Maccarinelli L PTS 4 Cardiff
28.04.02	Scott Lansdowne W RSC 4 Southwark
10.05.02	Paul Buttery L PTS 4 Preston
23.06.02	Neil Linford L PTS 5 Southwark
03.08.02	Mark Krence L PTS 4 Derby
17.08.02	Enzo Maccarinelli L RTD 2 Cardiff
23.09.02	Slick Miller W PTS 6 Cleethorpes
05.10.02	Phill Day W PTS 4 Coventry
19.10.02	James Zikic L PTS 4 Norwich
27.10.02	Hughie Doherty L PTS 4 Southwark
21.11.02	Jamie Warters W PTS 8 Hull
28.11.02	Roman Greenberg L PTS 4 Finchley
08.12.02	David Haye L RTD 2 Bethnal Green

30.01.03	Mohammed Benguesmia L RTD 4 Algiers, Algeria
05.04.03	Jason Callum L PTS 6 Coventry
17.05.03	Tony Moran L PTS 6 Liverpool
26.07.03	Kelly Oliver L PTS 4 Plymouth
26.09.03	Radcliffe Green W PTS 6 Millwall
14.11.03	Paul Bonson W PTS 6 Hull
14.02.04	Oneal Murray W PTS 8 Holborn
01.05.04	Elvis Michailenko L RTD 4 Gravesend
15.08.04	Bash Ali L RSC 4 Lagos, Nigeria
	(WBF Cruiserweight Title Challenge)
26.11.04	Paul Bonson W PTS 6 Hull
11.12.04	Hovik Keuchkerian L CO 1 Madrid, Spain
05.03.05	Junior MacDonald L PTS 4 Southwark
15.04.05	Johny Jensen L PTS 6 Copenhagen, Denmark
04.06.05	Martin Rogan L RSC 2 Manchester

Career: 136 contests, won 45, drew 8, lost 83.

Alan Bosworth

Northampton. *Born* Northampton, 31 December, 1967
L.Welterweight. Former Undefeated English Lightweight Champion. Former Undefeated British Masters L.Welterweight Champion. Ht. 5'7"
Manager M. Hennessy

17.10.95	Simon Hamblett W RSC 2 Wolverhampton
29.10.95	Shaun Gledhill W PTS 6 Shaw
16.11.95	Brian Coleman W PTS 6 Evesham
23.11.95	David Thompson W RSC 4 Tynemouth
13.01.96	Jason Blanche W PTS 6 Halifax
31.01.96	Arv Mittoo W PTS 6 Stoke
16.02.96	John Docherty W PTS 6 Irvine
24.03.96	Scott Walker DREW 6 Shaw
16.05.96	Yifru Retta W PTS 6 Dunstable
07.03.97	Wayne Rigby L RSC 5 Northampton
09.09.97	Colin Dunne L RSC 8 Bethnal Green
31.10.98	Alan Temple L PTS 6 Basingstoke
26.02.99	Des Sowden W PTS 6 Longford
13.03.99	Paul Burke L PTS 6 Manchester
24.04.99	Jan Bergman L RSC 6 Munich, Germany
02.07.99	Keith Jones W PTS 6 Bristol
24.09.99	Woody Greenaway L PTS 6 Merthyr
03.12.99	Darren Underwood W CO 5 Peterborough
20.01.00	Brian Coleman W PTS 6 Piccadilly
24.03.00	Allan Vester L PTS 12 Aarhus, Denmark
	(IBF Inter-Continental L. Welterweight Title Challenge)
28.04.00	George Scott L PTS 8 Copenhagen, Denmark
02.06.00	Mohamed Helel W PTS 6 Ashford
25.07.00	Shea Neary L PTS 10 Southwark
01.12.00	David Kirk DREW 8 Peterborough
13.03.01	Eamonn Magee L RSC 5 Plymouth
23.06.01	Keith Jones W PTS 6 Peterborough
23.11.01	Daniel James W RSC 7 Bethnal Green
	(Elim. British L.Welterweight Title)
16.03.02	Junior Witter L RSC 3 Northampton
	(Vacant British L.Welterweight Title)
28.09.02	Eamonn Magee L RSC 5 Manchester
28.01.03	Oscar Hall L PTS 10 Nottingham
	(Elim. British L. Welterweight Title)
25.07.03	Gavin Down W RSC 5 Norwich
	(British Masters L.Welterweight Title Challenge. Elim. British L.Welterweight Title)

89

11.12.03 Stephen Smith W PTS 10 Bethnal Green
(Vacant English L.Welterweight Title)
12.11.04 Francis Barrett L PTS 10 Wembley
(European Union L.Welterweight Title Challenge)
27.05.05 Nigel Wright L PTS 10 Spennymoor
(English L.Welterweight Title Challenge)

Career: 34 contests, won 17, drew 2, lost 15.

John Bothwell

Ballieston. *Born* Glasgow, 8 August, 1981
Featherweight. Ht. 5'5"
Manager A. Morrison/K. Morrison

17.10.03 Marty Kayes W PTS 6 Glasgow
30.10.03 Colin Moffett DREW 4 Belfast
07.12.03 Ian Reid W PTS 6 Glasgow
06.03.04 Fred Janes DREW 4 Renfrew
08.04.04 Chris Hooper L CO 2 Peterborough
28.05.04 Jason Nesbitt L RSC 3 Glasgow
01.04.05 Michael Crossan L PTS 6 Glasgow
20.05.05 Buster Dennis L RTD 4 Glasgow

Career: 8 contests, won 2, drew 2, lost 4.

Omid Bourzo

Sheffield. *Born* Tehran, Iran, 1 September, 1979
L. Heavyweight. Ht. 6'1"
Manager J. Ingle

11.10.04 Peter McCormack L PTS 6 Birmingham
09.04.05 Danny McIntosh L PTS 6 Norwich
24.04.05 Jonjo Finnegan W PTS 6 Derby

Career: 3 contests, won 1, lost 2.

Mickey Bowden

Forest Hill. *Born* Lewisham, 30 June, 1975
Featherweight. Ht. 5'8"
Manager J. Rooney

25.02.99 Kevin Gerowski W PTS 4 Kentish Town
09.05.99 Graham McGrath W RSC 4 Bracknell
07.08.99 Brendan Bryce W PTS 4 Dagenham
26.05.01 Anthony Hanna W PTS 4 Bethnal Green
25.02.02 Jimmy Beech L PTS 4 Slough
25.04.02 Nelson Valez L PTS 4 Las Vegas, Nevada, USA
30.10.02 Anthony Hanna W PTS 4 Leicester Square
12.12.02 Richmond Asante W PTS 6 Leicester Square
20.09.03 Stephen Chinnock L PTS 8 Nottingham
14.11.03 Anthony Hanna W PTS 4 Bethnal Green
19.06.04 John Mackay L PTS 8 Muswell Hill
10.09.04 Daniel Thorpe L PTS 6 Wembley
05.03.05 David Bailey W PTS 6 Southwark

Career: 13 contests, won 8, lost 5.

Michael Brodie

Manchester. *Born* Manchester, 10 May, 1974
Featherweight. Former Undefeated IBO & WBF Featherweight Champion. Former Undefeated British, European & Commonwealth S. Bantamweight Champion. Ht. 5'6"
Manager Self

03.10.94 Graham McGrath W RSC 5 Manchester
20.10.94 Chip O'Neill W CO 3 Middleton
28.11.94 Muhammad Shaffique W CO 2 Manchester
13.12.94 Pete Buckley W PTS 6 Potters Bar
16.02.95 G. G. Goddard W PTS 6 Bury
03.04.95 Garry Burrell W RSC 4 Manchester
05.05.95 G. G. Goddard W PTS 6 Swansea
17.05.95 Ian Reid W RSC 3 Ipswich
10.06.95 Chris Clarkson W PTS 6 Manchester
14.11.95 Niel Leggett W CO 1 Bury
25.11.95 Karl Morling W RSC 1 Dagenham
18.12.95 Marty Chestnut W RTD 3 Mayfair
26.02.96 Bamana Dibateza W PTS 6 Manchester
13.04.96 John Sillo W CO 1 Liverpool
07.05.96 Elvis Parsley W RSC 1 Mayfair
06.07.96 Colin Innes W RSC 2 Manchester
19.09.96 Ervine Blake W RSC 4 Manchester
09.11.96 Miguel Matthews W PTS 6 Manchester
22.03.97 Neil Swain W RSC 10 Wythenshawe
(Vacant British S. Bantamweight Title)
30.08.97 Pete Buckley W PTS 8 Cheshunt
01.11.97 Wilson Docherty W CO 4 Glasgow
(British S. Bantamweight Title Defence. Vacant Commonwealth S. Bantamweight Title)
31.01.98 Brian Carr W RSC 10 Edmonton
(British & Commonwealth S. Bantamweight Title Defences)
23.05.98 Simon Ramoni W PTS 12 Bethnal Green
(Commonwealth S. Bantamweight Title Defence)
17.10.98 Sergei Devakov W PTS 12 Manchester
(European S. Bantamweight Title Challenge)
13.03.99 Salim Medjkoune W RSC 9 Manchester
(European S. Bantamweight Title Defence)
31.07.99 Serge Poilblan W RSC 12 Carlisle
(European S. Bantamweight Title Defence)
01.10.99 Drew Docherty W RSC 6 Bethnal Green
(European S. Bantamweight Title Defence)
26.02.00 Salim Medjkoune W RSC 9 Carlisle
(European S. Bantamweight Title Defence)
01.07.00 Mustapha Hame W CO 4 Manchester
(European S.Bantamweight Title Defence)
09.09.00 Willie Jorrin L PTS 12 Manchester
(Vacant WBC S.Bantamweight Title)
03.02.01 Sergio Aguila W RSC 4 Manchester
06.10.01 Frederic Bonifai W RSC 5 Manchester
26.11.01 Sean Fletcher W CO 2 Manchester
18.05.02 Pastor Maurin W PTS 12 Millwall
(Vacant WBF Featherweight Title)
09.11.02 Luis Fuente W PTS 12 Altrincham
(WBF Featherweight Title Defence)
21.06.03 Juan Cabrera W PTS 12 Manchester
(Vacant IBO Featherweight Title)
18.10.03 In-Jin Chi DREW 12 Manchester
(Vacant WBC Featherweight Title)
10.04.04 In-Jin Chi L CO 7 Manchester
(Vacant WBC Featherweight Title)
03.06.05 Scott Harrison L CO 4 Manchester
(WBO Featherweight Title Challenge)

Career: 39 contests, won 35, drew 1, lost 3.

Craig Bromley

Sheffield. *Born* Sheffield, 28 June, 1986
Featherweight. Ht. 5'5"
Manager J. Ingle

10.12.04 Darren Broomhall L PTS 6 Mansfield
19.12.04 Paddy Folan DREW 6 Bolton
13.02.05 Paddy Folan W PTS 6 Bradford
15.04.05 Neil Marston W RSC 1 Shrewsbury

Career: 4 contests, won 2, drew 1, lost 1.

(Ezekiel) Kell Brook

Sheffield. *Born* Sheffield, 3 May, 1986
Lightweight. Ht. 5'9"
Manager J. Ingle

17.09.04 Pete Buckley W PTS 6 Sheffield
29.10.04 Andy Cosnett W CO 1 Worksop
09.11.04 Lee Williamson W RSC 2 Leeds
10.12.04 Brian Coleman W RSC 1 Sheffield
19.12.04 Karl Taylor W PTS 6 Bolton
04.03.05 Lea Handley W PTS 6 Rotherham
15.05.05 Ernie Smith W PTS 6 Sheffield

Career: 7 contests, won 7.

Kell Brook Les Clark

Casey Brooke

Great Wyrley. *Born* Birmingham, 8 July, 1971
Welterweight. Ht. 5'11"
Manager Self

06.06.00 Arv Mittoo L PTS 6 Brierley Hill
07.07.00 John Tiftik L RSC 2 Chigwell
10.10.00 Rene Grayel L PTS 6 Brierley Hill
28.11.00 Rene Grayel L PTS 6 Brierley Hill
03.02.01 Gary Harrison L PTS 6 Brighton
12.03.01 Tony Smith L PTS 6 Birmingham
26.09.03 Nathan Ward L RSC 1 Reading
26.10.03 Danny Cooper L PTS 6 Longford
30.11.03 Chris Brophy L PTS 6 Swansea
20.02.04 Tony Smith L PTS 6 Doncaster
30.03.04 Jay Morris L RSC 1 Southampton
24.04.05 Scott Conway L PTS 6 Derby

Career: 12 contests, lost 12.

Mark Brookes

Swinton. *Born* Doncaster, 1 December, 1979
L. Heavyweight. Ht. 6'0"
Manager D. Hobson

21.10.00 Rob Galloway W RSC 5 Sheffield
11.12.00 Jimmy Steel W PTS 6 Sheffield
24.03.01 Matthew Pepper W RSC 1 Sheffield
18.06.01 Clint Johnson W PTS 6 Bradford
27.07.01 Michael Pinnock W PTS 4 Sheffield
13.09.01 Darren Ashton W PTS 4 Sheffield
22.09.01 Valery Odin L PTS 4 Canning Town
15.12.01 Clint Johnson W PTS 4 Sheffield
11.05.02 Paul Bonson W PTS 4 Chesterfield
05.10.02 Darren Ashton W PTS 4 Chesterfield
05.12.02 Simeon Cover W RSC 3 Sheffield
18.03.03 Peter Haymer L PTS 6 Reading
10.06.03 Michael Pinnock W PTS 4 Sheffield
31.07.03 Hastings Rasani W PTS 6 Sheffield
10.12.03 Peter Haymer DREW 6 Sheffield
06.02.04 Simeon Cover W RSC 4 Sheffield
20.04.04 Neil Simpson W PTS 10 Sheffield
    (Elim. British L.Heavyweight Title)
17.09.04 Hastings Rasani W PTS 6 Sheffield
10.12.04 Peter Haymer L RSC 10 Sheffield
    *(English L.Heavyweight Title
    Challenge)*
Career: 19 contests, won 15, drew 1, lost 3.

Stuart Brookes
Mexborough. *Born* Mexborough, 31
August, 1982
L.Middleweight. Ht. 5'9"
Manager D. Hobson

15.05.05 Geraint Harvey W PTS 6 Sheffield
Career: 1 contest, won 1.

Darren Broomhall
Alfreton. *Born* Chesterfield, 13 May, 1982
Lightweight. Ht. 6'0"
Manager M. Scriven

10.12.04 Craig Bromley W PTS 6 Mansfield
24.04.05 Steve Gethin L CO 5 Derby
18.06.05 Rendall Munroe L RSC 3 Barnsley
Career: 3 contests, won 1, lost 2.

Chris Brophy   Les Clark

Chris Brophy
Swansea. *Born* Preston, 28 January, 1979
Welterweight. Ht. 5'10"
Manager N. Hodges

29.10.03 Aidan Mooney L RSC 5 Leicester
    Square

30.11.03 Casey Brooke W PTS 6 Swansea
21.12.03 Gary O'Connor L PTS 6 Bolton
21.02.04 Tony Doherty L RSC 2 Cardiff
02.04.04 Tommy Marshall DREW 6 Plymouth
26.04.04 Scott Haywood L RSC 5 Cleethorpes
05.06.04 Ashley Theophane L RSC 3 Bethnal
    Green
17.09.04 Tommy Marshall W PTS 6 Plymouth
21.11.04 Jay Morris L RSC 1 Bracknell
31.01.05 George McIlroy L RSC 6 Glasgow
Career: 10 contests, won 2, drew 1, lost 7.

Barrington Brown
Nottingham. *Born* Nottingham, 11 May,
1982
Featherweight. Ht. 5'7"
Manager J. Gill/T. Harris

06.03.05 Paddy Folan W RSC 6 Shaw
Career: 1 contest, won 1.

Cathy Brown
Peckham. *Born* Leeds, 28 July, 1970
Former WBF European Flyweight
Champion. Ht. 5'2"
Manager Self

31.10.99 Veerle Braspenningsx W PTS 5 Raynes
    Park
05.02.00 Veerle Braspenningsx W RSC 6 Sint-
    Truiden, Belgium
01.07.00 Jan Wild W PTS 6 Southwark
    *(Vacant WBF European Flyweight
    Title)*
31.10.00 Viktoria Vargal W RSC 3
    Hammersmith
28.02.01 Marietta Ivanova W PTS 4 Kensington
26.04.01 Oksana Vasilieva L PTS 4 Kensington
16.06.01 Romona Gughie W RSC 3 Wembley
22.11.01 Audrey Guthrie W PTS 6 Mayfair
    *(WBF European Flyweight Title
    Defence)*
13.12.01 Ilina Boneva W RSC 5 Leicester
    Square
13.03.02 Svetla Taskova W PTS 4 Mayfair
13.06.02 Alina Shaternikova L PTS 10 Leicester
    Square
    (Vacant WBF Womens Flyweight Title)
30.10.02 Monica Petrova W PTS 6 Leicester
    Square
20.03.03 Juliette Winter L PTS 4 Queensway
26.04.03 Regina Halmich L PTS 10 Schwerin,
    Germany
    (WIBF Flyweight Title Challenge)
17.12.03 Stefania Bianchini L PTS 10 Bergamo,
    Italy
    (European Flyweight Title Challenge)
06.11.04 Bettina Csabi L PTS 10 Szentes,
    Hungary
    *(WBF/GBU Bantamweight Title
    Challenges)*
02.12.04 Viktoria Varga W RSC 3 Crystal
    Palace
12.06.05 Svetla Taskova W RSC 6 Leicester
    Square
Career: 18 contests, won 12, lost 6.

Denzil Browne
Leeds. *Born* Leeds, 21 January, 1969
Central Area Cruiserweight Champion.
Ht. 6'2½"
Manager Self

18.10.90 Mark Bowen W PTS 6 Dewsbury
29.11.90 R. F. McKenzie L PTS 6 Sunderland
13.12.90 Gary Railton W RSC 2 Dewsbury
21.02.91 Mark Bowen W PTS 6 Walsall
21.03.91 R. F. McKenzie L PTS 6 Dewsbury
09.05.91 Darren McKenna W PTS 6 Leeds
27.06.91 Steve Yorath W PTS 6 Leeds
01.08.91 Tony Colclough W RSC 1 Dewsbury
09.10.91 R. F. McKenzie L PTS 6 Manchester
30.10.91 Gus Mendes W RSC 6 Leeds
23.01.92 Darren McKenna W PTS 6 York
19.03.92 Ian Bulloch W PTS 8 York
23.09.92 Steve Yorath W PTS 8 Leeds
29.10.92 Sean O'Phoenix W RSC 4 Leeds
25.02.93 Cordwell Hylton W PTS 8 Bradford
22.04.93 Dave Muhammed W PTS 8 Mayfair
01.07.93 Steve Osborne W RSC 1 York
07.10.93 Tony Booth DREW 8 York
01.12.93 Lennie Howard W RSC 6 Kensington
26.10.94 Steve Lewsam W CO 2 Leeds
21.01.95 Dennis Andries L RSC 11 Glasgow
    (Vacant British Cruiserweight Title)
08.07.95 Bobbi Joe Edwards L PTS 8 York
11.11.95 John Keeton L RSC 4 Halifax
13.01.96 Albert Call W PTS 6 Halifax
04.06.96 Bobbi Joe Edwards W PTS 10 York
    *(Vacant Central Area Cruiserweight
    Title)*
25.03.97 Chris Okoh L PTS 12 Lewisham
    *(Commonwealth Cruiserweight Title
    Challenge)*
05.02.01 Tony Booth W RSC 5 Hull
    *(Vacant Central Area Cruiserweight
    Title)*
02.06.01 Lee Swaby DREW 8 Wakefield
31.07.03 Phill Day W RSC 6 Sheffield
05.09.03 Tony Dowling L PTS 6 Sheffield
11.11.03 Hastings Rasani W PTS 6 Leeds
24.10.04 Lee Swaby L RSC 7 Sheffield
    (Elim. British Cruiserweight Title)
Career: 32 contests, won 22, drew 2, lost 8.

Steve Brumant
Birmingham. *Born* Birmingham, 18 May,
1971
L. Middleweight. Ht. 5'7"
Manager Self

18.09.97 Gerard Lawrence W CO 1 Alfreton
24.01.98 Anthony Farnell L PTS 4 Cardiff
28.04.98 Nicky Bardle W RSC 5 Brentford
24.03.99 Paul Dyer L PTS 4 Bayswater
20.05.99 David Kirk L PTS 4 Kensington
30.09.99 Delroy Mellis W PTS 6 Kensington
26.11.99 Scott Garrett W RSC 4 Bayswater
19.12.99 Wahid Fats L PTS 6 Salford
19.04.00 Karim Hussine L PTS 4 Kensington
24.06.00 Gerard Murphy L PTS 4 Glasgow
10.10.00 Jason Samuels L PTS 6 Brierley Hill
22.09.03 Davey Jones W PTS 6 Cleethorpes
31.01.04 Michael Lomax L PTS 6 Bethnal Green
13.03.04 Reggie Robshaw W PTS 4 Huddersfield
08.07.04 Ernie Smith W PTS 8 Birmingham
25.11.04 Gavin Down L PTS 10 Birmingham
    *(Vacant Midlands Area L.Middleweight
    Title)*
Career: 16 contests, won 7, lost 9.

Andrew Buchanan
West Denton. *Born* Newcastle, 24 March,
1980
Middleweight. Ht. 6'0"
Manager Self

01.12.00　Paul Johnson W PTS 4 Peterborough
28.03.01　Wayne Shepherd W RSC 2 Piccadilly
26.04.01　Steve Timms W RSC 4 Gateshead
18.03.02　Jason Collins L PTS 4 Crawley
27.05.05　Howard Clarke W PTS 4 Spennymoor
Career: 5 contests, won 4, lost 1.

Paul Buchanan

West Denton. *Born* Newcastle, 23 October, 1981
S.Middleweight. Ht. 5'10"
Manager T. Conroy

31.01.01　Gary Jones W RTD 1 Piccadilly
26.04.01　Lee Woodruff W PTS 6 Gateshead
08.03.02　Neil Bonner W PTS 6 Ellesmere Port
25.03.02　Dean Cockburn W PTS 6 Sunderland
06.03.04　Davey Jones W PTS 4 Renfrew
01.05.04　Gareth Lawrence W PTS 4 Gravesend
05.11.04　Jason McKay W PTS 6 Hereford
27.05.05　Ojay Abrahams W PTS 6 Spennymoor
Career: 8 contests, won 8.

Garry Buckland

Cardiff. *Born* Cardiff, 12 June 1986
L.Welterweight. Ht. 5'7"
Manager B. Powell

05.03.05　Warren Dunkley W PTS 4 Dagenham
Career: 1 contest, won 1.

Garry Buckland　　　　　　　　Les Clark

Paul Buckley

Welling. *Born* London, 20 September, 1977
L. Welterweight. Ht. 5'9¹/₄"
Manager F. Maloney

05.03.05　Pete Buckley W PTS 6 Southwark
29.04.05　Fred Janes W PTS 4 Southwark
Career: 2 contests, won 2.

Pete Buckley

Birmingham. *Born* Birmingham, 9 March, 1969
L. Welterweight. Former Undefeated Midlands Area S. Featherweight Champion. Former Midlands Area S. Bantamweight Champion. Ht. 5'8"
Manager Self

04.10.89　Alan Baldwin DREW 6 Stafford

10.10.89　Ronnie Stephenson L PTS 6 Wolverhampton
30.10.89　Robert Braddock W PTS 6 Birmingham
14.11.89　Neil Leitch W PTS 6 Evesham
22.11.89　Peter Judson W PTS 6 Stafford
11.12.89　Stevie Woods W PTS 6 Bradford
21.12.89　Wayne Taylor W PTS 6 Kings Heath
10.01.90　John O'Meara W PTS 6 Kensington
19.02.90　Ian McGirr L PTS 6 Birmingham
27.02.90　Miguel Matthews DREW 6 Evesham
14.03.90　Ronnie Stephenson DREW 6 Stoke
04.04.90　Ronnie Stephenson L PTS 8 Stafford
23.04.90　Ronnie Stephenson W PTS 6 Birmingham
30.04.90　Chris Clarkson L PTS 8 Mayfair
17.05.90　Johnny Bredahl L PTS 6 Aars, Denmark
04.06.90　Ronnie Stephenson W PTS 8 Birmingham
28.06.90　Robert Braddock W RSC 5 Birmingham
01.10.90　Miguel Matthews W PTS 8 Cleethorpes
09.10.90　Miguel Matthews L PTS 8 Wolverhampton
17.10.90　Tony Smith W PTS 6 Stoke
29.10.90　Miguel Matthews W PTS 8 Birmingham
21.11.90　Drew Docherty L PTS 8 Solihull
10.12.90　Neil Leitch W PTS 8 Birmingham
10.01.91　Duke McKenzie L RSC 5 Wandsworth
18.02.91　Jamie McBride L PTS 8 Glasgow
04.03.91　Brian Robb W RSC 7 Birmingham
26.03.91　Neil Leitch DREW 8 Wolverhampton
01.05.91　Mark Geraghty W PTS 8 Solihull
05.06.91　Brian Robb W PTS 10 Wolverhampton
(Vacant Midlands Area S. Featherweight Title)
09.09.91　Mike Deveney L PTS 8 Glasgow
24.09.91　Mark Bates W RTD 5 Basildon
29.10.91　John Armour L PTS 6 Kensington
14.11.91　Mike Deveney L PTS 6 Edinburgh
28.11.91　Craig Dermody L PTS 6 Liverpool
19.12.91　Craig Dermody L PTS 6 Oldham
18.01.92　Alan McKay DREW 8 Kensington
20.02.92　Brian Robb W RSC 10 Oakengates
(Midlands Area S. Featherweight Title Defence)
27.04.92　Drew Docherty L PTS 8 Glasgow
15.05.92　Ruben Condori L PTS 10 Augsburg, Germany
29.05.92　Donnie Hood L PTS 8 Glasgow
07.09.92　Duke McKenzie L RTD 3 Bethnal Green
12.11.92　Prince Naseem Hamed L PTS 6 Liverpool
19.02.93　Harald Geier L PTS 12 Vienna, Austria
(Vacant WBA Penta-Continental S. Bantamweight Title)
26.04.93　Bradley Stone L PTS 8 Lewisham
18.06.93　Eamonn McAuley L PTS 6 Belfast
01.07.93　Tony Silkstone L PTS 8 York
06.10.93　Jonjo Irwin L PTS 8 Solihull
25.10.93　Drew Docherty L PTS 8 Glasgow
06.11.93　Michael Alldis L PTS 8 Bethnal Green
30.11.93　Barry Jones L PTS 4 Cardiff
19.12.93　Shaun Anderson L PTS 6 Glasgow
22.01.94　Barry Jones L PTS 6 Cardiff
29.01.94　Prince Naseem Hamed L RSC 4 Cardiff
10.03.94　Tony Falcone L PTS 4 Bristol
29.03.94　Conn McMullen W PTS 6 Bethnal Green
05.04.94　Mark Bowers L PTS 6 Bethnal Green
13.04.94　James Murray L PTS 6 Glasgow

06.05.94　Paul Lloyd L RTD 4 Liverpool
03.08.94　Greg Upton L PTS 6 Bristol
26.09.94　John Sillo L PTS 6 Liverpool
05.10.94　Matthew Harris L PTS 6 Wolverhampton
07.11.94　Marlon Ward L PTS 4 Piccadilly
23.11.94　Justin Murphy L PTS 4 Piccadilly
29.11.94　Neil Swain L PTS 6 Cardiff
13.12.94　Michael Brodie L PTS 6 Potters Bar
20.12.94　Michael Alldis L PTS 6 Bethnal Green
10.02.95　Matthew Harris W RSC 6 Birmingham
(Midlands Area S. Bantamweight Title Challenge)
23.02.95　Paul Ingle L PTS 8 Southwark
20.04.95　John Sillo L PTS 6 Liverpool
27.04.95　Paul Ingle L PTS 8 Bethnal Green
09.05.95　Ady Lewis L PTS 4 Basildon
23.05.95　Spencer Oliver L PTS 4 Potters Bar
01.07.95　Dean Pithie L PTS 4 Kensington
21.09.95　Patrick Mullings L PTS 6 Battersea
29.09.95　Marlon Ward L PTS 4 Bethnal Green
25.10.95　Matthew Harris L PTS 10 Telford
(Midlands Area S. Bantamweight Title Defence)
08.11.95　Vince Feeney L PTS 8 Bethnal Green
28.11.95　Barry Jones L PTS 6 Cardiff
15.12.95　Patrick Mullings L PTS 4 Bethnal Green
05.02.96　Patrick Mullings L PTS 8 Bexleyheath
09.03.96　Paul Griffin L PTS 4 Millstreet
21.03.96　Colin McMillan L RSC 3 Southwark
14.05.96　Venkatesan Deverajan L PTS 4 Dagenham
29.06.96　Matt Brown W RSC 1 Erith
03.09.96　Vince Feeney L PTS 4 Bethnal Green
28.09.96　Fabrice Benichou L PTS 8 Barking
09.10.96　Gary Marston DREW 8 Stoke
06.11.96　Neil Swain L PTS 4 Tylorstown
29.11.96　Alston Buchanan L PTS 8 Glasgow
22.12.96　Brian Carr L PTS 6 Glasgow
11.01.97　Scott Harrison L PTS 4 Bethnal Green
29.01.97　Carl Allen L PTS 8 Stoke
12.02.97　Ronnie McPhee L PTS 6 Glasgow
25.02.97　Dean Pithie L PTS 4 Sheffield
07.03.97　Jason Booth L PTS 6 Northampton
20.03.97　Thomas Bradley W PTS 6 Newark
08.04.97　Sergei Devakov L PTS 6 Bethnal Green
25.04.97　Matthew Harris L PTS 6 Cleethorpes
08.05.97　Gregorio Medina L RTD 2 Mansfield
13.06.97　Mike Deveney L PTS 6 Paisley
19.07.97　Richard Evatt L PTS 4 Wembley
30.08.97　Michael Brodie L PTS 8 Cheshunt
06.10.97　Brendan Bryce W PTS 6 Piccadilly
20.10.97　Kelton McKenzie L PTS 6 Leicester
20.11.97　Ervine Blake L PTS 8 Solihull
06.12.97　Danny Adams L PTS 4 Wembley
13.12.97　Gary Thornhill L PTS 6 Sheffield
31.01.98　Scott Harrison L PTS 4 Edmonton
05.03.98　Steve Conway L PTS 5 Leeds
18.03.98　Ervine Blake L PTS 8 Stoke
26.03.98　Graham McGrath W RTD 4 Solihull
11.04.98　Salim Medjkoune L PTS 6 Southwark
18.04.98　Tony Mulholland L PTS 4 Manchester
27.04.98　Alston Buchanan L PTS 8 Glasgow
11.05.98　Jason Squire W RTD 2 Leicester
21.05.98　Lee Armstrong L PTS 6 Bradford
06.06.98　Tony Mulholland L PTS 6 Liverpool
14.06.98　Lee Armstrong L PTS 6 Shaw
21.07.98　David Burke L PTS 6 Widnes
05.09.98　Michael Gomez L PTS 6 Telford
17.09.98　Brian Carr L PTS 6 Glasgow
03.10.98　Justin Murphy L PTS 6 Crawley
05.12.98　Lehlohonolo Ledwaba L PTS 8 Bristol

19.12.98	Acelino Freitas L RTD 3 Liverpool	
09.02.99	Chris Jickells L PTS 6 Wolverhampton	
16.02.99	Franny Hogg L PTS 6 Leeds	
26.02.99	Richard Evatt L RSC 5 Coventry	
17.04.99	Martin O'Malley L RSC 3 Dublin	
29.05.99	Richie Wenton L PTS 6 Halifax	
14.06.99	Carl Allen L PTS 6 Birmingham	
26.06.99	Paul Halpin L PTS 4 Millwall	
15.07.99	Salim Medjkoune L PTS 6 Peterborough	
07.08.99	Steve Murray L PTS 6 Dagenham	
12.09.99	Kevin Gerowski L PTS 6 Nottingham	
20.09.99	Mat Zegan L PTS 6 Peterborough	
02.10.99	Jason Cook L PTS 4 Cardiff	
09.10.99	Brian Carr L PTS 6 Manchester	
19.10.99	Gary Steadman L PTS 4 Bethnal Green	
27.10.99	Miguel Matthews W PTS 8 Birmingham	
20.11.99	Carl Greaves L PTS 10 Grantham	
	(*British Masters S. Featherweight Title Challenge*)	
11.12.99	Gary Thornhill L PTS 6 Liverpool	
29.01.00	Bradley Pryce L PTS 4 Manchester	
19.02.00	Gavin Rees L PTS 4 Dagenham	
29.02.00	Tony Mulholland L PTS 4 Widnes	
20.03.00	Carl Greaves L PTS 4 Mansfield	
27.03.00	James Rooney L PTS 4 Barnsley	
08.04.00	Delroy Pryce L PTS 4 Bethnal Green	
17.04.00	Franny Hogg L PTS 8 Glasgow	
11.05.00	Craig Spacie L PTS 4 Newark	
25.05.00	Jimmy Phelan DREW 6 Hull	
19.06.00	Delroy Pryce L PTS 4 Burton	
01.07.00	Richard Evatt L PTS 4 Manchester	
16.09.00	Lee Meager L PTS 4 Bethnal Green	
23.09.00	Gavin Rees L PTS 4 Bethnal Green	
02.10.00	Brian Carr L PTS 4 Glasgow	
14.10.00	Gareth Jordan L PTS 4 Wembley	
13.11.00	Kevin Lear L PTS 6 Bethnal Green	
24.11.00	Lee Williamson L PTS 6 Hull	
09.12.00	Leo O'Reilly L PTS 4 Southwark	
15.01.01	Eddie Nevins L PTS 4 Manchester	
23.01.01	David Burke L PTS 4 Crawley	
31.01.01	Tony Montana L PTS 6 Piccadilly	
19.02.01	Kevin England W PTS 6 Glasgow	
12.03.01	Carl Allen L PTS 6 Birmingham	
19.03.01	Duncan Armstrong L PTS 6 Glasgow	
27.03.01	Carl Allen L PTS 8 Brierley Hill	
05.05.01	Danny Hunt L PTS 4 Edmonton	
09.06.01	Gary Thornhill L PTS 4 Bethnal Green	
21.07.01	Scott Miller L PTS 4 Sheffield	
28.07.01	Kevin Lear L PTS 4 Wembley	
25.09.01	Ricky Eccleston L PTS 4 Liverpool	
07.10.01	Nigel Senior L PTS 6 Wolverhampton	
31.10.01	Woody Greenaway L PTS 6 Birmingham	
16.11.01	Jimmy Beech L PTS 6 West Bromwich	
01.12.01	Chill John L PTS 4 Bethnal Green	
09.12.01	Nigel Senior W PTS 6 Shaw	
26.01.02	Scott Lawton L PTS 4 Bethnal Green	
09.02.02	Sam Gorman L PTS 6 Coventry	
23.02.02	Alex Moon L PTS 4 Nottingham	
04.03.02	Leo Turner L PTS 6 Bradford	
11.03.02	Martin Watson L PTS 4 Glasgow	
26.04.02	Scott Lawton L PTS 4 Coventry	
10.05.02	Lee Meager L PTS 6 Bethnal Green	
08.06.02	Bradley Pryce L RSC 1 Renfrew	
20.07.02	Jeff Thomas L PTS 4 Bethnal Green	
23.08.02	Ben Hudson DREW 4 Bethnal Green	
06.09.02	Dave Stewart L PTS 6 Bethnal Green	
14.09.02	Peter McDonagh L PTS 4 Bethnal Green	
20.10.02	James Paisley L PTS 4 Southwark	
12.11.02	Martin Hardcastle DREW 6 Leeds	
29.11.02	Daniel Thorpe L PTS 6 Hull	

09.12.02	Nicky Leech L PTS 6 Nottingham	
16.12.02	Joel Viney L PTS 6 Cleethorpes	
28.01.03	Billy Corcoran L PTS 6 Nottingham	
08.02.03	Colin Toohey L PTS 6 Liverpool	
15.02.03	Terry Fletcher L PTS 4 Wembley	
22.02.03	Dean Lambert L PTS 4 Huddersfield	
05.03.03	Billy Corcoran L PTS 6 Bethnal Green	
18.03.03	Nathan Ward L PTS 4 Reading	
05.04.03	Baz Carey L PTS 4 Manchester	
15.05.03	Mike Harrington W PTS 4 Clevedon	
27.05.03	Dave Stewart L PTS 4 Dagenham	
07.06.03	Rimell Taylor DREW 6 Coventry	
12.07.03	George Telfer L PTS 4 Renfrew	
22.07.03	Chas Symonds L PTS 6 Bethnal Green	
01.08.03	Jas Malik W PTS 4 Bethnal Green	
06.09.03	John Murray L PTS 4 Huddersfield	
13.09.03	Isaac Ward L PTS 6 Wakefield	
25.09.03	Gary Woolcombe L PTS 6 Bethnal Green	
06.10.03	Scott Haywood L PTS 6 Barnsley	
20.10.03	Joel Viney W PTS 6 Bradford	
29.10.03	David Kehoe L PTS 6 Leicester Square	
07.11.03	Femi Fehintola L PTS 6 Sheffield	
14.11.03	Dave Stewart L PTS 4 Bethnal Green	
21.11.03	Henry Castle L PTS 4 Millwall	
28.11.03	Lee Meager L PTS 4 Derby	
13.12.03	Derry Matthews L PTS 4 Manchester	
21.12.03	Daniel Thorpe L PTS 6 Bolton	
16.01.04	Nadeem Siddique L PTS 4 Bradford	
16.02.04	Scott Haywood L PTS 6 Scunthorpe	

29.02.04	Gary O'Connor L PTS 6 Shaw	
03.04.04	Steve Bell L PTS 4 Manchester	
16.04.04	Isaac Ward L PTS 6 Hartlepool	
23.04.04	Colin Bain L PTS 6 Glasgow	
06.05.04	Amir Ali L PTS 4 Barnsley	
13.05.04	Lee Beavis L PTS 4 Bethnal Green	
04.06.04	Tristan Davies L PTS 6 Dudley	
03.07.04	Barrie Jones L PTS 4 Newport	
03.09.04	Stefy Bull L PTS 6 Doncaster	
10.09.04	Tiger Matthews L PTS 4 Liverpool	
17.09.04	Kell Brook L PTS 6 Sheffield	
24.09.04	Ceri Hall L PTS 6 Dublin	
11.10.04	Darren Johnstone L PTS 6 Glasgow	
22.10.04	Jonathan Whiteman L PTS 6 Mansfield	
29.10.04	Colin Bain L PTS 6 Renfrew	
09.11.04	Tom Hogan L PTS 6 Leeds	
21.11.04	Chris McDonagh L PTS 4 Bracknell	
10.12.04	Craig Johnson L PTS 6 Mansfield	
17.12.04	Steve Mullin L PTS 4 Liverpool	
12.02.05	Jay Morris L PTS 6 Portsmouth	
21.02.05	Stuart Green L PTS 6 Glasgow	
05.03.05	Paul Buckley L PTS 6 Southwark	
23.03.05	Ryan Barrett L PTS 6 Leicester Square	
09.04.05	Nadeem Siddique L PTS 6 Norwich	
25.04.05	Jimmy Gilhaney L PTS 6 Glasgow	
14.05.05	James Gorman L PTS 6 Dublin	
27.05.05	Alan Temple L PTS 6 Spennymoor	
04.06.05	Patrick Hyland L PTS 4 Dublin	
25.06.05	Sean Hughes DREW 6 Wakefield	

Career: 249 contests, won 31, drew 11, lost 207.

Stefy Bull

Les Clark

(Andrew) Stefy Bull (Bullcroft)

Doncaster. *Born* Doncaster, 10 May, 1977
Central Area Lightweight Champion.
Former Undefeated Central Area
Featherweight Champion. Ht. 5'10"
Manager J. Rushton

30.06.95	Andy Roberts W PTS 4 Doncaster
11.10.95	Michael Edwards W PTS 6 Stoke
18.10.95	Alan Hagan W RSC 1 Batley
28.11.95	Kevin Sheil W PTS 6 Wolverhampton
26.01.96	Robert Grubb W PTS 6 Doncaster
12.09.96	Benny Jones W PTS 6 Doncaster
15.10.96	Kevin Sheil DREW 6 Wolverhampton
24.10.96	Graham McGrath W PTS 6 Birmingham
17.12.96	Robert Braddock W RSC 4 Doncaster
	(Vacant Central Area Featherweight Title)
10.07.97	Carl Greaves W PTS 6 Doncaster
11.10.97	Dean Pithie L RSC 11 Sheffield
	(Vacant WBO Inter-Continental S. Featherweight Title)
19.03.98	Chris Lyons W RSC 4 Doncaster
08.04.98	Alex Moon L RSC 3 Liverpool
31.07.99	Jason Dee L RSC 4 Carlisle
09.05.03	Joel Viney W RTD 3 Doncaster
02.06.03	Jason Nesbitt W PTS 6 Cleethorpes
05.09.03	Dave Hinds W PTS 6 Doncaster
20.02.04	Anthony Christopher W PTS 6 Doncaster
07.05.04	Daniel Thorpe W PTS 10 Doncaster
	(Central Area Lightweight Title Challenge)
03.09.04	Pete Buckley W PTS 6 Doncaster
29.10.04	Haroon Din W RSC 2 Doncaster
	(Central Area Lightweight Title Defence)
04.02.05	Gwyn Wale W PTS 10 Doncaster
	(Central Area Lightweight Title Defence)
11.03.05	Jimmy Beech W PTS 4 Doncaster
20.05.05	Billy Smith W PTS 6 Doncaster

Career: 24 contests, won 20, drew 1, lost 3.

David Burke

Liverpool. *Born* Liverpool, 3 February, 1975
Lightweight. Former Undefeated
Commonwealth & WBU Lightweight
Champion. Ht. 5'9"
Manager S. Vaughan

01.03.97	Ervine Blake W PTS 4 Liverpool
21.05.97	Carl Allen W PTS 4 Liverpool
26.09.97	Rudy Valentino W PTS 4 Liverpool
12.03.98	Bamana Dibateza W PTS 6 Liverpool
08.04.98	John O. Johnson W RSC 1 Liverpool
23.05.98	Mike Deveney W PTS 6 Bethnal Green
21.07.98	Pete Buckley W PTS 6 Widnes
24.10.98	Gary Flear W PTS 6 Liverpool
12.12.98	Justin Murphy W RSC 4 Southwark
05.03.99	Alan Temple W PTS 8 Liverpool
15.05.99	Marian Leonardu L RSC 3 Blackpool
19.06.99	Chris Williams W RTD 1 Dublin
13.12.99	Chris Jickells W PTS 6 Glasgow
09.03.00	Woody Greenaway W RSC 2 Liverpool
23.01.01	Pete Buckley W PTS 4 Crawley
03.02.01	Keith Jones W PTS 4 Manchester
03.03.01	Marco Fattore W RSC 1 Wembley
24.04.01	Jason Dee W RSC 1 Liverpool
26.05.01	Matthew Zulu W PTS 6 Bethnal Green
25.09.01	Richard Howard W PTS 6 Liverpool

09.03.02	Anthony Maynard W PTS 6 Manchester
07.09.02	Gary Hibbert W RSC 10 Liverpool
	(Vacant Commonwealth Lightweight Title)
07.12.02	Colin Dunne W PTS 12 Brentwood
	(WBU Lightweight Title Challenge)
07.06.03	Stefano Zoff L PTS 12 Trieste, Italy
	(Vacant European Lightweight Title)
10.09.04	Keith Jones W PTS 6 Liverpool
19.11.04	Peter McDonagh W PTS 8 Bethnal Green
17.12.04	Alan Temple W RSC 4 Liverpool
13.05.05	Duncan Cottier W PTS 6 Liverpool

Career: 28 contests, won 26, lost 2.

Stephen Burke

Liverpool. *Born* Liverpool, 18 March, 1979
Welterweight. Ht. 5'8"
Manager S. Vaughan

13.05.05	Ahmed Kharif W RSC 3 Liverpool

Career: 1 contest, won 1.

Paul Burns

Uddingston. *Born* Rutherglen, 5 January, 1983
Welterweight. Ht. 6'2"
Manager T. Gilmour

06.06.05	Terry Carruthers DREW 6 Glasgow

Career: 1 contest, drew 1.

Ricky Burns

Coatbridge. *Born* Bellshill, 13 April, 1983
S.Featherweight. Ht. 5'10"
Manager R. Bannan/A. Morrison

20.10.01	Woody Greenaway W PTS 4 Glasgow
15.03.02	Peter Allen W PTS 6 Glasgow
08.06.02	Gary Harrison W RSC 1 Renfrew
06.09.02	Ernie Smith W PTS 6 Glasgow
19.10.02	Neil Murray W RSC 2 Renfrew
08.12.02	No No Junior W PTS 8 Glasgow
08.10.04	Daniel Thorpe W PTS 6 Glasgow
29.10.04	Jeff Thomas W PTS 4 Renfrew
12.12.04	Colin Bain W PTS 6 Glasgow
25.02.05	Graham Earl W PTS 8 Wembley
08.04.05	Buster Dennis W PTS 6 Edinburgh
17.06.05	Haider Ali W PTS 8 Glasgow

Career: 12 contests, won 12.

Chris Burton

Darlington. *Born* Darlington, 27 February, 1981
Heavyweight. Ht. 6'5"
Manager D. Garside

02.06.05	David Ingleby W RSC 3 Yarm

Career: 1 contest, won 1.

Pinky Burton

Selby. *Born* Perth, 13 December, 1979
Cruiserweight. Former Undefeated British
Masters Cruiserweight Champion.
Ht. 5'11½"
Manager Self

28.04.01	Nathan King L PTS 4 Cardiff
28.01.02	Rob Galloway W RSC 4 Barnsley
02.03.02	Darren Ashton W PTS 6 Wakefield
17.02.03	Eamonn Glennon W PTS 6 Glasgow
24.03.03	Michael Pinnock W PTS 4 Barnsley
02.06.03	Ovill McKenzie W PTS 8 Glasgow

06.10.03	Paul Bonson W PTS 6 Barnsley
25.03.04	Ryan Walls W PTS 10 Longford
	(British Masters Cruiserweight Title Challenge)
11.10.04	Valery Odin W PTS 6 Glasgow

Career: 9 contests, won 8, lost 1.

Robert Burton

Barnsley. *Born* Barnsley, 1 April, 1971
Middleweight. Former Central Area
L.Middleweight Champion. Former Central
Area Welterweight Champion. Ht. 5'9"
Manager T. Schofield

05.02.01	Gavin Pearson W RSC 3 Bradford
23.02.01	Scott Millar W CO 5 Irvine
20.03.01	Peter Dunn W PTS 6 Leeds
08.05.01	Arv Mittoo W PTS 4 Barnsley
10.06.01	Martyn Bailey DREW 6 Ellesmere Port
08.10.01	Gavin Pearson W RSC 2 Barnsley
16.11.01	Martyn Bailey DREW 4 Preston
24.11.01	Peter Dunn L PTS 6 Wakefield
28.01.02	Peter Dunn W RSC 8 Barnsley
	(Vacant Central Area Welterweight Title)
23.08.02	David Walker L RSC 2 Bethnal Green
19.10.02	John Humphrey L RTD 4 Norwich
09.02.03	Donovan Smillie L PTS 6 Bradford
24.03.03	Andy Halder L PTS 6 Barnsley
31.05.03	David Keir W RSC 9 Barnsley
	(Central Area Welterweight Title Defence)
01.11.03	Scott Dixon L PTS 6 Glasgow
08.12.03	Jed Tytler W PTS 6 Barnsley
10.02.04	Paul Lomax W PTS 6 Barnsley
06.05.04	Matthew Hatton L PTS 10 Barnsley
	(Central Area Welterweight Title Defence)
08.06.04	Lee Murtagh W CO 3 Sheffield
	(Vacant Central Area L.Middleweight Title)
12.11.04	Matthew Hatton L PTS 10 Halifax
	(Central Area L.Middleweight Title Defence)
11.02.05	Paul Smith L CO 1 Manchester
22.04.05	John Marshall L RTD 4 Barnsley

Career: 22 contests, won 10, drew 2, lost 10.

Andrew Butlin

Huddersfield. *Born* Huddersfield, 31 January, 1982
L. Middleweight. Ht. 5'10"
Manager W. Barker

12.11.04	Martin Concepcion L RSC 1 Halifax

Career: 1 contest, lost 1.

Paul Butlin

Oakham. *Born* Oakham, 16 March, 1976
Heavyweight. Ht. 6'1½"
Manager Self

05.10.02	Dave Clarke W PTS 4 Coventry
16.11.02	Gary Williams W RSC 1 Coventry
09.12.02	Slick Miller W PTS 6 Nottingham
08.03.03	Dave Clarke W PTS 6 Coventry
19.04.03	Paul Buttery L RSC 3 Liverpool
27.04.04	Ebrima Secka W PTS 6 Leeds
26.09.04	Lee Mountford W PTS 6 Stoke
06.12.04	David Ingleby W CO 5 Leicester
30.04.05	David Ingleby L PTS 6 Coventry
25.06.05	Mal Rice W PTS 4 Melton Mowbray

Career: 10 contests, won 8, lost 2.

Daniel Cadman

Waltham Abbey. *Born* Harlow, 25 June, 1980
S.Middleweight. Ht. 5'10"
Manager M. Hennessy

25.07.03	Leigh Wicks W PTS 4 Norwich
04.10.03	Patrick Cito W PTS 6 Muswell Hill
28.11.03	Harry Butler W PTS 4 Derby
30.01.04	Mike Duffield W RSC 1 Dagenham
02.06.04	Joel Ani W CO 2 Nottingham
12.11.04	Howard Clarke W PTS 6 Wembley
26.03.05	Lee Williamson W PTS 4 Hackney
10.04.05	Howard Clarke W PTS 4 Brentwood

Career: 8 contests, won 8.

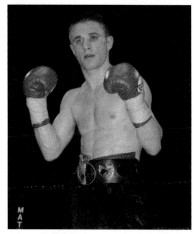

Marc Callaghan   Les Clark

Marc Callaghan

Barking. *Born* Barking, 13 November, 1977
Southern Area S. Bantamweight Champion.
Ht. 5'6"
Manager Self

08.09.98	Kevin Sheil W PTS 4 Bethnal Green
31.10.98	Nicky Wilders W RSC 1 Southend
12.01.99	Nicky Wilders W RTD 2 Bethnal Green
12.03.99	Peter Allen W PTS 4 Bethnal Green
25.05.99	Simon Chambers L RSC 1 Mayfair
16.10.99	Nigel Leake W PTS 4 Bethnal Green
20.12.99	Marc Smith W PTS 4 Bethnal Green
05.02.00	Steve Brook W RSC 2 Bethnal Green
01.04.00	John Barnes W PTS 4 Bethnal Green
19.08.00	Anthony Hanna W PTS 4 Brentwood
09.10.00	Jamie McKeever L PTS 6 Liverpool
04.11.00	Nigel Senior W RSC 4 Bethnal Green
03.03.01	Anthony Hanna W PTS 6 Wembley
26.05.01	Roy Rutherford L RSC 3 Bethnal Green
01.12.01	Nigel Senior L CO 1 Bethnal Green
26.01.02	Richmond Asante W PTS 4 Dagenham
18.03.02	Michael Hunter DREW 6 Crawley
11.05.02	Andrew Ferrans W PTS 6 Dagenham
21.09.02	Steve Gethin W PTS 6 Brentwood
07.12.02	Stevie Quinn L PTS 4 Brentwood
08.03.03	Dazzo Williams L PTS 8 Bethnal Green
05.07.03	Mark Payne L PTS 6 Brentwood
08.05.04	Baz Carey W PTS 6 Dagenham
27.05.04	Steve Gethin W PTS 6 Huddersfield
20.09.04	John Simpson L PTS 8 Glasgow
19.11.04	Michael Hunter L RSC 10 Hartlepool
	(British S.Bantamweight Title Challenge)
16.06.05	Ian Napa W PTS 10 Dagenham
	(Vacant Southern Area S.Bantamweight Title)

Career: 27 contests, won 17, drew 1, lost 9.

Jason Callum

Coventry. *Born* Coventry, 5 April, 1977
Heavyweight. Ht. 6'3"
Manager Self

05.04.03	Tony Booth W PTS 6 Coventry
15.11.03	Slick Miller W PTS 4 Coventry
01.05.04	David Ingleby W PTS 6 Coventry
06.12.04	Scott Lansdowne L CO 1 Leicester

Career: 4 contests, won 3, lost 1.

Joe Calzaghe

Newbridge. *Born* Hammersmith, 23 March, 1972
WBO S. Middleweight Champion. Former
Undefeated British S. Middleweight
Champion. Ht. 5'11"
Manager F. Warren

01.10.93	Paul Hanlon W RSC 1 Cardiff
10.11.93	Stinger Mason W RSC 1 Watford
16.12.93	Spencer Alton W RSC 2 Newport
22.01.94	Martin Rosamond W RSC 1 Cardiff
01.03.94	Darren Littlewood W RSC 1 Dudley
04.06.94	Karl Barwise W RSC 1 Cardiff
01.10.94	Mark Dawson W RSC 1 Cardiff
30.11.94	Trevor Ambrose W RSC 2 Wolverhampton
14.02.95	Frank Minton W CO 1 Bethnal Green
22.02.95	Bobbi Joe Edwards W PTS 8 Telford
19.05.95	Robert Curry W RSC 1 Southwark
08.07.95	Tyrone Jackson W RSC 4 York
30.09.95	Nick Manners W RSC 4 Basildon
28.10.95	Stephen Wilson W RSC 8 Kensington
	(Vacant British S. Middleweight Title)
13.02.96	Guy Stanford W RSC 1 Cardiff
13.03.96	Anthony Brooks W RSC 2 Wembley
20.04.96	Mark Delaney W RSC 5 Brentwood
	(British S. Middleweight Title Defence)
04.05.96	Warren Stowe W RTD 2 Dagenham
15.05.96	Pat Lawlor W RSC 2 Cardiff
21.01.97	Carlos Christie W CO 2 Bristol
22.03.97	Tyler Hughes W CO 1 Wythenshawe
05.06.97	Luciano Torres W RSC 3 Bristol
11.10.97	Chris Eubank W PTS 12 Sheffield
	(Vacant WBO S. Middleweight Title)
24.01.98	Branco Sobot W RSC 3 Cardiff
	(WBO S.Middleweight Title Defence)
25.04.98	Juan Carlos Gimenez W RTD 9 Cardiff
	(WBO S.Middleweight Title Defence)
13.02.99	Robin Reid W PTS 12 Newcastle
	(WBO S.Middleweight Title Defence)
05.06.99	Rick Thornberry W PTS 12 Cardiff
	(WBO S.Middleweight Title Defence)
29.01.00	David Starie W PTS 12 Manchester
	(WBO S, Middleweight Title Defence)
12.08.00	Omar Sheika W RSC 5 Wembley
	(WBO S.Middleweight Title Defence)
16.12.00	Richie Woodhall W RSC 10 Sheffield
	(WBO S. Middleweight Title Defence)
28.04.01	Mario Veit W RSC 1 Cardiff
	(WBO S.Middleweight Title Defence)
13.10.01	Will McIntyre W RSC 4 Copenhagen, Denmark
	(WBO S.Middleweight Title Defence)
20.04.02	Charles Brewer W PTS 12 Cardiff
	(WBO S.Middleweight Title Defence)
17.08.02	Miguel Jimenez W PTS 12 Cardiff
	(WBO S.Middleweight Title Defence)
14.12.02	Tocker Pudwill W RSC 2 Newcastle
	(WBO S.Middleweight Title Defence)
28.06.03	Byron Mitchell W RSC 2 Cardiff
	(WBO S.Middleweight Title Defence)
21.02.04	Mger Mkrtchian W RSC 7 Cardiff
	(WBO S.Middleweight Title Defence)
22.10.04	Kabary Salem W PTS 12 Edinburgh
	(WBO S.Middleweight Title Defence)
07.05.05	Mario Veit W RSC 6 Braunschweig, Germany
	(WBO S.Middleweight Title Defence)

Career: 39 contests, won 39.

Joe Calzaghe   Les Clark

Tom Cannon

Coatbridge. *Born* Bellshill, 18 March, 1980
Scottish S.Middleweight Champion.
Ht. 5'11½"
Manager R. Bannon

15.06.01	Valery Odin L PTS 4 Millwall
20.10.01	Andrew Lowe L PTS 4 Glasgow
26.01.02	Arthur Shekhmurzov DREW 4 Bethnal Green
15.03.02	Harry Butler W PTS 6 Glasgow
08.06.02	Ty Browne W PTS 4 Renfrew
06.09.02	Gary Dixon W PTS 6 Glasgow
21.10.02	Dean Cockburn DREW 4 Glasgow
19.06.04	Lee Woodruff W PTS 4 Renfrew
29.10.04	Ojay Abrahams W PTS 4 Renfrew
21.11.04	Jamie Hearn L PTS 6 Bracknell
12.12.04	Karl Wheeler W PTS 6 Glasgow
21.02.05	Cello Renda L PTS 6 Peterborough
01.04.05	Barry Connell W RTD 7 Glasgow
	(Vacant Scottish S.Middleweight Title)

Career: 13 contests, won 7, drew 2, lost 4.

Tom Cannon　　　　　Les Clark

(Barry) Baz Carey

Coventry. *Born* Coventry, 11 March, 1971
Lightweight. Ht. 5'4½"
Manager J. Griffin

19.12.01 J.J. Moore L PTS 4 Coventry
18.01.02 J.J. Moore DREW 4 Coventry
25.02.02 Chris McDonagh L PTS 6 Slough
19.03.02 Ilias Miah W PTS 6 Slough
21.09.02 Jackson Williams L PTS 6 Norwich
10.10.02 Dean Scott W RSC 2 Stoke
19.10.02 Lee McAllister L PTS 4 Renfrew
21.11.02 Chris Hooper L RTD 3 Hull
22.03.03 Dave Hinds W PTS 6 Coventry
05.04.03 Pete Buckley W PTS 4 Manchester
12.05.03 Matthew Marshall L PTS 6 Southampton
07.06.03 Joel Viney W PTS 6 Coventry
26.07.03 Andrew Ferrans DREW 4 Plymouth
13.09.03 Paul McIlwaine W RTD 2 Coventry
12.10.03 Daniel Thorpe DREW 6 Sheffield
08.11.03 Carl Allen L RSC 2 Coventry
15.03.04 Andrew Ferrans L PTS 10 Glasgow
　　　　　　(Vacant British Masters S.Featherweight Title)
17.04.04 Michael Kelly L PTS 4 Belfast
26.04.04 Rendall Munroe L PTS 6 Cleethorpes
08.05.04 Marc Callaghan L PTS 6 Dagenham
06.11.04 Daniel Thorpe L PTS 6 Coventry
20.11.04 Dave Hinds W RSC 4 Coventry
17.12.04 Kristian Laight W PTS 6 Coventry
30.04.05 Billy Smith W PTS 6 Coventry
26.05.05 Daniel Thorpe L PTS 6 Mayfair
Career: 25 contests, won 9, drew 3, lost 13.

Terry Carruthers

Birmingham. *Born* Birmingham, 4 February, 1986
L. Welterweight. Ht. 5'8"
Manager N. Nobbs

21.02.05 Andy Cosnett L PTS 6 Birmingham
06.03.05 Jonathan Whiteman DREW 6 Mansfield
25.04.05 Darren Gethin W RSC 3 Cleethorpes
16.05.05 Andy Cosnett DREW 6 Birmingham
06.06.05 Paul Burns DREW 6 Glasgow
26.06.05 Justin Murphy L RSC 1 Southampton
Career: 6 contests, won 1, drew 3, lost 2.

Henry Castle

Salisbury. *Born* Southampton, 7 February, 1979
S.Featherweight. Ht. 5'6¾"
Manager Self

29.01.01 Jason Nesbitt W CO 6 Peterborough
26.03.01 Eddie Nevins W RSC 2 Peterborough
23.11.01 Jimmy Beech W PTS 4 Bethnal Green
11.03.02 David Lowry W RSC 1 Glasgow
20.04.02 Jason Nesbitt W PTS 4 Cardiff
25.05.02 Jimmy Beech W PTS 4 Portsmouth
17.08.02 Joel Viney W RSC 1 Cardiff
23.11.02 John Mackay L RTD 8 Derby
29.03.03 Jus Wallie L RSC 2 Portsmouth
25.09.03 Mark Alexander W PTS 6 Bethnal Green
21.11.03 Pete Buckley W PTS 4 Millwall
20.02.04 Daleboy Rees W RSC 4 Bethnal Green
26.06.05 Karl Taylor W PTS 6 Southampton
Career: 13 contests, won 11, lost 2.

Henry Castle　　　　　Les Clark

Stephen Chinnock

Rugeley. *Born* Lichfield, 4 December, 1975
S.Featherweight. Midlands Area Featherweight Champion. Ht. 5'10"
Manager Self

10.09.00 Neil Read W RSC 5 Walsall
06.11.00 Jason Nesbitt W PTS 6 Wolverhampton
27.11.00 Jason White W PTS 4 Birmingham
20.05.01 Gareth Wiltshaw W PTS 6 Wolverhampton
07.10.01 Kevin Gerowski W PTS 10 Wolverhampton
　　　　　　(Vacant Midlands Area Featherweight Title)
18.01.02 John Mackay W PTS 4 Coventry
13.04.02 Neil Read W CO 3 Wolverhampton
　　　　　　(Midlands Area Featherweight Title Defence)
08.09.02 Nigel Senior W PTS 6 Wolverhampton
17.05.03 Dazzo Williams L PTS 10 Liverpool
　　　　　　(Elim. British Featherweight Title)

20.09.03 Mickey Bowden W PTS 8 Nottingham
14.02.04 Roy Rutherford L RSC 4 Nottingham
　　　　　　(Vacant English S.Featherweight Title)
26.02.05 Andrew Ferrans L RTD 5 Burton
Career: 12 contests, won 9, lost 3.

Stephen Chinnock　　　　　Les Clark

Karl Chiverton

Mansfield. *Born* Sutton in Ashfield, 1 March, 1986
L.Middleweight. Ht. 5'9¾"
Manager H. Rainey

18.09.04 Karl Taylor W PTS 6 Newark
10.12.04 Cafu Santos L RSC 4 Mansfield
Career: 2 contests, won 1, lost 1.

Anthony Christopher

Aberystwyth. *Born* Aberystwyth, 18 August, 1981
L.Welterweight. Ht. 5'8¼"
Manager Self

23.09.01 Arv Mittoo DREW 6 Shaw
29.09.02 Ernie Smith W PTS 6 Shrewsbury
03.12.02 Ernie Smith L PTS 6 Shrewsbury
23.02.03 Dean Larter L PTS 6 Aberystwyth
20.02.04 Stefy Bull L PTS 6 Doncaster
06.03.04 Gary Young L CO 1 Renfrew
08.05.05 Dwayne Hill L PTS 6 Sheffield
20.06.05 Ryan Barrett L RSC 1 Longford
Career: 8 contests, won 1, drew 1, lost 6.

Marco Cittadini

Glasgow. *Born* Glasgow, 12 September, 1977
L.Welterweight. Ht. 5'7¾"
Manager R. Bannan

17.06.05 Barrie Jones L RSC 2 Glasgow
Career: 1 contest, lost 1.

Dave Clarke

Blackpool. *Born* Dover, 20 June, 1976
Heavyweight. Ht. 6'1"
Manager W. Barker

22.11.01 Roman Greenberg L RSC 5 Paddington

11.02.02	Colin Kenna L RSC 4 Southampton
15.03.02	Shaun Bowes L PTS 6 Spennymoor
24.03.02	Tommy Eastwood L PTS 6 Streatham
11.05.02	Ivan Botton L PTS 6 Newark
03.06.02	Tony Moran L PTS 6 Glasgow
25.06.02	Carl Wright L PTS 6 Rugby
20.07.02	Matt Legg L RSC 2 Bethnal Green
05.10.02	Paul Butlin L PTS 4 Coventry
12.10.02	Enzo Maccarinelli L RSC 2 Bethnal Green
20.11.02	Costi Marin W RSC 2 Leeds
30.11.02	Ahmad Cheleh W RSC 1 Liverpool
05.12.02	Roman Greenberg L RSC 1 Sheffield
08.01.03	Scott Gammer L PTS 4 Aberdare
08.03.03	Paul Butlin L PTS 6 Coventry
17.03.03	Costi Marin W PTS 6 Glasgow
24.03.03	Neil Dawson L PTS 4 Barnsley
13.04.03	Oneal Murray W PTS 4 Streatham
28.04.03	Shane Woollas L PTS 6 Cleethorpes
15.05.03	Matt Skelton L RSC 1 Mayfair
28.06.03	Scott Gammer L RSC 1 Cardiff
06.09.03	Carl Baker L RSC 1 Aberdeen
06.10.03	Neil Dawson L PTS 6 Barnsley
01.12.03	Lee Mountford L PTS 6 Bradford
24.01.04	Augustin N'Gou L PTS 6 Wembley
16.02.04	Chris Woollas L PTS 6 Scunthorpe
12.03.04	Coleman Barrett L PTS 6 Nottingham
25.04.04	Luke Simpkin L RSC 2 Nottingham
07.06.04	Dave McKenna L PTS 6 Glasgow
20.09.04	David Ingleby L RTD 5 Glasgow
04.06.05	Darren Morgan L RSC 1 Manchester
Career: 31 contests, won 4, lost 27.

Howard Clarke

Warley. *Born* London, 23 September, 1967
Middleweight. Ht. 5'10"
Manager N. Nobbs

15.10.91	Chris Mylan W PTS 4 Dudley
09.12.91	Claude Rossi W RSC 3 Brierley Hill
04.02.92	Julian Eavis W PTS 4 Alfreton
03.03.92	Dave Andrews W RSC 3 Cradley Heath
21.05.92	Richard O'Brien W CO 1 Cradley Heath
29.09.92	Paul King W PTS 6 Stoke
27.10.92	Gordon Blair L RSC 4 Cradley Heath
16.03.93	Paul King W PTS 6 Edgbaston
07.06.93	Dean Bramhald W RTD 2 Walsall
29.06.93	Paul King W PTS 6 Edgbaston
06.10.93	Julian Eavis L PTS 8 Solihull
30.11.93	Julian Eavis W PTS 8 Wolverhampton
08.02.94	Nigel Bradley W RTD 6 Wolverhampton
18.04.94	Andy Peach W PTS 6 Walsall
28.06.94	Dennis Berry L RSC 3 Edgbaston
12.10.94	Julian Eavis W PTS 8 Stoke
25.10.94	Andy Peach W RSC 3 Edgbaston
02.11.94	Julian Eavis W PTS 8 Birmingham
29.11.94	Julian Eavis W PTS 6 Cannock
07.12.94	Peter Reid W PTS 8 Stoke
25.01.95	Dennis Berry L PTS 8 Stoke
08.03.95	Andrew Jervis W PTS 6 Solihull
11.05.95	David Bain W RSC 1 Dudley
20.09.95	Michael Smyth DREW 6 Ystrad
02.10.95	Nigel Wenton L PTS 6 Mayfair
02.12.96	Martin Smith L PTS 8 Birmingham
29.01.97	Gary Beardsley W PTS 6 Stoke
11.02.97	Prince Kasi Kaihau L RSC 4 Wolverhampton
19.03.97	Mark Cichocki W PTS 6 Stoke
15.04.97	Prince Kasi Kaihau W PTS 6 Edgbaston

30.04.97	Allan Gray W PTS 8 Acton
22.05.97	Michael Alexander W RSC 3 Solihull
21.06.97	Paul Samuels L PTS 8 Cardiff
09.09.97	Harry Dhami L PTS 8 Bethnal Green
05.11.97	Andras Galfi W PTS 8 Tenerife
27.01.98	Mack Razor L PTS 8 Hammanskraal, South Africa
23.03.98	Lindon Scarlett DREW 6 Crystal Palace
18.07.98	Jason Papillion W PTS 8 Sheffield
13.03.99	Fernando Vargas L RSC 4 NYC, New York, USA
	(IBF L. Middleweight Title Challenge)
05.11.99	Michael Rask L PTS 12 Aalberg, Denmark
	(WBA Inter-Continental L. Middleweight Title Challenge)
29.05.00	Anthony Farnell L PTS 12 Manchester
	(WBO Inter-Continental L. Middleweight Title Challenge)
12.08.00	Takaloo L PTS 12 Wembley
	(Vacant IBF Inter-Continental L.Middleweight Title)
04.11.00	Richard Williams L CO 4 Bethnal Green
16.12.00	Ryan Rhodes L PTS 6 Sheffield
03.02.01	Michael Jones L PTS 4 Manchester
26.02.01	Jawaid Khaliq L PTS 6 Nottingham
07.04.01	Gary Lockett L RSC 2 Wembley
06.05.01	Ian Cooper L PTS 6 Hartlepool
04.06.01	James Docherty L PTS 6 Hartlepool
14.07.01	Gary Lockett L CO 1 Wembley
15.09.01	Thomas McDonagh L PTS 6 Manchester
10.11.01	Ossie Duran L PTS 6 Wembley
26.11.01	Wayne Pinder L PTS 6 Manchester
16.12.01	Erik Teymour L PTS 6 Southwark
27.01.02	Paul Samuels L PTS 6 Streatham
03.03.02	Lee Murtagh NC 2 Shaw
20.04.01	Wayne Elcock L PTS 4 Cardiff
25.05.02	Ross Minter W RSC 2 Portsmouth
08.06.02	Alexander Vetoux L RSC 4 Renfrew
27.07.02	Mihaly Kotai L RSC 1 Nottingham
08.12.02	Matthew Tait L PTS 6 Bethnal Green
21.12.02	Matthew Thirlwall L PTS 6 Dagenham
25.01.03	Paul Samuels L PTS 6 Bridgend
08.02.03	Michael Jones L PTS 6 Liverpool
05.03.03	Gilbert Eastman L PTS 6 Bethnal Green
05.04.03	Paul Smith L PTS 4 Manchester
21.06.03	Wayne Pinder L PTS 4 Manchester
01.08.03	Arthur Shekhmurzov L PTS 6 Bethnal Green
17.10.03	Scott Dixon L PTS 6 Glasgow
25.10.03	Lawrence Murphy L PTS 6 Edinburgh
14.11.03	Sonny Pollard L PTS 6 Hull
07.02.04	Wayne Alexander L RSC 2 Bethnal Green
03.04.04	Paul Smith L PTS 4 Manchester
10.04.04	Wayne Pinder L PTS 4 Manchester
08.05.04	Allan Foster L PTS 4 Dagenham
04.06.04	Andrew Facey L PTS 6 Hull
17.06.04	Patrick J. Maxwell L RSC 1 Sheffield
24.09.04	Darren Barker L PTS 6 Nottingham
01.10.04	Matthew Hall L RSC 5 Manchester
12.11.04	Daniel Cadman L PTS 6 Wembley
20.11.04	Jason Collins L DIS 3 Coventry
10.12.04	Anthony Small L PTS 4 Sheffield
17.12.04	Paul Smith L CO 1 Liverpool
04.02.05	Jason Rushton L PTS 4 Doncaster
12.02.05	Gary Woolcombe L PTS 6 Portsmouth
20.02.05	Michael Monaghan L PTS 6 Sheffield
06.03.05	Lee Blundell L PTS 6 Shaw

23.03.05	Gareth Lawrence L PTS 6 Leicester Square
10.04.05	Daniel Cadman L PTS 4 Brentwood
21.04.05	Darren McDermott L RTD 1 Dudley
27.05.05	Andrew Buchanan L PTS 4 Spennymoor
16.06.05	Anthony Small L PTS 6 Mayfair
Career: 92 contests, won 27, drew 2, lost 62, no contest 1.

Dean Cockburn

Doncaster. *Born* Doncaster, 28 March, 1979
Central Area S.Middleweight Champion.
Ht. 5'9¹/₂"
Manager T. Gilmour

17.09.01	Mark Chesters W RSC 4 Glasgow
17.11.01	Paul Wesley W PTS 4 Glasgow
25.03.02	Paul Buchanan L PTS 6 Sunderland
21.06.02	Darren Stubbs W RSC 1 Leeds
08.10.02	Jason McKay L PTS 4 Glasgow
21.10.02	Tom Cannon DREW 4 Glasgow
01.11.02	Neil Bonner W PTS 4 Preston
20.11.02	Harry Butler W PTS 6 Leeds
17.03.03	Barry Thorogood W PTS 4 Southampton
10.05.03	George Robshaw L PTS 6 Huddersfield
07.05.04	Simeon Cover W PTS 6 Doncaster
14.06.04	Terry Morrill W RTD 4 Cleethorpes
03.09.04	Dean Walker W PTS 10 Doncaster
	(Vacant Central Area S.Middleweight Title)
29.10.04	Lee Nicholson W RSC 2 Doncaster
13.12.04	Lee Nicholson W RSC 3 Cleethorpes
04.02.05	Jason Collins W RSC 8 Doncaster
	(Central Area S.Middleweight Title Defence)
11.03.05	Gary Thompson W RSC 4 Doncaster
20.05.05	Jason Collins W PTS 10 Doncaster
	(Central Area S.Middleweight Title Defence)
Career: 18 contests, won 14, drew 1, lost 3.

Dean Cockburn　　　　　Les Clark

Brian Coleman

Birmingham. *Born* Birmingham, 27 July, 1969
L. Middleweight. Ht. 5'11"
Manager N. Nobbs

21.11.91	Jamie Morris DREW 6 Stafford
11.12.91	Craig Hartwell DREW 6 Leicester
22.01.92	John O. Johnson L PTS 6 Stoke
20.02.92	Davy Robb L PTS 6 Oakengates
31.03.92	Blue Butterworth L PTS 6 Stockport
17.05.92	Korso Aleain L RSC 5 Harringay
17.09.92	Nicky Bardle L RSC 4 Watford
21.10.92	Jason Barker W PTS 6 Stoke
10.12.92	A. M. Milton DREW 4 Bethnal Green
31.03.93	A. M. Milton L PTS 4 Bethnal Green
26.04.93	Jason Beard L PTS 6 Lewisham
06.05.93	Mark Allen W PTS 6 Walsall
18.05.93	Sean Metherell DREW 6 Kettering
27.05.93	Blue Butterworth L PTS 6 Burnley
23.06.93	Jonathan Thaxton L PTS 8 Gorleston
11.08.93	Steve Howden L RSC 4 Mansfield
13.09.93	Mick Hoban L PTS 6 Middleton
01.12.93	A. M. Milton L PTS 4 Bethnal Green
08.12.93	Chris Pollock W PTS 6 Stoke
16.12.93	Mark Newton L PTS 6 Newport
11.01.94	Paul Knights L RSC 4 Bethnal Green
08.02.94	Andy Peach W PTS 6 Wolverhampton
18.02.94	Cam Raeside L PTS 6 Leicester
08.03.94	Chris Pollock L PTS 6 Edgbaston
29.03.94	P. J. Gallagher L PTS 6 Bethnal Green
14.04.94	Cham Joof L CO 3 Battersea
02.06.94	Scott Walker L CO 1 Middleton
12.09.94	Shabba Edwards L PTS 6 Mayfair
19.09.94	Mark Breslin L CO 1 Glasgow
09.11.94	Kenny Scott L PTS 6 Stafford
23.11.94	Billy McDougall W PTS 4 Piccadilly
29.11.94	Warren Stephens W PTS 6 Wolverhampton
09.12.94	Danny Stevens L RTD 2 Bethnal Green
24.01.95	Wayne Jones L PTS 6 Piccadilly
07.02.95	Alan Temple L PTS 6 Ipswich
23.02.95	Darren Covill L PTS 4 Southwark
16.03.95	Paul Knights L RSC 2 Basildon
02.07.95	Tommy Lawler L PTS 6 Dublin
08.09.95	George Naylor L PTS 6 Liverpool
27.09.95	Allan Gray L PTS 6 Bethnal Green
20.10.95	Mikael Nilsson L PTS 4 Ipswich
02.11.95	Marco Fattore W PTS 6 Mayfair
16.11.95	Alan Bosworth L PTS 6 Evesham
24.11.95	Chris Barnett L PTS 6 Manchester
02.12.95	Neil Sinclair L RTD 1 Belfast
20.01.96	James Hare L PTS 6 Mansfield
29.01.96	Dave Fallon L PTS 6 Piccadilly
13.02.96	Martin Holgate L PTS 4 Bethnal Green
21.02.96	Marco Fattore W PTS 6 Piccadilly
13.03.96	Paul Samuels L PTS 6 Wembley
03.04.96	Ian Honeywood L PTS 6 Bethnal Green
20.04.96	Ray Robinson L PTS 6 Brentwood
24.05.96	Scott Dixon L PTS 6 Glasgow
08.06.96	Mark Winters L PTS 4 Newcastle
06.07.96	Nick Boyd L PTS 4 Manchester
16.08.96	Charlie Paine W PTS 6 Liverpool
27.08.96	Dave Brazil L PTS 6 Windsor
19.09.96	Ricky Sackfield W RSC 3 Manchester
27.09.96	Nicky Bardle L PTS 4 Stevenage
08.10.96	Marcus McCrae W PTS 6 Battersea
09.11.96	Mark Haslam L PTS 6 Manchester
27.11.96	Bernard Paul L PTS 6 Bethnal Green
09.12.96	Wayne Windle L PTS 6 Chesterfield
18.01.97	Paul Burke L PTS 6 Manchester
19.02.97	Anthony Campbell L PTS 6 Acton
25.03.97	Craig Stanley DREW 4 Lewisham
03.04.97	Kevin McCarthy L PTS 6 Wembley
22.04.97	Georgie Smith L PTS 6 Bethnal Green
19.05.97	John O.Johnson DREW 6 Cleethorpes
02.06.97	Steve McLevy W RSC 5 Glasgow
02.08.97	Junior Witter L PTS 4 Barnsley
13.09.97	Jason Rowland L PTS 8 Millwall
04.10.97	Everald Williams L PTS 4 Muswell Hill
24.10.97	Anthony Maynard L CO 1 Birmingham
27.01.98	Kevin McCarthy L PTS 6 Streatham
23.02.98	Kevin McKillan L PTS 6 Salford
05.03.98	Junior Witter L PTS 6 Leeds
24.03.98	Jon Harrison DREW 6 Wolverhampton
03.04.98	Peter Nightingale L PTS 6 West Bromwich
23.04.98	Marc Smith W PTS 6 Edgbaston
06.05.98	Stuart Rimmer L PTS 6 Blackpool
18.05.98	Steve Conway L PTS 6 Cleethorpes
26.05.98	Rimvidas Billius L PTS 4 Mayfair
06.06.98	Jamie McKeever L PTS 4 Liverpool
18.06.98	Shaun Stokes L PTS 6 Sheffield
12.09.98	Graham Earl L PTS 4 Bethnal Green
03.10.98	Peter Nightingale L PTS 6 West Bromwich
12.10.98	Christian Brady L PTS 6 Birmingham
22.10.98	Colin Lynes L RSC 2 Barking
25.11.98	Arv Mittoo W PTS 6 Clydach
07.12.98	Gavin Down L PTS 6 Manchester
21.01.99	Dennis Griffin W PTS 6 Piccadilly
06.02.99	Tontcho Tontchev L PTS 6 Halifax
26.02.99	Peter Nightingale L PTS 6 West Bromwich
08.03.99	Sammy Smith W PTS 8 Birmingham
25.03.99	Ernie Smith W PTS 6 Edgbaston
03.04.99	Ricky Hatton L CO 2 Kensington
27.05.99	Ernie Smith L PTS 6 Mayfair
04.06.99	Steve Conway L PTS 6 Hull
26.06.99	Steve Murray L PTS 6 Millwall
07.08.99	Jonathan Thaxton L PTS 6 Dagenham
13.09.99	Bobby Vanzie L PTS 6 Bethnal Green
27.09.99	Steve Conway L PTS 6 Leeds
24.10.99	Peter Nightingale L PTS 10 Wolverhampton *(Midlands Area Welterweight Title Challenge)*
06.11.99	Jacek Bielski L PTS 4 Bethnal Green
22.11.99	Sonny Thind W RSC 5 Piccadilly
30.11.99	Ernie Smith W PTS 8 Wolverhampton
11.12.99	Oscar Hall L PTS 6 Liverpool
20.01.00	Alan Bosworth L PTS 6 Piccadilly
12.02.00	Shaun Stokes W PTS 4 Sheffield
24.02.00	Ernie Smith W PTS 6 Edgbaston
09.03.00	Paul Burns L PTS 6 Liverpool
25.03.00	Michael Jennings L PTS 6 Liverpool
16.05.00	Michael Jennings L PTS 6 Warrington
25.05.00	Lee Molyneux L PTS 6 Peterborough
19.06.00	Gavin Down L PTS 4 Burton
19.08.00	Glenn McClarnon L PTS 6 Brentwood
25.09.00	Derek Roche L PTS 6 Barnsley
14.10.00	Colin Lynes L PTS 6 Wembley
31.10.00	Ivan Kirpa L RSC 3 Hammersmith
02.12.00	John Tiftik L PTS 4 Chigwell
11.12.00	Lee Bird W CO 4 Cleethorpes
23.01.01	Paul Knights L PTS 6 Crawley
03.02.01	Darren Spencer L PTS 6 Manchester
10.02.01	Carl Wall L RSC 1 Widnes
17.03.01	Bradley Pryce L PTS 4 Manchester
26.03.01	Ross Minter L PTS 4 Wembley
28.04.01	Ismail Khalil L PTS 4 Cardiff
08.05.01	Gavin Wake L PTS 4 Barnsley
21.05.01	Ernie Smith L PTS 6 Birmingham
09.06.01	Matthew Hatton L RTD 2 Bethnal Green
08.12.01	Gavin Down L RSC 1 Chesterfield
23.02.02	Young Muttley L PTS 4 Nottingham
22.03.02	Sam Gorman L PTS 6 Coventry
26.04.02	Andy Egan L PTS 6 Coventry
08.06.02	Ronnie Nailen L PTS 4 Renfrew
23.08.02	Brett James L PTS 6 Bethnal Green
28.09.02	Thomas McDonagh L RSC 1 Manchester
18.02.03	Ben Hudson L PTS 6 Bethnal Green
09.03.03	Wayne Shepherd L PTS 6 Shaw
22.03.03	Andy Egan L PTS 6 Coventry
05.04.03	Matthew Hall L RSC 1 Manchester
09.05.03	Sammy Smith L PTS 6 Longford
31.05.03	Terry Fletcher L PTS 4 Barnsley
15.06.03	Lee McAllister L PTS 6 Bradford
22.07.03	Ashley Theophane L PTS 6 Bethnal Green
03.08.03	Lee McAllister L PTS 4 Stalybridge
13.09.03	Ady Clegg L PTS 6 Wakefield
25.09.03	Elvis Mbwakongo L PTS 6 Bethnal Green
05.10.03	Steve Conway L PTS 6 Bradford
18.10.03	Colin Lynes L PTS 4 Manchester
26.10.03	Kevin Phelan L PTS 6 Longford
18.11.03	Mark Stupple L PTS 6 Bethnal Green
29.11.03	Barrie Lee L PTS 4 Renfrew
07.12.03	Ali Nuumembe L RTD 2 Bradford
16.02.04	Dave Pearson W PTS 6 Scunthorpe
29.02.04	Mark Paxford L PTS 6 Shaw
16.04.04	Franny Jones L PTS 6 Hartlepool
23.04.04	Barry Hughes L PTS 8 Glasgow
01.05.04	Richard Mazurek L PTS 6 Coventry
08.05.04	Michael Rennie L PTS 4 Dagenham
28.05.04	Barrie Lee L PTS 6 Glasgow
10.07.04	Richard Swallow W RSC 7 Coventry
30.07.04	Martin Concepcion L RSC 1 Bethnal Green
20.09.04	Luke Teague L PTS 6 Cleethorpes
30.09.04	Luke Teague L PTS 6 Hull
09.10.04	Danny Smith L PTS 6 Norwich
22.10.04	Chris Black L PTS 4 Edinburgh
29.10.04	Jason Rushton L PTS 6 Doncaster
06.11.04	Dave Pearson L PTS 6 Coventry
10.12.04	Kell Brook L RSC 1 Sheffield
21.01.05	Kerry Hope L PTS 4 Bridgend

Career: 172 contests, won 24, drew 7, lost 141.

Jason Collins

Walsall. *Born* Walsall, 5 December, 1972
Middleweight. Former Undefeated British Masters S. Middleweight Champion.
Ht. 5'9"
Manager B. Ingle

18.02.99	Biagio Falcone L PTS 6 Glasgow
17.03.99	Stuart Harper W RSC 2 Stoke
06.06.99	Jon Foster DREW 6 Nottingham
15.08.99	Matt Galer W PTS 6 Derby
28.10.99	Lee Blundell DREW 6 Burnley
20.11.99	Dennis Berry L PTS 6 Grantham
14.12.99	Jorge Araujo L PTS 6 Telde, Gran Canaria, Spain
15.01.00	Martin Jolley W RTD 1 Doncaster
18.02.00	Oscar Hall DREW 6 West Bromwich
27.02.00	Jawaid Khaliq L PTS 6 Leeds
05.03.00	Wayne Shepherd W PTS 6 Shaw
21.03.00	Sharden Ansoula W PTS 6 Telde, Gran Canaria
21.05.00	Neville Brown L RSC 2 Derby
08.07.00	Darren Rhodes DREW 4 Widnes
04.09.00	Darren Rhodes W PTS 4 Manchester
01.10.00	Juergen Braehmer L CO 1 Hamburg, Germany
13.11.00	Takaloo L RSC 2 Bethnal Green

16.12.00 Louis Swales DREW 4 Sheffield
27.01.01 Spencer Fearon W PTS 4 Bethnal Green
26.03.01 Patrick J. Maxwell W PTS 4 Wembley
20.04.01 Jim Rock L PTS 6 Dublin
08.06.01 Leigh Wicks W PTS 4 Hull
21.06.01 Lester Jacobs L CO 9 Earls Court
 (WBF Middleweight Title Challenge)
07.09.01 Delroy Mellis W DIS 5 Bethnal Green
22.09.01 Ian Cooper L PTS 10 Newcastle
 (Vacant British Masters Middleweight Title)
27.10.01 Ryan Rhodes L PTS 4 Manchester
17.11.01 Gerard Murphy L PTS 4 Glasgow
08.12.01 Steven Bendall L CO 12 Dagenham
 (Vacant WBU Inter-Continental Middleweight Title)
12.02.02 Delroy Leslie L RSC 1 Bethnal Green
18.03.02 Andrew Buchanan L PTS 4 Crawley
01.06.02 Wayne Elcock L RSC 2 Manchester
17.08.02 Jeff Lacy L CO 1 Cardiff
21.09.02 Wayne Asker DREW 6 Norwich
10.10.02 Mike Duffield W PTS 4 Piccadilly
25.10.02 Matthew Thirlwall L RSC 5 Bethnal Green
23.11.02 Wayne Elcock L RSC 1 Derby
24.02.03 Michael Monaghan L PTS 8 Birmingham
20.03.03 Kreshnik Qato L PTS 4 Queensway
29.03.03 Gary Lockett L CO 1 Portsmouth
12.05.03 Ojay Abrahams W PTS 10 Birmingham
 (Vacant British Masters S.Middleweight Title)
06.06.03 Danny Thornton L PTS 10 Hull
 (Vacant Central Area Middleweight Title)
12.07.03 Lawrence Murphy L PTS 4 Renfrew
25.07.03 Gilbert Eastman L RSC 1 Norwich
06.10.03 Alan Jones L PTS 8 Birmingham
28.11.03 Danny Thornton L PTS 10 Hull
 (Central Area Middleweight Title Challenge)
25.04.04 Michael Monaghan L PTS 6 Nottingham
10.05.04 Hamed Jamali L PTS 8 Birmingham
02.06.04 Alan Jones L PTS 6 Hereford
30.05.04 Jonathan O'Brian NC 3 Dublin
02.06.04 Alan Jones L PTS 6 Hereford
17.09.04 Andrew Facey L PTS 4 Sheffield
24.09.04 Matthew Thirlwall W PTS 6 Nottingham
01.10.04 Paul Smith L RSC 1 Manchester
20.11.04 Howard Clarke W DIS 3 Coventry
03.12.04 Matthew Hall L PTS 6 Edinburgh
04.02.05 Dean Cockburn L RSC 8 Doncaster
 (Central Area S.Middleweight Title Challenge)
09.04.05 Danny Smith L PTS 6 Norwich
20.05.05 Dean Cockburn L PTS 10 Doncaster
 (Central Area S.Middleweight Title Challenge)
Career: 56 contests, won 15, drew 6, lost 35.

Martin Concepcion

Leicester. *Born* Leicester, 11 August, 1981
L. Middleweight. Ht. 5'9"
Manager F. Maloney

06.12.03 Danny Gwilym W RSC 2 Cardiff
07.02.04 Jed Tytler W RSC 2 Bethnal Green
27.03.04 Joel Ani W RTD 3 Edinburgh
05.06.04 William Webster W RSC 1 Bethnal Green

30.07.04 Brian Coleman W RSC 1 Bethnal Green
10.09.04 Rob MacDonald W RSC 2 Bethnal Green
12.11.04 Andrew Butlin W RSC 1 Halifax
03.12.04 David Kirk W PTS 4 Edinburgh
11.12.04 Bertrand Souleyras W RSC 1 Canning Town
25.02.05 Craig Lynch W PTS 6 Wembley
03.06.05 Ernie Smith W PTS 4 Manchester
Career: 11 contests, won 11.

Barry Connell

Glasgow. *Born* Glasgow, 25 July, 1979
S. Middleweight. Ht. 6'1"
Manager A. Morrison

24.02.00 Colin Vidler W PTS 6 Glasgow
07.04.00 Ernie Smith W PTS 6 Glasgow
26.05.00 Harry Butler W PTS 4 Glasgow
14.03.03 Paul Owen W PTS 4 Glasgow
22.03.03 Simeon Cover W PTS 4 Renfrew
16.05.03 Martin Thompson DREW 4 Glasgow
17.10.03 Simeon Cover W PTS 6 Glasgow
07.12.03 Paul Owen W PTS 6 Glasgow
29.02.04 Gary Dixon L RTD 3 Shaw
01.04.05 Tom Cannon L RTD 7 Glasgow
 (Vacant Scottish S.Middleweight Title)
Career: 10 contests, won 7, drew 1, lost 2.

Gary Connolly

Worksop. *Born* Rotherham, 27 April, 1981
Welterweight. Ht. 5'7"
Manager J. Ingle

29.10.04 Arv Mittoo L RSC 5 Worksop
09.12.04 Sujad Elahi L RSC 2 Sunderland
25.06.05 Tye Williams L CO 4 Wakefield
Career: 3 contests, lost 3.

Scott Conway

Derby. *Born* Derby, 27 October, 1979
Welterweight. Ht. 6'0"
Manager M. Shinfield

27.09.04 Rocky Flanagan W RSC 2 Cleethorpes
16.12.04 Tony Randell L PTS 6 Cleethorpes
20.02.05 Sujad Elahi DREW 6 Sheffield
24.04.05 Casey Brooke W PTS 6 Derby
18.06.05 Joe Mitchell L RSC 5 Barnsley
Career: 5 contests, won 2, drew 1, lost 2.

Steve Conway

Dewsbury. *Born* Hartlepool, 6 October, 1977
L.Welterweight. Ht. 5'8"
Manager M. Marsden

21.02.96 Robert Grubb W PTS 6 Batley
24.04.96 Ervine Blake W PTS 6 Solihull
20.05.96 Chris Lyons W PTS 6 Cleethorpes
30.05.96 Ram Singh W PTS 6 Lincoln
03.02.97 Jason Squire W PTS 6 Leicester
11.04.97 Marc Smith W PTS 4 Barnsley
22.09.97 Arv Mittoo W PTS 6 Cleethorpes
09.10.97 Arv Mittoo W PTS 6 Leeds
01.11.97 Brian Carr L PTS 6 Glasgow
14.11.97 Brendan Bryce W PTS 6 Mere
04.12.97 Kid McAuley W RSC 6 Doncaster
15.12.97 Nicky Wilders W PTS 6 Cleethorpes
05.03.98 Pete Buckley W PTS 6 Leeds
25.04.98 Dean Phillips W PTS 6 Cardiff

09.05.98 Gary Flear W PTS 4 Sheffield
18.05.98 Brian Coleman W PTS 6 Cleethorpes
05.09.98 Benny Jones W PTS 4 Telford
19.12.98 Gary Thornhill L RSC 9 Liverpool
 (WBO Inter-Continental S. Featherweight Title Challenge)
04.06.99 Brian Coleman W PTS 6 Hull
27.09.99 Brian Coleman W PTS 6 Leeds
27.02.00 Chris Price W RTD 3 Leeds
21.03.00 Pedro Miranda L RSC 3 Telde, Gran Canaria
15.07.00 Arv Mittoo W PTS 6 Norwich
20.10.00 Junior Witter L RTD 4 Belfast
25.02.01 Ram Singh W RSC 2 Derby
02.06.01 Jimmy Phelan W PTS 4 Wakefield
18.08.01 Keith Jones W PTS 8 Dewsbury
17.11.01 Carl Allen W PTS 8 Dewsbury
27.04.02 Steve Robinson W PTS 8 Huddersfield
05.10.02 Rakheem Mingaleev W RSC 4 Huddersfield
19.10.02 Alex Arthur L CO 4 Renfrew
 (Vacant British S. Featherweight Title)
05.07.03 Dariusz Snarski W RSC 4 Brentwood
05.10.03 Brian Coleman W PTS 6 Bradford
06.11.03 Yuri Romanov L PTS 8 Sheffield
23.11.03 Gareth Wiltshaw W RSC 5 Rotherham
16.04.04 Norman Dhalie W CO 3 Hartlepool
23.10.04 Ernie Smith W PTS 6 Wakefield
Career: 37 contests, won 31, lost 6.

Jason Cook

Maesteg. *Born* Maesteg, 27 February, 1975
Lightweight. Former IBO Lightweight Champion. Former Undefeated Welsh L.Welterweight Champion. Former Undefeated European Lightweight Champion. Ht. 5'9"
Manager B. Hearn

11.10.96 Brian Robb W RSC 2 Mayfair
27.11.96 Andrew Reed W RSC 3 Bethnal Green
27.05.97 Marc Smith W PTS 4 Mayfair
31.10.97 Marc Smith W PTS 4 Mayfair
24.01.98 David Kirk W RSC 3 Cardiff
26.05.98 Trevor Smith W RSC 1 Mayfair
23.02.99 Darren Woodley W RSC 4 Cardiff
28.05.99 Dave Hinds W RSC 1 Liverpool
02.10.99 Pete Buckley W PTS 4 Cardiff
11.12.99 Woody Greenaway W RSC 1 Merthyr
 (Vacant Welsh L. Welterweight Title)
26.02.00 Harry Butler W PTS 6 Swansea
17.04.00 Andrei Sinepupov W RTD 3 Birmingham
12.05.00 Keith Jones W PTS 10 Swansea
 (Welsh L. Welterweight Title Defence)
09.10.00 Assen Vasilev W PTS 6 Liverpool
17.02.01 Dariusz Snarski W PTS 8 Kolbrzeg, Poland
18.03.02 Nono Junior W RSC 1 Crawley
11.05.02 Andrei Devyataykin W PTS 6 Dagenham
29.06.02 Viktor Baranov W PTS 6 Brentwood
03.08.02 Sandro Casamonica W RSC 3 San Mango D'Aquino, Italy
 (Vacant European Lightweight Title)
26.10.02 Nasser Lakrib W RSC 5 Maesteg
 (European Lightweight Title Defence)
25.01.03 Stefano Zoff W PTS 12 Bridgend
06.09.03 Vincent Howard W RTD 3 Huddersfield
08.11.03 Ariel Oliveira W RSC 7 Bridgend
 (Vacant IBO Lightweight Title)

Mark Dane

Peterborough. *Born* Peterborough, 9 January, 1977
L.Welterweight. Ht. 5'3¹/₂"
Manager I. Pauly

17.09.04   John Fewkes L RSC 2 Sheffield
Career: 1 contest, lost 1.

Scott Dann

Plymouth. *Born* Plymouth, 23 July, 1974
British Middleweight Champion.
Former Undefeated English & IBO
Inter-Continental Middleweight Champion.
Ht. 5'10¹/₂"
Manager C. Sanigar

15.11.97   Jon Rees W RSC 1 Bristol
25.04.98   Israel Khumalo W RSC 3 Cardiff
30.05.98   Michael Alexander W PTS 4 Bristol
14.07.98   Richard Glaysher W RSC 1 Reading
24.10.98   James Donoghue W PTS 6 Bristol
27.02.00   James Donoghue W RSC 1 Plymouth
07.04.00   Martin Jolley W RSC 2 Bristol
08.09.00   Sean Pritchard W RSC 5 Bristol
06.10.00   Peter Mitchell W RSC 3 Maidstone
03.11.00   Anthony Ivory W PTS 8 Ebbw Vale
13.03.01   Jason Hart W RSC 2 Plymouth
12.05.01   Elvis Adonesi W CO 7 Plymouth
               (Vacant IBO Inter-Continental
               Middleweight Title)
13.09.01   Jon Penn L RSC 5 Sheffield
10.05.02   Mark Phillips W PTS 6 Bethnal Green
10.07.02   Mark Phillips W PTS 4 Wembley
29.11.02   Delroy Leslie W RSC 1 Liverpool
               (Final Elim. British Middleweight Title)
16.04.03   Howard Eastman L RSC 3 Nottingham
               (British, Commonwealth & European
               Middleweight Title Challenges)
26.07.03   Kreshkik Qato W RSC 2 Plymouth
09.10.03   Hussain Osman W PTS 8 Bristol
02.04.04   Ojay Abrahams W RSC 6 Plymouth
08.05.04   Danny Thornton W RSC 3 Bristol
               (Vacant English Middleweight Title)
17.09.04   Steven Bendall W RSC 6 Plymouth
               (Vacant British Middleweight Title)
04.02.05   Alan Jones W CO 3 Plymouth
               (British Middleweight Title Defence)
29.04.05   Andy Halder W CO 1 Plymouth
               (British Middleweight Title Defence)
Career: 24 contests, won 22, lost 2.

John Davidson

Manchester. *Born* Manchester, 13 April, 1986
S. Featherweight. Ht. 5'8¹/₂"
Manager J. Trickett

26.11.04   Jason Nesbitt L RSC 1 Altrincham
Career: 1 contest, lost 1.

Dai Davies

Merthyr Tydfil. *Born* Merthyr Tydfil, 20 April, 1983
S. Featherweight. Ht. 5'6"
Manager D. Gardiner

08.07.04   Neil Marston W PTS 6 Birmingham
01.10.04   Riaz Durgahed W PTS 4 Bristol
02.12.04   Martin Lindsay L RSC 1 Crystal Palace
25.02.05   Matthew Marsh L PTS 4 Wembley
Career: 4 contests, won 2, lost 2.

Dai Davies   Les Clark

Tristan Davies

Telford. *Born* Shrewsbury, 13 October, 1978
L. Welterweight. Ht. 5'10"
Manager Self

04.06.04   Pete Buckley W PTS 6 Dudley
05.10.04   Gavin Tait W PTS 6 Dudley
17.02.05   Stuart Phillips W PTS 6 Dudley
Career: 3 contests, won 3.

Tristan Davies   Les Clark

Gary Davis (Harding)

St Helens. *Born* Liverpool, 17 October, 1982
S. Bantamweight. Ht. 5'6"
Manager Self

01.06.02   Steve Gethin L RSC 2 Manchester
05.10.02   Jason Thomas W RSC 5 Liverpool
29.11.02   Simon Chambers W RSC 2 Liverpool
15.11.04   Furhan Rafiq W PTS 6 Glasgow
Career: 4 contests, won 3, lost 1.

Varuzhan Davtyan

Birmingham. *Born* Armenia, 11 August, 1972
L. Heavyweight. Ht. 5'8¹/₂"
Manager Self

Previous record unknown
09.03.02   Tony Dodson W PTS 6 Manchester
09.05.02   Rasmus Ojemaye W RSC 3 Leicester
               Square
29.06.02   Elvis Michailenko L PTS 6 Brentwood
08.09.02   Paul Bonson W PTS 4 Wolverhampton
05.10.02   Mark Hobson L RSC 3 Huddersfield
30.11.02   Eric Teymour L PTS 6 Liverpool
14.12.02   Tomasz Adamek L RTD 4 Newcastle
05.03.03   Carl Froch L RSC 5 Bethnal Green
17.05.03   Jason McKay L PTS 6 Liverpool
24.05.03   Eric Teymour L PTS 4 Bethnal Green
28.06.03   Nathan King L PTS 4 Cardiff
26.07.03   Tony Dodson L RTD 3 Plymouth
20.09.03   Adrian Dodson W PTS 4 Nottingham
20.03.04   Andrew Lowe L PTS 6 Wembley
30.03.04   Jamie Hearn W PTS 4 Southampton
02.06.04   Steven Spartacus L RSC 1 Nottingham
28.10.04   Sam Price L PTS 6 Sunderland
08.12.04   Ryan Walls L PTS 4 Longford
17.12.04   Courtney Fry L RTD 2 Liverpool
12.02.05   Tony Oakey L RTD 5 Portsmouth
10.04.05   Andrew Lowe L PTS 6 Brentwood
29.04.05   Leigh Allis L PTS 4 Plymouth
03.06.05   Tony Quigley L PTS 4 Manchester
11.06.05   Steve McGuire L PTS 6 Kirkcaldy
Career: 24 contests, won 5, lost 19.

Lenny Daws

Morden. *Born* Carshalton, 29 December, 1978
L. Welterweight. Ht. 5'10¹/₂"
Manager M. Hennessy

16.04.03   Danny Gwilym W RSC 2 Nottingham
27.05.03   Ben Hudson W RSC 2 Dagenham
25.07.03   Karl Taylor W RTD 2 Norwich
04.10.03   Ernie Smith W PTS 4 Muswell Hill
28.11.03   Tony Montana W PTS 6 Derby
11.12.03   Keith Jones W PTS 6 Bethnal Green
30.01.04   Denis Alekseev W CO 3 Dagenham
24.09.04   Ernie Smith W PTS 6 Nottingham
12.11.04   Keith Jones W PTS 8 Wembley
10.04.05   Silence Saheed W PTS 6 Brentwood
Career: 10 contests, won 10.

Neil Dawson

Rotherham. *Born* Rotherham, 1 July, 1980
Cruiserweight. Ht. 6'4"
Manager C. Aston

12.11.02   Eamonn Glennon W PTS 6 Leeds
24.03.03   Dave Clarke W PTS 4 Barnsley
06.10.03   Dave Clarke W PTS 6 Barnsley
04.12.03   Wlodek Kopec W PTS 4 Huddersfield
13.03.04   Paul Bonson W PTS 4 Huddersfield
08.06.04   Greg Scott-Briggs W RSC 3 Sheffield
20.02.05   Gary Thompson W PTS 6 Sheffield
Career: 7 contests, won 7.

Rocky Dean

Thetford. *Born* Bury St Edmonds, 17 June, 1978
Southern Area Featherweight Champion.
Ht. 5'5"
Manager A. Bowers

14.10.99 Lennie Hodgkins W PTS 6 Bloomsbury
30.10.99 Lennie Hodgkins W PTS 6 Southwark
18.05.00 Danny Lawson W RSC 1 Bethnal Green
29.09.00 Anthony Hanna W PTS 4 Bethnal Green
10.11.00 Chris Jickells L RSC 1 Mayfair
19.04.02 Peter Svendsen W PTS 6 Aarhus, Denmark
19.10.02 Sean Grant W RSC 3 Norwich
21.12.02 Darren Cleary W PTS 4 Millwall
08.02.03 Steve Gethin DREW 4 Norwich
11.07.03 Isaac Ward DREW 4 Darlington
26.07.03 Michael Hunter L RSC 1 Plymouth
10.10.03 Isaac Ward L PTS 6 Darlington
06.11.03 Martin Power L PTS 6 Dagenham
07.12.03 Michael Crossan L PTS 6 Glasgow
24.09.04 Simon Wilson W PTS 4 Millwall
19.12.04 Jim Betts W PTS 8 Bethnal Green
05.03.05 Mickey Coveney W PTS 10 Dagenham
(Vacant Southern Area Featherweight Title)
20.05.05 Andy Morris L PTS 10 Southwark
(Vacant English Featherweight Title)
Career: 18 contests, won 10, drew 2, lost 6.

Garry Delaney

West Ham. *Born* Newham, 12 August, 1970
Heavyweight. Former Undefeated Southern
Area & British Masters Cruiserweight
Champion. Former Commonwealth, WBO
Inter-Continental & Southern Area
L.Heavyweight Champion. Ht. 6'3"
Manager A. Bowers

02.10.91 Gus Mendes W RSC 1 Barking
23.10.91 Joe Frater W RSC 1 Bethnal Green
13.11.91 John Kaighin W PTS 6 Bethnal Green
11.12.91 Randy B. Powell W RSC 1 Basildon
11.02.92 Simon Harris DREW 8 Barking
12.05.92 John Williams W PTS 6 Crystal Palace
16.06.92 Nigel Rafferty W CO 5 Dagenham
15.09.92 Gil Lewis W CO 2 Crystal Palace
06.10.92 Simon McDougall W PTS 8 Antwerp, Belgium
10.11.92 John Oxenham W CO 5 Dagenham
12.12.92 Simon McDougall W PTS 8 Muswell Hill
30.01.93 Simon Collins W PTS 8 Brentwood
28.09.93 Glazz Campbell W CO 6 Bethnal Green

(Southern Area L. Heavyweight Title Challenge)
06.11.93 John Kaighin W CO 1 Bethnal Green
21.12.93 Ray Albert W RSC 3 Mayfair
(Vacant WBO Inter-Continental L. Heavyweight Title)
11.01.94 Jim Murray W RSC 7 Bethnal Green
(WBO Inter-Continental L. Heavyweight Title Defence)
09.04.94 Simon Harris W CO 6 Bethnal Green
(WBO Inter-Continental & Southern Area L. Heavyweight Title Defences)
09.07.94 Sergio Merani W PTS 12 Earls Court
(WBO Inter-Continental L. Heavyweight Title)
30.09.94 Arigoma Chiponda W CO 2 Bethnal Green
(Vacant Commonwealth L. Heavyweight Title)
18.03.95 Ernest Mateen W RTD 7 Millstreet
(Vacant WBO Inter-Continental L. Heavyweight Title)
09.05.95 Noel Magee L RTD 7 Basildon
(Commonwealth L. Heavyweight Title Defence)
06.02.96 Francis Wanyama W PTS 6 Basildon
09.04.96 Joey Paladino W RSC 1 Stevenage
07.02.97 John Kiser W PTS 6 Las Vegas, Nevada, USA
04.03.97 Peter Oboh W DIS 8 Southwark
27.09.97 Julius Francis L RSC 6 Belfast
(Vacant British Heavyweight Title. Commonwealth Heavyweight Title Challenge)
05.06.98 Darron Griffiths W PTS 6 Southend
23.01.99 John Keeton L PTS 12 Cheshunt
(Vacant WBO Inter-Continental Cruiserweight Title)
01.05.99 Tim Brown W PTS 8 Crystal Palace
04.09.99 Lee Swaby W PTS 8 Bethnal Green
29.04.00 Jesper Kristiansen L RTD 10 Varde, Denmark
(Vacant WBO Inter-Continental Cruiserweight Title)
06.10.00 Dominic Negus W PTS 10 Maidstone
(Southern Area Cruiserweight Title Challenge)
10.03.01 Bruce Scott L RTD 3 Bethnal Green
(British Cruiserweight Title Challenge. Vacant Commonwealth Cruiserweight Title)
15.06.01 Darren Ashton W RTD 4 Millwall
(Vacant British Masters Cruiserweight Title)
14.07.01 Chris P. Bacon W RSC 10 Liverpool
(British Masters Cruiserweight Title Defence)
20.10.01 Tony Dowling W RSC 6 Glasgow
02.03.02 Sebastiaan Rothmann L PTS 12 Brakpan, South Africa
(WBU Cruiserweight Title Challenge)
26.09.03 Paul Bonson W PTS 6 Reading
21.02.04 Enzo Maccarinelli L RSC 8 Cardiff
(WBU Cruiserweight Title Challenge)
12.11.04 Steffen Nielsen L PTS 6 Copenhagen, Denmark
11.12.04 Konstantin Prizyuk L PTS 6 Madrid, Spain
21.01.05 David Haye L RTD 3 Brentford
19.04.05 Valery Checheнev L PTS 6 Bischofshofen, Austria
10.05.05 Alexey Mazikin L PTS 4 Palma de Mallorca, Spain
Career: 44 contests, won 31, drew 1, lost 12.

Rocky Dean   Les Clark

Graham Delehedy

Liverpool. *Born* Liverpool, 7 October, 1978
L.Middleweight. Ht. 5'8"
Manager T. Gilmour

17.05.03 Joel Ani W RSC 4 Liverpool
27.10.03 Rocky Muscus W RSC 2 Glasgow
01.12.03 Gary Cummings W RSC 1 Bradford
27.05.04 Ernie Smith W RSC 3 Huddersfield
08.10.04 David Kehoe W RSC 2 Brentwood
26.11.04 Tony Montana W PTS 6 Altrincham
30.04.05 Cafu Santos W RSC 1 Wigan
Career: 7 contests, won 7.

Graham Delehedy   Les Clark

(Dennis) Buster Dennis (Mwanze)

Canning Town. *Born* Mawokota, Uganda,
31 December, 1981
S.Featherweight. Ht. 5'0"
Manager A. Bowers

28.03.03 Vitali Makarov W RSC 2 Millwall
03.04.03 Chris Hooper L RSC 1 Hull
15.05.03 Mark Alexander L PTS 4 Mayfair
24.05.03 Haider Ali L PTS 4 Bethnal Green
21.11.03 Anthony Hanna W PTS 6 Millwall
30.11.03 Daleboy Rees W PTS 6 Swansea
20.02.04 Chris Hooper W RSC 2 Bethnal Green
01.04.04 Kevin O'Hara L PTS 4 Bethnal Green
19.06.04 Riaz Durgahed L PTS 4 Muswell Hill
03.09.04 Jamie Arthur L PTS 6 Newport
10.09.04 Derry Matthews L PTS 6 Liverpool
26.11.04 Eddie Hyland L PTS 4 Altrincham
13.12.04 Matt Teague W PTS 6 Cleethorpes
11.02.05 Andy Morris L PTS 6 Manchester
08.04.05 Ricky Burns L PTS 6 Edinburgh
20.05.05 John Bothwell W RTD 4 Glasgow
03.06.05 Steve Bell DREW 6 Manchester
Career: 17 contests, won 6, drew 1, lost 10.

Reagan Denton

Sheffield. *Born* Sheffield, 26 June, 1978
S. Middleweight. Ht. 5'11"
Manager D. Coldwell

15.05.99 Pedro Thompson W PTS 4 Sheffield
15.11.99 Colin Vidler W PTS 4 Bethnal Green
25.09.00 William Webster W PTS 4 Barnsley
08.10.01 Martyn Bailey W PTS 4 Barnsley
15.12.01 Darren Covill W PTS 4 Sheffield
24.03.03 Dave Pearson W PTS 6 Barnsley
06.10.03 Michael Pinnock W PTS 6 Barnsley
23.11.03 Gary Dixon L PTS 4 Rotherham
08.12.03 William Webster W RSC 6 Barnsley
15.12.04 Leigh Wicks W PTS 6 Sheffield
Career: 10 contests, won 9, lost 1.

Craig Dickson

Glasgow. *Born* Glasgow, 6 March, 1979
Welterweight. Ht. 5'11"
Manager T. Gilmour

21.10.02 Paul Rushton W RSC 2 Glasgow
18.11.02 Ernie Smith W PTS 6 Glasgow
17.02.03 Jon Hilton W RSC 2 Glasgow
14.04.03 Richard Inquieti W PTS 4 Glasgow
20.10.03 Danny Moir W RSC 3 Glasgow
19.01.04 Dean Nicholas W RSC 5 Glasgow
19.04.04 Ernie Smith W PTS 6 Glasgow
30.09.04 Taz Jones DREW 6 Glasgow
15.11.04 Tony Montana W PTS 8 Glasgow
21.03.05 David Keir W RTD 3 Glasgow
Career: 10 contests, won 9, drew 1.

Haroon Din

Sheffield. *Born* Middlesbrough, 21 May,
1978
Lightweight. Former Undefeated British
Masters L.Welterweight Champion.
Ht. 5'8"
Manager D. Ingle

21.09.98 Les Frost L PTS 6 Cleethorpes
14.12.98 Les Frost L RSC 1 Cleethorpes
02.05.99 Amjid Mahmood W PTS 6 Shaw
20.05.00 Dave Travers W PTS 6 Leicester
24.06.00 Willie Limond L PTS 4 Glasgow
30.08.00 Leon Dobbs W CO 1 Scunthorpe
19.11.00 Carl Greaves L RSC 4 Chesterfield
24.09.01 Nigel Senior W PTS 6 Cleethorpes
17.12.01 Nigel Senior W PTS 6 Cleethorpes
31.01.02 Ilias Miah W RSC 3 Piccadilly
20.04.02 Gareth Wiltshaw W PTS 6 Derby
17.11.02 Gareth Wiltshaw W PTS 6 Bradford
05.04.03 Andy Morris L RSC 1 Manchester
28.11.03 Billy Corcoran L RSC 3 Derby
05.03.04 Jason Nesbitt W PTS 6 Darlington
14.05.04 Jackson Williams W RSC 5 Sunderland
*(Vacant British Masters
L.Welterweight Title)*
29.10.04 Stefy Bull L RSC 2 Doncaster
*(Central Area Lightweight Title
Challenge)*
Career: 17 contests, won 10, lost 7.

Gary Dixon

Carlisle. *Born* Carlisle, 2 November, 1974
S. Middleweight. Ht. 5'10½"
Manager J. Doughty

18.03.01 Jamie Logan W PTS 6 Shaw
10.05.01 Paul Owen L RSC 3 Sunderland
26.07.01 Michael Thompson W PTS 6
Blackpool
23.09.01 Mark Sawyers DREW 6 Shaw
09.12.01 Danny Wray W RSC 4 Shaw
03.03.02 William Webster W PTS 6 Shaw
02.06.02 Simeon Cover L PTS 6 Shaw
06.09.02 Tom Cannon L PTS 6 Shaw
17.11.02 Conroy McIntosh L RSC 2 Shaw
09.03.03 Mike Duffield W PTS 6 Shaw
19.10.03 Farai Musiiwa L PTS 6 Shaw
23.11.03 Reagan Denton W PTS 4 Rotherham
29.02.04 Barry Connell W RTD 3 Shaw

23.09.04 Ryan Kerr L RSC 7 Gateshead
*(Northern Area S.Middleweight Title
Challenge)*
Career: 14 contests, won 7, drew 1, lost 6.

Terry Dixon

Harlesden. *Born* London, 29 July, 1966
Heavyweight. Ht. 5'11"
Manager Self

21.09.89 Dave Mowbray W RSC 1 Southampton
30.11.89 Brendan Dempsey W RSC 8 Barking
08.03.90 Cordwell Hylton W PTS 8 Watford
06.04.90 Prince Rodney W RSC 7 Stevenage
23.10.90 Dennis Bailey W PTS 6 Leicester
07.03.91 Carl Thompson L PTS 8 Basildon
22.04.91 Everton Blake L RSC 8 Mayfair
25.03.92 Mark Bowen W RTD 1 Kensington
27.04.92 Ian Bulloch W RSC 4 Mayfair
17.10.92 Darren McKenna L RSC 3 Wembley
04.10.93 Steve Yorath W RSC 4 Mayfair
03.08.94 Chemek Saleta L PTS 8 Bristol
09.05.02 Kevin Barrett DREW 4 Leicester Square
30.10.02 Leighton Morgan W RSC 1 Leicester
Square
29.03.03 Mal Rice W PTS 4 Wembley
12.06.05 Slick Miller W RSC 2 Leicester Square
Career: 16 contests, won 11, drew 1, lost 4.

Craig Docherty

Glasgow. *Born* Glasgow, 27 September,
1979
S.Featherweight. Former Commonwealth
S.Featherweight Champion. Ht. 5'7"
Manager T. Gilmour

16.11.98 Kevin Gerowski W PTS 6 Glasgow
22.02.99 Des Gargano W PTS 6 Glasgow
19.04.99 Paul Quarmby W RSC 4 Glasgow
07.06.99 Simon Chambers W PTS 6 Glasgow
20.09.99 John Barnes W PTS 6 Glasgow
15.11.99 Peter Allen W RSC 1 Glasgow
24.01.00 Lee Williamson W PTS 6 Glasgow
19.02.00 Steve Hanley W PTS 6 Prestwick
05.06.00 Sebastian Hart W RSC 1 Glasgow
23.10.00 Lee Armstrong DREW 8 Glasgow
22.01.01 Nigel Senior W RSC 4 Glasgow
20.03.01 Jamie McKeever W RSC 3 Glasgow
11.06.01 Rakhim Mingaleev W PTS 8
Nottingham
27.10.01 Michael Gomez L RSC 2 Manchester
*(British S.Featherweight Title
Challenge)*
18.03.02 Joel Viney W CO 1 Glasgow
13.07.02 Dariusz Snarski W PTS 6 Coventry
25.01.03 Nikolai Eremeev W PTS 6 Bridgend
12.04.03 Dean Pithie W CO 8 Bethnal Green
*(Commonwealth S. Featherweight
Title Challenge)*
01.11.03 Abdul Malik Jabir W PTS 12 Glasgow
*(Commonwealth S.Featherweight
Title Defence)*
22.04.04 Kpakpo Allotey W RSC 6 Glasgow
*(Commonwealth S.Featherweight
Title Defence)*
15.10.04 Boris Sinitsin L PTS 12 Glasgow
*(European S.Featherweight Title
Challenge)*
08.04.05 Alex Arthur L CO 9 Edinburgh
*(Vacant British S.Featherweight Title.
Commonwealth S.Featherweight Title
Defence)*
Career: 22 contests, won 18, drew 1, lost 3.

Craig Docherty   Les Clark

Tony Doherty

Pontypool. *Born* London, 8 April, 1983
Welterweight. Ht. 5'8"
Manager F. Warren

08.05.03	Karl Taylor W PTS 4 Widnes
28.06.03	Paul McIlwaine W RSC 1 Cardiff
13.09.03	Darren Covill W PTS 4 Newport
06.12.03	James Paisley W RSC 3 Cardiff
21.02.04	Chris Brophy W RSC 2 Cardiff
24.04.04	Keith Jones W PTS 6 Reading
22.05.04	Karl Taylor W RTD 2 Widnes
03.07.04	David Kirk W PTS 4 Newport
30.07.04	Ernie Smith W PTS 6 Bethnal Green
03.09.04	Keith Jones W PTS 6 Newport
10.09.04	Peter Dunn W RSC 2 Bethnal Green
19.11.04	Karl Taylor W RSC 2 Bethnal Green
21.01.05	Emmanuel Fleury W RSC 2 Bridgend
22.04.05	Belaid Yahiaoui W PTS 8 Barnsley

Career: 14 contests, won 14.

Tony Doherty   Les Clark

Dmitry Donetskiy

Southampton. *Born* Russia, 21 January,
1978
Middleweight. Ht. 5'9"
Manager J. Bishop

20.02.04	Isidro Gonzalez W RSC 6 Southampton
30.03.04	Steve Russell W PTS 6 Southampton
12.05.04	Geard Ajetovic L PTS 6 Reading
10.09.04	Gokhan Kazaz L RSC 4 Bethnal Green
24.04.05	Anthony Small L PTS 4 Leicester Square
12.06.05	Kreshnick Qato L RSC 6 Leicester Square

Career: 6 contests, won 2, lost 4.

Roddy Doran

Shrewsbury. *Born* Shrewsbury, 15 March,
1972
Middleweight. Former Undefeated
Midlands Area Middleweight Champion.
Former Undefeated British Masters
S.Middleweight Champion. Ht. 5'11"
Manager D. Bradley

08.10.01	Harry Butler W PTS 6 Birmingham
31.10.01	Harry Butler DREW 6 Birmingham
11.02.02	Freddie Yemofio W PTS 8 Shrewsbury
15.04.02	William Webster W PTS 8 Shrewsbury
13.05.02	Simeon Cover DREW 8 Birmingham
29.09.02	Simon Andrews W PTS 6 Shrewsbury
03.12.02	Harry Butler W PTS 6 Shrewsbury
23.02.03	Simeon Cover W PTS 10 Shrewsbury *(Vacant British Masters S.Middleweight Title)*
30.06.03	Mark Phillips W PTS 6 Shrewsbury
07.09.03	Conroy McIntosh W PTS 10 Shrewsbury *(Vacant Midlands Area Middleweight Title)*
28.11.03	Damon Hague W PTS 10 Derby *(Elim. WBF S.Middleweight Title)*
12.03.04	Damon Hague L PTS 12 Nottingham *(Vacant WBF S.Middleweight Title)*
12.09.04	Andy Halder L PTS 10 Shrewsbury *(Vacant WBF Inter-Continental Middleweight Title)*
18.11.04	Donovan Smillie L RSC 7 Shrewsbury *(Vacant English Middleweight Title)*
18.06.05	Andy Halder L RTD 7 Coventry *(WBF Inter-Continental Middleweight Title Challenge)*

Career: 15 contests, won 9, drew 2, lost 4.

Jenny Dowell

Coventry. *Born* Leicester, 8 September,
1973
Flyweight. Ht. 5'2"
Manager A. Phillips

30.04.05	Iliana Boneva W RSC 4 Coventry

Career: 1 contest, won 1.

Tony Dowling

Lincoln. *Born* Lincoln, 5 January, 1976
Cruiserweight. Ht. 6'2"
Manager J. Ashton

22.03.96	Slick Miller W RSC 4 Mansfield
30.05.96	Nigel Rafferty W PTS 6 Lincoln
29.07.96	Albert Call L RSC 4 Skegness
12.02.00	Adam Cale W PTS 4 Sheffield

20.03.00   Danny Southam W PTS 4 Mansfield
11.05.00   Jason Brewster W RSC 2 Newark
08.07.00   Slick Miller W PTS 4 Widnes
09.09.00   Lee Swaby L RSC 9 Newark
            (Vacant British Masters Cruiserweight
            Title)
20.04.01   Cathal O'Grady L RSC 1 Dublin
15.09.01   Michael Pinnock W PTS 6 Derby
20.10.01   Garry Delaney L RSC 6 Glasgow
11.05.02   Gary Thompson W RSC 3 Newark
29.09.02   Paul Bonson W PTS 6 Shrewsbury
30.11.02   Scott Lansdowne L RSC 2 Newark
            (Vacant Midlands Area Cruiserweight
            Title)
05.09.03   Denzil Browne W PTS 6 Sheffield
14.11.03   David Haye L RSC 1 Bethnal Green
            (Vacant English Cruiserweight Title)
25.04.04   Slick Miller W RSC 2 Nottingham
17.12.04   Carl Wright L PTS 10 Coventry
            (Vacant Midlands Area Cruiserweight
            Title)
Career: 18 contests, won 11, lost 7.

Gavin Down

Bolsover. *Born* Chesterfield, 2 February,
1977
Welterweight. Midlands Area
L.Middleweight Champion. Former British
Masters L.Welterweight Champion. Former
Undefeated Midlands Area L.Welterweight
Champion. Ht. 5'9"
Manager D. Ingle

21.09.98   Peter Lennon W RSC 1 Cleethorpes
27.11.98   Trevor Tacy L PTS 6 Nottingham
07.12.98   Brian Coleman W PTS 6 Manchester
26.02.99   Brian Gifford W PTS 6 West
            Bromwich
27.03.99   Lee Molyneux W PTS 4 Derby
15.05.99   Les Frost W RSC 1 Sheffield
27.06.99   Lee Molyneux W PTS 6 Alfreton
03.10.99   Ernie Smith W RSC 1 Chesterfield
28.11.99   Dave Gibson W PTS 6 Chesterfield
09.04.00   Sammy Smith W PTS 6 Alfreton
21.05.00   Arv Mittoo W PTS 6 Derby
19.06.00   Brian Coleman W PTS 4 Burton
13.08.00   Lee Bird W PTS 6 Nottingham
30.08.00   Ram Singh W PTS 6 Scunthorpe
04.11.00   Sebastian Hart W RSC 4 Derby
19.11.00   David Kirk W PTS 10 Chesterfield
            (Vacant British Masters
            L.Welterweight Title)
11.12.00   Dave Gibson W RSC 5 Cleethorpes
25.02.01   Jay Mahoney W RSC 1 Derby
01.04.01   Steve Saville W RSC 3 Alfreton
            (Vacant Midlands Area L.Welterweight
            Title)
16.06.01   Arv Mittoo W PTS 6 Derby
21.07.01   Tommy Peacock W RSC 1 Sheffield
15.09.01   Lee Williamson W PTS 6 Derby
08.12.01   Brian Coleman W RSC 1 Chesterfield
12.02.02   Bradley Pryce L RSC 9 Bethnal Green
            (Vacant IBF Inter-Continental
            L.Welterweight Title)
11.05.02   Woody Greenaway W RSC 3
            Chesterfield
05.10.02   Daniel Thorpe W RSC 2 Chesterfield
19.10.02   Daniel James W RTD 5 Norwich
28.01.03   Tony Montana W PTS 4 Nottingham
25.07.03   Alan Bosworth L RSC 5 Norwich
            (British Masters L.Welterweight Title
            Defence. Elim. British L.Welterweight
            Title)
16.01.04   Paul Denton W RSC 4 Bradford

12.03.04   Jon Hilton W RTD 1 Nottingham
02.06.04   Francis Barrett L PTS 10 Nottingham
            (Vacant European Union
            L.Welterweight Title)
05.10.04   Young Muttley L RSC 6 Dudley
            (English L.Welterweight Title
            Challenge. Vacant WBF Inter-
            Continental L.Welterweight Title)
25.11.04   Steve Brumant W PTS 10 Birmingham
            (Vacant Midlands Area L.Middleweight
            Title)
03.06.05   Michael Jennings L RSC 9 Manchester
            (English Welterweight Title Challenge)
Career: 35 contests, won 29, lost 6.

Warren Dunkley

Dartford. *Born* Dartford, 18 July, 1971
Lightweight. Ht. 5'5½"
Manager M. Roe

16.10.04   Fred Janes W PTS 6 Dagenham
19.12.04   Ian Reid W PTS 4 Bethnal Green
05.03.05   Garry Buckland L PTS 4 Dagenham
20.05.05   David Bailey L PTS 4 Southwark
Career: 4 contests, won 2, lost 2.

Warren Dunkley   Les Clark

Peter Dunn

Pontefract. *Born* Doncaster, 15 February,
1975
Middleweight. Ht. 5'8"
Manager Self

08.12.97   Leigh Daniels W PTS 6 Bradford
15.05.98   Peter Lennon W PTS 6 Nottingham
18.09.98   Jan Cree L RSC 5 Belfast
23.10.98   Bobby Lyndon W PTS 6 Wakefield
03.12.98   Craig Smith L RSC 3 Sunderland
17.03.99   Des Sowden W PTS 6 Kensington
15.05.99   Ray Wood DREW 4 Blackpool
29.05.99   Dean Nicholas L PTS 6 South Shields
01.10.99   Jon Honney L PTS 4 Bethnal Green
18.10.99   Jan Cree W PTS 6 Glasgow
26.11.99   Gavin Pearson DREW 6 Wakefield
18.02.00   John T. Kelly L PTS 6 Pentre Halkyn
11.03.00   Iain Eldridge L RSC 2 Kensington
18.09.00   Joe Miller L PTS 6 Glasgow
26.10.00   Ram Singh W PTS 6 Stoke
27.11.00   Young Muttley L RSC 3 Birmingham
22.02.01   Darren Spencer W PTS 6 Sunderland
03.03.01   Glenn McClarnon L PTS 4 Wembley
20.03.01   Robert Burton L PTS 6 Leeds

08.04.01   Martyn Bailey L PTS 6 Wrexham
17.05.01   Gavin Pearson L PTS 6 Leeds
25.09.01   Darren Spencer L PTS 6 Liverpool
06.10.01   Lee Byrne L RSC 4 Manchester
13.11.01   Richard Inquieti DREW 6 Leeds
24.11.01   Robert Burton W PTS 6 Wakefield
28.01.02   Robert Burton L RSC 8 Barnsley
            (Vacant Central Area Welterweight
            Title)
23.03.02   Colin Lynes L PTS 4 Southwark
19.04.02   Oscar Hall L PTS 6 Darlington
28.05.02   Matt Scriven L PTS 8 Leeds
29.06.02   Darren Bruce L PTS 6 Brentwood
28.09.02   Surinder Sekhon L PTS 6 Wakefield
13.09.03   Wayne Shepherd W PTS 6 Wakefield
20.09.03   Michael Lomax L PTS 4 Nottingham
04.10.03   Andy Gibson L PTS 6 Belfast
25.10.03   Gary Young L PTS 6 Edinburgh
13.12.03   Michael Jennings L PTS 6 Manchester
19.02.04   Young Muttley L PTS 4 Dudley
26.02.04   Matthew Hatton L PTS 6 Widnes
06.03.04   Jason Rushton L PTS 6 Renfrew
10.04.04   Ali Nuumembe L PTS 6 Manchester
22.04.04   Jamie Coyle L PTS 6 Glasgow
06.05.04   Jason Rushton L PTS 4 Barnsley
19.06.04   Chris Saunders L PTS 4 Muswell Hill
03.07.04   Oscar Hall L PTS 6 Blackpool
10.09.04   Tony Doherty L RSC 2 Bethnal Green
09.10.04   Steve Russell W PTS 6 Norwich
23.10.04   Geraint Harvey L PTS 6 Wakefield
11.12.04   Gary Woolcombe L PTS 4 Canning
            Town
19.12.04   Freddie Luke L PTS 4 Bethnal Green
25.02.05   Chas Symonds L PTS 4 Wembley
07.04.05   Jonjo Finnegan L PTS 6 Birmingham
26.04.05   Tyrone McInerney L RSC 6 Leeds
03.06.05   Oscar Hall L PTS 6 Hull
19.06.05   Gary Woolcombe L RSC 6 Bethnal
            Green
Career: 54 contests, won 10, drew 3, lost 41.

Riaz Durgahed

Bristol. *Born* Mauritius, 4 May, 1977
S.Featherweight. Ht. 5'6"
Manager C. Sanigar

29.02.04   Jason Thomas W RSC 1 Bristol
19.06.04   Buster Dennis W PTS 4 Muswell Hill
01.10.04   Dai Davies L PTS 4 Bristol
02.12.04   Lloyd Otte L PTS 6 Crystal Palace
08.04.05   Scott Flynn L PTS 4 Edinburgh
02.06.05   Jason Nesbitt W PTS 6 Peterborough
Career: 6 contests, won 3, lost 3.

Riaz Durgahed   Les Clark

Graham Earl

Luton. *Born* Luton, 26 August, 1978
British & Commonwealth Lightweight
Champion. Former Undefeated Southern
Area Lightweight Champion. Ht. 5'5³/₄"
Manager F. Maloney

02.09.97	Mark O'Callaghan W RSC 2 Southwark
06.12.97	Mark McGowan W PTS 4 Wembley
11.04.98	Danny Lutaaya W RSC 2 Southwark
23.05.98	David Kirk W PTS 4 Bethnal Green
12.09.98	Brian Coleman W PTS 4 Bethnal Green
10.12.98	Marc Smith W RSC 1 Barking
16.01.99	Lee Williamson W RSC 4 Bethnal Green
08.05.99	Benny Jones W PTS 6 Bethnal Green
15.07.99	Simon Chambers W CO 6 Peterborough
04.03.00	Ivo Golakov W RSC 1 Peterborough
29.04.00	Marco Fattore W PTS 6 Wembley
21.10.00	Lee Williamson W RSC 3 Wembley
10.03.01	Brian Gentry W RSC 8 Bethnal Green *(Vacant Southern Area Lightweight Title)*
22.09.01	Liam Maltby W CO 1 Bethnal Green *(Southern Area Lightweight Title Defence)*
15.12.01	Mark Winters W PTS 10 Wembley *(Elim. British Lightweight Title)*
12.10.02	Chill John W PTS 10 Bethnal Green *(Southern Area Lightweight Title Defence)*
15.02.03	Steve Murray W RSC 2 Wembley *(Southern Area Lightweight Title Defence. Final Elim. British Lightweight Title)*
24.05.03	Nikolai Eremeev W PTS 8 Bethnal Green
17.07.03	Bobby Vanzie W PTS 12 Dagenham *(British Lightweight Title Challenge)*
11.10.03	Jon Honney W PTS 8 Portsmouth
05.06.04	Bobby Vanzie W PTS 12 Bethnal Green *(Vacant British Lightweight Title)*
30.07.04	Steve Murray W RSC 6 Bethnal Green *(British Lightweight Title Defence)*
25.02.05	Ricky Burns L PTS 8 Wembley
19.06.05	Kevin Bennett W RSC 9 Bethnal Green *(Commonwealth Lightweight Title Challenge. British Lightweight Title Defence)*

Career: 24 contests, won 23, lost 1.

Gilbert Eastman

Battersea. *Born* Guyana, 16 November, 1972
Southern Area L Middleweight Champion.
Ht. 5'10"
Manager M. Hennessy

22.04.96	Wayne Shepherd W PTS 4 Crystal Palace
09.07.96	Costas Katsantonis W RSC 1 Bethnal Green
11.01.97	Mike Watson W RSC 1 Bethnal Green
25.03.97	Danny Quacoe W RSC 3 Lewisham
30.08.97	Karl Taylor W PTS 4 Cheshunt
08.11.97	Ray Newby W PTS 6 Southwark
14.02.98	Cam Raeside W RSC 5 Southwark
21.04.98	Dennis Berry W RSC 6 Edmonton
23.05.98	Shaun O'Neill W RSC 1 Bethnal Green
12.09.98	Everald Williams W RTD 5 Bethnal Green
21.11.98	Lindon Scarlett W RTD 3 Southwark
06.03.99	Kofi Jantuah L RSC 11 Southwark *(Commonwealth Welterweight Title Challenge)*
25.10.02	Ojay Abrahams W PTS 4 Bethnal Green
21.12.02	Pedro Thompson W RSC 2 Dagenham
05.03.03	Howard Clarke W PTS 6 Bethnal Green
16.04.03	Andrew Facey L RSC 3 Nottingham
25.07.03	Jason Collins W RSC 1 Norwich
04.10.03	Spencer Fearon W RSC 4 Muswell Hill *(Vacant Southern Area L.Middleweight Title)*
28.11.03	Eugenio Monteiro L PTS 8 Derby
30.01.04	Craig Lynch W PTS 6 Dagenham
16.04.04	Delroy Mellis W RSC 5 Bradford *(Southern Area L.Middleweight Title Defence)*
24.09.04	Clive Johnson W PTS 6 Nottingham

Career: 22 contests, won 19, lost 3.

Howard Eastman

Battersea. *Born* New Amsterdam, Guyana,
8 December, 1970
Middleweight. Former Undefeated British,
Commonwealth, European, IBO Inter-
Continental, WBA Inter-Continental &
Southern Area Middleweight Champion.
Ht. 5'11"
Manager M. Hennessy

06.03.94	John Rice W RSC 1 Southwark
14.03.94	Andy Peach W PTS 6 Mayfair
22.03.94	Steve Phillips W RSC 5 Bethnal Green
17.10.94	Barry Thorogood W RSC 6 Mayfair
06.03.95	Marty Duke W RSC 1 Mayfair
20.04.95	Stuart Dunn W RSC 2 Mayfair
23.06.95	Peter Vosper W RSC 1 Bethnal Green
16.10.95	Carlo Colarusso W RSC 1 Mayfair
29.11.95	Brendan Ryan W RSC 2 Mayfair
31.01.96	Paul Wesley W RSC 1 Birmingham
13.03.96	Steve Goodwin W RSC 5 Wembley
29.04.96	John Duckworth W RSC 5 Mayfair
11.12.96	Sven Hamer W RSC 10 Southwark *(Vacant Southern Area Middleweight Title)*
18.02.97	John Duckworth W CO 7 Cheshunt
25.03.97	Rachid Serdjane W RSC 7 Lewisham
14.02.98	Vitali Kopitko W PTS 8 Southwark
28.03.98	Terry Morrill W RTD 4 Hull
23.05.98	Darren Ashton W RSC 4 Bethnal Green
30.11.98	Steve Foster W RSC 7 Manchester *(Vacant British Middleweight Title)*
04.02.99	Jason Barker W RSC 6 Lewisham
06.03.99	Jon Penn W RSC 3 Southwark *(Vacant IBO Inter-Continental S. Middleweight Title)*
22.05.99	Roman Babaev W RSC 6 Belfast *(WBA Inter-Continental Middleweight Title Challenge)*
10.07.99	Teimouraz Kikelidze W RSC 6 Southwark *(WBA Inter-Continental Middleweight Title Defence)*
13.09.99	Derek Wormald W RSC 3 Bethnal Green *(British Middleweight Title Defence)*
13.11.99	Mike Algoet W RSC 8 Hull *(WBA Inter-Continental Middleweight Title Defence)*
18.01.00	Ojay Abrahams W RSC 2 Mansfield
04.03.00	Viktor Fesetchko W RTD 4 Peterborough
29.04.00	Anthony Ivory W RTD 6 Wembley
25.07.00	Ahmet Dottouev W RTD 5 Southwark *(WBA Inter-Continental Middleweight Title Defence)*
16.09.00	Sam Soliman W PTS 12 Bethnal Green *(Commonwealth Middleweight Title Challenge)*
05.02.01	Mark Baker W RTD 5 Hull
10.04.01	Robert McCracken W RSC 10 Wembley *(British & Commonwealth Middleweight Title Defences. Vacant European Middleweight Title)*
17.11.01	William Joppy L PTS 12 Las Vegas, Nevada, USA *(Vacant WBA Interim Middleweight Title)*
25.10.02	Chardan Ansoula W RSC 1 Bethnal Green
21.12.02	Hussain Osman W RTD 4 Dagenham
28.01.03	Christophe Tendil W RTD 4 Nottingham *(Vacant European Middleweight Title)*
05.03.03	Gary Beardsley W RSC 2 Bethnal Green
16.04.03	Scott Dann W RSC 3 Nottingham *(British, Commonwealth & European Middleweight Title Defences)*
25.07.03	Hacine Cherifi W RTD 8 Norwich *(European Middleweight Title Defence)*
30.01.04	Sergei Tatevosyan W PTS 12 Dagenham *(European Middleweight Title Defence)*
24.09.04	Jerry Elliott W PTS 10 Nottingham
19.02.05	Bernard Hopkins L PTS 12 Los Angeles, California, USA *(WBC, WBA, IBF & WBO Middleweight Title Challenges)*

Career: 42 contests, won 40, lost 2.

Tommy Eastwood

Epsom. *Born* Epsom, 16 May, 1979
Cruiserweight. Ht. 5'11¹/₂"
Manager Self

09.09.01	Tony Booth W PTS 4 Southwark

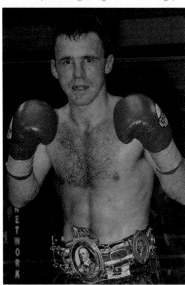

Graham Earl Les Clark

16.12.01	Paul Bonson W PTS 4 Southwark
12.02.02	Adam Cale W PTS 4 Bethnal Green
24.03.02	Dave Clarke W PTS 6 Streatham
23.06.02	Brodie Pearmaine W PTS 4 Southwark
24.01.03	Lee Swaby L PTS 6 Sheffield
26.11.03	Brian Gascoigne W RSC 2 Mayfair
10.09.04	Ovill McKenzie W PTS 8 Wembley

Career: 8 contests, won 7, lost 1.

Steve Ede

Gosport. *Born* Southampton, 22 June,1976
Middleweight. Ht. 5'10"
Manager J. Bishop

06.02.05	Jed Tytler W RSC 4 Southampton
26.06.05	Mark Wall W PTS 6 Southampton

Career: 2 contests, won 2.

Steve Ede   Les Clark

Chris Edwards

Stoke. *Born* Stoke, 6 May, 1976
British Masters S.Bantamweight Champion.
Ht. 5'3"
Manager Self

03.04.98	Chris Thomas W RSC 2 Ebbw Vale
21.09.98	Russell Laing L PTS 6 Glasgow
26.02.99	Delroy Spencer L PTS 6 West Bromwich
17.04.99	Stevie Quinn L RSC 4 Dublin
19.10.99	Lee Georgiou L RSC 2 Bethnal Green
03.12.99	Daniel Ring L PTS 4 Peterborough
15.05.00	Paddy Folan L PTS 6 Bradford
07.10.00	Andy Roberts W PTS 4 Doncaster
27.11.00	Levi Pattison W PTS 4 Birmingham
16.03.01	Jamie Evans L PTS 6 Portsmouth
03.06.01	Darren Taylor DREW 6 Hanley
08.10.01	Levi Pattison L PTS 4 Barnsley
06.12.01	Neil Read W PTS 8 Stoke
10.10.02	Neil Read W PTS 6 Stoke
13.06.03	Lee Haskins L PTS 6 Bristol
23.04.04	Delroy Spencer DREW 6 Leicester
26.09.04	Neil Read W RSC 2 Stoke
	(*Vacant British Masters S.Bantamweight Title*)
28.10.04	Colin Moffett L PTS 4 Belfast

Career: 18 contests, won 6, drew 2, lost 10.

Lee Edwards

Sheffield. *Born* Huntingdon, 25 May, 1984
L.Middleweight. Ht. 5'11"
Manager G. Rhodes

08.05.05	Sergey Haritonov W PTS 6 Sheffield

Career: 1 contest, won 1.

Andy Egan

Coventry. *Born* Coventry, 16 September, 1977
Welterweight. Ht. 5'8³/₄"
Manager A. Phillips

02.01.01	Gareth Jones L PTS 4 Coventry
19.12.01	Brian Gifford W RSC 1 Coventry
18.01.02	Marcus Portman L PTS 4 Coventry
09.02.02	Tony Smith W PTS 4 Coventry
26.04.02	Brian Coleman W PTS 6 Coventry
30.11.02	Wayne Wheeler W RSC 1 Coventry
22.03.03	Brian Coleman W PTS 6 Coventry
07.06.03	Lee Williamson W PTS 6 Coventry
30.04.05	Ernie Smith DREW 6 Coventry

Career: 9 contests, won 6, drew 1, lost 2.

Sujad Elahi

Bradford. *Born* Bradford, 13 October, 1982
Welterweight. Ht. 5'11"
Manager G. Rhodes

23.09.04	David Pinkney L PTS 6 Gateshead
09.12.04	Gary Connolly W RSC 2 Sunderland
20.02.05	Scott Conway DREW 6 Sheffield
08.05.05	Lance Verallo W PTS 6 Sheffield
25.06.05	Andy Cosnett W CO 2 Wakefield

Career: 5 contests, won 3, drew 1, lost 1.

Wayne Elcock

Birmingham. *Born* Birmingham, 12 February, 1974
Middleweight. Former WBU Middleweight Champion. Ht. 5'9¹/₂"
Manager Self

02.12.99	William Webster W PTS 6 Peterborough
04.03.00	Sonny Pollard W RSC 3 Peterborough
07.07.01	Darren Rhodes W PTS 4 Manchester
09.10.01	Valery Odin W PTS 4 Cardiff
02.03.02	Charles Shodiya W RSC 1 Bethnal Green
20.04.02	Howard Clarke W PTS 4 Cardiff
01.06.02	Jason Collins W RSC 2 Manchester
17.08.02	Ojay Abrahams W PTS 4 Cardiff
23.11.02	Jason Collins W RSC 1 Derby
15.02.03	Yuri Tsarenko W PTS 10 Wembley
05.04.03	Anthony Farnell W PTS 12 Manchester
	(*WBU Middleweight Title Challenge*)
29.11.03	Lawrence Murphy L CO 1 Renfrew
	(*WBU Middleweight Title Defence*)
07.02.04	Farai Musiiwa W PTS 6 Bethnal Green
05.06.04	Michael Monaghan W PTS 4 Bethnal Green
07.04.05	Darren Rhodes W CO 1 Birmingham

Career: 15 contests, won 14, lost 1.

Keith Ellwood

Edinburgh. *Born* Edinburgh, 14 December, 1979
S.Middleweight. Ht. 6'1"
Manager A. Morrison

02.10.00	Pedro Thompson W RSC 3 Glasgow
15.02.01	Chris Nembhard L RSC 2 Glasgow
19.04.04	Ady Clegg L CO 5 Glasgow
15.11.04	Ali Mateen L PTS 6 Glasgow
11.06.05	Martin Marshall L PTS 6 Kirkcaldy

Career: 5 contests, won 1, lost 4.

Mark Ellwood

Hull. *Born* Hull, 13 June, 1963
L.Heavyweight. Former Undefeated British Masters L.Heavyweight Champion.
Ht. 5'9¹/₂"
Manager S. Pollard

01.11.01	Adam Cale W PTS 6 Hull
25.04.02	Mark Phillips L PTS 6 Hull
26.09.02	Shpetim Hoti W PTS 6 Hull
21.11.02	Martin Thompson W PTS 6 Hull
11.12.02	William Webster W PTS 6 Hull
17.04.03	Mike Duffield W PTS 10 Hull
	(*Vacant British Masters L.Heavyweight Title*)
14.11.03	Mike Duffield W PTS 6 Hull
30.09.04	Cello Renda L RSC 2 Hull

Career: 8 contests, won 7, lost 1.

Declan English

Burton. *Born* Burton, 28 March, 1981
Lightweight. Ht. 5'7"
Manager Self

17.06.04	David Pereira L PTS 6 Sheffield
25.06.04	Rob Jeffries L PTS 6 Bethnal Green
10.07.04	Joe McCluskey L RSC 4 Coventry

Career: 3 contests, lost 3.

Declan English   Les Clark

Chris Evans

Conisbrough. *Born* Doncaster, 20 November, 1975
L.Middleweight. Ht. 5'9"
Manager J. Rushton

03.09.04	Tony Smith W RSC 2 Doncaster

Career: 1 contest, won 1.

F

Andrew Facey

Sheffield. *Born* Wolverhampton, 20 May, 1972
English L.Middleweight Champion. Former Undefeated Central Area Middleweight Champion. Ht. 6'0"
Manager B. Ingle

06.12.99	Peter McCormack W CO 2 Birmingham	
09.06.00	Matthew Pepper W RSC 1 Hull	
04.11.00	Earl Ling W PTS 6 Derby	
11.12.00	Gary Jones W PTS 6 Cleethorpes	
10.02.01	Louis Swales W RSC 3 Widnes	
17.03.01	Darren Rhodes L PTS 4 Manchester	
24.03.01	Matthew Tait W PTS 4 Chigwell	
16.06.01	Earl Ling DREW 6 Derby	
09.12.01	Michael Pinnock W PTS 6 Shaw	
02.03.02	Darren Rhodes W RSC 6 Wakefield *(Vacant Central Area Middleweight Title)*	
20.04.02	Darren Ashton W PTS 6 Derby	
13.04.02	Leigh Wicks W PTS 6 Norwich	
03.08.02	Damon Hague L CO 5 Derby *(Final Elim. WBF Middleweight Title)*	
25.10.02	William Webster W PTS 4 Cotgrave	
16.04.03	Gilbert Eastman W RSC 3 Nottingham	
06.11.03	Matthew Macklin W PTS 10 Dagenham *(Vacant English L.Middleweight Title)*	
22.11.03	Jamie Moore L RSC 7 Belfast *(British & Commonwealth L.Middleweight Title Challenges)*	
04.06.04	Howard Clarke W PTS 6 Hull	
17.09.04	Jason Collins W PTS 4 Sheffield	

Career: 19 contests, won 15, drew 1, lost 3.

Femi Fehintola

Bradford. *Born* Bradford, 1 July, 1982
S. Featherweight. Ht. 5'7"
Manager D. Hobson

26.09.03	John-Paul Ryan W PTS 6 Reading
07.11.03	Pete Buckley W PTS 6 Sheffield
10.12.03	Jason Nesbitt W PTS 6 Sheffield
06.02.04	Jason Nesbitt W PTS 6 Sheffield
20.04.04	Kristian Laight W PTS 6 Sheffield
17.06.04	Anthony Hanna W PTS 6 Sheffield
24.10.04	John-Paul Ryan W PTS 6 Sheffield
10.12.04	Philippe Meheust W PTS 6 Sheffield
04.03.05	Daniel Thorpe W PTS 6 Rotherham

Career: 9 contests, won 9.

Andrew Ferrans

New Cumnock. *Born* Irvine, 4 February, 1981
British Master S.Featherweight Champion. Ht. 5'9"
Manager T. Gilmour

19.02.00	Chris Lyons W PTS 6 Prestwick
03.03.00	Gary Groves W RSC 1 Irvine
20.03.00	John Barnes DREW 6 Glasgow
06.06.00	Duncan Armstrong W PTS 6 Motherwell
18.09.00	Steve Brook W PTS 6 Glasgow

20.11.00	Duncan Armstrong W PTS 6 Glasgow
23.02.01	Dave Cotterill L RSC 2 Irvine
30.04.01	Dave Cotterill W RSC 1 Glasgow
04.06.01	Jason Nesbitt W RSC 2 Glasgow
17.09.01	Gary Flear W PTS 8 Glasgow
10.12.01	Jamie McKeever L PTS 6 Liverpool
21.01.02	Joel Viney W PTS 8 Glasgow
01.03.02	Peter Allen W PTS 8 Irvine
13.04.02	Tony Mulholland L PTS 4 Liverpool
11.05.02	Marc Callaghan L PTS 6 Dagenham
23.09.02	Greg Edwards W RTD 4 Glasgow
08.10.02	Peter Allen W PTS 8 Glasgow
18.11.02	Joel Viney W PTS 6 Glasgow
30.11.02	Colin Toohey L PTS 6 Liverpool
28.02.03	Simon Chambers W PTS 7 Irvine
28.04.03	Craig Spacie L PTS 6 Nottingham
26.07.03	Baz Carey DREW 4 Plymouth
01.11.03	Anthony Hanna W PTS 4 Glasgow
19.01.04	Dariusz Snarski W PTS 6 Glasgow
15.03.04	Baz Carey W PTS 10 Glasgow *(Vacant British Masters S.Featherweight Title)*
08.05.04	Carl Johanneson L RSC 6 Bristol *(WBF S.Featherweight Title Challenge)*
26.02.05	Stephen Chinnock W RTD 5 Burton

Career: 27 contests, won 18, drew 2, lost 7.

John Fewkes

Sheffield. *Born* Sheffield, 16 July, 1985
Lightweight. Ht. 5'8"
Manager T. Gilmour/G. Rhodes

17.09.04	Mark Dane W RSC 2 Sheffield
24.10.04	Lea Handley W PTS 6 Sheffield
10.12.04	Jason Nesbitt W PTS 6 Sheffield
04.03.05	Jason Nesbitt W PTS 6 Rotherham
08.05.05	Chris Long W PTS 8 Sheffield
25.06.05	Billy Smith W PTS 6 Wakefield

Career: 6 contests, won 6.

John Fewkes   Les Clark

(John Joseph) Jonjo Finnegan

Burton on Trent. *Born* Burton on Trent, 25 April, 1980
S.Middleweight. Ht. 6'1"
Manager D. Bradley/E. Johnson

08.07.04	Paul Billington W PTS 6 Birmingham
25.11.04	Nick Okoth DREW 6 Birmingham
26.02.05	Arv Mittoo W PTS 4 Burton
07.04.05	Peter Dunn W PTS 6 Birmingham
24.04.05	Omid Bourzo L PTS 6 Derby

Career: 5 contests, won 3, drew 1, lost 1.

(Scott) Rocky Flanagan

Blackpool. *Born* Doncaster, 28 July, 1979
Lightweight. Ht. 5'3"
Manager L. Veitch

20.09.04	Amir Ali L PTS 4 Glasgow
27.09.04	Scott Conway L RSC 2 Cleethorpes
26.11.04	Muhsen Nasser L PTS 6 Hull
21.03.05	Jamie McIlroy L PTS 6 Glasgow

Career: 4 contests, lost 4.

Andrew Flute

Coseley. Born Wolverhampton, 5 March, 1970
L.Heavyweight. Ht. 6'1"
Manager Self

24.05.89	Stinger Mason W PTS 6 Hanley
24.10.89	Paul Murray W RSC 3 Wolverhampton
22.03.90	Dave Maxwell W RSC 5 Wolverhampton
24.05.90	Spencer Alton L RSC 1 Dudley
18.09.90	Tony Hodge W CO 2 Wolverhampton
24.10.90	Nigel Rafferty W CO 6 Dudley
27.11.90	Paul Burton L PTS 6 Stoke
13.03.91	Robert Peel W PTS 6 Stoke
10.04.91	Russell Washer W PTS 6 Wolverhampton
14.05.91	Alan Richards W PTS 8 Dudley
16.10.91	Karl Barwise L RSC 8 Stoke
05.12.91	Richard Okumu DREW 8 Cannock
17.03.92	Graham Burton W PTS 8 Wolverhampton
28.04.92	Paul Smith W RSC 5 Wolverhampton
20.01.93	Glen Payton W RSC 4 Wolverhampton
16.03.93	Mark Hale W RSC 2 Wolverhampton
24.04.93	Steve Thomas W RSC 1 Birmingham
21.10.93	Terry Magee W RSC 6 Bayswater
26.01.94	Neville Brown L RTD 7 Birmingham *(British Middleweight Title Challenge)*
16.03.94	Graham Burton W PTS 6 Birmingham
29.10.94	Carlos Christie L PTS 8 Cannock
29.11.94	Mark Dawson W PTS 8 Cannock
17.01.95	Chris Richards W PTS 6 Worcester
11.05.95	Paul Murray W PTS 6 Dudley
30.09.95	Mark Delaney L PTS 12 Basildon *(Vacant WBO Inter-Continental S. Middleweight Title)*
16.03.96	Robin Reid L RSC 7 Glasgow
25.05.96	Norbert Nieroba L RTD 4 Leipzig, Germany
28.09.96	Leif Keiski L PTS 8 Barking
24.10.96	Carlos Christie L PTS 10 Mayfair *(Midlands Area S. Middleweight Title Challenge)*
15.02.97	Markus Beyer L PTS 6 Vienna, Austria
01.06.97	Sven Ottke L PTS 6 Riesa, Germany
03.04.98	Octavian Stoica W PTS 6 West Bromwich
04.06.98	Martin Jolley W PTS 6 Dudley
03.10.98	Darren Littlewood W PTS 6 West Bromwich
05.12.98	Glenn Catley L RSC 5 Bristol *(Vacant IBF Inter-Continental S. Middleweight Title)*
26.02.99	Errol McDonald W RSC 4 West Bromwich
24.03.01	David Starie L RTD 3 Sheffield
05.10.04	Simeon Cover L PTS 4 Dudley

Career: 38 contests, won 22, drew 1, lost 15.

Scott Flynn

Edinburgh. *Born* Edinburgh, 27 March, 1984
Featherweight. Ht. 5'8"
Manager F. Warren/D. Powell

19.06.04   Henry Janes L RSC 4 Renfrew
22.10.04   Abdul Mougharbel W PTS 4
           Edinburgh
28.01.05   Neil Marston W RSC 2 Renfrew
08.04.05   Riaz Durgahead W PTS 4 Edinburgh
Career: 4 contests, won 3, lost 1.

(Patrick) Paddy Folan (Powders)

Huddersfield. *Born* Birmingham, 25 June, 1972
Featherweight. Ht. 5'7"
Manager C. Aston

25.10.98   Waj Khan W PTS 6 Shaw
26.11.98   Daniel Ring DREW 6 Bradford
07.12.98   Kevin Gerowski L PTS 6 Bradford
21.02.99   Chris Emanuele DREW 6 Bradford
19.04.99   Gary Groves L CO 1 Bradford
19.09.99   Gary Ford L PTS 6 Shaw
14.11.99   Shane Mallon W PTS 6 Bradford
26.11.99   Chris Emanuele L RSC 5 Wakefield
05.03.00   Gary Ford L PTS 6 Shaw
15.05.00   Chris Edwards W PTS 6 Bradford
25.06.00   Levi Pattison L PTS 6 Wakefield
30.11.00   Neil Read W PTS 6 Blackpool
07.12.00   John-Paul Ryan L PTS 6 Stoke
11.02.01   Michael Hunter L RSC 6 Hartlepool
20.03.01   Sean Grant DREW 6 Leeds
01.04.01   Dafydd Carlin L PTS 4 Southwark
09.04.01   Sean Grant L PTS 6 Bradford
10.06.01   Lee Holmes L PTS 6 Ellesmere Port
31.07.01   Jamie Yelland L RSC 5 Bethnal Green
22.10.01   Sean Grant L PTS 6 Glasgow
19.11.01   Gary Groves W PTS 6 Glasgow
09.12.01   Joel Viney L PTS 6 Blackpool
21.02.02   Gypsy Boy Mario W PTS 6 Sunderland
02.03.02   Sean Hughes L PTS 6 Wakefield
28.05.02   John Paul Ryan L PTS 6 Leeds
24.06.02   Gary Groves W RSC 2 Bradford
20.07.02   Steve Foster L CO 1 Bethnal Green
05.10.02   Sean Hughes L PTS 4 Huddersfield
05.10.03   Sean Hughes L RSC 4 Bradford
           (Vacant Central Area S.Bantamweight Title)
23.11.03   Fred Janes L RSC 5 Rotherham
19.04.04   Furhan Rafiq L PTS 6 Glasgow
12.09.04   Neil Marston L PTS 6 Shrewsbury
18.11.04   Neil Marston L PTS 6 Shrewsbury
06.12.04   Neil Marston L PTS 6 Bradford
19.12.04   Craig Bromley DREW 6 Bolton
13.02.05   Craig Bromley L PTS 6 Bradford
06.03.05   Barrington Brown L RSC 6 Shaw
03.06.05   Kyle Simpson L RSC 3 Hull
Career: 38 contests, won 7, drew 4, lost 27.

Gary Ford

Oldham. *Born* Oldham, 27 July, 1973
S.Bantamweight. Ht. 5'1"
Manager J. Doughty

19.09.99   Paddy Folan W PTS 6 Shaw
05.03.00   Paddy Folan W PTS 6 Shaw
21.05.00   Andy Roberts DREW 6 Shaw
24.09.00   Nicky Booth L PTS 6 Shaw
18.03.01   Andrew Greenaway W RSC 1 Shaw
17.05.01   Levi Pattison L RSC 5 Leeds
20.09.04   Wayne Bloy L PTS 6 Cleethorpes
31.10.04   Neil Read W PTS 6 Shaw
06.06.05   Abdul Mougharbel L PTS 6 Glasgow
Career: 9 contests, won 4, drew 1, lost 4.

Scott Forsyth

Edinburgh. *Born* Edinburgh, 23 July, 1982
S.Middleweight. Ht. 6'0"
Manager A., Morrison

27.03.04   Neil Addis W RSC 3 Edinburgh
12.12.04   Cello Renda L RSC 1 Glasgow
Career: 2 contests, won 1, lost 1.

Jon Foster

Oldham. *Born* Nottingham, 18 October, 1979
Middleweight. Ht. 6'1"
Manager M. Shinfield

31.10.97   David Thompson W RSC 4 Ilkeston
26.11.97   Billy McDougall W RSC 2 Stoke
20.03.98   Phil Molyneux W PTS 6 Ilkeston
03.04.98   Harry Butler W PTS 6 Ebbw Vale
23.04.98   Hughie Davey L PTS 8 Newcastle
11.09.98   Brian Dunn W RTD 3 Cleethorpes
07.12.98   Darren Christie W RSC 6 Cleethorpes
06.06.99   Jason Collins DREW 6 Nottingham
20.09.99   Joe Townsley L PTS 6 Glasgow
11.12.99   Jacek Bielski L PTS 6 Merthyr
12.02.00   Zoltan Sarossy L RSC 1 Sheffield
06.06.00   James Docherty L PTS 6 Motherwell
24.09.00   Lee Murtagh L PTS 6 Shaw
25.04.05   Jed Tytler L RSC 2 Cleethorpes
Career: 14 contests, won 6, drew 1, lost 7.

Steve Foster

Salford. *Born* Salford, 16 September, 1980
WBU Featherweight Champion. Former
Undefeated English Featherweight
Champion. Ht. 5'6"
Manager S.Foster/S.Wood/F.Warren

15.09.01   Andy Greenaway W PTS 4 Manchester
27.10.01   Gareth Wiltshaw W PTS 4 Manchester
02.03.02   Andy Greenaway W RSC 1 Bethnal Green
04.05.02   Gareth Wiltshaw W PTS 4 Bethnal Green
08.07.02   Ian Turner W RSC 1 Mayfair
20.07.02   Paddy Folan W CO 1 Bethnal Green
28.09.02   Jason White W RSC 3 Manchester
14.12.02   Sean Green W RSC 3 Newcastle
22.03.03   David McIntyre W PTS 4 Renfrew
24.05.03   Henry Janes W PTS 6 Bethnal Green
12.07.03   David McIntyre W RTD 3 Renfrew
18.09.03   Alexander Abramenko W RTD 4 Dagenham
06.11.03   Vladimir Borov W RSC 8 Dagenham
13.12.03   Steve Gethin W RTD 3 Manchester

Steve Foster   Paul Speak

26.02.04 Sean Hughes W RSC 6 Widnes
(Vacant English Featherweight Title)
30.07.04 Jean-Marie Codet W PTS 8 Bethnal Green
01.10.04 Gary Thornhill W RSC 9 Manchester
(English Featherweight Title Defence)
11.02.05 Livinson Ruiz W CO 10 Manchester
(Vacant WBU Featherweight Title)
Career: 18 contests, won 18.

Julius Francis

Woolwich. *Born* Peckham, 8 December, 1964
Heavyweight. Former Undefeated Commonwealth Heavyweight Champion. Former British Heavyweight Champion. Former Undefeated Southern Area Heavyweight Champion. Ht. 6'2"
Manager Self

23.05.93 Graham Arnold W RSC 5 Brockley
23.06.93 Joey Paladino W CO 4 Edmonton
24.07.93 Andre Tisdale W PTS 4 Atlantic City, New Jersey, USA
28.08.93 Don Sargent W RSC 2 Bismark, USA
01.12.93 John Keeton W PTS 4 Bethnal Green
27.04.94 Manny Burgo W PTS 4 Bethnal Green
25.05.94 John Ruiz L CO 4 Bristol
12.11.94 Conroy Nelson W RSC 4 Dublin
23.11.94 Gary Charlton W RSC 1 Piccadilly
23.02.05 Damien Caesar W RSC 8 Southwark
(Vacant Southern Area Heavyweight Title)
27.04.95 Keith Fletcher W PTS 10 Bethnal Green
(Southern Area Heavyweight Title Defence)
25.05.95 Steve Garber W PTS 8 Reading
01.07.95 Scott Welch L RSC 10 Kensington
(Southern Area Heavyweight Title Defence. Final Elim. British Heavyweight Title)
24.10.95 Neil Kirkwood W RSC 7 Southwark
30.11.95 Nikolai Kulpin L PTS 10 Saratov, Russia
05.02.96 Michael Murray L PTS 10 Bexleyheath
(Elim. British Heavyweight Title)
09.04.96 Damien Caesar W CO 1 Stevenage
(Vacant Southern Area Heavyweight Title)
07.05.96 Darren Fearn W PTS 8 Mayfair
09.07.96 Mike Holden W PTS 10 Bethnal Green
28.09.96 James Oyebola W RSC 5 Barking
(Southern Area Heavyweight Title Defence)
15.02.97 Zeljko Mavrovic L RSC 8 Vienna, Austria
(European Heavyweight Title Challenge)
30.06.97 Joseph Chingangu W PTS 12 Bethnal Green
(Vacant Commonwealth Heavyweight Title)
27.09.97 Garry Delaney W RSC 6 Belfast
(Commonwealth Heavyweight Title Defence. Vacant British Heavyweight Title)
28.02.98 Axel Schulz L PTS 12 Dortmund, Germany
18.04.98 Vitali Klitschko L RSC 2 Aachen, Germany
30.01.99 Pele Reid W RSC 3 Bethnal Green
(British & Commonwealth Heavyweight Title Defences)
03.04.99 Danny Williams W PTS 12 Kensington
(British & Commonwealth Heavyweight Title Defences)

26.06.99 Scott Welch W PTS 12 Millwall
(British & Commonwealth Heavyweight Title Defences)
29.01.00 Mike Tyson L RSC 2 Manchester
13.03.00 Mike Holden L PTS 12 Bethnal Green
(British Heavyweight Title Defence)
03.04.01 Mike Holden W PTS 12 Bethnal Green
(Final Elim. British Heavyweight Title)
28.07.01 Danny Williams L CO 4 Wembley
(British & Commonwealth Heavyweight Title Challenges)
10.05.02 Luke Simpkin DREW 6 Millwall
13.09.02 Steffen Nielsen W CO 6 Randers, Denmark
26.04.03 Sinan Samil Sam L RSC 7 Schwerin, Germany
(European Heavyweight Title Challenge)
13.06.03 Steffen Nielsen L PTS 10 Aalborg, Denmark
(Vacant European Union Heavyweight Title)
06.09.03 Vladimir Virchis L PTS 12 Kiev, Ukraine
(Vacant IBF Inter-Continental Interim Heavyweight Title)
18.10.03 Luan Krasniqi L PTS 8 Hamburg, Germany
27.11.03 Oleg Maskaev L RSC 2 Moscow, Russia
07.02.04 Matt Skelton L PTS 10 Bethnal Green
(English Heavyweight Title Challenge)
08.05.04 Audley Harrison L PTS 12 Bristol
(WBF Heavyweight Title Challenge)
31.07.04 Alexander Dimitrenko L PTS 8 Stuttgart, Germany
21.09.04 Taras Bidenko L PTS 10 Hamburg, Germany
10.12.04 Roman Greenberg L PTS 10 Sheffield
24.04.05 Micky Steeds L PTS 8 Leicester Square
26.06.05 Colin Kenna L PTS 4 Southampton
Career: 46 contests, won 23, drew 1, lost 22.

Simon Francis

Sheffield. *Born* Sheffield, 2 October, 1981
Cruiserweight. Ht. 6'2"
Manager D. Coldwell

06.05.04 Gary Thompson W PTS 4 Barnsley
08.06.04 Gary Thompson W RTD 2 Sheffield
24.06.04 Slick Miller W PTS 6 Gibralter
12.11.04 Brian Gascoigne W RSC 1 Halifax
15.12.04 Radcliffe Green W PTS 6 Sheffield
20.02.05 Greg Scott-Briggs W RSC 4 Sheffield
Career: 6 contests, won 6.

Mark Franks (Whitemore)

Wakefield. *Born* Hannover, Germany, 29 September, 1975
L. Middleweight. Ht. 5'7¾"
Manager K. Walker

06.12.04 Tommy Marshall L PTS 6 Leeds
18.04.05 Kaye Rehman DREW 6 Bradford
30.04.05 Rob MacDonald W RSC 6 Wigan
01.06.05 Geraint Harvey W PTS 6 Leeds
Career: 4 contests, won 2, drew 1, lost 1.

Carl Froch

Nottingham. *Born* Nottingham, 2 July, 1977
British & Commonwealth S.Middleweight Champion. Former Undefeated English S.Middleweight Champion. Ht. 6'4"
Manager Self

16.03.02 Michael Pinnock W RSC 4 Bethnal Green
10.05.02 Ojay Abrahams W RSC 1 Bethnal Green
23.08.02 Darren Covill W RSC 1 Bethnal Green
25.10.02 Paul Bonson W PTS 6 Bethnal Green
21.12.02 Mike Duffield W RSC 1 Dagenham
28.01.03 Valery Odin W RSC 6 Nottingham
05.03.03 Varuzhan Davtyan W RSC 5 Bethnal Green
16.04.03 Michael Monaghan W RSC 3 Nottingham
04.10.03 Vage Kocharyan W PTS 8 Muswell Hill
28.11.03 Alan Page W RSC 7 Derby
(Vacant English S.Middleweight Title. Elim. British S.Middleweight Title)
30.01.04 Dmitri Adamovich W RSC 2 Dagenham
12.03.04 Charles Adamu W PTS 12 Nottingham
(Commonwealth S.Middleweight Title Challenge)
02.06.04 Mark Woolnough W RSC 11 Nottingham
(Commonwealth S.Middleweight Title Defence)
24.09.04 Damon Hague W RSC 1 Nottingham
(Vacant British S.Middleweight Title. Commonwealth S.Middleweight Title Defence)
21.04.05 Henry Porras W RSC 8 Hollywood, California, USA
Career: 15 contests, won 15.

Carl Froch   Les Clark

Courtney Fry

Wood Green. *Born* Enfield, 19 May, 1975
L. Heavyweight. Ht. 6'1½"
Manager Self

29.03.03 Harry Butler W RSC 3 Wembley
31.05.03 Darren Ashton W PTS 4 Bethnal Green
24.10.03 Ovill McKenzie W PTS 4 Bethnal Green
20.03.04 Clint Johnson W RSC 2 Wembley
02.04.04 Paulie Silva W PTS 4 Plymouth
08.05.04 Radcliffe Green W PTS 6 Bristol
19.06.04 Valery Odin W PTS 8 Muswell Hill
17.12.04 Varuzhan Davtyan W RTD 2 Liverpool
13.05.05 Ovill McKenzie L PTS 4 Liverpool
Career: 9 contests, won 8, lost 1.

Matt Galer

Burton. *Born* Burton, 15 December, 1973
Middleweight. Ht. 5'8"
Manager Self

30.09.97	Martin Cavey W CO 1 Edgbaston
18.11.97	Chris Pollock W PTS 6 Mansfield
16.03.98	Mike Duffield W PTS 6 Nottingham
14.05.98	Freddie Yemofio W RSC 4 Acton
14.10.98	Carlton Williams L PTS 6 Stoke
25.03.99	Gordon Behan L RSC 9 Edgbaston
	(Midlands Area Middleweight Title
	Challenge)
15.08.99	Jason Collins L PTS 6 Derby
13.11.01	Danny Thornton W RSC 4 Leeds
09.02.02	Anthony Farnell L RSC 3 Manchester
23.02.04	Ojay Abrahams W PTS 4 Nottingham
12.06.04	Gary Lockett L RSC 4 Manchester
24.09.04	Jim Rock L PTS 6 Dublin
26.02.05	Mark Phillips W PTS 6 Burton

Career: 13 contests, won 7, lost 6.

Scott Gammer

Pembroke Dock. *Born* Pembroke Dock, 24
October, 1976
Heavyweight. Ht. 6'2"
Manager P. Boyce

15.09.02	Leighton Morgan W RSC 1 Swansea
26.10.02	James Gilbert W RSC 1 Maesteg
08.01.03	Dave Clarke W PTS 4 Aberdare
25.01.03	Ahmad Cheleh W CO 1 Bridgend
28.06.03	Dave Clarke W RSC 1 Cardiff
13.09.03	Derek McCafferty W PTS 6 Newport
08.11.03	Mendauga Kulikauskas DREW 6 Bridgend
28.02.04	James Zikic W PTS 6 Bridgend
01.05.04	Paul Buttery W CO 1 Bridgend
02.06.04	Paul King W RSC 3 Hereford
17.09.04	Carl Baker W PTS 4 Plymouth
05.11.04	Roman Bugaj W RSC 2 Hereford
18.02.05	Micky Steeds W PTS 6 Brighton
15.05.05	Mark Krence W RSC 8 Sheffield
	(Elim. British Heavyweight Title)

Career: 14 contests, won 13, drew 1.

Brian Gascoigne

Kirkby in Ashfield. *Born* Kirkby in
Ashfield, 4 June, 1970
Cruiserweight. Ht. 6'5"
Manager M. Scriven

23.11.98	Lennox Williams W RSC 3 Piccadilly
30.04.99	Shane Woollas DREW 6 Scunthorpe
03.10.99	Lee Swaby DREW 6 Chesterfield
06.12.99	Mark Hobson L RSC 3 Bradford
09.04.00	Nigel Rafferty W PTS 6 Alfreton
25.06.00	Danny Southam L RSC 4 Wakefield
04.12.00	Huggy Osman L PTS 6 Bradford
10.04.01	Kevin Barrett L RSC 1 Wembley
26.09.02	Adam Cale W PTS 4 Fulham
17.02.03	Tony Moran L RSC 1 Glasgow
31.05.03	Nate Joseph W RTD 1 Barnsley
02.06.03	Costi Marin W PTS 6 Glasgow
26.11.03	Tommy Eastwood L RSC 2 Mayfair
12.11.04	Simon Francis L RSC 1 Halifax

Career: 14 contests, won 5, drew 2, lost 7.

Darren Gethin

Walsall. *Born* Walsall, 19 August, 1976
Welterweight. Ht. 5'8"
Manager D. Bradley/E. Johnson

08.07.04	Joe Mitchell DREW 6 Birmingham
12.09.04	Joe Mitchell W PTS 6 Shrewsbury
12.11.04	Tyrone McInerney L PTS 4 Halifax
26.02.05	Tye Williams DREW 4 Burton
18.04.05	Joe Mitchell W PTS 6 Bradford
25.04.05	Terry Carruthers L RSC 3 Cleethorpes
02.06.05	Franny Jones L PTS 8 Yarm

Career: 7 contests, won 2, drew 2, lost 3.

Martin Gethin

Walsall. *Born* Walsall, 16 November, 1983
Lightweight. Ht. 5'6"
Manager E. Johnson/D. Bradley

18.11.04	Kristian Laight W RSC 4 Shrewsbury
15.04.05	Jason Nesbitt W PTS 6 Shrewsbury

Career: 2 contests, won 2.

Steve Gethin

Walsall. *Born* Walsall, 30 July, 1978
Featherweight. Ht. 5'9"
Manager Self

03.09.99	Ike Halls W RSC 3 West Bromwich
24.10.99	Ricky Bishop W RSC 4 Wolverhampton
22.01.00	Sebastian Hart L PTS 4 Birmingham
10.09.00	Nigel Senior DREW 6 Walsall
03.06.01	Richmond Asante L PTS 4 Southwark
28.11.01	Mickey Coveney L PTS 4 Bethnal Green
09.12.01	Gary Groves W PTS 6 Shaw
17.02.02	Gary Groves W PTS 6 Wolverhampton
01.06.02	Gary Davis W RSC 2 Manchester
21.09.02	Marc Callaghan L PTS 6 Brentwood
02.12.02	Neil Read W RTD 3 Leicester
14.12.02	Isaac Ward L PTS 4 Newcastle
08.02.03	Rocky Dean DREW 4 Norwich
15.02.03	Anthony Hanna W PTS 6 Wolverhampton
08.05.03	Derry Matthews L RSC 3 Widnes
07.09.03	Henry Janes L PTS 4 Shrewsbury
02.10.03	Mark Moran L PTS 4 Liverpool
20.10.03	John Simpson L PTS 8 Glasgow
30.10.03	Gareth Payne W PTS 6 Dudley
13.12.03	Steve Foster L RTD 3 Manchester
05.03.04	Isaac Ward L PTS 6 Darlington
27.05.04	Marc Callaghan L PTS 6 Huddersfield
30.07.04	Chris Hooper L PTS 4 Bethnal Green
08.10.04	Ian Napa L PTS 6 Brentwood
22.10.04	Andy Bell L RSC 5 Mansfield
17.12.04	Mark Moran L PTS 4 Liverpool
13.02.05	Patrick Hyland L PTS 4 Brentwood
24.04.05	Darren Broomhall W CO 5 Derby

Career: 28 contests, won 9, drew 2, lost 17.

Alan Gilbert

Crawley. *Born* Bromley, 17 November,
1970
Middleweight. Ht. 5'11"
Manager Self

02.12.97	Martin Cavey W RSC 1 Windsor
06.01.98	Harry Butler W PTS 4 Brighton
23.02.98	Jon Harrison W PTS 6 Windsor
21.04.98	Paul Henry L PTS 4 Edmonton
08.08.98	Lee Murtagh L PTS 4 Scarborough
03.10.98	C. J. Jackson W RSC 3 Crawley
25.02.99	Justin Simmons W RSC 5 Kentish Town
01.05.99	Anthony Farnell L RSC 8 Crystal Palace

Jimmy Gilhaney

Newmains. *Born* Lanark, 8 April, 1982
Lightweight. Ht. 5'7"
Manager T. Gilmour

25.04.05	Pete Buckley W PTS 6 Glasgow

Career: 1 contest, won 1.

Michael Gomez (Armstrong)

Manchester. *Born* Dublin, 21 June, 1977
S.Featherweight. Former WBU
S.Featherweight Champion. Former
Undefeated WBO Inter-Continental &
British S.Featherweight Champion. Former
WBO Inter-Continental S.Featherweight
Champion. Former Undefeated Central
Area & IBF Inter-Continental
Featherweight Champion. Ht. 5'5"
Manager F. Warren/T. Jones

07.08.99	Wayne Shepherd DREW 8 Dagenham
	(Vacant British Masters L.Middleweight Title)
11.03.00	Michael Jones L RTD 3 Kensington
12.06.00	Jim Rock L PTS 6 Belfast
22.07.00	Delroy Mellis L RSC 3 Watford
	(Vacant Southern Area L.Middleweight Title)
23.01.01	Delroy Mellis L RSC 3 Crawley
	(Southern Area L. Middleweight Title Challenge)
29.09.01	Steven Bendall L RTD 3 Southwark
10.02.02	Allan Gray DREW 4 Southwark
28.04.02	Allan Gray L PTS 10 Southwark
	(Vacant Southern Area Middleweight Title)
03.08.02	Lee Blundell L RSC 6 Blackpool
	(IBF Inter-Continental Middleweight Title Challenge)
15.10.02	Dean Powell W PTS 4 Bethnal Green
28.04.03	Ben Ogden L RSC 1 Nottingham
20.06.03	Leigh Wicks W PTS 4 Gatwick
25.07.03	Ryan Rhodes L RSC 5 Norwich
21.02.04	Leigh Wicks W PTS 4 Brighton
17.04.04	Jason McKay L PTS 6 Belfast
13.05.04	Gokhan Kazaz L PTS 4 Bethnal Green
24.04.05	Ruben Groenewald L RSC 10 Leicester Square
	(Vacant WBF Inter-Continental S.Middleweight Title)
19.06.05	Gokhan Kazaz L PTS 6 Bethnal Green

Career: 26 contests, won 8, drew 2, lost 16.

10.06.95	Danny Ruegg W PTS 6 Manchester
15.09.95	Greg Upton L PTS 4 Mansfield
24.11.95	Danny Ruegg L PTS 4 Manchester
19.09.96	Martin Evans W RSC 1 Manchester
09.11.96	David Morris W PTS 4 Manchester
22.03.97	John Farrell W RSC 2 Wythenshawe
03.05.97	Chris Williams L PTS 4 Manchester
11.09.97	Wayne Jones W RSC 2 Widnes
18.04.98	Benny Jones W PTS 4 Manchester
16.05.98	Craig Spacie W RSC 3 Bethnal Green
05.09.98	Pete Buckley W PTS 6 Telford
14.11.98	David Jeffrey W RSC 1 Cheshunt
19.12.98	Kevin Sheil W RSC 4 Liverpool
13.02.99	Dave Hinds W PTS 6 Newcastle
27.02.99	Chris Jickells W RSC 5 Oldham
	(Vacant Central Area Featherweight Title)
29.05.99	Nigel Leake W RSC 2 Halifax
	(Vacant IBF Inter-Continental Featherweight Title)

07.08.99 William Alverzo W PTS 6 Atlantic
City, New Jersey, USA
04.09.99 Gary Thornhill W RSC 2 Bethnal Green
(Vacant British S. Featherweight Title)
06.11.99 Jose Juan Manjarrez W PTS 12 Widnes
*(WBO Inter-Continental
S. Featherweight Title Defence)*
11.12.99 Oscar Galindo W RSC 11 Liverpool
*(WBO Inter-Continental
S. Featherweight Title Defence)*
29.01.00 Chris Jickells W RSC 4 Manchester
29.02.00 Dean Pithie W PTS 12 Widnes
(British S. Featherweight Title Defence)
24.06.00 Carl Allen W CO 2 Glasgow
08.07.00 Carl Greaves W CO 2 Widnes
(British S. Featherweight Title Defence)
19.10.00 Awel Abdulai W PTS 8 Harrisburg,
USA
11.12.00 Ian McLeod W PTS 12 Widnes
(British S.Featherweight Title Defence)
10.02.01 Laszlo Bognar L RSC 9 Widnes
*(WBO Inter-Continental
S. Featherweight Title Defence)*
07.07.01 Laszlo Bognar W RSC 3 Manchester
*(WBO Inter-Continental
S. Featherweight Title Challenge)*
27.10.01 Craig Docherty W RSC 2 Manchester
(British S.Featherweight Title Defence)
01.06.02 Kevin Lear L RTD 8 Manchester
(Vacant WBU S. Featherweight Title)
28.09.02 Jimmy Beech W RSC 4 Manchester
18.01.03 Rakhim Mingaleev W RTD 4 Preston
05.04.03 Vladimir Borov W RSC 3 Manchester
25.10.03 Alex Arthur W RSC 5 Edinburgh
*(British S.Featherweight Title
Challenge)*
03.04.04 Ben Odamattey W RSC 3 Manchester
(Vacant WBU S.Featherweight Title)
22.05.04 Justin Juuko W RSC 2 Widnes
(WBU S.Featherweight Title Defence)
01.10.04 Leva Kirakosyan W RTD 6 Manchester
(WBU S.Featherweight Title Defence)
11.02.05 Javier Osvaldo Alvarez L RSC 6
Manchester
(WBU S.Featherweight Title Defence)
Career: 38 contests, won 32, lost 6.

Danny Goode   Les Clark

Danny Goode

New Milton. *Born* Wimbledon, 15 January,
1980
Middleweight. Ht. 5'8"
Manager M. Roe

16.10.04 Geraint Harvey W PTS 4 Dagenham
06.02.05 Neil Jarmolinski W PTS 4
Southampton
23.03.05 Tony Randell W PTS 6 Leicester
Square
30.04.05 John-Paul Temple W PTS 4 Dagenham
26.06.05 John-Paul Temple W PTS 4
Southampton
Career: 5 contests, won 5.

Simon Goodwin

Cambridge. *Born* Cambridge, 13 January,
1979
Heavyweight. Ht. 6'2"
Manager Self

28.07.03 Marcus Lee L PTS 4 Plymouth
06.12.04 Billy Wilson L PTS 6 Leeds
Career: 2 contests, lost 2.

James Gorman

Belfast. *Born* Belfast, 1 August, 1979
Welterweight. Ht. 5'8"
Manager A. Wilton

28.06.03 Jamie Arthur L PTS 4 Cardiff
11.10.03 Lee Beavis L PTS 4 Portsmouth
25.10.03 George Telfer L PTS 4 Edinburgh
22.11.03 Peter McDonagh W PTS 4 Belfast
28.02.04 Ceri Hall L PTS 6 Bridgend
01.04.04 Lee Beavis L RTD 2 Bethnal Green
24.09.04 Silence Saheed L PTS 6 Millwall
12.11.04 Jas Malik W RTD 2 Belfast
18.03.05 Stephen Haughian L PTS 4 Belfast
14.05.05 Pete Buckley W PTS 6 Dublin
24.06.05 Daniel Thorpe W PTS 6 Belfast
Career: 11 contests, won 4, lost 7.

Jimmy Gould

Coseley. *Born* Wolverhampton, 8 July,
1977
Welterweight. Ht. 5'10"
Manager Self

23.06.99 Benny Jones W PTS 6 West Bromwich
03.09.99 Dave Travers W PTS 6 West
Bromwich
06.11.00 Jon Honney W PTS 6 Wolverhampton
28.01.01 David White W PTS 6 Wolverhampton
20.05.01 Keith Jones W PTS 6 Wolverhampton
07.09.01 Woody Greenaway W PTS 6 West
Bromwich
07.10.01 Steve Hanley W PTS 6
Wolverhampton
13.04.02 Keith Jones W PTS 8 Wolverhampton
25.05.02 Raymond Narh L RSC 3 Portsmouth
08.09.02 Tony Montana L PTS 8
Wolverhampton
08.03.03 Tony Conroy W PTS 4 Coventry
08.05.03 Michael Jennings L RTD 6 Widnes
*(Vacant WBU Inter-Continental
Welterweight Title)*
30.10.03 Richard Swallow L PTS 10 Dudley
*(Vacant British Masters Welterweight
Title)*
21.04.05 Ernie Smith W PTS 4 Dudley
Career: 14 contests, won 10, lost 4.

Nathan Graham

Aylesbury. *Born* Aylesbury, 21 September,
1982
L.Middleweight. Ht. 5'9"
Manager D. Williams

24.04.04 Tom Price W RSC 2 Reading
02.12.04 David Payne W RSC 3 Crystal Palace
26.03.05 Gatis Skuja W RSC 1 Hackney
Career: 3 contests, won 3.

Danny Grainger

Chesterfield. *Born* Chesterfield, 1
September, 1979
L. Heavyweight. Ht. 5'11"
Manager Self

05.10.02 Jamie Wilson W PTS 6 Chesterfield
21.10.02 Jamie Wilson W PTS 6 Cleethorpes
29.11.02 Gary Jones W PTS 6 Hull
08.06.03 Darren Stubbs W RSC 2 Shaw
12.10.03 Paul Billington W PTS 6 Sheffield
03.04.04 Terry Morrill W RSC 5 Sheffield
04.06.04 Patrick Cito W PTS 6 Hull
15.05.05 Hastings Rasani L RSC 5 Sheffield
Career: 8 contests, won 7, lost 1.

Michael Graydon

Bristol. *Born* Bristol, 30 October, 1985
Lightweight. Ht. 5'9"
Manager C. Sanigar

13.02.04 Fred Janes DREW 6 Bristol
08.05.04 Peter Allen W PTS 6 Bristol
03.07.04 Henry Jones DREW 6 Bristol
01.10.04 Daleboy Rees W PTS 6 Bristol
Career: 4 contests, won 2, drew 2.

Carl Greaves

Newark. *Born* Nottingham, 12 June, 1976
S.Featherweight. Former WBF
S.Featherweight Champion. Former
Undefeated British Masters & Midlands
Area S. Featherweight Champion. Ht. 5'7"
Manager Self

22.03.96 Paul Hamilton W PTS 6 Mansfield
30.05.96 Kevin Sheil W PTS 6 Lincoln
02.10.96 Robert Grubb W PTS 8 Stoke
01.11.96 Benny Jones W PTS 6 Mansfield
26.11.96 Danny Ruegg W RTD 4 Sheffield
04.12.96 Des Gargano W PTS 6 Stoke
20.02.97 Lee Armstrong L RSC 4 Mansfield
10.04.97 Kevin Sheil W PTS 6 Sheffield
08.05.97 Benny Jones L RSC 4 Mansfield
10.07.97 Stefy Bull L PTS 6 Doncaster
18.08.97 Graham McGrath W PTS 6 Nottingham
06.10.97 Ervine Blake L PTS 10 Birmingham
*(Vacant Midlands Area
S. Featherweight Title)*
30.10.97 Graham McGrath W PTS 6 Newark
18.11.97 Garry Burrell W CO 4 Mansfield
07.05.98 John T. Kelly W PTS 6 Sunderland
14.10.98 Andy Robinson W PTS 6 Stoke
02.12.98 Graham McGrath W PTS 6 Stoke
18.03.99 Ernie Smith W PTS 6 Doncaster
27.06.99 Chris Jickells W PTS 10 Alfreton
*(British Masters S. Featherweight
Final)*
20.11.99 Pete Buckley W PTS 10 Grantham
*(British Masters S. Featherweight Title
Defence)*
18.01.00 Keith Jones W PTS 6 Mansfield
19.02.00 Marc Smith W PTS 6 Newark
20.03.00 Pete Buckley W PTS 4 Mansfield
11.05.00 Marco Fattore W PTS 8 Newark
08.07.00 Michael Gomez L CO 2 Widnes
*(British S. Featherweight Title
Challenge)*

09.09.00 Dave Hinds W PTS 6 Newark
19.11.00 Haroon Din W RSC 4 Chesterfield
24.03.01 Nigel Senior W CO 6 Newark
          *(Vacant Midlands Area
          S. Featherweight Title)*
16.06.01 Dave Hinds W PTS 6 Derby
11.05.02 Wayne Wheeler W PTS 6 Newark
14.09.02 Peter Allen W PTS 6 Newark
14.12.02 Alex Arthur L RSC 6 Newcastle
          *(British S. Featherweight Title
          Challenge)*
16.04.03 Ben Odamattey W PTS 12 Nottingham
          (Vacant WBF S.Featherweight Title)
24.10.03 Keith Jones W PTS 6 Bethnal Green
28.11.03 Carl Allen W PTS 4 Derby
23.02.04 Jason Nesbitt W PTS 6 Nottingham
20.03.04 Carl Johanneson L RTD 3 Wembley
          (WBF S.Featherweight Title Defence)
24.06.04 Rakhim Mingaleev W PTS 6 Gibralter
18.09.04 Daniel Thorpe W PTS 6 Newark
Career: 39 contests, won 32, lost 7.

(Roger) Radcliffe Green

Balham. *Born* Jamaica, 24 November, 1973
Cruiserweight. Ht. 5'9¹/₂"
Manager Self

26.03.01 Peter Haymer L PTS 4 Wembley
22.04.01 Adam Cale W CO 5 Streatham
03.06.01 Rob Hayes-Scott W RSC 4 Southwark
21.07.01 John Keeton L PTS 4 Sheffield
28.10.01 Michael Pinnock W PTS 4 Southwark
16.11.01 Darren Corbett L PTS 8 Dublin
10.02.02 Valery Odin L PTS 6 Southwark
20.04.02 Nathan King L PTS 6 Cardiff
04.05.02 Andrew Lowe L PTS 4 Bethnal Green
22.09.02 Mark Baker L PTS 6 Southwark
27.10.02 Neil Linford DREW 10 Southwark
          *(Vacant British Masters L.Heavyweight
          Title)*
08.02.03 Eric Teymour L RTD 1 Norwich
29.03.03 Andrew Lowe L PTS 10 Wembley
          *(Vacant Southern Area L. Heavyweight
          Title)*
26.09.03 Tony Booth L PTS 6 Millwall
07.11.03 Andrew Lowe L PTS 6 Sheffield
07.02.04 Bruce Scott L PTS 6 Bethnal Green
08.05.04 Courtney Fry L PTS 6 Bristol
15.12.04 Simon Francis L PTS 6 Sheffield
04.02.05 Gareth Hogg L PTS 4 Plymouth
20.02.05 Henry Smith L PTS 6 Bristol
08.04.05 Neil Hosking W RSC 2 Bristol
19.06.05 Junior MacDonald L RTD 1 Bethnal
          Green
Career: 22 contests, won 4, drew 1, lost 17.

Stuart Green

Glenrothes. *Born* Kirkcaldy, 13 December,
1984
L. Welterweight. Ht. 5'6"
Manager T. Gilmour

17.11.03 Chris Long W PTS 6 Glasgow
12.03.04 Jason Nesbitt W PTS 8 Irvine
07.06.04 Gavin Tait W PTS 6 Glasgow
11.10.04 Paul Holborn L PTS 6 Glasgow
21.02.05 Pete Buckley W PTS 6 Glasgow
11.06.05 Dave Hinds W PTS 6 Kirkcaldy
Career: 6 contests, won 5, lost 1.

Roman Greenberg

Finchley. *Born* Russia, 18 May, 1982
Heavyweight. Ht. 6'2¹/₂"
Manager Self

22.11.01 Dave Clarke W RSC 5 Paddington
25.02.02 Paul Bonson W PTS 6 Slough
25.04.02 Jakarta Nakyru W RSC 4 Las Vegas,
          Nevada, USA
28.11.02 Tony Booth W PTS 4 Finchley
05.12.02 Dave Clarke W RSC 1 Sheffield
20.12.02 Derek McCafferty W PTS 4 Bracknell
24.01.03 Piotr Jurczk W CO 1 Sheffield
04.03.03 Calvin Miller W RSC 2 Miami,
          Florida, USA
18.03.03 Gary Williams W RSC 1 Reading
15.05.03 Tracy Williams W RTD 2 Miami,
          Florida, USA
29.05.03 Troy Beets W RSC 3 Miami, Florida,
          USA
05.09.03 Luke Simpkin W RTD 4 Sheffield
18.09.03 Konstanin Prizyuk W RSC 1 Mayfair
26.11.03 Mendauga Kulikauskas W RSC 5
          Mayfair
15.04.04 Jason Gethers W RSC 6 NYC, New
          York, USA
10.09.04 Vitaly Shkraba W PTS 6 Wembley
10.12.04 Julius Francis W PTS 10 Sheffield
28.01.05 Marcus McGee W RSC 4 NYC, New
          York, USA
11.06.05 Josh Gutcher W RSC 4 Las Vegas,
          Nevada, USA
Career: 19 contests, won 19.

Ruben Groenewald

Beckton. *Born* Brakpan, South Africa, 13
October, 1977
WBF Inter-Continental S.Middleweight
Champion. Former Undefeated WBU
Middleweight Champion. Former
Undefeated British Masters S.Middleweight
Champion. Former Undefeated All-African
Middleweight Champion. Ht. 5'11"
Manager Self

27.03.96 Andries Gogome DREW 4
          Johannesburg, South Africa
21.04.96 Clifford Smith W PTS 4 Thabong,
          South Africa
03.07.96 Michael Ramabele W PTS 4
          Johannesburg, South Africa
11.08.96 Alpheus Phungula W PTS 4 Durban,
          South Africa
01.09.96 Andries Gogome L PTS 4
          Johannesburg, South Africa
22.06.97 Edward Ramathape W RSC 2
          Johannesburg, South Africa
25.11.97 David Ramantsi W RSC 1 Temba,
          South Africa
31.05.98 Roland Francis DREW 6 Durban,
          South Africa
24.06.98 Sipho Ndele W RSC 4 Johannesburg,
          South Africa
26.08.98 Boyisela Mashalele W PTS 6
          Johannesburg, South Africa
14.10.98 Mondi Mbonambi W PTS 8 Secunda,
          South Africa
03.08.99 Sipho Sibeko DREW 6 Temba, South
          Africa
23.11.99 John Tshabalala W PTS 6 Temba,
          South Africa
10.03.00 Delroy Leslie L PTS 12 Bethnal Green
          *(Vacant Interim WBF Middleweight
          Title)*
20.09.00 Elvis Adonisi W CO 10 Carnival City,
          South Africa

24.10.00 Cyprian Emeti W RSC 11 Carnival
          City, South Africa
          *(Vacant All-African L.Middleweight
          Title)*
24.02.01 Ojay Abrahams W PTS 6 Bethnal
          Green
03.04.01 Paul Bowen W PTS 6 Bethnal Green
21.07.01 Terry Morrill W RSC 4 Sheffield
20.09.01 Harry Butler W PTS 4 Blackfriars
09.10.01 Leigh Wicks W PTS 6 Cardiff
10.02.02 Wayne Asker W PTS 10 Southwark
          *(Vacant British Masters
          S.Middleweight Title)*
01.06.02 Anthony Farnell W PTS 12 Manchester
          (Vacant WBU Middleweight Title)
28.09.02 Anthony Farnell L PTS 12 Manchester
          (WBU Middleweight Title Defence)
23.10.04 Danilo Haussler L PTS 8 Berlin,
          Germany
24.04.05 Alan Gilbert W RSC 10 Leicester
          Square
          *(Vacant WBF Inter-Continental
          S.Middleweight Title)*
Career: 26 contests, won 19, drew 3, lost 4.

Ruben Groenewald　　　　　Les Clark

Jake Guntert

Abingdon. *Born* Oxford, 14 January, 1983
Middleweight. Ht. 5'10"
Manager F. Maloney

07.05.04 Lee Williamson W PTS 6 Bethnal
          Green
25.06.04 Mark Wall W CO 1 Bethnal Green
24.09.04 Neil Addis W PTS 6 Bethnal Green
26.11.04 Dean Powell W PTS 4 Bethnal Green
12.02.05 Leigh Wicks W PTS 4 Portsmouth
Career: 5 contests, won 5.

Dan Guthrie

Yeovil. *Born* Taunton, 23 July, 1982
S. Middleweight. Ht. 6'2"
Manager C. Sanigar

03.12.04 Mark Phillips W RSC 1 Bristol
04.02.05 Egbui Ikeagwo DREW 4 Plymouth
08.04.05 Nick Okoth W RSC 2 Bristol
Career: 3 contests, won 2, drew 1.

Richard Hackney

Nottingham. *Born* Derby, 10 November, 1976
Middleweight. Ht. 5'8"
Manager J. Gill

09.12.04	Danny Parkinson L PTS 6 Stockport
26.02.05	Paul McInnes L PTS 6 Burton

Career: 2 contests, lost 2.

Damon Hague (Wheatley)

Derby. *Born* Derby, 29 October, 1970
S.Middleweight. Former Undefeated WBF
S.Middleweight Champion. Former
Undefeated WBF Middleweight Champion.
Former Undefeated WBF European &
Midlands Area S.Middleweight Champion.
Ht. 6'0"
Manager Self

27.11.98	Jimmy Steel DREW 6 Nottingham
14.12.98	Dean Ashton W PTS 6 Cleethorpes
26.02.99	Adrian Houldey W RSC 5 West Bromwich
27.03.99	Mark Owens W RSC 2 Derby
15.05.99	Michael Pinnock W PTS 4 Sheffield
27.06.99	Mark Owens W RSC 5 Alfreton
15.08.99	Ian Toby W PTS 6 Derby
03.10.99	Simon Andrews W PTS 6 Chesterfield
20.11.99	Simon Andrews W RSC 4 Grantham
15.01.00	Matthew Pepper W CO 1 Doncaster
09.04.00	Matthew Pepper W RSC 3 Alfreton
21.05.00	Martin Jolley W PTS 6 Derby
19.06.00	William Webster W PTS 4 Burton
13.08.00	Martin Jolley W RTD 1 Nottingham
04.11.00	Mike Duffield W RSC 3 Derby
	(Vacant WBF European S. Middleweight Title)
25.02.01	Rob Stevenson W PTS 8 Derby
16.06.01	Dean Ashton L DIS 1 Derby
21.07.01	Leigh Wicks W PTS 4 Sheffield
15.09.01	Dean Ashton W RTD 2 Derby
	(Vacant Midlands Area S.Middleweight Title)
08.12.01	Rob Stevenson W RSC 7 Chesterfield
20.04.02	Jimmy Steel W PTS 6 Derby
03.08.02	Andrew Facey W CO 5 Derby
	(Final Elim. WBF Middleweight Title)
23.11.02	Leigh Wicks W PTS 6 Derby
28.01.03	Wayne Pinder L RSC 7 Nottingham
	(Vacant WBF Middleweight Title)
16.04.03	Wayne Pinder W RSC 2 Nottingham
	(WBF Middleweight Title Challenge)
28.11.03	Roddy Doran L PTS 10 Derby
	(Elim. WBF S.Middleweight Title)
12.03.04	Roddy Doran W PTS 10 Nottingham
	(Vacant WBF S.Middleweight Title)
24.09.04	Carl Froch L RSC 1 Nottingham
	(Vacant British S.Middleweight Title. Commonwealth S.Middleweight Title Challenge)

Career: 28 contests, won 23, drew 1, lost 4.

Andy Halder

Coventry. *Born* Coventry, 22 August, 1973
Midlands Area & WBF Inter-Continental
Middleweight Champion. Ht. 5'11"
Manager Self

13.07.02	Martin Scotland W PTS 4 Coventry
05.10.02	Andrei Ivanov W PTS 6 Coventry
25.10.02	Jon Hilton W PTS 6 Cotgrave
18.11.02	Andy Gibson L PTS 4 Glasgow
30.11.02	Conroy McIntosh W PTS 4 Coventry
24.01.03	Chris Steele W PTS 4 Sheffield
08.03.03	Conroy McIntosh W PTS 4 Coventry
24.03.03	Robert Burton W PTS 6 Barnsley
10.06.03	Patrick J. Maxwell L RSC 1 Sheffield
13.09.03	Lee Williamson W PTS 6 Coventry
08.11.03	Lee Williamson W PTS 6 Coventry
21.02.04	Michael Thomas W RSC 3 Brighton
10.07.04	Conroy McIntosh W PTS 10 Coventry
	(Vacant Midlands Area Middleweight Title)
12.09.04	Roddy Doran W PTS 10 Shrewsbury
	(Vacant WBF Inter-Continental Middleweight Title)
29.04.05	Scott Dann L CO 1 Plymouth
	(British Middleweight Title Challenge)
18.06.05	Roddy Doran W RTD 7 Coventry
	(WBF Inter-Continental Middleweight Title Defence)

Career: 16 contests, won 13, lost 3.

Eddie Haley

South Shields. *Born* South Shields, 25
August, 1965
Northern Area Middleweight Champion.
Ht. 5'9"
Manager T. Conroy

06.06.94	Brian Dunn W PTS 6 Glasgow
25.10.94	Sven Hamer L RSC 4 Southwark
30.11.94	Roy Chipperfield W RSC 3 Solihull
23.01.95	Billy Collins L RSC 4 Glasgow
01.03.95	Gary Beardsley L RSC 1 Glasgow
27.04.95	Gary Silvester W RSC 2 Hull
19.05.95	James Lowther L RSC 5 Leeds
21.05.98	Jon Penn L RSC 2 Bradford
29.10.98	Ian Toby W PTS 10 Newcastle
	(Vacant Northern Area Middleweight Title)
13.02.99	Ian Toby W RSC 6 Newcastle
	(Northern Area Middleweight Title Defence)
29.05.99	Mike Duffield W RSC 6 South Shields
23.10.99	Toks Owoh L RSC 3 Telford
15.01.00	Ryan Rhodes L RSC 5 Doncaster
17.04.00	Dave Johnson W RSC 6 Glasgow
	(Northern Area Middleweight Title Defence)
03.11.00	Steven Bendall L RSC 1 Ebbw Vale
02.10.03	Ryan Kerr L PTS 8 Sunderland
26.02.04	Ryan Kerr L RSC 5 Sunderland
	(Vacant Northern Area S.Middleweight Title)
28.10.04	Mo DREW 6 Sunderland
09.12.04	Vince Baldassara L PTS 6 Sunderland

Career: 19 contests, won 7, drew 1, lost 11.

Ceri Hall

Loughor. *Born* Swansea, 25 March, 1980
L. Welterweight. Ht. 5'10"
Manager P. Boyce

15.09.02	Martin Turner W RSC 1 Swansea

10.04.03	Silence Saheed DREW 4 Clydach
08.11.03	Peter McDonagh W PTS 4 Bridgend
28.02.04	James Gorman W PTS 6 Bridgend
19.06.04	Chris Long W PTS 4 Muswell Hill
24.09.04	Pete Buckley W PTS 6 Dublin
25.11.04	Dean Hickman L PTS 4 Birmingham
19.02.05	Robbie Murray L PTS 8 Dublin
28.04.05	Jason Nesbitt W RTD 2 Clydach

Career: 9 contests, won 6, drew 1, lost 2.

Ceri Hall   Les Clark

Matthew Hall

Manchester. *Born* Manchester, 5 July, 1984
L. Middleweight. Ht. 5'7¾"
Manager F. Warren/B. Hughes

28.09.02	Pedro Thompson W RSC 1 Manchester
14.12.02	Pedro Thompson W PTS 4 Newcastle
18.01.03	Clive Johnson W PTS 4 Preston
05.04.03	Brian Coleman W RSC 1 Manchester
08.05.03	Patrick Cito W PTS 4 Widnes
06.05.04	Craig Lynch W PTS 6 Barnsley
12.06.04	Isidro Gonzalez W RSC 3 Manchester
01.10.04	Howard Clarke W RSC 5 Manchester
12.11.04	Ojay Abrahams W RSC 1 Halifax
03.12.04	Jason Collins W PTS 6 Edinburgh
21.01.05	Leigh Wicks W PTS 4 Bridgend
11.02.05	Sylvestre Marianini W CO 1 Manchester
04.06.05	Matt Scriven W RSC 2 Manchester

Career: 13 contests, won 13.

(Michael) Oscar Hall

Darlington. *Born* Darlington, 8 November, 1974
L. Welterweight. Northern Area
Welterweight Champion. Ht. 5'9"
Manager Self

09.05.98	Trevor Smith W PTS 4 Sheffield
27.02.99	Lee Molyneux W PTS 4 Oldham
15.05.99	Chris Price W PTS 4 Sheffield
29.05.99	Brian Gifford W RSC 1 Halifax
04.06.99	Arv Mittoo W PTS 6 Hull
27.09.99	Dave Gibson W PTS 6 Leeds
11.12.99	Brian Coleman W PTS 6 Liverpool
18.02.00	Jason Collins DREW 6 West Bromwich
02.03.00	Ernie Smith W PTS 6 Birkenhead
09.06.00	Dave Gibson W PTS 6 Hull
19.06.00	Paul Denton W PTS 4 Burton
13.08.00	Lee Molyneux W PTS 6 Nottingham

04.11.00	Ram Singh W PTS 6 Derby
24.11.00	Dean Nicholas W PTS 6 Darlington
11.12.00	Ram Singh W CO 4 Cleethorpes
16.06.01	David Kirk W PTS 6 Derby
18.08.01	David White W PTS 6 Dewsbury
22.09.01	Dean Nicholas W DIS 9 Newcastle
	(Vacant Northern Area Welterweight Title)
17.11.01	Paul Lomax W PTS 4 Dewsbury
15.03.02	Stuart Rimmer W RSC 4 Spennymoor
19.04.02	Peter Dunn W PTS 6 Darlington
10.05.02	Arv Mittoo W PTS 4 Bethnal Green
28.01.03	Alan Bosworth W PTS 10 Nottingham
	(Elim. British L.Welterweight Title)
11.07.03	William Webster W PTS 8 Darlington
10.10.03	Gary Reid L RSC 2 Darlington
11.12.03	Francis Barrett L PTS 10 Bethnal Green
05.03.04	Karl Taylor W PTS 6 Darlington
16.04.04	Junior Witter L RSC 3 Bradford
04.06.04	Lee Williamson W PTS 6 Hull
03.07.04	Peter Dunn W PTS 6 Blackpool
21.04.05	Young Muttley L PTS 10 Dudley
	(English & WBF Inter-Continental L.Welterweight Title Challenges)
03.06.05	Peter Dunn W PTS 6 Hull

Career: 32 contests, won 27, drew 1, lost 4.

Lea Handley

Peterborough. *Born* Peterborough, 29 June 1985
L. Welterweight. Ht. 5'9"
Manager I. Pauly

17.09.04	Matthew Marshall L RSC 6 Plymouth
16.10.04	Freddie Luke L PTS 4 Dagenham
24.10.04	John Fewkes L PTS 6 Sheffield
09.11.04	Tye Williams W RSC 1 Leeds
26.11.04	Nathan Ward L CO 2 Bethnal Green
21.01.05	Barrie Jones L PTS 4 Bridgend
21.02.05	Gary Coombes W PTS 6 Peterborough
04.03.05	Kell Brook L PTS 6 Rotherham

Career: 8 contests, won 2, lost 6.

Lea Handley   Les Clark

Anthony Hanna

Birmingham. *Born* Birmingham, 22 September, 1974
Lightweight. Former Undefeated Midlands Area Flyweight Champion. Ht. 5'6"
Manager Self

19.11.92	Nick Tooley L PTS 6 Evesham
10.12.92	Daren Fifield L RSC 6 Bethnal Green
11.05.93	Tiger Singh W PTS 6 Norwich
24.05.93	Lyndon Kershaw L PTS 6 Bradford
16.09.93	Chris Lyons W PTS 6 Southwark
06.10.93	Tiger Singh W PTS 6 Solihull
03.11.93	Mickey Cantwell L PTS 8 Bristol
25.01.94	Marty Chestnut W PTS 4 Picaddilly
10.02.94	Allan Mooney W RTD 1 Glasgow
13.04.94	Allan Mooney L PTS 6 Glasgow
22.04.94	Jesper Jensen L PTS 6 Aalborg, Denmark
03.08.94	Paul Ingle L PTS 6 Bristol
01.10.94	Mark Hughes L PTS 4 Cardiff
30.11.94	Shaun Norman W PTS 10 Solihull
	(Vacant Midlands Area Flyweight Title)
24.02.95	Darren Greaves W RSC 5 Weston super Mare
06.03.95	Mark Hughes L PTS 6 Mayfair
27.04.95	Mickey Cantwell L PTS 6 Bethnal Green
05.05.95	Mark Cokely W RSC 4 Swansea
04.06.95	Mark Reynolds L PTS 10 Bethnal Green
	(Elim. British Flyweight Title)
02.07.95	Mickey Cantwell L PTS 6 Dublin
02.11.95	Shaun Norman DREW 10 Mayfair
	(Midlands Area Flyweight Title Defence)
31.01.96	Marty Chestnut DREW 6 Stoke
20.03.96	Harry Woods L PTS 6 Cardiff
22.04.96	Neil Parry W PTS 6 Manchester
14.05.96	Dharmendra Singh Yadav L PTS 4 Dagenham
08.10.96	Marty Chestnut W PTS 6 Battersea
11.12.96	Mark Reynolds DREW 8 Southwark
28.01.97	Colin Moffett L PTS 4 Belfast
28.02.97	Paul Weir L PTS 8 Kilmarnock
14.03.97	Jesper Jensen L PTS 6 Odense, Denmark
30.04.97	Clinton Beeby DREW 6 Acton
10.05.97	Jason Booth L PTS 6 Nottingham
02.06.97	Keith Knox L PTS 6 Glasgow
14.10.97	Louis Veitch L PTS 6 Kilmarnock
27.10.97	Russell Laing W PTS 4 Musselburgh
13.11.97	Noel Wilders L PTS 6 Bradford
24.11.97	Shaun Anderson L PTS 8 Glasgow
20.12.97	Damaen Kelly L PTS 4 Belfast
31.01.98	Jason Booth L PTS 6 Edmonton
23.02.98	David Coldwell W PTS 6 Salford
19.03.98	Andy Roberts L PTS 6 Doncaster
18.05.98	Chris Emanuele W RSC 3 Cleethorpes
11.09.98	Nicky Booth DREW 6 Cleethorpes
18.09.98	Colin Moffett DREW 4 Belfast
29.10.98	Nick Tooley W RTD 6 Bayswater
25.11.98	Nicky Booth W PTS 6 Clydach
21.01.99	Ola Dali W PTS 6 Piccadilly
13.03.99	Damaen Kelly L PTS 12 Manchester
	(Vacant British Flyweight Title. Commonwealth Flyweight Title Challenge)
24.04.99	Noel Wilders L PTS 6 Peterborough
07.06.99	Alston Buchanan W RSC 3 Glasgow
29.06.99	Tommy Waite L PTS 4 Bethnal Green
16.10.99	Stevie Quinn W PTS 4 Belfast
22.11.99	Frankie DeMilo L PTS 6 Piccadilly
04.12.99	Ady Lewis L PTS 6 Manchester
19.02.00	Ian Napa L PTS 6 Dagenham
13.03.00	Mzukisi Sikali L PTS 6 Bethnal Green
27.05.00	Nicky Cook L PTS 6 Mayfair
25.07.00	David Lowry L PTS 4 Southwark
19.08.00	Marc Callaghan L PTS 4 Brentwood
29.09.00	Rocky Dean L PTS 4 Bethnal Green

07.10.00	Oleg Kiryukhin L PTS 6 Doncaster
14.10.00	Danny Costello DREW 4 Wembley
31.10.00	Dmitri Kirilov L PTS 6 Hammersmith
10.02.01	Tony Mulholland L PTS 4 Widnes
19.02.01	Alex Moon L PTS 6 Glasgow
03.03.01	Marc Callaghan L PTS 6 Wembley
24.04.01	Silence Mabuza L PTS 6 Liverpool
06.05.01	Michael Hunter L PTS 4 Hartlepool
26.05.01	Mickey Bowden L PTS 4 Bethnal Green
04.06.01	Michael Hunter L PTS 4 Hartlepool
01.11.01	Nigel Senior L PTS 6 Hull
24.11.01	Martin Power L PTS 4 Bethnal Green
08.12.01	Faprakob Rakkiatgym L PTS 8 Dagenham
24.03.02	Mickey Coveney L PTS 4 Streatham
23.06.02	Johannes Maisa L PTS 4 Southwark
30.10.02	Mickey Bowden L PTS 4 Leicester Square
08.11.02	Sean Green L PTS 6 Doncaster
17.11.02	Shinny Bayaar L PTS 6 Shaw
14.12.02	Michael Hunter L PTS 8 Newcastle
15.02.03	Steve Gethin L PTS 6 Wolverhampton
24.02.03	Jackson Williams W PTS 6 Birmingham
08.06.03	Darryn Walton L PTS 6 Shaw
25.09.03	Rob Jeffries L PTS 6 Bethnal Green
01.11.03	Andrew Ferrans L PTS 4 Glasgow
14.11.03	Mickey Bowden L PTS 4 Bethnal Green
21.11.03	Buster Dennis L PTS 6 Millwall
29.11.03	Willie Limond L PTS 4 Renfrew
09.04.04	Rendall Munroe L PTS 6 Rugby
16.04.04	Billy Corcoran L PTS 4 Bradford
24.04.04	Lee Beavis L PTS 4 Reading
12.05.04	Chris McDonagh L PTS 4 Reading
02.06.04	John Murray L PTS 4 Nottingham
17.06.04	Femi Fehintola L PTS 6 Sheffield
03.07.04	Jeff Thomas L PTS 6 Blackpool

Career: 94 contests, won 19, drew 7, lost 68.

James Hare

Robertown. *Born* Dewsbury, 16 July, 1976
Welterweight. Former WBF Welterweight Champion. Former Undefeated Commonwealth & European Union Welterweight Champion. Ht. 5'6"
Manager T. Gilmour/C. Aston

20.01.96	Brian Coleman W PTS 6 Mansfield
25.06.96	Mike Watson W PTS 4 Mansfield
13.07.96	Dennis Griffin W RSC 4 Bethnal Green
14.09.96	Paul Salmon W RSC 4 Sheffield
14.12.96	Jon Harrison W PTS 4 Sheffield
25.02.97	Kid McAuley W PTS 4 Sheffield
12.04.97	Andy Peach W RSC 1 Sheffield
13.12.97	Costas Katsantonis W RSC 3 Sheffield
09.05.98	Peter Nightingale W PTS 4 Sheffield
18.07.98	Karl Taylor W PTS 4 Sheffield
28.11.98	Peter Nightingale W PTS 6 Sheffield
15.05.99	Lee Williamson W RSC 2 Sheffield
23.10.99	Mark Winters DREW 6 Telford
23.10.00	Dean Nicholas W RSC 1 Glasgow
23.01.01	Mark Ramsey W PTS 6 Crawley
26.02.01	Paul Denton W PTS 6 Nottingham
08.05.01	Jessy Moreaux W RSC 3 Barnsley
26.05.01	John Humphrey W RSC 7 Bethnal Green
	(Elim. British Welterweight Title)
08.10.01	John Ameline W PTS 8 Barnsley
26.11.01	Paul Denton W RTD 4 Manchester
28.01.02	Monney Seka W PTS 10 Barnsley
	(Vacant European Union Welterweight Title)

27.04.02	Julian Holland W RSC 6 Huddersfield	
	(Commonwealth Welterweight Title	
	Challenge)	
15.06.02	Abdel Mehidi W PTS 8 Leeds	
05.10.02	Farai Musiiwa W RSC 8 Huddersfield	
	(Commonwealth Welterweight Title	
	Defence)	
30.11.02	Earl Foskin W RSC 1 Liverpool	
	(Commonwealth Welterweight Title	
	Defence)	
22.02.03	Frans Hantindi W RSC 1 Huddersfield	
	(Commonwealth Welterweight Title	
	Defence)	
21.06.03	Roman Dzuman W PTS 12 Manchester	
	(Vacant WBF Welterweight Title)	
06.09.03	Jan Bergman W RSC 2 Huddersfield	
	(WBF Welterweight Title Defence)	
18.10.03	Jozsef Matolcsi W RSC 10 Manchester	
	(WBF Welterweight Title Defence)	
04.12.03	Cosme Rivera L RSC 10 Huddersfield	
	(WBF Welterweight Title Defence)	
01.05.04	Jason Williams W RSC 2 Bridgend	
27.05.04	Moise Cherni W RSC 5 Huddersfield	
12.11.04	David Barnes L RSC 6 Halifax	
	(British Welterweight Title Challenge)	

Career: 33 contests, won 30, drew 1, lost 2.

Audley Harrison

Wembley. *Born* Park Royal, 26 October, 1971

Heavyweight. Former Undefeated WBF Heavyweight Champion. Ht. 6'4¾"

Manager Self

19.05.01	Michael Middleton W RSC 1 Wembley	
22.09.01	Derek McCafferty W PTS 6 Newcastle	
20.10.01	Piotr Jurczyk W RSC 2 Glasgow	
20.04.02	Julius Long W CO 2 Wembley	
21.05.02	Mark Krence W PTS 6 Custom House	
10.07.02	Dominic Negus W PTS 6 Wembley	
05.10.02	Wade Lewis W RSC 2 Liverpool	
23.11.02	Shawn Robinson W RSC 1 Atlantic City, New Jersey, USA	
08.02.03	Rob Calloway W RSC 5 Brentford	
29.03.03	Ratko Draskovic W PTS 8 Wembley	
31.05.03	Matthew Ellis W RSC 2 Bethnal Green	
09.09.03	Quinn Navarre W RSC 3 Miami, Florida, USA	
03.10.03	Lisandro Diaz W RSC 4 Las Vegas, Nevada, USA	
12.12.03	Brian Nix W RSC 3 Laughlin, Nevada, USA	
20.03.04	Richel Hersisia W CO 4 Wembley	
	(WBF Heavyweight Title Challenge)	
08.05.04	Julius Francis W PTS 12 Bristol	
	(WBF Heavyweight Title Defence)	
19.06.04	Tomasz Bonin W RSC 9 Muswell Hill	
	(WBF Heavyweight Title Defence)	
09.06.05	Robert Davis W RSC 7 Temecula, California, USA	

Career: 18 contests, won 18.

Jon Harrison

Plymouth. *Born* Scunthorpe, 18 March, 1977

L.Middleweight. Ht. 5'11½"

Manager Self

13.01.96	Mark Haslam L PTS 6 Manchester	
13.02.96	Paul Samuels L CO 1 Cardiff	
16.05.96	Dave Fallon W RSC 4 Dunstable	
03.07.96	Allan Gray L PTS 6 Wembley	
01.10.96	Cam Raeside L PTS 6 Birmingham	

07.11.96	Nicky Bardle L PTS 6 Battersea	
14.12.96	James Hare L PTS 4 Sheffield	
19.04.97	Jason Williams W PTS 6 Plymouth	
11.07.97	Pat Larner L PTS 6 Brighton	
07.10.97	Paul Salmon L PTS 6 Plymouth	
23.02.98	Alan Gilbert L PTS 6 Windsor	
24.03.98	Brian Coleman DREW 6 Wolverhampton	
14.07.98	Jason Williams L RTD 2 Reading	
12.05.01	Ernie Smith W PTS 4 Plymouth	
15.09.01	Darren Williams L PTS 6 Swansea	
02.04.04	Nathan Wyatt W PTS 6 Plymouth	
27.05.04	Ady Clegg W PTS 4 Huddersfield	
17.09.04	Geraint Harvey W PTS 6 Plymouth	
13.12.04	Simon Sherrington L RSC 5 Birmingham	
04.02.05	Joe Mitchell W PTS 6 Plymouth	
29.04.05	Neil Jarmolinski W PTS 6 Plymouth	

Career: 21 contests, won 8, drew 1, lost 12.

Jon Harrison Les Clark

Scott Harrison

Glasgow. *Born* Bellshill, 19 August, 1977

WBO Featherweight Champion. Former Undefeated British, Commonwealth & IBO Inter-Continental Featherweight Champion. Ht. 5'7"

Manager F. Maloney

07.10.96	Eddie Sica W RSC 2 Lewisham	
11.01.97	Pete Buckley W PTS 4 Bethnal Green	
25.03.97	David Morris W PTS 4 Lewisham	
04.10.97	Miguel Matthews L RSC 4 Muswell Hill	
16.12.97	Stephane Fernandez DREW 6 Grand Synthe, France	
31.01.98	Pete Buckley W PTS 4 Edmonton	
09.06.98	Carl Allen W RSC 6 Hull	
17.10.98	Rakhim Mingaleev W PTS 8 Manchester	
06.03.99	John Matthews W RSC 4 Southwark	
10.07.99	Smith Odoom W PTS 12 Southwark	
	(IBO Inter-Continental Featherweight Title Challenge)	
24.01.00	Patrick Mullings W PTS 12 Glasgow	
	(Commonwealth Featherweight Title Challenge)	
29.04.00	Tracy Harris Patterson W PTS 10 NYC, New York, USA	
15.07.00	Tom Johnson W PTS 12 Millwall	

	(IBO Inter-Continental Featherweight Title Defence)	
11.11.00	Eric Odumasi W RSC 12 Belfast	
	(Commonwealth Featherweight Title Defence)	
24.03.01	Richie Wenton W RSC 4 Sheffield	
	(Vacant British Featherweight Title. Commonwealth Featherweight Title Defence)	
15.09.01	Gary Thornhill W RSC 5 Manchester	
	(British & Commonwealth Featherweight Title Defences)	
17.11.01	Steve Robinson W RSC 3 Glasgow	
	(British & Commonwealth Featherweight Title Defences)	
11.03.02	Tony Wehbee W RSC 3 Glasgow	
	(Commonwealth Featherweight Title Defence)	
08.06.02	Victor Santiago W RSC 6 Renfrew	
	(Vacant WBO Interim Featherweight Title)	
19.10.02	Julio Pablo Chacon W PTS 12 Renfrew	
	(WBO Featherweight Title Challenge)	
22.03.03	Wayne McCullough W PTS 12 Renfrew	
	(WBO Featherweight Title Defence)	
12.07.03	Manuel Medina L PTS 12 Renfrew	
	(WBO Featherweight Title Defence)	
29.11.03	Manuel Medina W RSC 11 Renfrew	
	(WBO Featherweight Title Challenge)	
06.03.04	Walter Estrada W RSC 5 Renfrew	
	(WBO Featherweight Title Defence)	
19.06.04	William Abelyan W RSC 3 Renfrew	
	(WBO Featherweight Title Defence)	
29.10.04	Samuel Kebede W RSC 1 Renfrew	
	(WBO Featherweight Title Defence)	
28.01.05	Victor Polo DREW 12 Renfrew	
	(WBO Featherweight Title Defence)	
03.06.05	Michael Brodie W CO 4 Manchester	
	(WBO Featherweight Title Defence)	

Career: 28 contests, won 24, drew 2, lost 2.

Geraint Harvey

Mountain Ash. *Born* Pontypridd, 1 September, 1979

Welterweight. Ht. 5'9"

Manager D. Davies

22.09.03	Steve Scott W PTS 6 Cleethorpes	
29.10.03	Darren Covill W PTS 4 Leicester Square	
21.12.03	Danny Moir L PTS 6 Bolton	
14.02.04	Arek Malek L PTS 4 Nottingham	
28.02.04	Jamie Coyle L PTS 4 Bridgend	
15.04.04	Terry Adams L PTS 6 Dudley	
24.04.04	Chas Symonds L PTS 4 Reading	
08.07.04	Terry Adams L RSC 6 Birmingham	
17.09.04	Jon Harrison L PTS 6 Plymouth	
24.09.04	Gary Woolcombe L PTS 4 Bethnal Green	
16.10.04	Danny Goode L PTS 4 Dagenham	
23.10.04	Peter Dunn W PTS 6 Wakefield	
21.11.04	Robert-Lloyd Taylor L PTS 4 Bracknell	
03.12.04	Colin McNeil L PTS 6 Edinburgh	
28.01.05	Chris Black L PTS 4 Renfrew	
17.02.05	Young Muttley L PTS 6 Dudley	
05.03.05	Duncan Cottier L PTS 4 Dagenham	
29.04.05	Courtney Thomas L PTS 6 Plymouth	
15.05.05	Stuart Brookes L PTS 6 Sheffield	
01.06.05	Mark Franks L PTS 6 Leeds	
16.06.05	George Hillyard L RSC 1 Dagenham	

Career: 21 contests. won 3, lost 18.

Lee Haskins

Bristol. *Born* Bristol, 29 November, 1983
English Flyweight Champion. Ht. 5'5"
Manager C. Sanigar

06.03.03	Ankar Miah W RSC 1 Bristol	
13.06.03	Chris Edwards W PTS 6 Bristol	
09.10.03	Neil Read W PTS 4 Bristol	
05.12.03	Jason Thomas W PTS 6 Bristol	
13.02.04	Marty Kayes W PTS 6 Bristol	
08.05.04	Colin Moffett W RSC 2 Bristol	
03.07.04	Sergei Tasimov W RSC 5 Bristol	
01.10.04	Junior Anderson W CO 3 Bristol	
03.12.04	Delroy Spencer W RTD 3 Bristol	
	(Vacant English Flyweight Title)	
18.02.05	Hugo Cardinale W CO 1 Torrevieja, Spain	
08.04.05	Moses Kinyua W PTS 10 Bristol	
29.04.05	Andrzej Ziora W RSC 1 Plymouth	

Career: 12 contests, won 12.

Matthew Hatton   Paul Speak

Matthew Hatton

Manchester. *Born* Stockport, 15 May, 1981
Welterweight. Former Undefeated Central
Area L.Middleweight Champion. Former
Undefeated Central Area Welterweight
Champion. Ht. 5'8½"
Manager Self

23.09.00	David White W PTS 4 Bethnal Green	
25.11.00	David White W PTS 4 Manchester	
11.12.00	Danny Connelly W PTS 4 Widnes	
15.01.01	Keith Jones W PTS 4 Manchester	
10.02.01	Karl Taylor W PTS 4 Widnes	
17.03.01	Assen Vassilev W RSC 5 Manchester	
09.06.01	Brian Coleman W RTD 2 Bethnal Green	
21.07.01	Ram Singh W RSC 2 Sheffield	
15.09.01	Marcus Portman W RSC 3 Manchester	
15.12.01	Dafydd Carlin W PTS 6 Wembley	
09.02.02	Paul Denton W PTS 6 Manchester	
04.05.02	Karl Taylor W RSC 3 Bethnal Green	
20.07.02	Karl Taylor W RTD 2 Bethnal Green	
28.09.02	David Kirk L PTS 6 Manchester	

14.12.02	Paul Denton W PTS 6 Newcastle	
15.02.03	David Keir L RSC 4 Wembley	
08.05.03	Jay Mahoney W PTS 6 Widnes	
17.07.03	Jay Mahoney W RSC 1 Dagenham	
27.09.03	Taz Jones W PTS 6 Manchester	
13.12.03	Franny Jones DREW 6 Manchester	
26.02.04	Peter Dunn W PTS 6 Widnes	
06.05.04	Robert Burton W PTS 10 Barnsley	
	(Central Area Welterweight Title Challenge)	
12.06.04	Matt Scriven W RSC 4 Manchester	
01.10.04	Lee Armstrong W PTS 8 Manchester	
12.11.04	Robert Burton W PTS 10 Halifax	
	(Central Area L.Middleweight Title Challenge)	
11.03.05	Franny Jones W RTD 6 Doncaster	
03.06.05	Adnan Hadoui W PTS 8 Manchester	

Career: 27 contests, won 24, drew 1, lost 2.

Ricky Hatton

Manchester. *Born* Stockport, 6 October, 1978
IBF & WBU L.Welterweight Champion.
Former Undefeated British, WBO Inter-
Continental & Central Area L.Welterweight
Champion. Ht. 5'7½"
Manager Self

11.09.97	Kid McAuley W RTD 1 Widnes	
19.12.97	Robert Alvarez W PTS 4 NYC, New York, USA	
17.01.98	David Thompson W RSC 1 Bristol	
27.03.98	Paul Salmon W RSC 1 Telford	
18.04.98	Karl Taylor W RSC 1 Manchester	
30.05.98	Mark Ramsey W PTS 6 Bristol	
18.07.98	Anthony Campbell W PTS 6 Sheffield	
19.09.98	Pascal Montulet W CO 2 Oberhausen, Germany	

Ricky Hatton   Les Clark

31.10.98	Kevin Carter W RSC 1 Atlantic City, New Jersey, USA
19.12.98	Paul Denton W RSC 6 Liverpool
27.02.99	Tommy Peacock W RSC 2 Oldham
	(Vacant Central Area L. Welterweight Title)
03.04.99	Brian Coleman W CO 2 Kensington
29.05.99	Dillon Carew W RSC 5 Halifax
	(Vacant WBO Inter-Continental L. Welterweight Title)
17.07.99	Mark Ramsey W PTS 6 Doncaster
09.10.99	Bernard Paul W RTD 4 Manchester
	(WBO Inter-Continental L. Welterweight Title Defence)
11.12.99	Mark Winters W RSC 4 Liverpool
	(WBO Inter-Continental L. Welterweight Title Defence)
29.01.00	Leoncio Garces W RSC 3 Manchester
25.03.00	Pedro Teran W RSC 4 Liverpool
	(WBO Inter-Continental L. Welterweight Title Defence)
16.05.00	Ambioris Figuero W RSC 4 Warrington
	(WBO Inter-Continental L. Welterweight Title Defence)
10.06.00	Gilbert Quiros W CO 2 Detroit, Michigan, USA
	(WBO Inter-Continental L. Welterweight Title Defence)
23.09.00	Giuseppe Lauri W RSC 5 Bethnal Green
	(WBO Inter-Continental L.Welterweight Title Defence. WBA Inter-Continental L.Welterweight Title Challenge)
21.10.00	Jonathan Thaxton W PTS 12 Wembley
	(Vacant British L.Welterweight Title)
26.03.01	Tony Pep W CO 4 Wembley
	(Vacant WBU L. Welterweight Title)
07.07.01	Jason Rowland W CO 4 Manchester
	(WBU L.Welterweight Title Defence)
15.09.01	John Bailey W RSC 5 Manchester
	(WBU L.Welterweight Title Defence)
27.10.01	Fred Pendleton W CO 2 Manchester
	(WBU L.Welterweight Title Defence)
15.12.01	Justin Rowsell W RSC 2 Wembley
	(WBU L.Welterweight Title Defence)
09.02.02	Mikhail Krivolapov W RSC 9 Manchester
	(WBU L. Welterweight Title Defence)
01.06.02	Eamonn Magee W PTS 12 Manchester
	(WBU L.Welterweight Title Defence)
28.09.02	Stephen Smith W DIS 2 Manchester
	(WBU L.Welterweight Title Defence)
14.12.02	Joe Hutchinson W CO 4 Newcastle
	(WBU L. Welterweight Title Defence)
05.04.03	Vince Phillips W PTS 12 Manchester
	(WBU L.Welterweight Title Defence)
27.09.03	Aldi Rios W RTD 9 Manchester
	(WBU L.Welterweight Title Defence)
13.12.03	Ben Tackie W PTS 12 Manchester
	(WBU L.Welterweight Title Defence)
03.04.04	Dennis Holbaek Pedersen W RSC 6 Manchester
	(WBU L.Welterweight Title Defence)
12.06.04	Wilfredo Carlos Vilches W PTS 12 Manchester
	(WBU L.Welterweight Title Defence)
01.10.04	Michael Stewart W RSC 5 Manchester
	(WBU L.Welterweight Title Defence. Final Elim. IBF L.Welterweight Title)
11.12.04	Ray Oliveira W CO 10 Canning Town
	(WBU L.Welterweight Title Defence)
04.06.05	Kostya Tszyu W RSC 11 Manchester
	(IBF L.Welterweight Title Challenge)

Career: 39 contests, won 39.

Stephen Haughian

Lurgan Co. Armagh. *Born* Craigavon, 20 November, 1984
L.Welterweight. Ht. 5'10½"
Manager J. Breen/M. Callaghan/F. Warren

18.03.05	James Gorman W PTS 4 Belfast

Career: 1 contest, won 1.

David Haye

Bermondsey. *Born* London, 13 October, 1980
Cruiserweight. Former Undefeated English Cruiserweight Champion. Ht. 6'3"
Manager A. Booth

08.12.02	Tony Booth W RTD 2 Bethnal Green
24.01.03	Saber Zairi W RSC 4 Sheffield
04.03.03	Roger Bowden W RSC 2 Miami, Florida, USA
18.03.03	Phill Day W RSC 2 Reading
15.07.03	Vance Wynn W RSC 1 Los Angeles, California, USA
01.08.03	Greg Scott-Briggs W CO 1 Bethnal Green
26.09.03	Lolenga Mock W RSC 4 Reading
14.11.03	Tony Dowling W RSC 1 Bethnal Green
	(Vacant English Cruiserweight Title)
20.03.04	Hastings Rasani W RSC 1 Wembley
12.05.04	Arthur Williams W RSC 3 Reading
10.09.04	Carl Thompson L RSC 5 Wembley
	(IBO Cruiserweight Title Challenge)
10.12.04	Valery Semishkur W RSC 1 Sheffield
21.01.05	Garry Delaney W RTD 3 Brentford
04.03.05	Glen Kelly W CO 2 Rotherham

Career: 14 contests, won 13, lost 1.

Peter Haymer   Les Clark

Peter Haymer

Enfield. *Born* London, 10 July, 1978
English L.Heavyweight. Champion.
Ht. 6'1¼"
Manager Self

25.11.00	Adam Cale W RSC 1 Manchester
27.01.01	Darren Ashton W PTS 4 Bethnal Green
10.03.01	Daniel Ivanov W CO 2 Bethnal Green
26.03.01	Radcliffe Green W PTS 4 Wembley
05.05.01	Terry Morrill W PTS 4 Edmonton
22.09.01	Tony Booth W PTS 4 Bethnal Green
24.11.01	Nathan King L PTS 4 Bethnal Green
12.02.02	Nathan King L PTS 4 Bethnal Green
09.05.02	Mark Snipe W PTS 4 Leicester Square
15.06.02	Paul Bonson W PTS 4 Tottenham
30.10.02	Jimmy Steel W PTS 4 Leicester Square
18.03.03	Mark Brookes W PTS 6 Reading
18.09.03	Ovill McKenzie W PTS 4 Mayfair
10.12.03	Mark Brookes DREW 6 Sheffield
12.11.04	Steven Spartacus W PTS 10 Wembley
	(English L.Heavyweight Title Challenge)
10.12.04	Mark Brookes W RSC 10 Sheffield
	(English L.Heavyweight Title Defence)
24.04.05	Ryan Walls W PTS 6 Leicester Square
19.06.05	Tony Oakey W PTS 10 Bethnal Green
	(English L.Heavyweight Title Defence)

Career: 18 contests, won 15, drew 1, lost 2.

Scott Haywood

Derby. *Born* Derby, 5 June, 1981
L. Welterweight. Ht. 6'0"
Manager M. Shinfield

06.10.03	Pete Buckley W PTS 6 Barnsley
23.11.03	Arv Mittoo W PTS 6 Rotherham
16.02.04	Pete Buckley W PTS 6 Scunthorpe
26.04.04	Chris Brophy W RSC 5 Cleethorpes
27.09.04	Judex Meemea W PTS 6 Cleethorpes
16.12.04	Tony Montana L PTS 6 Cleethorpes
26.02.05	Jimmy Beech W PTS 6 Burton
24.04.05	Chris Long W PTS 6 Derby

Career: 8 contests, won 7, lost 1.

Ciaran Healy

Belfast. *Born* Belfast, 25 December, 1974
Middleweight. Ht. 5'11"
Manager Self

05.04.03	Tomas da Silva W PTS 4 Belfast
18.09.03	Patrick Cito W PTS 4 Mayfair
04.10.03	Joel Ani W PTS 4 Belfast
22.11.03	Neil Addis W RSC 1 Belfast
26.06.04	Jason McKay L PTS 6 Belfast
25.04.05	Vince Baldassara L RSC 4 Glasgow
17.06.05	Chris Black DREW 4 Glasgow

Career: 7 contests, won 4, drew 1, lost 2.

Jamie Hearn   Les Clark

Jamie Hearn

Colnbrook. *Born* Taplow, 4 June, 1982
S.Middleweight. Ht. 5'11½"
Manager J. Evans

27.09.02	Jimmy Steel W PTS 4 Bracknell
03.12.02	Mark Phillips W PTS 4 Bethnal Green
20.12.02	Danny Norton W PTS 4 Bracknell
18.03.03	Darren Stubbs L RSC 3 Reading
13.06.03	Liam Lathbury W RSC 4 Bristol
04.10.03	Jason McKay L PTS 8 Belfast
14.11.03	Harry Butler W PTS 4 Bethnal Green
30.03.04	Varuzhan Davtyan L PTS 4 Southampton
12.05.04	Hastings Rasani W RSC 4 Reading
10.09.04	Lee Woodruff W RSC 1 Wembley
21.11.04	Tom Cannon W PTS 6 Bracknell
21.01.05	Simeon Cover W PTS 4 Brentford
23.03.05	Simeon Cover L CO 7 Leicester Square
	(Vacant British Masters S.Middleweight Title)

Career: 13 contests, won 9, lost 4.

Paul Henry

Bristol. *Born* Bristol, 23 February, 1969
Middleweight. Ht. 5'9"
Manager C. Sanigar

11.04.98	Lee Simpkin W PTS 4 Southwark
21.04.98	Alan Gilbert W PTS 4 Edmonton
18.10.99	Danny Thornton L PTS 4 Bradford
03.12.04	Nick Okoth L RSC 5 Bristol

Career: 4 contests, won 2, lost 2.

(Jack) Jak Hibbert

Sheffield. *Born* Sheffield, 21 September, 1985
L. Middleweight. Ht. 6'0"
Manager D. Hobson

12.12.04	Chris Black L RSC 2 Glasgow
04.03.05	Neil Jarmolinski W PTS 6 Rotherham
17.06.05	Vince Baldassara L RSC 1 Glasgow

Career: 3 contests, won 1, lost 2.

Jak Hibbert   Les Clark

Dean Hickman

West Bromwich. *Born* West Bromwich, 24 November, 1979
Midlands Area L.Welterweight Champion. Ht. 5'7"
Manager Self

17.02.02	Wayne Wheeler DREW 6 Wolverhampton
13.04.02	Wayne Wheeler W PTS 6 Wolverhampton
13.07.02	Dai Bando W RSC 1 Wolverhampton
02.11.02	Darren Goode W RSC 2 Wolverhampton
15.02.03	Gareth Wiltshaw W PTS 6 Wolverhampton
21.03.03	David Vaughan W PTS 6 West Bromwich
30.06.03	Dave Hinds W RSC 4 Shrewsbury
17.07.03	Lee McAllister W PTS 6 Walsall
30.10.03	John-Paul Ryan W PTS 6 Dudley
15.04.04	Tony Montana W PTS 6 Dudley
04.06.04	Adnan Amar W RSC 8 Dudley
	(Vacant Midlands Area L.Welterweight Title)
25.11.04	Ceri Hall W PTS 4 Birmingham
17.02.05	Gary Reid W PTS 10 Dudley
	(Midlands Area L.Welterweight Title Defence)
11.03.05	Nigel Wright L CO 7 Doncaster
	(Vacant English L.Welterweight Title)

Career: 14 contests, won 12, drew 1, lost 1.

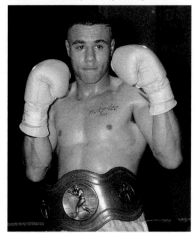

Dean Hickman   Les Clark

Justin Hicks

Yeovil. *Born* Yeovil, 15 July, 1976
L. Welterweight. Ht. 6'0"
Manager C. Sanigar

05.12.03	Kristian Laight W PTS 6 Bristol
13.02.04	Chris Long L RSC 4 Bristol
15.04.04	Gary Coombes DREW 6 Dudley
03.07.04	Gavin Tait L RSC 5 Bristol

Career: 4 contests, won 1, drew 1, lost 2.

Dwayne Hill

Sheffield. *Born* Sheffield, 31 January, 1986
Lightweight. Ht. 5'8"
Manager G. Rhodes

08.05.05	Anthony Christopher W PTS 6 Sheffield

Career: 1 contest, won 1.

George Hillyard

Canning Town. *Born* Forest Gate, 19 November, 1984
L.Middleweight. Ht. 5'9¼"
Manager R. Callaghan

16.06.05	Geraint Harvey W RSC 1 Dagenham

Career: 1 contest, won 1.

Dave Hinds

Birmingham. *Born* Leicester, 5 January, 1971
L. Welterweight. Ht. 5'5"
Manager Self

19.09.95	Martin Evans W RSC 5 Plymouth
08.11.95	Wayne Pardoe L CO 4 Walsall
04.04.96	Paul Salmon L RTD 5 Plymouth
06.10.97	Eddie Sica L RSC 1 Piccadilly
25.11.97	Graham McGrath W PTS 6 Wolverhampton
06.12.97	Adam Spelling W RSC 1 Wembley
27.01.98	Malcolm Thomas L PTS 6 Piccadilly
06.03.98	Jon Dodsworth W RSC 1 Hull
12.03.98	Jamie McKeever L PTS 4 Liverpool
20.03.98	John O'Johnson L PTS 6 Ilkeston
23.04.98	Roy Rutherford L RSC 5 Edgbaston
26.05.98	David Kehoe L RSC 5 Mayfair
07.10.98	Steve Saville L PTS 6 Stoke
26.10.98	Eddie Nevins L PTS 6 Manchester
26.11.98	Steve Saville L PTS 6 Edgbaston
07.12.98	Danny Bell L PTS 6 Nottingham
13.02.99	Michael Gomez L PTS 6 Newcastle
23.04.99	Mark Ramsey L PTS 6 Clydach
17.05.99	Jesse James Daniel L PTS 6 Cleethorpes
28.05.99	Jason Cook L RSC 1 Liverpool
17.07.99	Bradley Pryce L PTS 4 Doncaster
03.09.99	Young Muttley L RSC 4 West Bromwich
13.11.99	Humberto Soto L PTS 6 Hull
11.12.99	Gavin Rees L RSC 2 Liverpool
07.02.00	Liam Maltby L PTS 4 Peterborough
13.03.00	Danny Hunt L PTS 4 Bethnal Green
23.03.00	Marco Fattore L PTS 6 Bloomsbury
13.05.00	Alan Kershaw L PTS 4 Barnsley
22.05.00	Tony Conroy L PTS 4 Coventry
09.06.00	Elias Boswell W RSC 5 Blackpool
24.06.00	Brian Carr L PTS 4 Glasgow
01.07.00	Ricky Eccleston L PTS 4 Manchester
25.07.00	Kevin Lear L PTS 6 Southwark
09.09.00	Carl Greaves L PTS 6 Newark
16.09.00	Leo O'Reilly L RSC 2 Bethnal Green
27.11.00	Ricky Eccleston L PTS 4 Birmingham
04.12.00	Gavin Pearson L PTS 6 Bradford
11.12.00	Miguel Matthews W PTS 6 Birmingham
11.02.01	James Rooney L PTS 6 Hartlepool
26.03.01	Kevin Lear L CO 1 Wembley
03.06.01	Dafydd Carlin L PTS 4 Southwark
16.06.01	Carl Greaves L PTS 6 Derby
29.09.01	Scott Lawton L RSC 2 Southwark
15.12.01	Danny Hunt L PTS 4 Wembley
26.01.02	Chris McDonagh L PTS 4 Bethnal Green
03.03.02	Mally McIver L PTS 6 Shaw
11.03.02	Willie Limond L PTS 6 Glasgow
11.05.02	Craig Spacie L PTS 6 Chesterfield
15.06.02	Dave Stewart L PTS 6 Tottenham
23.06.02	Peter McDonagh L PTS 6 Southwark
13.07.02	Tony McPake L RSC 3 Coventry
22.03.03	Baz Carey L PTS 6 Coventry
29.03.03	Martin Power L PTS 4 Portsmouth
13.04.03	Nadeem Siddique L PTS 4 Bradford
06.06.03	Paul Rushton W PTS 6 Hull
20.06.03	Steve Mullin L PTS 4 Liverpool
30.06.03	Dean Hickman L RSC 4 Shrewsbury
05.09.03	Stefy Bull L PTS 6 Doncaster
13.09.03	Jamie Arthur L RTD 1 Newport
25.10.03	Colin Bain L PTS 4 Edinburgh
06.11.03	Andy Morris L PTS 4 Dagenham
18.11.03	Rob Jeffries L PTS 6 Bethnal Green

15.12.03	Matt Teague L PTS 6 Cleethorpes
27.03.04	Colin Bain L PTS 4 Edinburgh
23.04.04	Daniel Thorpe L PTS 6 Leicester
12.05.04	Nathan Ward L PTS 4 Reading
02.06.04	John O'Donnell L PTS 4 Nottingham
03.07.04	Isaac Ward L PTS 6 Blackpool
03.09.04	Barrie Jones L PTS 4 Newport
24.09.04	Nadeem Siddique L PTS 4 Nottingham
09.10.04	Jackson Williams L PTS 6 Norwich
20.11.04	Baz Carey L RSC 4 Coventry
15.04.05	Shaun Walton L PTS 6 Shrewsbury
28.04.05	Craig Morgan L PTS 4 Clydach
13.05.05	Tiger Matthews L CO 1 Liverpool
11.06.05	Stuart Green L PTS 6 Kirkcaldy

Career: 76 contests, won 7, lost 69.

Mark Hobson

Huddersfield. *Born* Workington, 7 May, 1976
British & Commonwealth Cruiserweight Champion. Ht. 6'5"
Manager C. Aston/T. Gilmour

09.06.97	Michael Pinnock W PTS 6 Bradford
06.10.97	P. R. Mason W PTS 6 Bradford
13.11.97	P. R. Mason W PTS 6 Bradford
27.02.98	Colin Brown DREW 6 Irvine
21.05.98	Paul Bonson W PTS 6 Bradford
15.06.98	Martin Jolley W RSC 3 Bradford
25.10.98	Mark Snipe W RSC 3 Shaw
26.11.98	Danny Southam W RSC 5 Bradford
19.04.99	Mark Levy L PTS 8 Bradford
11.09.99	Paul Bonson W PTS 4 Sheffield
06.12.99	Brian Gascoigne W RSC 3 Bradford
11.03.00	Nikolai Ermenkov W RSC 3 Kensington
27.03.00	Luke Simpkin W PTS 4 Barnsley
13.05.00	Paul Bonson W PTS 4 Barnsley
25.09.00	Mark Dawson W CO 1 Barnsley
26.02.01	Billy Bessey W PTS 4 Nottingham
24.04.01	Sebastiaan Rothmann L RTD 9 Liverpool
	(WBU Cruiserweight Title Challenge)
08.10.01	Firat Arslan L RSC 7 Barnsley
10.12.01	Luke Simpkin W RTD 3 Liverpool
23.02.02	Valery Semishkur W PTS 6 Nottingham
27.04.02	Lee Swaby W PTS 10 Huddersfield
	(Final Elim. British Cruiserweight Title)
05.10.02	Varuzhan Davtyan W RSC 3 Huddersfield
25.01.03	Abdul Kaddu W RSC 4 Bridgend
	(Vacant Commonwealth Cruiserweight Title)
10.05.03	Muslim Biarslanov W RSC 2 Huddersfield
05.09.03	Robert Norton W PTS 12 Sheffield
	(Commonwealth Cruiserweight Title Defence. Vacant British Cruiserweight Title)
13.03.04	Tony Moran W RSC 3 Huddersfield
	(British & Commonwealth Cruiserweight Title Defences)
27.05.04	Lee Swaby W RSC 6 Huddersfield
	(British & Commonwealth Cruiserweight Title Defences)
17.12.04	Bruce Scott W PTS 12 Huddersfield
	(British & Commonwealth Cruiserweight Title Defences)

Career: 28 contests, won 24, drew 1, lost 3.

Tom Hogan

Carlisle. *Born* Wigan, 2 May, 1977
L.Welterweight. Ht. 5'9½"
Manager T. Conroy

09.11.04	Pete Buckley W PTS 6 Leeds
21.02.05	Mike Reid L PTS 6 Glasgow

Career: 2 contests, won 1, lost 1.

Gareth Hogg

Torquay. *Born* Newton Abbott, 21 October, 1977
Cruiserweight. Ht. 6'2"
Manager C. Sanigar

13.02.98	Harry Butler W RSC 3 Weston super Mare
09.05.99	Matthew Barney L PTS 4 Bracknell
07.08.99	Clive Johnson W PTS 4 Dagenham
27.02.00	Darren Covill W RSC 3 Plymouth
29.03.00	Simon Andrews W RSC 5 Piccadilly
12.05.01	Oddy Papantoniou W RSC 2 Plymouth
10.07.01	Kevin Rainey W RSC 1 Montreal, Canada
23.06.02	Mark Phillips W PTS 4 Southwark
08.01.03	Darren Ashton W RSC 2 Aberdare
13.02.04	Dale Nixon W RTD 4 Bristol
04.02.05	Radcliffe Green W PTS 4 Plymouth

Career: 11 contests, won 10, lost 1.

Paul Holborn

Sunderland. *Born* Sunderland, 1 March, 1984
L. Welterweight. Ht. 5'8½"
Manager T. Conroy

11.10.04	Stuart Green W PTS 6 Glasgow
15.12.04	Amir Ali L PTS 6 Sheffield

Career: 2 contests, won 1, lost 1.

Jon Honney

Basingstoke. *Born* Basingstoke, 6 August, 1975
Lightweight. Ht. 5'7"
Manager Self

01.10.99	Peter Dunn W PTS 4 Bethnal Green
18.12.99	Marco Fattore W PTS 4 Southwark
21.02.00	Costas Katsantonis L RSC 1 Southwark
13.07.00	Mickey Yikealo L PTS 4 Bethnal Green
29.09.00	Manzo Smith L PTS 4 Bethnal Green
06.11.00	Jimmy Gould L PTS 6 Wolverhampton
16.03.01	Woody Greenaway W PTS 6 Portsmouth
07.09.01	Young Muttley L RSC 1 West Bromwich
20.10.01	Martin Watson L RSC 3 Glasgow
23.02.02	Darrell Grafton L RTD 1 Nottingham
28.11.02	Henry Jones W PTS 4 Finchley
20.12.02	Martin Hardcastle W PTS 4 Bracknell
05.03.03	Francis Barrett L PTS 10 Bethnal Green
	(Vacant Southern Area L.Welterweight Title)
27.05.03	Stephen Smith L PTS 8 Dagenham
26.07.03	Michael Ayers W PTS 6 Plymouth
11.10.03	Graham Earl L PTS 8 Portsmouth
07.04.04	Peter McDonagh L PTS 10 Leicester Square
	(Vacant Southern Area Lightweight Title)
12.05.04	John Alldis W PTS 6 Reading

22.05.04	Nigel Wright L RSC 2 Widnes
26.11.04	Rob Jeffries L PTS 8 Bethnal Green
25.02.05	Lee Beavis L PTS 6 Wembley

Career: 21 contests, won 7, lost 14.

Chris Hooper

Scarborough. *Born* Barking, 28 September, 1977
Featherweight. Ht. 5'9"
Manager Self

01.11.01	Jason Nesbitt W RSC 6 Hull
28.01.02	Greg Edwards W RSC 2 Barnsley
27.02.02	John Mackay L PTS 4 Nottingham
26.09.02	Sid Razak W PTS 6 Hull
21.11.02	Baz Carey W RTD 3 Hull
03.04.03	Buster Dennis W RSC 1 Hull
20.02.04	Buster Dennis L RSC 2 Bethnal Green
08.04.04	John Bothwell W CO 2 Peterborough
30.07.04	Steve Gethin W PTS 4 Bethnal Green
01.10.04	Andy Morris L RSC 3 Manchester

Career: 10 contests, won 7, lost 3.

Kerry Hope

Merthyr Tydfil. *Born* Merthyr Tydfil, 21 October, 1981
L.Middleweight. Ht. 5'10"
Manager F. Warren

21.01.05	Brian Coleman W PTS 4 Bridgend
08.04.05	Ernie Smith W PTS 4 Edinburgh
27.05.05	Lee Williamson W PTS 4 Spennymoor

Career: 3 contests, won 3.

Neil Hosking

Plymouth. *Born* Plymouth, 6 December, 1972
Heavyweight. Ht. 6'4"
Manager C. Sanigar

31.07.01	Slick Miller W RSC 2 Bethnal Green
17.09.04	Greg Scott-Briggs W RSC 2 Plymouth
08.04.05	Radcliffe Green L RSC 2 Bristol

Career: 3 contests, won 2, lost 1.

Shpetim Hoti

New Cross. *Born* Montenegro, 29 November, 1974
S.Middleweight. Ht. 5'11½"
Manager J. Evans

21.09.00	Elvis Michailenko L PTS 4 Bloomsbury
30.11.00	Harry Butler L PTS 4 Bloomsbury
21.06.01	Harry Butler L PTS 4 Earls Court
31.01.02	Simeon Cover L PTS 6 Piccadilly
26.09.02	Mark Ellwood L PTS 6 Hull
17.11.02	Darren Stubbs L RTD 2 Shaw
20.06.03	David Louzan W RSC 5 Gatwick
05.09.03	Amer Khan L RTD 4 Sheffield
19.02.04	Danny Norton L PTS 4 Dudley
01.05.04	Scott Baker W PTS 4 Gravesend
11.02.05	Tony Quigley L CO 1 Manchester

Career: 11 contests, won 2, lost 9.

Matthew Hough

Walsall. *Born* Walsall, 5 January, 1977
S.Middleweight. Ht. 6'2"
Manager E. Johnson

17.02.05	Paddy Ryan W PTS 6 Dudley
21.04.05	Mark Phillips W PTS 4 Dudley

Career: 2 contests, won 2.

Matthew Hough   Les Clark

Sean Hughes

Pontefract. *Born* Pontefract, 5 June, 1982
Central Area S. Bantamweight Champion.
Ht. 5'9"
Manager M. Marsden

02.03.02	Paddy Folan W PTS 6 Wakefield	
25.06.02	John Paul Ryan W PTS 6 Rugby	
05.10.02	Paddy Folan W PTS 4 Huddersfield	
10.02.03	Neil Read W PTS 6 Sheffield	
24.05.03	John-Paul Ryan W PTS 6 Sheffield	
13.09.03	Daniel Thorpe W PTS 6 Wakefield	
05.10.03	Paddy Folan W RSC 4 Bradford	
	(Vacant Central Area S.Bantamweight Title)	
07.12.03	Marty Kayes W PTS 6 Bradford	
26.02.04	Steve Foster L RSC 6 Widnes	
	(Vacant English Featherweight Title)	
23.10.04	Kristian Laight W PTS 6 Wakefield	
04.03.05	Michael Hunter L RSC 6 Hartlepool	
	(British S.Bantamweight Title Challenge)	
08.05.05	Billy Smith W PTS 6 Bradford	
25.06.05	Pete Buckley DREW 6 Wakefield	

Career: 13 contests, won 10, drew 1, lost 2.

John Humphrey

Newmarket. *Born* Kings Lynn, 24 July, 1980
L.Middleweight. Former Southern Area
L.Middleweight Champion. Former
Undefeated British Masters Welterweight
Champion. Ht. 6'2"
Manager J. Bowers

20.05.99	Arv Mittoo W PTS 6 Barking	
13.09.99	Les Frost W CO 1 Bethnal Green	
05.10.99	David Kehoe W PTS 4 Bloomsbury	
06.11.99	Emmanuel Marcos W PTS 4 Bethnal Green	
25.02.00	Matthew Barr L RSC 1 Newmarket	
18.05.00	Lee Molyneux W PTS 6 Bethnal Green	
29.09.00	Chris Henry W RSC 4 Bethnal Green	
15.02.01	Kevin McIntyre W RSC 4 Glasgow	
09.03.01	Harry Butler W RSC 1 Millwall	
20.04.01	Mark Ramsey W PTS 10 Millwall	
	(Vacant British Masters Welterweight Title)	
26.05.01	James Hare L RSC 7 Bethnal Green	
	(Elim. British Welterweight Title)	

28.09.01	Clive Johnson W PTS 6 Millwall	
23.11.01	Matthew Barr W RSC 2 Bethnal Green	
16.03.02	Ojay Abrahams W PTS 10 Bethnal Green	
	(Vacant Southern Area L.Middleweight Title)	
19.10.02	Robert Burton W RSC 4 Norwich	
08.02.03	Delroy Leslie W RSC 2 Norwich	
	(Southern Area L.Middleweight Title Defence)	
27.05.03	David Walker L CO 2 Dagenham	
	(Southern Area L.Middleweight Title Defence. Elim. British L. Middleweight Title)	
05.03.05	Dean Powell W RSC 3 Dagenham	
30.04.05	Michael Monaghan W PTS 6 Dagenham	

Career: 19 contests, won 16, lost 3.

Danny Hunt

Southend. *Born* Rochford, 1 May, 1981
English Lightweight Champion. Ht. 5'7"
Manager F. Maloney

29.11.99	Chris Lyons W PTS 4 Wembley	
13.03.00	Dave Hinds W PTS 4 Bethnal Green	
13.04.00	Steve Hanley W PTS 4 Holborn	
13.07.00	Dave Travers W PTS 4 Bethnal Green	
27.01.01	Lee Williamson L RSC 2 Bethnal Green	
03.04.01	Lee Williamson W PTS 4 Bethnal Green	
05.05.01	Pete Buckley W PTS 4 Edmonton	
22.09.01	Dafydd Carlin W PTS 4 Bethnal Green	
15.12.01	Dave Hinds W PTS 4 Wembley	
02.03.02	Gary Flear W PTS 4 Bethnal Green	
04.05.02	Jason Nesbitt W PTS 4 Bethnal Green	
14.09.02	David Kehoe W RSC 3 Bethnal Green	
15.02.03	Mark Bowen W RSC 1 Wembley	
29.03.03	Daniel Thorpe W PTS 6 Portsmouth	
02.10.03	Chill John W PTS 10 Liverpool	
	(Vacant English Lightweight Title)	
07.02.04	Anthony Maynard W PTS 10 Bethnal Green	
	(English Lightweight Title Defence)	
05.06.04	Chris McDonagh W CO 3 Bethnal Green	
19.11.04	Lee Meager W PTS 10 Bethnal Green	
	(English Lightweight Title Defence)	

Career: 18 contests, won 17, lost 1.

Michael Hunter

Hartlepool. *Born* Hartlepool, 5 May, 1978
British S.Bantamweight Champion. Former
Undefeated WBF & Northern Area
S.Bantamweight Champion. Ht. 5'7½"
Manager D. Garside

23.07.00	Sean Grant W PTS 6 Hartlepool	
01.10.00	Chris Emanuele W PTS 6 Hartlepool	
24.11.00	Gary Groves W RSC 2 Darlington	
09.12.00	Chris Jickells W PTS 4 Southwark	
11.02.01	Paddy Folan W RSC 6 Hartlepool	
06.05.01	Anthony Hanna W PTS 4 Hartlepool	
04.06.01	Anthony Hanna W PTS 4 Hartlepool	
09.09.01	John Barnes W RSC 8 Hartlepool	
	(Vacant Northern Area S.Bantamweight Title)	
29.11.01	Joel Viney W PTS 6 Hartlepool	
26.01.02	Stevie Quinn W CO 2 Dagenham	
18.03.02	Marc Callaghan DREW 6 Crawley	
18.05.02	Mark Payne W PTS 8 Millwall	

18.10.02	Frankie DeMilo W PTS 12 Hartlepool	
	(Vacant WBF S. Bantamweight Title)	
14.12.02	Anthony Hanna W PTS 8 Newcastle	
07.06.03	Afrim Mustafa W RSC 5 Trieste, Italy	
26.07.03	Rocky Dean W RSC 1 Plymouth	
04.10.03	Nikolai Eremeev W PTS 6 Belfast	
08.11.03	Gennadiy Delisandru W PTS 6 Bridgend	
16.04.04	Mark Payne W RSC 7 Hartlepool	
	(Vacant British S.Bantamweight Title)	
02.06.04	Vladimir Borov W PTS 6 Hereford	
19.11.04	Marc Callaghan W RSC 10 Hartlepool	
	(British S.Bantamweight Title Defence)	
04.03.05	Sean Hughes W RSC 6 Hartlepool	
	(British S.Bantamweight Title Defence)	
27.05.05	Kamel Guerfi W RSC 6 Spennymoor	

Career: 23 contests, won 22, drew 1.

Eddie Hyland

Wellingborough. *Born* Dublin, 24 April, 1981
S.Featherweight. Ht. 5'6½"
Manager J. Harding

26.11.04	Buster Dennis W PTS 4 Altrincham	
04.06.05	Stefan Berza W RSC 1 Dublin	

Career: 2 contests, won 2.

Patrick Hyland

Wellingborough. *Born* Dublin, 16 September, 1983
S.Bantamweight. Ht. 5'7¼"
Manager J. Harding

24.09.04	Dean Ward W PTS 4 Dublin	
13.02.05	Steve Gethin W PTS 4 Brentwood	
04.06.05	Pete Buckley W PTS 4 Dublin	

Career: 3 contests, won 3.

Patrick Hyland   Les Clark

Paul Hyland

Wellingborough. *Born* Dublin, 19 November, 1984
Featherweight. Ht. 5'7"
Manager J. Harding

05.11.04	Janos Garai W RSC 2 Hereford	
19.02.05	Vladimir Bukovy W RSC 3 Dublin	
04.06.05	Ferenc Szabo W PTS 6 Dublin	

Career: 3 contests, won 3.

Jon Ibbotson

Sheffield. *Born* Sheffield, 2 September, 1982
S.Middleweight. Ht. 6'3½"
Manager D. Coldwell

15.12.04 Paul Billington W PTS 4 Sheffield
20.02.05 Nick Okoth W PTS 6 Sheffield
22.04.05 Daniel Teasdale W RSC 1 Barnsley
18.06.05 Ojay Abrahams W PTS 4 Barnsley
Career: 4 contests, won 4.

Egbui Ikeagwo

Luton. *Born* Ibaden, Nigeria, 14 October, 1975
S.Middleweight. Ht. 6'0½"
Manager P. Rees

12.05.03 Michael Matthewsian W PTS 6 Southampton
13.06.03 Leigh Alliss L PTS 6 Bristol
06.02.04 Paul Owen W PTS 4 Sheffield
27.01.05 Joey Vegas L PTS 4 Piccadilly
04.02.05 Dan Guthrie DREW 4 Plymouth
26.03.05 Joey Vegas L PTS 4 Hackney
Career: 6 contests, won 2, drew 1, lost 3.

Egbui Ikeagwo   Les Clark

David Ingleby

Lancaster. *Born* Lancaster, 14 June, 1980
Heavyweight. Ht. 6'3"
Manager B. Myers

09.06.03 Costi Marin L RSC 1 Bradford
01.12.03 Paul Bonson L PTS 6 Leeds
28.02.04 Paul King L RSC 3 Manchester
01.05.04 Jason Callum L PTS 6 Coventry
10.07.04 Scott Lansdowne L RSC 4 Coventry
20.09.04 Dave Clarke W RTD 5 Glasgow
06.12.04 Paul Butlin L CO 5 Leicester
30.04.05 Paul Butlin W PTS 6 Coventry
02.06.05 Chris Burton L RSC 3 Yarm
Career: 9 contests, won 2, lost 7.

Richard Inquieti

Eastwood. *Born* Langley Mill, 19 October, 1968
L.Middleweight. Ht. 6'3¼"
Manager Self

30.09.96 Peter Varnavas L CO 2 Manchester
20.02.97 Paul Johnson W PTS 6 Mansfield
12.03.97 Tony Smith W RSC 2 Stoke
19.03.97 Andy Peach L RSC 1 Stoke
18.08.97 Jawaid Khaliq L RSC 5 Nottingham
18.09.97 Danny Bell L RSC 1 Alfreton
11.11.97 Trevor Smith L RSC 3 Edgbaston
08.12.97 Danny Bell L RSC 1 Nottingham
07.10.98 Sean O'Sullivan W PTS 6 Stoke
29.10.98 Dean Nicholas L RSC 1 Newcastle
02.12.98 Martyn Thomas L RSC 3 Stoke
25.03.99 Shane Junior L CO 2 Edgbaston
06.03.00 Martyn Bailey W RSC 5 Bradford
28.03.00 David Smales W PTS 6 Hartlepool
05.05.00 Martyn Bailey W PTS 6 Pentre Halkyn
20.11.00 Darren Spencer L RSC 1 Glasgow
04.02.01 Neil Bonner L PTS 6 Queensferry
23.02.01 Dean Nicholas L PTS 6 Irvine
08.03.01 Alan Campbell L PTS 6 Blackpool
01.04.01 Stuart Elwell L PTS 6 Wolverhampton
09.04.01 Gavin Wake L PTS 6 Bradford
20.04.01 Darren Williams L PTS 6 Dublin
03.06.01 Nicky Leech L PTS 6 Hanley
15.09.01 Andrei Ivanov DREW 6 Nottingham
23.09.01 Wayne Shepherd L PTS 6 Shaw
04.10.01 Danny Moir L PTS 6 Sunderland
15.10.01 Danny Parkinson L RSC 1 Bradford
13.11.01 Peter Dunn DREW 6 Leeds
24.11.01 Gavin Wake L PTS 6 Wakefield
06.12.01 John Jackson W RSC 3 Sunderland
08.02.02 Mark Paxford L PTS 6 Preston
18.03.02 Gavin Pearson L PTS 6 Glasgow
22.04.02 Ciaran Duffy L PTS 6 Glasgow
29.04.02 Gavin Pearson L PTS 6 Bradford
09.05.02 Lee Armstrong W RSC 5 Sunderland
03.06.02 Gary Porter L PTS 6 Glasgow
03.08.02 Dean Walker L PTS 6 Derby
28.09.02 Gavin Wake L PTS 6 Wakefield
10.10.02 Mark Paxford L PTS 6 Stoke
18.10.02 Franny Jones L PTS 6 Hartlepool
01.11.02 Michael Jennings L RSC 2 Preston
22.12.02 Danny Moir L RTD 3 Salford
20.01.03 Andy Gibson L RSC 5 Glasgow
14.04.03 Craig Dickson L PTS 4 Glasgow
02.06.03 Jamie Coyle L RSC 2 Glasgow
06.10.03 Ady Clegg L PTS 6 Barnsley
10.02.04 Chris Steele W RSC 4 Barnsley
20.02.04 Brett James L PTS 6 Southampton
15.03.04 Ady Clegg L PTS 6 Bradford
26.04.04 Richard Swallow L RSC 1 Cleethorpes
10.07.04 Richard Mazurek L RSC 1 Coventry
23.09.04 Martin Marshall L PTS 6 Gateshead
30.09.04 Rocky Muscus L PTS 4 Glasgow
28.10.04 Martin Marshall L PTS 6 Sunderland
Career: 54 contests, won 8, drew 2, lost 44.

Peter Jackson

Halesowen. *Born* Wordsley, 27 January, 1976
Midlands Area S.Middleweight Champion. Ht. 5'11"
Manager Self

28.01.01 Harry Butler W PTS 6 Wolverhampton
01.04.01 Jamie Logan W PTS 6 Wolverhampton
20.05.01 Jamie Logan W PTS 6 Wolverhampton
09.09.01 Neil Bonner W PTS 6 Hartlepool
16.11.01 Andrei Ivanov W PTS 6 West Bromwich
17.02.02 Alan Jones L PTS 6 Wolverhampton
13.04.02 Simon Andrews W PTS 4 Wolverhampton
03.08.02 Jimmy Steel W PTS 4 Blackpool

08.09.02 Mike Duffield W PTS 4 Wolverhampton
02.11.02 Mike Duffield L PTS 10 Wolverhampton
(Vacant Midlands Area S.Middleweight Title)
15.02.03 Simeon Cover L RSC 2 Wolverhampton
17.07.03 Mike Duffield W PTS 10 Walsall
(Midlands Area S.Middleweight Title Challenge)
11.12.03 Ryan Rhodes L PTS 6 Bethnal Green
19.02.04 Patrick Cito DREW 4 Dudley
19.02.05 Jim Rock L CO 7 Dublin
(Irish S.Middleweight Title Challenge)
22.04.05 Ryan Rhodes L PTS 6 Barnsley
Career: 16 contests, won 9, drew 1, lost 6.

Hamed Jamali

Birmingham. *Born* Iran, 23 November, 1973
S. Middleweight. Ht. 5'9"
Manager Self

09.12.02 Dale Nixon W CO 1 Birmingham
24.02.03 Harry Butler W PTS 6 Birmingham
06.10.03 Simeon Cover W PTS 6 Birmingham
08.12.03 Gary Ojuederie W PTS 6 Birmingham
08.03.04 Ojay Abrahams W PTS 8 Birmingham
10.05.04 Jason Collins W PTS 8 Birmingham
11.10.04 Hastings Rasani W PTS 8 Birmingham
13.12.04 Simeon Cover L PTS 10 Birmingham
(Vacant British Masters S.Middleweight Title)
21.02.05 Michael Pinnock W PTS 8 Birmingham
Career: 9 contests, won 8, lost 1.

Fred Janes

Cardiff. *Born* Cardiff, 17 December, 1984
Featherweight. Ht. 5'9"
Manager D. Gardiner

23.11.03 Paddy Folan W RSC 5 Rotherham
13.12.03 Steve Bell L PTS 4 Manchester
13.02.04 Michael Graydon DREW 6 Bristol
06.03.04 John Bothwell DREW 4 Renfrew
01.04.04 Martin Power L RSC 2 Bethnal Green
02.06.04 John Simpson L PTS 6 Hereford
10.09.04 Matthew Marsh L PTS 4 Bethnal Green
16.10.04 Warren Dunkley L PTS 6 Dagenham
06.12.04 Danny Wallace L RSC 2 Leeds
29.04.05 Paul Buckley L PTS 4 Southwark
Career: 10 contests, won 1, drew 2, lost 7.

Henry Janes

Cardiff. *Born* Cardiff, 24 May, 1983
Lightweight. Ht. 5'7"
Manager D. Gardiner

24.05.03 Steve Foster L PTS 6 Bethnal Green
02.06.03 Matt Teague L PTS 6 Cleethorpes
20.06.03 Derry Matthews L RSC 1 Liverpool
07.09.03 Steve Gethin W PTS 4 Shrewsbury
30.10.03 Kevin O'Hara L PTS 6 Belfast
30.11.03 Ian Reid W PTS 6 Swansea
13.12.03 Andy Morris L PTS 4 Manchester
19.01.04 John Simpson L PTS 8 Glasgow
07.02.04 Lee Whyatt W PTS 4 Bethnal Green
06.03.04 Kevin O'Hara L PTS 6 Renfrew
13.03.04 Danny Wallace L PTS 4 Huddersfield
03.04.04 Derry Matthews L PTS 4 Manchester
22.04.04 Barry Hawthorne L PTS 6 Glasgow
19.06.04 Scott Flynn W RSC 4 Renfrew

16.10.04 John Mackay W PTS 4 Dagenham
04.11.04 Sam Rukundo L PTS 6 Piccadilly
19.11.04 Lee Beavis L PTS 4 Bethnal Green
11.12.04 Kevin Mitchell L PTS 4 Canning Town
11.02.05 Steve Bell L RTD 3 Manchester
Career: 19 contests, won 6, lost 13.

Tony Janes
Cardiff. *Born* Cardiff, 30 January, 1986
Middleweight. Ht. 5'7"
Manager D. Gardiner

19.12.04 Gareth Lawrence L PTS 4 Bethnal
Green

Career: 1 contest, lost 1.

Neil Jarmolinski
Aldershot. *Born* Doncaster, 13 October,
1977
L. Middleweight. Ht. 5'9"
Manager J. Evans

30.09.04 Ivor Bonavic DREW 4 Glasgow
21.11.04 John-Paul Temple DREW 4 Bracknell
06.02.05 Danny Goode L PTS 4 Southampton
04.03.05 Jak Hibbert L PTS 6 Rotherham
08.04.05 Courtney Thomas L PTS 6 Bristol
29.04.05 Jon Harrison L PTS 6 Plymouth
Career: 6 contests, drew 2, lost 4.

Neil Jarmolinski   Les Clark

(Robin) Rob Jeffries (Jeffrey)
Bexleyheath. *Born* Crayford, 25 June, 1973
Southern Area Lightweight Champion.
Ht. 5'8"
Manager Self

22.07.03 Jaz Virdee W PTS 6 Bethnal Green
25.09.03 Anthony Hanna W PTS 6 Bethnal
Green
18.11.03 Dave Hinds W PTS 6 Bethnal Green
20.02.04 Chris McDonagh W RSC 2 Bethnal
Green
25.06.04 Declan English W PTS 6 Bethnal
Green
24.09.04 Chris McDonagh W PTS 4 Bethnal
Green
26.11.04 Jon Honney W PTS 8 Bethnal Green
05.03.05 Chill John W PTS 8 Southwark
30.04.05 Peter McDonagh W PTS 10 Dagenham
*(Southern Area Lightweight Title
Challenge)*
Career: 9 contests, won 9.

Rob Jeffries   Les Clark

Michael Jennings
Chorley. *Born* Preston, 9 September, 1977
English Welterweight Champion. Former
Undefeated WBU Inter-Continental
Welterweight Champion. Ht. 5'9½"
Manager F. Warren/B. Hughes

15.05.99 Tony Smith W RSC 1 Blackpool
11.12.99 Lee Molyneux W PTS 4 Liverpool
29.02.00 Lee Molyneux W PTS 6 Widnes
25.03.00 Brian Coleman W PTS 6 Liverpool
16.05.00 Brian Coleman W PTS 6 Warrington
29.05.00 William Webster W PTS 6 Manchester
08.07.00 Paul Denton W PTS 6 Widnes
04.09.00 Mark Ramsey W PTS 6 Manchester
25.11.00 Ernie Smith W PTS 4 Manchester
11.12.00 Paul Denton W PTS 4 Widnes
10.02.01 Mark Haslam W RSC 2 Widnes
07.07.01 David Kirk W PTS 6 Manchester
15.09.01 Gary Harrison W PTS 6 Manchester
09.02.02 James Paisley W RSC 3 Manchester
01.06.02 Lee Williamson W PTS 4 Manchester
28.09.02 Karl Taylor W RSC 4 Manchester
01.11.02 Richard Inquieti W RSC 2 Preston
18.01.03 Lee Williamson W RTD 4 Preston
08.05.03 Jimmy Gould W RTD 6 Widnes
*(Vacant WBU Inter-Continental
Welterweight Title)*
27.09.03 Sammy Smith W RTD 4 Manchester
*(WBU Inter-Continental Welterweight
Title Defence)*
13.12.03 Peter Dunn W PTS 6 Manchester
01.04.04 Brett James W RTD 5 Bethnal Green
*(WBU Inter-Continental Welterweight
Title Defence)*
22.05.04 Rafal Jackiewicz W PTS 8 Widnes
01.10.04 Chris Saunders W RTD 5 Manchester
(English Welterweight Title Challenge)
11.02.05 Vasile Dragomir W CO 3 Manchester
03.06.05 Gavin Down W RSC 9 Manchester
(English Welterweight Title Defence)
Career: 26 contests, won 26.

Carl Johanneson
Leeds. *Born* Leeds, 1 August, 1978
WBF S.Featherweight Champion. Ht. 5'5"
Manager R. Manners

08.07.00 Calvin Sheppard W PTS 3 North
Carolina, USA

15.09.00 Sean Thomassen W RSC 1 Paterson,
New Jersey, USA
14.10.00 Hiep Bui W RSC 1 Scranton,
Pennsylvania, USA
08.12.00 Walusimbi Kizito W PTS 4 Atlantic
City, New Jersey, USA
12.04.01 Efrain Guzman W PTS 4 Melville,
New York, USA
04.05.01 Calvin Sheppard W RSC 4 Atlantic
City, New Jersey, USA
26.06.01 Joey Figueroa W PTS 6 NYC, New
York, USA
26.10.01 Jose Ramon Disla W RSC 5 Atlantic
City, New Jersey, USA
14.12.01 Angel Rios W PTS 6 Uncasville,
Connecticut, USA
03.03.02 Kema Muse W PTS 6 Scranton,
Pennsylvania, USA
02.07.02 James Baker W RSC 4 Washington
DC, USA
16.01.03 Juan R. Llopis W RSC 5 Philadelphia,
Pennsylvania, USA
05.06.03 Koba Gogoladze L PTS 8 Detroit,
Michigan, USA
18.07.03 Reggie Sanders W PTS 6 Dover,
Delaware, USA
21.08.03 Steve Trumble W RSC 2 Philadelphia,
Pennsylvania, USA
30.01.04 Harold Grey W RSC 5 Philadelphia,
Pennsylvania, USA
20.03.04 Carl Greaves W RTD 3 Wembley
(WBF S.Featherweight Title Challenge)
08.05.04 Andrew Ferrans W RSC 6 Bristol
(WBF S.Featherweight Title Defence)
19.06.04 Alexander Abramenko W RSC 5
Muswell Hill
(WBF S.Featherweight Title Defence)
02.12.04 Leva Kirakosyan L RSC 1 Crystal
Palace
08.05.05 Jimmy Beech W CO 2 Bradford
Career: 21 contests, won 19, lost 2.

(Garnet) Chill John
Brighton. *Born* St Vincent, 11 August, 1977
Lightweight. Ht. 5'7"
Manager R. Davies

22.10.00 Paul Philpott W PTS 6 Streatham
03.02.01 Dave Travers W PTS 4 Brighton
25.02.01 Scott Hocking W RSC 4 Streatham
05.05.01 Woody Greenaway W PTS 6 Brighton
04.07.01 Steve Hanley W PTS 4 Bloomsbury
20.10.01 Mark Halstead W PTS 4 Portsmouth
01.12.01 Pete Buckley W PTS 4 Bethnal Green
13.04.02 Jonathan Thaxton L RSC 2 Norwich
12.07.02 Daniel Thorpe W PTS 4 Southampton
22.09.02 Jason Hall L PTS 6 Southwark
12.10.02 Graham Earl L PTS 10 Piccadilly
*(Southern Area Lightweight Title
Challenge)*
21.12.02 Lee Meager L RSC 5 Dagenham
02.10.03 Danny Hunt L PTS 10 Liverpool
(Vacant English Lightweight Title)
21.02.04 Peter McDonagh L RTD 2 Brighton
05.03.05 Rob Jeffries L PTS 8 Southwark
Career: 15 contests, won 8, lost 7.

Clive Johnson
Basingstoke. *Born* Botswana, 18 October,
1977
L. Middleweight. Ht. 5'10"
Manager C. Sanigar

18.02.99 Harry Butler W PTS 6 Barking

20.05.99	Joe Skeldon W PTS 6 Barking
07.08.99	Gareth Hogg L PTS 4 Dagenham
09.10.99	Jamie Moore L RSC 3 Manchester
07.04.00	Kevin Lang W RSC 1 Bristol
08.09.00	Chris Henry L PTS 4 Bristol
06.10.00	Colin Vidler L PTS 6 Maidstone
26.03.01	David Baptiste W PTS 6 Peterborough
28.09.01	John Humphrey L PTS 6 Millwall
09.02.02	Darren McInulty L PTS 8 Coventry
18.01.03	Matthew Hall L PTS 4 Preston
27.03.04	Alexander Sipos L PTS 6 Magdeburg, Germany
24.09.04	Gilbert Eastman L PTS 6 Nottingham
23.10.04	Sebastian Sylvester L RSC 2 Berlin, Germany

Career: 14 contests, won 4, lost 10.

Craig Johnson

Clay Cross. *Born* Chesterfield, 10 November, 1980
Lightweight. Ht. 5'7"
Manager Self

25.04.04	Peter Allen W PTS 6 Nottingham
18.09.04	David Bailey L PTS 6 Newark
22.10.04	Carl Allen W PTS 6 Mansfield
10.12.04	Pete Buckley W PTS 6 Mansfield
06.03.05	Ian Reid W PTS 6 Mansfield

Career: 5 contests, won 4, lost 1.

Danny Johnston

Stoke. *Born* Stoke, 19 May, 1981
Welterweight. Ht. 5'10"
Manager P. Dykes

26.09.04	Karl Taylor W PTS 6 Stoke

Career: 1 contest, won 1.

Darren Johnstone

Larkhall. *Born* Motherwell, 30 March, 1982
Lightweight. Ht. 5'9"
Manager T. Gilmour

17.11.03	Jamie Hill W PTS 6 Glasgow
15.03.04	Ian Reid W PTS 6 Glasgow
07.06.04	Joel Viney W PTS 6 Glasgow
11.10.04	Pete Buckley W PTS 6 Glasgow
27.05.05	Gavin Tait W PTS 6 Motherwell

Career: 5 contests, won 5.

Alan Jones

Aberystwyth. *Born* Aberystwyth, 6 October, 1976
Middleweight. Ht. 6'1"
Manager T. Gilmour

15.09.01	Martyn Woodward W CO 3 Swansea
21.10.01	Kenny Griffith W RSC 4 Pentre Halkyn
17.02.02	Peter Jackson W PTS 6 Wolverhampton
16.03.02	Allan Foster DREW 6 Northampton
07.10.02	Donovan Smillie W RSC 6 Birmingham
23.02.03	Leigh Wicks W PTS 8 Aberystwyth
06.10.03	Jason Collins W PTS 8 Birmingham
30.10.03	Jim Rock W PTS 8 Belfast
02.06.04	Jason Collins W PTS 6 Hereford
05.11.04	Szabolcs Rimovszky W PTS 6 Hereford
04.02.05	Scott Dann L CO 3 Plymouth
	(*British Middleweight Title Challenge*)

Career: 11 contests, won 9, drew 1, lost 1.

Barrie Jones

Rhondda. *Born* Tylorstown, 1 March, 1985
L.Welterweight. Ht. 5'11"
Manager D. Powell/F. Warren

03.07.04	Pete Buckley W PTS 4 Newport
03.09.04	Dave Hinds W PTS 4 Newport
21.01.05	Lea Handley W PTS 4 Bridgend
17.06.05	Marco Cittadini W RSC 2 Glasgow

Career: 4 contests, won 4.

Davey Jones

Epworth. *Born* Grimsby, 30 May, 1977
Middleweight. Ht. 5'11"
Manager Self

23.09.02	William Webster W PTS 6 Cleethorpes
08.11.02	William Webster W PTS 6 Doncaster
30.11.02	Matt Scriven W PTS 6 Newark
16.12.02	Gary Jones W PTS 6 Cleethorpes
21.02.03	Jimi Hendricks W PTS 6 Doncaster
09.05.03	Wayne Shepherd W PTS 6 Doncaster
22.09.03	Steve Brumant L PTS 6 Cleethorpes
26.02.04	Paul Smith L PTS 4 Widnes
06.03.04	Paul Buchanan L PTS 4 Renfrew
23.05.05	Ernie Smith DREW 6 Cleethorpes

Career: 10 contests, won 6, drew 1, lost 3.

Franny Jones

Darlington. *Born* Burnley, 7 February, 1981
L. Middleweight. Ht. 5'9½"
Manager Self

05.05.02	Surinder Sekhon W PTS 6 Hartlepool
28.09.02	Martin Scotland W PTS 6 Wakefield
18.10.02	Richard Inquieti W PTS 6 Hartlepool
27.02.03	Danny Moir DREW 6 Sunderland
17.03.03	Gary Porter W PTS 6 Glasgow
11.07.03	Gary Cummings W RSC 2 Darlington
10.10.03	Pedro Thompson W PTS 6 Darlington
13.12.03	Matthew Hatton DREW 6 Manchester
05.03.04	Danny Moir NC 3 Darlington
	(*Vacant Northern Area L.Middleweight Title*)
16.04.04	Brian Coleman W PTS 6 Hartlepool
19.11.04	Paul Lomax W RSC 2 Hartlepool
04.03.05	Ali Nuumbembe L PTS 6 Hartlepool
11.03.05	Matthew Hatton L RTD 6 Doncaster
02.06.05	Darren Gethin W PTS 8 Yarm

Career: 14 contests, won 9, drew 2, lost 2, no contest 1.

Franny Jones　　　　　Les Clark

Henry Jones

Pembroke. *Born* Haverfordwest, 23 December, 1975
Lightweight. Ht. 5'0"
Manager Self

17.06.95	Abdul Mannon W PTS 6 Cardiff
07.07.95	Harry Woods L PTS 4 Cardiff
07.10.95	Frankie Slane L PTS 4 Belfast
28.11.95	Jason Thomas L PTS 4 Cardiff
20.12.95	Brendan Bryce W PTS 6 Usk
20.03.96	Danny Lawson W CO 1 Cardiff
29.05.96	Ian Turner L PTS 6 Ebbw Vale
02.10.96	Jason Thomas W PTS 4 Cardiff
26.10.96	Danny Costello L RSC 3 Liverpool
29.04.97	Tommy Waite L PTS 4 Belfast
19.05.97	Francky Leroy L RSC 1 Coudekerque, France
02.12.97	Ian Turner L RSC 8 Swansea
	(*Vacant Welsh Bantamweight Title*)
30.10.98	Tiger Singh W CO 4 Peterborough
05.05.00	Jason Edwards L PTS 6 Pentre Halkyn
28.11.02	Jon Honney L PTS 4 Finchley
23.02.03	David Vaughan L PTS 6 Aberystwyth
10.04.03	Daleboy Rees L PTS 4 Clydach
07.05.03	Jason Nesbitt W PTS 6 Ellesmere Port
15.06.03	Dean Lambert L RSC 4 Bradford
20.04.04	Scott Lawton L PTS 4 Sheffield
19.06.04	Colin Bain L PTS 4 Renfrew
03.07.04	Michael Graydon DREW 6 Bristol

Career: 22 contests, won 6, drew 1, lost 15.

Jonathan Jones

Merthyr Tydfil. *Born* Merthyr Tydfil, 13 December, 1985
Lightweight. Ht. 5'10"
Manager B. Coleman

17.12.04	Peter Sesmo L RSC 1 Coventry
04.02.05	Matthew Marshall W PTS 6 Plymouth
05.03.05	Jed Syger L PTS 4 Dagenham
18.03.05	Andrew Murray L RSC 4 Belfast

Career: 4 contests, won 1, lost 3.

Jonathan Jones　　　　　Les Clark

Keith Jones

Cefn Hengoed. *Born* Bradwell, 4 December, 1968
Welterweight. Former Undefeated British Masters Lightweight Champion. Ht. 5'5¾"
Manager Self

17.05.94	Abdul Mannon L PTS 6 Kettering
13.06.94	G. G. Goddard L PTS 6 Liverpool
21.07.94	G. G. Goddard L RSC 1 Battersea
12.09.94	Marco Fattore L PTS 6 Mayfair
29.09.94	Marlon Ward L PTS 4 Bethnal Green
21.10.94	James Murray L CO 3 Glasgow
27.11.94	Daniel Lutaaya L CO 1 Southwark
03.09.96	Benny May W RSC 2 Bethnal Green
18.09.96	Kevin Sheil W PTS 4 Tylorstown
04.10.96	Andy Ross DREW 6 Pentre Halkyn
18.10.96	Wayne Jones DREW 6 Barnstaple
06.11.96	Robert Grubb W PTS 4 Tylorstown
22.11.96	Tony Mulholland L PTS 4 Liverpool
03.12.96	Alex Moon L RTD 5 Liverpool
21.01.97	Greg Upton DREW 6 Bristol
26.02.97	Greg Upton L PTS 4 Cardiff
07.03.97	Dean Murdoch L PTS 6 Weston super Mare
20.03.97	Kevin Sheil DREW 8 Solihull
04.04.97	Tony Mulholland L PTS 4 Liverpool
22.05.97	Darrell Easton L PTS 4 Southwark
02.10.98	Dean Pithie L PTS 8 Cheshunt
10.10.98	Steve Murray L RSC 4 Bethnal Green
21.11.98	Mat Zegan L PTS 4 Southwark
30.11.98	Eddie Nevins L PTS 4 Manchester
14.12.98	Roy Rutherford L PTS 6 Birmingham
12.01.99	Richard Evatt L CO 3 Bethnal Green
23.02.99	Simon Chambers DREW 4 Cardiff
12.03.99	Maurycy Gojko L PTS 4 Bethnal Green
09.04.99	Brian Carr L PTS 8 Glasgow
23.04.99	Dewi Roberts W PTS 6 Clydach
01.05.99	Steve Murray L RSC 6 Crystal Palace
04.06.99	Luis Navarro L RSC 5 Malaga, Spain
02.07.99	Alan Bosworth L PTS 6 Bristol
15.07.99	Tomas Jansson L PTS 4 Peterborough
20.08.99	Jason Hall L PTS 6 Bloomsbury
02.10.99	Jason Dee L RSC 5 Cardiff
06.11.99	Isaac Sebaduka W PTS 4 Bethnal Green
14.11.99	Lee Armstrong L PTS 6 Bradford
04.12.99	Franny Hogg L PTS 4 Manchester
14.12.99	Roy Rutherford L PTS 4 Coventry
18.01.00	Carl Greaves L PTS 6 Mansfield
29.01.00	Steve Murray L PTS 4 Manchester
27.02.00	Mark McGowan W RSC 7 Plymouth (British Masters Lightweight Title Challenge)
25.03.00	Alex Moon L PTS 6 Liverpool
12.05.00	Jason Cook L PTS 10 Swansea (Welsh L. Welterweight Title Challenge)
01.07.00	Matty Leonard W RSC 4 Southwark
25.07.00	Koba Gogoladze L PTS 4 Southwark
19.08.00	Richard Evatt L PTS 6 Brentwood
16.09.00	David Walker L PTS 6 Bethnal Green
21.10.00	Francis Barrett L PTS 4 Wembley
16.11.00	Jimmy Phelan DREW 6 Hull
27.11.00	Kevin Bennett L PTS 8 Birmingham
11.12.00	Steve Saville L PTS 8 Birmingham
02.01.01	Mark Payne L PTS 6 Coventry
15.01.01	Matthew Hatton L PTS 4 Manchester
03.02.01	David Burke L PTS 4 Manchester
10.02.01	Nigel Wright L PTS 4 Widnes
23.02.01	Darren Melville L PTS 4 Barking
29.03.01	Ted Bami L PTS 4 Hammersmith
10.04.01	Dean Pithie L PTS 4 Wembley
22.04.01	Brian Gentry L PTS 8 Streatham
08.05.01	Kevin Bennett L PTS 6 Barnsley
20.05.01	Jimmy Gould L PTS 6 Wolverhampton
02.06.01	Mally McIver L PTS 6 Wakefield
23.06.01	Alan Bosworth L PTS 6 Peterborough
14.07.01	Wayne Rigby L CO 3 Wembley

18.08.01	Steve Conway L PTS 8 Dewsbury
28.09.01	Daniel James L PTS 6 Millwall
20.10.01	Ronnie Nailen L PTS 4 Glasgow
10.11.01	Colin Lynes L PTS 6 Wembley
17.11.01	Willie Limond L PTS 4 Glasgow
24.11.01	Steve Murray L RSC 4 Bethnal Green
13.04.02	Jimmy Gould L PTS 8 Wolverhampton
27.04.02	Lee Armstrong L PTS 6 Huddersfield
09.05.02	Martin Holgate L PTS 6 Leicester Square
13.06.02	Ajose Olusegun L PTS 6 Leicester Square
23.06.02	Ted Bami L RSC 4 Southwark
15.09.02	Ross McCord W RSC 4 Swansea (Vacant Welsh Welterweight Title)
05.10.02	Tony Conroy W RSC 4 Coventry
02.11.02	Gary Young L PTS 4 Belfast
16.11.02	Glenn McClarnon L PTS 6 Nottingham
09.12.02	Steve Saville L PTS 8 Birmingham
21.12.02	Francis Barrett L PTS 6 Dagenham
23.02.03	Jason Williams L PTS 10 Aberystwyth (Welsh Welterweight Title Defence)
08.03.03	Leo O'Reilly L PTS 6 Bethnal Green
21.03.03	Kevin Bennett L PTS 4 West Bromwich
05.04.03	Gary Greenwood DREW 8 Coventry
12.04.03	Barry Morrison L PTS 4 Bethnal Green
26.04.03	Ajose Olusegun L PTS 6 Brentford
15.05.03	Brett James L PTS 4 Mayfair
05.10.03	Ali Nuumembe L PTS 6 Bradford
24.10.03	Carl Greaves L PTS 6 Bethnal Green
07.11.03	Bobby Vanzie L PTS 6 Sheffield
27.11.03	Sammy Smith L PTS 10 Longford (Vacant British Masters L.Welterweight Title)
11.12.03	Lenny Daws L PTS 6 Bethnal Green
27.03.04	Gary Young L PTS 6 Edinburgh
07.04.04	John Alldis L PTS 6 Leicester Square
24.04.04	Tony Doherty L PTS 6 Reading
02.06.04	Kevin McIntyre L PTS 6 Hereford
03.07.04	Bradley Pryce L RSC 8 Newport (Vacant Welsh Welterweight Title)
03.09.04	Tony Doherty L PTS 6 Newport
10.09.04	David Burke L PTS 6 Liverpool
24.09.04	Chas Symonds L PTS 10 Bethnal Green (Vacant British Masters Welterweight Title)
12.11.04	Lenny Daws L PTS 8 Wembley
19.11.04	Gary Woolcombe L PTS 4 Bethnal Green
02.12.04	Ashley Theophane L PTS 6 Crystal Palace
07.04.05	Terry Adams L PTS 6 Birmingham

Career: 107 contests, won 9, drew 7, lost 91.

Michael Jones

Liverpool. *Born* Liverpool, 14 November, 1974
British L.Middleweight Champion. Former Commonwealth L.Middleweight Champion. Ht. 6'0¼"
Manager Self

15.11.97	Harry Butler W PTS 4 Bristol
17.01.98	Martin Cavey W CO 1 Bristol
07.03.98	Darren McInulty W PTS 4 Reading
25.04.98	Koba Kulu W RSC 3 Cardiff
06.06.98	G. L. Booth W RSC 2 Liverpool
10.10.98	Takaloo W PTS 6 Bethnal Green
19.12.98	Ojay Abrahams W PTS 6 Liverpool

26.06.99	Paul King W PTS 6 Glasgow
11.03.00	Alan Gilbert W RTD 3 Kensington
02.06.00	Mohammed Boualleg W PTS 8 Ashford
03.02.01	Howard Clarke W PTS 4 Manchester
24.04.01	Judicael Bedel W PTS 6 Liverpool
06.10.01	Delroy Mellis W PTS 8 Manchester
10.12.01	Piotr Bartnicki W RSC 4 Liverpool
13.04.02	Mark Richards W RSC 1 Liverpool
28.05.02	Joshua Onyango W RSC 6 Liverpool (Commonwealth L. Middleweight Title Challenge)
08.02.03	Howard Clarke W PTS 6 Liverpool
19.04.03	Jamie Moore L PTS 12 Liverpool (Commonwealth L.Middleweight Title Defence. Vacant British L.Middleweight Title)
18.10.03	Ojay Abrahams W PTS 6 Manchester
13.03.04	Jason Williams W PTS 6 Huddersfield
10.04.04	Darren Rhodes W RSC 3 Manchester (Final Elim. British L.Middleweight Title)
26.11.04	Jamie Moore W DIS 3 Altrincham (British L.Middleweight Title Challenge)

Career: 22 contests, won 21, lost 1.

(Lee) Taz Jones

Abercynon. *Born* Aberdare, 24 August, 1982
British Masters L.Middleweight Champion. Ht. 5'11"
Manager B. Coleman

15.09.02	David White DREW 4 Swansea
02.11.02	Gerard McAuley DREW 4 Belfast
21.12.02	Luke Rudd W RTD 1 Millwall
08.01.03	Elroy Edwards W PTS 6 Aberdare
27.09.03	Matthew Hatton L PTS 6 Manchester
06.12.03	Ernie Smith W PTS 4 Cardiff
21.02.04	Craig Lynch W PTS 4 Cardiff
17.04.04	Andy Gibson W PTS 6 Belfast
03.09.04	Karl Taylor W PTS 4 Newport
30.09.04	Craig Dickson DREW 6 Glasgow
08.12.04	Kevin Phelan W PTS 10 Longford (British Masters L.Middleweight Title Challenge)
18.03.05	Neil Sinclair W RSC 1 Belfast

Career: 12 contests, won 8, drew 3, lost 1.

(Nathaniel) Nate Joseph

Bradford. *Born* Bradford, 6 June, 1979
Cruiserweight. Ht. 5'10"
Manager C. Aston

20.11.02	Lee Mountford L PTS 6 Leeds
03.02.03	Gary Thompson W PTS 4 Bradford
13.04.03	Eamonn Glennon W PTS 6 Bradford
13.05.03	Lee Mountford W PTS 6 Leeds
31.05.03	Brian Gascoigne L RTD 1 Barnsley
07.12.03	Earl Ling DREW 6 Bradford
16.01.04	Terry Morrill L PTS 6 Bradford
16.04.04	Michael Pinnock W PTS 4 Bradford
09.10.04	Earl Ling L PTS 6 Norwich
06.12.04	Gary Thompson W PTS 6 Bradford
13.02.05	Lee Mountford W PTS 6 Bradford
08.05.05	Hastings Rasani L RSC 4 Bradford
18.06.05	Carl Wright L CO 1 Coventry (Vacant British Masters Cruiserweight Title)

Career: 13 contests, won 5, drew 1, lost 7.

Gokhan Kazaz

Walthamstow. *Born* Turkey, 21 November, 1977
Middleweight. Ht. 5'9"
Manager F. Maloney

17.07.03	Joel Ani W PTS 4 Dagenham	
18.09.03	Jimi Hendricks W PTS 4 Dagenham	
06.11.03	Tomas da Silva W PTS 4 Dagenham	
07.02.04	Patrick Cito W PTS 4 Bethnal Green	
13.05.04	Alan Gilbert W PTS 4 Bethnal Green	
30.07.04	Dean Powell W RSC 2 Bethnal Green	
10.09.04	Dmitry Donetskiy W RSC 4 Bethnal Green	
11.12.04	Darren McDermott DREW 4 Canning Town	
19.06.05	Alan Gilbert W PTS 6 Bethnal Green	

Career: 9 contests, won 8, drew 1.

Gokhan Kazaz   Les Clark

John Keeton

Sheffield. *Born* Sheffield, 19 May, 1972
Cruiserweight. Former Undefeated WBF & WBO Inter-Continental Cruiserweight Champion. Ht. 6'0"
Manager D. Ingle

11.08.93	Tony Colclough W RSC 1 Mansfield
15.09.93	Val Golding L PTS 6 Ashford
27.10.93	Darren McKenna W RSC 3 Stoke
01.12.93	Julius Francis L PTS 4 Bethnal Green
19.01.94	Dennis Bailey W RTD 2 Stoke
17.02.94	Dermot Gascoyne L RSC 1 Dagenham
09.04.94	Eddie Knight W RTD 5 Mansfield
11.05.94	John Rice W RSC 5 Sheffield
02.06.94	Devon Rhooms W RSC 2 Tooting
06.09.94	Mark Walker W RSC 5 Stoke
24.09.94	Dirk Wallyn L CO 3 Middlekerke, Belgium
26.10.94	Lee Archer W PTS 6 Stoke
09.12.94	Bruce Scott L CO 2 Bethnal Green
11.02.95	Rudiger May L PTS 6 Frankfurt, Germany
06.03.95	Simon McDougall W RSC 5 Mayfair
07.07.95	Nicky Piper L RTD 2 Cardiff
15.09.95	Steve Osborne W RSC 4 Mansfield
27.10.95	Nicky Wadman W RSC 1 Brighton
03.11.95	Monty Wright W RSC 4 Dudley
11.11.95	Denzil Browne W RSC 4 Halifax
30.01.96	Cesar Kazadi W RSC 3 Lille, France
11.05.96	Terry Dunstan L RSC 1 Bethnal Green *(British Cruiserweight Title Challenge)*
14.09.96	John Pierre W PTS 4 Sheffield
14.12.96	Nigel Rafferty W RTD 3 Sheffield
12.04.97	Nigel Rafferty W RSC 6 Sheffield
11.10.97	Kelly Oliver L RSC 8 Sheffield *(Vacant WBO Inter-Continental Cruiserweight Title)*
16.05.98	Jacob Mofokeng L RTD 4 Hammanskraal, South Africa
18.07.98	Kelly Oliver W RSC 2 Sheffield
23.01.99	Garry Delaney W PTS 12 Cheshunt *(Vacant WBO Inter-Continental Cruiserweight Title)*
15.05.99	William Barima W RTD 3 Sheffield
29.02.00	Tony Booth W RSC 2 Widnes
16.12.00	Bruce Scott L CO 6 Sheffield *(Vacant British Cruiserweight Title)*
21.07.01	Radcliffe Green W RSC 4 Sheffield
19.03.02	Butch Lesley W PTS 12 Slough *(Vacant WBF Cruiserweight Title)*
16.04.04	Paul Bonson W PTS 4 Bradford
14.05.05	Paul Bonson W PTS 4 Aberdeen
11.06.05	Krzysztof Wlodarczyk L RTD 3 Gorzow Wielkopolski, Poland *(WBC Youth Cruiserweight Title Challenge)*

Career: 37 contests, won 25, lost 12.

David Kehoe

Northampton. *Born* Northampton, 24 December, 1972
Welterweight. Ht. 5'10½"
Manager Self

06.02.96	Simon Frailing W CO 1 Basildon
20.04.96	Paul Salmon W PTS 6 Brentwood
12.11.96	Peter Nightingale L PTS 6 Dudley
28.04.97	Craig Kelley L DIS 3 Enfield
18.11.97	Peter Nightingale DREW 4 Mansfield
27.01.98	Paul Miles L PTS 4 Bethnal Green
11.03.98	Trevor Tacy W RTD 1 Bethnal Green
28.03.98	David Thompson W PTS 6 Crystal Palace
26.05.98	Dave Hinds W RSC 5 Mayfair
08.09.98	Marc Smith W PTS 6 Bethnal Green
12.01.99	Gary Flear L PTS 4 Bethnal Green
25.01.99	Roger Sampson L PTS 4 Glasgow
12.03.99	Jamie McKeever L RSC 2 Bethnal Green
02.07.99	Mark McGowan L RSC 3 Bristol *(Vacant British Masters Lightweight Title)*
13.09.99	Stephen Smith L DIS 2 Bethnal Green
05.10.99	John Humphrey L PTS 4 Bloomsbury
24.10.99	Young Muttley L RTD 1 Wolverhampton
02.12.99	Liam Maltby L PTS 4 Peterborough
19.02.00	Dariusz Snarski DREW 6 Prestwick
10.03.00	Ted Bami L PTS 4 Bethnal Green
17.04.00	Mark Hawthorne L PTS 4 Birmingham
25.07.00	P.J.Gallagher L PTS 6 Southwark
08.09.00	Dariusz Snarski W PTS 4 Hammersmith
27.11.00	Anthony Maynard L RSC 5 Birmingham
16.03.02	Wayne Wheeler DREW 6 Northampton
28.05.02	Ricky Eccleston L RSC 4 Liverpool
14.09.02	Danny Hunt L RSC 3 Bethnal Green
16.11.02	Gwyn Wale L PTS 4 Nottingham
01.02.03	Mark Winters L RSC 2 Belfast
29.10.03	Pete Buckley W PTS 6 Leicester Square
08.07.04	Rocky Muscus W PTS 6 The Strand
08.10.04	Graham Delehedy L RSC 2 Brentwood
18.03.05	Paul McCloskey L RSC 3 Belfast
24.04.05	Ashley Theophane L PTS 4 Leicester Square
26.06.05	Jay Morris L PTS 4 Southampton

Career: 35 contests, won 9, drew 3, lost 23.

David Keir

Liverpool. *Born* Liverpool, 23 September, 1977
Welterweight. Ht. 5'9½"
Manager Self

10.12.01	Lee Williamson DREW 4 Liverpool
11.02.02	Sammy Smith L PTS 6 Southampton
13.04.02	Lee Williamson W PTS 4 Liverpool
03.06.02	Paul McIlwaine W CO 2 Glasgow
23.09.02	Gary Porter L PTS 8 Glasgow
15.10.02	Costas Katsantonis W PTS 6 Bethnal Green
15.02.03	Matthew Hatton W RSC 4 Wembley
28.04.03	Darrell Grafton L DIS 5 Nottingham
31.05.03	Robert Burton L RSC 9 Barnsley *(Central Area Welterweight Title Challenge)*
08.05.04	Michael Lomax L RTD 4 Dagenham
21.03.05	Craig Dickson L RTD 3 Glasgow

Career: 11 contests, won 4, drew 1, lost 6.

Damaen Kelly

Belfast. *Born* Belfast, 3 April, 1973
Flyweight. IBO S.Flyweight Champion. Former Undefeated WBF & IBO Flyweight Champion. Former Undefeated European Flyweight Champion. Former Undefeated WBC International S.Flyweight Champion. Former British & Commonwealth Flyweight Champion. Ht. 5'5"
Manager Self

27.09.97	Chris Thomas W RSC 1 Belfast
22.11.97	Bojidar Ivanov W CO 1 Manchester
20.12.97	Anthony Hanna W PTS 4 Belfast
14.02.98	Hristo Lessov W RSC 2 Southwark
14.03.98	Mark Reynolds W RSC 4 Bethnal Green
02.05.98	Krasimir Tcholakov W RSC 3 Kensington
26.09.98	Mike Thomas W PTS 6 Uncasville, Connecticut, USA
12.12.98	Alfonso Zvenyika W PTS 12 Chester *(Commonwealth Flyweight Title Challenge)*
13.03.99	Anthony Hanna W PTS 12 Manchester *(Vacant British Flyweight Title. Commonwealth Flyweight Title Defence)*
22.05.99	Keith Knox L RTD 6 Belfast *(British & Commonwealth Flyweight Title Defences)*
16.10.99	Igor Gerasimov W RSC 4 Belfast *(Vacant WBC International S. Flyweight Title)*
12.02.00	Alexander Mahmutov W PTS 12 Sheffield *(European Flyweight Title Challenge)*
12.06.00	Jose Antonio Lopez Bueno W PTS 12 Belfast *(European Flyweight Title Defence)*
30.09.00	Zolile Mbitye W PTS 12 Peterborough *(IBO Flyweight Title Challenge)*

17.02.01	Paulino Villabos W PTS 12 Bethnal Green
	(IBO Flyweight Title Defence)
31.07.01	Sipho Mantyi W RSC 4 Bethnal Green
18.01.02	Simphewe Xabendini W RSC 1 Coventry
21.05.02	Celso Dangud W PTS 12 Custom House
	(Vacant WBF Flyweight Title)
05.10.02	Jovy Oracion W PTS 8 Liverpool
27.09.03	Irene Pacheco L RSC 7 Barranquilla, Colombia,
	(IBF Flyweight Title Challenge)
17.04.04	Andrei Kostin W RSC 1 Belfast
26.06.04	Delroy Spencer W RSC 4 Belfast
17.12.04	Jason Booth W PTS 12 Huddersfield
	(IBO S.Flyweight Title Challenge)

Career: 23 contests, won 21, lost 2.

Colin Kenna

Southampton. *Born* Dublin, 28 July, 1976
Heavyweight. Ht. 6'1"
Manager J. Bishop

25.02.01	Slick Miller W RSC 3 Streatham
22.04.01	Eamonn Glennon W PTS 4 Streatham
15.10.01	Tony Booth W PTS 6 Southampton
11.02.02	Dave Clarke W RSC 4 Southampton
08.04.02	James Gilbert W RSC 1 Southampton
12.07.02	Gary Williams W RSC 3 Southampton
01.11.02	Paul Buttery DREW 6 Preston

Damaen Kelly   Les Clark

17.03.03	Derek McCafferty W PTS 6 Southampton
12.05.03	Paul Bonson W PTS 6 Southampton
01.08.03	Michael Sprott L RSC 1 Bethnal Green
	(Southern Area Heavyweight Title Challenge)
26.10.03	Darren Ashton W CO 1 Longford
20.02.04	Paul Bonson W PTS 6 Southampton
30.03.04	Chris Woollas W PTS 6 Southampton
12.05.04	Mark Krence L RTD 3 Reading
06.02.05	Oneal Murray W RTD 3 Southampton
19.02.05	Paul King DREW 6 Dublin
26.06.05	Julius Francis W PTS 4 Southampton

Career: 17 contests, won 13, drew 2, lost 2.

Ryan Kerr

Bannockburn. *Born* Falkirk, 19 March, 1982
English & Northern Area S.Middleweight Champion. Ht. 5'9"
Manager T. Conroy

17.09.01	Pedro Thompson W RSC 1 Glasgow
04.10.01	Colin McCash W PTS 6 Sunderland
03.11.01	Tomas da Silva W PTS 4 Glasgow
21.02.02	Wayne Shepherd W PTS 6 Sunderland
03.10.02	Steve Timms W RSC 1 Sunderland
05.12.02	Martin Thompson W RSC 4 Sunderland
27.02.03	Surinder Sekhon W PTS 6 Sunderland

17.03.03	Lee Molloy W PTS 8 Glasgow
02.10.03	Eddie Haley W PTS 8 Sunderland
26.02.04	Eddie Haley W RSC 5 Sunderland
	(Vacant Northern Area S.Middleweight Title)
23.09.04	Gary Dixon W RSC 7 Gateshead
	(Northern Area S.Middleweight Title Defence)
24.02.05	Ryan Walls W PTS 10 Sunderland
	(Vacant English S.Middleweight Title)

Career: 12 contests, won 12.

Imad Khamis

Manchester. *Born* Egypt, 9 March, 1977
L. Welterweight. Ht. 5'11¼"
Manager W. Barker

17.06.05	Martin McDonagh L DIS 4 Glasgow

Career: 1 contest, lost 1.

Amer Khan

Sheffield. *Born* Sheffield, 21 February, 1981
L. Heavyweight. Ht. 6'2"
Manager Self

06.06.03	Gary Jones W PTS 6 Hull
31.07.03	Michael Pinnock W PTS 6 Sheffield
05.09.03	Shpetim Hoti W RTD 4 Sheffield
04.12.03	Terry Morrill W PTS 6 Sunderland
06.02.04	Terry Morrill W PTS 6 Sheffield
03.04.04	Michael Pinnock W PTS 6 Sheffield
17.06.04	Hastings Rasani W PTS 6 Sheffield
24.10.04	Paulie Silva W PTS 6 Sheffield
04.03.05	Karl Wheeler W PTS 6 Rotherham

Career: 9 contests, won 9.

Nathan King

Mountain Ash. *Born* Aberdare, 19 March, 1981
S.Middleweight. Ht. 6'3"
Manager B. Coleman

27.01.01	Tony Oakey L PTS 6 Bethnal Green
28.04.01	Pinky Burton W PTS 4 Cardiff
09.06.01	Michael Pinnock W PTS 4 Bethnal Green
09.10.01	Darren Ashton W PTS 6 Cardiff
24.11.01	Peter Haymer W PTS 4 Bethnal Green
12.02.02	Peter Haymer W PTS 4 Bethnal Green
20.04.02	Radcliffe Green W PTS 6 Cardiff
17.08.02	Valery Odin L PTS 6 Cardiff
14.12.02	Paul Bonson L PTS 4 Newcastle
10.04.03	Ovill McKenzie L PTS 4 Clydach
28.06.03	Varuzhan Davtyan W PTS 4 Cardiff
21.02.04	Daniel Sackey L PTS 4 Cardiff
12.03.04	Elvis Michailenko L PTS 6 Millwall
03.07.04	Nick Okoth W PTS 4 Newport
22.10.04	Hastings Rasani W PTS 6 Edinburgh
24.11.04	Eric Teymour L PTS 12 Mayfair
	(Vacant WBU S.Middleweight Title)
13.02.05	Malik Dziarra W PTS 6 Brentwood
28.06.05	Malik Dziarra L PTS 8 Cuaxhaven, Germany

Career: 18 contests, won 10, lost 8.

Paul King

Sheffield. *Born* Sheffield, 9 August, 1974
Heavyweight. Ht. 6'3"
Manager G. Rhodes

10.02.04	Billy Wilson L PTS 6 Barnsley
28.02.04	David Ingleby W RSC 3 Manchester

12.03.04	Micky Steeds L PTS 6 Millwall	
03.04.04	Carl Baker W PTS 6 Sheffield	
10.04.04	Albert Sosnowski L PTS 4 Manchester	
02.06.04	Scott Gammer L RSC 3 Hereford	
18.09.04	Luke Simpkin W PTS 6 Newark	
30.09.04	Chris Woollas W PTS 4 Glasgow	
12.11.04	Leif Larsen L CO 1 Copenhagen, Denmark	
06.02.05	Billy Bessey W PTS 6 Southampton	
19.02.05	Colin Kenna DREW 6 Dublin	
04.03.05	Carl Baker L RSC 2 Rotherham	
30.04.05	Wayne Llewelyn L PTS 6 Dagenham	

Career: 13 contests, won 5, drew 1, lost 7

Paul King   Les Clark

David Kirk

Sutton in Ashfield. *Born* Mansfield, 5 October, 1974
L.Middleweight. Former Undefeated WBF European Welterweight Champion. Ht. 5'8"
Manager Self

01.11.96	Arv Mittoo W PTS 6 Mansfield
04.12.96	Stuart Rimmer W PTS 6 Stoke
20.02.97	Chris Price W PTS 6 Mansfield
16.03.97	Gary Hibbert L PTS 6 Shaw
25.03.97	Miguel Matthews W PTS 6 Wolverhampton
28.04.97	Mark Breslin L PTS 8 Glasgow
06.10.97	Christian Brady L PTS 6 Birmingham
30.10.97	Trevor Tacy L PTS 6 Newark
08.12.97	Nick Hall L PTS 6 Nottingham
12.01.98	Juha Temonen DREW 6 Helsinki, Finland
24.01.98	Jason Cook L RSC 3 Cardiff
24.02.98	Roy Rutherford L PTS 6 Edgbaston
11.03.98	Patrick Gallagher L PTS 6 Bethnal Green
27.04.98	Tommy Peacock L PTS 6 Manchester
08.05.98	Chris Barnett L PTS 6 Manchester
23.05.98	Graham Earl L PTS 4 Bethnal Green
04.06.98	Mark Richards L PTS 6 Dudley
21.09.98	Steve McLevy L PTS 8 Glasgow
12.10.98	Malcolm Melvin L PTS 10 Birmingham
	(Midlands Area L. Welterweight Title Challenge)
31.10.98	Bernard Paul L PTS 6 Southend
28.11.98	Glenn McClarnon L PTS 4 Belfast
11.12.98	Charlie Kane L PTS 8 Prestwick
20.02.99	Dennis Berry L PTS 10 Thornaby
	(Vacant Continental European Welterweight Title)

09.05.99	Sammy Smith L PTS 6 Bracknell
20.05.99	Steve Brumant W PTS 4 Kensington
05.06.99	Neil Sinclair L PTS 8 Cardiff
11.09.99	Glenn McClarnon L PTS 6 Sheffield
20.10.99	Dave Gibson W PTS 6 Stoke
18.11.99	Adrian Chase W PTS 10 Mayfair
	(Vacant WBF European Welterweight Title)
26.11.99	Gerard Murphy L RTD 3 Hull
25.03.00	Jacek Bielski L PTS 6 Liverpool
29.04.00	Eamonn Magee L RSC 8 Wembley
13.08.00	Ram Singh W PTS 6 Nottingham
09.09.00	Mally McIver L PTS 6 Newark
23.09.00	Steve Murray L PTS 4 Bethnal Green
09.10.00	Steve Saville W PTS 8 Birmingham
19.11.00	Gavin Down L PTS 10 Chesterfield
	(Vacant British Masters L.Welterweight Title)
01.12.00	Alan Bosworth DREW 8 Peterborough
04.02.01	Mark Winters L PTS 6 Queensferry
28.02.01	Ossie Duran L PTS 8 Kensington
	(Vacant WBF European Welterweight Title)
10.03.01	Junior Witter L RSC 2 Bethnal Green
10.04.01	Colin Lynes L PTS 6 Wembley
20.04.01	Mark Winters L PTS 6 Dublin
16.06.01	Oscar Hall L PTS 6 Derby
07.07.01	Michael Jennings L PTS 6 Manchester
28.07.01	Jonathan Thaxton L PTS 4 Wembley
13.09.01	David Walker DREW 8 Sheffield
17.11.01	Kevin McIntyre L PTS 4 Glasgow
24.11.01	Ivan Kirpa L PTS 4 Bethnal Green
08.12.01	Chris Saunders L CO 2 Chesterfield
26.01.02	Colin Lynes L PTS 6 Dagenham
09.02.02	David Barnes L RTD 1 Manchester
11.03.02	Matthew Macklin L PTS 4 Glasgow
25.05.02	Francis Barrett L PTS 6 Portsmouth
08.06.02	Kevin McIntyre L RTD 4 Renfrew
28.09.02	Matthew Hatton W PTS 6 Manchester
22.03.03	Kevin McIntyre L RSC 1 Renfrew
24.05.03	Nigel Wright L PTS 4 Bethnal Green
31.05.03	Sammy Smith L PTS 4 Bethnal Green
08.06.03	Adnan Amar L PTS 6 Nottingham
04.10.03	Francis Barrett L PTS 6 Muswell Hill
10.04.04	Albert Sosnowski L PTS 4 Manchester
07.05.04	Gary Woolcombe L PTS 4 Bethnal Green
19.06.04	Gary Young L PTS 4 Renfrew
03.07.04	Tony Doherty L PTS 4 Newport
19.11.04	Ross Minter L PTS 6 Bethnal Green
03.12.04	Martin Concepcion L PTS 4 Edinburgh

Career: 67 contests, won 10, drew 3, lost 54.

Mark Krence

Chesterfield. *Born* Chesterfield, 24 August, 1976
English & Midlands Area Heavyweight Champion. Ht. 6'5"
Manager D. Hobson

09.04.00	Slick Miller W PTS 6 Alfreton
21.10.00	Neil Kirkwood W PTS 6 Sheffield
11.12.00	Tony Booth W PTS 6 Sheffield
20.01.01	Nigel Rafferty W PTS 4 Bethnal Green
24.03.01	Mark Williams W PTS 4 Sheffield
27.07.01	Shane Woollas W PTS 4 Sheffield
13.09.01	Luke Simpkin W PTS 4 Sheffield
25.09.01	Darren Chubbs W PTS 4 Liverpool
15.12.01	Eamonn Glennon W RSC 2 Sheffield
16.03.02	Neil Kirkwood L RSC 4 Bethnal Green
11.05.02	Gary Williams W PTS 6 Chesterfield
21.05.02	Audley Harrison L PTS 6 Custom House

03.08.02	Tony Booth W PTS 4 Derby
05.10.02	Gary Williams W RSC 4 Chesterfield
24.01.03	Petr Horacek W RSC 4 Sheffield
18.03.03	Paul Bonson W PTS 4 Reading
10.06.03	Luke Simpkin W RTD 8 Sheffield
	(Vacant Midlands Area Heavyweight Title)
01.08.03	Derek McCafferty W PTS 4 Bethnal Green
05.09.03	Collice Mutizwa W CO 2 Sheffield
06.02.04	Mendauga Kulikauskas W PTS 8 Sheffield
12.05.04	Colin Kenna W RTD 3 Reading
10.09.04	Konstantin Prizyuk L RSC 6 Wembley
11.12.04	John McDermott W PTS 10 Canning Town
	(Vacant English Heavyweight Title)
15.05.05	Scott Gammer L RSC 8 Sheffield
	(Elim. British Heavyweight Title)

Career: 24 contests, won 21, lost 3.

Mark Krence   Les Clark

Eder Kurti

Kennington. *Born* Albania, 29 August, 1984
Middleweight. Ht. 5'10¾"
Manager B. Baker

04.11.04	Cafu Santos W RSC 1 Piccadilly
02.12.04	Craig Lynch W DIS 4 Crystal Palace
27.01.05	Ojay Abrahams W PTS 6 Piccadilly

Career: 3 contests, won 3.

Eder Kurti   Les Clark

129

Kristian Laight

Nuneaton. *Born* Nuneaton, 15 June, 1980
Lightweight. Ht. 5'10"
Manager J. Gill

26.09.03 James Paisley L PTS 6 Millwall
14.11.03 Matt Teague L PTS 6 Hull
05.12.03 Justin Hicks L PTS 6 Bristol
07.02.04 Kevin Mitchell L PTS 4 Bethnal Green
30.03.04 Chris McDonagh L PTS 6
Southampton
08.04.04 Jaz Virdee W PTS 6 Peterborough
20.04.04 Femi Fehintola L PTS 6 Sheffield
04.06.04 Gary Coombes DREW 6 Dudley
19.06.04 Ryan Barrett L PTS 4 Muswell Hill
23.10.04 Sean Hughes L PTS 6 Wakefield
18.11.04 Martin Gethin L RSC 4 Shrewsbury
17.12.04 Baz Carey L PTS 6 Coventry
08.05.05 Nadeem Siddique L RSC 7 Bradford
25.06.05 John-Paul Ryan DREW 6 Melton
Mowbray

Career: 14 contests, won 1, drew 2, lost 11.

Mervyn Langdale

Southampton. *Born* Hythe, Hull, 11 May,
1977
Cruiserweight. Ht. 6'4"
Manager J. Bishop

06.02.05 Nick Okoth DREW 6 Southampton
Career: 1 contest, drew 1

Mervyn Langdale   Les Clark

Scott Lansdowne

Leicester. *Born* Leicester, 11 August, 1972
Heavyweight. Former Undefeated Midlands
Area Cruiserweight Champion. Former
Undefeated WBF European
S.Cruiserweight Champion. Ht. 5'10"
Manager D. Coldwell

15.12.98 Gary Williams W PTS 6 Sheffield
11.09.99 Luke Simpkin W PTS 4 Sheffield
09.12.99 Geoff Hunter W PTS 6 Sheffield
20.05.00 Gary Williams W RSC 1 Leicester
*(Vacant WBF European
S. Cruiserweight Title)*
21.10.00 Adam Cale W RSC 5 Sheffield
29.01.01 Nigel Rafferty W PTS 4 Peterborough
28.04.02 Tony Booth L RSC 4 Southwark
23.06.02 Paul Bonson L PTS 4 Southwark
30.11.02 Tony Dowling W RSC 2 Newark
*(Vacant Midlands Area Cruiserweight
Title)*
16.03.03 Michael Pinnock W PTS 6 Nottingham
12.10.03 Clint Johnson W PTS 4 Sheffield
11.12.03 Steven Spartacus L RSC 3 Bethnal
Green
(Vacant English L.Heavyweight Title)
10.07.04 David Ingleby W RSC 4 Coventry
06.12.04 Jason Callum W CO 1 Leicester
25.06.05 Carl Baker L RSC 8 Melton Mowbray
*(Vacant British Masters Heavyweight
Title)*

Career: 15 contests, won 11, lost 4.

Gareth Lawrence

Sidcup. *Born* Barking, 21 August, 1980
S. Middleweight. Ht. 6'2"
Manager M. Roe

01.05.04 Paul Buchanan L PTS 4 Gravesend
16.10.04 Dean Powell W PTS 4 Dagenham
19.12.04 Tony Janes W PTS 4 Bethnal Green
21.01.05 Matthew Barr L RSC 2 Brentford
05.03.05 Leigh Wicks W PTS 4 Dagenham
23.03.05 Howard Clarke W PTS 6 Leicester
Square
30.04.05 Michael Banbula W PTS 6 Dagenham
26.05.05 Joey Vegas L PTS 4 Mayfair

Career: 8 contests, won 5, lost 3.

Gareth Lawrence   Les Clark

Scott Lawton

Stoke. *Born* Stoke, 23 September, 1976
Midlands Area Lightweight Champion.
Ht. 5'10"
Manager Self

29.09.01 Dave Hinds W RSC 2 Southwark
08.12.01 Ilias Miah W PTS 4 Dagenham
26.01.02 Pete Buckley W PTS 4 Bethnal Green
26.04.02 Pete Buckley W PTS 4 Coventry
06.09.02 Ben Hudson W PTS 4 Bethnal Green

30.01.03 Dave Stewart L PTS 6 Piccadilly
26.04.03 Chris McDonagh W RSC 2 Brentford
13.06.03 Jason Nesbitt W PTS 6 Queensway
14.11.03 Jimmy Beech W RSC 5 Bethnal
Green
20.04.04 Henry Jones W PTS 6 Sheffield
17.06.04 Carl Allen W PTS 10 Sheffield
*(Vacant Midlands Area Lightweight
Title)*
17.09.04 Silence Saheed W PTS 6 Sheffield
10.12.04 Roger Sampson W PTS 6 Sheffield
04.03.05 Peter McDonagh W PTS 6 Rotherham
15.05.05 Carl Allen W PTS 6 Sheffield

Career: 15 contests, won 14, lost 1.

Barrie Lee

Arbroath. *Born* Arbroath, 29 March, 1982
Scottish L. Middleweight Champion.
Ht. 5'8"
Manager A. Morrison/K. Morrison

25.10.03 Dave Wakefield W PTS 4 Edinburgh
29.11.03 Brian Coleman W PTS 4 Renfrew
27.03.04 Arv Mittoo W PTS 4 Edinburgh
23.04.04 William Webster W PTS 6 Glasgow
28.05.04 Brian Coleman W PTS 6 Glasgow
19.06.04 Craig Lynch W PTS 6 Renfrew
08.10.04 Vince Baldassara DREW 6 Glasgow
22.10.04 Craig Lynch W PTS 10 Edinburgh
(Vacant Scottish L.Middleweight Title)
03.12.04 John-Paul Temple W PTS 4 Edinburgh
08.04.05 Vince Baldassara W PTS 4 Edinburgh
03.06.05 Thomas McDonagh L RSC 7
Manchester
*(WBU Inter-Continental
L.Middleweight Title Challenge)*

Career: 11 contests, won 9, drew 1, lost 1.

Willie Limond

Glasgow. *Born* Glasgow, 2 February, 1979
Celtic & European Union S.Featherweight
Champion. Ht. 5'7"
Manager Self

12.11.99 Lennie Hodgkins W RTD 1 Glasgow
13.12.99 Steve Hanley W PTS 6 Glasgow
24.02.00 Nigel Senior W RSC 6 Glasgow
18.03.00 Phil Lashley W RSC 1 Glasgow
07.04.00 Jimmy Beech W RSC 2 Glasgow
26.05.00 Billy Smith W PTS 4 Glasgow
24.06.00 Haroon Din W PTS 4 Glasgow
10.11.00 Danny Connelly W PTS 6 Glasgow
17.12.00 Billy Smith W PTS 6 Glasgow
15.02.01 Marcus Portman W PTS 6 Glasgow
03.04.01 Trevor Smith W PTS 4 Bethnal Green
27.04.01 Choi Tseveenpurev W PTS 6 Glasgow
07.09.01 Gary Reid W PTS 8 Glasgow
03.11.01 Rakhim Mingaleev W PTS 6 Glasgow
17.11.01 Keith Jones W PTS 4 Glasgow
11.03.02 Dave Hinds W PTS 6 Glasgow
06.09.02 Assen Vassilev W RSC 3 Glasgow
22.03.03 Jimmy Beech W CO 4 Renfrew
12.07.03 Alex Arthur L RSC 8 Renfrew
*(British S.Featherweight Title
Challenge)*
01.11.03 Dariusz Snarski W RSC 1 Glasgow
29.11.03 Anthony Hanna W PTS 4 Renfrew
06.03.04 Dafydd Carlin W RSC 1 Renfrew
19.06.04 Youssouf Djibaba W PTS 10 Renfrew
*(Vacant European Union
S.Featherweight Title)*
29.10.04 Frederic Bonifai W PTS 8 Glasgow

03.12.04 Alberto Lopez W PTS 10 Edinburgh
(European Union S.Featherweight Title Defence)
20.05.05 John Mackay W RSC 5 Glasgow
17.06.05 Kevin O'Hara W PTS 10 Glasgow
(Vacant Celtic S.Featherweight Title)
Career: 27 contests, won 26, lost 1.

Willie Limond   Les Clark

Martin Lindsay

Belfast. *Born* Belfast, 10 May, 1982
S.Featherweight. Ht. 5'7"
Manager J. Rooney

02.12.04 Dai Davies W RSC 1 Crystal Palace
24.04.05 Rakhim Mingaleev W PTS 4 Leicester Square
Career: 2 contests, won 2.

Martin Lindsay   Les Clark

Neil Linford

Leicester. *Born* Leicester, 29 September, 1977
L. Heavyweight. Ht. 5'10¾"
Manager Self

30.10.98 Israel Khumalo W RSC 2 Peterborough
30.11.98 David Baptiste W PTS 4 Peterborough
15.12.98 Johannes Ngiba W CO 2 Durban, South Africa
16.01.99 Dean Powell W RSC 1 Bethnal Green
22.02.99 Leigh Wicks W PTS 4 Peterborough
24.04.99 Adrian Houldey W RSC 2 Peterborough
17.05.99 Jason Barker L RSC 3 Peterborough
15.07.99 Hussain Osman L RSC 5 Peterborough
07.02.00 Mark Dawson W PTS 4 Peterborough
04.03.00 Darren Ashton W PTS 6 Peterborough
25.05.00 Michael Pinnock W PTS 4 Peterborough
30.09.00 Matthew Barney W PTS 10 Peterborough
(Elim. British S. Middleweight Title)
30.11.00 Darren Ashton W PTS 4 Peterborough
29.01.01 Brian Magee L PTS 12 Peterborough
(Vacant IBO Inter-Continental S. Middleweight Title)
23.06.01 Jon Penn W RSC 3 Peterborough
29.09.01 David Starie L RSC 6 Southwark
(British & Commonwealth S.Middleweight Title Challenges)
26.01.02 Ali Forbes W PTS 6 Bethnal Green
23.06.02 Tony Booth W RSC 5 Southwark
22.09.02 Paul Bonson W PTS 6 Southwark
27.10.02 Radcliffe Green DREW 10 Southwark
(Vacant British Masters L.Heavyweight Title)
29.03.03 Tony Oakey L PTS 12 Portsmouth
(WBU L. Heavyweight Title Challenge)
31.05.03 Andrew Lowe L PTS 10 Bethnal Green
(Elim. British L. Heavyweight Title)
26.11.04 Brian Magee L RSC 7 Altrincham
Career: 23 contests, won 15, drew 1, lost 7.

Earl Ling

Ipswich. *Born* Kings Lynn, 9 March, 1972
Cruiserweight. Ht. 5'10"
Manager Self

08.09.92 Eddie Collins W PTS 6 Norwich
11.05.93 Mark Hale L RSC 2 Norwich
12.12.94 Clinton Woods L RSC 5 Cleethorpes
04.12.95 Jeff Finlayson L PTS 6 Manchester
26.02.96 Peter Waudby L PTS 6 Hull
19.03.96 James Lowther L RSC 4 Leeds
16.05.98 Dean Ashton DREW 6 Chigwell
02.07.98 Dean Ashton L RSC 2 Ipswich
17.09.98 Jimmy Steel DREW 6 Brighton
19.01.99 Israel Khumalo L RSC 1 Ipswich
15.07.00 Mike Duffield W PTS 6 Norwich
04.11.00 Andrew Facey L PTS 6 Derby
16.06.01 Andrew Facey DREW 6 Derby
04.07.01 Calvin Stonestreet L PTS 4 Bloomsbury
13.04.02 Simeon Cover W CO 4 Norwich
25.04.02 Lee Whitehead W PTS 6 Hull
21.11.02 Michael Pinnock W PTS 6 Hull
12.04.03 Ryan Walls L RSC 4 Norwich
07.12.03 Nate Joseph DREW 6 Bradford
21.02.04 Hastings Rasani DREW 6 Norwich
09.10.04 Nate Joseph W PTS 6 Norwich
Career: 21 contests, won 6, drew 5, lost 10.

Wayne Llewelyn

Beckenham. *Born* Greenwich, 20 April, 1970
Heavyweight. Ht. 6'3½"
Manager Self

18.01.92 Chris Coughlan W RSC 3 Kensington
30.03.92 Steve Stewart W RSC 4 Eltham
23.04.92 Gary Charlton W RSC 6 Eltham
10.12.92 Gary McCrory W RSC 2 Glasgow
23.05.93 Cordwell Hylton W PTS 6 Brockley
01.12.93 Manny Burgo W PTS 6 Bethnal Green
14.04.94 Vance Idiens W RSC 1 Battersea
22.05.94 Cordwell Hylton W CO 2 Crystal Palace
03.05.95 Mitch Rose W PTS 4 NYC, New York, USA
07.07.95 Vance Idiens W RSC 1 Cardiff
11.08.95 Carlos Monroe W RSC 3 New Orleans, Louisiana, USA
26.04.96 Steve Garber W CO 1 Cardiff
08.06.96 Dermot Gascoyne W RSC 4 Newcastle
22.03.97 Mike Sedillo W CO 2 Wythenshawe
20.09.97 Michael Murray W RTD 4 Aachen, Germany
21.03.98 Everton Davis W PTS 8 Bethnal Green
06.06.98 Pele Reid L CO 1 Liverpool
(Elim. British Heavyweight Title)
18.02.99 Derek Williams W RSC 3 Bossier City, Louisiana, USA
03.06.99 Frankie Swindell L CO 2 Mount Pleasant, Michigan, USA
21.08.99 Terry Veners W RSC 3 Coachella, California, USA
28.11.99 Terry Veners W CO 2 Monterey, California, USA
10.03.00 William Barima W CO 1 Bethnal Green
19.03.00 Augustin Corpus L PTS 8 Tunica, Mississippi, USA
14.10.00 Michael Sprott W RSC 3 Wembley
08.12.00 Alex Vasiliev L RSC 1 Crystal Palace
01.04.01 Luke Simpkin W PTS 6 Southwark
19.01.02 Andreas Sidon W CO 1 Berlin, Germany
22.03.02 Ladislav Husarik W PTS 6 Berlin, Germany
25.08.02 Ergin Solmaz W RSC 3 Berlin, Germany
07.09.02 Vladislav Druso W PTS 6 Munich, Germany
11.10.03 Ervin Slonka W RSC 2 Velten, Germany
15.04.04 Jameel McCline L RSC 1 NYC, New York, USA
26.11.04 Roman Kaloczai W CO 1 Berlin, Germany
15.01.05 Vladislav Druso W RSC 1 Berlin, Germany
30.04.05 Paul King W PTS 6 Dagenham
Career: 35 contests, won 30, lost 5.

Robert Lloyd-Taylor (Lloyd)

Northolt. *Born* Perivale, 1 September, 1980
Welterweight. Ht. 5'11¼"
Manager Self

27.09.02 Wayne Wheeler W PTS 6 Bracknell
25.10.02 Nicky Leech L PTS 6 Cotgrave
20.12.02 Dean Larter W PTS 4 Bracknell
26.04.03 Ben Hudson L PTS 4 Brentford
31.05.03 Aidan Mooney W PTS 4 Bethnal Green

26.10.03 Arv Mittoo W PTS 6 Longford
14.11.03 Michael Lomax L PTS 6 Bethnal Green
07.04.04 Joe Mitchell W RSC 5 Leicester Square
07.05.04 Chas Symonds L RTD 5 Bethnal Green
08.07.04 Ivor Bonavic W PTS 4 The Strand
18.09.04 Matt Scriven W RTD 4 Newark
21.11.04 Geraint Harvey W PTS 4 Bracknell
21.01.05 Ivor Bonavic W CO 2 Brentford
16.06.05 Duncan Cottier W RSC 1 Mayfair
Career: 14 contests, won 10, lost 4.

Gary Lockett

Cwmbran. *Born* Pontypool, 25 November, 1976
Middleweight. Former WBO Inter-Continental L. Middleweight Champion. Ht. 5'10"
Manager Self

06.09.96 Ernie Loveridge W PTS 4 Liverpool
26.10.96 Charlie Paine W RSC 4 Liverpool
24.10.98 Lee Bird W RSC 2 Liverpool
27.02.99 Carl Smith W RSC 2 Bethnal Green
15.05.99 Mike Whittaker W RSC 2 Blackpool
19.06.99 Kid Halls W CO 1 Dublin
09.03.00 Kevin Thompson W CO 2 Liverpool
04.11.00 David Baptiste W PTS 4 Bethnal Green
23.01.01 Abdul Mehdi W RSC 2 Crawley
03.03.01 Hussain Osman W CO 2 Wembley
07.04.01 Howard Clarke W RSC 2 Wembley
08.05.01 Mike Algoet W PTS 6 Barnsley
14.07.01 Howard Clarke W CO 1 Wembley
25.09.01 Denny Dalton W RSC 1 Liverpool
24.11.01 Chris Nembhard W RSC 2 Bethnal Green
09.02.02 Kevin Kelly W CO 4 Manchester
(Vacant WBO Inter-Continental L.Middleweight Title)
20.04.02 Youri Tsarenko L PTS 12 Cardiff
(WBO Inter-Continental L.Middleweight Title Defence)
23.11.02 Viktor Fesetchko W PTS 8 Derby
29.03.03 Jason Collins W CO 1 Portsmouth
08.05.03 Yuri Tsarenko W PTS 10 Widnes
28.06.03 Michael Monaghan W PTS 10 Cardiff
21.02.04 Kreshnik Qato W RSC 2 Cardiff
12.06.04 Matt Galer W RSC 4 Manchester
03.09.04 Michael Monaghan W RSC 3 Newport
Career: 24 contests, won 23, lost 1.

Michael Lomax

Chingford. *Born* London, 25 September, 1978
Welterweight. Ht. 6'0"
Manager Self

05.07.03 Ernie Smith W PTS 4 Brentwood
20.09.03 Peter Dunn W PTS 4 Nottingham
14.11.03 Robert Lloyd-Taylor W PTS 6 Bethnal Green
16.01.04 Craig Lynch W PTS 6 Bradford
31.01.04 Steve Brumant W PTS 6 Bethnal Green
08.05.04 David Keir W RTD 4 Dagenham
13.02.05 Terry Adams W RSC 1 Brentwood
16.06.05 Jamie Coyle W PTS 6 Dagenham
Career: 8 contests, won 8.

Paul Lomax

Sunderland. *Born* Sunderland, 11 May, 1974
L.Middleweight. Ht. 6'0½"
Manager Self

23.07.00 Reece McAllister L PTS 6 Hartlepool
10.06.01 Tony Byrne L PTS 6 Ellesmere Port
17.11.01 Oscar Hall L PTS 4 Dewsbury
09.12.01 Tony Byrne L PTS 6 Blackpool
15.03.02 Andrei Ivanov W PTS 6 Spennymoor
29.04.02 Martyn Bailey DREW 6 Bradford
28.05.02 James Davenport W CO 3 Liverpool
07.05.03 Martyn Bailey L RTD 3 Ellesmere Port
(British Masters Middleweight Title Challenge)
12.10.03 Dean Walker L PTS 6 Sheffield
10.02.04 Robert Burton L PTS 6 Barnsley
19.11.04 Franny Jones L RSC 2 Hartlepool
Career: 11 contests, won 2, drew 1, lost 8.

Gerard London

Gospel Oak. *Born* London, 16 December, 1980
S.Middleweight. Ht 6'0½"
Manager Self

25.06.04 David Pearson W PTS 4 Bethnal Green
24.09.04 Paddy Ryan L PTS 4 Bethnal Green
26.11.04 Paddy Ryan W PTS 4 Bethnal Green
Career: 3 contests, won 2, lost 1.

Gerard London　　　　　Les Clark

Chris Long

Calne. *Born* Gloucester, 5 March, 1980
Lightweight. Ht. 5'9"
Manager T. Woodward

15.05.03 Darren Goode W RSC 1 Clevedon
21.09.03 Daniel Thorpe L PTS 6 Bristol
17.11.03 Stuart Green L PTS 6 Glasgow
13.02.04 Justin Hicks W RSC 4 Bristol
29.02.04 Gareth Perkins L PTS 6 Bristol
12.03.04 Ivor Bonavic W PTS 6 Millwall
01.05.04 Stuart Phillips W RSC 1 Bridgend
19.06.04 Ceri Hall L PTS 4 Muswell Hill
12.09.04 Ernie Smith DREW 6 Shrewsbury
24.09.04 John O'Donnell L RSC 4 Nottingham
02.12.04 Gavin Tait W PTS 6 Bristol

27.01.05 Sam Rukundo L PTS 4 Piccadilly
24.04.05 Scott Haywood L PTS 6 Derby
08.05.05 John Fewkes L PTS 8 Sheffield
Career: 14 contests, won 5, drew 1, lost 8.

Keith Long

Brixton. *Born* Greenwich, 30 July, 1968
Heavyweight. Ht. 5'11½"
Manager D. Williams/F. Warren

15.02.97 Steve Cranston W PTS 4 Tooting
04.02.99 Gordon Minors W PTS 6 Lewisham
24.04.99 Derek McCafferty L PTS 4 Peterborough
07.08.99 Israel Ajose DREW 6 Dagenham
29.11.99 Mark Potter W PTS 8 Wembley
13.04.00 Harry Senior W PTS 10 Holborn
18.11.00 Luke Simpkin W RSC 3 Dagenham
13.09.01 Mike Holden W PTS 10 Sheffield
(Elim.British Heavyweight Title)
08.07.02 Alexei Varakin W RSC 4 Mayfair
17.09.02 Danny Williams L PTS 12 Bethnal Green
(British & Commonwealth Heavyweight Title Challenges)
15.02.03 Slick Miller W RSC 1 Wembley
24.01.04 Denis Bakhtov L PTS 12 Wembley
(WBC International Heavyweight Title Challenge)
19.11.04 Matt Skelton L RSC 11 Bethnal Green
(British & Commonwealth Heavyweight Title Challenges)
Career: 13 contests, won 8, drew 1, lost 4.

Andrew Lowe

Hackney. *Born* Hackney, 23 June, 1974
Southern Area L. Heavyweight Champion. Ht. 5'10"
Manager Self

19.05.01 Rob Stevenson W PTS 4 Wembley
16.06.01 William Webster W RSC 2 Dagenham
20.10.01 Tom Cannon W PTS 4 Glasgow
24.11.01 Paul Wesley W PTS 4 Bethnal Green
15.12.01 Mark Snipe W PTS 4 Chigwell
12.02.02 Ali Forbes W PTS 4 Bethnal Green
04.05.02 Radcliffe Green W PTS 4 Bethnal Green
12.10.02 Paul Bonson W PTS 4 Bethnal Green
08.02.03 Clint Johnson W PTS 6 Brentford
29.03.03 Radcliffe Green W PTS 10 Wembley
(Vacant Southern Area L.Heavyweight Title)
31.05.03 Neil Linford W PTS 10 Bethnal Green
(Elim. British L. Heavyweight Title)
07.11.03 Radcliffe Green W PTS 6 Sheffield
20.03.04 Varuzhan Davtyan W PTS 6 Wembley
12.05.04 Peter Oboh L RTD 10 Reading
(British & Commonwealth L.Heavyweight Title Challenges)
10.04.05 Varuzhan Davtyan W PTS 6 Brentwood
Career: 15 contests, won 14, lost 1.

Freddie Luke

West Kingsdown. *Born* Dartford, 2 February, 1977
L. Welterweight. Ht. 5'7"
Manager M. Roe

01.05.04 Wayne Wheeler W RSC 1 Gravesend
16.10.04 Lea Handley W PTS 4 Dagenham
19.12.04 Peter Dunn W PTS 4 Bethnal Green
Career: 3 contests, won 3.

Freddie Luke   Les Clark

Craig Lynch

Edinburgh. *Born* Edinburgh, 22 July, 1974
L. Middleweight. Ht. 6'1"
Manager Self

13.05.95 James Clamp DREW 6 Glasgow
08.06.95 Gary Silvester W RSC 3 Glasgow
15.09.95 Adam Baldwin W PTS 6 Glasgow
25.11.95 Jim Rock L PTS 4 Dublin
02.03.96 Hughie Davey L PTS 4 Newcastle
08.06.96 Hughie Davey L PTS 4 Newcastle
24.10.96 Pat Wright L PTS 6 Wembley
21.02.02 Gary Firby W RSC 3 Sunderland
26.04.02 Kevin McIntyre L PTS 10 Glasgow
                (Vacant Scottish Welterweight Title)
25.10.02 Joel Ani W PTS 6 Millwall
23.11.02 Bradley Pryce L CO 4 Derby
16.01.04 Michael Lomax L PTS 6 Bradford
30.01.04 Gilbert Eastman L PTS 6 Dagenham
21.02.04 Taz Jones L PTS 4 Cardiff
03.04.04 Thomas McDonagh L PTS 6
                Manchester
06.05.04 Matthew Hall L PTS 6 Barnsley
19.06.04 Barrie Lee L PTS 6 Renfrew
30.07.04 Neil Sinclair L PTS 6 Bethnal Green
22.10.04 Barrie Lee L PTS 10 Edinburgh
                (Vacant Scottish L.Middleweight
                Title)
02.12.04 Eder Kurti L DIS 4 Crystal Palace
25.02.05 Martin Concepcion L PTS 6 Wembley
03.06.05 Ryan Rhodes L RSC 3 Manchester
Career: 22 contests, won 4, drew 1, lost 17.

Colin Lynes

Hornchurch. *Born* Whitechapel, 26
November, 1977
IBO L.Welterweight Champion. Former
IBO Inter-Continental L.Welterweight
Champion. Ht. 5'7½"
Manager Self

04.06.98 Les Frost W CO 1 Barking
23.07.98 Ram Singh W CO 1 Barking
22.10.98 Brian Coleman W RSC 2 Barking
31.10.98 Marc Smith W PTS 4 Basingstoke
10.12.98 Trevor Smith W RSC 1 Barking
25.02.99 Dennis Griffin W PTS 6 Kentish
                Town
20.05.99 Mark Haslam W PTS 4 Barking
18.05.00 Jason Vlasman W RSC 2 Bethnal
                Green
16.09.00 Karl Taylor W PTS 6 Bethnal Green
14.10.00 Brian Coleman W PTS 6 Wembley
09.12.00 Jimmy Phelan W PTS 6 Southwark
17.02.01 Mark Ramsey W PTS 6 Bethnal
                Green
10.04.01 David Kirk W PTS 6 Wembley
10.11.01 Keith Jones W PTS 6 Wembley
01.12.01 Leonti Voronchuk W PTS 6 Bethnal
                Green
26.01.02 David Kirk W PTS 6 Dagenham

23.03.02 Peter Dunn W PTS 4 Southwark
18.05.02 Kevin Bennett W RSC 4 Millwall
29.06.02 Ian Smith W RSC 7 Brentwood
21.09.02 Abdelilah Touil W CO 7 Brentwood
07.12.02 Richard Kiley W RSC 9 Brentwood
                (Vacant IBO Inter-Continental
                L.Welterweight Title)
08.03.03 Samuel Malinga L RTD 8 Bethnal
                Green
                (IBO Inter-Continental L.Welterweight
                Title Defence)
18.10.03 Brian Coleman W PTS 4 Manchester
22.11.03 Fabrice Colombel W PTS 6 Belfast
31.01.04 Cesar Levia W PTS 8 Bethnal Green
08.05.04 Pablo Sarmiento W PTS 12 Dagenham
                (IBO L.Welterweight Title Challenge)
13.02.05 Juaquin Gallardo W PTS 12
                Brentwood
                (IBO L.Welterweight Title Defence)
Career: 27 contests, won 26, lost 1.

Colin Lynes   Les Clark

133

Lee McAllister

Aberdeen. *Born* Aberdeen, 5 October, 1982
L.Welterweight. Former Undefeated British
Masters L.Welterweight Champion.
Ht. 5'9"
Manager B. Ingle/F. Warren

19.10.02	Baz Carey	W PTS 4 Renfrew
17.11.02	Arv Mittoo	W PTS 6 Bradford
23.02.03	Lee Williamson	W PTS 6 Shrewsbury
13.04.03	Ernie Smith	W PTS 4 Bradford
12.05.03	Ernie Smith	W PTS 6 Birmingham
15.06.03	Brian Coleman	W PTS 6 Bradford
11.07.03	John-Paul Ryan	W RTD 2 Darlington
17.07.03	Dean Hickman	L PTS 6 Walsall
03.08.03	Brian Coleman	W PTS 4 Stalybridge
06.09.03	Jeff Thomas	W PTS 10 Aberdeen
	(Vacant British Masters	
	L.Welterweight Title)	
28.11.03	Ernie Smith	W PTS 6 Hull
30.01.04	Karl Taylor	W PTS 6 Dagenham
08.03.04	Lee Williamson	W PTS 6 Birmingham
15.05.04	Martin Hardcastle	W PTS 8 Aberdeen
13.02.05	Daniel Thorpe	W PTS 4 Bradford
26.04.05	Mark Wall	W PTS 6 Leeds
14.05.05	Karl Taylor	W RTD 3 Aberdeen

Career: 17 contests, won 16, lost 1.

Kevin McBride

Clones. *Born* Monaghan, 10 May, 1973
All-Ireland Heavyweight Champion.
Ht. 6'5"
Manager Self

17.12.92	Gary Charlton	DREW 6 Barking
13.02.93	Gary Williams	W PTS 4 Manchester
15.09.93	Joey Paladino	W CO 2 Bethnal Green
13.10.93	Chris Coughlan	W PTS 4 Bethnal Green
01.12.93	John Harewood	W RSC 3 Bethnal Green
06.05.94	Edgar Turpin	W RSC 1 Atlantic City, New Jersey, USA
04.06.94	Roger Bryant	W CO 1 Reno, Nevada, USA
17.06.94	Stanley Wright	W PTS 6 Atlantic City, New Jersey, USA
26.08.94	James Truesdale	W RSC 3 Upper Marlboro, Maryland, USA
24.09.94	Graham Arnold	W RSC 2 Wembley
12.11.94	Dean Storey	W RSC 3 Dublin
10.12.94	John Lamphrey	W RSC 1 Portland, Maine, USA
07.02.95	Carl Gaffney	W RSC 1 Ipswich
03.03.95	Carl McGrew	W RSC 5 Boston, Mass, USA
22.04.95	Jimmy Harrison	W RSC 1 Boston, Mass, USA
13.05.95	Atelea Kalhea	W CO 1 Sacramento, California, USA
02.07.95	Steve Garber	W RSC 7 Dublin
06.11.96	Shane Woollas	W RSC 2 Hull
03.12.96	R.F. McKenzie	W RSC 6 Liverpool
21.01.97	Tui Toia	W RSC 2 Kansas City, Missouri, USA
07.02.97	Louis Monaco	L RSC 5 Las Vegas, Nevada, USA

28.04.97	Stoyan Stoyanov	W RSC 1 Hull
02.06.97	Paul Douglas	W RSC 5 Belfast
	(Vacant All-Ireland Heavyweight Title)	
30.08.97	Axel Schulz	L RSC 9 Berlin, Germany
22.11.97	Yuri Yelistratov	W RSC 1 Manchester
11.04.98	Michael Murray	L RSC 3 Southwark
26.06.99	Domingo Monroe	W CO 1 Boston, Mass, USA
11.08.01	Willie Phillips	W PTS 10 Little Rock, Arkansas, USA
01.11.01	Rodney McSwain	W PTS 10 Little Rock, Arkansas, USA
18.01.02	Davarryl Williamson	L RSC 5 Las Vegas, Nevada, USA
27.05.02	Gary Winmon	W RSC 2 Revere, Mass, USA
26.07.02	Reynaldo Minus	W RSC 3 Boston, Mass, USA
26.10.02	Craig Tomlinson	W RSC 3 Revere, Mass, USA
17.03.03	Najee Shaheed	W RSC 7 Brockton, Mass, USA
09.08.03	Lenzie Morgan	W CO 1 Brockton, Mass, USA
04.12.03	Marcus Rhode	W RSC 3 Boston, Mass, USA
18.03.05	Kevin Montiy	W RSC 5 Mashantucket, Connecticut, USA
11.06.05	Mike Tyson	W RSC 6 Washington DC, USA

Career: 38 contests, won 33, drew 1, lost 4.

Enzo Maccarinelli   Les Clark

Enzo Maccarinelli

Swansea. *Born* Swansea, 20 August, 1980
WBU Cruiserweight Champion. Ht. 6'4"
Manager F. Warren/C. Pearson

02.10.99	Paul Bonson	W PTS 4 Cardiff
11.12.99	Mark Williams	W RSC 1 Merthyr
26.02.00	Nigel Rafferty	W RSC 3 Swansea
12.05.00	Lee Swaby	L CO 3 Swansea
11.12.00	Chris Woollas	W PTS 4 Widnes
28.04.01	Darren Ashton	W CO 1 Cardiff

09.10.01	Eamonn Glennon	W RSC 2 Cardiff
15.12.01	Kevin Barrett	W RSC 2 Wembley
12.02.02	James Gilbert	W RSC 2 Bethnal Green
20.04.02	Tony Booth	W PTS 4 Cardiff
17.08.02	Tony Booth	W RTD 2 Cardiff
12.10.02	Dave Clarke	W RSC 2 Bethnal Green
18.01.03	Paul Bonson	W PTS 4 Preston
29.03.03	Valery Shemishkur	W RSC 1 Portsmouth
28.06.03	Bruce Scott	W RSC 4 Cardiff
	(Vacant WBU Cruiserweight Title)	
13.09.03	Andrei Kiarsten	W CO 1 Newport
	(WBU Cruiserweight Title Defence)	
06.12.03	Earl Morais	W RSC 1 Cardiff
	(WBU Cruiserweight Title Defence)	
21.02.04	Garry Delaney	W RSC 8 Cardiff
	(WBU Cruiserweight Title Defence)	
03.07.04	Ismail Abdoul	W PTS 12 Newport
	(WBU Cruiserweight Title Defence)	
03.09.04	Jesper Kristiansen	W CO 3 Newport
	(WBU Cruiserweight Title Defence)	
21.01.05	Rich LaMontagne	W RSC 4 Bridgend
	(WBU Cruiserweight Title Defence)	
04.06.05	Roman Bugaj	W RSC 1 Manchester

Career: 22 contests, won 21, lost 1.

Glenn McClarnon

Lurgan. *Born* Carrickfergus, 1 July, 1974
Welterweight. Ht. 5'9"
Manager J. Breen/M. Callahan

20.12.97	Marc Smith	W PTS 4 Belfast
21.02.98	Andrew Reed	W CO 1 Belfast
28.04.98	Brian Robb	W RSC 2 Belfast
18.09.98	Mark Ramsey	W PTS 4 Belfast
28.11.98	David Kirk	W PTS 4 Belfast
12.01.99	Ram Singh	W RSC 1 Bethnal Green
25.01.99	Dean Nicholas	W CO 1 Glasgow
12.03.99	Mark Ramsey	W PTS 6 Bethnal Green
25.05.99	Steve Tuckett	W PTS 6 Mayfair
11.09.99	David Kirk	W PTS 6 Sheffield
27.11.99	Chris Barnett	L PTS 12 Liverpool
	(Vacant IBO International L.Welterweight Title)	
01.04.00	Bernard Paul	W RTD 5 Bethnal Green
19.08.00	Brian Coleman	W PTS 6 Brentwood
13.10.00	Allan Vester	L PTS 12 Aarhus, Denmark
	(IBF Inter-Continental L.Welterweight Title Challenge)	
02.12.00	John Ameline	L PTS 4 Bethnal Green
03.03.01	Peter Dunn	W PTS 4 Wembley
28.04.01	Jacek Bielski	L PTS 12 Wroclaw, Poland
	(Vacant IBO Inter-Continental Welterweight Title)	
25.09.01	Gary Ryder	L PTS 8 Liverpool
10.11.01	Rosalin Nasibulin	W PTS 6 Wembley
26.01.02	Kevin Bennett	W PTS 8 Dagenham
16.11.02	Keith Jones	W PTS 6 Nottingham
22.03.03	Ossie Duran	L RSC 2 Huddersfield
30.10.03	Ronnie Nailen	W RSC 1 Belfast
03.04.04	David Barnes	L PTS 12 Manchester
	(British Welterweight Title Challenge)	
31.01.05	Kevin Anderson	L RSC 4 Glasgow
	(Vacant Celtic Welterweight Title)	

Career: 25 contests, won 17, lost 8.

Paul McCloskey

Dungiven. *Born* Londonderry, 3 August, 1979
L. Welterweight. Ht. 5'8½"
Manager J. Breen/M. Callaghan/F. Warren

18.03.05 David Kehoe W RSC 3 Belfast
17.06.05 Oscar Milkitas W PTS 4 Glasgow
Career: 2 contests, won 2.

Billy McClung

Kilmarnock. *Born* Irvine, 13 March, 1982
Cruiserweight. Ht. 6'3"
Manager Self

19.11.01 Darren Ashton W PTS 6 Glasgow
18.02.02 Clint Johnson W PTS 6 Glasgow
01.03.02 Clint Johnson W PTS 6 Irvine
18.03.02 Shane White L RTD 4 Glasgow
25.02.05 Csaba Andras W PTS 6 Irvine
21.03.05 Henry Smith W PTS 6 Glasgow
Career: 6 contests, won 5, lost 1.

Joe McCluskey

Coventry. *Born* Coventry, 26 November,
1977
L. Welterweight. Ht. 5'9"
Manager O. Delargy

01.05.04 John-Paul Ryan W RTD 2 Coventry
10.07.04 Declan English W RSC 4 Coventry
20.11.04 Judex Meemea DREW 6 Coventry
18.06.05 Carl Allen W PTS 6 Coventry
Career: 4 contests, won 3, drew 1.

Peter McCormack

Erdington. *Born* Birmingham, 9 March,
1974
S.Middleweight. Ht. 5'10"
Manager P. Cowdell

07.10.96 Paul Webb DREW 6 Birmingham
21.11.96 Ozzy Orrock W RSC 2 Solihull
04.12.96 Lee Simpkin L PTS 6 Stoke
11.02.97 Mark Sawyers L RSC 2
            Wolverhampton
11.10.99 Andy Vickers L PTS 6 Birmingham
27.10.99 Paul Bonson L PTS 6 Birmingham
06.12.99 Andrew Facey L CO 2 Birmingham
28.03.00 William Webster W PTS 6
            Wolverhampton
11.10.04 Omid Bourzo W PTS 6 Birmingham
16.12.04 Dave Pearson L PTS 6 Cleethorpes
25.04.05 Dave Pearson L PTS 6 Cleethorpes
Career: 11 contests, won 3, drew 1, lost 7.

Darren McDermott   Les Clark

Darren McDermott

Dudley. *Born* Dudley, 17 July, 1978
Middleweight. Ht. 6'1"
Manager D. Powell

26.04.03 Leigh Wicks W PTS 4 Brentford
13.06.03 Gary Jones W RSC 1 Queensway
30.10.03 Harry Butler W PTS 4 Dudley
21.02.04 Freddie Yemofio W RSC 3 Cardiff
15.04.04 Mark Phillips W PTS 4 Dudley
03.07.04 Neil Addis W PTS 4 Newport
11.12.04 Gokhan Kazaz DREW 4 Canning
            Town
21.04.05 Howard Clarke W RTD 1 Dudley
Career: 8 contests, won 7, drew 1.

John McDermott

Horndon. *Born* Basildon, 26 February,
1980
Heavyweight. Ht. 6'3"
Manager J. Branch

23.09.00 Slick Miller W RSC 1 Bethnal Green
21.10.00 Gary Williams W PTS 4 Wembley
13.11.00 Geoff Hunter W RSC 1 Bethnal Green
27.01.01 Eamonn Glennon W RSC 1 Bethnal
            Green
24.02.01 Alexei Osokin W PTS 4 Bethnal Green
26.03.01 Mal Rice W RSC 2 Wembley
09.06.01 Luke Simpkin W PTS 6 Bethnal Green
22.09.01 Gary Williams W RSC 4 Bethnal
            Green
24.11.01 Gordon Minors W RSC 3 Bethnal
            Green
19.01.02 Tony Booth W RSC 1 Bethnal Green
04.05.02 Martin Roothman W RSC 1 Bethnal
            Green
14.09.02 Alexander Mileiko W RSC 2 Bethnal
            Green
12.10.02 Mendauga Kulikauskas W PTS 6
            Bethnal Green
14.12.02 Jason Brewster W RSC 1 Newcastle
15.02.03 Derek McCafferty W PTS 4 Wembley
08.05.03 Konstantin Prizyuk W PTS 8 Widnes
18.09.03 Nicolai Popov L RSC 2 Dagenham
13.05.04 James Zikic W RSC 4 Bethnal Green
30.07.04 Suren Kalachyan W CO 7 Bethnal
            Green
11.12.04 Mark Krence L PTS 10 Canning Town
            (Vacant English Heavyweight Title)
08.04.05 Slick Miller W RSC 1 Edinburgh
Career: 21 contests, won 19, lost 2.

Chris McDonagh

Maidenhead. *Born* Ascot, 9 July, 1978
Lightweight. Ht. 5'10"
Manager Self

22.11.01 Jason Gonzales W PTS 6 Paddington
26.01.02 Dave Hinds W PTS 4 Bethnal Green
25.02.02 Baz Carey W PTS 6 Slough
19.03.02 Ray Wood W PTS 4 Slough
25.04.02 Vatche Wartanian L PTS 4 Las Vegas,
            Nevada, USA
21.05.02 Daniel Thorpe W PTS 6 Custom House
12.07.02 Tony Montana L PTS 4 Southampton
27.09.02 Gareth Wiltshaw L RSC 1 Bracknell
20.12.02 Jason Nesbitt W PTS 6 Bracknell
26.04.03 Scott Lawton L RSC 2 Brentford
27.11.03 David Vaughan DREW 4 Longford
20.02.04 Rob Jeffries L RSC 2 Bethnal Green
30.03.04 Kristian Laight W PTS 6 Southampton

12.05.04 Anthony Hanna W PTS 4 Reading
05.06.04 Danny Hunt L CO 3 Bethnal Green
24.09.04 Rob Jeffries L PTS 4 Bethnal Green
21.11.04 Pete Buckley W PTS 4 Bracknell
11.12.04 Lee Beavis L RSC 6 Canning Town
Career: 18 contests, won 9, drew 1, lost 8.

Martin McDonagh

Coatbridge. *Born* Bellshill, 30 October,
1982
Lightweight. Ht. 5'8"
Manager A. Morrison/R. Bannan

01.04.05 Jason Nesbitt W PTS 6 Glasgow
17.06.05 Imad Khamis W DIS 4 Glasgow
Career: 2 contests, won 2.

Peter McDonagh

Bermondsey. *Born* Galway, 21 December,
1977
L.Welterweight. Former Southern Area
Lightweight Champion. Ht. 5'9"
Manager Self

28.04.02 Arv Mittoo W PTS 6 Southwark
23.06.02 Dave Hinds W PTS 6 Southwark
14.09.02 Pete Buckley W PTS 4 Bethnal Green
27.10.02 Ben Hudson L PTS 6 Southwark
18.02.03 Daffyd Carlin L PTS 4 Bethnal Green
08.04.03 Ben Hudson W PTS 4 Bethnal Green
08.11.03 Ceri Hall L PTS 4 Bridgend
22.11.03 James Gorman L PTS 4 Belfast
21.02.04 Chill John W RTD 2 Brighton
06.03.04 Barry Hughes L PTS 6 Renfrew
07.04.04 Jon Honney W PTS 10 Leicester
            Square
            *(Vacant Southern Area Lightweight
            Title)*
19.11.04 David Burke L PTS 8 Bethnal Green
21.01.05 Ryan Barrett L PTS 8 Brentford
04.03.05 Scott Lawton L PTS 6 Rotherham
30.04.05 Rob Jeffries L PTS 10 Dagenham
            *(Southern Area Lightweight Title
            Defence)*
14.05.05 Robbie Murray L PTS 10 Dublin
            (Vacant Irish L.Welterweight Title)
Career: 16 contests, won 6, lost 10.

Thomas McDonagh

Manchester. *Born* Manchester, 8 December,
1980
WBU Inter-Continental L.Middleweight
Champion. Ht. 6'0"
Manager F. Warren/B. Hughes

09.10.99 Lee Molyneux W PTS 4 Manchester
06.11.99 Lee Molyneux W PTS 4 Widnes
11.12.99 Arv Mittoo W RSC 2 Liverpool
29.01.00 Emmanuel Marcos W PTS 4
            Manchester
29.02.00 William Webster W RTD 2 Widnes
25.03.00 Lee Molyneux W PTS 6 Liverpool
16.05.00 Richie Murray W PTS 4 Warrington
29.05.00 David Baptiste W PTS 6 Manchester
04.09.00 Colin Vidler W PTS 6 Manchester
11.12.00 Richie Murray W PTS 6 Widnes
15.01.01 Kid Halls W RSC 4 Manchester
10.02.01 Harry Butler W PTS 6 Widnes
17.03.01 David Baptiste W PTS 4 Manchester
07.07.01 Paul Denton W PTS 6 Manchester
15.09.01 Howard Clarke W PTS 6 Manchester
27.10.01 Mark Richards DREW 4 Manchester

135

30.11.00 Jimmy Phelan L RSC 4 Bloomsbury
29.03.01 Darren Melville L RSC 1 Hammersmith
26.09.02 Ben Hudson L CO 3 Fulham
01.08.03 Pete Buckley L PTS 4 Bethnal Green
24.10.03 Lance Hall L RSC 1 Bethnal Green
12.11.04 James Gorman L RTD 2 Belfast
Career: 8 contests, won 2, lost 6.

Emmanuel Marcos

Haringey. *Born* Luanda, 13 July, 1976
Welterweight. Ht. 5'4"
Manager Self

06.11.99 John Humphrey L PTS 4 Bethnal Green
29.01.00 Thomas McDonagh L PTS 4 Manchester
21.10.00 Isam Khalil L RSC 1 Wembley
22.10.01 Darrell Grafton L RSC 2 Glasgow
29.11.01 Andrew Close L PTS 6 Hartlepool
10.09.04 Anthony Small L RSC 1 Wembley
Career: 6 contests, lost 6.

Matthew Marsh

West Ham. *Born* Sidcup, 1 August, 1982
S.Bantamweight. Ht. 5'5³/₄"
Manager F. Warren/F. Maloney

10.09.04 Fred Janes W PTS 4 Bethnal Green
19.11.04 Dean Ward W PTS 4 Bethnal Green
11.12.04 Abdul Mougharbel W PTS 4 Canning Town
25.02.05 Dai Davies W PTS 4 Wembley
Career: 4 contests, won 4

John Marshall

Glossop. *Born* Australia, 28 May, 1975
L.Middleweight. Ht. 5'6"
Manager Self

07.09.01 Dave Stewart L PTS 6 Glasgow
23.12.01 Arv Mittoo W RSC 1 Salford
21.01.02 Gary Hamilton W PTS 4 Glasgow
17.02.02 Joel Viney W RSC 6 Salford
31.05.02 Tony Montana W PTS 6 Hull
21.07.02 Daniel Thorpe W RSC 1 Salford
02.11.02 Mark Winters L RSC 5 Belfast
28.04.03 Young Muttley L RSC 5 Nottingham
18.09.03 Ross Minter DREW 6 Dagenham
09.12.04 Tony Montana L PTS 4 Stockport
19.12.04 Martin Marshall W CO 5 Bolton
22.04.05 Robert Burton W RTD 4 Barnsley
12.05.05 Danny Moir W RSC 5 Sunderland
Career: 13 contests, won 8, drew 1, lost 4.

Martin Marshall

Sunderland. *Born* Sunderland, 28 January, 1983
L. Middleweight. Ht. 6'1"
Manager T. Conroy

14.05.04 Richard Mazurek DREW 6 Sunderland
23.09.04 Richard Inquieti W PTS 6 Gateshead
28.10.04 Richard Inquieti W PTS 6 Sunderland
09.12.04 Gary Porter L PTS 6 Sunderland
19.12.04 John Marshall L CO 5 Bolton
12.05.05 Muhsen Nasser L PTS 6 Sunderland
27.05.05 Gary Porter L PTS 6 Motherwell
11.06.05 Keith Ellwood W PTS 6 Kirkcaldy
Career: 8 contests, won 3, drew 1, lost 4.

Matthew Marshall

Torquay. *Born* Torquay, 6 February, 1979
Lightweight. Ht. 5'7"
Manager C. Sanigar

12.05.03 Baz Carey W PTS 6 Southampton
17.09.04 Lea Handley W RSC 6 Plymouth
04.02.05 Jonathan Jones L PTS 6 Plymouth
Career: 3 contests, won 2, lost 1.

Tommy Marshall

Plymouth. *Born* Aberystwyth, 22 August, 1984
Welterweight. Ht. 6'0"
Manager C. Sanigar

02.04.04 Chris Brophy DREW 6 Plymouth
03.07.04 Arv Mittoo W PTS 6 Bristol
17.09.04 Chris Brophy L PTS 6 Plymouth
06.12.04 Mark Franks W PTS 6 Leeds
18.02.05 William Imoro L PTS 4 Torrevieja, Spain
Career: 5 contests, won 2, drew 1, lost 2.

Neil Marston

Shrewsbury. *Born* Shrewsbury, 8 February, 1977
Featherweight. Ht. 5'7"
Manager E. Johnson/D. Bradley

08.07.04 Dai Davies L PTS 6 Birmingham
12.09.04 Paddy Folan W PTS 6 Shrewsbury
18.11.04 Paddy Folan W PTS 6 Shrewsbury
06.12.04 Paddy Folan W PTS 6 Bradford
28.01.05 Scott Flynn L RSC 2 Renfrew
15.04.05 Craig Bromley L RSC 1 Shrewsbury
23.05.05 Wayne Bloy L PTS 6 Cleethorpes
Career: 7 contests, won 3, lost 4.

Shanee Martin

Colchester. *Born* Dagenham, 31 January, 1982
S.Flyweight. Ht. 5'2"
Manager M. Roe

16.10.04 Iliana Boneva W RSC 4 Dagenham
05.03.05 Svetla Taskova W PTS 6 Dagenham
Career: 2 contests, won 2

Shanee Martin   Les Clark

Ali Mateen

Sheffield. *Born* Sheffield, 2 June, 1986
L.Middleweight. Ht. 5'11¹/₂"
Manager J. Ingle

15.11.04 Keith Ellwood W PTS 6 Glasgow
26.11.04 Glen Matsell L RTD 3 Hull
06.03.05 Rob MacDonald W PTS 6 Shaw
Career: 3 contests, won 2, lost 1.

Glen Matsell

Hull. *Born* Hull, 24 March, 1975
L.Middleweight. Ht. 5'9"
Manager S. Smith

26.11.04 Ali Mateen W RTD 3 Hull
Career: 1 contest, won 1.

Derry Matthews

Liverpool. *Born* Liverpool, 23 September, 1983
Featherweight. Ht. 5'8¹/₂"
Manager F. Warren/S. Vaughan

18.01.03 Sergei Tasimov W CO 1 Preston
05.04.03 Jus Wallie W PTS 4 Manchester
08.05.03 Steve Gethin W RSC 3 Widnes
20.06.03 Henry Janes W RSC 1 Liverpool
29.08.03 Marty Kayes W RTD 2 Liverpool
02.10.03 Alexei Volchan W RSC 2 Liverpool
13.12.03 Pete Buckley W PTS 4 Manchester
26.02.04 Gareth Payne W RSC 4 Widnes
03.04.04 Henry Janes W PTS 4 Manchester
10.09.04 Buster Dennis W PTS 6 Liverpool
17.12.04 Dean Ward W RSC 1 Liverpool
13.05.05 John Mackay W PTS 6 Liverpool
Career: 12 contests, won 12.

(Steven) Tiger Matthews

Liverpool. *Born* Liverpool, 1 April, 1981
Lightweight. Ht. 5'9¹/₂"
Manager S. Vaughan

10.09.04 Pete Buckley W PTS 4 Liverpool
13.05.05 Dave Hinds W CO 1 Liverpool
Career: 2 contests, won 2.

Anthony Maynard

Birmingham. *Born* Birmingham, 12 January, 1972
L.Welterweight. Former Undefeated Midlands Area Lightweight Champion. Ht. 5'8"
Manager Self

17.10.94 Malcolm Thomas W PTS 6 Birmingham
02.11.94 Dean Phillips W PTS 6 Birmingham
25.01.95 Neil Smith L PTS 6 Stoke
07.02.95 Anthony Campbell W PTS 8 Wolverhampton
08.03.95 Scott Walker W PTS 6 Solihull
28.03.95 Kid McAuley W PTS 8 Wolverhampton
11.05.95 Gary Hiscox W RSC 4 Dudley
06.06.95 Richard Swallow L RSC 2 Leicester
02.10.95 Jay Mahoney W PTS 8 Birmingham
26.10.95 Ray Newby W PTS 8 Birmingham
17.01.96 Tom Welsh W RSC 8 Solihull
06.03.96 G. G. Goddard W RSC 3 Solihull
20.03.97 Richard Swallow W PTS 6 Solihull
24.10.97 Brian Coleman W CO 1 Birmingham
27.03.98 Gary Flear W RSC 9 Telford
       (Vacant Midlands Area Lightweight Title)

30.05.98	Michael Ayers W PTS 8 Bristol
21.11.98	Stephen Smith L PTS 10 Southwark
27.11.00	David Kehoe W RSC 5 Birmingham
07.04.01	Alfred Kotey L RTD 6 Wembley
	(Vacant WBF Inter-Continental
	Lightweight Title)
11.06.01	Woody Greenaway W PTS 4
	Nottingham
08.10.01	Bobby Vanzie L RSC 1 Barnsley
	(British Lightweight Title Challenge)
09.03.02	David Burke L PTS 6 Manchester
09.11.02	Chris Barnett W PTS 6 Altrincham
08.02.03	Gary Hibbert DREW 6 Liverpool
18.10.03	Gary Hibbert L PTS 6 Manchester
07.02.04	Danny Hunt L PTS 10 Bethnal Green
	(English Lightweight Title Challenge)
07.04.05	Tony Montana W PTS 4 Birmingham

Career: 27 contests, won 18, drew 1, lost 8.

Richard Mazurek

Leamington. *Born* Leamington, 20 January, 1977
L. Middleweight. Ht. 5'10"
Manager O. Delargy

15.11.03	Neil Addis W PTS 6 Coventry
21.02.04	Simon Hopkins W RSC 3 Brighton
01.05.04	Brian Coleman W PTS 6 Coventry
14.05.04	Martin Marshall DREW 6 Sunderland
10.07.04	Richard Inquieti W RSC 1 Coventry
20.11.04	David Payne W PTS 6 Coventry
18.06.05	Ernie Smith L PTS 6 Coventry

Career: 7 contests, won 5, drew 1, lost 1.

Lee Meager

Salford. *Born* Salford, 18 January, 1978
Lightweight. Ht. 5'8"
Manager Self

16.09.00	Pete Buckley W PTS 4 Bethnal Green
14.10.00	Chris Jickells W PTS 4 Wembley
18.11.00	Billy Smith W RSC 1 Dagenham
09.12.00	Jason Nesbitt W RSC 2 Southwark
05.02.01	Carl Allen DREW 6 Hull
13.03.01	Lennie Hodgkins W RSC 3 Plymouth
12.05.01	Jason White W PTS 4 Plymouth
31.07.01	Steve Hanley W PTS 6 Bethnal Green
13.09.01	Arv Mittoo W PTS 6 Sheffield
16.03.02	Jason Nesbitt W PTS 6 Bethnal Green
10.05.02	Pete Buckley W PTS 6 Bethnal Green
25.10.02	Iain Eldridge W RSC 5 Bethnal Green
21.12.02	Chill John W RSC 5 Dagenham
28.01.03	Carl Allen W PTS 8 Nottingham
28.11.03	Pete Buckley W PTS 4 Derby
11.12.03	Charles Shepherd W RTD 7 Bethnal
	Green
02.06.04	Michael Muya W PTS 8 Nottingham
19.11.04	Danny Hunt L PTS 10 Bethnal Green
	(English Lightweight Title Challenge)

Career: 18 contests, won 16, drew 1, lost 1.

Judex Meemea

Walthamstow. *Born* Mauritius, 24 November, 1973
L.Welterweight. Ht. 5'10"
Manager C. Sanigar

21.02.04	Jay Morris DREW 4 Brighton
08.06.04	Tyrone McInerney DREW 6 Sheffield
27.09.04	Scott Haywood L PTS 6 Cleethorpes
20.11.04	Joe McCluskey DREW 6 Coventry
26.03.05	Ashley Theophane W PTS 6 Hackney
02.06.05	Andy Cosnett W PTS 6 Peterborough
18.06.05	Gwyn Wale L RSC 5 Barnsley

Career: 7 contests, won 2, drew 3, lost 2.

Delroy Mellis

Brixton. *Born* Jamaica, 7 January, 1971
L. Middleweight. Former Undefeated
Southern Area L. Middleweight Champion.
Ht. 5'8"
Manager B. Baker

27.02.98	Pat Larner L PTS 4 Brighton
16.04.98	Sonny Thind L RTD 5 Mayfair
09.06.98	Darren Christie L PTS 4 Hull
10.09.98	Paul Miles W RSC 3 Acton
03.10.98	Wayne Asker L PTS 6 Crawley
06.11.98	Darren Bruce L RTD 3 Mayfair
21.01.99	Darren Christie L PTS 6 Piccadilly
04.02.99	Sergei Dzindziruk L RSC 3 Lewisham
24.03.99	Martyn Thomas L RSC 3 Bayswater
20.05.99	Daniel James L PTS 4 Barking
02.07.99	Jason Williams L PTS 6 Bristol
30.09.99	Steve Brumant L PTS 6 Kensington
16.10.99	Jacek Bielski L PTS 4 Bethnal Green
18.11.99	Dennis Griffin W RSC 5 Mayfair
29.11.99	George Scott L PTS 6 Wembley
20.03.00	Lance Crosby L PTS 4 Mansfield
01.04.00	Paul Knights W RSC 3 Bethnal Green
15.05.00	Christian Brady W RSC 6 Birmingham
01.07.00	Cham Joof DREW 6 Southwark
22.07.00	Alan Gilbert W RSC 3 Watford
	(Vacant Southern Area L.Middleweight
	Title)
22.10.00	Allan Gray W RSC 6 Streatham
	(Southern Area L.Middleweight Title
	Defence)
23.01.01	Alan Gilbert W RSC 3 Crawley
	(Southern Area L. Middleweight Title
	Defence)
20.04.01	Chris Nembhard W RSC 8 Millwall
	(Southern Area L. Middleweight Title
	Defence)
07.09.01	Jason Collins L DIS 5 Bethnal Green
06.10.01	Michael Jones L PTS 8 Manchester
13.12.01	Ossie Duran L PTS 10 Leicester Square
	(WBF European Welterweight Title
	Challenge)
01.06.02	Thomas McDonagh L PTS 4
	Manchester
15.06.02	Chardan Ansoula L RTD 4 Tottenham
07.09.02	Jamie Moore L CO 6 Liverpool
06.12.03	Wayne Alexander W RSC 8 Cardiff
16.04.04	Gilbert Eastman L RSC 5 Bradford
	(Southern Area L.Middleweight Title
	Challenge)
11.12.04	Wayne Alexander L PTS 10 Canning
	Town
23.03.05	Ernie Smith W PTS 6 Leicester Square

Career: 33 contests, won 11, drew 1, lost 21.

Darren Melville

Belfast. *Born* Tobago, 13 September, 1975
L. Welterweight. Ht. 5'8"
Manager J. Breen/M. Callahan

29.09.00	Lee Williamson W RSC 4 Bethnal
	Green
10.11.00	Jason McElligott W RSC 2 Mayfair
23.02.01	Keith Jones W PTS 4 Barking
09.03.01	Billy Smith W PTS 4 Millwall
29.03.01	Jas Malik W RSC 1 Hammersmith
20.04.01	Marcus Portman W RSC 3 Millwall
15.06.01	Isaac Sebaduka W RSC 6 Millwall
22.09.01	Steve Murray L PTS 8 Bethnal Green
08.12.01	Christian Hodoragea W PTS 4
	Millwall
15.03.02	Mark Ramsey W PTS 6 Millwall
19.04.02	Jan Jensen DREW 6 Aarhus, Denmark

25.10.02	Sergei Starkov W PTS 6 Millwall
21.12.02	Alan Temple W PTS 8 Millwall
29.03.03	Nigel Wright L PTS 6 Portsmouth
14.05.05	Oscar Milkitas W PTS 6 Dublin

Career: 15 contests, won 12, drew 1, lost 2.

(Elviss) Elvis Michailenko

Beckton. *Born* Jormala, Latvia, 13
September, 1976
European Union & Latvian L.Heavyweight
Champion. Former Undefeated WBF
European L.Heavyweight Champion.
Former WBA Inter-Continental
L.Heavyweight Champion. Ht. 5'11¹/₂"
Manager Self

18.05.00	Adam Cale W PTS 4 Bethnal Green
21.09.00	Shpetim Hoti W PTS 4 Bloomsbury
09.10.00	Tony Dodson DREW 6 Liverpool
02.11.00	Freddie Yemofio W PTS 6 Kensington
28.02.01	Tommy Matthews W PTS 4 Kensington
09.03.01	Tommy Matthews W PTS 4 Millwall
20.04.01	Dean Ashton W RSC 4 Millwall
16.06.01	Sven Hamer W RSC 6 Wembley
	(Vacant WBF European
	L. Heavyweight Title)
28.09.01	Paul Bonson W PTS 6 Millwall
23.11.01	Paul Bonson W PTS 6 Bethnal Green
15.03.02	Hastings Rasani W RSC 5 Millwall
29.06.02	Varuzhan Davtyan W PTS 6 Brentwood
03.10.02	Alejandro Lakatus W PTS 12 Madrid,
	Spain
	(Vacant WBA Inter-Continental
	L.Heavyweight Title)
24.05.03	Hastings Rasini W RSC 4 Bethnal
	Green
14.11.03	Peter Oboh L RSC 11 Bethnal Green
	(WBA Inter-Continental L.Heavyweight
	Title Defence)
12.03.04	Nathan King W PTS 6 Millwall
01.05.04	Tony Booth W RTD 4 Gravesend
11.06.04	Giovanni Alvarez W PTS 10
	Copenhagen, Denmark
	(European Union L.Heavyweight Title
	Challenge)
25.09.04	Roman Dobolinsh W PTS 10 Riga,
	Latvia
	(Vacant Latvian L.Heavyweight Title)
12.03.05	Kai Kurzawa W PTS 10 Zwickau,
	Germany
	(European Union L.Heavyweight Title
	Defence)

Career: 20 contests, won 18, drew 1, lost 1.

Oscar Milkitas

Canning Town. *Born* Lithuania, 24
December, 1972
Welterweight. Ht. 5'8"
Manager M. Roe

07.06.00	Ciro Canales W PTS 4 Miami, Florida,
	USA
21.07.00	Andre Cody W CO 1 Miami, Florida,
	USA
16.08.00	Elvin Peluyera W PTS 4 Davie,
	Florida, USA
20.09.00	Hamilton Verano W PTS 4 Davie,
	Florida, USA
19.12.04	Gareth Couch L PTS 6 Bethnal Green
19.02.05	Francis Barrett L PTS 6 Dublin
14.05.05	Darren Melville L PTS 6 Dublin
17.06.05	Paul McCloskey L PTS 4 Glasgow

Career: 8 contests, won 4, lost 4.

139

Ian Millarvie

Hamilton. *Born* Bellshill, 7 April, 1980
Heavyweight. Ht. 6'5¾"
Manager T. Gilmour

31.01.05	Mal Rice W RTD 3 Glasgow
21.02.05	Luke Simpkin W PTS 6 Glasgow
27.05.05	Sergey Voron W RSC 1 Motherwell

Career: 3 contests, won 3.

(Alvin) Slick Miller

Doncaster. *Born* Doncaster, 12 May, 1968
Heavyweight. Ht. 6'2"
Manager Self

28.04.94	Declan Faherty L RSC 2 Hull
06.10.94	Kent Davis L PTS 6 Hull
17.11.94	Graham Wassell L RSC 1 Sheffield
29.09.95	Mark Richardson L PTS 6 Hartlepool
13.01.96	Geoff Hunter DREW 6 Halifax
13.02.96	Danny Williams L RSC 1 Bethnal Green
15.03.96	Tony Booth L PTS 6 Hull
22.03.96	Tony Dowling L RSC 4 Mansfield
26.09.96	Steve Pettit L PTS 6 Walsall
22.11.96	Tony Booth L RSC 5 Hull
17.03.97	Michael Sprott L CO 1 Mayfair
25.04.97	Pele Lawrence L PTS 6 Mere
16.05.97	Edwin Cleary DREW 6 Hull
20.10.97	Neil Simpson L RTD 1 Leicester
16.04.98	Kevin Mitchell L RSC 2 Mayfair
08.06.98	Stevie Pettit W CO 1 Birmingham
30.11.98	Neil Simpson L CO 3 Leicester
23.01.99	Faisal Mohammed L RSC 2 Cheshunt
25.03.99	Nigel Rafferty L PTS 8 Edgbaston
17.04.99	Ahmet Oner L RSC 1 Dublin
24.10.99	Nigel Rafferty W RSC 4 Wolverhampton
25.03.00	Brian Kilbride W RSC 1 Liverpool
09.04.00	Mark Krence L PTS 6 Alfreton
11.06.00	Glenn Williams L PTS 4 Salford
08.07.00	Tony Dowling L PTS 4 Widnes
23.09.00	John McDermott L RSC 1 Bethnal Green
03.02.01	Scott Baker W RSC 4 Brighton
18.02.01	Hughie Robertson W RSC 2 Southwark
25.02.01	Colin Kenna L RSC 3 Streatham
05.05.01	Danny Percival W CO 1 Edmonton
31.07.01	Neil Hosking L RSC 2 Bethnal Green
07.09.01	Jason Brewster L PTS 6 West Bromwich
22.09.01	Dennis Bakhtov L CO 1 Bethnal Green
22.11.01	Petr Horacek L PTS 4 Paddington
26.01.02	Fola Okesola L RSC 1 Dagenham
23.09.02	Tony Booth L PTS 6 Cleethorpes
12.10.02	Matt Legg W RSC 2 Bethnal Green
27.10.02	Matt Skelton L CO 1 Southwark
09.12.02	Paul Butlin L PTS 6 Nottingham
15.02.03	Keith Long L RSC 1 Wembley
18.09.03	Micky Steeds L PTS 4 Mayfair
15.11.03	Jason Callum L PTS 4 Coventry
28.11.03	Carl Baker L CO 1 Hull
25.04.04	Tony Dowling L RSC 2 Nottingham
24.06.04	Simon Francis L PTS 6 Gibralter
21.01.05	Joe Young L RSC 2 Brentford
08.04.05	John McDermott L RSC 1 Edinburgh
23.05.05	Lee Nicholson L PTS 6 Cleethorpes
12.06.05	Terry Dixon L RSC 2 Leicester Square

Career: 49 contests, won 7, drew 2, lost 40.

Ross Minter

Crawley. *Born* Crawley, 10 November, 1978
Southern Area Welterweight Champion.
Ht. 5'7¾"
Manager Self

26.03.01	Brian Coleman W PTS 4 Wembley
05.05.01	Trevor Smith W RTD 3 Edmonton
28.07.01	Lee Williamson W PTS 4 Wembley
24.11.01	Karl Taylor W PTS 4 Bethnal Green
15.12.01	Ernie Smith W RSC 2 Wembley
02.03.02	Paul Denton W PTS 6 Bethnal Green
25.05.02	Howard Clarke L RSC 2 Portsmouth
12.10.02	Dafydd Carlin W RSC 1 Bethnal Green
15.02.03	Karl Taylor W PTS 6 Wembley
29.03.03	Jay Mahoney W RSC 2 Portsmouth
24.05.03	Jay Mahoney W PTS 6 Bethnal Green
18.09.03	John Marshall DREW 6 Dagenham
19.11.04	David Kirk W PTS 6 Bethnal Green
25.02.05	Ernie Smith W PTS 4 Wembley
29.04.05	Chas Symonds W RSC 3 Southwark *(Southern Area Welterweight Title Challenge)*

Career: 15 contests, won 13, drew 1, lost 1.

Ross Minter   Les Clark

Joe Mitchell

Birmingham. *Born* Birmingham, 8 February, 1971
Welterweight. Ht. 5'9"
Manager T. Nerwal

20.02.04	Steve Scott W PTS 6 Doncaster
07.04.04	Robert Lloyd-Taylor L RSC 5 Leicester Square
08.07.04	Darren Gethin DREW 6 Birmingham
12.09.04	Darren Gethin L PTS 6 Shrewsbury
05.10.04	Mark Wall DREW 6 Dudley
22.10.04	Dennis Corpe W PTS 6 Mansfield
25.11.04	Ernie Smith L PTS 6 Birmingham
04.02.05	Jon Harrison L PTS 6 Plymouth
18.04.05	Darren Gethin L PTS 6 Bradford
18.06.05	Scott Conway W RSC 5 Barnsley

Career: 10 contests, won 3, drew 2, lost 5.

Kevin Mitchell

Dagenham. *Born* Dagenham, 29 October, 1984
S. Featherweight. Ht. 5'8"
Manager F. Warren/F. Maloney

17.07.03	Stevie Quinn W CO 1 Dagenham
18.09.03	Csabi Ladanyi W RSC 1 Dagenham
06.11.03	Vlado Varhegyi W RSC 3 Dagenham
24.01.04	Jaz Virdee W RSC 1 Wembley
07.02.04	Kristian Laight W PTS 4 Bethnal Green
24.04.04	Eric Patrac W RSC 1 Reading

13.05.04	Slimane Kebaili W RSC 1 Bethnal Green
05.06.04	Jason Nesbitt W RSC 3 Bethnal Green
10.09.04	Arpad Toth W RSC 3 Bethnal Green
22.10.04	Mounir Guebbas W PTS 6 Edinburgh
19.11.04	Alain Rakow W CO 1 Bethnal Green
11.12.04	Henry Janes W PTS 4 Canning Town
08.04.05	Frederic Bonifai W PTS 6 Edinburgh
29.04.05	Karim Chakim W PTS 8 Southwark

Career: 14 contests, won 14.

Kevin Mitchell   Philip Sharkey

(Arvill) Arv Mittoo

Birmingham. *Born* Birmingham, 8 July, 1971
Welterweight. Ht. 5'8"
Manager Self

31.01.96	Alan Bosworth L PTS 6 Stoke
13.02.96	Tommy Janes L PTS 6 Cardiff
21.02.96	Danny Lutaaya L PTS 6 Piccadilly
20.05.96	Terry Whittaker L CO 5 Cleethorpes
29.06.96	Craig Stanley L PTS 4 Erith
23.09.96	Thomas Bradley DREW 6 Cleethorpes
03.10.96	John T. Kelly L PTS 6 Sunderland
01.11.96	David Kirk L PTS 6 Mansfield
14.11.96	Thomas Bradley L RSC 4 Sheffield
22.05.97	Craig Stanley W RSC 3 Southwark
02.09.97	Trevor Tacy L PTS 6 Manchester
22.09.97	Steve Conway L PTS 6 Cleethorpes
09.10.97	Steve Conway L PTS 6 Leeds
23.10.97	Marco Fattore W PTS 6 Mayfair
11.11.97	Kevin McCarthy L PTS 6 Bethnal Green
03.12.97	Marc Smith W PTS 6 Stoke
31.01.98	Harry Andrews L PTS 4 Edmonton
06.03.98	Gavin McGill W PTS 6 Hull
18.03.98	Marc Smith W PTS 6 Stoke
26.03.98	Danny Lutaaya DREW 6 Piccadilly
11.04.98	Charlie Rumbol L PTS 4 Southwark
21.04.98	Adam Spelling W PTS 4 Edmonton
02.10.98	Sammy Smith L PTS 4 Cheshunt
16.10.98	Mark Haslam L PTS 6 Salford
25.11.98	Brian Coleman L PTS 6 Clydach

27.01.99	Ernie Smith DREW 6 Stoke
26.02.99	Mark Payne L PTS 4 Coventry
17.03.99	Marc Smith L PTS 6 Stoke
20.05.99	John Humphrey L PTS 6 Barking
28.05.99	Jamie McKeever L PTS 6 Liverpool
04.06.99	Oscar Hall L PTS 6 Hull
02.07.99	Wahid Fats L PTS 6 Manchester
21.07.99	Brian Gentry L RSC 4 Bloomsbury
20.10.99	Steve Saville L PTS 8 Stoke
31.10.99	Ross McCord L PTS 6 Raynes Park
15.11.99	Lee Sharp L PTS 6 Glasgow
22.11.99	Mohamed Helel L PTS 6 Piccadilly
29.11.99	Peter Swinney L PTS 4 Wembley
11.12.99	Thomas McDonagh L RSC 2 Liverpool
12.02.00	Mally McIver L PTS 4 Sheffield
10.03.00	Jason Hall W RSC 3 Bethnal Green
08.04.00	Junior Witter L PTS 4 Bethnal Green
17.04.00	Gavin Pearson L PTS 6 Glasgow
13.05.00	Chris Steele W RSC 3 Barnsley
21.05.00	Gavin Down L PTS 6 Derby
06.06.00	Casey Brooke W PTS 6 Brierley Hill
15.07.00	Steve Conway L PTS 6 Norwich
30.09.00	Mark Florian L PTS 4 Peterborough
07.10.00	Jesse James Daniel L PTS 4 Doncaster
16.11.00	Lance Crosby L RSC 3 Hull
28.01.01	Stuart Elwell L PTS 6 Wolverhampton
19.02.01	Lee Sharp L PTS 6 Glasgow
26.02.01	Gavin Wake L PTS 4 Nottingham
24.03.01	Richard Holden L PTS 6 Newark
01.04.01	Babatunde Ajayi L PTS 6 Southwark
20.04.01	Manzo Smith L PTS 4 Millwall
08.05.01	Robert Burton L PTS 4 Barnsley
04.06.01	Gary Porter L PTS 6 Glasgow
16.06.01	Gavin Down L PTS 6 Derby
14.07.01	Lee Byrne L PTS 4 Wembley
13.09.01	Lee Meager L PTS 6 Sheffield
23.09.01	Anthony Christopher DREW 6 Shaw
28.10.01	Peter Swinney L PTS 4 Southwark
16.11.01	Terry Ham L PTS 6 Preston
10.12.01	Lee Armstrong L PTS 6 Bradford
23.12.01	John Marshall L RSC 1 Salford
15.04.02	Chris Duggan L PTS 6 Shrewsbury
28.04.02	Peter McDonagh L PTS 6 Southwark
10.05.02	Oscar Hall L PTS 4 Bethnal Green
15.06.02	Chris Saunders L PTS 6 Norwich
23.06.02	Mark Stupple L PTS 6 Southwark
17.09.02	Gwyn Wale L PTS 6 Bethnal Green
05.10.02	Dean Lambert L PTS 4 Huddersfield
17.11.02	Lee McAllister L PTS 6 Bradford
30.11.02	Richard Swallow L PTS 4 Coventry
08.12.02	Elvis Mbwakongo L PTS 6 Bethnal Green
20.12.02	Nathan Ward L PTS 6 Bracknell
23.02.03	Adnan Amar L PTS 6 Shrewsbury
16.03.03	Jonathan Woollins L PTS 4 Nottingham
08.04.03	Justin Hudson L PTS 4 Bethnal Green
28.04.03	Barry Morrison L RSC 3 Nottingham
03.06.03	Chas Symonds L PTS 6 Bethnal Green
13.06.03	Gary Steadman L PTS 4 Queensway
22.07.03	Gary Woolcombe L PTS 6 Bethnal Green
01.08.03	Mark Alexander L PTS 4 Bethnal Green
26.10.03	Robert Lloyd-Taylor L PTS 6 Longford
23.11.03	Scott Haywood L PTS 6 Rotherham
21.02.04	Steve Russell L PTS 6 Norwich
06.03.04	Colin McNeil L PTS 4 Renfrew
27.03.04	Barrie Lee L PTS 4 Edinburgh
16.04.04	Nadeem Siddique L PTS 6 Bradford
19.06.04	Ashley Theophane L PTS 4 Muswell Hill
03.07.04	Tommy Marshall L PTS 6 Bristol
29.10.04	Gary Connolly W RSC 5 Worksop
08.12.04	Sammy Smith L PTS 6 Longford
17.12.04	Jamie Coyle L RSC 5 Huddersfield
26.02.05	Jonjo Finnegan L PTS 4 Burton

Career: 97 contests, won 10, drew 4, lost 83.

(Qais) Mo (Ariya)

Sheffield. *Born* Kabul, Afghanistan, 15 February, 1979
Middleweight. Ht. 5'9"
Manager Self

12.07.02	Danny Gwilym L PTS 6 Southampton
27.09.02	Freddie Yemofio W PTS 4 Bracknell
09.05.03	Freddie Yemofio W PTS 4 Longford
12.10.03	Danny Gwilym W PTS 6 Sheffield
10.02.04	Danny Thornton L PTS 6 Barnsley
28.10.04	Eddie Haley DREW 6 Sunderland
20.02.05	Dean Walker L PTS 6 Sheffield

Career: 7 contests, won 3, drew 1, lost 3.

Colin Moffett

Belfast. *Born* Belfast, 15 April, 1975
Bantamweight. Ht. 5'6"
Manager Self

05.11.96	Shane Mallon W RSC 2 Belfast
28.01.97	Anthony Hanna W PTS 4 Belfast
29.04.97	Gary Hickman W PTS 4 Belfast
02.06.97	Jason Thomas L RSC 3 Belfast
20.12.97	Graham McGrath DREW 4 Belfast
18.09.98	Anthony Hanna DREW 4 Belfast
28.11.98	Shaun Norman W PTS 4 Belfast
31.07.99	Waj Khan W CO 1 Carlisle
16.10.99	Delroy Spencer L PTS 4 Bethnal Green
31.03.00	Steffen Norskov L PTS 4 Esbjerg, Denmark
05.06.00	Keith Knox L RSC 3 Glasgow
02.12.00	Dale Robinson L PTS 4 Bethnal Green
15.09.01	Chris Emanuele L RSC 4 Nottingham
27.04.02	Levi Pattison L RSC 2 Huddersfield
27.07.02	Jim Betts L RSC 3 Nottingham
30.10.03	John Bothwell DREW 4 Renfrew
08.05.04	Lee Haskins L RSC 2 Bristol
19.06.04	Michael Crossan DREW 4 Renfrew
28.10.04	Chris Edwards W PTS 4 Belfast

Career: 19 contests, won 6, drew 4, lost 9.

Danny Moir

Gateshead. *Born* Gateshead, 21 January, 1972
L.Middleweight. Former British Masters
L.Middleweight Champion. Ht. 5'11"
Manager T. Conroy

04.10.01	Richard Inquieti W PTS 6 Sunderland
20.10.01	Lee Minter W RSC 1 Portsmouth
06.12.01	Gary Jones W PTS 6 Sunderland
08.02.02	Colin McCash W RSC 3 Preston
08.03.02	Martyn Bailey L PTS 6 Ellesmere Port
25.03.02	Gavin Pearson L PTS 6 Sunderland
03.10.02	Andy Gibson L RTD 4 Sunderland
22.12.02	Richard Inquieti W RTD 3 Salford
20.01.03	Gary Porter W PTS 6 Glasgow
27.02.03	Franny Jones DREW 6 Sunderland
17.03.03	Ciaran Duffy L PTS 6 Glasgow
29.05.03	Eugenio Monteiro L PTS 6 Sunderland
09.06.03	Danny Parkinson L PTS 6 Bradford
02.10.03	Omar Gumati W PTS 6 Sunderland
20.10.03	Craig Dickson L RSC 3 Glasgow
04.12.03	Wayne Shepherd W PTS 6 Sunderland

21.12.03	Geraint Harvey W PTS 6 Bolton
05.03.04	Franny Jones NC 3 Darlington
	(Vacant Northern Area L.Middleweight Title)
12.03.04	Gary Porter DREW 6 Irvine
25.03.04	Kevin Phelan W PTS 10 Longford
	(Vacant British Masters L.Middleweight Title)
27.05.04	Kevin Anderson L RSC 1 Huddersfield
23.09.04	Kevin Phelan L RTD 3 Gateshead
	(British Masters L.Middleweight Title Defence)
12.11.04	David Walker L RSC 5 Wembley
24.02.05	Gary Porter W PTS 6 Sunderland
04.03.05	Kevin Bennett L RSC 3 Hartlepool
12.05.05	John Marshall L RSC 5 Sunderland

Career: 26 contests, won 11, drew 2, lost 12, no contest 1.

Danny Moir Les Clark

Michael Monaghan

Nottingham. *Born* Nottingham, 31 May, 1976
Middleweight. Ht. 5'10³/₄"
Manager Self

23.09.96	Lee Simpkin W PTS 6 Cleethorpes
24.10.96	Lee Bird W RSC 6 Lincoln
09.12.96	Lee Simpkin W PTS 6 Chesterfield
16.12.96	Carlton Williams W PTS 6 Cleethorpes
20.03.97	Paul Miles W PTS 6 Newark
26.04.97	Paul Ryan L RSC 2 Swadlincote
05.07.97	Ali Khattab W PTS 4 Glasgow
18.08.97	Trevor Meikle W PTS 6 Nottingham
12.09.97	Willie Quinn L PTS 6 Glasgow
19.09.97	Roy Chipperfield W PTS 6 Salford
30.09.97	George Richards L PTS 6 Edgbaston
10.03.98	Anthony van Niekirk L RTD 6 Hammanskraal, South Africa
23.04.98	Darren Sweeney L PTS 10 Edgbaston
	(Midlands Area Middleweight Title Challenge)
19.09.98	Jim Rock L PTS 12 Dublin
	(Vacant WAA Inter-Continental S. Middleweight Title)
27.11.98	Mark Dawson W PTS 6 Nottingham
07.12.98	Mike Whittaker L PTS 6 Manchester
14.09.02	Paul Billington W RSC 4 Newark
30.11.02	Gary Beardsley W PTS 6 Newark
24.02.03	Jason Collins W PTS 8 Birmingham
16.04.03	Carl Froch L RSC 3 Nottingham
28.06.03	Gary Lockett L PTS 10 Cardiff
13.09.03	Tomas da Silva W PTS 6 Newport

141

25.04.04 Jason Collins W PTS 6 Nottingham
05.06.04 Wayne Elcock L PTS 4 Bethnal Green
03.09.04 Gary Lockett L RSC 3 Newport
29.10.04 Lawrence Murphy L PTS 6 Renfrew
20.02.05 Howard Clarke W PTS 6 Sheffield
18.03.05 Jim Rock L PTS 8 Belfast
27.03.05 Michal Bilak W PTS 6 Prague, Czech Republic
30.04.05 John Humphrey L PTS 6 Dagenham
14.05.05 Matthew Macklin L CO 5 Dublin
(Vacant Irish Middleweight Title)

Career: 31 contests, won 16, lost 15.

(Elton) Tony Montana (Gashi)

Sheffield. *Born* Yugoslavia, 5 August, 1982
Welterweight. Central Area L.Welterweight
Champion. Ht. 5'8"
Manager Self

24.11.00 Dave Gibson W PTS 6 Hull
03.12.00 Gary Greenwood DREW 6 Shaw
31.01.01 Pete Buckley W PTS 6 Piccadilly
13.02.01 Barrie Kelley L PTS 6 Brierley Hill
06.03.01 Chris Price W PTS 6 Yarm
18.03.01 Ray Wood DREW 6 Shaw
26.03.01 Francis Barrett L PTS 4 Wembley
24.05.01 Ajose Olusegun L RSC 1 Kensington
07.09.01 Mark Hawthorne L CO 3 Bethnal Green
16.11.01 Young Muttley L PTS 6 West Bromwich
30.11.01 Brian Gifford W PTS 6 Hull
17.12.01 Andrei Ivanov DREW 6 Cleethorpes
31.01.02 James Paisley W PTS 6 Piccadilly
11.02.02 Ernie Smith W PTS 6 Shrewsbury
13.04.02 Nicky Leech L PTS 6 Wolverhampton
11.05.02 Robbie Sivyer L PTS 6 Chesterfield
31.05.02 John Marshall L PTS 6 Hull
12.07.02 Chris McDonagh W PTS 4 Southampton
08.09.02 Jimmy Gould W PTS 8 Wolverhampton
21.09.02 Christophe de Busillet L PTS 6 Norwich
02.11.02 Young Muttley L PTS 4 Wolverhampton
22.12.02 Mark Haslam W PTS 6 Salford
28.01.03 Gavin Down L PTS 4 Nottingham
22.03.03 George Telfer W PTS 4 Renfrew
17.07.03 Young Muttley L PTS 4 Walsall
28.11.03 Lenny Daws L PTS 6 Derby
06.02.04 Bobby Vanzie L PTS 6 Sheffield
14.02.04 Gary Hibbert W PTS 6 Nottingham
15.04.04 Dean Hickman L PTS 6 Dudley
23.04.04 Lee Williamson W PTS 6 Leicester
22.05.04 Wayne Rigby W PTS 10 Manchester
(Vacant Central Area L.Welterweight Title)
26.09.04 Gary Reid L PTS 10 Stoke
(Vacant British Masters L.Welterweight Title)
15.11.04 Craig Dickson L PTS 8 Glasgow
26.11.04 Graham Delehedy L PTS 6 Altrincham
09.12.04 John Marshall W PTS 4 Stockport
16.12.04 Scott Haywood W PTS 6 Cleethorpes
07.04.05 Anthony Maynard L PTS 4 Birmingham
25.04.05 Jamie Coyle L RSC 3 Glasgow
20.06.05 Sammy Smith L PTS 10 Longford
(Vacant WBF Continental Welterweight Title)

Career: 39 contests, won 15, drew 3, lost 21.

Jamie Moore

Salford. *Born* Salford, 4 November, 1978
L.Middleweight. Former British &
Commonwealth L.Middleweight
Champion. Ht. 5'8"
Manager S. Wood

09.10.99 Clive Johnson W RSC 3 Manchester
13.11.99 Peter Nightingale W PTS 4 Hull
19.12.99 Paul King W PTS 6 Salford
29.02.00 David Baptiste W RSC 3 Manchester
20.03.00 Harry Butler W RSC 2 Mansfield
14.04.00 Jimmy Steel W PTS 6 Manchester
27.05.00 Koba Kulu W RTD 3 Southwark
07.10.00 Leigh Wicks W PTS 4 Doncaster
12.11.00 Prince Kasi Kaihau W RSC 2 Manchester
25.11.00 Wayne Shepherd W RSC 3 Manchester
17.03.01 Richie Murray W RSC 1 Manchester
27.05.01 Paul Denton W RSC 3 Manchester
07.07.01 Scott Dixon L CO 5 Manchester
(Vacant WBO Inter-Continental L.Middleweight Title)
26.01.02 Harry Butler W RSC 3 Dagenham
09.03.02 Andrzej Butowicz W RSC 5 Manchester
07.09.02 Delroy Mellis W CO 6 Liverpool
08.02.03 Akhmed Oligov W PTS 6 Liverpool
19.04.03 Michael Jones W PTS 12 Liverpool
(Vacant British L. Middleweight Title. Commonwealth L. Middleweight Title Challenge)
18.10.03 Gary Logan W CO 5 Manchester
(British & Commonwealth L.Middleweight Title Defences)
22.11.03 Andrew Facey W RSC 7 Belfast
(British & Commonwealth L.Middleweight Title Defences)
10.04.04 Adam Katumwa W RSC 5 Manchester
(Vacant Commonwealth L.Middleweight Title)
26.06.04 Ossie Duran L RSC 3 Belfast
(Commonwealth L.Middleweight Title Defence)
26.11.04 Michael Jones L DIS 3 Altrincham
(British L.Middleweight Title Defence)

Career: 23 contests, won 20, lost 3.

Mark Moran

Liverpool. *Born* Liverpool, 16 February, 1982
Featherweight. Ht. 5'6"
Manager S. Vaughan/F. Warren

02.10.03 Steve Gethin W PTS 4 Liverpool
13.12.03 Delroy Spencer W PTS 4 Manchester
26.02.04 Darren Cleary W PTS 4 Widnes
03.04.04 Neil Read W RSC 2 Manchester
22.05.04 Darren Cleary DREW 4 Widnes
17.12.04 Steve Gethin W PTS 4 Liverpool

Career: 6 contests, won 5, drew 1.

Tony Moran

Liverpool. *Born* Liverpool, 4 July, 1973
Cruiserweight. Ht. 6'6"
Manager Self

26.04.01 Shaun Bowes L PTS 6 Gateshead
13.11.01 Paul Bonson L PTS 6 Leeds
19.03.02 Graham Nolan W PTS 6 Slough
10.05.02 Eamonn Glennon W RTD 1 Preston
03.06.02 Dave Clarke W PTS 6 Glasgow
07.09.02 Adam Cale W PTS 4 Liverpool

05.10.02 Jason Brewster W PTS 4 Liverpool
29.11.02 Adam Cale W RSC 1 Liverpool
08.02.03 Michael Pinnock W PTS 4 Liverpool
17.02.03 Brian Gascoigne W RSC 1 Glasgow
19.04.03 Paul Bonson W PTS 4 Liverpool
17.05.03 Tony Booth W PTS 6 Liverpool
27.10.03 Matthew Ellis W RSC 4 Glasgow
13.03.04 Mark Hobson L RSC 3 Huddersfield
(British & Commonwealth Cruiserweight Title Challenges)
30.04.05 Paul Bonson W PTS 6 Wigan
13.05.05 Lee Mountford W RSC 1 Liverpool

Career: 16 contests, won 13, lost 3.

Craig Morgan

Llanharan. *Born* Church Village, 9 April, 1983
Lightweight. Ht. 5'7"
Manager P. Boyce

28.04.05 Dave Hinds W PTS 4 Clydach

Career: 1 contest, won 1.

Darren Morgan

Swansea. *Born* Swansea, 26 October, 1976
Heavyweight. Ht. 6'1½"
Manager F. Warren

21.01.05 Ebrima Secka W RSC 1 Bridgend
04.06.05 Dave Clarke W RSC 1 Manchester

Career: 2 contests, won 2.

Andy Morris

Wythenshawe. *Born* Manchester, 10 March, 1983
English Featherweight Champion. Ht. 5'6½"
Manager F. Warren/F. Maloney

18.01.03 Jason Nesbitt W PTS 4 Preston
05.04.03 Haroon Din W RSC 1 Manchester
08.05.03 Daniel Thorpe W PTS 4 Widnes
06.11.03 Dave Hinds W PTS 4 Dagenham
13.12.03 Henry Janes W PTS 4 Manchester
26.02.04 Daniel Thorpe W RSC 3 Widnes
03.04.04 Carl Allen W PTS 4 Manchester
12.06.04 Jus Wallie W PTS 6 Manchester
01.10.04 Chris Hooper W RSC 3 Manchester
11.02.05 Buster Dennis W PTS 6 Manchester
20.05.05 Rocky Dean W PTS 10 Southwark
(Vacant English Featherweight Title)

Career: 11 contests, won 11.

Jay Morris   Les Clark

Jay Morris

Newport, IoW. *Born* Newport, IoW, 8 May, 1978
Welterweight. Ht. 5'7"
Manager R. Davies

21.02.04	Judex Meemea DREW 4 Brighton
30.03.04	Casey Brooke W RSC 1 Southampton
21.11.04	Chris Brophy W RSC 1 Bracknell
12.02.05	Pete Buckley W PTS 6 Portsmouth
26.06.05	David Kehoe W PTS 4 Southampton

Career: 5 contests, won 4, drew 1.

Barry Morrison

Motherwell. *Born* Bellshill, 8 May, 1980
British Masters L.Welterweight Champion.
Ht. 5'7"
Manager T. Gilmour

12.04.03	Keith Jones W PTS 4 Bethnal Green
28.04.03	Arv Mittoo W RSC 3 Nottingham
05.07.03	Cristian Hodorogea W RSC 3 Brentwood
06.09.03	Jay Mahoney W RSC 2 Huddersfield
04.10.03	Sergei Starkov W PTS 6 Belfast
01.11.03	Tarik Amrous W PTS 8 Glasgow
28.02.04	Zoltan Surman W RSC 3 Bridgend
22.04.04	Andrei Devyataykin W PTS 8 Glasgow
15.10.04	Adam Zadworny W RSC 2 Glasgow
27.05.04	Gary Reid W RTD 8 Motherwell *(British Masters L.Welterweight Title Challenge)*

Career: 10 contests, won 10.

Abdul Mougharbel (Almgharbel)

Dewsbury. *Born* Syria, 10 November, 1975
S.Bantamweight. Ht. 5'4"
Manager C. Aston

15.03.04	Hussain Nasser W RTD 3 Bradford
19.04.04	Sandy Bartlett W PTS 6 Glasgow
11.10.04	Sandy Bartlett L PTS 6 Glasgow
22.10.04	Scott Flynn L PTS 4 Edinburgh
19.11.04	Isaac Ward L PTS 4 Hartlepool
11.12.04	Matthew Marsh L PTS 4 Canning Town
06.03.05	Andy Bell L PTS 4 Mansfield
18.04.05	Neil Read W PTS 6 Bradford
27.05.05	Kevin Townsley L PTS 6 Motherwell
06.06.05	Gary Ford W PTS 6 Glasgow

Career: 10 contests, won 4, lost 6.

Lee Mountford

Pudsey. *Born* Leeds, 1 September, 1972
Heavyweight. Ht. 6'2"
Manager T. O'Neill/D. Coldwell

19.04.02	Gary Thompson DREW 4 Darlington
24.06.02	Eamonn Glennon L PTS 6 Bradford
20.11.02	Nate Joseph W PTS 6 Leeds
03.02.03	Eamonn Glennon DREW 6 Bradford
28.02.03	Gary Thompson W PTS 6 Irvine
13.05.03	Nate Joseph L PTS 6 Leeds
01.12.03	Dave Clarke W PTS 6 Bradford
15.03.04	Greg Scott-Briggs DREW 6 Bradford
09.04.04	Carl Wright L PTS 4 Rugby
20.04.04	Lee Swaby L RSC 1 Sheffield
26.09.04	Paul Butlin L PTS 6 Stoke
28.10.04	Martin Rogan L RSC 1 Belfast
13.02.05	Nate Joseph L PTS 6 Bradford
13.05.05	Tony Moran L RSC 1 Liverpool
18.06.05	John Anthony L RSC 5 Barnsley

Career: 15 contests, won 3, drew 3, lost 9.

Steve Mullin

Liverpool. *Born* Liverpool, 7 July, 1983
Lightweight. Ht. 5'7"
Manager S. Vaughan

19.04.03	Daniel Thorpe L RSC 1 Liverpool
20.06.03	Dave Hinds W PTS 4 Liverpool
29.08.03	Peter Allen W PTS 6 Liverpool
08.12.03	Sid Razak W PTS 6 Birmingham
08.03.04	Sid Razak W PTS 6 Birmingham
10.09.04	Peter Allen W PTS 4 Liverpool
17.12.04	Pete Buckley W PTS 4 Liverpool

Career: 7 contests, won 6, lost 1.

Rendall Munroe

Leicester. *Born* Leicester, 1 June, 1980
Featherweight. Ht. 5'7"
Manager M. Shinfield/D. Coldwell

20.09.03	Joel Viney W RTD 3 Nottingham
23.11.03	John-Paul Ryan W PTS 6 Rotherham
14.02.04	Neil Read W RSC 1 Nottingham
09.04.04	Anthony Hanna W PTS 6 Rugby
26.04.04	Baz Carey W PTS 6 Cleethorpes
27.09.04	David Bailey W PTS 6 Cleethorpes
08.10.04	David Killu W PTS 6 Brentwood
18.06.05	Darren Broomhall W RSC 3 Barnsley

Career: 8 contests, won 8.

Rendall Munroe   Les Clark

Justin Murphy

Hove. *Born* Brighton, 21 February, 1974
Lightweight. Ht. 5'7"
Manager R. Davies

15.09.93	Andrew Bloomer W PTS 4 Bethnal Green
13.10.93	Thomas Bernard W RSC 1 Bethnal Green
01.12.93	Mark Hargreaves W PTS 4 Bethnal Green
25.01.94	Jobie Tyers W RSC 3 Piccadilly
29.03.94	Tony Falcone W RSC 2 Bethnal Green
15.06.94	Mike Deveney W PTS 6 Southwark
23.11.94	Pete Buckley W PTS 4 Piccadilly
25.05.95	Barry Jones L PTS 10 Reading *(Elim. British Featherweight Title)*
16.06.95	Paul Webster L PTS 6 Southwark
08.11.95	P. J. Gallagher L RSC 6 Bethnal Green *(Vacant Southern Area S.Featherweight Title & Elim. British S.Featherweight Title)*

30.01.96	Colin McMillan L RSC 4 Barking
17.09.98	David Morris W PTS 4 Brighton
03.10.98	Pete Buckley W PTS 6 Crawley
12.12.98	David Burke L RSC 4 Southwark
26.02.99	Paul Halpin L RSC 2 Bethnal Green *(Vacant Southern Area Featherweight Title)*
18.02.05	Ian Reid W PTS 6 Brighton
26.06.05	Terry Carruthers W RSC 1 Southampton

Career: 17 contests, won 11, lost 6.

Lawrence Murphy

Uddingston. *Born* Bellshill, 9 February, 1976
Middleweight. Former WBU Middleweight Champion. Ht. 6'1"
Manager A. Morrison

15.05.98	Mark Owens W RSC 2 Edinburgh
17.09.98	Lee Bird W RSC 3 Glasgow
13.11.98	Ian Toby W PTS 6 Glasgow
18.02.99	Mike Duffield W RSC 2 Glasgow
26.06.99	Harry Butler W RSC 1 Glasgow
17.12.00	Michael Alexander W PTS 6 Glasgow
07.09.01	Chris Nembhard DREW 6 Glasgow
17.11.01	Leigh Wicks W PTS 4 Glasgow
16.12.01	Kreshnik Qato W PTS 6 Glasgow
11.03.02	Rob Stevenson W RSC 1 Glasgow
22.03.03	Leigh Wicks W PTS 4 Renfrew
12.07.03	Jason Collins W PTS 4 Renfrew
25.10.03	Howard Clarke W PTS 6 Edinburgh
29.11.03	Wayne Elcock W CO 1 Renfrew *(WBU Middleweight Title Challenge)*
06.03.04	Anthony Farnell L RSC 3 Renfrew *(WBU Middleweight Title Defence)*
29.10.04	Michael Monaghan W PTS 6 Renfrew

Career: 16 contests, won 14, drew 1, lost 1.

Andrew Murray

Cavan. *Born* Cavan, 10 September, 1982
Lightweight. Ht. 5'10"
Manager M. Helliet

18.03.05	Jonathan Jones W RSC 4 Belfast

Career: 1 contest, won 1.

John Murray

Manchester. *Born* Manchester, 20 December, 1984
S. Featherweight. Ht. 5'8"
Manager S. Wood

06.09.03	Pete Buckley W PTS 4 Huddersfield
18.10.03	Matthew Burke W RSC 1 Manchester
21.12.03	Jason Nesbitt W PTS 6 Bolton
30.01.04	Norman Dhalie W CO 2 Dagenham
12.03.04	John-Paul Ryan W RSC 1 Nottingham
02.06.04	Anthony Hanna W PTS 4 Nottingham
24.09.04	Dariusz Snarski W RSC 2 Nottingham
31.10.04	Ernie Smith W PTS 4 Shaw
26.11.04	Daniel Thorpe W RSC 2 Altrincham
09.12.04	Harry Ramogoadi W RSC 4 Stockport
06.03.05	Karl Taylor W PTS 6 Shaw

Career: 11 contests, won 11.

Oneal Murray

Brixton. *Born* Jamaica, 8 March, 1973
Cruiserweight. Ht. 6'0"
Manager B. Baker

29.03.01 Oddy Papantoniou L PTS 4 Hammersmith
04.10.01 Michael Pinnock W PTS 6 Finsbury
15.10.01 Joe Brame W RSC 2 Southampton
15.12.01 Steven Spartacus L RSC 4 Chigwell
27.01.02 Adam Cale W PTS 6 Streatham
23.02.03 Brodie Pearmaine L PTS 4 Streatham
13.04.03 Dave Clarke L PTS 4 Streatham
14.02.04 Tony Booth L PTS 8 Holborn
06.02.05 Colin Kenna L RTD 3 Southampton
28.06.05 Denis Boytsov L RSC 1 Cuaxhaven, Germany

Career: 10 contests, won 3, lost 7.

Steve Murray

Harlow. *Born* Harlow, 5 October, 1975
Lightweight. Former WBO Inter-
Continental Lightweight Champion.
Former Undefeated IBF Inter-Continental
Lightweight Champion. Ht. 5'6"
Manager F. Warren

10.10.98 Keith Jones W RSC 4 Bethnal Green
14.11.98 Dave Travers W RSC 2 Cheshunt
23.01.99 Marc Smith W PTS 6 Cheshunt
30.01.99 Dewi Roberts W RSC 1 Bethnal Green
03.04.99 Woody Greenaway W CO 2 Kensington
01.05.99 Keith Jones W RSC 6 Crystal Palace
26.06.99 Brian Coleman W PTS 6 Millwall
07.08.99 Pete Buckley W PTS 6 Dagenham
15.11.99 Karl Taylor W RSC 1 Bethnal Green
29.01.00 Keith Jones W PTS 4 Manchester
19.02.00 Juan Carlos Zummaraga W RSC 1 Dagenham
(Vacant IBF Inter-Continental Lightweight Title)
29.05.00 Wahid Fats W RSC 3 Manchester
24.06.00 Nono Junior W RSC 4 Glasgow
12.08.00 Alan Temple W RSC 2 Wembley
(IBF Inter-Continental Lightweight Title Defence. Elim. British Lightweight Title)
23.09.00 David Kirk W PTS 4 Bethnal Green
24.02.01 Sergei Starkov W PTS 8 Bethnal Green
05.05.01 Bobby Vanzie L RSC 7 Edmonton
(British Lightweight Title Challenge)
22.09.01 Darren Melville W PTS 8 Bethnal Green
24.11.01 Keith Jones W RSC 4 Bethnal Green
15.12.01 Jason Hall W RSC 4 Wembley
(Elim. British Lightweight Title)
02.03.02 Viktor Baranov W RSC 5 Bethnal Green
(Vacant WBO Inter-Continental Lightweight Title)
04.05.02 Rosalin Nasibulin W CO 5 Bethnal Green
14.09.02 Yuri Romanov L RSC 10 Bethnal Green
(WBO Inter-Continental Lightweight Title Defence)
15.02.03 Graham Earl L RSC 2 Wembley
(Southern Area Lightweight Title Challenge. Final Elim. British Lightweight Title)
24.01.04 Jimmy Beech W RSC 4 Wembley
01.04.04 Martin Watson W PTS 10 Bethnal Green
30.07.04 Graham Earl L RSC 6 Bethnal Green
(British Lightweight Title Challenge)
25.02.05 Jeff Thomas W RTD 3 Wembley

Career: 28 contests, won 24, lost 4.

Lee Murtagh

Leeds. *Born* Leeds, 30 September, 1973
Central Area L.Middleweight Champion.
Former Undefeated Central Area
Middleweight Champion. Former British
Masters Middleweight Champion. Former
British Masters L.Middleweight Champion.
Ht. 5'9¼"
Manager Self

12.06.95 Dave Curtis W PTS 6 Bradford
25.09.95 Roy Gbasai W PTS 6 Bradford
30.10.95 Cam Raeside L PTS 6 Bradford
11.12.95 Donovan Davey W PTS 6 Bradford
13.01.96 Peter Varnavas W PTS 6 Halifax
05.02.96 Shamus Casey W PTS 6 Bradford
20.05.96 Shaun O'Neill W PTS 6 Bradford
24.06.96 Michael Alexander W PTS 6 Bradford
28.10.96 Jimmy Vincent L RSC 2 Bradford
14.04.97 Lee Simpkin W PTS 6 Bradford
09.10.97 Brian Dunn W PTS 6 Leeds
05.03.98 Wayne Shepherd W PTS 6 Leeds
08.08.98 Alan Gilbert W PTS 4 Scarborough
13.03.99 Keith Palmer DREW 6 Manchester
27.09.99 Jawaid Khaliq L RSC 5 Leeds
(Vacant WBF European L. Middleweight Title)
27.02.00 Gareth Lovell W PTS 6 Leeds
24.09.00 Jon Foster W PTS 6 Shaw
03.12.00 Michael Alexander W PTS 6 Shaw
17.05.01 Ojay Abrahams L RSC 2 Leeds
(Vacant British Masters L. Middleweight Title)
03.03.02 Howard Clarke NC 2 Shaw
19.04.02 Neil Bonner W PTS 6 Darlington
21.06.02 Wayne Shepherd W PTS 10 Leeds
(Vacant British Masters Middleweight Title)
02.12.02 Martyn Bailey L RSC 6 Leeds
(British Masters Middleweight Title Defence)
10.05.03 Darren Rhodes L PTS 6 Huddersfield
15.09.03 Matt Scriven W DIS 9 Leeds
(British Masters L.Middleweight Title Challenge)
01.12.03 Gary Beardsley L RSC 6 Leeds
(British Masters L.Middleweight Title Defence)
08.06.04 Robert Burton L CO 3 Sheffield
(Vacant Central Area L.Middleweight Title)
15.12.04 Dean Walker W PTS 10 Sheffield
(Vacant Central Area Middleweight Title)
20.05.05 Jason Rushton W PTS 10 Doncaster
(Central Area L.Middleweight Title Challenge)

Career: 29 contests, won 19, drew 1, lost 8, no contest 1.

(Nikos) Rocky Muscus (Agrapidis Israel)

Chertsey. *Born* Athens, Greece, 5 August, 1983
L. Middleweight. Ht. 5'6½"
Manager J. Evans

12.05.03 Danny Cooper L PTS 6 Southampton
18.09.03 Wayne Wheeler L PTS 6 Mayfair
27.10.03 Graham Delehedy L RSC 2 Glasgow
08.07.04 David Kehoe L PTS 6 The Strand

30.09.04 Richard Inquieti W PTS 4 Glasgow
23.10.04 Tye Williams L PTS 6 Wakefield
24.11.04 Ivor Bonavic L PTS 4 Mayfair

Career: 7 contests, won 1, lost 6.

(Lee) Young Muttley (Woodley)

West Bromwich. *Born* West Bromwich, 17 May, 1976
WBF Inter-Continental L.Welterweight
Champion. Former Undefeated English &
Midlands Area L.Welterweight Champion.
Ht. 5'8½"
Manager Self

03.09.99 Dave Hinds W RSC 4 West Bromwich
24.10.99 David Kehoe W RTD 1 Wolverhampton
22.01.00 Wahid Fats L PTS 4 Birmingham
18.02.00 Stuart Rimmer W RSC 1 West Bromwich
27.11.00 Peter Dunn W RSC 3 Birmingham
07.09.01 Jon Honney W RSC 1 West Bromwich
16.11.01 Tony Montana W PTS 6 West Bromwich
26.11.01 Lee Byrne W RSC 1 Manchester
23.02.02 Brian Coleman W PTS 4 Nottingham
23.03.02 Adam Zadworny W RSC 3 Southwark
02.11.02 Tony Montana W PTS 4 Wolverhampton
21.03.03 Gary Reid W RSC 7 West Bromwich
(Vacant Midlands Area L.Welterweight Title)
28.04.03 John Marshall W RSC 5 Nottingham
17.07.03 Tony Montana W PTS 4 Walsall
19.02.04 Peter Dunn W PTS 4 Dudley
08.05.04 Sammy Smith W RSC 1 Bristol
(Vacant English L.Welterweight Title)
05.10.04 Gavin Down W RSC 6 Dudley
(English L.Welterweight Title Defence. Vacant WBF Inter-Continental L.Welterweight Title)
17.02.05 Geraint Harvey W PTS 6 Dudley
21.04.05 Oscar Hall W PTS 10 Dudley
(WBF Inter-Continental L.Welterweight Title Defence)

Career: 19 contests, won 18, lost 1.

Young Muttley   Les Clark

Ian Napa

Hackney. *Born* Zimbabwe, 14 March, 1978
S.Bantamweight. Former Undefeated
Southern Area Flyweight Champion.
Ht. 5'1"
Manager B. Lawrence

06.06.98	Nick Tooley W PTS 6 Liverpool
14.07.98	Nicky Booth W PTS 6 Reading
10.10.98	Sean Green W PTS 6 Bethnal Green
30.01.99	Delroy Spencer W PTS 6 Bethnal Green
15.11.99	Mark Reynolds W PTS 10 Bethnal Green
	(Southern Area Flyweight Title Challenge)
19.02.00	Anthony Hanna W PTS 6 Dagenham
08.04.00	Delroy Spencer W PTS 8 Bethnal Green
15.07.00	Jamie Evans W PTS 4 Millwall
13.11.00	Jason Booth L PTS 12 Bethnal Green
	(British & Commonwealth Flyweight Title Challenges)
24.02.01	Oleg Kiryukhin W PTS 6 Bethnal Green
09.06.01	Peter Culshaw L RSC 8 Bethnal Green
	(WBU Flyweight Title Challenge)
08.05.04	Danny Costello W PTS 4 Dagenham
08.10.04	Steve Gethin W PTS 6 Brentwood
13.02.05	Alexey Volchan W PTS 4 Brentwood
16.06.05	Marc Callaghan L PTS 10 Dagenham
	(Vacant Southern Area S.Bantamweight Title)

Career: 15 contests, won 12, lost 3.

Muhsen Nasser

Sheffield. *Born* Yemen, 10 April, 1986
L.Middleweight. Ht. 5'11"
Manager J. Ingle

11.10.04	Andy Cosnett W PTS 6 Birmingham
26.11.04	Rocky Flanagan W PTS 6 Hull
27.01.05	Ernie Smith W PTS 6 Piccadilly
12.05.05	Martin Marshall W PTS 6 Sunderland

Career: 4 contests, won 4.

Muhsen Nasser   Les Clark

Johnny Nelson

Sheffield. *Born* Sheffield, 4 January, 1967
WBO Cruiserweight Champion. Former
Undefeated British & European
Cruiserweight Champion. Former
Undefeated WBU Heavyweight Champion.
Former WBF Heavyweight Champion.
Former WBF Cruiserweight Champion.
Former Undefeated Central Area
Cruiserweight Champion. Ht. 6'2"
Manager D. Ingle

18.03.86	Peter Brown L PTS 6 Hull
15.05.86	Tommy Taylor L PTS 6 Dudley
03.10.86	Magne Havnaa L PTS 4 Copenhagen, Denmark
20.11.86	Chris Little W PTS 6 Bredbury
19.01.87	Gypsy Carman W PTS 6 Mayfair
02.03.87	Doug Young W PTS 6 Huddersfield
10.03.87	Sean Daly W RSC 1 Manchester
28.04.87	Brian Schumacher L PTS 8 Halifax
03.06.87	Byron Pullen W RSC 3 Southwark
14.12.87	Jon McBean W RSC 6 Edgbaston
01.02.88	Dennis Bailey L PTS 8 Northampton
24.02.88	Cordwell Hylton W RSC 1 Sheffield
25.04.88	Kenny Jones W CO 1 Liverpool
04.05.88	Crawford Ashley W PTS 8 Solihull
06.06.88	Lennie Howard W CO 2 Mayfair
31.08.88	Andrew Gerrard W PTS 8 Stoke
26.10.88	Danny Lawford W RSC 2 Sheffield
	(Vacant Central Area Cruiserweight Title)
04.04.89	Steve Mormino W RSC 2 Sheffield
21.05.89	Andy Straughn W CO 8 Finsbury Park
	(British Cruiserweight Title Challenge)
02.10.89	Ian Bulloch W CO 2 Hanley
	(British Cruiserweight Title Defence)
27.01.90	Carlos de Leon DREW 12 Sheffield
	(WBC Cruiserweight Title Challenge)
14.02.90	Dino Homsey W RSC 7 Brentwood
28.03.90	Lou Gent W CO 4 Bethnal Green
	(British Cruiserweight Title Defence)
27.06.90	Arthur Weathers W RSC 2 Kensington
05.09.90	Andre Smith W PTS 8 Brighton
14.12.90	Markus Bott W RSC 12 Karlsruhe, Germany
	(Vacant European Cruiserweight Title)
12.03.91	Yves Monsieur W RTD 8 Mansfield
	(European Cruiserweight Title Defence)
16.05.92	James Warring L PTS 12 Fredericksburg, USA
	(IBF Cruiserweight Title Challenge)
15.08.92	Norbert Ekassi L RSC 3 Ajaccio, France
29.10.92	Corrie Sanders L PTS 10 Morula, South Africa
30.04.93	Dave Russell W RSC 11 Melbourne, Australia
	(WBF Cruiserweight Title Challenge)
11.08.93	Tom Collins W RSC 1 Mansfield
	(WBF Cruiserweight Title Defence)
01.10.93	Francis Wanyama L DIS 10 Waregem, Belgium
	(WBF Cruiserweight Title Defence)
20.11.93	Jimmy Thunder W PTS 12 Auckland, New Zealand
	(WBF Heavyweight Title Challenge)
05.04.94	Henry Akinwande L PTS 10 Bethnal Green
05.11.94	Nikolai Kulpin W PTS 12 Bangkok, Thailand
	(WBF Heavyweight Title Defence)
22.08.95	Adilson Rodrigues L PTS 12 Sao Paulo, Brazil
	(WBF Heavyweight Title Defence)

03.12.95	Adilson Rodrigues L PTS 12 Sao Paulo, Brazil
	(WBF Heavyweight Title Challenge)
20.01.96	Tony Booth W RSC 2 Mansfield
14.12.96	Dennis Andries W RSC 7 Sheffield
	(Vacant British Cruiserweight Title)
22.02.97	Patrice Aouissi W RSC 7 Berck sur Mer, France
	(Vacant European Cruiserweight Title)
19.07.97	Michael Murray W PTS 4 Wembley
11.10.97	Dirk Wallyn W RSC 1 Sheffield
	(European Cruiserweight Title Defence)
18.07.98	Peter Oboh W RTD 6 Sheffield
27.03.99	Carl Thompson W RSC 5 Derby
	(WBO Cruiserweight Title Challenge)
15.05.99	Bruce Scott W PTS 12 Sheffield
	(WBO Cruiserweight Title Defence)
07.08.99	Willard Lewis W RTD 4 Dagenham
	(WBO Cruiserweight Title Defence)
18.09.99	Sione Asipeli W PTS 12 Las Vegas, Nevada, USA
	(WBO Cruiserweight Title Defence)
06.11.99	Christophe Girard W CO 4 Widnes
	(WBO Cruiserweight Title Defence)
08.04.00	Pietro Aurino W RTD 7 Bethnal Green
	(WBO Cruiserweight Title Defence)
07.10.00	Adam Watt W RSC 5 Doncaster
	(WBO Cruiserweight Title Defence)
27.01.01	George Arias W PTS 12 Bethnal Green
	(WBO Cruiserweight Title Defence)
21.07.01	Marcelo Dominguez W PTS 12 Sheffield
	(WBO Cruiserweight Title Defence)
24.11.01	Alex Vasiliev W PTS 12 Bethnal Green
	(Vacant WBU Heavyweight Title)
06.04.02	Ezra Sellers W CO 8 Copenhagen, Denmark
	(WBO Cruiserweight Title Defence)
23.11.02	Guillermo Jones DREW 12 Derby
	(WBO Cruiserweight Title Defence)
15.11.03	Alexander Petkovic W PTS 12 Bayreuth, Germany
	(WBO Cruiserweight Title Defence)
04.09.04	Rudiger May W RSC 7 Essen, Germany
	(WBO Cruiserweight Title Defence)

Career: 58 contests, won 44, drew 2, lost 12.

Johnny Nelson   Les Clark

Robert Nelson

Bradford. *Born* Bradford, 15 January, 1980
Bantamweight. Ht. 5'5"
Manager M. Marsden

27.05.05 Delroy Spencer W PTS 4 Spennymoor
25.06.05 Delroy Spencer W PTS 6 Wakefield
Career: 2 contests, won 2.

Jason Nesbitt

Nuneaton. *Born* Birmingham, 15
December, 1973
Lightweight. Ht. 5'9"
Manager Self

06.11.00 Stephen Chinnock L PTS 6
Wolverhampton
09.12.00 Lee Meager L RSC 2 Southwark
29.01.01 Henry Castle L CO 6 Peterborough
27.03.01 Billy Smith W PTS 6 Brierley Hill
21.05.01 Sid Razak L PTS 4 Birmingham
04.06.01 Andrew Ferrans L RSC 2 Glasgow
07.07.01 Colin Toohey L PTS 4 Manchester
15.09.01 Colin Toohey L PTS 4 Manchester
22.09.01 John Mackay L PTS 4 Canning Town
01.11.01 Chris Hooper L RSC 6 Hull
16.03.02 Lee Meager L PTS 6 Bethnal Green
27.03.02 Greg Edwards W RSC 5 Mayfair
20.04.02 Henry Castle L PTS 4 Cardiff
04.05.02 Danny Hunt L PTS 4 Bethnal Green
15.06.02 Jesse James Daniel L PTS 4 Leeds
27.07.02 Craig Spacie L PTS 4 Nottingham
23.08.02 Billy Corcoran L PTS 4 Bethnal Green
25.10.02 Billy Corcoran L RSC 2 Bethnal Green
03.12.02 Mark Bowen L PTS 6 Shrewsbury
11.12.02 Matt Teague L PTS 6 Hull
20.12.02 Chris McDonagh L PTS 6 Bracknell
18.01.03 Andy Morris L PTS 4 Preston
09.02.03 Mally McIver L PTS 6 Bradford
09.03.03 Choi Tseveenpurev L PTS 8 Shaw
29.03.03 Kevin O'Hara L RSC 3 Portsmouth
07.05.03 Henry Jones L PTS 6 Ellesmere Port
02.06.03 Stefy Bull L PTS 6 Cleethorpes
13.06.03 Scott Lawton L PTS 6 Queensway
17.07.03 Haider Ali L PTS 4 Dagenham
29.08.03 Gary Thornhill L CO 1 Liverpool
05.10.03 Nadeem Siddique L PTS 6 Bradford
08.11.03 Harry Ramogoadi L PTS 6 Coventry
23.11.03 Amir Ali L PTS 6 Rotherham
10.12.03 Femi Fehintola L PTS 6 Sheffield
21.12.03 John Murray L PTS 6 Bolton
06.02.04 Femi Fehintola L PTS 6 Sheffield
23.02.04 Carl Greaves L PTS 6 Nottingham
05.03.04 Haroon Din L PTS 6 Darlington
12.03.04 Stuart Green L PTS 8 Irvine
03.04.04 Daniel Thorpe L PTS 6 Sheffield
16.04.04 John O'Donnell L PTS 4 Bradford
27.04.04 Jim Betts L PTS 6 Leeds
07.05.04 Jus Wallie L PTS 6 Bethnal Green
28.05.04 John Bothwell W RSC 3 Glasgow
05.06.04 Kevin Mitchell L RSC 3 Bethnal Green
30.07.04 Lee Beavis L PTS 6 Bethnal Green
20.09.04 Matt Teague L PTS 6 Cleethorpes
30.09.04 Eddie Nevins L PTS 6 Hull
18.11.04 Joel Viney W PTS 6 Blackpool
26.11.04 John Davidson W RSC 1 Altrincham
10.12.04 John Fewkes L PTS 6 Sheffield
17.12.04 Gwyn Wale L PTS 4 Huddersfield
13.02.05 Nadeem Siddique L PTS 6 Bradford
04.03.05 John Fewkes L PTS 6 Rotherham
01.04.05 Martin McDonagh L PTS 6 Glasgow
15.04.05 Martin Gethin L PTS 6 Shrewsbury

28.04.05 Ceri Hall L RTD 2 Clydach
02.06.05 Riaz Durgahed L PTS 6 Peterborough
Career: 58 contests, won 5, lost 53.

Eddie Nevins

Manchester. *Born* Manchester, 17 April,
1975
Central Area S. Featherweight Champion.
Ht. 5'6"
Manager J. Ingle

17.10.98 Simon Chambers W RSC 4 Manchester
26.10.98 Dave Hinds W PTS 6 Manchester
30.11.98 Keith Jones W PTS 4 Manchester
13.03.99 Gary Jenkinson W PTS 4 Manchester
02.07.99 Ram Singh W CO 1 Manchester
06.11.99 Bradley Pryce L RSC 2 Widnes
21.05.00 Lennie Hodgkins W RSC 1 Shaw
12.08.00 Paul Halpin L PTS 6 Wembley
12.11.00 Mohamed Helel W PTS 4 Manchester
15.01.01 Pete Buckley W PTS 4 Manchester
10.02.01 Alex Arthur L RSC 1 Widnes
26.03.01 Henry Castle L RSC 2 Peterborough
21.07.02 Carl Allen W PTS 4 Salford
09.11.02 Gareth Wiltshaw W PTS 4 Altrincham
16.02.03 Daniel Thorpe W RSC 8 Salford
(*Vacant Central Area S. Featherweight
Title*)
30.09.04 Jason Nesbitt W PTS 6 Hull
31.10.04 Ian Reid W PTS 6 Shaw
30.04.05 Peter Allen L PTS 6 Wigan
Career: 18 contests, won 14, lost 4.

Lee Nicholson

Doncaster. *Born* Mexborough, 10
November, 1976
Cruiserweight. Ht. 5'11"
Manager Self

24.09.01 Jason Brewster L PTS 6 Cleethorpes
17.02.02 Jason Brewster L PTS 6 Wolverhampton
11.05.02 Fola Okesola L RSC 1 Dagenham
07.09.03 Stewart West L RSC 2 Shrewsbury
01.12.03 Mike Duffield W PTS 6 Barnsley
15.12.03 Simeon Cover L RSC 4 Cleethorpes
29.10.04 Dean Cockburn L RSC 2 Doncaster
13.12.04 Dean Cockburn L RSC 3 Cleethorpes
23.05.05 Slick Miller W PTS 6 Cleethorpes
Career: 9 contests, won 2, lost 7.

Laura Norton

London. *Born* Glasgow, 18 August, 1976
Bantamweight. Ht. 5'5½"
Manager H. Foster

12.12.02 Krampe Reva W PTS 4 Leicester
Square
28.08.04 Mirasol Miranda W PTS 4 Boynton
Beach, Florida, USA
09.04.05 Tiliena Perez W PTS 4 Boynton Beach,
Florida, USA
27.05.05 Lisa Zeringue W RSC 1 Pompano
Beach, Florida, USA
Career: 4 contests, won 4.

Robert Norton

Stourbridge. *Born* Dudley, 20 January, 1972
Cruiserweight. Former Undefeated British
Masters Cruiserweight Champion. Former
WBU Cruiserweight Champion. Ht. 6'2"
Manager J. Weaver

30.09.93 Stuart Fleet W CO 2 Walsall
27.10.93 Kent Davis W PTS 6 West Bromwich
02.12.93 Eddie Pyatt W RSC 2 Walsall
26.01.94 Lennie Howard W PTS 6 Birmingham
17.05.94 Steve Osborne W PTS 6 Kettering
05.10.94 Chris Woollas DREW 6 Wolverhampton
30.11.94 L. A. Williams W RSC 2
Wolverhampton
10.02.95 Newby Stevens W RSC 3 Birmingham
22.02.95 Steve Osborne W PTS 6 Telford
21.04.95 Cordwell Hylton W PTS 6 Dudley
25.10.95 Nigel Rafferty W RSC 6 Telford
31.01.96 Gary Williams W RSC 2 Birmingham
25.04.96 Steve Osborne W RSC 5 Mayfair
01.10.96 Andrew Benson W RSC 6 Birmingham
12.11.96 Nigel Rafferty W PTS 8 Dudley
11.02.97 Touami Benhamed W RSC 5 Bethnal
Green
16.04.97 Tony Booth W RSC 4 Bethnal Green
20.12.97 Darren Corbett L PTS 12 Belfast
(*Commonwealth Cruiserweight Title
Challenge*)
03.04.98 Adrian Nicolai W RSC 2 West
Bromwich
03.10.98 Tim Brown W CO 3 West Bromwich
01.04.99 Jacob Mofokeng W PTS 12
Birmingham
(*WBU Cruiserweight Title Challenge*)
24.09.99 Sebastiaan Rothmann L RSC 8 Merthyr
(*WBU Cruiserweight Title Defence*)
30.09.00 Tony Booth W RSC 3 Peterborough
18.11.00 Darron Griffiths W PTS 10 Dagenham
(*Elim. British Cruiserweight Title*)
05.02.01 Lee Swaby W PTS 8 Hull
30.11.02 Paul Bonson W PTS 6 Coventry
05.09.03 Mark Hobson L PTS 12 Sheffield
(*Commonwealth Cruiserweight Title
Challenge. Vacant British
Cruiserweight Title*)
09.04.04 Greg Scott-Briggs W CO 1 Rugby
10.07.04 Chris Woollas W RSC 4 Coventry
06.12.04 Paul Bonson W CO 6 Leicester
(*Vacant British Masters Cruiserweight
Title*)
Career: 30 contests, won 26, drew 1, lost 3.

(Paulus) Ali Nuumbembe

Glossop. *Born* Oshakati, Namibia, 24 June,
1978
Namibian Welterweight Champion.
Ht. 5'8½"
Manager Self

16.04.03 Dai Bando W PTS 4 Nottingham
15.06.03 Ernie Smith W PTS 4 Bradford
03.08.03 Lee Williamson W PTS 6 Stalybridge
29.08.03 Ernie Smith W PTS 6 Liverpool
05.10.03 Keith Jones W PTS 6 Bradford
07.12.03 Brian Coleman W RTD 2 Bradford
16.01.04 Wayne Wheeler W RSC 1 Bradford
29.02.04 William Webster W RSC 3 Shaw
10.04.04 Peter Dunn W PTS 6 Manchester
09.10.04 Bethuel Ushona L PTS 10 Windhoek,
Namibia
(*Vacant Namibian Welterweight Title*)
09.12.04 Lee Armstrong W PTS 6 Stockport
04.03.05 Franny Jones W PTS 6 Hartlepool
22.04.05 David Barnes DREW 12 Barnsley
(*Vacant WBO Inter-Continental
Welterweight Title*)
Career: 13 contests, won 11, drew 1, lost 1.

Tony Oakey

Portsmouth. *Born* Portsmouth, 2 January, 1976
L.Heavyweight. Former WBU L.Heavyweight Champion. Former Undefeated Commonwealth & Southern Area L.Heavyweight Champion. Ht. 5'8"
Manager Self

12.09.98	Smokey Enison W RSC 2 Bethnal Green
21.11.98	Zak Chelli W RSC 1 Southwark
16.01.99	Jimmy Steel W PTS 4 Bethnal Green
06.03.99	Mark Dawson W PTS 4 Southwark
10.07.99	Jimmy Steel W PTS 4 Southwark
01.10.99	Michael Pinnock W PTS 4 Bethnal Green
21.02.00	Darren Ashton W PTS 4 Southwark
13.03.00	Martin Jolley W PTS 6 Bethnal Green
21.10.00	Darren Ashton W PTS 4 Wembley
27.01.01	Nathan King W PTS 6 Bethnal Green
26.03.01	Butch Lesley W PTS 10 Wembley
	(Southern Area L. Heavyweight Title Challenge)
08.05.01	Hastings Rasani W RSC 10 Barnsley
	(Vacant Commonwealth L. Heavyweight Title)
09.09.01	Konstantin Ochrej W RSC 4 Southwark
20.10.01	Chris Davies W PTS 12 Portsmouth
	(Commonwealth L.Heavyweight Title Defence)
02.03.02	Konstantin Shvets W PTS 12 Bethnal Green
	(Vacant WBU L. Heavyweight Title)
25.05.02	Neil Simpson W PTS 12 Portsmouth
	(WBU L. Heavyweight Title Defence)
12.10.02	Andrei Kaersten W PTS 12 Bethnal Green
	(WBU L. Heavyweight Title Defence)
29.03.03	Neil Linford W PTS 12 Portsmouth
	(WBU L. Heavyweight Title Defence)
11.10.03	Matthew Barney L PTS 12 Portsmouth
	(WBU L.Heavyweight Title Defence)
12.02.05	Varuzhan Davtyan W RTD 5 Portsmouth
19.06.05	Peter Haymer L PTS 10 Bethnal Green
	(English L.Heavyweight Title Challenge)

Career: 21 contests, won 19, lost 2.

Valery Odin

Canning Town. *Born* Guadeloupe, 23 December, 1974
Cruiserweight. Ht. 6'2½"
Manager P. McCausland

15.06.01	Tom Cannon W PTS 4 Millwall
22.09.01	Mark Brookes W PTS 4 Canning Town
09.10.01	Wayne Ellcock L PTS 4 Cardiff
10.11.01	Tony Dodson L RSC 4 Wembley
13.12.01	Calvin Stonestreet W RSC 2 Leicester Square
10.02.02	Radcliffe Green W PTS 6 Southwark
20.04.02	Toks Owoh W PTS 8 Wembley
21.05.01	Mark Smallwood L RSC 4 Custom House
17.08.02	Nathan King W PTS 6 Cardiff

17.09.02	Charden Ansoula L PTS 6 Bethnal Green
26.10.02	Chris Davies L PTS 6 Maesteg
28.01.03	Carl Froch L RSC 6 Nottingham
06.09.03	Kai Kurzawa L PTS 8 Efurt, Germany
19.06.04	Courtney Fry L PTS 8 Muswell Hill
11.10.04	Pinky Burton L PTS 6 Glasgow
05.11.04	Gyorgy Hidvegi L PTS 6 Hereford
03.12.04	Leigh Allis W RSC 5 Bristol

Career: 17 contests, won 7, lost 10.

John O'Donnell

Shepherds Bush. *Born* Croydon, 13 November, 1985
Welterweight. Ht. 5'11"
Manager R. McCracken

16.04.04	Jason Nesbitt W PTS 4 Bradford
02.06.04	Dave Hinds W PTS 4 Nottingham
24.09.04	Chris Long W RSC 4 Nottingham
12.11.04	Ernie Smith W PTS 6 Wembley
10.04.05	Duncan Cottier W PTS 4 Brentwood

Career: 5 contests, won 5.

John O'Donnell   Les Clark

Kevin O'Hara

Belfast. *Born* Belfast, 21 September, 1981
S.Featherweight. Ht. 5'6"
Manager M.Callahan/J.Breen/F.Warren

02.11.02	Mike Harrington W RSC 1 Belfast
01.02.03	Jus Wallie W RSC 2 Belfast
29.03.03	Jason Nesbitt W RSC 3 Portsmouth
14.06.03	Piotr Niesporek W PTS 4 Magdeburg, Germany
02.10.03	Vladimir Borov W PTS 6 Liverpool
30.10.03	Henry Janes W PTS 6 Belfast
29.11.03	Gareth Payne W PTS 4 Renfrew
06.03.04	Henry Janes W PTS 6 Renfrew
01.04.04	Buster Dennis W PTS 4 Bethnal Green
06.05.04	Choi Tsveenpurev L PTS 8 Barnsley
28.10.04	Jean-Marie Codet W PTS 8 Belfast
17.06.05	Willie Limond L PTS 10 Glasgow
	(Vacant Celtic S.Featherweight Title)

Career: 12 contests, won 10, lost 2.

Nick Okoth

Battersea. *Born* Camden Town, 19 July, 1973
L. Heavyweight. Ht. 5'11"
Manager J. Evans

18.09.03	Mark Phillips W PTS 4 Mayfair
28.02.04	Paulie Silva L PTS 6 Manchester
08.04.04	Karl Wheeler L PTS 6 Peterborough
24.04.04	Daniel Sackey L RSC 2 Reading
03.07.04	Nathan King L PTS 4 Newport
31.10.04	Darren Stubbs L PTS 6 Shaw
25.11.04	Jonjo Finnegan DREW 6 Birmingham
03.12.04	Paul Henry W RSC 5 Bristol
21.01.05	Sam Price L PTS 6 Brentford
06.02.05	Mervyn Langdale DREW 6 Southampton
20.02.05	Jon Ibbotson L PTS 6 Sheffield
08.04.05	Dan Guthrie L RSC 2 Bristol

Career: 12 contests, won 2, drew 2, lost 8.

Ajose Olusegun

Kentish Town. *Born* Nigeria, 6 December, 1979
ABU L.Welterweight Champion. Ht. 5'9"
Manager Self

24.05.01	Tony Montana W RSC 1 Kensington
21.06.01	Woody Greenaway W RSC 1 Earls Court
09.09.01	Sunni Ajayi W PTS 6 Lagos, Nigeria
04.10.01	Stuart Rimmer W RTD 2 Finsbury
13.03.02	Gary Flear W PTS 4 Mayfair
13.06.02	Keith Jones W PTS 6 Leicester Square
30.10.02	Martin Holgate W RSC 7 Leicester Square
27.11.02	Vladimir Kortovski W RSC 1 Tel Aviv, Israel
15.12.02	Adewale Adegbusi W RSC 6 Lagos, Nigeria
20.03.03	Cristian Hodorogea W PTS 4 Queensway
26.04.03	Keith Jones W PTS 6 Brentford
29.10.03	Karl Taylor W PTS 6 Leicester Square
10.04.04	Victor Kpadenue W PTS 12 Carabas, Nigeria
	(ABU L.Welterweight Title Challenge)
03.09.04	Bradley Pryce W RSC 4 Newport
26.03.05	Vasile Dragomir W PTS 8 Hackney

Career: 15 contests, won 15.

Lloyd Otte

West Ham. *Born* Australia, 26 June, 1981
S.Featherweight. Ht. 5'6½"
Manager T. Sims

02.12.04	Riaz Durgahed W PTS 6 Crystal Palace
10.04.05	Peter Allen W PTS 6 Brentwood

Career: 2 contests, won 2.

Damian Owen

Swansea. *Born* Swansea, 7 May, 1985
Lightweight. Ht. 5'7"
Manager N. Hodges

01.10.04	Darren Payne W RSC 4 Bristol
05.11.04	Peter Allen W RSC 1 Hereford
08.04.05	Jus Wallie W PTS 4 Bristol

Career: 3 contests, won 3.

Ricky Owen

Swansea. Born Swansea, 10 May, 1985
Featherweight. Ht. 5'6"
Manager A. Gower

05.11.04	Sandy Bartlett W RSC 2 Hereford
16.06.05	Billy Smith W PTS 4 Dagenham

Career: 2 contests, won 2.

PQ

James Paisley

Mile End. *Born* Ballymena, 4 January 1980
Welterweight. Ht. 5'8"
Manager Self

09.09.01	Babatunde Ajayi L PTS 4 Southwark
28.10.01	Carl Walton W PTS 4 Southwark
15.12.01	David Barnes L RTD 2 Wembley
31.01.02	Tony Montana L PTS 6 Piccadilly
09.02.02	Michael Jennings L RSC 3 Manchester
11.03.02	Nigel Wright L PTS 4 Glasgow
23.06.02	Jason Gonzales W PTS 6 Southwark
17.09.02	Dave Stewart L RSC 5 Bethnal Green
20.10.02	Pete Buckley W PTS 4 Southwark
27.10.02	Elvis Mbwakongo L RSC 2 Southwark
22.02.03	Gwyn Wale L RSC 1 Huddersfield
26.09.03	Kristian Laight W PTS 6 Millwall
06.12.03	Tony Doherty L RSC 3 Cardiff
20.02.04	Justin Hudson W PTS 4 Bethnal Green
24.09.04	Nathan Ward L PTS 4 Bethnal Green
19.12.04	Ryan Barrett L DIS 5 Bethnal Green
19.06.05	Nathan Ward L RSC 4 Bethnal Green
	(Vacant British Masters Welterweight Title)

Career: 17 contests, won 5, lost 12.

Danny Parkinson

Bradford. *Born* Bradford, 6 August, 1980
Welterweight. Ht. 5'11"
Manager C. Aston

12.06.00	Ram Singh W RSC 3 Bradford
04.12.00	Ram Singh W PTS 6 Bradford
05.02.01	Dean Nicholas W PTS 6 Bradford
19.03.01	Lee Sharp L PTS 6 Glasgow
15.10.01	Richard Inquieti W RSC 1 Bradford
04.03.02	Matt Scriven W PTS 6 Bradford
09.06.03	Danny Moir W PTS 6 Bradford
05.10.03	Wayne Shepherd W RSC 5 Bradford
20.10.03	Pedro Thompson W RSC 3 Bradford
04.12.03	Dean Nicholas L RSC 4 Huddersfield
26.02.04	Gary Porter W PTS 6 Sunderland
09.12.04	Richard Hackney W PTS 6 Stockport
13.02.05	Lee Williamson W PTS 4 Bradford
08.05.05	Ernie Smith W PTS 6 Bradford
20.05.05	Gary Woolcombe L RSC 3 Southwark

Career: 15 contests, won 12, lost 3.

Darren Payne   Les Clark

Darren Payne

Bristol. *Born* Bristol, 20 April, 1983
Welterweight. Ht. 5'11½"
Manager C. Sanigar

01.10.04	Damian Owen L RSC 4 Bristol

Career: 1 contest, lost 1

David Payne

Wellingborough. *Born* Kettering, 1 August,
1984
Middleweight. Ht. 5'8½"
Manager S. James

05.10.04	Paul McInnes W RSC 1 Dudley
20.11.04	Richard Mazurek L PTS 6 Coventry
02.12.04	Nathan Graham L RSC 3 Crystal Palace

Career: 3 contests, won 1, lost 2

David Payne   Les Clark

Dave Pearson   Les Clark

Dave Pearson

Middlesbrough. *Born* Middlesbrough, 1
April, 1974
S. Middleweight. Ht. 6'2¾"
Manager M. Shinfield

15.04.02	Ian Thomas L CO 3 Shrewsbury

03.10.02	Gary Firby W CO 3 Sunderland
21.10.02	Gary Jones L RSC 3 Cleethorpes
05.12.02	Chris Steele W PTS 6 Sunderland
24.03.03	Reagan Denton L PTS 6 Barnsley
31.05.03	Gary Jones L RSC 2 Barnsley
11.07.03	Ben Coward L PTS 6 Darlington
16.02.04	Brian Coleman L PTS 6 Scunthorpe
26.02.04	Tony Quigley L RSC 1 Widnes
26.04.04	Mark Phillips L RSC 6 Cleethorpes
25.06.04	Gerard London L PTS 4 Bethnal Green
06.11.04	Brian Coleman W PTS 6 Coventry
16.12.04	Peter McCormack W PTS 6 Cleethorpes
25.04.05	Peter McCormack W PTS 6 Cleethorpes

Career: 14 contests, won 5, lost 9.

David Pereira

Kennington. *Born* Lambeth, 22 May, 1981
Lightweight. Ht. 5'8"
Manager A. Booth

17.06.04	Declan English W PTS 6 Sheffield
24.11.04	Gavin Tait W PTS 6 Mayfair
21.01.05	David Bailey W PTS 6 Brentford
16.06.05	Gareth Couch L PTS 4 Mayfair

Career: 4 contests, won 3, lost 1.

Kevin Phelan

Slough. *Born* Slough, 11 June, 1977
L.Middleweight. Former British Masters
L.Middleweight Champion. Ht. 6'1"
Manager G. Carmen

27.09.02	Lee Hodgson L RSC 1 Bracknell
21.03.03	Jimi Hendricks W RSC 6 Longford
12.04.03	Steve Russell W PTS 4 Norwich
26.04.03	Dave Wakefield W PTS 4 Brentford
09.05.03	Leigh Wicks W PTS 6 Longford
26.10.03	Brian Coleman W PTS 6 Longford
27.11.03	Dave Wakefield W PTS 6 Longford
25.03.04	Danny Moir L PTS 10 Longford
	(Vacant British Masters L.Middleweight Title)
02.06.04	David Walker L PTS 6 Nottingham
23.09.04	Danny Moir W RTD 3 Gateshead
	(British Masters L.Middleweight Title Challenge)
08.12.04	Taz Jones L PTS 10 Longford
	(British Masters L.Middleweight Title Defence)

Career: 11 contests, won 7, lost 4.

Dean Phillips

Llanelli. *Born* Swansea, 1 February, 1976
Lightweight. Ht. 5'6"
Manager Self

10.03.94	Paul Richards L PTS 6 Bristol
23.03.94	Phil Janes W RSC 1 Cardiff
27.08.94	Craig Kelley W RSC 4 Cardiff
21.09.94	Steve Edwards W RTD 4 Cardiff
02.11.94	Anthony Maynard L PTS 6 Birmingham
04.02.95	Greg Upton W PTS 6 Cardiff
04.03.95	Mike Deveney W PTS 8 Livingston
24.03.95	Bamana Dibateza W PTS 6 Swansea
16.06.95	Danny Luutaya W RSC 2 Southwark
22.07.95	Colin McMillan L PTS 8 Millwall
20.09.95	Mervyn Bennett W PTS 6 Ystrad
16.03.96	Mike Anthony Brown W RSC 6 Glasgow

26.04.96	Bamana Dibateza W PTS 6 Cardiff	
19.09.96	Peter Judson L RSC 10 Manchester	
	(Vacant IBF Inter-Continental	
	S. Featherweight Title)	
24.01.98	Jimmy Phelan W PTS 6 Cardiff	
25.04.98	Steve Conway L PTS 6 Cardiff	
30.11.03	Nigel Senior W CO 1 Swansea	
28.02.04	Gary Hibbert W RSC 5 Bridgend	
01.05.04	Michael Muya W PTS 8 Bridgend	
19.11.04	Kevin Bennett L PTS 12 Hartlepool	
	(Commonwealth Lightweight Title	
	Challenge)	

Career: 20 contests, won 14, lost 6.

Mark Phillips

St Clare's. *Born* Carmarthen, 28 April, 1975
S.Middleweight. Ht. 6'0"
Manager Self

26.10.00	Shayne Webb W PTS 6 Clydach
12.12.00	Tommy Matthews W PTS 6 Clydach
13.03.01	William Webster W RTD 1 Plymouth
07.10.01	Danny Norton L PTS 6 Wolverhampton
12.12.01	Simon Andrews W PTS 6 Clydach
25.04.02	Mark Ellwood L PTS 6 Hull
10.05.02	Scott Dann L PTS 6 Bethnal Green
23.06.02	Gareth Hogg L PTS 4 Southwark
10.07.02	Scott Dann L PTS 4 Wembley
03.12.02	Jamie Hearn L PTS 4 Bethnal Green
20.12.02	Ryan Walls L PTS 4 Bracknell
06.03.03	Darren Dorrington L PTS 8 Bristol
21.03.03	Steve Timms L PTS 6 West Bromwich
05.04.03	Dale Nixon L PTS 6 Coventry
13.04.03	Donovan Smillie L PTS 6 Bradford
12.05.03	Leigh Alliss L PTS 6 Southampton
27.05.03	Steven Spartacus L RSC 2 Dagenham
30.06.03	Roddy Doran L PTS 6 Shrewsbury
06.09.03	Alan Page L PTS 6 Huddersfield
18.09.03	Nick Okoth L PTS 4 Mayfair
09.10.03	Leigh Alliss L PTS 4 Bristol
30.11.03	Jimi Hendricks W PTS 6 Swansea
16.01.04	Donovan Smillie L PTS 4 Bradford
07.04.04	Christian Imaga L PTS 6 Leicester Square
15.04.04	Darren McDermott L PTS 4 Dudley
26.04.04	Dave Pearson W RSC 6 Cleethorpes
04.06.04	Steve Timms L PTS 6 Dudley
03.12.04	Dan Guthrie L RSC 1 Bristol
26.02.05	Matt Galer L PTS 6 Burton
21.04.05	Matthew Hough L PTS 4 Dudley

Career: 30 contests, won 6, lost 24.

Stuart Phillips

Port Talbot. *Born* Abergavenny, 24 January, 1981
Welterweight. Ht. 5'8"
Manager D. Davies

08.11.03	Lance Hall W PTS 4 Bridgend
30.11.03	Wayne Wheeler W PTS 4 Swansea
01.05.04	Chris Long L RSC 1 Bridgend
17.02.05	Tristan Davies L PTS 6 Dudley
28.04.05	Duncan Cottier DREW 4 Clydach

Career: 5 contests, won 2, drew 1, lost 2.

Esham Pickering

Newark. *Born* Newark, 7 August, 1976
European & Commonwealth
S.Bantamweight Champion. Former
Undefeated British Masters Bantamweight
Champion. Ht. 5'5"
Manager J. Ingle

23.09.96	Brendan Bryce W RSC 5 Cleethorpes
24.10.96	Kevin Sheil W PTS 6 Lincoln
22.11.96	Amjid Mahmood W RSC 2 Hull
09.12.96	Des Gargano W RTD 2 Chesterfield
16.12.96	Graham McGrath W PTS 6 Cleethorpes
20.03.97	Robert Braddock W RSC 6 Newark
12.04.97	Graham McGrath W PTS 4 Sheffield
26.04.97	Mikc Deveney W PTS 4 Swadlincote
16.05.97	Chris Price W PTS 6 Hull
26.06.97	Graham McGrath W PTS 6 Salford
01.11.97	Mike Deveney W RSC 8 Glasgow
	(Elim. British Featherweight Title)
09.05.98	Jonjo Irwin L PTS 12 Sheffield
	(Vacant British Featherweight Title)
11.09.98	Louis Veitch W PTS 6 Newark
15.08.99	Chris Lyons W RSC 2 Derby

23.10.99	Ian Turner W PTS 6 Telford
20.11.99	Marc Smith W PTS 6 Grantham
19.02.00	Kevin Gerowski W PTS 10 Newark
	(Vacant British Masters Bantamweight Title. Elim. British Bantamweight Title)
13.08.00	Lee Williamson W PTS 6 Nottingham
16.12.00	Mauricio Martinez L RSC 1 Sheffield
	(WBO Bantamweight Title Challenge)
15.09.01	Carl Allen W PTS 6 Derby
08.12.01	Carl Allen W PTS 8 Chesterfield
20.04.02	Carl Allen W PTS 6 Derby
24.09.02	Alejandro Monzon L PTS 12 Gran Canaria, Spain
	(Vacant WBA Inter-Continental S.Featherweight Title)
02.12.02	Carl Allen W PTS 6 Leicester
08.02.03	Duncan Karanja W CO 5 Brentford
	(Vacant Commonwealth S.Bantamweight Title)
12.07.03	Brian Carr W RSC 4 Renfrew
	(Vacant British S.Bantamweight Title. Commonwealth S.Bantamweight Title Defence)
24.10.03	Alfred Tetteh W RSC 7 Bethnal Green
	(Commonwealth S.Bantamweight Title Defence)
16.01.04	Vincenzo Gigliotti W CO 10 Bradford
	(Vacant European S.Bantamweight Title)
12.05.04	Juan Garcia Martin W RSC 8 Reading
	(European S.Bantamweight Title Defence)
08.05.05	Noel Wilders W PTS 8 Bradford
09.06.05	Miguel Mallon W RSC 10 Alcobendas, Madrid, Spain
	(European S.Bantamweight Title Defence)

Career: 31 contests, won 28, lost 3.

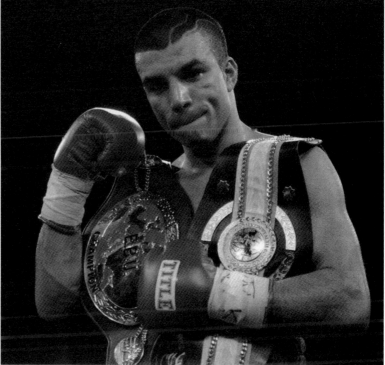

Stuart Phillips   Les Clark

Esham Pickering   Les Clark

David Pinkney

South Shields. *Born* South Shields, 14 August, 1975
L.Welterweight. Ht. 5'9"
Manager M. Gates

23.09.04 Sujad Elahi W PTS 6 Gateshead
Career: 1 contest, won 1.

Michael Pinnock

Birmingham. *Born* Birmingham, 6 June, 1965
Cruiserweight. Ht. 6'0"
Manager Self

19.05.95 David Flowers L PTS 6 Leeds
13.06.95 Mark Snipe L PTS 6 Basildon
20.06.95 Darren Sweeney L PTS 8 Birmingham
06.09.95 Steve Loftus L PTS 6 Stoke
21.09.95 Luan Morena L PTS 4 Battersea
24.10.95 Graham Townsend L PTS 4 Southwark
17.11.95 Graham Townsend L PTS 4 Bethnal Green
03.12.95 Neville Smith L RSC 5 Southwark
23.01.96 Butch Lesley L PTS 4 Bethnal Green
05.03.96 Panayiotis Panayiotiou L PTS 4 Bethnal Green
16.03.96 Mark Hickey L PTS 6 Barnstaple
25.03.96 Lee Simpkin W PTS 6 Birmingham
03.04.96 Jason Hart L PTS 6 Bethnal Green
24.04.96 Gordon Behan L PTS 6 Solihull
03.05.96 David Larkin DREW 6 Sheffield
14.05.96 Mervyn Penniston L RSC 2 Dagenham
19.07.96 Chris Davies L PTS 6 Ystrad
29.07.96 Stuart Fleet L RSC 3 Skegness
04.10.96 Paul Bonson L PTS 6 Wakefield
28.10.96 Zak Goldman DREW 6 Leicester
14.11.96 Paul Bonson DREW 6 Sheffield
21.11.96 Darren Sweeney W RSC 5 Solihull
26.11.96 Mark Smallwood L PTS 6 Wolverhampton
03.02.97 Neil Simpson L PTS 6 Leicester
09.06.97 Mark Hobson L PTS 6 Bradford
05.07.97 Paschal Collins L PTS 6 Glasgow
02.09.97 Mike Gormley L PTS 6 Manchester
18.09.97 Martin Jolley DREW 6 Alfreton
04.10.97 Zoltan Sarossy L PTS 6 Muswell Hill
27.10.97 Johnny Hooks DREW 6 Nottingham
11.11.97 Graham Townsend L PTS 8 Bethnal Green
25.11.97 Barry Thorogood L PTS 8 Wolverhampton
15.12.97 Greg Scott-Briggs L PTS 6 Nottingham
02.02.98 Glenn Williams L CO 5 Manchester
30.04.98 Bobby Banghar L PTS 6 Purfleet
18.05.98 Jon O'Brien L PTS 6 Cleethorpes
22.10.98 Paul Carr L PTS 6 Barking
29.10.98 Paul Carr DREW 6 Bayswater
05.12.98 Dave Stenner W RSC 3 Bristol
03.04.99 Robert Zlotkowski L PTS 4 Carlisle
15.05.99 Damon Hague L PTS 4 Sheffield
05.06.99 Leif Keiski L PTS 6 Cardiff
02.07.99 Mike Gormley L RSC 6 Manchester
01.10.99 Tony Oakey L PTS 4 Bethnal Green
16.10.99 Brian Magee L RSC 3 Belfast
17.04.00 Gordon Behan L PTS 6 Birmingham
15.05.00 Tony Booth L PTS 6 Cleethorpes
25.05.00 Neil Linford L PTS 4 Peterborough
08.09.00 Steven Spartacus L PTS 4 Hammersmith
10.11.00 Tony Griffiths L PTS 4 Mayfair
01.12.00 Allan Foster L PTS 4 Peterborough
29.01.01 Ivan Botton W PTS 4 Peterborough
20.03.01 Joe Gillon L PTS 6 Glasgow
28.03.01 Darren Ashton DREW 6 Piccadilly

09.06.01 Nathan King L PTS 4 Bethnal Green
21.06.01 Paul Bonson L PTS 6 Sheffield
27.07.01 Mark Brookes L PTS 4 Sheffield
15.09.01 Tony Dowling L PTS 6 Derby
04.10.01 Oneal Murray L PTS 6 Finsbury
21.10.01 Peter Merrall DREW 6 Pentre Halkyn
28.10.01 Radcliffe Green L PTS 4 Southwark
24.11.01 Steven Spartacus L PTS 4 Bethnal Green
09.12.01 Andrew Facey L PTS 6 Shaw
16.12.01 Sam Price L PTS 4 Southwark
16.03.02 Carl Froch L RSC 4 Bethnal Green
21.11.02 Earl Ling L PTS 6 Hull
16.12.02 Eamonn Glennon DREW 6 Cleethorpes
08.02.03 Tony Moran L PTS 4 Liverpool
23.02.03 Ryan Walls L PTS 6 Streatham
16.03.03 Scott Lansdowne L PTS 6 Nottingham
24.03.03 Pinky Burton L PTS 4 Barnsley
10.06.03 Mark Brookes L PTS 4 Sheffield
31.07.03 Amer Khan L PTS 6 Sheffield
06.10.03 Reagan Denton L PTS 6 Barnsley
26.10.03 Ryan Walls L PTS 10 Longford
          (Vacant British Masters Cruiserweight Title)
11.11.03 Keiran O'Donnell L PTS 6 Leeds
03.04.04 Amer Khan L PTS 6 Sheffield
16.04.04 Nate Joseph L PTS 6 Bradford
08.05.04 Leigh Alliss L PTS 4 Bristol
07.06.04 Sandy Robb L PTS 6 Glasgow
19.12.04 Lee Blundell L PTS 6 Bolton
13.02.05 Donovan Smillie L PTS 6 Bradford
21.02.05 Hamed Jamali L PTS 8 Birmingham
22.04.05 Rod Anderton L PTS 6 Barnsley
13.05.05 Lee Blundell L PTS 4 Liverpool
Career: 85 contests, won 4, drew 9, lost 72.

Gary Porter

Glasgow. *Born* Glasgow, 12 September, 1978
L. Middleweight. Ht. 5'9"
Manager Self

04.06.01 Arv Mittoo W PTS 6 Glasgow
17.09.01 Carl Walton W PTS 6 Glasgow
03.11.01 Sam Mottram W PTS 4 Glasgow
22.04.02 Matt Scriven W PTS 6 Glasgow
03.06.02 Richard Inquieti W PTS 6 Glasgow
23.09.02 David Keir W PTS 8 Glasgow
20.01.03 Danny Moir L PTS 6 Glasgow
17.03.03 Franny Jones L PTS 6 Glasgow
26.02.04 Danny Parkinson L PTS 6 Sunderland
12.03.04 Danny Moir DREW 6 Irvine
09.12.04 Martin Marshall W PTS 6 Sunderland
24.02.05 Danny Moir L PTS 6 Sunderland
27.05.05 Martin Marshall W PTS 6 Motherwell
Career: 13 contests, won 8, drew 1, lost 4.

Dean Powell

Peckham. *Born* Salisbury, 4 June, 1970
Middleweight. Ht. 5'9"
Manager Self

17.12.96 Matthew Tait L PTS 6 Bethnal Green
11.02.97 Matthew Tait L RSC 4 Bethnal Green
26.09.98 Brian Knudsen L PTS 4 York
12.12.98 Jeff Mills W RSC 3 Southwark
16.01.99 Neil Linford L RSC 1 Bethnal Green
22.11.01 Darren Covill W PTS 4 Mayfair
15.10.02 Alan Gilbert L PTS 4 Bethnal Green
03.12.02 Tomas da Silva W PTS 4 Bethnal Green
08.02.03 Lee Hodgson L PTS 4 Brentford

13.04.03 Michael Thomas L RSC 1 Streatham
20.06.03 Mark Thornton L PTS 6 Gatwick
04.10.03 Matthew Thirlwall L RSC 2 Muswell Hill
30.07.04 Gokhan Kazaz L RSC 2 Bethnal Green
16.10.04 Gareth Lawrence L PTS 4 Dagenham
26.11.04 Jake Guntert L PTS 4 Bethnal Green
05.03.05 John Humphrey L RSC 3 Dagenham
Career: 16 contests, won 3, lost 13.

Martin Power

St Pancras. *Born* London, 14 February, 1980
British Bantamweight Champion. Ht. 5'6"
Manager F. Maloney

09.06.01 Sean Grant W PTS 4 Bethnal Green
28.07.01 Andrew Greenaway W RSC 3 Wembley
22.09.01 Stevie Quinn W RSC 2 Bethnal Green
24.11.01 Anthony Hanna W PTS 4 Bethnal Green
19.01.02 Gareth Wiltshaw W PTS 4 Bethnal Green
08.07.02 Darren Cleary W PTS 4 Mayfair
12.10.02 Stevie Quinn W RSC 4 Bethnal Green
15.02.03 Stevie Quinn W RTD 1 Wembley
29.03.03 Dave Hinds W PTS 4 Portsmouth
17.07.03 Darren Cleary W PTS 6 Dagenham
06.11.03 Rocky Dean W PTS 6 Dagenham
24.01.04 Delroy Spencer W RTD 1 Wembley
01.04.04 Fred Janes W RSC 2 Bethnal Green
13.05.04 Jean-Marie Codet W PTS 8 Bethnal Green
30.07.04 Delroy Spencer W CO 2 Bethnal Green
11.12.04 Shinny Bayaar W PTS 10 Canning Town
20.05.05 Dale Robinson W PTS 12 Southwark
          (Vacant British Bantamweight Title)
Career: 17 contests, won 17.

Sam Price

Reading. *Born* Hillingdon, 6 July, 1981
L. Heavyweight. Ht. 6'0½"
Manager G. Carman

16.12.01 Michael Pinnock W PTS 4 Southwark
10.02.02 Calvin Stonestreet W PTS 4 Southwark
19.03.02 Jimmy Steel W PTS 4 Slough
21.03.03 Harry Butler W PTS 4 Longford
25.03.04 Terry Morrill L RSC 3 Longford
28.10.04 Varuzhan Davtyan W PTS 6 Sunderland
08.12.04 Hastings Rasani W PTS 6 Longford
21.01.05 Nick Okoth W PTS 6 Brentford
10.04.05 Steven Spartacus L RSC 6 Brentwood
          (British Masters L.Heavyweight Title Challenge)
Career: 9 contests, won 7, lost 2.

Bradley Pryce (Price)

Newbridge. *Born* Newport, 15 March, 1981
Welsh Welterweight Champion. Former Undefeated IBF Inter-Continental L.Welterweight Champion. Former Undefeated WBO Inter-Continental Lightweight Champion. Ht. 5'11"
Manager Self

17.07.99	Dave Hinds W PTS 4 Doncaster
23.10.99	David Jeffrey W RSC 3 Telford
06.11.99	Eddie Nevins W RSC 2 Widnes
29.01.00	Pete Buckley W PTS 4 Manchester
29.02.00	Carl Allen W PTS 4 Widnes
16.05.00	Carl Allen W RSC 3 Warrington
15.07.00	Gary Flear W RSC 1 Millwall
07.10.00	Gary Reid W RSC 5 Doncaster
27.01.01	Joel Viney W RSC 3 Bethnal Green
17.03.01	Brian Coleman W PTS 4 Manchester
28.04.01	Jason Hall W PTS 4 Cardiff
	(Vacant WBO Inter-Continental Lightweight Title)
21.07.01	Stuart Patterson W RSC 5 Sheffield
09.10.01	Lucky Sambo W PTS 12 Cardiff
	(WBO Inter-Continental Lightweight Title Defence)
12.02.02	Gavin Down W RSC 9 Bethnal Green
	(Vacant IBF Inter-Continental L.Welterweight Title)
20.04.02	Dafydd Carlin W RSC 8 Cardiff

Martin Power

Philip Sharkey

08.06.02	Pete Buckley W RSC 1 Renfrew
17.08.02	Ted Bami L RSC 6 Cardiff
23.11.02	Craig Lynch W CO 4 Derby
01.02.03	Neil Sinclair L RSC 8 Belfast
	(British Welterweight Title Challenge)
08.05.03	Ivan Kirpa W PTS 10 Widnes
21.02.04	Farai Musiiwa L PTS 6 Cardiff
06.05.04	Thomas McDonagh L PTS 12 Barnsley
	(WBU International L.Middleweight Title Challenge)
03.07.04	Keith Jones W RSC 8 Newport
	(Vacant Welsh Welterweight Title)
03.09.04	Ajose Olusegun L RSC 4 Newport
11.12.04	Sergey Styopkin W RSC 10 Canning Town

Career: 25 contests, won 20, lost 5.

Kreshnik Qato

Wembley. *Born* Albania, 13 August, 1978
Eastern European Boxing Association
S.Middleweight Champion. Ht. 5'9½"

Manager Self

28.09.01	Erik Teymour L PTS 6 Millwall
16.12.01	Lawrence Murphy L PTS 6 Glasgow
08.04.02	Ty Browne W PTS 4 Southampton
10.05.02	Paul Jones L PTS 6 Millwall
20.03.03	Jason Collins W PTS 4 Queensway
13.04.03	Mark Thornton W RSC 3 Streatham
13.05.03	Danny Thornton W PTS 6 Leeds
26.07.03	Scott Dann L RSC 2 Plymouth
26.09.03	Joel Ani W PTS 6 Millwall
14.11.03	Steven Bendall L PTS 8 Bethnal Green
21.02.04	Gary Lockett L RSC 2 Cardiff
16.10.04	Vladimir Zavgorodniy W PTS 10 Yalta, Ukraine
	(Vacant Eastern European Boxing Association S.Middleweight Title)
05.03.05	Rizvan Magomedov W PTS 12 Durres, Albania
	(Eastern European Boxing Association S.Middleweight Title Defence)
12.06.05	Dmitry Donetskiy W RSC 6 Leicester Square

Career: 14 contests, won 8, lost 6.

Tony Quigley

Liverpool. *Born* Liverpool, 1 October, 1984
L.Heavyweight. Ht. 5'10"
Manager F. Warren/D. Powell

26.02.04	Dave Pearson W RSC 1 Widnes
22.05.04	Patrick Cito W PTS 4 Widnes
01.10.04	Leigh Wicks W PTS 4 Manchester
11.02.05	Shpetim Hoti W CO 1 Manchester
03.06.05	Varuzhan Davtyan W PTS 4 Manchester

Career: 5 contests, won 5.

Stevie Quinn

Newtownards. *Born* Newtonards, 14 November, 1969
Bantamweight. Ht. 5'7"
Manager Self

07.02.98	Stephen Oates L PTS 4 Cheshunt
28.04.98	Tommy Waite L RSC 3 Belfast
11.12.98	Mark Payne L RSC 2 Cheshunt
17.04.99	Chris Edwards W RSC 4 Dublin
22.05.99	Ross Cassidy W PTS 4 Belfast
16.10.99	Anthony Hanna L PTS 4 Belfast
19.02.00	Barry Hawthorne W RSC 5 Prestwick
12.06.00	Mickey Coveney L PTS 4 Belfast
20.10.00	Sean Grant W RSC 2 Belfast
11.11.00	Paul Weir W PTS 4 Belfast
27.01.01	Hussein Hussein L RTD 2 Bethnal Green
01.04.01	Richmond Asante W PTS 4 Southwark
28.04.01	Noel Wilders L RTD 6 Cardiff
22.09.01	Martin Power L RSC 2 Bethnal Green
19.12.01	Mark Payne L RTD 2 Coventry
26.01.02	Michael Hunter L CO 2 Dagenham
12.10.02	Martin Power L RSC 4 Bethnal Green
07.12.02	Marc Callaghan W PTS 4 Brentwood
01.02.03	Marty Kayes W PTS 4 Belfast
15.02.03	Martin Power L RTD 1 Wembley
05.04.03	Marty Kayes W RSC 5 Belfast
17.07.03	Kevin Mitchell L CO 1 Dagenham
12.11.04	Delroy Spencer W PTS 6 Belfast

Career: 23 contests, won 10, lost 13.

151

R

Furhan Rafiq
Glasgow. *Born* Glasgow, 16 December, 1977
Featherweight. Ht. 5'8"
Manager T. Gilmour

19.04.04 Paddy Folan W PTS 6 Glasgow
15.11.04 Gary Davis L PTS 6 Glasgow
Career: 2 contests, won 1, lost 1.

Harry Ramogoadi
Coventry. *Born* South Africa, 21 March, 1976
S. Featherweight. Ht. 5'6"
Manager J. Weaver/D. Lutaaya

20.11.98 Dan Ngweyna W PTS 4 Thembisa, South Africa
24.01.99 Zachariah Madau W PTS 4 Johannesburg, South Africa
26.03.99 Jan van Rooyen DREW 4 Witbank, South Africa
27.06.99 Kenneth Buhlalu W PTS 4 Durban, South Africa
23.07.99 Bethule Machedi W PTS 4 Johannesburg, South Africa
25.09.99 Malepa Levi W PTS 6 Nelspruit, South Africa
01.12.99 Mandla Mashiane L PTS 6 Johannesburg, South Africa
13.07.00 Martin Mnyandu L PTS 6 Johannesburg, South Africa
28.10.00 Trevor Gouws W PTS 6 Johannesburg, South Africa
18.02.01 Thomas Mashaba DREW 6 Johannesburg, South Africa
15.04.01 Malepa Levi W PTS 8 Johannesburg, South Africa
02.11.01 Malcolm Klaasen W PTS 6 Benoni, South Africa
08.02.02 Takalani Kwinda W PTS 8 Johannesburg, South Africa
09.10.02 Ariel Mathebula W PTS 6 Sandton, South Africa
24.10.03 Stephen Oates W PTS 6 Bethnal Green
08.11.03 Jason Nesbitt W PTS 6 Coventry
09.04.04 Nigel Senior W RSC 1 Rugby
10.07.04 Choi Tseveenpurev L RTD 6 Coventry
(British Masters Featherweight Title Challenge)
09.12.04 John Murray L RSC 4 Stockport
06.03.05 Choi Tseveenpurev L RSC 5 Shaw
(British Masters Featherweight Title Challenge)
01.06.05 Danny Wallace W PTS 6 Leeds
Career: 21 contests, won 14, drew 2, lost 5.

Tony Randell (Webster)
Birmingham. *Born* Peterborough, 11 April, 1982
Middleweight. Ht. 5'11½"
Manager N. Nobbs

16.12.04 Scott Conway W PTS 6 Cleethorpes
13.02.05 Gavin Smith L PTS 6 Bradford

23.03.05 Danny Goode L PTS 6 Leicester Square
01.04.05 Chris Black L PTS 6 Glasgow
16.05.05 Sergey Haritonov W RSC 4 Birmingham
Career: 5 contests, won 2, lost 3.

Tony Randell　　　　Les Clark

Hastings Rasani
Birmingham. *Born* Zimbabwe, 16 April, 1974
L. Heavyweight. Ht. 6'2"
Manager Self

21.12.97 Elias Chikwanda W RSC 4 Harare, Zimbabwe
28.02.98 Victor Ndebele W CO 1 Harare, Zimbabwe
04.04.98 William Mpoku W PTS 8 Harare, Zimbabwe
03.05.98 Nightshow Mafukidze W CO 3 Harare, Zimbabwe
30.05.98 Frank Mutiyaya W RSC 4 Harare, Zimbabwe
24.07.98 Ambrose Mlilo L RSC 9 Harare, Zimbabwe
13.01.99 Tobia Wede W RSC 4 Harare, Zimbabwe
27.02.99 Ambrose Mlilo L CO 9 Harare, Zimbabwe
17.04.99 Eric Sauti W RSC 2 Harare, Zimbabwe
05.06.99 Gibson Mapfumo W RSC 2 Harare, Zimbabwe
02.01.01 Neil Simpson L CO 4 Coventry
(Vacant Commonwealth L.Heavyweight Title)
28.04.01 Arigoma Chiponda W DIS Harare, Zimbabwe
08.05.01 Tony Oakey L RSC 10 Barnsley
(Vacant Commonwealth L.Heavyweight Title)
06.10.01 Sipho Moyo L CO 9 Harare, Zimbabwe
15.03.02 Elvis Michailenko L RSC 5 Millwall
24.05.03 Elvis Michailenko L RSC 4 Bethnal Green
31.07.03 Mark Brookes L PTS 6 Sheffield
05.09.03 Carl Thompson L RSC 1 Sheffield

04.10.03 Steven Spartacus L RSC 1 Muswell Hill
11.11.03 Denzil Browne L PTS 6 Leeds
13.02.04 Leigh Alliss L PTS 6 Bristol
21.02.04 Earl Ling DREW 6 Norwich
12.03.04 Simeon Cover W CO 6 Irvine
20.03.04 David Haye L RSC 1 Wembley
12.05.04 Jamie Hearn L RSC 4 Reading
17.06.04 Amer Khan L PTS 6 Sheffield
17.09.04 Mark Brookes L PTS 6 Sheffield
11.10.04 Hamed Jamali L PTS 8 Birmingham
22.10.04 Nathan King L PTS 6 Edinburgh
08.12.04 Sam Price L PTS 6 Longford
17.12.04 Neil Simpson L PTS 6 Coventry
21.02.05 Karl Wheeler L PTS 6 Peterborough
24.04.05 Nicki Taylor W RTD 4 Askern
08.05.05 Nate Joseph W RSC 4 Bradford
15.05.05 Danny Grainger W RSC 5 Sheffield
02.06.05 Karl Wheeler W RSC 5 Peterborough
Career: 36 contests, won 14, drew 1, lost 21.

Neil Read
Bilston. *Born* Wolverhampton, 9 February, 1972
S. Bantamweight. Ht. 5'4"
Manager P. Bowen

08.02.00 Gary Groves W PTS 6 Wolverhampton
10.09.00 Stephen Chinnock L RSC 5 Walsall
30.11.00 Paddy Folan L PTS 6 Blackpool
13.02.01 Sid Razak L PTS 6 Brierley Hill
08.03.01 John-Paul Ryan W PTS 6 Stoke
26.08.01 Lee Holmes L PTS 6 Warrington
06.12.01 Chris Edwards L PTS 8 Stoke
28.01.02 Jamil Hussain L CO 2 Barnsley
13.04.02 Stephen Chinnock L CO 3 Wolverhampton
(Midlands Area Featherweight Title Challenge)
29.06.02 Jamie Yelland L PTS 6 Brentwood
03.08.02 Isaac Ward L RSC 1 Blackpool
23.09.02 Andy Roberts L PTS 6 Cleethorpes
10.10.02 Chris Edwards L PTS 6 Stoke
08.11.02 Andy Roberts L PTS 6 Doncaster
02.12.02 Steve Gethin L RTD 3 Leicester
10.02.03 Sean Hughes L PTS 6 Sheffield
17.03.03 Junior Anderson W CO 2 Southampton
07.06.03 Gareth Payne L RSC 5 Coventry
(Vacant Midlands Area S.Bantamweight Title)
05.09.03 Andy Roberts L PTS 6 Doncaster
09.10.03 Lee Haskins L PTS 4 Bristol
08.11.03 Gareth Payne L PTS 4 Coventry
14.02.04 Rendall Munroe L RSC 1 Nottingham
03.04.04 Mark Moran L RSC 2 Manchester
14.06.04 Wayne Bloy DREW 6 Cleethorpes
26.09.04 Chris Edwards L RSC 2 Stoke
(Vacant British Masters S.Bantamweight Title)
31.10.04 Gary Ford L PTS 6 Shaw
18.04.05 Abdul Mougharbel L PTS 6 Bradford
Career: 27 contests, won 3, drew 1, lost 23.

(Dale) Daleboy Rees
Swansea. *Born* Swansea, 7 July, 1979
Lightweight. Ht. 5'7"
Manager D. Williams

15.09.02 Greg Edwards W PTS 4 Swansea
08.01.03 Joel Viney W RSC 5 Aberdare
25.01.03 Pavel Potipko W PTS 4 Bridgend
10.04.03 Henry Jones W PTS 4 Clydach

30.11.03 Buster Dennis L PTS 6 Swansea
20.02.04 Henry Castle L RSC 4 Bethnal Green
01.10.04 Michael Graydon L PTS 6 Bristol
Career: 7 contests, won 4, lost 3.

Daleboy Rees   Les Clark

Gavin Rees

Newbridge. *Born* Newport, 10 May, 1980
Lightweight. Former Undefeated WBO
Inter-Continental Featherweight Champion.
Ht. 5'7"
Manager Self

05.09.98 John Farrell W PTS 4 Telford
05.12.98 Ernie Smith W PTS 4 Bristol
27.03.99 Graham McGrath W RSC 2 Derby
05.06.99 Wayne Jones W RSC 2 Cardiff
11.12.99 Dave Hinds W RSC 2 Liverpool
19.02.00 Pete Buckley W PTS 4 Dagenham
29.05.00 Willie Valentine W RSC 3 Manchester
23.09.00 Pete Buckley W PTS 4 Bethnal Green
13.11.00 Steve Hanley W RSC 1 Bethnal Green
15.01.01 Chris Jickells W RSC 2 Manchester
28.04.01 Vladimir Borov W RSC 4 Cardiff
          *(Vacant WBO Inter-Continental
          Featherweight Title)*
21.07.01 Nigel Senior W RSC 2 Sheffield
09.10.01 Nikolai Eremeev W PTS 12 Cardiff
          *(WBO Inter-Continental Featherweight
          Title Defence)*
12.02.02 Rakhim Mingaleev W PTS 6 Bethnal
          Green
20.04.02 Gary Flear W RTD 4 Cardiff
08.07.02 Ernie Smith W RSC 5 Mayfair
17.08.02 Sergei Andreychikov W RTD 1 Cardiff
14.12.02 Jimmy Beech W PTS 4 Newcastle
15.02.03 Andrei Devyataykin W PTS 6
          Wembley
28.06.03 Daniel Thorpe W RSC 1 Cardiff
03.07.04 Michael Muya W RSC 2 Newport
03.09.04 Carl Allen W PTS 6 Newport
Career: 22 contests, won 22.

(Khatib) Kaye Rehman (Khan)

Bradford. *Born* Pakistan, 8 September,
1974
Middleweight. Ht. 5'7³/₄"
Manager C. Aston

18.04.05 Mark Franks DREW 6 Bradford
Career: 1 contest, drew 1.

Gary Reid

Stoke. *Born* Jamaica, 20 November, 1972
L.Welterweight. Former British Masters
L.Welterweight Champion. Ht. 5'5¹/₂"
Manager Self

09.12.98 Carl Tilley W CO 1 Stoke
11.02.99 Ted Bami L RSC 2 Dudley
23.03.99 Lee Williamson W PTS 6
          Wolverhampton
07.10.99 Stuart Rimmer W RSC 2 Mere
19.12.99 No No Junior L PTS 6 Salford
14.04.00 Lee Molyneux W PTS 6 Manchester
18.05.00 Sammy Smith W RSC 1 Bethnal Green
23.07.00 Kevin Bennett L RSC 4 Hartlepool
21.09.00 Karim Bouali L PTS 4 Bloomsbury
07.10.00 Bradley Pryce L RSC 5 Doncaster
07.09.01 Willie Limond L PTS 8 Glasgow
22.09.01 Francis Barrett L PTS 4 Bethnal Green
17.02.02 Richie Caparelli W PTS 6 Salford
02.03.02 Paul Halpin L RSC 3 Bethnal Green
26.04.02 Martin Watson L PTS 6 Glasgow
28.05.02 Gareth Jordan DREW 6 Liverpool
13.07.02 Gary Greenwood L RSC 5 Coventry
05.10.02 Joel Viney W CO 2 Coventry
18.11.02 Martin Watson L RSC 4 Glasgow
21.03.03 Young Muttley L RSC 7 West
          Bromwich
          *(Vacant Midlands Area L.Welterweight
          Title)*
10.10.03 Oscar Hall W RSC 2 Darlington
26.09.04 Tony Montana W PTS 10 Stoke
          *(Vacant British Masters
          L.Welterweight Title)*
17.02.05 Dean Hickman L PTS 10 Dudley
          *(Midlands Area L.Welterweight Title
          Challenge)*
27.05.05 Barry Morrison L RTD 8 Motherwell
          *(British Masters L.Welterweight Title
          Defence)*
Career: 24 contests, won 9, drew 1, lost 14.

Ian Reid

Battersea. *Born* Lambeth, 30 August, 1972
Lightweight. Ht. 5'2"
Manager Self

30.03.93 Russell Rees L PTS 6 Cardiff
31.08.93 Jason Hutson W RSC 6 Croydon
10.11.93 Marcus McCrae L PTS 6 Bethnal
          Green
09.12.94 Mark Bowers L PTS 6 Bethnal Green
17.05.95 Michael Brodie L RSC 3 Ipswich
30.11.03 Henry Janes L PTS 6 Swansea
07.12.03 John Bothwell L PTS 6 Glasgow
15.03.04 Darren Johnstone L PTS 6 Glasgow
31.10.04 Eddie Nevins L PTS 6 Shaw
12.11.04 Simon Wilson L PTS 6 Belfast
19.12.04 Warren Dunkley L PTS 4 Bethnal
          Green
18.02.05 Justin Murphy L PTS 6 Brighton
06.03.05 Craig Johnson L PTS 6 Mansfield
23.03.05 Gareth Couch L RSC 6 Leicester
          Square
30.04.05 Jed Syger L PTS 4 Dagenham
20.05.05 Lee Cook L PTS 4 Southwark
Career: 16 contests, won 1, lost 15.

Mike Reid

Aberdeen. *Born* Inverurie, 4 November,
1983
L. Welterweight. Ht. 5'8"
Manager T. Gilmour

15.11.04 Willie Valentine W PTS 6 Glasgow
21.02.05 Tom Hogan W PTS 6 Glasgow
11.06.05 Lance Verallo W PTS 6 Kirkcaldy
Career: 3 contests, won 3.

Robin Reid

Runcorn. Liverpool, 19 February, 1971
IBO S.Middleweight Champion. Former
Undefeated WBF S.Middleweight
Champion. Former WBC S.Middleweight
Champion. Ht. 5'9"
Manager Self

27.02.93 Mark Dawson W RSC 1 Dagenham
06.03.93 Julian Eavis W RSC 2 Glasgow
10.04.93 Andrew Furlong W PTS 6 Swansea
10.09.93 Juan Garcia W PTS 6 San Antonio,
          Texas, USA
09.10.93 Ernie Loveridge W PTS 4 Manchester
18.12.93 Danny Juma DREW 6 Manchester
09.04.94 Kesem Clayton W RSC 1 Mansfield
04.06.94 Andrew Furlong W RSC 2 Cardiff
17.08.94 Andrew Jervis W RSC 1 Sheffield
19.11.94 Chris Richards W RSC 3 Cardiff
04.02.95 Bruno Westenberghs W RSC 1 Cardiff
04.03.95 Marvin O'Brien W RSC 6 Livingston
06.05.95 Steve Goodwin W CO 1 Shepton
          Mallet
10.06.95 Martin Jolley W CO 1 Manchester
22.07.95 John Duckworth W PTS 8 Millwall
15.09.95 Trevor Ambrose W CO 5 Mansfield
10.11.95 Danny Juma W PTS 8 Derby
26.01.96 Stinger Mason W RSC 2 Brighton
16.03.96 Andrew Flute W RSC 7 Glasgow
26.04.96 Hunter Clay W RSC 1 Cardiff
08.06.96 Mark Dawson W RSC 5 Newcastle
31.08.96 Don Pendleton W RTD 4 Dublin
12.10.96 Vincenzo Nardiello W CO 7 Milan,
          Italy
          *(WBC S. Middleweight Title
          Challenge)*
08.02.97 Giovanni Pretorius W RSC 7 Millwall
          (WBC S. Middleweight Title Defence)
03.05.97 Henry Wharton W PTS 12 Manchester
          (WBC S. Middleweight Title Defence)
11.09.97 Hassine Cherifi W PTS 12 Widnes
          (WBC S. Middleweight Title Defence)
19.12.97 Thulani Malinga L PTS 12 Millwall
          (WBC S. Middleweight Title Defence)
18.04.98 Graham Townsend W RSC 6
          Manchester
13.02.99 Joe Calzaghe L PTS 12 Newcastle
          *(WBO S. Middleweight Title
          Challenge)*
24.06.00 Silvio Branco L PTS 12 Glasgow
          *(WBU S. Middleweight Title
          Challenge)*
08.12.00 Mike Gormley W RSC 1 Crystal
          Palace
          (Vacant WBF S. Middleweight Title)
19.05.01 Roman Babaev W RSC 3 Wembley
          (WBF S. Middleweight Title Defence)
14.07.01 Soon Botes W RSC 4 Liverpool
          (WBF S.Middleweight TitleDefence)
20.10.01 Jorge Sclarandi W CO 3 Glasgow
          (WBF S. Middleweight Title Defence)
19.12.01 Julio Cesar Vasquez W PTS 12
          Coventry
          (WBF S. Middleweight Title Defence)
10.07.02 Francisco Mora W PTS 12 Wembley
          (WBF S. Middleweight Title Defence)

29.11.02	Mondili Mbonambi W RSC 2 Liverpool
05.04.03	Enrique Carlos Campos W RSC 8 Leipzig, Germany
04.10.03	Willard Lewis W RSC 6 Zwickau, Germany
24.10.03	Dmitri Adamovich W CO 4 Bethnal Green
13.12.03	Sven Ottke L PTS 12 Nuremberg, Germany
	(WBA & IBF S.Middleweight Title Challenges)
26.06.04	Brian Magee W PTS 12 Belfast
	(IBO S.Middleweight Title Challenge)
13.02.05	Ramdane Serdjane W PTS 6 Brentwood

Career: 43 contests, won 38, drew 1, lost 4.

(Marcello) Cello Renda

Peterborough. *Born* Peterborough, 4 June, 1985
S. Middleweight. Ht. 5'11"
Manager I. Pauly

30.09.04	Mark Ellwood W RSC 2 Hull
04.11.04	Joey Vegas L RSC 3 Piccadilly
12.12.04	Scott Forsyth W RSC 1 Glasgow
21.02.05	Tom Cannon W PTS 6 Peterborough
11.03.05	Ricardo Samms L PTS 4 Doncaster
02.06.05	Michael Banbula DREW 6 Peterborough

Career: 6 contests, won 3, drew 1, lost 2.

Michael Rennie

Margate. *Born* Lambeth, 10 September, 1982
L. Middleweight. Ht. 5'10"
Manager Self

08.05.04	Brian Coleman W PTS 4 Dagenham
08.10.04	Neil Addis W RSC 2 Brentwood

Career: 2 contests, won 2.

Darren Rhodes

Leeds. *Born* Leeds, 16 September, 1975
L. Middleweight. Ht. 5'11"
Manager Self

18.07.98	Andy Kemp W RSC 1 Sheffield
10.10.98	Perry Ayres W CO 2 Bethnal Green
27.02.99	Gareth Lovell W PTS 4 Oldham
01.05.99	Carlton Williams W RSC 4 Crystal Palace
29.05.99	Sean Pritchard DREW 4 Halifax
09.10.99	Leigh Wicks W PTS 4 Manchester
11.12.99	Leigh Wicks W PTS 4 Liverpool
25.03.00	Leigh Wicks W PTS 4 Liverpool
29.05.00	Dean Ashton W RSC 3 Manchester
08.07.00	Jason Collins DREW 4 Widnes
04.09.00	Jason Collins L PTS 4 Manchester
11.12.00	Paul Wesley W PTS 4 Widnes
17.03.01	Andrew Facey W PTS 4 Manchester
07.07.01	Wayne Elcock L PTS 4 Manchester
24.11.01	Simeon Cover W RSC 5 Wakefield
02.03.02	Andrew Facey L RSC 6 Wakefield
	(Vacant Central Area Middleweight Title)
21.05.02	Hussain Osman L PTS 10 Custom House
15.06.02	Harry Butler W PTS 4 Leeds
28.09.02	Martin Thompson W PTS 8 Wakefield
09.11.02	Wayne Pinder L RSC 4 Altrincham

12.04.03	Mihaly Kotai L PTS 10 Bethnal Green
10.05.03	Lee Murtagh W PTS 6 Huddersfield
05.07.03	Darren Bruce W RSC 3 Brentwood
06.09.03	Scott Dixon DREW 6 Huddersfield
04.12.03	Steve Roberts W CO 6 Huddersfield
10.04.04	Michael Jones L RSC 3 Manchester
	(Final Elim. British L.Middleweight Title)
12.11.04	Thomas McDonagh L PTS 10 Halifax
	(Elim. British L.Middleweight Title)
07.04.05	Wayne Elcock L CO 1 Birmingham

Career: 28 contests, won 16, drew 3, lost 9.

Ryan Rhodes

Sheffield. *Born* Sheffield, 20 November, 1976
Middleweight. Former Undefeated WBO Inter-Continental Middleweight Champion. Former Undefeated British & IBF Inter-Continental L. Middleweight Champion. Ht. 5'8½"
Manager F. Warren/D. Coldwell

04.02.95	Lee Crocker W RSC 2 Cardiff
04.03.95	Shamus Casey W CO 1 Livingston
06.05.95	Chris Richards W PTS 6 Shepton Mallet
15.09.95	John Rice W RSC 2 Mansfield
10.11.95	Mark Dawson W PTS 6 Derby
20.01.96	John Duckworth W RSC 2 Mansfield
26.01.96	Martin Jolley W CO 3 Brighton
11.05.96	Martin Jolley W RSC 2 Bethnal Green
25.06.96	Roy Chipperfield W RSC 1 Mansfield
14.09.96	Del Bryan W PTS 6 Sheffield
14.12.96	Paul Jones W RSC 8 Sheffield
	(Vacant British L. Middleweight Title)
25.02.97	Peter Waudby W CO 1 Sheffield
	(British L. Middleweight Title Defence)
14.03.97	Del Bryan W RSC 7 Reading
	(British L. Middleweight Title Defence)
12.04.97	Lindon Scarlett W RSC 1 Sheffield
	(Vacant IBF Inter-Continental L. Middleweight Title)
02.08.97	Ed Griffin W RSC 2 Barnsley
	(IBF Inter-Continental L. Middleweight Title Defence. Vacant WBO L. Middleweight Title)
11.10.97	Yuri Epifantsev W RSC 2 Sheffield
	(Final Elim. WBO Middleweight Title)
13.12.97	Otis Grant L PTS 12 Sheffield
	(Vacant WBO Middleweight Title)
18.07.98	Lorant Szabo W RSC 8 Sheffield
	(WBO Inter-Continental Middleweight Title Challenge)
28.11.98	Fidel Avendano W RSC 1 Sheffield
	(WBO Inter-Continental Middleweight Title Defence)
27.03.99	Peter Mason W RSC 1 Derby
17.07.99	Jason Matthews L CO 2 Doncaster
	(Vacant WBO Middleweight Title)
15.01.00	Eddie Haley W RSC 5 Doncaster
16.05.00	Ojay Abrahams W PTS 6 Warrington
21.10.00	Michael Alexander W PTS 6 Wembley
16.12.00	Howard Clarke W PTS 6 Sheffield
21.07.01	Youri Tsarenko W PTS 6 Sheffield
27.10.01	Jason Collins W PTS 4 Manchester
16.03.02	Lee Blundell L RSC 3 Bethnal Green
	(Vacant WBF Inter-Continental Middleweight Title)
16.04.03	Paul Wesley W CO 3 Nottingham
25.07.03	Alan Gilbert W RSC 5 Norwich
11.12.03	Peter Jackson W PTS 6 Bethnal Green

12.03.04	Scott Dixon W PTS 8 Nottingham
16.04.04	Tomas da Silva W RSC 4 Bradford
22.04.05	Peter Jackson W PTS 6 Barnsley
03.06.05	Craig Lynch W RSC 3 Manchester

Career: 35 contests, won 32, lost 3.

Mal Rice

Flint. *Born* Mancot, 19 July, 1975
Heavyweight. Ht. 6'2"
Manager Self

26.11.97	Gary Cavey W CO 2 Stoke
29.01.98	Lennox Williams W PTS 6 Pentre Halkyn
30.03.98	Bruno Foster L PTS 6 Bradford
30.04.98	Lennox Williams W PTS 6 Pentre Halkyn
21.06.98	Shane Woollas L PTS 6 Liverpool
18.02.00	Gary Williams L PTS 6 Pentre Halkyn
13.03.00	Patrick Halberg W RSC 2 Bethnal Green
05.05.00	Gary Williams L PTS 4 Pentre Halkyn
27.05.00	Mark Potter L CO 1 Southwark
26.03.01	John McDermott L RSC 2 Wembley
28.07.01	Matt Legg L PTS 4 Wembley
13.09.01	Petr Horacek W RSC 1 Sheffield
04.10.01	Pele Reid L PTS 4 Finsbury
16.12.01	Greg Wedlake L RSC 3 Bristol
18.05.02	Danny Watts L RTD 3 Millwall
29.03.03	Terry Dixon L PTS 4 Wembley
31.01.05	Ian Millarvie L RTD 3 Glasgow
12.06.05	Micky Steeds L PTS 6 Leicester Square
25.06.05	Paul Butlin L PTS 4 Melton Mowbray

Career: 19 contests, won 5, lost 14.

Wayne Rigby

Manchester. *Born* Manchester, 19 July, 1973
L.Welterweight. Former WBF L.Welterweight Champion. Former Undefeated IBO Inter-Continental Lightweight Champion. Former British Lightweight Champion. Former Undefeated Central Area Lightweight Champion. Ht. 5'6"
Manager Self

27.02.92	Lee Fox L PTS 6 Liverpool
08.06.92	Leo Turner W PTS 6 Bradford
02.07.92	Leo Turner W CO 5 Middleton
05.10.92	Colin Innes W PTS 6 Manchester
01.12.92	John T. Kelly L PTS 6 Hartlepool
02.06.94	Kid McAuley W PTS 6 Middleton
13.06.94	Chris Clarkson W PTS 6 Liverpool
22.09.94	Mark Hargreaves W PTS 6 Bury
06.03.95	Kelton McKenzie L PTS 8 Leicester
18.05.95	John T. Kelly W PTS 6 Middleton
05.06.95	Hugh Collins W RSC 4 Glasgow
17.01.96	Kid McAuley W PTS 6 Solihull
24.03.96	Steve Tuckett W PTS 6 Shaw
27.09.96	Jimmy Phelan W PTS 10 Hull
	(Central Area Lightweight Title Challenge)
07.03.97	Alan Bosworth W RSC 5 Northampton
10.01.98	Tanveer Ahmed W PTS 12 Bethnal Green
	(Vacant British Lightweight Title)
11.04.98	Matt Brown W RTD 8 Southwark
	(British Lightweight Title Defence)
17.10.98	Bobby Vanzie L RSC 10 Manchester
	(British Lightweight Title Defence)
31.07.99	Mark McGowan W RSC 4 Carlisle

11.09.99 Alan Temple L PTS 8 Sheffield
04.12.99 Mark Haslam W CO 3 Peterborough
27.05.00 Dariusz Snarski W RSC 8 Mayfair
(*Vacant IBO Inter-Continental Lightweight Title*)
01.07.00 Michael Ayers L RSC 10 Manchester
(*IBO Lightweight Title Challenge*)
03.03.01 Michael Ayers L PTS 12 Wembley
(*IBO Lightweight Title Challenge*)
14.07.01 Keith Jones W CO 3 Wembley
26.11.01 Antonio Ramirez W PTS 12 Manchester
(*Vacant WBF L.Welterweight Title*)
09.03.02 Sedat Puskulla W CO 1 Manchester
(*Vacant WBF L. Welterweight Title*)
18.05.02 Colin Dunne L RTD 10 Millwall
(*WBU Lightweight Title Challenge. Vacant WBF Lightweight Title*)
09.11.02 Gary Ryder L PTS 12 Altrincham
(*WBF L. Welterweight Title Defence*)
22.05.04 Tony Montana L PTS 10 Manchester
(*Vacant Central Area L.Welterweight Title*)
24.10.04 Roger Sampson L PTS 6 Sheffield
Career: 31 contests, won 20, lost 11.

(Alexander) Sandy Robb

Nairn. *Born* Irvine, 5 April, 1981
L.Heavyweight. Ht. 6'0"
Manager T. Gilmour

07.06.04 Michael Pinnock W PTS 6 Glasgow
20.09.04 Nicki Taylor W RSC 5 Glasgow
25.02.05 John Smith W RSC 5 Irvine
21.03.05 Shane White W RSC 4 Glasgow
Career: 4 contests, won 4.

Dale Robinson

Huddersfield. *Born* Huddersfield, 9 April, 1980
Bantamweight. Former Undefeated Commonwealth Flyweight Champion. Former Undefeated Central Area Flyweight Champion. Ht. 5'4"
Manager T. Gilmour/C. Aston

25.09.00 John Barnes W PTS 4 Barnsley
28.10.00 Delroy Spencer W RSC 4 Coventry
02.12.00 Colin Moffett W PTS 4 Bethnal Green
26.02.01 Christophe Rodrigues W PTS 6 Nottingham
07.04.01 Andrei Kostin W PTS 6 Wembley
08.05.01 Terry Gaskin W RTD 3 Barnsley
(*Central Area Flyweight Title Challenge*)
27.04.02 Jason Thomas W RSC 4 Huddersfield
18.05.02 Sergei Tasimov W RSC 3 Millwall
15.06.02 Kakhar Sabitov W PTS 6 Leeds
05.10.02 Alain Bonnel W PTS 8 Huddersfield
30.11.02 Marc Dummett W RSC 3 Liverpool
22.02.03 Spencer Matsangura W PTS 12 Huddersfield
(*Vacant Commonwealth Flyweight Title*)
10.05.03 Zolile Mbityi W PTS 12 Huddersfield
(*Commonwealth Flyweight Title Defence*)
09.10.03 Emil Stoica W RSC 3 Bristol
04.12.03 Pavel Kubasov W CO 4 Huddersfield
13.03.04 Jason Booth L PTS 12 Huddersfield
(*IBO S.Flyweight Title Challenge*)
27.05.04 Moses Kinyau W PTS 6 Huddersfield

17.12.04 Lahcene Zemmouri W RSC 8 Huddersfield
20.05.05 Martin Power L PTS 12 Southwark
(*Vacant British Bantamweight Title*)
Career: 19 contests, won 17, lost 2.

Jim Rock

Dublin. *Born* Dublin, 12 March, 1972
All-Ireland S.Middleweight Champion. Former Undefeated All-Ireland L.Middleweight Champion. Former Undefeated WAA Inter-Continental S.Middleweight Champion. WBF European L.Middleweight Champion. Ht. 5'11"
Manager M. O'Callaghan

25.11.95 Craig Lynch W PTS 4 Dublin
09.03.96 Peter Mitchell W PTS 6 Millstreet
03.09.96 Rob Stevenson W PTS 6 Belfast
05.11.96 Danny Quacoe W RSC 4 Belfast
28.01.97 Roy Chipperfield W RTD 2 Belfast
12.04.97 George Richards W PTS 6 Sheffield
13.09.97 Robert Njie W CO 3 Millwall
18.04.98 Ensley Bingham L RSC 7 Manchester
19.09.98 Michael Monaghan W PTS 12 Dublin
(*Vacant WAA Inter-Continental S. Middleweight Title*)
14.12.98 Perry Ayres W RTD 3 Cleethorpes
22.01.99 Jimmy Vincent W PTS 10 Dublin
20.02.99 Pedro Carragher W RSC 3 Thornaby
(*Vacant WBF European L. Middleweight Title*)
17.04.99 Michael Alexander W RSC 1 Dublin
(*Vacant All-Ireland S. Middleweight Title*)
19.06.99 Kevin Thompson W PTS 4 Dublin
15.04.00 Allan Gray W PTS 10 Bethnal Green

(*Vacant All-Ireland L. Middleweight Title*)
12.06.00 Alan Gilbert W PTS 6 Belfast
20.10.00 Brooke Welby W RSC 3 Belfast
11.11.00 David Baptiste W PTS 4 Belfast
08.12.00 Tommy Attardo W PTS 8 Worcester, Mass, USA
24.03.01 Hollister Elliott W CO 6 Worcester, Mass, USA
20.04.01 Jason Collins W PTS 6 Dublin
01.12.01 Ian Cooper L PTS 6 Bethnal Green
24.04.02 Harry Butler W PTS 6 Dublin
01.02.03 Takaloo L RSC 9 Belfast
(*Vacant WBU L. Middleweight Title*)
30.10.03 Alan Jones L PTS 8 Belfast
24.09.04 Matt Galer W PTS 6 Dublin
28.10.04 Sylvestre Marianini W PTS 6 Belfast
19.02.05 Peter Jackson W CO 7 Dublin
(*Irish S.Middleweight Title Defence*)
18.03.05 Michael Monaghan W PTS 8 Belfast
Career: 29 contests, won 25, lost 4.

Martin Rogan

Belfast. *Born* Belfast, 1 May, 1971
Heavyweight. Ht. 6'3"
Manager J. Breen/M. Callahan/F. Warren

28.10.04 Lee Mountford W RSC 1 Belfast
18.03.05 Billy Bessey W PTS 4 Belfast
04.06.05 Tony Booth W RSC 2 Manchester
Career: 3 contests, won 3.

Sam Rukundo

Tottenham. *Born* Kampala Uganda, 18 May, 1980
Lightweight. Ht. 5'7¼"
Manager M. Helliet

Sam Rukundo   Les Clark

04.11.04 Henry Janes W PTS 6 Piccadilly
27.01.05 Chris Long W PTS 4 Piccadilly
23.03.05 Billy Smith W RSC 3 Leicester Square
26.05.05 John-Paul Ryan W RSC 4 Mayfair
Career: 4 contests, won 4.

Vinesh Rungea

Brentford. *Born* Mauritius, 25 December, 1980
Featherweight. Ht. 5'5³/₄"
Manager C. Sanigar

26.03.05 Lee Whyatt W PTS 4 Hackney
Career: 1 contest, won 1.

Jason Rushton

Doncaster. *Born* Doncaster, 15 February, 1983
L.Middleweight. Former Central Area L.Middleweight Champion. Ht. 5'10"
Manager J. Rushton/F. Warren

27.10.01 Ram Singh W PTS 6 Manchester
09.02.02 Brian Gifford W RSC 1 Manchester
01.06.02 Tony Smith W PTS 4 Manchester

08.11.02 Gary Hadwin W CO 4 Doncaster
21.02.03 Wayne Shepherd W PTS 6 Doncaster
05.09.03 Harry Butler W PTS 4 Doncaster
27.09.03 Jimi Hendricks W PTS 4 Manchester
06.03.04 Peter Dunn W PTS 6 Renfrew
06.05.04 Peter Dunn W PTS 4 Barnsley
03.09.04 Ernie Smith W PTS 4 Doncaster
29.10.04 Brian Coleman W PTS 6 Doncaster
04.02.05 Howard Clarke W PTS 4 Doncaster
11.03.05 Lee Armstrong W PTS 10 Doncaster
(Vacant Central Area L.Middleweight Title)
20.05.05 Lee Murtagh L PTS 10 Doncaster
(Central Area L.Middleweight Title Defence)
Career: 14 contests, won 13, lost 1.

Steve Russell

Norwich. *Born* Norwich, 1 September, 1979
Middleweight. Ht. 5'10"
Manager J. Ingle

12.04.03 Kevin Phelan L PTS 4 Norwich
06.06.03 Jimi Hendricks L PTS 6 Norwich

20.06.03 Carl Wall L PTS 4 Liverpool
21.02.04 Arv Mittoo W PTS 6 Norwich
30.03.04 Dmitry Donetskiy L PTS 6 Southampton
09.10.04 Peter Dunn L PTS 6 Norwich
Career: 6 contests, won 1, lost 5.

John-Paul Ryan

Northampton. *Born* Enfield, 1 April, 1971
L. Welterweight. Ht. 5'5"
Manager Self

07.12.00 Paddy Folan W PTS 6 Stoke
08.03.01 Neil Read L PTS 6 Stoke
28.05.02 Paddy Folan W PTS 6 Leeds
25.06.02 Sean Hughes L PTS 6 Rugby
18.10.02 Isaac Ward L PTS 6 Hartlepool
20.01.03 John Simpson L PTS 6 Glasgow
16.02.03 Simon Chambers L RSC 2 Salford
22.03.03 Gareth Payne L PTS 4 Coventry
24.05.03 Sean Hughes L PTS 6 Sheffield
11.07.03 Lee McAllister L RTD 2 Darlington
13.09.03 Joel Viney L PTS 6 Coventry
26.09.03 Femi Fehintola L PTS 6 Reading
30.10.03 Dean Hickman L PTS 6 Dudley
23.11.03 Rendall Munroe L PTS 6 Rotherham
12.03.04 John Murray L RSC 1 Nottingham
01.05.04 Joe McCluskey L RTD 2 Coventry
24.10.04 Femi Fehintola L PTS 6 Sheffield
25.02.05 Jamie McIlroy L PTS 6 Irvine
26.05.05 Sam Rukundo L RSC 4 Mayfair
25.06.05 Kristian Laight DREW 6 Melton Mowbray
Career: 20 contests, won 2, drew 1, lost 17.

(Patrick) Paddy Ryan

Nottingham. *Born* Nottingham, 30 November, 1974
S.Middleweight. Ht. 6'4"
Manager J. Gill

24.09.04 Gerard London W PTS 4 Bethnal Green
26.11.04 Gerard London L PTS 4 Bethnal Green
17.02.05 Matthew Hough L PTS 6 Dudley
Career: 3 contests, won 1, lost 2.

Jason Rushton   Les Clark   *Paddy Ryan*   Les Clark

(Saheed) Silence Saheed (Salawu)

Canning Town. *Born* Ibadan, Nigeria, 1 January, 1978
L. Welterweight. Ht. 5'6"
Manager Self

28.03.03	Martin Hardcastle W PTS 4 Millwall
10.04.03	Ceri Hall DREW 4 Clydach
27.05.03	Francis Barrett W RSC 1 Dagenham
11.10.03	Wayne Wheeler W RSC 1 Portsmouth
15.11.03	Gary Greenwood W RTD 1 Coventry
21.11.03	Jaz Virdee W RSC 2 Millwall
01.05.04	Alan Temple L DIS 8 Gravesend
	(Vacant British Masters Lightweight Title)
17.09.04	Scott Lawton L PTS 6 Sheffield
24.09.04	James Gorman W PTS 6 Millwall
09.10.04	Jonathan Thaxton L PTS 6 Norwich
22.10.04	Nigel Wright L PTS 8 Edinburgh
10.04.05	Lenny Daws L PTS 6 Brentwood

Career: 12 contests, won 6, drew 1, lost 5.

Ricardo Samms

Nottingham. *Born* Nottingham, 2 June, 1982
S.Middleweight. Ht. 6'1"
Manager D. Coldwell/F. Warren

11.03.05	Cello Renda W PTS 4 Doncaster
04.06.05	Ojay Abrahams W PTS 4 Manchester

Career: 2 contests, won 2.

Ricardo Samms   Les Clark

Roger Sampson

Sheffield. *Born* Sheffield, 3 July, 1972
Lightweight. Ht. 5'7¼"
Manager Self

26.06.97	Robbie Sivyer W PTS 6 Sheffield
06.10.97	Lee Armstrong W PTS 6 Bradford
09.02.98	Gary Jenkinson L PTS 6 Bradford
17.03.98	Gary Jenkinson W PTS 6 Sheffield
20.09.98	John T. Kelly W PTS 6 Sheffield
19.10.98	Bradley Welsh L PTS 8 Glasgow
03.12.98	Michael Ayers W PTS 6 Mayfair

25.01.99	David Kehoe W PTS 4 Glasgow
28.11.99	Chris Price W PTS 4 Chesterfield
24.03.01	Jimmy Phelan W PTS 4 Sheffield
24.10.04	Wayne Rigby W PTS 6 Sheffield
10.12.04	Scott Lawton L PTS 6 Sheffield

Career: 12 contests, won 9, lost 3.

Cafu Santos

Wellingborough. *Born* Kettering, 27 December, 1982
Middleweight. Ht. 6'1½"
Manager S. James

22.10.04	Andiano Aubrey W PTS 6 Mansfield
04.11.04	Eder Kurti L RSC 1 Piccadilly
10.12.04	Karl Chiverton W RSC 4 Mansfield
21.02.05	Vince Baldassara L CO 2 Glasgow
30.04.05	Graham Delehedy L RSC 1 Wigan

Career: 5 contests, won 2, lost 3.

Chris Saunders

Barnsley. *Born* Barnsley, 15 August, 1969
Welterweight. Former British & English Welterweight Champion. Ht. 5'8"
Manager Self

22.02.90	Malcolm Melvin W PTS 4 Hull
10.04.90	Mike Morrison W PTS 6 Doncaster
20.05.90	Justin Graham W RSC 3 Sheffield
29.11.90	Ross Hale L PTS 6 Bayswater
05.03.91	Rocky Ferrari L PTS 4 Glasgow
19.03.91	Richard Woolgar W RSC 3 Leicester
26.03.91	Felix Kelly L PTS 6 Bethnal Green
17.04.91	Billy Schwer L RSC 1 Kensington
16.05.91	Richard Burton L PTS 6 Liverpool
06.06.91	Mark Tibbs W RSC 6 Barking
30.06.91	Billy Schwer L RSC 3 Southwark
01.08.91	James Jiora W RSC 6 Dewsbury
03.10.91	Gary Flear L PTS 6 Burton
24.10.91	Ron Shinkwin W PTS 6 Dunstable
21.11.91	J. P. Matthews L RSC 4 Burton
30.01.92	John O. Johnson L PTS 6 Southampton
11.02.92	Eddie King W RSC 4 Wolverhampton
27.02.92	Richard Burton L PTS 10 Liverpool
	(Vacant Central Area L. Welterweight Title)
09.09.92	John O. Johnson DREW 6 Stoke
01.10.92	Mark McCreath L RSC 4 Telford
01.12.92	Shea Neary L PTS 6 Liverpool
22.02.93	Cham Joof L PTS 4 Eltham
16.03.93	Mark Elliot L PTS 6 Wolverhampton
26.04.93	Dean Hollington W RSC 5 Lewisham
23.10.93	Michael Smyth L PTS 6 Cardiff
02.12.93	Rob Stewart L PTS 4 Sheffield
03.03.94	Kevin Lueshing W RSC 4 Ebbw Vale
04.06.94	Jose Varela W CO 2 Dortmund, Germany
26.08.94	Julian Eavis W PTS 6 Barnsley
26.09.94	Julian Eavis W RSC 6 Cleethorpes
26.10.94	Lindon Scarlett W PTS 8 Leeds
17.12.94	Roberto Welin W RSC 7 Cagliari, Italy
15.09.95	Del Bryan W PTS 12 Mansfield
	(British Welterweight Title Challenge)
13.02.96	Kevin Lueshing L RSC 3 Bethnal Green
	(British Welterweight Title Defence)
25.06.96	Michael Carruth L RSC 10 Mansfield
09.06.97	Derek Roche L RSC 4 Bradford
	(Central Area Welterweight Title Challenge. Elim. British Welterweight Title)
27.02.98	Scott Dixon L PTS 10 Glasgow
	(Elim. British Welterweight Title)

17.04.99	Michael Carruth L RSC 5 Dublin
08.12.01	David Kirk W CO 2 Chesterfield
15.06.02	Arv Mittoo W PTS 6 Norwich
24.09.02	Robert Pacuraru W RTD 4 Gran Canaria, Spain
09.02.03	Richard Swallow W PTS 4 Bradford
03.04.04	Marcus Portman W RSC 1 Sheffield
	(Vacant English Welterweight Title)
19.06.04	Peter Dunn W PTS 4 Muswell Hill
01.10.04	Michael Jennings L RTD 5 Manchester
	(English Welterweight Title Defence)

Career: 45 contests, won 22, drew 1, lost 22.

Bruce Scott

Hackney. *Born* Jamaica, 16 August, 1969
Cruiserweight. Former Undefeated British, Commonwealth & WBU Inter-Continental Cruiserweight Champion. Former Undefeated Southern Area Cruiserweight Champion. Ht. 5'9½"
Manager F. Warren

25.04.91	Mark Bowen L PTS 6 Mayfair
16.09.91	Randy B. Powell W RSC 5 Mayfair
21.11.91	Steve Osborne W PTS 6 Burton
27.04.92	John Kaighin W CO 4 Mayfair
07.09.92	Lee Prudden W PTS 6 Bethnal Green
03.12.92	Mark Pain W RSC 5 Lewisham
15.02.93	Paul McCarthy W PTS 6 Mayfair
22.04.93	Sean O'Phoenix W RSC 3 Mayfair
14.06.93	John Oxenham W RSC 1 Bayswater
04.10.93	Simon McDougall W PTS 6 Mayfair
16.12.93	Bobby Mack W RSC 4 Newport
05.04.94	Steve Osborne W RSC 5 Bethnal Green
17.10.94	Bobbi Joe Edwards W PTS 8 Mayfair
09.12.94	John Keeton W CO 2 Bethnal Green
19.04.95	Nigel Rafferty W RSC 2 Bethnal Green
19.05.95	Cordwell Hylton W RSC 1 Southwark
11.11.95	Tony Booth W RSC 3 Halifax
05.03.96	Nick Manners W RSC 5 Bethnal Green
13.07.96	Tony Booth W PTS 8 Bethnal Green
30.11.96	Nicky Piper L RSC 7 Tylorstown
	(Commonwealth L. Heavyweight Title Challenge)
15.05.97	Grant Briggs W RSC 2 Reading
04.10.97	Tony Booth L PTS 8 Muswell Hill
21.04.98	Dominic Negus W RSC 9 Edmonton
	(Southern Area Cruiserweight Title Challenge)
28.11.98	Darren Corbett W RSC 10 Belfast
	(Commonwealth Cruiserweight Title Challenge. Vacant British Cruiserweight Title)
15.05.99	Johnny Nelson L PTS 12 Sheffield
	(WBO Cruiserweight Title Challenge)
17.07.99	Juan Carlos Gomez L RSC 6 Dusseldorf, Germany
	(WBC Cruiserweight Title Challenge)
08.04.00	Chris Woollas W RSC 2 Bethnal Green
24.06.00	Adam Watt L RSC 4 Glasgow
	(Vacant Commonwealth Cruiserweight Title)
16.12.00	John Keeton W CO 6 Sheffield
	(Vacant British Cruiserweight Title)
10.03.01	Garry Delaney W RTD 3 Bethnal Green
	(British Cruiserweight Title Defence. Vacant Commonwealth Cruiserweight Title)
28.07.01	Rene Janvier W PTS 12 Wembley
	(Vacant WBU Inter-Continental Cruiserweight Title)
28.06.03	Enzo Maccarinelli L RSC 4 Cardiff

(Vacant WBU Cruiserweight Title)

07.02.04	Radcliffe Green W PTS 6 Bethnal Green
17.12.04	Mark Hobson L PTS 12 Huddersfield

(British & Commonwealth Cruiserweight Title Challenges)

Career: 34 contests, won 26, lost 8.

Greg Scott-Briggs

Chesterfield. *Born* Swaziland, 6 February, 1966
Cruiserweight. Ht. 6'1"
Manager Self

04.02.92	Mark McBiane W PTS 6 Alfreton
03.03.92	Tony Colclough W RSC 2 Cradley Heath
30.03.92	Carl Smallwood L PTS 6 Coventry
27.04.92	Richard Atkinson L PTS 6 Bradford
28.05.92	Steve Walton W PTS 6 Gosforth
04.06.92	Joe Frater L PTS 6 Cleethorpes
30.09.92	Carl Smallwood L PTS 6 Solihull
17.03.93	Carl Smallwood L PTS 8 Stoke
26.04.93	Tony Colclough W RSC 4 Glasgow
08.06.93	Peter Flint W RSC 1 Derby
07.09.93	Steve Loftus W RSC 2 Stoke
22.09.93	Paul Hanlon W PTS 6 Chesterfield
04.11.93	Lee Archer L PTS 8 Stafford
24.11.93	Tony Colclough W PTS 6 Solihull
08.12.93	Lee Archer W RTD 6 Stoke
08.02.94	Nigel Rafferty L PTS 6 Wolverhampton
17.02.94	Lee Archer L PTS 8 Walsall
11.03.94	Monty Wright L CO 1 Bethnal Green
26.09.94	Dave Battey W RSC 4 Cleethorpes
11.10.94	Mark Smallwood L PTS 8 Wolverhampton
29.10.94	Mark Smallwood L PTS 6 Cannock
12.11.94	Thomas Hansvoll L PTS 4 Randers, Denmark
30.11.94	Monty Wright L PTS 6 Wolverhampton
06.03.95	Neil Simpson L RTD 5 Leicester
15.09.95	David Flowers L PTS 6 Darlington
29.11.95	Neil Simpson L DIS 7 Solihull

(Vacant Midlands Area L. Heavyweight Title)

20.03.96	Stinger Mason W PTS 6 Stoke
26.10.96	Danny Peters L PTS 6 Liverpool
13.06.97	Jamie Warters L RSC 5 Leeds
15.12.97	Michael Pinnock W PTS 6 Nottingham
11.05.98	Neil Simpson L PTS 6 Leicester
25.11.98	Sven Hamer L CO 2 Streatham
13.03.99	Ole Klemetsen L CO 4 Manchester
24.04.99	Monty Wright W RSC 3 Peterborough
20.05.99	Sven Hamer L RSC 5 Kensington
03.10.99	Carl Smallwood W PTS 6 Chesterfield
09.04.00	Tony Booth L PTS 10 Alfreton

(Vacant British Masters L. Heavyweight Title)

15.07.00	Clinton Woods L RSC 3 Millwall
03.08.02	Lee Swaby L RSC 4 Derby
21.10.02	Chris Woollas L PTS 6 Cleethorpes
02.12.02	Clint Johnson L PTS 6 Leeds
01.08.03	David Haye L CO 1 Bethnal Green
31.01.04	Albert Sosnowski L CO 2 Bethnal Green
15.03.04	Lee Mountford DREW 6 Bradford
09.04.04	Robert Norton L CO 1 Rugby
08.06.04	Neil Dawson L RSC 3 Sheffield
17.09.04	Neil Hosking L RSC 2 Plymouth
20.02.05	Simon Francis L RSC 4 Sheffield

Career: 48 contests, won 15, drew 1, lost 32.

Matt Scriven

Nottingham. *Born* Nottingham, 1 September, 1973
L.Middleweight. Former Undefeated Midlands Area L.Middleweight Champion. Former British Masters L.Middleweight Champion. Ht. 5'10"
Manager T. Harris

26.11.97	Shamus Casey W PTS 6 Stoke
08.12.97	Shane Thomas W PTS 6 Bradford
20.03.98	C. J. Jackson L PTS 6 Ilkeston
15.05.98	Lee Bird W RSC 5 Nottingham
08.10.98	Stevie McCready L RTD 3 Sunderland
01.04.99	Adrian Houldey W PTS 6 Birmingham
25.04.99	Danny Thornton L RSC 4 Leeds
27.06.99	Shane Junior L RSC 2 Alfreton
11.09.99	David Arundel L RTD 1 Sheffield
20.03.00	James Docherty L PTS 8 Glasgow
27.03.00	Matt Mowatt L PTS 4 Barnsley
09.04.00	David Matthews W PTS 6 Alfreton
06.06.00	Jackie Townsley L RSC 3 Motherwell
04.11.00	Brett James L RTD 1 Bethnal Green
04.02.01	Mark Paxford L PTS 6 Queensferry
26.02.01	Pedro Thompson W RTD 1 Nottingham
12.03.01	Ernie Smith W PTS 6 Birmingham
20.03.01	James Docherty L RSC 1 Glasgow
21.05.01	Christian Brady L RSC 5 Birmingham

(Vacant Midlands Area Welterweight Title)

21.10.01	Neil Bonner NC 1 Glasgow
04.03.02	Danny Parkinson L PTS 6 Bradford
22.04.02	Gary Porter L PTS 6 Glasgow
28.05.02	Peter Dunn W PTS 8 Leeds
14.09.02	Ernie Smith W PTS 6 Newark
29.09.02	James Lee L RTD 4 Shrewsbury
30.11.02	Davey Jones L PTS 6 Newark
16.03.03	Lee Williamson W PTS 10 Nottingham

(Vacant Midlands Area & British Masters L. Middleweight Titles)

08.06.03	Wayne Shepherd W PTS 10 Nottingham

(British Masters L.Middleweight Title Defence)

15.09.03	Lee Murtagh L DIS 9 Leeds

(British Masters L.Middleweight Title Defence)

12.03.04	David Walker L RSC 3 Nottingham
12.06.04	Matthew Hatton L RSC 4 Manchester
18.09.04	Robert Lloyd-Taylor L RTD 4 Newark
28.01.05	Colin McNeil L PTS 4 Renfrew
06.03.05	Mark Wall W PTS 4 Mansfield
29.04.05	Gary Woolcombe L RSC 4 Southwark
04.06.05	Matthew Hall L RSC 2 Manchester

Career: 36 contests, won 12, lost 23, no contest 1.

Ebrima Secka

Brighton. *Born* Gambia, 1 March, 1975
Heavyweight. Ht. 6'0"
Manager Self

27.04.04	Paul Butlin L PTS 6 Leeds
21.11.04	Billy Bessey L PTS 6 Bracknell
21.01.05	Darren Morgan L RSC 1 Bridgend

Career: 3 contests, lost 3.

Simon Sherrington

Birmingham. *Born* Birmingham, 14 July, 1971
L. Middleweight. Ht. 5'9½"
Manager Self

09.10.00	Paddy Martin W RSC 5 Birmingham
28.11.00	Pedro Thompson W RSC 5 Brierley Hill
13.12.04	Jon Harrison W RSC 5 Birmingham
21.02.05	Lee Williamson DREW 6 Birmingham
16.05.05	Lee Williamson W PTS 8 Birmingham

Career: 5 contests, won 4, drew 1.

Nadeem Siddique

Bradford. *Born* Bradford, 28 October, 1977
L. Welterweight. Ht. 5'8"
Manager J. Ingle

17.11.02	Daniel Thorpe W PTS 4 Bradford
09.02.03	Norman Dhalie W PTS 4 Bradford
13.04.03	Dave Hinds W PTS 4 Bradford
15.06.03	Nigel Senior W PTS 6 Bradford
05.10.03	Jason Nesbitt W PTS 6 Bradford
27.10.03	Daniel Thorpe W PTS 6 Glasgow
07.12.03	Chris Duggan W RSC 2 Bradford
16.01.04	Pete Buckley W PTS 4 Bradford
16.04.04	Arv Mittoo W PTS 6 Bradford
15.05.04	Joel Viney W PTS 6 Aberdeen
24.09.04	Dave Hinds W PTS 4 Nottingham
13.02.05	Jason Nesbitt W PTS 6 Bradford
09.04.05	Pete Buckley W PTS 6 Norwich
08.05.05	Kristian Laight W RSC 7 Bradford
03.06.05	Daniel Thorpe W PTS 6 Hull

Career: 15 contests, won 15.

(Paulino) Paulie Silva

Droylsden. *Born* Almada, Portugal, 29 April, 1978
L. Heavyweight. Ht. 5'10"
Manager W. Barker

16.06.00	Adolfo Marcelo Trinidad L CO 4 Santa Rita, Argentina
28.02.04	Nick Okoth W PTS 6 Manchester
02.04.04	Courtney Fry L PTS 4 Plymouth
24.04.04	Giovanni Diniz L DIS 2 Sao Paulo, Brazil
24.10.04	Amer Khan L PTS 6 Sheffield

Career: 5 contests, won 1, lost 4.

Luke Simpkin

Swadlincote. *Born* Derby, 5 May, 1979
Heavyweight. Ht. 6'2"
Manager Self

24.09.98	Simon Taylor W CO 3 Edgbaston
16.10.98	Chris P. Bacon L PTS 6 Salford
10.12.98	Jason Flisher W RSC 5 Barking
04.02.99	Danny Watts L CO 3 Lewisham
28.05.99	Tommy Bannister W RSC 4 Liverpool
07.08.99	Owen Beck L PTS 4 Dagenham
11.09.99	Scott Lansdowne L PTS 4 Sheffield
11.03.00	Albert Sosnowski L PTS 4 Kensington
27.03.00	Mark Hobson L PTS 4 Barnsley
29.04.00	Johan Thorbjoernsson L PTS 4 Wembley
23.09.00	Mark Potter L PTS 6 Bethnal Green
30.09.00	Gordon Minors DREW 4 Peterborough
18.11.00	Keith Long L RSC 3 Dagenham
03.02.01	Paul Buttery W RSC 1 Manchester
01.04.01	Wayne Llewelyn L PTS 6 Southwark
24.04.01	Darren Chubbs L PTS 4 Liverpool
06.05.01	Billy Bessey L PTS 6 Hartlepool
09.06.01	John McDermott L PTS 6 Bethnal Green
13.09.01	Mark Krence L PTS 4 Sheffield
10.12.01	Mark Hobson L RTD 3 Liverpool

27,.01.02 Pele Reid DREW 4 Streatham
15.03.02 Mike Holden L PTS 6 Millwall
13.04.02 Fola Okesola W PTS 4 Liverpool
10.05.02 Julius Francis DREW 6 Millwall
23.08.02 Mark Potter L PTS 6 Bethnal Green
10.06.03 Mark Krence L RTD 8 Sheffield
          (Vacant Midlands Area Heavyweight
          Title)
05.09.03 Roman Greenberg L RTD 4 Sheffield
25.04.04 Dave Clarke W RSC 2 Nottingham
18.09.04 Paul King L PTS 6 Newark
02.12.04 Micky Steeds L RSC 3 Crystal Palace
21.02.05 Ian Millarvie L PTS 6 Glasgow
26.04.05 Carl Baker W RSC 4 Leeds
Career: 32 contests, won 7, drew 3, lost 22.

John Simpson

Greenock. *Born* Greenock, 26 July, 1983
Featherweight. Ht. 5'7"
Manager T. Gilmour

23.09.02 Simon Chambers W RSC 1 Glasgow
06.10.02 Lee Holmes L PTS 6 Rhyl
07.12.02 Matthew Burke W PTS 4 Brentwood
20.01.03 John-Paul Ryan W PTS 6 Glasgow
17.02.03 Joel Viney W RTD 1 Glasgow
14.04.03 Simon Chambers W PTS 6 Glasgow
20.10.03 Steve Gethin W PTS 8 Glasgow
01.11.03 Mark Alexander W PTS 4 Glasgow
19.01.04 Henry Janes W PTS 8 Glasgow
31.01.04 Gennadiy Delisandru W PTS 4 Bethnal
          Green
22.04.04 Jus Wallie W PTS 6 Glasgow
02.06.04 Fred Janes W PTS 6 Hereford
20.09.04 Marc Callaghan W PTS 8 Glasgow
05.11.04 Dazzo Williams L PTS 12 Hereford
          (British Featherweight Title
          Challenge)
06.06.05 Dariusz Snarski W RSC 3 Glasgow
Career: 15 contests, won 13, lost 2.

John Simpson   Les Clark

Kyle Simpson

Bridlington. *Born* Bradford, 2 January,
1986
Featherweight. Ht. 5'8"
Manager J. Ingle

03.06.05 Paddy Folan W RSC 3 Hull
Career: 1 contest, won 1

Neil Simpson

Coventry. *Born* London, 5 July, 1970
L.Heavyweight. Former Undefeated British
& Commonwealth L.Heavyweight
Champion. Former Midlands Area
L.Heavyweight Champion. Ht. 6'2"
Manager Self

04.10.94 Kenny Nevers W PTS 4 Mayfair
20.10.94 Johnny Hooks W RSC 2 Walsall
05.12.94 Chris Woollas L PTS 6 Cleethorpes
15.12.94 Paul Murray W PTS 6 Walsall
06.03.95 Greg Scott-Briggs W RTD 5 Leicester
17.03.95 Thomas Hansvold L PTS 4
          Copenhagen, Denmark
26.04.95 Craig Joseph L PTS 6 Solihull
11.05.95 Andy McVeigh L CO 2 Dudley
24.06.95 Dave Owens W RSC 1 Cleethorpes
25.09.95 Tony Booth L PTS 8 Cleethorpes
11.10.95 Darren Ashton W RSC 3 Solihull
29.11.95 Greg Scott-Briggs W DIS 7 Solihull
          (Vacant Midlands Area L. Heavyweight
          Title)
19.02.96 Stephen Wilson L PTS 6 Glasgow
27.03.96 Tony Booth W PTS 6 Whitwick
26.04.96 Dean Francis L RSC 3 Cardiff
02.10.96 Chris Davies W PTS 4 Cardiff
28.10.96 Nigel Rafferty W PTS 8 Leicester
03.12.96 Danny Peters L PTS 6 Liverpool
03.02.97 Michael Pinnock W PTS 6 Leicester
25.04.97 Stuart Fleet L PTS 10 Cleethorpes
          (Midlands Area L. Heavyweight Title
          Defence)
20.10.97 Slick Miller W RTD 1 Leicester
15.12.97 Chris Woollas L PTS 6 Cleethorpes
11.05.98 Greg Scott-Briggs W PTS 6 Leicester
30.11.98 Slick Miller W CO 3 Leicester
26.02.99 Adam Cale W RSC 3 Coventry
12.07.99 Tony Booth W PTS 10 Coventry
          (Elim. British L. Heavyweight Title)
14.12.99 Darren Corbett L PTS 12 Coventry
          (Vacant IBO Inter-Continental
          L. Heavyweight Title)
22.05.00 Mark Baker W PTS 12 Coventry
          (Vacant British & Commonwealth
          L. Heavyweight Titles)
18.11.00 Mark Delaney W RSC 1 Dagenham
          (British L. Heavyweight Title Defence)
02.01.01 Hastings Rasani W CO 4 Coventry
          (Vacant Commonwealth
          L. Heavyweight Title)
06.04.01 Yawe Davis L RSC 3 Grosseto, Italy
          (Vacant European L. Heavyweight
          Title)
25.05.02 Tony Oakey L PTS 12 Portsmouth
          (WBU L. Heavyweight Title Challenge)
08.03.03 Peter Oboh L RSC 11 Coventry
          (Commonwealth L.Heavyweight Title
          Challenge. Vacant British
          L.Heavyweight Title)
20.04.04 Mark Brookes L PTS 10 Sheffield
          (Elim. British L.Heavyweight Title)
17.12.04 Hastings Rasani W PTS 6 Coventry
18.06.05 Paul Bonson W PTS 6 Coventry
Career: 36 contests, won 21, lost 15.

Neil Sinclair

Belfast. *Born* Belfast, 23 February, 1974
Welterweight. Former Undefeated British
Welterweight Champion. Ht. 5'10½"
Manager Self

14.04.95 Marty Duke W RSC 2 Belfast

27.05.95 Andrew Jervis L RSC 3 Belfast
17.07.95 Andy Peach W RSC 1 Mayfair
26.08.95 George Wilson W PTS 4 Belfast
07.10.95 Wayne Shepherd W RSC 6 Belfast
02.12.95 Brian Coleman W RTD 1 Belfast
13.04.96 Hughie Davey W PTS 6 Liverpool
28.05.96 Prince Kasi Kaihau W RSC 2 Belfast
03.09.96 Dennis Berry L PTS 6 Belfast
27.09.97 Trevor Meikle W RSC 5 Belfast
20.12.97 Chris Pollock W RTD 3 Belfast
21.02.98 Leigh Wicks W RSC 1 Belfast
19.09.98 Paul Denton W RSC 1 Dublin
07.12.98 Michael Smyth W CO 1 Acton
22.01.99 Mark Ramsey W CO 3 Dublin
05.06.99 David Kirk W PTS 8 Cardiff
16.10.99 Paul Dyer W RSC 8 Belfast
18.03.00 Dennis Berry W RSC 2 Glasgow
16.05.00 Paul Dyer W RSC 6 Warrington
24.06.00 Chris Henry W RSC 1 Glasgow
12.08.00 Adrian Chase W RSC 2 Wembley
16.12.00 Daniel Santos L CO 2 Sheffield
          (WBO Welterweight Title Challenge)
28.04.01 Zoltan Szilii W CO 2 Cardiff
22.09.01 Viktor Fesetchko W PTS 6 Bethnal
          Green
19.11.01 Harry Dhami W RSC 5 Glasgow
          (British Welterweight Title Challenge)
20.04.02 Leonti Voronchuk W RSC 4 Cardiff
15.06.02 Derek Roche W CO 1 Leeds
          (British Welterweight Title Defence)
17.08.02 Dmitri Kashkan W RSC 4 Cardiff
02.11.02 Paul Knights W RSC 2 Belfast
          (British Welterweight Title Defence)
01.02.03 Bradley Pryce W RSC 8 Belfast
          (British Welterweight Title Defence)
30.07.04 Craig Lynch W PTS 6 Bethnal Green
18.03.05 Taz Jones L RSC 1 Belfast
Career: 32 contests, won 28, lost 4.

Matt Skelton

Bedford. *Born* Bedford, 23 January, 1968
British Heavyweight Champion. Former
Undefeated WBU & Commonwealth
Heavyweight Champion. Former
Undefeated English Heavyweight
Champion. Ht. 6'3"
Manager K. Sanders/F. Maloney

22.09.02 Gifford Shillingford W RSC 2
          Southwark
27.10.02 Slick Miller W CO 1 Southwark
08.12.02 Neil Kirkwood W RSC 1 Bethnal
          Green
18.02.03 Jacklord Jacobs W RSC 4 Bethnal
          Green
08.04.03 Alexei Varakin W CO 2 Bethnal Green
15.05.03 Dave Clarke W RSC 1 Mayfair
17.07.03 Antoine Palatis W RSC 4 Dagenham
18.09.03 Mike Holden W RSC 6 Dagenham
          (Vacant English Heavyweight Title)
11.10.03 Costi Marin W RSC 1 Portsmouth
25.10.03 Ratko Draskovic W RSC 3 Edinburgh
15.11.03 Patriche Costel W CO 1 Bayreuth,
          Germany
07.02.04 Julius Francis W PTS 10 Bethnal Green
          (English Heavyweight Title Defence)
24.04.04 Michael Sprott W CO 12 Reading
          (British & Commonwealth
          Heavyweight Title Challenges)
05.06.04 Bob Mirovic W RTD 4 Bethnal Green
          (Commonwealth Heavyweight Title
          Defence)

19.11.04 Keith Long W RSC 11 Bethnal Green
(British & Commonwealth Heavyweight Title Defences)
25.02.05 Fabio Eduardo Moli W RSC 6 Wembley
(Vacant WBU Heavyweight Title)

Career: 16 contests, won 16.

Matt Skelton   Les Clark

Gatis Skuja

Bethnal Green. *Born* Latvia, 23 June, 1982
Welterweight. Ht. 5'9"
Manager C. Sanigar

26.03.05 Nathan Graham L RSC 1 Hackney

Career: 1 contest, lost 1.

Anthony Small

Deptford. *Born* London, 28 June, 1981
L.Middleweight. Ht. 5'9"
Manager A. Booth

12.05.04 Lance Hall W RSC 1 Reading
10.09.04 Emmanuel Marcos W RSC 1 Wembley
10.12.04 Howard Clarke W PTS 4 Sheffield
21.01.05 Andrei Sherel W RSC 3 Brentford
24.04.05 Dmitry Donetskiy W PTS 4 Leicester Square
16.06.05 Howard Clarke W PTS 6 Mayfair

Career: 6 contests, won 6.

Anthony Small   Les Clark

Donovan Smillie

Bradford. *Born* Bradford, 9 August, 1975
English Middleweight Champion. Former Undefeated British Masters S.Middleweight Champion. Ht. 5'10½"
Manager Self

10.04.99 Sean Pritchard W RSC 1 Manchester
02.05.99 Mark Dawson W PTS 6 Shaw
04.12.99 Mark Dawson W PTS 4 Manchester
14.04.00 Dennis Doyley W PTS 4 Manchester
25.11.00 Ojay Abrahams L RSC 2 Manchester
30.11.01 Rob Stevenson W PTS 6 Hull
17.12.01 Mark Chesters W PTS 6 Cleethorpes
17.02.02 William Webster W PTS 6 Salford
20.04.02 Mike Duffield L PTS 4 Derby
15.06.02 Wayne Asker DREW 6 Norwich
07.10.02 Alan Jones L RSC 6 Birmingham
17.11.02 William Webster W PTS 6 Bradford
09.02.03 Robert Burton W PTS 6 Bradford
13.04.03 Mark Phillips W PTS 6 Bradford
15.06.03 Mike Duffield W RSC 3 Bradford
(Vacant British Masters S.Middleweight Title)
03.08.03 William Webster W RSC 4 Stalybridge
05.10.03 Gary Jones W CO 2 Bradford
07.12.03 Patrick Cito W PTS 6 Bradford
16.01.04 Mark Phillips W PTS 4 Bradford
16.04.04 Patrick Cito W RSC 3 Bradford
18.11.04 Roddy Doran W RSC 7 Shrewsbury
(Vacant English Middleweight Title)
13.02.05 Michael Pinnock W PTS 6 Bradford
08.05.05 Ryan Walls L PTS 6 Bradford

Career: 23 contests, won 18, drew 1, lost 4.

Billy Smith

Stourport. *Born* Kidderminster, 10 June, 1978
L.Welterweight. Ht. 5'7"
Manager E. Johnson

28.03.00 Marcus Portman L PTS 6 Wolverhampton
07.04.00 Barry Hughes L PTS 6 Glasgow
18.05.00 Manzo Smith L PTS 4 Bethnal Green
26.05.00 Willie Limond L PTS 4 Glasgow
07.07.00 Gareth Jordan L PTS 6 Chigwell
15.07.00 David Walker L RTD 2 Millwall
09.09.00 Ricky Eccleston L PTS 4 Manchester
24.09.00 Choi Tsveenpurev L RTD 2 Shaw
18.11.00 Lee Meager L RSC 1 Dagenham
17.12.00 Willie Limond L PTS 6 Glasgow
03.02.01 Scott Spencer L PTS 6 Brighton
09.03.01 Darren Melville L PTS 4 Millwall
27.03.01 Jason Nesbitt L PTS 6 Brierley Hill
05.03.05 Lee Cook L PTS 4 Southwark
23.03.05 Sam Rukundo L RSC 3 Leicester Square
30.04.05 Baz Carey L PTS 6 Coventry
08.05.05 Sean Hughes L PTS 6 Bradford
20.05.05 Stefy Bull L PTS 6 Doncaster
02.06.05 Isaac Ward L PTS 8 Yarm
16.06.05 Ricky Owen L PTS 4 Dagenham
25.06.05 John Fewkes L PTS 6 Wakefield

Career: 21 contests, lost 21.

Clint Smith

Desborough. *Born* Kettering, 1 July, 1981
L. Middleweight. Ht. 5'11½"
Manager K. Sanders/F. Maloney

05.03.05 Lee Williamson W PTS 6 Southwark

Career: 1 contest, won 1.

Danny Smith

Lowestoft. *Born* Great Yarmouth, 6 October, 1979
Middleweight. Ht. 6'0"
Manager Self

15.07.00 Gary Jones W RSC 1 Norwich
04.11.00 Rob Stevenson DREW 6 Derby
28.03.01 Simeon Cover W PTS 6 Piccadilly
08.06.01 Rob Stevenson W PTS 6 Hull
13.04.02 Freddie Yemofio W PTS 6 Norwich
15.06.02 William Webster W PTS 6 Norwich
21.09.02 Mike Duffield W PTS 6 Norwich
12.04.03 Simeon Cover W CO 5 Norwich
06.06.03 Gary Cummings W PTS 6 Norwich
25.07.03 William Webster W PTS 4 Norwich
21.02.04 Lee Williamson W PTS 6 Norwich
09.10.04 Brian Coleman W PTS 6 Norwich
09.04.05 Jason Collins W PTS 6 Norwich

Career: 13 contests, won 12, drew 1.

Ernie Smith

Stourport. *Born* Kidderminster, 10 June, 1978
L.Middleweight. Ht. 5'8"
Manager Self

24.11.98 Woody Greenaway L PTS 6 Wolverhampton
05.12.98 Gavin Rees L PTS 4 Bristol
27.01.99 Arv Mittoo DREW 6 Stoke
11.02.99 Tony Smith W PTS 6 Dudley
22.02.99 Liam Maltby W PTS 4 Peterborough
08.03.99 Wayne Jones W PTS 6 Birmingham
18.03.99 Carl Greaves L PTS 6 Doncaster
25.03.99 Brian Coleman L PTS 6 Edgbaston
27.05.99 Brian Coleman W PTS 6 Edgbaston
14.06.99 Dave Gibson W PTS 6 Birmingham
22.06.99 Koba Gogoladze L RSC 1 Ipswich
03.10.99 Gavin Down L RSC 1 Chesterfield
30.11.99 Brian Coleman L PTS 8 Wolverhampton
13.12.99 Richie Murray L RSC 5 Cleethorpes
24.02.00 Brian Coleman L PTS 6 Edgbaston
02.03.00 Oscar Hall L PTS 6 Birkenhead
10.03.00 John Tiftik L PTS 4 Chigwell
18.03.00 Biagio Falcone L PTS 4 Glasgow
07.04.00 Barry Connell L PTS 6 Glasgow
14.04.00 Jose Luis Castro L PTS 6 Madrid, Spain
06.05.00 Matthew Barr L PTS 4 Southwark
15.05.00 Harry Butler L PTS 6 Birmingham
26.05.00 Biagio Falcone L PTS 4 Glasgow
06.06.00 Chris Henry L PTS 8 Brierley Hill
08.07.00 Takaloo L RSC 4 Widnes
13.08.00 Jawaid Khaliq L RSC 4 Nottingham
(Vacant Midlands Area Welterweight Title)
24.09.00 Shaun Horsfall L PTS 6 Shaw
09.10.00 Dave Gibson W PTS 6 Birmingham
22.10.00 Matthew Barr L PTS 4 Streatham
06.11.00 Stuart Elwell L PTS 6 Wolverhampton
25.11.00 Michael Jennings L PTS 4 Manchester
03.12.00 Shaun Horsfall L PTS 6 Shaw
17.12.00 Kevin McIntyre L PTS 6 Glasgow
20.01.01 David Walker L RTD 1 Bethnal Green
12.03.01 Matt Scriven L PTS 6 Birmingham
24.03.01 Bobby Banghar L PTS 4 Chigwell
12.05.01 Jon Harrison L PTS 4 Plymouth
21.05.01 Brian Coleman W PTS 6 Birmingham
03.06.01 Babatunde Ajayi L PTS 4 Southwark
16.06.01 Bobby Banghar L PTS 4 Dagenham
26.07.01 Andy Abrol L PTS 6 Blackpool
13.09.01 Leo O'Reilly L PTS 6 Sheffield

29.09.01	Brett James L PTS 6 Southwark
01.11.01	Lance Crosby L PTS 6 Hull
17.11.01	Nigel Wright L PTS 4 Glasgow
15.12.01	Ross Minter L RSC 2 Wembley
11.02.02	Tony Montana L PTS 6 Shrewsbury
13.05.02	Martin Scotland W RTD 2 Birmingham
15.06.02	Gavin Wake L PTS 4 Leeds
08.07.02	Gavin Rees L RSC 5 Mayfair
06.09.02	Ricky Burns L PTS 6 Glasgow
14.09.02	Matt Scriven L PTS 6 Newark
29.09.02	Anthony Christopher L PTS 6 Shrewsbury
18.11.02	Craig Dickson L PTS 6 Glasgow
03.12.02	Anthony Christopher W PTS 6 Shrewsbury
23.02.03	Gary Greenwood L PTS 4 Shrewsbury
24.03.03	Darrell Grafton L PTS 6 Barnsley
13.04.03	Lee McAllister L PTS 4 Bradford
28.04.03	Adnan Amar L PTS 6 Cleethorpes
12.05.03	Lee McAllister L PTS 6 Birmingham
31.05.03	Robbie Sivyer L PTS 6 Barnsley
08.06.03	Jonathan Woollins W PTS 4 Nottingham
15.06.03	Ali Nuumembe L PTS 4 Bradford
05.07.03	Michael Lomax L PTS 4 Brentwood
29.08.03	Ali Nuumembe L PTS 6 Liverpool
04.10.03	Lenny Daws L PTS 4 Muswell Hill
18.11.03	Chas Symonds L PTS 6 Bethnal Green
28.11.03	Lee McAllister L PTS 6 Hull
06.12.03	Taz Jones L PTS 4 Cardiff
07.02.04	Gary Woolcombe L PTS 4 Bethnal Green
09.04.04	Richard Swallow L PTS 4 Rugby
19.04.04	Craig Dickson L PTS 6 Glasgow
10.05.04	Adnan Amar L PTS 6 Birmingham
27.05.04	Graham Delehedy L RSC 3 Huddersfield
08.07.04	Steve Brumant L PTS 8 Birmingham
30.07.04	Tony Doherty L PTS 6 Bethnal Green
03.09.04	Jason Rushton L PTS 4 Doncaster
12.09.04	Chris Long DREW 6 Shrewsbury
24.09.04	Lenny Daws L PTS 6 Nottingham
23.10.04	Steve Conway L PTS 6 Wakefield
31.10.04	John Murray L PTS 4 Shaw
12.11.04	John O'Donnell L PTS 6 Wembley
25.11.04	Joe Mitchell W PTS 6 Birmingham
03.12.04	George Telfer L PTS 4 Edinburgh
13.12.04	Luke Teague L PTS 6 Cleethorpes

27.01.05	Muhsen Nasser L PTS 6 Piccadilly
12.02.05	Nathan Ward L PTS 6 Portsmouth
25.02.05	Ross Minter L PTS 4 Wembley
05.03.05	Gary Woolcombe L PTS 6 Southwark
23.03.05	Delroy Mellis L PTS 6 Leicester Square
08.04.05	Kerry Hope L PTS 4 Edinburgh
21.04.05	Jimmy Gould L PTS 4 Dudley
30.04.05	Andy Egan DREW 6 Coventry
08.05.05	Danny Parkinson L PTS 6 Bradford
15.05.05	Kell Brook L PTS 6 Sheffield
23.05.05	Davey Jones DREW 6 Cleethorpes
03.06.05	Martin Concepcion L PTS 4 Manchester
18.06.05	Richard Mazurek W PTS 6 Coventry
25.06.05	Adnan Amar L PTS 6 Melton Mowbray

Career: 99 contests, won 12, drew 4, lost 83.

Gavin Smith

Bradford. *Born* Bradford, 16 December, 1981
Welterweight. Ht. 5'7¾"
Manager D. Hobson

23.10.04	Mark Wall W PTS 6 Wakefield
10.12.04	Mark Wall W PTS 4 Sheffield
13.02.05	Tony Randell W PTS 6 Bradford

Career: 3 contests, won 3.

Henry Smith

Bristol. *Born* Bristol, 24 September, 1978
Heavyweight. Ht. 5'11½"
Manager T. Woodward

20.02.05	Radcliffe Green W PTS 6 Bristol
21.03.05	Billy McClung L PTS 6 Glasgow

Career: 2 contests, won 1, lost 1.

John Smith

Weston super Mare. *Born* Bristol, 2 February, 1980
Cruiserweight. Ht. 5'11"
Manager T. Woodward

25.02.05	Sandy Robb L RSC 5 Irvine

Career: 1 contest, lost 1.

Paul Smith

Liverpool. *Born* Liverpool, 6 October, 1982
Middleweight. Ht. 5'11"
Manager F. Warren

05.04.03	Howard Clarke W PTS 4 Manchester
08.05.03	Andrei Ivanov W RSC 2 Widnes
20.06.03	Elroy Edwards W RSC 2 Liverpool
29.08.03	Patrick Cito W PTS 4 Liverpool
02.10.03	Mike Duffield W RSC 1 Liverpool
13.12.03	Joel Ani W PTS 4 Manchester
26.02.04	Davey Jones W PTS 4 Widnes
03.04.04	Howard Clarke W PTS 4 Manchester
12.06.04	Steve Timms W RSC 1 Manchester
10.09.04	Ojay Abrahams W PTS 4 Liverpool
01.10.04	Jason Collins W RSC 1 Manchester
17.12.04	Howard Clarke W CO 1 Liverpool
11.02.05	Robert Burton W CO 1 Manchester
03.06.05	Simeon Cover W PTS 6 Manchester

Career: 14 contests, won 14.

Sammy Smith

Bracknell. *Born* Chichester, 12 May, 1978
WBF Continental Welterweight Champion. Former Undefeated British Masters L.Welterweight Champion. Ht. 5'6"
Manager G. Carmen

26.03.98	Shaba Edwards W PTS 6 Acton
28.04.98	Les Frost W CO 2 Brentford
02.10.98	Arv Mittoo W PTS 4 Cheshunt
27.10.98	Rudy Valentino W PTS 6 Brentford
07.12.98	Ross McCord W RSC 5 Acton
25.02.99	Trevor Smith W RSC 2 Kentish Town
08.03.99	Brian Coleman L PTS 8 Birmingham
09.05.99	David Kirk W PTS 6 Bracknell
09.04.00	Gavin Down L PTS 6 Alfreton
18.05.00	Gary Reid L RSC 1 Bethnal Green
11.02.02	David Keir W PTS 6 Southampton
25.02.02	Marcus Portman L PTS 6 Slough
09.05.03	Brian Coleman W PTS 6 Longford
31.05.03	David Kirk W PTS 4 Bethnal Green
01.08.03	Brett James L PTS 10 Bethnal Green *(Vacant Southern Area Welterweight Title)*
27.09.03	Michael Jennings L RTD 4 Manchester *(WBU Inter-Continental Welterweight Title Challenge)*
27.11.03	Keith Jones W PTS 10 Longford *(Vacant British Masters L.Welterweight Title)*
08.05.04	Young Muttley L RSC 1 Bristol *(Vacant English L.Welterweight Title)*
08.12.04	Arv Mittoo W PTS 6 Longford
20.06.05	Tony Montana W PTS 10 Longford *(Vacant WBF Continental Welterweight Title)*

Career: 20 contests, won 13, lost 7.

Tony Smith

Rotherham. *Born* Sheffield, 15 August, 1967
L. Middleweight. Ht. 5'8"
Manager Self

12.03.97	Richard Inquieti L RSC 2 Stoke
25.04.97	Dean Bramhald L PTS 6 Cleethorpes
03.05.97	Anas Oweida L RSC 1 Manchester
09.06.97	Christian Brady L RSC 4 Birmingham
10.07.97	Mark Allen L PTS 6 Doncaster
08.10.97	Marc Smith L PTS 6 Stoke

Ernie Smith   Les Clark

20.11.97 Marc Smith W PTS 6 Solihull
04.12.97 Dean Bramhald L PTS 6 Doncaster
15.01.98 Marc Smith L PTS 6 Solihull
13.05.98 Chris Price W PTS 6 Scunthorpe
21.05.98 Marc Smith L PTS 6 Solihull
21.09.98 Dave Gibson L RSC 6 Cleethorpes
09.12.98 Sean O'Sullivan L PTS 6 Stoke
11.02.99 Ernie Smith L PTS 6 Dudley
18.03.99 Rene Grayel DREW 6 Doncaster
15.05.99 Michael Jennings L RSC 1 Blackpool
04.10.99 Barry Hughes L RSC 5 Glasgow
30.11.99 Craig Clayton L PTS 6 Wolverhampton
08.12.99 Craig Clayton L PTS 6 Stoke
21.05.00 Shaun Horsfall L RSC 4 Shaw
03.02.01 Danny Wray L RSC 1 Brighton
12.03.01 Casey Brooke W PTS 6 Birmingham
01.04.01 Marcus Portman L PTS 6 Wolverhampton
03.06.01 Sam Mottram L PTS 6 Hanley
07.09.01 Marcus Portman L PTS 6 West Bromwich
15.09.01 Ross McCord L PTS 6 Swansea
10.10.01 Jamie Logan L PTS 6 Stoke
10.12.01 Sam Mottram L PTS 6 Nottingham
09.02.02 Andy Egan L PTS 4 Coventry
01.06.02 Jason Rushton L PTS 4 Manchester
20.02.04 Casey Brooke W PTS 6 Doncaster
03.09.04 Chris Evans L RSC 2 Doncaster
Career: 32 contests, won 4, drew 1, lost 27.

Steven Spartacus (Smith)

Ipswich. *Born* Bury St Edmunds, 3
November, 1976
British Masters L.Heavyweight Champion
Former English L.Heavyweight Champion.
Ht. 5'10¹/₂"
Manager Self

08.09.00 Michael Pinnock W PTS 4 Hammersmith
30.09.00 Martin Jolley W PTS 6 Chigwell
24.03.01 Calvin Stonestreet W PTS 4 Chigwell
16.06.01 Kevin Burton W RSC 1 Dagenham
07.09.01 Rob Stevenson W RSC 4 Bethnal Green
27.10.01 Darren Ashton W PTS 4 Manchester
24.11.01 Michael Pinnock W PTS 4 Bethnal Green
15.12.01 Oneal Murray W RSC 4 Chigwell
19.01.02 Darren Ashton W PTS 4 Bethnal Green
14.09.02 Calvin Stonestreet W RSC 3 Bethnal Green
08.02.03 Paul Bonson W PTS 6 Norwich
27.05.03 Mark Phillips W RSC 2 Dagenham
25.07.03 Simeon Cover W CO 3 Norwich
(Vacant British Masters L.Heavyweight Title)
04.10.03 Hastings Rasani W RSC 1 Muswell Hill
11.12.03 Scott Lansdowne W RSC 3 Bethnal Green
(Vacant English L.Heavyweight Title)
30.01.04 Ovill McKenzie L PTS 6 Dagenham
02.06.04 Varuzhan Davtyan W RSC 1 Nottingham
12.11.04 Peter Haymer L PTS 10 Wembley
(English L.Heavyweight Title Defence)
10.04.05 Sam Price W RSC 6 Brentwood
(British Masters L.Heavyweight Title Defence)
Career: 19 contests, won 17, lost 2.

Delroy Spencer

Walsall. *Born* Walsall, 25 July, 1968
British Masters Flyweight Champion.
Ht. 5'4"
Manager Self

30.10.98 Gwyn Evans L PTS 4 Peterborough
21.11.98 Jamie Evans W PTS 4 Southwark
30.01.99 Ian Napa L PTS 6 Bethnal Green
26.02.99 Chris Edwards W PTS 6 West Bromwich
30.04.99 Nicky Booth L PTS 6 Scunthorpe
06.06.99 Nicky Booth L PTS 4 Nottingham
19.06.99 Willie Valentine L PTS 4 Dublin
16.10.99 Colin Moffett W PTS 4 Bethnal Green
31.10.99 Shane Mallon W PTS 6 Raynes Park
29.11.99 Lee Georgiou L PTS 4 Wembley
19.02.00 Steffen Norskov L PTS 4 Aalborg, Denmark
08.04.00 Ian Napa L PTS 8 Bethnal Green
15.04.00 Lee Georgiou L PTS 4 Bethnal Green
04.07.00 Ankar Miah W RSC 3 Tooting
13.07.00 Darren Hayde W PTS 4 Bethnal Green
30.09.00 Paul Weir L PTS 8 Chigwell
28.10.00 Dale Robinson L RSC 4 Coventry
02.12.00 Keith Knox W PTS 6 Bethnal Green
08.05.01 Levi Pattison L PTS 4 Barnsley
22.05.01 Mimoun Chent L DIS 5 Telde, Gran Canaria
16.06.01 Sunkanmi Ogunbiyi L PTS 4 Wembley
22.11.01 Darren Taylor W PTS 8 Paddington
(Vacant British Masters Flyweight Title)
09.12.01 Shinny Bayaar L PTS 4 Shaw
19.12.01 Gareth Payne L PTS 4 Coventry
18.01.02 Gareth Payne W PTS 4 Coventry
28.01.02 Levi Pattison L RSC 5 Barnsley
19.10.03 Shinny Bayaar L PTS 6 Shaw
13.12.03 Mark Moran L PTS 4 Manchester
24.01.04 Martin Power L RTD 1 Wembley
23.04.04 Chris Edwards DREW 6 Leicester
26.06.04 Damaen Kelly L RSC 4 Belfast
30.07.04 Martin Power L CO 2 Bethnal Green
31.10.04 Shinny Bayaar L PTS 6 Shaw
12.11.04 Stevie Quinn L PTS 6 Belfast
03.12.04 Lee Haskins L RTD 3 Bristol
(Vacant English Flyweight Title)
27.05.05 Robert Nelson L PTS 4 Spennymoor
25.06.05 Robert Nelson L PTS 6 Wakefield
Career: 37 contests, won 9, drew 1, lost 27.

Michael Sprott

Reading. *Born* Reading, 16 January, 1975
European Union Heavyweight Champion.
Former British & Commonwealth
Heavyweight Champion. Former
Undefeated Southern Area & WBF
European Heavyweight Champion.
Ht. 6'0³/₄"
Manager D. Powell/F. Warren

20.11.96 Geoff Hunter W RSC 1 Wembley
19.02.97 Johnny Davison W CO 2 Acton
17.03.97 Slick Miller W CO 1 Mayfair
16.04.97 Tim Redman W CO 2 Bethnal Green
20.05.97 Waldeck Fransas W PTS 6 Edmonton
02.09.97 Gary Williams W PTS 6 Southwark
08.11.97 Darren Fearn W PTS 6 Southwark
06.12.97 Nick Howard W RSC 1 Wembley
10.01.98 Johnny Davison W RSC 2 Bethnal Green
14.02.98 Ray Kane W RTD 1 Southwark
14.03.98 Michael Murray W PTS 6 Bethnal Green
12.09.98 Harry Senior L RSC 6 Bethnal Green

(Vacant Southern Area Heavyweight Title)
16.01.99 Gary Williams W PTS 6 Bethnal Green
10.07.99 Chris Woollas W RTD 4 Southwark
18.01.00 Tony Booth W PTS 6 Mansfield
14.10.00 Wayne Llewelyn L RSC 3 Wembley
17.02.01 Timo Hoffmann W PTS 8 Bethnal Green
24.03.01 Timo Hoffmann L PTS 8 Magdeburg, Germany
03.11.01 Corrie Sanders L RSC 1 Brakpan, South Africa
20.12.01 Jermell Lamar Barnes W PTS 8 Rotterdam, Holland
12.02.02 Danny Williams L RTD 8 Bethnal Green
(British & Commonwealth Heavyweight Title Challenges)
09.05.02 Pele Reid W RSC 7 Leicester Square
(Vacant WBF European Heavyweight Title)
10.07.02 Garing Lane W PTS 6 Wembley
17.09.02 Derek McCafferty W PTS 8 Bethnal Green
12.12.02 Tamas Feheri W RSC 2 Leicester Square
24.01.03 Mike Holden W RSC 4 Sheffield
18.03.03 Mark Potter W RSC 3 Reading
(Southern Area Heavyweight Title Challenge. Elim. British Heavyweight Title)
10.06.03 Petr Horacek W CO 1 Sheffield
01.08.03 Colin Kenna W RSC 1 Bethnal Green
(Southern Area Heavyweight Title Defence)
26.09.03 Danny Williams L RSC 5 Reading
(British & Commonwealth Heavyweight Title Challenges)
24.01.04 Danny Williams W PTS 12 Wembley
(British & Commonwealth Heavyweight Title Challenges)
24.04.04 Matt Skelton L CO 12 Reading
(British & Commonwealth Heavyweight Title Defences)
10.09.04 Robert Sulgan W RSC 1 Bethnal Green
23.04.05 Cengiz Koc W PTS 10 Dortmund, Germany
(Vacant European Union Heavyweight Title)
Career: 34 contests, won 27, lost 7.

Micky Steeds   Les Clark

Micky Steeds

Isle of Dogs. *Born* London, 14 September, 1983
Heavyweight. Ht. 6'0"
Manager J. Rooney

18.09.03	Slick Miller W PTS 4 Mayfair	
21.02.04	Brodie Pearmaine W RSC 1 Brighton	
12.03.04	Paul King W PTS 6 Millwall	
02.12.04	Luke Simpkin W RSC 3 Crystal Palace	
18.02.05	Scott Gammer L PTS 6 Brighton	
24.04.05	Julius Francis W PTS 8 Leicester Square	
12.06.05	Mal Rice W PTS 6 Leicester Square	

Career: 7 contests, won 6, lost 1.

Dave Stewart

Ayr. *Born* Irvine, 5 September, 1975
Lightweight. Former Undefeated British Masters Lightweight Champion. Ht. 6'0¼"
Manager Self

15.02.01	Danny Connelly W PTS 6 Glasgow
27.04.01	Woody Greenaway W PTS 6 Glasgow
07.09.01	John Marshall W PTS 6 Glasgow
15.06.02	Dave Hinds W PTS 6 Tottenham
06.09.02	Pete Buckley W PTS 6 Bethnal Green
17.09.02	James Paisley W RSC 5 Bethnal Green
30.01.03	Scott Lawton W PTS 6 Piccadilly
26.04.03	Nigel Senior W RSC 2 Brentford
	(British Masters Lightweight Title Challenge)
27.05.03	Pete Buckley W PTS 4 Dagenham
01.08.03	Norman Dhalie W RTD 2 Bethnal Green
26.09.03	Jimmy Beech W RTD 2 Reading
14.11.03	Pete Buckley W PTS 4 Bethnal Green
16.04.04	Carl Allen W PTS 6 Dagenham
10.09.04	Bobby Vanzie W PTS 4 Wembley
10.04.05	Daniel Thorpe W RSC 3 Brentwood

Career: 15 contests, won 15.

Darren Stubbs

Oldham. *Born* Manchester, 16 October, 1971
S. Middleweight. Ht. 5'10"
Manager J. Doughty

02.06.02	Adam Cale W RSC 6 Shaw
21.06.02	Dean Cockburn L RSC 1 Leeds
17.11.02	Shpetim Hoti W RTD 2 Shaw
29.11.02	Jamie Wilson W PTS 6 Hull
09.03.03	Martin Thompson W RSC 3 Shaw
18.03.03	Jamie Hearn W RSC 3 Reading
08.06.03	Danny Grainger L RSC 2 Shaw
19.10.03	Paul Wesley W PTS 6 Shaw
29.02.04	Patrick Cito W PTS 6 Shaw
10.04.04	Alan Page L PTS 4 Manchester
20.04.04	Paul Owen W PTS 6 Sheffield
31.10.04	Nick Okoth W PTS 6 Shaw

Career: 12 contests, won 9, lost 3.

Lee Swaby

Lincoln. *Born* Lincoln, 14 May, 1976
Cruiserweight. Former Undefeated British Masters Cruiserweight Champion. Ht. 6'2"
Manager Self

29.04.97	Naveed Anwar W PTS 6 Manchester
19.06.97	Liam Richardson W RSC 4 Scunthorpe
30.10.97	Phil Ball W RSC 3 Newark
17.11.97	L. A. Williams W PTS 6 Manchester
02.02.98	Tim Redman L PTS 6 Manchester
27.02.98	John Wilson W CO 3 Glasgow
07.03.98	Phill Day L PTS 4 Reading
08.05.98	Chris P. Bacon L RSC 3 Manchester
17.07.98	Chris P. Bacon L PTS 6 Mere
19.09.98	Cathal O'Grady L RSC 1 Dublin
20.12.98	Mark Levy L RTD 5 Salford
23.06.99	Lee Archer W PTS 6 West Bromwich
04.09.99	Garry Delaney L PTS 8 Bethnal Green
03.10.99	Brian Gascoigne DREW 6 Chesterfield
11.12.99	Owen Beck L PTS 4 Liverpool
05.03.00	Kelly Oliver L PTS 10 Peterborough
	(Vacant British Masters Cruiserweight Title)
15.04.00	Mark Levy W PTS 4 Bethnal Green
12.05.00	Enzo Maccarinelli W CO 3 Swansea
26.05.00	Steffen Nielsen L PTS 4 Holbaek, Denmark
09.09.00	Tony Dowling W RSC 9 Newark
	(Vacant British Masters Cruiserweight Title)
05.02.01	Robert Norton L PTS 8 Hull
24.03.01	Crawford Ashley L PTS 8 Sheffield
30.04.01	Eamonn Glennon W PTS 6 Glasgow
02.06.01	Denzil Browne DREW 8 Wakefield
31.07.01	Stephane Allouane W PTS 4 Bethnal Green
13.09.01	Kevin Barrett W PTS 4 Sheffield
15.12.01	Chris Woollas W RSC 4 Sheffield
27.04.02	Mark Hobson L PTS 10 Huddersfield
	(Final Elim. British Cruiserweight Title)
03.08.02	Greg Scott-Briggs W RSC 4 Derby
05.12.02	Eamonn Glennon W PTS 4 Sheffield
24.01.03	Tommy Eastwood W PTS 6 Sheffield
10.06.03	Paul Bonson W PTS 6 Sheffield
05.09.03	Brodie Pearmaine W RTD 4 Sheffield
20.04.04	Lee Mountford W RSC 1 Sheffield
27.05.04	Mark Hobson L RSC 6 Huddersfield
	(British & Commonwealth Cruiserweight Title Challenges)
24.10.04	Denzil Browne W RSC 7 Sheffield
	(Elim. British Cruiserweight Title)

Career: 36 contests, won 20, drew 2, lost 14.

Richard Swallow

Northampton. *Born* Northampton, 10 February, 1970
Welterweight. Former British Masters Welterweight Champion. Ht. 5'8"
Manager Self

15.10.90	Richard O'Brien L RTD 1 Kettering
14.02.91	Dave Fallon W RSC 4 Southampton
06.03.91	Carl Brasier W PTS 6 Croydon
02.05.91	Mike Morrison W PTS 6 Northampton
24.03.92	Dean Bramhald W PTS 8 Wolverhampton
06.04.92	Dean Bramhald W PTS 6 Northampton
29.04.92	Chris Aston W RSC 3 Solihull
14.10.92	Wayne Shepherd W PTS 8 Stoke
24.11.92	Chris Mulcahy W PTS 6 Wolverhampton
20.01.93	Ray Newby W PTS 8 Solihull
03.03.93	Ray Newby L PTS 8 Solihull
11.06.93	Soren Sondergaard L RTD 3 Randers, Denmark
08.02.94	Billy McDougall W PTS 6 Wolverhampton
30.09.94	Bernard Paul W PTS 8 Bethnal Green
31.10.94	Carl Wright L PTS 6 Liverpool
09.12.94	Jason Rowland L RSC 2 Bethnal Green
14.02.95	Jason Beard L PTS 6 Bethnal Green
17.03.95	Frank Olsen L RSC 1 Copenhagen, Denmark
06.06.95	Anthony Maynard W RSC 2 Leicester
23.10.95	Shaun Stokes L PTS 6 Leicester
22.11.95	Gary Beardsley DREW 6 Sheffield
17.01.96	Shaun Stokes W PTS 6 Solihull
12.02.96	Nicky Bardle W RSC 4 Heathrow
28.10.96	Bobby Vanzie L PTS 6 Bradford
20.03.97	Anthony Maynard L PTS 6 Solihull
12.05.97	Nigel Bradley W PTS 6 Leicester
16.11.02	Lee Williamson W PTS 4 Coventry
30.11.02	Arv Mittoo W PTS 4 Coventry
09.12.02	Jon Hilton W PTS 6 Nottingham
09.02.03	Chris Saunders L PTS 4 Bradford
07.06.03	Tony Conroy L RSC 5 Coventry
	(Vacant Midlands Area Welterweight Title)
30.10.03	Jimmy Gould W PTS 10 Dudley
	(Vacant British Masters Welterweight Title)
19.02.04	Marcus Portman L PTS 10 Dudley
	(British Masters Welterweight Title Defence)
09.04.04	Ernie Smith W PTS 4 Rugby
26.04.04	Richard Inquieti W RSC 1 Cleethorpes
10.07.04	Brian Coleman L RSC 7 Coventry

Career: 36 contests, won 21, drew 1, lost 14.

(Cevdet) Jed Syger (Saygi)

Mile End. *Born* Iskendurun, Turkey, 15 July, 1983
Lightweight. Ht. 5'8"
Manager C. Magri

10.07.04	Frank Layz W PTS 4 Asbury Park, New Jersey, USA
11.09.04	Adam Allen W RSC 3 Philadelphia, Pennsylvania, USA
05.03.05	Jonathan Jones W PTS 4 Dagenham
30.04.05	Ian Reid W PTS 4 Dagenham
16.06.05	Junior Anderson W CO 2 Mayfair

Career: 5 contests, won 5.

Chas Symonds

Croydon. *Born* Croydon, 8 July, 1982
Welterweight. Former Undefeated British Masters Welterweight Champion. Former Southern Area Welterweight Champion. Ht. 5'6"
Manager F. Maloney

18.02.03	Darren Goode W RSC 2 Bethnal Green
08.04.03	Lee Bedell W PTS 4 Bethnal Green
03.06.03	Arv Mittoo W PTS 6 Bethnal Green
22.07.03	Pete Buckley W PTS 6 Bethnal Green
25.09.03	Ben Hudson W PTS 6 Bethnal Green
18.11.03	Ernie Smith W PTS 6 Bethnal Green
20.02.04	Dave Wakefield W RSC 5 Bethnal Green
24.04.04	Geraint Harvey W PTS 4 Reading
07.05.04	Robert Lloyd-Taylor W RTD 5 Bethnal Green
25.06.04	Brett James W RSC 4 Bethnal Green
	(Southern Area Welterweight Title Challenge)
24.09.04	Keith Jones W PTS 10 Bethnal Green
	(Vacant British Masters Welterweight Title)
25.02.05	Peter Dunn W PTS 4 Wembley
29.04.05	Ross Minter L RSC 3 Southwark
	(Southern Area Welterweight Title Defence)

Career: 13 contests, won 12, lost 1.

T

Gavin Tait

Carmarthen. *Born* Carmarthen, 2 March, 1976
L. Welterweight. Ht. 5'7"
Manager N. Hodges

07.06.04 Stuart Green L PTS 6 Glasgow
03.07.04 Justin Hicks W RSC 5 Bristol
05.10.04 Tristan Davies L PTS 6 Dudley
24.11.04 David Pereira L PTS 6 Mayfair
02.12.04 Chris Long L PTS 6 Bristol
07.04.05 Gary Coombes W RSC 3 Birmingham
27.05.05 Darren Johnstone L PTS 6 Motherwell
Career: 7 contests, won 2, lost 5.

Gavin Tait   Les Clark

(Mehrdud) Takaloo (Takalobigashi)

Margate. *Born* Iran, 23 September, 1975
L.Middleweight. Former Undefeated WBU
L.Middleweight Champion. Former
Undefeated IBF Inter-Continental
L.Middleweight Champion. Ht. 5'9"
Manager F. Warren

19.07.97 Harry Butler W RSC 1 Wembley
13.09.97 Michael Alexander W PTS 4 Millwall
15.11.97 Koba Kulu W RSC 3 Bristol
19.12.97 Mark Sawyers W PTS 4 Millwall
07.02.98 Jawaid Khaliq L RSC 4 Cheshunt
16.05.98 Anas Oweida W RSC 1 Bethnal Green
10.10.98 Michael Jones L PTS 6 Bethnal Green
30.01.99 Darren McInulty W RSC 5 Bethnal Green
03.04.99 Gareth Lovell W RSC 6 Kensington
26.06.99 Leigh Wicks W CO 3 Millwall
04.09.99 Carlton Williams W RSC 4 Bethnal Green
23.10.99 Prince Kasi Kaihau W RSC 3 Telford
29.01.00 Paul King W RSC 2 Manchester
08.04.00 Biagio Falcone W RTD 4 Bethnal Green
08.07.00 Ernie Smith W RSC 4 Widnes
12.08.00 Howard Clarke W PTS 12 Wembley

(Vacant IBF Inter-Continental L.Middleweight Title)
13.11.00 Jason Collins W RSC 2 Bethnal Green
24.02.01 James Lowther W PTS 12 Bethnal Green
(IBF Inter-Continental L.Middleweight Title Defence)
07.07.01 Anthony Farnell W RSC 1 Manchester
(Vacant WBU L.Middleweight Title)
22.09.01 Scott Dixon W CO 1 Bethnal Green
(WBU L. Middleweight Title Defence)
04.05.02 Gary Logan W RSC 10 Bethnal Green
(WBU L. Middleweight Title Defence)
17.08.02 Daniel Santos L PTS 12 Cardiff
(WBO L.Middleweight Title Challenge. WBU L.Middleweight Title Defence)
01.02.03 Jim Rock W RSC 9 Belfast
(Vacant WBU L. Middleweight Title)
24.05.03 Jose Rosa W PTS 12 Bethnal Green
(WBU L.Middleweight Title Defence)
13.09.03 Vladimir Borovski W CO 3 Newport
24.01.04 Eugenio Monteiro L PTS 8 Wembley
10.09.04 Wayne Alexander L RSC 2 Bethnal Green
(Vacant WBU L.Middleweight Title)
Career: 27 contests, won 22, lost 5.

Karl Taylor

Birmingham. *Born* Birmingham, 5 January, 1966
Welterweight. Former Undefeated
Midlands Area Lightweight Champion.
Ht. 5'5"
Manager Self

18.03.87 Steve Brown W PTS 6 Stoke
06.04.87 Paul Taylor L PTS 6 Southampton
12.06.87 Mark Begley W RSC 1 Leamington
18.11.87 Colin Lynch W RSC 4 Solihull
29.02.88 Peter Bradley L PTS 8 Birmingham
04.10.89 Mark Antony W CO 2 Stafford
30.10.89 Tony Feliciello L PTS 8 Birmingham
06.12.89 John Davison L PTS 8 Leicester
23.12.89 Regilio Tuur L RTD 1 Hoogvliet, Holland
22.02.90 Mark Ramsey L RSC 4 Hull
29.10.90 Steve Walker DREW 6 Birmingham
10.12.90 Elvis Parsley L PTS 6 Birmingham
16.01.91 Wayne Windle W PTS 8 Stoke
02.05.91 Billy Schwer L RSC 2 Northampton
25.07.91 Peter Till L RSC 4 Dudley
(Midlands Area Lightweight Title Challenge)
24.02.92 Charlie Kane L PTS 8 Glasgow
28.04.92 Richard Woolgar W PTS 6 Wolverhampton
29.05.92 Alan McDowall L PTS 6 Glasgow
25.07.92 Michael Armstrong L RSC 3 Manchester
02.11.92 Hugh Forde L PTS 6 Wolverhampton
23.11.92 Dave McHale L PTS 8 Glasgow
22.12.92 Patrick Gallagher L RSC 3 Mayfair
13.02.93 Craig Dermody L RSC 5 Manchester
31.03.93 Craig Dermody W PTS 6 Barking
07.06.93 Mark Geraghty W PTS 8 Glasgow
13.08.93 Giorgio Campanella L CO 6 Arezzo, Italy
05.10.93 Paul Harvey W PTS 6 Mayfair
21.10.93 Charles Shepherd L RTD 5 Bayswater
21.12.93 Patrick Gallagher L PTS 6 Mayfair
09.02.94 Alan Levene W RSC 2 Brentwood
01.03.94 Shaun Cogan L PTS 6 Dudley
15.03.94 Patrick Gallagher L PTS 6 Mayfair

18.04.94 Peter Till W PTS 10 Walsall
(Midlands Area Lightweight Title Challenge)
24.05.94 Michael Ayers DREW 8 Sunderland
12.11.94 P. J. Gallagher L PTS 6 Dublin
29.11.94 Dingaan Thobela W PTS 8 Cannock
31.03.95 Michael Ayers L RSC 8 Crystal Palace
(British Lightweight Title Challenge)
06.05.95 Cham Joof W PTS 8 Shepton Mallet
23.06.95 Poli Diaz L PTS 8 Madrid, Spain
02.09.95 Paul Ryan L RSC 3 Wembley
04.11.95 Carl Wright L PTS 6 Liverpool
15.12.95 Peter Richardson L PTS 8 Bethnal Green
23.01.96 Paul Knights DREW 6 Bethnal Green
05.03.96 Andy Holligan L PTS 6 Barrow
20.03.96 Mervyn Bennett W PTS 8 Cardiff
21.05.96 Malcolm Melvin L PTS 10 Edgbaston
(Midlands Area L. Welterweight Title Challenge)
07.10.96 Joshua Clottey L RSC 2 Lewisham
20.12.96 Anatoly Alexandrov L RSC 7 Bilbao, Spain
28.01.97 Eamonn Magee L PTS 6 Belfast
28.02.97 Mark Breslin L RSC 6 Kilmarnock
30.08.97 Gilbert Eastman L PTS 4 Cheshunt
25.10.97 Tontcho Tontchev L PTS 4 Queensferry
22.11.97 Bobby Vanzie L PTS 6 Manchester
18.04.98 Ricky Hatton L RSC 1 Manchester
18.07.98 James Hare L PTS 4 Sheffield
26.09.98 Oktay Urkal L PTS 8 Norwich
28.11.98 Junior Witter L PTS 4 Sheffield
06.03.99 George Scott L RSC 4 Southwark
15.05.99 Jon Thaxton L PTS 6 Sheffield
10.07.99 Eamonn Magee L RTD 3 Southwark
06.11.99 Alan Sebire W PTS 6 Widnes
15.11.99 Steve Murray L RSC 1 Bethnal Green
19.08.00 Iain Eldridge L PTS 4 Brentwood
04.09.00 Tomas Jansson L PTS 6 Manchester
16.09.00 Colin Lynes L PTS 6 Bethnal Green
09.12.00 David Walker L PTS 6 Southwark
10.02.01 Matthew Hatton L PTS 4 Widnes
10.03.01 Francis Barrett L RSC 3 Bethnal Green
10.04.01 Costas Katsantonis L PTS 4 Wembley
16.06.01 Brett James DREW 4 Wembley
15.09.01 David Barnes L PTS 4 Manchester
28.10.01 Babatunde Ajayi L PTS 4 Southwark
24.11.01 Ross Minter L PTS 4 Bethnal Green
15.12.01 Alexandra Vetoux L PTS 4 Wembley
12.02.02 Brett James DREW 4 Bethnal Green
11.03.02 Kevin McIntyre L PTS 4 Glasgow
04.05.02 Matthew Hatton L RSC 3 Bethnal Green
25.06.02 Rimell Taylor DREW 6 Rugby
20.07.02 Matthew Hatton L RTD 2 Bethnal Green
28.09.02 Michael Jennings L RSC 4 Manchester
16.11.02 Gavin Wake L PTS 4 Nottingham
30.11.02 Tony Conroy L PTS 4 Coventry
14.12.02 Alexander Vetoux L RTD 3 Newcastle
15.02.03 Ross Minter L PTS 6 Wembley
29.03.03 Alexander Vetoux L RSC 1 Portsmouth
08.05.03 Tony Doherty L PTS 4 Widnes
25.07.03 Lenny Daws L RTD 2 Norwich
06.10.03 Jonathan Woollins W PTS 6 Birmingham
29.10.03 Ajose Olusegun L PTS 6 Leicester Square
29.11.03 Gary Young L RSC 3 Renfrew
30.01.04 Lee McAllister L PTS 4 Dagenham
05.03.04 Oscar Hall L PTS 6 Darlington
27.03.04 Jamie Arthur L PTS 6 Edinburgh
06.05.04 Ashley Theophane L PTS 4 Barnsley

22.05.04 Tony Doherty L RTD 2 Widnes
03.09.04 Taz Jones L PTS 4 Newport
18.09.04 Karl Chiverton L PTS 6 Newark
26.09.04 Danny Johnston L PTS 6 Stoke
19.11.04 Tony Doherty L RSC 2 Bethnal Green
19.12.04 Kell Brook L PTS 6 Bolton
06.03.05 John Murray L PTS 6 Shaw
14.05.05 Lee McAllister L RTD 3 Aberdeen
26.06.05 Henry Castle L PTS 6 Southampton
Career: 103 contests, won 16, drew 6, lost 81.

Nicki Taylor
Askern. *Born* Doncaster, 6 July, 1979
L.Heavyweight. Ht. 5'11"
Manager M. Scriven

20.09.04 Sandy Robb L RSC 5 Glasgow
24.04.05 Hastings Rasani L RTD 4 Askern
18.06.05 Rod Anderton L RSC 4 Barnsley
Career: 3 contests, lost 3.

Luke Teague
Grimsby. *Born* Grimsby, 7 December, 1972
L. Middleweight. Ht. 6'1"
Manager S. Fleet/S. Pollard

22.09.03 Lance Hall W RSC 1 Cleethorpes
14.11.03 William Webster W PTS 6 Hull
15.12.03 Simon Hopkins DREW 6 Cleethorpes
20.09.04 Brian Coleman W PTS 6 Cleethorpes
30.09.04 Brian Coleman W PTS 6 Hull
13.12.04 Ernie Smith W PTS 6 Cleethorpes
Career: 6 contests, won 5, drew 1.

Matt Teague
Grimsby. *Born* Grimsby, 14 July, 1980
S.Featherweight. Ht. 5'9"
Manager S. Fleet/S. Pollard

21.11.02 Andy Robinson W RTD 3 Hull
11.12.02 Jason Nesbitt W PTS 6 Hull
17.04.03 Martin Hardcastle L PTS 6 Hull
02.06.03 Henry Janes W PTS 6 Cleethorpes
22.09.03 Tom Price W PTS 6 Cleethorpes
14.11.03 Kristian Laight W PTS 6 Hull
15.12.03 Dave Hinds W PTS 6 Cleethorpes
14.06.04 Dean Ward W PTS 6 Cleethorpes
20.09.04 Jason Nesbitt W PTS 6 Cleethorpes
13.12.04 Buster Dennis L PTS 6 Cleethorpes
Career: 10 contests, won 8, lost 2.

Daniel Teasdale   Les Clark

Daniel Teasdale
Rotherham. *Born* Rotherham, 4 September, 1982
L.Heavyweight. Ht. 6'1"
Manager T. Gilmour/G. Rhodes

23.11.03 Patrick Cito NC 1 Rotherham
10.02.04 Ojay Abrahams W PTS 6 Barnsley
01.04.04 Tomas da Silva W PTS 4 Bethnal Green
06.05.04 Ojay Abrahams W PTS 4 Barnsley
22.04.05 Jon Ibbotson L RSC 1 Barnsley
Career: 5 contests, won 3, lost 1, no contest 1.

George Telfer
Hawick. *Born* Hawick, 26 May, 1979
Welterweight. Ht. 5'7"
Manager K. Morrison

14.03.03 Vince Baldassara W PTS 4 Glasgow
22.03.03 Tony Montana L PTS 4 Renfrew
12.07.03 Pete Buckley W PTS 4 Renfrew
25.10.03 James Gorman W PTS 4 Edinburgh
07.12.03 Dave Hill W RSC 4 Glasgow
06.03.04 Nigel Wright L RSC 3 Renfrew
29.10.04 Ivor Bonavic W PTS 4 Renfrew
03.12.04 Ernie Smith W PTS 4 Edinburgh
Career: 8 contests, won 6, lost 2.

Alan Temple
Hartlepool. *Born* Hartlepool, 21 October, 1972
British Masters Lightweight Champion. Ht. 5'8"
Manager Self

29.09.94 Stevie Bolt W CO 2 Bethnal Green
22.11.94 Phil Found W PTS 6 Bristol
07.02.95 Brian Coleman W PTS 6 Ipswich
27.04.95 Everald Williams L PTS 6 Bethnal Green
29.09.95 Kevin McKillan W PTS 6 Hartlepool
23.11.95 Rudy Valentino L RSC 3 Marton
02.03.96 Tony Foster W PTS 6 Newcastle
08.06.96 Micky Hall W RSC 2 Newcastle
20.09.96 Scott Dixon L PTS 4 Glasgow
24.10.96 Billy Schwer L PTS 8 Wembley
04.12.96 Harry Escott W PTS 8 Hartlepool
12.02.97 Tanveer Ahmed L RSC 8 Glasgow
(*Elim. British Lightweight Title*)
13.02.98 Bobby Vanzie L CO 3 Seaham
(*Elim. British Lightweight Title*)
21.03.98 Michael Ayers L RSC 2 Bethnal Green
31.10.98 Alan Bosworth W PTS 6 Basingstoke
20.02.99 Ivan Walker W PTS 4 Thornaby
05.03.99 David Burke L PTS 8 Liverpool
01.05.99 Jason Rowland L PTS 6 Crystal Palace
22.05.99 Eamonn Magee L CO 3 Belfast
26.06.99 Steve McLevy W RSC 6 Glasgow
11.09.99 Wayne Rigby W PTS 8 Sheffield
02.11.99 Souleymane M'Baye L RTD 7 Ciudad Real, Spain
12.08.00 Steve Murray L RSC 2 Wembley
(*IBF Inter-Continental Lightweight Title Challenge. Elim. British Lightweight Title*)
26.03.01 Jonathan Thaxton L PTS 4 Wembley
04.06.01 Gary Hibbert W PTS 6 Hartlepool
21.07.01 Junior Witter L CO 5 Sheffield
10.11.01 Colin Dunne L RSC 7 Wembley
09.03.02 Gary Hibbert L RSC 1 Manchester
26.10.02 Leo O'Reilly W RSC 4 Maesteg
21.12.02 Darren Melville L PTS 8 Millwall

01.05.04 Silence Saheed W DIS 8 Gravesend
(*Vacant British Masters Lightweight Title*)
17.12.04 David Burke L RSC 4 Liverpool
27.05.05 Pete Buckley W PTS 4 Spennymoor
Career: 33 contests, won 15, lost 18.

John-Paul Temple
Brighton. *Born* London, 30 May, 1973
L.Middleweight. Ht. 5'11"
Manager R. Davies

11.02.97 Mark O'Callaghan W PTS 6 Bethnal Green
17.03.97 Les Frost W CO 4 Mayfair
24.04.97 Chris Lyons W PTS 6 Mayfair
23.10.97 Chris Lyons W PTS 8 Mayfair
26.03.98 Trevor Smith L RSC 5 Piccadilly
28.04.98 Chris Price L PTS 6 Brentford
05.10.99 Jason Hall L PTS 6 Bloomsbury
25.02.00 Daniel James L PTS 10 Newmarket
(*Vacant Southern Area L.Welterweight Title*)
21.11.04 Neil Jarmolinski DREW 4 Bracknell
03.12.04 Barrie Lee L PTS 4 Edinburgh
30.04.05 Danny Goode L PTS 4 Dagenham
26.06.05 Danny Goode L PTS 4 Southampton
Career: 12 contests, won 4, drew 1, lost 7.

(Eranos) Erik Teymour (Teymurazov)
Canning Town. *Born* Moscow, Russia, 1 March, 1979
WBU S.Middleweight Champion. Ht. 5'8 1/2"
Manager Self

14.07.01 Dean Ashton W RSC 2 Liverpool
31.07.01 Leigh Wicks W RSC 1 Bethnal Green
28.09.01 Kreshnik Qato W PTS 6 Millwall
23.11.01 Harry Butler W RSC 2 Bethnal Green
16.12.01 Howard Clarke W PTS 6 Southwark
15.03.02 Darren Littlewood W RSC 1 Millwall
26.04.02 Sam Soliman L PTS 8 Wembley
21.05.02 Toks Owoh W PTS 6 Custom House
25.10.02 Donatas Bondarevas W RSC 3 Millwall
30.11.02 Varuzhan Davtyan W PTS 6 Liverpool
08.02.03 Radcliffe Green W RTD 1 Norwich
28.03.03 Paul Bonson W PTS 6 Millwall
24.05.03 Varuzhan Davtyan W PTS 4 Bethnal Green
13.09.03 Vage Kocharyan W PTS 4 Newport
06.12.03 Farai Musiiwa W PTS 6 Cardiff
01.04.04 Hussain Osman W RSC 8 Bethnal Green
08.07.04 Lee Woodruff W RSC 2 The Strand
16.10.04 Artem Vychkin W RSC 2 Dagenham
24.11.04 Nathan King W PTS 12 Mayfair
(*Vacant WBU S.Middleweight Title*)
Career: 19 contests, won 18, lost 1.

Jonathan Thaxton
Norwich. *Born* Norwich, 10 September, 1974
WBF Lightweight Champion. Former Southern Area, IBF & WBO Inter-Continental L.Welterweight Champion. Ht. 5'6"
Manager Self

09.12.92 Scott Smith W PTS 6 Stoke

03.03.93 Dean Hiscox W PTS 6 Solihull
17.03.93 John O. Johnson W PTS 6 Stoke
23.06.93 Brian Coleman W PTS 8 Gorleston
22.09.93 John Smith W PTS 6 Wembley
07.12.93 Dean Hollington W RSC 3 Bethnal Green
10.03.94 B. F. Williams W RSC 4 Watford
(Vacant Southern Area L. Welterweight Title)
18.11.94 Keith Marner L PTS 10 Bracknell
(Southern Area L. Welterweight Title Defence)
26.05.95 David Thompson W RSC 6 Norwich
23.06.95 Delroy Leslie W PTS 6 Bethnal Green
12.08.95 Rene Prins L PTS 8 Zaandam, Holland
08.12.95 Colin Dunne L RSC 5 Bethnal Green
(Vacant Southern Area Lightweight Title)
20.01.96 John O. Johnson W RSC 4 Mansfield
13.02.96 Paul Ryan W RSC 1 Bethnal Green
25.06.96 Mark Elliot W CO 5 Mansfield
(Vacant IBF Inter-Continental L. Welterweight Title)
14.09.96 Bernard Paul W PTS 12 Sheffield
(Vacant WBO Inter-Continental L. Welterweight Title)
27.03.97 Paul Burke W RSC 9 Norwich
(IBF & WBO Inter-Continental L. Welterweight Title Defences)
28.06.97 Gagik Chachatrian W RSC 2 Norwich
(IBF & WBO Inter-Continental L. Welterweight Title Defences)
29.11.97 Rimvidas Billius W PTS 12 Norwich
(IBF & WBO Inter-Continental L. Welterweight Title Defences)
26.09.98 Emanuel Burton L RSC 7 Norwich
(IBF & WBO Inter-Continental L. Welterweight Title Defences)
15.05.99 Karl Taylor W PTS 6 Sheffield
07.08.99 Brian Coleman W PTS 6 Dagenham
15.11.99 Jason Rowland L RSC 5 Bethnal Green
(British L. Welterweight Title Challenge)
15.07.00 Kimoun Kouassi W RSC 3 Norwich
21.10.00 Ricky Hatton L PTS 12 Wembley
(Vacant British L.Welterweight Title)
26.03.01 Alan Temple W PTS 4 Wembley
28.07.01 David Kirk W PTS 4 Wembley
09.02.02 Eamonn Magee L RSC 6 Manchester
(Commonwealth L.Welterweight Title Challenge)
13.04.02 Chill John W RSC 2 Norwich
15.06.02 Marc Waelkens W RSC 7 Norwich
21.09.02 Viktor Baranov W RSC 1 Norwich
09.10.04 Silence Saheed W PTS 6 Norwich
13.12.04 Carl Allen W RSC 1 Birmingham
09.04.05 Christophe De Busillet W CO 4 Norwich
(Vacant WBF Lightweight Title)
Career: 34 contests, won 27, lost 7.

Ashley Theophane

Kilburn. *Born* London, 20 August, 1980
L. Welterweight. Ht. 5'7"
Manager I. Akay/D. Coldwell

03.06.03 Lee Bedell W RSC 4 Bethnal Green
22.07.03 Brian Coleman W PTS 6 Bethnal Green
25.04.04 David Kirk W PTS 6 Nottingham
06.05.04 Karl Taylor W PTS 4 Barnsley
05.06.04 Chris Brophy W RSC 3 Bethnal Green
19.06.04 Arv Mittoo W PTS 4 Muswell Hill
02.12.04 Keith Jones W PTS 6 Crystal Palace

26.03.05 Judex Meemea L PTS 6 Hackney
24.04.05 David Kehoe W PTS 4 Leicester Square
12.06.05 Jus Wallie W PTS 4 Leicester Square
Career: 10 contests, won 9, lost 1.

Ashley Theophane   Les Clark

Matthew Thirlwall

Bermondsey. *Born* Middlesbrough, 28 November, 1980
Middleweight. Ht. 5'9½"
Manager Self

16.03.02 William Webster W RSC 1 Bethnal Green
10.05.02 Leigh Wicks W PTS 4 Bethnal Green
23.08.02 Harry Butler W RSC 3 Bethnal Green
25.10.02 Jason Collins W RSC 5 Bethnal Green
21.12.02 Howard Clarke W PTS 6 Dagenham
28.01.03 Gary Beardsley L PTS 6 Nottingham
16.04.03 Gary Beardsley W PTS 6 Nottingham
27.05.03 Leigh Wicks W PTS 6 Dagenham
04.10.03 Dean Powell W RSC 2 Muswell Hill
11.12.03 Harry Butler W PTS 6 Bethnal Green
12.03.04 Patrick Cito W RSC 3 Nottingham
24.09.04 Jason Collins L PTS 6 Nottingham
Career: 12 contests, won 10, lost 2.

Courtney Thomas

Taunton. *Born* Taunton, 17 March, 1976
L. Middleweight. Ht. 5'8"
Manager C. Sanigar

08.04.05 Neil Jarmolinski W PTS 6 Bristol
29.04.05 Geraint Harvey W PTS 6 Plymouth
Career: 2 contests, won 2.

Jeff Thomas

St Annes. *Born* Holland, 30 October, 1981
Lightweight. Ht. 5'10"
Manager Self

09.12.01 Peter Allen W PTS 6 Blackpool
20.07.02 Pete Buckley W PTS 4 Bethnal Green
03.08.02 Gareth Wiltshaw W DIS 2 Blackpool
26.10.02 Dave Curran W RSC 6 Wigan
28.04.03 Daniel Thorpe W PTS 6 Cleethorpes
09.05.03 Carl Allen DREW 6 Doncaster
08.06.03 Norman Dhalie W PTS 6 Shaw

06.09.03 Lee McAllister L PTS 10 Aberdeen
(Vacant British Masters L.Welterweight Title)
07.12.03 Martin Hardcastle L PTS 10 Bradford
(Vacant British Masters S.Featherweight Title)
03.07.04 Anthony Hanna W PTS 6 Blackpool
29.10.04 Ricky Burns L PTS 4 Renfrew
25.02.05 Steve Murray L RTD 3 Wembley
Career: 12 contests, won 7, drew 1, lost 4.

Jeff Thomas   Les Clark

(Adrian) Carl Thompson

Manchester. *Born* Manchester, 26 May, 1964
IBO Cruiserweight Champion. Former WBO Cruiserweight Champion. Former Undefeated European, British & WBC International Cruiserweight Champion. Ht. 6'0"
Manager Self

06.06.88 Darren McKenna W RSC 2 Manchester
11.10.88 Paul Sheldon W PTS 6 Wolverhampton
13.02.89 Steve Osborne W PTS 6 Manchester
07.03.89 Sean O'Phoenix W RSC 4 Manchester
04.04.89 Keith Halliwell W RSC 1 Manchester
04.05.89 Tenko Ernie W CO 4 Mayfair
12.06.89 Steve Osborne W PTS 8 Manchester
11.07.89 Peter Brown W RSC 5 Batley
31.10.89 Crawford Ashley L RSC 6 Manchester
(Vacant Central Area L. Heavyweight Title)
21.04.90 Francis Wanyama L PTS 6 St Amandsberg, Belgium
07.03.91 Terry Dixon W PTS 8 Basildon
01.04.91 Yawe Davis L RSC 2 Monaco, Monte Carlo
04.09.91 Nicky Piper W RSC 3 Bethnal Green
04.06.92 Steve Lewsam W RSC 8 Cleethorpes
(Vacant British Cruiserweight Title)
17.02.93 Arthur Weathers W CO 2 Bethnal Green
(Vacant WBC International Cruiserweight Title)
31.03.93 Steve Harvey W CO 1 Bethnal Green
25.07.93 Willie Jake W CO 3 Oldham

02.02.94	Massimiliano Duran W CO 8 Ferrara, Italy *(European Cruiserweight Title Challenge)*
14.06.94	Akim Tafer W RSC 6 Epernay, France *(European Cruiserweight Title Defence)*
10.09.94	Dionisio Lazario W RSC 1 Birmingham
13.10.94	Tim Knight W RSC 5 Paris, France
10.06.95	Ralf Rocchigiani L RSC 11 Manchester *(Vacant WBO Cruiserweight Title)*
13.04.96	Albert Call W RTD 4 Wythenshawe
09.11.96	Jason Nicholson W PTS 8 Manchester
26.04.97	Keith McMurray W RSC 4 Zurich, Switzerland
04.10.97	Ralf Rocchigiani W PTS 12 Hannover, Germany *(WBO Cruiserweight Title Challenge)*
18.04.98	Chris Eubank W PTS 12 Manchester *(WBO Cruiserweight Title Defence)*
18.07.98	Chris Eubank W RSC 9 Sheffield *(WBO Cruiserweight Title Defence)*

27.03.99	Johnny Nelson L RSC 5 Derby *(WBO Cruiserweight Title Defence)*
03.12.99	Terry Dunstan W CO 12 Peterborough *(Vacant British Cruiserweight Title)*
13.05.00	Alain Simon W RSC 6 Barnsley *(Vacant European Cruiserweight Title)*
25.09.00	Alexei Illiin W RSC 2 Barnsley *(European Cruiserweight Title Defence)*
03.02.01	Uriah Grant W RSC 5 Manchester *(IBO Cruiserweight Title Challenge)*
26.11.01	Ezra Sellers L RSC 4 Manchester *(IBO Cruiserweight Title Defence)*
10.06.03	Phill Day W CO 4 Sheffield
05.09.03	Hastings Rasani W RSC 1 Sheffield
07.11.03	Paul Bonson W PTS 6 Sheffield
06.02.04	Sebastiaan Rothmann W RSC 9 Sheffield *(IBO Cruiserweight Title Challenge)*
10.09.04	David Haye W RSC 5 Wembley *(IBO Cruiserweight Title Defence)*

Career: 39 contests, won 33, lost 6.

Gary Thompson

Blackburn. *Born* Darwen, 22 June, 1981
Cruiserweight. Ht. 5'9"
Manager Self

22.09.01	Michael Thompson L RSC 3 Newcastle
16.11.01	Adam Cale W PTS 6 Preston
10.12.01	Rob Galloway W PTS 6 Bradford
23.12.01	Lee Whitehead L PTS 4 Salford
08.02.02	Shane White DREW 6 Preston
17.02.02	Lee Whitehead DREW 6 Salford
19.04.02	Lee Mountford DREW 4 Darlington
11.05.02	Tony Dowling L RSC 3 Newark
18.10.02	Michael Thompson L PTS 4 Hartlepool
26.10.02	Paul Richardson DREW 6 Wigan
02.12.02	Danny Thornton L PTS 6 Leeds
03.02.03	Nate Joseph L PTS 4 Bradford
28.02.03	Lee Mountford L PTS 6 Irvine
07.06.03	Carl Wright L RTD 2 Coventry
06.05.04	Simon Francis L PTS 4 Barnsley
15.05.04	Simeon Cover L PTS 6 Aberdeen
08.06.04	Simon Francis L RTD 2 Sheffield
04.11.04	Simeon Cover L PTS 6 Piccadilly
06.12.04	Nate Joseph W PTS 6 Bradford
20.02.05	Neil Dawson L PTS 6 Sheffield
11.03.05	Dean Cockburn L RSC 4 Doncaster
22.04.05	John Anthony L PTS 4 Barnsley
29.04.05	Junior MacDonald L RSC 1 Southwark
01.06.05	Danny Thornton L PTS 4 Leeds

Career: 24 contests, won 3, drew 4, lost 17.

Gary Thornhill

Liverpool. *Born* Liverpool, 11 February, 1968
Featherweight. Former Undefeated British Featherweight Champion. Former Undefeated WBO Inter-Continental & Central Area S. Featherweight Champion. Ht. 5'6½"
Manager S. Vaughan

27.02.93	Brian Hickey W CO 4 Ellesmere Port
02.07.93	Dougie Fox W CO 1 Liverpool
30.10.93	Miguel Matthews W PTS 6 Chester
01.12.93	Wayne Windle W PTS 6 Stoke
25.02.94	Edward Lloyd DREW 6 Chester
06.05.94	Derek Amory W RSC 1 Liverpool
25.03.95	Craig Kelley W PTS 6 Chester
20.04.95	Michael Hermon W RSC 6 Liverpool
30.06.95	Chip O'Neill W RTD 3 Liverpool
04.11.95	Kid McAuley W PTS 6 Liverpool
08.12.95	Des Gargano W RTD 2 Liverpool *(Vacant Central Area S. Featherweight Title)*
13.04.96	Dominic McGuigan W RSC 3 Liverpool
25.06.96	Chris Jickells W PTS 6 Stevenage
11.12.96	Justin Juuko L RSC 8 Southwark *(Commonwealth S. Featherweight Title Challenge)*
13.12.97	Pete Buckley W PTS 6 Sheffield
06.06.98	Dean Pithie W CO 8 Liverpool *(WBO Inter-Continental S. Featherweight Title Challenge)*
19.12.98	Steve Conway W RSC 9 Liverpool *(WBO Inter-Continental S. Featherweight Title Defence)*
07.08.99	Chris Jickells W RSC 4 Dagenham
04.09.99	Michael Gomez L RSC 2 Bethnal Green *(Vacant British S. Featherweight Title)*
06.11.99	Marc Smith W PTS 6 Widnes
11.12.99	Pete Buckley W PTS 6 Liverpool
29.02.00	Benny Jones W PTS 6 Widnes

Carl Thompson   Les Clark

16.05.00	Richie Wenton W RTD 8 Warrington

(Vacant British Featherweight Title)

16.05.00   Richie Wenton W RTD 8 Warrington
(Vacant British Featherweight Title)
09.06.01   Pete Buckley W PTS 4 Bethnal Green
15.09.01   Scott Harrison L RSC 5 Manchester
*(British & Commonwealth
Featherweight Title Challenges)*
06.09.02   Rakhim Mingaleev W PTS 6 Glasgow
05.10.02   Nicky Cook L RSC 7 Liverpool
*(WBF Inter-Continental
S.Featherweight Title Challenge)*
29.08.03   Jason Nesbitt W CO 1 Liverpool
22.05.04   Daniel Thorpe W RSC 4 Manchester
01.10.04   Stephen Foster L RSC 9 Manchester
*(English Featherweight Title
Challenge)*

Career: 30 contests, won 24, drew 1, lost 5.

Danny Thornton

Leeds. *Born* Leeds, 20 July, 1978
Middleweight. Former Undefeated Central
Area Middleweight Champion. Ht. 5'10"
Manager Self

06.10.97   Pedro Carragher L PTS 6 Bradford
13.11.97   Shaun O'Neill DREW 6 Bradford
08.12.97   Shaun O'Neill DREW 6 Bradford
09.02.98   Roy Chipperfield W RSC 4 Bradford
17.03.98   Patrick J. Maxwell L PTS 6 Sheffield
30.03.98   Mark Owens W PTS 6 Bradford
15.05.98   Danny Bell W PTS 6 Nottingham
15.06.98   Jimmy Hawk W PTS 6 Bradford
12.10.98   Wayne Shepherd W PTS 6 Bradford
21.02.99   Shaun O'Neill W PTS 6 Bradford
25.04.99   Matt Scriven W RSC 4 Leeds
14.06.99   Martin Thompson W PTS 6 Bradford
18.10.99   Paul Henry W PTS 4 Bradford
14.11.99   Dean Ashton W PTS 4 Bradford
06.12.99   Lee Blundell L PTS 6 Bradford
05.02.00   Steve Roberts L PTS 6 Bethnal Green
25.03.00   Lee Molloy W RSC 2 Liverpool
06.06.00   Joe Townsley L RSC 7 Motherwell
*(IBO Inter-Continental
L. Middleweight Title Challenge)*
30.11.00   Lee Blundell L RSC 8 Blackpool
*(Vacant Central Area L. Middleweight
Title)*
20.03.01   Ian Toby W PTS 8 Leeds
13.11.01   Matt Galer L RSC 4 Leeds
02.12.02   Gary Thompson W PTS 6 Leeds
13.05.03   Kreshnik Qato L PTS 6 Leeds
06.06.03   Jason Collins W PTS 10 Hull
*(Vacant Central Area Middleweight
Title)*
28.11.03   Jason Collins W PTS 10 Hull
*(Central Area Middleweight Title
Defence)*
10.02.04   Mo W PTS 6 Barnsley
08.05.04   Scott Dann L RSC 3 Bristol
(Vacant English Middleweight Title)
14.05.05   Simeon Cover DREW 6 Aberdeen
01.06.05   Gary Thompson W PTS 4 Leeds
Career: 29 contests, won 17, drew 3, lost 9.

Daniel Thorpe

Sheffield. *Born* Sheffield, 24 September,
1977
Lightweight. Former Central Area
Lightweight Champion. Ht. 5'7½"
Manager Self

07.09.01   Brian Gifford DREW 4 Bethnal Green
24.09.01   Ram Singh W RSC 4 Cleethorpes
17.11.01   Mally McIver L PTS 6 Dewsbury
10.12.01   Jason Gonzales W RSC 2 Birmingham
17.12.01   Joel Viney L RSC 2 Cleethorpes
11.02.02   Gareth Wiltshaw L PTS 6 Shrewsbury
04.03.02   Dave Travers W PTS 6 Birmingham
13.04.02   Jackson Williams L PTS 6 Norwich
11.05.02   Dean Scott W RSC 1 Chesterfield
21.05.02   Chris McDonagh L PTS 6 Custom
House
08.06.02   Gary Young L RSC 1 Renfrew
12.07.02   Chill John L PTS 4 Southampton
21.07.02   John Marshall L RSC 1 Salford
22.09.02   Albi Hunt L PTS 6 Southwark
05.10.02   Gavin Down L RSC 2 Chesterfield
17.11.02   Nadeem Siddique L PTS 4 Bradford
29.11.02   Pete Buckley W PTS 6 Hull
21.12.02   Billy Corcoran L CO 2 Dagenham
16.02.03   Eddie Nevins L RSC 8 Salford
*(Vacant Central Area S.Featherweight
Title)*
22.03.03   Jamie Arthur L PTS 4 Renfrew
29.03.03   Danny Hunt L PTS 6 Portsmouth
12.04.03   Jackson Williams L PTS 6 Norwich
19.04.03   Steve Mullin W RSC 1 Liverpool
28.04.03   Jeff Thomas L PTS 6 Cleethorpes
08.05.03   Andy Morris L PTS 4 Widnes
08.06.03   Choi Tseveenpurev L PTS 8 Shaw
20.06.03   Colin Toohey L PTS 6 Liverpool
28.06.03   Gavin Rees L RSC 1 Cardiff
03.08.03   Joel Viney L PTS 6 Stalybridge
06.09.03   Joel Viney W PTS 6 Aberdeen
13.09.03   Sean Hughes L PTS 6 Wakefield
21.09.03   Chris Long W PTS 6 Bristol
12.10.03   Baz Carey DREW 6 Sheffield
19.10.03   Charles Shepherd L PTS 6 Shaw
27.10.03   Nadeem Siddique L PTS 6 Glasgow
06.11.03   Lee Beavis L PTS 4 Dagenham
07.12.03   Mally McIver W PTS 10 Bradford
*(Vacant Central Area Lightweight
Title)*
21.12.03   Pete Buckley W PTS 6 Bolton
26.02.04   Andy Morris L RSC 3 Widnes
03.04.04   Jason Nesbitt W PTS 6 Sheffield
23.04.04   Dave Hinds W PTS 6 Leicester
07.05.04   Stefy Bull L PTS 10 Doncaster
*(Central Area Lightweight Title
Defence)*
22.05.04   Gary Thornhill L RSC 4 Manchester
03.07.04   Joel Viney W RSC 1 Blackpool
10.09.04   Mickey Bowden W PTS 6 Wembley
18.09.04   Carl Greaves L PTS 6 Newark
01.10.04   Steve Bell L PTS 6 Manchester
08.10.04   Ricky Burns L PTS 6 Glasgow
16.10.04   Ryan Barrett L PTS 4 Dagenham
29.10.04   Adnan Amar L PTS 4 Worksop
06.11.04   Baz Carey W PTS 6 Coventry
26.11.04   John Murray L RSC 2 Altrincham
13.02.05   Lee McAllister L PTS 4 Bradford
04.03.05   Femi Fehintola L PTS 6 Rotherham
10.04.05   Dave Stewart L RSC 3 Brentwood
14.05.05   Tye Williams L RSC 3 Aberdeen
26.05.05   Baz Carey W PTS 6 Mayfair
03.06.05   Nadeem Siddique L PTS 6 Hull
24.06.05   James Gorman L PTS 6 Belfast
Career: 59 contests, won 16, drew 2, lost 41.

Neil Tidman

Bedworth. *Born* Nuneaton, 16 April, 1978
S.Middleweight. Ht. 5'10"
Manager O. Delargy

18.06.05   Lee Williamson W PTS 6 Coventry
Career: 1 contest, won 1.

Kevin Townsley

Cleland. *Born* Lanark, 21 September, 1982
S.Bantamweight. Ht. 5'8"
Manager T. Gilmour

27.05.05   Abdul Mougharbel W PTS 6
Motherwell

Career: 1 contest, won 1.

Choi Tseveenpurev

Oldham. *Born* Mongolia, 6 October, 1971
British Masters Featherweight Champion.
Ht. 5'5¾"
Manager J. Doughty

22.11.96   Jeun-Tae Kim W CO 8 Seoul, South
Korea
19.08.98   Veeraphol Sahaprom L PTS 10
Bangkok, Thailand
02.10.98   Surapol Sithnaruepol W CO 1
Bangkok, Thailand
07.01.99   Ekarat 13Reintower W CO 2 Krabi,
Thailand
18.04.99   Bulan Bugiarso L PTS 12 Jakarta,
Indonesia
01.05.99   Bulan Bugiarso L PTS 12 Kalimanton,
Indonesia
12.08.99   Jiao Hasabayar W RSC 4 Ulan-Bator,
Mongolia
22.08.99   Con Roksa W CO 3 Seinyeng, China
22.08.99   Thongdang Sorvoraphin W CO 4
Seinyeng, China
21.05.00   David Jeffrey W RSC 2 Shaw
24.09.00   Billy Smith W RTD 2 Shaw
03.12.00   Chris Williams W PTS 4 Shaw
27.04.01   Willie Limond L PTS 6 Glasgow
23.09.01   Steve Hanley W PTS 6 Shaw
06.10.01   Livinson Ruiz W PTS 4 Manchester
09.12.01   Kevin Gerowski W RSC 5 Shaw
*(Vacant British Masters Featherweight
Title)*
22.03.02   Chris Emanuele W PTS 4 Coventry
02.06.02   John Mackay W RSC 5 Shaw
17.11.02   Peter Allen W RSC 4 Shaw
09.03.03   Jason Nesbitt W PTS 8 Shaw
08.06.03   Daniel Thorpe W PTS 8 Shaw
29.02.04   John Mackay W RSC 3 Shaw
13.03.04   Lehlohonolo Ledwaba L PTS 8
Copenhagen, Denmark
06.05.04   Kevin O'Hara W PTS 8 Barnsley
10.07.04   Harry Ramogoadi W RTD 6 Coventry
*(British Masters Featherweight Title
Defence)*
06.03.05   Harry Ramogoadi W RSC 5 Shaw
*(British Masters Featherweight Title
Defence)*

Career: 26 contests, won 21, lost 5.

(Jeremy) Jed Tytler

Hartlepool. *Born* Beverley, 8 September,
1972
Middleweight. Ht. 5'9¼"
Manager T. O'Neill/D. Coldwell

16.03.01   James Lee L RSC 3 Portsmouth
24.05.01   Charden Ansoula L RSC 2 Kensington
20.10.03   Jamie Coyle L RSC 2 Glasgow
08.12.03   Robert Burton L PTS 6 Barnsley
07.02.04   Martin Concepcion L RSC 2 Bethnal
Green
06.02.05   Steve Ede L RSC 4 Southampton
25.04.05   Jon Foster W RSC 2 Cleethorpes
Career: 7 contests, won 1, lost 6.

UV

Bobby Vanzie

Bradford. *Born* Bradford, 11 January, 1974
Lightweight. Former British &
Commonwealth Lightweight Champion.
Former Undefeated Central Area
Lightweight Champion. Ht. 5'5"
Manager J. Doughty

22.05.95 Alan Peacock W RSC 1 Morecambe
29.10.95 Steve Tuckett W RSC 2 Shaw
14.11.95 John Smith W PTS 6 Bury
07.03.96 John Smith W PTS 6 Bradford
02.06.96 Anthony Campbell W PTS 6 Shaw
28.10.96 Richard Swallow W PTS 6 Bradford
24.02.97 Mark Ramsey DREW 8 Glasgow
08.06.97 C. J. Jackson W RSC 3 Shaw
23.10.97 Stuart Rimmer W RTD 8 Mayfair
　　　　　*(Vacant Central Area Lightweight
　　　　　Title)*
22.11.97 Karl Taylor W PTS 6 Manchester
13.02.98 Alan Temple W CO 3 Seaham
　　　　　(Elim. British Lightweight Title)
01.06.98 Gary Flear W PTS 6 Manchester
17.10.98 Wayne Rigby W RSC 10 Manchester
　　　　　(British Lightweight Title Challenge)
01.04.99 Anthony Campbell W PTS 12
　　　　　Birmingham
　　　　　(British Lightweight Title Defence)
28.05.99 Athanus Nzau W RSC 10 Liverpool
　　　　　*(Vacant Commonwealth Lightweight
　　　　　Title)*
13.09.99 Brian Coleman W PTS 6 Bethnal
　　　　　Green
04.12.99 Vincent Howard W PTS 12
　　　　　Manchester
　　　　　*(Commonwealth Lightweight Title
　　　　　Defence)*
21.02.00 Stephen Smith W RSC 9 Southwark
　　　　　*(British & Commonwealth Lightweight
　　　　　Title Defences)*
17.04.00 Paul Kaoma W RSC 2 Birmingham
　　　　　*(Commonwealth Lightweight Title
　　　　　Defence)*
09.09.00 Joseph Charles W RSC 6 Manchester
　　　　　*(Commonwealth Lightweight Title
　　　　　Defence)*
09.10.00 Laatekwei Hammond W RSC 8
　　　　　Liverpool
　　　　　*(Commonwealth Lightweight Title
　　　　　Defence)*
03.02.01 James Armah L PTS 12 Manchester
　　　　　*(Commonwealth Lightweight Title
　　　　　Defence)*
05.05.01 Steve Murray W RSC 7 Edmonton
　　　　　(British Lightweight Title Defence)
08.10.01 Anthony Maynard W RSC 1 Barnsley
　　　　　(British Lightweight Title Defence)
01.06.02 Viktor Baranov W PTS 8 Manchester
12.10.02 Andrei Devyataykin W PTS 8 Bethnal
　　　　　Green
18.01.03 Yuri Romanov L RSC 8 Preston
　　　　　*(WBO Inter-Continental Lightweight
　　　　　Title Challenge)*
17.07.03 Graham Earl L PTS 12 Dagenham
　　　　　(British Lightweight Title Defence)

07.11.03 Keith Jones W PTS 6 Sheffield
06.02.04 Tony Montana W PTS 6 Sheffield
05.06.04 Graham Earl L PTS 12 Bethnal Green
　　　　　(Vacant British Lightweight Title)
10.09.04 Dave Stewart L PTS 4 Wembley
Career: 32 contests, won 26, drew 1, lost 5.

Bobby Vanzie　　　　　　　　Les Clark

Joey Vegas (Lubega)

Tottenham. *Born* Namirembe Uganda, 1
January, 1982
S.Middleweight. Ht. 5'8¹/₂"
Manager M. Helliet

04.11.04 Cello Renda W RSC 3 Piccadilly
27.01.05 Egbui Ikeagwo W PTS 4 Piccadilly
26.03.05 Egbui Ikeagwo W PTS 4 Hackney
26.05.05 Gareth Lawrence W PTS 4 Mayfair
Career: 4 contests, won 4.

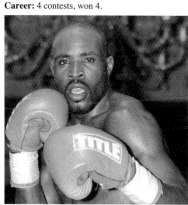

Joey Vegas　　　　　　　　Les Clark

Lance Verallo

Birmingham. *Born* Cardiff, 25 July, 1984
Lightweight. Ht. 5'11"
Manager N. Nobbs

08.05.05 Sujad Elahi L PTS 6 Sheffield
11.06.05 Mike Reid L PTS 6 Kirkcaldy
19.06.05 Ian Wilson L PTS 4 Bethnal Green
Career: 3 contests, lost 3.

Lance Verallo　　　　　　　　Les Clark

Joel Viney

Blackpool. *Born* Manchester, 25
September, 1973
Lightweight. Ht. 5'7³/₄"
Manager Self

02.03.00 Duncan Armstrong W PTS 6 Blackpool
09.06.00 Gareth Wiltshaw W PTS 6 Blackpool
30.11.00 Dave Cotterill L RSC 1 Blackpool
27.01.01 Bradley Pryce L RSC 3 Bethnal Green
10.03.01 Kevin Lear L RSC 2 Bethnal Green
04.06.01 Barry Hawthorne L PTS 8 Glasgow
11.06.01 Inderpaul Sandhu L PTS 4 Nottingham
26.07.01 Mark Winters L RSC 4 Blackpool
15.10.01 Tasawar Khan L PTS 6 Bradford
29.11.01 Michael Hunter L PTS 6 Hartlepool
09.12.01 Paddy Folan W PTS 6 Blackpool
17.12.01 Daniel Thorpe W RSC 2 Cleethorpes
21.01.02 Andrew Ferrans L PTS 8 Glasgow
17.02.02 John Marshall L RSC 6 Salford
18.03.02 Craig Docherty L CO 1 Glasgow
05.05.02 Andy McLean L PTS 6 Hartlepool
28.05.02 Tony McPake L RSC 1 Liverpool
29.06.02 Matthew Burke L PTS 4 Brentwood
17.08.02 Henry Castle L RSC 1 Cardiff
23.09.02 Sean Green L PTS 6 Cleethorpes
05.10.02 Gary Reid L CO 2 Coventry
09.11.02 Darryn Walton L PTS 6 Altrincham
18.11.02 Andrew Ferrans L PTS 6 Glasgow
02.12.02 Gareth Wiltshaw W PTS 6 Bradford
16.12.02 Pete Buckley W PTS 6 Cleethorpes
08.01.03 Daleboy Rees L RSC 5 Aberdare
08.02.03 Jackson Williams L PTS 4 Norwich
17.02.03 John Simpson L RTD 1 Glasgow
22.03.03 Martin Watson L RSC 2 Renfrew
09.05.03 Stefy Bull L RTD 3 Doncaster
07.06.03 Baz Carey L PTS 6 Coventry
03.08.03 Daniel Thorpe W PTS 6 Stalybridge
06.09.03 Daniel Thorpe L PTS 6 Aberdeen
13.09.03 John-Paul Ryan W PTS 6 Coventry
20.09.03 Rendall Munroe L RTD 3 Nottingham
20.10.03 Pete Buckley L PTS 6 Bradford
27.10.03 Barry Hawthorne L RSC 1 Glasgow
15.05.04 Nadeem Siddique L PTS 6 Aberdeen
22.05.04 Nigel Senior L PTS 6 Manchester
07.06.04 Darren Johnstone L PTS 6 Glasgow
03.07.04 Daniel Thorpe L RSC 1 Blackpool
18.11.04 Jason Nesbitt L PTS 6 Blackpool
10.12.04 Jonathan Whiteman L RSC 4
　　　　　Mansfield
Career: 43 contests, won 8, lost 35.

Gwyn Wale

Barnsley. *Born* Barnsley, 24 August, 1984
L. Welterweight. Ht. 5'8"
Manager T. Gilmour/C. Aston

17.09.02	Arv Mittoo W PTS 6 Bethnal Green
05.10.02	Martin Hardcastle W PTS 4 Huddersfield
16.11.02	David Kehoe W PTS 4 Nottingham
22.02.03	James Paisley W RSC 1 Huddersfield
10.05.03	David Vaughan DREW 4 Huddersfield
13.09.03	Gary Cummings L PTS 6 Wakefield
17.12.04	Jason Nesbitt W PTS 4 Huddersfield
04.02.05	Stefy Bull L PTS 10 Doncaster
	(Central Area Lightweight Title Challenge)
18.06.05	Judex Meemea W RSC 5 Barnsley

Career: 9 contests, won 6, drew 1, lost 2.

Gwyn Wale   Les Clark

David Walker

Sidcup. *Born* Bromley, 17 June, 1976
L.Middleweight. Former Undefeated
Southern Area L.Middleweight Champion.
Former Undefeated Southern Area
Welterweight Champion. Ht. 5'10"
Manager Self

29.04.00	Dave Fallon W RSC 1 Wembley
27.05.00	Stuart Rimmer W RSC 2 Southwark
15.07.00	Billy Smith W RTD 2 Millwall
16.09.00	Keith Jones W PTS 6 Bethnal Green
14.10.00	Jason Vlasman W RSC 1 Wembley
18.11.00	Gary Flear W PTS 4 Dagenham
09.12.00	Karl Taylor W PTS 6 Southwark
20.01.01	Ernie Smith W RTD 1 Bethnal Green
17.02.01	Paul Denton W PTS 4 Bethnal Green
19.05.01	Mark Ramsey W PTS 4 Wembley
14.07.01	David White W PTS 4 Liverpool
13.09.01	David Kirk DREW 8 Sheffield
16.03.02	Paul Dyer W RSC 6 Bethnal Green
	(Vacant Southern Area Welterweight Title)

10.05.02	Pedro Thompson W RSC 3 Bethnal Green
23.08.02	Robert Burton W RSC 2 Bethnal Green
25.10.02	Brett James W RSC 4 Bethnal Green
	(Southern Area Welterweight Title Defence)
21.12.02	Jimmy Vincent L RSC 8 Dagenham
	(Final Elim. British Welterweight Title)
05.03.03	Ojay Abrahams W PTS 6 Bethnal Green
16.04.03	Leigh Wicks W PTS 6 Nottingham
27.05.03	John Humphrey W CO 2 Dagenham
	(Southern Area L.Middleweight Title Challenge. Elim. British L.Middleweight Title)
25.07.03	Spencer Fearon W RSC 4 Norwich
	(Southern Area L.Middleweight Title Defence)
04.10.03	Roman Karmazin L RTD 3 Muswell Hill
	(European L.Middleweight Title Challenge)
12.03.04	Matt Scriven W RSC 3 Nottingham
02.06.04	Kevin Phelan W PTS 6 Nottingham
12.11.04	Danny Moir W RSC 5 Wembley

Career: 25 contests, won 22, drew 1, lost 2.

Dean Walker

Sheffield. *Born* Sheffield, 25 April, 1979
Middleweight. Ht. 5'11"
Manager D. Coldwell

21.10.00	Colin McCash DREW 6 Sheffield
11.12.00	James Lee L PTS 6 Sheffield
27.07.01	Chris Duggan W RSC 4 Sheffield
15.12.01	William Webster W PTS 6 Sheffield
03.03.02	Shaun Horsfall W PTS 6 Shaw
02.06.02	Wayne Shepherd W PTS 6 Shaw
03.08.02	Richard Inquieti W PTS 6 Derby
05.10.02	Martin Scotland W PTS 6 Chesterfield
24.05.03	Neil Bonner W PTS 6 Sheffield
12.10.03	Paul Lomax W PTS 6 Sheffield
10.02.04	Neil Addis W PTS 6 Barnsley
21.02.04	Matthew Macklin L CO 1 Cardiff
08.06.04	Andrei Ivanov W PTS 6 Sheffield
03.09.04	Dean Cockburn L PTS 10 Doncaster
	(Vacant Central Area S.Middleweight Title)
15.12.04	Lee Murtagh L PTS 10 Sheffield
	(Vacant Central Central Area Middleweight Title)
20.02.05	Mo W PTS 6 Sheffield
19.03.05	Jozsef Nagy L RTD 8 Tapolca, Hungary
	(IBF Inter-Continental Middleweight Title Challenge)

Career: 17 contests, won 11, drew 1, lost 5.

Mark Wall

Dudley. *Born* Sandwell, 1 September, 1978
Middleweight. Ht. 5'8"
Manager Self

09.04.04	Dean Lloyd W PTS 6 Rugby
27.04.04	Andrei Ivanov L CO 6 Leeds
25.06.04	Jake Guntert L CO 1 Bethnal Green
05.10.04	Joe Mitchell DREW 6 Dudley
23.10.04	Gavin Smith L PTS 6 Wakefield
10.12.04	Gavin Smith L PTS 4 Sheffield
06.03.05	Matt Scriven L PTS 4 Mansfield
26.04.05	Lee McAllister L PTS 6 Leeds
20.05.05	Vince Baldassara L PTS 6 Glasgow
26.06.05	Steve Ede L PTS 6 Southampton

Career: 10 contests, won 1, drew 1, lost 8.

Mark Wall   Les Clark

Danny Wallace

Leeds. *Born* Leeds, 12 July, 1980
Featherweight. Ht. 5'7"
Manager K. Walker

24.08.01	Roger Glover W PTS 4 Atlantic City, USA
12.04.02	Michael Weaver DREW 4 Philadelphia, USA
22.02.03	Jamil Hussain W RSC 1 Huddersfield
12.04.03	Ian Turner W RSC 4 Bethnal Green
10.05.03	Marcel Kasimov L RSC 3 Huddersfield
06.09.03	Alexei Volchan W PTS 4 Huddersfield
31.01.04	Jamie Yelland W PTS 6 Bethnal Green
13.03.04	Henry Janes L PTS 4 Huddersfield
11.09.04	Joseph Barela W RSC 2 Philadelphia, Pennsylvania, USA
06.12.04	Fred Janes W RSC 2 Leeds
01.06.05	Harry Ramogoadi L PTS 6 Leeds

Career: 10 contests, won 6, drew 1, lost 3.

(Walisundra) Jus Wallie (Mudiyanselage)

Balham. *Born* Sri Lanka, 14 May, 1976
Lightweight. Ht. 5'5"
Manager Self

01.02.03	Kevin O'Hara L RSC 2 Belfast
29.03.03	Henry Castle W RSC 2 Portsmouth
05.04.03	Derry Matthews L PTS 4 Manchester
08.05.03	Steve Bell DREW 4 Widnes
31.05.03	J.J.Moore W RSC 1 Bethnal Green
29.11.03	Haider Ali L PTS 4 Renfrew
06.12.03	Jamie Arthur L PTS 6 Cardiff
21.02.04	Samuel Kebede L PTS 8 Cardiff
22.04.04	John Simpson L PTS 6 Glasgow
07.05.04	Jason Nesbitt W PTS 6 Bethnal Green
12.06.04	Andy Morris L PTS 6 Manchester
19.06.04	Martin Watson L PTS 6 Renfrew
24.09.04	Lee Cook L RSC 2 Bethnal Green
08.04.05	Damian Owen L PTS 4 Bristol
12.06.05	Ashley Theophane L PTS 4 Leicester Square
19.06.05	Craig Watson L PTS 4 Bethnal Green

Career: 16 contests, won 3, drew 1, lost 12.

Ryan Walls

Slough. *Born* Reading, 29 January, 1979
WBF International S.Middleweight
Champion. Former British Masters
Cruiserweight Champion. Ht. 6'0½"
Manager G. Carmen

20.12.02	Mark Phillips W PTS 4 Bracknell
23.02.03	Michael Pinnock W PTS 6 Streatham
21.03.03	Jimmy Steel W PTS 6 Longford
12.04.03	Earl Ling W RSC 4 Norwich
09.05.03	Darren Ashton W PTS 6 Longford
01.08.03	Darren Ashton W PTS 4 Bethnal Green
26.10.03	Michael Pinnock W PTS 10 Longford
	(Vacant British Masters Cruiserweight
	Title)
25.03.04	Pinky Burton L PTS 10 Longford
	(British Masters Cruiserweight Title
	Defence)
08.05.04	Toks Owoh W PTS 6 Bristol
08.12.04	Varuzhan Davtyan W PTS 4 Longford
24.02.05	Ryan Kerr L PTS 10 Sunderland
	(Vacant English S.Middleweight Title)
24.04.05	Peter Haymer L PTS 6 Leicester Square
08.05.05	Donovan Smillie W PTS 6 Bradford
20.06.05	Simeon Cover W RSC 8 Longford
	(Vacant WBF International
	S.Middleweight Title)

Career: 14 contests, won 11, lost 3.

Ryan Walls   Les Clark

Shaun Walton
Telford. *Born* West Bromwich, 2 January, 1975
S.Featherweight. Ht. 5'10"
Manager D. Bradley/E. Johnson

15.04.05	Dave Hinds W PTS 6 Shrewsbury

Career: 1 contest, won 1.

Dean Ward
Birmingham. *Born* Birmingham, 12 August, 1975
S.Featherweight. Ht. 5'6"
Manager Self

23.04.04	Michael Crossan L PTS 6 Glasgow
07.05.04	David Bailey L PTS 6 Bethnal Green
14.06.04	Matt Teague L PTS 6 Cleethorpes
24.09.04	Patrick Hyland L PTS 4 Dublin
19.11.04	Matthew Marsh L PTS 4 Bethnal Green
10.12.04	Andy Bell L PTS 6 Mansfield
17.12.04	Derry Matthews L RSC 1 Liverpool

Career: 7 contests, lost 7.

Isaac Ward
Darlington. *Born* Darlington, 7 April, 1977
Featherweight. Ht. 5'5"
Manager M. Marsden

03.08.02	Neil Read W RSC 1 Blackpool
18.10.02	John-Paul Ryan W PTS 6 Hartlepool
14.12.02	Steve Gethin W PTS 4 Newcastle
11.07.03	Rocky Dean DREW 4 Darlington
13.09.03	Pete Buckley W PTS 6 Wakefield
10.10.03	Rocky Dean W PTS 6 Darlington
04.12.03	Jamie Yelland W PTS 6 Huddersfield
05.03.04	Steve Gethin W PTS 6 Darlington
16.04.04	Pete Buckley W PTS 6 Hartlepool
03.07.04	Dave Hinds W PTS 6 Blackpool
19.11.04	Abdul Mougharbel W PTS 4 Hartlepool
04.03.05	Peter Allen DREW 6 Hartlepool
02.06.05	Billy Smith W PTS 8 Yarm

Career: 13 contests, won 11, drew 2.

Nathan Ward
Reading. *Born* Reading, 19 July, 1979
L.Welterweight. British Masters Welterweight Champion. Ht. 5'10"
Manager Self

27.09.02	Darren Goode W RSC 1 Bracknell
03.12.02	Dean Larter W PTS 4 Bethnal Green
20.12.02	Arv Mittoo W PTS 6 Bracknell
18.03.03	Pete Buckley W PTS 4 Reading
26.04.03	Cristian Hodorogea L RSC 1 Brentford
26.09.03	Casey Brooke W RSC 1 Reading
26.11.03	Lance Hall L PTS 4 Mayfair
12.05.04	Dave Hinds W PTS 4 Reading
24.09.04	James Paisley W PTS 4 Bethnal Green
26.11.04	Lea Handley W CO 2 Bethnal Green
12.02.05	Ernie Smith W PTS 6 Portsmouth
19.06.05	James Paisley W RSC 4 Bethnal Green
	(Vacant British Masters Welterweight
	Title)

Career: 12 contests, won 10, lost 2.

Craig Watson
Manchester. *Born* Oldham, 7 February, 1983
L.Welterweight. Ht. 5'10"
Manager F. Maloney

20.05.05	Willie Valentine W RTD 2 Southwark
19.06.05	Jus Wallie W PTS 4 Bethnal Green

Career: 2 contests, won 2.

Martin Watson
Coatbridge. *Born* Bellshill, 12 May, 1981
Celtic & Scottish Lightweight Champion. Ht. 5'8"
Manager R. Bannon/A. Morrison

24.05.01	Shaune Danskin W RSC 3 Glasgow
20.10.01	Jon Honney W RSC 3 Glasgow
16.12.01	Richie Caparelli W PTS 6 Glasgow
11.03.02	Pete Buckley W PTS 4 Glasgow
26.04.02	Gary Reid W PTS 6 Glasgow
08.06.02	Scott Miller W RSC 2 Renfrew
18.11.02	Gary Reid W RSC 4 Glasgow
22.03.03	Joel Viney W RSC 2 Renfrew
16.05.03	Barry Hughes W RTD 8 Glasgow
	(Vacant Scottish Lightweight Title)
30.10.03	Mark Winters DREW 8 Belfast
01.04.04	Steve Murray L PTS 10 Bethnal Green
19.06.04	Jus Wallie W PTS 6 Renfrew
29.10.04	Mark Winters W PTS 10 Renfrew
	(Vacant Celtic Lightweight Title)
28.01.05	Jimmy Beech W PTS 4 Renfrew

Career: 14 contests, won 12, drew 1, lost 1.

Karl Wheeler
Peterborough. *Born* Peterborough, 30 May, 1982
L. Heavyweight. Ht. 6'3"
Manager I. Pauly

07.05.03	Martin Thompson W PTS 6 Ellesmere Port
29.05.03	Paul Billington W PTS 6 Sunderland
14.02.04	Gary Jones W RSC 1 Holborn
08.04.04	Nick Okoth W PTS 6 Peterborough
03.07.04	Leigh Allis L PTS 4 Bristol
15.10.04	Steve McGuire L PTS 4 Glasgow
02.12.04	Shane White W PTS 6 Bristol
12.12.04	Tom Cannon L PTS 6 Glasgow
21.02.05	Hastings Rasani W PTS 6 Peterborough
04.03.05	Amer Khan L PTS 6 Rotherham
02.06.05	Hastings Rasani L RSC 5 Peterborough

Career: 11 contests, won 6, lost 5.

Karl Wheeler   Les Clark

David White
Cardiff. *Born* Cardiff, 18 April, 1975
Middleweight. Ht. 5'9"
Manager D. Gardiner

23.09.00	Matthew Hatton L PTS 4 Bethnal Green
25.11.00	Matthew Hatton L PTS 4 Manchester
28.01.01	Jimmy Gould L PTS 6 Wolverhampton
05.02.01	Lance Crosby DREW 6 Hull
24.02.01	Francis Barrett L PTS 4 Bethnal Green
28.04.01	Ahmet Kaddour L PTS 4 Cardiff
12.05.01	Leo O'Reilly L PTS 4 Plymouth
24.05.01	Ronnie Nailen L PTS 6 Glasgow
14.07.01	David Walker L PTS 4 Liverpool
18.08.01	Oscar Hall L PTS 6 Dewsbury
15.09.02	Taz Jones DREW 4 Swansea
05.10.02	Gary Ryder L PTS 6 Liverpool
12.11.04	Darren Barker L RSC 2 Wembley

Career: 13 contests, drew 2, lost 11.

Shane White
Wells. *Born* Bristol, 27 January, 1972
L. Heavyweight. Ht. 5'9"
Manager Self

08.02.02	Gary Thompson DREW 6 Preston
18.03.02	Billy McClung W RTD 4 Glasgow
21.09.03	Paul Billington DREW 6 Bristol
17.11.03	Steve McGuire L CO 2 Glasgow
21.12.03	Paul Billington W RSC 2 Bristol
29.02.04	Harry Butler W PTS 6 Bristol

01.10.04 Leigh Allis L RSC 2 Bristol
(Vacant Western Area L.Heavyweight Title)
02.12.04 Karl Wheeler L PTS 6 Bristol
20.02.05 Sergey Haritonov W RSC 3 Bristol
21.03.05 Sandy Robb L RSC 4 Glasgow
Career: 10 contests, won 4, drew 2, lost 4.

Shane White   Les Clark

Jonathan Whiteman

Mansfield. *Born* Sutton in Ashfield, 1 May, 1984
L.Welterweight. Ht. 5'11"
Manager M. Scriven

22.10.04 Pete Buckley W PTS 6 Mansfield
10.12.04 Joel Viney W RSC 4 Mansfield
06.03.05 Terry Carruthers DREW 6 Mansfield
24.04.05 Dave Curran L DIS 2 Askern
Career: 4 contests, won 2, drew 1, lost 1.

Lee Whyatt

Morden. *Born* Croydon, 16 September, 1977
S. Bantamweight. Ht. 5'7"
Manager D. Williams/F. Warren

07.02.04 Henry Janes L PTS 4 Bethnal Green
26.03.05 Vinesh Rungea L PTS 4 Hackney
Career: 2 contests, lost 2.

Leigh Wicks

Brighton. *Born* Worthing, 29 July, 1965
S. Middleweight. Ht. 5'6¼"
Manager Self

29.04.87 Fidel Castro W PTS 6 Hastings
26.09.87 Jason Rowe W PTS 6 Hastings
18.11.87 Lou Ayres W PTS 6 Holborn
26.01.88 Theo Marius L PTS 8 Hove
15.02.88 Shamus Casey W PTS 6 Copthorne
26.04.88 Franki Moro DREW 8 Hove
04.05.88 Tony Britton W PTS 8 Wembley
18.05.88 Mark Howell W RSC 4 Portsmouth
25.05.88 Newton Barnett DREW 8 Hastings
22.11.88 Roy Callaghan L PTS 8 Basildon
16.03.89 Tony Britland W PTS 8 Southwark
12.10.89 Tony Gibbs W CO 2 Southwark
08.02.90 Ernie Noble W PTS 8 Southwark
26.04.90 Julian Eavis DREW 8 Mayfair
06.11.90 Gordon Blair W PTS 8 Mayfair
10.01.91 Barry Messam W PTS 6 Wandsworth

14.02.91 Kevin Thompson W PTS 8 Southampton
21.10.91 Tony Britland W RSC 3 Mayfair
20.02.92 Mick Duncan L PTS 8 Glasgow
30.04.92 Darren Morris DREW 6 Mayfair
19.10.92 Bozon Haule W PTS 8 Mayfair
20.01.93 Robert McCracken L PTS 8 Wolverhampton
17.02.93 Kevin Lueshing L PTS 6 Bethnal Green
22.04.93 Warren Stowe L PTS 6 Bury
27.10.95 Danny Quacoe W RSC 4 Brighton
18.11.95 Gary Jacobs L RTD 3 Glasgow
26.01.96 Wayne Appleton L PTS 6 Brighton
05.03.96 Kevin Thompson L PTS 6 Bethnal Green
24.03.97 Ross Hale L PTS 6 Bristol
08.04.97 Ahmet Dottuev L RSC 1 Bethnal Green
29.05.97 Nicky Thurbin L PTS 8 Mayfair
11.07.97 Darren Covill L RSC 2 Brighton
27.11.97 Lester Jacobs L PTS 6 Bloomsbury
06.12.97 Rhoshi Wells L PTS 4 Wembley
21.02.98 Neil Sinclair L RSC 1 Belfast
24.03.98 Ojay Abrahams L PTS 6 Bethnal Green
05.06.98 Darren Bruce L PTS 6 Southend
25.11.98 Darren Covill W PTS 4 Streatham
22.02.99 Neil Linford L PTS 4 Peterborough
26.06.99 Takaloo L CO 3 Millwall
09.10.99 Darren Rhodes L PTS 4 Manchester
27.11.99 Geoff McCreesh L PTS 6 Lubeck, Germany
11.12.99 Darren Rhodes L PTS 4 Liverpool
21.02.00 Sergei Dzinziruk L RSC 2 Southwark
25.03.00 Darren Rhodes L PTS 4 Liverpool
08.04.00 Spencer Fearon L PTS 4 Bethnal Green
02.06.00 Allan Foster L PTS 4 Ashford
24.06.00 Scott Dixon L PTS 4 Glasgow
01.07.00 Karim Hussine L PTS 6 Southwark
30.09.00 Bobby Banghar L PTS 4 Peterborough
07.10.00 Jamie Moore L PTS 4 Doncaster
11.11.00 Brian Knudsen L RSC 5 Belfast
17.03.01 Wayne Pinder L PTS 4 Manchester
29.03.01 Lester Jacobs L PTS 6 Hammersmith
05.05.01 Ty Browne L PTS 6 Brighton
08.06.01 Jason Collins L PTS 4 Hull
21.07.01 Damon Hague L PTS 4 Sheffield
31.07.01 Erik Teymour L RSC 1 Bethnal Green
30.09.01 Liam Lathbury L PTS 4 Bristol
09.10.01 Ruben Groenewald L PTS 6 Cardiff
28.10.01 Allan Gray L PTS 4 Southwark
17.11.01 Lawrence Murphy L PTS 4 Glasgow
08.12.01 Wayne Asker L PTS 4 Dagenham
16.12.01 Allan Gray L PTS 4 Southwark
31.01.02 Freddie Yemofio W PTS 6 Piccadilly
09.02.02 Patrick J. Maxwell L PTS 4 Manchester
13.04.02 Andrew Facey L PTS 6 Norwich
10.05.02 Matthew Thirlwall L PTS 4 Bethnal Green
17.09.02 Kenroy Lambert L PTS 6 Bethnal Green
23.11.02 Damon Hague L PTS 6 Derby
03.12.02 Lee Hodgson L PTS 4 Bethnal Green
08.02.03 Spencer Fearon L PTS 6 Brentford
23.02.03 Alan Jones L PTS 8 Aberystwyth
22.03.03 Lawrence Murphy L PTS 4 Renfrew
16.04.03 David Walker L PTS 6 Nottingham
26.04.03 Darren McDermott L PTS 4 Brentford
09.05.03 Kevin Phelan L PTS 6 Longford
27.05.03 Matthew Thirlwall L PTS 6 Dagenham
20.06.03 Alan Gilbert L PTS 4 Gatwick
25.07.03 Daniel Cadman L PTS 4 Norwich
27.11.03 Matthew Barr L PTS 4 Longford
21.02.04 Alan Gilbert L PTS 4 Brighton

12.03.04 Wayne Pinder L PTS 4 Nottingham
01.10.04 Tony Quigley L PTS 4 Manchester
15.12.04 Reagan Denton L PTS 6 Sheffield
21.01.05 Matthew Hall L PTS 4 Bridgend
12.02.05 Jake Guntert L PTS 4 Portsmouth
05.03.05 Gareth Lawrence L PTS 4 Dagenham
26.03.05 Darren Barker L RTD 4 Hackney
Career: 89 contests, won 17, drew 4, lost 68.

Noel Wilders

Castleford. *Born* Castleford, 4 January, 1975
S.Bantamweight. Former European Bantamweight Champion. Former Undefeated IBO, British & Central Area Bantamweight Champion. Ht. 5'5"
Manager Self

16.03.96 Neil Parry W RTD 4 Sheffield
04.06.96 Graham McGrath W PTS 6 York
04.10.96 Tiger Singh W PTS 6 Wakefield
23.10.96 Jason Thomas W PTS 6 Halifax
12.03.97 John Matthews W PTS 6 Stoke
20.04.97 Shaun Anderson W PTS 6 Leeds
13.11.97 Anthony Hanna W PTS 6 Bradford
06.02.98 Marcus Duncan W RSC 6 Wakefield
(Vacant Central Area Bantamweight Title)
21.05.98 Matthew Harris W PTS 6 Bradford
18.07.98 Sean Grant W RSC 4 Sheffield
23.10.98 Fondil Madani W DIS 7 Wakefield
28.11.98 Ross Cassidy W PTS 8 Sheffield
06.02.99 Jason Thomas W PTS 10 Halifax
(Elim. British Bantamweight Title)
24.04.99 Anthony Hanna W PTS 6 Peterborough
22.06.99 Ady Lewis W RSC 6 Ipswich
(Final Elim. British Bantamweight Title)
30.10.99 Francis Ampofo W PTS 12 Peterlee
(Vacant British Bantamweight Title)
18.01.00 Steve Williams W RTD 11 Mansfield
(British Bantamweight Title Defence)
20.03.00 Kamel Guerfi W PTS 12 Mansfield
(Vacant IBO Bantamweight Title)
15.07.00 Paul Lloyd W PTS 12 Millwall
(IBO Bantamweight Title Defence)
28.04.01 Stevie Quinn W RTD 6 Cardiff
21.07.01 Chris Emanuele W PTS 6 Sheffield
15.06.02 Sean Grant W RSC 3 Leeds
28.01.03 Fabien Guillerme W PTS 12 Nice, France
(Vacant European Bantamweight Title)
18.03.03 Frederic Patrac DREW 4 Reading
(European Bantamweight Title Defence)
10.06.03 David Guerault L RSC 7 Sheffield
(European Bantamweight Title Defence)
06.02.04 Vladimir Borov W PTS 4 Sheffield
07.08.04 Silence Mabuza L CO 5 Temba, South Africa
(IBO Bantamweight Title Challenge)
08.05.05 Esham Pickering L PTS 8 Bradford
Career: 28 contests, won 24, drew 1, lost 3.

Danny Williams

Brixton. *Born* London, 13 July, 1973
WBU Inter-Continental Heavyweight Champion. Former British & Commonwealth Heavyweight Champion. Former Undefeated WBO Inter-Continental Heavyweight Champion. Ht. 6'3"
Manager F. Warren

21.10.95	Vance Idiens W CO 2 Bethnal Green
09.12.95	Joey Paladino W RSC 1 Bethnal Green
13.02.96	Slick Miller W RSC 1 Bethnal Green
09.03.96	James Wilder W PTS 4 Millstreet
13.07.96	John Pierre W PTS 4 Bethnal Green
31.08.96	Andy Lambert W RSC 2 Dublin
09.11.96	Michael Murray W CO 1 Manchester
08.02.97	Shane Woollas W RSC 2 Millwall
03.05.97	Albert Call W RSC 4 Manchester
19.07.97	R. F. McKenzie W RSC 2 Wembley
15.11.97	Bruce Douglas W RSC 2 Bristol
19.12.97	Derek Amos W RSC 4 NYC, New York, USA
21.02.98	Shane Woollas W RSC 2 Belfast
16.05.98	Antonio Diaz W CO 3 Bethnal Green
10.10.98	Antoine Palatis W PTS 12 Bethnal Green
	(Vacant WBO Inter-Continental Heavyweight Title)
03.04.99	Julius Francis L PTS 12 Kensington
	(British & Commonwealth Heavyweight Title Challenges)
02.10.99	Ferenc Deak W RTD 1 Namur, Belgium
18.12.99	Harry Senior W PTS 12 Southwark
	(Vacant Commonwealth Heavyweight Title)
19.02.00	Anton Nel W CO 5 Dagenham
06.05.00	Michael Murray W RSC 6 Frankfurt, Germany
24.06.00	Craig Bowen-Price W CO 1 Glasgow
23.09.00	Quinn Navarre W RSC 6 Bethnal Green
21.10.00	Mark Potter W RSC 6 Wembley
	(Commonwealth & WBO Inter-Continental Heavyweight Title Defences. Vacant British Heavyweight Title)
09.06.01	Kali Meehan W RSC 1 Bethnal Green
	(Commonwealth Heavyweight Title Defence)
28.07.01	Julius Francis W CO 4 Wembley
	(British & Commonwealth Heavyweight Title Defences)
15.12.01	Shawn Robinson W RSC 2 Mashantucket Connecticut, USA
12.02.02	Michael Sprott W RTD 7 Bethnal Green
	(British & Commonwealth Heavyweight Title Defences)
17.09.02	Keith Long W PTS 12 Bethnal Green
	(British & Commonwealth Heavyweight Title Defences)
08.02.03	Sinan Samil Sam L RSC 6 Berlin, Germany
	(European Heavyweight Title Challenge)
26.04.03	Bob Mirovic W RSC 4 Brentford
	(Commonwealth Heavyweight Title Defence)
26.09.03	Michael Sprott W RSC 5 Reading
	(British & Commonwealth Heavyweight Title Defences)
24.01.04	Michael Sprott L PTS 12 Wembley
	(British & Commonwealth Heavyweight Title Defences)
01.04.04	Ratko Draskovic W RSC 1 Bethnal Green
13.05.04	Augustin N'Gou W RTD 3 Bethnal Green
	(Vacant WBU Inter-Continental Heavyweight Title)
30.07.04	Mike Tyson W CO 4 Louisville, Kentucky, USA

11.12.04	Vitali Klitschko L RSC 8 Las Vegas, USA
	(WBC Heavyweight Title Challenge)
04.06.05	Zoltan Petranyi W RSC 3 Manchester

Career: 37 contests, won 33, lost 4.

(Darren) Dazzo Williams

Hereford. *Born* Lambeth, 19 March, 1974
Featherweight. Former British
Featherweight Champion. Ht. 5'8"
Manager T. Gilmour

24.02.01	Mickey Coveney W CO 1 Bethnal Green
19.05.01	Mark Payne W PTS 8 Wembley
14.07.01	Dimitri Gorodetsky W RSC 3 Liverpool
19.12.01	Mark Alexander W PTS 6 Coventry
18.01.02	Zolani Msolo W RSC 2 Coventry
20.04.02	John Mackay L PTS 6 Wembley
26.10.02	Carl Allen L RSC 2 Maesteg
25.01.03	Vladimir Borov W PTS 6 Bridgend
08.03.03	Marc Callaghan W PTS 8 Bethnal Green
17.05.03	Stephen Chinnock W PTS 10 Liverpool
	(Elim. British Featherweight Title)
22.11.03	Roy Rutherford W PTS 12 Belfast
	(British Featherweight Title Challenge)
28.02.04	Jamie McKeever W PTS 12 Bridgend
	(British Featherweight Title Defence)
02.06.04	Roy Rutherford W PTS 12 Hereford
	(British Featherweight Title Defence)
05.11.04	John Simpson W PTS 12 Hereford
	(British Featherweight Title Defence)
16.06.05	Nicky Cook L CO 2 Dagenham
	(European & Commonwealth Featherweight Title Challenges. British Featherweight Title Defence)

Career: 15 contests, won 12, lost 3.

Jackson Williams

Norwich. *Born* Norwich, 19 June, 1981
Lightweight. Ht. 5'6½"
Manager Self

13.04.02	Daniel Thorpe W PTS 6 Norwich
15.06.02	Jason Gonzales W PTS 6 Norwich
21.09.02	Baz Carey W PTS 6 Norwich
10.10.02	Jason Gonzales W PTS 4 Piccadilly
08.02.03	Joel Viney W PTS 4 Norwich
24.02.03	Anthony Hanna L PTS 6 Birmingham
12.04.03	Daniel Thorpe W PTS 6 Norwich
06.06.03	Nigel Senior W PTS 8 Norwich
25.07.03	Paul Rushton W PTS 4 Norwich
21.02.04	Nigel Senior W PTS 6 Norwich
14.05.04	Haroon Din L RSC 5 Sunderland
	(Vacant British L.Welterweight Title)
09.10.04	Dave Hinds W PTS 6 Norwich

Career: 12 contests, won 10, lost 2.

Richard Williams

Stockwell. *Born* London, 9 May, 1971
L.Middleweight. Former IBO
L.Middleweight Champion. Former
Undefeated Commonwealth & WBF
L.Middleweight Champion. Ht. 5'9½"
Manager Self

08.03.97	Marty Duke W RSC 3 Brentwood
30.06.97	Danny Quacoe W PTS 4 Bethnal Green
02.09.97	Michael Alexander L PTS 4 Southwark

16.10.99	Pedro Carragher W RSC 2 Bethnal Green
06.11.99	Lee Bird W RSC 4 Bethnal Green
20.12.99	Harry Butler W RSC 1 Bethnal Green
17.04.00	Kevin Thompson W CO 1 Birmingham
16.06.00	Piotr Bartnicki W RSC 3 Bloomsbury
08.09.00	Dean Ashton W RSC 1 Hammersmith
04.11.00	Howard Clarke W CO 4 Bethnal Green
02.12.00	Aziz Daari W RSC 2 Bethnal Green
23.01.01	Tony Badea W RSC 3 Crawley
	(Commonwealth L. Middleweight Title Challenge)
04.06.01	Hussain Osman W PTS 10 Hartlepool
25.09.01	Andrew Murray W RSC 3 Liverpool
	(Commonwealth L. Middleweight Title Defence)
20.10.01	Viktor Fesetchko W RSC 6 Portsmouth
01.12.01	Shannan Taylor W RSC 4 Bethnal Green
	(Commonwealth L. Middleweight Title Defence. Vacant IBO L. Middleweight Title)
29.06.02	Paul Samuels T DRAW 3 Brentwood
	(IBO L. Middleweight Title Defence)
07.12.02	Paul Samuels W RSC 10 Brentwood
	(IBO L. Middleweight Title Defence)
08.03.03	Andrei Pestriaev W PTS 12 Bethnal Green
	(IBO L. Middleweight Title Defence. WBF L. Middleweight Title Challenge)
21.06.03	Sergio Martinez L PTS 12 Manchester
	(IBO L.Middleweight Title Defence)
31.01.04	Ayittey Powers W RSC 7 Bethnal Green
	(Vacant Commonwealth L.Middleweight Title)
17.04.04	Sergio Martinez L RTD 9 Belfast
	(IBO L.Middleweight Title Challenge)
26.11.04	Szabolcs Rimovszky W RSC 3 Altrincham

Career: 23 contests, won 19, drew 1, lost 3.

Tye Williams

Dewsbury. *Born* London, 9 June, 1976
Welterweight. Ht. 5'9"
Manager M. Marsden

23.10.04	Rocky Muscus W PTS 6 Wakefield
09.11.04	Lea Handley L RSC 1 Leeds
26.02.05	Darren Gethin DREW 4 Burton
14.05.05	Daniel Thorpe W RSC 3 Aberdeen
25.06.05	Gary Connolly W CO 4 Wakefield

Career: 5 contests, won 3, drew 1, lost 1.

Lee Williamson

Worcester. *Born* Worcester, 3 February, 1974
Middleweight. Ht. 5'9"
Manager Self

26.10.98	Trevor Tacy L PTS 6 Manchester
26.11.98	David Smales W PTS 6 Bradford
16.01.99	Graham Earl L RSC 4 Bethnal Green
23.03.99	Gary Reid L PTS 6 Wolverhampton
22.04.99	Brian Gifford W PTS 6 Dudley
15.05.99	James Hare L RSC 2 Sheffield
11.10.99	Carl Allen W PTS 6 Birmingham
28.10.99	Mark Hargreaves L PTS 6 Burnley
30.11.99	Marc Smith W PTS 6 Wolverhampton
11.12.99	Brian Carr DREW 6 Liverpool
24.01.00	Craig Docherty L PTS 6 Glasgow
08.02.00	Carl Allen L PTS 8 Wolverhampton
19.02.00	Kevin Lear L PTS 4 Dagenham

04.03.00	Liam Maltby L PTS 6 Peterborough
28.03.00	Carl Allen L PTS 8 Wolverhampton
06.06.00	Dave Travers W PTS 6 Brierley Hill
24.06.00	Kevin McIntyre L PTS 4 Glasgow
08.07.00	Tony Mulholland L PTS 8 Widnes
13.08.00	Esham Pickering L PTS 6 Nottingham
29.09.00	Darren Melville L RSC 4 Bethnal Green
21.10.00	Graham Earl L RSC 3 Wembley
24.11.00	Pete Buckley W PTS 6 Hull
09.12.00	Terry Butwell L PTS 4 Southwark
27.01.01	Danny Hunt W RSC 2 Bethnal Green
10.02.01	Geir Inge Jorgensen L RSC 3 Widnes
20.03.01	James Rooney L PTS 4 Glasgow
26.03.01	Liam Maltby L PTS 6 Peterborough
03.04.01	Danny Hunt L PTS 4 Bethnal Green
06.05.01	James Rooney L PTS 6 Hartlepool
21.06.01	Gavin Wake L PTS 6 Sheffield
14.07.01	Brett James L PTS 6 Wembley
28.07.01	Ross Minter L PTS 4 Wembley
15.09.01	Gavin Down L PTS 6 Derby
10.12.01	David Keir DREW 4 Liverpool
04.03.02	Pedro Thompson W PTS 6 Bradford
13.04.02	David Keir L PTS 4 Liverpool
13.05.02	Chris Duggan W RSC 3 Birmingham
01.06.02	Michael Jennings L PTS 4 Manchester
23.06.02	Brett James L PTS 6 Southwark
28.09.02	Mickey Quinn L RSC 2 Manchester
16.11.02	Richard Swallow L PTS 4 Coventry
30.11.02	Mark Dillon W PTS 4 Liverpool
18.01.03	Michael Jennings L RTD 4 Preston
23.02.03	Lee McAllister L PTS 6 Shrewsbury
16.03.03	Matt Scriven L PTS 10 Nottingham
	(Vacant Midlands Area & British
	Masters L. Middleweight Titles)
07.06.03	Andy Egan L PTS 6 Coventry
12.07.03	Gary Young L PTS 4 Renfrew
03.08.03	Ali Nuumembe L PTS 6 Stalybridge
13.09.03	Andy Halder L PTS 6 Coventry
19.10.03	Mark Paxford L PTS 6 Shaw
08.11.03	Andy Halder L PTS 6 Coventry
21.11.03	Darren Covill W PTS 6 Millwall
01.12.03	Andrei Ivanov W RSC 4 Barnsley
14.02.04	Gary Woolcombe L PTS 6 Holborn
21.02.04	Danny Smith L PTS 6 Norwich
08.03.04	Lee McAllister L PTS 6 Birmingham
27.03.04	Colin McNeil L PTS 4 Edinburgh
23.04.04	Tony Montana L PTS 6 Leicester
07.05.04	Jake Guntert L PTS 6 Bethnal Green
04.06.04	Oscar Hall L PTS 6 Hull
09.11.04	Kell Brook L RSC 2 Leeds
13.02.05	Danny Parkinson L PTS 4 Bradford
21.02.05	Simon Sherrington DREW 6 Birmingham
05.03.05	Clint Smith L PTS 6 Southwark
26.03.05	Daniel Cadman L PTS 4 Hackney
16.05.05	Simon Sherrington L PTS 8 Birmingham
27.05.05	Kerry Hope L PTS 4 Spennymoor
18.06.05	Neil Tidman L PTS 6 Coventry

Career: 68 contests, won 12, drew 3, lost 53.

Billy Wilson

York. *Born* York, 28 December, 1980
Heavyweight. Ht. 6'6"
Manager T. O'Neill/D. Coldwell

15.09.03	Carl Baker L RSC 2 Leeds
11.11.03	Brodie Pearmaine W PTS 6 Leeds
10.02.04	Paul King W PTS 6 Barnsley
06.12.04	Simon Goodwin W PTS 6 Leeds
16.12.04	Chris Woollas L PTS 6 Cleethorpes

Career: 5 contests, won 3, lost 2.

Ian Wilson

Camden. *Born* London, 9 June, 1981
S.Featherweight. Ht. 5'10½"
Manager F. Maloney

19.06.05	Lance Verallo W PTS 4 Bethnal Green

Career: 1 contest, won 1.

Simon Wilson

Belfast. *Born* Carrickfergus, 2 June, 1970
Lightweight. Ht. 5'7"
Manager A. Wilton

26.06.04	Michael Kelly L PTS 4 Belfast
24.09.04	Rocky Dean L PTS 4 Millwall
12.11.04	Ian Reid W PTS 6 Belfast

Career: 3 contests, won 1, lost 2.

Mark Winters

Antrim. *Born* Antrim, 29 December, 1971
Lightweight. Former British
L. Welterweight Champion. Ht. 5'8"
Manager Self

04.03.95	Trevor Smith W PTS 6 Livingston
10.06.95	Mark McGowan W PTS 6 Manchester
09.09.95	Anthony Campbell W PTS 4 Cork
25.11.95	John O. Johnson W RSC 2 Dublin
13.01.96	Rick North W PTS 4 Manchester
09.03.96	Danny Quacoe W RSC 2 Millstreet
08.06.96	Brian Coleman W PTS 4 Newcastle
31.08.96	John Smith W PTS 4 Dublin
30.11.96	Paul Dyer W PTS 6 Tylorstown
14.03.97	Paul Denton W PTS 8 Reading
03.05.97	Jimmy Phelan W PTS 4 Manchester
11.10.97	Carl Wright W PTS 12 Sheffield
	(Vacant British L. Welterweight Title)
21.02.98	Bernard Paul W PTS 12 Belfast
	(British L. Welterweight Title Defence)
16.05.98	Jason Rowland L PTS 12 Bethnal Green
	(British L. Welterweight Title Defence)
05.09.98	Junior Witter L PTS 8 Telford
23.10.99	James Hare DREW 6 Telford
11.12.99	Ricky Hatton L RSC 4 Liverpool
	(WBO Inter-Continental
	L.Welterweight Title Challenge)
04.02.01	David Kirk W PTS 6 Queensferry
20.04.01	David Kirk W PTS 6 Dublin
26.07.01	Joel Viney W RSC 4 Blackpool
15.12.01	Graham Earl L PTS 10 Wembley
	(Elim. British Lightweight Title)
02.11.02	John Marshall W RSC 5 Belfast
01.02.03	David Kehoe W RSC 2 Belfast
30.10.03	Martin Watson DREW 8 Belfast
29.10.04	Martin Watson L PTS 10 Renfrew
	(Vacant Celtic Lightweight Title)

Career: 25 contests, won 18, drew 2, lost 5.

Junior Witter

Bradford. *Born* Bradford, 10 March, 1974
British, Commonwealth & European
L.Welterweight Champion. Former
Undefeated European Union, WBU Inter-
Continental & WBF L.Welterweight
Champion. Ht. 5'7"
Manager J. Ingle

Junior Witter   Les Clark

18.01.97	Cam Raeside DREW 6 Swadlincote	
04.03.97	John Green W PTS 6 Yarm	
20.03.97	Lee Molyneux W RSC 6 Salford	
25.04.97	Trevor Meikle W PTS 6 Mere	
15.05.97	Andreas Panayi W RSC 5 Reading	
02.08.97	Brian Coleman W PTS 4 Barnsley	
04.10.97	Michael Alexander W PTS 4 Hannover, Germany	
07.02.98	Mark Ramsey DREW 6 Cheshunt	
05.03.98	Brian Coleman W PTS 6 Leeds	
18.04.98	Jan Bergman W PTS 6 Manchester	
05.09.98	Mark Winters W PTS 8 Telford	
28.11.98	Karl Taylor W PTS 4 Sheffield	
13.02.99	Malcolm Melvin W RSC 2 Newcastle *(Vacant WBF L. Welterweight Title)*	
17.07.99	Isaac Cruz W PTS 8 Doncaster	
06.11.99	Harry Butler W PTS 6 Widnes	
21.03.00	Mrhai Iourgh W RSC 1 Telde, Gran Canaria	
08.04.00	Arv Mittoo W PTS 4 Bethnal Green	
24.06.00	Zab Judah L PTS 12 Glasgow *(IBF L. Welterweight Title Challenge)*	
20.10.00	Steve Conway W PTS 6 Sheffield	
25.11.00	Chris Henry W RSC 3 Manchester	
10.03.01	David Kirk W RSC 2 Bethnal Green	
22.05.01	Fabrice Faradji W RSC 1 Telde, Gran Canaria	
21.07.01	Alan Temple W CO 5 Sheffield	
27.10.01	Colin Mayisela W RSC 2 Manchester *(Vacant WBU Inter-Continental L.Welterweight Title)*	
16.03.02	Alan Bosworth W RSC 3 Northampton *(Vacant British L.Welterweight Title)*	
08.07.02	Laatekwi Hammond W RSC 2 Mayfair *(Vacant Commonwealth L.Welterweight Title)*	
19.10.02	Lucky Samba W RSC 2 Renfrew	
23.11.02	Giuseppe Lauri W RSC 2 Derby *(Final Elim. WBO L. Welterweight Title)*	
05.04.03	Jurgen Haeck W RTD 4 Manchester *(Vacant European Union L.Welterweight Title)*	
27.09.03	Fred Kinuthia W RSC 2 Manchester *(Commonwealth L.Welterweight Title Defence)*	
16.04.04	Oscar Hall W RSC 3 Bradford	
02.06.04	Salvatore Battaglia W RSC 2 Nottingham *(Vacant European L.Welterweight Title)*	
12.11.04	Krzysztof Bienias W RSC 2 Wembley *(European L.Welterweight Title Defence)*	
19.02.05	Lovemore N'Dou W PTS 12 Los Angeles, California, USA *(Commonwealth L.Welterweight Title Defence)*	

Career: 34 contests, won 31, drew 2, lost 1.

Lee Woodruff

Lancaster. *Born* Lancaster, 27 February, 1980
S. Middleweight. Ht. 5'11"
Manager Self

18.03.01	Tommy Matthews W RSC 2 Shaw	
26.04.01	Paul Buchanan L PTS 6 Gateshead	
26.07.01	Paul Martin W RSC 1 Blackpool	
23.09.01	Louis Swales W RSC 4 Shaw	
08.02.02	Paul Owen L RSC 2 Preston	
19.06.04	Tom Cannon L PTS 4 Renfrew	
08.07.04	Eric Teymour L RSC 2 The Strand	
10.09.04	Jamie Hearn L RSC 1 Wembley	

Career: 8 contests, won 3, lost 5.

Clinton Woods

Sheffield. *Born* Sheffield, 1 May, 1972
IBF L.Heavyweight Champion. Former Undefeated British, European, WBC International & Commonwealth L.Heavyweight Champion. Former Commonwealth S.Middleweight Champion. Former Undefeated Central Area S.Middleweight Champion. Ht. 6'2"
Manager D. Hobson

17.11.94	Dave Proctor W PTS 6 Sheffield	
12.12.94	Earl Ling W RSC 5 Cleethorpes	
23.02.95	Paul Clarkson W RSC 1 Hull	
06.04.95	Japhet Hans W RSC 3 Sheffield	
16.05.95	Kevin Burton W PTS 6 Cleethorpes	
14.06.95	Kevin Burton W RSC 6 Batley	
21.09.95	Paul Murray W PTS 6 Sheffield	
20.10.95	Phil Ball W RSC 4 Mansfield	
22.11.95	Andy Ewen W RSC 3 Sheffield	
05.02.96	Chris Walker W RSC 6 Bradford	
16.03.96	John Duckworth W PTS 8 Sheffield	
13.06.96	Ernie Loveridge W PTS 6 Sheffield	
14.11.96	Craig Joseph W PTS 10 Sheffield *(Vacant Central Area S. Middleweight Title)*	
20.02.97	Rocky Shelly W RSC 2 Mansfield	
10.04.97	Darren Littlewood W RSC 6 Sheffield *(Central Area S.Middleweight Title Defence)*	
26.06.97	Darren Ashton W PTS 6 Sheffield	
25.10.97	Danny Juma W PTS 8 Queensferry	
26.11.97	Jeff Finlayson W PTS 8 Sheffield	
06.12.97	Mark Baker W PTS 12 Wembley *(Vacant Commonwealth S.Middleweight Title)*	
28.03.98	David Starie L PTS 12 Hull *(Commonwealth S. Middleweight Title Defence)*	
18.06.98	Peter Mason W RTD 4 Sheffield	
30.11.98	Mark Smallwood W RSC 7 Manchester	
13.03.99	Crawford Ashley W RSC 8 Manchester *(British, Commonwealth & European L. Heavyweight Title Challenges)*	

Clinton Woods   Les Clark

10.07.99	Sam Leuii W RSC 6 Southwark	
	(Commonwealth L. Heavyweight Title	
	Defence)	
11.09.99	Lenox Lewis W RSC 10 Sheffield	
	(Commonwealth L. Heavyweight Title	
	Defence)	
10.12.99	Terry Ford W RTD 4 Warsaw, Poland	
12.02.00	Juan Perez Nelongo W PTS 12	
	Sheffield	
	(European L. Heavyweight Title	
	Defence)	
29.04.00	Ole Klemetsen W RSC 9 Wembley	
	(European L. Heavyweight Title	
	Defence)	
15.07.00	Greg Scott-Briggs W RSC 3 Millwall	
24.03.01	Ali Forbes W RTD 10 Sheffield	
	(Vacant WBC International	
	L. Heavyweight Title)	
27.07.01	Paul Bonson W PTS 6 Sheffield	
13.09.01	Yawe Davis W PTS 12 Sheffield	
	(Final Elim.WBC L.Heavyweight Title)	
16.03.02	Clint Johnson W RSC 3 Bethnal Green	
07.09.02	Roy Jones L RSC 6 Portland, Oregon,	
	USA	
	(WBC, WBA & IBF L.Heavyweight	
	Title Challenges)	
24.01.03	Sergio Martin Beaz W RSC 3 Sheffield	
18.03.03	Arturo Rivera W RSC 2 Reading	
10.06.03	Demetrius Jenkins W RSC 7 Sheffield	
07.11.03	Glengoffe Johnson DREW 12 Sheffield	
	(Vacant IBF L.Heavyweight Title)	
06.02.04	Glengoffe Johnson L PTS 12 Sheffield	
	(Vacant IBF L.Heavyweight Title)	
24.10.04	Jason DeLisle W RSC 12 Sheffield	
	(Elim. IBF L.Heavyweight Title)	
04.03.05	Rico Hoye W RSC 5 Rotherham	
	(Vacant IBF L.Heavyweight Title)	

Career: 41 contests, won 37, drew 1, lost 3.

Gary Woolcombe

Welling. *Born* London, 4 August, 1982
L.Middleweight. Ht. 5'10¾"
Manager F. Maloney

15.05.03	Paul McIlwaine W RSC 2 Mayfair
22.07.03	Arv Mittoo W PTS 6 Bethnal Green
25.09.03	Pete Buckley W PTS 6 Bethnal Green
18.11.03	John Butler W PTS 4 Bethnal Green
07.02.04	Ernie Smith W PTS 4 Bethnal Green
14.02.04	Lee Williamson W PTS 6 Holborn
07.05.04	David Kirk W PTS 4 Bethnal Green
05.06.04	Ivor Bonavic W PTS 4 Bethnal Green
24.09.04	Geraint Harvey W PTS 4 Bethnal Green
19.11.04	Keith Jones W PTS 4 Bethnal Green
11.12.04	Peter Dunn W PTS 4 Canning Town
12.02.05	Howard Clarke W PTS 6 Portsmouth
05.03.05	Ernie Smith W PTS 6 Southwark
29.04.05	Matt Scriven W RSC 2 Southwark
20.05.05	Danny Parkinson W RSC 3 Southwark
19.06.05	Peter Dunn W RSC 6 Bethnal Green

Career: 16 contests, won 16.

Chris Woollas

Epworth. *Born* Scunthorpe, 22 November, 1973
Heavyweight. Former Undefeated Midlands Area Cruiserweight Champion. Ht. 5'11"
Manager M. Shinfield

17.08.94	Darren Littlewood W RSC 4 Sheffield
05.10.94	Robert Norton DREW 6 Wolverhampton

05.12.94	Neil Simpson W PTS 6 Cleethorpes
10.02.95	Monty Wright L RSC 4 Birmingham
30.06.95	Kenny Nevers L RSC 2 Doncaster
25.09.95	Cliff Elden DREW 6 Cleethorpes
08.11.95	Stevie Pettit W PTS 6 Walsall
17.11.95	Markku Salminen L PTS 6 Helsinki, Finland
11.12.95	Cliff Elden DREW 6 Cleethorpes
15.02.96	Pele Lawrence W RSC 6 Sheffield
29.02.96	John Pierre DREW 6 Scunthorpe
16.03.96	David Jules W PTS 6 Sheffield
22.04.96	Jacklord Jacobs DREW 4 Crystal Palace
30.05.96	Martin Langtry L RSC 6 Lincoln
	(Midlands Area Cruiserweight Title Challenge)
03.09.96	Darren Corbett L RSC 7 Belfast
02.10.96	Rocky Shelly W RSC 6 Stoke
09.10.96	Nigel Rafferty W PTS 6 Stoke
28.10.96	Colin Brown L PTS 8 Glasgow
10.11.96	Michael Gale DREW 6 Glasgow
25.11.96	Albert Call L PTS 6 Cleethorpes
17.12.96	Darren Corbett L RSC 1 Doncaster
16.01.97	Mark Smallwood L PTS 8 Solihull
31.01.97	Tim Redman L PTS 6 Pentre Halkyn
14.03.97	Kelly Oliver L PTS 6 Reading
24.03.97	Mikael Lindblad L RSC 7 Helsinki, Finland
19.06.97	Ian Henry W PTS 6 Scunthorpe
02.08.97	Kelly Oliver L RSC 3 Barnsley
15.12.97	Neil Simpson W PTS 6 Cleethorpes
26.01.98	Colin Brown W PTS 6 Glasgow
26.03.98	Cliff Elden L PTS 4 Scunthorpe
06.05.98	Simon McDougall W PTS 6 Blackpool
21.07.98	Matthew Ellis L RSC 5 Widnes
11.09.98	Lennox Williams W PTS 6 Cleethorpes
12.03.99	Albert Sosnowski L PTS 4 Bethnal Green
27.05.99	Nigel Rafferty W PTS 10 Edgbaston
	(Midlands Area Cruiserweight Title Challenge)
10.07.99	Michael Sprott L RTD 4 Southwark
13.09.99	Dominic Negus L PTS 10 Bethnal Green
	(Elim. British Cruiserweight Title)
09.10.99	Chris P. Bacon L PTS 4 Manchester
30.10.99	Terry Dunstan L RSC 1 Southwark
08.04.00	Bruce Scott L RSC 2 Bethnal Green
13.07.00	Firat Aslan L RSC 2 Bethnal Green
08.09.00	Petr Horacek L PTS 4 Hammersmith
21.10.00	Danny Percival L PTS 4 Wembley
18.11.00	Matthew Ellis L PTS 4 Dagenham
11.12.00	Enzo Maccarinelli L PTS 4 Widnes
15.12.01	Lee Swaby L RSC 4 Sheffield
21.10.02	Greg Scott-Briggs W PTS 6 Cleethorpes
01.11.02	Spencer Wilding DREW 6 Preston
28.04.03	Eamonn Glennon W PTS 6 Cleethorpes
22.11.03	Albert Sosnowski L RSC 1 Belfast
16.02.04	Dave Clarke W PTS 6 Scunthorpe
30.03.04	Colin Kenna L PTS 6 Southampton
10.07.04	Robert Norton L RSC 4 Coventry
30.09.04	Paul King L PTS 4 Glasgow
06.11.04	Carl Wright L RSC 1 Coventry
16.12.04	Billy Wilson W PTS 6 Cleethorpes

Career: 56 contests, won 17, drew 7, lost 32.

Carl Wright

Rugby. *Born* Rugby, 26 April, 1978
Midlands Area & British Masters Cruiserweight Champion. Ht. 6'1¼"
Manager Self

25.06.02	Dave Clarke W PTS 6 Rugby
05.10.02	Adam Cale W PTS 6 Coventry
16.11.02	Jimmy Steel W PTS 6 Coventry
08.03.03	Gary Williams W PTS 6 Coventry
16.03.03	Darren Ashton DREW 6 Nottingham
07.06.03	Gary Thompson W RTD 2 Coventry
13.09.03	Darren Ashton W PTS 4 Coventry
09.04.04	Lee Mountford W PTS 4 Rugby
01.05.04	Paul Bonson W PTS 6 Coventry
06.11.04	Chris Woollas W RSC 1 Coventry
17.12.04	Tony Dowling W PTS 10 Coventry
	(Vacant Midlands Area Cruiserweight Title)
18.06.05	Nate Joseph W CO 1 Coventry
	(Vacant British Masters Cruiserweight Title)

Career: 12 contests, won 11, drew 1.

Nigel Wright

Crook. *Born* Bishop Auckland, 22 June, 1979
English L.Welterweight Champion. Ht. 5'9"
Manager G. Robinson

10.02.01	Keith Jones W PTS 4 Widnes
15.09.01	Tommy Peacock W RSC 1 Manchester
17.11.01	Ernie Smith W PTS 4 Glasgow
19.01.02	Woody Greenaway W CO 2 Bethnal Green
11.03.02	James Paisley W PTS 4 Glasgow
19.10.02	Kevin McIntyre L PTS 6 Renfrew
29.03.03	Darren Melville W PTS 6 Portsmouth
24.05.03	David Kirk W PTS 4 Bethnal Green
02.10.03	Nigel Senior W RSC 5 Liverpool
29.11.03	Jason Hall W PTS 6 Renfrew
06.03.04	George Telfer W RSC 3 Renfrew
22.05.04	Jon Honney W RSC 2 Widnes
22.10.04	Silence Saheed W PTS 8 Edinburgh
11.03.05	Dean Hickman W CO 7 Doncaster
	(Vacant English L.Welterweight Title)
27.05.05	Alan Bosworth W PTS 10 Spennymoor
	(English L.Welterweight Title Defence)

Career: 15 contests, won 14, lost 1.

Gary Young

Edinburgh. *Born* Edinburgh, 23 May, 1983
Welterweight. Ht. 5'7"
Manager Self

11.03.02	Paul McIlwaine W CO 2 Glasgow
08.06.02	Daniel Thorpe W RSC 1 Renfrew
02.11.02	Keith Jones W PTS 4 Belfast
22.03.03	Dean Larter W RSC 2 Renfrew
12.07.03	Lee Williamson W PTS 4 Renfrew
25.10.03	Peter Dunn W PTS 6 Edinburgh
29.11.03	Karl Taylor W RSC 3 Renfrew
06.03.04	Anthony Christopher W CO 1 Renfrew
27.03.04	Keith Jones W PTS 6 Edinburgh
19.06.04	David Kirk W PTS 4 Renfrew
22.10.04	Lionel Saraille W RSC 3 Edinburgh
28.01.05	Thomas Hengstberger W RSC 3 Renfrew
08.04.05	Viktor Baranov W PTS 8 Edinburgh

Career: 13 contests, won 13.

Joe Young

Kilburn. *Born* Paddington, 23 February, 1972
Heavyweight. Ht. 6'3"
Manager C. McMillan

21.01.05	Slick Miller W RSC 2 Brentford

Career: 1 contest, won 1.

British Area Title Bouts, 2004-2005

Central Area

Titleholders at 30 June 2005

Fly: *vacant.* **Bantam:** *vacant.* **S.Bantam:** Sean Hughes. **Feather:** *vacant.* **S.Feather:** Eddie Nevins. **Light:** Stefy Bull. **L.Welter:** Tony Montana. **Welter:** Matthew Hatton. **L.Middle:** Lee Murtagh. **Middle:** *vacant.* **S.Middle:** Dean Cockburn. **L.Heavy:** *vacant.* **Cruiser:** Denzil Browne. **Heavy:** *vacant.*

3 September — Dean Cockburn W PTS 10 Dean Walker, Doncaster (Vacant S.Middleweight Title)

29 October — Stefy Bull W RSC 2 Haroon Din, Doncaster (Lightweight Title Defence)

12 November — Robert Burton L PTS 10 Matthew Hatton, Halifax (L.Middleweight Title Defence)

4 February — Dean Cockburn W RSC 8 Jason Collins, Doncaster (S.Middleweight Title Defence)

15 December — Lee Murtagh W PTS 10 Dean Walker, Sheffield (Vacant Middleweight Title)

4 February — Stefy Bull W PTS 10 Gwyn Wale, Doncaster (Lightweight Title Defence)

11 March — Jason Rushton W PTS 10 Lee Armstrong, Doncaster (Vacant L.Middleweight Title)

20 May — Dean Cockburn W PTS 10 Jason Collins, Doncaster (S.Middleweight Title Defence)

20 May — Jason Rushton L PTS 10 Lee Murtagh, Doncaster (L.Middleweight Title Defence)

Between 1 July 2004 and 30 June 2005, Danny Thornton (Middle) and Matthew Hatton (L.Middle) relinquished their titles.

Midlands Area

Titleholders at 30 June 2005

Fly: *vacant.* **Bantam:** *vacant.* **S.Bantam:** *vacant.* **Feather:** Stephen Chinnock. **S.Feather:** *vacant.* **Light:** Scott Lawton. **L.Welter:** Dean Hickman. **Welter:** *vacant.* **L.Middle:** Gavin Down. **Middle:** Andy Halder. **S.Middle:** Peter Jackson. **L.Heavy:** *vacant.* **Cruiser:** Carl Wright. **Heavy:** Mark Krence.

Jason Rushton (right) picked up the Central Area light-middleweight title on outpointing Lee Armstrong   Les Clark

10 July	Andy Halder W PTS 10 Conroy McIntosh, Coventry (Vacant Middleweight Title)
25 November	Gavin Down W PTS 10 Steve Brumant, Birmingham (Vacant L.Middleweight Title)
17 December	Carl Wright W PTS 10 Tony Dowling, Coventry (Vacant Cruiserweight Title)
17 February	Dean Hickman W PTS 10 Gary Reid, Dudley (L.Welterweight Title Defence)

Between 1 July 2004 and 30 June 2005, Matt Scriven (L.Middle) and Scott Lansdowne (Cruiser) relinquished their titles, while Gareth Payne (S.Bantam) retired and Tony Conroy (Welter) forfeited.

Northern Area

Titleholders at 30 June 2005

Fly: *vacant.* **Bantam:** *vacant.* **S.Bantam:** *vacant.* **Feather:** *vacant.* **S.Feather:** *vacant.* **Light:** *vacant.* **L.Welter:** *vacant.* **Welter:** Oscar Hall. **L.Middle:** *vacant.* **Middle:** Eddie Haley. **S.Middle:** Ryan Kerr. **L.Heavy:** *vacant.* **Cruiser:** *vacant.* **Heavy:** *vacant.*

23 September	Ryan Kerr W RSC 7 Gary Dixon, Gateshead (S.Middleweight Title Defence)

Northern Ireland Area

Titleholders at 30 June 2005

Fly: *vacant.* **Bantam:** *vacant.* **S.Bantam:** *vacant.* **Feather:** *vacant.* **S.Feather:** *vacant.* **Light:** Dafydd Carlin. **L.Welter:** *vacant.* **Welter:** *vacant.* **L.Middle:** *vacant.* **Middle:** *vacant.* **S.Middle:** *vacant.* **L.Heavy:** *vacant.* **Cruiser:** *vacant.* **Heavy:** *vacant.*

There were no title bouts held in 2004-2005.

Scottish Area

Titleholders at 30 June 2005

Fly: *vacant.* **Bantam:** *vacant.* **S.Bantam:** *vacant.* **Feather:** *vacant.* **S.Feather:** *vacant.* **Light:** Martin Watson. **L.Welter:** *vacant.* **Welter:** Kevin McIntyre. **L.Middle:** Barrie Lee. **Middle:** *vacant.* **S.Middle:** Tom Cannon. **L.Heavy:** *vacant.* **Cruiser:** *vacant.* **Heavy:** *vacant.*

22 October	Barrie Lee W PTS 10 Craig Lynch, Edinburgh (Vacant L.Middleweight Title)
1 April	Tom Cannon W RTD 7 Barry Connell, Glasgow (Vacant S.Middleweight Title)

Between 1 July 2004 and 30 June 2005, Brian Carr (Feather) retired.

Southern Area

Titleholders at 30 June 2005

Fly: *vacant.* **Bantam:** *vacant.* **S.Bantam:** Marc Callaghan. **Feather:** Rocky Dean. **S.Feather:** *vacant.* **Light:** Rob Jeffries. **L.Welter:** Francis Barrett. **Welter:** Ross Minter. **L.Middle:** Gilbert Eastman. **Middle:** *vacant.* **S.Middle:** *vacant.* **L.Heavy:** Andrew Lowe. **Cruiser:** *vacant.* **Heavy:** *vacant.*

16 June	Marc Callaghan W PTS 10 Ian Napa, Dagenham (Vacant S.Bantamweight Title)
5 March	Rocky Dean W PTS 10 Mickey Coveney, Dagenham (Vacant Featherweight Title)
29 April	Chas Symonds L RSC 3 Ross Minter, Southwark (Welterweight Title Defence)
30 April	Peter McDonagh L PTS 10 Rob Jeffries, Dagenham (Lightweight Title Defence)

Between 1 July 2004 and 30 June 2005, Allan Gray (Middle) and Garry Delaney (Cruiser) relinquished their titles.

Welsh Area

Titleholders at 30 June 2005

Fly: *vacant.* **Bantam:** *vacant.* **S.Bantam:** *vacant.* **Feather:** *vacant.* **S.Feather:** *vacant.* **Light:** *vacant.* **L.Welter:** *vacant.* **Welter:** Bradley Pryce. **L.Middle:** *vacant.* **Middle:** *vacant.* **S.Middle:** *vacant.* **L.Heavy:** *vacant.* **Cruiser:** *vacant.* **Heavy:** *vacant.*

3 July	Bradley Pryce W RSC 8 Keith Jones, Newport (Vacant Welterweight Title)

Western Area

Titleholders at 30 June 2005

Fly: *vacant.* **Bantam:** *vacant.* **S.Bantam:** *vacant.* **Feather:** *vacant.* **S.Feather:** *vacant.* **Light:** *vacant.* **L.Welter:** *vacant.* **Welter:** *vacant.* **L.Middle:** *vacant.* **Middle:** *vacant.* **S.Middle:** *vacant.* **L.Heavy:** Leigh Alliss. **Cruiser:** *vacant.* **Heavy:** *vacant.*

1 October	Leigh Alliss W RSC 2 Shane White, Bristol (Vacant L.Heavyweight Title)

Between 1 July 2004 and 30 June 2005, Darren Dorrington (S.Middle) relinquished his title.

English and Celtic Title Bouts, 2004-2005

English Title Bouts

Due to the fact that was often a dearth of competition for certain weights at Area level, the BBBoC had long felt the need for an English championship competition and, having taken the necessary steps, Matt Skelton and Matt Holden were matched to contest the innaugural English title, at heavyweight, on 18 September, 2003.

Titleholders at 30 June 2005

Fly: Lee Haskins. **Bantam:** *vacant.* **S.Bantam:** *vacant.* **Feather:** Andy Morris. **S.Feather:** Roy Rutherford. **Light:** Danny Hunt. **L.Welter:** Nigel Wright. **Welter:** Michael Jennings. **L.Middle:** Andrew Facey. **Middle:** Donovan Smillie. **S.Middle:** Ryan Kerr. **L.Heavy:** Peter Haymer. **Cruiser:** *vacant.* **Heavy:** Mark Krence.

1 October	Steve Foster W RSC 9 Gary Thornhill, Manchester (Featherweight Title Defence)
1 October	Chris Saunders L RTD 5 Michael Jennings, Manchester (Welterweight Title Defence)
5 October	Young Muttley W RSC 6 Gavin Down, Dudley (L.Welterweight Title Defence)
12 November	Steven Spartacus L PTS 10 Peter Haymer, Wembley (L.Heavyweight Title Defence)
18 November	Donovan Smillie W RSC 7 Roddy Doran, Shrewsbury (Vacant Middleweight Title)
19 November	Danny Hunt W PTS 10 Lee Meager, Bethnal Green (Lightweight Title Defence)
3 December	Lee Haskins W RTD 3 Delroy Spencer, Bristol (Vacant Flyweight Title)
10 December	Peter Haymer W RSC 10 Mark Brookes, Sheffield (L.Heavyweight Title Defence)
11 December	Mark Krence W PTS 10 John McDermott, Canning Town (Vacant Heavyweight Title)
25 February	Ryan Kerr W PTS 10 Ryan Walls, Sunderland (Vacant S.Middleweight Title)
11 March	Nigel Wright W CO 7 Dean Hickman, Doncaster (Vacant L.Welterweight Title)
20 May	Andy Morris W PTS 10 Rocky Dean, Southwark (Vacant Featherweight Title)
27 May	Nigel Wright W PTS 10 Alan Bosworth, Spennymoor (L.Welterweight Title Defence)
19 June	Peter Haymer W PTS 10 Tony Oakey, Bethnal Green (L.Heavyweight Title Defence)
30 June	Michael Jennings W RSC 9 Gavin Down, Manchester (Welterweight Title Defence)

Between 1 July 2004 and 30 June 2005, Steve Foster (Feather), Young Muttley (L.Welter) and Scott Dann (Middle) relinquished their titles.

Celtic Title Bouts

Following the successful introduction of English titles, in August 2004 the BBBoC introduced the Celtic title to accommodate boxers from Ireland, Scotland and Wales, with the inaugural title bout being contested by Martin Watson and Mark Winters at the lightweight limit.

Titleholders at 30 June 2005

Fly: *vacant.* **Bantam:** *vacant.* **S.Bantam:** *vacant.* **Feather:** *vacant.* **S.Feather:** Willie Limond. **Light:** Martin Watson. **L.Welter:** *vacant.* **Welter:** Kevin Anderson. **L.Middle:** *vacant.* **Middle:** *vacant.* **S.Middle:** *vacant.* **L.Heavy:** *vacant.* **Cruiser:** *vacant.* **Heavy:** *vacant.*

29 October	Martin Watson W PTS 10 Mark Winters, Renfrew (Vacant Lightweight Title)
31 January	Kevin Anderson W RSC 4 Glenn McClarnon, Glasgow (Vacant Welterweight Title)
17 June	Willie Limond W PTS 10 Kevin O'Hara, Glasgow (Vacant S.Featherweight Title)

Nigel Wright, the English light-welterweight champion

Les Clark

British Title Bouts, 2004-2005

All of last season's title bouts are shown in date order within their weight divisions and give the contestants' respective weights, along with the scorecard if going to a decision. Every contest is summarised briefly and all referees are named.

Flyweight

Jason Booth (England) handed back his belt in December 2003 after winning the IBO championship on 20 September and deciding to concentrate on defending that title. With no title bouts taking place during 2004-2005, the title remained vacant.

Bantamweight

20 May   Martin Power 8.5 (England) W PTS 12 Dale Robinson 8.5 (England), Elephant & Castle Leisure Centre, Southwark, London. Referee: Paul Thomas 116-113. Contested for the vacant title after Nicky Booth (England) forfeited his crown in June 2004 after being convicted of criminal offences outside the ring, Power eventually got home to avenge an amateur loss against Robinson, who was up against it from the moment he was badly cut over the left eye in the second round. Despite the cut, during the middle sessions Robinson was doing the better work, his body punching excellent and he even had Power over in the 11th, although it appeared to be more of a push than a punch. In what was a close fight, many thinking that Robinson had done enough, it was only in the last four rounds that Power came through with short bursts of punches and better defensive work to sway the referee.

S. Bantamweight

19 November   Michael Hunter 8.9¾ (England) W RSC 10 Marc Callaghan 8.8¼ (England), Borough Hall, Hartlepool. Referee: Ian John-Lewis. In an absorbing contest, it was the heavier punching power of the champion that prevailed over the clever Callaghan, who was deducted a point for low blows in the eighth. Although Callaghan had stayed with Hunter up to a fashion, it was from hereon that he began to crumble as the local man started to unload and, at 2.31 of round ten, the referee rescued the brave challenger, who was being pounded without return.

Opposing a man who had beaten him in the amateurs, Martin Power (right) was adjudged to have outscored Dale Robinson to win the vacant British bantamweight title last May

Les Clark

4 March   Michael Hunter 8.9¹/₂ (England) W RSC 6 Sean Hughes 8.8 (England), Borough Hall, Hartlepool. Referee: John Keane. Starting well behind the southpaw jab, the challenger held Hunter at bay for a while, but once the champion got into his stride in the second session he was soon punching his man around the ring. Under pressure, Hughes came back well in the fifth, but was again under the cosh in the sixth and after being bowled over for a count he was rescued at 1.34 of the round when he was reeling against the ropes as more punches got to him.

Featherweight

5 November   Dazzo Williams 8.13³/₄ (Wales) W PTS 12 John Simpson 8.13¹/₂ (Scotland), The Leisure Centre, Hereford. Referee: Phil Edwards 115-114. Having earned his title opportunity when beating Marc Callaghan, the unheralded Scot proceeded to give the champion all the trouble he could handle as he began to take over in the middle rounds, his better boxing picking up points, his defences remaining sound. Williams had started reasonably well and he needed to finish well, but although he came on strongly in the last couple of rounds to have his arm lifted at the final bell there were many who thought the decision favoured the wrong man.

16 June   Dazzo Williams 8.13¹/₄ (Wales) L CO 2 Nicky Cook 9.0 (England), Goresbrook Leisure Centre, Dagenham. Referee: John Keane. Judges: Larry O'Connell, Terry O'Connor, Richie Davies. With Cook's European and Commonwealth titles also on the line, he was quick to impose himself on the British champion with jabs and solid shots to the body putting him in the driving seat in the first before starting the second with much of the same. Then it happened. Having missed with a solid right to the head, Cook instinctively threw a left hook to the body, the effects of which saw Williams counted out on all fours.

S. Featherweight

9 April   Alex Arthur 9.3³/₄ (Scotland) W CO 9 Craig Docherty 9.3¹/₄ (Scotland), Meadowbank Leisure Centre, Edinburgh. Referee: Richie Davies. Contested for the vacant title that Michael Gomez had relinquished after winning the WBU crown on 3 April 2004, Docherty, whose Commonwealth crown was also at stake, made the early running before Arthur came on strong in the fourth round. Putting his punches together for the first time in the fight, Arthur broke his rival's nose and generally picked it up with blows to both head and body. There was no way back after that and Arthur's better boxing saw him take over, his combinations especially effective, as Docherty gradually wilted. Having taken a pounding in the seventh and eighth rounds, Docherty was soon caught again in the ninth and was counted out 46 seconds into the session after a series of punches, followed by a left hook to the body, dropped him and left him with nothing in the tank.

Lightweight

30 July   Graham Earl 9.8¹/₂ (England) W RSC 6 Steve Murray 9.8 (England), York Hall, Bethnal Green, London. Referee: Howard Foster. Trying to put their previous fight behind him, Murray set a cracking pace in the first two rounds before a bad cut on the right cheek and then a cut on the left eye in the fourth session made his task even more difficult. It had been punch for punch until then, despite Murray suffering a flash knockdown in the third, but with the eye in a parlous state he went for broke and accepted the consequences. Although the corner did a good job with the injuries, with the eyebrow worsening it was clear that Murray had little time left and while he certainly hurt the champion with some heavy hooks to the head, once he was again under pressure the referee called it off with 23 seconds of round six remaining.

19 June   Graham Earl 9.7¹/₂ (England) W RSC 9 Kevin Bennett 9.8¹/₂ (England), York Hall, Bethnal Green, London. Referee: Howard Foster. Outboxed from the opening bell and dropped from a right to the head in the sixth, it seemed that Earl's days as a champion were virtually over, especially with the challenger continuing to hammer in blows that looked to end the contest summarily. However, after somehow regrouping in the seventh, it was noticeable that Bennett, whose Commonwealth title was also at stake, was breathing heavily and the eighth saw a dramatic turnaround as Earl, his left eye swelling ominously, forced his rival around the ring. Early in the ninth, Earl again had Bennett stumbling around the ring and after two heavy rights weakened him further the referee called it off on the 2.10 mark.

L. Welterweight

On 8 May, Junior Witter (England) was presented with the Lonsdale Belt for keeps after no challenger had been deemed worthy enough to challenge him during the past three years.

Welterweight

12 November   David Barnes 10.6¹/₂ (England) W RSC 6 James Hare 10.6³/₄ (England), North Bridge Leisure Centre, Halifax. Referee: Marcus McDonnell. In winning a Lonsdale Belt outright, Barnes proved the master of the pre-fight favourite, Hare, whose days looked numbered after he was sent stumbling from a heavy left in the third and ended the round with damage over both eyes. It was Barnes' hand speed which was controlling the fight and in the fourth a southpaw left cross put Hare down heavily for a count of eight. Despite him coming back in the fifth the end was in sight when a solid left cross had Hare down again in the sixth. Although he somehow beat the count the referee judged him to be in no position to defend himself and the contest was over with 1.41 on the clock. Barnes was stripped of the title on 8 June, having undertaken to defend against Jimmy Vincent on 16 July. That was before he received a 45-day suspension after being stopped by Joshua Okine in a Commonwealth title bout on 4 June, at which point the Board considered that Vincent had waited long enough and acted accordingly.

L. Middleweight

26 November   Jamie Moore 11.0 (England) L DIS 3 Michael Jones 11.0 (England), The Sports Centre, Altrincham. Referee: Dave Parris. Having beaten Jones to win the vacant British title, Moore was expected to retain this time and was somewhat unfortunate not to do so. Following a first round where Jones had hurt Moore with a big right, but had also required time to recover from low blows, when both threw low blows in the second session it was clear that this was going to be a difficult one to control. After 1.16 of the third it was all over when the referee had no alternative but to disqualify Moore. The champion, who had been ordered to stop boxing after knocking out Jones' gumshield and delivering a low blow, seemingly ignored the instruction to drop Jones with an instinctive left hook and when the latter stated that he was unable to continue it was all over.

Middleweight

17 September   Scott Dann 11.5³/₄ (England) W RSC 6 Steven Bendall 11.6 (England), The Pavilions, Plymouth. Referee: Marcus McDonnell. In a contest between southpaws for the vacant title, Howard Eastman having relinquished in May 2004 to concentrate on his European crown and securing a world title shot, Dann came out on top, his left hand being the main difference between the two. With Bendall deciding to charge in regardless, Dann picked him off and by the fourth round it was looking ominous for the Coventry man as lefts, both long and short, rattled home. In the sixth, with Bendall cornered after being hit by a cracking left hand and having to soak up a barrage of leather as Dann followed up, once another mighty left had again found its mark the referee stopped the contest at 2.05 of the round.

4 February   Scott Dann 11.5 (England) W CO 3 Alan Jones 11.4¹/₂ (Wales), The Pavilions, Plymouth. Referee: Mark Green. Having stalked the unfortunate challenger for two rounds, and having cut him over the right eye, Dann went to work in the third with a vengeance. Following two cracking lefts he sent in another heavy right, followed by a crunching left cross, and Jones finished up with his head hanging over the bottom strand. Although the Welshman somehow got to his feet he failed to make the count and it was all over for him.

29 April   Scott Dann 11.4¹/₂ (England) W CO 1 Andy Halder 11.3 (England), The Pavilions, Plymouth. Referee: Ian John-Lewis. Having won the title when beating a fellow southpaw, this time he was making his second defence against another one in Andy Halder, who lasted just 165 seconds. Despite being anxious to land a Lonsdale Belt in quick time, Dann waited for Halder, who was trying to keep it at distance, to leave an opening and when he did the champion stepped in with a three-punch combination, a left to the head being the final blow. Although the challenger went down on his back and looked well out of it, he made a monumental effort to get to his feet before being ultimately counted out in the act of rising.

S. Middleweight

24 September   Carl Froch 11.13 (England) W RSC 1 Damon Hague 12.0 (England), The Arena, Nottingham. Referee: Mickey Vann. Contested for the vacant title after Tony Dodson (England) had handed back his belt in September, having been unable to meet Froch on three occasions due to injury, it also involved Froch's Commonwealth crown. While Hague may have been tense, Froch was extremely relaxed and it showed as he moved around the ring to make his rival miss before setting him up with a couple of big rights to the head that were followed up with more of the same, this time to the body. Towards the end of the first, Froch put Hague down for an 'eight' count with a short right to the temple and with the latter back on shaky legs, but allowed to box on, a right cross-left hook sent him crashing again just as the bell went to end the round. Although Hague managed to get up at 'four', knowing that he was in no fit condition to continue even allowing for the break, the referee called it off.

L. Heavyweight

Peter Oboh failed to defend during the period.

Cruiserweight

17 December   Mark Hobson 14.1 (England) W PTS 12 Bruce Scott 14.3³/₄ (England), The Sports Centre, Huddersfield. Referee: Paul Thomas 118-112. In the first British cruiserweight championship fight at the new weight of 200lbs, with Hobson's Commonwealth title also on the line, the champion outboxed the smaller Scott for most of the fight. Apart from the fourth round, when the challenger hurt Hobson with several right hands, it was much of the same as the latter kept the left jab going, while crossing the right and looking to land left hooks when the opportunity arose. It was pretty mundane stuff, but Hobson did more than enough to ensure that he would take home a Lonsdale Belt for keeps.

Heavyweight

19 November   Matt Skelton 17.11 (England) W RSC 11 Keith Long 14.12 (England), York Hall, Bethnal Green, London. Referee: Howard Foster. In what was a boring affair, Skelton, whose Commonwealth title was also at risk, made hard work of a 'difficult' opponent in Long before getting the job done with just 15 seconds of the 11th round remaining. At times there was more wrestling than boxing and Skelton had a point deducted in the seventh for holding and hitting before he began to get more distance in an effort to place his punches. Finally, in the 11th, Skelton picked out a solid right uppercut to put Long down and when the latter got up, but wasn't fighting back when hit by several right hands, the referee had seen enough.

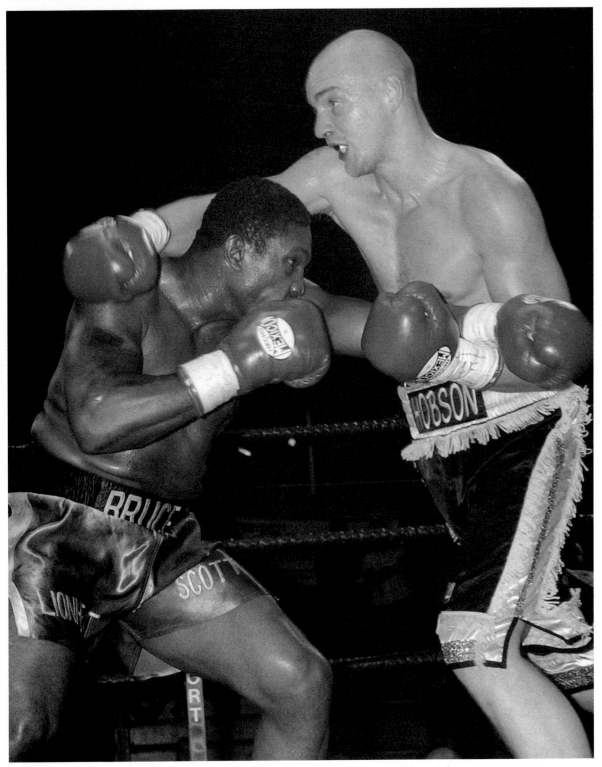

Mark Hobson (right) had no difficulty in outscoring Bruce Scott to win a Lonsdale Belt outright

Les Clark

Lord Lonsdale Challenge Belts: Outright Winners

Outright Winners of the National Sporting Club's Challenge Belt, 1909-1935 (21)

Under pressure from other promoters with bigger venues, and in an effort to sustain their monopoly – having controlled championship fights in Britain up until that point in time – the National Sporting Club launched the belt in 1909. They did so on the proviso that there should be eight weight divisions – fly, bantam, feather, light, welter, middle, light-heavy, and heavy – and that to win a belt outright a champion must score three title-match victories at the same weight, but not necessarily consecutively. Worth a substantial amount of money, and carrying a £1 a week pension from the age of 50, the President of the NSC, Lord Lonsdale, donated the first of 22 belts struck. Known as the Lonsdale Belt, despite the inscription reading: 'The National Sporting Club's Challenge Belt', the first man to put a notch on a belt was Freddie Welsh, who outpointed Johnny Summers for the lightweight title on 8 November 1909, while Jim Driscoll became the first man to win one outright. The record time for winning the belt is held by Jim Higgins (279 days).

FLYWEIGHT	Jimmy Wilde; Jackie Brown
BANTAMWEIGHT	Digger Stanley; Joe Fox; Jim Higgins; Johnny Brown; Dick Corbett; Johnny King
FEATHERWEIGHT	Jim Driscoll; Tancy Lee; Johnny Cuthbert; Nel Tarleton
LIGHTWEIGHT	Freddie Welsh
WELTERWEIGHT	Johnny Basham; Jack Hood
MIDDLEWEIGHT	Pat O'Keefe; Len Harvey; Jock McAvoy
L. HEAVYWEIGHT	Dick Smith
HEAVYWEIGHT	Bombardier Billy Wells; Jack Petersen

Note: Both Dick Corbett and Johnny King – with one notch apiece on the 'special' British Empire Lonsdale Belt that was struck in 1933 and later presented to the winner of the Tommy Farr v Joe Louis fight – were allowed to keep their Lonsdale Belts with just two notches secured; Freddie Welsh, also with two notches, was awarded a belt due to his inability to defend because of the First World War; the first bantam belt came back into circulation and was awarded to Johnny Brown; Al Foreman, with just one notch on the second lightweight belt, took it back to Canada with him without the consent of the BBBoC; while the second light-heavy belt was awarded to Jack Smith of Worcester for winning a novices heavyweight competition. Having emigrated to New Zealand, Smith later presented the visiting Her Majesty The Queen with the belt and it now hangs in the BBBoC's offices.

Outright Winners of the BBBoC Lord Lonsdale Challenge Belt, 1936-2005 (116)

Re-introduced by the British Boxing Board of Control as the Lord Lonsdale Challenge Belt, but of less intrinsic value – Benny Lynch's eight-round win over Pat Palmer (16 September 1936 at Shawfield Park, Glasgow) got the new version underway – Eric Boon became the first man to win one outright, in 1939, following victories over Dave Crowley (2) and Arthur Danahar. Since those early days, six further weight divisions have been added and, following on from Henry Cooper's feat of winning three Lonsdale Belts outright, on 10 June 1981 the BBBoC's rules and regulations were amended to read that no boxer shall receive more than one belt as his own property, in any one weight division. From 1 September 1999, any boxer putting a notch on a Lonsdale Belt for the first time will require three more notches at the same weight before he can call the belt his own. However, men who already had a notch on the Lonsdale Belt prior to 1 September 1999 could contest it under the former ruling of three winning championship contests at the same weight. Incidentally, the fastest of the modern belt winners is Ryan Rhodes (90 days), while Chris and Kevin Finnegan are the only brothers to have each won a belt outright.

FLYWEIGHT	Jackie Paterson; Terry Allen; Walter McGowan; John McCluskey; Hugh Russell; Charlie Magri; Pat Clinton; Robbie Regan; Francis Ampofo; Ady Lewis
BANTAMWEIGHT	Johnny King; Peter Keenan (2); Freddie Gilroy; Alan Rudkin; Johnny Owen; Billy Hardy; Drew Docherty; Nicky Booth
S. BANTAMWEIGHT	Richie Wenton; Michael Brodie; Michael Alldis
FEATHERWEIGHT	Nel Tarleton; Ronnie Clayton (2); Charlie Hill; Howard Winstone (2); Evan Armstrong; Pat Cowdell; Robert Dickie; Paul Hodkinson; Colin McMillan; Sean Murphy; Jonjo Irwin; Dazzo Williams
S. FEATHERWEIGHT	Jimmy Anderson; John Doherty; Floyd Havard; Charles Shepherd; Michael Gomez; Alex Arthur

185

LIGHTWEIGHT	Eric Boon; Billy Thompson; Joe Lucy; Dave Charnley; Maurice Cullen; Ken Buchanan; Jim Watt; George Feeney; Tony Willis; Carl Crook; Billy Schwer; Michael Ayers; Bobby Vanzie; Graham Earl
L. WELTERWEIGHT	Joey Singleton; Colin Power; Clinton McKenzie; Lloyd Christie; Andy Holligan; Ross Hale; Junior Witter
WELTERWEIGHT	Ernie Roderick; Wally Thom; Brian Curvis (2); Ralph Charles; Colin Jones; Lloyd Honeyghan; Kirkland Laing; Del Bryan; Geoff McCreesh; Derek Roche; Neil Sinclair; David Barnes
L. MIDDLEWEIGHT	Maurice Hope; Jimmy Batten; Pat Thomas; Prince Rodney; Andy Till; Robert McCracken; Ryan Rhodes; Ensley Bingham
MIDDLEWEIGHT	Pat McAteer; Terry Downes; Johnny Pritchett; Bunny Sterling; Alan Minter; Kevin Finnegan; Roy Gumbs; Tony Sibson; Herol Graham; Neville Brown; Howard Eastman
S. MIDDLEWEIGHT	Sammy Storey; David Starie
L. HEAVYWEIGHT	Randy Turpin; Chic Calderwood; Chris Finnegan; Bunny Johnson; Tom Collins; Dennis Andries; Tony Wilson; Crawford Ashley
CRUISERWEIGHT	Johnny Nelson; Terry Dunstan; Bruce Scott; Mark Hobson
HEAVYWEIGHT	Henry Cooper (3); Horace Notice; Lennox Lewis; Julius Francis; Danny Williams

Note: Walter McGowan, Charlie Magri and Junior Witter, with one notch apiece, kept their belts under the three years/no available challengers' ruling, while Johnny King, with two notches, was awarded the belt on the grounds that the Second World War stopped him from making further defences. Incidentally, King and Nel Tarleton are the only men to have won both the NSC and BBBoC belts outright.

Junior Witter, seen here having his hand raised in victory, became the first man since Charlie Magri to be awarded the Lonsdale Belt for keeps under the three years/no available challengers' ruling   Les Clark

British Champions Since Gloves, 1878-2005

The listings below show the tenure of all British champions at each weight since gloves (two ounces or more) were introduced to British rings under Queensberry Rules. Although Charley Davis (147 lbs) had beaten Ted Napper (140 lbs) with gloves in 1873, we start with Denny Harrington, who defeated George Rooke for both the English and world middleweight titles in London on 12 March 1878. We also make a point of ignoring competition winners, apart from Anthony Diamond who beat Dido Plumb for the middles title over 12 rounds, basically because full championship conditions or finish fights of three-minute rounds were not applied. Another point worth bearing in mind, is that prior to the 1880s there were only five weights – heavy, middle, light, feather and bantam. Anything above 154 lbs, the middleweight limit, was classified a heavyweight contest, whereas lightweight, feather and bantamweight poundages were much looser. Therefore, to put things into current perspective, in many cases we have had to ascertain the actual poundage of fighters concerned and relate them to the modern weight classes. Another point worth remembering is that men born outside Britain who won international titles in this country, are not recorded for fear of added confusion and, although many of the champions or claimants listed before 1909 were no more than English titleholders, having fought for the 'championship of England', for our purposes they carry the 'British' label.

Prior to 1909, the year that the Lord Lonsdale Challenge Belt was introduced and weight classes subsequently standardised, poundages within divisions could vary quite substantially, thus enabling men fighting at different weights to claim the same 'title' at the same time. A brief history of the weight fluctuations between 1891 and 1909, shows:

Bantamweight   With the coming of gloves, the division did not really take off until Nunc Wallace established himself at 112 lbs on beating (small) Bill Goode after nine rounds in London on 12 March 1889. Later, with Wallace fighting above the weight, Billy Plimmer was generally recognised as the country's leading eight stoner, following victories over Charles Mansford and Jem Stevens, and became accepted as world champion when George Dixon, the number one in America's eyes, gradually increased his weight. In 1895, Pedlar Palmer took the British title at 112 lbs, but by 1900 he had developed into a 114 pounder. Between 1902 and 1904, Joe Bowker defended regularly at 116 lbs and in 1909 the NSC standardised the weight at 118 lbs, even though the USA continued for a short while to accept only 116 lbs.

Featherweight   Between 1886 and 1895, one of the most prestigious championship belts in this country was fought for at 126 lbs and, although George Dixon was recognised in the USA as world featherweight champion – gradually moving from 114 to 122 lbs – no major international contests took place in Britain during the above period at his weight. It was only in 1895, when Fred Johnson took the British title at 120 lbs, losing it to Ben Jordan two years later, that we came into line with the USA. Ben Jordan became an outstanding champion who, between 1898 and 1899, was seen by the NSC as world champion at 120 lbs. However, first Harry Greenfield, then Jabez White and Will Curley, continued to claim the 126 lbs version of the British title and it was only in 1900, when Jack Roberts beat Curley, that the weight limit was finally standardised at nine stone.

Lightweight   Outstanding champions often carried their weights as they grew in size. A perfect example of this was Dick Burge, the British lightweight champion from 1891-1901, who gradually increased from 134 to 144 lbs, while still maintaining his right to the title. It was not until 1902 that Jabez White brought the division into line with the USA. Later, both White, and then Goldswain, carried their weight up to 140 lbs and it was left to Johnny Summers to set the current limit of 135 lbs.

Welterweight   The presence of Dick Burge fighting from 134 to 144 lbs plus up until 1900, explains quite adequately why the welterweight division, although very popular in the USA, did not take off in this country until 1902. The championship was contested between 142 and 146 lbs in those days and was not really supported by the NSC, but by 1909 with their backing it finally became established at 147 lbs.

On 8 September 1970, Bunny Sterling became the first immigrant to win a British title under the ten-year residential ruling, while earlier, on 28 June 1948, Dick Turpin won the British middleweight title and, in doing so, became the first coloured fighter to win the title, thus breaking down the so-called 'colour bar'.

Note that the Lonsdale Belt notches (title bout wins) relate to NSC, 1909-1935, and BBBoC, 1936-2005.

Champions in **bold** are accorded national recognition.

*Undefeated champions (Does not include men who forfeited titles).

Title Holder	Lonsdale Belt Notches	Tenure	Title Holder	Lonsdale Belt Notches	Tenure	Title Holder	Lonsdale Belt Notches	Tenure
Flyweight (112 lbs)			**Percy Jones**	1	1914	**Joe Symonds**	1	1915-1916
Sid Smith		1911	Joe Symonds		1914	**Jimmy Wilde***	3	1916-1923
Sid Smith	1	1911-1913	**Tancy Lee**	1	1914-1915	**Elky Clark***	2	1924-1927
Bill Ladbury		1913-1914	Jimmy Wilde		1914-1915	**Johnny Hill***	1	1927-1929

Title Holder	Lonsdale Belt Notches	Tenure
Jackie Brown		1929-1930
Bert Kirby	1	1930-1931
Jackie Brown	3	1931-1935
Benny Lynch*	2	1935-1938
Jackie Paterson	4	1939-1948
Rinty Monaghan*	1	1948-1950
Terry Allen	1	1951-1952
Teddy Gardner*	1	1952
Terry Allen*	2	1952-1954
Dai Dower*	1	1955-1957
Frankie Jones	2	1957-1960
Johnny Caldwell*	1	1960-1961
Jackie Brown	1	1962-1963
Walter McGowan*	1	1963-1966
John McCluskey*	3	1967-1977
Charlie Magri*	1	1977-1981
Kelvin Smart	1	1982-1984
Hugh Russell*	3	1984-1985
Duke McKenzie*	2	1985-1986
Dave Boy McAuley*	1	1986-1988
Pat Clinton*	3	1988-1991
Robbie Regan	1	1991
Francis Ampofo	1	1991
Robbie Regan*	2	1991-1992
Francis Ampofo	3	1992-1996
Mickey Cantwell*	1	1996-1997
Ady Lewis*	3	1997-1998
Damaen Kelly	1	1999
Keith Knox	1	1999
Jason Booth*	2	1999-2003

Bantamweight (118 lbs)

Title Holder	Lonsdale Belt Notches	Tenure
Nunc Wallace*		1889-1891
Billy Plimmer		1891-1895
Tom Gardner		1892
Willie Smith		1892-1896
Nunc Wallace		1893-1895
George Corfield		1893-1896
Pedlar Palmer		1895-1900
Billy Plimmer		1896-1898
Harry Ware		1899-1900
Harry Ware		1900-1902
Andrew Tokell		1901-1902
Jim Williams		1902
Andrew Tokell		1902
Harry Ware		1902
Joe Bowker		1902-1910
Owen Moran		1905-1907
Digger Stanley		1906-1910
Digger Stanley	2	1910-1913
Bill Beynon	1	1913
Digger Stanley	1	1913-1914
Curley Walker*	1	1914-1915
Joe Fox*	3	1915-1917
Tommy Noble	1	1918-1919
Walter Ross*	1	1919-1920
Jim Higgins	3	1920-1922
Tommy Harrison		1922-1923
Bugler Harry Lake	1	1923
Johnny Brown	3	1923-1928
Alf Pattenden	2	1928-1929
Johnny Brown		1928
Teddy Baldock		1928-1929
Teddy Baldock*	1	1929-1931
Dick Corbett	1	1931-1932
Johnny King	1	1932-1934
Dick Corbett*	1	1934

Title Holder	Lonsdale Belt Notches	Tenure
Johnny King	1+2	1935-1947
Jackie Paterson	2	1947-1949
Stan Rowan*	1	1949
Danny O'Sullivan	1	1949-1951
Peter Keenan	3	1951-1953
John Kelly	1	1953-1954
Peter Keenan	3	1954-1959
Freddie Gilroy*	4	1959-1963
Johnny Caldwell	1	1964-1965
Alan Rudkin	1	1965-1966
Walter McGowan	1	1966-1968
Alan Rudkin*	4	1968-1972
Johnny Clark*	1	1973-1974
Dave Needham	1	1974-1975
Paddy Maguire	1	1975-1977
Johnny Owen*	4	1977-1980
John Feeney	1	1981-1983
Hugh Russell	1	1983
Davy Larmour	1	1983
John Feeney	1	1983-1985
Ray Gilbody	2	1985-1987
Billy Hardy*	5	1987-1991
Joe Kelly	1	1992
Drew Docherty	4	1992-1997
Paul Lloyd	2	1997-1999
Noel Wilders*	2	1999-2000
Ady Lewis	1	2000
Tommy Waite	1	2000
Nicky Booth	5	2000-2004
Martin Power	1	2005-

S. Bantamweight (122 lbs)

Title Holder	Lonsdale Belt Notches	Tenure
Richie Wenton*	3	1994-1996
Michael Brodie*	3	1997-1999
Patrick Mullings	1	1999
Drew Docherty*	1	1999
Michael Alldis	3	1999-2001
Patrick Mullings	1	2001
Michael Alldis*	1	2002
Esham Pickering*	1	2003-2004
Michael Hunter	3	2004-

Featherweight (126 lbs)

Title Holder	Lonsdale Belt Notches	Tenure
Bill Baxter		1884-1891
Harry Overton		1890-1891
Billy Reader		1891-1892
Fred Johnson		1891-1895
Harry Spurden		1892-1895
Jack Fitzpatrick		1895-1897
Fred Johnson		1895-1897
Harry Greenfield		1896-1899
Ben Jordan*		1897-1900
Jabez White		1899-1900
Will Curley		1900-1901
Jack Roberts		1901-1902
Will Curley		1902-1903
Ben Jordan*		1902-1905
Joe Bowker		1905
Johnny Summers		1906
Joe Bowker		1905-1906
Jim Driscoll		1906-1907
Spike Robson		1906-1907
Jim Driscoll*	3	1907-1913
Spike Robson		1907-1910
Ted Kid Lewis*	1	1913-1914
Llew Edwards*	1	1915-1917
Charlie Hardcastle	1	1917

Title Holder	Lonsdale Belt Notches	Tenure
Tancy Lee*	3	1917-1919
Mike Honeyman	2	1920-1921
Joe Fox*	1	1921-1922
George McKenzie	2	1924-1925
Johnny Curley	2	1925-1927
Johnny Cuthbert	1	1927-1928
Harry Corbett	1	1928-1929
Johnny Cuthbert	2	1929-1931
Nel Tarleton	1	1931-1932
Seaman Tommy Watson	2	1932-1934
Nel Tarleton	2	1934-1936
Johnny McGrory	1	1936-1938
Jim Spider Kelly	1	1938-1939
Johnny Cusick	1	1939-1940
Nel Tarleton*	3	1940-1947
Ronnie Clayton	6	1947-1954
Sammy McCarthy	1	1954-1955
Billy Spider Kelly	1	1955-1956
Charlie Hill	3	1956-1959
Bobby Neill	1	1959-1960
Terry Spinks	2	1960-1961
Howard Winstone*	7	1961-1969
Jimmy Revie	2	1969-1971
Evan Armstrong	2	1971-1972
Tommy Glencross	1	1972-1973
Evan Armstrong*	2	1973-1975
Vernon Sollas	1	1975-1977
Alan Richardson	2	1977-1978
Dave Needham	2	1978-1979
Pat Cowdell*	3	1979-1982
Steve Sims*	1	1982-1983
Barry McGuigan*	2	1983-1986
Robert Dickie	3	1986-1988
Peter Harris	1	1988
Paul Hodkinson*	3	1988-1990
Sean Murphy	2	1990-1991
Gary de Roux	1	1991
Colin McMillan*	3	1991-1992
John Davison*	1	1992-1993
Sean Murphy	1	1993
Duke McKenzie*	1	1993-1994
Billy Hardy*	1	1994
Michael Deveney	1	1995
Jonjo Irwin	2	1995-1996
Colin McMillan	1	1996-1997
Paul Ingle*	3	1997-1998
Jonjo Irwin*	2	1998-1999
Gary Thornhill	1	2000
Scott Harrison*	3	2001-2002
Jamie McKeever	1	2003
Roy Rutherford	1	2003
Dazzo Williams	4	2003-2005
Nicky Cook	1	2005-

S. Featherweight (130 lbs)

Title Holder	Lonsdale Belt Notches	Tenure
Jimmy Anderson*	3	1968-1970
John Doherty	1	1986
Pat Cowdell	1	1986
Najib Daho	1	1986-1987
Pat Cowdell	1	1987-1988
Floyd Havard	1	1988-1989
John Doherty	1	1989-1990
Joey Jacobs	1	1990
Hugh Forde	1	1990
Kevin Pritchard	1	1990-1991
Robert Dickie	1	1991
Sugar Gibiliru	1	1991

Title Holder	Lonsdale Belt Notches	Tenure
John Doherty	1	1991-1992
Michael Armstrong	1	1992
Neil Haddock	2	1992-1994
Floyd Havard*	3	1994-1995
P. J. Gallagher	2	1996-1997
Charles Shepherd	3	1997-1999
Michael Gomez*	5	1999-2002
Alex Arthur	3	2002-2003
Michael Gomez	1	2003-2004
Alex Arthur	1	2005-

Lightweight (135 lbs)

Title Holder	Lonsdale Belt Notches	Tenure
Dick Burge		1891-1897
Harry Nickless		1891-1894
Tom Causer		1894-1897
Tom Causer		1897
Dick Burge*		1897-1901
Jabez White		1902-1906
Jack Goldswain		1906-1908
Johnny Summers		1908-1909
Freddie Welsh	1	1909-1911
Matt Wells	1	1911-1912
Freddie Welsh*	1	1912-1919
Bob Marriott*	1	1919-1920
Ernie Rice	1	1921-1922
Seaman Nobby Hall		1922-1923
Harry Mason		1923-1924
Ernie Izzard	2	1924-1925
Harry Mason		1924-1925
Harry Mason*	1	1925-1928
Sam Steward		1928-1929
Fred Webster		1929-1930
Al Foreman*	1	1930-1932
Johnny Cuthbert		1932-1934
Harry Mizler		1934
Jackie Kid Berg		1934-1936
Jimmy Walsh	1	1936-1938
Dave Crowley	1	1938
Eric Boon	3	1938-1944
Ronnie James*	1	1944-1947
Billy Thompson	3	1947-1951
Tommy McGovern	1	1951-1952
Frank Johnson	1	1952-1953
Joe Lucy	1	1953-1955
Frank Johnson	1	1955-1956
Joe Lucy	2	1956-1957
Dave Charnley*	3	1957-1965
Maurice Cullen	4	1965-1968
Ken Buchanan*	2	1968-1971
Willie Reilly*	1	1972
Jim Watt	1	1972-1973
Ken Buchanan*	1	1973-1974
Jim Watt*	2	1975-1977
Charlie Nash*	1	1978-1979
Ray Cattouse	2	1980-1982
George Feeney*	3	1982-1985
Tony Willis	3	1985-1987
Alex Dickson	1	1987-1988
Steve Boyle	2	1988-1990
Carl Crook	5	1990-1992
Billy Schwer	1	1992-1993
Paul Burke	1	1993
Billy Schwer*	2	1993-1995
Michael Ayers*	5	1995-1997
Wayne Rigby	2	1998
Bobby Vanzie	5	1998-2003
Graham Earl	1	2003-2004
Graham Earl	3	2004-

Michael Ayers, the former undefeated British lightweight champion

Les Clark

L. Welterweight (140 lbs)

Title Holder	Lonsdale Belt Notches	Tenure
Des Rea	1	1968-1969
Vic Andreetti*	2	1969-1970
Des Morrison	1	1973-1974
Pat McCormack	1	1974
Joey Singleton	3	1974-1976
Dave Boy Green*	1	1976-1977
Colin Power*	2	1977-1978
Clinton McKenzie	1	1978-1979
Colin Power	1	1979
Clinton McKenzie	5	1979-1984
Terry Marsh*	1	1984-1986
Tony Laing*	1	1986
Tony McKenzie	2	1986-1987
Lloyd Christie	3	1987-1989
Clinton McKenzie*	1	1989
Pat Barrett*	2	1989-1990
Tony Ekubia	1	1990-1991
Andy Holligan	3	1991-1994
Ross Hale	4	1994-1995
Paul Ryan	1	1995-1996
Andy Holligan*	1	1996-1997
Mark Winters	2	1997-1998
Jason Rowland*	2	1998-2000
Ricky Hatton*	1	2000-2001
Junior Witter	1	2002-

Welterweight (147 lbs)

Title Holder	Lonsdale Belt Notches	Tenure
Charlie Allum		1903-1904
Charlie Knock		1904-1906
Curly Watson		1906-1910
Young Joseph		1908-1910
Young Joseph	1	1910-1911
Arthur Evernden		1911-1912
Johnny Summers		1912
Johnny Summers	2	1912-1914
Tom McCormick		1914
Matt Wells		1914
Johnny Basham	3	1914-1920
Matt Wells		1914-1919
Ted Kid Lewis		1920-1924
Tommy Milligan*		1924-1925

Title Holder	Lonsdale Belt Notches	Tenure
Hamilton Johnny Brown		1925
Harry Mason		1925-1926
Jack Hood*	3	1926-1934
Harry Mason		1934
Pat Butler*		1934-1936
Dave McCleave		1936
Jake Kilrain	1	1936-1939
Ernie Roderick	5	1939-1948
Henry Hall	1	1948-1949
Eddie Thomas	2	1949-1951
Wally Thom	1	1951-1952
Cliff Curvis*	1	1952-1953
Wally Thom	2	1953-1956
Peter Waterman*	2	1956-1958
Tommy Molloy	2	1958-1960
Wally Swift	1	1960
Brian Curvis*	7	1960-1966
Johnny Cooke	2	1967-1968
Ralph Charles	3	1968-1972
Bobby Arthur	1	1972-1973
John H. Stracey*	1	1973-1975
Pat Thomas	2	1975-1976
Henry Rhiney	2	1976-1979
Kirkland Laing	1	1979-1980
Colin Jones*	3	1980-1982
Lloyd Honeyghan*	2	1983-1985
Kostas Petrou	1	1985
Sylvester Mittee	1	1985
Lloyd Honeyghan*	1	1985-1986
Kirkland Laing	4	1987-1991
Del Bryan	2	1991-1992
Gary Jacobs*	2	1992-1993
Del Bryan	4	1993-1995
Chris Saunders	1	1995-1996
Kevin Lueshing	1	1996-1997
Geoff McCreesh*	4	1997-1999
Derek Roche	3	1999-2000
Harry Dhami	3	2000-2001
Neil Sinclair*	4	2001-2003
David Barnes	4	2003-2005

L. Middleweight (154 lbs)

Title Holder	Lonsdale Belt Notches	Tenure
Larry Paul	2	1973-1974
Maurice Hope*	3	1974-1977
Jimmy Batten	3	1977-1979
Pat Thomas	3	1979-1981
Herol Graham*	2	1981-1983
Prince Rodney*	1	1983-1984
Jimmy Cable	2	1984-1985
Prince Rodney	2	1985-1986
Chris Pyatt*	1	1986
Lloyd Hibbert*	1	1987
Gary Cooper	1	1988
Gary Stretch	2	1988-1990
Wally Swift Jnr	2	1991-1992
Andy Till	3	1992-1994
Robert McCracken*	3	1994-1995
Ensley Bingham*	2	1996
Ryan Rhodes*	3	1996-1997
Ensley Bingham	3	1997-1999
Wayne Alexander*	2	2000-2003
Jamie Moore	3	2003-2004
Michael Jones	1	2004-

Middleweight (160 lbs)

Title Holder	Lonsdale Belt Notches	Tenure
Denny Harrington		1878-1880
William Sheriff*		1880-1883
Bill Goode		1887-1890

Title Holder	Lonsdale Belt Notches	Tenure
Toff Wall*		1890
Ted Pritchard		1890-1895
Ted White		1893-1895
Ted White*		1895-1896
Anthony Diamond*		1898
Dick Burge*		1898-1900
Jack Palmer		1902-1903
Charlie Allum		1905-1906
Pat O'Keefe		1906
Tom Thomas	1	1906-1910
Jim Sullivan*	1	1910-1912
Jack Harrison*	1	1912-1913
Pat O'Keefe	2	1914-1916
Bandsman Jack Blake	1	1916-1918
Pat O'Keefe*	1	1918-1919
Ted Kid Lewis		1920-1921
Tom Gummer	1	1920-1921
Gus Platts		1921
Johnny Basham		1921
Ted Kid Lewis	2	1921-1923
Johnny Basham		1921
Roland Todd		1923-1925
Roland Todd		1925-1927
Tommy Milligan	1	1926-1928
Frank Moody		1927-1928
Alex Ireland		1928-1929
Len Harvey	5	1929-1933
Jock McAvoy	3+2	1933-1944
Ernie Roderick	1	1945-1946
Vince Hawkins	1	1946-1948
Dick Turpin	2	1948-1950
Albert Finch	1	1950
Randy Turpin*	1	1950-1954
Johnny Sullivan	1	1954-1955
Pat McAteer*	3	1955-1958
Terry Downes	1	1958-1959
John Cowboy McCormack	1	1959
Terry Downes	2	1959-1962
George Aldridge	1	1962-1963
Mick Leahy	1	1963-1964
Wally Swift	1	1964-1965
Johnny Pritchett*	4	1965-1969
Les McAteer	1	1969-1970
Mark Rowe	1	1970
Bunny Sterling	4	1970-1974
Kevin Finnegan*	1	1974
Bunny Sterling*	1	1975
Alan Minter	3	1975-1977
Kevin Finnegan	1	1977
Alan Minter*	1	1977-1978
Tony Sibson	1	1979
Kevin Finnegan*	1	1979-1980
Roy Gumbs	3	1981-1983
Mark Kaylor	1	1983-1984
Tony Sibson*	1	1984
Herol Graham*	1	1985-1986
Brian Anderson	1	1986-1987
Tony Sibson*	1	1987-1988
Herol Graham	4	1988-1992
Frank Grant	2	1992-1993
Neville Brown	6	1993-1998
Glenn Catley*	1	1998
Howard Eastman*	4	1998-2004
Scott Dann	3	2004-

S. Middleweight (168 lbs)

Title Holder	Lonsdale Belt Notches	Tenure
Sammy Storey	2	1989-1990
James Cook*	1	1990-1991
Fidel Castro	2	1991-1992
Henry Wharton*	1	1992-1993
James Cook	1	1993-1994
Cornelius Carr*	1	1994
Ali Forbes	1	1995
Sammy Storey*	1	1995
Joe Calzaghe*	2	1995-1997
David Starie	1	1997
Dean Francis*	2	1997-1998
David Starie*	5	1998-2003
Matthew Barney*	1	2003
Tony Dodson*	1	2003-2004
Carl Froch	1	2004-

L. Heavyweight (175lbs)

Title Holder	Lonsdale Belt Notches	Tenure
Dennis Haugh		1913-1914
Dick Smith	2	1914-1916
Harry Reeve*	1	1916-1917
Dick Smith*	1	1918-1919
Boy McCormick*	1	1919-1921
Jack Bloomfield*	1	1922-1924
Tom Berry	1	1925-1927
Gipsy Daniels*	1	1927
Frank Moody	1	1927-1929
Harry Crossley	1	1929-1932
Jack Petersen*	1	1932
Len Harvey*	1	1933-1934
Eddie Phillips		1935-1937
Jock McAvoy	1	1937-1938
Len Harvey	2	1938-1942
Freddie Mills*	1	1942-1950
Don Cockell	2	1950-1952
Randy Turpin*	1	1952
Dennis Powell	1	1953
Alex Buxton	2	1953-1955
Randy Turpin*	1	1955
Ron Barton*	1	1956
Randy Turpin*	2	1956-1958
Chic Calderwood	3	1960-1963
Chic Calderwood*	1	1964-1966
Young John McCormack	2	1967-1969
Eddie Avoth	2	1969-1971
Chris Finnegan	2	1971-1973
John Conteh*	2	1973-1974
Johnny Frankham	1	1975
Chris Finnegan*	1	1975-1976
Tim Wood	1	1976-1977
Bunny Johnson*	3	1977-1981
Tom Collins	3	1982-1984
Dennis Andries*	5	1984-1986
Tom Collins*	1	1987
Tony Wilson	3	1987-1989
Tom Collins*	1	1989-1990
Steve McCarthy	1	1990-1991
Crawford Ashley*	3	1991-1992
Maurice Core*	2	1992-1994
Crawford Ashley	3	1994-1999
Clinton Woods*	1	1999-2000
Neil Simpson*	2	2000-2002
Peter Oboh	2	2003-

Cruiserweight (200 lbs)

Title Holder	Lonsdale Belt Notches	Tenure
Sam Reeson*	1	1985-1986
Andy Straughn	1	1986-1987
Roy Smith	1	1987
Tee Jay	1	1987-1988
Glenn McCrory*	2	1988
Andy Straughn	1	1988-1989
Johnny Nelson*	3	1989-1991
Derek Angol*	2	1991-1992
Carl Thompson*	1	1992-1994
Dennis Andries	1	1995
Terry Dunstan*	3	1995-1996
Johnny Nelson*	1	1996-1998
Bruce Scott	1	1998-1999
Carl Thompson*	1	1999-2000
Bruce Scott	2	2000-2003
Mark Hobson	4	2003-

Heavyweight (200 lbs +)

Title Holder	Lonsdale Belt Notches	Tenure
Tom Allen*		1878-1882
Charlie Mitchell*		1882-1894
Jem Smith		1889-1891
Ted Pritchard		1891-1895
Jem Smith		1895-1896
George Chrisp		1901
Jack Scales		1901-1902
Jack Palmer		1903-1906
Gunner Moir		1906-1909
Iron Hague		1909-1910
P.O. Curran		1910-1911
Iron Hague		1910-1911
Bombardier Billy Wells	3	1911-1919
Joe Beckett		1919
Frank Goddard	1	1919
Joe Beckett*	1	1919-1923
Frank Goddard		1923-1926
Phil Scott*		1926-1931
Reggie Meen		1931-1932
Jack Petersen	3	1932-1933
Len Harvey		1933-1934
Jack Petersen		1934-1936
Ben Foord		1936-1937
Tommy Farr*	1	1937-1938
Len Harvey*	1	1938-1942
Jack London	1	1944-1945
Bruce Woodcock	2	1945-1950
Jack Gardner	1	1950-1952
Johnny Williams	1	1952-1953
Don Cockell*	1	1953-1956
Joe Erskine	2	1956-1958
Brian London	1	1958-1959
Henry Cooper*	9	1959-1969
Jack Bodell	1	1969-1970
Henry Cooper	1	1970-1971
Joe Bugner	1	1971
Jack Bodell	1	1971-1972
Danny McAlinden	1	1972-1975
Bunny Johnson	1	1975
Richard Dunn	2	1975-1976
Joe Bugner*	1	1976-1977
John L. Gardner*	2	1978-1980
Gordon Ferris	1	1981
Neville Meade	1	1981-1983
David Pearce*	1	1983-1985
Hughroy Currie	1	1985-1986
Horace Notice*	4	1986-1988
Gary Mason	2	1989-1991
Lennox Lewis*	3	1991-1993
Herbie Hide*	1	1993-1994
James Oyebola	1	1994-1995
Scott Welch*	1	1995-1996
Julius Francis	4	1997-2000
Mike Holden*	1	2000
Danny Williams	5	2000-2004
Michael Sprott	1	2004
Matt Skelton	2	2004-

Retired or Inactive Post-War British Champions: Career Summary

Includes all British champions, along with British boxers who have won major international titles since 1945, who had retired by July 2004 or have been inactive since that date. The section does not include champions still active (for their records see under Active British-Based Boxers), while undefeated champions are those who relinquished their titles, not forfeited them. *Current Champions.

George Aldridge British Middleweight Champion, 1962-1963. *Born* 01.02.36. *From* Market Harborough. *Pro Career* 1956-1963 (52 contests, won 36, drew 2, lost 14).

Michael Alldis British S. Bantamweight Champion, 1999-2001. Undefeated British and Commonwealth S. Bantamweight Champion, 2002. *Born* 25.05.68. *From* Crawley. *Pro Career* 1992-2002 (21 contests, won 24, lost 8).

Terry Allen British Flyweight Champion, 1951-1952. Undefeated British Flyweight Champion, 1952-1954. European and World Flyweight Champion, 1950. *Born* 18.06.24. *From* Islington. *Birthname* Edward Govier. *Deceased* 1987. *Pro Career* 1942-1954 (74 contests, won 60, drew 1, lost 13).

Francis Ampofo British Flyweight Champion, 1991. Undefeated British Flyweight Champion, 1992-1996. Undefeated Commonwealth Flyweight Champion, 1993. Commonwealth Flyweight Champion, 1994-1995. *Born* Ghana 05.06.67. *From* Bethnal Green. *Pro Career* 1990-2002 (28 contests, won 17, lost 11).

Brian Anderson British Middleweight Champion, 1986-1987. *Born* 09.07.61. *From* Sheffield. *Pro Career* 1980-1987 (39 contests, won 27, drew 3, lost 9).

Jimmy Anderson Undefeated British S. Featherweight Champion, 1968-1970. *Born* 01.10.42. *From* Waltham Cross. *Pro Career* 1964-1971 (37 contests, won 27, drew 1, lost 9).

Vic Andreetti Undefeated British L. Welterweight Champion, 1969-1970. *Born* 29.01.42. *From* Hoxton. *Pro Career* 1961-1969 (67 contests, won 51, drew 3, lost 13).

Dennis Andries Undefeated British L. Heavyweight Champion, 1984-86. World L. Heavyweight Champion (WBC version), 1986-1987, 1989, and 1990-1991. British Cruiserweight Champion, 1995. *Born* Guyana 05.11.53. *From* Hackney. *Pro Career* 1978-1996 (65 contests, won 49, drew 2, lost 14).

Derek Angol Undefeated British Cruiserweight Champion, 1991-1992. Undefeated Commonwealth Cruiserweight Champion, 1989-1993. *Born* 28.11.64. *From* Camberwell. *Pro Career* 1986-1996 (31 contests, won 28, lost 3).

Evan Armstrong British Featherweight Champion, 1971-1972. Undefeated British Featherweight Champion, 1973-1975. Commonwealth Featherweight Champion, 1974. *Born* 15.02.43. *From* Ayr. *Pro Career* 1963-1974 (54 contests, won 39, drew 1, lost 14).

Michael Armstrong British S. Featherweight Champion, 1992. *Born* 18.12.68. *From* Moston. *Birthname* Morris. *Pro Career* 1987-1994 (26 contests, won 18, drew 1, lost 7).

Bobby Arthur British Welterweight Champion, 1972-1973. *Born* 25.07.47. *From* Coventry. *Pro Career* 1967-1976 (41 contests, won 26, lost 15).

Crawford Ashley Undefeated British L. Heavyweight Champion, 1991-1992. British L. Heavyweight Champion, 1994-1999. European L. Heavyweight Champion, 1997 and 1998-1999. Commonwealth L. Heavyweight Champion, 1998-1999. *Born* 20.05.64. *From* Leeds. *Birthname* Gary Crawford. *Pro Career* 1987-2001 (44 contests, won 33, drew 1, lost 10).

Eddie Avoth British L. Heavyweight Champion, 1969-1971. Commonwealth L. Heavyweight Champion, 1970-1971. *Born* 02.05.45. *From* Cardiff. *Pro Career* 1963-1972 (53 contests, won 44, lost 9).

Michael Ayers Undefeated British Lightweight Champion, 1995-1997. *Born* 26.01.65. *From* Tooting. *Pro-Career* 1989-2003 (37 contests, won 31, drew 1, lost 5).

Pat Barrett Undefeated British L. Welterweight Champion, 1989-1990.

European L. Welterweight Champion, 1990-1992. Born 22.07.67. *From* Manchester. *Pro Career* 1987-1994 (42 contests, won 37, drew 1, lost 4).

Ron Barton Undefeated British L. Heavyweight Champion, 1956. *Born* 25.02.33. *From* West Ham. *Pro Career* 1954-1961 (31 contests, won 26, lost 5).

Jimmy Batten British L. Middleweight Champion, 1977-1979. *Born* 07.11.55. *From* Millwall. *Pro Career* 1974-1983 (49 contests, won 40, lost 9).

Nigel Benn Commonwealth Middleweight Champion, 1988-1989. World Middleweight Champion (WBO version), 1990. World S. Middleweight Champion (WBC version), 1992-1996. *Born* 22.01.64. *From* Ilford. *Pro Career* 1987-1996 (48 contests, won 42, drew 1, lost 5).

Ensley Bingham Undefeated British L. Middleweight Champion, 1996. British L. Middleweight Champion, 1997-1999. *Born* 27.05.63. *From* Manchester. *Pro Career* 1986-1999 (28 contests, won 20, lost 8).

Jack Bodell British Heavyweight Champion, 1969-1970 and 1971-1972. Commonwealth Heavyweight Champion, 1971-1972. European Heavyweight Champion, 1971. *Born* 11.08.40. *From* Swadlincote. *Pro Career* 1962-1972 (71 contests, won 58, lost 13).

Nicky Booth British Bantamweight Champion, 2000-2004. Commonwealth Bantamweight Champion, 2000-2002. *Born* 21.01.80. *From* Nottingham. *Pro Career* 1998-2003 (23 contersts, won 17, drew 1, lost 5).

Steve Boyle British Lightweight Champion, 1988-1990. *Born* 28.11.62. *From* Glasgow. *Pro Career* 1983-1993 (33 contests, won 25, drew 2, lost 6).

Cornelius Boza-Edwards Undefeated European S. Featherweight Champion, 1982. World S. Featherweight Champion, 1981 (WBC version). *Born* Uganda, 27.05.56. *From* London. *Pro Career* 1976-1987 (53 contests, won 45, drew 1, lost 7).

Jim Brady British Empire Bantamweight Championship Claimant, 1941-1945. *From* Dundee. *Deceased* 1980. *Pro Career* 1932-1947 (169 contests, won 104, drew 15, lost 50).

Jackie Brown British and British Empire Flyweight Champion, 1962-1963. *Born* 02.03.35. *From* Edinburgh. *Pro Career* 1958-1966 (44 contests, won 32, drew 1, lost 10, no contest 1).

Neville Brown British Middleweight Champion, 1993-1998. *Born* 26.02.66. *From* Burton. *Pro Career* 1989-2000 (40 contests, won 32, lost 8).

Frank Bruno Undefeated European Heavyweight Champion, 1985-1986. World Heavyweight Champion (WBC version), 1995-96. *Born* 16.11.61. *From* Wandsworth. *Pro Career* 1982-1996 (45 contests, won 40, lost 5).

Del Bryan British Welterweight Champion, 1991-1992 and 1993-1995. *Born* 16.04.1967. *From* Birmingham. *Pro Career* 1986-1998 (52 contests, won 32, drew 1, lost 19).

Ken Buchanan Undefeated British Lightweight Champion, 1968-1971, and 1973-1974. Undefeated European Lightweight Champion, 1974-1975. World Lightweight Champion, 1970-1971. World Lightweight Champion, (WBA version), 1971-1972. *Born* 28.06.45. *From* Edinburgh. *Pro Career* 1965-1982 (69 contests, won 61, lost 8).

Joe Bugner British, Commonwealth and European Heavyweight Champion, 1971. Undefeated European Heavyweight Champion, 1972-1975. European Heavyweight Champion, 1976-1977. Undefeated British and Commonwealth Heavyweight Champion, 1976-1977. *Born* Hungary, 13.03.50. *From* Bedford. *Pro Career* 1967-1999 (83 contests, won 69, drew 1, lost 13).

Paul Burke British and Commonwealth Lightweight Champion, 1993. Commonwealth L. Welterweight Champion, 1997 and 1998-1999. *Born* 25.07.66. *From* Preston. *Pro Career* 1987-1999 (43 contests, won 28, drew 2, lost 13).

Alex Buxton British L. Heavyweight Champion, 1953-1955. *Born* 10.05.25. *From* Watford. *Pro Career* 1942-1963 (125 contests, won 78, drew 4, lost 43).

Jimmy Cable British L. Middleweight Champion, 1984-1985. European L. Middleweight Champion, 1984. *Born* 07.09.57. *From* Crawley. *Pro Career* 1980-1988 (41 contests, won 30, drew 2, lost 9).

Chic Calderwood British and British Empire L. Heavyweight Champion, 1960-1963. Undefeated British L. Heavyweight Champion, 1964-1966. *Born* 09.01.37. *From* Craigneuk. *Birthname* Charles Calderwood. *Deceased* 1966. *Pro Career* 1957-1966 (55 contests, won 44, drew 1, lost 9, no contest 1).

Johnny Caldwell Undefeated British Flyweight Champion, 1960-1961. British and British Empire Bantamweight Champion, 1964-1965. World Bantamweight Champion (EBU version), 1961-1962. *Born* 07.05.38. *From* Belfast. *Pro Career* 1958-1965 (35 contests, won 29, drew 1, lost 5).

Mickey Cantwell Undefeated British Flyweight Champion, 1996-1997. *Born* 23.11.64. *From* Eltham. *Pro Career* 1991-2001 (22 contests, won 14, drew 1, lost 7).

Brian Carr Commonwealth S.Bantamweight Champion, 2001-2002. *Born* 20.06.69. *From* Moodiesburn. *Pro Career* 1994-2003 (33 contests, won 25, drew 1, lost 7).

Cornelius Carr Undefeated British S. Middleweight Champion, 1994. *Born* 09.04.69. *From* Middlesbrough. *Pro Career* 1987-2001 (38 contests, won 34, lost 4).

Fidel Castro British S. Middleweight Champion, 1991-1992. *Born* 17.04.63. *From* Nottingham. *Birthname* Smith. *Pro Career* 1987-1995 (30 contests, won 22, lost 8).

Glenn Catley Undefeated British Middleweight Champion, 1998. World S. Middleweight Champion (WBC version), 2000. *Born* 15.03.72. *From* Bristol. *Pro Career* 1993-2003 (34 contests, won 27, lost 7).

Ray Cattouse British Lightweight Champion, 1980-1982. *Born* 24.07.52. *From* Balham. *Pro Career* 1975-1983 (31 contests, won 26, drew 3, lost 2).

Ralph Charles Undefeated British and British Empire/Commonwealth Welterweight Champion, 1968-1972. European Welterweight Champion, 1970-1971. *Born* 05.02.43. *From* West Ham. *Pro Career* 1963-1972 (43 contests, won 39, lost 4).

Dave Charnley Undefeated British Lightweight Champion, 1957-1965. British Empire Lightweight Champion, 1959-1962. European Lightweight Champion, 1960-1963. *Born* 10.10.35. *From* Dartford. *Pro Career* 1954-1964 (61 contests, won 48, drew 1, lost 12).

Lloyd Christie British L. Welterweight Champion, 1987-1989. *Born* 28.02.62. *From* Wolverhampton. *Pro Career* 1981-1989 (46 contests, won 24, drew 1, lost 21).

Johnny Clark Undefeated British and European Bantamweight Champion, 1973-1974. *Born* 10.09.47. *From* Walworth. *Pro Career* 1966-1974 (43 contests, won 39, drew 1, lost 3).

Ronnie Clayton British Featherweight Champion, 1947-1954. British Empire Featherweight Championship Claimant, 1947-1951. European Featherweight Champion, 1947-1948. *Born* 09.02.23. *From* Blackpool. *Deceased* 1999. *Pro Career* 1941-1954 (113 contests, won 79, drew 8, lost 26).

Pat Clinton Undefeated British Flyweight Champion, 1988-1991. Undefeated European Flyweight Champion, 1990-1991. World Flyweight Champion (WBO version), 1992-1993. *Born* 04.04.64. *From* Croy. *Pro Career* 1985-1991 (23 contests, won 20, lost 3).

Ray Close Undefeated European S. Middleweight Champion, 1993. *Born* 20.01.69. *From* Belfast. *Pro Career* 1988-1997 (29 contests, won 25, drew 1, lost 3).

Don Cockell British L. Heavyweight Champion, 1950-1952. Undefeated European L. Heavyweight Champion, 1951-1952. Undefeated British Heavyweight Champion, 1953-1956. British Empire Heavyweight Championship Claimant, 1953-1954. Undefeated British Empire Heavyweight Champion, 1954-1956. *Born* 22.09.28. *From* Battersea. *Deceased* 1983. *Pro Career* 1946-1956 (80 contests, won 65, drew 1, lost 14).

Steve Collins Undefeated World Middleweight Champion (WBO version), 1994-1995. Undefeated World S. Middleweight Champion (WBO version), 1995-1997. *Born* 21.07.64. *From* Dublin. *Pro Career* 1986-1997 (39 contests, won 36, lost 3).

Tom Collins British L. Heavyweight Champion, 1982-1984. Undefeated British L. Heavyweight Champion, 1987 and 1989-1990. European L. Heavyweight Champion, 1987-1988 and 1990-1991. *Born* Curacao, 01.07.55. *From* Leeds. *Pro Career* 1977-1993 (50 contests, won 26, drew 2, lost 22).

John Conteh Undefeated British, Commonwealth and European L. Heavyweight Champion, 1973-1974. World L. Heavyweight Champion (WBC version), 1974-1977. *Born* 27.05.51. *From* Liverpool. *Pro Career* 1971-1980 (39 contests, won 34, drew 1, lost 4).

James Cook Undefeated British S. Middleweight Champion, 1990-1991. British S. Middleweight Champion, 1993-1994. European S. Middleweight Champion, 1991-1992. *Born* Jamaica, 17.05.59. *From* Peckham. *Pro Career* 1982-1994 (35 contests, won 25, lost 10).

Johnny Cooke British and British Empire Welterweight Champion, 1967-1968. *Born* 17.12.34. *From* Bootle. *Pro Career* 1960-1971 (93 contests, won 52, drew 7, lost 34).

Gary Cooper British L. Middleweight Champion, 1988. *Born* 31.05.57. *From* Lymington. *Pro Career* 1978-1989 (27 contests, won 16, drew 2, lost 9).

Henry Cooper Undefeated British Heavyweight Champion, 1959-1969. British Heavyweight Champion, 1970-1971. British Empire/Commonwealth Heavyweight Champion, 1959-1971. Undefeated European Heavyweight Champion, 1964 and 1968-1969. European Heavyweight Champion, 1970-1971. *Born* 03.05.34. *From* Bellingham. *Pro Career* 1954-1971 (55 contests, won 40, drew 1, lost 14).

Darren Corbett Commonwealth Cruiserweight Champion, 1997-1998. *Born* 08.07.72. *From* Belfast. *Pro Career* 1994-2004 (31 contests, won 26, drew 1, lost 4).

Maurice Core Undefeated British L. Heavyweight Champion, 1992-1994. *Born* 22.06.65. *From* Manchester. *Birthname* Maurice Coore. *Pro Career* 1990-1996 (18 contests, won 15, drew 1, lost 2).

Pat Cowdell Undefeated British Featherweight Champion, 1979-1982. Undefeated European Featherweight Champion, 1982-1983. British S. Featherweight Champion, 1986 and 1987-1988. European S. Featherweight Champion, 1984-1985. *Born* 18.08.53. *From* Warley. *Pro Career* 1977-1988 (42 contests, won 36, lost 6).

Carl Crook British and Commonwealth Lightweight Champion, 1990-1992. *Born* 10.11.63. *From* Chorley. *Pro Career* 1985-1993 (31 contests, won 26, drew 1, lost 4).

Maurice Cullen British Lightweight Champion, 1965-1968. *Born* 30.12.37. *From* Shotton. *Deceased* 2001. *Pro Career* 1959-1970 (55 contests, won 45, drew 2, lost 8).

Peter Culshaw Commonwealth Flyweight Champion, 1996-1997. *Born* 15.05.73. *From* Liverpool. *Pro Career* (27 contests, won 24, drew 1, lost 2).

Hughroy Currie British Heavyweight Champion, 1985-1986. *Born* Jamaica, 09.02.59. *From* Catford. *Pro Career* 1981-1989 (29 contests, won 17, drew 1, lost 11).

Brian Curvis Undefeated British and British Empire Welterweight Champion, 1960-1966. *Born* 14.08.37. *From* Swansea. *Birthname* Brian Nancurvis. *Pro Career* 1959-1966 (41 contests, won 37, lost 4).

Cliff Curvis Undefeated British Welterweight Champion, 1952-1953. British Empire Welterweight Championship Claimant, 1952. *Born* 02.11.27. *From* Swansea. *Birthname* Cliff Nancurvis. *Pro Career* 1944-1953 (55 contests, won 42, drew 1, lost 12).

Najib Daho British S. Featherweight Champion, 1986-1987. Commonwealth Lightweight Champion, 1989-1990. *Born* Morocco, 13.01.59. *From* Manchester. *Deceased* 1993. *Pro Career* 1977-1991 (60 contests, won 34, drew 1, lost 25).

John Davison Undefeated British Featherweight Champion, 1992-1993. *Born* 30.09.58. *From* Newcastle. *Pro Career* 1988-1993 (20 contests, won 15, lost 5).

Gary DeRoux British Featherweight Champion, 1991. *Born* 04.11.62. *From* Peterborough. *Pro Career* 1986-1993 (22 contests, won 13, drew 1, lost 8).

Mike Deveney British Featherweight Champion, 1995. *Born* 14.12.65. *From* Paisley. *Pro Career* 1991-1998 (42 contests, won 22, drew 1, lost 19).

Harry Dhami British Welterweight Champion, 2000-2001. *Born* 17.04.72. *From* Gravesend. *Pro Career* 1993-2003 (23 contests, won 17, drew 1, lost 5).

Robert Dickie British Featherweight Champion, 1986-1988. British S. Featherweight Champion, 1991. *Born* 23.06.64. *From* Swansea. *Pro Career* 1983-1993 (28 contests, won 22, drew 2, lost 4).

Alex Dickson British Lightweight Champion, 1987-1988. *Born* 01.10.62. *From* Larkhall. *Pro Career* 1985-1989 (22 contests, won 18, drew 1, lost 3).

Scott Dixon Undefeated Commonwealth Welterweight Champion, 2000. *Born* 28.09.76. *From* Hamilton. *Pro Career* 1995-2004 (40 contests, won 27, drew 3, lost 10).

Drew Docherty Undefeated British S. Bantamweight Champion, 1999. British Bantamweight Champion, 1992-1997. *Born* 29.11.65. *From* Condorrat. *Pro Career* 1989-2000 (24 contests, won 16, drew 1, lost 7).

John Doherty British S. Featherweight Champion, 1986, 1989-1990, and 1991-1992. *Born* 17.07.62. *From* Bradford. *Pro Career* 1982-1992 (39 contests, won 28, drew 3, lost 8).

Pat Doherty Commonwealth Lightweight Champion, 1989. *Born* 12.04.62. *From* Croydon. *Pro Career* 1981-1989 (32 contests, won 18, drew 3, lost 11).

Dai Dower Undefeated British Flyweight Champion, 1955-1957. Undefeated British Empire Flyweight Champion, 1954-1957. European Flyweight Champion, 1955. *Born* 26.06.33. *From* Abercynon. *Pro Career* 1953-1958 (37 contests, won 34, lost 3).

Terry Downes British Middleweight Champion, 1958-1959 and 1959-1962. World Middleweight Champion (NY/EBU version), 1961-1962. *Born* 09.05.36. *From* Paddington. *Pro Career* 1957-1964 (44 contests, won 35, lost 9).

Richard Dunn British and Commonwealth Heavyweight Champion, 1975-1976. European Heavyweight Champion, 1976. *Born* 19.01.45. *From* Bradford. *Pro Career* 1969-1977 (45 contests, won 33, lost 12).

Terry Dunstan Undefeated British Cruiserweight Champion, 1995-1996. Undefeated European Cruiserweight Champion, 1998. *Born* 21.10.68. *From* Vauxhall. *Pro Career* 1992-1999 (21 contests, won 19, lost 2).

Tony Ekubia British L. Welterweight Champion, 1990-1991. Commonwealth L. Welterweight Champion, 1989-1991. *Born* Nigeria, 06.03.60. *From* Manchester. *Pro Career* 1986-1993 (25 contests, won 21, lost 4).

Joe Erskine British Heavyweight Champion, 1956-1958. British Empire Heavyweight Champion, 1957-1958. *Born* 26.01.34. *From* Cardiff. *Deceased* 1990. *Pro Career* 1954-1964 (54 contests, won 45, drew 1, lost 8).

Chris Eubank Undefeated WBO Middleweight Champion, 1990-1991. WBO S. Middleweight Title, 1991-1995. *Born* 08.08.1966. *From* Brighton. *Pro Career* 1985-1998 (52 contests, won 45, drew 2, lost 5).

George Feeney Undefeated British Lightweight Champion, 1982-1985. *Born* 09.02.57. *From* West Hartlepool. *Pro Career* 1977-1984 (29 contests, won 19, lost 10).

John Feeney British Bantamweight Champion, 1981-1983 and 1983-1985. *Born* 15.05.58. *From* West Hartlepool. *Pro Career* 1977-1987 (48 contests, won 35, lost 13).

Gordon Ferris British Heavyweight Champion, 1981. *Born* 21.11.52. *From* Enniskillen. *Pro Career* 1977-1982 (26 contests, won 20, lost 6).

Darren Fifield Commonwealth Flyweight Champion, 1993-1994. *Born* 09.10.69. *From* Henley. *Pro Career* 1992-1996 (13 contests, won 7, drew 2, lost 4).

Albert Finch British Middleweight Champion, 1950. *Born* 16.05.26. *From* Croydon. *Deceased* 2003. *Pro Career* 1945-1958 (103 contests, won 72, drew 9, lost 21, no contest 1).

Chris Finnegan British L. Heavyweight Champion, 1971-1973. Undefeated

British L. Heavyweight Champion, 1975-1976. Commonwealth L. Heavyweight Champion, 1971-1973. European L. Heavyweight Champion, 1972. *Born* 05.06.44. *From* Iver. *Pro Career* 1968-1975 (37 contests, won 29, drew 1, lost 7).

Kevin Finnegan British Middleweight Champion, 1977. Undefeated British Middleweight Champion, 1974 and 1979-1980. European Middleweight Champion, 1974-1975 and 1980. *Born* 18.04.48. *From* Iver. *Pro Career* 1970-1980 (47 contests, won 35, drew 1, lost 11).

Ali Forbes British S. Middleweight Champion, 1995. *Born* 07.03.61. *From* Sydenham. *Pro Career* 1989-2002 (25 contests, won 14, drew 1, lost 10).

Hugh Forde British S. Featherweight Champion, 1990. Commonwealth S. Featherweight Champion, 1991. *Born* 07.05.64. *From* Birmingham. *Pro Career* 1986-1995 (31 contests, won 24, lost 7).

Steve Foster Commonwealth L. Middleweight Champion, 1996-1997. *Born* 28.12.60. *From* Salford. *Pro Career* 1981-1999 (39 contests, won 20, drew 2, lost 17).

Dean Francis Undefeated British and European S.Middleweight Champion, 1997-1998. *Born* 23.01.74. *From* Basingstoke. *Pro Career* 1994-2003 (25 contests, won 22, lost 3).

Johnny Frankham British L. Heavyweight Champion, 1975. *Born* 06.06.48. *From* Reading. *Pro Career* 1970-1976 (40 contests, won 28, drew 1, lost 11).

P.J. Gallagher British S. Featherweight Champion, 1996-1997. *Born* 14.02.73. *From* Wood Green. *Pro Career* 1993-2000 (20 contests, won 19, lost 1).

Jack Gardner British Heavyweight Champion, 1950-1952. British Empire Heavyweight Championship Claimant, 1950-1952. European Heavyweight Champion, 1951. *Born* 06.11.26. *From* Market Harborough. *Deceased* 1978. *Pro Career* 1948-1956 (34 contests, won 28, lost 6).

John L. Gardner Undefeated British Heavyweight Champion, 1978-1980. Undefeated Commonwealth Heavyweight Champion, 1978-1981. Undefeated European Heavyweight Champion, 1980-1981. *Born* 19.03.53. *From* Hackney. *Pro Career* 1973-1983 (39 contests, won 35, lost 4).

Teddy Gardner Undefeated British and European Flyweight Champion, 1952. British Empire Flyweight Championship Claimant, 1952. *Born* 27.01.22. *From* West Hartlepool. *Deceased* 1977. *Pro Career* 1938-1952 (66 contests, won 55, drew 3, lost 8).

Sugar Gibiliru British S. Featherweight Champion, 1991. *Born* 13.07.66. *From* Liverpool. *Pro Career* 1984-1995 (55 contests, won 16, drew 7, lost 32).

Ray Gilbody British Bantamweight Champion, 1985-1987. *Born* 21.03.60. *From* Warrington. *Pro Career* 1983-1987 (16 contests, won 11, drew 1, lost 4).

Freddie Gilroy Undefeated British and British Empire Bantamweight Champion, 1959-1963. European Bantamweight Champion, 1959-1960. *Born* 07.03.36. *From* Belfast. *Pro Career* 1957-1962 (31 contests, won 28, lost 3).

Tommy Glencross British Featherweight Champion, 1972-1973. *Born* 31.07.47. *From* Glasgow. *Pro Career* 1967-1978 (48 contests, won 31, drew 1, lost 16).

Herol Graham Undefeated British L. Middleweight Champion, 1981-1983. Undefeated Commonwealth L. Middleweight Champion, 1981-1984. Undefeated European L. Middleweight Champion, 1983-1984. Undefeated British Middleweight Champion, 1985-1986. British Middleweight Champion, 1988-1992. European Middleweight Champion, 1986-1987. *Born* 13.09.59. *From* Sheffield. *Pro Career* 1978-1998 (54 contests, won 48, lost 6).

Frank Grant British Middleweight Champion, 1992-1993. *Born* 22.05.65. *From* Bradford. *Pro Career* 1986-1993 (26 contests, won 22, lost 4).

Dave Boy Green Undefeated British and European L. Welterweight Champion, 1976-1977. European Welterweight Champion, 1979. *Born* 02.06.53. *From* Chatteris. *Pro Career* 1974-1981 (41 contests, won 37, lost 4).

Roy Gumbs British Middleweight Champion, 1981-1983. Commonwealth

Middleweight Champion, 1983. *Born* St Kitts, 05.09.54. *From* Tottenham. *Pro Career* 1976-1985 (40 contests, won 26, drew 3, lost 11).

Neil Haddock British S. Featherweight Champion, 1992-1994. *Born* 22.06.64. *From* Llanelli. *Pro Career* 1987-1994 (26 contests, won 14, drew 1, lost 11).

Ross Hale British and Commonwealth L. Welterweight Champion, 1994-1995. *Born* 28.02.1967. *From* Bristol. *Pro Career* 1989-1998 (33 contests, won 29, lost 4).

Henry Hall British Welterweight Champion, 1948-1949. *Born* 06.09.22. *From* Sheffield. *Deceased* 1979. *Pro Career* 1945-1952 (66 contests, won 43, drew 3, lost 20).

Prince Naseem Hamed Undefeated European Bantamweight Champion, 1994-1995. Undefeated WBO Featherweight Champion, 1997-2000. Undefeated IBF Featherweight Champion, 1997. WBC Featherweight Champion, 1999-2000. *Born* 12.02.74. *From* Sheffield. *Pro Career* 1992-2002 (37 contests, won 36, lost 1).

Billy Hardy Undefeated British Bantamweight Champion, 1987-1991. Undefeated British Featherweight Champion, 1994. Undefeated Commonwealth Featherweight Champion, 1992-1996. European Featherweight Champion, 1995-1998. *Born* 05.09.1964. *From* Sunderland. *Pro Career* 1983-1998 (48 contests, won 37, drew 2, lost 9).

Peter Harris British Featherweight Champion, 1988. *Born* 23.08.62. *From* Swansea. *Pro Career* 1983-1996 (33 contests, won 16, drew 2, lost 15).

Paul Harvey Commonwealth S. Featherweight Champion, 1991-1992. *Born* 10.11.64. *From* Ilford. *Pro Career* 1989-1994 (22 contests, won 16, drew 1, lost 5).

Floyd Havard British S. Featherweight Champion, 1988-1989. Undefeated British S. Featherweight Champion, 1994-1995. *Born* 16.10.65. *From* Swansea. *Pro Career* 1985-1996 (36 contests, won 34, lost 2).

Vince Hawkins British Middleweight Champion, 1946-1948. *Born* 15.04.23. *From* Eastleigh. *Pro Career* 1940-1950 (86 contests, won 75, drew 1, lost 10).

Lloyd Hibbert Undefeated British L. Middleweight Champion, 1987. Commonwealth L. Middleweight Champion, 1987. *Born* 29.06.59. *From* Birmingham. *Pro Career* 1979-1987 (23 contests, won 19, lost 4).

Herbie Hide Undefeated British Heavyweight Champion, 1993-1994. World Heavyweight Champion (WBO version), 1997-1999. *Born* Nigeria 27.08.71. *From* Norwich. *Pro Career* 1989-2004 (39 contests, won 35, lost 4).

Charlie Hill British Featherweight Champion, 1956-1959. *Born* 20.06.30. *From* Cambuslang. *Pro Career* 1953-1959 (36 contests, won 31, lost 5).

Paul Hodkinson Undefeated British Featherweight Champion, 1988-1990. Undefeated European Featherweight Champion, 1989-1991. World Featherweight Champion, 1991-1993 (WBC version). *Born* 14.09.65. *From* Liverpool. *Pro Career* 1986-1994 (26 contests, won 22, drew 1, lost 3).

Mike Holden Undefeated British Heavyweight Champion, 2000. *Born* 13.03.68. *From* Manchester. *Pro Career* 1994-2003 (19 contests, won 10, lost 9).

Andy Holligan British and Commonwealth L. Welterweight Champion, 1991-1994 and 1996-1997. *Born* 06.06.67. *From* Liverpool. *Pro Career* 1987-1998 (30 contests, won 27, lost 3).

Lloyd Honeyghan Undefeated British Welterweight Champion, 1983-1985 and 1985-1986. Undefeated Commonwealth & European Champion, 1985-1986. World Welterweight Champion, 1986. World Welterweight Champion (WBC version), 1986-1987 and 1988-1989. World Welterweight Champion (IBF version), 1986-1987. Commonwealth L. Middleweight Champion, 1993-1994. *Born* 22.04.60, Jamaica. *From* Bermondsey. *Pro Career* 1980-1995 (48 contests, won 43, lost 5).

Maurice Hope Undefeated British L. Middleweight Champion, 1974-1977. Undefeated Commonwealth L. Middleweight Champion, 1976-1979. Undefeated European L. Middleweight Champion, 1976-1978. World L. Middleweight Champion (WBC version), 1979-1981. *Born* Antigua, 06.12.51. *From* Hackney. *Pro Career* 1973-1982 (35 contests, won 30, drew 1, lost 4).

Mickey Hughes Commonwealth L. Middleweight Champion, 1992-1993. *Born* 13.06.62. *From* St Pancras. *Pro Career* 1985-1993 (31 contests, won 24, lost 7).

Mo Hussein Commonwealth Lightweight Champion, 1987-1989. *Born* 17.11.62. *From* West Ham. *Pro Career* 1982-1989 (27 contests, won 23, lost 4).

Paul Ingle World Featherweight Champion (IBF Version), 1999-2000. Undefeated British Featherweight Champion, 1997-1998. Undefeated Commonwealth and European Champion, 1997-1999. *Born* 22.06.72. *From* Scarborough. *Pro Career* (25 contests, won 23, lost 2).

Jonjo Irwin British Featherweight Champion, 1995-1996. Undefeated British Featherweight Champion, 1998-1999. Commonwealth Featherweight Champion, 1996-1997. *Born* 31.05.69. *From* Doncaster. *Pro Career* 1992-1999 (24 contests, won 19, lost 5).

Gary Jacobs Undefeated British Welterweight Champion, 1992-1993. Commonwealth Welterweight Champion, 1988-1989. European Welterweight Champion, 1993-1994. *Born* 10.12.65. *From* Glasgow. *Pro Career* 1985-1997 (53 contests, won 45, lost 8).

Joey Jacobs British S. Featherweight Champion, 1990. *Born* 01.10.60. *From* Manchester. *Pro Career* 1986-1991 (15 contests, won 10, lost 5).

Ronnie James Undefeated British Lightweight Champion, 1944-1947. *Born* 08.10.17. *From* Swansea. *Deceased* 1977. *Pro Career* 1933-1947 (119 contests, won 98, drew 5, lost 16).

Tee Jay British Cruiserweight Champion, 1987-1988. *Born* Ghana, 21.01.62. *Birthname* Taju Akay. *From* Notting Hill. *Pro Career* 1985-1991 (19 contests, won 14, drew 1, lost 4).

Bunny Johnson British and Commonwealth Heavyweight Champion, 1975. Undefeated British L. Heavyweight Champion, 1977-1981. *Born* Jamaica, 10.05.47. *From* Birmingham. *Birthname* Fitzroy Johnson. *Pro Career* 1968-1981 (73 contests, won 55, drew 1, lost 17).

Frank Johnson British Lightweight Champion, 1952-1953 and 1955-1956. British Empire Lightweight Championship Claimant, 1953. *Born* 27.11.28. *From* Manchester. *Birthname* Frank Williamson. *Deceased* 1970. *Pro Career* 1946-1957 (58 contests, won 47, lost 11).

Barry Jones Undefeated WBO S. Featherweight Champion, 1997-1998. *Born* 03.05.74. *From* Cardiff. *Pro Career* 1992-2000 (20 contests, won 18, drew 1, lost 1).

Colin Jones Undefeated British Welterweight Champion, 1980-1982. Undefeated Commonwealth Welterweight Champion, 1981-1984. Undefeated European Welterweight Champion, 1982-1983. *Born* 21.03.59. *From* Gorseinon. *Pro Career* 1977-1985 (30 contests, won 26, drew 1, lost 3).

Frankie Jones British Flyweight Champion, 1957-1960. British Empire Flyweight Champion, 1957. *Born* 12.02.33. *From* Plean. *Deceased* 1991. *Pro Career* 1955-1960 (25 contests, won 17, lost 8).

Paul Jones Commonwealth Middleweight Champion, 1998-1999. *Born* 19.11.66. *From* Sheffield. *Pro Career* 1986-2002 (44 contests, won 31, drew 1, lost 12).

Peter Kane Undefeated World Flyweight Champion, 1938-1939. European Bantamweight Champion, 1947-1948. *Born* 28.04.18. *From* Golborne. *Birthname* Peter Cain. *Deceased* 1991. *Pro Career* 1934-1948 (102 contests, won 92, drew 2, lost 7, no contest 1).

Mark Kaylor British and Commonwealth Middleweight Champion, 1983-1984. *Born* 11.05.61. *From* West Ham. *Pro Career* 1980-1991 (48 contests, won 40, drew 1, lost 7).

Peter Keenan British Bantamweight Champion, 1951-1953 and 1954-1959. British Empire Bantamweight Champion, 1955-1959. European Bantamweight Champion, 1951-1952 and 1953. *Born* 08.08.28. *From* Glasgow. *Deceased* 2000. *Pro Career* 1948-1959 (66 contests, won 54, drew 1, lost 11).

Billy Spider Kelly British Featherweight Champion, 1955-1956. British Empire Featherweight Championship Claimant, 1954. British Empire Featherweight Champion, 1954-1955. *Born* 21.04.32. *From* Londonderry. *Pro Career* 1950-1962 (83 contests, won 56, drew 4, lost 23).

Joe Kelly British Bantamweight Champion, 1992. *Born* 18.05.64. *From* Glasgow. *Pro Career* 1985-1992 (27 contests, won 18, drew 2, lost 7).

John Kelly British and European Bantamweight Champion, 1953-1954. *Born* 17.01.32. *From* Belfast. *Pro Career* 1951-1957 (28 contests, won 24, lost 4).

Jawaid Khaliq Undefeated Commonwealth Welterweight Champion, 2000-2001. *Born* 30.07.70. *From* Nottingham. *Pro Career* 1997-2004 (25 contests, won 23, drew 1, lost 1).

Johnny King British Bantamweight Champion, 1932-1934 and 1935-1947. British Empire Bantamweight Championship Claimant, 1932-1934. *Born* 08.01.12. *From* Manchester. *Deceased* 1963. *Pro Career* 1926-1947 (222 contests, won 158, drew 15, lost 48, no contest 1).

Keith Knox British and Commonwealth Flyweight Champion, 1999. *Born* 20.06.67. *From* Bonnyrigg. *Pro Career* 1994-2001 (23 contests, won 13, drew 2, lost 8).

Kirkland Laing British Welterweight Champion, 1987-1991. European Welterweight Champion, 1990. *Born* 20.06.54, Jamaica. *From* Nottingham. *Pro Career* 1975-1994 (56 contests, won 43, drew 1, lost 12).

Tony Laing Undefeated British L. Welterweight Champion, 1986. Commonwealth L. Welterweight Champion, 1987-1988. *Born* 22.09.57. *From* Nottingham. *Pro Career* 1977-1988 (18 contests, won 13, drew 1, lost 4).

Davy Larmour British Bantamweight Champion, 1983. *Born* 02.04.52. *From* Belfast. *Pro Career* 1977-1983 (18 contests, won 11, lost 7).

Mick Leahy British Middleweight Champion, 1963-1964. *Born* Cork, 12.03.35. *From* Coventry. *Pro Career* 1956-1965 (72 contests, won 46, drew 7, lost 19).

Ady Lewis Undefeated British and Commonwealth Flyweight Champion, 1997-1998. British and Commonwealth Bantamweight Champion, 2000. *Born* 31.05.75. *From* Bury. *Pro Career* 1994-2001 (25 contests, won 19, drew 1, lost 5).

Lennox Lewis Undefeated British Heavyweight Champion, 1991-1993. Undefeated Commonwealth Heavyweight Champion, 1992-1993. Undefeated European Heavyweight Champion, 1990-1992. World Heavyweight Champion (WBC version), 1992-1994 and 1997-2001. Undefeated World Heavyweight Champion (IBF version), 2001-2002. Undefeated World Heavyweight Champion (WBA version), 1999-2000. Undefeated World Heavyweight Champion (WBC version), 2001-2004. *Born* 02.09.65. *From* London. *Pro Career* 1989-2004 (44 contests, won 41, drew 1, lost 2).

Stewart Lithgo Commonwealth Cruiserweight Champion, 1984. *Born* 02.06.57. *From* West Hartlepool. *Pro Career* 1977-1987 (30 contests, won 16, drew 2, lost 12).

Paul Lloyd British Bantamweight Champion, 1997-1999. Undefeated Commonwealth Bantamweight Champion, 1996-2000. Undefeated European Bantamweight Champion, 1998-1999. *Born* 07.12.68. *From* Ellesmere Port. *Pro Career* 1992-2000 (27 contests, won 20, lost 7).

Brian London British and British Empire Heavyweight Champion, 1958-1959. *Born* 19.06.34. *From* Blackpool. *Birthname* Brian Harper. *Pro Career* 1955-1970 (58 contests, won 37, drew 1, lost 20).

Jack London British Heavyweight Champion, 1944-1945. British Empire Heavyweight Championship Claimant, 1944-1945. *Born* 23.06.13. *From* West Hartlepool. *Birthname* Jack Harper. *Deceased* 1964. *Pro Career* 1931-1949 (141 contests, won 95, drew 5, lost 39, no contest 2).

Eamonn Loughran Undefeated Commonwealth Welterweight Champion, 1992-1993. WBO Welterweight Champion, 1993-1996. *Born* 05.06.70. *Fron* Ballymena. *Pro Career* 1987-1996 (30 contests, won 26, drew 1, lost 2, no contest 1).

Joe Lucy British Lightweight Champion, 1953-1955 and 1956-1957. *Born* 09.02.30. *From* Mile End. *Deceased* 1991. *Pro Career* 1950-1957 (37 contests, won 27, lost 10).

Kevin Lueshing British Welterweight Champion, 1996-1997. *Born* 17.04.1968. *From* Beckenham. *Pro Career* 1991-1999 (25 contests, won 21, lost 4).

Danny McAlinden British and Commonwealth Heavyweight Champion, 1972-1975. *Born* Newry, 01.06.47. *From* Coventry. *Pro Career* 1969-1981 (45 contests, won 31, drew 2, lost 12).

Les McAteer British and British Empire Middleweight Champion, 1969-1970. *Born* 19.08.45. *From* Birkenhead. *Pro Career* 1965-1979 (39 contests, won 27, drew 2, lost 10).

Pat McAteer Undefeated British Middleweight Champion, 1955-1958. British Empire Middleweight Champion, 1955-1958. *Born* 17.03.32. *From* Birkenhead. *Pro Career* 1952-1958 (57 contests, won 49, drew 2, lost 6).

Dave McAuley Undefeated British Flyweight Champion, 1986-1988. World Flyweight Champion (IBF version), 1989-1992. *Born* 15.06.61. *From* Larne. *Pro Career* 1983-1992 (23 contests, won 18, drew 2, lost 3).

Sammy McCarthy British Featherweight Champion, 1954-1955. *Born* 05.11.31. *From* Stepney. *Pro Career* 1951-1957 (53 contests, won 44, drew 1, lost 8).

Steve McCarthy British L. Heavyweight Champion, 1990-1991. *Born* 30.07.62. *From* Southampton. *Pro Career* 1987-1994 (17 contests, won 12, drew 1, lost 4).

John McCluskey Undefeated British Flyweight Champion, 1967-1977. Commonwealth Flyweight Champion, 1970-1971. *Born* 23.01.44. *From* Hamilton. *Pro Career* 1965-1975 (38 contests, won 23, lost 15).

John Cowboy McCormack British Middleweight Champion, 1959. European Middleweight Champion, 1961-1962. *Born* 09.01.35. *From* Maryhill. *Pro Career* 1957-1966 (45 contests, won 38, lost 7).

Young John McCormack British L. Heavyweight Champion, 1967-1969. *Born* Dublin, 11.12.44. *From* Brixton. *Pro Career* 1963-1970 (42 contests, won 33, drew 1, lost 8).

Pat McCormack British L. Welterweight Champion, 1974. *Born* Dublin, 28.04.46. *From* Brixton. *Pro Career* 1968-1975 (49 contests, won 30, drew 1, lost 18).

Robert McCracken Undefeated British L. Middleweight Champion, 1994-1995. Commonwealth Middleweight Champion, 1995-1997. *Born* 31.05.68. *From* Birmingham. *Pro Career* 1991-2001 (35 contests, won 33, lost 2).

Geoff McCreesh Undefeated British Welterweight Champion, 1997-1999. *Born* 12.06.70. *From* Bracknell. *Pro Career* 1994-2001 (30 contests, won 23, lost 7).

Glenn McCrory Undefeated British Cruiserweight Champion, 1988. Undefeated Commonwealth Cruiserweight Champion, 1987-1989. World Cruiserweight Champion (IBF version), 1989-1990. *Born* 23.09.64. *From* Annfield Plain. *Pro Career* 1984-1993 (39 contests, won 30, drew 1, lost 8).

Jim McDonnell Undefeated European Featherweight Champion, 1985-1987. *Born* 12.09.60. *From* Camden Town. *Pro Career* 1983-1998 (30 contests, won 26, lost 4).

Tommy McGovern British Lightweight Champion, 1951-1952. *Born* 05.02.24. *From* Bermondsey. *Deceased* 1989. *Pro Career* 1947-1953 (66 contests, won 45, drew 4, lost 17).

Walter McGowan Undefeated British Flyweight Champion, 1963-1966. Undefeated British Empire Flyweight Champion, 1963-1969. World Flyweight Champion (WBC version), 1966. British and British Empire Bantamweight Champion, 1966-1968. *Born* 13.10.42. *From* Hamilton. *Pro Career* 1961-1969 (40 contests, won 32, drew 1, lost 7).

Barry McGuigan Undefeated British Featherweight Champion, 1983-1986. Undefeated European Featherweight Champion, 1983-1985. World Featherweight Champion (WBA version), 1985-1986. *Born* 28.02.61. *From* Clones. *Pro Career* 1981-1989 (35 contests, won 32, lost 3).

Jamie McKeever British Featherweight Champion, 2003. *Born* 07.07.79. *From* Birkenhead. *Pro Career* 1998-2004 (21 contests, won 15, drew 1, lost 5).

Clinton McKenzie British L. Welterweight Champion, 1978-1979 and 1979-1984. Undefeated British L. Welterweight Champion, 1989. European L. Welterweight Champion, 1981-1982. *Born* 15.09.55. *From* Croydon. *Pro Career* 1976-1989 (50 contests, won 36, lost 14).

Duke McKenzie Undefeated British Flyweight Champion, 1985-1986.

Undefeated European Flyweight Champion, 1986-1988. World Flyweight Champion (IBF version), 1988-1989. World Bantamweight Champion (WBO version), 1991-1992. World S. Bantamweight Champion (WBO version), 1992-1993. Undefeated British Featherweight Champion, 1993-1994. *Born* 05.05.63. *From* Croydon. *Pro Career* 1982-1998 (46 contests, won 39, lost 7).

Tony McKenzie British L. Welterweight Champion, 1986-1987. *Born* 04.03.63. *From* Leicester. *Pro Career* 1983-1993 (34 contests, won 26, drew 1, lost 7).

Ian McLeod Undefeated Commonwealth S. Featherweight Champion, 2000. *Born* 11.06.69. *From* Kilmarnock. *Pro Career* 1992-2000 (14 contests, won 11, drew 1, lost 2).

Colin McMillan Undefeated British Featherweight Champion, 1991-1992. British Featherweight Champion, 1996-1997. Undefeated Commonwealth Featherweight Champion, 1992. World Featherweight Champion (WBO version), 1992. *Born* 12.02.66. *From* Barking. *Pro Career* 1988-1997 (35 contests, won 31, lost 4).

Noel Magee Commonwealth L. Heavyweight Champion, 1995. *Born* 16.12.65. *From* Belfast. *Pro Career* 1985-1997 (37 contests, won 27, drew 2, lost 8).

Charlie Magri Undefeated British Flyweight Champion, 1977-1981. Undefeated European Flyweight Champion, 1979-1983 and 1984-1985. European Flyweight Champion, 1985-1986. World Flyweight Champion (WBC version), 1983. *Born* Tunisia, 20.07.56. *From* Stepney. *Pro Career* 1977-1986 (35 contests, won 30, lost 5).

Paddy Maguire British Bantamweight Champion, 1975-1977. *Born* 26.09.48. *From* Belfast. *Pro Career* 1969-1977 (35 contests, won 26, drew 1, lost 8).

Terry Marsh Undefeated British L. Welterweight Champion, 1984-1986. European L. Welterweight Champion, 1985-1986. Undefeated World L. Welterweight Champion (IBF version), 1987. *Born* 07.02.58. *From* Basildon. *Pro Career* 1981-1987 (27 contests, won 26, drew 1).

Gary Mason British Heavyweight Champion, 1989-1991. *Born* Jamaica, 15.12.62. *From* Wandsworth. *Pro Career* 1984-1991 (36 contests, won 35, lost 1).

Jason Matthews Undefeated Commonwealth Middleweight Champion, 1999. WBO Middleweight Champion, 1999. *Born* 20.07.70. *From* Hackney. *Pro Career* 1995-1999 (23 contests, won 21, lost 2).

Neville Meade British Heavyweight Champion, 1981-1983. *Born* Jamaica, 12.09.48. *From* Swansea. *Pro Career* 1974-1983 (34 contests, won 20, drew 1, lost 13).

Freddie Mills Undefeated British L. Heavyweight Champion, 1942-1950. British Empire L. Heavyweight Championship Claimant, 1942-1950. Undefeated European L. Heavyweight Champion, 1947-1950. World L. Heavyweight Champion (GB version), 1942-1946. World L. Heavyweight Champion, 1948-1950. *Born* 26.06.19. *From* Bournemouth. *Deceased* 1965. *Pro Career* 1936-1950 (101 contests, won 77, drew 6, lost 18).

Alan Minter British Middleweight Champion, 1975-1977. Undefeated British Middleweight Champion, 1977-1978. European Middleweight Champion, 1977. Undefeated European Middleweight Champion, 1978-1979. World Middleweight Champion, 1980. *Born* 17.08.51. *From* Crawley. *Pro Career* 1972-1981 (49 contests, won 39, lost 9, no contest 1).

Sylvester Mittee British Welterweight Champion, 1985. Commonwealth Welterweight Champion, 1984-1985. *Born* St Lucia, 29.10.56. *From* Bethnal Green. *Pro Career* 1977-1988 (33 contests, won 28, lost 5).

Tommy Molloy British Welterweight Champion, 1958-1960. *Born* 02.02.34. *From* Birkenhead. *Pro Career* 1955-1963 (43 contests, won 34, drew 2, lost 6, no contest 1).

Rinty Monaghan Undefeated British and World Flyweight Champion, 1948-1950. British Empire Flyweight Championship Claimant, 1948-1950. Undefeated European Flyweight Champion, 1949-1950. World Flyweight Champion (NBA version), 1947-1948. *Born* 21.08.20. *From* Belfast. *Birthname* John Monaghan. *Deceased* 1984. *Pro Career* 1934-1949 (66 contests, won 51, drew 6, lost 9).

Alex Moon Commonwealth S. Featherweight Champion, 2001-2002. *Born*

17.11.71. *From* Liverpool. *Pro Career* 1995-2003 (27 contests, won 19, drew 2, lost 6).

Des Morrison British L. Welterweight Champion, 1973-1974. *Born* Jamaica, 01.02.50. *From* Bedford. *Pro Career* 1970-1982 (50 contests, won 36, drew 2, lost 12).

Patrick Mullings British S. Bantamweight Champion, 1999 and 2001. Commonwealth Featherweight Champion, 1999-2000. *Born* 19.10.70. *From* Harlesden. *Pro Career* 1994-2001 (30 contests, won 24, lost 6).

Sean Murphy British Featherweight Champion, 1990-1991 and 1993. *Born* 01.12.64. *From* St Albans. *Pro Career* 1986-1994 (27 contests, won 22, lost 5).

Charlie Nash Undefeated British Lightweight Champion, 1978-1979. Undefeated European Lightweight Champion, 1979-1980. European Lightweight Champion, 1980-1981. *Born* 10.05.51. *From* Derry. *Pro Career* 1975-1983 (30 contests, won 25, lost 5).

Dave Needham British Bantamweight Champion, 1974-1975. British Featherweight Champion, 1978-1979. *Born* 15.08.51. *From* Nottingham. *Pro Career* 1971-1980 (39 contests, won 30, drew 1, lost 8).

Bobby Neill British Featherweight Champion, 1959-1960. *Born* 10.10.33. *From* Edinburgh. *Pro Career* 1955-1960 (35 contests, won 28, lost 7).

Horace Notice Undefeated British and Commonwealth Heavyweight Champion, 1986-1988. *Born* 07.08.57. *From* Birmingham. *Pro Career* 1983-1988 (16 contests, won 16).

Peter Oboh* Undefeated British L.Heavyweight Champion, 2003-2005. Undefeated Commonwealth L.Heavyweight Champion, 2002-2005. *Born* Nigeria 06.09.68. *From* Brockley. *Pro Career* 1993-2004 (19 contests, won 14, lost 5).

John O'Brien British Empire Featherweight Champion, 1967. *Born* 20.02.37. *From* Glasgow. *Deceased* 1979. *Pro Career* 1956-1971 (47 contests, won 30, lost 17).

Chris Okoh Commonwealth Cruiserweight Champion, 1995-1997. *Born* 18.04.69. *From* Croydon. *Pro Career* 1993-1999 (16 contests, won 14, lost 2).

Spencer Oliver European S. Bantamweight Champion, 1997-1998. *Born* 27.03.75. *From* Barnet. *Pro Career* 1995-1998 (15 contests, won 14, lost 1).

Danny O'Sullivan British Bantamweight Champion, 1949-1951. *Born* 06.01.23. *From* Finsbury Park. *Deceased* 1990. *Pro Career* 1947-1951 (43 contests, won 33, drew 1, lost 9).

Johnny Owen Undefeated British Bantamweight Champion, 1977-1980. Undefeated Commonwealth Bantamweight Champion, 1978-1980. Undefeated European Bantamweight Champion, 1980. *Born* 07.01.56. *From* Merthyr. *Deceased* 1980. *Pro Career* 1976-1980 (28 contests, won 25, drew 1, lost 2).

James Oyebola British Heavyweight Champion, 1994-1995. *Born* Nigeria 10.06.61. *From* Paddington. *Pro Career* 1987-1996 (23 contests, won 18, drew 1, lost 4).

Jackie Paterson British Flyweight Champion, 1939-1948. British Empire Flyweight Championship Claimant, 1940-1948. World Flyweight Champion, 1943-1947. World Flyweight Champion (GB/NY version), 1947-1948. British Bantamweight Champion, 1947-1949. British Empire Bantamweight Championship Claimant, 1945-1949. European Bantamweight Champion, 1946. *Born* 05.09.20. *From* Springfield. *Deceased* 1966. *Pro Career* 1938-1950 (92 contests, won 64, drew 3, lost 25).

Bernard Paul Commonwealth L. Welterweight Champion, 1997-1999. *Born* 22.20.65. *From* Tottenham. *Pro Career* 1991-2000 (35 contests, won 21, drew 4, lost 10).

Larry Paul British L. Middleweight Champion, 1973-1974. *Born* 19.04.52. *From* Wolverhampton. *Pro Career* 1973-1978 (40 contests, won 30, drew 1, lost 9).

David Pearce Undefeated British Heavyweight Champion, 1983-1985. *Born* 08.05.59. *From* Newport. *Deceased* 2000. *Pro Career* 1978-1984 (21 contests, won 17, drew 1, lost 3).

Kostas Petrou British Welterweight Champion, 1985. *Born* 17.04.59. *From* Birmingham. *Pro Career* 1981-1988 (37 contests, won 30, lost 7).

Tiger Al Phillips European Featherweight Champion, 1947. British Empire Featherweight Championship Claimant, 1947. *Born* 25.01.20. *From* Aldgate. *Deceased* 1999. *Pro Career* 1938-1951 (89 contests, won 72, drew 3, lost 14).

Nicky Piper Undefeated Commonwealth L. Heavyweight Champion, 1995-1997. *Born* 05.05.66. *From* Cardiff. *Pro Career* 1989-1997 (33 contests, won 26, drew 2, lost 5).

Dean Pithie Commonwealth S. Featherweight Champion, 2002-2003. *Born* 18.01.74. *From* Coventry. *Pro Career* 1995-2003 (32 contests, won 25, drew 2, lost 5).

Dennis Powell British L. Heavyweight Champion, 1953. *Born* 12.12.24. *From* Four Crosses. *Deceased* 1993. *Pro Career* 1947-1954 (68 contests, won 42, drew 4, lost 22).

Colin Power Undefeated British L. Welterweight Champion, 1977-1978. British L. Welterweight Champion, 1979. European L. Welterweight Champion, 1978. *Born* 02.02.56. *From* Paddington. *Pro Career* 1975-1983 (34 contests, won 28, drew 1, lost 5).

Kevin Pritchard British S. Featherweight Champion, 1990-1991. *Born* 26.09.61. *From* Liverpool. *Pro Career* 1981-1991 (48 contests, won 23, drew 3, lost 22).

Johnny Pritchett Undefeated British Middleweight Champion, 1965-1969. Undefeated British Empire Middleweight Champion, 1967-1969. *Born* 15.02.43. *From* Bingham. *Pro Career* 1963-1969 (34 contests, won 32, drew 1, lost 1).

Chris Pyatt Undefeated British L. Middleweight Champion, 1986. European L. Middleweight Champion, 1986-1987. Undefeated Commonwealth L. Middleweight Champion, 1991-1992. Commonwealth L. Middleweight Champion, 1995-1996. World Middleweight Champion (WBO version), 1993-1994. *Born* 03.07.63. *From* Leicester. *Pro Career* 1983-1997 (51 contests, won 46, lost 5).

Des Rea British L. Welterweight Champion, 1968-1969. *Born* 09.01.44. *From* Belfast. *Pro Career* 1964-1974 (69 contests, won 28, drew 5, lost 36).

Mark Reefer Undefeated Commonwealth S. Featherweight Champion, 1989-1990. *Born* 16.03.64. *Birthname* Mark Thompson. *From* Dagenham. *Pro Career* 1983-1992 (32 contests, won 23, drew 1, lost 8).

Sam Reeson Undefeated British Cruiserweight Champion, 1985-1986. Undefeated European Cruiserweight Champion, 1987-1988. *Born* 05.01.63. *From* Battersea. *Pro Career* 1983-1989 (26 contests, won 24, lost 2).

Robbie Regan Undefeated World Bantamweight Champion (WBO version), 1996-1997. British Flyweight Champion, 1991. Undefeated British Flyweight Champion, 1991-1992. Undefeated European Flyweight Champion, 1992-1993 and 1994-1995. *Born* 30.08.68. *From* Cefn Forest. *Pro Career* 1989-1996 (22 contests, won 17, drew 3, lost 2).

Willie Reilly Undefeated British Lightweight Champion, 1972. *Born* 25.03.47. *From* Glasgow. *Pro Career* 1968-1972 (23 contests, won 13, drew 3, lost 7).

Jimmy Revie British Featherweight Champion, 1969-1971. *Born* 08.07.47. *From* Stockwell. *Pro Career* 1966-1976 (48 contests, won 38, drew 1, lost 9).

Henry Rhiney British Welterweight Champion, 1976-1979. European Welterweight Champion, 1978-1979. *Born* Jamaica, 28.11.51. *From* Luton. *Pro Career* 1973-1980 (57 contests, won 32, drew 6, lost 19).

Alan Richardson British Featherweight Champion, 1977-1978. *Born* 04.11.48. *From* Fitzwilliam. *Pro Career* 1971-1978 (27 contests, won 17, drew 1, lost 9).

Dick Richardson European Heavyweight Champion, 1960-1962. *Born* 01.06.34. *From* Newport. *Deceased* 1999. *Pro Career* 1954-1963 (47 contests, won 31, drew 2, lost 14).

Steve Robinson European Featherweight Champion, 1999-2000. WBO Featherweight Champion, 1993-1995. *Born* 13.12.68. *From* Cardiff. *Pro Career* 1989-2002 (51 contests, won 32, drew 2, lost 17).

Derek Roche British Welterweight Champion, 1999-2000. *Born* 19.07.72. *From* Leeds. *Pro Career* 1994-2004 (34 contests, won 29, lost 5).

Ernie Roderick British Welterweight Champion, 1939-1948. European Welterweight Champion, 1946-1947. British Middleweight Champion, 1945-1946. *Born* 25.01.14. *From* Liverpool. *Deceased* 1986. *Pro Career* 1931-1950 (142 contests, won 114, drew 4, lost 24).

Prince Rodney Undefeated British L. Middleweight Champion, 1983-1984. British L. Middleweight Champion, 1985-1986. *Born* 31.10.58. *From* Huddersfield. *Pro Career* 1977-1990 (41 contests, won 31, drew 1, lost 9).

Stan Rowan Undefeated British Bantamweight Champion, 1949. British Empire Bantamweight Championship Claimant, 1949. *Born* 06.09.24. *From* Liverpool. *Deceased* 1997. *Pro Career* 1942-1953 (67 contests, won 46, drew 5, lost 16).

Mark Rowe British and Commonwealth Middleweight Champion, 1970. *Born* 12.07.47. *Born* 12.07.47. *From* Camberwell. *Pro Career* 1966-1973 (47 contests, won 38, drew 1, lost 8).

Jason Rowland Undefeated British L. Welterweight Champion, 1998-2000. *Born* 06.08.70. *From* West Ham. *Pro Career* 1989-2003 (28 contests, won 26, lost 2).

Alan Rudkin British Bantamweight Champion, 1965-1966. Undefeated British Bantamweight Champion, 1968-1972. British Empire Bantamweight Champion, 1965-1966 and 1968-1969. European Bantamweight Champion, 1971. Undefeated Commonwealth Bantamweight Champion, 1970-1972. *Born* 18.11.41. *From* Liverpool. *Pro Career* 1962-1972 (50 contests, won 42, lost 8).

Hugh Russell Undefeated British Flyweight Champion, 1984-1985. British Bantamweight Champion, 1983. *Born* 15.12.59. *From* Belfast. *Pro Career* 1981-1985 (19 contests, won 17, lost 2).

Roy Rutherford British Featherweight Champion, 2003. *Born* 04.08.73. *From* Coventry. *Pro Career* 1998-2004 (21 contests, won 17, drew 1, lost 3).

Paul Ryan British and Commonwealth L. Welterweight Champion, 1995-1996. *Born* 02.02.65. *From* Hackney. *Pro Career* 1991-1997 (28 contests, won 25, lost 3).

Billy Schwer British Lightweight Champion, 1992-1993. Undefeated British Lightweight Champion, 1993-1995. Commonwealth Lightweight Champion, 1992-1993 and 1993-1995. Undefeated European Lightweight Champion, 1997-1999. *Born* 12.04.69. *From* Luton. *Pro Career* 1990-2001 (45 contests, won 39, lost 6).

Charles Shepherd British S.Featherweight Champion, 1997-1999. Undefeated Commonwealth S.Featherweight Champion, 1999. *Born* 28.06.70. *From* Carlisle. *Pro Career* 1991-2004 (34 contests, won 21, drew 1, lost 12).

Tony Sibson British Middleweight Champion, 1979. Undefeated British Middleweight Champion, 1984 and 1987-1988. Undefeated Commonwealth Middleweight Champion, 1980-1983 and 1984-1988. Undefeated European Middleweight Champion, 1980-1982. European Middleweight Champion, 1984-1985. *Born* 09.04.58. *From* Leicester. *Pro Career* 1976-1988 (63 contests, won 55, drew 1, lost 7).

Steve Sims Undefeated British Featherweight Champion, 1982-1983. *Born* 10.10.58. *From* Newport. *Pro Career* 1977-1987 (29 contests, won 14, drew 1, lost 14).

Joey Singleton British L. Welterweight Champion, 1974-1976. *Born* 06.06.51. *From* Kirkby. *Pro Career* 1973-1982 (40 contests, won 27, drew 2, lost 11).

Kelvin Smart British Flyweight Champion, 1982-1984. *Born* 18.12.60. *From* Caerphilly. *Pro Career* 1979-1987 (29 contests, won 17, drew 2, lost 10).

Roy Smith British Cruiserweight Champion, 1987. *Born* 31.08.61. *From* Nottingham. *Pro Career* 1985-1991 (26 contests, won 18, lost 8).

Vernon Sollas British Featherweight Champion, 1975-1977. *Born* 14.08.54. *From* Edinburgh. *Pro Career* 1973-1977 (33 contests, won 25, drew 1, lost 7).

Terry Spinks British Featherweight Champion, 1960-1961. *Born* 28.02.38. *From* Canning Town. *Pro Career* 1957-1962 (49 contests, won 41, drew 1, lost 7).

David Starie British S. Middleweight Champion, 1997. Undefeated British S. Middleweight Champion, 1998-2003. Commonwealth S. Middleweight Champion, 1998-2003. *Born* 11.06.74. *From* Bury St Edmunds. *Pro Career* 1994-2003 (35 contests, won 31, lost 4).

Bunny Sterling British Middleweight Champion, 1970-1974. Undefeated British Middleweight Champion, 1975. Commonwealth Middleweight Champion, 1970-1972. European Middleweight Champion, 1976. *Born* Jamaica, 04.04.48. *From* Finsbury Park. *Pro Career* 1966-1977 (57 contests, won 35, drew 4, lost 18).

Sammy Storey British S. Middleweight Champion, 1989-1990. Undefeated British S. Middleweight Champion, 1995. *Born* 09.08.63. *From* Belfast. *Pro Career* 1985-1997 (31 contests, won 25, lost 6).

John H. Stracey Undefeated British Welterweight Champion, 1973-1975. Undefeated European Welterweight Champion, 1974-1975. World Welterweight Champion (WBC version), 1975-1976. *Born* 22.09.50. *From* Bethnal Green. *Pro Career* 1969-1978 (51 contests, won 45, drew 1, lost 5).

Andy Straughn British Cruiserweight Champion, 1986-1987 and 1988-1989. *Born* Barbados, 25.12.59. *From* Hitchin. *Pro Career* 1982-1990 (27 contests, won 18, drew 2, lost 7).

Gary Stretch British L. Middleweight Champion, 1988-1990. *Born* 04.11.65. *From* St Helens. *Pro Career* 1985-1993 (25 contests, won 23, lost 2).

Johnny Sullivan British Empire Middleweight Championship Claimant, 1954. British and British Empire Middleweight Champion, 1954-1955. *Born* 19.12.32. *From* Preston. *Deceased* 2003. *Birthname* John Hallmark. *Pro Career* 1948-1960 (97 contests, won 68, drew 3, lost 26).

Neil Swain Undefeated Commonwealth S. Bantamweight Champion, 1995 and 1996-1997. *Born* 04.09.71. *From* Gilfach Goch. *Pro Career* 1993-1997 (24 contests, won 17, lost 7).

Wally Swift British Welterweight Champion, 1960. British Middleweight Champion, 1964-1965. *Born* 10.08.36. *From* Nottingham. *Pro Career* 1957-1969 (88 contests, won 68, drew 3, lost 17).

Wally Swift Jnr British L. Middleweight Champion, 1991-1992. *Born* 17.02.66. *From* Birmingham. *Pro Career* 1985-1994 (38 contests, won 26, drew 1, lost 11).

Nel Tarleton British Featherweight Champion, 1931-1932 and 1934-1936. Undefeated British Featherweight Champion, 1940-1947. Undefeated British Empire Featherweight Championship Claimant, 1940-1947. *Born* 14.01.06. *From* Liverpool. *Deceased* 1956. *Pro Career* 1926-1945 (144 contests, won 116, drew 8, lost 20).

Wally Thom British Welterweight Champion, 1951-1952 and 1953-1956. British Empire Welterweight Championship Claimant, 1951-1952. European Welterweight Champion, 1954-1955. *Born* 14.06.26. *From* Birkenhead. *Deceased* 1980. *Pro Career* 1949-1956 (54 contests, won 42, drew 1, lost 11).

Eddie Thomas British Welterweight Champion, 1949-1951. European Welterweight Champion, 1951. British Empire Welterweight Championship Claimant, 1951. *Born* 27.07.26. *From* Merthyr. *Deceased* 1997. *Pro Career* 1946-1954 (48 contests, won 40, drew 2, lost 6).

Pat Thomas British Welterweight Champion, 1975-1976. British L. Middleweight Champion, 1979-1981. *Born* St Kitts, 05.05.50. *From* Cardiff. *Pro Career* 1970-1984 (57 contests, won 35, drew 3, lost 18, no contest 1).

Billy Thompson British Lightweight Champion, 1947-1951. European Lightweight Champion, 1948-1949. *Born* 20.12.25. *From* Hickleton Main. *Pro Career* 1945-1953 (63 contests, won 46, drew 4, lost 13).

Andy Till British L. Middleweight Champion, 1992-1994. *Born* 22.08.63. *From* Northolt. *Pro Career* 1986-1995 (24 contests, won 19, lost 5).

Dick Turpin British Middleweight Champion, 1948-1950. British Empire Middleweight Championship Claimant, 1948-1949. *Born* 26.11.20. *From* Leamington Spa. *Deceased* 1990. *Pro Career* 1937-1950 (103 contests, won 76, drew 6, lost 20, no contest 1).

Randy Turpin Undefeated British Middleweight Champion, 1950-1954. British Empire Middleweight Championship Claimant, 1952-1954. European Middleweight Champion, 1951-1954. World Middleweight Champion, 1951. World Middleweight Champion (EBU version), 1953. Undefeated British L. Heavyweight Champion, 1952, 1955, and 1956-1958. British Empire L. Heavyweight Championship Claimant, 1952-1954. Undefeated British Empire L. Heavyweight Champion, 1954-1955. *Born*

07.06.28. *From* Leamington Spa. *Deceased* 1966. *Pro Career* 1946-1958 (73 contests, won 64, drew 1, lost 8).

Tommy Waite British and Commonwealth Bantamweight Champion, 2000. *Born* 11.03.72. *From* Belfast. *Pro Career* 1996-2001 (15 contests, won 11, lost 4).

Keith Wallace Undefeated Commonwealth Flyweight Champion, 1983-1984. *Born* 29.03.61. *From* Liverpool. *Deceased* 2000. *Pro Career* 1982-1990 (25 contests, won 20, lost 5).

Peter Waterman Undefeated British Welterweight Champion, 1956-1958. Undefeated European Welterweight Champion, 1958. *Born* 08.12.34. *From* Clapham. *Deceased* 1986. *Pro Career* 1952-1958 (46 contests, won 41, drew 2, lost 3).

Michael Watson Undefeated Commonwealth Middleweight Champion, 1989-1991. *Born* 15.03.65. *From* Islington. *Pro Career* 1984-1991 (30 contests, won 25, drew 1, lost 4).

Jim Watt British Lightweight Champion, 1972-1973. Undefeated British Lightweight Champion, 1975-1977. Undefeated European Lightweight Champion, 1977-1979. World Lightweight Champion (WBC version), 1979-1981. *Born* 18.07.48. *From* Glasgow. *Pro Career* 1968-1981 (46 contests, won 38, lost 8).

Paul Weir Undefeated WBO M. Flyweight Champion, 1993-1994. WBO L. Flyweight Champion, 1994-1995. *Born* 16.09.67. *From* Irvine. *Pro Career* 1992-2000 (20 contests, won 14, lost 6).

Scott Welch Undefeated British Heavyweight Champion, 1995-1996. Commonwealth Heavyweight Champion, 1995-1997. *Born* 21.04.1968. *From* Shoreham. *Pro Career* 1992-1999 (26 contests, won 22, lost 4).

Richie Wenton Undefeated British S. Bantamweight Champion, 1994-1996. *Born* 28.10.67. *From* Liverpool. *Pro Career* 1988-2001 (30 contests, won 24, lost 6).

Henry Wharton Undefeated British S. Middleweight Champion, 1992-1993. Undefeated Commonwealth Champion, 1991-1997. Undefeated European S. Middleweight Champion, 1995-1996. *Born* 23.11.1967. *From* York. *Pro Career* 1989-1998 (31 contests, won 27, drew 1, lost 3).

Derek Williams Commonwealth Heavyweight Champion, 1988-1992. European Heavyweight Champion, 1989-1992. *Born* 11.03.65. *From* Peckham. *Pro Career* 1984-1999 (35 contests, won 22, lost 13).

Johnny Williams British Heavyweight Champion, 1952-1953. British Empire Heavyweight Championship Claimant, 1952-1953. *Born* 25.12.26. *From* Rugby. *Pro Career* 1946-1956 (75 contests, won 60, drew 4, lost 11).

Tony Willis British Lightweight Champion, 1985-1987. *Born* 17.06.60. *From* Liverpool. *Pro Career* 1981-1989 (29 contests, won 25, lost 4).

Nick Wilshire Commonwealth L. Middleweight Champion, 1985-1987. *Born* 03.11.61. *From* Bristol. *Pro Career* 1981-1987 (40 contests, won 36, lost 4).

Tony Wilson British L. Heavyweight Champion, 1987-1989. *Born* 25.04.64. *From* Wolverhampton. *Pro Career* 1985-1993 (29 contests, won 20, drew 1, lost 8).

Howard Winstone Undefeated British Featherweight Champion, 1961-1969. European Featherweight Champion, 1963-1967. World Featherweight Champion (WBC version), 1968. *Born* 15.04.39. *From* Merthyr. *Deceased* 2000. *Pro Career* 1959-1968 (67 contests, won 61, lost 6).

Tim Wood British L. Heavyweight Champion, 1976-1977. *Born* 10.08.51. *From* Leicester. *Pro Career* 1972-1979 (31 contests, won 19, drew 1, lost 11).

Bruce Woodcock British Heavyweight Champion, 1945-1950. British Empire Heavyweight Championship Claimant, 1945-1950. European Heavyweight Champion, 1946-1949. *Born* 18.01.21. *From* Doncaster. *Deceased* 1997. *Pro Career* 1942-1950 (39 contests, won 35, lost 4).

Richie Woodhall WBC S. Middleweight Champion, 1998-1999. Commonwealth Middleweight Champion, 1992-1995. Undefeated European Middleweight Champion, 1995-1996. *Born* 17.04.68. *From* Telford. *Pro Career* 1990-2000 (29 contests, won 26, lost 3).

Commonwealth Title Bouts, 2004-2005

All of last season's title bouts are shown in date order within their weight divisions and give the contestants' respective weights, along with the scorecard if going to a decision. Every contest involving a British fighter is summarised briefly and all British officials are named.

Flyweight

Dale Robinson (England) forfeited the title in November after failing to make a defence since winning it in February 2003.

Bantamweight

29 October   Joseph Agbeko (Ghana) W PTS 12 Sumaila Badu (Ghana), Accra, Ghana. Scorecards: 120-106, 120-107, 120-107. Contested for the vacant title after Steve

Molitor (Canada) was stripped in April 2004 for failing to meet the deadlines for a defence.

S.Bantamweight

Esham Pickering (England) failed to defend during the period.

Featherweight

16 June   Nicky Cook 9.0 (England) W CO 2 Dazzo

Graham Earl (left) came back in dramatic fashion to retain his British lightweight title and land the Commonwealth crown when stopping Kevin Bennett in the ninth round

Les Clark

Williams 8.13¼ (Wales), Goresbrook Leisure Centre, Dagenham, England. Referee: John Keane. Judges: Larry O'Connell, Terry O'Connor, Richie Davies. Williams was defending the British title, while Cook's European and Commonwealth titles were on the line. For a summary, see under British Title Bouts During 2004-2005.

S.Featherweight

9 April   Craig Docherty 9.3¼ (Scotland) L CO 9 Alex Arthur 9.3¾ (Scotland), Meadowbank Sports Centre, Edinburgh, Scotland. Referee: Richie Davies. The vacant British title was also involved. For a summary, see under British Title Bouts During 2004-2005.

Lightweight

19 November   Kevin Bennett 9.8 (England) W PTS 12 Dean Phillips 9.7 (Wales), Borough Hall, Hartlepool, England. Referee: Phil Edwards 118-111. Shown incorrectly in last year's book as having relinquished his Commonwealth title in April 2004, Bennett was made to work hard for his victory by the resilient Welshman, who survived a knockdown in the second round after taking a left hook to the head. Although the champion looked to be close to a stoppage win on several occasions, Phillips always managed to fight back and even in the final round when he was rocked quite a few times and nearly went over he somehow managed to make it to the bell.

19 June   Kevin Bennett 9.8½ (England) L RSC 9 Graham Earl 9.7½ (England), York Hall, Bethnal Green, London, England. Referee: Howard Foster. Earl's British title was also on the line. For a summary, see under British Title Bouts During 2004-2005.

L.Welterweight

19 February   Junior Witter 9.13¾ (England) W PTS 12 Lovemore Ndou 9.12½ (Australia, via South Africa), Staples Center, Los Angeles, California, USA. Scorecards: 114-112, 114-112, 115-111. Although America seemed to be a strange place to defend the Commonwealth title, Witter, despite damaging his left hand, killed two birds with one stone when he outpointed a dangerous opponent in front of a large audience to earn himself a promotional deal with Oscar de la Hoya's promotional team. After dropping the tough Ndou twice, in the third and fourth rounds, it looked as though the champion might just stop the hardman from Australia, but, being forced to conserve his damaged hand, allowed the challenger back into the fight and Witter took some solid shots in the process. Still, it was a worthy victory and one that strengthened his position in the world ratings.

Welterweight

17 September   Fatai Onikeke (Nigeria) W PTS 12 Hassan Matumla (Tanzania), Lorin, Nigeria. Scorecards: 118-112, 119-114, 117-113. Contested for the vacant title after Ossie

Duran (Ghana) vacated on winning the Commonwealth welterweight crown on 26 June 2004.

4 March   Fatai Onikeke (Nigeria) L RSC 8 Joshua Okine (Ghana), Accra, Ghana.

4 June   Joshua Okine 10.7 (Ghana) W RSC 12 David Barnes 19.5¾ (England), MEN Arena, Manchester, England. Referee: Phil Edwards. Finding it difficult to fathom out Okine, a southpaw like himself, Barnes began to get outgunned and in the fifth round a right-left combination set him up for a knockdown, from which he never really recovered. Not wishing to trade punches with Okine on a regular basis, the challenger backed off, but was hurt several times and although he rallied sporadically it was noticeable that he was having great difficulty in getting through the fight. Come the last session, Okine again got to Barnes, now suffering from facial swellings, and although the Mancunian gave it a go, with the champion smashing in lefts and rights the referee had seen enough and called it off with 49 seconds remaining.

L.Middleweight

Ossie Duran (Ghana) failed to defend during the period.

Middleweight

3 July   James Obede Toney (Ghana) W PTS 12 Ayittey Powers (Ghana), Accra, Ghana. Scorecards: 118-109, 118-108, 111-107. Contested for the vacant crown after Howard Eastman (England, via Guyana) relinquished the title in May 2004 to concentrate on European and world title shots.

S.Middleweight

24 September   Carl Froch 11.13 (England) W RSC 1 Damon Hague 12.0 (England), The Arena, Nottingham, England. Referee: Mickey Vann. The vacant British title was also up for grabs. For a summary, see under British Title Bouts During 2004-2005.

L.Heavyweight

Peter Oboh (England, via Nigeria) failed to defend during the period.

Cruiserweight

17 December   Mark Hobson 14.1 (England) W PTS 12 Bruce Scott 14.3¾ (England, via Jamaica), The Sports Centre, Huddersfield, England. Referee: Paul Thomas 118-112. Hobson's British title was also at risk. For a summary, see under British Title Bouts During 2004-2005.

Heavyweight

19 November   Matt Skelton 17.11 (England) W RSC 11 Keith Long 14.12 (England), York Hall, Bethnal Green, London, England. Referee: Howard Foster. Skelton's British title was also on the line. Skelton relinquished the title after winning the WBU crown on 25 February. For a summary, see under British Title Bouts During 2004-2005.

Commonwealth Champions, 1887-2005

Since the 1997 edition, Harold Alderman's magnificent research into Imperial British Empire title fights has introduced many more claimants/champions than were shown previously. Prior to 12 October 1954, the date that the British Commonwealth and Empire Boxing Championships Committee was formed, there was no official body as such and the Australian and British promoters virtually ran the show, with other members of the British Empire mainly out in the cold. We have also listed Canadian representatives, despite championship boxing in that country being contested over ten or 12 rounds at most, but they are not accorded the same kind of recognition that their British and Australian counterparts are. On 8 September 1970, Bunny Sterling became the first immigrant to win a British title under the ten-year residential ruling and from that date on champions are recorded by domicile rather than by birthplace. Reconstituted as the British Commonwealth Boxing Championships Committee on 22 November 1972, and with a current membership that includes Australia, Bahamas, Canada, Ghana, Guyana, Jamaica, Kenya, Namibia, New Zealand, Nigeria, South Africa, Tanzania, Uganda and Zambia, in 1989 the 'British' tag was dropped.

COMMONWEALTH COUNTRY CODE

A = Australia; BAH = Bahamas; BAR = Barbados; BER = Bermuda; C = Canada; E = England; F = Fiji; GH = Ghana; GU = Guyana; I = Ireland; J = Jamaica; K = Kenya; N = Nigeria; NZ = New Zealand; NI = Northern Ireland; PNG = Papua New Guinea; SA = South Africa; SAM = Samoa; S = Scotland; T = Tonga; TR = Trinidad; U = Uganda; W = Wales; ZA = Zambia; ZI = Zimbabwe.

Champions in **bold** denote those recognised by the British Commonwealth and Empire Boxing Championships Committee (1954 to date) and, prior to that, those with the best claims

*Undefeated champions (Does not include men who forfeited titles)

Title Holder	Birthplace/ Domicile	Tenure	Title Holder	Birthplace/ Domicile	Tenure	Title Holder	Birthplace/ Domicile	Tenure
Flyweight (112 lbs)			**Bantamweight (118 lbs)**			Ray Minus*	BAH	1986-1991
Elky Clark*	S	1924-1927	**Digger Stanley**	E	1904-1905	**John Armour***	E	1992-1996
Harry Hill	E	1929	**Owen Moran**	E	1905	**Paul Lloyd***	E	1996-2000
Frenchy Belanger	C	1929	**Ted Green**	A	1905-1911	**Ady Lewis**	E	2000
Vic White	A	1929-1930	**Charlie Simpson***	A	1911-1912	**Tommy Waite**	NI	2000
Teddy Green	A	1930-1931	**Jim Higgins**	S	1920-1922	**Nicky Booth**	E	2000-2002
Jackie Paterson	S	1940-1948	**Tommy Harrison**	E	1922-1923	**Steve Molitor**	C	2002-2004
Rinty Monaghan*	NI	1948-1950	**Bugler Harry Lake**	E	1923	**Joseph Agbeko**	GH	2004-
Teddy Gardner	E	1952	**Johnny Brown**	E	1923-1928			
Jake Tuli	SA	1952-1954	Billy McAllister	A	1928-1930	**S. Bantamweight (122 lbs)**		
Dai Dower*	W	1954-1957	**Teddy Baldock***	E	1928-1930	Neil Swain	W	1995
Frankie Jones	S	1957	Johnny Peters	E	1930	**Neil Swain**	W	1996-1997
Dennis Adams*	SA	1957-1962	**Dick Corbett**	E	1930-1932	**Michael Brodie**	E	1997-1999
Jackie Brown	S	1962-1963	**Johnny King**	E	1932-1934	**Nedal Hussein***	A	2000-2001
Walter McGowan*	S	1963-1969	**Dick Corbett**	E	1934	**Brian Carr**	S	2001-2002
John McCluskey	S	1970-1971	Frankie Martin	C	1935-1937	**Michael Alldis**	E	2002
Henry Nissen	A	1971-1974	Baby Yack	C	1937	**Esham Pickering**	E	2003-
Big Jim West*	A	1974-1975	Johnny Gaudes	C	1937-1939			
Patrick Mambwe	ZA	1976-1979	Lefty Gwynn	C	1939	**Featherweight (126 lbs)**		
Ray Amoo	N	1980	Baby Yack	C	1939-1940	**Jim Driscoll***	W	1908-1913
Steve Muchoki	K	1980-1983	**Jim Brady**	S	1941-1945	**Llew Edwards**	W	1915-1916
Keith Wallace*	E	1983-1984	**Jackie Paterson**	S	1945-1949	**Charlie Simpson***	A	1916
Richard Clarke	J	1986-1987	**Stan Rowan**	E	1949	Tommy Noble	E	1919-1921
Nana Yaw Konadu*	GH	1987-1989	**Vic Toweel**	SA	1949-1952	**Bert Spargo**	A	1921-1922
Alfred Kotey*	GH	1989-1993	**Jimmy Carruthers***	A	1952-1954	**Bert McCarthy**	A	1922
Francis Ampofo*	E	1993	**Peter Keenan**	S	1955-1959	**Bert Spargo**	A	1922-1923
Daren Fifield	E	1993-1994	**Freddie Gilroy***	NI	1959-1963	**Billy Grime**	A	1923
Francis Ampofo	E	1994-1995	**Johnny Caldwell**	NI	1964-1965	**Ernie Baxter**	A	1923
Danny Ward	SA	1995-1996	**Alan Rudkin**	E	1965-1966	Leo Kid Roy	C	1923
Peter Culshaw	E	1996-1997	**Walter McGowan**	S	1966-1968	**Bert Ristuccia**	A	1923-1924
Ady Lewis*	E	1997-1998	**Alan Rudkin**	E	1968-1969	Barney Wilshur	C	1923
Alfonso Zvenyika	ZI	1998	**Lionel Rose***	A	1969	Benny Gould	C	1923-1924
Damaen Kelly	NI	1998-1999	**Alan Rudkin***	E	1970-1972	**Billy Grime**	A	1924
Keith Knox	S	1999	**Paul Ferreri**	A	1972-1977	Leo Kid Roy	C	1924-1932
Jason Booth*	E	1999-2003	**Sulley Shittu**	GH	1977-1978	**Johnny McGrory**	S	1936-1938
Dale Robinson	E	2003-2004	**Johnny Owen***	W	1978-1980	**Jim Spider Kelly**	NI	1938-1939
			Paul Ferreri	A	1981-1986	**Johnny Cusick**	E	1939-1940

201

Title Holder	Birthplace/ Domicile	Tenure
Nel Tarleton	E	1940-1947
Tiger Al Phillips	E	1947
Ronnie Clayton	E	1947-1951
Roy Ankrah	GH	1951-1954
Billy Spider Kelly	NI	1954-1955
Hogan Kid Bassey*	N	1955-1957
Percy Lewis	TR	1957-1960
Floyd Robertson	GH	1960-1967
John O'Brien	S	1967
Johnny Famechon*	A	1967-1969
Toro George	NZ	1970-1972
Bobby Dunne	A	1972-1974
Evan Armstrong	S	1974
David Kotey*	GH	1974-1975
Eddie Ndukwu	N	1977-1980
Pat Ford*	GU	1980-1981
Azumah Nelson*	GH	1981-1985
Tyrone Downes	BAR	1986-1988
Thunder Aryeh	GH	1988-1989
Oblitey Commey	GH	1989-1990
Modest Napunyi	K	1990-1991
Barrington Francis*	C	1991
Colin McMillan*	E	1992
Billy Hardy*	E	1992-1996
Jonjo Irwin	E	1996-1997
Paul Ingle*	E	1997-1999
Patrick Mullings	E	1999-2000
Scott Harrison*	S	2000-2002
Nicky Cook	E	2003-

Title Holder	Birthplace/ Domicile	Tenure
S. Featherweight (130 lbs)		
Billy Moeller	A	1975-1977
Johnny Aba*	PNG	1977-1982
Langton Tinago	ZI	1983-1984
John Sichula	ZA	1984
Lester Ellis*	A	1984-1985
John Sichula	ZA	1985-1986
Sam Akromah	GH	1986-1987
John Sichula	ZA	1987-1989
Mark Reefer*	E	1989-1990
Thunder Aryeh	GH	1990-1991
Hugh Forde	E	1991
Paul Harvey	E	1991-1992
Tony Pep	C	1992-1995
Justin Juuko*	U	1995-1998
Charles Shepherd*	E	1999
Mick O'Malley	A	1999-2000
Ian McLeod*	S	2000
James Armah*	GH	2000-2001
Alex Moon	E	2001-2002
Dean Pithie	E	2002-2003
Craig Docherty	S	2003-2004
Alex Arthur	S	2004-
Lightweight (135 lbs)		
Jim Burge	A	1890
George Dawson*	A	1890
Harry Nickless	E	1892-1894
Arthur Valentine	E	1894-1895

Title Holder	Birthplace/ Domicile	Tenure
Dick Burge*	E	1894-1895
Jim Murphy*	NZ	1894-1897
Eddie Connolly*	C	1896-1897
Jack Goldswain	E	1906-1908
Jack McGowan	A	1909
Hughie Mehegan	A	1909-1910
Johnny Summers*	E	1910
Hughie Mehegan	A	1911
Freddie Welsh*	W	1912-1914
Ernie Izzard	E	1928
Tommy Fairhall	A	1928-1930
Al Foreman	E	1930-1933
Jimmy Kelso	A	1933
Al Foreman*	E	1933-1934
Laurie Stevens*	SA	1936-1937
Dave Crowley	E	1938
Eric Boon	E	1938-1944
Ronnie James*	W	1944-1947
Arthur King	C	1948-1951
Frank Johnson	E	1953
Pat Ford	A	1953-1954
Ivor Germain	BAR	1954
Pat Ford	A	1954-1955
Johnny van Rensburg	SA	1955-1956
Willie Toweel	SA	1956-1959
Dave Charnley	E	1959-1962
Bunny Grant	J	1962-1967
Manny Santos*	NZ	1967
Love Allotey	GH	1967-1968

Nicky Cook (left) added the British featherweight title to his Commonwealth and European honours when stopping Dazzo Williams inside two rounds at Dagenham in June

Les Clark

202

Title Holder	Birthplace/ Domicile	Tenure
Percy Hayles	J	1968-1975
Jonathan Dele	N	1975-1977
Lennox Blackmore	GU	1977-1978
Hogan Jimoh	N	1978-1980
Langton Tinago	ZI	1980-1981
Barry Michael	A	1981-1982
Claude Noel	T	1982-1984
Graeme Brooke	A	1984-1985
Barry Michael*	A	1985-1986
Langton Tinago	ZI	1986-1987
Mo Hussein	E	1987-1989
Pat Doherty	E	1989
Najib Daho	E	1989-1990
Carl Crook	E	1990-1992
Billy Schwer	E	1992-1993
Paul Burke	E	1993
Billy Schwer	E	1993-1995
David Tetteh	GH	1995-1997
Billy Irwin	C	1997
David Tetteh	GH	1997-1999
Bobby Vanzie	E	1999-2001
James Armah*	GH	2001-2002
David Burke*	E	2002
Michael Muya	K	2003
Kevin Bennett	E	2003-2005
Graham Earl	E	2005-

L. Welterweight (140 lbs)

Title Holder	Birthplace/ Domicile	Tenure
Joe Tetteh	GH	1972-1973
Hector Thompson	A	1973-1977
Baby Cassius Austin	A	1977-1978
Jeff Malcolm	A	1978-1979
Obisia Nwankpa	N	1979-1983
Billy Famous	N	1983-1986
Tony Laing	E	1987-1988
Lester Ellis	A	1988-1989
Steve Larrimore	BAH	1989
Tony Ekubia	E	1989-1991
Andy Holligan	E	1991-1994
Ross Hale	E	1994-1995
Paul Ryan	E	1995-1996
Andy Holligan	E	1996-1997
Bernard Paul	E	1997-1999
Eamonn Magee	NI	1999-
Paul Burke	E	1997
Felix Bwalya*	ZA	1997
Paul Burke	E	1998-1999
Eamonn Magee*	NI	1999-2002
Junior Witter	E	2002-

Welterweight (147 lbs)

Title Holder	Birthplace/ Domicile	Tenure
Tom Williams	A	1892-1895
Dick Burge	E	1895-1897
Eddie Connelly*	C	1903-1905
Joe White*	C	1907-1909
Johnny Summers	E	1912-1914
Tom McCormick	I	1914
Matt Wells	E	1914-1919
Fred Kay	A	1915
Tommy Uren	A	1915-1916
Fritz Holland	A	1916
Tommy Uren	A	1916-1919
Fred Kay	A	1919-1920
Johnny Basham	W	1919-1920
Bermondsey Billy Wells	E	1922

Title Holder	Birthplace/ Domicile	Tenure
Ted Kid Lewis	E	1920-1924
Tommy Milligan*	S	1924-1925
Jack Carroll	A	1928
Charlie Purdie	A	1928-1929
Wally Hancock	A	1929-1930
Tommy Fairhall*	A	1930
Jack Carroll	A	1934-1938
Eddie Thomas	W	1951
Wally Thom	E	1951-1952
Cliff Curvis	W	1952
Gerald Dreyer	SA	1952-1954
Barry Brown	NZ	1954
George Barnes	A	1954-1956
Darby Brown	A	1956
George Barnes	A	1956-1958
Johnny van Rensburg	SA	1958
George Barnes	A	1958-1960
Brian Curvis*	W	1960-1966
Johnny Cooke	E	1967-1968
Ralph Charles*	E	1968-1972
Clyde Gray	C	1973-1979
Chris Clarke	C	1979
Clyde Gray*	C	1979-1980
Colin Jones*	W	1981-1984
Sylvester Mittee	E	1984-1985
Lloyd Honeyghan*	E	1985-1986
Brian Janssen	A	1987
Wilf Gentzen	A	1987-1988
Gary Jacobs	S	1988-1989
Donovan Boucher	C	1989-1992
Eamonn Loughran*	NI	1992-1993
Andrew Murray*	GU	1993-1997
Kofi Jantuah*	GH	1997-2000
Scott Dixon	S	2000
Jawaid Khaliq*	E	2000-2001
Julian Holland	A	2001-2002
James Hare*	E	2002-2003
Ossie Duran*	GH	2003-2004
Fatai Onikeke	NI	2004-2005
Joshua Okine	GH	2005-

L. Middleweight (154 lbs)

Title Holder	Birthplace/ Domicile	Tenure
Charkey Ramon*	A	1972-1975
Maurice Hope*	E	1976-1979
Kenny Bristol	GU	1979-1981
Herol Graham*	E	1981-1984
Ken Salisbury	A	1984-1985
Nick Wilshire	E	1985-1987
Lloyd Hibbert	E	1987
Troy Waters*	A	1987-1991
Chris Pyatt	E	1991-1992
Mickey Hughes	E	1992-1993
Lloyd Honeyghan	E	1993-1994
Leo Young	A	1994-1995
Kevin Kelly	A	1995
Chris Pyatt	E	1995-1996
Steve Foster	E	1996-1997
Kevin Kelly	A	1997-1999
Tony Badea	C	1999-2001
Richard Williams*	E	2001
Joshua Onyango	K	2002
Michael Jones	E	2002-2003
Jamie Moore*	E	2003-2004
Richard Williams*	E	2004
Jamie Moore	E	2004
Ossie Duran	GH	2004-

Middleweight (160 lbs)

Title Holder	Birthplace/ Domicile	Tenure
Chesterfield Goode	E	1887-1890
Toff Wall	E	1890-1891
Jim Hall	A	1892-1893
Bill Heffernan	NZ	1894-1896
Bill Doherty	A	1896-1897
Billy Edwards	A	1897-1898
Dido Plumb*	E	1898-1901
Tom Duggan	A	1901-1903
Jack Palmer*	E	1902-1904
Jewey Cooke	E	1903-1904
Tom Dingey	C	1904-1905
Jack Lalor	SA	1905
Ted Nelson	A	1905
Tom Dingey	C	1905
Sam Langford*	C	1907-1911
Ed Williams	A	1908-1910
Arthur Cripps	A	1910
Dave Smith	A	1910-1911
Jerry Jerome	A	1913
Arthur Evernden	E	1913-1914
Mick King	A	1914-1915
Les Darcy*	A	1915-1917
Ted Kid Lewis	E	1922-1923
Roland Todd	E	1923-1926
Len Johnson	E	1926-1928
Tommy Milligan	S	1926-1928
Alex Ireland	S	1928-1929
Len Harvey	E	1929-1933
Del Fontaine	C	1931
Ted Moore	E	1931
Jock McAvoy	E	1933-1939
Ron Richards*	A	1940
Ron Richards*	A	1941-1942
Bos Murphy	NZ	1948
Dick Turpin	E	1948-1949
Dave Sands*	A	1949-1952
Randy Turpin	E	1952-1954
Al Bourke	A	1952-1954
Johnny Sullivan	E	1954-1955
Pat McAteer	E	1955-1958
Dick Tiger	N	1958-1960
Wilf Greaves	C	1960
Dick Tiger	N	1960-1962
Gomeo Brennan	BAH	1963-1964
Tuna Scanlon*	NZ	1964
Gomeo Brennan	BAH	1964-1966
Blair Richardson*	C	1966-1967
Milo Calhoun	J	1967
Johnny Pritchett*	E	1967-1969
Les McAteer	E	1969-1970
Mark Rowe	E	1970
Bunny Sterling	E	1970-1972
Tony Mundine*	A	1972-1975
Monty Betham	NZ	1975-1978
Al Korovou	A	1978
Ayub Kalule	U	1978-1980
Tony Sibson*	E	1980-1983
Roy Gumbs	E	1983
Mark Kaylor	E	1983-1984
Tony Sibson*	E	1984-1988
Nigel Benn	E	1988-1989
Michael Watson*	E	1989-1991
Richie Woodhall	E	1992-1995
Robert McCracken	E	1995-1997

Title Holder	Birthplace/ Domicile	Tenure
Johnson Tshuma	SA	1997-1998
Paul Jones	E	1998-1999
Jason Matthews*	E	1999
Alain Bonnamie*	C	1999-2000
Sam Soliman	A	2000
Howard Eastman*	E	2000-2004
James Obede Toney	GH	2004-

S. Middleweight (168 lbs)

Title Holder	Birthplace/ Domicile	Tenure
Rod Carr	A	1989-1990
Lou Cafaro	A	1990-1991
Henry Wharton*	E	1991-1997
Clinton Woods	E	1997-1998
David Starie	E	1998-2003
Andre Thysse	SA	2003
Charles Adamu	GH	2003-2004
Carl Froch	E	2004-

L. Heavyweight (175 lbs)

Title Holder	Birthplace/ Domicile	Tenure
Dave Smith*	A	1911-1915
Jack Bloomfield*	E	1923-1924
Tom Berry	E	1927
Gipsy Daniels*	W	1927
Len Harvey	E	1939-1942
Freddie Mills*	E	1942-1950
Randy Turpin*	E	1952-1955
Gordon Wallace	C	1956-1957
Yvon Durelle*	C	1957-1959
Chic Calderwood	S	1960-1963
Bob Dunlop*	A	1968-1970
Eddie Avoth	W	1970-1971
Chris Finnegan	E	1971-1973
John Conteh*	E	1973-1974
Steve Aczel	A	1975
Tony Mundine	A	1975-1978
Gary Summerhays	C	1978-1979
Lottie Mwale	ZA	1979-1985
Leslie Stewart*	TR	1985-1987
Willie Featherstone	C	1987-1989
Guy Waters*	A	1989-1993
Brent Kosolofski	C	1993-1994
Garry Delaney	E	1994-1995
Noel Magee	I	1995
Nicky Piper*	W	1995-1997
Crawford Ashley	E	1998-1999
Clinton Woods*	E	1999-2000
Neil Simpson	E	2001
Tony Oakey*	E	2001-2002
Peter Oboh	E	2002-

Cruiserweight (200 lbs)

Title Holder	Birthplace/ Domicile	Tenure
Stewart Lithgo	E	1984
Chisanda Mutti	ZA	1984-1987
Glenn McCrory*	E	1987-1989
Apollo Sweet	A	1989
Derek Angol*	E	1989-1993
Francis Wanyama	U	1994-1995
Chris Okoh	E	1995-1997
Darren Corbett	NI	1997-1998
Bruce Scott	E	1998-1999
Adam Watt*	A	2000-2001
Bruce Scott*	E	2001-2003
Mark Hobson	E	2003-

Heavyweight (200 lbs +)

Title Holder	Birthplace/ Domicile	Tenure
Peter Jackson*	A	1889-1901
Dan Creedon	NZ	1896-1903
Billy McColl	A	1902-1905
Tim Murphy	A	1905-1906
Bill Squires	A	1906-1909
Bill Lang	A	1909-1910
Tommy Burns*	C	1910-1911
P.O. Curran	I	1911
Dan Flynn	I	1911
Bombardier Billy Wells	E	1911-1919
Bill Lang	A	1911-1913
Dave Smith	A	1913-1917
Joe Beckett*	E	1919-1923
Phil Scott	E	1926-1931
Larry Gains	C	1931-1934
Len Harvey	E	1934
Jack Petersen	W	1934-1936
Ben Foord	SA	1936-1937
Tommy Farr	W	1937
Len Harvey*	E	1939-1942
Jack London	E	1944-1945
Bruce Woodcock	E	1945-1950
Jack Gardner	E	1950-1952
Johnny Williams	W	1952-1953
Don Cockell	E	1953-1956
Joe Bygraves	J	1956-1957
Joe Erskine	W	1957-1958
Brian London	E	1958-1959
Henry Cooper	E	1959-1971
Joe Bugner	E	1971
Jack Bodell	E	1971-1972
Danny McAlinden	NI	1972-1975
Bunny Johnson	E	1975
Richard Dunn	E	1975-1976
Joe Bugner*	E	1976-1977
John L. Gardner*	E	1978-1981
Trevor Berbick	C	1981-1986
Horace Notice*	E	1986-1988
Derek Williams	E	1988-1992
Lennox Lewis*	E	1992-1993
Henry Akinwande	E	1993-1995
Scott Welch	E	1995-1997
Julius Francis*	E	1997-1999
Danny Williams	E	1999-2004
Michael Sprott	E	2004
Matt Skelton*	E	2004-2005

Peter Oboh, the current Commonwealth light-heavyweight champion   Les Clark

European Title Bouts, 2004-2005

All of last season's title bouts are shown in date order within their weight divisions and give the boxers' respective weights, along with the scorecards if going to a decision. There is also a short summary of any bout that involved a British contestant and British officials are listed where applicable.

Flyweight

10 July   Brahim Asloum 7.12½ (France) W PTS 12 Alexander Mahmutov 7.12¾ (Russia), Le Cannet, France. Scorecards: 118-111, 115-113, 115-114.
14 March   Brahim Asloum 7.12½ (France) W RSC 3 Jose Antonio Bueno 7.13¼ (Spain), Paris, France. Asloum relinquished the title on 13 June to concentrate on winning the WBA title.

Bantamweight

18 September   Frederic Patrac 8.3¾ (France) L PTS 12 Simone Maludrottu 8.5¼ (Italy), Olbia, Italy. Scorecards: 110-119, 110-118, Terry O'Connor 113-116.
29 October   Simone Maludrottu 8.5¾ (Italy) W PTS 12 Karim Quibir Lopes 8.5¾ (Spain), Madrid, Spain. Scorecards: Larry O'Connell 115-114, 115-115, 115-114.
27 May   Simone Maludrottu 8.4¾ (Italy) W CO 4 Hassan Naji 8.5 (Belgium), Cagliari, Italy. Judge: Mark Green.

S.Bantamweight

9 June   Esham Pickering 8.9½ (England) W RSC 10 Miguel Mallon 8.9½ (Spain), Madrid, Spain. After making a good start, the champion saw Mallon get back into the fight after four rounds and was forced into a 'battle' as the locals got behind their man. However, Pickering was the better man and eventually, in the eighth, began to put his punches together. After a messy ninth, Mallon, who had just got up from being thrown through the ropes, was dropped heavily by a right to the head and, on getting to his feet in some disarray, the referee called it off.

Featherweight

8 October   Nicky Cook 8.13¾ (England) W PTS 12 Johnny Begue 8.13 (France), International Centre, Brentwood. Scorecards: 119-118, 118-109, 119-108. Although he was in control throughout, and had floored his challenger in the second round with a combination of left hooks to head and body, Cook was forced to go the distance against an extremely tough opponent. Try as he might the champion couldn't put his man away, despite Begue's left eye almost closing towards the end, and his biggest problem was whether his hands would stand up to the constant pounding he was handing out. The hands did make it to the final bell, but, not surprisingly, were badly swollen.
16 June   Nicky Cook 9.0 (England) W CO 2 Dazzo Williams 8.13¼ (Wales), Goresbrook Leisure Centre, Dagenham, England. Referee: John Keane. Judges: Larry

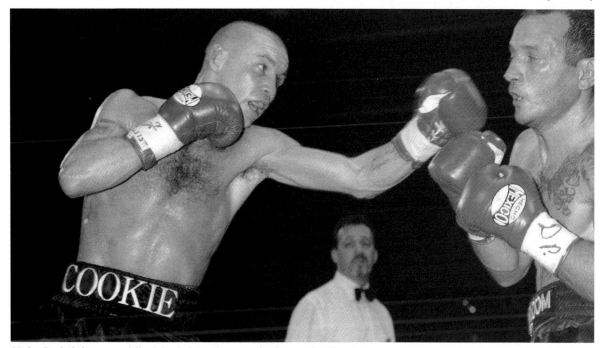

Nicky Cook (left) successfully defended the European featherweight title when outscoring the tough Frenchman, Johnny Begue
Les Clark

O'Connell, Terry O'Connor, Richie Davies. For a summary, see under British Title Bouts During 2004-2005.

S.Featherweight

15 October Boris Sinitsin 9.2½ (Russia) W PTS 12 Craig Docherty 9.3½ (Scotland), Kelvin Hall, Glasgow, Scotland. Scorecards: 115-113, 115-115, 117-111. Despite giving it his best shot, once the challenger was badly cut over the right eye from a head clash in the sixth round the odds against him finishing the fight shortened, let alone him winning. Sinitsin, a knowing pro with all the tricks of the trade at his disposal, was always just in front and always doing just enough to retain his title. When Docherty closed in to work the body he was often tied up by the clever champion, who worked on the damaged eye whenever he could and, ultimately, proved too experienced for the game Scot.

Lightweight

16 October Stefano Zoff 9.8¼ (Italy) W RSC 10 Michele Delli Paoli 9.9 (Italy), Verbania, Italy.
12 March Stefano Zoff 9.6¾ (Italy) W PTS 12 Martin Kristjansen 9.7 (Denmark), Milan, Italy. Scorecards: 117-111, 116-112, 116-112. Zoff relinquished the title on 11 April in order to dispute the IBF crown.

L.Welterweight

12 November Junior Witter 9.13¾ (England) W RSC 2 Krsztof Bienias 9.13½ (Poland), The Conference Centre, Wembley, England. No match for the champion, as early as the opening round Bienias was being picked off and when a long left, half uppercut, half cross, landed flush he was badly cut over the right eye. With Witter upping the pace, there was no way back for the Pole and, as soon as the second was underway, he was quickly under the cosh. All Bienias could do was to retreat and when he was sent staggering into the ropes with Witter in hot pursuit, it was obvious that he had little to offer and the referee called a halt on the 2.04 mark.

Welterweight

17 July Frederic Klose 10.6½ (France) W PTS 12 Michael Trabant 10.6½ (Germany), Zwickau, Germany. Scorecards: 115-113, 111-117, 115-113.
14 May Frederic Klose 10.6½ (France) L PTS 12 Oktay Urkal 10.6¾ (Germany), Bayreuth, Germany. Scorecards: Mickey Vann 111-117, 113-116, 114-116.

L.Middleweight

17 July Sergei Dzindziruk 10.13¾ (Ukraine) W RSC 3 Mamadou Thiam 10.12¾ (France), Zwickau, Germany. Judge: Dave Parris. Contested for the vacant title after Roman Karmazin (Russia) handed back his belt in April 2004 in order to campaign in the USA for a world title opportunity.
6 November Sergei Dzindziruk 10.13¼ (Ukraine) W CO 11 Hussein Bayram 10.13¾ (France), Riesa, Germany.
16 April Sergei Dzindziruk 10.13¾ (Ukraine) W PTS 12 Jimmy Colas 10.12½ (France), Magdeburg, Germany. Referee: Dave Parris. Scorecards: 119-108, 117-111, 118-109.

Middleweight

26 March Morrade Hakkar 11.5¾ (France) W PTS 12 Jorge Sendra 11.5¾ (Spain), Besancon, France. Scorecards: 116-112, 115-114, John Coyle 114-115. Contested for the vacant title after Howard Eastman (England) handed in his belt on 9 December to concentrate of a world title shot against Bernard Hopkins.

S.Middleweight

24 July Rudy Markussen 11.13¼ (Denmark) W PTS 12 Danilo Haussler 12.0 (Germany), Frankfurt Oder, Germany. Referee: Mickey Vann. Scorecards: John Coyle 115-111, 113-112, 115-111. Having won the title that Mads Larsen (Denmark) had relinquished in June 2004 due to medical problems associated with his neck, Markussen handed in his belt on 18 March to concentrate on winning the WBO crown.

L.Heavyweight

17 July Thomas Ulrich 12.6½ (Germany) W CO 11 Silvio Branco 12.6½ (Italy), Zwickau, Germany. Referee: Dave Parris. Contested for the vacant title after Stipe Drews (Croatia) handed in his belt in June 2004 to pursue world title opportunities.
26 March Thomas Ulrich 12.6½ (Germany) W PTS 12 Matthew Barney 12.6½ (England), Riesa, Germany. Scorecards: 116-112, 115-114, 115-114. Boxing well behind an admirable left hand and showing excellent movement, Barney looked on the way to landing the title, especially with the champion seemingly unable to catch up with him. Although the middle rounds were hard to call, by the ninth Ulrich's right eye was closed and it seemed that all Barney needed to do was more of the same. However, the last three sessions saw the Englishman barely working the jab, being mainly content to move and avoid being hit, and the judges marked the champion ahead on aggression, but how one of them saw it as 116-112 was strange to say the least. Ulrich relinquished the title on 15 June to concentrate on his world title ambitions.

Cruiserweight

27 November Alexander Gurov 13.11¼ (Ukraine) W RSC 2 Vincenzo Rossitto 13.10¾ (Italy), Chiavari, Italy. Contested for the vacant title after Vincenzo Cantatore handed in his belt on 6 September to concentrate on getting a crack at the WBO crown.

Heavyweight

31 July Luan Krasniqi 16.6¼ (Germany) W RTD 7 Rene Monse 16.4 (Germany), Stuttgart, Germany. Judge: Paul Thomas.
4 December Luan Krasniqi 16.5½ (Germany) DREW 12 Timo Hoffmann 18.8 (Germany), Berlin, Germany. Scorecards: Ian John-Lewis 114-114, 113-115, 114-114. Krasniqi was stripped on 4 May for refusing to sign the contract for a return against Hoffmann.
11 June Paolo Vidoz 17.4¼ (Italy) W PTS 12 Timo Hoffmann 18.10 (Germany), Kempten, Germany. Scorecards: 112-115, 115-113, 113-114.

European Champions, 1909-2005

Prior to 1946, the championship was contested under the auspices of the International Boxing Union, re-named that year as the European Boxing Union (EBU). The IBU had come into being when Victor Breyer, a Paris-based journalist and boxing referee who later edited the Annuaire du Ring (first edition in 1910), warmed to the idea of an organisation that controlled boxing right across Europe, regarding rules and championship fights between the champions of the respective countries. He first came to London at the end of 1909 to discuss the subject with the NSC, but went away disappointed. However, at a meeting between officials from Switzerland and France in March 1912, the IBU was initially formed and, by June of that year, had published their first ratings. By April 1914, Belgium had also joined the organisation, although it would not be until the war was over that the IBU really took off. Many of the early champions shown on the listings were the result of promoters, especially the NSC, billing their own championship fights. Although the (French dominated) IBU recognised certain champions, prior to being re-formed in May 1920, they did not find their administrative 'feet' fully until other countries such as Italy (1922), Holland (1923), and Spain (1924), produced challengers for titles. Later in the 1920s, Germany (1926), Denmark (1928), Portugal (1929) and Romania (1929) also joined the fold. Unfortunately, for Britain, its representatives (Although the BBBoC, as we know it today, was formed in 1929, an earlier attempt to form a Board of Control had been initiated in April 1918 by the NSC and it was that body who were involved here) failed to reach agreement on the three judges' ruling, following several meetings with the IBU early in 1920 and, apart from Elky Clark (fly), Ernie Rice and Alf Howard (light), and Jack Hood (welter), who conformed to that stipulation, fighters from these shores would not be officially recognised as champions until the EBU was formed in 1946. This led to British fighters claiming the title after beating IBU titleholders, or their successors, under championship conditions in this country. The only men who did not come into this category were Kid Nicholson (bantam), and Ted Kid Lewis and Tommy Milligan (welter), who defeated men not recognised by the IBU. For the record, the first men recognised and authorised, respectively, as being champions of their weight classes by the IBU were: Sid Smith and Michel Montreuil (fly), Charles Ledoux (bantam), Jim Driscoll and Louis de Ponthieu (feather), Freddie Welsh and Georges Papin (light), Georges Carpentier and Albert Badoud (welter), Georges Carpentier and Ercole Balzac (middle), Georges Carpentier and Battling Siki (light-heavy and heavy).

EUROPEAN COUNTRY CODE

AU = Austria; BEL = Belgium; BUL = Bulgaria; CRO = Croatia; CZ = Czechoslovakia; DEN = Denmark; E = England; FIN = Finland; FR = France; GER = Germany; GRE = Greece; HOL = Holland; HUN = Hungary; ITA = Italy; KAZ = Kazakhstan; LUX = Luxembourg; NI = Northern Ireland; NOR = Norway; POL = Poland; POR = Portugal; ROM = Romania; RUS = Russia; S = Scotland; SP = Spain; SWE = Sweden; SWI = Switzerland; TU = Turkey; UK = Ukraine; W = Wales; YUG = Yugoslavia.

Champions in **bold** denote those recognised by the IBU/EBU

*Undefeated champions (Does not include men who may have forfeited titles)

Title Holder	Birthplace/ Domicile	Tenure	Title Holder	Birthplace/ Domicile	Tenure	Title Holder	Birthplace/ Domicile	Tenure
Flyweight (112 lbs)			Nazzareno Giannelli	ITA	1954-1955	**Brahim Asloum***	FR	2003-2005
Sid Smith	E	1913	**Dai Dower**	W	1955			
Bill Ladbury	E	1913-1914	Young Martin	SP	1955-1959	**Bantamweight (118 lbs)**		
Percy Jones	W	1914	Risto Luukkonen	FIN	1959-1961	Joe Bowker	E	1910
Joe Symonds	E	1914	**Salvatore Burruni***	ITA	1961-1965	Digger Stanley	E	1910-1912
Tancy Lee	S	1914-1916	**Rene Libeer**	FR	1965-1966	**Charles Ledoux**	FR	1912-1921
Jimmy Wilde	W	1914-1915	**Fernando Atzori**	ITA	1967-1972	Bill Beynon	W	1913
Jimmy Wilde*	W	1916-1923	**Fritz Chervet**	SWI	1972-1973	Tommy Harrison	E	1921-1922
Michel Montreuil	BEL	1923-1925	Fernando Atzori	ITA	1973	**Charles Ledoux**	FR	1922-1923
Elky Clark*	S	1925-1927	**Fritz Chervet***	SWI	1973-1974	Bugler Harry Lake	E	1923
Victor Ferrand	SP	1927	Franco Udella	ITA	1974-1979	Johnny Brown	E	1923-1928
Emile Pladner	FR	1928-1929	**Charlie Magri***	E	1979-1983	**Henry Scillie***	BEL	1925-1928
Johnny Hill	S	1928-1929	**Antoine Montero**	FR	1983-1984	Kid Nicholson	E	1928
Eugene Huat	FR	1929	**Charlie Magri***	E	1984-1985	Teddy Baldock	E	1928-1931
Emile Degand	BEL	1929-1930	**Franco Cherchi**	ITA	1985	**Domenico Bernasconi**	ITA	1929
Kid Oliva	FR	1930	**Charlie Magri**	E	1985-1986	**Carlos Flix**	SP	1929-1931
Lucien Popescu	ROM	1930-1931	**Duke McKenzie***	E	1986-1988	**Lucien Popescu**	ROM	1931-1932
Jackie Brown	E	1931-1935	**Eyup Can***	TU	1989-1990	**Domenico Bernasconi**	ITA	1932
Praxile Gyde	FR	1932-1935	**Pat Clinton***	S	1990-1991	**Nicholas Biquet**	BEL	1932-1935
Benny Lynch	S	1935-1938	**Salvatore Fanni**	ITA	1991-1992	**Maurice Dubois**	SWI	1935-1936
Kid David*	BEL	1935-1936	**Robbie Regan***	W	1992-1993	**Joseph Decico**	FR	1936
Ernst Weiss	AU	1936	**Luigi Camputaro**	ITA	1993-1994	**Aurel Toma**	ROM	1936-1937
Valentin Angelmann*	FR	1936-1938	**Robbie Regan***	W	1994-1995	**Nicholas Biquet**	BEL	1937-1938
Enrico Urbinati*	ITA	1938-1943	**Luigi Camputaro***	ITA	1995-1996	**Aurel Toma**	ROM	1938-1939
Raoul Degryse	BEL	1946-1947	**Jesper Jensen**	DEN	1996-1997	**Ernst Weiss**	AU	1939
Maurice Sandeyron	FR	1947-1949	**David Guerault***	FR	1997-1999	**Gino Cattaneo**	ITA	1939-1941
Rinty Monaghan*	NI	1949-1950	**Alexander Mahmutov**	RUS	1999-2000	**Gino Bondavilli***	ITA	1941-1943
Terry Allen	E	1950	**Damaen Kelly***	NI	2000	**Jackie Paterson**	S	1946
Jean Sneyers*	BEL	1950-1951	**Alexander Mahmutov**	RUS	2000-2002	**Theo Medina**	FR	1946-1947
Teddy Gardner*	E	1952	**Mimoun Chent**	FR	2002-2003	**Peter Kane**	E	1947-1948
Louis Skena*	FR	1953-1954	**Alexander Mahmutov***	RUS	2003	**Guido Ferracin**	ITA	1948-1949

Title Holder	Birthplace/Domicile	Tenure
Luis Romero	SP	1949-1951
Peter Keenan	S	1951-1952
Jean Sneyers*	BEL	1952-1953
Peter Keenan	S	1953
John Kelly	NI	1953-1954
Robert Cohen*	FR	1954-1955
Mario D'Agata	ITA	1955-1958
Piero Rollo	ITA	1958-1959
Freddie Gilroy	NI	1959-1960
Pierre Cossemyns	BEL	1961-1962
Piero Rollo	ITA	1962
Alphonse Halimi	FR	1962
Piero Rollo	ITA	1962-1963
Mimoun Ben Ali	SP	1963
Risto Luukkonen	FIN	1963-1964
Mimoun Ben Ali	SP	1965
Tommaso Galli	ITA	1965-1966
Mimoun Ben Ali	SP	1966-1968
Salvatore Burruni*	ITA	1968-1969
Franco Zurlo	ITA	1969-1971
Alan Rudkin	E	1971
Agustin Senin*	SP	1971-1973
Johnny Clark*	E	1973-1974
Bob Allotey	SP	1974-1975
Daniel Trioulaire	FR	1975-1976
Salvatore Fabrizio	ITA	1976-1977
Franco Zurlo	ITA	1977-1978
Juan Francisco Rodriguez	SP	1978-1980
Johnny Owen*	W	1980
Valerio Nati	ITA	1980-1982
Giuseppe Fossati	ITA	1982-1983
Walter Giorgetti	ITA	1983-1984
Ciro de Leva*	ITA	1984-1986
Antoine Montero	FR	1986-1987
Louis Gomis*	FR	1987-1988
Fabrice Benichou	FR	1988
Vincenzo Belcastro*	ITA	1988-1990
Thierry Jacob*	FR	1990-1992
Johnny Bredahl*	DEN	1992
Vincenzo Belcastro	ITA	1993-1994
Prince Naseem Hamed*	E	1994-1995
John Armour*	E	1995-1996
Johnny Bredahl	DEN	1996-1998
Paul Lloyd*	E	1998-1999
Johnny Bredahl*	DEN	1999-2000
Luigi Castiglione	ITA	2000-2001
Fabien Guillerme	FR	2001
Alex Yagupov	RUS	2001
Spend Abazi	SWE	2001-2002
Noel Wilders	E	2003
David Guerault	FR	2003-2004
Frederic Patrac	FR	2004
Simone Maludrottu	ITA	2004-

S. Bantamweight (122 lbs)

Title Holder	Birthplace/Domicile	Tenure
Vincenzo Belcastro	ITA	1995-1996
Salim Medjkoune	FR	1996
Martin Krastev	BUL	1996-1997
Spencer Oliver	E	1997-1998
Sergei Devakov	UK	1998-1999
Michael Brodie*	E	1999-2000
Vladislav Antonov	RUS	2000-2001
Salim Medjkoune*	FR	2001-2002
Mahyar Monshipour*	FR	2002-2003
Esham Pickering	E	2003-

Featherweight (126 lbs)

Title Holder	Birthplace/Domicile	Tenure
Young Joey Smith	E	1911
Jean Poesy	FR	1911-1912
Jim Driscoll*	W	1912-1913
Ted Kid Lewis*	E	1913-1914
Louis de Ponthieu*	FR	1919-1920
Arthur Wyns	BEL	1920-1922
Billy Matthews	E	1922
Eugene Criqui*	FR	1922-1923
Edouard Mascart	FR	1923-1924
Charles Ledoux	FR	1924
Henri Hebrans	BEL	1924-1925
Antonio Ruiz	SP	1925-1928
Luigi Quadrini	ITA	1928-1929
Knud Larsen	DEN	1929
Jose Girones	SP	1929-1934
Maurice Holtzer*	FR	1935-1938
Phil Dolhem	BEL	1938-1939
Lucien Popescu	ROM	1939-1941
Ernst Weiss	AU	1941
Gino Bondavilli	ITA	1941-1945
Ermanno Bonetti*	ITA	1945-1946
Tiger Al Phillips	E	1947
Ronnie Clayton	E	1947-1948
Ray Famechon	FR	1948-1953
Jean Sneyers	BEL	1953-1954
Ray Famechon	FR	1954-1955
Fred Galiana*	SP	1955-1956
Cherif Hamia	FR	1957-1958
Sergio Caprari	ITA	1958-1959
Gracieux Lamperti	FR	1959-1962
Alberto Serti	ITA	1962-1963
Howard Winstone	W	1963-1967
Jose Legra*	SP	1967-1968
Manuel Calvo	SP	1968-1969
Tommaso Galli	ITA	1969-1970
Jose Legra*	SP	1970-1972
Gitano Jiminez	SP	1973-1975
Elio Cotena	ITA	1975-1976
Nino Jimenez	SP	1976-1977
Manuel Masso	SP	1977
Roberto Castanon*	SP	1977-1981
Salvatore Melluzzo	ITA	1981-1982
Pat Cowdell*	E	1982-1983
Loris Stecca*	ITA	1983
Barry McGuigan*	NI	1983-1985
Jim McDonnell*	E	1985-1987
Valerio Nati	ITA	1987
Jean-Marc Renard*	BEL	1988-1989
Paul Hodkinson*	E	1989-1991
Fabrice Benichou	FR	1991-1992
Maurizio Stecca	ITA	1992-1993
Herve Jacob	FR	1993
Maurizio Stecca	ITA	1993
Stephane Haccoun	FR	1993-1994
Stefano Zoff	ITA	1994
Medhi Labdouni	FR	1994-1995
Billy Hardy	E	1995-1998
Paul Ingle*	E	1998-1999
Steve Robinson	W	1999-2000
Istvan Kovacs*	HUN	2000-2001
Manuel Calvo*	SP	2001-2002
Cyril Thomas	FR	2002-2004
Nicky Cook	E	2004-

S. Featherweight (130 lbs)

Title Holder	Birthplace/Domicile	Tenure
Tommaso Galli	ITA	1971-1972
Domenico Chiloiro	ITA	1972
Lothar Abend	GER	1972-1974
Sven-Erik Paulsen*	NOR	1974-1976
Roland Cazeaux	FR	1976
Natale Vezzoli	ITA	1976-1979
Carlos Hernandez	SP	1979
Rodolfo Sanchez	SP	1979
Carlos Hernandez	SP	1979-1982
Cornelius Boza-Edwards*	E	1982
Roberto Castanon	SP	1982-1983
Alfredo Raininger	ITA	1983-1984
Jean-Marc Renard	BEL	1984
Pat Cowdell	E	1984-1985
Jean-Marc Renard*	BEL	1986-1987
Salvatore Curcetti	ITA	1987-1988
Piero Morello	ITA	1988
Lars Lund Jensen	DEN	1988
Racheed Lawal	DEN	1988-1989
Daniel Londas*	FR	1989-1991
Jimmy Bredahl*	DEN	1992
Regilio Tuur	HOL	1992-1993
Jacobin Yoma	FR	1993-1995
Anatoly Alexandrov*	KAZ	1995-1996
Julian Lorcy*	FR	1996
Djamel Lifa	FR	1997-1998
Anatoly Alexandrov*	RUS	1998
Dennis Holbaek Pedersen	DEN	1999-2000
Boris Sinitsin	RUS	2000
Dennis Holbaek Pedersen*	DEN	2000
Tontcho Tontchev*	BUL	2001
Boris Sinitsin	RUS	2001-2002
Pedro Oscar Miranda	SP	2002
Affif Djelti	FR	2002-2003
Boris Sinitsin	RUS	2003-

Lightweight (135 lbs)

Title Holder	Birthplace/Domicile	Tenure
Freddie Welsh	W	1909-1911
Matt Wells	E	1911-1912
Freddie Welsh*	W	1912-1914
Georges Papin	FR	1920-1921
Ernie Rice	E	1921-1922
Seaman Nobby Hall	E	1922-1923
Harry Mason	E	1923-1926
Fred Bretonnel	FR	1924
Lucien Vinez	FR	1924-1927
Luis Rayo*	SP	1927-1928
Aime Raphael	FR	1928-1929
Francois Sybille	BEL	1929-1930
Alf Howard	E	1930
Harry Corbett	E	1930-1931
Francois Sybille	BEL	1930-1931
Bep van Klaveren	HOL	1931-1932
Cleto Locatelli	ITA	1932
Francois Sybille	BEL	1932-1933
Cleto Locatelli*	ITA	1933
Francois Sybille	BEL	1934
Carlo Orlandi*	ITA	1934-1935
Enrico Venturi*	ITA	1935-1936
Vittorio Tamagnini	ITA	1936-1937
Maurice Arnault	FR	1937
Gustave Humery	FR	1937-1938
Aldo Spoldi*	ITA	1938-1939
Karl Blaho	AU	1940-1941
Bruno Bisterzo	ITA	1941
Ascenzo Botta	ITA	1941
Bruno Bisterzo	ITA	1941-1942
Ascenzo Botta	ITA	1942
Roberto Proietti	ITA	1942-1943
Bruno Bisterzo	ITA	1943-1946
Roberto Proietti*	ITA	1946
Emile Dicristo	FR	1946-1947
Kid Dussart	BEL	1947
Roberto Proietti	ITA	1947-1948
Billy Thompson	E	1948-1949
Kid Dussart	BEL	1949
Roberto Proietti*	ITA	1949-1950
Pierre Montane	FR	1951
Elis Ask	FIN	1951-1952
Jorgen Johansen	DEN	1952-1954
Duilio Loi*	ITA	1954-1959
Mario Vecchiatto	ITA	1959-1960
Dave Charnley	E	1960-1963
Conny Rudhof*	GER	1963-1964
Willi Quatuor*	GER	1964-1965
Franco Brondi	ITA	1965
Maurice Tavant	FR	1965-1966
Borge Krogh	DEN	1966-1967

Title Holder	Birthplace/Domicile	Tenure
Pedro Carrasco*	SP	1967-1969
Miguel Velazquez	SP	1970-1971
Antonio Puddu	ITA	1971-1974
Ken Buchanan*	S	1974-1975
Fernand Roelandts	BEL	1976
Perico Fernandez*	SP	1976-1977
Jim Watt*	S	1977-1979
Charlie Nash*	NI	1979-1980
Francisco Leon	SP	1980
Charlie Nash	NI	1980-1981
Joey Gibilisco	ITA	1981-1983
Lucio Cusma	ITA	1983-1984
Rene Weller	GER	1984-1986
Gert Bo Jacobsen	DEN	1986-1988
Rene Weller*	GER	1988
Policarpo Diaz*	SP	1988-1990
Antonio Renzo	ITA	1991-1992
Jean-Baptiste Mendy*	FR	1992-1994
Racheed Lawal	DEN	1994
Jean-Baptiste Mendy*	FR	1994-1995
Angel Mona	FR	1995-1997
Manuel Carlos Fernandes	FR	1997
Oscar Garcia Cano	SP	1997
Billy Schwer*	E	1997-1999
Oscar Garcia Cano	SP	1999-2000
Lucien Lorcy*	FR	2000-2001
Stefano Zoff*	ITA	2001-2002
Jason Cook	W	2002-2003
Stefano Zoff*	ITA	2003-2005

L. Welterweight (140 lbs)

Title Holder	Birthplace/Domicile	Tenure
Olli Maki	FIN	1964-1965
Juan Sombrita-Albornoz	SP	1965
Willi Quatuor*	GER	1965-1966
Conny Rudhof	GER	1967
Johann Orsolics	AU	1967-1968
Bruno Arcari*	ITA	1968-1970
Rene Roque	FR	1970-1971
Pedro Carrasco*	SP	1971-1972
Roger Zami	FR	1972
Cemal Kamaci	TU	1972-1973
Toni Ortiz	SP	1973-1974
Perico Fernandez*	SP	1974
Jose Ramon Gomez-Fouz	SP	1975
Cemal Kamaci*	TU	1975-1976
Dave Boy Green*	E	1976-1977
Primo Bandini	ITA	1977
Jean-Baptiste Piedvache	FR	1977-1978
Colin Power	E	1978
Fernando Sanchez	SP	1978-1979
Jose Luis Heredia	SP	1979
Jo Kimpuani	FR	1979-1980
Giuseppe Martinese	ITA	1980
Antonio Guinaldo	SP	1980-1981
Clinton McKenzie	E	1981-1982
Robert Gambini	FR	1982-1983
Patrizio Oliva*	ITA	1983-1985
Terry Marsh	E	1985-1986
Tusikoleta Nkalankete	FR	1987-1989
Efren Calamati	ITA	1989-1990
Pat Barrett	E	1990-1992
Valery Kayumba	ITA	1992-1993
Christian Merle	FR	1993-1994
Valery Kayumba	FR	1994
Khalid Rahilou*	FR	1994-1996
Soren Sondergaard*	DEN	1996-1998
Thomas Damgaard*	DEN	1998-2000
Oktay Urkal*	GER	2000-2001
Gianluca Branco*	ITA	2001-2002
Oktay Urkal*	GER	2002-2003
Junior Witter	E	2004-

Welterweight (147 lbs)

Title Holder	Birthplace/Domicile	Tenure
Young Joseph	E	1910-1911
Georges Carpentier*	FR	1911-1912
Albert Badoud*	SWI	1915-1921

Title Holder	Birthplace/Domicile	Tenure
Johnny Basham	W	1919-1920
Ted Kid Lewis	E	1920-1924
Piet Hobin	BEL	1921-1925
Billy Mack	E	1923
Tommy Milligan	S	1924-1925
Mario Bosisio*	ITA	1925-1928
Leo Darton	BEL	1928
Alf Genon	BEL	1928-1929
Gustave Roth	BEL	1929-1932
Adrien Aneet	BEL	1932-1933
Jack Hood*	E	1933
Gustav Eder	GER	1934-1936
Felix Wouters	BEL	1936-1938
Saverio Turiello	ITA	1938-1939
Marcel Cerdan*	FR	1939-1942
Ernie Roderick	E	1946-1947
Robert Villemain*	FR	1947-1948
Livio Minelli	ITA	1949-1950
Michele Palermo	ITA	1950-1951
Eddie Thomas	W	1951
Charles Humez*	FR	1951-1952
Gilbert Lavoine	FR	1953-1954
Wally Thom	E	1954-1955
Idrissa Dione	FR	1955-1956
Emilio Marconi	ITA	1956-1958
Peter Waterman*	E	1958
Emilio Marconi	ITA	1958-1959
Duilio Loi*	ITA	1959-1963
Fortunato Manca*	ITA	1964-1965
Jean Josselin	FR	1966-1967
Carmelo Bossi	ITA	1967-1968
Fighting Mack	HOL	1968-1969
Silvano Bertini	ITA	1969
Jean Josselin	FR	1969
Johann Orsolics	AU	1969-1970
Ralph Charles	E	1970-1971
Roger Menetrey	FR	1971-1974
John H. Stracey*	E	1974-1975
Marco Scano	ITA	1976-1977
Jorgen Hansen	DEN	1977
Jorg Eipel	GER	1977
Alain Marion	FR	1977-1978
Jorgen Hansen	DEN	1978
Josef Pachler	AU	1978
Henry Rhiney	E	1978-1979
Dave Boy Green	E	1979
Jorgen Hansen*	DEN	1979-1981
Hans-Henrik Palm	DEN	1982
Colin Jones*	W	1982-1983
Gilles Elbilia	FR	1983-1984
Gianfranco Rosi	ITA	1984-1985
Lloyd Honeyghan*	E	1985-1986
Jose Varela	GER	1986-1987
Alfonso Redondo	SP	1987
Mauro Martelli*	SWI	1987-1988
Nino la Rocca	ITA	1989
Antoine Fernandez	FR	1989-1990
Kirkland Laing	E	1990
Patrizio Oliva*	ITA	1990-1992
Ludovic Proto	FR	1992-1993
Gary Jacobs*	S	1993-1994
Jose Luis Navarro	SP	1994-1995
Valery Kayumba	FR	1995
Patrick Charpentier*	FR	1995-1996
Andrei Pestriaev*	RUS	1997
Michele Piccirillo*	ITA	1997-1998
Maxim Nesterenko	RUS	1998-1999
Alessandro Duran	ITA	1999
Andrei Pestriaev	RUS	1999-2000
Alessandro Duran	ITA	2000
Thomas Damgaard	DEN	2000-2001
Alessandro Duran	ITA	2001-2002
Christian Bladt	DEN	2002
Michel Trabant*	GER	2002-2003
Frederic Klose	FR	2003-

L. Middleweight (154 lbs)

Title Holder	Birthplace/Domicile	Tenure
Bruno Visintin	ITA	1964-1966
Bo Hogberg	SWE	1966
Yolande Leveque	FR	1966
Sandro Mazzinghi*	ITA	1966-1968
Remo Golfarini	ITA	1968-1969
Gerhard Piaskowy	GER	1969-1970
Jose Hernandez	SP	1970-1972
Juan Carlos Duran	ITA	1972-1973
Jacques Kechichian	FR	1973-1974
Jose Duran	SP	1974-1975
Eckhard Dagge	GER	1975-1976
Vito Antuofermo	ITA	1976
Maurice Hope*	E	1976-1978
Gilbert Cohen	FR	1978-1979
Marijan Benes	YUG	1979-1981
Louis Acaries	FR	1981
Luigi Minchillo*	ITA	1981-1983
Herol Graham*	E	1983-1984
Jimmy Cable	E	1984
Georg Steinherr	GER	1984-1985
Said Skouma*	FR	1985-1986
Chris Pyatt	E	1986-1987
Gianfranco Rosi*	ITA	1987
Rene Jacquot*	FR	1988-1989
Edip Secovic	AU	1989
Giuseppe Leto	ITA	1989
Gilbert Dele*	FR	1989-1990
Said Skouma	FR	1991
Mourad Louati	HOL	1991
Jean-Claude Fontana	FR	1991-1992
Laurent Boudouani	FR	1992-1993
Bernard Razzano	FR	1993-1994
Javier Castillejos	SP	1994-1995
Laurent Boudouani*	FR	1995-1996
Faouzi Hattab	FR	1996
Davide Ciarlante*	ITA	1996-1997
Javier Castillejo*	SP	1998
Mamadou Thiam*	FR	1998-2000
Roman Karmazin*	RUS	2000
Mamadou Thiam*	FR	2001
Wayne Alexander*	E	2002
Roman Karmazin*	RUS	2003-2004
Sergei Dzindziruk	UK	2004-

Middleweight (160 lbs)

Title Holder	Birthplace/Domicile	Tenure
Georges Carpentier*	FR	1912-1918
Ercole Balzac	FR	1920-1921
Gus Platts	E	1921
Willem Westbroek	HOL	1921
Johnny Basham	W	1921
Ted Kid Lewis	E	1921-1923
Roland Todd	E	1923-1924
Ted Kid Lewis	E	1924-1925
Bruno Frattini	ITA	1924-1925
Tommy Milligan	S	1925-1928
Rene Devos	BEL	1926-1927
Barthelemy Molina	FR	1928
Alex Ireland	S	1928-1929
Mario Bosisio	ITA	1928
Leone Jacovacci	ITA	1928-1929
Len Johnson	E	1928-1929
Marcel Thil	FR	1929-1930
Mario Bosisio	ITA	1930-1931
Poldi Steinbach	AU	1931
Hein Domgoergen	GER	1931-1932
Ignacio Ara	SP	1932-1933
Gustave Roth	BEL	1933-1934
Marcel Thil*	FR	1934-1938
Edouard Tenet	FR	1938
Bep van Klaveren	HOL	1938
Anton Christoforidis	GRE	1938-1939
Edouard Tenet	FR	1939
Josef Besselmann*	GER	1942-1943
Marcel Cerdan	FR	1947-1948

209

EUROPEAN CHAMPIONS, 1909-2005

Title Holder	Birthplace/Domicile	Tenure
Cyrille Delannoit	BEL	1948
Marcel Cerdan*	FR	1948
Cyrille Delannoit	BEL	1948-1949
Tiberio Mitri*	ITA	1949-1950
Randy Turpin	E	1951-1954
Tiberio Mitri	ITA	1954
Charles Humez	FR	1954-1958
Gustav Scholz*	GER	1958-1961
John Cowboy McCormack	S	1961-1962
Chris Christensen	DEN	1962
Laszlo Papp*	HUN	1962-1965
Nino Benvenuti*	ITA	1965-1967
Juan Carlos Duran	ITA	1967-1969
Tom Bogs	DEN	1969-1970
Juan Carlos Duran	ITA	1970-1971
Jean-Claude Bouttier	FR	1971-1972
Tom Bogs*	DEN	1973
Elio Calcabrini	ITA	1973-1974
Jean-Claude Bouttier	FR	1974
Kevin Finnegan	E	1974-1975
Gratien Tonna*	FR	1975
Bunny Sterling	E	1976
Angelo Jacopucci	ITA	1976
Germano Valsecchi	ITA	1976-1977
Alan Minter	E	1977
Gratien Tonna	FR	1977-1978
Alan Minter*	E	1978-1979
Kevin Finnegan	E	1980
Matteo Salvemini	ITA	1980
Tony Sibson*	E	1980-1982
Louis Acaries	FR	1982-1984
Tony Sibson	E	1984-1985
Ayub Kalule	DEN	1985-1986
Herol Graham	E	1986-1987
Sumbu Kalambay*	ITA	1987
Pierre Joly	FR	1987-1988
Christophe Tiozzo*	FR	1988-1989
Francesco dell' Aquila	ITA	1989-1990
Sumbu Kalambay*	ITA	1990-1993
Agostino Cardamone*	ITA	1993-1994
Richie Woodhall*	E	1995-1996
Alexandre Zaitsev	RUS	1996
Hassine Cherifi*	FR	1996-1998
Agostino Cardamone*	ITA	1998
Erland Betare*	FR	1999-2000
Howard Eastman*	E	2001
Christian Sanavia	ITA	2001-2002
Morrade Hakkar*	FR	2002
Howard Eastman*	E	2003-2004
Morrade Hakkar	FR	2005-

S. Middleweight (168 lbs)

Title Holder	Birthplace/Domicile	Tenure
Mauro Galvano*	ITA	1990-1991
James Cook	E	1991-1992
Franck Nicotra*	FR	1992
Vincenzo Nardiello	ITA	1992-1993
Ray Close*	NI	1993
Vinzenzo Nardiello	ITA	1993-1994
Frederic Seillier*	FR	1994-1995
Henry Wharton*	E	1995-1996
Frederic Seillier*	FR	1996
Andrei Shkalikov*	RUS	1997
Dean Francis*	E	1997-1998
Bruno Girard*	FR	1999
Andrei Shkalikov	RUS	2000-2001
Danilo Haeussler	GER	2001-2003
Mads Larsen*	DEN	2003-2004
Rudy Markussen*	DEN	2004-2005

L. Heavyweight (175 lbs)

Title Holder	Birthplace/Domicile	Tenure
Georges Carpentier	FR	1913-1922
Battling Siki	FR	1922-1923
Emile Morelle	FR	1923
Raymond Bonnel	FR	1923-1924
Louis Clement	SWI	1924-1926
Herman van T'Hof	HOL	1926
Fernand Delarge	BEL	1926-1927
Max Schmeling*	GER	1927-1928
Michele Bonaglia*	ITA	1929-1930
Ernst Pistulla*	GER	1931-1932
Adolf Heuser	GER	1932
John Andersson	SWE	1933
Martinez de Alfara	SP	1934
Marcel Thil	FR	1934-1935
Merlo Preciso	ITA	1935
Hein Lazek	AU	1935-1936
Gustave Roth	BEL	1936-1938
Adolf Heuser*	GER	1938-1939
Luigi Musina*	ITA	1942-1943
Freddie Mills*	E	1947-1950
Albert Yvel	FR	1950-1951
Don Cockell*	E	1951-1952
Conny Rux*	GER	1952
Jacques Hairabedian	FR	1953-1954
Gerhard Hecht	GER	1954-1955
Willi Hoepner	GER	1955
Gerhard Hecht	GER	1955-1957
Artemio Calzavara	ITA	1957-1958
Willi Hoepner	GER	1958
Erich Schoeppner	GER	1958-1962
Giulio Rinaldi	ITA	1962-1964
Gustav Scholz*	GER	1964-1965
Giulio Rinaldi	ITA	1965-1966
Piero del Papa	ITA	1966-1967
Lothar Stengel	GER	1967-1968
Tom Bogs*	DEN	1968-1969
Yvan Prebeg	YUG	1969-1970
Piero del Papa	ITA	1970-1971
Conny Velensek	GER	1971-1972
Chris Finnegan	E	1972
Rudiger Schmidtke	GER	1972-1973
John Conteh*	E	1973-1974
Domenico Adinolfi	ITA	1974-1976
Mate Parlov*	YUG	1976-1977
Aldo Traversaro	ITA	1977-1979
Rudi Koopmans	HOL	1979-1984
Richard Caramonolis	FR	1984
Alex Blanchard	HOL	1984-1987
Tom Collins	E	1987-1988
Pedro van Raamsdonk	HOL	1988
Jan Lefeber	HOL	1988-1989
Eric Nicoletta	FR	1989-1990
Tom Collins	E	1990-1991
Graciano Rocchigiani*	GER	1991-1992
Eddie Smulders	HOL	1993-1994
Fabrice Tiozzo*	FR	1994-1995
Eddy Smulders	HOL	1995-1996
Crawford Ashley	E	1997
Ole Klemetsen*	NOR	1997-1998
Crawford Ashley	E	1998-1999
Clinton Woods*	E	1999-2000
Yawe Davis	ITA	2001-2002
Thomas Ulrich*	GER	2002-2003
Stipe Drews*	CRO	2003-2004
Thomas Ulrich	GER	2004-

Cruiserweight (200 lbs)

Title Holder	Birthplace/Domicile	Tenure
Sam Reeson*	E	1987-1988
Angelo Rottoli	ITA	1989
Anaclet Wamba*	FR	1989-1990
Johnny Nelson*	E	1990-1992
Akim Tafer*	FR	1992-1993
Massimiliano Duran	ITA	1993-1994
Carl Thompson	E	1994
Alexander Gurov	UK	1995
Patrice Aouissi	FR	1995
Alexander Gurov*	UK	1995-1996
Akim Tafer*	FR	1996-1997
Johnny Nelson	E	1997-1998
Terry Dunstan*	E	1998
Alexei Iliin	RUS	1999
Torsten May*	GER	1999-2000
Carl Thompson*	E	2000-2001
Alexander Gurov*	UK	2001-2002
Pietro Aurino*	ITA	2002-2003
Vincenzo Cantatore	ITA	2004
Alexander Gurov	UK	2004-

Heavyweight (200 lbs +)

Title Holder	Birthplace/Domicile	Tenure
Georges Carpentier	FR	1913-1922
Battling Siki	FR	1922-1923
Erminio Spalla	ITA	1923-1926
Paolino Uzcudun	SP	1926-1928
Harry Persson	SWE	1926
Phil Scott	E	1927
Pierre Charles	BEL	1929-1931
Hein Muller	GER	1931-1932
Pierre Charles	BEL	1932-1933
Paolino Uzcudun	SP	1933
Primo Carnera	ITA	1933-1935
Pierre Charles	BEL	1935-1937
Arno Kolblin	GER	1937-1938
Hein Lazek	AU	1938-1939
Adolf Heuser	GER	1939
Max Schmeling*	GER	1939-1941
Olle Tandberg	SWE	1943
Karel Sys*	BEL	1943-1946
Bruce Woodcock	E	1946-1949
Joe Weidin	AU	1950-1951
Jack Gardner	E	1951
Hein Ten Hoff	GER	1951-1952
Karel Sys	BEL	1952
Heinz Neuhaus	GER	1952-1955
Franco Cavicchi	ITA	1955-1956
Ingemar Johansson*	SWE	1956-1959
Dick Richardson	W	1960-1962
Ingemar Johansson*	SWE	1962-1963
Henry Cooper*	E	1964
Karl Mildenberger	GER	1964-1968
Henry Cooper*	E	1968-1969
Peter Weiland	GER	1969-1970
Jose Urtain	SP	1970
Henry Cooper	E	1970-1971
Joe Bugner	E	1971
Jack Bodell	E	1971
Jose Urtain	SP	1971-1972
Jurgen Blin	GER	1972
Joe Bugner*	E	1972-1975
Richard Dunn	E	1976
Joe Bugner	E	1976-1977
Jean-Pierre Coopman	BEL	1977
Lucien Rodriguez	FR	1977
Alfredo Evangelista	SP	1977-1979
Lorenzo Zanon*	SP	1979-1980
John L. Gardner*	E	1980-1981
Lucien Rodriguez	FR	1981-1984
Steffen Tangstad	NOR	1984-1985
Anders Eklund	SWE	1985
Frank Bruno*	E	1985-1986
Steffen Tangstad	NOR	1986
Alfredo Evangelista	SP	1987
Anders Eklund	SWE	1987
Francesco Damiani	ITA	1987-1989
Derek Williams	E	1989-1990
Jean Chanet	FR	1990
Lennox Lewis	E	1990-1992
Henry Akinwande*	E	1993-1995
Zeljko Mavrovic*	CRO	1995-1998
Vitali Klitschko*	UK	1998-1999
Vladimir Klitschko*	UK	1999-2000
Vitali Klitschko*	UK	2000-2001
Luan Krasniqi	GER	2002
Przemyslaw Saleta	POL	2002
Sinan Samil Sam	TU	2002-2004
Luan Krasniqi	GER	2004-2005
Paolo Vidoz	ITA	2005-

A-Z of Current World Champions

by Eric Armit

Shows the record since 1 July 2004, plus career summary and pen portrait, of all men holding IBF, WBA, WBC and WBO titles as at 30 June 2005. The author has also produced the same data for those who first won titles between 1 July 2004 and 30 June 2005, but were no longer champions at the end of the period in question. Incidentally, the place name given is the respective boxer's domicile and may not necessarily be his birthplace, while all nicknames are shown where applicable in brackets. Not included are British fighters, Joe Calzaghe (WBO super-middleweight champion), Johnny Nelson (WBO cruiserweight champion), Scott Harrison (WBO featherweight champion) and Clinton Woods (IBF light-heavyweight champion). Their full records can be found among the Active British-Based Boxers: Career Records' section.

Tomasz (Goral) Adamek

Bielsko Biala, Poland. *Born* 1 December, 1976
WBC L.Heavyweight Champion

Major Amateur Honours: Having won a bronze medal in the 1996 Copenhagen Cup and Acropolis tournament, he competed in the 1997 World Championships, before winning a bronze medal in the 1998 European Championships
Turned Pro: March 1999
Significant Results: Rudi Lupo W PTS 10, Zdravko Kostic W PTS 10, Sergei Karanevich W PTS 10, Roberto Coelho W PTS 8, Jabrail Jabrailov W CO 5
Type/Style: An upright, tough battler with a good jab and a hard right-hand punch
Points of Interest: 6'1" tall. Turned pro in Manchester and had his first two fights in England. Has 19 wins by stoppage or kayo. Suffered a broken nose whilst preparing for the Paul Briggs fight, but concealed it and then had it broken again during the fight

10.09.04	Ismail Abdoul W PTS 8 Warsaw	
21.05.05	Paul Briggs W PTS 12 Chicago *(Vacant WBC Heavyweight Title)*	
Career: 29 contests, won 29.		

Mike (The Powerful) Anchondo

La Puente, USA. *Born* 15 April, 1982
Former WBO S.Featherweight Champion

Major Amateur Honours: The winner of a gold medal in the 1998 US Junior Championships, he was a runner-up in the 1999 United States Junior Championships
Turned Pro: May 2000
Significant Results: Ever Beleno W PTS 10, Isidro Tejedor W RSC 2, Roque Cassiani W CO 10, Silverio Ortiz W RSC 4, Gregorio Vargas W PTS 10
Type/Style: Powerful, fast-handed, hard puncher
Points of Interest: 5'5" tall. Won his first ten fights by knockout and has 18 wins inside the distance. Promoted by Oscar De La Hoya's Golden Boy group, he was recognised as the full WBO champion when Diego Corrales relinquished the title. Lost the title on the scales when he failed to make the weight for his first defence against Jorge Luis Barrios

15.07.04	Julio Pablo Chacon W PTS 12 Dallas *(Vacant WBO Interim S.Featherweight Title)*	
08.04.05	Jorge Luis Barrios L RSC 4 Miami	
Career: 26 contests, won 25, lost 1.		

Mike Anchondo   Les Clark

Marco Antonio (Baby Faced Assassin) Barrera

Mexico City, Mexico. *Born* 17 January, 1974
WBC S.Featherweight Champion.
Former Undefeated WBO S.Bantamweight Champion. Former Undefeated Mexican S.Flyweight Champion

Major Amateur Honours: None known, but claims only four losses in 60 fights
Turned Pro: November 1989
Significant Results: Carlos Salazar W PTS 10, Frankie Toledo W RSC 2, Kennedy McKinney W CO 12, Jesse Benavides W CO 3, Junior Jones L DIS 5 & L PTS 12, Richie Wenton W RTD 3, Paul Lloyd W RTD 1, Erik Morales L PTS 12 & W PTS 12, Jesus Salud W RSC 6, Prince Naseem Hamed W PTS 12, Enrique Sanchez W RSC 6, Johnny Tapia W PTS 12, Kevin Kelley W RSC 4, Manny Pacquiao L RSC 11, Paulie Ayala W CO 10
Type/Style: Is a terrific box-fighter with a hard punch in both hands
Points of Interest: 5'7" tall. Attended the University of Mexico. A natural southpaw who fights right handed, despite losing a hotly disputed decision to Erik Morales in 2000, in a match for both the WBC and WBO super-bantamweight titles, the WBO reinstated him as champion. Moved up to lift the WBC featherweight title with a revenge win over Morales and is 2-1 up in one of boxing's great fight series. Bounced back from a shock loss to Manny Pacquiao in November 2003 to beat Morales again and has taken part in 22 world title fights. Has 42 wins inside the distance

27.11.04	Erik Morales W PTS 12 Las Vegas *(WBC S.Featherweight Title Challenge)*	
09.04.05	Mzonke Fana W RSC 2 El Paso *(WBC S.Featherweight Title Defence)*	
Career: 65 contests, won 60, lost 4, no decision 1.		

211

Marco Antonio Barrera

Jorge (La Hiena) Barrios

Tigre, Argentina. *Born* 1 August, 1976
WBO S.Featherweight Champion.
Former Undefeated Argentinian
S.Featherweight Champion

Major Amateur Honours: None known,
but claims a record of 35 wins, ten
losses and two draws
Turned Pro: August 1996
Significant Results: Cesar Domine L
DIS 4 & W CO 2, Silvano Usini W
RSC 8, Affif Djelti W PTS 12, Carlos
Rios W TD 6, Orlando Soto W RSC 4,
Acelino Freitas L RSC 12
Type/Style: Is rugged, rough and
aggressive, with a crude but effective
style and a heavy punch
Points of Interest: Once trained by
Amilcar Brusa, who also trained
Carlos Monzon, he lost only one of his
first 42 fights and that was on
disqualification. Has 31 wins by
stoppage or kayo and had Acelino
Freitas on the floor in a challenge for
the WBO title in August 2003. A
reformed bad boy of Argentinian
boxing, he won the WBO title on
beating Mike Anchondo, who had
failed to make the weight for their bout

08.10.04	Carlos Uribe W RSC 7 Cordoba
08.04.05	Mike Anchondo W RSC 4 Miami
	(Vacant WBO S.Featherweight Title)
Career:	47 contests, 43, drew 1, lost 2, no decision 1.

O'Neil (Give'em Hell) Bell

Atlanta, USA. *Born* Jamaica, 29
December, 1974
IBF Cruiserweight Champion

Major Amateur Honours: None known
Turned Pro: February 1998
Significant Results: Mohamed Ben
Guesmia, Jason Robinson W PTS 10,
Ka-Dy King W RSC 3, Ernest Mateen
T DRAW 4, Arthur Williams W RSC
11 & W RSC 9, Kelvin Davis W RSC
11, Derrick Harmon W CO 8
Type/Style: A lanky, loose limbed
boxer with an awkward leaning style
Points of Interest: 6'2" tall. Lost to
Ben Guesmia in only his second paid
fight. Has 22 wins inside the distance
and, in fact, has only once won a fight
on points

04.09.04	Ezra Sellers W CO 2 Las Vegas
20.05.05	Dale Brown W PTS 12 Hollywood
	(Vacant IBF cruiserweight title)
Career:	26 contests, won 24, drew 1, lost 1.

Markus (Boom Boom) Beyer

Eriabrunn, Germany. *Born* 28 April,
1971
WBC S.Middleweight Champion.
Former German S.Middleweight
Champion

Major Amateur Honours: A gold
medallist in the 1988 European Junior
Championships, he competed in the
1992 and 1996 Olympics and won a
bronze medal in the 1995 World
Championships and a silver medal in
the 1996 European Championships
Turned Pro: November 1996
Significant Results: Juan Carlos
Viloria W PTS 12, Richie Woodhall W
PTS 10, Leif Keiski W CO 7, Glenn
Catley L RSC 12, Eric Lucas W PTS
12, Danny Green W DIS 5, Andre
Thysse W PTS 12, Cristian Sanavia L
PTS 12
Type/Style: Is a smart boxing southpaw
and a real tactician, but not a puncher
Points of Interest: 5'9" tall. Won his
European Junior Championship gold
medal at flyweight. Now in his third
reign as the WBC champion, having
beaten Richie Woodhall for the title in
October 1999 before losing it to Glenn
Catley in his second defence in May
2000. Regained the title with a close
points win over Eric Lucas in April

2003, only to lose it again to Cristian
Sanavia in June 2004. Was on the floor
twice and looked to be on the way to
defeat until Danny Green was
disqualified in their 2003 fight. With
just 12 wins by kayo or stoppage, he
has made seven title defences in his
three reigns

09.10.04	Cristian Sanavia W CO 6 Erfurt *(WBC S.Middleweight Title Challenge)*
18.12.04	Yoshinori Nishizawa W PTS 12 Bayreuth *(WBC S.Middleweight Title Defence)*
12.03.05	Danny Green W PTS 12 Zwickau *(WBC S.Middleweight Title Defence)*
Career:	34 contests, won 32, lost 2.

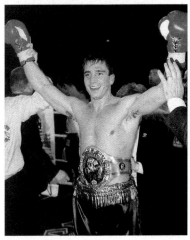

Markus Beyer　　　　　　Les Clark

Lamon (Relentless) Brewster

Indianapolis, USA. *Born* 5 June, 1973
WBO Heavyweight Champion

Major Amateur Honours: The
Californian State Golden Gloves
champion in 1992 and 1993, he won a
gold medal in the 1995 US Champion-
ships, a silver medal in the 1995 Pan-
American Games, a bronze medal in the
1994 US Championships and a gold
medal in the 1995 US Championships
Turned Pro: November 8, 1996
Significant Results: Clifford Etienne L
PTS 10, Charles Shufford L PTS 10,
Nate Jones W RSC 3, Tommy Martin
W RSC 3, Vladimir Klitschko W RSC 5
Type/Style: Has a powerful, relaxed
style with good hand speed and a hard
punch

Points of Interest: 6'1" tall. A high school graduate, who started boxing at the age of eight, he is devoutly religious. Inactive for 13 months before climbing off the floor to beat Vladimir Klitschko in April 2004, he later raised his profile greatly with his quick stoppage of Andrew Golota. Trained by Jesse Reid, an ex pro, he has 28 wins inside the distance and has made two title defences

04.09.04	Kali Meehan W PTS 12 Las Vegas
	(WBO Heavyweight Title Defence)
21.05.05	Andrew Golota W RSC 1 Chicago
	(WBO Heavyweight Title Defence)

Career: 34 contests, won 32, lost 2.

Lamon Brewster　　　　　　Les Clark

Isaac (Tortas) Bustos

Mexico City, Mexico. *Born* 16 February, 1975
Former WBC M.Flyweight Champion

Major Amateur Honours: None, having just three amateur fights
Turned Pro: February 1995
Significant Results: Fernando Luna W PTS 12 & W RSC 1, Valentin Leon W RSC 10, Edgar Sosa W PTS 12
Type/Style: Is a durable fighter with good stamina, but one paced and a bit crude
Points of Interest: 5'4" tall. Lost his first paid fight and won only six of his first 14 before going unbeaten in his next 19. Has 13 stoppages or kayos. Won the WBC title when Eagle Akakura had to retire in their fight with an injured arm

18.12.04	Eagle Akakura W RSC 4 Tokyo
	(WBC M.Flyweight Title Challenge)
04.04.05	Katsunari Takayama L PTS 12 Osaka
	(WBC M.Flyweight Title Defence)

Career: 34 contests, won 24, drew 3, lost 7.

Chris (Rapid Fire) Byrd

Flint, Michigan, USA. *Born* 15 August, 1970
IBF Heavyweight Champion. Former WBO Heavyweight Champion

Major Amateur Honours: The United States champion in 1989 at 156lbs and at 165lbs in 1991 and 1992, he won a silver medal in the 1992 Olympic Games
Turned Pro: January 1993
Significant Results: Arthur Williams W PTS 10, Phil Jackson W PTS 12, Lionel Butler W RSC 8, Uriah Grant W PTS 10, Ike Ibeabuchi L RSC 5, Vitali Klitschko W RTD 9, Vladimir Klitschko L PTS 12, David Tua W PTS 12, Evander Holyfield W PTS 12, Fres Oquendo W PTS 12, Andrew Golota DREW 12
Type/Style: Is a slick, fast moving southpaw
Points of Interest: Coming from a family of boxers, his father was the head coach for the United States amateur team and other members of his family, including a sister, have also fought as professionals. Became the WBO champion by beating Vitali Klitschko in April 2000, losing the title in his first defence six months later to Vladimir Klitschko before winning the vacant IBF title in December 2002 by outpointing Holyfield. Since then he has made only three defences

| 13.11.04 | Jameel McCline W PTS 12 New York |
| | *(IBF Heavyweight Title Defence)* |

Career: 41 contests, won 38, lost 2 drew 1.

Ivan (Iron Boy) Calderon

Guaynabo, Puerto Rico. *Born* 7 January, 1975
WBO M.Flyweight Champion

Major Amateur Honours: A bronze medallist in the 1999 Pan-American Games, he also competed in the World Championships that year. Won a silver medal in the 1999 Central American Games before competing in the 2000 Olympic Games. Claims 110 wins in 130 bouts
Turned Pro: February 2001
Significant Results: Jorge Romero W RTD 4, Alejandro Moreno W PTS 10, Eduardo Marquez W TD 9, Lorenzo Trejo W PTS 12, Alex Sanchez W PTS 12, Edgar Cardenas W CO 11
Type/Style: Southpaw. Although an excellent boxer technically and a good counter-puncher, he lacks power
Points of Interest: 5'0" tall. Won the WBO title with a technical verdict over Eduardo Marquez in May 2003 and has made five defences. An extrovert who is tremendously popular in Puerto Rico, being voted Boxer of the Year there in 2002, he has six wins by stoppage or kayo

31.07.04	Roberto Leyva W PTS 12 Las Vegas
	(WBO M.Flyweight Title Defence)
27.11.04	Carlos Fajardo W PTS 12 Las Vegas
	(WBO M.Flyweight Title Defence)
30.04.05	Noel Tunacao W RSC 8 Hato Rey
	(WBO M.Flyweight Title Defence)
25.06.05	Gerardo Verde W PTS 12 Atlantic City
	(WBO M.Flyweight Title Defence)

Career: 23 contests won 23.

Javier (The Lynx of Parla) Castillejo

Madrid, Spain. *Born* 22 March 1968
Former WBC L.Middleweight Champion. Former Undefeated European L.Middleweight Champion. Former Undefeated Spanish L.Middleweight & Welterweight Champion

Major Amateur Honours: None known
Turned Pro: July 1988
Significant Results: Julio Cesar Vazquez L PTS 12, Bernard Razzano W RSC 6, Laurent Boudouani L RSC 6, Ahmet Dottuev W RSC 12, Keith Mullings W PTS 12, Paolo Roberto W RSC 7, Mikael Rask RSC 7, Tony Marshall W PTS 10. Oscar De La Hoya L PTS 12, Roman Karmazin W PTS 12
Type/Style: Is aggressive and strong, and a heavy puncher
Points of Interest: 5'9" tall. Failed in a bid for the WBA title against Julio Cesar Vazquez in 1993 before winning the WBC title in January 1999 and making six defences prior to losing the title to Oscar De La Hoya in June

2001. He became the WBC interim champion on beating Roman Karmazin in July 2002 and when Ronnie Wright relinquished the title in May 2005 he was then recognised as the full champion. However, he was quickly stripped for refusing to meet Ricardo Mayorga in a title defence. Twice the European champion at light-middleweight, he has 40 wins inside the distance. Was inactive during the period covered

Career: 63 contests, won 58, lost 5.

Martin (Gallo) Castillo

Mexico City. Mexico. *Born* 13 January, 1977
WBA S.Flyweight Champion

Major Amateur Honours: The Mexican junior champion in 1993 and the silver medallist in the 1993 Pan-American Games, he became the Mexican champion in 1995 before competing in the 1996 Olympics. In 1997 he won a gold medal in the Central American Games, a bronze medal in the Pan-American Games and competed in the World Championships
Turned Pro: July 1998
Significant Results: Oscar Andrade W PTS 10, Gabriel Munoz W PTS 10, Francisco Tejedor W CO 1, Evangelista Perez W RSC 3, Ricardo Vargas W TD 6, Felix Machado L TD 6, Hideyasu Ishihara W RSC 11
Type/Style: A compact, intelligent and patient boxer with a long, fast jab, he has excellent reflexes
Points of Interest: 5'4" tall. Beat both Floyd Mayweather and Eric Morel in the same month as an amateur. Was unsuccessful in a challenge for the IBF title when losing to Felix Machado in March 2002, but won the interim WBA title on stopping Hideyasu Ishihara in May 2004 and the full title when beating Alexander Munoz. Has 16 wins by kayo or stoppage

03.12.04	Alexander Munoz W PTS 12 Laredo *(WBA S.Flyweight Title Challenge)*
19.03.05	Eric Morel W PTS 12 Las Vegas *(WBA S.Flyweight Title Defence)*
26.06.05	Hideyasu Ishihara W PTS 12 Nagoya *(WBA S.Flyweight Title Defence)*

Career: 30 contests, won 29, lost 1.

Hugo (Fidel) Cazares

Los Mochis, Mexico. *Born* 24 March, 1978
WBO L.Flyweight Champion. Former Undefeated Mexican L.Flyweight Champion

Major Amateur Honours: None known
Turned Pro: February 1997
Significant Results: Sergio Perez L CO 1, Gerson Guerrero L RSC 5, Rafael Orozco W CO 6, Eric Jamili W CO 3, Valentin Leon W RSC 3, Juan Keb-Baas W CO 9
Type/Style: Is a tough, aggressive switch-hitter
Points of Interest: Was already fighting over ten-rounds by only his sixth fight. Has 14 wins by stoppage or kayo and is unbeaten in his last 11 contests, with eight of those ending by kayo or stoppage

29.01.05	Miguel Del Valle W PTS 10 Bayamon
30.04.05	Nelson Dieppa W TD 10 Hato Rey *(WBO L.Flyweight Title Challenge)*

Career: 24 contests, won 20, drew 1, lost 3.

In-Jin Chi

Seoul, South Korea. *Born* 18 July, 1973
WBC Featherweight Champion. Former Undefeated South Korean Bantamweight Champion

Major Amateur Honours: None known
Turned Pro: November 1991
Significant Results: Jesse Maca W PTS 10 & W PTS 12, Baby Lorona W PTS 10, Erik Morales L PTS 12, Sammy Duran W RSC 3, Michael Brodie DREW 12 & W CO 9
Type/Style: A tough, raw, aggressive fighter, he is a good body puncher with a strong chin
Points of Interest: 5'7" tall with a 67" reach. Lost his first paid fight, but since then only Erik Morales has beaten him. Has made two title defences since winning the title following his victory over Michael Brodie in April 2004. There are 18 wins inside the distance on his record

24.07.04	Eiichi Sugama W RSC 10 Seoul *(WBC Featherweight Title Defence)*
30.01.05	Tommy Browne W PTS 12 Seoul *(WBC Featherweight Title Defence)*

Career: 33 contests, won 30, drew 1, lost 2.

In-Jin Chi   Les Clark

Diego (Chico) Corrales

Columbia, USA. *Born* 25 August, 1977
WBC & WBO Lightweight Champion. Former Undefeated WBO & IBF S.Featherweight Champion

Major Amateur Honours: Won a silver medal in the US Junior and Senior Championships in 1994 and a bronze medal in the 1995 Pan-American Games
Turned Pro: March 1996
Significant Results: Steve Quinones W RSC 4, Rafael Meran W CO 2, Hector Arroyo W RSC 5, Gary St Clair W PTS 12, Roberto Garcia W RSC 7, John Brown W PTS 12, Derrick Gainer W RSC 3, Justin Juuko W RSC 10, Angel Manfredy W RSC 3, Floyd Mayweather L RSC 10, Joel Casamayor L RSC 6 & W PTS 12
Type/Style: Although a strong, heavy hitter and a good combination puncher, his defence is not too sound
Points of Interest: 5'11" tall with a 73" reach. His father was a pro and Diego started boxing at the age of 12. Won the IBF title in October 1999 by stopping Roberto Garcia and made four defences. When losing to Floyd Mayweather for the WBC title in January 2001, he was on the floor five times. Was jailed in 2001 for spousal assault and inactive for two years before returning to win the WBO super-featherweight title by beating Joel Casamayor in March 2004. Has stopped or knocked out 33 opponents

07.08.04	Acelino Freitas W RSC 10 Mashantucket *(WBO Lightweight Title Challenge)*
07.05.05	Jose Luis Castillo W RSF 10 Las Vegas *(WBO Lightweight Title Defence. WBC Lightweight Title Challenge)*

Career: 42 contests, won 40, lost 2.

Diego Corrales   Les Clark

Miguel Cotto

Caguas, Puerto Rico. *Born* 29 October, 1980

WBO L.Welterweight Champion

Major Amateur Honours: A bronze medallist in the 1997 Central American Games and a silver medallist in the 1998 World Junior Championships, he went on to compete in the 1999 World Championships and Pan-American Games. Won a gold medal in the 2002 Central American Games, having earlier competed in the 2000 Olympics, where he lost to Mohamad Abdulaev

Turned Pro: February 2001

Significant Results: Justin Juuko W RSC 5, John Brown W PTS 10, Cesar Bazan W RSC 11, Joel Perez W CO 4, Demetrio Ceballos W RSC 7, Carlos Maussa W RSC 8, Victoriano Sosa W RSC 4, Lovemore Ndou W PTS 12

Type/Style: Miguel is a classy, hard-hitting box puncher with an exciting style

Points of Interest: 5'8" tall with a 67" reach. His father, uncle and cousin all boxed and his brother, Jose Miguel, is also an unbeaten pro. Is trained by his

uncle, Evangelista, and has 20 wins inside the distance

11.09.04	Kelson Pinto W RSC 6 Hato Rey *(Vacant WBO L.Welterweight Title)*
11.12.04	Randall Bailey W RSC 6 Las Vegas *(WBO L.Welterweight Title Defence)*
26.02.05	DeMarcus Corley W RSC 5 Bayamon *(WBO L.Welterweight Title Defence)*
11.06.05	Muhamad Abdullaev W RSC 9 New York *(WBO L.Welterweight Title Defence)*

Career: 24 contests, won 24.

Vic (Raging Bull) Darchinyan

Australia. *Born* Vanadvor, Armenia, 7 January, 1976

IBF Flyweight Champion. Former Undefeated Australian Flyweight Champion

Major Amateur Honours: Competed in the 1997 World Championships before winning bronze medals in the 1998 Goodwill Games and World Cup. He then competed in the 2000 European Championships and was a quarter-finalist in the 2000 Olympics

Turned Pro: November 2000

Significant Results: Raul Medina W TD 8, Wandee Chor Chareon W CO 4 & W CO 5, Alejandro Montiel W PTS 10

Type/Style: Southpaw. Is a good boxer and a hard puncher with both hands

Points of Interest: 5'5" tall. His real first name is Vakhtang and he stayed and settled in Australia after representing Armenia in the Sydney Olympics. Trained and managed by Jeff Fenech, he won the Australian title in only his seventh fight. Has stopped or kayoed 17 opponents

16.12.04	Irene Pacheco W RSC 11 Hollywood *(IBF Flyweight Title Challenge)*
27.03.05	Mzukisi Sikali W RSC 8 Sydney *(IBF Flyweight Title Defence)*

Career: 23 contests, won 23.

Juan (Baby Bull) Diaz

Houston, USA. *Born* 17 September, 1983

WBA Lightweight Champion

Major Amateur Honours: The Mexican junior and senior champion in 1999, he

claims 105 wins in 110 fights, but was too young for the Sydney Olympics

Turned Pro: June 2002

Significant Results: John Bailey W RSC 7, Eleazar Contreras W PTS 10, Joel Perez W RSC 6, Martin O'Malley W CO 2

Type/Style: Juan is a solid, busy fighter with great hand speed, but is not a big puncher

Points of Interest: 5'6" tall. Becoming the fourth youngest fighter to win a version of the lightweight title, and still a high school student at the time, he is now at College taking Government studies. He is trained by the ex-pro, Ronnie Shields, and managed by Shelly Finkel

17.07.04	Lakva Sim W PTS 12 Houston *(WBA Lightweight Title Challenge)*
04.11.04	Julien Lorcy W PTS 12 San Antonio *(WBA Lightweight Title Defence)*
21.01.05	Billy Irwin W RSC 9 Houston *(WBA Lightweight Title Defence)*

Career: 27 contests, won 27.

Juan Diaz   Les Clark

Zsolt (Fire) Erdei

Budapest, Hungary. *Born* 31 May, 1974

WBO L.Heavyweight Champion

Major Amateur Honours: The European junior champion in 1992, he competed in the 1995 World Championships and won a gold medal in the 1997 World Championships, having earlier won a silver in the 1996 European Championships and competed in the Olympics that year. He then won a gold medal in both

the 1998 and 2000 European Championships, before winning a bronze in the 2000 Olympics
Turned Pro: December 2000
Significant Results: Jim Murray W CO 5, Juan Carlos Gimenez W RSC 8, Massimiliano Saiani W RSC 7, Julio Gonzalez W PTS 12, Hugo Garay W PTS 12
Type/Style: Although an excellent, clever technical craftsman and quick combination puncher with a strong, accurate jab, he is not a puncher
Points of Interest: 5'10" tall with a 72" reach. Floored twice in early fights. Based in Germany, in beating Julio Gonzalez in January 2004 he brought the WBO title back to his stable after fellow Universum fighter, Dariusz Michalczweski had lost to Gonzalez. Has 13 wins inside the distance and has made three title defences

| 11.09.04 | Alejandro Lakatus W PTS 12 Budapest *(WBO L.Heavyweight Title Defence)* |
| 26.02.05 | Hugo Garay W PTS 12 Hamburg *(WBO L.Heavyweight Title Defence)* |

Career: 22 contests, won 22.

Arturo (Thunder) Gatti

New Jersey, USA. *Born* Canada, 15 April, 1972
Former WBC L.Welterweight Champion. Former Undefeated IBF S.Featherweight Champion

Major Amateur Honours: Was a three-times Canadian Golden Gloves champion
Turned Pro: June 1991
Significant Results: Tracy Harris Patterson W PTS 12 (twice), Jose Sanabria W PTS 12, Wilson Rodriguez W RSC 6, Calvin Grove W RTD 7, Gabriel Ruelas W RSC 5, Angel Manfredy L PTS 10, Ivan Robinson L PTS 10 (twice), Joey Gamache W CO 2, Oscar De La Hoya L RSC 5, Terronn Millett W RSC 4, Mickey Ward L PTS 10 & W PTS 10 (twice), Gianluca Branco W PTS 12
Type/Style: Arturo is a fast starter and big hitter with a huge heart and a good chin
Points of Interest: 5'8" tall. Brother Joe was also a pro. Won the IBF super-featherweight title by beating Tracy

Harris Patterson in December 1995 and made three defences before moving up due to weight problems in 1998. With 30 wins inside the distance,14 coming in the first round, it was no surprise that his three fights with Mickey Ward were all classics

24.07.04	Leonardo Dorin W CO 2 Atlantic City *(WBC L.Welterweight Title Defence)*
29.01.05	James Leija W CO 5 Atlantic City *(WBC L.Welterweight Title Defence)*
25.06.05	Floyd Mayweather L RTD 6 Atlantic City *(WBC L.Welterweight Title Defence)*

Career: 46 contests, won 39, lost 7.

Will (Steel Will) Grigsby

St Paul, USA. *Born* 19 March,1970
IBF L.Flyweight Champion. Former WBO L. Flyweight Champion

Major Amateur Honours: A trialist for the US team for 1988 Olympic Games, having been a quarter-finalist in the National Golden Gloves that year
Turned Pro: November 1988
Significant Results: Michael Carbajal L PTS 4, Jesus Lopez W PTS 12, Ratanapol Sowvoraphin W PTS 12, Carmelo Caceres W PTS 12, Ricardo Lopez L PTS 12, Nelson Dieppa ND 12
Type/Style: Has fast footwork and quick hands, but is not a puncher
Points of Interest: 5'4" tall. Lost in his second paid fight to Michael Carbajal and was inactive from 1989 to 1994. Raises pit bull terriers. Won the IBF title for the first time in December 1998 by beating Ratanapol Sowvoraphin, but lost it to Ricardo Lopez in his second defence, in October 1999. Beat Nelson Dieppa for the WBO title in July 2000, but was stripped for failing a drug test for marijuana and the verdict was changed to that of no-decision. Was in jail for two years before returning to the ring in 2002

27.11.04	Ruben Poma W RSC 1 Lafayette
28.01.05	Ruben Contreras W PTS 8 Indianapolis
14.05.05	Jose Victor Burgos W PTS 12 Las Vegas *(IBF L.Flyweight Title Challenge)*

Career: 22 contests, won 18, drew 1, lost 2, no decision 1.

Joan (Little Tyson) Guzman

Santo Domingo, Dominican Republic.
Born 1 May, 1976
WBO S.Bantamweight Champion. Former Undefeated Dominican Featherweight & S. Bantamweight Champion

Major Amateur Honours: : Competed in the 1995 Pan-American Games and 1996 Olympics and was a three-time Central American champion
Turned Pro: September 1997
Significant Results: Francisco De Leon W CO 11, Hector Avila W CO 2, Edgar Ruiz W PTS 12, Fabio Oliva W KO 3, Jorge Monsalvo W CO 1, Agapito Sanchez W RSC 7
Type/Style: Is a compact, powerful, short-armed fighter with good movement and a strong body puncher, who could be a star of the future if more active
Points of Interest: 5'7" tall. Won the vacant WBO title in Cardiff in August 2002 by knocking out Fabio Oliva and has 17 wins inside the distance. Contract problems and postponed title fights mean he has made only two defences in three years, but is now managed by the Sycuan Native American group. Lost to current WBO flyweight champion, Omar Narvaez, in the 1996 Olympics

| 06.11.04 | Joe Morales W PTS 10 Phoenix |
| 22.04.05 | Fernando Beltran W PTS 12 Hidalgo *(WBO S.Bantamweight Title Defence)* |

Career: 23 contests, won 23.

Hozumi Hasegawa

Nishiwaki City. Japan. *Born* 16 December, 1980
WBC Bantamweight Champion

Major Amateur Honours: None known
Turned Pro: November 1999
Significant Results: Jess Maca W PTS 12, Gunao Uno W PTS 12, Alvin Felisilda W CO 10, Jun Toriumi W PTS 10
Type/Style: Southpaw. Is a tall, fast and stylish fighter
Points of Interest: 5'5" tall. Has only five wins inside the distance. Once known as the 'Japanese Pernell', due to his boxing skills, he lost two of his first five fights but is now unbeaten in

15. Veeraphol Sahaprom was unbeaten in his last 45 fights when Hozumi beat him

30.10.04	Jun Toriumi W PTS 10 Tokyo
16.04.05	Veeraphol Sahaprom W PTS 12 Tokyo *(WBC Bantamweight Title Challenge)*
Career: 20 contests, won 18, lost 2.	

Ivan (Choko) Hernandez
Mexico City, Mexico. *Born* 24 November, 1982
Former WBO S.Flyweight Champion

Major Amateur Honours: None known
Turned Pro: April 2000
Significant Results: Victor Hernandez W RSC 7, Gabriel Munoz W PTS 10, Rafael Chavez DREW 8
Type/Style: Is a fast-punching, lanky, loose-limbed banger
Points of Interest: With 13 wins inside the distance, he is tall for the division and has had trouble making the weight. Was only just inside the super-bantamweight limit against Lee Cargle

25.09.04	Mark Johnson W CO 8 Memphis *(WBO S.Flyweight Title Challenge)*
19.02.05	Lee Cargle W PTS 8 Lula
09.04.05	Fernando Montiel L RSC 7 El Paso *(WBO S.Flyweight Title Defence)*
Career: 23 contests, won 21, drew 1, lost 1.	

Bernard (The Executioner) Hopkins
Philadelphia, USA. *Born* 15 January, 1965
WBC, WBA, WBO & IBF Middleweight Champion

Major Amateur Honours: None, but claims 95 wins in 99 fights
Turned Pro: October 1988
Significant Results: Roy Jones L PTS 12, Lupe Aquino W PTS 12, Segundo Mercado DREW 12 & W PTS 12, Robert Allen NC 4, W RSC 7 & W PTS 12, Antwun Echols W PTS 12, Syd Vanderpool W PTS 12, Antwun Echols W RSC 10, Keith Holmes W PTS 12, Felix Trinidad W RSC 12, Carl Daniels W RTD 10, Morrade Hakkar W RTD 8, William Joppy W PTS 12
Type/Style: Is a strong, mechanical boxer, but is a good tactician and a powerful puncher with fast hands
Points of Interest: 6'0" tall with a 71"

reach. The nephew of former pro, Art McCloud, he spent five years in jail. Entering the ring wearing an executioner's mask and a cape, and despite losing his first paid fight, he can boast of 29 wins inside the distance. Lost to Roy Jones in his first attempt to win the IBF title and drew with Segundo Mercado for the vacant title before beating Mercado in a return in April 1995. He made 15 defences of his IBF title and carried off the WBC title when outpointing Keith Holmes in April 2001 and then the WBA title by halting Felix Trinidad in September 2001. Injured his ankle in first fight with Robert Allen when he was pushed out of the ring and bout declared a no-contest. Has 32 wins inside the distance and has taken part in 22 world title fights

18.09.04	Oscar de la Hoya W CO 9 Las Vegas *(IBF,WBA & WBC Middleweight Titles Defences. WBO Middleweight Title Challenge)*
19.02.05	Howard Eastman W PTS 12 Los Angeles *(IBF, WBA, WBC & WBO Middleweight Title Defences)*
Career: 50 contests, won 46, drew 1, lost 2, no contests 1.	

Bernard Hopkins

Leavander Johnson
Atlantic City, USA. *Born* 24 December, 1969
IBF Lightweight Champion

Major Amateur Honours: Was a quarter-finalist in the 1988 National Golden Gloves
Turned Pro: February 1989

Significant Results: Sharmba Mitchell W CO 8, Miguel Angel Gonzalez L RSC 8, Hector Tejeda W CO 6, Orzubek Nazarov L RSC 7, Juan Polo Perez W RSC 3, Sean Fletcher W RSC 4, Ray Minus W RSC 8, Mike Clark L TD 5, Emanuel Augustus DREW 10, Javier Jauregui L RSC 11, Roque Cassiani W PTS 10
Type/Style: Recognised as a rangy craftsman and a hard puncher
Points of Interest: 5'9" tall. Started boxing at the age of eight and has always been trained by his father. Early in his career had a run of 16 straight wins inside the distance, before losing in challenges for the WBC title against Miguel Angel Gonzalez, for the WBA title against Orzubek Nazarov and for the vacant IBF title against Javier Jauregui prior to winning at the fourth attempt. With only three fights in the past 32 months, and inactive for 15 months before beating Stefano Zoff, he has 26 wins by stoppage or kayo

| 17.06.05 | Stefano Zoff W RSC 7 Milan *(Vacant IBF Lightweight Title)* |
| **Career:** 41 contests, won 34, drew 2, lost 4, no decision 1. | |

Zab Judah
New York, USA. *Born* 27 October, 1977
IBF, WBC & WBA Welterweight Champion. Former Undefeated WBO L. Welterweight Champion. Former IBF L.Welterweight Champion

Major Amateur Honours: A three-time New York Golden Gloves champion, he won a bronze medal in the 1995 National Golden Gloves and was a reserve for the United States team at the 1996 Olympic Games. Claims 110 wins in 115 fights
Turned Pro: September 1996
Significant Results: Mickey Ward W PTS 12, Darryl Tyson W RSC 11, Wilfredo Negron W RSC 4, Jan Bergman W CO 4, Junior Witter W PTS 12, Terron Millett WRSC 4, Hector Quiroz W RSC 8, Reggie Green W RSC 10, Allan Vester W RSC 3, Kostya Tszyu L RSC 2, Omar Weiss W PTS 10, DeMarcus Corley W PTS 12, Cory Spinks L PTS 12, Rafael Pineda W PTS 12

Type/Style: Has shown himself to be a stylish, classy very fast and flashy southpaw. Has tremendous talent but is brash and arrogant

Points of Interest: 5'7" tall. From a boxing family, his dad, Yoel, was former world kickboxing champion and trained Zab, who started boxing at the age of six, at the Judah Brothers Gym. Earlier known as 'Pernell Whitaker junior' because of the time he spent sparring with the former world champion, two of his brothers also won New York Golden Gloves titles and Daniel is now a world-rated cruiserweight. Won the IBF Interim title in January 1999 by beating Wilfredo Negron and the vacant title by beating Jan Bergman in February 2000. Made five defences of his IBF title before losing to Kostya Tszyu in 2001 in a unification match for the WBC, WBA and IBF titles. Moved up to welterweight to challenge Cory Spinks but lost in the first attempt in April 2004. Has 25 wins inside the distance on his record

02.10.04	Wayne Martell W RSC 1 New York
05.02.05	Cory Spinks W RSC 9 St Louis *(IBF, WBC & WBA Welterweight Titles Challenge)*
14.05.05	Cosme Rivera W RSC 3 Las Vegas *(IBF, WBC & WBA Welterweight Titles Defence)*

Career: 37 contests, won 34, lost 2, no contest 1.

Zab Judah

Katsushige Kawashima

Chiba, Japan. *Born* 6 October, 1974
WBC S.Flyweight Champion. Former Undefeated Japanese S.Flyweight Champion

Major Amateur Honours: None known
Turned Pro: February 1997
Significant Results: Samuth Sithnarupol W CO 2, Jess Maca L PTS 12, Yokthai Sith-Oar W PTS 10, Shingo Sasaki W PTS 10, Masamori Tokuyama L PTS 12 and W RSC 1
Type/Style: A game, aggressive banger with a hard punch in his right hand, he has good stamina
Points of Interest: Managed and promoted by the former WBC and WBA mini-flyweight champion, Hideyuki Ohashi, at the start of his career he was the runner-up in the Japanese Novice Championships in 1997. Moved up to bantamweight to challenge Jess Maca for the OPBF title then back down to his natural weight. Having lost to Masamori Tokuyama in a challenge for the WBC title in June 2003, he gained ample revenge by stopping Tokuyama in one round to win the WBC title in June 2004. Has 18 wins inside the distance, but has yet to impress as a champion in his two defences. Is susceptible to cuts

20.09.04	Raul Juarez W PTS 12 Yokohama *(WBC S.Flyweight Title Defence)*
03.01.05	Jose Navarro W PTS 12 Tokyo *(WBC S.Flyweight Title Defence)*

Career: 31 contests, won 28, lost 3.

Mikkel (Viking Warrior) Kessler

Copenhagen, Denmark. *Born* 1 March, 1979
WBA S.Middleweight Champion

Major Amateur Honours: Was the European junior champion in 1996 and the Danish junior champion in 1996 and 1997
Turned Pro: March 1998
Significant Results: Elicier Julio W CO 3, Manny Sobral W RTD 5, Dingaan Thobela W PTS 12, Henry Porras W RSC 9, Julio Cesar Green W CO 1, Andre Thysse W PTS 12
Type/Style: A tall, strong, quality box fighter, with a good jab, he has been unfortunate to have had trouble with hand injuries in the past
Points of Interest: 6'1" tall with a 73"

reach. Heavily tattooed, he came in against Manny Siaca for the title as a late substitute when Mads Larsen dropped out and made the most of his opportunity. With 26 wins by stoppage or kayo, he is managed by Team Palle and was voted the Danish Fighter of the Year for 2004

12.11.04	Manny Siaca W RTD 7 Copenhagen *(WBA S.Middleweight Title Challenge)*
08.06.05	Anthony Mundine W PTS 12 Sydney *(WBA S.Middleweight Title Defence)*

Career: 36 contests, won 36.

Vitali (Iron Fist) Klitschko

Belovodsk, Ukraine. *Born* 19 February, 1971
WBC Heavyweight Champion. Former WBO Heavyweight Champion. Former Undefeated European Heavyweight Champion

Major Amateur Honours: The European junior champion in 1993, a silver medallist in the 1995 World Championships and the winner of the World Military Championship in 1995, he claims 195 wins in 210 fights
Turned Pro: November 1996
Significant Results: Julius Francis W RSC 2, Mario Schiesser W CO 2, Herbie Hide W CO 2, Obed Sullivan W RSC 9, Chris Byrd L RTD 9, Timo Hoffmann W PTS 12, Orlin Norris W RTD 1, Ross Puritty W RSC 11, Vaughan Bean W RSC 11, Larry Donald W RSC 10, Lennox Lewis L RSC 6, Kirk Johnson W RSC 2, Corrie Sanders W RSC 8
Type/Style: Tall and upright, he has a heavy punch in his right hand
Points of Interest: 6'7" tall with an 80" reach. The brother of the Olympic gold medal winner and former WBO champion, Vladimir, he won the WBO title in June 1999 when beating Herbie Hide and made three defences before losing to Chris Byrd in April 2000, when he suffered a torn rotator cuff. Apart from the Timo Hoffmann fight, every other fight has ended inside the distance and the judges had him ahead against Lennox Lewis when cuts forced the stoppage. Won the vacant WBC title by beating Corrie Sanders

in April 2004 and has 34 wins inside the distance

11.12.04	Danny Williams W RSC 8 Las Vegas
	(WBC Heavyweight Title Defence)
Career: 37 contests, won 35, lost 2.	

Vitali Klitschko   Les Clark

Jeff (Mini Holyfield) Lacy

St Petersburg, USA. *Born* 12 May, 1977

IBF S.Middleweight Champion

Major Amateur Honours: The winner of a bronze medal in the 1993 US Junior Championships, a silver medal in the 1994 US Junior Championships, a silver medal in the 1997 Ali Cup, a bronze medal in the 1997 National Golden Gloves, he competed in the 1997 World Championships. Went on to win a gold medal in the 1998 US and PAL Championships, a silver medal in the 1999 US Championships and a gold medal in the1999 PAL. Was a quarter-finalist in the 2000 Olympics
Turned Pro: February 2001
Significant Results: Ross Thompson W PTS 12, James Crawford W RSC 2, Anwar Oshana W RSC 2, Richard Grant W PTS 12, Donnell Wiggins W RSC 8, Vitali Tsypko ND 2
Type/Style: Is a strong, aggressive fighter, with a powerful punch, who wears the opposition down
Points of Interest: Also known as 'Left Hook', he won six of his first eight pro fights in the first round. Jeff's father competed in the trials for the US team for the 1968 Olympic Games and also

fought as a pro, so it was no surprise when he started boxing at the age of eight. Lost to Brian Magee in the Ali Cup. Has 15 wins by stoppage or kayo

02.10.04	Syd Vanderpool W RSC 8 Las Vegas
	(Vacant IBF S.Middleweight Title)
04.12.04	Omar Sheika W PTS 12 Las Vegas
	(IBF S.Middleweight Title Defence)
05.03.05	Rubin Williams W RSC 7 Las Vegas
	(IBF S.Middleweight Title Defence)
Career: 20 contests won 19, no decision 1.	

Oscar (Chololo) Larios

Guadalajara, Mexico. *Born* 1 November, 1976

WBC S.Bantamweight Champion. Former Undefeated Mexican S.Bantamweight Champion

Major Amateur Honours: None known, but claims 48 wins in 50 fights
Turned Pro: January 1994
Significant Results: Agapito Sanchez L RSC 5, Cesar Soto W PTS 12, Willie Jorrin L PTS 12 & W RSC 1, John Lowey W PTS 10, Angel Chacon W PTS 12, Israel Vazquez L RSC 1 & W KO 12, Marcos Licona W PTS 10, Shigeru Nakazato W PTS 12 (twice), Kozo Ishii W RSC 2, Napapol Kiatisakchokchai W RSC 10
Type/Style: Tall and skinny, he is a (fast) jab and move fighter
Points of Interest: 5'7" tall. Trained at one time by the former WBC featherweight champion, Marcos Villasana, he once worked as a stonemason. Made seven defences of his Mexican title before moving into world class, he suffered a broken jaw against Shigeru Nakazato in their first fight. Was the WBC Interim champion from May 2002 until beating Willie Jorrin for the full title in November 2002 and has made six defences, four of them in Japan. Has 35 wins inside the distance

20.08.04	Ivan Alvarez W PTS 10 Albuquerque
27.11.04	Nedal Hussein W PTS 12 Las Vegas
	(WBC S.Bantamweight Title Defence)
10.02.05	Wayne McCullough W PTS 12 Lemoore
	(WBC S.Bantamweight Title Defence)
Career: 59 contests, won 55, drew 1, lost 3.	

Antonio Margarito

Tijuana, Mexico. *Born* 18 March, 1978
WBO Welterweight Champion

Major Amateur Honours: None known
Turned Pro: January 1994
Significant Results: Larry Dixon L PTS 10, Rodney Jones L PTS 10, Alfred Ankamah W CO 4, Danny Perez W PTS 8 & W PTS 12, David Kamau W CO 2, Frankie Randall W RSC 4, Daniel Santos NC 1, Antonio Diaz W RSC 10, Andrew Lewis W RSC 2, Hercules Kyvelos W RSC 2
Type/Style: Is a tall, strong, aggressive banger, although a bit one-paced, and has a good jab and a strong chin
Points of Interest: 6'0" tall. Turned pro at the age of 15 and suffered three early defeats. His first fight with Daniel Santos for the WBO welterweight title was stopped and declared a no-contest, due to Antonio suffering a bad cut, and when Santos handed in the belt he won the vacant title by beating Antonio Diaz in March 2002. His challenge against Santos for the WBO light-middleweight title also had to go to a technical decision due to a cut. Has made six defences and has 23 wins inside the distance

11.09.04	Daniel Santos L TD 9 Hato Rey
	(WBO L.Middleweight Title Challenge)
18.02.05	Sebastian Lujan W RSC 10 Atlantic City
	(WBO Welterweight Title Defence)
23.04.05	Kermit Cintron W RSC 5 Las Vegas
	(WBO Welterweight Title Defence)
Career: 36 contests, won 31, lost4, no contests 1.	

Juan Manuel (Dinamita) Marquez

Mexico City, Mexico. *Born* 23 August, 1973

IBF & WBA Featherweight Champion

Major Amateur Honours: None known, but claims 32 wins in 33 bouts
Turned Pro: May 1993
Significant Results: Julian Wheeler W RSC 10, Julio Gervacio W CO 10, Agapito Sanchez W PTS 12, Alfred Kotey W PTS 12, Freddy Norwood L PTS 12, Daniel Jimenez W RTD 7, Julio Gamboa W RTD 6, Robbie Peden W RSC 10, Manuel Medina W RSC 7, Derrick Gainer W TD 7, Manny Pacquiao DREW 12

Type/Style: A solid, compact stylist, he is also a hard puncher with either hand
Points of Interest: 5'7" tall. Despite studying to be an accountant, having been an amateur since the age of 12 he took up pro boxing, following in the footsteps of his father, who had boxed as a pro. He is also the brother of the IBF bantamweight champion, Rafael Martinez. Although he lost his first pro fight on a disqualification, he was not deterred and battled his way to a world title shot, losing to Freddy Norwood in a challenge for the WBA title in September 1999. He then went on to win the IBF title by beating Manuel Medina in February 2003. Floored three times in the first round of his fight with Manny Pacquiao in May last year, he has 33 wins by stoppage or kayo

| 18.09.04 | Orlando Salido W PTS 12 Las *(IBF & WBA Featherweight Title Defences)* |
| 07.05.05 | Victor Polo W PTS 12 Las Vegas *(IBF & WBA Featherweight Title Defences)* |

Career: 47 contests, won 44, drew 1, lost 2.

Rafael Marquez

Mexico City, Mexico. *Born* 25 March, 1975
IBF Bantamweight Champion

Major Amateur Honours: None known, but claims only one loss in 57 fights
Turned Pro: September 1995
Significant Results: Victor Rabanales L CO 8, Francisco Mateos L RSC 3, Tomas Rivera W CO 2, Genaro Garcia L RSC 2, Aquilies Guzman W RSC 7, Gerardo Espinoza W RSC 4, Mark Johnson W PTS 10 & W RSC 8, Tim Austin W RSC 8, Mauricio Pastrana, Peter Frissina W RSC 2
Type/Style: Although being compact and solid, and a big puncher with the right hand, his defence sometimes lets him down
Points of Interest: 5'5" tall. Lost his first pro fight against Victor Rabanales, who was a former WBC bantamweight champion with more than 50 fights to his name at the time, and eventually won the IBF title by stopping Tim Austin in February 2003, just two weeks after his brother, Juan

Manuel Marquez, won the IBF featherweight title. Their father, also Rafael, was a pro in the 1950s. Has 30 wins inside the distance and all of his losses have also come inside the distance. Is trained by the top Mexican, Nacho Beristan, and has made four defences

31.07.04	Heriberto Ruiz W CO 3 Las Vegas *(IBF Bantamweight Title Defence)*
27.11.04	Mauricio Pastrana W RTD 8 Las Vegas *(IBF Bantamweight Title Defence)*
28.05.05	Ricardo Vargas W PTS 12 Los Angeles *(IBF Bantamweight Title Defence)*

Career: 37 contests, won 34, lost 3.

Carlos Maussa

Monteria, Colombia. *Born* 29 April, 1971
WBA L.Welterweight Champion

Major Amateur Honours: Won a silver medal in the 1997 Central American Games
Turned Pro: July 2000
Significant Results: Freddy Cruz W RSC 2, Jeff Resto W RSC 6, Miguel Cotto L RSC 8, Masakazu Satake W PTS 10
Type/Style: Very upright with a messy style jerky style, he is very effective and a deceptively hard puncher
Points of Interest: 5'11" tall with a 73" reach. The winner Won 15 of his first 16 fights inside the distance before losing to the fast-rising Miguel Cotto for the WBC International title and then to Arturo Morua for the vacant WBO Latino title, both at light-welter. It was a huge shock when the 33-year-old wild punching delivery boy took out Vivian Harris to win the WBO crown

17.12.04	Arturo Morua L PTS 12 Miami *(Vacant WBO Latino L.Welterweight Title)*
19.03.05	Antonio Espitia W CO 4 Arbolete
25.06.05	Vivian Harris W CO 7 Atlantic City *(WBA L.Welterweight Title Challenge)*

Career: 21 contests, won 19, lost 2.

Floyd (Little Stone) Mayweather

Grand Rapids, Michigan, USA. *Born* 24 February, 1977
WBC L.Welterweight Champion.

Former Undefeated WBC Lightweight Champion. Former Undefeated WBC S.Featherweight Champion

Major Amateur Honours: A National Golden Gloves champion in 1993, 1994 and 1996, his first US title was at 106lbs in 1995.Competed in the 1995 World Championships and won a bronze Medal in the 1996 Olympics. Won 84 of 90 fights
Turned Pro: October 1996
Significant Results: Genaro Hernandez W RTD 8,Angel Manfredy W RSC 2,Carlos Rios W PTS 12,Justin Juuko W RSC 9, Carlos Gerena W RTD 7, Gregorio Vargas W PTS 12, Diego Corrales W RSC 10, Carlos Hernandez W PTS 12, Jesus Chavez W RTD 9, Jose Luis Castillo W PTS 12 (twice), Victoriano Sosa W PTS 12, Phillip Ndou W RSC 7, DeMarcus Corley W PTS 12
Type/Style: Very talented, he is a flashy fighter with fast hands, great reflexes and a hard punch
Points of Interest: 5'8" tall. Floyd's father, also named Floyd, was a good professional and Floyd's uncle, Roger, was the WBA super-featherweight and WBC light-welterweight champion, so boxing is well and truly in the blood. He won the super-featherweight title in October 1998, beating Carlos Hernandez, and made eight defences before winning the lightweight title when defeating Jose Luis Castillo in April 2002 and making two defences before moving on. Has 23 wins inside the distance

| 22.01.05 | Henry Bruseles W RSC 8 Miami |
| 25.06.05 | Arturo Gatti W RTD 6 Atlantic City *(WBC L.Welterweight Title Challenge)* |

Career: 33 contests, won 33.

Mahyar (Little Tyson) Monshipour

Poitiers, France. *Born* Tehran, Iran, 21 March, 1975
WBA S.Bantamweight Champion.
Former Undefeated French & European S.Bantamweight Champion

Major Amateur Honours: None known
Turned Pro: October 1996
Significant Results: Sandor Koczak L RSC 3, German Guartos DRAW 6 & W RSC 3, Turkay Kaya W PTS 8 & W RSC 6, Michael Alldis W PTS 8,

Salim Bouaita W RSC 9, Mustapha Hame W RSC 6, Salim Medjkoune W CO 12 & W RSC 8, Jairo Tagliaferro W RTD 7

Type/Style: Although a crude brawler at times, he is an extremely strong all-action fighter

Points of Interest: 5'5" tall. Sent to France as a safety measure from Iran by his parents in 1986, he won the European title by stopping Turkay Kaya in July 2002 and made two defences. Won the WBA super-bantam title by beating Salim Medjkoune for the first time in July 2003 and has made five defences. Has 17 wins inside the distance and is now also promoting fights

08.11.04	Yoddamrong Sithyodthong W RSC 6 Paris
	(WBA S.Bantamweight Title Defence)
29.04.05	Shigeru Nakazato W RSC 6 Marseille
	(WBA S.Bantamweight Title Defence)
25.06.05	Julio Zarate W RTD 8 Poitiers
	(WBA S.Bantamweight Title Defence)
Career: 32 contests, won 28, drew 2, lost 2.	

Fernando (Cochulito) Montiel

Los Mochis, Mexico. *Born* 1 March, 1979

WBO S. Flyweight Champion. Former Undefeated WBO Flyweight Champion

Major Amateur Honours: Claiming 33 wins in 36 fights, he was a local Golden Gloves champion
Turned Pro: December 1996
Significant Results: Paulino Villalobos DREW 10 & W PTS 10, Sergio Millan W PTS 10, Cruz Carbajal W RSC 4, Isidro Garcia W RSC 7, Zoltan Lunka W RSC 7, Juan Domingo Cordoba W CO 1, Jose Lopez W PTS 12, Pedro Alcazar W RSC 6, Roy Doliguez W RSC 3, Mark Johnson L PTS 12,
Type/Style: Is a clever and stylish boxer. Also has a good uppercut
Points of Interest: 5'4" tall. The youngest of a fighting family, his father and four brothers were all boxers, he won his first 11 bouts inside the distance. Jointly trained by his father, Manuel, and a Japanese trainer based in Mexico, Fernando has 24

wins by knockout or stoppage. Won the WBO flyweight title by stopping Isidro Garcia in December 2000 and made three defences before moving up to win the super-flyweight title, defeating Pedro Alcazar in June 2002. Sadly, Alcazar collapsed and died after the fight. Having lost the title in his second defence, against Mark Johnson, he came back to regain it last April when stopping Ivan Hernandez

03.09.04	Reynaldo Hurtado W CO 7 Phoenix
09.04.05	Ivan Hernandez W RSC 7 El Paso
	(WBO S.Flyweight Title Challenge)
Career: 32 contests, won 30, drew 1, lost 1.	

Fernando Montiel

Erik (The Terrible) Morales

Tijuana, Mexico. *Born* 1 September, 1976

Former IBF & WBC S.Featherweight Champion. Former Undefeated WBC Featherweight Champion. Former Undefeated WBC & WBO S.Bantamweight Champion. Former Undefeated Mexican S.Bantamweight Champion

Major Amateur Honours: None, but claims 108 wins in 114 fights
Turned Pro: March 1993
Significant Results: Daniel Zaragoza W CO 11, Jose Luis Bueno W CO 2, Hector Acero Sanchez W PTS 12, Junior Jones W RSC 4, Angel Chacon W RSC 2, Juan Carlos Ramirez W RSC 9, Reynante Jamili W RSC 6, Wayne McCullough W PTS 12, Marco

Antonio Barrera W PTS 12 & L PTS 12, Guty Espadas W PTS 12, In-Jin Chi W PTS 12, Paulie Ayala W PTS 12, Jesus Chavez W PTS 12

Type/Style: Is a cool, upright pressure fighter who can bang hard with both hands

Points of Interest: 5'8" tall. From a boxing family, his dad fought Orlando Canizales as a pro and his brother, Diego, is a former WBO S.Flyweight champion, he turned pro at the age of 16. Made nine defences of his WBC super-bantamweight title before relinquishing and after he beat Marco Antonio Barrera for the WBO title on a hotly disputed decision he also vacated that title. Won the WBC title by decisioning Guty Espadas in February 2001, but lost it to Barrera in a return bout in June 2002. He regained the title by outpointing Paulie Ayala in November 2002 and made two defences before moving up to super-featherweight. Won the WBC super-featherweight title in February 2004 by beating Jesus Chavez and then the IBF title when outpointing Hernandez. Has taken part in 19 WBC title fights and has 34 wins inside the distance

31.07.04	Carlos Hernandez W PTS 12 Las Vegas
	(WBC S.Featherweight Title Defence & IBF S.Featherweight Title Challenge)
27.11.04	Marco Antonio Barrera L PTS 12 Las Vegas
	(WBC S.Featherweight Title Defence)
19.03.05	Manny Pacquiao W PTS 12 Las Vegas
Career: 50 contests, won 48, lost 2.	

Jean-Marc Mormeck

Pointe-A-Pitre, Guadeloupe. *Born* 3 June, 1972

WBA & WBC Cruiserweight Champion. Former Undefeated French L.Heavyweight Champion

Major Amateur Honours: None, but claims 13 wins in 15 fights
Turned Pro: March 1995
Significant Results: Lee Manuel Osie L PTS 4, Alain Simon W PTS 10, Pascual Warusfel W PTS 10, Valery Vikhor W RSC 3, Virgil Hill W RTD 8, Dale Brown W RSC 8, Alexander Gurov W RSC 8

Type/Style: Although a strong, stocky, aggressive pressure fighter with a hard clubbing right hand who just keeps rumbling forward, he is not a devastating puncher

Points of Interest: 6'0" tall. Only took up boxing after being injured at football when 15 and later worked as Security Guard at McDonalds. Although he has had three operations on his right hand, he won the WBA title by beating Virgil Hill in February 2002. Has 21 wins by stoppage or kayo and is now based in the USA with Don King as his promoter

02.04.05	Wayne Braithwaite W PTS 12 Worcester *(WBA Cruiserweight Title Defence. WBC Cruiserweight Title Challenge)*
Career: 33 contests, won 31, lost 2.	

Vicente (El Loco) Mosquera

Puerto Caimito, Panama. *Born* 9 December, 1979
WBA S.Featherweight Champion

Major Amateur Honours: None known, but had 33 fights
Turned Pro: February 1998
Significant Results: Armando Cordova DREW 12 & L PTS 12, Ali Oubaali W PTS 10, Edgar Ilarraza W PTS 12
Type/Style: A skilful boxer and a good tactician who can fight on the inside and on the outside, he is a sharp but not hard puncher
Points of Interest: 5'8" tall. Starting boxing at the age of 16, he became the first Panamanian to win a world title in Madison Square Garden since Roberto Duran in 1972, depite being inactive between April 2000 and February 2003. Has just ten wins inside the distance

28.08.04	Victor Julio W RSC 3 Panama City
01.10.04	Edison Garcia W RSC 8 Panama City
03.12.04	Esteban DeJesus W DIS 9 Panama City
30.04.05	Yodesnan Sornontachai W PTS 12 New York *(WBA S.Featherweight Title Challenge)*
Career: 23 contests, won 21, drew 1, lost 1.	

Omar (Huracan) Narvaez

Trelew, Argentina. *Born* 7 October, 1975
WBO Flyweight Champion

Major Amateur Honours: Won a bronze medal in the 1997 World Championships, a silver in the 1999 World Championships, a gold in the 1999 Pan-American Games and competed in the 1996 and 2000 Olympics
Turned Pro: December 2000
Significant Results: Carlos Montiveros DREW 4, Wellington Vicente W PTS 10, Marcos Obregon W PTS 10, Adonis Rivas W PTS 12, Luis Lazarate W DIS 10, Andrea Sarritzu W PTS 12 & DREW 12, Everardo Morales W RSC 5, Alexander Mahmutov W RSC 10
Type/Style: A stocky and aggressive, southpaw, he has fast hands
Points of Interest: Became the first of the 2000 Olympians to win a version of a world title, having beaten the current WBO super-bantamweight champion, Joan Guzman, in the 1996 Games. Trained by the Cuban, Sarbelio Fuentes, he won the WBO title in only his 12th fight by beating Adonis Rivas in July 2002. Has made six defences and has 13 wins inside the distance

29.10.04	Wellington Vicente Da Silva W RSC 10 Cordoba
10.12.04	Marcos Obregon W CO 5 Cordoba
08.04.05	Wellington Vicente W CO 7 Trelew
Career: 21 contests, won 19, drew 2.	

Yutaka Niida

Kanagawa, Japan. *Born* 2 October, 1978
WBA M.Flyweight Champion. Former Undefeated Japanese M. Flyweight Champion

Major Amateur Honours: None known
Turned Pro: November 1996
Significant Results: Makoto Suzuki W RSC 9, Daisuke Iida DREW 10, Chana Porpaoin W PTS 12, Nohel Arambulet L PTS 12
Type/Style: Aggressive, with good speed and a big right hand punch, but has a suspect chin
Points of Interest: Managed by Mitsunori Seki, who failed in five attempts to win versions of the world featherweight title, he climbed off the floor twice in the first round for his draw with Daisuke Iida. Although surprisingly retiring immediately after winning the WBA title by beating

Chana Porpaoin in August 2001, he returned to action in July 2003, losing to Nohel Arambulet for the WBA title. However, Arambulet failed to make the weight for their return fight in July 2004 and Yutaka won the vacant title after outpointing the Venezuelan

03.07.04	Nohel Arambulet W PTS 12 Tokyo
30.10.04	Juan Landaeta W PTS 12 Tokyo *(WBA M.Flyweight Title Defence)*
16.04.05	Jae-Won Kim W PTS 12 Tokyo *(WBA M.Flyweight Title Defence)*
Career: 22 contests, won 18, drew 3, lost 1.	

Erick Ortiz

Mexico City, Mexico. *Born* 19 May, 1977
WBC L.Flyweight Champion

Major Amateur Honours: None known
Turned Pro: February 1996
Significant Results: Rafael Chavez L RSC 3, Alfredo Virgen W RSC 11, Rafael Orozco W RSC 5, Fred Valdez W RSC 5, Paulino Villalbos W PTS 12, Luis Valdez L RSC 4
Type/Style: A sharp-punching, aggressive boxer, who has had problems with cuts
Points of Interest: 5'2" tall. Starting boxing at the age of 12, he later studied as an account and also practiced karate. Inactive at the end of 2001 after suffering a career threatening eye injury in a mugging, he has won 16 fights by stoppage or kayo. Has lost only one of his last 22 fights and that was on cuts

04.09.04	Wendyl Janiola W TD 5 Tijuana
11.03.05	Jose Antonio Aguirre W RSC 7 Mexico City *(Vacant WBC L.Flyweight Title)*
Career: 29 contests, won 24, drew 1, lost 4.	

Kassim (The Dream) Ouma

Kampala, Uganda. *Born* 12 December, 1978
IBF L.Middleweight Champion

Major Amateur Honours: Qualified for the 1996 Olympics, but Uganda could not afford to send him. He did compete in the 1997 World Military Games, however
Turned Pro: July 1998
Significant Results: Agustin Silva L RSC 1, Alex Bunema W RSC 5, Kuvanych Toygonbaye W PTS 6,

Tony Marshall W PTS 10, Verno Phillips W PTS 10, Michael Lerma W PTS 10, Jason Papillion W RSC 8, Darrell Woods ND11, Carlos Bojorquez W RSC 8, Juan Candelo W RSC 10

Type/Style: Is an all-action, relentlessly aggressive southpaw

Points of Interest: Was kidnapped into the Ugandan army at the age of seven, but defected when competing in the World Military Games in the USA. He then worked as a dishwasher and lived on the streets for a while, even when sparring with Zab Judah. Tested positive for marijuana after stopping Darrell Woods in their 2002 fight and the verdict was changed to no decision. Was then shot in a drive-by shooting later the same year. Trained by the former WBA light-welterweight champion, Johnny Bumphus, he has 13 wins by stoppage or kayo

02.10.04	Verno Phillips W PTS 12 Las Vegas *(IBF L.Middleweight Title Challenge)*
29.01.05	Kofi Jantuah W PTS 12 Atlantic City *(IBF L.Middleweight Title Defence)*
Career: 24 contests, won 21, drew 1, lost 1, no decision 1.	

Lorenzo (Lencho) Parra

Aragua, Venezuela. *Born* 19 August, 1978

WBA Flyweight Champion

Major Amateur Honours: Competed in the 1996 World Junior Championships and claims 268 wins in 278 fights
Turned Pro: March 1999
Significant Results: Edicson Torres W RSC 12, Jose Lopez W CO 11, Edgar Velazquez W PTS 12, Eric Morel W PTS 12, Takefumi Sakata W PTS 12
Type/Style: A clever, stringy little fighter, he is recognised for his excellent movement and a sharp punch
Points of Interest: 5'5" tall with a 66" reach. Trained by Pedro Gamarro, who won a silver medal in the 1976 Olympics, he was fighting ten rounds in only his sixth bout. Has 17 wins by stoppage or kayo. Won the WBA title by beating Eric Morel in December 2003 and has made three defences, all in the Far East. Has 17 wins by stoppage or kayo

09.09.04	Yo-Sam Choi W PTS 12 Seoul *(WBA Flyweight Title Defence)*
03.01.05	Masaki Nakanuma W PTS 12 Tokyo *(WBA Flyweight Title Defence)*
Career: 25 contests, won 25.	

Robbie (The Bomber) Peden

Brisbane, Australia. *Born* 11 November, 1973

IBF S.Featherweight Champion

Major Amateur Honours: Competed in the 1991 and 1993 World Championships and in the 1992 Olympics as a flyweight. A five-time Australian champion, he won a gold medal in the 1994 Commonwealth Games
Turned Pro: December 1996
Significant Results: Carlos Rios W PTS 12, John Brown L PTS 12, Juan Manuel Marquez L RSC 10, Lamon Pearson W RSC 7, Nate Campbell W CO 5
Type/Style: A classy boxer with a reasonable punch and a good technician with a solid chin, he has struggled to make the weight
Points of Interest: 5'8" tall with a 69" reach. His career was held up briefly in 1999 when he was injured by a burglar. Interestingly, he had never fought in Australia as a pro until winning the IBF title and although he was technically 1/4lb over the weight limit for the contest with Nate Campbell, it went ahead as a title fight under local rules. Is self managed and has 14 wins by stoppage or kayo

31.07.04	Armando Cordova W PTS 8 Las Vegas
23.02.05	Nate Campbell W RSC 8 Melbourne *(Vacant IBF S.Featherweight Title)*
Career: 27 contests, won 25, lost 2.	

Luis (The Demolisher) Perez

Managua, Nicaragua. *Born* 6 April, 1978

IBF S.Flyweight Champion

Major Amateur Honours: None known
Turned Pro: November 1996

Significant Results: Leon Salazar W RSC 4, Justo Zuniga W CO 1, Vernie Torres L PTS 12, Moises Castro W PTS 10, Edicson Torres W PTS 12 (twice), Felix Machado W PTS 12
Type/Style: Is a skinny skilful southpaw with a strong jab, but is not a big puncher
Points of Interest: 5'5" tall with a 67" reach. Had only five days notice of the first fight with Felix Machado in January 2003 when he won the IBF title, but showed it had been no fluke in the rematch. Managed by Anna Alvarez, the wife of the former WBA light-flyweight champion, Rosendo Alvarez, he has 15 wins inside the distance. Strangely inactive, Luis has made only one defence in 18 months

30.04.05	Luis Bolano W RSC 6 New York *(IBF S.Flyweight Title Defence)*
Career: 24 contests, won 23, lost 1.	

Muhammad (Rock Breaker) Rachman

Papua, Indonesia. *Born* 23 December, 1972

IBF M.Flyweight Champion. Former Undefeated Indonesian M.Flyweight Champion

Major Amateur Honours: None known
Turned Pro: January 1993
Significant Results: Jin-Ho Kim W PTS 10, Lindi Memani W PTS 12, Patrick Twala W PTS 10, Ernesto Rubillar W PTS 10, Jun Arlos W PTS 10, Noel Tunacao W RSC 2
Type/Style: Is a busy southpaw, but not a puncher
Points of Interest: 5'3" tall with a 59" reach. Gaining his nickname after beating a Filipino boxer known as 'The Rock', he is unbeaten in his last 35 bouts, with 25 wins by stoppage or kayo. Has only fought outside Indonesia four times and lost all four fights

14.09.04	Daniel Reyes W PTS 12 Jakarta *(IBF M.Flyweight Title Challenge)*
05.04.05	Fahlan Sakkriren T Draw 3 Merauke City *(IBF M.Flyweight Title Defence)*
Career: 67 contests, won 56, drew 4, lost 7.	

John Ruiz   Les Clark

John (The Quite Man) Ruiz

Chelsea, USA. *Born* 4 January, 1972
WBA Heavyweight Champion

Major Amateur Honours: Competed in the 1991 World Championships and won a gold medal in the 1991 Olympic Festival, prior to losing in the 1992 Olympic trials
Turned Pro: August 1992
Significant Results: Sergei Kobozev L PTS 10, Julius Francis W CO 4, Danell Nicholson L PTS 12, Boris Powell W PTS 10, David Tua L RSC 1, Tony Tucker W RSC 11, Jerry Ballard W RSC 4, Evander Holyfield L PTS 12, W PTS 12, & DREW 12, Kirk Johnson W DIS 10, Roy Jones L PTS 12,Hasim Rahman W PTS 12,Fres Oquendo W RSC 9
Type/Style: Strong with an awkward forward leaning style, he has a solid jab
Points of Interest: 6'2" tall. Became the first boxer of Puerto Rican origin to win a world heavyweight title when he outpointed Evander Holyfield in March 2001. Made two defences, including a draw with Holyfield, before losing the title to Roy Jones in March 2003. Won the WBA interim title by beating Hasim Rahman in December 2003 and became full champion when Jones moved back down to light-heavyweight. Named after John Kennedy, he has been plagued by hand problems throughout his career. The fight with James Toney was originally declared as a win for Toney, however, Toney later tested

positive for a banned substance and on May 11 the decision was changed to that of no-contest and Ruiz was reinstated as champion. Has 28 wins by stoppage or kayo

13.11.04	Andrew Golota W PTS 12 New York *(WBA Heavyweight Title Defence)*
30.04.05	James Toney L PTS 12 New York *(WBA Heavyweight Title Defence)*

Career: 48 contests, won 41, drew 1, lost 5, no contest 1.

Daniel Santos

San Juan, Puerto Rico. *Born* 10 October, 1975
WBO L. Middleweight Champion. Former Undefeated WBO Welterweight Champion

Major Amateur Honours: Won a bronze medal in the 1992 World Junior Championships, competed in the 1993 World Championship and the 1994 Goodwill Games, won a silver medal in the 1995 Pan-American Games, competed in the 1995 World Championships and was a bronze medallist in the 1996 Olympic Games
Turned Pro: September 1996
Significant Results: Luis Verdugo T DRAW 1, William Ruiz W RSC 3, Ray Lovato W RSC 2, Kofi Jantuah L RSC 5, Ahmed Katajev L PTS 12 & W CO 5, Giovanni Parisi W RSC 4, Neil Sinclair W CO 2, Antonio Margarito NC 1, Yori Boy Campas W RSC 11, Mehrdud Takaloo W PTS 12, Fulgencio Zuniga W PTS 12, Michael Lerma W PTS 12
Type/Style: Although a fast, clever, flashy southpaw, and a heavy left hand puncher, his chin questionable and so is stamina
Points of Interest: 6'0" tall. After losing to David Reid in the Pan-American Games, he went unbeaten in his first 21 fights. Having lost a disputed decision to Ahmed Katajev in his first challenge for the WBO welterweight title, the WBO ordered a rematch, which he won in May 2000. Made three defences of his welterweight title before winning the vacant light-middleweight title, when beating Yori Boy Campas in March 2002, and has made four defences. Has 20 wins inside the distance

11.09.04	Antonio Margarito W TD 9 Hato Rey *(WBO L.Middleweight Title Defence)*

Career: 33 contests, won 29,drew 1,lost 2, no contest 1.

Wladimir Sidorenko

Energodar, Ukraine. *Born* 23 September, 1975
WBA Bantamweight Champion

Major Amateur Honours: Competed in the 1997 and 1999 World Championships and won a silver medal in the 2001 Championships. Won the World Military Championships three times, won a gold medal in the 1998 European Championships and was a quarter-finalist in the 2000 Olympics
Turned Pro: November 2001
Significant Results: Giovanni Andrade, Sergey Tasimov W PTS 8, Moises Castro W PTS 12, Joseph Agbeko W PTS 12
Type/Style: Is a short, sturdy, busy counter-puncher with a tight guard
Points of Interest: 5'4" tall. Starting boxing in 1988, he comes from a boxing family, with his brother also a pro, and had 310 amateur fights before punching for pay. Has only five wins inside the distance

26.10.04	Leo Gamez W PTS 12 Rostock
26.02.05	Julio Zarate W PTS 12 Hamburg *(WBA Bantamweight Title Challenge)*

Career: 17 contests, won 17.

Travis Simms

Norwalk, USA. *Born* 1 May, 1971
Former WBA L.Middleweight Champion

Major Amateur Honours: Won a silver medal in the 1993 National Golden Gloves Championships, a bronze medal in the 1995 US Championships and gold medals in the 1995 and 1996 PAL. Competed in the 1996 Olympic Trials and vied with David Reid for a position on the Olympic team
Turned Pro: February 1998
Significant Results: Kevin Kelly W PTS 8, Antoine Robinson W RSC 8, Alejandro Garcia W CO 5
Type/Style: A southpaw who can

switch, he has fast hands and a solid jab

Points of Interest: From a boxing family, and one of nine children, he has an identical twin brother, Tarvis, who is a pro at middleweight, and Dad was also a pro. Although troubled by hand injuries and tight at the weight, he won the WBA interim title when beating Alejandro Garcia in December 2003 and achieved full recognition as WBA champion when the WBA super champion, Ronnie Wright, relinquished the title in April 2005. However, in late June he was stripped due to contractual problems

02.10.04	Bronco McKart W PTS 12 New York
	(WBA Interim L.Middleweight Title Defence)
Career: 24 contests, won 24.	

Ratanchai Sowvoraphin

Korat, Thailand. *Born* 1 November, 1976
WBO Bantamweight Champion.
Former Thai L.Flyweight Champion.
Former Undefeated Thai S.Flyweight Champion

Major Amateur Honours: None known
Turned Pro: April 1992
Significant Results: Abdi Pohan W PTS 12 & L TD 4, Somsak Singchachawan W PTS 10, Mark Johnson L PTS 12, Gerry Penalosa L RSC 6, Yoddamrong Sithyodthong L PTS 10, Danny Romero W PTS 10, Tim Austin L PTS 12, Chris John L PTS 10, Cruz Carbajal W PTS 12
Type/Style: A southpaw and a counter puncher, he is tough but limited
Points of Interest: 5'5" tall. Real name is Chaiya Phothong. His younger brother, Ratanapol, was IBF mini-flyweight champion and made 20 title defences. Ratanchai, who won the Thai light-flyweight title in his sixth fight, lost to Mark Johnson for the vacant IBF super-flyweight title in 1999 and Tim Austin for the IBF bantamweight title in 2001 before beating Cruz Carbajal in May 2004 to become the first Thai fighter to win a WBO title in the first WBO title fight held in Thailand. Has not yet defended the title

16.07.04	Rashid Ally W CO 2 Tachaom
25.08.04	Rajabu Maojabu W CO 1 Buriram
04.10.04	Lontar Simanjant W CO 4 Korat
19.11.04	Joel Bauya W PTS 6 Chacheongsao
01.02.05	Takhir Ibragimov W RSC 5 Supanburi
24.03.05	Joven Jorda W PTS 6 Phrae
19.04.05	Ayon Naranjo W PTS 6 Bangkok
Career: 71 contests, won 63, lost 8.	

Katsunari Takayama

Osaka, Japan. *Born* 12 May, 1983
WBC M.Flyweight Champion

Major Amateur Honours: None known
Turned Pro: October 2000
Significant Results: Daisaku Kashiwagi W CO 4, Songkram Porpaoin W PTS 8, Masato Hatakeyama L RSC 9
Type/Style: Short and elusive, he is a classy boxer with fast footwork and fast hands
Points of Interest: 5'2" tall. Lost to Masato Hatakeyama for the Japanese light-flyweight title in April 2003 and then moved down to mini-flyweight. Wins over Songkram Porpaoin and Elmer Gejon were both majority verdicts and seven of his victories have come inside the distance

08.08.04	Elmer Gejon W PTS 10 Osaka
08.12.04	Namchai Taksinisan W CO 3 Osaka
04.04.05	Isaac Bustos W PTS 12 Osaka
	(WBC M. Flyweight Title Challenge)
Career: 16 contests, won 15, lost 1.	

Fabrice Tiozzo

Saint Denis, France. *Born* 8 May, 1969
WBA L.Heavyweight Champion.
Former WBA Cruiserweight Champion. Former Undefeated WBC L.Heavyweight Champion. Former Undefeated European & French L.Heavyweight Champion

Major Amateur Honours: None known
Turned Pro: October 1988
Significant Results: Michael Nunn W RSC 11, Reggie Johnson W PTS 12, Mike McCallum DREW 12 & W PTS 12, Iran Barkley W RSC 9, Roy Jones L PTS 12, Montell Griffin L PTS 12, Ramon Garbey W PTS 10, Evander Holyfield W RSC 9, Jason Robinson W CO 7, Vassily Jirov W PTS 12
Type/Style: Has an upright style and is strong and skilful with a solid chin

Points of Interest: 6'1" tall. Another from a boxing family, his brother, Christophe, was a WBA super-middleweight champion. Fabrice, who made only two defences of his WBC light-heavyweight title before weight problems forced him to move up to cruiserweight, won the WBA title by beating Nate Miller in 1997 and made four defences before losing to Virgil Hill in December 2000. Had only one fight in 27 months before returning as a light-heavyweight in March 2003 and won the WBA title by coming off the floor to decision Silvio Branco in March 2004. Has 31 wins inside the distance and when beating Dariusz Michalczewski he gained revenge for a loss suffered when they were amateurs

26.02.05	Dariusz Michalczewski W RSC 6 Hamburg
	(WBA L.Heavyweight Title Defence)
Career: 49 contests, won 47, lost 2.	

James (Lights Out) Toney

Grand Rapids, Michigan, USA. *Born* 24 August, 1968
Former WBA Heavyweight Champion. Former Undefeated IBF Cruiserweight Champion. Former Undefeated IBF Middleweight champion. Former IBF S.Middleweight Champion

Major Amateur Honours: None known
Turned Pro: October 1988
Significant Results: Michael Nunn W RSC 11, Reggie Johnson W PTS 12, Mike McCallum DREW 12 & W PTS 12, Iran Barkley W RSC 9, Roy Jones L PTS 12, Montell Griffin L PTS 12, Ramon Garbey W PTS 10, Evander Holyfield W RSC 9, Jason Robinson W CO 7, Vassily Jirov W PTS 12
Type/Style: Has a lazy, laid back style and often does just enough to win, often relying on an excellent defence, a great chin and his punching ability with either hand
Points of Interest: Having a dad who was a pro in the 1940s, he first won the IBF middleweight title in 1991 by beating Michael Nunn and then made six defences. He then won the IBF super-middleweight title in 1993 when

stopping Iran Barkley and made four defences. In April 2003, he won the IBF cruiserweight title, but did not defend the title and moved up to heavy to defeat John Ruiz for the WBA crown. However, his drug test showed positive for steroids and the verdict was later changed to a no decision and he was stripped of the title. Has 43 wins inside the distance and has never been stopped

23.09.04	Rydell Booker W PTS 12 Temecula
30.04.05	John Ruiz W PTS 12 New York (WBA Heavyweight Title Challenge)
Career: 75 contests, won 68, drew 2, lost 4, o decision 1.	

Israel (Magnifico) Vazquez

Mexico City, Mexico. *Born* 25 December, 1977
IBF S.Bantamweight Champion

Major Amateur Honours: None known, although he claims 58 wins
Turned Pro: March 1995
Significant Results: Marcos Licona L PTS 12, Eddy Saenz W CO 3, Ever Beleno W CO 2, Osvaldo Guerrero W PTS 10, Oscar Larios L CO 12, Jorge Julio W RSC 10, Trinidad Mendoza W CO 7, Jose Luis Valbuena W RSC 12
Type/Style: Is a quick, but upright boxer with a high, tight guard and a hard punch
Points of Interest: 5'6" tall with a 66" reach. Gave up karate to concentrate on boxing, his inspiration being the great Ruben Olivares. Lost to Oscar Larios for the vacant WBC interim super-bantamweight title in May 2002, but kept going to win the vacant IBF title in March 2004 by beating Jose Luis Valbuena and has made two defences. Has 28 wins inside the distance

28.12.04	Art Simonyan W RSC 5 El Cajon (*IBF S.Bantamweight Title Defence*)
31.05.05	Armando Guerrero W PTS 12 Lynwood (*IBF S.Bantamweight Title Defence*)
Career: 41 contests, won 38, lost 3.	

Roberto (La Arana) Vasquez

Panama City, Panama. *Born* 26 May, 1983

WBA L.Flyweight Champion

Major Amateur Honours: Was the Panamanian junior champion in 1998 and the senior champion in 2000
Turned Pro: March 2001
Significant Results: Eduardo Marquez W RSC 2, Luis Doria W RSC 7, Jose Garcia W RSC 11
Type/Style: Is a skinny, slick southpaw who is a good body puncher
Points of Interest: 5'4" tall with a 72" reach. With a nickname meaning 'Spiderman', he was voted the Panamanian Boxer of the Year in 2004. Started boxing at the age of nine, having been inspired to take up the sport by his idol the former WBC light-flyweight champion, Hilario Zapata, he has two elder brothers who also fought as pros. Lost his first pro fight, but has won all 19 since, including 16 inside the distance

16.07.04	Edgar Velasquez W CO 5 Panama City
01.10.04	Freddy Beleno W PTS 12 Panama City
11.12.04	Farid Cassiani W RSC 1 Panama City
29.04.05	Beibis Mendoza W RSC 10 Panama City (*Vacant WBA L.Flyweight Title*)
Career: 20 contests, won 19, lost 1.	

Pongsaklek Wonjongkam

Nakhornatchaseema, Thailand. *Born* 11 August, 1977
WBC Flyweight Champion

Major Amateur Honours: None
Turned Pro: December 1994
Significant Results: Randy Mangubat W CO 3, Mzukisi Sikali W RSC 1, Juanito Rubillar W PTS 10, Malcolm Tunacao W RSC 1, Daisuke Naito W CO 1, Jesus Martinez W PTS 12, Hidenobu Honda W PTS 12, Hussein Hussein W PTS 12, Masaki Nakanuma W PTS 12
Type/Style: A tough, aggressive pressure fighter, he is also a southpaw with a wicked right hook
Points of Interest: 5'1" tall. Real name is Dongskorn Wonjongkan. Pongsaklek's last loss was in December 1995 and he is unbeaten in his last 47 bouts, having also boxed under the names of Nakornthong Parkview and Sithkanongsak. Won the

WBC title by halting Malcolm Tunacao in March 2001 and has made 11 defences. With 30 wins by stoppage or kayo, his quickest victory came when he put Daisuke Naito away in just 34 seconds

15.07.04	Luis Angel Martinez W RSC 5 Khonkaen (*WBC Flyweight Title Defence*)
29.01.05	Noriyuki Komatsu W RSC 5 Osaka (*WBC Flyweight Title Defence*)
29.04.05	Daniel Diolan W RSC 3 Petchaburi
Career: 58 contests, won 56, lost 2.	

Julio (La Sombra) Zarate

Ixtapa, Mexico. *Born* 23 August, 1975
Former WBA Bantamweight Champion. Former Undefeated Mexican Bantamweight Champion

Major Amateur Honours: None known, but claims just two losses in 48 fights
Turned Pro: March 1997
Significant Results: Erik Lopez W RSC 10, Francisco Mateos W CO 7, Oscar Arciniega W RSC 5, Oscar Andrade W PTS 10, Hideki Todaka W PTS 12
Type/Style: Orthodox and clever, but limited
Points of Interest: 5'7" tall. With a nickname meaning 'The Shadow', he starting boxing at the age of 13, following in the footsteps of his uncle, the former WBC bantamweight champion, Rafael Herrera. Inactive for over a year in 2001/ 2002 due to contract problems, Julio won recognition as interim WBA champion by beating Hideki Todaka in March 2004 and was recognised as full champion when Johnny Bredahl retired. Having had Mahyar Monshipour on the floor before losing, 15 of his 21 wins have come inside the distance

26.02.05	Wladimir Sidorenko L PTS 12 Hamburg (*WBA Bantamweight Title Defence*)
25.06.05	Mahyar Monshipour L RTD 8 Poitiers (*WBA S.Bantamweight Title Challenge*)
Career: 26 contests, won 21, drew 1, lost 4.	

World Title Bouts, 2004-2005

by Bob Yalen

All of last season's title bouts for the IBF, WBA, WBC and WBO are shown in date order within their weight division and give the boxers' respective weights, along with the scorecard if going to a decision. There is also a short summary of every bout that involved a British contestant, and British officials, where applicable, are listed. Yet again there were no WORLD TITLE FIGHTS as such – even if you allow for Zab Judah (Welter) and Bernard Hopkins (Middle), who hold three and four of the four major titles, respectively – just a proliferation of champions recognised by the above four commissions and spread over 17 weight divisions. Below the premier league, come other commissions such as the WBU, IBO, IBC and WBF, etc, etc, which would devalue the world championships even further if one recognised their champions as being the best in the world. Right now, the WBA have decided to continue recognising their champions who move on to claim other commissions' titles as super champions – despite vacating the title and creating a new champion, who, for our purposes, will be classified as a secondary champion – which if taken up in general could eventually lead to the best man at his weight being recognised universally as a world champion if the fights can be made.

M.Flyweight

IBF

14 September   Daniel Reyes 7.7 (Colombia) L PTS 12 Muhammad Rachman 7.7 (Indonesia), Jakarta, Indonesia. Scorecards: 116-113, 113-115, 112-116.

5 April Muhammad Rachman 7.5^1/$_2$ (Indonesia) T.DRAW 3 Fahlan Sakkriren 7.7 (Thailand), Merauke City, Papua, Indonesia. Scorecards: 20-18, 20-18, 19-19.

WBA

30 October   Yutaka Niida 7.6^3/$_4$ (Japan) W PTS 12 Juan Landaeta 7.6^3/$_4$ (Venezuela), Tokyo, Japan. Scorecards: 115-113, 113-115, 115-114. Earlier, on 3 July, in Tokyo, Japan, Niida (7.6^3/$_4$) was awarded the title after outpointing the former champion, Nohel Arambulet (7.7^3/$_4$), who had failed to make 105lbs at the weigh-in the previous day

16 April   Yutaka Niida 7.7 (Japan) W PTS 12 Jae-Won Kim 7.7 (South Korea), Tokyo, Japan. Scorecards: 117-112, 118-110, 119-111.

WBC

18 December   Eagle Akakura 7.7 (Thailand) L RSC 4 Isaac Bustos 7.6^3/$_4$ (Mexico), Tokyo, Japan.

4 April   Isaac Bustos 7.7 (Mexico) L PTS 12 Katsunari Takayama 7.7 (Japan), Osaka, Japan. Scorecards: 111-117, 112-117, 113-115.

WBO

31 July   Ivan Calderon 7.6^1/$_2$ (Puerto Rico) W PTS 12 Roberto Leyva 7.7 (Mexico), Las Vegas, Nevada, USA. Scorecards: 116-112, 116-112, 116-112.

27 November   Ivan Calderon 7.6^1/$_2$ (Puerto Rico) W PTS 12 Carlos Fajardo 7.7 (Nicaragua), Las Vegas, Nevada, USA. Scorecards: 120-107, 118-109, 119-108.

30 April   Ivan Calderon 7.7 (Puerto Rico) W RSC 8 Noel Tunacao 7.7 (Philippines), Hato Rey, Puerto Rico.

25 June   Ivan Calderon 7.6 (Puerto Rico) W PTS 12 Gerardo Verde 7.5 (Mexico), Atlantic City, New Jersey, USA. Scorecards: 117-111, 117-111, 115-113.

L.Flyweight

IBF

14 May   Jose Victor Burgos 7.9 (Mexico) L PTS 12 Will Grigsby 7.8 (USA), Las Vegas, Nevada, USA. Scorecards: 112-116, 110-118, 111-117.

WBA

29 April   Roberto Vasquez 7.10 (Panama) W RSC 10 Beibis Mendoza 7.10 (Colombia), Panama City, Panama. Earlier, on 2 October, in NYC, New York, Rosendo Alvarez (Nicaragua) forfeited title on the scales when he came in just under eight stone for a defence against Mendoza, the reigning interim champion. Despite that, the fight went ahead with Alvarez winning on points over 12 rounds, with Mendoza promised a crack at the vacant title against Vasquez.

WBC

4 September   Jorge Arce 7.9^3/$_4$ (Mexico) W PTS 12 Juanito Rubillar 7.9 (Philippines), Tijuana, Mexico. Scorecards: 115-112, 119-108, 115-112.

18 December   Jorge Arce 7.10 (Mexico) W RSC 3 Juan Centeno 7.10 (Nicaragua), Culiacan, Sinaloa, Mexico. Arce vacated the title in January to move up a weight division.

11 March   Erick Ortiz 7.7^3/$_4$ (Mexico) W RSC 7 Jose Antonio Aguirre 7.8^1/$_4$ (Mexico), Mexico City, Mexico

WBO

30 July   Nelson Dieppa 7.10 (Puerto Rico) W PTS 12 Ulises Solis 7.9^3/$_4$ (Mexico), Louisville, Kentucky, USA. Scorecards: 114-114, 120-108, 120-108.

29 January   Nelson Dieppa 7.10 (Puerto Rico) W CO 11 Alex Sanchez 7.10 (Puerto Rico), Bayamon, Puerto Rico.

30 April   Nelson Dieppa 7.10 (Puerto Rico) L TD 10 Hugo Cazares 7.9^3/$_4$ (Mexico), Hato Rey, Puerto Rico. Scorecards: 94-96, 94-96, 92-98.

Flyweight

IBF

16 December   Irene Pacheco 8.0 (Colombia) L RSC 11

Vic Darchinyan 7.13½ (Australia), Hollywood, Florida, USA.
27 March   Vic Darchinyan 8.0 (Australia) W RSC 8 Mzukisi Sikali 7.13¾ (South Africa), Sydney, Australia.

WBA
9 September   Lorenzo Parra 8.0 (Venezuela) W PTS 12 Yo-Sam Choi 8.0 (South Korea), Seoul, South Korea. Scorecards: 116-113, 117-111, 116-112.
3 January   Lorenzo Parra 7.13¼ (Venezuela) W PTS 12 Masaki Nakanuma 7.13½ (Japan), Tokyo, Japan. Scorecards: 116-112, 116-112, 115-113.

WBC
15 July   Pongsaklek Wonjongkam 8.0 (Thailand) W RSC 5 Luis Angel Martinez 8.0 (Mexico), Khonkaen, Thailand.
29 January   Pongsaklek Wonjongkam 8.0 (Thailand) W RSC 5 Noriyuki Komatsu 8.0 (Japan), Osaka, Japan.

WBO
Omar Narvaez (Argentina), although fighting three times during the past 12 months, was not called upon to make a title defence.

S.Flyweight
IBF
30 April   Luis Perez 8.3 (Nicaragua) W RSC 6 Luis Bolano 8.1¼ (Colombia), NYC, New York, USA.

WBA
3 December   Alexander Munoz 8.3 (Venezuela) L PTS 12 Martin Castillo 8.3 (Mexico), Laredo, Texas, USA. Scorecards: 109-117, 110-116, 109-117.
19 March   Martin Castillo 8.3 (Mexico) W PTS 12 Eric Morel 8.3 (USA), Las Vegas, Nevada, USA. Scorecards: 119-109, 119-109, 119-109.
26 June   Martin Castillo 8.2½ (Mexico) W PTS 12 Hideyasu Ishihara 8.3 (Japan), Nagoya, Japan. Scorecards: 116-112, 116-111, 116-111.

WBC
20 September   Katsushige Kawashima 8.3 (Japan) W PTS 12 Raul Juarez 8.2¼ (Mexico), Yokohama, Japan. Scorecards: 114-110, 113-111, 117-107.
3 January   Katsushige Kawashima 8.3 (Japan) W PTS 12 Jose Navarro 8.2½ (USA), Tokyo, Japan. Scorecards: 109-120, 115-114, 115-113. Referee: Mark Green.

WBO
25 September   Mark Johnson 8.3 (USA) L CO 8 Ivan Hernandez 8.3 (Mexico), Memphis, Tennessee, USA.
9 April   Ivan Hernandez 8.1½ (Mexico) L RSC 7 Fernando Montiel 8.3 (Mexico), El Paso, Texas, USA.

Bantamweight
IBF
31 July   Rafael Marquez 8.6 (Mexico) W CO 3 Heriberto Ruiz 8.6 (Mexico), Las Vegas, Nevada, USA.

27 November   Rafael Marquez 8.6 (Mexico) W RTD 8 Mauricio Pastrana 8.5 (Colombia), Las Vegas, Nevada, USA.
28 May   Rafael Marquez 8.4½ (Mexico) W PTS 12 Ricardo Vargas 8.6 (Mexico), Los Angeles, California, USA. Scorecards: 118-109, 116-111, 116-111.

WBA
26 February   Julio Zarate 8.6 (Mexico) L PTS 12 Wladimir Sidorenko 8.5¼ (Ukraine), Hamburg, Germany. Scorecards: 114-116, 112-117, 111-118. Zarate, the interim titleholder, had been promoted to champion on Johnny Bredahl's retirement in October.

WBC
11 September   Veeraphol Sahaprom 8.6 (Thailand) W PTS 12 Cecilio Santos 8.5¼ (Mexico), Chainart Province, Thailand. Scorecards: 118-110, 119-109, 117-111.
16 April   Veeraphol Sahaprom 8.6 (Thailand) L PTS 12 Hozumi Hasegawa 8.6 (Japan), Tokyo, Japan. Scorecards: 113-115, 113-115, 112-116.

WBO
Ratanchai Sowvoraphin (Thailand), despite boxing seven times during the period, was not called upon to make a defence.

S.Bantamweight
IBF
28 December   Israel Vazquez 8.9 (Mexico) W RSC 5 Art Simonyan 8.9½ (Armenia), El Cajon, California, USA.
31 May   Israel Vazquez 8.9½ (Mexico) W PTS 12 Armando Guerrero 8.10 (Mexico), Lynwood, Illinois, USA. Scorecards: 116-112, 116-112, 116-112.

WBA
8 November   Mahyar Monshipour 8.9¼ France) W RSC 6 Yoddamrong Sithyodthong 8.9¾ (Thailand), Paris, France.
29 April   Mahyar Monshipour 8.9 (France) W RSC 6 Shigeru Nakazato 8.9 (Japan), Marseille, France.
25 June   Mahyar Monshipour 8.9¼ (France) W RTD 8 Julio Zarate 8.9¼ (Mexico), Poitiers, France.

WBC
27 November   Oscar Larios 8.9 (Mexico) W PTS 12 Nedal Hussein 8.10 (Australia), Las Vegas, Nevada, USA. Scorecards: 118-110, 119-109, 120-108.
10 February   Oscar Larios 8.9¾ (Mexico) W PTS 12 Wayne McCullough 8.9 (Ireland), Lemoore, California, USA. Scorecards: 118-110, 118-110, 116-112.

WBO
22 April   Joan Guzman 8.9 (Dominican Republic) W PTS 12 Fernando Beltran 8.9 (Mexico), Hidalgo, Texas, USA. Scorecards: 115-113, 116-112, 117-111.

Featherweight
IBF/WBA
18 September   Juan Manuel Marquez 9.0 (Mexico) W

PTS 12 Orlando Salido 9.0 (Mexico), Las Vegas, Nevada, USA. Scorecards: 118-110, 117-111, 117-111. On 3 December, in Borneo, Indonesia, Chris John (Indonesia) retained the WBA secondary title on a fourth-round technical draw against Jose Rojas (Venezuela). John again successfully defended the WBA secondary title in Jakarta when outpointing Derrick Gainer (USA) over 12 rounds on 22 April.

7 May Juan Manuel Marquez 8.13 (Mexico) W PTS 12 Victor Polo 9.0 (Colombia), Las Vegas, Nevada, USA. Scorecards: 119-108, 118-109, 120-107.

WBC

24 July In-Jin Chi 9.0 (South Korea) W RSC 10 Eiichi Sugama 9.0 (Japan), Seoul, South Korea.

30 January In-Jin Chi 9.0 (South Korea) W PTS 12 Tommy Browne 8.13¾ (Australia), Seoul, South Korea. Scorecards: 120-107, 119-108, 117-112.

WBO

29 October Scott Harrison 8.13¾ (Scotland) W CO 1 Samuel Kebede 8.12 (Ethiopia), Braehead Arena, Glasgow, Scotland. Referee: Mickey Vann. Judge: Dave Parris. Lasting just 59 seconds, this was a total mismatch and, thus, bad for boxing. The fight had barely begun when the challenger was decked from a right to the temple and when he got up he looked unsteady. When a short left hook from Harrison put Kebede down again, despite the latter getting up, it was obvious that the contest was almost over and it came as no surprise when the referee called it off moments later.

28 January Scott Harrison 8.13¾ (Scotland) DREW 12 Victor Polo 8.13¾ (Colombia), Braehead Arena, Glasgow, Scotland. Scorecards: 115-113, John Coyle 113-116, 114-114. Denied from winning a major title for the fourth time by a verdict that hardly favoured him, at the finish the Colombian southpaw challenger had given it everything and more. Although he made a reasonable start, Harrison, cut and swollen on his left eye from a raking left hand in the sixth, was up against it from then on as Polo gained in confidence and as the rounds went by the challenger began to take over, especially after his body punches began to have an effect on the champion. However, it wasn't to be and Harrison survived to fight another day.

3 June Scott Harrison 9.0 (Scotland) W CO 4 Michael Brodie 9.0 (England), MEN Arena, Manchester, England. Referee: Mickey Vann. Judges: Dave Parris, John Coyle, Roy Francis. Putting his last defence behind him, Harrison settled down quickly and following a short skirmish in the third round realised that body punches were the answer. From then on there was only going to be one winner and it wasn't going to be Brodie, despite him having done well up until then. Coming out fast in the fourth and giving the challenger no chance to find any rhythm, Harrison set up a concerted body attack which eventually put Brodie down on one knee and saw him counted out in the act of rising after 46 seconds.

S.Featherweight

IBF

31 July Carlos Hernandez 9.4 (USA) L PTS 12 Erik Morales 9.4 (Mexico), Las Vegas, Nevada, USA. Scorecards: 113-115, 109-119, 109-119. In late September, Morales forfeited the title when he failed to ask for an exception to defend against Marco Antonio Barrera on 27 November, the fight going ahead for the WBC crown only.

23 February Robbie Peden 9.4 (Australia) W RSC 8 Nate Campbell 9.3½ (USA), Melbourne, Australia.

WBA

7 August Yodesnan Sornontachai 9.4 (Thailand) W PTS 12 Steve Forbes 9.4 (USA), Mashantucket, Connecticut, USA. Scorecards: 117-111, 117-111, 117-111.

30 April Yodesnan Sornontachai 9.3½ (Thailand) L PTS 12 Vicente Mosquera 9.3 (Panama), NYC, New York, USA. Scorecards: 112-115, 108-118, 111-116.

WBC

31 July Erik Morales 9.4 (Mexico) W PTS 12 Carlos Hernandez 9.4 (USA), Las Vegas, Nevada, USA. Scorecards: 115-113, 119-109, 119-109.

27 November Erik Morales 9.4 (Mexico) L PTS 12 Marco Antonio Barrera 9.3½ (Mexico), Las Vegas, Nevada, USA. Scorecards: 113-115, 114-114, Larry O'Connell 114-115.

9 April Marco Antonio Barrera 9.4 (Mexico) W RSC 2 Mzonke Fana 9.2¾ (South Africa), El Paso, Texas, USA.

WBO

In a fight to decide the interim title on 15 July, in Dallas, Texas, Mike Anchondo (USA) outpointed Julio Pablo Chacon (Argentina) over 12 rounds, before being upgraded to full championship status when Diego Corrales vacated the title on winning the WBO lightweight crown on 7 August. Later, on 8 April, in Miami, Florida, Anchondo (9.8½) failed to make the weight for a defence against the Argentinian, Jorge Barrios (9.2½), who was awarded the title following a fourth-round stoppage win after the fight went ahead.

Lightweight

IBF

17 June Leavander Johnson 9.8¼ (USA) W RSC 7 Stefano Zoff 9.8¼ (Italy), Milan, Italy. Contested for the vacant title after Julio Diaz (Mexico) handed in his belt in February to challenge Jose Luis Castillo for the WBC crown in favour of making a defence against Johnson for less money.

WBA

17 July Lakva Sim 9.9 (Mongolia) L PTS 12 Juan Diaz 9.8¾ (USA), Houston, Texas, USA. Scorecards: 110-118, 112-116, 111-118.

4 November Juan Diaz 9.9 (USA) W PTS 12 Julien Lorcy 9.7¾ (France), San Antonio, Texas, USA. Scorecards: 119-109, 118-110, 118-110.

21 January   Juan Diaz 9.8$^{1}/_{2}$ (USA) W RSC 9 Billy Irwin 9.7$^{1}/_{2}$ (Canada), Houston, Texas, USA.

WBC

4 December   Jose Luis Castillo 9.7$^{1}/_{2}$ (Mexico) W PTS 12 Joel Casamayor 9.9 (Cuba), Las Vegas, Nevada, USA. Scorecards: 116-112, 113-115, 117-111.

5 March   Jose Luis Castillo 9.9 (Mexico) W RSC 10 Julio Diaz 9.8$^{1}/_{2}$ (Mexico), Las Vegas, Nevada, USA.

7 May   Jose Luis Castillo 9.9 (Mexico) L RSC 10 Diego Corrales 9.9 (USA), Las Vegas, Nevada, USA.

WBO

7 August   Acelino Freitas 9.8$^{1}/_{2}$ (Brazil) L RSC 10 Diego Corrales 9.9 (USA), Mashantucket, Connecticut, USA.

7 May   Diego Corrales 9.9 (USA) W RSC 10 Jose Luis Castillo 9.9 (Mexico), Las Vegas, Nevada, USA.

L.Welterweight

IBF

6 November   Kostya Tszyu 10.0 (Russia) W RSC 3 Sharmba Mitchell 10.0 (USA), Phoenix, Arizona, USA.

4 June   Kostya Tszyu 10.0 (Russia) L RTD 11 Ricky Hatton 10.0 (England), MEN Arena, Manchester, England. Referee: Dave Parris. In one of the great British fight nights, Hatton forced the once great champion to retire on his stool at the end of the 11th, having beaten him to a standstill and leaving him with nothing in the tank. It was a sad end to Tszyu's reign, but the challenger had taken everything that was thrown at him before coming on like a train to control the last few rounds and, ultimately, destroy whatever chances remained for the champion. He had outboxed and outpunched his rival, shown many of the qualities that great fighters need and had achieved his dream of becoming a champion by fighting the best.

WBA

23 October   Vivian Harris 9.13$^{3}/_{4}$ (Guyana) W RSC 11 Oktay Urkal 9.13 (Germany), Berlin, Germany.

25 June   Vivian Harris 9.13 (Guyana) L CO 7 Carlos Maussa 9.13 (Colombia), Atlantic City, New Jersey, USA. After Kostya Tszyu (Russia) forfeited the title in June 2004, the secondary champion, Harris, was given full championship status.

WBC

24 July   Arturo Gatti 9.13$^{1}/_{4}$ (Canada) W CO 2 Leonardo Dorin 9.13 (Romania), Atlantic City, New Jersey, USA. Earlier, following Gatti's win over Italy's Gianluca Branco (w pts 12 in Atlantic City on 24 January 2004) it was clear that the WBC's 'Emeritus' status given to Kostya Tszyu in August 2003 was just what it implied and should be seen as an honorary title only.

29 January   Arturo Gatti 10.0 (Canada) W CO 5 James Leija 10.0 (USA), Atlantic City, New Jersey, USA.

25 June   Arturo Gatti 10.0 (Canada) L RTD 6 Floyd Mayweather 9.13 (USA), Atlantic City, New Jersey, USA. After losing to Ricky Hatton for the IBF belt, Kostya Tszyu

was automatically deprived of his WBC 'Emeritus' title and Gatti, the 'secondary' champion, who had made successful defences during the period in Atlantic City against Leonard Dorin (w co 2 on 24 July) and James Leija (w co 5 on 29 January) was handed full title status on 5 June.

WBO

11 September   Miguel Cotto 9.13 (Puerto Rico) W RSC 6 Kelson Pinto 10.0 (Brazil), Hato Rey, Puerto Rico. Contested for the vacant title following Zab Judah's decision to hand back his belt on beating Rafael Pineda for the WBO Inter-Continental crown on 15 May 2004.

11 December   Miguel Cotto 10.0 (Puerto Rico) W RSC 6 Randall Bailey 9.13$^{1}/_{2}$ (USA), Las Vegas, Nevada, USA.

26 February   Miguel Cotto 10.0 (Puerto Rico) W RSC 5 DeMarcus Corley 9.11 (USA), Bayamon, Puerto Rico.

11 June   Miguel Cotto 9.10$^{3}/_{4}$ (Puerto Rico) W RSC 9 Mohammad Abdullaev 9.10$^{3}/_{4}$ (Uzbekhistan), NYC, New York, USA.

Welterweight

IBF/WBA/WBC

4 September   Cory Spinks 10.7 (USA) W PTS 12 Miguel Angel Gonzalez 10.6$^{1}/_{2}$ (Mexico), Las Vegas, Nevada, USA. Scorecards: 118-109, 118-109, 118-109.

5 February   Cory Spinks 10.7 (USA) L RSC 9 Zab Judah 10.6 (USA), St Louis, Missouri, USA.

14 May   Zab Judah 10.6$^{1}/_{2}$ (USA) W RSC 3 Cosme Rivera 10.7 (Mexico), Las Vegas, Nevada, USA. On 2 April, in Worcester, Massachusetts, Jose Antonio Rivera (Puerto Rico) lost the WBA secondary title to Luis Collazo (USA) when he was outpointed over 12 rounds.

WBO

18 February   Antonio Margarito 10.7 (Mexico) W RSC 10 Sebastian Lujan 10.6 (Argentina), Atlantic City, New Jersey, USA. Earlier, on 17 July, in Houston, Texas, Kermit Cintron (USA) stopped Teddy Reid (USA), in the eighth round of a contest to decide the vacant interim title.

23 April   Antonio Margarito 10.7 (Mexico) W RSC 5 Kermit Cintron (USA), Las Vegas, Nevada, USA.

L.Middleweight

IBF

2 October   Verno Phillips 10.12$^{1}/_{2}$ (USA) L PTS 12 Kassim Ouma 10.12 (Uganda), Las Vegas, Nevada, USA. Scorecards: 113-114, 113-114, 110-117.

29 January   Kassim Ouma 10.12 (Uganda) W PTS 12 Kofi Jantuah 10.13 (Ghana), Atlantic City, New Jersey, USA. Scorecards: 117-111, 116-112, 118-110.

WBA

20 November   Ronald Wright 11.0 (USA) W PTS 12 Shane Mosley 11.0 (USA), Las Vegas, Nevada, USA. Scorecards: 115-113, 114-114, 115-113. Wright forfeited the title in April after signing to meet Felix Trinidad in an official WBC middleweight eliminator on 14 May and Travis Simms, the interim champion was handed the belt, having earlier made a successful defence against Bronco McKart (W PTS 12) on 2 October in NYC, New York. The vacant interim title was then contested by Rhoshi Wells (USA) and the Mexican, Alejandro Garcia, in Chicago, Illinois on 21 May, being won by the latter on a ninth-round stoppage. When Simms was stripped by the WBA in late June, due to a contractual problem, Garcia was awarded the title.

WBC

20 November Ronald Wright 11.0 (USA) W PTS 12 Shane Mosley 11.0 (USA), Las Vegas, Nevada, USA. Scorecards: 115-113, 114-114, 115-113. Having decided to move up a weight, Wright relinquished the title in April and the interim titleholder, Javier Castillejo (Spain) was accorded full championship status despite being inactive for a long period. However, having signed up for a fight against Fernando Vargas instead of making required defence against Ricardo Mayorga he was stripped at the end of May.

WBO

11 September Daniel Santos 11.0 (Puerto Rico) W TD 9 Antonio Margarito 10.13 (Mexico), Hato Rey, Puerto Rico. Scorecards: 85-86, 86-85, 87-84.

Middleweight
IBF/WBA/WBC

18 September Bernard Hopkins 11.2 (USA) W CO 9 Oscar de la Hoya 11.1 (USA), Las Vegas, Nevada, USA. De la Hoya lost his WBO crown on the result

19 February Bernard Hopkins 11.5^1/$_2$ (USA) W PTS 12 Howard Eastman 11.5^1/$_2$ (England), Los Angeles, California, USA. Scorecards: 119-110, 117-111, 116-112. Unable to find the answer to the ageless champion's ability to control a fight, Eastman was beaten by a fairly substantial points margin, never having really shown. It was a case of Hopkins having just too much of everything and although Eastman took the fight to his rival he never forced home any attack, which might have left him open to the counters. With Hopkins picking his punches before moving out of range as the challenger predictably stalked him, the contest was never exciting and although Eastman was never embarrassed it appeared to be a bridge too far for him.

WBO

18 September Oscar de la Hoya 11.1 (USA) L CO 9 Bernard Hopkins 11.2 (USA), Las Vegas, Nevada, USA.

S.Middleweight
IBF

2 October Jeff Lacey 11.13 (USA) W RSC 8 Syd Vanderpool 12.0 (Canada), Las Vegas, Nevada, USA. Contested for the vacant title after Sven Ottke (Germany) retired in March 2004.

4 December Jeff Lacey 12.0 (USA) W PTS 12 Omar

Sheika 11.12 (USA), Las Vegas, Nevada, USA. Scorecards: 115-113, 117-111, 115-113.

5 March Jeff Lacey 11.13 (USA) W RSC 7 Rubin Williams 11.13 (USA), Las Vegas, Nevada, USA.

WBA

12 November Manny Siaca 12.0 (Puerto Rico) L RTD 7 Mikkel Kessler 12.0 (Denmark), Copenhagen, Denmark.

8 June Mikkel Kessler 11.13^1/$_2$ (Denmark) W PTS 12 Anthony Mundine 11.12^3/$_4$ (Australia), Sydney, Australia. Scorecards: 116-112, 120-108, 117-113.

WBC

9 October Cristian Sanavia 11.11^3/$_4$ (Italy) L CO 6 Markus Beyer 11.13^1/$_4$ (Germany), Erfurt, Germany. Referee: Ian-John Lewis.

18 December Markus Beyer 11.12^3/$_4$ (Germany) W PTS 12 Yoshinori Nishizawa 11.13 (Japan), Bayreuth, Germany. Scorecards: 116-111, 117-111, 118-109. Referee: John Keane.

12 March Markus Beyer 11.13 (Germany) W PTS 12 Danny Green 11.12 (Australia), Zwickau, Germany. Scorecards: 114-113, 115-112, 114-114.

WBO

22 October Joe Calzaghe 12.0 (Wales) W PTS 12 Kabary Salem 11.13^3/$_4$ (Egypt), Royal Highland Showground, Edinburgh, Scotland. Scorecards: 117-109, 118-107, 116-109. Referee: Paul Thomas. There is no doubt that on a good day Calzaghe is possibly the best super-middle around, but unfortunately this wasn't a good day. However, it was obvious that Kabary came to spoil and in that he succeeded, but there was no way he was ever going to win the title, despite putting the champion down in the fourth after cutting him with his head in round two. Rising above the lethargy, Calzaghe got himself going to cut Salem over the right eye in the seventh and generally work him over before nearly putting him away in the final session following a solid straight left that dropped the Egyptian for eight. On 6 November, in Riesa, Germany, Mario Veit (Germany) successfully defended the interim title when stopping Charles Brewer (USA) in the ninth round.

7 May Joe Calzaghe 11.13^3/$_4$ (Wales) W RSC 6 Mario Veit 11.13^3/$_4$ (Germany), Braunschweig, Germany. Although Calzaghe had beaten Veit inside two minutes previously, the German was much improved and Calzaghe was firing smoothly on all cylinders for this one as he looked to put the Salem fight behind him. It was soon apparent that the challenger's best chance of winning lay in keeping his distance as he stuck to the task well, his left jab popping out consistently, but once Calzaghe began to work the body, his hand speed blistering, to the initiated it seemed to be just a matter of time. And so it proved as Calzaghe dropped the challenger with a smashing left at the end of the fifth. Storming out for the sixth, the champion soon had Veit down again, following a barrage of heavy shots, and although the German got his feet he was soon rescued by the referee, with just 42 seconds of the session gone.

L.Heavyweight
IBF

25 September Glengoffe Johnson 12.6 (Jamaica) W CO 9 Roy Jones 12.7 (USA), Memphis, Tennessee, USA. Johnson vacated the title in November in favour of a big money fight against Antoine Tarver for the vacant IBO crown.

4 March Clinton Woods 12.6 (England) W RSC 5 Rico Hoye 12.6$^1/_2$ (USA), Magna Centre, Rotherham, England. Referee: Ian John-Lewis. Judge: Dave Parris. In taking on the dangerous, heavy-handed American in a battle for the vacant title, Woods showed he was really up for it by first outboxing his rival and then outpunching him. While Hoye, who had spent ten years in prison for a gangland killing, tried to blast his way through Woods, the Sheffield man kept his defences together, despite taking a number of low blows which saw Hoye deducted two points, and bided his time. In the fifth, he eventually upped the pace, correctly believing his time had come, and was driving Hoye before him without reply when the refereee called it off with just one second of the round remaining.

WBA

26 February Fabrice Tiozzo 12.6$^1/_4$ (France) W RSC 6 Dariusz Michalczewski 12.7 (Germany), Hamburg, Germany.

WBC

21 May Tomasz Adamek 12.7 (Poland) W PTS 12 Paul Briggs 12.7 (Australia), Chicago, Illinois, USA. Scorecards: John Keane 117-113, 115-113, 114-114. Contested for the vacant title after Antonio Tarver had vacated in November in favour of match against Glengoffe Johnson for the vacant IBO crown.

WBO

11 September Zsolt Erdei 12.6 (Hungary) W PTS 12 Alejandro Lakatus 12.6$^1/_4$ (Romania), Budapest, Hungary. Scorecards: Dave Parris 116-112, 118-109, Roy Francis 116-111.

26 February Zsolt Erdei 12.5 (Hungary) W PTS 12 Hugo Garay 12.7 (Argentina), Hamburg, Germany. Scorecards: 110-118, 116-112, 115-113.

Cruiserweight
IBF

20 May O'Neil Bell 14.3 (USA) W PTS 12 Dale Brown 14.2$^3/_4$ (Canada), Hollywood, Florida, USA. Scorecards: 115-113, 116-112, 117-111. Contested for the vacant title after Kelvin Davis (USA) had been stripped on 9 February for failing to agree a defence against Bell.

WBA

2 April Jean-Marc Mormeck 13.6 (France) W PTS 12 Wayne Braithwaite 14.2 (Guyana), Worcester, Massachusetts, USA. Scorecards: 116-110, 114-112, 115-111.

WBC

2 April Wayne Braithwaite 14.2 (Guyana) L PTS 12 Jean-Marc Mormeck 13.6 (France), Worcester, Massachusetts, USA. Scorecards: 110-116, 112-114, 111-115.

WBO

4 September Johnny Nelson 14.3$^1/_2$ (England) W RSC 7 Rudiger May 14.2$^3/_4$ (Germany), Essen, Germany. Despite being firm friends, it counted for nothing once the action got underway as May took the early iniative. However, by the the the third round, the champion was beginning to go on the offensive, getting in solid combinations, and was starting to control and following a situation where he was deducted two points for pushing in the sixth he cut loose. From thereon, it was all Nelson as the challenger tired and in the seventh he dropped May with a heavy right to the head. Up again, it was apparent that May was through as Nelson stormed in with damaging blows hitting the target and with May all over the place the referee called it off on the 2.29 mark.

Heavyweight
IBF

13 November Chris Byrd 15.4 (USA) W PTS 12 Jameel McCline 19.4 (USA), NYC, New York, USA. Scorecards: 115-112, 114-113, 112-114.

WBA

13 November John Ruiz 17.1 (Puerto Rico) W PTS 12 Andrew Golota 17.0 (Poland), NYC, New York, USA. Scorecards: 114-111, 113-112, 114-111.

30 April John Ruiz 17.6 (Puerto Rico) L PTS 12 James Toney 16.7 (USA), NYC, New York, USA. Scorecards: 112-115, 111-116, 111-116. Following the fight, the result was accorded 'No Decision' status when it was learned that Toney had failed the post-fight drug test and Ruiz was reinstated a few weeks later.

WBC

11 December Vitali Klitschko 17.12 (Ukraine) W RSC 8 Danny Williams 19.4 (England), Las Vegas, Nevada, USA. Although he showed great bravery in the face of a one-way thrashing, the challenger had no answers to the hard-punching Klitschko and was put down four times before the referee had seen enough and brought matters to a halt at 1.26 of the eighth round. If nothing else, Williams, who strangely came in at a weight which hindered his speed, certainly disproved the British 'horizontal' heavyweight theory prevalent in America over the years, but courage doesn't win contests and the man famous for beating Mike Tyson had to be rescued, almost from himself.

WBO

4 September Lamon Brewster 16.3 (USA) W PTS 12 Kali Meehan 16.12 (New Zealand), Las Vegas, Nevada, USA. Scorecards: 115-113, 113-114, 114-113.

21 May Lamon Brewster 16.0 (USA) W RSC 1 Andrew Golota 17.10 (Poland), Chicago, Illinois, USA.

World Champions Since Gloves, 1889-2005

Since I began to carry out extensive research into world championship boxing from the very beginnings of gloved action, I discovered much that needed to be amended regarding the historical listings as we know them, especially prior to the 1920s. Although yet to finalise my researches, despite making considerable changes, the listings are the most comprehensive ever published. Bearing all that in mind, and using a wide range of American newspapers, the aim has been to discover just who had claims, valid or otherwise. Studying the records of all the recognised champions, supplied by Professor Luckett Davis and his team, fights against all opposition have been analysed to produce the ultimate data. Because there were no boxing commissions as such in America prior to the 1920s, the yardstick used to determine valid claims were victories over the leading fighters of the day and recognition given within the newspapers. Only where that criteria has been met have I adjusted previous information.

Championship Status Code:

AU = Austria; AUST = Australia; CALIF = California; CAN = Canada; CLE = Cleveland Boxing Commission; EBU = European Boxing Union; FL = Florida; FR = France; GB = Great Britain; GEO = Georgia; H = Hawaii; IBF = International Boxing Federation; IBU = International Boxing Union; ILL = Illinois; LOUIS = Louisiana; MARY = Maryland; MASS = Massachusetts; MICH = Michigan; NBA = National Boxing Association; NC = North Carolina; NY = New York; PEN = Pennsylvania; SA = South Africa; TBC = Territorial Boxing Commission; USA = United States; WBA = World Boxing Association; WBC = World Boxing Council; WBO = World Boxing Organisation.

Champions in **bold** are accorded universal recognition.

*Undefeated champions (Only relates to universally recognised champions prior to 1962 and thereafter WBA/WBC/IBF/WBO champions. Does not include men who forfeited titles).

Title Holder	Birthplace	Tenure	Status	Title Holder	Birthplace	Tenure	Status
M. Flyweight (105 lbs)				Eduardo Marquez	Nicaragua	2003	WBO
Kyung-Yung Lee*	S Korea	1987	IBF	Ivan Calderon	Puerto Rico	2003-	WBO
Hiroki Ioka	Japan	1987-1988	WBC	Edgar Cardenas	Mexico	2003	IBF
Silvio Gamez*	Venezuela	1988-1989	WBA	Daniel Reyes	Colombia	2003-2004	IBF
Samuth Sithnaruepol	Thailand	1988-1989	IBF	Eagle Akakura	Thailand	2004	WBC
Napa Kiatwanchai	Thailand	1988-1989	WBC	Muhammad Rachman	Indonesia	2004-	IBF
Bong-Jun Kim	S Korea	1989-1991	WBA	Yutaka Niida	Japan	2004-	WBA
Nico Thomas	Indonesia	1989	IBF	Isaac Bustos	Mexico	2004-2005	WBC
Rafael Torres	Dom Republic	1989-1992	WBO	Katsunari Takayama	Japan	2005-	WBC
Eric Chavez	Philippines	1989-1990	IBF				
Jum-Hwan Choi	S Korea	1989-1990	WBC	**L. Flyweight (108 lbs)**			
Hideyuki Ohashi	Japan	1990	WBC	Franco Udella	Italy	1975	WBC
Fahlan Lukmingkwan	Thailand	1990-1992	IBF	Jaime Rios	Panama	1975-1976	WBA
Ricardo Lopez*	Mexico	1990-1997	WBC	Luis Estaba	Venezuela	1975-1978	WBC
Hi-Yon Choi	S Korea	1991-1992	WBA	Juan Guzman	Dom Republic	1976	WBA
Manny Melchor	Philippines	1992	IBF	Yoko Gushiken	Japan	1976-1981	WBA
Hideyuki Ohashi	Japan	1992-1993	WBA	Freddie Castillo	Mexico	1978	WBC
Ratanapol Sowvoraphin	Thailand	1992-1996	IBF	Sor Vorasingh	Thailand	1978	WBC
Chana Porpaoin	Thailand	1993-1995	WBA	Sun-Jun Kim	S Korea	1978-1980	WBC
Paul Weir*	Scotland	1993-1994	WBO	Shigeo Nakajima	Japan	1980	WBC
Alex Sanchez	Puerto Rico	1993-1997	WBO	Hilario Zapata	Panama	1980-1982	WBC
Rosendo Alvarez	Nicaragua	1995-1998	WBA	Pedro Flores	Mexico	1981	WBA
Ratanapol Sowvoraphin	Thailand	1996-1997	IBF	Hwan-Jin Kim	S Korea	1981	WBA
Ricardo Lopez*	Mexico	1997-1998	WBC/WBO	Katsuo Tokashiki	Japan	1981-1983	WBA
Zolani Petelo*	S Africa	1997-2000	IBF	Amado Ursua	Mexico	1982	WBC
Ricardo Lopez*	Mexico	1998	WBC	Tadashi Tomori	Japan	1982	WBC
Eric Jamili	Philippines	1998	WBO	Hilario Zapata	Panama	1982-1983	WBC
Kermin Guardia*	Colombia	1998-2002	WBO	Jung-Koo Chang*	S Korea	1983-1988	WBC
Ricardo Lopez*	Mexico	1998-1999	WBA/WBC	Lupe Madera	Mexico	1983-1984	WBA
Wandee Chor Chareon	Thailand	1999-2000	WBC	Dodie Penalosa	Philippines	1983-1986	IBF
Nohel Arambulet	Venezuela	1999-2000	WBA	Francisco Quiroz	Dom Republic	1984-1985	WBA
Jose Antonio Aguirre	Mexico	2000-2004	WBC	Joey Olivo	USA	1985	WBA
Jomo Gamboa	Philippines	2000	WBA	Myung-Woo Yuh	S Korea	1985-1991	WBA
Keitaro Hoshino	Japan	2000-2001	WBA	Jum-Hwan Choi	S Korea	1986-1988	IBF
Chana Porpaoin	Thailand	2001	WBA	Tacy Macalos	Philippines	1988-1989	IBF
Roberto Levya	Mexico	2001-2003	IBF	German Torres	Mexico	1988-1989	WBC
Yutaka Niida*	Japan	2001	WBA	Yul-Woo Lee	S Korea	1989	WBC
Keitaro Hoshino	Japan	2002	WBA	Muangchai Kitikasem	Thailand	1989-1990	IBF
Jorge Mata	Spain	2002-2003	WBO	Jose de Jesus	Puerto Rico	1989-1992	WBO
Nohel Arambulet	Venezuela	2002-2004	WBA	Humberto Gonzalez	Mexico	1989-1990	WBC
Miguel Barrera	Colombia	2002-2003	IBF	Michael Carbajal*	USA	1990-1993	IBF

Title Holder	Birthplace	Tenure	Status
Rolando Pascua	Philippines	1990-1991	WBC
Melchor Cob Castro	Mexico	1991	WBC
Humberto Gonzalez	Mexico	1991-1993	WBC
Hiroki Ioka	Japan	1991-1992	WBA
Josue Camacho	Puerto Rico	1992-1994	WBO
Myung-Woo Yuh*	S Korea	1992-1993	WBA
Michael Carbajal	USA	1993-1994	IBF/WBC
Silvio Gamez	Venezuela	1993-1995	WBA
Humberto Gonzalez	Mexico	1994-1995	WBC/IBF
Michael Carbajal*	USA	1994	WBO
Paul Weir	Scotland	1994-1995	WBO
Hi-Yong Choi	S Korea	1995-1996	WBA
Saman Sorjaturong*	Thailand	1995	WBC/IBF
Jacob Matlala*	South Africa	1995-1997	WBO
Saman Sorjaturong	Thailand	1995-1999	WBC
Carlos Murillo	Panama	1996	WBA
Michael Carbajal	USA	1996-1997	IBF
Keiji Yamaguchi	Japan	1996	WBA
Pichitnoi Chor Siriwat	Thailand	1996-2000	WBA
Mauricio Pastrana	Colombia	1997-1998	IBF
Jesus Chong	Mexico	1997	WBO
Melchor Cob Castro	Mexico	1997-1998	WBO
Mauricio Pastrana	Colombia	1997-1998	IBF
Juan Domingo Cordoba	Argentina	1998	WBO
Jorge Arce	Mexico	1998-1999	WBO
Will Grigsby	USA	1998-1999	IBF
Michael Carbajal*	USA	1999-2000	WBO
Ricardo Lopez*	Mexico	1999-2002	IBF
Yo-Sam Choi	S Korea	1999-2002	WBC
Masibuleke Makepula*	S Africa	2000	WBO
Will Grigsby	USA	2000	WBO
Beibis Mendoza	Colombia	2000-2001	WBA
Rosendo Alvarez	Nicaragua	2001-2004	WBA
Nelson Dieppa	Puerto Rico	2001-2005	WBO
Jorge Arce*	Mexico	2002-2005	WBC
Jose Victor Burgos	Mexico	2003-2004	IBF
Erick Ortiz	Mexico	2005-	WBC
Roberto Vasquez	Panama	2005-	WBA
Hugo Cazares	Mexico	2005-	WBO
Will Grigsby	USA	2005-	IBF

Flyweight (112 lbs)

Title Holder	Birthplace	Tenure	Status
Johnny Coulon	Canada	1910	USA
Sid Smith	England	1911-1913	GB
Sid Smith	England	1913	GB/IBU
Bill Ladbury	England	1913-1914	GB/IBU
Percy Jones	Wales	1914	GB/IBU
Tancy Lee	Scotland	1915	GB/IBU
Joe Symonds	England	1915-1916	GB/IBU
Jimmy Wilde	Wales	1916	GB/IBU
Jimmy Wilde	Wales	1916-1923	
Pancho Villa*	Philippines	1923-1925	
Fidel la Barba	USA	1925-1927	NBA/CALIF
Fidel la Barba*	USA	1927	
Pinky Silverberg	USA	1927	NBA
Johnny McCoy	USA	1927-1928	CALIF
Izzy Schwartz	USA	1927-1928	NY
Frenchy Belanger	Canada	1927-1928	NBA
Newsboy Brown	Russia	1928	CALIF
Johnny Hill	Scotland	1928-1929	GB
Frankie Genaro	USA	1928-1929	NBA
Emile Pladner	France	1929	NBA/IBU
Frankie Genaro	USA	1929-1931	NBA/IBU
Midget Wolgast	USA	1930-1935	NY
Young Perez	Tunisia	1931-1932	NBA/IBU
Jackie Brown	England	1932-1935	NBA/IBU
Jackie Brown	England	1935	GB/NBA
Benny Lynch	Scotland	1935-1937	GB/NBA
Small Montana	Philippines	1935-1937	NY/CALIF
Valentin Angelmann	France	1936-1938	IBU
Peter Kane*	England	1938-1939	NBA/NY/GB/IBU

Title Holder	Birthplace	Tenure	Status
Little Dado	Philippines	1938-1939	CALIF
Little Dado	Philippines	1939-1943	NBA/CALIF
Jackie Paterson	Scotland	1943-1947	
Jackie Paterson	Scotland	1947-1948	GB/NY
Rinty Monaghan	Ireland	1947-1948	NBA
Rinty Monaghan*	Ireland	1948-1950	
Terry Allen	England	1950	
Dado Marino	Hawaii	1950-1952	
Yoshio Shirai	Japan	1952-1954	
Pascual Perez	Argentina	1954-1960	
Pone Kingpetch	Thailand	1960-1962	
Fighting Harada	Japan	1962-1963	
Pone Kingpetch	Thailand	1963	
Hiroyuki Ebihara	Japan	1963-1964	
Pone Kingpetch	Thailand	1964-1965	
Salvatore Burruni	Italy	1965	
Salvatore Burruni	Italy	1965-1966	WBC
Horacio Accavallo*	Argentina	1966-1968	WBA
Walter McGowan	Scotland	1966	WBC
Chartchai Chionoi	Thailand	1966-1969	WBC
Efren Torres	Mexico	1969-1970	WBC
Hiroyuki Ebihara	Japan	1969	WBA
Bernabe Villacampo	Philippines	1969-1970	WBA
Chartchai Chionoi	Thailand	1970	WBC
Berkrerk Chartvanchai	Thailand	1970	WBA
Masao Ohba*	Japan	1970-1973	WBA
Erbito Salavarria	Philippines	1970-1971	WBC
Betulio Gonzalez	Venezuela	1971-1972	WBC
Venice Borkorsor*	Thailand	1972-1973	WBC
Chartchai Chionoi	Thailand	1973-1974	WBA
Betulio Gonzalez	Venezuela	1973-1974	WBC
Shoji Oguma	Japan	1974-1975	WBC
Susumu Hanagata	Japan	1974-1975	WBA
Miguel Canto	Mexico	1975-1979	WBC
Erbito Salavarria	Philippines	1975-1976	WBA
Alfonso Lopez	Panama	1976	WBA
Guty Espadas	Mexico	1976-1978	WBA
Betulio Gonzalez	Venezuela	1978-1979	WBA
Chan-Hee Park	S Korea	1979-1980	WBC
Luis Ibarra	Panama	1979-1980	WBA
Tae-Shik Kim	S Korea	1980	WBA
Shoji Oguma	Japan	1980-1981	WBC
Peter Mathebula	S Africa	1980-1981	WBA
Santos Laciar	Argentina	1981	WBA
Antonio Avelar	Mexico	1981-1982	WBC
Luis Ibarra	Panama	1981	WBA
Juan Herrera	Mexico	1981-1982	WBA
Prudencio Cardona	Colombia	1982	WBC
Santos Laciar*	Argentina	1982-1985	WBA
Freddie Castillo	Mexico	1982	WBC
Eleonicio Mercedes	Dom Republic	1982-1983	WBC
Charlie Magri	Tunisia	1983	WBC
Frank Cedeno	Philippines	1983-1984	WBC
Soon-Chun Kwon	S Korea	1983-1985	IBF
Koji Kobayashi	Japan	1984	WBC
Gabriel Bernal	Mexico	1984	WBC
Sot Chitalada	Thailand	1984-1988	WBC
Hilario Zapata	Panama	1985-1987	WBA
Chong-Kwan Chung	S Korea	1985-1986	IBF
Bi-Won Chung	S Korea	1986	IBF
Hi-Sup Shin	S Korea	1986-1987	IBF
Fidel Bassa	Colombia	1987-1989	WBA
Dodie Penalosa	Philippines	1987	IBF
Chang-Ho Choi	S Korea	1987-1988	IBF
Rolando Bohol	Philippines	1988	IBF
Yong-Kang Kim	S Korea	1988-1989	WBC
Duke McKenzie	England	1988-1989	IBF
Elvis Alvarez*	Colombia	1989	WBO
Sot Chitalada	Thailand	1989-1991	WBC
Dave McAuley	Ireland	1989-1992	IBF
Jesus Rojas	Venezuela	1989-1900	WBA

Title Holder	Birthplace	Tenure	Status
Yukihito Tamakuma	Japan	1990-1991	WBA
Isidro Perez	Mexico	1990-1992	WBO
Yul-Woo Lee	S Korea	1990	WBA
Muangchai Kitikasem	Thailand	1991-1992	WBC
Elvis Alvarez	Colombia	1991	WBA
Yong-Kang Kim	S Korea	1991-1992	WBA
Pat Clinton	Scotland	1992-1993	WBO
Rodolfo Blanco	Colombia	1992	IBF
Yuri Arbachakov	Russia	1992-1997	WBC
Aquiles Guzman	Venezuela	1992	WBA
Pichit Sitbangprachan*	Thailand	1992-1994	IBF
David Griman	Venezuela	1992-1994	WBA
Jacob Matlala	S Africa	1993-1995	WBO
Saen Sorploenchit	Thailand	1994-1996	WBA
Alberto Jimenez	Mexico	1995-1996	WBO
Francisco Tejedor	Colombia	1995	IBF
Danny Romero*	USA	1995-1996	IBF
Mark Johnson*	USA	1996-1998	IBF
Jose Bonilla	Venezuela	1996-1998	WBA
Carlos Salazar	Argentina	1996-1998	WBO
Chatchai Sasakul	Thailand	1997-1998	WBC
Hugo Soto	Argentina	1998-1999	WBA
Ruben Sanchez	Mexico	1998-1999	WBO
Manny Pacquiao	Philippines	1998-1999	WBC
Silvio Gamez	Venezuela	1999	WBA
Irene Pacheco	Colombia	1999-2004	IBF
Jose Antonio Lopez	Spain	1999	WBO
Sompichai Pisanurachan	Thailand	1999-2000	WBA
Medgoen Singsurat	Thailand	1999-2000	WBC
Isidro Garcia	Mexico	1999-2000	WBO
Malcolm Tunacao	Philippines	2000-2001	WBC
Eric Morel	USA	2000-2003	WBA
Fernando Montiel*	Mexico	2000-2002	WBO
Pongsaklek Wonjongkam	Thailand	2001-	WBC
Adonis Rivas	Nicaragua	2002	WBO
Omar Narvaez	Argentina	2002-	WBO
Lorenzo Parra	Venezuela	2003-	WBA
Vic Darchinyan	Armenia	2004-	IBF

S. Flyweight (115 lbs)

Title Holder	Birthplace	Tenure	Status
Rafael Orono	Venezuela	1980-1981	WBC
Chul-Ho Kim	S Korea	1981-1982	WBC
Gustavo Ballas	Argentina	1981	WBA
Rafael Pedroza	Panama	1981-1982	WBA
Jiro Watanabe	Japan	1982-1984	WBA
Rafael Orono	Venezuela	1982-1983	WBC
Payao Poontarat	Thailand	1983-1984	WBC
Joo-Do Chun	S Korea	1983-1985	IBF
Jiro Watanabe	Japan	1984-1986	WBC
Kaosai Galaxy*	Thailand	1984-1992	WBA
Elly Pical	Indonesia	1985-1986	IBF
Cesar Polanco	Dom Republic	1986	IBF
Gilberto Roman	Mexico	1986-1987	WBC
Elly Pical	Indonesia	1986-1987	IBF
Santos Laciar	Argentina	1987	WBC
Tae-Il Chang	S Korea	1987	IBF
Jesus Rojas	Colombia	1987-1988	WBC
Elly Pical	Indonesia	1987-1989	IBF
Gilberto Roman	Mexico	1988-1989	WBC
Jose Ruiz	Puerto Rico	1989-1992	WBO
Juan Polo Perez	Colombia	1989-1990	IBF
Nana Yaw Konadu	Ghana	1989-1990	WBC
Sung-Il Moon	S Korea	1990-1993	WBC
Robert Quiroga	USA	1990-1993	IBF
Jose Quirino	Mexico	1992	WBO
Katsuya Onizuka	Japan	1992-1994	WBA
Johnny Bredahl	Denmark	1992-1994	WBO
Julio Cesar Borboa	Mexico	1993-1994	IBF
Jose Luis Bueno	Mexico	1993-1994	WBC
Hiroshi Kawashima	Japan	1994-1997	WBC
Harold Grey	Colombia	1994-1995	IBF

Title Holder	Birthplace	Tenure	Status
Hyung-Chul Lee	S Korea	1994-1995	WBA
Johnny Tapia*	USA	1994-1997	WBO
Alimi Goitia	Venezuela	1995-1996	WBA
Carlos Salazar	Argentina	1995-1996	IBF
Harold Grey	Colombia	1996	IBF
Yokthai Sith-Oar	Thailand	1996-1997	WBA
Danny Romero	USA	1996-1997	IBF
Gerry Penalosa	Philippines	1997-1998	WBC
Johnny Tapia*	USA	1997-1998	IBF/WBO
Satoshi Iida	Japan	1997-1998	WBA
In-Joo Cho	S Korea	1998-2000	WBC
Victor Godoi	Argentina	1998-1999	WBO
Jesus Rojas	Venezuela	1998-1999	WBA
Mark Johnson	USA	1999-2000	IBF
Diego Morales	Mexico	1999	WBO
Hideki Todaka	Japan	1999-2000	WBA
Adonis Rivas	Nicaragua	1999-2001	WBO
Felix Machado	Venezuela	2000-2003	IBF
Masamori Tokuyama	Japan	2000-2004	WBC
Silvio Gamez	Venezuela	2000-2001	WBA
Celes Kobayashi	Japan	2001-2002	WBA
Pedro Alcazar	Panama	2001-2002	WBO
Alexander Munoz	Venezuela	2002-2004	WBA
Fernando Montiel	Mexico	2002-2003	WBO
Luis Perez	Nicaragua	2003-	IBF
Mark Johnson	USA	2003-2004	WBO
Katsushige Kawashima	Japan	2004-	WBC
Ivan Hernandez	Mexico	2004-2005	WBO
Martin Castillo	Mexico	2004-	WBA
Fernando Montiel	Mexico	2005-	WBO

Bantamweight (118 lbs)

Title Holder	Birthplace	Tenure	Status
Tommy Kelly	USA	1889	
George Dixon	Canada	1889-1890	
Chappie Moran	England	1889-1890	
Tommy Kelly	USA	1890-1892	
Billy Plimmer	England	1892-1895	
Pedlar Palmer	England	1895-1899	
Terry McGovern	USA	1899	USA
Pedlar Palmer	England	1899-1900	GB
Terry McGovern*	USA	1899-1900	
Clarence Forbes	USA	1900	
Johnny Reagan	USA	1900-1902	
Harry Ware	England	1900-1902	GB
Harry Harris	USA	1901	
Harry Forbes	USA	1901-1902	
Kid McFadden	USA	1901	
Dan Dougherty	USA	1901	
Andrew Tokell	England	1902	GB
Harry Ware	England	1902	GB
Harry Forbes	USA	1902-1903	USA
Joe Bowker	England	1902-1904	GB
Frankie Neil	USA	1903-1904	USA
Joe Bowker*	England	1904-1905	
Frankie Neil	USA	1905	USA
Digger Stanley	England	1905-1907	
Owen Moran	England	1905-1907	
Jimmy Walsh	USA	1905-1908	USA
Owen Moran	England	1907	GB
Monte Attell	USA	1908-1910	
Jimmy Walsh	USA	1908-1911	
Digger Stanley	England	1909-1912	GB
Frankie Conley	Italy	1910-1911	
Johnny Coulon	Canada	1910-1911	
Monte Attell	USA	1910-1911	
Johnny Coulon	Canada	1911-1913	USA
Charles Ledoux	France	1912-1913	GB/IBU
Eddie Campi	USA	1913-1914	
Johnny Coulon	Canada	1913-1914	
Kid Williams	Denmark	1913-1914	
Kid Williams	Denmark	1914-1915	

WORLD CHAMPIONS SINCE GLOVES, 1889-2005

Title Holder	Birthplace	Tenure	Status	Title Holder	Birthplace	Tenure	Status
Kid Williams	Denmark	1915-1917		**Rafael Herrera**	Mexico	1972	
Johnny Ertle	USA	1915-1918		**Enrique Pinder**	Panama	1972	
Pete Herman	USA	1917-1919		Enrique Pinder	Panama	1972-1973	WBC
Pal Moore	USA	1918-1919		Romeo Anaya	Mexico	1973	WBA
Pete Herman	USA	1919-1920		Rafael Herrera	Mexico	1973-1974	WBC
Joe Lynch	USA	1920-1921		Arnold Taylor	S Africa	1973-1974	WBA
Pete Herman	USA	1921		Soo-Hwan Hong	S Korea	1974-1975	WBA
Johnny Buff	USA	1921-1922		Rodolfo Martinez	Mexico	1974-1976	WBC
Joe Lynch	USA	1922-1923		Alfonso Zamora	Mexico	1975-1977	WBA
Joe Lynch	USA	1923-1924	NBA	Carlos Zarate	Mexico	1976-1979	WBC
Joe Burman	England	1923	NY	Jorge Lujan	Panama	1977-1980	WBA
Abe Goldstein	USA	1923-1924	NY	Lupe Pintor*	Mexico	1979-1983	WBC
Joe Lynch	USA	1924		Julian Solis	Puerto Rico	1980	WBA
Abe Goldstein	USA	1924		Jeff Chandler	USA	1980-1984	WBA
Eddie Martin	USA	1924-1925		Albert Davila	USA	1983-1985	WBC
Charley Rosenberg	USA	1925-1926		Richard Sandoval	USA	1984-1986	WBA
Charley Rosenberg	USA	1926-1927	NY	Satoshi Shingaki	Japan	1984-1985	IBF
Bud Taylor*	USA	1926-1928	NBA	Jeff Fenech*	Australia	1985-1987	IBF
Bushy Graham*	Italy	1928-1929	NY	Daniel Zaragoza	Mexico	1985	WBC
Al Brown	Panama	1929-1931		Miguel Lora	Colombia	1985-1988	WBC
Al Brown	Panama	1931	NY/IBU	Gaby Canizales	USA	1986	WBA
Pete Sanstol	Norway	1931	CAN	Bernardo Pinango*	Venezuela	1986-1987	WBA
Al Brown	Panama	1931-1933		Takuya Muguruma	Japan	1987	WBA
Al Brown	Panama	1933-1934	NY/NBA/IBU	Kelvin Seabrooks	USA	1987-1988	IBF
Speedy Dado	Philippines	1933	CALIF	Chang-Yung Park	S Korea	1987	WBA
Baby Casanova	Mexico	1933-1934	CALIF	Wilfredo Vasquez	Puerto Rico	1987-1988	WBA
Sixto Escobar	Puerto Rico	1934	CAN	Kaokor Galaxy	Thailand	1988	WBA
Sixto Escobar	Puerto Rico	1934-1935	NBA	Orlando Canizales*	USA	1988-1994	IBF
Al Brown	Panama	1934-1935	NY/IBU	Sung-Il Moon	S Korea	1988-1989	WBA
Lou Salica	USA	1935	CALIF	Raul Perez	Mexico	1988-1991	WBC
Baltazar Sangchilli	Spain	1935-1938	IBU	Israel Contrerras*	Venezuela	1989-1991	WBO
Lou Salica	USA	1935	NBA/NY	Kaokor Galaxy	Thailand	1989	WBA
Sixto Escobar	Puerto Rico	1935-1937	NBA/NY	Luisito Espinosa	Philippines	1989-1991	WBA
Harry Jeffra	USA	1937-1938	NY/NBA	Greg Richardson	USA	1991	WBC
Sixto Escobar	Puerto Rico	1938-1939	NY/NBA	Gaby Canizales	USA	1991	WBO
Al Brown	Panama	1938	IBU	Duke McKenzie	England	1991-1992	WBO
Sixto Escobar	Puerto Rico	1939		Joichiro Tatsuyoshi*	Japan	1991-1992	WBC
George Pace	USA	1939-1940	NBA	Israel Contrerras	Venezuela	1991-1992	WBA
Lou Salica	USA	1939	CALIF	Eddie Cook	USA	1992	WBA
Tony Olivera	USA	1939-1940	CALIF	Victor Rabanales	Mexico	1992-1993	WBC
Little Dado	Philippines	1940	CALIF	Rafael del Valle	Puerto Rico	1992-1994	WBO
Lou Salica	USA	1940-1941		Jorge Elicier Julio	Colombia	1992-1993	WBA
Kenny Lindsay	Canada	1941	CAN	Il-Jung Byun	S Korea	1993	WBC
Lou Salica	USA	1942	NY	Junior Jones	USA	1993-1994	WBA
David Kui Kong Young	Hawaii	1941-1943	TBC	Yasuei Yakushiji	Japan	1993-1995	WBC
Lou Salica	USA	1941-1942	NY/NBA	John Michael Johnson	USA	1994	WBA
Manuel Ortiz	USA	1942-1943	NBA	Daorung Chuwatana	Thailand	1994-1995	WBA
Manuel Ortiz	USA	1943-1945	NY/NBA	Alfred Kotey	Ghana	1994-1995	WBO
David Kui Kong Young	Hawaii	1943	TBC	Harold Mestre	Colombia	1995	IBF
Rush Dalma	Philippines	1943-1945	TBC	Mbulelo Botile	S Africa	1995-1997	IBF
Manuel Ortiz	USA	1945-1947		Wayne McCullough	Ireland	1995-1997	WBC
Harold Dade	USA	1947		Veeraphol Sahaprom	Thailand	1995-1996	WBA
Manuel Ortiz	USA	1947-1950		Daniel Jimenez	Puerto Rico	1995-1996	WBO
Vic Toweel	S Africa	1950-1952		Nana Yaw Konadu	Ghana	1996	WBA
Jimmy Carruthers*	Australia	1952-1954		Robbie Regan*	Wales	1996-1998	WBO
Robert Cohen	Algeria	1954		Daorung Chuwatana	Thailand	1996-1997	WBA
Robert Cohen	Algeria	1954-1956	NY/EBU	Sirimongkol Singmanassak	Thailand	1997	WBC
Raton Macias	Mexico	1955-1957	NBA	Nana Yaw Konadu	Ghana	1997-1998	WBA
Mario D'Agata	Italy	1956-1957	NY/EBU	Tim Austin	USA	1997-2003	IBF
Alphonse Halimi	Algeria	1957	NY/EBU	Joichiro Tatsuyoshi	Japan	1997-1998	WBC
Alphonse Halimi	Algeria	1957-1959		Jorge Elicier Julio	Colombia	1998-2000	WBO
Joe Becerra*	Mexico	1959-1960		Johnny Tapia	USA	1998-1999	WBA
Alphonse Halimi	Algeria	1960-1961	EBU	Veeraphol Sahaprom	Thailand	1998-2005	WBC
Eder Jofre	Brazil	1960-1962	NBA	Paulie Ayala	USA	1999-2001	WBA
Johnny Caldwell	Ireland	1961-1962	EBU	Johnny Tapia*	USA	2000	WBO
Eder Jofre	Brazil	1962-1965		Mauricio Martinez	Panama	2000-2002	WBO
Fighting Harada	Japan	1965-1968		Eidy Moya	Venezuela	2001-2002	WBA
Lionel Rose	Australia	1968-1969		Cruz Carbajal	Mexico	2002-2004	WBO
Ruben Olivares	Mexico	1969-1970		Johnny Bredahl*	Denmark	2002-2004	WBA
Chuchu Castillo	Mexico	1970-1971		Rafael Marquez	Mexico	2003-	IBF
Ruben Olivares	Mexico	1971-1972		Ratanchai Sowvoraphin	Thailand	2004-	WBO

Title Holder	Birthplace	Tenure	Status
Julio Zarate	Mexico	2004-2005	WBA
Wladimir Sidorenko	Ukraine	2005-	WBA
Hozumi Hasegawa	Japan	2005-	WBC

S. Bantamweight (122 lbs)

Title Holder	Birthplace	Tenure	Status
Rigoberto Riasco	Panama	1976	WBC
Royal Kobayashi	Japan	1976	WBC
Dong-Kyun Yum	S Korea	1976-1977	WBC
Wilfredo Gomez*	Puerto Rico	1977-1983	WBC
Soo-Hwan Hong	S Korea	1977-1978	WBA
Ricardo Cardona	Colombia	1978-1980	WBA
Leo Randolph	USA	1980	WBA
Sergio Palma	Argentina	1980-1982	WBA
Leonardo Cruz	Dom Republic	1982-1984	WBA
Jaime Garza	USA	1983-1984	WBC
Bobby Berna	Philippines	1983-1984	IBF
Loris Stecca	Italy	1984	WBA
Seung-In Suh	S Korea	1984-1985	IBF
Victor Callejas	Puerto Rico	1984-1986	WBA
Juan Meza	Mexico	1984-1985	WBC
Ji-Won Kim*	S Korea	1985-1986	IBF
Lupe Pintor	Mexico	1985-1986	WBC
Samart Payakarun	Thailand	1986-1987	WBC
Louie Espinosa	USA	1987	WBA
Seung-Hoon Lee*	S Korea	1987-1988	IBF
Jeff Fenech*	Australia	1987-1988	WBC
Julio Gervacio	Dom Republic	1987-1988	WBA
Bernardo Pinango	Venezuela	1988	WBA
Daniel Zaragoza	Mexico	1988-1990	WBC
Jose Sanabria	Venezuela	1988-1989	IBF
Juan J. Estrada	Mexico	1988-1989	WBA
Fabrice Benichou	Spain	1989-1990	IBF
Kenny Mitchell	USA	1989	WBO
Valerio Nati	Italy	1989-1990	WBO
Jesus Salud	USA	1989-1990	WBA
Welcome Ncita	S Africa	1990-1992	IBF
Paul Banke	USA	1990	WBC
Orlando Fernandez	Puerto Rico	1990-1991	WBO
Luis Mendoza	Colombia	1990-1991	WBA
Pedro Decima	Argentina	1990-1991	WBC
Kiyoshi Hatanaka	Japan	1991	WBC
Jesse Benavides	USA	1991-1992	WBO
Daniel Zaragoza	Mexico	1991-1992	WBC
Raul Perez	Mexico	1991-1992	WBA
Thierry Jacob	France	1992	WBC
Wilfredo Vasquez	Puerto Rico	1992-1995	WBA
Tracy Harris Patterson	USA	1992-1994	WBC
Duke McKenzie	England	1992-1993	WBO
Kennedy McKinney	USA	1992-1994	IBF
Daniel Jimenez	Puerto Rico	1993-1995	WBO
Vuyani Bungu *	S Africa	1994-1999	IBF
Hector Acero-Sanchez	Dom Republic	1994-1995	WBC
Marco Antonio Barrera	Mexico	1995-1996	WBO
Antonio Cermeno *	Venezuela	1995-1997	WBA
Daniel Zaragoza	Mexico	1995-1997	WBC
Junior Jones	USA	1996-1997	WBO
Erik Morales*	Mexico	1997-2000	WBC
Kennedy McKinney*	USA	1997-1998	WBO
Enrique Sanchez	Mexico	1998	WBA
Marco Antonio Barrera	Mexico	1998-2000	WBO
Nestor Garza	Mexico	1998-2000	WBA
Lehlohonolo Ledwaba	S Africa	1999-2001	IBF
Erik Morales	Mexico	2000	WBC/WBO
Erik Morales*	Mexico	2000	WBC
Marco Antonio Barrera*	Mexico	2000-2001	WBO
Clarence Adams	USA	2000-2001	WBA
Willie Jorrin	USA	2000-2002	WBC
Manny Pacquiao*	Philippines	2001-2003	IBF
Agapito Sanchez*	Dom Republic	2001-2002	WBO
Yober Ortega	Venezuela	2001-2002	WBA
Yoddamrong Sithyodthong	Thailand	2002	WBA

Title Holder	Birthplace	Tenure	Status
Osamu Sato	Japan	2002	WBA
Joan Guzman	Dom Republic	2002-	WBO
Salim Medjkoune	France	2002-2003	WBA
Oscar Larios	Mexico	2002-	WBC
Mahyar Monshipour	Iran	2003-	WBA
Israel Vazquez	Mexico	2004-	IBF

Featherweight (126 lbs)

Title Holder	Birthplace	Tenure	Status
Ike Weir	Ireland	1889-1890	
Billy Murphy	New Zealand	1890-1893	
George Dixon	Canada	1890-1893	
Young Griffo	Australia	1890-1893	
Johnny Griffin	USA	1891-1893	
Solly Smith	USA	1893	
George Dixon	Canada	1893-1896	
Solly Smith	USA	1896-1898	
Frank Erne	USA	1896-1897	
George Dixon	Canada	1896-1900	
Harry Greenfield	England	1897-1899	
Ben Jordan	England	1897-1899	
Will Curley	England	1897-1899	
Dave Sullivan	Ireland	1898	
Ben Jordan	England	1899-1905	GB
Eddie Santry	USA	1899-1900	
Terry McGovern	USA	1900	
Terry McGovern	USA	1900-1901	USA
Young Corbett II	USA	1901-1903	USA
Eddie Hanlon	USA	1903	
Young Corbett II	USA	1903-1904	
Abe Attell	USA	1903-1904	
Abe Attell	USA	1904-1911	USA
Joe Bowker	England	1905-1907	GB
Jim Driscoll	Wales	1907-1912	GB
Abe Attell	USA	1911-1912	
Joe Coster	USA	1911	
Joe Rivers	Mexico	1911	
Johnny Kilbane	USA	1911-1912	
Jim Driscoll*	Wales	1912-1913	GB/IBU
Johnny Kilbane	USA	1912-1922	USA
Johnny Kilbane	USA	1922-1923	NBA
Johnny Dundee	Italy	1922-1923	NY
Eugene Criqui	France	1923	
Johnny Dundee*	Italy	1923-1924	
Kid Kaplan	Russia	1925	NY
Kid Kaplan*	Russia	1925-1926	
Honeyboy Finnegan	USA	1926-1927	MASS
Benny Bass	Russia	1927-1928	NBA
Tony Canzoneri	USA	1928	
Andre Routis	France	1928-1929	
Bat Battalino	USA	1929-1932	
Bat Battalino	USA	1932	NBA
Tommy Paul	USA	1932-1933	NBA
Kid Chocolate*	Cuba	1932-1934	NY
Baby Arizmendi	Mexico	1932-1933	CALIF
Freddie Miller	USA	1933-1936	NBA
Baby Arizmendi	Mexico	1934-1935	NY
Baby Arizmendi	Mexico	1935-1936	NY/MEX
Baby Arizmendi	Mexico	1936	MEX
Petey Sarron	USA	1936-1937	NBA
Henry Armstrong	USA	1936-1937	CALIF/MEX
Mike Belloise	USA	1936	NY
Maurice Holtzer	France	1937-1938	IBU
Henry Armstrong*	USA	1937-1938	NBA/NY
Leo Rodak	USA	1938	MARY
Joey Archibald	USA	1938-1939	NY
Leo Rodak	USA	1938-1939	NBA
Joey Archibald	USA	1939-1940	
Joey Archibald	USA	1940	NY
Petey Scalzo	USA	1940-1941	NBA
Jimmy Perrin	USA	1940	LOUIS
Harry Jeffra	USA	1940-1941	NY/MARY

Title Holder	Birthplace	Tenure	Status
Joey Archibald	USA	1941	NY/MARY
Richie Lemos	USA	1941	NBA
Chalky Wright	Mexico	1941-1942	NY/MARY
Jackie Wilson	USA	1941-1943	NBA
Willie Pep	USA	1942-1946	NY
Jackie Callura	Canada	1943	NBA
Phil Terranova	USA	1943-1944	NBA
Sal Bartolo	USA	1944-1946	NBA
Willie Pep	USA	1946-1948	
Sandy Saddler	USA	1948-1949	
Willie Pep	USA	1949-1950	
Sandy Saddler*	USA	1950-1957	
Hogan Kid Bassey	Nigeria	1957-1959	
Davey Moore	USA	1959-1963	
Sugar Ramos	Cuba	1963-1964	
Vicente Saldivar*	Mexico	1964-1967	
Raul Rojas	USA	1967	CALIF
Howard Winstone	Wales	1968	WBC
Raul Rojas	USA	1968	WBA
Johnny Famechon	France	1968-1969	AUST
Jose Legra	Cuba	1968-1969	WBC
Shozo Saijyo	Japan	1968-1971	WBA
Johnny Famechon	France	1969-1970	WBC
Vicente Saldivar	Mexico	1970	WBC
Kuniaki Shibata	Japan	1970-1972	WBC
Antonio Gomez	Venezuela	1971-1972	WBA
Clemente Sanchez	Mexico	1972	WBC
Ernesto Marcel*	Panama	1972-1974	WBA
Jose Legra	Cuba	1972-1973	WBC
Eder Jofre	Brazil	1973-1974	WBC
Ruben Olivares	Mexico	1974	WBA
Bobby Chacon	USA	1974-1975	WBC
Alexis Arguello*	Nicaragua	1974-1977	WBA
Ruben Olivares	Mexico	1975	WBC
David Kotey	Ghana	1975-1976	WBC
Danny Lopez	USA	1976-1980	WBC
Rafael Ortega	Panama	1977	WBA
Cecilio Lastra	Spain	1977-1978	WBA
Eusebio Pedroza	Panama	1978-1985	WBA
Salvador Sanchez*	Mexico	1980-1982	WBC
Juan Laporte	Puerto Rico	1982-1984	WBC
Min-Keun Oh	S Korea	1984-1985	IBF
Wilfredo Gomez	Puerto Rico	1984	WBC
Azumah Nelson*	Ghana	1984-1988	WBC
Barry McGuigan	Ireland	1985-1986	WBA
Ki-Yung Chung	S Korea	1985-1986	IBF
Steve Cruz	USA	1986-1987	WBA
Antonio Rivera	Puerto Rico	1986-1988	IBF
Antonio Esparragoza	Venezuela	1987-1991	WBA
Calvin Grove	USA	1988	IBF
Jeff Fenech*	Australia	1988-1989	WBC
Jorge Paez*	Mexico	1988-1990	IBF
Maurizio Stecca	Italy	1989	WBO
Louie Espinosa	USA	1989-1990	WBO
Jorge Paez*	Mexico	1990-1991	IBF/WBO
Marcos Villasana	Mexico	1990-1991	WBC
Kyun-Yung Park	S Korea	1991-1993	WBA
Troy Dorsey	USA	1991	IBF
Maurizio Stecca	Italy	1991-1992	WBO
Manuel Medina	Mexico	1991-1993	IBF
Paul Hodkinson	England	1991-1993	WBC
Colin McMillan	England	1992	WBO
Ruben Palacio	Colombia	1992-1993	WBO
Tom Johnson	USA	1993-1997	IBF
Steve Robinson	Wales	1993-1995	WBO
Gregorio Vargas	Mexico	1993	WBC
Kevin Kelley	USA	1993-1995	WBC
Eloy Rojas	Venezuela	1993-1996	WBA
Alejandro Gonzalez	Mexico	1995	WBC
Manuel Medina	Mexico	1995	WBC
Prince Naseem Hamed*	England	1995-1997	WBO

Title Holder	Birthplace	Tenure	Status
Luisito Espinosa	Philippines	1995-1999	WBC
Wilfredo Vasquez	Puerto Rico	1996-1998	WBA
Prince Naseem Hamed *	England	1997	WBO/IBF
Prince Naseem Hamed*	England	1997-1999	WBO
Hector Lizarraga	Mexico	1997-1998	IBF
Freddie Norwood	USA	1998	WBA
Manuel Medina	Mexico	1998-1999	IBF
Antonio Cermeno	Venezuela	1998-1999	WBA
Cesar Soto	Mexico	1999	WBC
Freddie Norwood	USA	1999-2000	WBA
Prince Naseem Hamed	England	1999-2000	WBC/WBO
Paul Ingle	England	1999-2000	IBF
Prince Naseem Hamed*	England	2000	WBO
Gustavo Espadas	Mexico	2000-2001	WBC
Derrick Gainer	USA	2000-2003	WBA
Mbulelo Botile	S Africa	2000-2001	IBF
Istvan Kovacs	Hungary	2001	WBO
Erik Morales	Mexico	2001-2002	WBC
Frankie Toledo	USA	2001	IBF
Julio Pablo Chacon	Argentina	2001-2002	WBO
Manuel Medina	Mexico	2001-2002	IBF
Johnny Tapia	USA	2002	IBF
Marco Antonio Barrera*	Mexico	2002	WBC
Scott Harrison	Scotland	2002-	WBO
Erik Morales*	Mexico	2002-2003	WBC
Juan Manuel Marquez*	Mexico	2003	IBF
Juan Manuel Marquez	Mexico	2003-	IBF/WBA
In-Jin Chi	South Korea	2004-	WBC

S. Featherweight (130 lbs)

Title Holder	Birthplace	Tenure	Status
Johnny Dundee	Italy	1921-1923	NY
Jack Bernstein	USA	1923	NY
Jack Bernstein	USA	1923	NBA/NY
Johnny Dundee	Italy	1923-1924	NBA/NY
Kid Sullivan	USA	1924-1925	NBA/NY
Mike Ballerino	USA	1925	NBA/NY
Tod Morgan	USA	1925-1929	NBA/NY
Benny Bass	Russia	1929-1930	NBA/NY
Benny Bass	Russia	1930-1931	NBA
Kid Chocolate	Cuba	1931-1933	NBA
Frankie Klick	USA	1933-1934	NBA
Sandy Saddler	USA	1949-1950	NBA
Sandy Saddler	USA	1950-1951	CLE
Harold Gomes	USA	1959-1960	NBA
Flash Elorde	Philippines	1960-1962	NBA
Flash Elorde	Philippines	1962-1967	WBA
Raul Rojas	USA	1967	CALIF
Yoshiaki Numata	Japan	1967	WBA
Hiroshi Kobayashi	Japan	1967-1971	WBA
Rene Barrientos	Philippines	1969-1970	WBC
Yoshiaki Numata	Japan	1970-1971	WBC
Alfredo Marcano	Venezuela	1971-1972	WBA
Ricardo Arredondo	Mexico	1971-1974	WBC
Ben Villaflor	Philippines	1972-1973	WBA
Kuniaki Shibata	Japan	1973	WBA
Ben Villaflor	Philippines	1973-1976	WBA
Kuniaki Shibata	Japan	1974-1975	WBC
Alfredo Escalera	Puerto Rico	1975-1978	WBC
Sam Serrano	Puerto Rico	1976-1980	WBA
Alexis Arguello*	Nicaragua	1978-1980	WBC
Yasutsune Uehara	Japan	1980-1981	WBA
Rafael Limon	Mexico	1980-1981	WBC
Cornelius Boza-Edwards	Uganda	1981	WBC
Sam Serrano	Puerto Rico	1981-1983	WBA
Rolando Navarrete	Philippines	1981-1982	WBC
Rafael Limon	Mexico	1982	WBC
Bobby Chacon	USA	1982-1983	WBC
Roger Mayweather	USA	1983-1984	WBA
Hector Camacho*	Puerto Rico	1983-1984	WBC
Rocky Lockridge	USA	1984-1985	WBA
Hwan-Kil Yuh	S Korea	1984-1985	IBF

Title Holder	Birthplace	Tenure	Status
Julio Cesar Chavez*	Mexico	1984-1987	WBC
Lester Ellis	England	1985	IBF
Wilfredo Gomez	Puerto Rico	1985-1986	WBA
Barry Michael	England	1985-1987	IBF
Alfredo Layne	Panama	1986	WBA
Brian Mitchell*	S Africa	1986-1991	WBA
Rocky Lockridge	USA	1987-1988	IBF
Azumah Nelson	Ghana	1988-1994	WBC
Tony Lopez	USA	1988-1989	IBF
Juan Molina*	Puerto Rico	1989	WBO
Juan Molina	Puerto Rico	1989-1990	IBF
Kamel Bou Ali	Tunisia	1989-1992	WBO
Tony Lopez	USA	1990-1991	IBF
Joey Gamache*	USA	1991	WBA
Brian Mitchell*	S Africa	1991-1992	IBF
Genaro Hernandez	USA	1991-1995	WBA
Juan Molina*	Puerto Rico	1992-1995	IBF
Daniel Londas	France	1992	WBO
Jimmy Bredahl	Denmark	1992-1994	WBO
Oscar de la Hoya*	USA	1994	WBO
James Leija	USA	1994	WBC
Gabriel Ruelas	USA	1994-1995	WBC
Regilio Tuur*	Surinam	1994-1997	WBO
Eddie Hopson	USA	1995	IBF
Tracy Harris Patterson	USA	1995	IBF
Yong-Soo Choi	S Korea	1995-1998	WBA
Arturo Gatti*	Canada	1995-1997	IBF
Azumah Nelson	Ghana	1996-1997	WBC
Genaro Hernandez	USA	1997-1998	WBC
Barry Jones*	Wales	1997-1998	WBO
Roberto Garcia	USA	1998-1999	IBF
Anatoly Alexandrov	Kazakhstan	1998-1999	WBO
Takenori Hatakeyama	Japan	1998-1999	WBA
Floyd Mayweather*	USA	1998-2002	WBC
Lakva Sim	Mongolia	1999	WBA
Acelino Freitas*	Brazil	1999-2002	WBO
Diego Corrales*	USA	1999-2000	IBF
Jong-Kwon Baek	S Korea	1999-2000	WBA
Joel Casamayor	Cuba	2000-2002	WBA
Steve Forbes	USA	2000-2002	IBF
Acelino Freitas*	Brazil	2002-2004	WBO/WBA
Sirimongkol Singmanassak	Thailand	2002-2003	WBC
Carlos Hernandez	USA	2003-2004	IBF
Jesus Chavez	Mexico	2003-2004	WBC
Yodesnan Sornontachai	Thailand	2004-2005	WBA
Erik Morales	Mexico	2004	WBC
Diego Corrales*	USA	2004	WBO
Erik Morales	Mexico	2004	IBF
Mike Anchondo	USA	2004-2005	WBO
Marco Antonio Barrera	Mexico	2004-	WBC
Robbie Peden	Australia	2005-	IBF
Jorge Barrios	Argentina	2005-	WBO
Vincente Mosquera	Panama	2005-	WBA

Lightweight (135 lbs)

Title Holder	Birthplace	Tenure	Status
Jack McAuliffe	Ireland	1889-1894	USA
Jem Carney	England	1889-1891	
Jimmy Carroll	England	1889-1891	
Dick Burge	England	1891-1896	GB
George Lavigne	USA	1894-1896	USA
George Lavigne	USA	1896	
George Lavigne	USA	1896-1897	
Eddie Connolly	Canada	1896-1897	
George Lavigne	USA	1897-1899	
Frank Erne	Switzerland	1899-1902	
Joe Gans	USA	1902	
Joe Gans	USA	1902-1906	
Jabez White	England	1902-1905	GB
Jimmy Britt	USA	1902-1905	
Battling Nelson	Denmark	1905-1907	
Joe Gans	USA	1906-1908	

Title Holder	Birthplace	Tenure	Status
Battling Nelson	Denmark	1908-1910	
Ad Wolgast	USA	1910-1912	
Willie Ritchie	USA	1912	
Freddie Welsh	Wales	1912-1914	GB
Willie Ritchie	USA	1912-1914	USA
Freddie Welsh	Wales	1914-1917	
Benny Leonard*	USA	1917-1925	
Jimmy Goodrich	USA	1925	NY
Rocky Kansas	USA	1925-1926	
Sammy Mandell	USA	1926-1930	
Al Singer	USA	1930	
Tony Canzoneri	USA	1930-1933	
Barney Ross*	USA	1933-1935	
Tony Canzoneri	USA	1935-1936	
Lou Ambers	USA	1936-1938	
Henry Armstrong	USA	1938-1939	
Lou Ambers	USA	1939-1940	
Sammy Angott	USA	1940-1941	NBA
Lew Jenkins	USA	1940-1941	NY
Sammy Angott*	USA	1941-1942	
Beau Jack	USA	1942-1943	NY
Slugger White	USA	1943	MARY
Bob Montgomery	USA	1943	NY
Sammy Angott	USA	1943-1944	NBA
Beau Jack	USA	1943-1944	NY
Bob Montgomery	USA	1944-1947	NY
Juan Zurita	Mexico	1944-1945	NBA
Ike Williams	USA	1945-1947	NBA
Ike Williams	USA	1947-1951	
Jimmy Carter	USA	1951-1952	
Lauro Salas	Mexico	1952	
Jimmy Carter	USA	1952-1954	
Paddy de Marco	USA	1954	
Jimmy Carter	USA	1954-1955	
Wallace Bud Smith	USA	1955-1956	
Joe Brown	USA	1956-1962	
Carlos Ortiz	Puerto Rico	1962-1963	
Carlos Ortiz*	Puerto Rico	1963-1964	WBA/WBC
Kenny Lane	USA	1963-1964	MICH
Carlos Ortiz	Puerto Rico	1964-1965	
Ismael Laguna	Panama	1965	
Carlos Ortiz	Puerto Rico	1965-1966	
Carlos Ortiz*	Puerto Rico	1966-1967	WBA
Carlos Ortiz	Puerto Rico	1967-1968	
Carlos Teo Cruz	Dom Republic	1968-1969	
Mando Ramos	USA	1969-1970	
Ismael Laguna	Panama	1970	
Ismael Laguna	Panama	1970	WBA
Ken Buchanan*	Scotland	1970-1971	WBA
Ken Buchanan	Scotland	1971	
Ken Buchanan	Scotland	1971-1972	WBA
Pedro Carrasco	Spain	1971-1972	WBC
Mando Ramos	USA	1972	WBC
Roberto Duran*	Panama	1972-1978	WBA
Chango Carmona	Mexico	1972	WBC
Rodolfo Gonzalez	Mexico	1972-1974	WBC
Guts Ishimatsu	Japan	1974-1976	WBC
Esteban de Jesus	Puerto Rico	1976-1978	WBC
Roberto Duran*	Panama	1978-1979	
Jim Watt	Scotland	1979-1981	WBC
Ernesto Espana	Venezuela	1979-1980	WBA
Hilmer Kenty	USA	1980-1981	WBA
Sean O'Grady	USA	1981	WBA
Alexis Arguello*	Nicaragua	1981-1983	WBC
Claude Noel	Trinidad	1981	WBA
Arturo Frias	USA	1981-1982	WBA
Ray Mancini	USA	1982-1984	WBA
Edwin Rosario	Puerto Rico	1983-1984	WBC
Charlie Choo Choo Brown	USA	1984	IBF
Harry Arroyo	USA	1984-1985	IBF
Livingstone Bramble	USA	1984-1986	WBA

WORLD CHAMPIONS SINCE GLOVES, 1889-2005

Title Holder	Birthplace	Tenure	Status
Jose Luis Ramirez	Mexico	1984-1985	WBC
Jimmy Paul	USA	1985-1986	IBF
Hector Camacho*	Puerto Rico	1985-1987	WBC
Edwin Rosario	Puerto Rico	1986-1987	WBA
Greg Haugen	USA	1986-1987	IBF
Vinny Pazienza	USA	1987-1988	IBF
Jose Luis Ramirez	Mexico	1987-1988	WBC
Julio Cesar Chavez*	Mexico	1987-1988	WBA
Greg Haugen	USA	1988-1989	IBF
Julio Cesar Chavez*	Mexico	1988-1989	WBA/WBC
Mauricio Aceves	Mexico	1989-1990	WBO
Pernell Whitaker*	USA	1989	IBF
Edwin Rosario	Puerto Rico	1989-1990	WBA
Pernell Whitaker*	USA	1989-1990	IBF/WBC
Juan Nazario	Puerto Rico	1990	WBA
Pernell Whitaker*	USA	1990-1992	IBF/WBC/WBA
Dingaan Thobela*	S Africa	1990-1992	WBO
Joey Gamache	USA	1992	WBA
Miguel Gonzalez*	Mexico	1992-1996	WBC
Giovanni Parisi*	Italy	1992-1994	WBO
Tony Lopez	USA	1992-1993	WBA
Fred Pendleton	USA	1993-1994	IBF
Dingaan Thobela	S Africa	1993	WBA
Orzubek Nazarov	Kyrghyzstan	1993-1998	WBA
Rafael Ruelas	USA	1994-1995	IBF
Oscar de la Hoya*	USA	1994-1995	WBO
Oscar de la Hoya*	USA	1995	WBO/IBF
Oscar de la Hoya*	USA	1995-1996	WBO
Phillip Holiday	S Africa	1995-1997	IBF
Jean-Baptiste Mendy	France	1996-1997	WBC
Artur Grigorian	Uzbekistan	1996-2004	WBO
Steve Johnston	USA	1997-1998	WBC
Shane Mosley*	USA	1997-1999	IBF
Jean-Baptiste Mendy	France	1998-1999	WBA
Cesar Bazan	Mexico	1998-1999	WBC
Steve Johnston	USA	1999-2000	WBC
Julien Lorcy	France	1999	WBA
Stefano Zoff	Italy	1999	WBA
Paul Spadafora*	USA	1999-2003	IBF
Gilberto Serrano	Venezuela	1999-2000	WBA
Takanori Hatakeyama	Japan	2000-2001	WBA
Jose Luis Castillo	Mexico	2000-2002	WBC
Julien Lorcy	France	2001	WBA
Raul Balbi	Argentina	2001-2002	WBA
Leonardo Dorin	Romania	2002-2003	WBA
Floyd Mayweather*	USA	2002-2004	WBC
Javier Jauregui	Mexico	2003-2004	IBF
Acelino Freitas	Brazil	2004	WBO
Lakva Sim	Mongolia	2004	WBA
Julio Diaz*	Mexico	2004-2005	IBF
Jose Luis Castillo	Mexico	2004-2005	WBC
Juan Diaz	USA	2004-	WBA
Diego Corrales*	USA	2004-2005	WBO
Diego Corrales	USA	2005-	WBC/WBO
Leavander Johnson	USA	2005-	IBF

L. Welterweight (140 lbs)

Title Holder	Birthplace	Tenure	Status
Pinkey Mitchell	USA	1922-1926	NBA
Mushy Callahan	USA	1926-1927	NBA
Mushy Callahan	USA	1927-1930	NBA/NY
Mushy Callahan	USA	1930	NBA
Jackie Kid Berg	England	1930-1931	NBA
Tony Canzoneri	USA	1931-1932	NBA
Johnny Jadick	USA	1932	NBA
Johnny Jadick	USA	1932-1933	PEN
Battling Shaw	Mexico	1933	LOUIS
Tony Canzoneri	USA	1933	LOUIS
Barney Ross*	USA	1933-1935	ILL
Maxie Berger	Canada	1939	CAN
Harry Weekly	USA	1941-1942	LOUIS
Tippy Larkin	USA	1946-1947	NY/NBA

Title Holder	Birthplace	Tenure	Status
Carlos Ortiz	Puerto Rico	1959-1960	NBA
Duilio Loi	Italy	1960-1962	NBA
Duilio Loi	Italy	1962	WBA
Eddie Perkins	USA	1962	WBA
Duilio Loi*	Italy	1962-1963	WBA
Roberto Cruz	Philippines	1963	WBA
Eddie Perkins	USA	1963-1965	WBA
Carlos Hernandez	Venezuela	1965-1966	WBA
Sandro Lopopolo	Italy	1966-1967	WBA
Paul Fujii	Hawaii	1967-1968	WBA
Nicolino Loche	Argentina	1968-1972	WBA
Pedro Adigue	Philippines	1968-1970	WBC
Bruno Arcari*	Italy	1970-1974	WBC
Alfonso Frazer	Panama	1972	WBA
Antonio Cervantes	Colombia	1972-1976	WBA
Perico Fernandez	Spain	1974-1975	WBC
Saensak Muangsurin	Thailand	1975-1976	WBC
Wilfred Benitez	USA	1976	WBA
Miguel Velasquez	Spain	1976	WBC
Saensak Muangsurin	Thailand	1976-1978	WBC
Antonio Cervantes	Colombia	1977-1980	WBA
Wilfred Benitez*	USA	1977-1978	NY
Sang-Hyun Kim	S Korea	1978-1980	WBC
Saoul Mamby	USA	1980-1982	WBC
Aaron Pryor*	USA	1980-1984	WBA
Leroy Haley	USA	1982-1983	WBC
Bruce Curry	USA	1983-1984	WBC
Johnny Bumphus	USA	1984	WBA
Bill Costello	USA	1984-1985	WBC
Gene Hatcher	USA	1984-1985	WBA
Aaron Pryor	USA	1984-1985	IBF
Ubaldo Sacco	Argentina	1985-1986	WBA
Lonnie Smith	USA	1985-1986	WBC
Patrizio Oliva	Italy	1986-1987	WBA
Gary Hinton	USA	1986	IBF
Rene Arredondo	Mexico	1986	WBC
Tsuyoshi Hamada	Japan	1986-1987	WBC
Joe Manley	USA	1986-1987	IBF
Terry Marsh*	England	1987	IBF
Juan M. Coggi	Argentina	1987-1990	WBA
Rene Arredondo	Mexico	1987	WBC
Roger Mayweather	USA	1987-1989	WBC
James McGirt	USA	1988	IBF
Meldrick Taylor	USA	1988-1990	IBF
Hector Camacho	Puerto Rico	1989-1991	WBO
Julio Cesar Chavez*	Mexico	1989-1990	WBC
Julio Cesar Chavez*	Mexico	1990-1991	IBF/WBC
Loreto Garza	USA	1990-1991	WBA
Greg Haugen	USA	1991	WBO
Hector Camacho	Puerto Rico	1991-1992	WBO
Edwin Rosario	Puerto Rico	1991-1992	WBA
Julio Cesar Chavez	Mexico	1991-1994	WBC
Rafael Pineda	Colombia	1991-1992	IBF
Akinobu Hiranaka	Japan	1992	WBA
Carlos Gonzalez	Mexico	1992-1993	WBO
Pernell Whitaker*	USA	1992-1993	IBF
Morris East	Philippines	1992-1993	WBA
Juan M. Coggi	Argentina	1993-1994	WBA
Charles Murray	USA	1993-1994	IBF
Zack Padilla*	USA	1993-1994	WBO
Frankie Randall	USA	1994	WBC
Jake Rodriguez	USA	1994-1995	IBF
Julio Cesar Chavez	Mexico	1994-1996	WBC
Frankie Randall	USA	1994-1996	WBA
Konstantin Tszyu	Russia	1995-1997	IBF
Sammy Fuentes	Puerto Rico	1995-1996	WBO
Juan M. Coggi	Argentina	1996	WBA
Giovanni Parisi	Italy	1996-1998	WBO
Oscar de la Hoya*	USA	1996-1997	WBC
Frankie Randall	USA	1996-1997	WBA
Khalid Rahilou	France	1997-1998	WBA

Title Holder	Birthplace	Tenure	Status
Vince Phillips	USA	1997-1999	IBF
Carlos Gonzalez	Mexico	1998-1999	WBO
Sharmba Mitchell	USA	1998-2001	WBA
Terron Millett	USA	1999	IBF
Randall Bailey	USA	1999-2000	WBO
Kostya Tszyu*	Russia	1999-2001	WBC
Zab Judah	USA	2000-2001	IBF
Ener Julio	Colombia	2000-2001	WBO
Kostya Tszyu*	Russia	2001	WBA/WBC
DeMarcus Corley	USA	2001-2003	WBO
Kostya Tszyu*	Russia	2001-2004	WBA/WBC/IBF
Zab Judah*	USA	2003-2004	WBO
Kostya Tszyu	Russia	2004-2005	IBF
Arturo Gatti	Canada	2004-2005	WBC
Vivien Harris	Guyana	2004-2005	WBA
Miguel Cotto	Puerto Rico	2004-	WBO
Ricky Hatton	England	2005-	IBF
Carlos Maussa	Colombia	2005-	WBA
Floyd Mayweather	USA	2005-	WBC

Welterweight (147 lbs)

Title Holder	Birthplace	Tenure	Status
Paddy Duffy	USA	1889-1890	
Tommy Ryan	USA	1891-1894	
Mysterious Billy Smith	USA	1892-1894	
Tommy Ryan	USA	1894-1897	USA
Tommy Ryan	USA	1897-1899	
Dick Burge	GB	1897	
George Green	USA	1897	
Tom Causer	GB	1897	
Joe Walcott	Barbados	1897	
George Lavigne	USA	1897-1899	
Dick Burge	GB	1897-1898	
Mysterious Billy Smith	USA	1898-1900	
Bobby Dobbs	USA	1898-1902	
Rube Ferns	USA	1900	
Matty Matthews	USA	1900	
Eddie Connolly	Canada	1900	
Matty Matthews	USA	1900-1901	
Rube Ferns	USA	1901	
Joe Walcott	Barbados	1901-1906	
Eddie Connolly	Canada	1902-1903	GB
Matty Matthews	USA	1902-1903	
Rube Ferns	USA	1903	
Martin Duffy	USA	1903-1904	
Honey Mellody	USA	1904	
Jack Clancy	USA	1904-1905	GB
Dixie Kid	USA	1904-1905	
Buddy Ryan	USA	1904-1905	
Sam Langford	Canada	1904-1905	
George Petersen	USA	1905	
Jimmy Gardner	USA	1905	
Mike Twin Sullivan	USA	1905-1906	
Joe Gans	USA	1906	
Joe Walcott	Barbados	1906	USA
Honey Mellody	USA	1906	USA
Honey Mellody	USA	1906-1907	
Joe Thomas	USA	1906-1907	
Mike Twin Sullivan	USA	1907-1911	
Jimmy Gardner	USA	1907-1908	
Frank Mantell	USA	1907-1908	
Harry Lewis	USA	1908-1910	
Jack Blackburn	USA	1908	
Jimmy Gardner	USA	1908-1909	
Willie Lewis	USA	1909-1910	
Harry Lewis	USA	1910-1911	GB/FR
Jimmy Clabby	USA	1910-1911	
Dixie Kid	USA	1911-1912	GB/FR
Ray Bronson	USA	1911-1914	
Marcel Thomas	France	1912-1913	FR
Wildcat Ferns	USA	1912-1913	
Spike Kelly	USA	1913-1914	

Title Holder	Birthplace	Tenure	Status
Mike Glover	USA	1913-1915	
Mike Gibbons	USA	1913-1914	
Waldemar Holberg	Denmark	1914	
Tom McCormick	Ireland	1914	
Matt Wells	England	1914-1915	AUSTR
Kid Graves	USA	1914-1917	
Jack Britton	USA	1915	
Ted Kid Lewis	England	1915-1916	
Jack Britton	USA	1916-1917	
Ted Kid Lewis	England	1917	
Ted Kid Lewis	England	1917-1919	
Jack Britton	USA	1919-1922	
Mickey Walker	USA	1922-1923	
Mickey Walker	USA	1923-1924	NBA
Dave Shade	USA	1923	NY
Jimmy Jones	USA	1923	NY/MASS
Mickey Walker	USA	1924-1926	
Pete Latzo	USA	1926-1927	
Joe Dundee	Italy	1927-1928	
Joe Dundee	Italy	1928-1929	NY
Jackie Fields	USA	1929	NBA
Jackie Fields	USA	1929-1930	
Young Jack Thompson	USA	1930	
Tommy Freeman	USA	1930-1931	
Young Jack Thompson	USA	1930	
Lou Brouillard	Canada	1931-1932	
Jackie Fields	USA	1932-1933	
Young Corbett III	Italy	1933	
Jimmy McLarnin	Ireland	1933-1934	
Barney Ross	USA	1934	
Jimmy McLarnin	Ireland	1934-1935	
Barney Ross	USA	1935-1938	
Barney Ross	USA	1938	NY/NBA
Felix Wouters	Belgium	1938	IBU
Henry Armstrong	USA	1938-1940	
Fritzie Zivic	USA	1940	
Fritzie Zivic	USA	1940-1941	NY/NBA
Izzy Jannazzo	USA	1940-1942	MARY
Red Cochrane	USA	1941-1942	NY/NBA
Red Cochrane	USA	1942-1946	
Marty Servo	USA	1946	
Sugar Ray Robinson*	USA	1946-1951	
Johnny Bratton	USA	1951	NBA
Kid Gavilan	Cuba	1951-1952	NBA/NY
Kid Gavilan	Cuba	1952-1954	
Johnny Saxton	USA	1954-1955	
Tony de Marco	USA	1955	
Carmen Basilio	USA	1955-1956	
Johnny Saxton	USA	1956	
Carmen Basilio*	USA	1956-1957	
Virgil Akins	USA	1957-1958	MASS
Virgil Akins	USA	1958	
Don Jordan	Dom Republic	1958-1960	
Benny Kid Paret	Cuba	1960-1961	
Emile Griffith	Virgin Islands	1961	
Benny Kid Paret	Cuba	1961-1962	
Emile Griffith	Virgin Islands	1962-1963	
Luis Rodriguez	Cuba	1963	
Emile Griffith*	Virgin Islands	1963-1966	
Willie Ludick	S Africa	1966-1968	SA
Curtis Cokes*	USA	1966	WBA
Curtis Cokes*	USA	1966-1967	WBA/WBC
Charley Shipes	USA	1966-1967	CALIF
Curtis Cokes	USA	1968-1969	
Jose Napoles	Cuba	1969-1970	
Billy Backus	USA	1970-1971	
Jose Napoles	Cuba	1971-1972	
Jose Napoles*	Cuba	1972-1974	WBA/WBC
Hedgemon Lewis	USA	1972-1974	NY
Jose Napoles	Cuba	1974-1975	
Jose Napoles	Cuba	1975	WBC

WORLD CHAMPIONS SINCE GLOVES, 1889-2005

Title Holder	Birthplace	Tenure	Status	Title Holder	Birthplace	Tenure	Status
Angel Espada	Puerto Rico	1975-1976	WBA	Miguel de Oliveira	Brazil	1975	WBC
John H. Stracey	England	1975-1976	WBC	Jae-Do Yuh	S Korea	1975-1976	WBA
Carlos Palomino	Mexico	1976-1979	WBC	Elisha Obed	Bahamas	1975-1976	WBC
Pipino Cuevas	Mexico	1976-1980	WBA	Koichi Wajima	Japan	1976	WBA
Wilfred Benitez	USA	1979	WBC	Jose Duran	Spain	1976	WBA
Sugar Ray Leonard	USA	1979-1980	WBC	Eckhard Dagge	Germany	1976-1977	WBC
Roberto Duran	Panama	1980	WBC	Miguel Castellini	Argentina	1976-1977	WBA
Thomas Hearns	USA	1980-1981	WBA	Eddie Gazo	Nicaragua	1977-1978	WBA
Sugar Ray Leonard	USA	1980-1981	WBC	Rocky Mattioli	Italy	1977-1979	WBC
Sugar Ray Leonard*	USA	1981-1982		Masashi Kudo	Japan	1978-1979	WBA
Don Curry*	USA	1983-1984	WBA	Maurice Hope	Antigua	1979-1981	WBC
Milton McCrory	USA	1983-1985	WBC	Ayub Kalule	Uganda	1979-1981	WBA
Don Curry*	USA	1984-1985	WBA/IBF	Wilfred Benitez	USA	1981-1982	WBC
Don Curry	USA	1985-1986		Sugar Ray Leonard*	USA	1981	
Lloyd Honeyghan	Jamaica	1986		Tadashi Mihara	Japan	1981-1982	WBA
Lloyd Honeyghan	Jamaica	1986-1987	WBC/IBF	Davey Moore	USA	1982-1983	WBA
Mark Breland	USA	1987	WBA	Thomas Hearns*	USA	1982-1986	WBC
Marlon Starling	USA	1987-1988	WBA	Roberto Duran*	Panama	1983-1984	WBA
Jorge Vaca	Mexico	1987-1988	WBC	Mark Medal	USA	1984	IBF
Lloyd Honeyghan	Jamaica	1988-1989	WBC	Mike McCallum*	Jamaica	1984-1987	WBA
Simon Brown*	Jamaica	1988-1991	IBF	Carlos Santos	Puerto Rico	1984-1986	IBF
Tomas Molinares	Colombia	1988-1989	WBA	Buster Drayton	USA	1986-1987	IBF
Mark Breland	USA	1989-1990	WBA	Duane Thomas	USA	1986-1987	WBC
Marlon Starling	USA	1989-1990	WBC	Matthew Hilton	Canada	1987-1988	IBF
Genaro Leon*	Mexico	1989	WBO	Lupe Aquino	Mexico	1987	WBC
Manning Galloway	USA	1989-1993	WBO	Gianfranco Rosi	Italy	1987-1988	WBC
Aaron Davis	USA	1990-1991	WBA	Julian Jackson*	Virgin Islands	1987-1990	WBA
Maurice Blocker	USA	1990-1991	WBC	Don Curry	USA	1988-1989	WBC
Meldrick Taylor	USA	1991-1992	WBA	Robert Hines	USA	1988-1989	IBF
Simon Brown*	Jamaica	1991	WBC/IBF	John David Jackson*	USA	1988-1993	WBO
Simon Brown	Jamaica	1991	WBC	Darrin van Horn	USA	1989	IBF
Maurice Blocker	USA	1991-1993	IBF	Rene Jacqot	France	1989	WBC
James McGirt	USA	1991-1993	WBC	John Mugabi	Uganda	1989-1990	WBC
Crisanto Espana	Venezuela	1992-1994	WBA	Gianfranco Rosi	Italy	1989-1994	IBF
Gert Bo Jacobsen*	Denmark	1993	WBO	Terry Norris	USA	1990-1993	WBC
Pernell Whitaker	USA	1993-1997	WBC	Gilbert Dele	France	1991	WBA
Felix Trinidad*	Puerto Rico	1993-2000	IBF	Vinny Pazienza*	USA	1991-1992	WBA
Eamonn Loughran	Ireland	1993-1996	WBO	Julio Cesar Vasquez	Argentina	1992-1995	WBA
Ike Quartey	Ghana	1994-1998	WBA	Verno Phillips	USA	1993-1995	WBO
Jose Luis Lopez	Mexico	1996-1997	WBO	Simon Brown	USA	1993-1994	WBC
Michael Loewe*	Romania	1997-1998	WBO	Terry Norris	USA	1994	WBC
Oscar de la Hoya	USA	1997-1999	WBC	Vince Pettway	USA	1994-1995	IBF
Ahmed Kotiev	Russia	1998-2000	WBO	Luis Santana	Dom Republic	1994-1995	WBC
James Page	USA	1998-2000	WBA	Pernell Whitaker*	USA	1995	WBA
Oscar de la Hoya	USA	2000	WBC	Gianfranco Rosi	Italy	1995	WBO
Daniel Santos*	Puerto Rico	2000-2002	WBO	Carl Daniels	USA	1995	WBA
Shane Mosley	USA	2000-2002	WBC	Verno Phillips	USA	1995	WBO
Andrew Lewis	Guyana	2001-2002	WBA	Paul Vaden	USA	1995	IBF
Vernon Forrest	USA	2001	IBF	Terry Norris*	USA	1995	WBC
Vernon Forrest	USA	2002-2003	WBC	Paul Jones	England	1995-1996	WBO
Antonio Margarito	Mexico	2002-	WBO	Terry Norris	USA	1995-1997	IBF/WBC
Ricardo Mayorga*	Nicaragua	2002-2003	WBA	Julio Cesar Vasquez	Argentina	1995-1996	WBA
Michele Piccirillo	Italy	2002-2003	IBF	Bronco McKart	USA	1996	WBO
Ricardo Mayorga	Nicaragua	2003	WBA/WBC	Ronald Wright	USA	1996-1998	WBO
Cory Spinks*	USA	2003	IBF	Laurent Boudouani	France	1996-1999	WBA
Cory Spinks	USA	2003-2005	IBF/WBA/WBC	Terry Norris	USA	1997	WBC
Zab Judah	USA	2005-	IBF/WBA/WBC	Raul Marquez	USA	1997	IBF
				Luis Campas	Mexico	1997-1998	IBF

L. Middleweight (154 lbs)

Title Holder	Birthplace	Tenure	Status	Title Holder	Birthplace	Tenure	Status
Emile Griffith*	USA	1962-1963	AU	Keith Mullings	USA	1997-1999	WBC
Denny Moyer	USA	1962-1963	WBA	Harry Simon*	Namibia	1998-2001	WBO
Ralph Dupas	USA	1963	WBA	Fernando Vargas	USA	1998-2000	IBF
Sandro Mazzinghi	Italy	1963-1965	WBA	Javier Castillejo	Spain	1999-2001	WBC
Nino Benvenuti	Italy	1965-1966	WBA	David Reid	USA	1999-2000	WBA
Ki-Soo Kim	S Korea	1966-1968	WBA	Felix Trinidad*	Puerto Rico	2000	WBA
Sandro Mazzinghi	Italy	1968-1969	WBA	Felix Trinidad*	Puerto Rico	2000-2001	IBF/WBA
Freddie Little	USA	1969-1970	WBA	Oscar de la Hoya*	USA	2001-2002	WBC
Carmelo Bossi	Italy	1970-1971	WBA	Fernando Vargas	USA	2001-2002	WBA
Koichi Wajima	Japan	1971-1974	WBA	Ronald Wright*	USA	2001-2004	IBF
Oscar Albarado	USA	1974-1975	WBA	Daniel Santos	Puerto Rico	2002-	WBO
Koichi Wajima	Japan	1975	WBA	Oscar de la Hoya	USA	2002-2003	WBA/WBC
				Shane Mosley	USA	2003-2004	WBA/WBC

Title Holder	Birthplace	Tenure	Status
Ronald Wright	USA	2004	IBF/WBA/WBC
Ronald Wright	USA	2004-2005	WBA/WBC
Verno Phillips	USA	2004	IBF
Kassim Ouma	Uganda	2004-	IBF
Ronald Wright*	USA	2005	WBC
Travis Simms	USA	2005	WBA
Javier Castillejo	Spain	2005	WBC
Alejandro Garcia	Mexico	2005-	WBA

Middleweight (160 lbs)

Title Holder	Birthplace	Tenure	Status
Nonpareil Jack Dempsey	Ireland	1889-1891	USA
Bob Fitzsimmons	England	1891-1893	USA
Jim Hall	Australia	1892-1893	GB
Bob Fitzsimmons	England	1893-1894	
Bob Fitzsimmons	England	1894-1899	
Frank Craig	USA	1894-1895	GB
Dan Creedon	New Zealand	1895-1897	GB
Tommy Ryan	USA	1895-1896	
Kid McCoy	USA	1896-1898	
Tommy Ryan	USA	1898-1905	
Charley McKeever	USA	1900-1902	
George Gardner	USA	1901-1902	
Jack O'Brien	USA	1901-1905	
George Green	USA	1901-1902	
Jack Palmer	England	1902-1903	GB
Hugo Kelly	USA	1905-1908	
Jack Twin Sullivan	USA	1905-1908	
Sam Langford	Canada	1907-1911	
Billy Papke	USA	1908	
Stanley Ketchel	USA	1908	
Billy Papke	USA	1908	
Stanley Ketchel	USA	1908-1910	
Billy Papke	USA	1910-1913	
Stanley Ketchel*	USA	1910	
Hugo Kelly	USA	1910-1912	
Cyclone Johnny Thompson	USA	1911-1912	
Harry Lewis	USA	1911	
Leo Houck	USA	1911-1912	
Georges Carpentier	France	1911-1912	
Jack Dillon	USA	1912	
Frank Mantell	USA	1912-1913	
Frank Klaus	USA	1912-1913	
Georges Carpentier	France	1912	IBU
Jack Dillon	USA	1912-1915	
Eddie McGoorty	USA	1912-1913	
Frank Klaus	USA	1913	IBU
Jimmy Clabby	USA	1913-1914	
George Chip	USA	1913-1914	
Joe Borrell	USA	1913-1914	
Jeff Smith	USA	1913-1914	
Eddie McGoorty	USA	1914	AUSTR
Jeff Smith	USA	1914	AUSTR
Al McCoy	USA	1914-1917	
Jimmy Clabby	USA	1914-1915	
Mick King	Australia	1914	AUSTR
Jeff Smith	USA	1914-1915	AUSTR
Young Ahearn	England	1915-1916	
Les Darcy*	Australia	1915-1917	AUSTR
Mike Gibbons	USA	1916-1917	
Mike O'Dowd	USA	1917-1920	
Johnny Wilson	USA	1920-1921	
Johnny Wilson	USA	1921-1922	NBA/NY
Bryan Downey	USA	1921-1922	OHIO
Johnny Wilson	USA	1922-1923	NBA
Dave Rosenberg	USA	1922	NY
Jock Malone	USA	1922-1923	OHIO
Mike O'Dowd	USA	1922-1923	NY
Johnny Wilson	USA	1923	
Harry Greb	USA	1923-1926	
Tiger Flowers	USA	1926	
Mickey Walker	USA	1926-1931	

Title Holder	Birthplace	Tenure	Status
Gorilla Jones	USA	1932	NBA
Marcel Thil	France	1932-1933	NBA/IBU
Marcel Thil	France	1933-1937	IBU
Ben Jeby	USA	1933	NY
Lou Brouillard	Canada	1933	NY
Lou Brouillard	Canada	1933	NY/NBA
Vearl Whitehead	USA	1933	CALIF
Teddy Yarosz	USA	1933-1934	PEN
Vince Dundee	USA	1933-1934	NY/NBA
Teddy Yarosz	USA	1934-1935	NY/NBA
Babe Risko	USA	1935-1936	NY/NBA
Freddie Steele	USA	1936-1938	NY/NBA
Fred Apostoli	USA	1937-1938	IBU
Edouard Tenet	France	1938	IBU
Young Corbett III	Italy	1938	CALIF
Freddie Steele	USA	1938	NBA
Al Hostak	USA	1938	NBA
Solly Krieger	USA	1938-1939	NBA
Fred Apostoli	USA	1938-1939	NY
Al Hostak	USA	1939-1940	NBA
Ceferino Garcia	Philippines	1939-1940	NY
Ken Overlin	USA	1940-1941	NY
Tony Zale	USA	1940-1941	NBA
Billy Soose	USA	1941	NY
Tony Zale	USA	1941-1947	
Rocky Graziano	USA	1947-1948	
Tony Zale	USA	1948	
Marcel Cerdan	Algeria	1948-1949	
Jake la Motta	USA	1949-1950	
Jake la Motta	USA	1950-1951	NY/NBA
Sugar Ray Robinson	USA	1950-1951	PEN
Sugar Ray Robinson	USA	1951	
Randy Turpin	England	1951	
Sugar Ray Robinson*	USA	1951-1952	
Randy Turpin	England	1953	GB/EBU
Carl Bobo Olson	Hawaii	1953-1955	
Sugar Ray Robinson	USA	1955-1957	
Gene Fullmer	USA	1957	
Sugar Ray Robinson	USA	1957	
Carmen Basilio	USA	1957-1958	
Sugar Ray Robinson	USA	1958-1959	
Sugar Ray Robinson	USA	1959-1960	NY/EBU
Gene Fullmer	USA	1959-1962	NBA
Paul Pender	USA	1960-1961	NY/EBU
Terry Downes	England	1961-1962	NY/EBU
Paul Pender	USA	1962	NY/EBU
Dick Tiger	Nigeria	1962-1963	NBA
Dick Tiger	Nigeria	1963	
Joey Giardello	USA	1963-1965	
Dick Tiger	Nigeria	1965-1966	
Emile Griffith	Virgin Islands	1966-1967	
Nino Benvenuti	Italy	1967	
Emile Griffith	Virgin Islands	1967-1968	
Nino Benvenuti	Italy	1968-1970	
Carlos Monzon	Argentina	1970-1974	
Carlos Monzon*	Argentina	1974-1976	WBA
Rodrigo Valdez	Colombia	1974-1976	WBC
Carlos Monzon*	Argentina	1976-1977	
Rodrigo Valdez	Colombia	1977-1978	
Hugo Corro	Argentina	1978-1979	
Vito Antuofermo	Italy	1979-1980	
Alan Minter	England	1980	
Marvin Hagler	USA	1980-1987	
Marvin Hagler	USA	1987	WBC/IBF
Sugar Ray Leonard	USA	1987	WBC
Frank Tate	USA	1987-1988	IBF
Sumbu Kalambay	Zaire	1987-1989	WBA
Thomas Hearns	USA	1987-1988	WBC
Iran Barkley	USA	1988-1989	WBC
Michael Nunn	USA	1988-1991	IBF
Roberto Duran	Panama	1989-1990	WBC

WORLD CHAMPIONS SINCE GLOVES, 1889-2005

Title Holder	Birthplace	Tenure	Status		Title Holder	Birthplace	Tenure	Status
Doug de Witt	USA	1989-1990	WBO		Markus Beyer	Germany	1999-2000	WBC
Mike McCallum	Jamaica	1989-1991	WBA		Bruno Girard	France	2000-2001	WBA
Nigel Benn	England	1990	WBO		Glenn Catley	England	2000	WBC
Chris Eubank*	England	1990-1991	WBO		Dingaan Thobela	S Africa	2000	WBC
Julian Jackson	Virgin Islands	1990-1993	WBC		Dave Hilton	Canada	2000-2001	WBC
James Toney*	USA	1991-1993	IBF		Byron Mitchell	USA	2001-2003	WBA
Gerald McClellan*	USA	1991-1993	WBO		Eric Lucas	Canada	2001-2003	WBC
Reggie Johnson	USA	1992-1993	WBA		Sven Ottke*	Germany	2003-2004	IBF/WBA
Gerald McClellan*	USA	1993-1995	WBC		Markus Beyer	Germany	2003-2004	WBC
Chris Pyatt	England	1993-1994	WBO		Anthony Mundine	Australia	2004	WBA
Roy Jones*	USA	1993-1994	IBF		Manny Sica	Puerto Rico	2004	WBA
John David Jackson	USA	1993-1994	WBA		Cristian Sanavia	Italy	2004	WBC
Steve Collins*	Ireland	1994-1995	WBO		Jeff Lacey	USA	2004-	IBF
Jorge Castro	Argentina	1994	WBA		Markus Beyer	Germany	2004-	WBC
Julian Jackson	Virgin Islands	1995	WBC		Mikkel Kessler	Denmark	2004-	WBA
Bernard Hopkins*	USA	1995-2001	IBF					
Lonnie Bradley*	USA	1995-1998	WBO		**L. Heavyweight (175 lbs)**			
Quincy Taylor	USA	1995-1996	WBC		Jack Root	Austria	1903	
Shinji Takehara	Japan	1995-1996	WBA		George Gardner	Ireland	1903	
Keith Holmes	USA	1996-1998	WBC		George Gardner	Ireland	1903	USA
William Joppy	USA	1996-1997	WBA		Bob Fitzsimmons	England	1903-1905	USA
Julio Cesar Green	Dom Republic	1997-1998	WBA		Jack O'Brien	USA	1905-1911	
William Joppy	USA	1998-2001	WBA		Sam Langford	Canada	1911-1913	
Hassine Cherifi	France	1998-1999	WBC		Georges Carpentier	France	1913-1920	IBU
Otis Grant*	Canada	1998	WBO		Jack Dillon	USA	1914-1916	USA
Bert Schenk	Germany	1999	WBO		Battling Levinsky	USA	1916-1920	USA
Keith Holmes	USA	1999-2001	WBC		**Georges Carpentier**	France	1920-1922	
Jason Matthews	England	1999	WBO		**Battling Siki**	Senegal	1922-1923	
Armand Krajnc	Slovenia	1999-2002	WBO		**Mike McTigue**	Ireland	1923-1925	
Bernard Hopkins*	USA	2001	WBC/IBF		**Paul Berlenbach**	USA	1925-1926	
Felix Trinidad	Puerto Rico	2001	WBA		**Jack Delaney***	Canada	1926-1927	
Bernard Hopkins*	USA	2001-2004	WBC/WBA/IBF		Jimmy Slattery	USA	1927	NBA
Harry Simon	Namibia	2002-2003	WBO		Tommy Loughran	USA	1927	NY
Hector Javier Velazco	Argentina	2003	WBO		**Tommy Loughran***	USA	1927-1929	
Felix Sturm	Germany	2003-2004	WBO		Jimmy Slattery	USA	1930	NY
Oscar de la Hoya	USA	2004	WBO		**Maxie Rosenbloom**	USA	1930-1931	
Bernard Hopkins	USA	2004-	IBF/WBA/WBC/		Maxie Rosenbloom	USA	1931-1933	NY
			WBO		George Nichols	USA	1932	NBA
					Bob Godwin	USA	1933	NBA
S. Middleweight (168 lbs)					**Maxie Rosenbloom**	USA	1933-1934	
Murray Sutherland	Scotland	1984	IBF		Maxie Rosenbloom	USA	1934	NY
Chong-Pal Park*	S Korea	1984-1987	IBF		Joe Knight	USA	1934-1935	FL/NC/GEO
Chong-Pal Park	S Korea	1987-1988	WBA		Bob Olin	USA	1934-1935	NY
Graciano Rocchigiani*	Germany	1988-1989	IBF		Al McCoy	Canada	1935	CAN
Fully Obelmejias	Venezuela	1988-1989	WBA		Bob Olin	USA	1935	NY/NBA
Sugar Ray Leonard*	USA	1988-1990	WBC		John Henry Lewis	USA	1935-1938	NY/NBA
Thomas Hearns*	USA	1988-1991	WBO		Gustav Roth	Belgium	1936-1938	IBU
In-Chul Baek	S Korea	1989-1990	WBA		Ad Heuser	Germany	1938	IBU
Lindell Holmes	USA	1990-1991	IBF		**John Henry Lewis**	USA	1938	
Christophe Tiozzo	France	1990-1991	WBA		John Henry Lewis	USA	1938-1939	NBA
Mauro Galvano	Italy	1990-1992	WBC		Melio Bettina	USA	1939	NY
Victor Cordoba	Panama	1991-1992	WBA		Len Harvey	England	1939-1942	GB
Darrin van Horn	USA	1991-1992	IBF		Billy Conn	USA	1939-1940	NY/NBA
Chris Eubank	England	1991-1995	WBO		Anton Christoforidis	Greece	1941	NBA
Iran Barkley	USA	1992-1993	IBF		Gus Lesnevich	USA	1941	NBA
Michael Nunn	USA	1992-1994	WBA		Gus Lesnevich	USA	1941-1946	NY/NBA
Nigel Benn	England	1992-1996	WBC		Freddie Mills	England	1942-1946	GB
James Toney	USA	1993-1994	IBF		**Gus Lesnevich**	USA	1946-1948	
Steve Little	USA	1994	WBA		**Freddie Mills**	England	1948-1950	
Frank Liles	USA	1994-1999	WBA		**Joey Maxim**	USA	1950-1952	
Roy Jones*	USA	1994-1997	IBF		**Archie Moore**	USA	1952-1960	
Steve Collins*	Ireland	1995-1997	WBO		Archie Moore	USA	1960-1962	NY/EBU
Thulani Malinga	S Africa	1996	WBC		Harold Johnson	USA	1961-1962	NBA
Vincenzo Nardiello	Italy	1996	WBC		**Harold Johnson**	USA	1962-1963	
Robin Reid	England	1996-1997	WBC		**Willie Pastrano**	USA	1963	
Charles Brewer	USA	1997-1998	IBF		Willie Pastrano*	USA	1963-1964	WBA/WBC
Joe Calzaghe	Wales	1997-	WBO		Eddie Cotton	USA	1963-1964	MICH
Thulani Malinga	S Africa	1997-1998	WBC		**Willie Pastrano**	USA	1964-1965	
Richie Woodhall	England	1998-1999	WBC		**Jose Torres**	Puerto Rico	1965-1966	
Sven Ottke*	Germany	1998-2003	IBF		**Dick Tiger**	Nigeria	1966-1968	
Byron Mitchell	USA	1999-2000	WBA		**Bob Foster**	USA	1968-1970	

Title Holder	Birthplace	Tenure	Status
Bob Foster*	USA	1970-1972	WBC
Vicente Rondon	Venezuela	1971-1972	WBA
Bob Foster*	USA	1972-1974	
John Conteh	England	1974-1977	WBC
Victor Galindez	Argentina	1974-1978	WBA
Miguel Cuello	Argentina	1977-1978	WBC
Mate Parlov	Yugoslavia	1978	WBC
Mike Rossman	USA	1978-1979	WBA
Marvin Johnson	USA	1978-1979	WBC
Victor Galindez	Argentina	1979	WBA
Matt Saad Muhammad	USA	1979-1981	WBC
Marvin Johnson	USA	1979-1980	WBA
Mustafa Muhammad	USA	1980-1981	WBA
Michael Spinks*	USA	1981-1983	WBA
Dwight Muhammad Qawi	USA	1981-1983	WBC
Michael Spinks*	USA	1983-1985	
J. B. Williamson	USA	1985-1986	WBC
Slobodan Kacar	Yugoslavia	1985-1986	IBF
Marvin Johnson	USA	1986-1987	WBA
Dennis Andries	Guyana	1986-1987	WBC
Bobby Czyz	USA	1986-1987	IBF
Thomas Hearns*	USA	1987	WBC
Leslie Stewart	Trinidad	1987	WBA
Virgil Hill	USA	1987-1991	WBA
Charles Williams	USA	1987-1993	IBF
Don Lalonde	Canada	1987-1988	WBC
Sugar Ray Leonard*	USA	1988	WBC
Michael Moorer*	USA	1988-1991	WBO
Dennis Andries	Guyana	1989	WBC
Jeff Harding	Australia	1989-1990	WBC
Dennis Andries	Guyana	1990-1991	WBC
Leonzer Barber	USA	1991-1994	WBO
Thomas Hearns	USA	1991-1992	WBA
Jeff Harding	Australia	1991-1994	WBC
Iran Barkley*	USA	1992	WBA
Virgil Hill*	USA	1992-1996	WBA
Henry Maske	Germany	1993-1996	IBF

Title Holder	Birthplace	Tenure	Status
Mike McCallum	Jamaica	1994-1995	WBC
Dariusz Michalczewski*	Poland	1994-1997	WBO
Fabrice Tiozzo	France	1995-1997	WBC
Virgil Hill	USA	1996-1997	IBF/WBA
Roy Jones	USA	1997	WBC
Montell Griffin	USA	1997	WBC
Dariusz Michalczewski*	Poland	1997	WBO/IBF/WBA
Dariusz Michalczewski	Poland	1997-2003	WBO
William Guthrie	USA	1997-1998	IBF
Roy Jones*	USA	1997-1998	WBC
Lou del Valle	USA	1997-1998	WBA
Reggie Johnson	USA	1998-1999	IBF
Roy Jones*	USA	1998-1999	WBC/WBA
Roy Jones*	USA	1999-2002	WBC/WBA/IBF
Roy Jones*	USA	2002-2003	WBA/WBC
Mehdi Sahnoune	France	2003	WBA
Antonio Tarver*	USA	2003	IBF/WBC
Silvio Branco	Italy	2003-2004	WBA
Julio Gonzalez	Mexico	2003-2004	WBO
Antonio Tarver*	USA	2003-2004	WBC
Zsolt Erdei	Hungary	2004-	WBO
Glengoffe Johnson*	Jamaica	2004	IBF
Fabrice Tiozzo	France	2004-	WBA
Clinton Woods	England	2005-	IBF
Tomasz Adamek	Poland	2005-	WBC

Cruiserweight (200 lbs)

Title Holder	Birthplace	Tenure	Status
Marvin Camel	USA	1979-1980	WBC
Carlos de Leon	Puerto Rico	1980-1982	WBC
Ossie Ocasio	Puerto Rico	1982-1984	WBA
S. T. Gordon	USA	1982-1983	WBC
Marvin Camel	USA	1983-1984	IBF
Carlos de Leon	Puerto Rico	1983-1985	WBC
Lee Roy Murphy	USA	1984-1986	IBF
Piet Crous	S Africa	1984-1985	WBA
Alfonso Ratliff	USA	1985	WBC
Dwight Muhammad Qawi	USA	1985-1986	WBA
Bernard Benton	USA	1985-1986	WBC
Carlos de Leon	Puerto Rico	1986-1988	WBC
Evander Holyfield*	USA	1986-1987	WBA
Rickey Parkey	USA	1986-1987	IBF
Evander Holyfield*	USA	1987-1988	WBA/IBF
Evander Holyfield*	USA	1988	
Taoufik Belbouli*	France	1989	WBA
Carlos de Leon	Puerto Rico	1989-1990	WBC
Glenn McCrory	England	1989-1990	IBF
Robert Daniels	USA	1989-1991	WBA
Boone Pultz	USA	1989-1990	WBO
Jeff Lampkin*	USA	1990-1991	IBF
Magne Havnaa*	Norway	1990-1992	WBO
Masimilliano Duran	Italy	1990-1991	WBC
Bobby Czyz	USA	1991-1993	WBA
Anaclet Wamba	Congo	1991-1995	WBC
James Warring	USA	1991-1992	IBF
Tyrone Booze	USA	1992-1993	WBO
Al Cole*	USA	1992-1996	IBF
Marcus Bott	Germany	1993	WBO
Nestor Giovannini	Argentina	1993-1994	WBO
Orlin Norris	USA	1993-1995	WBA
Dariusz Michalczewski*	Poland	1994-1995	WBO
Ralf Rocchigiani	Germany	1995-1997	WBO
Nate Miller	USA	1995-1997	WBA
Marcelo Dominguez	Argentina	1995-1998	WBC
Adolpho Washington	USA	1996-1997	IBF
Uriah Grant	USA	1997	IBF
Carl Thompson	England	1997-1999	WBO
Imamu Mayfield	USA	1997-1998	IBF
Fabrice Tiozzo	France	1997-2000	WBA
Juan Carlos Gomez*	Cuba	1998-2002	WBC
Arthur Williams	USA	1998-1999	IBF
Johnny Nelson	England	1999-	WBO

England's Clinton Woods (right) made it fourth time lucky when stopping America's Rico Hoye to win the vacant IBF light-heavyweight crown   Les Clark

Name	Country	Years	Org
Vassily Jirov	Kazakhstan	1999-2003	IBF
Virgil Hill	USA	2000-2002	WBA
Jean-Marc Mormeck*	Guadeloupe	2002-2005	WBA
Wayne Braithwaite	Guyana	2002-2005	WBC
James Toney*	USA	2003-2004	IBF
Kelvin Davis	USA	2004-2005	IBF
Jean-Marc Mormeck	Guadaloupe	2005-	WBA/WBC
O'Neil Bell	USA	2005-	IBF

Heavyweight (200 lbs+)

Name	Country	Years	Org
John L. Sullivan	USA	1889-1892	USA
Peter Jackson	Australia	1889-1892	
Frank Slavin	Australia	1890-1892	GB/AUST
Peter Jackson	Australia	1892-1893	GB/AUST
James J. Corbett	USA	1892-1894	USA
James J. Corbett	USA	1894-1895	
James J. Corbett	USA	1895-1897	
Peter Maher	Ireland	1895-1896	
Bob Fitzsimmons	England	1896-1897	
Bob Fitzsimmons	England	1897-1899	
James J. Jeffries	USA	1899-1902	
James J. Jeffries	USA	1902-1905	
Denver Ed Martin	USA	1902-1903	
Jack Johnson	USA	1902-1908	
Bob Fitzsimmons	England	1905	
Marvin Hart	USA	1905-1906	
Jack O'Brien	USA	1905-1906	
Tommy Burns	Canada	1906-1908	
Jack Johnson	USA	1908-1909	
Jack Johnson	USA	1909-1915	
Sam Langford	USA	1909-1911	
Sam McVey	USA	1911-1912	
Sam Langford	USA	1912-1914	
Luther McCarty	USA	1913	
Arthur Pelkey	Canada	1913-1914	
Gunboat Smith	USA	1914	
Harry Wills	USA	1914	
Georges Carpentier	France	1914	
Sam Langford	USA	1914-1915	
Jess Willard	USA	1915-1919	
Joe Jeannette	USA	1915	
Sam McVey	USA	1915	
Harry Wills	USA	1915-1916	
Sam Langford	USA	1916-1917	
Bill Tate	USA	1917	
Sam Langford	USA	1917-1918	
Harry Wills	USA	1918-1926	
Jack Dempsey	USA	1919-1926	
Gene Tunney*	USA	1926-1928	
Max Schmeling	Germany	1930-1932	
Jack Sharkey	USA	1932-1933	
Primo Carnera	Italy	1933-1934	
Max Baer	USA	1934-1935	
James J. Braddock	USA	1935	
James J. Braddock	USA	1935-1936	NY/NBA
George Godfrey	USA	1935-1936	IBU
James J. Braddock	USA	1936-1937	
Joe Louis*	USA	1937-1949	
Ezzard Charles	USA	1949-1950	NBA
Lee Savold	USA	1950-1951	GB/EBU
Ezzard Charles	USA	1950-1951	NY/NBA
Joe Louis	USA	1951	GB/EBU
Jersey Joe Walcott	USA	1951	NY/NBA
Jersey Joe Walcott	USA	1951-1952	
Rocky Marciano*	USA	1952-1956	
Floyd Patterson	USA	1956-1959	
Ingemar Johansson	Sweden	1959-1960	
Floyd Patterson	USA	1960-1962	
Sonny Liston	USA	1962-1964	
Muhammad Ali	USA	1964	
Muhammad Ali*	USA	1964-1967	WBC
Ernie Terrell	USA	1965-1967	WBA
Muhammad Ali	USA	1967	
Muhammad Ali	USA	1967-1968	WBC
Joe Frazier*	USA	1968-1970	NY/MASS
Jimmy Ellis	USA	1968-1970	WBA
Joe Frazier	USA	1970-1973	
George Foreman	USA	1973-1974	
Muhammad Ali	USA	1974-1978	
Leon Spinks	USA	1978	
Leon Spinks	USA	1978	WBA
Larry Holmes*	USA	1978-1983	WBC
Muhammad Ali*	USA	1978-1979	WBA
John Tate	USA	1979-1980	WBA
Mike Weaver	USA	1980-1982	WBA
Michael Dokes	USA	1982-1983	WBA
Gerrie Coetzee	S Africa	1983-1984	WBA
Larry Holmes	USA	1983-1985	IBF
Tim Witherspoon	USA	1984	WBC
Pinklon Thomas	USA	1984-1986	WBC
Greg Page	USA	1984-1985	WBA
Tony Tubbs	USA	1985-1986	WBA
Michael Spinks	USA	1985-1987	IBF
Tim Witherspoon	USA	1986	WBA
Trevor Berbick	Jamaica	1986	WBC
Mike Tyson*	USA	1986-1987	WBC
James Smith	USA	1986-1987	WBA
Mike Tyson*	USA	1987	WBA/WBC
Tony Tucker	USA	1987	IBF
Mike Tyson	USA	1987-1989	
Mike Tyson	USA	1989-1990	IBF/WBA/WBC
Francesco Damiani	Italy	1989-1991	WBO
James Douglas	USA	1990	IBF/WBA/WBC
Evander Holyfield	USA	1990-1992	IBF/WBA/WBC
Ray Mercer	USA	1991-1992	WBO
Michael Moorer*	USA	1992-1993	WBO
Riddick Bowe	USA	1992	IBF/WBA/WBC
Riddick Bowe	USA	1992-1993	IBF/WBA
Lennox Lewis	England	1992-1994	WBC
Tommy Morrison	USA	1993	WBO
Michael Bentt	England	1993-1994	WBO
Evander Holyfield	USA	1993-1994	WBA/IBF
Herbie Hide	England	1994-1995	WBO
Michael Moorer	USA	1994	WBA/IBF
Oliver McCall	USA	1994-1995	WBC
George Foreman	USA	1994-1995	WBA/IBF
Riddick Bowe*	USA	1995-1996	WBO
George Foreman*	USA	1995	IBF
Bruce Seldon	USA	1995-1996	WBA
Frank Bruno	England	1995-1996	WBC
Frans Botha	S Africa	1995-1996	IBF
Mike Tyson	USA	1996	WBC
Michael Moorer	USA	1996-1997	IBF
Henry Akinwande*	England	1996-1997	WBO
Mike Tyson	USA	1996	WBA
Evander Holyfield*	USA	1996-1997	WBA
Lennox Lewis*	England	1997-1999	WBC
Herbie Hide	England	1997-1999	WBO
Evander Holyfield	USA	1997-1999	IBF/WBA
Vitali Klitschko	Ukraine	1999-2000	WBO
Lennox Lewis*	England	1999-2000	IBF/WBA/WBC
Chris Byrd	USA	2000	WBO
Lennox Lewis	England	2000-2001	IBF/WBC
Evander Holyfield	USA	2000-2001	WBA
Vladimir Klitschko	Ukraine	2000-2003	WBO
John Ruiz	USA	2001-2003	WBA
Hasim Rahman	USA	2001	WBC/IBF
Lennox Lewis*	England	2001-2002	WBC/IBF
Lennox Lewis*	England	2002-2004	WBC
Chris Byrd	USA	2002-	IBF
Roy Jones*	USA	2003	WBA
Corrie Sanders*	S Africa	2003	WBO
Lamon Brewster	USA	2004-	WBO
John Ruiz	Puerto Rico	2004-2005	WBA
Vitali Klitschko	Ukraine	2004-	WBC
James Toney	USA	2005	WBA
John Ruiz	Puerto Rico	2005-	WBA

Early Gloved Championship Boxing: The 'True' Facts (The Final Part)

by Harold Alderman

Following on from our previous exploration of how the weight classes came into being in the early days of gloved boxing, this time round we examine heavyweights in excess of 170lbs. Recognising that many fights listed by weight divisions prior to the advent of the named-weight divisions and weight limits announced by the National Sporting Club on 11 February 1909 did not add up, I started my research in the early 1960s, using world-wide newspaper reports, which included a thorough examination of the *Sporting Life*, *Bells Life*, *Mirror of Life*, *Sportsman*, and *Police Gazette*, etc. It did not take long to discover that the vast majority of fights, certainly in this country, were made at every two pounds, plus or minus two pounds. This is how it was as boxing transferred from the bare-knuckle days to gloves, passing through phases of driving gloves, kid gloves, and two-ounce gloves to what we have today, and takes us through to 1909. Although Australian title fights are shown within, because the 'Black' heavyweight title sequence was published in the 1997 Yearbook we have only built it in to this exercise when it was deemed to be of international importance.

1877

2 March F. Milsom w pts 4 J. Hope, The Music Hall, Hoxton, London. Referee: Jim Goode. The final of a heavyweight competition that had just four entries, in the previous round Milsom forced H. Gadson to retire in the second round, while Hope knocked out H. Britten.

19 May John Knifeton w pts 3 Tom Tulley, Sadlers Wells Theatre, Clerkenwell, London. The final of a novices heavyweight competition for £10 and a silver cup, there were eight entries, most of whom were complete novices. *Bells Life* stated that the decision didn't please all. In the second round both fell down together and both stayed down for 30 seconds. Also given as a world heavyweight championship competition, in previous rounds Knifeton, who was stated to be 6ft 2in tall and 16 stone (224lbs), showing only strength and size and no skill at all, beat Jim Madden (w co 2) and Walter Watson (w rtd 1), while Tulley, who was initially named as Sulley, beat J. Pennock and John Grover on points. Knifeton's ring debut show was given very poor coverage by the sporting press. The other two entries in the competition were Tom Hope, who lost to Grover and Tom Watson, who lost to his namesake, Walter Watson.

26 May *Bells Life* reported that the amateur, Mr Tom Scutton, who stated that his name had been sent in for the above competition without his knowledge, challenged the winner for a £10 silver cup or would stake a cup of equal value against that in the above competition – winner to take both cups. Scutton, although a well-known amateur, had only ever boxed in exhibition bouts.

2 June Tom Allen (Birmingham), aged 37, who arrived back in the UK after a long spell in America, is the true English heavyweight champion reported *Bells Life*. The paper went on to say that although he had never competed with gloves, Allen was still in possession of his championship belt and cups and would box anyone in England with gloves under MoQ Rules for the English championship.

16 June John (Jack) Knifeton stated that he'd never received the cup he won, so he can't state it, but will put £12-10 shillings to a like sum of Tom Scrutton and winner to buy a £25 cup – *Bells Life*. In the same Issue, Tom Allen stated that he will not agree to a charge being made as he is the true champion, who just wants to box for honour and to prove who is the true champion.

30 June Mr Tom Scrutton left money for his half of the cup, but there was no sign of Knifeton's money. Knifeton must send £15 or £20 to *Bells Life* to cover his half of the cup – *Bells Life*.

2 July Tom Allen, calling himself the heavyweight champion of England and America, was called to task by the *Sportsman*, who stated that this was a misnomer as Allen had never won any English honours up to this date, only assumed them.

14 July Tom Allen, remembering that when he was in USA Mr Galpin challenged Jem Mace or any other man in the world, states that he will make a match to box Mr Galpin for either a belt or a cup to the value of £100 or £200, under MoQ Rules, with gloves – *Bells Life*. On 21 July, in *Bells Life*, Mr Galpin stated that the above was all false as he had never issued such

a challenge. He went on to say that as he's got a regular business he hadn't got time to waste for the benefit of such men as Tom Allen – *Bells Life*.

20 July At the *Bells Life* office, the well-known amateur Mr Tom Scrutton and Ted Napper's amateur, Mr John Knifeton, signed to 'spar' for a cup on 4 September at the Cambridge Hall in Newman St, off Oxford Street, London.

29 August Thompkin Gilbert from Lincoln, aged 30, challenges Tom Allen with gloves, under MoQ Rules, for £50 a-side. Gilbert was stated to be completely unknown outside of some rough and tumbles in the Lincoln district – *Bells Life*. In the same issue, James (Jem) Stewart (Glasgow), aged 33, was still repeating his challenge to meet Tom Allen in Glasgow under MoQ Rules and would accept Allen's request that if they did meet the bout would be restricted to one hour.

1 September The champion, Tom Allen (Birmingham), has transferred £10 to put down as a deposit to bind a match with James (Jem) Stewart (Glasgow) and to cover the challenge of the novice, Thompkin Gilbert (from 'The Browncow Inn' Lincoln), who could make his own rules as long as the bout was with gloves – *Sporting Life*.

3 September Thompkin Gilbert (Lincoln) has covered Tom Allen's deposit for the bout to be with gloves in a 24ft ring at a London venue – *Sporting Life*.

4 September Mr John Knifeton no decision 9 Mr Tom Scrutton, The Cambridge Hall, Newman Street, off Oxford Street, London. Promoter: Charlie Franks. Referee: Mr J.Jenn. Contested in a 16$\frac{1}{2}$ ft x 14 ft ring and billed for 25 rounds or more, £25 a-side, the winner was to receive a £50 silver cup. Advertised in the *Sportsman* and *Bells Life* as an amateur bout, both the *Sportsman* and the *Sporting Life* mentioned that it involved the English title, despite it being Tom Scrutton's first ever actual contest. Although a well known amateur boxer, Scrutton had only ever engaged in exhibition bouts and was badly out of condition. Both men were completely exhausted after just one round and had to be carried to their respective corners. It was the same in the second round, but in the third, the ring was invaded by east-end roughs, with both mens' seconds, Jack Baldock for Knifeton and Ned Donnelly for Scrutton, also entering the ring. The bout carried on amidst much yelling and screaming and continued from then on with both men fighting how they liked, while breaking every rule in the book. At end of the eighth round the gas was turned down and Knifeton dealt his man a foul blow, perhaps unintentionally. The ninth round was fought in semi-darkness, amidst much confusion, and at its conclusion the referee refused to give a decision and left the hall after what had been the most disgusting spectacle ever seen under (supposedly) MoQ Rules. The seconds were Ned Donnelly and Mike Cockling for Scrutton and Ted Napper and Jack Baldock for Knifeton. The *Sportsman* reported the ring invasion as being after five or six rounds, with the bout being halted in the ninth, when the lights went out, before being resumed when the lights came back on again. The *Sportsman's* reporter, whose second boxing show this was, called it disgraceful, even worse than the first show he had attended, and reported that glove fighting, like prize fighting, was a disgusting sport and should rank as a thing of the past. On 6 September, the referee, Mr J.Jenn, ordered both men to meet at the City Gym at 6.0 p.m. to settle the match, but Scrutton refused, so the stakes for the silver cup were awarded to Knifeton.

8 September Seeing so much talk of who is the champion boxer, John Knifeton informed one and all that, in the absence of Jem Mace, he intended to defend the title and would box any man in the world, bar Jem Mace, for a cup or a money prize to the value of £100, under MoQ Rules with gloves, Tom Allen (Birmingham) preferred – *Bells Life*.

29 October Tom Allen (Birmingham) w rtd 7 Thompkin (Tomkin also given) Gilbert (Lincoln), Sadlers Wells Theatre, Clerkenwell, London. Weighing 12-7, Thompkin's real first name was stated to be Thomas in the 1881 census. Billed as for the world and English heavyweight championship under MoQ Rules, with gloves, for a £100 silver cup, the bout should never have been allowed as the 30-year-old Gilbert, 5' 7¹/₂" tall, was a complete 'novice' who had taken part in just one 'rough and tumble' bout in the Lincoln District and had neither skill nor courage and no idea of boxing at all. At the end of the seventh round, Gilbert left the ring and ran to the dressing room. Robert Watson, the well-known referee, tried to get him to return to the ring as Allen (168lbs) wished the bout to continue, but Gilbert refused. All the sporting press agreed that this sort of bout must never be allowed to happen again and that only tried and tested men should be allowed to contest an English championship. *Bells Life* stated that 'Punch' Dowsett of Hackney, the 108lbs bantamweight champion, would have no trouble beating Thompkin Gilbert. *The Daily Telegraph* gave a completely different report to any other newspaper and had the result as Gilbert winning on a foul in the seventh, with the result not being announced for fear of causing a riot. This was copied by the *Lincolnshire Chronicle* of 2 November 1877, which had it been true would have given Lincoln a 'world' heavyweight champion, let alone a man who held the English heavyweight title as well !!

27 December At the Lincoln Police Court, Cabman Thompkin Gilbert, who recently fought Tom Allen, was convicted of refusing to leave the Great Northern Hotel and assault on William Thomas West, the publican, and was fined two pounds, five shillings for each offense. Gilbert then asked for protection from the police as, since the Allen bout, he had been given a hard time by various people who threatened "to bring Tom Allen" every time he went out.

1878
16 March *Bells Life* reported that a bout had been made for 4 April for the English heavyweight title and £200 – under MoQ Rules with gloves – between the holder, Tom Allen, and the former 11 stone champion, Charlie Davis. The paper went on to say that once again it was a match which could do much to harm boxing as Davis had been a very sick man, despite him claiming to have recovered.

4 April Tom Allen (Birmingham) w disq 5 Charlie Davis (Stepney), The Cambridge Heath Skating Rink, Hackney, London. Promoter: John Fleming. Referee: Mr Charles Conquest. Contested in a 22 foot ring to a finish and billed for the English heavyweight championship and £200, once again it was a bout that was slated by the sporting press as one that should never have been allowed. Davis, once a very muscular 160lbs, was wasted by illness and it was very doubtful if he weighed above 132lbs. It was inhuman that he was allowed to box and it was no surprise that he was put down in the second and third, before being dropped again in the fifth. Down for well over ten seconds he got up and was again floored for over ten seconds, leading to his second, Jack Hicks, entering the ring and picking him up. Allen's second, Tom Tyler, claimed a foul, which was upheld, but Davis should have been deemed 'counted out' in any case, on the first knockdown of the round. Charges for the show were ten shillings and £1, which kept the rough element out.

10 April Jack Knifeton (Shoreditch) challenges Tom Allen, £50 a-side and the world championship, winner take all. On 19 April, Allen, the champion, withdrew his long-standing deposit from the *Sporting Life* as no one had covered it. Allen stated that he hadn't got the time to remain in London waiting for matters with second-class men, but any time a first-class man put down a deposit it would be covered – *Sporting Life*.

2 December Larry Foley (Sydney) drew 16 (18 also given) Peter Newton (Melbourne), Thompson's Athletic Hall, Melbourne, Australia. Promoter: Jem Mace. Billed as being for the Australian heavyweight title under MoQ Rules with gloves. in the *Sportsman's* 1879 summary of 1878 results it was given as a 48-round draw, which was a certain misprint. The police's explanation for stopping the bout was that there had been complaints about the noise the crowd were making. With Foley on top throughout, it was the first ever gloved (MoQ) championship bout held in Australia.

19 December Carney (Canadian Artillery, Quebec) w rtd 4 Labossiere (Quebec), The Music Hall, Quebec, Canada. Reported in the *Montreal Gazette*, it was billed as being for the Canadian heavyweight championship, with the winner to get about $800. Labossiere was billed as a French wrestler.

1879
22 April Tom Allen (Birmingham) drew 25 James 'Jem' Stewart (Glasgow), St James Hall, Piccadilly, London. Referee: Charlie Conquest. the editor of *Sporting Life*. Allen weighed 184lbs to Stewart's 170. Contested in a 24' ring under MoQ Rules, for a £100 cup, and billed as for world and English heavyweight championship, with Allen (aged 39) termed the holder, it was agreed with the management that the contest would finish at 11p.m., which it did, and the referee would give his decision at 12 noon the next day at the *Sporting Life* office. Prices were £1 and £1-10 shillings for reserved seats, but 50 'roughs' gained free admission by rushing the doors in what was stated to be the most disgraceful affair ever remembered and would set boxing back 20 years. Stewart (aged 35) seemed scared stiff and Allen, although a poor champion, could have knocked out his man any time he liked, but was content to 'carry him'. Stewart, who was another fifth-rate challenger, had participated in his first bout 17 years earlier, which he won, but apart from one competition bout seven years previously he had never won and had mainly engaged in exhibition bouts since then.

5 July James 'Jem' Stewart (Glasgow) challenges any man in the world for £100 a-side and a cup in a match of one hour's duration made between 12 August and 6 September – *Sporting Life*.

6 September James 'Jem' Stewart (Glasgow) w disq 13 Thompkin Gilbert (Lincoln), The Springfield Grounds, Glasgow. Referee: John Riddell. With just 200 people in attendance, Gilbert (168lbs) was disqualified for hitting his man while down, according to *Bells Life*, while the *Sporting Life* reported that the disqualification was for cross buttocking and throwing. Contested under MoQ Rules for a limit of one hour, it involved £25 a-side with the winner to buy a £50 silver cup from the proceeds.

1880
17 January Tom Allen, the champion, had put his £100 deposit down for a month, but no one has yet covered it. Allen repeated his challenge to anyone under MoQ Rules, with gloves, in a 16' ring – *Sporting Life*.

20 January James 'Jem' Stewart (Glasgow) calls himself the champion of England – *Sportsman*.

25 February Alf Greenfield (Birmingham, born in Northampton) w disq 20 James 'Jem' Stewart (Glasgow), Chelsea Baths Gym, Kings Road, London. Referee: Mr Charles Bedford. Attended by 500, this one was contested under MoQ Rules with gloves and, although there was no title billing attached, Greenfield (157lbs) laid claim to the English title despite Tom Allen never losing the title or announcing his retirement, It later transpired that the 11 April 1879 bout was, in fact, Allen's last serious bout. The above fight saw Greenfield's glove burst at the end of the fifth round and had to be replaced. In the sixth he broke his right arm but, although boxing one-handed from then on, he still contained Stewart (166lbs) and wore him down until the latter was disqualified for throwing his man. There was no doubting that with two good hands Greenfield would have stopped his man, as Stewart was nothing but a fifth rater with no pretension to any class. Stewart was outclassed from start to finish by a man who for the majority of the bout could only use one arm.

3 March Alf Greenfield challenges any man in the world for a £500 cup within six months, Tom Allen preferred – *Sporting Life*.

6 March Tom Allen is due to return to Australia in May, but will stay to box Alf Greenfield for a £200 trophy, stating that

Greenfield's talk of £1,000 was just talk in his book. Allen put down £5 deposit for contest to be held in 16' ring, with the match to be within three months of 8 March.

12 March On this day, Tom Allen exhibited his English championship belt, his American gold championship belt and the English championship cup presented to him by the Marquis of Queensberry and Sir J.D. Astley-Bart, before returning to the USA.

4 August Alf Greenfield (Birmingham) challenges the world, £50 up to £500 a-side – *Sporting Life*. On 7 August, this was accepted by the veteran Bat Mullins for a cup valued at £1000. In the same issue, Joe Collins, alias 'Tug Wilson', Leicester, also accepted Greenfield's challenge, £100 up to a £500 a-side.

16 August Alf Greenfield's 'backer', Jack McDonald, puts down £100 at the *Sporting Life* offices for Greenfield to box any man in world, £300 up to £500 a-side, Joe Collins preferred – *Sporting Life*.

13 September Ben Smith w rtd 3 Louis Leard, Pelhams Station, Alabama, USA. For the coloured championship of Alabama.

19 October The well known amateur boxer, Mr Tom Scrutton, has now got a new public house, 'The Ship Tavern' at Shadwell – *Sporting Life*.

1881

30 April New York's Richard K.Fox, of the *Police Gazette*, has ordered the making of a £200 valued silver championship belt to be put up for the world heavyweight championship. The first two men to box for this are expected to be Paddy Ryan and John L.Sullivan (Boston, Mass). Sullivan, aged 22, 6' tall and weighing 212lbs, challenges any man in the world for £100 or £200 a-side – *Sporting Life*.

19 May Jack Burke w pts 3 William Middings, The East Central Boxing Club HQ, 'The Griffin', High Street, Shoreditch, London. The final of Mr Reeland's £5 silver cup competition. The prize was a silver cup on an ebony stand under a glass shade and was given by Mr T.W. Hawkins of 'The Black Horse', The Barbican. With just four entries, in the previous round, Burke, 'The Irish Lad', beat Pat Condon, while Middings beat Obe Atterbury. The final was called one on the best and greatest 'spars' seen for some time.

1 August The *Sporting Life* stated that Alf Greenfield would be laid up for at least a year, as the broken right arm he suffered in an unreported 26 May bare-knuckle bout, versus Tug Wilson, was worse than at first thought. The reason the Wilson bout went unreported was because the Prince of Wales, the Duke of Beaufort, Lord Aylesford, Captain Wyndham and Lord Lonsdale, etc, all of whom were present, didn't want their names in the press. The report of the bout was also carried in the *Sportsman* of May 1881, but mens' names not given.

1882

13 March Mr Richard K.Fox of the *Police Gazette* made an offer for a world heavyweight title match between John L.Sullivan, the American champion, and Alf Greenfield, the English champion – *Sporting Life*.

19 March The death in 35th year of John L.Dwyer (Brooklyn, New York, USA. Born in St Johns, Newfoundland) was reported. Dwyer was a former American heavyweight championship claimant.

25 March Alf Greenfield is stated to be going to USA to make the match with John L.Sullivan – *Sporting Life*.

28 March Tug Wilson challenges any man in England for the English heavyweight championship, £100 a-side. On 10 May in the *Sporting Life*, Collins is called the English champion. This was repeated in the 19 October issue.

6 April Jack Knifeton challenges any heavyweight in the world, £200 a-side. In the same issue of the *Sporting Life*, a letter from Tug Wilson was printed, stating he was winning easily in his bout with Alf Greenfield, but agreed to a draw at the request of Lords and Baronetts at the show. This was pointed out as being all wrong as, although Greenfield had broke his arm in the fifth round, he had carried on for another 16 rounds and had so badly punished Wilson that he was unable to continue and was the first to agree to the bout being called a draw. It had nothing at all to do with Lords and Baronetts at the show. The *Sportsman* report of 28 May 1891 stated that although the Birmingham man's arm was injured in the fifth, he so badly punished the other man that he couldn't go on and the bout was declared a draw. Later reports gave it as a bare-knuckle bout. In the same edition of the *Sporting Life*, it was reported that Alf Greenfield was now doing so well in his pub, 'The Swan with Two Necks' in Livery Street (near

where it joined Constitutional Hill), Birmingham, that he was retiring from boxing.

26 April Tug Wilson, the English 161lbs middleweight champion, challenges Alf Greenfield for the English heavyweight title with bare-knuckles, £100 up to £500 a-side, before Greenfield goes to the USA – *Sporting Life*.

4 May The *Police Gazette's* Mr Richard K.Fox stated that he would match Tug Wilson with John L.Sullivan for the world heavyweight title and sent $100 to the *Sporting Life* to cover Wilson's expense.

27 June John L. Sullivan offered Tug Wilson $1,000 if he, Wilson, could stay four rounds with him under MoQ Rules with gloves. Richard K. Fox, of the *Police Gazette*, who was also still willing to match Wilson with Sullivan for the world heavyweight title and $2,500 a-side, posted $1,000 on Wilson's behalf.

17 July Tug Wilson w pts 4 John L. Sullivan (Boston), Madison Square Garden, NYC, USA. Referee: Billy Hill. With 12,000 people in attendance, wearing gloves, Wilson became first man to stay four rounds with Sullivan, thus winning $1,000 and the decision. Wilson did it by the simple trick of 'dropping down' every time Sullivan came near him and was down 27 times in all. Wilson was down nine times in the first, with Sullivan claiming that he was down for 28 seconds on the first knockdown, eight times in the second and four times in the third. In the third, Sullivan appeared 'done in' and Wilson laughed at him, as he did throughout the bout. Wilson was down six times in the fourth, but was called the winner as Sullivan, who had to sit down at the end, had failed to stop him. Wilson, who was still standing, was also on half the gate receipts, so got $8,000 in all. With 200 policemen present to keep order, it became the first ever boxing match to get police protection. Following the fight, Wilson and Sullivan were matched to box for the world bare-knuckles title, but didn't happen, which was the same with a proposed four-round return glove bout at Madison Square Garden. Wilson then received many challenges and also issued several, but they were all pertaining to bare-knuckle bouts.

11 September Tug Wilson arrived back in England on 'The Indiana', having left the USA on 30 August, and was greeted by a band playing 'See the Conquering Hero Comes', in honour of his win over John L.Sullivan. Prior to the Sullivan bout, Wilson was a 'fight for what he could get' man in England, but was now a £500 a-side or nothing man in the USA. His stay in the UK looked to be only a short one as, on 26 August, he signed to box Jimmy Elliott (bare-knuckles) on 28 November for $2,500 a-side, plus contracting for bouts with Joe Goss and a return with John L.Sullivan. On 14 October, the bout scheduled for 28 November was called off as Wilson hadn't returned to the USA. In fact, Wilson never did return to the USA and forfeited the $500 deposit which Richard K.Fox had put up for him. Wilson had been paid $25 a week by Fox, who also gave him a $500 gold medal as a present and did all he could to make him popular. Later, Fox stated that he wouldn't sue Wilson for the $500.

9 November The *Sporting Life* stated that Wilson's action in 'running out' on his American 'backer' has made it almost impossible for English boxers in the USA to now get support.

23 December Charlie Mitchell (Birmingham) w pts 3 Dick Roberts (Clerkenwell), St George's Hall (opposite the 'Langham Hotel'), Regent Street, London. This was the final of Billy Madden's English heavyweight championship competition that started on 21 December at the King's Road Baths, Chelsea, having been moved from original choice – Bermondsey Drill Hall. Mitchell weighed 143lbs to Roberts' 142. The decision, thought to be a bad one, was on the referees casting vote after the two judges disagreed. Contested for a £40 trophy, with the runner up getting a £10 plate, in previous rounds Mitchell beat George Cox (Holloway), a novice, Bill Springhall (Battersea), the 11 stone champion who was right off form and not trying, Joe Stubbins (Nottingham) and W. Heal, alias 'Cully', in the semi-final. Roberts, who drew a bye in first series, then beat W.Shaw (Manchester), Pat Condon (Haggerston) and Jem Goode (Mile End). Of the 21 men who took part in this competition (out of 32 entries) the only genuine class men beside the two in final were, Jem Goode, Bill Springhall, Bill 'Coddy' Middings, Jack Massey and Pat Condon.

1883

2 January Thompkin Gilbert (Lincoln) stated that the challenge in 2

January issue of the *Sporting Life* in his name wasn't from him.

10 January   Bat Mullins challenges Charlie Mitchell again, £50 or £100 a-side, for the English heavyweight title (£10 deposit) – *Sporting Life*.

23 January   In a three-round exhibition held at Leicester's Floral Hall Rink, Tug Wilson (Leicester), who was much heavier, had much the better of Charlie Mitchell, nearly stopping the Birmingham man in the third.

13 February   Tug Wilson stated that the challenge to Charlie Mitchell in the 10 February issue of the *Sporting Life*, purporting to come from him, wasn't, as he had now retired from boxing. Mitchell's 'backer' was stated to be angry that the challenge was a hoax as he'd gone to the paper in order to make the match. It later transpired that the challenge had come from Mitchell's camp and was just a publicity stunt, at which Mitchell was a past master. In later years he was to claim that, following his 23 December 1882 win, he toured the UK defeating all his challenges in defense of his title, which was nonsense. What he did do was to undertake an exhibition tour (of which 23 January bout was one) in which he met mainly Wilson, who trained with him. He also met Alf Greenfield on one occasion.

22 February   George Godfrey (USA) w co 6 Charles Hadley (USA), The Crib Club, Boston, Mass, USA. Billed as a battle for the 'coloured' heavyweight title to a finish, using two-ounce gloves.

14 May   John L. Sullivan (Boston, Mass) w rsc 3 Charlie Mitchell (England), Madison Square Garden, NYC, USA. In a bout scheduled for four rounds, Mitchell was put down in the third just as the police arrived and the referee stopped the contest in favour of Sullivan on the orders of Captain Williams. Mitchell had been down twice in the first round, then floored Sullivan, before being put down four times in the second, the last knockdown seeing him knocked off the stage.

28 May   'Professor' Billy Miller (Melbourne) drew 40 Larry Foley (Sydney), The Academy of Music, Castle Reach Street, Sydney, Australia. Billed for the Australian heavyweight title with gloves, Foley was kayoed in the 40th round by a right to the jaw, but instead of Miller (191lbs) being returned the winner roughs broke into the ring and the police had to break it up. The referee, Mr William Forrester and Larry Foley had left the ring and Forrester stated he would give his decision at 10pm on Tuesday, 29 May at 'Tattersalls Hotel' in Sydney. Prior to that, Foley's 'backers' and 'seconds' all prevailed on Miller to agree to a draw, which he did even though he'd won the bout fair and square. Miller, who was born in Liscard, Cheshire, England in 1847, was aged 36, while Foley was 34.

29 June   Alf Greenfield (Birmingham) w pts 3 Jack Burke (England), The Free Trade Hall, Peter Street, Manchester. The final of Jem Mace's English heavyweight championship belt competition saw Burke looking a good winner and the decision almost caused a riot, Jem Mace having to calm the crowd down. Burke, who gave his £5 runners-up prize to the 'Manchester Guardians of the Poor' fund, accepted Greenfield's offer of a return bout. In the previous round, with four entries only, Greenfield beat Mick Galligan, while Burke beat J. Nixey.

30 June   Charlie Mitchell (Birmingham), who is on tour with Billy Madden, is being billed as the English heavyweight champion – *Sporting Life*.

10 November   Jack Davis (Birmingham), Jem Mace's novice, challenges the world for a trophy to the value of £50, £200 or more, either under MoQ Rules or bare-knuckles. This was accepted in the 16 November issue of the *Sporting Life* by Alf Greenfield, the English heavyweight champion and holder of Jem Mace's championship belt.

31 December   Jack Knifeton challenges Alf Greenfield or Dick Collier (Birmingham), £25, £50 or £100 a-side – *Sporting Life*.

1884

8 February   Charlie Mitchell, now weighing 13 stone (182lbs), challenges John L. Sullivan and is to reside permanently in the USA. Mitchell sailed for the USA on 16 February – *Sporting Life*.

3 April   Jack Knifeton challenges all-England, £25 a-side, and was accepted on 12 April by Jack Davis, if Knifeton were confined to 188lbs – *Sporting Life*.

10 May   George Godfrey (USA) drew 4 McHenry Johnson (USA), The Crib Club, Boston, Mass, USA. Billed for a finish to decide the 'coloured' title, police stopped it after Godfrey was well on top.

26 July   Bill Farnan (South Melbourne) w rtd 4 Peter Jackson (St Croix, British West Indies) , The Victoria Hall, Bourke Street, Melbourne, Australia. Billed as an Australian heavyweight championship fight, it was the first official bout for this title and the first official MoQ Rules, with gloves, heavyweight title bout held outside of England. Jackson, a negro, couldn't come out at the bell to start the fourth round.

4 September   Bill Farnan (South Melbourne) drew 6 (stopped police) Peter Jackson (born B.W.I.), The Haymarket, Sydney, Australia. Billed for the Australian heavyweight title under MoQ Rules, with gloves, Farnan was to lose this title in a bare-knuckle bout on 20 March 1885 to Tom Lees.

12 September   The *Sporting Life* reported that Jack Knifeton and Woolf Bendoff had signed to box for the English championship belt. In the same issue, in a letter to the *New York Herald*, Jack Burke (England), 'The Irish Lad', again challenges Charlie Mitchell (who still claimed to be the English heavyweight champion) to a championship bout as he had done repeatedly since their draw at Newmarket in 1876 in a bare-knuckle bout. However, Mitchell just didn't want to know.

27 September   Jack Knifeton challenges Alf Greenfield through the *Sporting Life* and on 1 October Greenfield stated that on his return from the USA he would defend his Jem Mace English heavyweight championship belt against Knifeton.

14 October   Jack Knifeton (Shoreditch) w rtd 10 Wolf Bendoff (London). Contested in The London District. Prior to the bout taking place, it was advertised as being for the English heavyweight title and championship belt, but not mentioned in the reports. The *Sporting Life* stated that Knifeton's size was too much for Bendoff (165lbs), who was little more than a novice and mainly known only as a 'sparrer', despite claiming several wins in the USA, of which none can be traced. Knifeton (197lbs), who was reported to be the English champion in the *Sporting Life* four days later, was said to be strong and durable with great size, but very slow.

22 October   The bout for Richard K.Fox's *Police Gazette* heavyweight championship belt and $2,000 between Jack Burke (England) and Hail H.Stoddard (Syracuse) is now off as a stake holder couldn't be agreed upon – *Sporting Life*.

23 October   Jack Knifeton, the English heavyweight champion, who stated that he'd won the world heavyweight championship 40 guinea cup competition in 1877 and is undefeated in his entire career, will pay his own expenses to the USA in order to meet Alf Greenfield – *Sporting Life*.

18 November   A four-round exhibition spar with gloves between John L.Sullivan (Boston, Mass) and Alf Greenfield (England) in Madison Square Garden, NYC, USA was stopped by the police (due to a cut eye) in the second round. Although billed as a sparring match, which the first round was, in the second round both started fighting in earnest, leaving Greenfield with a badly cut left eye and Sullivan cut on his neck. With blood everywhere, the police, led by Captain Williams, invaded the ring and the bout was stopped. Despite it not being a proper bout, the MC was ordered to announce Sullivan as the winner, which he did, before both men were arrested.

17 December   Jem Smith (Cripplegate) w rtd 12 Woolf Bendoff. Contested at a private show in London's west-end, for a £50 trophy (not £100 as first reported), no title billing was attached and Bendoff, who was down in the 12th before being saved by the bell, retired in the interval.

1885

12 January   John L.Sullivan (Boston) w pts 4 Alf Greenfield (Birmingham, England), New England Institute Hall, Boston, Mass, USA. The referee and timekeeper were both chosen by Sullivan's manager but not named. Although Greenfield – who since their first bout had become a good friend and drinking buddy of Sullivan – was down twice in the second round, according to reports he held his own. However, at this time English heavyweights were not given a fair deal in the USA, often being 'fobbed off' with meaningless four-round bouts.

21 February   In the USA, Dominic McCaffrey (Pittsburgh), the heavyweight champion of Pennsylvania, claimed to have a $500 deposit down at the *Police Gazette* office for title a bout with the holder, John L. Sullivan, and also challenged the world, $2,500 a-side, but in Philadelphia. However, McCaffrey had turned down Bill Springall and George Fryer – both of England – who challenged him for £500 a-side – *Sporting Life*.

26 February Jem Smith (Cripplegate) w pts 3 Tom Longer (Clerkenwell), 'The Blue Anchor', Church Lane, Shoreditch, London. This was the final of a heavyweight (catchweights also given) championship competition for £25, after six of eight entries had been eliminated. In previous rounds, Smith beat 'Sugar' Goodson and the well-known wrestler, Jack Wannop, while Longer beat Jim Hurley and Tom Smith, Jem's brother.

14 April Jem Smith, the winner of an English heavyweight championship competition, has accepted the challenge made in the USA by the ex-amateur champion, George Fryer, and they will meet on Fryer's return to England for £200 a-side, old or new style – *Sporting Life*.

21 April Jack Knifeton claims to be the English heavyweight champion and later, on 25 May, offered to defend this title against anyone – *Sporting Life*.

20 May Tom Lees (Australia) w co 12 Bill Farnan (Australia), Lyceum Hall, Melbourne, Australia. Lees claimed the Australian heavyweight title on winning.

19 August Jack Davis (Newton Abbott, Devon), Jem Mace's novice, challenges any man in the world with gloves, under MoQ Rules, Jack Knifeton or Jem Smith preferred. This was repeated on 21 September – *Sporting Life*.

23 August Jack Knifeton, the English heavyweight champion, accepted the above, but he had repeatedly challenged Davis before without any reply – *Sporting Life*.

25 August Richard Matthews (Born San Bernardo, California, USA) w co 5 Bill Wilkinson (Auckland, New Zealand), New Zealand. Billed for the New Zealand heavyweight championship. Following this fight, Matthews, who had been in Australia for six years, returned to San Francisco, California and challenged the world, $1,000 a-side. It is highly possible the the above was a bare-knuckle bout.

28 August Jem Smith accepted the challenge of Jack Davis, £50 or £100 a-side, deposit put down, and in 27 September issue of the *Sporting Life*, Smith stated that he'd had his money down for some time for a bout with Davis, but Davis had never covered it. They did finally fight on 17 December 1885, but with bare-knuckles, Smith winning by a sixth-round kayo.

29 August John L. Sullivan (Boston, USA) w disq 7 Dominick McCaffrey (Pitsburg, Pennsylvania, USA), The Chester Park Driving Track, Cincinnati, Ohio, USA. Referee: Mr William Tate (Toledo). Scheduled for a finish, with McCaffrey's manager, Billy O'Brien, claiming his man was worth a draw, it was for the world heavyweight title and was not a six rounder as often given. The *Boston Globe* of 30 August stated that Sullivan won on a foul at one minute, 45 seconds of round seven and was to a finish, being four rounds lasting three minutes, one round of three minutes, 20 seconds and one of three minutes, 15 seconds, plus the seventh round of one minute, 42 seconds, with six intervals of one minute. However, the *Chicago Tribune* stated that it was six rounds for the world championship and that the contract was for a draw to be declared if it went the distance, but Billy Tate gave it to Sullivan.

1886

31 March Jem Smith disputed Alf Greenfield's claim to the English heavyweight championship, MoQ with gloves, which Greenfield had claimed on winning Jem Mace's English championship title competition with gloves, as he was the holder of the London prize ring (bare-knuckles) English championship and had also won an English (gloves) championship competition. Greenfield had first claimed the English MoQ with gloves heavyweight title back in 1880 after his win over Jim Stewart – *Sporting Life*.

19 April Tom Lees (Australia) drew 19 Bill Farnan (Australia), Williamstown Racecourse, Victoria, Australia. Police intervened in the 19th round and the fight continued the next day at Essenden, Lees successfully defending his Australian title with a fourth-round knockout.

31 July Jem Smith and Jack Knifeton have signed to box for the English heavyweight championship – *Sporting Life*.

25 September Peter Jackson (born St Croix, British West Indies) w rtd 3 Tom Lees Australia), Larry Foley's 'White Horse Hotel', George Street, Sydney, Australia. Billed for a finish to decide the Australian heavyweight title, with the ex-policeman Tom Lees named the holder, Jackson weighed 189lbs to Lees' 177.

2 October At Larry Foley's Gym in Sydney, Peter Jackson was presented with the Australian heavyweight championship belt, manufactured in London, England in 1846.

1887

10 January Charlie Mitchell (Birmingham), the winner of Billy Madden's English MoQ gloves heavyweight championship competition for a silver plate on 23 December 1882, who is now in the USA, has announced his retirement from boxing and as Alf Greenfield and Jack Knifeton have also retired, this leaves only Jem Smith, who was mainly a bare-knuckle fighter – *Sporting Life*. Despite the announcements, Mitchell continued to box and Knifeton, who was repeatedly shown up in exhibition bouts by much lighter men, stated that he'd had a gutful of boxing and he confirmed his retirement when a proposed March 1887 tour of the USA under his American manager, 'Parson' Davis, was cancelled when the latter was informed that Knifeton was little more than a fifth rater with size and no talent. This had come about after his three-day sparring show at the Agricultural Hall, Islington, on 15 to 17 February, in which he sparred each day, firstly with Charlie 'Toff' Wall, secondly with Mitchell, and finally with Alf Greenfield. On each day he was made to look foolish, each man 'playing with him' in turn. However, to be fair to Knifeton, he still only ever lost one of his recorded bouts - to 'Coddy' Middings - although some records show the Wall exhibition as being the final of a 'catchweights' competition, which it wasn't. On this same three-day show, on the final day, Wall also made a complete 'hack' of Jem Smith in another three-round exhibition. Wall had done the same with the ex-wrestler, Jack Wannop, earlier.

23 April On his arrival in the USA, with his wife, Charlie Mitchell stated that he would have just four more bouts, all under MoQ with gloves, before retiring for good – *Sportsman*.

17 May In the USA, Jake Kilrain, real name John Joseph Killion, challenged John L. Sullivan, $2,500 up to $5,000 a-side, for the *Police Gazette's* diamond championship belt and the championship of America to a finish, either with bare fists or two-ounce gloves, four to six weeks from signing. Sullivan not defended the title in five years. On 28 March, Kilrain had challenged Sullivan to glove bout of ten rounds, MoQ Rules, which had been refused.

4 June At the Monumental Theatre, in Baltimore, Jake Kilrain was awarded Richard K. Fox's *Police Gazette* world heavyweight championship belt by Mr W.R.Harding, representing Richard K.Fox, as John L. Sullivan had refused Kilrain's challenge and had failed to cover Kilrain's $1,000 deposit in the required time. The conditions required Kilrain to defend the belt, valued at $1,000, weighing nine pounds and measuring 15 inches, against all comers from either side of the Atlantic. In the same issue of the *Sporting Life*, under *American Notes*, it reported that Jake Kilrain may technically now be the American/world champion and holder of Richard K.Fox's *Police Gazette* championship belt, but all fights fans will still consider John L. Sullivan as the champion until he's beaten for the title, although he seems to have no interest in it after stating "if Kilrain wants the title, let him have it".

29 June Jem Smith (Cripplegate), through his backer, Charlie White of the 'The Dukes Motto' and John Fleming, his manager, accepted the challenge of Jake Kilrain to fight for the world heavyweight title and *Police Gazette* championship belt, with Kilrain to get £100 expenses for £500 a-side – *Sporting Life*.

24 July Richard Matthews (born California, USA) w disq 11 J.C. Richardson, Wellington, New Zealand. Billed for the New Zealand heavyweight championship, it was believed to have been a bare-knuckle bout, with Matthews stated to have been in Australia for eight years.

24 December Jack Burke, the 'Irish Lad', now in Australia, challenges Charlie Mitchell, £500 a-side, with gloves or bare-knuckles – *Sporting Mirror*.

1888

25 January George Godfrey (USA) w disq 4 McHenry Johnson, The Crib Club, Boston, Mass, USA. Billed for the 'coloured' title, Johnson was initially given the fight by disqualification, but later the decision was reversed.

14 April Bill 'Chesterfield' Goode (Shadwell) w pts 4 Ted Burchell (Shoreditch), Royal Agricultural Hall, High Street, Islington, London. The final of Ben Hyams' English 'catchweights' championship competition, and the debut of shows lasting six days, Goode, a shade over 12 stone, beat Charlie Parish and 'Baby' Jack Partridge, while Burchell beat Sam Breeze (Birmingham) and Mike Jennett (Leicester). Goode never made any pretence to being a heavyweight, let alone a champion at the weight.

24 August Peter Jackson (St Croix, DWI) w rtd 19 George Godfrey (USA), Californian AC, San Francisco, California, USA. Billed for the 'coloured' heavyweight title.

11 December Frank 'Paddy' Slavin (Maitland, NSW) w co 1 Mick Dooley (Sydney), Larry Foley's 'White Horse Hotel', Sydney, Australia. Referee: Mr Bloomfield. Billed for the Australian heavyweight championship, Slavin weighed 180lbs to Dooley's 174.

1889

30 September Jem Smith (Clerkenwell) w pts 10 Jack Wannop (New Cross), 'The Novelty Theatre', Long Acre, London. Referee: Mr W.J. King. Wannop, aged 32, weighing 178lbs, was a celebrated wrestler (Cumberland and Westmoreland style). With no title billing for £400, Smith, billed as the champion of England, staked £250 to Wannop's £200.

11 November Peter Jackson w disq 2 (throwing his man) Jem Smith (England), New Pelican Club Gym, Gerrard Street, Soho, London. Referee: George Vize. An international match, scheduled for ten rounds, with no actual title billing, as in *Sportsman*, etc, reports, it was made for £1,000 (£800 winner and £200 loser), with the attendance restricted to 95 club members.

16 November Charlie Mitchell, aged 28, who is signing himself off as the English heavyweight champion, has accepted the £1,000 challenge of Jem Mace, aged 58, and the ex bare-knuckle champion of the world. In the 20 November issue of the *Sporting Life*, this match was stated to have been made for the second week of January 1890 with six-ounce gloves, four judges, who had the power to order an extra round, and a referee. In fact, it was all a publicity stunt, dreamed up by Mitchell, which Mace went along with – *Sporting Life*.

1890

29 January The exhibition spar between Jem Mace and Charlie Mitchell, which was being billed as for the English boxing championship, was moved from 31 January to 5 February to take place at the Princes Hall, Piccadilly, London. However, in the 1 February issue of the *Sporting Life* it was stated that last named venue had refused to have anything to do with it and the match had been moved to Scotland, where boxing-wise fans at this time were more gullible and the bout was easier to sell.

7 February Charlie Mitchell (Birmingham) w pts 4 Jem Mace (Beeston), 'The Gaiety Theatre', Sauchie Hall Street, Glasgow. Referee: Mr Robert Watson. Judges: Mr Wellwood Maxwell and Mr E.Bailey. Timekeeper: Mr Jack Kidger. Although only an exhibition, with Jem Mace, aged 58, this was the con to end all cons, thought up by Mitchell. Having persuaded Mace to make a false challenge to him, running down modern fighters, which Mace went along with, Mitchell got it advertised as being for the English heavyweight title, which was swallowed by the press and advertised as for £1,000. In fact, there was no money involved between them, only expenses. The agreement signed on 15 November 1889 was for an exhibition, pure and simple, or at least that's what Mace thought. At the bell to start the first round, instead of touching gloves as agreed, Mitchell hit Mace on the jaw, knocking him down. Mace also broke the little finger of his left hand in this round and, still groggy, was also put down in the second before starting to recover. In the third, Mitchell slipped down as Mace held his own, but right at very end of round four, the Chief Constable, Mr Boyd, entered the ring ordering bout to be stopped (it was over in any case) as Mace was being badly punished. Meantime, Mitchell went to both judges telling them he had won and the decision was given in favour of Mitchell. They then boxed another round as an exhibition. Following this, both Mitchell and Mace went on sparring tour of Scotland, but so successful was Mitchell's publicity that it not only got reported as an English heavyweight title bout, but even went into the record books as such!!.

6 May Jake Kilrain (New York), the holder of the *Police Gazette* championship belt, was reported to be a very sick man (Kilrain continued to box up until 1899 and lived to be 78). In the same issue of the *Sporting Life*, Joe McAuliffe (San Francisco), known as 'The Mission Boy' and the Pacific Coast heavyweight champion, put down $500 forfeit money to bind a match with either John L.Sullivan, Jake Kilrain or Frank Slavin.

27 May John L.Sullivan stated it wasn't true that he was matched to box Joe McAuliffe for the championship, but Billy Madden

stated that Sullivan had accepted from him, the challenge of Joe McAuliffe, which was in reply to Sullivan's challenge to box any man in the world. There had been purse offers as high as $15,000 for the match and McAuliffe stated that Sullivan must either defend the championship or else forfeit any claim to it. That is what happened and McAuliffe claimed the title by forfeit – *Sporting Mirror*.

24 June Joe Goddard (Australia) w co 21 Mick Dooley (Australia), Sydney Amateur AC, Australia. Billed to a finish for the Australian heavyweight title.

15 July Joe McAuliffe and Frank 'Paddy' Slavin have signed to box 30 rounds or more under MoQ Rules with gloves, for the world heavyweight title and Richard K. Fox's *Police Gazette* championship belt – *Sporting Life*.

31 July Robert Wallis, 'Keenan's Big Un', challenges any man in England. It should be noted that Wallis was little more than a big strong novice and a very poor one at that, having only size in his favour – *Sporting Life*.

27 September Frank 'Paddy' Slavin (Australia) w co 2 Joe McAuliffe (San Francisco, California, USA), The Ormonde Club, Walworth Road, London. Scheduled for 15 rounds and the *Police Gazette* championship belt, with McAuliffe billed as the American champion, it had initially been billed for 30 rounds or more, but on the insistence of the police it had been reduced to 15 rounds, with four-ounce gloves. On winning, Slavin straight away challenged any man in the world to contest the world heavyweight title and *Police Gazette* championship belt. Following the bout, warrants were issued for the arrest of both men and both surrendered to police on Friday, 10 October. They were both committed for trail by Mr Partridge for partaking in a prize fight which was illegal, gloves or not. On Wednesday, 10 December, at the County of London Sessions Court, Newington, Frank Slavin and Joe McAuliffe were both found 'not guilty' at the insistence of the treasury department and discharged.

2 October Richard K.Fox is willing to back John L.Sullivan (Boston, Mass) £500 a-side, for a match with Frank 'Paddy' Slavin (Australia) involving the *Police Gazette* championship belt and world heavyweight title – *Sporting Life*.

20 October Joe Goddard drew 8 Peter Jackson, The Athletic Club, Melbourne, Australia. Although not a billed title fight, the Australian and Imperial titles were technically at stake.

1 November Joe Goddard (The Barrier Champion) w rtd 7 Mick Dooley (Sydney), Melbourne AC, Australia. Billed for the Australian heavyweight championship.

5 November The proposed bout on this date at the Lyceum Theatre, Pembroke Place, Liverpool (over 12 rounds for £100 a-side with four-ounce gloves) between Gus Lambert, the heavyweight champion of Canada, and Terry O'Neill (Liverpool), and promoted by Paddy Gill, was prevented by the police arresting both men prior to the bout. After both men were locked up for the night, the case was heard on Thursday, 6 November before Mr Raffles. In court, the bout was stated to have been one of ten rounds and both fighters were bound over to keep the peace in sum of £50 each.

11 November Jem Smith (Cripplegate) is stated to be the English heavyweight champion – *Sporting Life*.

3 December An offer has been made to the world heavyweight champion, and holder of the *Police Gazette* world championship belt, Frank Slavin, to defend both against James J. Corbett (San Francisco) in New Orleans to a finish for a purse of $6,000 – *Sporting Mirror*.

12 December In the USA, Jake Kilrain has turned down an offer of a $4,000 purse to box the negro, George Godfrey (Boston, Mass. Born Prince Edward Island). Godfrey had accepted the offer – *Sporting Life*.

1891

20 January Recently, John L. Sullivan stated he would give Frank Slavin, the holder of the *Police Gazette* world championship belt, $2,500 or $5,000 to stand before him for six rounds with five-ounce gloves as soon as his present theatre engagements were over. Sullivan also said that Slavin, James J. Corbett and Jake Kilrain could decide who is the champion among them, with the winner to meet him. On this same date, in Grand Rapids, Sullivan denied he had signed articles to meet Frank Slavin and formally announced his retirement from boxing as there was much more money to be made in the theatrical profession – *Sporting Life*.

31 January Frank Slavin (Australia) cabled his acceptance to J.L.

Sullivan's challenge of $5,000 that he would kayo' Slavin inside six rounds. Slavin would bet $5,000 that he won, plus a further $1,000 to $5,000 that he would kayo Sullivan inside six rounds. Unfortunately, this, like the majority of challenges to Sullivan, was refused. The Ormonde Club, London then offered a £2,000 purse for Sullivan to meet Slavin there, but this too was turned down – *Sporting Life*.

10 February Joe Goddard (Australia) w co 4 Joe Choynski (USA), The Athletic Club, Sydney, Australia. Regarded as being a contest involving the Australian open heavyweight title, it was to be contested to a finish.

25 February Frank Slavin (Australia), the world heavyweight champion and holder of Richard K. Fox's *Police Gazette* championship belt, will go to the USA to defend his title against the likes of John L. Sullivan, James J. Corbett or anyone else. In the same issue of the *Sporting Mirror*, Charlie Mitchell is called the English heavyweight champion.

28 February Jem Smith (Cripplegate) is called both the English Prize Ring (bare-knuckle) and MoQ gloves heavyweight champion – *Sporting Mirror*.

16 June Frank 'Paddy' Slavin (Australia) w rsc 9 Jake Kilrain (Baltimore, USA), The Granite Club, Hoboken, New Jersey. Referee: Jerry Dunn. Billed for the world heavyweight title, plus $10,000, $2,000 a-side, using four-ounce gloves and scheduled for ten rounds, no weights were given. Kilrain was down in the ninth and although the timekeeper, John Kelly, counted off ten seconds it was not picked up by the referee and the round ended in confusion. Dunn stated that he would give his decision the next day and did so in Slavin's favour, but would not allow a kayo verdict.

17 July Joe Goddard w co 4 Joe Choynski (USA), The Athletic Club, Melbourne, Australia. A rematch for the Australian open title, it was again billed for a finish.

27 July Ted Pritchard (Lambeth, born Wales) w rtd 3 Jem Smith (Cripplegate), Jack Wannop's Gym, Old Kent Road, New Cross, London. A private show in front of 40 people (only two from the press), Pritchard weighed 152lbs to Smith's 182. The match had been arranged as far back as March and when Smith went into training he was around 17 stone. In some reports it was shown as being billed for the English heavyweight title and £1,000, with Smith billed as the holder and Pritchard as the English 154lbs middleweight champion. It was an accepted fact that a heavyweight champion couldn't have non-title bout against an opponent eligible for his title, which was automatically at stake. Earlier, the venue was given out as being 'The Temple Club' in Fleet Street, but that was just a decoy. The *Sportsman* report stated that Pritchard, himself premier glove fighter in England, had Smith on the ropes in the third round and the latter just turned his back and refused to carry on (not a kayo as often given), leaving Pritchard as the winner. Following Smith's retirement, Pritchard's 'backer', Frank Carew, stated that his man wouldn't assume the heavyweight championship which he had won fair and square, as he wasn't big enough to meet all comers as a heavyweight.

21 September Joe Goddard drew 8 Tom Lees, The Athletic Club, Melbourne, Australia. Although just an eight rounder, the Australian title was technically at stake.

31 December Joe Goddard w co 4 Ned Ryan, The Athletic Club, Melbourne, Australia. Despite it being an eight rounder, it involved the Australian title and on winning, Goddard set sail for England.

1892
30 May Peter Jackson (Australia, born BWI) w co 10 Frank Slavin (Australia), NSC, King Street, Covent Garden, London. Slavin (188lbs) was billed as the holder of the world title and Richard K. Fox *Police Gazette* championship belt (and Imperial British Empire heavyweight title). Scheduled for 20 rounds, Jackson scaling 192lbs, advance billing called it "The Greatest Heavyweight Bout Ever Seen"!

7 September James J. Corbett (San Francisco, California) w co 21 John L. Sullivan (Boston, Mass), The Olympic Club, New Orleans, USA. Referee: Professor Duffy. The final day of a three-day tournament, with 8,000 in attendance, it was billed as being for the American/world heavyweight title and Sullivan was billed as the holder. Significantly, it was the first American heavyweight title bout under MoQ Rules with gloves, although several had been held in the UK since 1877 and also in Australia from the 1880s. Corbett's weight was stated to have been 178lbs, while Sullivan was given as being 212lbs.

1893
10 January Ted Prichard (Lambeth) challenges any man in England at any weight for £500 or £1,000 a-side – *Sporting Life*.

11 February Steve O'Donnell drew 10 Ned Ryan, Sydney, Australia. Billed for the Australian heavyweight title and a finish, a police intervention ended it after just ten rounds.

15 March Jem Smith (Cripplegate, Clerkenwell) is advertising himself as the English heavyweight champion, despite being defeated by Ted Pritchard – *Sporting Life*.

1894
1 January Harry Laing (Wanganus, New Zealand) w rtd 12 Joe Goddard (Australia), The Athletic Hall, Melbourne, Australia. Billed as involving the Commonwealth and Australian heavyweight championship, Laing was the New Zealand champion, while Goddard, the Barrier champion, was also billed as the Australian champion. Both men were 32.

25 January James J. Corbett (San Francisco, USA) w co 3 Charlie Mitchell (Birmingham, England), The Dubal AC, Old Fair Ground Buildings (only partially roofed), Jacksonville, Florida, USA. Referee: 'Honest' John Kelly. Scheduled for 20 rounds or more, bad weather kept the crowd down to under 2,000 in what was billed for the world heavyweight title in four-ounce gloves, $5,000 and a $20,000 purse, winner take all. Reports stated that Peter Jackson had a better claim to the world title than Corbett by holding the world 'coloured' championship. Jackson had a win over fellow coloured man, George Godfrey, who Sullivan refused to meet. He had also won a bout advertised as for the world title and with it Richard K. Fox's *Police Gazette* championship belt. He also held the Imperial Empire title, having beaten the English champion. In fact, he had beaten the best from three continents.

10 February Charlie Mitchell (Birmingham) announced his retirement – *Mirror of Life*.

17 February The death of 36-year-old Bob Wallis, 'Colonel Keenan's Big Un' is announced – *Sporting Life*.

7 April Bob Fitzsimmons challenges any man in the world, bar the negro, Peter Jackson – *Mirror of Life*.

2 June The *Mirror of Life* reported the death of Harry Laing, the New Zealand and Imperial heavyweight champion, who fell under the carriage while getting off a moving train. Laing, who had his legs cut off, was born in Blenheim, New Zealand.

25 June Mick Dooley w pts 20 Jim 'Tut' Ryan, Melbourne, Australia. Billed for the vacant Australian heavyweight title.

10 July Dai St John challenges any heavyweight in England, no one barred – *Sporting Life*. This was repeated on 9 and 11 October, when Frank Slavin and Jem Smith were named.

18 September Jem Smith is still advertising himself as the English heavyweight champion – *Sporting Life*.

6 November Peter Jackson (Australia) challenges the world, no one barred. His 'backer', Barney Barnato, is willing to lay £1,000 to £800 bout for a bout at the NSC within three months – *Sporting Life*. Jackson, who last boxed on 30 May 1892, didn't box again until 22 March 1898 when but a wreck of a man.

6 December In a court case in New York, USA on 'Police Corruption', James J. Corbett's manager, William Brady, stated: "that when Corbett sparred Charlie Mitchell in Madison Square Garden on 24 February 1894 they were compelled to give 25% of gate receipts to the police in order to prevent them from raiding the place". Brady said he also paid police captain, Schmitt Bergen, $1,200, to which Mitchell made strong objection.

1895
17 January Peter Jackson (Australia), who still holds Richard K. Fox's *Police Gazette* world heavyweight championship belt, challenges Charlie Mitchell (Birmingham), who claims to be the English heavyweight champion – *Sporting Life*. On 24 January, Mitchell accepted Jackson and the Bolingbroke Club of London offered a purse of £1,200 for the bout, but on 2 February Jackson refused the offer stating: "He would only box at the NSC and if they didn't offer a purse any notion of a bout was off". Jackson hadn't boxed since May 1892 and was to all intents retired, while Mitchell also had fought his last bout on 25 January 1894 and didn't box again outside of exhibitions, although he kept his name in the papers by issuing challenges to the various top heavyweights over the years.

10 May Jem Smith (St Lukes) w co 2 Ted Pritchard (Lambeth), Central Hall, Holborn, London. Referee: Joe Steers, the ex ABA heavyweight champion, who officiated from inside the ring. Scheduled for 20 rounds and billed for the English heavyweight title, the *Mirror of Life* report stated that the bout screamed 'fix'. In the first round, Pritchard had Smith at his mercy and when the referee stepped between them to give Smith time to recover, Smith hit Pritchard below the belt and everywhere else in order to kayo his man, without a word of warning from Joe Steers. Many more shows like this by the promoter, Jack Gorringe, and boxing will be killed off. However, the *Sporting Life* report insisted that bout was on the level and one of the fiercest ever seen in the short time it lasted.

10 July The death of the former English heavyweight champion and winner of Jem Mace's championship belt, Alf Greenfield (Birmingham, born Northampton), aged 42, was announced. Greenfield was buried in Yardley Cemetery, Birmingham.

8 August Peter Maher (Dublin), who is just back from the USA, challenges any man in the world, £2,000 a-side. This was repeated in the 29 August issue of the *Sporting Life*.

11 November Peter Maher (Dublin) w co 1 (63 seconds) Steve O'Donnell (Australia), Long Island, Maspeth, New York, USA. At the finish, James J. Corbett, the world heavyweight champion, congratulated the winner and formally resigned the world title in favour of Maher.

13 November Peter Maher, who'd just had the world title handed to him by the retiring champion, James J. Corbett, challenges any man in the world to box him for the title – *Sporting Life*. On 15 November, Frank Slavin (Australia) accepted the challenge, £300 up to £1,000 a-side.

26 November Jem Smith (Cripplegate) w disq 9 Dick Burge (Newcastle), The Bolingbroke Club, Clapham Junction, London. Scheduled for 20 rounds, it was billed for the English heavyweight title, involving a £300 purse, £200 a-side, using four-ounce gloves, and contested in a 14 foot ring. Heavily outweighed by Smith (178lbs), Burge (144lbs) was disqualified for going down without a blow.

1896

27 January Dan Creedon (Australia, born New Zealand) w co 2 Jem Smith (Clerkenwell), NSC, King Street, Covent Garden, London. Referee: Bernard J. Angle. Contested for the Imperial British Empire title, which was considered vacant as Peter Jackson hadn't fought since May 1892 and Harry Laing (New Zealand), who was a claimant, was dead. It was also given English title billing, but Creedon, who was billed as the world middleweight champion, was not eligible.

29 January Frank 'Paddy' Slavin challenges Peter Jackson, having waited four long years for the promised return bout with Jackson, who hadn't fought since their May 1892 bout – *Sporting Life*.

21 February Bob Fitzsimmons (Australia, born England) w co 1 Peter Maher (Dublin). Contested on Mexican soil across the Rio Grande River, opposite El Paso, Texas, USA. Referee: George Siler. Put back from 14 February, with Langtry, Texas also given as the venue in some reports, it was billed for the world heavyweight title and Richard K. Fox championship belt, plus $10,000 purse. It was later announced that Fitzsimmons had refused to accept Richard K. Fox's *Police Gazette* championship belt that James J. Corbett had presented to Peter Maher, just as John L. Sullivan had years earlier. Interestingly, in January 1895, Peter Jackson claimed to still hold the *Police Gazette* belt, so seemingly the one Corbett gave to Maher was a different one and there is no record of Corbett ever winning a *Police Gazette* belt for his wins over John L. Sullivan or Charlie Mitchell.

22 February Jem Smith (Cripplegate, Clerkenwell) aged 36, calls himself the world heavyweight champion – *Sporting Life*.

12 March In New York, USA, James J.Corbett signed articles sent by the NSC in London for a world heavyweight title bout against Bob Fitzsimmons, but Fitzsimmons refused to sign.

4 April Mick Dooley (Australia) w co 2 Peter Felix (St Croix, DWI), Melbourne, Australia. Billed for the Australian 'open' heavyweight title.

6 May The death of John 'Jack' Knifeton, aged 41, is announced. Knifeton, a former claimant of the MoQ Rules English heavyweight championship, was known as 'The 81 Tonner' – *Sporting Life*.

29 August Jem Smith, the English champion, challenges the world, £200 or £500 a-side, Frank Slavin preferred – *Sporting Life*.

9 November Joe Goddard (Australia) w co 4 'Denver' Ed Smith (USA), The Ampitheatre, Johannesburg, South Africa. Referee: Mr Clem D. Webb. Scheduled for 20 rounds and billed for the world heavyweight title, with Smith billed as the American champion.

25 November The *Mirror of Life* stated that Peter Jackson (Australia) is the world heavyweight champion. This was amazing, seeing that Jackson hadn't fought since May 1892.

2 December 'Sailor' Tom Sharkey (USA) w disq 8 Bob Fitzsimmons, The National Club, Mechanics Pavillion, San Francisco, California, USA. Referee: Wyatt Earp. Scheduled for ten rounds and given world title billing, reports state that Fizsimmons made a chopping block of Sharkey and knocked him out in the eighth round with a blow to the stomach, only for the referee, Wyatt Earp, to disqualify Fitzsimmons for deliberately kneeing Sharkey in the groin when falling on him. This was a foul that no one else saw and all reports agreed that Fitzsimmons was robbed. Rumours had been flying around, prior to the bout, that Earp, a gunfighter and gambler, had been paid to give the decision to Sharkey, come what may. Following the fight, the banks refused to cash the $10,000 cheque until the courts had given a decision as to whether Sharkey was entitled to the money. The *New York World* newspaper quoted 17 well-known men who were present, with 12 saying there wasn't a foul and five saying that there was. Earp gave a signed statement stating: "Sharkey was hit on the shoulder by a right and below the belt by a left, which was clearly a foul and before he moved I said the bout was over". There was no mention of a knee in the groin. Sharkey was reported to have been unconscious for 30 minutes, with his groin injured and swollen. Later reports from 12 December issue of the *New York Herald* stated that the kayo punch was a 'left to the jaw' and Sharkey was counted out and carried to his corner before Earp gave him the decision.

1897

10 February Mick Dooley drew 10 Peter Felix, Brisbane, Australia. Registered as a defence of the Australian 'open' title.

19 February George Chrisp (Newcastle) w disq 5 Jem Smith (Cripplegate), Ginnett's Circus, Newcastle. Referee: Ed Plummer of the *Sporting Life*. Made for £100 a-side and £80 purse, it was a handicap match with Smith having undertaken to stop Chrisp inside the scheduled eight rounds. Although the bout wasn't billed for the title and was over a non-championship distance, with the understanding that a heavyweight champion couldn't have a bout other than exhibitions without the title being at stake, this win gave Chrisp a claim to the English heavyweight title, despite it being more of a gimmick than a genuine bout. In the fifth, Smith's eye was badly cut, whereupon he seized Chrisp around the waist then landed a left uppercut which cut Chrisp's eyebrow. Then Smith held Chrisp with one hand, while hitting him with the other.

1 March In Carson City, Nevada, USA, A bill was introduced in the Nevada legislature, authorising the state to find $300 for a silver belt, studded with diamonds, to be presented to the winner of the James J. Corbett v Bob Fitzsimmons fight. The belt will bear a reproduction of the official seal of the state and a facsimile of the governors' autograph.

16 March George 'Pony' Moore, the father-in-law of Charlie Mitchell, put down a £500 deposit in an effort to meet the winner of Corbett v Fitzsimmons.

17 March Bob Fitzsimmons (late of Australia and New Zealand, born in Helston, Cornwall, England and now an American citizen) w co 14 James J. Corbett (San Francisco, California, USA), The Race Track Arena, Carson City, Nevada, USA. Referee: George Siler. Contested in the centre of the race track, it was a left to the solar plexus that finished Corbett in their battle for the undisputed world heavyweight championship. It should be noted that reports of the fight contradict all the stories carried over the years of Fitzsimmons getting a terrible beating before landing the kayo, stating that, although bleeding like a stuck pig from the sixth round, during which he was floored, Fitzsimmons then started to come on, while Corbett started to fade. Although winning the eighth round, Corbett had dropped behind in the ninth and Fitzsimmons, who was always the stronger of the two, looked certain to win, it being only a matter on time. Corbett did rally to win the 12th, but that was it. Throughout the bout, Mrs Fitzsimmons had been shouting out instructions for

Bob to go for the body. The win was very popular as Corbett had been an unpopular champion because of his bragging and boasting and high opinion of himself, but Fitzsimmons, after winning the bout, announced on the same day that he was retiring from boxing and resigning the title. It was stated that whoever dubbed Corbett 'Gentleman Jim' had a sense of humour, as he was anything but.

23 March Charlie Mitchell (England), who had long since retired, challenged Bob Fitzsimmons to meet him at The Bolingbroke Club in London, offering a purse of $12,500 plus $500 for Fitzsimmons – *Mirror of Life*.

10 April Bob Fitzsimmons sent a cablegram from Chicago to New York, stating that he was formally resigning the world heavyweight title.

26 April Charlie Mitchell, seeing that Peter Jackson is to come back, challenged him for £1000 and the best purse – *Sporting Life*.

27 April Peter Jackson challenged James J. Corbett to a bout for the vacant world heavyweight title as the retired champion, Bob Fitzsimmons, as always, refused to meet him – *Sporting Life*.

8 May Mr Tom Scrutton, the retired amateur boxer, who 20 years ago boxed Jack Knifeton, a professional, has now taken over the 'The Blue Post' public house in Southampton Buildings, Holborn, London – *Sporting Life*.

4 October Bob Fitzsimmons sent letters to the US press, again announcing his retirement and that he had relinquished the title, which was followed by James J. Corbett formally reclaiming the title and offering to defend it against all-comers.

20 October Joe Goddard (Australia), the Barrier champion, challenges the world, Bob Fitzsimmons preferred. In the same issue of the *Mirror of Life*, Peter Maher (Dublin) challenged James J. Corbett to a bout for the vacant world heavyweight title or any other man in the world, $5000 a-side.

27 October 'Sailor' Tom Sharkey (Boston) challenges any white man in the world for the world heavyweight title, but wouldn't box a black man as he drew the coloured line – *Mirror of Life*. On the same day in the *Police Gazette*, Bob Fitzsimmons yet again issued a statement that he was finished with boxing for good and had vacated the title. But Sam Austin of the *Police Gazette* stated: "Fitzsimmons was a man whose word the public had no faith in at all and time would soon prove the public right and show just what sort of man he is".

3 November Peter Maher (Dublin) again challenged the world to a bout for the vacant world heavyweight title, 'Sailor' Tom Sharkey (Boston) or Peter Jackson (Australia) preferred – *Police Gazette*.

17 November With Bob Fitzsimmons now retired and James J. Corbett refusing to meet Peter Maher, the latter is now being favoured by many as the world heavyweight champion – *Sporting Life*.

1898
10 January Charlie Mitchell, the English heavyweight champion, challenges Charles 'Kid' McCoy, £1000 a-side – *Mirror of Life*. On 21 January, Mitchell stated this wasn't from him and he was only interested in boxing Bob Fitzsimmons or James J. Corbett.

26 January Charles 'Kid' McCoy challenges either Bob Fitzsimmons or James J. Corbett to a bout for the world heavyweight title. If the challenge was not accepted, McCoy would claim the title. Corbett just ignored this challenge, while Fitzsimmons, after accepting, later stated that he would only box McCoy, if McCoy first met and beat Peter Maher (Dublin) – *Mirror of Life*.

12 March Jem Smith is still being called the English heavyweight champion, which is repeated in the 30 March and 6 April issues of the *Sporting Life*.

23 March Peter Jackson is now a physical wreck, according to a *Mirror of Life* report, and the planned bout with the unbeaten young giant, Jim Jeffries, should be stopped. However, it went ahead with Jeffries winning by a second-round kayo.

30 March Peter Maher (Dublin), who is now vastly improved, has $5,000 down to box any man in the world for the world heavyweight title, but Charles 'Kid' McCoy refuses point blank to box him, as does the coloured man, Bob Armstrong. In the same issue of the *Mirror of Life*, McCoy - now formally claiming the world heavyweight title – is to make his first defence, against Gus Ruhlin, thus avoiding both Joe Choynski and Peter Maher, who had both taken up his challenge.

21 May Charles 'Kid' McCoy w pts 20 Gus Ruhlin (Ohio), The Old Skating Rink, Syracuse, New York, USA. Referee: George Siler. Billed as the first defence of McCoy's claim to the world heavyweight title, no weights were given, but Ruhlin was stated to be 30lbs heavier.

7 September Mick Dooley w co 6 Bill Doherty, Freemantle, Australia. An Australian title fight, Dooley also knocked out Will Bell in the second round of a fight for the title later in the year, but the date and venue are unknown.

28 October Charlie Mitchell challenges the world, bar Bob Fitzsimmons, but in a repeat challenge in the 8 November issue of the *Sporting Life*, Mitchell stated that he'd never said that he barred Bob Fitzsimmons as he was included if he intended to come back to boxing. Mitchell, although he had no intentions of a comeback, kept throwing out these challenges to the world, as it kept his name in the public eye and shifted attention from his more 'shady' dealings.

1899
10 January 'Sailor' Tom Sharkey (Boston) w co 10 Charles 'Kid' McCoy, The Lennox Club, NYC, New York, USA. Scheduled for ten rounds and billed for the world heavyweight title claimed by McCoy, Sharkey (172lbs), born in Dundalk, Ireland, was down in the third before McCoy (158lbs) took a 'nine' count in the eighth. McCoy was then put down again in the tenth from a right to the head and was counted out by the referee, but got up and the bout continued. After McCoy was put down again, the referee stopped it in Sharkey's favour. The attendance was 10,000.

21 January Mick Dooley w co 2 Jim Fogarty, Perth, Australia. Billed for the Australian title.

25 February Bill Doherty w co 6 Mick Dooley, Kalgoorlie, Australia. The Australian title changed hands on this result.

22 April Bill Doherty w co 2 Mick Dooley, Kalgoorlie, Australia. Billed for the Australian title, Doherty made another defence, this time against Jim 'Tut' Ryan, who was disqualified during the 12th round in Kalgoorlie sometime in June.

9 June Jim Jeffries (California) w co 11 Bob Fitzsimmons, Coney Island AC, Brooklyn, New York, USA. Referee: George Siler. Contested in a 22 foot ring, for a $20,000 purse, and billed as being a world heavyweight championship fight, Jeffries weighed 206lbs to Fitzsimmons' 167. Just as Sam Austin had predicted earlier in the *Police Gazette*, all of Fitzsimmons' many announcements of his retirement had gone by the board. On winning, Jeffries was challenged to title bout by both 'Kid' McCoy and 'Sailor' Tom Sharkey.

7,8,9,11 and 12 August At the Royal Aquarium, Westminster, London, Jim Jeffries and George Chrisp (Newcastle) put on three-round exhibitions each night.

14 August Bill Doherty w co 8 Jim 'Tut' Ryan, Kalgoorlia, Australia. Billed for the Australian heavyweight title.

15 August At Westminster's Royal Aquarium, Jim Jeffries met Jack Scales (Bethnal Green) in a three-round exhibition and later stated that Scales was the best heavyweight in England, whereupon, Scales laid claim to the English heavyweight title.

14 September Jack Scales (Bethnal Green) challenges all England at catchweights or at heavyweight, wearing four-ounce gloves, over ten or 20 rounds, £25 up to £100 a-side, and an NSC purse, George Chrisp (Newcastle) preferred – *Sporting Life*.

29 September Jack Walsh (Canning Town) challenges all England at catchweights or heavyweight. This was not the same man as Jack Walsh (Brentwood) – *Sporting Life*.

16 October Jack Scales (Bethnal Green) is the English heavyweight champion – *Sporting Life*. This was repeated in the 21 November and 6 December issues, when he challenged all England, £200 up to £500 a-side.

3 November Jim Jeffries w pts 25 'Sailor' Tom Sharkey (Boston, born Dundalk), Coney Island AC, Brooklyn, New York, USA. Referee: George Siler. Billed for the world heavyweight title and called by the press as the greatest heavyweight title bout ever seen, many thought Sharkey had won, or was worth at least a draw. The bout was halted twice in the last round due to Sharkey pulling Jeffries' glove off.

4 November Jem Smith (Cripplegate), aged 36, is still claiming to be the English heavyweight champion – *Sporting Life*. Smith's last bout had been on 18 February 1897, prior to coming back for one bout in 1918, aged 55.

2 December Peter Felix w rtd 7 Bill Doherty, Kalgoorlie, Australia. Billed for the Australian 'open' heavyweight title.

5 December George Chrisp (Newcastle) failed to turn up at the NSC to sign for a bout with Jack Scales for the English heavyweight title, thus giving Scales a claim to the title by forfeit – *Sporting Life*.

13 December Jack Scales, the English heavyweight champion, challenges Dick Burge over ten or 15 rounds of three minutes each round at either the NSC or Goodwin Club, for a purse of £100 or £200 a-side, using four-ounce gloves in a 16 foot ring – *Sporting Life*.

1900

9 February Dick Burge (Newcastle) w co 1 Jack Scales (Bethnal Green), The New Palace Club (Formerly Wilcox's Dancing Acadamy), Westminster, London. Referee: Ed Plumber of the *Sporting Life*. Billed for the English heavyweight title, Burge weighing 146lbs to Scales' 174, it was scheduled for 20 rounds, £200 a-side and £300 purse. Once again, as with several of Burge's bouts it was an 'out and out fix', with Scales, the 65 to 50 favourite, in on it. With Scales being a 'self-styled' English heavyweight champion, the 'Fix' was common knowledge and as a consequence this became the first English heavyweight title bout that was pushed into the background.

16 February Jack Scales challenges all England at heavyweight, £200 up to £500 a- side – *Sporting Life*.

28 February The *Mirror of Life* stated that both of the sporting 'Dailys' still called Jem Smith the English heavyweight champion.

28 February John J. Jackson (Crewe), once the North of England heavyweight champion, challenges Jack Scales to a return over 20 rounds and would accept a bet of £100 to £75. Jackson had been knocked out inside two rounds by Scales on 26 February in first series of the Wonderland competition.

5 March Pat Daley (Westminster, born County Cork) w co 1 (75 sec) Jim Styles (Marylebone), Wonderland, Whitechapel Road, London. Referee: Ted White. Promoters: Tom 'Pedlar' Palmer and Harry Wright. Contested in a 14 foot ring over six rounds, and a full house with hundreds turned away, it was the final of 'Pedlar' Palmer's and Harry Wright's English heavyweight £100 gold and silver championship belt competition. The winner also got £50. The tournament had started on 26 February with eight entries, Daley coming in as a substitute for 'Dido' Plumb. In previous rounds, Daley, the claimant of the English ten stone lightweight title, had beaten the 12 stone Bill Shaw (Stepney) on a second-round stoppage and Jack Scales (Bethnal Green), weighing 13 stone, seven pounds, on the referee's casting vote, although Daley claimed he won on a three-round kayo. Styles, the claimant of the English 146lbs title, had beaten 'Ginger' Osbourne and Arthur Morris (Fulham) on points over three rounds. This venue was formerly 'The Effingham Theatre', then the 'East London Theatre', then a workshop for a clothing factory, until 'Pedlar' Palmer turned it into the above.

10 March Pat Daley challenges all England at heavyweight, no one barred – *Sporting Life*.

14 March Jack Scales challenges Pat Daley to a return over 20 rounds, £200 a-side upwards – *Sporting Life*. Because Daley refused to accept this challenge, although keeping the heavyweight championship belt, it left the way clear for Scales to reinstate himself as the English heavyweight champion, the fixed fight with Dick Burge being ignored.

7 April Jim Jeffries w rtd 1 (55sec) Jack Finnegan (Pittsburgh), Detroit, Michigan, USA. Given billing as a world heavyweight title bout, Finnegan was down three times before the towel was thrown in.

7 May Jack Scales is again claiming the English heavyweight title – *Sporting Life*.

11 May Jim Jeffries w co 3 James J. Corbett, Greater New York AC, Brooklyn, New York, USA. Referee: Charley White. Billed for the world heavyweight title.

16 July Bill Doherty (Melbourne) w pts 20 Peter Felix (Sydney, born British West Indies), Sydney, Australia. Billed for the Australian 'open' heavyweight title held by Felix.

31 July Jack Walsh (Canning Town) challenges any heavyweight in England, Jack Scales or Pat Daley preferred – *Sporting Life*.

11 August Bill Doherty w co 3 Mick Dooley, Sydney, Australia. Billed for the Australian heavyweight title.

17 August Jack Scales challenges Pat Daley with six-ounce gloves, £100 up to £200 a-side and an NSC purse – *Sporting Life*.

18 September Jack Scales calls himself the English heavyweight champion – *Sporting Life*. On 1 October, Scales repeated his claim and challenged any heavyweight in England, £500 or £1000 a-side and an NSC purse for the title, George Chrisp preferred.

6 October Pat Daley's English heavyweight championship belt is on show all week at 'The Artichoke', Clare Street, The Strand, London – *Sporting Life*.

12 November George Chrisp (Newcastle) challenges any man in the north at catchweights over 20 three-minute rounds for £25 a-side, Harry Smith (Birmingham) preferred – *Sporting Life*.

1 December Bill Doherty (Melbourne) drew 20 Peter Felix, The Summer Gardens, Kalgoorlie, Australia. Referee: Mr R.P.Bell. Billed for the Australian 'open' title, after the lights failed in the eighth round the bout was ordered to be resumed later. The remaining 12 rounds were fought and the decision was given as a draw. This resumption is believed to have been held on 3 December.

17 December George Chrisp (Newcastle) w co 14 Harry Smith (Birmingham, born Stoke), Ginnett's Circus, Northumberland Road, Newcastle. Referee: T.W. Gale. Scheduled for 20, three-minute rounds, made at catchweights and given English heavyweight title billing, for £50 a-side and £60 purse. Not large enough stakes for a major title bout, according to rules, it was the comeback of Chrisp (170lbs), who hadn't engaged in a serious bout since November 1898. He did, of course, have a claim of sorts on the English heavyweight title, stemming from his February 1897 win in a handicap match over the then champion, Jem Smith, by disqualification. Harry Smith weighed 163lbs.

19 December Jack Scales challenges George Chrisp over 15 three-minute rounds, £100 or £200 a-side and an NSC purse. Scales left a £5 deposit for the bout to be for the English heavyweight title – *Sporting Life*.

31 December Jack Scales is billed as the English heavyweight champion – *Sporting Life*.

1901

3 January Jack Scales calls himself the English heavyweight champion, which was repeated throughout the year – *Sporting Life*.

7 January Jack Scales (Bethnal Green) w co 2 George 'Cloggy' Saunders (Hammersmith), Wonderland, Whitechapel Road, London. Scheduled for ten, two-minute rounds there was no title billing and no weights given.

16 January A letter from Dick Burge stated: "How curious it was that Jack Scales and George Chrisp were to meet for English heavyweight title, when Jerry Driscoll (who Burge had met at 11-8 on 28 January) had beaten Chrisp on 18 February 1895, prior to Chrisp's win over Jem Smith, and he (Dick Burge) had scored a one-round kayo (Feb 9 1900) over Jack Scales in a billed English heavyweight title match on 9 February 1900. However, as this last bout was admitted to being 'arranged' it was ignored.

17 January Due to a mistake by one of his 'backers', George Chrisp forfeited to Jack Scales, although efforts were made to rematch them. But, just to confuse matters, in the 23 January issue of the *Sporting Life*, Scales challenged Chrisp to a bout at the 12 stone limit over 15 or 20 rounds, £200 up to £500 a-side and an NSC purse.

30 January 'Big' Ben Taylor (Woolwich) challenges Jack Scales for the English heavyweight title or any heavyweight in the world under the age of 21, no one barred – *Sporting Life*.

4 February In the USA, Jim Jeffries is suing Richard K. Fox of the *Police Gazette* over the $2,500 diamond studded gold championship belt, as Fox said that any man winning three bouts for the world heavyweight title would make the belt his own property. This Jeffries did by beating Fitzsimmons, Sharkey and Corbett, but he never received the belt.

11 February 'Big' Ben Taylor (Woolwich) challenges all England – *Sporting Life*. On 15 February, Jack Scales accepted the challenge, £200 up to £500 a-side, for the English heavyweight title – *Sporting Life*.

16 February From the Wonderland ring, Jack Scales challenged any heavyweight in England, the winner of George Chrisp v 'Big' Ben Taylor bout preferred. This was repeated in the 1 March issue of the *Sporting Life*.

26 February George Chrisp challenges 'Big' Ben Taylor over 20 rounds – *Sporting Life*.

18 March Pat Daley, the ten stone English champion and winner of the English heavyweight championship belt, challenges Jack Scales, £100 up to £200 a-side, with Daley to be 146lbs and Scales limited to 160lbs – *Sporting Life*.

1 April George Chrisp (Newcastle) w co 8 'Big' Ben Taylor

(Woolwich), The Standard Theatre, Gateshead. Referee: Eugene Corri. Scheduled for 20, three-minute rounds and billed for the English heavyweight title, but not by all the sporting press, for £50 a-side and £130 purse. Chrisp had a claim to the title with a win over Jem Smith, but had forfeited to Jack Scales through no fault of his own.

17 April   George Chrisp challenges all England for the English heavyweight title – *Sporting Life*.

22 April   Harry Neumier (St Georges) w co 4 Jack Scales, Wonderland, Whitechapel Road, London. Only a six rounder of two minutes a round, the *Sporting Life* gave the above result, but 'co 5' was given elsewhere and the *Mirror of Life* reported it as a first-round kayo.

30 May   'Big' Ben Taylor challenges all England – *Sporting Life*.

17 June   Peter Felix w co 2 Mick Dooley, Melbourne, Australia. Billed for the Australian 'open' heavyweight title.

19 June   Jim 'Tut' Ryan w co 3 Bill Doherty, Kalgoorlie, Australia. Billed for the Australian heavyweight title.

17 August   Jim 'Tut' Ryan w rtd 11 Tim Nolan, Kalgoorlie, Australia. Ryan defended the Australian heavyweight title in this one.

4 September Bill Doherty w co 7 Jim 'Tut' Ryan, Perth, Australia. Doherty reclaimed the Australian title on winning.

23 September Jack Scales (Bethnal Green) w co 11 Jack Palmer (Benwell), Ginnett's Circus, Newcastle. Referee: George T. Dunning of the *Sportsman*. Scheduled for 20 rounds at catchweights, for £170 (£50 a-side and £70 purse), it was also given as a defence of Scales' claim to the English heavyweight title. Palmer (154lbs), whose real surname was Liddell, was the winner, while the 'backer' of Scales (175lbs) lodged an unsuccessful objection that the count lasted only five seconds.

8 October   Jack Scales challenges George Chrisp at the NSC, not Newcastle, but Chrisp wanted Newcastle or nothing and Newcastle had offered the best purse. This being the one bout that Chrisp wanted before he retired. He also stipulated £100 a-side – *Sporting Life*. Prior to his 7 November bout in Liverpool, Scales, through his 'backer', challenged any man in England. He then got into the ring and was knocked out in the first round by the American, 'Philadelphia' Jack O'Brien, in a catchweights bout.

23 October   Pat Daley challenges all comers, no one barred – *Sporting Life*.

11 November Harry 'Slounch' Dixon (Stepney) w pts 6 Fred Barrett (Hackney), Wonderland, Whitechapel Road, London. Referee: Fred Hollingsworth. This was the final of an English 'novices' heavyweight championship belt competition.

15 November Jim Jeffries w rtd 5 Gus Ruhlin (Ohio), The 20th Century Club, Mechanics Pavilion, San Francisco, California, USA. Referee: George Siler. Billed for the world heavyweight title.

18 November Harry 'Slounch' Dixon (Stepney) w rtd 2 Fred Greenbank (Ascot), NSC, King Street, Covent Garden, London. The final of an English 'novices' heavyweight (catchweights also given) £50 silver championship belt competition, scheduled for three rounds.

20 November In the *Montreal Daily Star*, Jim Jeffries was quoted as saying: "that he refused to defend the world heavyweight title against 'Denver' Ed Martin as he wouldn't fight a coloured man, for if he lost that would mean a coloured heavyweight champion and that must never happen".

7 December   Bill Doherty w pts 20 Peter Felix, Melbourne, Australia. Billed for the Australian heavyweight title.

1902

15 January   Harry 'Slounch' Dixon (Stepney) is the winner of a heavyweight championship belt competition – *Sporting Life*.

6 February   'Big' Ben Taylor (Woolwich) challenges any heavyweight in England – *Sporting Life*.

3 March   John 'Sandy' Ferguson (Boston, Mass, born Canada) w pts 10 'Big' Ben Taylor (Woolwich), Wonderland, Whitechapel Road, London. An international match for £50 a-side and purse, it was contested under no type of title conditions other than three-minute rounds, yet the *Mirror of Life* wrote it up as being for the English heavyweight title, which it wasn't.

16 April   Jack Scales challenges Jack Palmer (Benwell) at catchweights, £25 or £50 a-side – *Sporting Life*.

14 May   'Big' Ben Taylor (Woolwich) is the English heavyweight champion – *Sporting Life*.

23 May   'Sailor' Tom Sharkey (Boston, Mass, born Dundalk, Ireland)

is the ex world heavyweight champion. The same issue of the *Sporting Life* reported that 'Denver' Ed Martin, the world coloured heavyweight champion, has been after a match with Jim Jeffries for the world heavyweight title, but Jeffries has refused on the grounds that he wouldn't box a coloured man.

18 June   Harry 'Slounch' Dixon (Stepney) challenges Jack Scales over 20 three-minute rounds, £25 or £50 a-side – *Sporting Life*.

25 June   'Denver' Ed Martin (USA) w rsc 5 John 'Sandy' Ferguson (Boston, Mass, born Canada), NSC, King Street, Covent Garden, London. Scheduled for 15 rounds and part of the Coronation Tournament, Ferguson was a substitute for Bob Armstrong (USA), who had been down to meet Martin in a billed world coloured heavyweight title match. With this win over Ferguson, Martin, who rightly claimed that the world champion had refused to meet him, laid claim to the world heavyweight title. The bout was also reported as being for the English heavyweight title, which it wasn't with neither man eligible.

25 June   Jack Scales (Bethnal Green) w pts 10 'Big' Ben Taylor (Woolwich), New Aldelphi Club, Maidens Lane, The Strand, London. Referee: Harry Cooper. The final day of a three-day show, the fight, billed for the English heavyweight championship belt, was originally scheduled for 15 rounds before being cut to ten. Scales was presented with the belt on 24 July by Mr E. Hart.

7 July   Bill Doherty w co 13 Peter Felix, Melbourne, Australia. Billed for the Australian 'open' title.

25 July   'Denver' Ed Martin (USA) w pts 15 Bob Armstrong (Washington, Indiana), The Crystal Palace, Sydenham, London. Referee: Tom Scott. Billed for the world 'coloured' heavyweight championship, Martin weighed 186lbs to Armstrong's 196.

25 July   Jim Jeffries (USA) w co 8 Bob Fitzsimmons, The Arena, San Francisco, California, USA. Referee: Ed Graney. Billed for the world heavyweight title and scheduled for 20 rounds.

13 September Jack Palmer (Benwell) w co 5 Harry 'Slounch' Dixon (Stepney), Ginnett's Circus, Newcastle. Scheduled for ten rounds at catchweights with no weights given and no title billing.

19 September Jack Walsh (Canning Town) challenges any heavyweight in England, Jack Palmer or 'Barney Scannell's Big Un' preferred – *Sporting Life*.

13 October   The *Mirror of Life* editorial stated that the new NSC Rules are farcical to the extreme.

13 October   Bill McColl (NSW) w co 5 Bill Doherty (Victoria), Sydney, Australia. Billed for the Commonwealth (Australian) heavyweight title.

13 October   Jack Scales (Bethnal Green) w co 7 Harry 'Slounch' Dixon (Stepney), NSC, King Street, Covent Garden, London. Scheduled for ten rounds and £10 a-side and purse, there was no title billing. Other than three-minute rounds, no championship conditions would be met in any case.

8 November   Charley Wilson (Notting Hill) w co 3 Jack Scales (Bethnal Green), Wonderland, Whitechapel Road, London. Although Scales was billed as the English heavyweight champion (which wasn't officially recognized as such by the NSC and many others), the bout was just a normal six-round bout with two-minute rounds and no championship conditions prevailing. No weights were given, but Wilson's future heavyweight title claims stemmed from this win.

12 November Harry 'Slounch' Dixon (Stepney) reported as the winner of the heavyweight championship belt – *Sporting Life*.

1 December   On this day, a ten-round bout advertised for English heavyweight title between Jack Scales and Harry 'Slounch' Dixon at the 'Tee To Tum' Club, Stamford Hill, London was cancelled due to Scales having an abcess on his shoulder.

22 December Jack Munroe (Butte, born Canada) w pts 4 Jim Jeffries, Butte, Montana, USA. The conditions were that if Jeffries, on tour taking on all comers, failed to stop his man inside the four rounds he would lose both the decision and $500, which is what happened. It was Munroe's first bout since winning an Olympic Club (San Francisco) amateur heavyweight competition in 1900. He turned down the offer to try and stay a further four rounds against either Jeffries or Bob Fitzsimmons on 27 December, stating that he'd prefer to get in better condition before undertaking such a task again.

1903

23 February Jack Mullen (Wrekenton) w co 10 George Chrisp

257

(Newcastle), Ginnett's Circus, Newcastle. Referee: J.R. Smith. Scheduled for 15 rounds with no title billing and no weights given. With both said to be about 172lbs, it involved £25 a-side (£50 also given) and an £80 purse. Prior to his retirement in the middle of 1901, Chrisp, making a comeback, had won a claim to the English heavyweight title in a bout under championship conditions and over the full championship course. However, the above bout didn't have a large enough monetary reward for title recognition and Mullen didn't make any title claims on winning.

3 March Bill McColl (NSW) w rtd 6 Dan Creedon, NSC, Sydney, Australia. Scheduled for 20 rounds and billed for the Australian Commonwealth heavyweight title.

16 March Harry 'Slounch' Dixon (Stepney) drew 13 'Big' Ben Taylor (Woolwich), Wonderland, Whitechapel Road, London. Billed for the English heavyweight title and £100, it was disqualified from title consideration as only over two-minute rounds and money stake not high enough.

21 March Pat Daley, the English 140lbs champion and winner of an English heavyweight championship belt competition, seeing that his challenge to the world at 140lbs has been ignored, now challenges any heavyweight in England, no one barred, over 15 or 20 three minute-rounds for the best purse – *Sporting Life*.

1 April Jack Palmer (Benwell) challenges any man in England for the English heavyweight title, £50 or £100 a-side, 'Big' Ben Taylor or Harry 'Slounch' Dixon preferred – *Sporting Life*.

2 May Jack Palmer (Benwell) w co 12 'Big' Ben Taylor (Woolwich), Ginnett's Circus, Newcastle. Referee: Sam Francis. Scheduled for 20 rounds and billed for the English heavyweight championship.

5 May Bill McColl w co 3 Jim Scanlon, Sydney, Australia. Billed for the Australian heavyweight title.

30 May 'Big' Ben Taylor (Woolwich) w co 16 Jack Mullen (Wrekenton), Ginnett's Circus, Newcastle. Scheduled for 20 rounds, no weights or title billing given. If Mullen had laid claim to the heavyweight title following his win over Chrisp, this would have involved that claim and, as it was, it let Taylor back into the English title picture.

6 June Mike Williams (Born Galway, Ireland) w co 3 Jim Speed (Born Belfast), Plunketts Pavilion, Johannesburg, South Africa. Scheduled for 20 rounds and billed for the South African heavyweight title, Williams weighed 164lbs to Speed's 155.

28 July Henry J.T. Placke, the Dutch heavyweight champion, challenges the winner of the Jim Jeffries v Jim Corbett world heavyweight title bout to defend the title against him – *Sporting Life*.

29 July Jack Palmer (Benwell) is claiming the English heavyweight title after beating 'Big' Ben Taylor, who in his next bout kayoed Jack Mullen, who in his previous bout had kayoed the lineal champion, George Chrisp. Following that, the *Sporting Life* then stated that 'Philadelphia' Jack O'Brien (USA) was the English heavyweight champion because of his 20 May 1901 stoppage win over Chrisp. This caused an angry outburst, with it being pointed out that it had always been laid down in the rules that only a man born in the British Isles of British born parents could contest an English title and O'Brien v Chrisp was nothing more than an international match. Previously the paper had run items on exactly the same lines, which made its comments in regard to O'Brien a real surprise. It is possible that the comments came from Eugene Corri, who was always pressing for all and sundry to contest English titles.

14 August Jim Jeffries w co 10 Jim Corbett, Mechanics Pavilion, San Francisco, California, USA. Referee: Ed Graney. Billed for the world heavyweight title and scheduled for 20 rounds.

22 September Peter Felix w disq 15 Jim Scanlon, Sydney, Australia. Billed for the Australian 'open' heavyweight title.

23 November Peter Felix w rtd 3 Alf James, Melbourne, Australia. Billed for the Australian 'open' title.

9 December Jack Palmer (Benwell) is the English heavyweight champion – *Mirror of Life*.

1904

25 March Gunner Hewitt (Royal Marines) is undoubtedly the best heavyweight in England. There was some dispute over Hewitt's christian name, with both George and Harry being given over the years – *Sporting Life*.

26 August Harry 'Slounch' Dixon (Stepney) won the English

heavyweight championship belt competition at Wonderland in 1902 and the NSC heavyweight competition in 1903 – *Sporting Life*. Both of these competitions were, in fact, in 1901 and within a week of each other on 11 and 18 November, with both being billed as English 'novices' championship competitions and both for a championship belt.

26 August Jim Jeffries w co 2 Jack Munroe (Butte, Montana, born Canada), Mechanics Pavilion, San Francisco, California, USA. Referee: Ed Graney. Scheduled for 20 rounds and billed for the world heavyweight championship.

27 September Peter Felix drew 20 Arthur Cripps, Sydney, Australia. Billed for the Australian 'open' heavyweight title.

22 November Bill Squires w co 2 Peter Felix, Sydney, Australia. Billed for the Australian 'open' title.

15 December Mike Shallow (St John's, Newfoundland) drew 10 Jack Scales, Artillery Barracks, Newport, Monmouth. Referee: Captain Lowing, RGA. For £75 (£25 a-side and £25 purse), wearing four-ounce gloves and articled for ten rounds of two minutes each, the *Mirror of Life*, *Sporting Mirror* and *Sporting Life* all reported it as being over eight rounds of two minutes each. For some strange reason it was given billing as an English heavyweight title fight, with Scales announced as the holder. Shallow, of course, was not eligible to contest the English title and with the bout under no championship conditions whatsoever, no weights were given.

31 December Jack Scales is the English heavyweight champion – *Sporting Life*.

1905

18 January Jack Palmer (Benwell) is the English heavyweight champion – *Mirror of Life*.

11 March Pasquilla Camera (Camberwell, born Italy) w pts 6 Harry Ramano (Born Italy), Beresford Street Hall, Woolwich, London. Billed for the Italian heavyweight title, it was a publicity gimmick to draw the large Italian community living in London, which it did.

15 March Jack Palmer (Benwell) is taken ill in South Africa, with enteric fever, an intestinal disorder – *Mirror of Life*.

13 May Jim Jeffries, the world heavyweight champion, announces his retirement from boxing and formally relinquished his world title.

5 June Bill McColl w co 1 Dan Creedon, Melbourne, Australia. Billed for the Australian heavyweight title.

3 July Marvin Hart (Louisville) w co 12 Jack Root (Chicago, born Austria), The Arena, Reno, Nevada. Referee: Jim Jeffries. Scheduled for 20 rounds and given world heavyweight championship billing by Jim Jeffries, who awarded his world championship belt to Hart at the end of the fight. Root's real name was Janos Ruthaly. It later transpired that Hart only had one eye, having lost his right eye as a child when hit with a stone. Jack Johnson called Hart the best man he ever met and that Hart beat him fair and square in their 28 March 1905 bout, which Hart won on points over 20 rounds.

10 July Bill Squires w co 5 Tom Fennessy, Melbourne, Australia. Billed for the Australian heavyweight title.

19 July The *Mirror of Life's* pen picture of Harry 'Slounch' Dixon (Stepney) reported him to be the English heavyweight champion and holder of the championship belt pertaining to same.

2 September Bill Squires (Australia) may go to South Africa for a series of bouts with army boxers – *Sporting Life*.

7 September Bill Squires w co 4 Dick Kernick, Melbourne, Australia. Billed for the Australian heavyweight title.

9 September Tim Murphy w co 11 Bill McColl, Sydney, Australia. Billed for the Australian and Imperial heavyweight titles.

27 October 'Philadelphia' Jack O'Brien w co 17 Al Kaufmann (San Francisco), Woodwards Pavilion, San Francisco, California, USA. Referee: Jack Welch. Scheduled for 20 rounds, with the 19-year-old Kaufman little more than a novice, but O'Brien still claimed the American/world heavyweight title with this win.

20 November Corporal J.R. Sunshine (Royal Fusilliers, born York) w co 2 Harry 'Slounch' Dixon (Stepney), NSC, King Street, Covent Garden, London. Dixon was a substitute for Harry Shearing (Walthamstow), while Sunshine was the Army and Navy champion of 1905. No weights were given and no title billing accorded.

9 December Jack Scales (Bethnal Green) says he will box any of the many claimants to the English heavyweight title, 'Big' Ben

Taylor, Geoffrey Thorne, Harry 'Slounch' Dixon, Corporal J.R. Sunshine, Charley Wilson and Jack Palmer (Benwell) preferred – *Sporting Life*. In the same paper it was stated that under the banner of the NSC a match had been made between Palmer and Thorne to decide the vacant English heavyweight title in an effort to clear up the confusion.

15 December The *Sporting Life* reported that 'Big' Ben Taylor, Jack Scales, Harry 'Slounch' Dixon, Harry Smith (Birmingham, born Stoke) and George Chrisp had all claimed the English heavyweight title and then lost to smaller men from overseas, such as 'Philadelphia' Jack O'Brien and the coloured man, 'Young' Peter Jackson, (Baltimore) in international bouts.

18 December Jack Palmer (Benwell) w co 4 Geoff Thorne (Greenwich), NSC, King Street, Covent Garden, London. Billed for the vacant English heavyweight title and scheduled for 20 rounds and £350. The choice of Thorne who, under his real name of G.L.Townsend, had won the ABA middleweight title in 1895 and 1898 and an ABA heavyweight title in 1897 and 1898, was heavily criticised. The press stated that as British heavyweights were of such poor standard he had as much right as anyone to meet Palmer, who was considered to be by far the best of a very poor bunch with the possible exception of 'Gunner' James Moir (Lambeth), who had just returned from Australia.

20 December 'Philadelphia' Jack O'Brien w co 13 Bob Fitzsimmons, Mechanics Pavilion, San Francisco, California, USA. Referee: Ed Graney. Scheduled for 20 rounds, O'Brien (164lbs) stated that this win cemented his claim to the world heavyweight championship on the theory that the title reverted to Fitzsimmons (165lbs) on Jim Jeffries' retirement.

1906

17 January Jack Palmer (Benwell), the English heavyweight champion, challenges the world at 157lbs – *Mirror of Life*.

3 February 'Philadelphia' Jack O'Brien is the world heavyweight champion – *Sporting Life*.

14 February Although 'Philadelphia' Jack O'Brien claims the world heavyweight title with his win over Bob Fitzsimmons, the title is really vacant – *Sporting Life*.

23 February Tommy Burns (Detroit, born Ontario, Canada) w pts 20 Marvin Hart (Louisville, Kentucky), Naud Junction Pavilion, Los Angeles, California, USA. Referee: Charles Eyton. Billed as an American/world heavyweight title fight, with Hart as holder. Burns, whose real name was Noah Brusso, was born in Chesley, Ontario, Canada on 17 June 1881.

26 February 'Gunner' James Moir (Lambeth) w co 8 Jim Casey (formerly Young Fitzsimmons, born County Clare, Ireland), NSC, King Street, Covent Garden, London. This was a final eliminator, scheduled for 20 rounds, for the English heavyweight title, with the winner to meet the holder, Jack Palmer, for the title.

28 March On this day, the world heavyweight champion, Tommy Burns, beat Jim O'Brien and Jim Walker inside a round apiece in San Diego, California, Although they have come to be known as exhibitions, both bouts were scheduled for ten rounds and were billed as involving the world title.

21 April Jack Palmer (Benwell) is willing to defend the English heavyweight title against anyone, over 20 rounds for an NSC purse, 'Gunner' James Moir (Lambeth) for choice – *Sporting Life*.

28 April Bill Squires w co 1 Tim Murphy, Carlton, Victoria, Australia. All over in one minute, 50 seconds, it was a billed Commonwealth and Australian heavyweight title bout over 20 rounds.

28 June Jack Palmer (Benwell) challenges any heavyweight in the world, 'Philadelphia' Jack O'Brien preferred – *Sporting Life*.

2 October Tommy Burns (Detroit, born Canada) w co 15 'Fireman' Jim Flynn, Naud Junction Pavilion, Los Angeles, California, USA. Referee: Eddie Robinson. Billed for the American/world heavyweight title.

29 October 'Gunner' James Moir (Lambeth) w disq 9 Jack Palmer (Benwell), NSC, King Street, Covent Garden, London. Scheduled for 20 rounds and billed for the English heavyweight title, the bout was filmed by Mr Charles Urban and the film showed clearly that Palmer did land two low blows in what was described as a terrible bout, typical of the heavyweights.

1 November 'Gunner' James Moir challenges 'Philadelphia' Jack O'Brien for the world heavyweight title – *Sporting Life*.

6 November Bill Squires (Newcastle, Australia) w co 3 Peter Kling (Sydney), Ascot Vale Race Course, Victoria, NSW,

Australia. Scheduled for 20 rounds and billed for the Australian heavyweight title and a £500 purse.

16 November Jack Palmer (Benwell) sought an injunction to stop the NSC showing the film of his bout with 'Gunner' James Moir as it would show him in a bad light, but the injunction was refused by Mr Justice Warrington – *Sporting Life*.

17 November Pat Daley is willing to defend his English heavyweight title and championship belt against any English heavyweight – *Sporting Life*.

24 November The *Mirror of Life* published a letter asking for the formation of a proper boxing control body to be set up, in order to provide genuine English championships. This would stop all and sundry claiming the championship, as at present, for as soon as a man wins a contest at a set poundage he claims the championship at that poundage.

28 November Tommy Burns drew 20 'Philadelphia' Jack O'Brien, Naud Junction Pavilion, Los Angeles, California, USA. Referee: Jim Jeffries. Billed for the American/world heavyweight title, the bout had been pre-arranged to be called a draw in order to set up a money making return, the winner of which was to meet the English Champion, 'Gunner' James Moir, for the world title in March. It had long been expected for O'Brien and Moir to meet in a title bout in Britain.

1 December A £1000 purse and £100 each for expenses has been offered by a South of England sportsman to set up a world heavyweight title bout between 'Philadelphia' Jack O'Brien, real name Joseph Hagen, and 'Gunner' James Moir – *Sporting Life*.

3 December Bill Squires w co 1 Bill Smith, Melbourne, Australia. Billed for the Australian and Imperial titles.

11 December Charles B.Cochrane, on behalf of 'Gunner' James Moir, has put down a £100 deposit with the *Sporting Life* to bind a match with 'Philadelphia' Jack O'Brien for the vacant world heavyweight title.

19 December 'Philadelphia' Jack O'Brien is still recognized in American as the world heavyweight champion – *Sporting Life*.

21 December The *Sporting Life* stated that the four men in the running to settle the vacant world heavyweight title are: 1. 'Philadelphia' Jack O'Brien (USA), 2. Tommy Burns (Canada), 3. 'Gunner' James Moir (England) and 4. James 'Tiger' Smith (real name Addis of the Army and Wales). The choice of Smith was astounding as he had done nothing to warrant a high standing on the world stage and was, arguably, the most over-rated boxer in history, However, as an Army champion he could do no wrong in the eyes of 'Peggy' Bettison of the NSC, who like most British officials and press men of the day, had an obsession with boxers from the Army. In their eyes these men could beat the world and no one more so than 'Tiger' Smith, who, in reality, was little more than a six-round prelim boxer with a big punch and a weak chin. Moir too, although much better class than Smith and the reigning English champion with good wins in Australia, still owed much of his high world ranking by the NSC to his Army background.

22 December Bill Squires (Australia) w co 1 Mike Williams (South Africa), Melbourne, Australia. Billed for the Imperial title.

29 December Contracts were signed on this date in San Francisco for a world heavyweight title bout in April between the holder Jim Jeffries, who will be coming out of retirement, and Bill Squires, the Australian champion, at the 'Rhyo Late Club', Nevada. This completely ignored the long pending 'Philadelphia' Jack O'Brien versus the winner of the 'Gunner' James Moir v James 'Tiger' Smith bout for the vacant title – *Sporting Life*.

1907

25 February 'Gunner' James Moir (Lambeth) w co 1 James 'Tiger' Smith (Merthyr, South Wales, late of the Army), NSC, King Street, Covent Garden, London. Scheduled for 20 rounds, Moir weighing 180lbs to Smith's 162 (170lbs also given), it was billed for the English heavyweight title for a total of £1,350. The bout, filmed by Mr Charles Urban, lasted two minutes and 49 seconds and showed Smith to be a third rater.

28 February Promoter Harry Jacobs offered a purse of £500 for a 'Gunner' James Moir (holder) v Charley Wilson (Notting Hill) title bout. This was repeated on 2 March. It should be noted that Wilson was really only a middleweight – *Sporting Life*.

2 March The promoter and ex-boxer, Harry Williams (Hatcham), has offered a £550 purse for a Moir v Wilson match, if for £200 a-side – *Sporting Life*.

15 April	Mike Schreck w co 19 John Willie, Tonopah Casino AC, Nevada, USA. Billed for the American heavyweight title over 20 rounds and a $10,000 purse.
26 April	Charley Wilson (Notting Hill) and Jem Roche (Wexford), the Irish heavyweight champion, are both claiming the English title as 'Gunner' James Moir hasn't met either of them – *Sporting Life*.
2 May	Jack Johnson, a negro from Galveston,Texas who weighs 180lbs, challenges any heavyweight in the world – *Sporting Life*.
8 May	Tommy Burns (Canada) w pts 20 'Philadelphia' Jack O'Brien, Naud Junction Pavilion, Los Angeles, California, USA. Referee: Charles Eyton. Billed for the American/world heavyweight title.
27 May	Bill Lang w rtd 9 Peter Kling, Melbourne, Australia. Lang claimed the Australian 'residential' heavyweight title on winning.
4 July	Tommy Burns (Canada) w co 1 Bill Squires(Australia), Mission Street Arena, Colma, California, USA. Referee: Jim Jeffries. Billed for the world title and scheduled for 20 rounds, it was all over in two minutes and eight seconds.
6 July	Charley Wilson (Notting Hill) once again challenged 'Gunner' James Moir (holder) to a bout for the English heavyweight title. Wilson's 'backer' had deposited £50, which had been down for two months, but Moir just refuses to box Wilson again. The pair had met early in Moir's career, Wilson winning by a second-round knockout, but Moir was vastly improved from those days – *Sporting Life*.
8 July	Bill Lang w co 2 Dick Kernick, Melbourne, Australia. Billed for the Australian 'residential' title.
10 July	'Gunner' James Moir challenges Tommy Burns to a bout for the world title for for the best purse in the USA. Moir also stated that he was only a novice when losing to Charley Wilson and got out of a sick bed to fight. He then twisted his leg and the bout was stopped by the referee, Harry Jacobs, in the second round. Adamant that he wasn't kaoyed, Moir stated that if Wilson's 'backer' put up £500 then an English title bout between them could be made for October – *Sporting Life*.
19 August	Bill Lang w co 1 Mike Williams (South Africa), Melbourne, Australia. Recognised as an Australian 'open' title fight.
24 August	Charley Wilson challenges any white man in England for £200 a-side and a Liverpool Gym Club purse – *Sporting Life*.
16 September	Bill Lang w disq 3 George Ruenalf, Broken Hill, Australia. Billed for the Australian 'residential' heavyweight title.
3 October	Bill Lang w co 12 Peter Felix, Broken Hill, Australia. Billed for the Australian 'residential' title.
6 November	Bill Lang w rtd 8 Arthur Cripps, Melbourne, Australia. Billed for the Australian title.
2 December	Tommy Burns (Canada) w co 10 'Gunner' James Moir, NSC, King Street, Covent Garden, London. Referee: Eugene Corri. Billed for the undisputed world heavyweight title, a total purse of £2,300, and scheduled for 20 rounds, Burns had turned down a list of six referees, asking for Bob Watson, but was informed that only NSC members could officiate then, so agreed to Eugene Corri. The bout was filmed and Moir was stated to have been outclassed in all but courage. Some reports tried to make out the English title was also at stake, but A.F. 'Peggy' Bettinson of the NSC, stated that only a British-born person of British-born parents could contest an English title and, with Burns not being eligible for this, Moir was still the English heavyweight champion.
21 December	'Gunner' James Moir will defend his English title against the Irish champion, Jem Roche (Wexford), for £500 up to £2,000 a-side – *Sporting Life*.
23 December	Bill Lang w co 3 Ed Williams, Melbourne, Australia. Billed for the Australian title.
1908	
10 February	Tommy Burns (Canada) w co 4 Jack Palmer (Benwell), Wonderland, Whitechapel Road, London. Referee: Bob Watson. Billed for the world heavyweight title and scheduled for 20 three-minute rounds, £500 a-side and 80% of gate, it was stated to have been the worst title fight ever seen. Palmer made no attempt whatsoever to win.
17 February	Bill Lang w rtd 7 Peter Felix, Melbourne, Australia. Billed for the Australian 'residential' title.
26 February	Tommy Burns offered to box any three Englishmen in the same night and named the southpaw, James 'Tiger' Smith,

	who had challenged Burns to a title bout, 'Gunner' James Moir and Bill Squires (Australia) to six or ten rounds each – *Sporting Life*.
9 March	Bill Lang w co 1 Bill Smith, Melbourne, Australia. Billed for the Australian title.
17 March	Tommy Burns (Canada) w co 1 Jem Roche (Wexford), The Theatre Royal, Dublin, Ireland. Referee: Bob Watson. Billed for the world heavyweight title and contested on St Patrick's Day over 20 rounds, it was all over in 88 seconds.
27 March	A world heavyweight title bout in Paris, France has been proposed between Tommy Burns and Charley Wilson (Notting Hill), but had to be called off as Burns wife was seriously ill – *Sporting Life*.
18 April	Tommy Burns (Canada) w co 5 'Jewey' Smith (South Africa, born Spitalfields, London), Nevilly Bowling Grounds, Paris, France. Referee: Dr Phelin Roux. Scheduled for ten rounds and billed for the world heavyweight title over ten rounds and a £2,500 purse, prior to the bout starting the ring canopy was set on fire by camera flashlights, unnerving even more an already nervous Jewey Smith. With Burns being just 5'7" tall and Smith 5'5½", this must have involved the smallest heavyweight title contestants of all time. The match-up really was scraping the bottom of the barrel, as Smith, little more than a novice in only his third traced professional bout, had only engaged in Army service bouts while serving with the 3rd Battalion Royal Fusilliers in South Africa. Smith had never had a glove on prior to going to South Africa and just five service bouts can be traced, all in the Middelburg Cape Colony Army Garrison, of which he won four and drew one. In South Africa until being demobbed at the end of 1907, he returned to London to live in Aldgate. For the bout with Burns, which involved 'the richest prize in sport', Smith got just £25, plus expenses for two. The Wonderland promoter, Harry Jacobs, then acting as Smith's manager, being the other party. Smith, who showed himself to be a real trier and a dedicated trainer, was still boxing in New York, aged 42, in 1925. If ever a fighter got 'ripped off' it was Smith.
30 April	Bill Squires (Australia) w co 1 Jem Roche (Ireland), Dublin, Ireland. Billed for the Imperial heavyweight title.
13 June	Tommy Burns (Canada) w co 8 Bill Squires (Australia), Nevilly Bowling Grounds, Paris, France. Referee: Dr Phelin Roux. Billed for the world heavyweight title and scheduled for ten rounds, prior to the bout the management of the Bowling Palace came up with the then new idea of both men training in public.
20 July	Bill Lang w co 6 Jim Griffin, Melbourne, Australia. Billed for the Australian title..
24 August	Tommy Burns (Canada) w co 13 Bill Squires (Australia), Rushcutters Bay Stadium, Sydney, Australia. Referee: H.C.Nathan. Scheduled for 20 rounds, it was billed for the world heavyweight title and involved a £1600 purse (£1,000 winner and £600 loser).
2 September	Tommy Burns w co 6 Bill Lang (Melbourne, born Carlton, Australia), The City Road New Stadium, South Melbourne, Australia. Referee: Hugh D.McIntosh. Billed for the world heavyweight title and scheduled for 20 rounds, Lang, whose real name was William Langfranchi, stopped Jim Griffin in five rounds (in Melbourne on 16 November) and knocked out Bill Squires (on 3 February 1909 in Sydney) in the 17th round to win the Australian and Imperial titles, but would never get another crack at Burns.
21 December	A.F. 'Peggy' Bettinson stated: "it had always been the rule that only a British born person could contest an English title". However, the NSC referee, Eugene Corri, was one of the few at the Club who wanted this changed so that anyone from anywhere could contest an English title – *Mirror of Life*.
26 December	Jack Johnson (Galveston, Texas, USA) w rsc 14 Tommy Burns (Canada). The Rushcutters Bay Stadium, Sydney, Australia. Promoter and Referee: Hugh D. McIntosh. Billed for the world heavyweight title and scheduled for 20 rounds, in the lead up to this bout many notable American experts called Tommy Burns: "The greatest heavyweight ever seen and a certainty to win", an opinion shared by many English and Australian experts.
1909	
11 February	On this day, the NSC renamed the English title as the 'British' title and introduced eight-named spread weight divisions with all over 175lbs being known as heavyweights.

Highlights from the 2004-2005 Amateur Season

by Chris Kempson

The Olympic year of 2004 was dominated by one boxer in much the same way that Audley Harrison MBE had done so in Australia in 2000. This time, a teenager from Bolton came, saw and conquered (well almost) and then in May 2005 decided to seek fame and fortune in the professional code. Amir Khan gave hope and inspiration through his deeds in the ring to many aspiring Olympic hopefuls. It is sad that he is no longer going to ply his trade in the vest and headguard, but he left many magical moments behind him for which the nation and its boxing fans in particular should be grateful.

Elsewhere the season was one of considerable change and new direction. For instance, amateurs appearing on professional shows that some forecast would never see the light of day, well they were wrong. BBC and ITV covered our sport and we can hope but for more of the same, while Channels 4 and 5 did their bit as well. Ian Irwin slipped into retirement after many years as England coach and the former world super-middleweight champion, Richie Woodhall, became 'High Performance Manager', raising eyebrows among some of the 'blazers'. Also, new administrative and funding arrangements for the sport are being introduced.

The latter includes the 'Talented Athletes Support Scheme' (TASS) and allocates £10,000 each to James Degale, Ryan Pickard, Danny Price and Bradley Saunders, to help with their training, medical and travelling expenses, etc. They have been identified as potential 2012 Olympics participants, although it is possible they may be candidates for Beijing 2008. After almost 60 years, the National Schoolboy Championships gave way to the Golden Gloves Championships, and while women's boxing continued to make considerable inroads into the male dominated sport, some sighed, frowned and questioned where will it all end?

Join me now in a detailed trip through the season to examine in more detail the historic events which made the amateur season of 2004-2005 one of the very best for many years.

JULY

The England team once again covered itself with glory at the annual International Junior Olympics, which were staged on this occasion at the Jacob Brown Auditorium in Brownsville, Texas from 5-8 July. In the searing heat and humidity, and only just 100 metres from the Mexican border, England's under-17 team landed two golds, four silvers and two bronze. Gold was claimed by southpaw, Luke Campbell (St Paul's, Hull), at 50kgs and Anthony Agogo (Lowestoft, Triple A) in the 66kgs division.

Ireland struck gold in the second European Schoolboys Championships for boxers aged 14-16 in Siofok, Hungary from 29 June – 4 July. Willie O'Reilly of St Paul's, Waterford was successful at 40kgs, while Stephen O'Reilly from Twintowns in Donegal was the kingpin at 68kgs. The Emerald Isle also claimed one silver and two bronze, while Wales weighed-in with two bronze. The event which saw 112 boxers from 14 nations did not include entrants from either England or Scotland.

AUGUST

The boxing tournament in the Athens Olympics opened on 14 August and was concluded with the finals, which were boxed off on 29 August. England's lightweight representative, Amir Khan and Ireland's southpaw middleweight, Andy Lee, met with mixed fortunes.

Khan won a fabulous silver medal, only being bested in the final by the legendary Cuban great, Mario Kindelan Mesa, 30-22 after a tremendous tussle. On his way to the final, the precocious Bolton teenager stopped Marios Kaperonis (Greece) in his first series bout in the third round on the outclassed rule (32-12); outpointed Bulgaria's Dimitar Stilianov 37-21 in his second series contest; stopped Baik Jong Sub (Korea) in the opening session of his quarter-final and trounced Serik Yeleuov of Kazakhstan 40-26 in the semi-final to set up his final encounter with the reigning Olympic champion and three times world champion. Lee, for his part, found life difficult in the 75kgs division and after winning his first series bout 38-23 against Alfredo Angulo Lopez from Mexico, he was eliminated on a countback by Hassan Ndam Njikam from Cameroon. Although it ended level at 27 points apiece, no details were given as such of Nikam's overall points advantage. Lee has vowed to make it to Beijing in 2008.

SEPTEMBER

England and Ireland were among the medals at the ninth European Cadet (under-17) Championships held in Saratov, Russia from 11-20 September, a tournament which was heavily dominated by the host nation among the 29 participating countries. Ireland's 70kgs representative Eamonn Corbett (Ligoniel) took silver, having been unfortunately unable to box in the final due to a broken thumb sustained in the semi-final. England's three bronze medals came via Luke Campbell (St Paul's, Hull) at 50kgs, Anthony Agogo (Lowestoft's Triple A Club) at 66kgs and George Groves (Dale Youth) in the 75kgs division.

Meanwhile, Young England just got the better of Young Ireland by the odd bout in nine (5-4) at Merseyside's Everton Park Sports Centre on 24 September.

The Nationen Cup multi-nations event held in Wiener Neustadt, Austria from 23-26 September, saw Ireland return home with two bronze medals, Eamonn Touhey (60kgs) and John Joe McDonagh (64kgs) being the recipients.

The Netherlands hosted Ireland, who drew the senior contests 1-1 and lost the junior matches 2-0, in a mixed-ages match on 26 September and took the overall spoils, 4-2.

OCTOBER

Scotland were decidedly on the gold standard at the Box Am multi-nations tournament stages in Almeira, Spain on 4-10 October. The men from north of the border were the only representatives from the Four Nations to compete in this tournament for the second year in a row. Gold went to Mitch Prince at lightweight, Craig McEwan, a southpaw, at middleweight and Steve Simmons at heavyweight on a walkover, when his opponent, a Madrid policeman, could not get off duty to box! Scotland's giant super-heavyweight Ian Millarvie weighed in with a bronze.

The Four Nations did extremely well at the annual Tammer multi-nations tournament held at Tamper in Finland from 14-17 October, England bagging four golds and a silver, Ireland landing one gold and two bronze, Wales a silver and two bronze and Scotland one bronze. English gold successes were achieved by Hollington's Langley brothers, Darran (48kgs) and Stewart (51kgs), Nick McDonald (Vauxhall Motors) at 54kgs and, at the other end of the scale, by David Dolan, a heavyweight from Plains Farm. Silver went to Merseyside's David Price (Salisbury) at super-heavyweight. Ireland's medals were claimed by Kenneth Egan, with a gold at 81kgs to go with the 'Best Technical Boxer' award and bronzes for Conor Ahern (48kgs) and Eamonn O'Kane (75kgs). The Welsh silver went to Kevin Evans (91kgs), while Mohamed Nasir (48kgs) and Matthew Edmonds (51kgs) each claimed bronze. Scotland's bronze went to Steve Simmons in the heavyweight division.

Ireland travelled to the Glamorgan Cricket Club on 29 October and triumphed by 7-2 over their Welsh hosts on a dinner show.

NOVEMBER

The Scottish NYAC Championships, part of the UK's NACYP, were boxed off at the North Merchiston Boys Club in Edinburgh on 6 November.

Ireland's juniors and seniors continued their rich winning vein with a 6-3 triumph over Holland in Dublin's National Stadium on 12 November, while two nights later (14 November) they were thumped by the Dutch visitors by a 5-2 margin in Dundalk.

The Irish Under-21 Championship finals were held at the National Stadium in Dublin on 27 November, the earlier rounds having taken place on 19 and 20 November. St Michael's Boxing Club from Athy in County Kildare took four of the nine finals contested, with three members of the Joyce family taking titles.

England and Ireland drew 7-7 in a Schoolboy international at Ipswich on 26 November.

On 26 November, Wales drew 5-5 with Scotland in a mixed-ages international match at Barry Leisure Centre, with four bouts contested at senior level, three at junior and three at cadet.

England squeezed home 4-3 against the United States at London's luxurious Metropole Hotel on 29 November. The heavyweight, David Dolan, from Plains Farm, sealed the English victory with a 20-point 'mercy' stoppage over Tim Skolnik.

DECEMBER

The national coach, Terry Edwards, was inducted into the UK 2004 'Coaching Hall of Fame', by picking up the 'Mussabini Medal' at the Café Royal on 2 December from HRH The Princess Royal. Mussabini was the trainer who coached the 1924 Olympic 100yds winner, Harold Abrahams, who was made famous by the film, Chariots of Fire.

The Welsh national team travelled to Stavanger and defeated Norway 5-4 on 4 December, their seniors winning 3-1, their juniors losing 3-0 and the cadets winning 2-0.

England won their second international against the United States by the slenderest of margins, this time 5-4 at the Liverpool Olympia on 3 December. Amir Khan, having his first bout since his silver medal success in Athens, was among the victors.

The city of Bendigo, in Victoria, Australia, hosted the inaugural Commonwealth Youth Games from 1-3 December and England's under-19 boxers won no fewer than six gold medals at these Games. Golds went to Liam Walsh (Kingfisher) at bantamweight, James McElvaney (South Bank) at featherweight, Gary Barker (Repton), a southpaw, at lightweight, South Durham's Bradley Saunders at light-welterweight, while another Reptonite, Ryan Pickard, triumphed at welterweight and Dale Youth's impressive southpaw, James Degale, weighed-in with gold at middleweight. Scotland and Northern Ireland also did well at these Games. Scotland got silver through Jason Hastie in the bantamweight division and David Appleby at lightweight, while bronze medals were achieved for the Scots by Joe Kelso at featherweight, Gary McMillan at light-welterweight and Andrew McKelvie in the middleweight division. Ireland's brace of medals were gleaned by Patrick Murphy, who won a silver at light-welterweight, and David McComb, with a bronze at lightweight.

A meeting, held on 5 December, of the Schools Amateur Boxing Association (SABA), resolved that it would not be practical to stage the annual SABA Championships this season. As the ABA were hosting a National Championship called the 'Golden Gloves' for boys born in 1990, 1991 and 1992, preliminary rounds of which would start next month.

This month is the traditional time for the NACYP finals and they were held as follows: Class 'A' at the Britannia Adelphi Hotel in Liverpool on 10 December; Class 'B' at Kirkby-in-Ashfield in Nottinghamshire on 13 December and Class 'C' in London's Royal Lancaster Hotel on 8 December.

The ABAE staged a fascinating series of England trials over three days (17-19 December) at the Crystal Palace National Sports Centre. Its purpose was to establish a pecking order for funding once the new four-year programme, underwritten by Sport England, comes into place early next year.

The inaugural National Novice Cadet Finals Class 'C' took place on 11 December at Crystal Palace.

An historic announcement was unveiled in London at the Strand Palace Hotel on 16 December, stating that amateur boxers will appear on professional shows for the first time, in England in 2005. Frank Warren's Sports Network company have clinched an arrangement with the ABAE Ltd to include 'elite' amateurs on his shows. It is a long-term deal, over three years.

As the New Year dawned, news broke that long-time top England coach, Ian Irwin, was retiring from the sport.

JANUARY 2005

The first major multi-nations tournament of the New Year, the Norway Box Cup which took place in Oslo 21-23 January proved lucrative, medal wise for the Scots and the Welsh. Scotland's Mark Hastie grabbed gold at his new weight of 64kgs, while bronze medals went to the Scots trio of Mitch Prince (lightweight), Fundo Mahura (welterweight) and Steve Simmons at heavyweight. Bronze for Wales came via the gloves of Vivian Bryan (64kgs) and Kevin Evans at heavyweight.

At the end of the month, Young Ireland, boxing on away territory, defeated their French equivalents 6-3 (29-31 January).

FEBRUARY

The times certainly are a changing, as on 1 February Kaleen Love and Teri Kleinberg contested the first all-female contest in over 120 years at the Oxford Union.

The Irish Intermediate Championships were held in the National Stadium in Dublin on 4 February, earlier rounds having taken place on 28 and 29 January. On finals night the boys had to share centre stage with the girls, as for the first time the Irish Womens' Championships were staged. Jennifer Campbell, a bantamweight from Limerick, became the first of her sex to win a national crown.

Young England beat Young Italy (Under-19) twice, with the same score 4-3 on each occasion, first in Lowestoft on 16 February and then, two days later, at Basingstoke (18 February).

A well publicised and well documented ticket row led to the Olympic silver medallist, Amir Khan, now competing at light-welterweight, pulling out of the ABA Senior Championships prior to the Eastern/Home Counties versus North West Counties ABA quarter finals in Gorleston on 26 February. The departure of Khan certainly threw the title into the melting pot for the competitors still remaining in the Championship mix.

The Ulster Senior Championships were concluded on 24 February at the Ulster Hall, while the preliminaries and the semi-finals took place on 15-17 February at the Belfast Dockworkers Club.

MARCH

The Welsh ABA Senior finals took place on 4 March at Newport Leisure Centre.

On 18 March, the Irish Senior Championships took place in the National Stadium in Dublin, earlier rounds having been boxed off on 4,5,11 and 12 March. The 20-year old Irish Olympian, Limerick's Andy Lee, won his third national senior middleweight title.

That same day, 18 March, also saw the Scottish Senior ABA finals take place at the Monklands Time Capsule in Coatbridge, while 24 hours later (19 March) the same venue hosted the Scottish Schoolboys and Cadets finals.

The 116th English ABA finals were staged, too, on 18 March in another London venue, this time in the Docklands at the ExCel Centre, and they proved to be a great occasion even if our Olympic silver medallist from Athens was no more than a well sought after ringside spectator on the night. London ABA had a good night with four champions crowned - the Langley twins from Hollington, Darran (48kgs) and Stewart (51kgs), Haringey Police Community's Michael Grant, who deservedly took over the Amir Khan mantle at 64kgs and Dale Youth's immensely promising James Degale in the 75kgs division. Arguably, the other two most notable triumphs came from Hall Green's Frankie Gavin (60kgs) and the gigantic Liverpudlian, David Price (Salisbury), at super-heavyweight. A special women's contest was also on the ExCel agenda on finals night and was won by Amanda Coulson (Hartlepool Catholic) over Eastside, Belfast's Alana Audley Murphy.

The Four Nations tournament took place at the Liverpool Olympia on 24 and 25 March. England came top with six gold, followed by Ireland with three, Wales two and, sadly, Scotland none. England also bagged four silver and a bronze, Ireland two silver and four bronze, Wales three silver and two bronze, with the Scots netting two silver and four bronze.

The finals of the inaugural National Golden Gloves Championships took place at Gateshead Leisure Centre on 26 and 27 March.

APRIL

On 1 April the start of a new four-year programme for English amateur boxing, backed by £4,271,000 from Sport England, came into being. Terry Edwards was given the role of 'High Performance Director', while the former world professional super-middleweight champion and former 1988 Olympic bronze medallist, Richie Woodhall, became 'High Performance Manager', an interesting choice, even if not apparently a universally welcome one by the rank and file of the sport. But then, this is nothing new.

The Cubans came to town, well the Liverpool Olympia to be precise, on 8 April and dished out a 7-1 drubbing to the Four Nations champions. Mario Kindelan Mesa was in the party and convincingly outpointed fellow southpaw and new ABA champion, Frankie Gavin. England's sole success came via David Price at super-heavyweight, with a fine points victory over Liosvan Hernandez.

The 24th GeeBee multi-nations tournament was held in Helsinki, Finland from 8-10 April and England's four-man team each came home with a medal. Don Broadhurst (51kgs) and Tony Jeffries (81kgs) bagged silver apiece, while bronze went to Stephen Smith (57kgs) and Gary Barr (75kgs). Wales got a bronze from Matthew Edmonds (51kgs) and Scotland, for their part, took one silver and three bronze. Craig McEwan (75kgs) got the silver, while bronze went to James Ancliff (54kgs), Sammy Carroll (57kgs) and Steve Simmons (91kgs).

The National Stadium in Dublin witnessed an historic success by the Four Nations team on 15 April as they turned the tables on their Cuban visitors and proceeded to thump them 6-2 in a sensational turnaround of fortune from their dismal performance a week earlier. Five out of the six winners were from Ireland. There were also two walkovers which were not included in the team score.

The Four Nations Boys Championships were held in the National Stadium, Dublin on 22 and 23 April. England came out on top with a most impressive 33-medal tally (nine gold, 11 silver and 13 bronze), Ireland achieved 28 medals (nine gold, ten silver and nine bronze) and Wales performed so well to amass 20 medals (ten gold, four silver and six bronze). The Scots in fourth place could only muster nine medals (three silver and six bronze).

The 32nd President's Cup was staged in Wroclawek, Poland from 27-30 April and England returned home with two bronze medals. They went to Joe Murray (bantamweight) and James McElvaney (featherweight). 66 boxers from ten nations took part in the event.

MAY

The fourth Women's European Championships were held in Tonsberg, Norway from 9-14 May. Eighteen-year-old Wicklow lightweight, Katie Taylor, became the first Irish girl to strike gold in this tournament, boxing three times for her triumph, and now is looking forward to the World Championships in Russia. England's team of four were beaten in the preliminary rounds, but the experience will stand the girls in good stead.

England travelled to Kaunas in Lithuania (12-15 May) for the ninth Algiras Socikas multi-nations tournament and what a lucrative event it proved to be for them. The Kirkdale southpaw, Neil Perkins, grabbed gold in the welterweight division, Sunderland's Tony Jeffries secured silver at light-heavyweight, while Danny Price (Westway) in his first senior international also won silver, at heavyweight.

On an emotional night (14 May) in Bolton's impressive Reebok Stadium, Amir Khan finally got his revenge over Mario Kindelan Mesa by 19 points to 13 over four-twos, as part of a four-bout dinner event involving England and Cuba. The contest was shown live on ITV1 and heralded their first venture back into boxing, albeit the amateur code in quite a while. Let us hope that more of the same will come in turn.

The Cuban maestro still held the final sway, however, with two victories against one loss to Khan in their three-fight series. The Cubans won the other three bouts against England in this mini-event, but the evening was all about Amir, who, following his great success, promptly waved goodbye to the amateur code and announced that he was turning professional with Frank Warren. No surprise really, the lure of Beijing in 2008 could not match the fame and fortune which this young 18-year-old seems certain to embark upon.

The Four Nations Cadets tournament took place at Ystrad Rhondda Leisure Centre in Wales from 19-22 May. With boxers born in 1989 and 1990 taking part, Ireland came out on top with 12 golds and six silvers, followed by England with ten gold and seven silvers. The host nation were in third place with two gold and seven silvers, with Scotland in fourth place with two gold and six silvers.

The finals of the Irish Junior Championships were held on 27 May at Dublin's National Stadium, the earlier rounds having taken place on 20 and 21 May. 17-year-old David Oliver Joyce, from a well-known boxing family, and boxing for St Michael's ABC in Athy, County Kildare, made history when he became the first boxer to win senior, junior, intermediate and under-21 titles in the same season. Congratulations to David and I am sure we will hear much more about him in the years to come.

Knottingley Leisure Centre was once again the venue for the National Novice finals, on 21 May Also, some of the Women's ABA Championships were boxed-off here, the remainder being completed on 28 May at Huddersfield Town Hall.

May 28 was also the date for the Junior ABA finals at the Huddersfield Town Hall and there was an unsavoury moment when a beaten boxer threw punches at the referee, Jack Goodwin. Thankfully, this is such a rarity in our sport these days that it only makes the headlines because it is so unusual.

JUNE

The first pro-am show in the Republic of Ireland took place on 4 June on Paddy Hyland's promotion at Dublin's, National Stadium.

The Four Nations for boxers born in 1987-88 were held in Aberdeen, Scotland on 3 and 4 June. The Irish won seven golds, six silver and six bronze; England also netted seven golds but only four silver and eight bronze; while the hosts, Scotland, got three gold, three silver and seven bronze. The other country, Wales, won two gold, six silver and six bronze.

The third European Union Championships in Ala Birdi, Sardinia (3-11 June) proved to be a successful hunting ground for England's boxers, who netted one gold, one silver and three bronze medals. Ireland also struck gold. At welterweight, the Kirkdale southpaw, Neil Perkins, boxed four times for his gold medal, while a silver went to Birtley middleweight, Gary Barr, who also had to box four times. Bronze medals went to Don Broadhurst (Birmingham Irish) at flyweight, the Hall Green southpaw, Frankie Gavin, at lightweight and to Sunderland's light-heavyweight, Tony Jeffries. Ireland's gold was claimed by Kenneth Egan at light-heavyweight.

Ireland hosted two junior internationals against Canada on 10 and 12 June. At the National Stadium in Dublin on 10 June they thumped the Canadians 8-2, while two days later at the St Joseph's Hall, Blessington, they achieved a much narrower success over their visitors by 5-4.

England came out on top in the Six Nations Junior tournament in Rome on 18 and 19 June. The three English golds went to James McElvaney (South Bank) at 57kgs, Jamie Cox (Walcot Boys) at 64kgs and George Groves (Dale Youth) at 75kgs. Ireland's two golds went to Carl Frampton (Midland City, Belfast) at flyweight and David Oliver Joyce (St Michael's, Athy) at featherweight.

The tenth European Cadet (under-17) Championships were boxed-off in Siofok, Hungary from 18-25 June and England secured two excellent silver medals, via Khalid Saeed (Birmingham City) at 48kgs and Michael Maguire (Kettering School of Boxing) at 50kgs. For Ireland, Michael Collins from the Darndale Club in Dublin, won bronze at 66kgs.

Well, there it is, this journey is over, but a new one will commence shortly. A good time for amateur boxing it has been and the future certainly looks assured too. And, with the Olympics bound for London in 2012, the challenges for our amateur boxers in the intervening years will be good for our sport. Once again, get behind the clubs and their boxers as they remain the lifeblood of the sport and its future.

ABA National Championships, 2004-2005

Note: Only men who actually fought are included.

Eastern Counties/Home Counties v North-West Counties

Eastern Counties
Essex Division   The Town Hall, Clacton – 28 January
L.Fly: no entries. **Fly:** no entries. **Bantam:** no entries. **Feather:** *final:* M.Poston (Harwich) wo. **Light:** no entries. **L.Welter:** *final:* J.Martin (Canvey) wo. **Welter:** no entries. **Middle:** *final:* G.Barton (Southend) wo. **L.Heavy:** no entries. **Heavy:** no entries. **S.Heavy:** no entries.

Mid-Anglia Division   The Sportsman, Chatteris – 21 January
L.Fly: no entries. **Fly:** no entries. **Bantam:** no entries. **Feather:** no entries. **Light:** no entries. **L.Welter:** no entries. **Welter:** *final:* P.McAleese (Haddenham) wo. **Middle:** no entries. **L.Heavy:** *final:* P.Wright (Chatteris) wo. **Heavy:** no entries. **S.Heavy:** no entries.

Norfolk Division   Ocean Room, Gorleston – 26 January
L.Fly: no entries. **Fly:** *final:* R.Walsh (Kingfisher) wo. **Bantam:** *final:* L.Walsh (Kingfisher) wo. **Feather:** no entries. **Light:** no entries. **L.Welter:** no entries. **Welter:** *final:* S.Rice (Dereham) wo. **Middle:** *final:* M.Cooper (Aylsham) wo. **L.Heavy:** *final:* M.Redhead (Kingfisher) wo. **Heavy:** no entries. **S.Heavy:** no entries.

Suffolk Division   Risby Village Hall, Bury St Edmunds – 12 December
L.Fly: no entries. **Fly:** no entries. **Bantam:** no entries. **Feather:** *final:* R.Mitchell (New Astley) wo. **Light:** *final:* K.Allen (Eastgate) wo. **L.Welter:** no entries. **Welter:** no entries. **Middle:** *final:* W.Bayliss (New Astley) wo. **L.Heavy:** *final:* P.Davis (Lowestoft) w rsc 2 L.Larmour (New Astley). **Heavy:** no entries. **S.Heavy:** no entries.

Eastern Counties Semi-Finals & Finals   Pontins Holiday Camp, Kessingland – 4 February
L.Fly: no entries. **Fly:** *final:* R.Walsh (Kingfisher) wo. **Bantam:** *final:* L.Walsh (Kingfisher) wo. **Feather:** *final:* M.Poston (Harwich) w pts R.Mitchell (New Astley). **Light:** *final:* K.Allen (Eastgate) wo. **L.Welter:** *final:* J.Martin (Canvey) wo. **Welter:** *final:* P.McAleese (Haddenham) w pts S.Rice (Dereham). **Middle:** *semi-finals:* G.Barton (Southend) wo, W.Bayliss (New Astley) w pts M.Cooper (Aylsham); *final:* G.Barton w pts W.Bayliss. **L.Heavy:** *semi-finals:* M.Redhead (Kingfisher) wo, P.Davis (Lowestoft) w pts P.Wright (Chatteris); *final:* M.Redhead w pts P.Davis. **Heavy:** no entries. **S.Heavy:** no entries.

Home Counties   Jumpin Jaks Nightclub, Dunstable – 31 January
L.Fly: *final:* J.Fowl (Haileybury) wo. **Fly:** *final:* D.Culling (Stevenage) w rsc 1 M.Kenright (Bushey). **Bantam:** *final:* L.Lewis (Wolvercote) wo. **Feather:** *final:* I.Bailey (Slough) wo. **Light:** *final:* A.Lever (Bedford) w pts D.Phillips (Luton Shamrock). **L.Welter:** *final:* W.Crotty (Cheshunt) w pts P.Steadman (Wolvercote). **Welter:** *final:* S.Ely (Lewsey) wo. **Middle:** *final:* S.Mullins (Wolvercote) wo. **L.Heavy:** no entries.

Heavy: *final:* L.Howkins (Pinewood Starr) wo. **S.Heavy:** no entries.

Home Counties v Eastern Counties   Windrush Leisure Centre, Witney – 12 February
L.Fly: J.Fowl (Haileybury) wo. **Fly:** R.Walsh (Kingfisher) w pts D.Culling (Stevenage). **Bantam:** L.Walsh (Kingfisher) w pts L.Lewis (Wolvercote). **Feather:** M.Poston (Harwich) w pts I.Bailey (Slough). **Light:** D.Phillips (Luton Shamrock) w pts K.Allen (Eastgate). **L.Welter:** J.Martin (Canvey) w pts W.Crotty (Cheshunt). **Welter:** P.McAleese (Haddenham) w pts S.Ely (Lewsey). **Middle:** S.Mullins (Wolvercote) w pts G.Barton (Southend). **L.Heavy:** M.Redhead (Kingfisher) wo. **Heavy:** L.Howkins (Pinewood Starr) wo. **S.Heavy:** no entries.

North-West Counties
East Lancs & Cheshire Division   The Guildhall, Preston – 7 February
L.Fly: no entries. **Fly:** *final:* J.Wilkinson (Fox) wo. **Bantam:** *final:* S.McFadden (Sandygate) wo. **Feather:** *final:* J.Kays (Arrow) w pts A.Crolla (Fox). **Light:** *final:* J.Cosgrove (Barton) w pts R.Burns (Cleator Moor). **L.Welter:** *quarter-finals:* A.Khan (Bury), C.Watson (Northside) wo, L.Dorrian (Arrow) wo, L.Graves (Chorley) w pts G.Higginson (Nichols Police); *semi-finals:* A.Khan w pts C.Watson, L.Dorrian w pts L.Graves; *final:* A.Khan w pts L.Dorrian. **Welter:** *final:* D.Vassell (Fox) w co 1 M.King (Cleator Moor). **Middle:** *final:* B.Rose (Blackpool & Fylde) w rsc 3 L.Newman (Bredbury). **L.Heavy:** *semi-finals:* E.Hanlungu (Viking, IoM), C.Chambers (Larches & Savick) w pts N.Travis (Tonge); *final:* C.Chambers w rsc 3 E.Hanlungu. **Heavy:** no entries. **S.Heavy:** no entries.

West Lancs & Cheshire Division   Everton Park Sports Centre, Liverpool – 4 & 11 February
L.Fly: *final:* C.Lyon (Wigan) wo. **Fly:** *final:* P.Edwards (Salisbury) wo. **Bantam:** *semi-finals:* N.McDonald (Vauxhall Motors) wo, S.Smith (Rotunda) w pts J.Donnelly (Croxteth); *final:* N.McDonald w pts S.Smith. **Feather:** *semi-finals:* R.Jockins (Rotunda) wo, M.Robinson (Tower Hill) w pts K.Buckley (Chester); *final:* M.Robinson w pts R.Jockins. **Light:** *final:* S.Jennings (Tower Hill) wo. **L.Welter:** *final:* S.Williams (Avalon) wo. **Welter:** *semi-finals:* J.Selkirk (Rotunda) wo, L.Kempster (Halewood) w pts A.Davies (Tower Hill); *final:* J.Selkirk w rsc 1 L.Kempster. **Middle:** *final:* J.McNally (Rotunda) w pts S.Birch (Lowe House). **L.Heavy:** *final:* J.Ainscough (Kirkdale) w pts M.Whitty (Rotunda). **Heavy:** *final:* T.Bellew (Rotunda) w rsc 4 P.Craig (Knowsley Vale). **S.Heavy:** *final:* D.Price (Salisbury) wo.

North-West Counties Finals   Olympia, Liverpool – 18 February
L.Fly: C.Lyon (Wigan) wo. **Fly:** P.Edwards (Salisbury) w pts J.Wilkinson (Fox). **Bantam:** N.McDonald (Vauxhall Motors) w rsc 3 S.McFadden (Sandygate). **Feather:** M.Robinson (Tower Hill) w pts J.Kays (Arrows). **Light:** S.Jennings (Tower Hill) w pts J.Cosgrove (Barton). **L.Welter:** A.Khan (Bury) w rsc 3 S.Williams (Avalon). **Welter:** J.Selkirk (Rotunda) w pts D.Vassell (Fox). **Middle:** J.McNally (Rotunda) w pts B.Rose (Blackpool & Fylde). **L.Heavy:** J.Ainscough (Kirkdale) w rsc 3 C.Chambers

(Larches & Savick). **Heavy:** T.Bellew (Rotunda) wo. **S.Heavy:** D.Price (Salisbury) wo.

Eastern Counties/Home Counties v North-Western Counties Ocean Rooms, Gorleston – 26 February
L.Fly: C.Lyon (Wigan) w pts J.Fowl (Haileybury). **Fly:** P.Edwards (Salisbury) w pts R.Walsh (Kingfisher). **Bantam:** N.McDonald (Vauxhall Motors) w pts L.Walsh (Kingfisher). **Feather:** M.Robinson (Tower Hill) w pts M.Poston (Harwich). **Light:** S.Jennings (Tower Hill) w rsc 4 D.Phillips (Luton Shamrock). **L.Welter:** S.Williams (Avalon) – replaced A.Khan (Bury) - wo J.Martin (Canvey). **Welter:** J.Selkirk (Rotunda) w rsc 3 P.McAleese (Haddenham). **Middle:** S.Mullins (Wolvercote) w pts J.McNally (Rotunda). **L.Heavy:** M.Redhead (Kingfisher) w pts J.Ainscough (Kirkdale). **Heavy:** T.Bellew (Rotunda) w pts L.Howkins (Pinewood Starr). **S.Heavy:** D.Price (Salisbury) wo.

London v Midland Counties

London
North-East Division Goresbrook Leisure Centre, Dagenham – 20 January
L.Fly: no entries. **Fly:** no entries. **Bantam:** *final:* A.Nabizadeh (Repton) wo. **Feather:** *final:* L.Ballard (Repton) wo. **Light:** *semi-finals:* B.Dodd (Hornchurch & Elm Park) wo, D.Smith (Dagenham) w pts A.Wallace (Repton); Final: B.Dodd w rsc 3 A.Wallace – replaced D.Smith, who had double vision. **L.Welter:** *final:* N.Weise (West Ham) w co 4 M.Idris (Repton). **Welter:** *semi-finals:* L.Calvert (Dagenham) w pts M.Lawrence (Fairbairn House), D.Herdman (Repton) w pts C.McDonagh (Dagenham); *final:* D.Herdman w pts L.Calvert. **Middle:** *semi-finals:* D.Happe (Repton) wo, D.Prevost (Debden) w pts A. Iqbal (County); *final:* D.Happe w pts D.Prevost. **L.Heavy:** *final:* D.Lewis (Peacock) w pts D.Sadler (Barking). **Heavy:** *final:* O.Ossai (Repton) wo. **S.Heavy:** *final:* D.Campbell (Repton) w pts R.McCallum (Broad Street).

North-West Division   The Town Hall, Brent – 25 January
L.Fly: no entries. **Fly:** no entries. **Bantam:** no entries. **Feather:** *final:* M.Mehmet (Finchley) wo. **Light:** *final:* P.Liggins (Trojan) w pts M.Child (Finchley). **L.Welter:** *final:* M.Grant (Haringey Police) w pts M.Sazish (Hanwell). **Welter:** *semi-finals:* J.Bacuku Islington) wo, Jemal Morrison (All Stars) w pts A.Neunie (Haringey Police); *final:* J.Bacuku w pts Jemal Morrison. **Middle:** *semi-finals:* R.Harris (Haringey Police) wo, J.Degale (Dale Youth) w rsc 3 Jamie Morrison (All Stars); *final:* J.Degale w rtd 1 R.Harris. **L.Heavy:** *final:* T.Salem (Camden Kronk) w rsc 2 D.Mohseni (All Stars). **Heavy:** *final:* D.Cunnage (Northolt) w pts A.Al-Sady (All Stars). **S.Heavy:** no entries.

South-East Division   National Sports Centre, Crystal Palace
L.Fly: *final:* D.Langley (Hollington) wo. **Fly:** *final:* S.Langley (Hollington) wo. **Bantam:** *final:* C.Brahmbhatt (Bexley) w pts S.Gregory (Samuel Montague). **Feather:** no entries. **Light:** no entries. **L.Welter:** *semi-finals:* D.Gregory (Fitzroy Lodge) wo, M.Cordici (Fitzroy Lodge) w pts D.Richards (Hollington); *final:* D.Gregory w co 1 M.Cordici. **Welter:** *semi-finals:* M.Welsh (Fitzroy Lodge) wo, S.Webb (Bromley & Downham) w pts F.Makenda; *final:* S.Webb w pts M.Welsh. **Middle:** *semi-finals:* B.Aird (Samuel Montague) wo, L.Senior (Fisher) w pts E.Kahlow (Bromley & Downham); *final:* L.Senior w pts B.Aird. **L.Heavy:** no entries. **Heavy:** *final:* J.Sawicki (St Peter's) w pts L.Williams

(Fitzroy Lodge). **S.Heavy:** *final:* D.Akinlade (Fitzroy Lodge) w pts I.Lewison (Miguel's).

South-West Division   Earlsfield Gym, Wandsworth – 31 January
L.Fly: no entries. **Fly:** no entries. **Bantam:** no entries. **Feather:** no entries. **Light:** no entries. **L.Welter:** *final:* D.Khan (Earlsfied) wo. **Welter:** *final:* S.Barr (Kingston) w co 4 C.Edu (Battersea). **Middle:** *final:* G.Dawson (Kingston) wo. **L.Heavy:** no entries. **Heavy:** no entries. **S.Heavy:** no entries.

London Semi-Finals & Finals   Goresbrook Leisure Centre, Dagenham – 4 & 10 February
L.Fly: *final:* D.Langley (Hollington) wo. **Fly:** *final:* S.Langley (Hollington) wo. **Bantam:** *final:* C.Brahmbhatt (Bexley) w pts A.Nabizadeh (Repton). **Feather:** *final:* L.Ballard (Repton) w pts M.Mehmet (Finchley). **Light:** *final:* B.Dodd (Hornchurch & Elm Park) w rsc 3 P.Liggins (Trojan). **L.Welter:** *semi-finals:* M.Grant (Haringey Police) w pts D.Khan (Earlsfield), D.Gregory (Fitzroy Lodge) w pts N.Weise (West Ham); *final:* M.Grant w pts D.Gregory. **Welter:** *semi-finals:* D.Herdman (Repton) w pts J.Bacuku (Islington), S.Webb (Bromley & Downham) wo S.Barr (Kingston); *final:* S.Webb w pts D.Herdman. **Middle:** *semi-finals:* J.Degale (Dale Youth) w rsc 1 G.Dawson (Kingston), D.Happe (Repton) w pts L.Senior (Fisher); *final:* J.Degale wo D.Happe. **L.Heavy:** *final:* T.Salem (Camden Kronk) w rsc 1 D.Lewis (Peacock). **Heavy:** *semi-finals:* J.Sawicki (St Peter's) wo, D.Cunnage (Northolt) w pts O.Ossai (Repton); *final:* J.Sawicki w rsc 2 D.Cunnage. **S.Heavy:** *final:* D.Campbell (Repton) w pts D.Akinlade (Fitzroy Lodge).

Midland Counties
Northern Zone Embassy Centre, Skegness – 29 January, The College, Grantham – 5 February & Oldbury RBL, Warley – 7 February
L.Fly: *final:* U.Ahmed (Merlin Youth) wo. **Fly:** no entries. **Bantam:** *final:* P.Walkman (Chadd) w pts A.Brennan (Triumph). **Feather:** *final:* J.Spring (Terry Allen Unique) w pts I.Ali (One Nation). **Light:** *final:* R.Bennett (Belgrave) wo. **L.Welter:** *semi-finals:* N.Asghar (Merlin Youth) wo, A.Hill (South Normanton SoB) w pts N.McQuade (Kettering SoB); *final:* A.Hill w pts N.Asghar. **Welter:** *semi-finals:* L.Morris (Phoenix) w rsc 4 J.Graham (Triumph), J.Elliott (South Normanton SoB) w pts S.McKervey (Bulkington); *final:* J.Elliott w rsc 1 L.Morris. **Middle:** *final:* C.Johnson (Terry Allen Unique) w pts M.Curley (Chelmsley Wood). **L.Heavy:** *quarter-finals:* A.Farrell (Triumph) wo, A.Javed (Phoenix) wo, N.Tidman (Bulkington) wo, V.Petkovic (One Nation) w pts E.Dube (Merlin Youth); *semi-finals:* A.Javed w pts N.Tidman, A.Farrell w rsc 2 V.Petkovic; *final:* A.Farrell w pts A.Javed. **Heavy:** no entries. **S.Heavy:** no entries.

Southern Zone   - Bidd's Nightclub, Stoke - 29 January & Oldbury RBL, Warley – 7 February
L.Fly: *final:* B.Lewis (Wolverhampton) wo. **Fly:** no entries. **Bantam:** *final:* A.Odud (Birmingham City) wo. **Feather:** *final:* M.Abbott (Hulton Abbey) wo. **Light:** *final:* F.Gavin (Hall Green) wo. **L.Welter:** *final:* J.Doherty (Hulton Abbey) w pts M.Gordon (Lions). **Welter:** *semi-finals:* J.Ball (Priory) M.Barney (Tamworth), J.Jeavons (Aston) w rsc 4 S.Myatt (Donnington Ex-Servicemens'); *final:* J.Ball w pts J.Jeavons. **Middle:** *semi-finals:* B.Murphy (Aston) wo, M.Lloyd (Telford) w pts A.Hough (Pleck); *final:* M.Lloyd w pts B.Murphy. **L.Heavy:** *final:* R.Collins (Lions) wo. **Heavy:** *semi-finals:* S.Warren (Wolverhampton) wo, E.Clayton (Donnington Ex-Servicemens') w pts K.Flower (Orme); *final:*

E.Clayton w pts S.Warren. **S.Heavy:** *final:* D.Smith (Donnington Ex-Servicemens') wo.

Midland Counties Finals   The Gym, Burton – 12 February
L.Fly: U.Ahmed (Merlin Youth) w pts B.Lewis (Wolverhampton). **Fly:** no entries. **Bantam:** P.Walkman (Chadd) w pts A.Odud (Birmingham City). **Feather:** J.Spring (Terry Allen Unique) w pts M.Abbott (Hulton Abbey). **Light:** F.Gavin (Hall Green) w pts R.Bennett (Belgrave). **L.Welter:** A.Hill (South Normanton SoB) w pts J.Doherty (Hulton Abbey). **Welter:** J.Elliott (South Normanton SoB) w pts J.Ball (Priory Park). **Middle:** C.Johnson (Terry Allen Unique) w pts M.Lloyd (Telford). **L.Heavy:** A.Farrell (Triumph) w pts R.Collins (Lions). **Heavy:** E.Clayton (Donnington Ex-Servicemens') wo. **S.Heavy:** D.Smith (Donnington Ex Servicemens') wo.

London v Midland Counties   Goresbrook Leisure Centre, Dagenham – 17 February
L.Fly: D.Langley w pts Y.Ahmed (Merlin Youth). **Fly:** S.Langley (Hollington) wo. **Bantam:** C.Brahmbhatt (Bexley) w pts P.Walkman (Chadd). **Feather:** L.Ballard (Repton) w pts J.Spring (Terry Allen Unique). **Light:** F.Gavin (Hall Green) wo B.Dodd (Hornchurch & Elm Park). **L.Welter:** M.Grant (Haringey Police) w rsc 2 A.Hill (South Normanton SoB). **Welter:** S.Webb (Bromley & Downham) w pts J.Elliott (South Normanton SoB). **Middle:** J.Degale (Dale Youth) w pts C.Johnson (Terry Allen Unique), **L.Heavy:** A.Farrell (Triumph) w disq 4 T.Salem (Camden Kronk). **Heavy:** E.Clayton (Donnington Ex-Servicemens') w pts J.Sawicki (St Peter's). **S.Heavy:** D.Campbell (Repton) wo D.Smith (Donnington Ex-Servicemens').

North-East Counties v Southern Counties

North-East Counties
Tyne, Tees & Wear Division   Borough Hall, Hartlepool – 21 January
L.Fly: no entries. **Fly:** no entries. **Bantam:** *final:* S.Hall (Spennymoor) wo. **Feather:** *final:* G.Reay (Spennymoor) wo. **Light:** *semi-finals:* G.Roberts (Hartlepool Catholic) wo, B.Saunders (South Durham) w pts C.Dixon (Birtley Police); *final:* B.Saunders w pts G.Roberts. **L.Welter:** *semi-finals:* R.Wainwright (Lambton Street) wo, P.Boyle (Halfpenny) w pts C.Woods (Halfpenny); *final:* P.Boyle w pts R.Wainwright. **Welter:** *final:* N.Gittus (Birtley Police) w rsc 4 A.Oliver (Spennymoor). **Middle:** *final:* S.McCrone (Spennymoor) w pts M.Denton (Headland). **L.Heavy:** *final:* D.Pendleton (Birtley Police) w pts O.Baker (Washington). **Heavy:** *final:* J-L. Dickinson (Birtley Police) wo. **S.Heavy:** *final:* C.Burton (Headland) wo.

Yorkshire & Humberside Division   The Metrodome, Barnsley – 4 February
L.Fly: no entries. **Fly:** no entries. **Bantam:** *semi-finals:* R.Nelson (Karmand) wo, S.Marcus (Sheffield) w pts S.Doherty (Bradford Police); *final:* R.Nelson w pts S.Marcus. **Feather:** *final:* G.Sykes (Cleckheaton) wo. **Light:** *final:* J.Dyer (Burmantofts) w pts A.McIver (Cleckheaton). **L.Welter:** *semi-finals:* D.Hill (Sheffield) wo, C.Sebine (Burmantofts) w pts L.Lothian (Unity); *final:* C.Sebine w pts D.Hill. **Welter:** *final:* T.Booth (Unity) wo. **Middle:** *final:* C.Denton (Handsworth Police) wo. **L.Heavy:** *semi-finals:* D.Slaney (Conisbrough) w pts R.Cunningham (Hard & Fast), N.McGarry (Doncaster Plant) w pts P.David (Unity); *final:*

N.McGarry w rsc 2 D.Slaney. **Heavy:** *final:* P.Clarke (Round One) w pts J.Anthony (Rotherham). **S.Heavy:** *final:* W.Crummack (Temple) wo.

North-East Counties Finals   The Leisure Centre, Gateshead – 11 February
L.Fly: no entries. **Fly:** no entries. **Bantam:** R.Nelson (Karmand) w pts S.Hall (Spennymoor). **Feather:** G.Sykes (Cleckheaton) w pts G.Reay (Spennymoor). **Light:** J.Dyer (Burmantofts) w rsc 3 G.Roberts (Hartlepool Catholic) – replaced B.Saunders (South Durham). **L.Welter:** C.Sebine (Burmantofts) w pts P.Boyle (Halfpenny). **Welter:** N.Gittus (Birtley Police) w pts T.Booth (Unity). **Middle:** S.McCrone (Spennymoor) w pts C.Denton (Handsworth Police). **L.Heavy:** D.Pendleton (Birtley Police) w pts N.McGarry (Doncaster Plant). **Heavy:** J-L. Dickinson (Birtley Police) w rsc 2 P.Clarke (Round One). **S.Heavy:** C.Burton (Headland) w rsc 3 W.Crummack (Temple).

Southern Counties   Prince of Wales Youth Centre, Folkestone – 5 February & Leas Cliff Hall, Folkestone – 11 February
L.Fly: no entries. **Fly:** no entries. **Bantam:** *final:* R.Smart (Southampton) wo. **Feather:** *final:* R.Deakin (Crawley) wo. **Light:** *semi-finals:* M.Tew (Southampton) wo, B.Jones (Crawley) w pts G.Chapman (Westhill); *final:* B.Jones w pts M.Tew. **L.Welter:** *quarter-finals:* A.Swan (Faversham) wo, J.Berry (Sandwich) wo, S.Watson (Golden Ring) w rsc 3 A.Leigh (City of Portsmouth), J.Leigh (City of Portsmouth) w pts B.Buchanan (Westhill); *semi-finals:* S.Watson w pts J.Berry, J.Leigh w pts A.Swan; *final:* S.Watson w co 4 J.Leigh. **Welter:** *quarter-finals:* J.Rogers (Golden Ring) wo, I.Hudson (St Mary's) wo, B.Madgewick (City of Portsmouth) w rtd 1 A.Martin (Foley), L.Pritchard (St Mary's) w pts S.Woolford (The Grange); *semi-finals:* B.Madgewick w pts J.Rogers, I.Hudson w pts L.Pritchard; *final:* B.Madgewick w rsc 1 I.Hudson. **Middle:** *quarter-finals:* M.Twyman (The Grange) wo, P.Morby (Bognor) wo, T.Hill (Golden Ring) w pts A.Young (Crawley), T.Maxwell (Shepway) w pts W.Kokhan (Faversham); *semi-finals:* T.Hill w pts M.Twyman, P.Morby w pts T.Maxwell; *final:* T.Hill w pts P.Morby. **L.Heavy:** no entries. **Heavy:** *final:* T.Dallas (St Mary's) wo. **S.Heavy:** no entries.

North-East Counties v Southern Counties   Manor Social Club, Sheffield – 17 February
L.Fly: no entries. **Fly:** no entries. **Bantam:** R.Nelson (Karmand) w pts R.Smart (Southampton). **Feather:** G.Sykes (Cleckheaton) w rsc 3 R.Deakin (Crawley). **Light:** B.Jones (Crawley) w pts J.Dyer (Burmantofts). **L.Welter:** C.Sebine (Burmantofts) w pts S.Watson (Golden Ring). **Welter:** N.Gittus (Birtley Police) w pts B.Madgewick (City of Portsmouth). **Middle:** S.McCrone (Spennymoor) w pts T.Hill (Golden Ring). **L.Heavy:** D.Pendleton (Birtley Police) wo. **Heavy:** J-L. Dickinson (Birtley Police) w rsc 4 T.Dallas (St Mary's). **S.Heavy:** C.Burton (Headland) wo.

Western Counties v Combined Services

Western Counties
Northern Division   Scotch Horn Leisure Centre, Nailsea – 29 January
L.Fly: no entries. **Fly:** no entries. **Bantam:** *final:* D.Webb (Broad Plain) wo. **Feather:** *final:* S.Hussain (Walcot Boys) wo. **Light:** no

entries. **L.Welter:** *semi-finals:* J.Cox (Walcot Boys) wo, J.Hicks (Yeovil) w pts T.Kirk (Broad Plain); *final:* J.Cox w rsc 1 J.Hicks. **Welter:** *final:* A.Woodward (Watchet) w pts J.Gardiner (Broad Plain). **Middle:** *final:* C.Woods (Penhill RBL) w pts L.Stinchcombe (Broad Plain). **L.Heavy:** no entries. **Heavy:** *final:* D.Poulson (Taunton) wo. **S.Heavy:** no entries.

Southern Division   The Rugby Club, Camborne – 29 January
L.Fly: no entries. **Fly:** no entries. **Bantam:** no entries. **Feather:** *final:* B.Zacharkiw (Pilgrims) wo. **Light:** *final:* B.Murray (Jersey Leonis) w pts J.Vannemenis (Bideford). **L.Welter:** *final:* A.Wyatt (Paignton) w pts D.O'Connor (Devonport Police). **Welter:** *quarter-finals:* B.Patrick (Devonport Police) wo, A.Coles (Camborne & Redruth) wo, P.Young (Jersey Leonis) w pts J.Houston (Portland), R.Warman (Camborne & Redruth) w pts R.Fearnley (Pilgrims); *semi-finals:* A.Coles w pts B.Patrick, R.Warman w pts P.Young; *final:* A.Coles wo R.Warman. **Middle:** *semi-finals:* P.Brown (Pilgrims) w pts R.Gammon (Camborne & Redruth), L.Whane (Apollo) w pts Y.Doumbia (Devonport Police); *final:* L.Whane w pts P.Brown. **L.Heavy:** no entries. **Heavy:** no entries. **S.Heavy:** *final:* D.Lund (Jersey Leonis) wo.

Western Counties Finals   Badger Hill Public House, Frome – 4 February
L.Fly: no entries. **Fly:** no entries. **Bantam:** D.Webb (Broad Plain) wo. **Feather:** B.Zacharkiw (Pilgrims) w disq 4 S.Hussain (Walcot Boys). **Light:** B.Murray (Jersey Leonis) wo. **L.Welter:** J.Cox (Walcot Boys) w rsc 2 A.Wyatt (Paignton). **Welter:** A.Woodward (Watchet) w pts A.Coles (Camborne & Redruth). **Middle:** L.Whane (Apollo) w C.Woods (Penhill RBL). **L.Heavy:** no entries. **Heavy:** D.Poulson (Taunton) wo. **S.Heavy:** D.Lund (Jersey Leonis) wo.

Combined Services
Nelson Barracks Gymnasium, Portsmouth – 10 February
L.Fly: no entries. **Fly:** *final:* R.Burkinshaw (Army) w rsc 1 M.Khan (RN). **Bantam:** *final:* A.Boyle (RN) w pts C.Sagar (Army). **Feather:** *final:* J.Allen (Army) w pts A.Urrutia (RN). **Light:** *final:* S.Turner (Army) wo. **L.Welter:** *final:* M.Stead (Army) w rsc 4 L.Wilson (RN). **Welter:** *final:* B.Flournoy (Army) w rsc 4 S.Elwell (RN). **Middle:** *final:* J.Summers (Army) w rsc 1 S.Tighe (RN). **L.Heavy:** *semi-finals:* S.McDonald (RN) wo, I.Aldridge (RAF) w rsc 3 D.Frost (Army); *final:* I.Aldridge w pts S.McDonald. **Heavy:** *final:* M.O'Connell (RN) w pts J.Whitfield (Army). **S.Heavy:** *final:* S.Scott (RN) w pts J.Tuiauta (Army).

Western Counties v Combined Services   National Sailing Centre, Portland – 19 February
L.Fly: no entries. **Fly:** R.Burkinshaw (Army) wo. **Bantam:** D.Webb (Broad Plain) w pts A.Boyle (RN). **Feather:** J.Allen (Army) wo B.Zacharkiw (Pilgrims). **Light:** S.Turner (Army) w pts B.Murray. **L.Welter:** J.Cox (Walcot Boys) w co 1 M.Stead (Army). **Welter:** B.Flournoy (Army) w pts A.Woodward (Watchet). **Middle:** L.Whane (Apollo) w rsc 1 J.Summers (Army). **L.Heavy:** S.McDonald (RN) – replaced I.Aldridge (RAF) – wo. **Heavy:** M.O'Connell (RN) w pts D.Poulson (Taunton). **S.Heavy:** S.Scott (RN) w pts D.Lund (Jersey Leonis).

English ABA Semi-Finals & Finals

The Guildhall, Preston – 4 March & ExCel Centre, Canning Town – 18 March
L.Fly: *final:* D.Langley (Hollington) w pts J.Fowl (Haileybury) – replaced C.Lyon (Wigan). **Fly:** *semi-finals:* R.Burkinshaw (Army) wo, S.Langley (Hollington) w pts P.Edwards (Salisbury); *final:* S.Langley w pts R.Burkinshaw. **Bantam:** *semi-finals:* R.Nelson (Karmand) w pts C.Brahmbhatt (Bexley), N.McDonald (Vauxhall Motors) w pts D.Webb (Broad Plain); *final:* N.McDonald w rsc 3 R.Nelson. **Feather:** *semi-finals:* G.Sykes (Cleckheaton) w pts J.Spring (Terry Allen Unique) – replaced L.Ballard (Repton), M.Robinson (Tower Hill) w pts J.Allen (Army); *final:* G.Sykes w pts M.Robinson. **Light:** *semi-finals:* F.Gavin (Hall Green) w pts S.Jennings (Tower Hill), S.Turner (Army) w pts B.Jones (Crawley); *final:* F.Gavin w pts S.Turner. **L.Welter:** *semi-finals:* J.Cox (Walcot Boys) w pts S.Williams (Avalon), M.Grant (Haringey Police) w pts C.Sebine (Burmantofts); *final:* M.Grant w pts J.Cox. **Welter:** *semi-finals:* J.Selkirk (Rotunda) w pts S.Webb (Bromley & Downham), B.Flournoy (Army) w pts N.Gittus (Birtley Police); *final:* B.Flournoy w pts J.Selkirk. **Middle:** *semi-finals:* S.Mullins (Wolvercote) w pts L.Whane (Apollo), J.Degale (Dale Youth) w pts S.McCrone (Spennymoor); *final:* J.Degale w pts S.Mullins. **L.Heavy:** *semi-finals:* D.Pendleton (Birtley Police) w pts A.Farrell (Triumph), M.Redhead (Kingfisher) w pts S.McDonald (RN); *final:* D.Pendleton w pts M.Redhead. **Heavy:** *semi-finals:* J-L. Dickinson (Birtley Police) w pts M.O'Connell (RN), T.Bellew (Rotunda) w rsc 4 E.Clayton (Donnington Ex-Servicemens'); *final:* T.Bellew w co 2 J-L. Dickinson. **S.Heavy:** *semi-finals:* D.Price (Salisbury) w pts C.Burton (Headland), D.Campbell (Repton) w rsc 4 S.Scott (RN); *final:* D.Price w pts D.Campbell.

Michael Grant wins the ABA light-welter title   Les Clark

Irish Championships, 2004-2005

Senior Tournament

The National Stadium, Dublin – 4,5,11,12 & 18 March

L.Fly: *semi-finals*: C. Ahern (Baldoyle, Dublin) w pts M. Myers (Brosna, Offaly), J. Moore (St. Francis, Limerick) w pts P. Barnes (Holy Family, Belfast); *final*: C. Ahern w rsc 3 J. Moore. **Fly**: *quarter-finals*: D. Thorpe (St. Aiden's, Ferns) wo, T.J. Doheny (Portlaoise, Laois) wo, D. McArdle (Dealgan, Louth) wo, C. Frampton (Midland White City, Belfast) w pts J. Conlan (St. John Bosco, Belfast); *semi-finals*: D. Thorpe w pts T.J. Doheny, C. Frampton w pts D. McArdle; *final*: C. Frampton w pts D. Thorpe; *box-off for third and fourth places*: T.J. Doheny w pts D. McArdle. **Bantam**: *semi-finals*: D.O. Joyce (St. Michael's, Athy) w rsc 2 J. Cooley (St. Joseph's, Derry), S. McKim (Abbey, Antrim) w pts B. Harkin (Twin Towns, Donegal); *final*: D.O. Joyce w pts S. McKim; *box-off for third and fourth places*: J. Cooley w pts B. Harkin. **Feather**: *quarter-finals*: E. Donovan (St. Michael's, Athy) wo, E. Touhey (Moate, Westmeath) wo, D. Lawlor (St. Fiach's, Carlow) w pts J.P. McDonagh (St. Paul's, Waterford); D. McCombe (Holy Trinity, Belfast) w pts P. Cowzer (Darndale, Dublin); *semi-finals*: E. Donovan w pts D. Lawlor, E. Touhey w pts D. McCombe; *final*: E. Donovan w pts E. Touhey. **Light**: *prelims*: D. Murphy (St. Saviour's OAB, Dublin) wo, N. Monteith (Dockers, Belfast) wo, P. Hendricks (Baldoyle, Dublin) wo, T. Carlyle (Crumlin, Dublin) wo, S. Ormonde (St. Matthew's, Dublin), A. Sadlier (St. Saviour's OAB, Dublin) wo, D.A. Joyce (St. Michael's, Athy) w rsc 4 T. Dillon (Drimnagh, Dublin), J.J. Joyce (St. Michael's, Athy) w pts D. Moore (St. Joseph's, Derry); *quarter-finals*: D. Murphy w pts N. Monteith, P. Hendricks w pts T. Carlyle, S. Ormonde w pts A. Sadlier, D.A. Joyce wo, J.J. Joyce src; *semi-finals*: D. Murphy w rsc 3 P. Hendricks, S. Ormonde w pts D.A. Joyce; *final*: S. Ormonde w pts D. Murphy. **L.Welter**: *prelims*: D. Byrne (Crumlin, Dublin) wo, E. McEneaney (Dealgan, Louth) wo, K. Boyle (St. Saviour's OAB, Dublin) wo, A. Carlyle (Crumlin, Dublin) wo, T. O'Neill (Mount Tallant, Dublin) w pts P. Connolly (Neilstown, Dublin), D. Joyce (St. Michael's, Athy) w rsc 3 W. McLaughlin (Illes Golden Gloves, Donegal), D. Nevin (Cavan) w pts G. Dunne (Neilstown, Dublin), J.J. McDonagh (Brosna, Offaly) w pts D. Hamill (All Saints, Belfast); *quarter-finals*: D. Byrne w pts E. McEneaney, K. Boyle w pts T. O'Neill, D. Joyce w pts D. Nevin, A. Carlyle w pts J.J. McDonagh; *semi-finals*: D. Joyce w pts A. Carlyle, K. Boyle w pts D. Byrne; *final*: D. Joyce w pts K. Boyle; *box-off for third and fourth places*: D. Byrne w pts J.J. McDonagh. **Welter**: *quarter-finals*: H. Coyle (Geesala, Mayo) w pts C. Curtis (Dealgan, Louth), K. Brabazon (St. Saviour's OAB, Dublin) w pts T. Hamill (All Saints, Belfast), R. Sheahan (St. Michael's, Athy) w pts R. Cardwell (Dockers, Belfast), O. Kelly (Portlaoise, Laois) w pts F. Redmond (Arklow, Wicklow); *semi-finals*: K. Brabazon w pts H. Coyle, O. Kelly w pts R. Sheahan; *final*: K. Brabazon w pts O. Kelly; *box-off for third and fourth places*: R. Sheahan wo, C. Curtis scr. **Middle**: *quarter-finals*: A. Lee (St. Francis, Limerick) wo, E. O'Kane (St. Canice's, Derry) wo, H. Joyce (St. Michael's, Athy) w pts G. Disha (St. Matthew's, Dublin), K. Whelan (St. Paul's, Waterford) w pts E. Healy (Portlaoise, Laois); *semi-finals*: A. Lee w pts H. Joyce, E. O'Kane w pts K. Whelan; *final*: A. Lee w pts E. O'Kane; *box-off for third and fourth places*: E. Healy w pts H. Joyce. **L.**

Heavy: *quarter-finals*: T. Sheahan (St. Michael's, Athy) wo, K. Egan (Neilstown, Dublin) wo, L. Senior (Crumlin, Dublin) wo, D. O'Neill (Paulstown, Kilkenny) w pts J. Waldron (Castlebar, Mayo); *semi-finals*: D. O'Neill w pts T. Sheahan, K. Egan w pts L. Senior; *final*: K. Egan w pts D. O'Neill; *box-off for third and fourth places*: J. Waldron wo, T. Sheahan scr. **Heavy**: *quarter-finals*: A. Reynolds (Ballina, Mayo) wo, J. Sweeney (Dungloe, Donegal) w pts P. Smyth (Keady, Armagh), I. Tims (St. Matthew's, Dublin) w pts S. Curran (Holy Trinity, Belfast), G. Smith (Cabra Panthers, Dublin) w pts M. Fouhy (St. Colman's, Cork); *semi-finals*: I. Tims w pts G. Smith, A. Reynolds w pts J. Sweeney; *final*: I. Tims w pts A. Reynolds; *box-off for third and fourth places*: J. Sweeney w pts M. Fouhy. **S.Heavy**: *quarter-finals*: S. Belshaw (City of Lisburn, Antrim) wo, T. Clare (Crumlin, Dublin) wo, J. Upton (Crumlin, Dublin) wo, C. McMonagle (Holy Trinity, Belfast) w pts M. McDonagh (Brosna, Offaly); *semi-finals*: S. Belshaw w pts T. Clare, C. McMonagle w pts J. Upton; *final*: C. McMonagle w pts S. Belshaw.

Intermediate Finals

The National Stadium, Dublin – 4 February

L.Fly: P. Barnes (Holy Family, Belfast) w pts C. McGuinness (Holy Trinity, Belfast). **Fly**: K. Fennessy (Clonmel, Tipperary) w rsc 3 P. Barbour (Shamrock, Omagh). **Bantam**: D.O. Joyce (St. Michael's, Athy) w pts P. Duncliffe (Leeside Lough, Cork). **Feather**: C. Bates (St. Mary's, Dublin) w pts P. Cowzer (Darndale, Dublin). **Light**: J.P. McDonagh (St. Paul's, Waterford) w pts J. Wallace (Dungloe, Donegal). **L.Welter**: D. Byrne (Crumlin, Dublin) w pts O. Gribben (Sacred Heart, Newry). **Welter**: O. Kelly (Portlaoise, Laois) w pts F. Redmond (Arklow, Wicklow). **Middle**: G. Disha (St. Matthew's, Dublin) w rtd 4 N. Higgins (Loughglynn, Roscommon). **L.Heavy**: S. Martin (St. John Bosco, Belfast) w pts M. Stokes (Crumlin, Dublin). **Heavy**: J. Sweeney (Dungloe, Donegal) w pts P. Lee (Oughterard, Galway). **S.Heavy**: S. Belshaw (Lisburn, Antrim) w pts P. O'Rourke (Ballybrack, Dublin).

Junior Finals

The National Stadium, Dublin – 27 May

L. Fly: P. Barnes (Holy Family, Belfast) w pts J. Quigley (St. Paul's, Waterford). **Fly**: K. Fennessy (Clonmel, Tipperary) w pts R. Lindberg (Immaculata, Belfast). **Bantam**: D.O. Joyce (St. Michael's, Athy) w rtd 2 P. Barbour (Shamrock, Omagh). **Feather**: P. Duncliffe (Sunnyside, Cork) w pts P. Magee (Ligoniel, Belfast). **Light**: J.J. Joyce (St. Michael's, Athy) w pts D. Ward (Loughglynn, Roscommon). **L.Welter**: P.A. Ward (Galway) w pts M.F. Ward (Galway). **Welter**: M. Lynch (Illes Golden Gloves, Donegal) w rsc 3 D. Trainor (St. Bronagh's, Down). **Middle**: E. Corbett (Sacred Heart, Antrim) w pts D. Nevin (Holy Family, Drogheda). **L.Heavy**: D. Joyce (Moate, Westmeath) w rsc 4 C. Mervyn (Oliver Plunkett, Belfast). **Heavy**: J.P. Reah (Shamrock, Omagh) wo. **S.Heavy**: C. Magee (Ballybrack, Dublin) wo.

Scottish and Welsh Senior Championships, 2004-2005

Scotland ABA

Monklands Time Capsule, Coatbridge – 5 & 18 March, Treetops Hotel, Aberdeen – 11 March & Bowhill War Memorial Club, Cardenden – 13 March

L.Fly: no entries. **Fly:** *final:* U. Hussain (Kinross) w pts S. Marshall (Inverness). **Bantam:** *semi-finals:* M. Steto (Kingdom) w pts K. Fleetham (Garnock Valley), J. Ancliffe (Granite City) w rsc 3 D. Davage (Argo); *final:* J. Ancliffe w pts M. Steto. **Feather:** quarter-finals: D. Taylor (Granite City) wo, S. Moles (Denny) wo, J. Hastie (Gilmerton) wo, J. Kelso (Blantyre) w pts S. Carroll (Granite City); *semi-finals:* D. Taylor w rsc 4 S. Moles, J. Hastie w pts J. Kelso; *final:* J. Hastie w pts D. Taylor. **Light:** *semi-finals:* G. McArthur (Blantyre) wo, M. Prince (Broadwood) w rsc 3 J. Watson (Barn); *final:* G. McArthur w pts M. Prince. **L.Welter:** *quarter-finals:* L. Burnett (Kincorth) wo, E. Doyle (Glenboig) wo, R. Scott (Springhill) w pts A. Barlow (Kingdom), M. Hastie (Broadwood) w pts M. Bett (Lanark); *semi-finals:* L. Burnett w rsc 3 E. Doyle, M. Hastie w pts R. Scott; *final:* M. Hastie w pts L. Burnett. **Welter:** *prelims:* K. Carslaw (Paisley) wo, A. Montgomery (Forgewood) wo, D. Campbell (Denbeath) wo, F. Mahura (Leith Victoria) wo, L. Murray (Kincorth), P. Deegan (Gilmerton) wo, P. Pollock (Lanark) wo, W. Bilan (Denbeath) w pts S. Kynoch (Dennistoun); *quarter-finals:* K. Carslaw w pts P. Pollock, W. Bilan wo P. Deegan, A. Montgomery (Forgewood) w pts D. Campbell (Denbeath), F. Mahura (Leith Victoria) w rsc 3 L. Murray (Kincorth); *semi-finals:* K. Carslaw wo A. Montgomery, W Bilan wo F. Mahura; *final:* K. Carslaw w pts W. Bilan. **Middle:** *final:* C. McEwen (Clovenstone) w rsc 2 P. Warner (Springhill). **L.Heavy:** *quarter-finals:* M. Donald (Kincorth) wo, K. Reynolds (Barn) wo, A. Dyer (Glasgow Phoenix) w pts K. Davidson (Cleland), K. Anderson (Craigmillar) w co 1 A. Imudia (Noble Art); *semi-finals:* M. Donald w pts K. Reynolds, K. Anderson w rsc 3 A. Dyer; *final:* K. Anderson w pts M. Donald. **Heavy:** *semi-finals:* S. Simmons (Leith Victoria) wo, B. Stewart (Inverness) w rsc 3 D. Anderson (Denbeath); *final:* S. Simmons w rsc 3 B. Stewart. **S.Heavy:** *quarter-finals:* J. Perry (Larkhall) wo, S. Topen (Lochee) wo, A. Boyle (Kinross) w rsc 3 J. Hutcheson (Kingdom), F. Thirde (Arbroath) w pts M. Anderson (Denbeath); *semi-finals:* J. Perry w pts S. Topen, F. Thirde w pts A. Boyle; *final:* J. Perry w pts F. Thirde.

Wales ABA

Pil Millenium Centre, Newport – 29 January, Ebbw Vale Bridge Club – 10 February, The Social Club, Baglan – 14 February & The Leisure Centre, Newport – 4 March

L.Fly: *semi-finals:* K. Spong (Army) wo, M. Nasir (St Joseph's) w rsc 1 D. Gethin (Kyber Colts); *final:* M. Nasir w pts K. Spong. **Fly:** *final:* M. Edmonds (St Joseph's) wo. **Bantam:** *semi-finals:* N. Probert (Pembroke) wo, L. Fortt (Jim Driscoll's) w pts L. Roberts (Cwmbran); *final:* L. Fortt w pts N. Probert. **Feather:** *semi-finals:* A. Davies (Kyber Colts) w pts P. Economides (Shotton), D. Edwards (Cwmavon Hornets) w pts A. Urrutia (RN); *final:* D. Edwards w pts A. Davies. **Light:** *quarter-finals:* D. Harty (Heads of the Valley) wo, J. Lloyd (Gelligaer) wo, P. Ashton (Cwmavon Hornets) wo, M. Roberts (Sports Connexion) w pts M. Evans (Red); *semi-finals:* P. Ashton w pts M. Roberts, J. Lloyd w pts D. Harty; *final:* P. Ashton w rsc 3 J. Lloyd. **L.Welter:** *quarter-finals:* S. Bowers (Rhondda) wo, V. Bryan (Army) w pts I. Ghandy (Grange Catholic), S. Jama (Prince of Wales) w pts C. Morgan (Llanharan), R. Saunders (Victoria Park) w pts A. Cazzo (RAF); *semi-finals:* R. Saunders w rsc 3 S. Jama (Prince of Wales), S. Bowers w pts V. Bryan; *final:* S. Bowers w pts R. Saunders. **Welter:** *semi-finals:* L. Trott (Towy) w pts R. Evans (Splott), A. Thomas (Clwd) w pts R. James (Merthyr); *final:* L. Trott w pts A. Thomas. **Middle:** *prelims:* J. Evans (Pontypool) wo, B. Alexandra (Crindau) wo, J. Phillips (Bonymaen) wo, D. Smith (Pontypool) wo, L. Owen (Blaenymaes/Portmead) w pts G. Summer (Army), L. Osman (Trelewis) w pts O. Lloyd (Caernarfon), G. Jones (Army) w pts S. Goody (Victoria Park), W. O'Sullivan (Merlins Bridge) w pts J. Way (Cwmcarn); *quarter-finals:* J. Evans w pts B. Alexandra, J. Phillips w pts D. Smith, L. Owen w pts L. Osman, W. O'Sullivan w pts G. Jones; *semi-finals:* W. O'Sullivan w pts L. Owen, J. Phillips w pts J. Evans; *final:* W. O'Sullivan w pts J. Phillips. **L.Heavy:** *quarter-finals:* R. Ellery (Splott) w rsc 3 J. Morris (Fleur de Lys), J. Jones (Clwyd) w pts L. Davies (Menai Bridge), W. Brooks (Ely Star) w rsc 2 G. Harvey (Crindau), J. Hugh (Newport) w pts I. Aldridge (RAF); *semi-finals:* R. Ellery w pts J. Jones, W. Brooks w pts J. Hugh; *final:* R. Ellery w pts W. Brooks. **Heavy:** *quarter-finals:* S. O'Connell (Pecoed) wo, R. Davies (Penyrheol) w rsc 2 A. Morris (Gelligaer), K. Evans (Carmarthen) w rsc 2 G. Vince (Clwyd), O. Harries (Trostre) w disq 3 G. Paders (Crindau); *semi-finals:* K. Evans w rtd 2 O. Harries, S. O'Connell w pts R. Davies; *final:* K. Evans w rsc 1 S. O'Connell. **S.Heavy:** *semi-finals:* A. Kasongo (Splott) wo, M. Flynn (Premier) w pts M-L. Griffiths (Caernarfon); *final:* A. Kasongo w rsc 2 M. Flynn.

Four Nations Tournament, 2005

Olympia, Liverpool – 24 & 25 March
L. Fly: *semi-finals:* D.Langley (England) wo, C.Ahern (Ireland) w pts M.Nasir (Wales); *final:* D.Langley w pts C.Ahern. **Fly:** *semi-finals:* M.Edmonds (Wales) wo, S.Langley (England) w pts C.Frampton (Ireland); *final:* S.Langley w pts M.Edmonds. **Bantam:** *semi-finals:* N.McDonald (England) w pts D.O.Joyce (Ireland), J.Ancliffe (Scotland) w pts L.Fortt (Wales); *final:* N.McDonald w pts D.O.Joyce. *Box-off:* D.O.Joyce wo L.Fortt. **Feather:** *semi-finals:* G.Sykes (England) w pts J.Hastie (Scotland), D.Edwards (Wales) w pts E.Donovan (Ireland); *final:* D.Edwards w pts G.Sykes. *Box-off:* E.Donovan w rsc 3 J.Hastie. **Light:** *semi-finals:* P.Ashton (Wales) wo, F.Gavin (England) w pts M.Prince (Scotland); *final:* F.Gavin w pts P.Ashton. **L.Welter:** *semi-finals:* D.Joyce (Ireland) wo, J.Cox (England) w pts M.Hastie (Scotland); *final:* J.Cox w pts D.Joyce. **Welter:** *semi-finals:* K.Brabazon (Ireland) w pts L.Trott (Wales), B.Flournoy (England) w pts K.Carslaw (Scotland); *final:* K.Brabazon w pts B.Flournoy. *Box-off:* K.Carslaw w pts L.Trott. **Middle:** *semi-finals:* A.Lee (Ireland) w pts S.Mullins (England), C.McEwen (Scotland) w rsc 2 B.Phillips (Wales); *final:* A.Lee w pts C.McEwen. *Box-off:* S.Mullins wo B.Phillips. **L.Heavy:** *semi-finals:* K.Egan (Ireland) w co 3 K.Anderson (Scotland), D.Pendleton (England) w pts R.Ellery (Wales); *final:* K.Egan w rsc 2 D.Pendleton. *Box-off:* R.Ellery wo K.Anderson. **Heavy:** *semi-finals:* D.Dolan (England) wo, K.Evans (Wales) w pts S.Simmons (Scotland); *final:* K.Evans w pts D.Dolan. **S.Heavy:** *semi-finals:* A.Kasongo (Wales) wo, D.Price (England) w co 2 C.McMonagle (Ireland); *final:* D.Price w pts A.Kasongo.

Note: The following national champions were either replaced or withdrew prior to the tournament.

England: M.Grant (L.Welter), J.Degale (Middle), T.Bellew (Heavy).

Ireland: S.Ormonde (Light), I.Tims (Heavy).

Scotland: U.Hussain (Fly), G.McArthur (Light), J.Perry (S.Heavy).

Wales: S.Bowers (L.Welter), W.O'Sullivan (Middle).

Darren Langley (left), seen outpointing James Fowl in the ABA light-flyweight final, won the Four Nations tournament when beating the Irishman, Conor Ahern

Les Clark

British and Irish International Matches, 2004-2005

Does not include Multi-nation or championship tournaments, despite them being recognised as international appearances, merely because space will not allow. British and Irish interest in the major tournaments can be found within the pages of Chris Kempson's 'Highlights from the 3004-2005 Amateur Season' elsewhere in the book. We apologise if any international matches have been missed, but we have covered all those we have been made aware of. Some of the matches listed below were mixed matches, but we have only included the junior and senior elements of them and have not listed schoolboy and cadet bouts.

Young England (5) v Young Ireland (4) Everton Park Sports Centre, Liverpool – 24 September
(English names first): **L. Fly:** J. Murray w rsc 3 K. Fennessey. **Fly:** P. Edwards l pts R. Hickey. **Bantam:** L. Walsh w rsc 3 D. O.Joyce. **Feather:** J. McElvaney l pts J.J. Joyce. **Light:** G. Barker w rtd 3 K. Bates. **L.Welter:** M. Ungi w pts David Joyce (St Michael's, Athy). **Welter:** R. Pickard l pts J. Sweeney. **Middle:** J. Degale w pts David Joyce (Moate). **L. Heavy:** M. Stanton l pts M. Stokes.

Ireland (1) v Holland (3) Holland – 26 September
(Irish names first): **Seniors: Light:** S. Ormond w pts K. Kocabas. **Middle:** H. Joyce l pts D. Kooij. **Juniors:** K. Doherty l pts M. Steenbakkers. **Welter:** D. O'Connor l rsc 4 M. de Snoo.

Wales (2) v Ireland (7) Glamorgan Gricket Club, Cardiff – 29 October
(Welsh names first): **L.Fly:** M. Nasir l pts C. Ahern. **Bantam:** L. Roberts l pts B. Gillen. **Feather:** D. Edwards l pts E. Donovan. **Light:** P. Ashton w pts E. Touhey, G. Buckland w pts R. O'Kane. **L.Welter:** C. Morgan l pts A. Carlyle. **Welter:** A. Thomas l pts R. Sheehan. **Middle:** S.Davies l pts E. O'Kane. **L.Heavy:** J. Jones l pts D. O'Neill.

Ireland (6) v Holland (3) National Stadium, Dublin – 12 November
(Irish names first): **Seniors: Light:** J.J. McDonagh l pts H. Kocabas. **Welter:** R. Sheahan l pts O. Ozturk. **Middle:** D. Joyce w pts V.Kersten, D. Sutherland w rsc 4 D. Serdjoek. **L. Heavy:** K. Egan w rsc 3 M. Uysal. **S.Heavy:** J. Upton l pts J. Ignacia. **Juniors:** J.J. Joyce w pts M. Steenbakkers. **Light:** D. O'Connor w pts P. Mullenberg. **Middle:** J. Sweeney w pts M. de Snoo.

Ireland (2) v Holland (5) Clann Naofa ABC, Dundalk, Co. Louth – 14 November
(Irish names first): **Seniors: Light:** A. Sadlier l pts H. Kocabas. **Welter:** C. Curtis l pts O. Ozturk. **Middle:** E. Healy l pts D. Serdjoek. **S.Heavy:** C. McMonagle w pts J. Ignacia. **Juniors:** A. Hopkins w pts M. Steenbakkers. **Welter:** M. Lynch l pts P. Mullenberg. **Middle:** B. Fitzpatrick l pts M. de Snoo.

Wales (3) v Scotland (3) The Leisure Centre, Barry - 26 November
(Welsh names first): **Seniors: Light:** P.Ashton l pts M.Hastie, D.Harty l rsc 2 M.Prince. **Welter:** L. Trott l pts E. Finney, R. James w pts S. Weir. **Juniors: Bantam:** L. Selby w pts J. Carne. **Welter:** T. Hearne w pts S. Kynoch.

England (4) v USA (3) Metropole Hotel, Paddington, London - 29 November

Bantam: C. Brahmbhatt l pts T. Wohosky. **Feather:** G. Sykes w td M. Remillard. **Light:** F. Gavin w pts R. Rivera. **L. Welter:** M. Stead l pts K. Dargan. **Welter:** M. Murray l pts D. Jacobs. **Middle:** G. Barr w pts K. Porter. **Heavy:** D. Dolan w rsc 3 T. Skolnik.

England (5) v USA (4) Olympia, Liverpool - 3 December
(English names first): **Fly:** D. Broadhurst l pts R. Warren. **Bantam:** S. Smith w pts C. Huerta. **Light:** A. Khan w pts M. Evans, F. Gavin w pts R. Rivera. **L. Welter:** N. Brough l pts K. Dargan. **Welter:** M. Murray l pts D. Jacobs. **Middle:** G. Barr l pts K. Porter. **Heavy:** T. Bellew w pts T. Skolnik. **S. Heavy:** D. Price w pts G. Corbin.

Wales (3) v Norway (4) Stavanger, Norway - 4 December
(Welsh names first): **Seniors: Feather:** D. Edwards w pts A. Evensen. **L. Welter:** C. Morgan l pts F. Amaru. **Welter:** A. Thomas w pts D. Eide. **L. Heavy:** J. Jones w pts M. Rogulj. **Juniors: L. Welter:** P. Davies l pts D. Halvorsen. **Welter:** N. Cleverly l pts N. Dubunin. **L.Heavy:** W. Brooks l pts J. Egil.

Young Ireland (6) v Young France (3) France – 29 & 31 January
(Irish names first): **L. Fly:** J. Conlon w pts N. Ait-Ihya. **Fly:** T.J. Doheny w pts M. Savary. **Bantam:** J. Cooley w pts Z. Saidj. **Feather:** J.J. Joyce w pts I. Mansri. **Light:** D.A. Joyce l pts R. Jacob. **L.Welter:** P. Murphy l rsc 3 A. Vastine. **Welter:** C. McCarthy l pts D. Gimenez. **Middle:** D. Joyce w rsc 2 A. Zabre. **Heavy:** J.P. Reah w pts Y. Saar.

Young England (4) v Young Italy (3) Waveney Sports Centre, Lowestoft - 16 February
(English names first): **Light:** A. Anwar w pts V. Ferrara. **Welter:** T. McDonagh l pts M. Ernesti, P. McAleese w pts L. Podda. **Middle:** J. Burnett l pts G. Pugliese, A. Agogo w rsc 2 E. Musone. **L.Heavy:** M. Fielding l rtd 2 F. Bevilacqua, R. Boardman w pts G. Iovine.

Young England (4) v Young Italy (3) The Rotary Club, Basingstoke - 18 February
(English names first): **Fly:** Y. Naseer w pts N. Cipoletta. **Light:** G. Barker w rsc 2 V. Ferrara. **Welter:** T. McDonagh l pts M. Ernesti. **Middle:** A. Agogo w pts L. Podda, J. Turner l rsc 3 G. Pugliese, J. Burnett w rsc 3 A. Sabatini. **L. Heavy:** R. Boardman l pts F. Bevilacqua.

England (1) v Cuba (3) Rebok Stadium, Bolton - 14 May
(English names first): **Feather:** G. Sykes l pts E. Flores. **L. Welter:** A. Khan w pts M. Kindelan. **Middle:** J. Degale l pts E. Correa. **L.Heavy:** T. Salem l pts Y. Gonzalez.

Young Ireland (8) v Young Canada (2)   National Stadium, Dublin – 10 June
(Irish names first): **Fly:** C. Frampton w pts J-M Kind. **Bantam:** D.O. Joyce w rsc 2 I. Shiba. **Feather:** P. Duncliffe w pts S. Drolet. **Light:** J.J. Joyce w pts S. Ali. **L.Welter:** P.A. Ward w pts S. Boyd, M.F. Ward l co 1 D. Lemieux. **Welter:** D. Trainor w pts J. Mills. **Middle:** E. Corbett w pts D. Lao. **L.Heavy:** D. Joyce wo, B. Gohar scr. **Heavy:** J.P. Reah l rtd 1 B. Didier.

Young Ireland (5) v Young Canada (4)   St. Joseph's Hall, Blessington, Co. Wicklow – 12 June
(Irish names first): **Fly:** K. Fennessy w pts J-M Kind. **Bantam:** R.Hickey w pts I. Shiba. **Feather:** P. Magee l pts S. Drolet. **Light:** D. Ward w pts S. Ali. **L.Welter:** M. Collins l rtd 1 D. Lemieux, E. Gibbons w pts S. Boyd. **Welter:** K. Holmes l pts J. Mills. **Middle:** D. Nevin w pts D.Lao. **Heavy:** M. Maguire l co 2 B. Didier.

Amir Khan receives the Boxing Writers' 'Best Young Boxer of the Year' award for 2005, the first time the trophy has ever gone to an amateur

Les Clark

British Junior Championship Finals, 2004-2005

National Association of Clubs for Young People (NACYP)

The Britannia Adelphi Hotel, Liverpool – 10 December

Class A: 46kg: K.Saeed (Birmingham City Police) w pts S.Upton (West Ham). 48kg: M.Maguire (Kettering SoB) w pts J.Gage (Cwmavon Hornets). 50kg: K.De'ath (Northside) w pts C.Evans (Fleur de Lys). 52kg: S.Cairns (Newarthill) w pts J.Smith (Splott Adventure). 54kg: T.Langford (Bideford) w pts G.Shields (Greenock). 57kg: B.Claydon (Guildford City) w pts T.Costello (Chelmsley Wood). 60kg: L.Buckley (Chorley) w pts J.Innes (Cwmbran). 63kg: B.J.Saunders (Cheshunt) w pts G.Broadhurst (Birmingham Irish). 66kg: N.Devlin (Repton) w pts S.Aluko (Pool of Life). 70kg: W.Evans (Splott Adventure) w pts L.Ward (Triumph).

The Festival Hall, Kirkby in Ashfield – 13 December

Class B: 48kg: A.Selby (Splott Adventure) w pts E.Finnegan (Oliver Plunkett). 51kg: M.Ward (Birtley Police Boys) w pts C.Jenkins (Cwmgors). 54kg: G.Hancock (Hartlepool Catholic) w pts J.Saeed (Eltham). 57kg: M.Fagan (Vauxhall Motors) w pts L.Turner (West Ham). 60kg: J.Jones (Stevenage) w pts J.McDonough (Larne). 64kg: J.Stalker (St Aloysius) w pts F.Holmes (Stevenage). 69kg: J.McCann (Kettering SoB) w pts M.Shinkwin (Bushey). 75kg: T.Dickensen (Birtley Police) w rsc 2 D.Gardener (Cheshunt). 81kg: P.Connors (Cheshunt) w pts J.Turner (Shildon).

The Royal Lancaster Hotel, Bayswater – 8 December

Class C: 48kg: J.Cole (Dagenham Police) w pts S.Smith (Kingsthorpe). 51kg: S.Marcus (Sheffield) w pts R.Palmer (Barnstaple). 57kg: R.Walsh (Kingfisher) w pts J.Boyle (Knowsley Vale). 57kg: C.Smith (Pinewood Starr) w pts C.Webb (Haileybury). 60kg: A.Anwar (Bateson's) w pts M.Murnane (Chalvedon). 64kg: J.Cox (Walcott Boys) w rsc 2 R.Douglas (Phil Thomas SoB). 69kg: J.Coyle (Fisher) w pts C.Bunn (Northside). 75kg: R.Ellery (Splott Adventure) w pts J.Turner (Kettering SoB). 81kg: R.Boardman (Broad Plain) w pts M.Fielding (Salisbury).

Schools

It was announced on 5 December that it was not practical to stage the SABA Championships this season, due to the ABA hosting the Golden Gloves Championships, which took in boys born in 1990, 1991 and 1992.

Golden Gloves

The Leisure Centre, Gateshead – 26 & 27 March

Class 1: 30kg: C.Watts (West Ham) w pts C.Jones (Croxteth). 32kg: C.Johnson (Tower Hill) w pts L.Chambers (Berry Boys). 34kg: C.Chadwick (Phoenix) w pts T.Price (West Ham). 36kg: H.Yaqoub (Bateson's) w pts A.Smith (New Astley). 38kg: R.Davison (South Durham) w pts J.Langford (Bideford). 40kg: J.Dignum (Newham) w pts M.Railton (Headland). 44kg: J.Ward (Repton) w pts J.Turner (Northside). 46kg: J.Smith (Tower Hill) w pts S.Cole (Golden Ring). 48kg: M.Bradbury (Devonport) w pts D.Robinson (Northside). 50kg: A.Yunus (Burton) w pts J.Hughes (Bexley). R.Smailes (Spennymoor) w pts D.Kelly (Kirkby). 54kg: M.Corcoran (Dale Youth) w rsc 2 K.Fisher (West Wirral).

Class 2: 34kg: A.Jevons (Golden Gloves) w pts R.Curry (Five Star). 36kg: C.Hoy (Cheshunt) w pts M.Ward (Repton). 38kg: R.Brodie (Golden Gloves) w pts B.Colebourne (Brompton). 40kg: T.Holmes (Stevenage) w pts T.Baker (Repton). 42kg: J.Saunders (South Durham) w pts G.Langley (Repton). 44kg: A.Fowler (Golden Gloves) w pts J.Day (Newham). 46kg:

G.Brown (Boarshaw) w pts J.Smith (Guildford City). 48kg: M.Docherty (Marvels Lane) w pts P.Fury (Heart of England). 50kg: S.Barnes (Manor) w pts A.Pullen (Dorking). 52kg: J.Kerr (West Ham) w rsc 1 T.Shinkwin (Bushey). 54kg: S.Kane (Meanwood) wo T.Scully (Bromley & Downham). 57kg: J.Lever (Lynn) w pts G.Mulholland (Leam Lane). 60kg: J.Coyle (Foley) w pts D.Kane (Birtley Police). 63kg: G.O'Neill (Horden) w pts S.Wall (Marlow). 66kg: J.Dennis (Brompton) w pts D.Deevey (Braunstone).

Class 3: 38kg: J.Warrington (Burmantofts) w pts L.Munday (Portsmouth). 40kg: R.Bradley (St Paul's) w rsc 1 D.Shannon (Brompton). 42kg: L.Driscoll (Eltham) w pts W.Williamson (Farley). 44kg: A.Leak (Northside) w pts B.Morgan (West Ham). 46kg: R.Heffron (Boarshaw) w pts C.Jacobs (Harwich). 48kg: J.Hughes (Malmesbury) w pts P.Gallagher (Kirby). 50kg: R.O'Rourke (Wednesbury) w pts J.Jones (Dorking). 52kg: D.Phillips (South Bank) w pts R.Williamson (Dagenham). 54kg: A.Price (Lions) w pts L.Thompson (Guildford City). 57kg: S.Cairns (St Mary's) w pts D.Docherty (Bushey). 60kg: R.Crotty (Cheshunt) w pts T.Smith (Wisbech). 63kg: G.Foot (Marley Potts) w pts J.Green (Hornchurch & Elm Park). 66kg: K.Garvey (Earlsfield) w pts M.Mallin (Hoyle Mill). 70kg: T.Qaddus (Peterborough Phoenix) w pts F.Jones (Haileybury). 75kg: R.Cowley (Lambton Street) w pts R.Sheppard (Malmesbury).

ABA Youth

The Town Hall, Huddersfield – 28 May

Class C: 46kg: M.Hadfield (Headland) w pts B.Evans (Stevenage). 48kg: K.Sahid (Birmingham City) w pts P.Lovell (Chester). 50kg: M.Maguire (Kettering SoB) w pts R.Roberts (Ardwick). 52kg: K.De'ath (Northside) w pts D.O'Shaughnessy (West Ham). 54kg: S.Hedges (New Astley) w pts R.Rose (St Mary's). 57kg: J.Purvis (Sunderland) w pts S.Levy (Ongar). 60kg: S.Cardle (Mill Farm) w rsc 2 B.Lawson (West Hill). 63kg: T.Costello (Chelmsley Wood) w pts J.Arnfield (Blackpool & Fylde). 66kg: J.Davies (Kingsthorpe) w pts A.Brazil (Kingfisher). 70kg: S.Aluko (Pool of Life) w pts N.Devlin (Repton). 75kg: S.Griffiths (Shrewsbury & Severnside) w pts M.Hanger (Southend). 80kg: O.Mkwakongo (Fisher) w disq 3 B.Eastwood (St Mary's).

Class 5: 48kg: L.Wood (Phoenix) w pts C.Williamson (Farley). 51kg: A.Whitfield (Sunderland) w pts K.Satchell (Everton Red Triangle). 54kg: M.Ward (Birtley Police) w pts S.Maxwell (Highersete). 57kg: L.Turner (West Ham) w pts M.Faggin (Vauxhall Motors). 60kg: L.Smith (Rotunda) w pts L.Smedley (Retford). 64kg: J.Stalker (St Aloysius) w pts J.Holmes (Kettering SoB). 69kg: A.Agogo (Triple A) w pts D.Fletcher (Karmand). 75kg: M.Shinkwin (Bushey) w pts T.Dickensen (Birtley Police). 81kg: C.Scott (Truro) w pts C.Pollock (Phil Thomas SoB).

Class 6: 48kg: J.Cole (Dagenham Police) w pts B.Fowl (Haileybury). 51kg: A.Al-Fadil (Phil Thomas SoB) w pts A.Sexton (Cheshunt). 54kg: C.Higgs (Lydney) w pts L.Campbell (St Paul's). 57kg: C.Smith (Stevenage) w pts D.Rogers (Kettering SoB). 60kg: G.Barker (Repton) w pts C.Howes (Stevenage). 64kg: M.Ungi (Golden Gloves) w pts G.Foot (Marley Potts). 69kg: D.Butler (Broad Plain) w pts L.Noble (Unity). 75kg: M.Fielding (Salisbury) w rsc 4 J.Turner (Kettering SoB). 81kg: S.Brookes (Wombwell) w pts M.Stanton (Kirkby). 91kg: M.Churcher (Thames Valley) w pts I.Askew (Lambton Street). C.Snell (Taunton). 91+ kg: E.Jegeni (Haringey Police) wo C.Smith (Pinewood Starr).

ABA Champions, 1881-2005

L. Flyweight
1971 M. Abrams
1972 M. Abrams
1973 M. Abrams
1974 C. Magri
1975 M. Lawless
1976 P. Fletcher
1977 P. Fletcher
1978 J. Dawson
1979 J. Dawson
1980 T. Barker
1981 J. Lyon
1982 J. Lyon
1983 J. Lyon
1984 J. Lyon
1985 M. Epton
1986 M. Epton
1987 M. Epton
1988 M. Cantwell
1989 M. Cantwell
1990 N. Tooley
1991 P. Culshaw
1992 D. Fifield
1993 M. Hughes
1994 G. Jones
1995 D. Fox
1996 R. Mercer
1997 I. Napa
1998 J. Evans
1999 G. Jones
2000 J. Mulherne
2001 C. Lyon
2002 D. Langley
2003 C. Lyon
2004 S. McDonald
2005 D. Langley

Flyweight
1920 H. Groves
1921 W. Cuthbertson
1922 E. Warwick
1923 L. Tarrant
1924 E. Warwick
1925 E. Warwick
1926 J. Hill
1927 J. Roland
1928 C. Taylor
1929 T. Pardoe
1930 T. Pardoe
1931 T. Pardoe
1932 T. Pardoe
1933 T. Pardoe
1934 P. Palmer
1935 G. Fayaud
1936 G. Fayaud
1937 P. O'Donaghue
1938 A. Russell
1939 D. McKay
1944 J. Clinton
1945 J. Bryce
1946 R. Gallacher
1947 J. Clinton
1948 H. Carpenter
1949 H. Riley
1950 A. Jones
1951 G. John
1952 D. Dower
1953 R. Currie
1954 R. Currie
1955 D. Lloyd
1956 T. Spinks
1957 R. Davies
1958 J. Brown
1959 M. Gushlow
1960 D. Lee
1961 W. McGowan
1962 M. Pye
1963 M. Laud
1964 J. McCluskey
1965 J. McCluskey
1966 P. Maguire
1967 S. Curtis
1968 J. McGonigle
1969 D. Needham
1970 D. Needham
1971 P. Wakefield
1972 M. O'Sullivan
1973 R. Hilton
1974 M. O'Sullivan
1975 C. Magri
1976 C. Magri
1977 C. Magri
1978 G. Nickels
1979 R. Gilbody
1980 K. Wallace
1981 K. Wallace
1982 J. Kelly
1983 S. Nolan
1984 P. Clinton
1985 P. Clinton
1986 J. Lyon
1987 J. Lyon
1988 J. Lyon
1989 J. Lyon
1990 J. Armour
1991 P. Ingle
1992 K. Knox
1993 P. Ingle
1994 D. Costello
1995 D. Costello
1996 D. Costello
1997 M. Hunter
1998 J. Hegney
1999 D. Robinson
2000 D. Robinson
2001 M. Marsh
2002 D. Barriball
2003 D. Broadhurst
2004 S. Langley
2005 S. Langley

Bantamweight
1884 A. Woodward
1885 A. Woodward
1886 T. Isley
1887 T. Isley
1888 H. Oakman
1889 H. Brown
1890 J. Rowe
1891 E. Moore
1892 F. Godbold
1893 E. Watson
1894 P. Jones
1895 P. Jones
1896 P. Jones
1897 C. Lamb
1898 F. Herring
1899 A. Avent
1900 J. Freeman
1901 W. Morgan
1902 A. Miner
1903 H. Perry
1904 H. Perry
1905 W. Webb
1906 T. Ringer
1907 E. Adams
1908 H. Thomas
1909 J. Condon
1910 W. Webb
1911 W. Allen
1912 W. Allen
1913 A. Wye
1914 W. Allen
1919 W. Allen
1920 G. McKenzie
1921 L. Tarrant
1922 W. Boulding
1923 A. Smith
1924 L. Tarrant
1925 A. Goom
1926 F. Webster
1927 E. Warwick
1928 J. Garland
1929 F. Bennett
1930 H. Mizler
1931 F. Bennett
1932 J. Treadaway
1933 G. Johnston
1934 A. Barnes
1935 L. Case
1936 A. Barnes
1937 A. Barnes
1938 J. Pottinger
1939 R. Watson
1944 J. Bissell
1945 P. Brander
1946 C. Squire
1947 D. O'Sullivan
1948 T. Profitt
1949 T. Miller
1950 K. Lawrence
1951 T. Nicholls
1952 T. Nicholls
1953 J. Smillie
1954 J. Smillie
1955 G. Dormer
1956 O. Reilly
1957 J. Morrissey
1958 H. Winstone
1959 D. Weller
1960 F. Taylor
1961 P. Benneyworth
1962 P. Benneyworth
1963 B. Packer
1964 B. Packer
1965 R. Mallon
1966 J. Clark
1967 M. Carter
1968 M. Carter
1969 M. Piner
1970 A. Oxley
1971 G. Turpin
1972 G. Turpin
1973 P. Cowdell
1974 S. Ogilvie
1975 S. Ogilvie
1976 J. Bambrick
1977 J. Turner
1978 J. Turner
1979 R. Ashton
1980 R. Gilbody
1981 P. Jones
1982 R. Gilbody
1983 J. Hyland
1984 J. Hyland
1985 S. Murphy
1986 S. Murphy
1987 J. Sillitoe
1988 K. Howlett
1989 K. Howlett
1990 P. Lloyd
1991 D. Hardie
1992 P. Mullings
1993 R. Evatt
1994 S. Oliver
1995 N. Wilders
1996 L. Eedle
1997 S. Oates
1998 L. Pattison
1999 M. Hunter
2000 S. Foster
2001 S. Foster
2002 D. Matthews
2003 N. McDonald
2004 M. Marsh
2005 N. McDonald

Featherweight
1881 T. Hill
1882 T. Hill
1883 T. Hill
1884 E. Hutchings
1885 J. Pennell
1886 T. McNeil
1887 J. Pennell
1888 J. Taylor
1889 G. Belsey
1890 G. Belsey
1891 F. Curtis
1892 F. Curtis
1893 T. Davidson
1894 R. Gunn
1895 R. Gunn
1896 R. Gunn
1897 N. Smith
1898 P. Lunn
1899 J. Scholes
1900 R. Lee
1901 C. Clarke
1902 C. Clarke
1903 J. Godfrey
1904 C. Morris
1905 H. Holmes
1906 A. Miner
1907 C. Morris
1908 T. Ringer
1909 A. Lambert
1910 C. Houghton
1911 H. Bowers
1912 G. Baker
1913 G. Baker
1914 G. Baker
1919 G. Baker
1920 J. Fleming
1921 G. Baker
1922 E. Swash
1923 E. Swash
1924 A. Beavis
1925 A. Beavis
1926 R. Minshull
1927 F. Webster
1928 F. Meachem
1929 F. Meachem
1930 J. Duffield
1931 B. Caplan
1932 H. Mizler
1933 J. Walters
1934 J. Treadaway
1935 E. Ryan
1936 J. Treadaway
1937 A. Harper
1938 C. Gallie
1939 C. Gallie
1944 D. Sullivan
1945 J. Carter
1946 P. Brander
1947 S. Evans
1948 P. Brander
1949 H. Gilliland
1950 P. Brander
1951 J. Travers
1952 P. Lewis
1953 P. Lewis
1954 D. Charnley
1955 T. Nicholls
1956 T. Nicholls
1957 M. Collins
1958 M. Collins
1959 G. Judge
1960 P. Lundgren
1961 P. Cheevers
1962 B. Wilson
1963 A. Riley
1964 R. Smith
1965 K. Buchanan
1966 H. Baxter
1967 K. Cooper
1968 J. Cheshire
1969 A. Richardson
1970 D. Polak
1971 T. Wright
1972 K. Laing
1973 J. Lynch
1974 G. Gilbody
1975 R. Beaumont
1976 P. Cowdell
1977 P. Cowdell
1978 M. O'Brien
1979 P. Hanlon
1980 M. Hanif
1981 P. Hanlon
1982 H. Henry
1983 P. Bradley
1984 K. Taylor
1985 F. Havard
1986 P. Hodkinson
1987 P. English
1988 D. Anderson
1989 P. Richardson
1990 B. Carr

1991 J. Irwin	1895 A. Randall	1930 J. Waples	1965 A. White	1996 K. Wing
1992 A. Temple	1896 A. Vanderhout	1931 D. McCleave	1966 J. Head	1997 M. Hawthorne
1993 J. Cook	1897 A. Vanderhout	1932 F. Meachem	1967 T. Waller	1998 A. McLean
1994 D. Pithie	1898 H. Marks	1933 H. Mizler	1968 J. Watt	1999 S. Burke
1995 D. Burrows	1899 H. Brewer	1934 J. Rolland	1969 H. Hayes	2000 A. McLean
1996 T. Mulholland	1900 G. Humphries	1935 F. Frost	1970 N. Cole	2001 S. Burke
1997 S. Bell	1901 A. Warner	1936 F. Simpson	1971 J. Singleton	2002 A. Morris
1998 D. Williams	1902 A. Warner	1937 A. Danahar	1972 N. Cole	2003 S. Burke
1999 S. Miller	1903 H. Fergus	1938 T. McGrath	1973 T. Dunn	2004 C. Pacy
2000 H. Castle	1904 M. Wells	1939 H. Groves	1974 J. Lynch	2005 F. Gavin
2001 S. Bell	1905 M. Wells	1944 W. Thompson	1975 P. Cowdell	
2002 D. Mulholland	1906 M. Wells	1945 J. Williamson	1976 S. Mittee	**L. Welterweight**
2003 K. Mitchell	1907 M. Wells	1946 E. Thomas	1977 G. Gilbody	1951 W. Connor
2004 D. Mulholland	1908 H. Holmes	1947 C. Morrissey	1978 T. Marsh	1952 P. Waterman
2005 G. Sykes	1909 F. Grace	1948 R. Cooper	1979 G. Gilbody	1953 D. Hughes
	1910 T. Tees	1949 A. Smith	1980 G. Gilbody	1954 G. Martin
Lightweight	1911 A. Spenceley	1950 R. Latham	1981 G. Gilbody	1955 F. McQuillan
1881 F. Hobday	1912 R. Marriott	1951 R. Hinson	1982 J. McDonnell	1956 D. Stone
1882 A. Bettinson	1913 R. Grace	1952 F. Reardon	1983 K. Willis	1957 D. Stone
1883 A. Diamond	1914 R. Marriott	1953 D. Hinson	1984 A. Dickson	1958 R. Kane
1884 A. Diamond	1919 F. Grace	1954 G. Whelan	1985 E. McAuley	1959 R. Kane
1885 A. Diamond	1920 F. Grace	1955 S. Coffey	1986 J. Jacobs	1960 R. Day
1886 G. Roberts	1921 G. Shorter	1956 R. McTaggart	1987 M. Ayers	1961 B. Brazier
1887 J. Hair	1922 G. Renouf	1957 J. Kidd	1988 C. Kane	1962 B. Brazier
1888 A. Newton	1923 G. Shorter	1958 R. McTaggart	1989 M. Ramsey	1963 R. McTaggart
1889 W. Neale	1924 W. White	1959 P. Warwick	1990 P. Gallagher	1964 R. Taylor
1890 A. Newton	1925 E. Viney	1960 R. McTaggart	1991 P. Ramsey	1965 R. McTaggart
1891 E. Dettmer	1926 T. Slater	1961 P. Warwick	1992 D. Amory	1966 W. Hiatt
1892 E. Dettmer	1927 W. Hunt	1962 B. Whelan	1993 B. Welsh	1967 B. Hudspeth
1893 W. Campbell	1928 F. Webster	1963 B. O'Sullivan	1994 A. Green	1968 E. Cole
1894 W. Campbell	1929 W. Hunt	1964 J. Dunne	1995 R. Rutherford	1969 J. Stracey

Frankie Gavin (right) on his way to winning the 2005 ABA lightweight title with a points victory over the Army's Steve Turner

Les Clark

1970 D. Davies
1971 M. Kingwell
1972 T. Waller
1973 N. Cole
1974 P. Kelly
1975 J. Zeraschi
1976 C. McKenzie
1977 J. Douglas
1978 D. Williams
1979 E. Copeland
1980 A. Willis
1981 A. Willis
1982 A. Adams
1983 D. Dent
1984 D. Griffiths
1985 I. Mustafa
1986 J. Alsop
1987 A. Holligan
1988 A. Hall
1989 A. Hall
1990 J. Pender
1991 J. Matthews
1992 D. McCarrick
1993 P. Richardson
1994 A. Temple
1995 A. Vaughan
1996 C. Wall
1997 R. Hatton
1998 N. Wright
1999 D. Happe
2000 N. Wright
2001 G. Smith
2002 L. Daws
2003 L. Beavis
2004 J. Watson
2005 M. Grant

Welterweight
1920 F. Whitbread
1921 A. Ireland
1922 E. White
1923 P. Green
1924 P. O'Hanrahan
1925 P. O'Hanrahan
1926 B. Marshall
1927 H. Dunn
1928 H. Bone
1929 T. Wigmore
1930 F. Brooman
1931 J. Barry
1932 D. McCleave
1933 P. Peters
1934 D. McCleave
1935 D. Lynch
1936 W. Pack
1937 D. Lynch
1938 C. Webster
1939 R. Thomas
1944 H. Hall
1945 R. Turpin
1946 J. Ryan
1947 J. Ryan
1948 M. Shacklady
1949 A. Buxton
1950 T. Ratcliffe
1951 J. Maloney
1952 J. Maloney
1953 L. Morgan
1954 N. Gargano
1955 N. Gargano
1956 N. Gargano

1957 R. Warnes
1958 B. Nancurvis
1959 J. McGrail
1960 C. Humphries
1961 A. Lewis
1962 J. Pritchett
1963 J. Pritchett
1964 M. Varley
1965 P. Henderson
1966 P. Cragg
1967 D. Cranswick
1968 A. Tottoh
1969 T. Henderson
1970 T. Waller
1971 D. Davies
1972 T. Francis
1973 T. Waller
1974 T. Waller
1975 W. Bennett
1976 C. Jones
1977 C. Jones
1978 E. Byrne
1979 J. Frost
1980 T. Marsh
1981 T. Marsh
1982 C. Pyatt
1983 R. McKenley
1984 M. Hughes
1985 E. McDonald
1986 D. Dyer
1987 M. Elliot
1988 M. McCreath
1989 M. Elliot
1990 A. Carew
1991 J. Calzaghe
1992 M. Santini
1993 C. Bessey
1994 K. Short
1995 M. Hall
1996 J. Khaliq
1997 F. Barrett
1998 D. Walker
1999 A. Cesay
2000 F. Doherty
2001 M. Macklin
2002 M. Lomax
2003 D. Happe
2004 M. Murray
2005 B. Flournoy

L. Middleweight
1951 A. Lay
1952 B. Foster
1953 B. Wells
1954 B. Wells
1955 B. Foster
1956 J. McCormack
1957 J. Cunningham
1958 S. Pearson
1959 S. Pearson
1960 W. Fisher
1961 J. Gamble
1962 J. Lloyd
1963 A. Wyper
1964 W. Robinson
1965 P. Dwyer
1966 T. Imrie
1967 A. Edwards
1968 E. Blake
1969 T. Imrie
1970 D. Simmonds

1971 A. Edwards
1972 L. Paul
1973 R. Maxwell
1974 R. Maxwell
1975 A. Harrison
1976 W. Lauder
1977 C. Malarkey
1978 E. Henderson
1979 D. Brewster
1980 J. Price
1981 E. Christie
1982 D. Milligan
1983 R. Douglas
1984 R. Douglas
1985 R. Douglas
1986 T. Velinor
1987 N. Brown
1988 W. Ellis
1989 N. Brown
1990 T. Taylor
1991 T. Taylor
1992 J. Calzaghe
1993 D. Starie
1994 W. Alexander
1995 C. Bessey
1996 S. Dann
1997 C. Bessey
1998 C. Bessey
1999 C. Bessey
2000 C. Bessey
2001 M. Thirwall
2002 P. Smith

Middleweight
1881 T. Bellhouse
1882 A. H. Curnick
1883 A. J. Curnick
1884 W. Brown
1885 M. Salmon
1886 W. King
1887 R. Hair
1888 R. Hair
1889 G. Sykes
1890 J. Hoare
1891 J. Steers
1892 J. Steers
1893 J. Steers
1894 W. Sykes
1895 G. Townsend
1896 W. Ross
1897 W. Dees
1898 G. Townsend
1899 R. Warnes
1900 E. Mann
1901 R. Warnes
1902 E. Mann
1903 R. Warnes
1904 E. Mann
1905 J. Douglas
1906 A. Murdock
1907 R. Warnes
1908 W. Child
1909 W. Child
1910 R. Warnes
1911 W. Child
1912 E. Chandler
1913 W. Bradley
1914 H. Brown
1919 H. Mallin
1920 H. Mallin
1921 H. Mallin

1922 H. Mallin
1923 H. Mallin
1924 J. Elliot
1925 J. Elliot
1926 F. P. Crawley
1927 F. P. Crawley
1928 F. Mallin
1929 F. Mallin
1930 F. Mallin
1931 F. Mallin
1932 F. Mallin
1933 A. Shawyer
1934 J. Magill
1935 J. Magill
1936 A. Harrington
1937 M. Dennis
1938 H. Tiller
1939 H. Davies
1944 J. Hockley
1945 R. Parker
1946 R. Turpin
1947 R. Agland
1948 J. Wright
1949 S. Lewis
1950 P. Longo
1951 E. Ludlam
1952 T. Gooding
1953 R. Barton
1954 K. Phillips
1955 F. Hope
1956 R. Redrup
1957 P. Burke
1958 P. Hill
1959 F. Elderfield
1960 R. Addison
1961 J. Caiger
1962 A. Matthews
1963 A. Matthews
1964 W. Stack
1965 W. Robinson
1966 C. Finnegan
1967 A. Ball
1968 P. McCann
1969 D. Wallington
1970 J. Conteh
1971 A. Minter
1972 F. Lucas
1973 F. Lucas
1974 D. Odwell
1975 D. Odwell
1976 E. Burke
1977 R. Davies
1978 H. Graham
1979 N. Wilshire
1980 M. Kaylor
1981 B. Schumacher
1982 J. Price
1983 T. Forbes
1984 B. Schumacher
1985 D. Cronin
1986 N. Benn
1987 R. Douglas
1988 M. Edwards
1989 S. Johnson
1990 S. Wilson
1991 M. Edwards
1992 L. Woolcock
1993 J. Calzaghe
1994 D. Starie
1995 J. Matthews
1996 J. Pearce

1997 I. Cooper
1998 J. Pearce
1999 C. Froch
2000 S. Swales
2001 C. Froch
2002 N. Perkins
2003 N. Perkins
2004 D. Guthrie
2005 J. Degale

L. Heavyweight
1920 H. Franks
1921 L. Collett
1922 H. Mitchell
1923 H. Mitchell
1924 H. Mitchell
1925 H. Mitchell
1926 D. McCorkindale
1927 A. Jackson
1928 A. Jackson
1929 J. Goyder
1930 J. Murphy
1931 J. Petersen
1932 J. Goyder
1933 G. Brennan
1934 G. Brennan
1935 R. Hearns
1936 J. Magill
1937 J. Wilby
1938 A. S. Brown
1939 B. Woodcock
1944 E. Shackleton
1945 A. Watson
1946 J. Taylor
1947 A. Watson
1948 D. Scott
1949 *Declared no contest*
1950 P. Messervy
1951 G. Walker
1952 H. Cooper
1953 H. Cooper
1954 A. Madigan
1955 D. Rent
1956 D. Mooney
1957 T. Green
1958 J. Leeming
1959 J. Ould
1960 J. Ould
1961 J. Bodell
1962 J. Hendrickson
1963 P. Murphy
1964 J. Fisher
1965 E. Whistler
1966 R. Tighe
1967 M. Smith
1968 R. Brittle
1969 J. Frankham
1970 J. Rafferty
1971 J. Conteh
1972 W. Knight
1973 W. Knight
1974 W. Knight
1975 M. Heath
1976 G. Evans
1977 C. Lawson
1978 V. Smith
1979 A. Straughn
1980 A. Straughn
1981 A. Straughn
1982 G. Crawford
1983 A. Wilson

277

1984 A. Wilson	1884 H. Dearsley	1923 E. Eagan	1962 R. Dryden	1997 B. Stevens
1985 J. Beckles	1885 W. West	1924 A. Clifton	1963 R. Sanders	1998 N. Hosking
1986 J. Moran	1886 A. Diamond	1925 D. Lister	1964 C. Woodhouse	1999 S. St John
1987 J. Beckles	1887 E. White	1926 T. Petersen	1965 W. Wells	2000 D. Dolan
1988 H. Lawson	1888 W. King	1927 C. Capper	1966 A. Brogan	2001 D. Dolan
1989 N. Piper	1889 A. Bowman	1928 J. L. Driscoll	1967 P. Boddington	2002 D. Dolan
1990 J. McCluskey	1890 J. Steers	1929 P. Floyd	1968 W. Wells	2003 M. O'Connell
1991 A. Todd	1891 V. Barker	1930 V. Stuart	1969 A. Burton	2004 T. Bellew
1992 K. Oliver	1892 J. Steers	1931 M. Flanagan	1970 J. Gilmour	2005 T. Bellew
1993 K. Oliver	1893 J. Steers	1932 V. Stuart	1971 L. Stevens	
1994 K. Oliver	1894 H. King	1933 C. O'Grady	1972 T. Wood	**S. Heavyweight**
1995 K. Oliver	1895 W. E. Johnstone	1934 P. Floyd	1973 G. McEwan	1982 A. Elliott
1996 C. Fry	1896 W. E. Johnstone	1935 P. Floyd	1974 N. Meade	1983 K. Ferdinand
1997 P. Rogers	1897 G. Townsend	1936 V. Stuart	1975 G. McEwan	1984 R. Wells
1998 C. Fry	1898 G. Townsend	1937 V. Stuart	1976 J. Rafferty	1985 G. Williamson
1999 J. Ainscough	1899 F. Parks	1938 G. Preston	1977 G. Adair	1986 J. Oyebola
2000 P. Haymer	1900 W. Dees	1939 A. Porter	1978 J. Awome	1987 J. Oyebola
2001 C. Fry	1901 F. Parks	1944 M. Hart	1979 A. Palmer	1988 K. McCormack
2002 T. Marsden	1902 F. Parks	1945 D. Scott	1980 F. Bruno	1989 P. Passley
2003 J. Boyd	1903 F. Dickson	1946 P. Floyd	1981 A. Elliott	1990 K. McCormack
2004 M. Abdusalem	1904 A. Horner	1947 G. Scriven	1982 H. Hylton	1991 K. McCormack
2005 D. Pendleton	1905 F. Parks	1948 J. Gardner	1983 H. Notice	1992 M. Hopper
	1906 F. Parks	1949 A. Worrall	1984 D. Young	1993 M. McKenzie
Cruiserweight	1907 H. Brewer	1950 P. Toch	1985 H. Hylton	1994 D. Watts
1998 T. Oakey	1908 S. Evans	1951 A. Halsey	1986 E. Cardouza	1995 R. Allen
1999 M. Krence	1909 C. Brown	1952 E. Hearn	1987 J. Moran	1996 D. Watts
2000 J. Dolan	1910 F. Storbeck	1953 J. Erskine	1988 H. Akinwande	1997 A. Harrison
2001 J. Dolan	1911 W. Hazell	1954 B. Harper	1989 H. Akinwande	1998 A. Harrison
2002 J. Dolan	1912 R. Smith	1955 D. Rowe	1990 K. Inglis	1999 W. Bessey
	1913 R. Smith	1956 D. Rent	1991 P. Lawson	2000 J. McDermott
	1914 E. Chandler	1957 D. Thomas	1992 S. Welch	2001 M. Grainger
Heavyweight	1919 H. Brown	1958 D. Thomas	1993 P. Lawson	2002 M. Grainger
1881 R. Frost-Smith	1920 R. Rawson	1959 D. Thomas	1994 S. Burford	2003 D. Price
1882 H. Dearsley	1921 R. Rawson	1960 L. Hobbs	1995 M. Ellis	2004 J. Young
1883 H. Dearsley	1922 T. Evans	1961 W. Walker	1996 T. Oakey	2005 D. Price

Tony Bellew (left) knocked out Jon-Lewis Dickensen to win the 2005 ABA heavyweight crown   Les Clark

International Amateur Champions, 1904-2005

Shows all Olympic, World, European & Commonwealth champions since 1904. British silver and bronze medal winners are shown throughout, where applicable.

Country Code

ALG = Algeria; ARG = Argentina; ARM = Armenia; AUS = Australia; AUT = Austria; AZE = Azerbaijan; BE = Belarus; BEL = Belgium; BUL = Bulgaria; CAN = Canada; CEY = Ceylon (now Sri Lanka); CI = Channel Islands; CUB = Cuba; DEN = Denmark; DOM = Dominican Republic; ENG = England; ESP = Spain; EST = Estonia; FIJ = Fiji Islands; FIN = Finland; FRA = France; GBR = United Kingdom; GDR = German Democratic Republic; GEO = Georgia; GER = Germany (but West Germany only from 1968-1990); GHA = Ghana; GUY = Guyana; HOL = Netherlands; HUN = Hungary; IND = India; IRL = Ireland; ITA = Italy; JAM = Jamaica; JPN = Japan; KAZ = Kazakhstan; KEN = Kenya; LIT = Lithuania; MAS = Malaysia; MEX = Mexico; MRI = Mauritius; NKO = North Korea; NIG = Nigeria; NIR = Northern Ireland; NOR = Norway; NZL = New Zealand; PAK = Pakistan; POL = Poland; PUR = Puerto Rico; ROM = Romania; RUS = Russia; SAF = South Africa; SCO = Scotland; SKO = South Korea; SR = Southern Rhodesia; STV = St Vincent; SWE = Sweden; TCH = Czechoslovakia; THA = Thailand; TUR = Turkey; UGA = Uganda; UKR = Ukraine; URS = USSR; USA = United States of America; UZB = Uzbekistan; VEN = Venezuela; WAL = Wales; YUG = Yugoslavia; ZAM = Zambia.

Olympic Champions, 1904-2004

St Louis, USA - 1904
Fly: G. Finnegan (USA). **Bantam:** O. Kirk (USA). **Feather:** O. Kirk (USA). **Light:** H. Spangler (USA). **Welter:** A. Young (USA). **Middle:** C. May (USA). **Heavy:** S. Berger (USA).

London, England - 1908
Bantam: H. Thomas (GBR). **Feather:** R. Gunn (GBR). **Light:** F. Grace (GBR). **Middle:** J.W.H.T. Douglas (GBR). **Heavy:** A. Oldman (GBR).
Silver medals: J. Condon (GBR), C. Morris (GBR), F. Spiller (GBR), S. Evans (GBR).
Bronze medals: W. Webb (GBR), H. Rodding (GBR), T. Ringer (GBR), H. Johnson (GBR), R. Warnes (GBR), W. Philo (GBR), F. Parks (GBR).

Antwerp, Belgium - 1920
Fly: F. Genaro (USA). **Bantam:** C. Walker (SAF). **Feather:** R. Fritsch (FRA). **Light:** S. Mossberg (USA). **Welter:** T. Schneider (CAN). **Middle:** H. Mallin (GBR). **L. Heavy:** E. Eagan (USA). **Heavy:** R. Rawson (GBR).
Silver medal: A. Ireland (GBR).
Bronze medals: W. Cuthbertson (GBR), G. McKenzie (GBR), H. Franks (GBR).

Paris, France - 1924
Fly: F. la Barba (USA). **Bantam:** W. Smith (SAF). **Feather:** J. Fields (USA). **Light:** H. Nielson (DEN). **Welter:** J. Delarge (BEL). **Middle:** H. Mallin (GBR). **L. Heavy:** H. Mitchell (GBR). **Heavy:** O. von Porat (NOR).
Silver medals: J. McKenzie (GBR), J. Elliot (GBR).

Amsterdam, Holland - 1928
Fly: A. Kocsis (HUN). **Bantam:** V. Tamagnini (ITA). **Feather:** B. van Klaveren (HOL). **Light:** C. Orlando (ITA). **Welter:** E. Morgan (NZL). **Middle:** P. Toscani (ITA). **L. Heavy:** V. Avendano (ARG). **Heavy:** A. Rodriguez Jurado (ARG).

Los Angeles, USA - 1932
Fly: I. Enekes (HUN). **Bantam:** H. Gwynne (CAN). **Feather:** C. Robledo (ARG). **Light:** L. Stevens (SAF). **Welter:** E. Flynn (USA). **Middle:** C. Barth (USA). **L. Heavy:** D. Carstens (SAF). **Heavy:** A. Lovell (ARG).

Berlin, West Germany - 1936
Fly: W. Kaiser (GER). **Bantam:** U. Sergo (ITA). **Feather:** O. Casanova (ARG). **Light:** I. Harangi (HUN). **Welter:** S. Suvio (FIN). **Middle:** J. Despeaux (FRA). **L. Heavy:** R. Michelot (FRA). **Heavy:** H. Runge (GER).

London, England - 1948
Fly: P. Perez (ARG). **Bantam:** T. Csik (HUN). **Feather:** E. Formenti (ITA). **Light:** G. Dreyer (SAF). **Welter:** J. Torma (TCH). **Middle:** L. Papp (HUN). **L. Heavy:** G. Hunter (SAF). **Heavy:** R. Iglesas (ARG).
Silver medals: J. Wright (GBR), D. Scott (GBR).

Helsinki, Finland - 1952
Fly: N. Brooks (USA). **Bantam:** P. Hamalainen (FIN). **Feather:** J. Zachara (TCH). **Light:** A. Bolognesi (ITA). **L. Welter:** C. Adkins (USA). **Welter:** Z. Chychla (POL). **L. Middle:** L. Papp (HUN). **Middle:** F. Patterson (USA). **L. Heavy:** N. Lee (USA). **Heavy:** E. Sanders (USA).
Silver medal: J. McNally (IRL).

Melbourne, Australia - 1956
Fly: T. Spinks (GBR). **Bantam:** W. Behrendt (GER). **Feather:** V. Safronov (URS). **Light:** R. McTaggart (GBR). **L. Welter:** V. Jengibarian (URS). **Welter:** N. Linca (ROM). **L. Middle:** L. Papp (HUN). **Middle:** G. Schatkov (URS). **L.**

Heavy: J. Boyd (USA). **Heavy:** P. Rademacher (USA).
Silver medals: T. Nicholls (GBR), F. Tiedt (IRL).
Bronze medals: J. Caldwell (IRL), F. Gilroy (IRL), A. Bryne (IRL), N. Gargano (GBR), J. McCormack (GBR).

Rome, Italy - 1960
Fly: G. Torok (HUN). **Bantam:** O. Grigoryev (URS). **Feather:** F. Musso (ITA). **Light:** K. Pazdzior (POL). **L. Welter:** B. Nemecek (TCH). **Welter:** N. Benvenuti (ITA). **L. Middle:** W. McClure (USA). **Middle:** E. Crook (USA). **L. Heavy:** C. Clay (USA). **Heavy:** F. de Piccoli (ITA).
Bronze medals: R. McTaggart (GBR), J. Lloyd (GBR), W. Fisher (GBR).

Tokyo, Japan - 1964
Fly: F. Atzori (ITA). **Bantam:** T. Sakurai (JPN). **Feather:** S. Stepashkin (URS). **Light:** J. Grudzien (POL). **L. Welter:** J. Kulej (POL). **Welter:** M. Kasprzyk (POL). **L. Middle:** B. Lagutin (URS). **Middle:** V. Popenchenko (URS). **L. Heavy:** C. Pinto (ITA). **Heavy:** J. Frazier (USA).
Bronze medal: J. McCourt (IRL).

Mexico City, Mexico - 1968
L. Fly: F. Rodriguez (VEN). **Fly:** R. Delgado (MEX). **Bantam:** V. Sokolov (URS). **Feather:** A. Roldan (MEX). **Light:** R. Harris (USA). **L. Welter:** J. Kulej (POL). **Welter:** M. Wolke (GDR). **L. Middle:** B. Lagutin (URS). **Middle:** C. Finnegan (GBR). **L. Heavy:** D. Poznyak (URS). **Heavy:** G. Foreman (USA).

Munich, West Germany - 1972
L. Fly: G. Gedo (HUN). **Fly:** G. Kostadinov (BUL). **Bantam:** O. Martinez (CUB). **Feather:** B. Kusnetsov (URS). **Light:** J. Szczepanski (URS). **L. Welter:** R. Seales (USA). **Welter:** E. Correa (CUB). **L. Middle:** D. Kottysch (GER). **Middle:** V. Lemeschev (URS). **L. Heavy:** M. Parlov (YUG). **Heavy:** T. Stevenson (CUB).
Bronze medals: R. Evans (GBR), G. Turpin (GBR), A. Minter (GBR).

Montreal, Canada - 1976
L. Fly: J. Hernandez (CUB). **Fly:** L. Randolph (USA). **Bantam:** Y-J. Gu (NKO). **Feather:** A. Herrera (CUB). **Light:** H. Davis (USA). **L. Welter:** R. Leonard (USA). **Welter:** J. Bachfield (GDR). **L. Middle:** J. Rybicki (POL). **Middle:** M. Spinks (USA). **L. Heavy:** L. Spinks (USA). **Heavy:** T. Stevenson (CUB).
Bronze medal: P. Cowdell (GBR).

Moscow, USSR - 1980
L. Fly: S. Sabirov (URS). **Fly:** P. Lessov (BUL). **Bantam:** J. Hernandez (CUB). **Feather:** R. Fink (GDR). **Light:** A. Herrera (CUB). **L. Welter:** P. Oliva (ITA). **Welter:** A. Aldama (CUB). **L. Middle:** A. Martinez (CUB). **Middle:** J. Gomez (CUB). **L. Heavy:** S. Kacar (YUG). **Heavy:** T. Stevenson (CUB).
Bronze medals: H. Russell (IRL), A. Willis (GBR).

Los Angeles, USA - 1984
L. Fly: P. Gonzalez (USA). **Fly:** S. McCrory (USA). **Bantam:** M. Stecca (ITA). **Feather:** M. Taylor (USA). **Light:** P. Whitaker (USA). **L. Welter:** J. Page (USA). **Welter:** M. Breland (USA). **L. Middle:** F. Tate (USA). **Middle:** J-S. Shin (SKO). **L. Heavy:** A. Josipovic (YUG). **Heavy:** H. Tillman (USA). **S. Heavy:** T. Biggs (USA).
Bronze medal: B. Wells (GBR).

Seoul, South Korea - 1988
L. Fly: I. Mustafov (BUL). **Fly:** H-S. Kim (SKO). **Bantam:** K. McKinney (USA). **Feather:** G. Parisi (ITA). **Light:** A. Zuelow (GDR). **L. Welter:** V. Yanovsky (URS). **Welter:** R. Wangila (KEN). **L. Middle:** S-H. Park (SKO). **Middle:** H. Maske (GDR). **L. Heavy:** A. Maynard (USA). **Heavy:** R. Mercer (USA). **S. Heavy:** L. Lewis (CAN).
Bronze medal: R. Woodhall (GBR).

Barcelona, Spain - 1992

L. Fly: R. Marcelo (CUB). **Fly:** C-C. Su (NKO). **Bantam:** J. Casamayor (CUB). **Feather:** A. Tews (GER). **Fly:** C-C. Su (NKO). **L. Welter:** H. Vinent (CUB). **Welter:** M. Carruth (IRL). **L. Middle:** J. Lemus (CUB). **Middle:** A. Hernandez (CUB). **L. Heavy:** T. May (GER). **Heavy:** F. Savon (CUB). **S. Heavy:** R. Balado (CUB).
Silver medal: W. McCullough (IRL).
Bronze medal: R. Reid (GBR).

Atlanta, USA - 1996

L. Fly: D. Petrov (BUL). **Fly:** M. Romero (CUB). **Bantam:** I. Kovaks (HUN). **Feather:** S. Kamsing (THA). **Light:** H. Soltani (ALG). **L. Welter:** H. Vinent (CUB). **Welter:** O. Saitov (RUS). **L. Middle:** D. Reid (USA). **Middle:** A. Hernandez (CUB). **L. Heavy:** V. Jirov (KAZ). **Heavy:** F. Savon (CUB). **S. Heavy:** Vladimir Klitschko (UKR).

Sydney, Australia - 2000

L. Fly: B. Aslom (FRA). **Fly:** W. Ponlid (THA). **Bantam:** G. Rigondeaux (CUB). **Feather:** B. Sattarkhanov (KAZ). **Light:** M. Kindelan (CUB). **L. Welter:** M. Abdullaev (UZB). **Welter:** O. Saitov (RUS). **L. Middle:** Y. Ibraimov (KAZ). **Middle:** J. Gutierrez Espinosa (CUB). **L. Heavy:** A. Lebziak (RUS). **Heavy:** F. Savon (CUB). **S. Heavy:** A. Harrison (ENG).

Athens, Greece - 2004

L. Fly: Y. Bartelemi (CUB). **Fly:** Y. Gamboa (CUB). **Bantam:** G. Rigondeaux (CUB). **Feather:** A. Tichtchenko (RUS). **Light:** M. Kindelan (CUB). **L. Welter:** M. Boonjumnong (THA). **Welter:** B. Artayev (KAZ). **Middle:** G. Gaiderbekov (RUS). **L. Heavy:** A. Ward (USA). **Heavy:** O. Solis (CUB). **S. Heavy:** A. Povetkin (RUS).
Silver medal: A. Khan (ENG).

World Champions, 1974-2003

Havana, Cuba - 1974

L. Fly: J. Hernandez (CUB). **Fly:** D. Rodriguez (CUB). **Bantam:** W. Gomez (PUR). **Feather:** H. Davis (USA). **Light:** V. Solomin (URS). **L. Welter:** A. Kalule (UGA). **Welter:** E. Correa (CUB). **L. Middle:** R. Garbey (CUB). **Middle:** R. Riskiev (URS). **L. Heavy:** M. Parlov (YUG). **Heavy:** T. Stevenson (CUB).

Belgrade, Yugoslavia - 1978

L. Fly: S. Muchoki (KEN). **Fly:** H. Strednicki (POL). **Bantam:** A. Horta (CUB). **Feather:** A. Herrera (CUB). **Light:** D. Andeh (NIG). **L. Welter:** V. Lvov (URS). **Welter:** V. Rachkov (URS). **L. Middle:** V. Savchenko (URS). **Middle:** J. Gomez (CUB). **L. Heavy:** S. Soria (CUB). **Heavy:** T. Stevenson (CUB).

Munich, West Germany - 1982

L. Fly: I. Mustafov (BUL). **Fly:** Y. Alexandrov (URS). **Bantam:** F. Favors (USA). **Feather:** A. Horta (CUB). **Light:** A. Herrera (CUB). **L. Welter:** C. Garcia (CUB). **Welter:** M. Breland (USA). **L. Middle:** A. Koshkin (URS). **Middle:** B. Comas (CUB). **L. Heavy:** P. Romero (CUB). **Heavy:** A. Jagubkin (URS). **S. Heavy:** T. Biggs (USA).
Bronze medal: T. Corr (IRL).

Reno, USA - 1986

L. Fly: J. Odelin (CUB). **Fly:** P. Reyes (CUB). **Bantam:** S-I. Moon (SKO). **Feather:** K. Banks (USA). **Light:** A. Horta (CUB). **L. Welter:** V. Shishov (URS). **Welter:** K. Gould (USA). **L. Middle:** A. Espinosa (CUB). **Middle:** D. Allen (USA). **L. Heavy:** P. Romero (CUB). **Heavy:** F. Savon (CUB). **S. Heavy:** T. Stevenson (CUB).

Moscow, USSR - 1989

L. Fly: E. Griffin (USA). **Fly:** Y. Arbachakov (URS). **Bantam:** E. Carrion (CUB). **Feather:** A. Khamatov (URS). **Light:** J. Gonzalez (CUB). **L. Welter:** I. Ruzinkov (URS). **Welter:** F. Vastag (Rom). **L. Middle:** I. Akopokhian (URS). **Middle:** A. Kurniavka (URS). **L. Heavy:** H. Maske (GDR). **Heavy:** F. Savon (CUB). **S. Heavy:** R. Balado (CUB).
Bronze medal: M. Carruth (IRL).

Sydney, Australia - 1991

L. Fly: E. Griffin (USA). **Fly:** I. Kovacs (HUN). **Bantam:** S. Todorov (BUL). **Feather:** K. Kirkorov (BUL). **Light:** M. Rudolph (GER). **L. Welter:** K. Tszyu (URS). **Welter:** J. Hernandez (CUB). **L. Middle:** J. Lemus (CUB). **Middle:** T. Russo (ITA). **L. Heavy:** T. May (GER). **Heavy:** F. Savon (CUB). **S. Heavy:** R. Balado (CUB).

Tampere, Finland - 1993

L. Fly: N. Munchian (ARM). **Fly:** W. Font (CUB). **Bantam:** A. Christov (BUL). **Feather:** S. Todorov (BUL). **Light:** D. Austin (CUB). **L. Welter:** H. Vinent (CUB). **Welter:** J. Hernandez (CUB). **L. Middle:** F. Vastag (ROM). **Middle:** A. Hernandez (CUB). **L. Heavy:** R. Garbey (CUB). **Heavy:** F. Savon (CUB). **S. Heavy:** R. Balado (CUB).
Bronze medal: D. Kelly (IRL).

Berlin, Germany - 1995

L. Fly: D. Petrov (BUL). **Fly:** Z. Lunka (GER). **Bantam:** R. Malachbekov (RUS). **Feather:** S. Todorov (BUL). **Light:** L. Doroftei (ROM). **L. Welter:** H. Vinent (CUB). **Welter:** J. Hernandez (CUB). **L. Middle:** F. Vastag (ROM). **Middle:** A. Hernandez (CUB). **L. Heavy:** A. Tarver (USA). **Heavy:** F. Savon (CUB). **S. Heavy:** A. Lezin (RUS).

Budapest, Hungary - 1997

L. Fly: M. Romero (CUB). **Fly:** M. Mantilla (CUB). **Bantam:** R Malakhbekov (RUS). **Feather:** I. Kovacs (HUN). **Light:** A. Maletin (RUS). **L. Welter:** D. Simion (ROM). **Welter:** O. Saitov (RUS). **L. Middle:** A. Duvergel (CUB). **Middle:** Z. Erdei (HUN). **L. Heavy:** A. Lebsiak (RUS). **Heavy:** F. Savon (CUB). **S. Heavy:** G. Kandelaki (GEO).
Bronze medal: S. Kirk (IRL).

Houston, USA - 1999

L. Fly: B. Viloria (USA). **Fly:** B. Jumadilov (KAZ). **Bantam:** R. Crinu (ROM). **Feather:** R. Juarez (USA). **Light:** M. Kindelan (CUB). **L. Welter:** M. Abdullaev (UZB). **Welter:** J. Hernandez (CUB). **L. Middle:** M. Simion (ROM). **Middle:** U. Haydarov (UZB). **L. Heavy:** M. Simms (USA). **Heavy:** M. Bennett (USA). **S. Heavy:** S. Samilsan (TUR).
Bronze medal: K. Evans (WAL).

Belfast, Northern Ireland - 2001

L. Fly: Y. Bartelemi (CUB). **Fly:** J. Thomas (FRA). **Bantam:** G. Rigondeaux (CUB). **Feather:** R. Palyani (TUR). **Light:** M. Kindelan (CUB). **L. Welter:** D. Luna Martinez (CUB). **Welter:** L. Aragon (CUB). **L. Middle:** D. Austin (CUB). **Middle:** A. Gogolev (RUS). **L. Heavy:** Y. Makarenko (RUS). **Heavy:** O. Solis (CUB). **S. Heavy:** R. Chagaev (UZB).
Silver medal: D. Haye (ENG).
Bronze medals: J. Moore (IRL), C. Froch (ENG).

Bangkok, Thailand - 2003

L. Fly: S. Karazov (RUS). **Fly:** S. Jongjohor (THA). **Bantam:** A. Mamedov (AZE). **Feather:** G. Jafarov (KAZ). **Light:** M. Kindelan (CUB). **L. Welter:** W. Blain (FRA). **Welter:** L. Aragon (CUB). **Middle:** G. Golovkin (KAZ). **L. Heavy:** Y. Makarenko (RUS). **Heavy:** O. Solis (CUB). **S. Heavy:** A. Povetkin (RUS).

World Junior Champions, 1979-2004

Yokohama, Japan - 1979

L. Fly: R. Shannon (USA). **Fly:** P. Lessov (BUL). **Bantam:** P-K. Choi (SKO). **Feather:** Y. Gladychev (URS). **Light:** R. Blake (USA). **L. Welter:** I. Akopokhian (URS). **Welter:** M. McCrory (USA). **L. Middle:** A. Mayes (USA). **Middle:** A. Milov (URS). **L. Heavy:** A. Lebedev (URS). **Heavy:** M. Frazier (USA).
Silver medals: N. Wilshire (ENG), D. Cross (ENG).
Bronze medal: I. Scott (SCO).

Santa Domingo, Dominican Republic - 1983

L. Fly: M. Herrera (DOM). **Fly:** J. Gonzalez (DOM). **Bantam:** J. Molina (PUR). **Feather:** A. Miesses (DOM). **Light:** A. Beltre (DOM). **L. Welter:** A. Espinoza (CUB). **Welter:** M. Watkins (USA). **L. Middle:** U. Castillo (CUB). **Middle:** R. Batista (CUB). **L. Heavy:** O. Pought (USA). **Heavy:** A. Williams (USA). **S. Heavy:** L. Lewis (CAN).

Bucharest, Romania - 1985

L. Fly: R-S. Hwang (SKO). **Fly:** T. Marcelica (ROM). **Bantam:** R. Diaz (CUB). **Feather:** D. Maeran (ROM). **Light:** J. Teiche (GDR). **L. Welter:** W. Saeger (GDR). **Welter:** A. Stoianov (BUL). **L. Middle:** M. Franek (TCH). **Middle:** O. Zahalotskih (URS). **L. Heavy:** B. Riddick (USA). **Heavy:** F. Savon (CUB). **S. Heavy:** A. Prianichnikov (URS).

Havana, Cuba - 1987

L. Fly: E. Paisan (CUB). **Fly:** C. Daniels (USA). **Bantam:** A. Moya (CUB). **Feather:** G. Iliyasov (URS). **Light:** J. Hernandez (CUB). **L. Welter:** L. Mihai (ROM). **Welter:** F. Vastag (ROM). **L. Middle:** A. Lobsyak (URS). **Middle:** W. Martinez (CUB). **L. Heavy:** D. Yeliseyev (URS). **Heavy:** R. Balado (CUB). **S. Heavy:** L. Martinez (CUB).
Silver medal: E. Loughran (IRL).
Bronze medal: D. Galvin (IRL).

San Juan, Puerto Rico - 1989

L. Fly: D. Petrov (BUL). **Fly:** N. Monchai (FRA). **Bantam:** J. Casamayor (CUB). **Feather:** C. Febres (PUR). **Light:** A. Acevedo (PUR). **L. Welter:** E. Berger (GDR). **Welter:** A. Hernandez (CUB). **L. Middle:** L. Bedey (CUB). **Middle:** R. Garbey (CUB). **L. Heavy:** R. Alvarez (CUB). **Heavy:** K. Johnson (CAN). **S. Heavy:** A. Burdiantz (URS).
Silver medals: E. Magee (IRL), R. Reid (ENG), S. Wilson (SCO).

Lima, Peru - 1990

L. Fly: D. Alicea (PUR). **Fly:** K. Pielert (GDR). **Bantam:** K. Baravi (URS). **Feather:** A. Vaughan (ENG). **Light:** J. Mendez (CUB). **L. Welter:** H. Vinent (CUB). **Welter:** A. Hernandez (CUB). **L. Middle:** A. Kakauridze (URS).

Middle: J. Gomez (CUB). **L. Heavy:** B. Torsten (GDR). **Heavy:** I. Andreev (URS). **S. Heavy:** J. Quesada (CUB).
Bronze medal: P. Ingle (ENG).

Montreal, Canada - 1992
L. Fly: W. Font (CUB). **Fly:** J. Oragon (CUB). **Bantam:** N. Machado (CUB). **Feather:** M. Stewart (CAN). **Light:** D. Austin (CUB). **L. Welter:** O. Saitov (RUS). **Welter:** L. Brors (GER). **L. Middle:** J. Acosta (CUB). **Middle:** I. Arsangaliev (RUS). **L. Heavy:** S. Samilsan (TUR). **Heavy:** G. Kandeliaki (GEO). **S. Heavy:** M. Porchnev (RUS).
Bronze medal: N. Sinclair (IRL).

Istanbul, Turkey - 1994
L. Fly: J. Turunen (FIN). **Fly:** A. Jimenez (CUB). **Bantam:** J. Despaigne (CUB). **Feather:** D. Simion (ROM). **Light:** L. Diogenes (CUB). **L. Welter:** V. Romero (CUB). **Welter:** E. Aslan (TUR). **L. Middle:** G. Ledsvanys (CUB). **Middle:** M. Genc (TUR). **L. Heavy:** P. Aurino (ITA). **Heavy:** M. Lopez (CUB). **S. Heavy:** P. Carrion (CUB).

Havana, Cuba - 1996
L. Fly: L. Hernandez (CUB). **Fly:** L. Cabrera (CUB). **Bantam:** P. Miradal (CUB). **Feather:** E. Rodriguez (CUB). **Light:** R. Vaillan (CUB). **L. Welter:** T. Mergadze (RUS). **Welter:** J. Brahmer (GER). **L. Middle:** L. Mezquia (CUB). **Middle:** V. Pletniov (RUS). **L. Heavy:** O. Simon (CUB). **Heavy:** A. Yatsenko (UKR). **S. Heavy:** S. Fabre (CUB).
Bronze medal: R. Hatton (ENG).

Buenos Aires, Argentina - 1998
L. Fly: S. Tanasie (ROM). **Fly:** S. Yeledov (KAZ). **Bantam:** S. Suleymanov (UKR). **Feather:** I. Perez (ARG). **Light:** A. Solopov (RUS). **L. Welter:** Y. Tomashov (UKR). **Welter:** K. Oustarkhanov (RUS). **L. Middle:** S. Kostenko (UKR). **Middle:** M. Kempe (GER). **L. Heavy:** H. Yohanson Martinez (CUB). **Heavy:** O. Solis Fonte (CUB). **S. Heavy:** B. Ohanyan (ARM).
Silver medal: H. Cunningham (IRL).
Bronze medal: D. Campbell (IRL).

Budapest, Hungary - 2000
L. Fly: Y. Leon Alarcon (CUB). **Fly:** O. Franco Vaszquez (CUB). **Bantam:** V. Tajbert (GER). **Feather:** G. Kate (HUN). **Light:** F. Adzsanalov (AZE). **L. Welter:** G. Galovkin (KAZ). **Welter:** S. Ustunel (TUR). **L. Middle:** D. Chernysh (RUS). **Middle:** F. Sullivan Barrera (CUB). **L. Heavy:** A. Shekmourov (RUS). **Heavy:** D. Medzhydov (UKR). **S. Heavy:** A. Dmitrienko (RUS).
Bronze medal: C. Barrett (IRL).

Santiago, Cuba - 2002
L. Fly: D. Acripitian (RUS). **Fly:** Y. Fabregas (CUB). **Bantam:** S. Bahodirijan (UZB). **Feather:** A. Tichtchenko (RUS). **Light:** S. Mendez (CUB). **L. Welter:** K. Iliyasov (KAZ). **Welter:** J. McPherson (USA). **L. Middle:** V. Diaz (CUB). **Middle:** A. Duarte (CUB). **L. Heavy:** R. Zavalnyuyk (UKR). **Heavy:** Y. P. Hernandez (CUB). **S. Heavy:** P. Portal (CUB).
Silver medal: A. Lee (IRL).
Bronze medal: N. Brough (ENG).

Jeju Island, South Korea - 2004
L. Fly: P. Bedak (Hun). **Fly:** I. Rahimov (UZB). **Bantam:** A. Abdimomunov (KAZ). **Feather:** E. Ambartsumyan (RUS). **Light:** A. Khan (ENG). **L. Welter:** C. Banteur (CUB). **Welter:** E. Rasulov (UZB). **Middle:** D. Tchudinov (RUS). **L. Heavy:** I. Perez (CUB). **Heavy:** E. Romanov (RUS). **S.Heavy:** D. Boytsov (RUS).
Bronze medal: D. Price (ENG).

European Champions, 1924-2004

Paris, France - 1924
Fly: J. McKenzie (GBR). **Bantam:** J. Ces (FRA). **Feather:** R. de Vergnie (BEL). **Light:** N. Nielsen (DEN). **Welter:** J. Delarge (BEL). **Middle:** H. Mallin (GBR). **L. Heavy:** H. Mitchell (GBR). **Heavy:** O. von Porat (NOR).

Stockholm, Sweden - 1925
Fly: E. Pladner (FRA). **Bantam:** A. Rule (GBR). **Feather:** P. Andren (SWE). **Light:** S. Johansson (SWE). **Welter:** H. Nielsen (DEN). **Middle:** F. Crawley (GBR). **L. Heavy:** T. Petersen (DEN). **Heavy:** B. Persson (SWE).
Silver medals: J. James (GBR), E. Viney (GBR), D. Lister (GBR).

Berlin, Germany - 1927
Fly: L. Boman (SWE). **Bantam:** K. Dalchow (GER). **Feather:** F. Dubbers (GER). **Light:** H. Domgoergen (GER). **Welter:** R. Caneva (ITA). **Middle:** J. Christensen (NOR). **L. Heavy:** H. Muller (GER). **Heavy:** N. Ramm (SWE).

Amsterdam, Holland - 1928
Fly: A. Kocsis (HUN). **Bantam:** V. Tamagnini (ITA). **Feather:** B. van Klaveren (HOL). **Light:** C. Orlandi (ITA). **Welter:** R. Galataud (FRA). **Middle:** P. Toscani (ITA). **L. Heavy:** E. Pistulla (GER). **Heavy:** N. Ramm (SWE).

Budapest, Hungary - 1930
Fly: I. Enekes (HUN). **Bantam:** J. Szeles (HUN). **Feather:** G. Szabo (HUN). **Light:** M. Bianchini (ITA). **Welter:** J. Besselmann (GER). **Middle:** C. Meroni (ITA). **L. Heavy:** T. Petersen (DEN). **Heavy:** J. Michaelson (DEN).

Los Angeles, USA - 1932
Fly: I. Enekes (HUN). **Bantam:** H. Ziglarski (GER). **Feather:** J. Schleinkofer (GER). **Light:** T. Ahlqvist (SWE). **Welter:** E. Campe (GER). **Middle:** R. Michelot (FRA). **L. Heavy:** G. Rossi (ITA). **Heavy:** L. Rovati (ITA).

Budapest, Hungary - 1934
Fly: P. Palmer (GBR). **Bantam:** I. Enekes (HUN). **Feather:** O. Kaestner GER). **Light:** E. Facchini (ITA). **Welter:** D. McCleave (GBR). **Middle:** S. Szigetti (HUN). **L. Heavy:** P. Zehetmayer (AUT). **Heavy:** G. Baerlund (FIN).
Bronze medal: P. Floyd (GBR).

Milan, Italy - 1937
Fly: I. Enekes (HUN). **Bantam:** U. Sergo (ITA). **Feather:** A. Polus (POL). **Light:** H. Nuremberg (GER). **Welter:** M. Murach (GER). **Middle:** H. Chmielewski (POL). **L. Heavy:** S. Szigetti (HUN). **Heavy:** O. Tandberg (SWE).

Dublin, Eire - 1939
Fly: J. Ingle (IRL). **Bantam:** U. Sergo (ITA). **Feather:** P. Dowdall (IRL). **Light:** H. Nuremberg (GER). **Welter:** A. Kolczyski (POL). **Middle:** A. Raadik (EST). **L. Heavy:** L. Musina (ITA). **Heavy:** O. Tandberg (SWE).
Bronze medal: C. Evenden (IRL).

Dublin, Eire - 1947
Fly: L. Martinez (ESP). **Bantam:** L. Bogacs (HUN). **Feather:** K. Kreuger (SWE). **Light:** J. Vissers (BEL). **Welter:** J. Ryan (ENG). **Middle:** A. Escudie (FRA). **L. Heavy:** H. Quentemeyer (HOL). **Heavy:** G. O'Colmain (IRL).
Silver medals: J. Clinton (SCO), P. Maguire (IRL), W. Thom (ENG), G. Scriven (ENG).
Bronze medals: J. Dwyer (SCO), A. Sanderson (ENG), W. Frith (SCO), E. Cantwell (IRL), K. Wyatt (ENG).

Oslo, Norway - 1949
Fly: J. Kasperczak (POL). **Bantam:** G. Zuddas (ITA). **Feather:** J. Bataille (FRA). **Light:** M. McCullagh (IRL). **Welter:** J. Torma (TCH). **Middle:** L. Papp (HUN). **L. Heavy:** G. di Segni (ITA). **Heavy:** L. Bene (HUN).
Bronze medal: D. Connell (IRL).

Milan, Italy - 1951
Fly: A. Pozzali (ITA). **Bantam:** V. Dall'Osso (ITA). **Feather:** J. Ventaja (FRA). **Light:** B. Visintin (ITA). **L. Welter:** H. Schelling (GER). **Welter:** Z. Chychla (POL). **L. Middle:** L. Papp (HUN). **Middle:** S. Sjolin (SWE). **L. Heavy:** M. Limage (BEL). **Heavy:** G. di Segni (ITA).
Silver medals: J. Kelly (IRL).
Bronze medals: D. Connell (IRL), T. Milligan (IRL), A. Lay (ENG).

Warsaw, Poland - 1953
Fly: H. Kukier (POL). **Bantam:** Z. Stefaniuk (POL). **Feather:** J. Kruza (POL). **Light:** V. Jengibarian (URS). **L. Welter:** L. Drogosz (POL). **Welter:** Z. Chychla (POL). **L. Middle:** B. Wells (ENG). **Middle:** D. Wemhoner (GER). **L. Heavy:** U. Nietchke (GER). **Heavy:** A. Schotzikas (URS).
Silver medal: T. Milligan (IRL).
Bronze medals: J. McNally (IRL), R. Barton (ENG).

Berlin, West Germany - 1955
Fly: E. Basel (GER). **Bantam:** Z. Stefaniuk (POL). **Feather:** T. Nicholls (ENG). **Light:** H. Kurschat (GER). **L. Welter:** L. Drogosz (POL). **Welter:** N. Gargano (ENG). **L. Middle:** Z. Pietrzykowski (POL). **Middle:** G. Schatkov (URS). **L. Heavy:** E. Schoeppner (GER). **Heavy:** A. Schotzikas (URS).

Prague, Czechoslovakia - 1957
Fly: M. Homberg (GER). **Bantam:** O. Grigoryev (URS). **Feather:** D. Venilov (BUL). **Light:** K. Pazdzior (POL). **L. Welter:** V. Jengibarian (URS). **Welter:** M. Graus (GER). **L. Middle:** N. Benvenuti (ITA). **Middle:** Z. Pietrzykowski (POL). **L. Heavy:** G. Negrea (ROM). **Heavy:** A. Abramov (URS).
Bronze medals: R. Davies (WAL), J. Morrissey (SCO), J. Kidd (SCO), F. Teidt (IRL).

Lucerne, Switzerland - 1959
Fly: M. Homberg (GER). **Bantam:** H. Rascher (GER). **Feather:** J. Adamski (POL). **Light:** O. Maki (FIN). **L. Welter:** V. Jengibarian (URS). **Welter:** L. Drogosz (POL). **L. Middle:** N. Benvenuti (ITA). **Middle:** G. Schatkov (URS). **L. Heavy:** Z. Pietrzykowski (POL). **Heavy:** A. Abramov (URS).
Silver medal: D. Thomas (ENG).
Bronze medals: A. McClean (IRL), H. Perry (IRL), C. McCoy (IRL), H. Scott (ENG).

Belgrade, Yugoslavia - 1961
Fly: P. Vacca (ITA). **Bantam:** S. Sivko (URS). **Feather:** F. Taylor (ENG). **Light:** R. McTaggart (SCO). **L. Welter:** A. Tamulis (URS). **Welter:** R. Tamulis

(URS). **L. Middle:** B. Lagutin (URS). **Middle:** T. Walasek (POL). **L. Heavy:** G. Saraudi (ITA). **Heavy:** A. Abramov (URS).
Bronze medals: P. Warwick (ENG), I. McKenzie (SCO), J. Bodell (ENG).

Moscow, USSR - 1963
Fly: V. Bystrov (URS). **Bantam:** O. Grigoryev (URS). **Feather:** S. Stepashkin (URS). **Light:** J. Kajdi (HUN). **L. Welter:** J. Kulej (POL). **Welter:** R. Tamulis (URS). **L. Middle:** B. Lagutin (URS). **Middle:** V. Popenchenko (URS). **L. Heavy:** Z. Pietrzykowski (POL). **Heavy:** J. Nemec (TCH).
Silver medal: A. Wyper (SCO).

Berlin, East Germany - 1965
Fly: H. Freisdadt (GER). **Bantam:** O. Grigoryev (URS). **Feather:** S. Stepashkin (URS). **Light:** V. Barranikov (URS). **L. Welter:** J. Kulej (POL). **Welter:** R. Tamulis (URS). **L. Middle:** V. Ageyev (URS). **Middle:** V. Popenchenko (URS). **L. Heavy:** D. Poznyak (URS). **Heavy:** A. Isosimov (URS).
Silver medal: B. Robinson (ENG).
Bronze medals: J. McCluskey (SCO), K. Buchanan (SCO), J. McCourt (IRL).

Rome, Italy - 1967
Fly: H. Skrzyczak (POL). **Bantam:** N. Giju (ROM). **Feather:** R. Petek (POL). **Light:** J. Grudzien (POL). **L. Welter:** V. Frolov (URS). **Welter:** B. Nemecek (TCH). **L. Middle:** V. Ageyev (URS). **Middle:** M. Casati (ITA). **L. Heavy:** D. Poznyak (URS). **Heavy:** M. Baruzzi (ITA).
Silver medal: P. Boddington (ENG).

Bucharest, Romania - 1969
L. Fly: G. Gedo (HUN). **Fly:** C. Ciuca (ROM). **Bantam:** A. Dumitrescu (ROM). **Feather:** L. Orban (HUN). **Light:** S. Cutov (ROM). **L. Welter:** V. Frolov (URS). **Welter:** G. Meier (GER). **L. Middle:** V. Tregubov (URS). **Middle:** V. Tarasenkov (URS). **L. Heavy:** D. Poznyak (URS). **Heavy:** I. Alexe (ROM).
Bronze medals: M. Dowling (IRL), M. Piner (ENG), A. Richardson (ENG), T. Imrie (SCO).

Madrid, Spain - 1971
L. Fly: G. Gedo (HUN). **Fly:** J. Rodriguez (ESP). **Bantam:** T. Badar (HUN). **Feather:** R. Tomczyk (POL). **Light:** J. Szczepanski (POL). **L. Welter:** U. Beyer (GDR). **Welter:** J. Kajdi (HUN). **L. Middle:** V. Tregubov (URS). **Middle:** J. Juotsiavitchus (URS). **L. Heavy:** M. Parlov (YUG). **Heavy:** V. Tchernishev (URS).
Bronze medals: N. McLaughlin (IRL), M. Dowling (IRL), B. McCarthy (IRL), M. Kingwell (ENG), L. Stevens (ENG).

Belgrade, Yugoslavia - 1973
L. Fly: V. Zasypko (URS). **Fly:** C. Gruescu (ROM). **Bantam:** A. Cosentino (FRA). **Feather:** S. Forster (GDR). **Light:** S. Cutov (ROM). **L. Welter:** M. Benes (YUG). **Welter:** S. Csjef (HUN). **L. Middle:** A. Klimanov (URS). **Middle:** V. Lemechev (URS). **L. Heavy:** M. Parlov (YUG). **Heavy:** V. Ulyanich (URS).
Bronze medal: J. Bambrick (SCO).

Katowice, Poland - 1975
L. Fly: A. Tkachenko (URS). **Fly:** V. Zasypko (URS). **Bantam:** V. Rybakov (URS). **Feather:** T. Badari (HUN). **Light:** S. Cutov (ROM). **L. Welter:** V. Limasov (URS). **Welter:** K. Marjaama (FIN). **L. Middle:** W. Rudnowski (POL). **Middle:** V. Lemechev (URS). **L. Heavy:** A. Klimanov (URS). **Heavy:** A. Biegalski (POL).
Bronze medals: C. Magri (ENG), P. Cowdell (ENG), G. McEwan (ENG).

Halle, East Germany - 1977
L. Fly: H. Srednicki (POL). **Fly:** L. Blazynski (POL). **Bantam:** S. Forster (GDR). **Feather:** R. Nowakowski (GDR). **Light:** A. Rusevski (YUG). **L. Welter:** B. Gajda (POL). **Welter:** V. Limasov (URS). **L. Middle:** V. Saychenko (URS). **Middle:** I. Shaposhnikov (URS). **L. Heavy:** D. Kvachadze (URS). **Heavy:** E. Gorstkov (URS).
Bronze medal: P. Sutcliffe (IRL).

Cologne, West Germany - 1979
L. Fly: S. Sabirov (URS). **Fly:** H. Strednicki (POL). **Bantam:** N. Khrapzov (URS). **Feather:** V. Rybakov (URS). **Light:** V. Demianenko (URS). **L. Welter:** S. Konakbaev (URS). **Welter:** E. Muller (GER). **L. Middle:** M. Perunovic (YUG). **Middle:** T. Uusiverta (FIN). **L. Heavy:** A. Nikolyan (URS). **Heavy:** E. Gorstkov (URS). **S. Heavy:** P. Hussing (GER).
Bronze medal: P. Sutcliffe (IRL).

Tampere, Finland - 1981
L. Fly: I. Mustafov (BUL). **Fly:** P. Lessov (BUL). **Bantam:** V. Miroschnichenko (URS). **Feather:** R. Nowakowski (GDR). **Light:** V. Rybakov (URS). **L. Welter:** V. Shisov (URS). **Welter:** S. Konakvbaev (URS). **L. Middle:** A. Koshkin (URS). **Middle:** J. Torbek (URS). **L. Heavy:** A Krupin (URS). **Heavy:** A. Jagupkin (URS). **S. Heavy:** F. Damiani (ITA).
Bronze medal: G. Hawkins (IRL).

Varna, Bulgaria - 1983
L. Fly: I. Mustafov (BUL). **Fly:** P. Lessov (BUL). **Bantam:** Y. Alexandrov

(URS). **Feather:** S. Nurkazov (URS). **Light:** E. Chuprenski (BUL). **L. Welter:** V. Shishov (URS). **Welter:** P. Galkin (URS). **L. Middle:** V. Laptev (URS). **Middle:** V. Melnik (URS). **L. Heavy:** V. Kokhanovski (URS). **Heavy:** A. Jagubkin (URS). **S. Heavy:** F. Damiani (ITA).
Bronze medal: K. Joyce (IRL).

Budapest, Hungary - 1985
L. Fly: R. Breitbarth (GDR). **Fly:** D. Berg (GDR). **Bantam:** L. Simic (YUG). **Feather:** S. Khachatrian (URS). **Light:** E. Chuprenski (BUL). **L. Welter:** S. Mehnert (GDR). **Welter:** I. Akopokhian (URS). **L. Middle:** M. Timm (GDR). **Middle:** H. Maske (GDR). **L. Heavy:** N. Shanavasov (URS). **Heavy:** A. Jagubkin (URS). **S. Heavy:** F. Somodi (HUN).
Bronze medals: S. Casey (IRL), J. Beckles (ENG).

Turin, Italy - 1987
L. Fly: N. Munchyan (URS). **Fly:** A. Tews (GDR). **Bantam:** A. Hristov (BUL). **Feather:** M. Kazaryan (URS). **Light:** O. Nazarov (URS). **L. Welter:** B. Abadjier (BUL). **Welter:** V. Shishov (URS). **L. Middle:** E. Richter (GDR). **Middle:** H. Maske (GDR). **L. Heavy:** Y. Vaulin (URS). **Heavy:** A. Vanderlijde (HOL). **S. Heavy:** U. Kaden (GDR).
Bronze medal: N. Brown (ENG).

Athens, Greece - 1989
L. Fly: I.Mustafov (BUL). **Fly:** Y. Arbachakov (URS). **Bantam:** S. Todorov (BUL). **Feather:** K. Kirkorov (BUL). **Light:** K. Tsziu (URS). **L. Welter:** I. Ruznikov (URS). **Welter:** S. Mehnert (GDR). **L. Middle:** I. Akopokhian (URS). **Middle:** H. Maske (GDR). **L. Heavy:** S. Lange (GDR). **Heavy:** A. Vanderlijde (HOL). **S. Heavy:** U. Kaden (GDR).
Bronze Medal: D. Anderson (SCO).

Gothenburg, Sweden - 1991
L. Fly: I. Marinov (BUL). **Fly:** I. Kovacs (HUN). **Bantam:** S. Todorov (BUL). **Feather:** P. Griffin (IRL). **Light:** V. Nistor (ROM). **L. Welter:** K. Tsziu (URS). **Welter:** R. Welin (SWE). **L. Middle:** I. Akopokhian (URS). **Middle:** S. Otke (GER). **L. Heavy:** D. Michalczewski (GER). **Heavy:** A. Vanderlijde (HOL). **S. Heavy:** E. Beloussov (URS).
Bronze medals: P. Weir (SCO), A. Vaughan (ENG).

Bursa, Turkey - 1993
L. Fly: D. Petrov (BUL). **Fly:** R. Husseinov (AZE). **Bantam:** R. Malakhbetov (RUS). **Feather:** S. Todorov (BUL). **Light:** J. Bielski (POL). **L. Welter:** N. Suleymanogiu (TUR). **Welter:** V. Karpaclauskas (LIT). **L. Middle:** F. Vastag (ROM). **Middle:** D. Eigenbrodt (GER). **L. Heavy:** I. Kshinin (RUS). **Heavy:** G. Kandelaki (GEO). **S. Heavy:** S. Rusinov (BUL).
Bronze medals: P. Griffin (IRL), D. Williams (ENG), K. McCormack (WAL).

Vejle, Denmark - 1996
L. Fly: D. Petrov (BUL). **Fly:** A. Pakeev (RUS). **Bantam:** I. Kovacs (HUN). **Feather:** R. Paliani (RUS). **Light:** L. Doroftei (ROM). **L. Welter:** O. Urkal (GER). **Welter:** H. Al (DEN). **L. Middle:** F. Vastag (ROM). **Middle:** S. Ottke (GER). **L. Heavy:** P. Aurino (ITA). **Heavy:** L. Krasniqi (GER). **S. Heavy:** A. Lezin (RUS).
Bronze medals: S. Harrison (SCO), D. Burke (ENG), D. Kelly (IRL).

Minsk, Belarus - 1998
L. Fly: S. Kazakov (RUS). **Fly:** V. Sidorenko (UKR). **Bantam:** S. Danilchenko (UKR). **Feather:** R. Paliani (TUR). **Light:** K. Huste (GER). **L. Welter:** D. Simion (ROM). **Welter:** O. Saitov (RUS). **L. Middle:** F. Esther (FRA). **Middle:** Z. Erdei (HUN). **L. Heavy:** A. Lebsiak (RUS). **Heavy:** G. Fragomeni (ITA). **S. Heavy:** A. Lezin (RUS).
Silver Medals: B. Magee (IRL), C. Fry (ENG).
Bronze medal: C. Bessey (ENG).

Tampere, Finland - 2000
L. Fly: Valeri Sidorenko (UKR). **Fly:** Vladimir Sidorenko (UKR). **Bantam:** A. Agagueloglu (TUR). **Feather:** R. Paliani (TUR). **Light:** A. Maletin (RUS). **L. Welter:** A. Leonev (RUS). **Welter:** B. Ueluesoy (TUR). **L. Middle:** A. Catic (GER). **Middle:** Z. Erdei (HUN). **L. Heavy:** A. Lebsiak (RUS). **Heavy:** J. Chanet (FRA). **S. Heavy:** A. Lezin (RUS).

Perm, Russia - 2002
L. Fly: S. Kazakov (RUS). **Fly:** G. Balakshin (RUS). **Bantam:** K. Khatsygov (BE). **Feather:** R. Malakhbekov (RUS). **Light:** A. Maletin (RUS). **L. Welter:** D. Panayotov (BUL). **Welter:** T. Gaidalov (RUS). **L. Middle:** A. Mishin (RUS). **Middle:** O. Mashkin (UKR). **L. Heavy:** M. Gala (RUS). **Heavy:** E. Makarenko (RUS). **S. Heavy:** A. Povetkin (RUS).

Pula, Croatia - 2004
L. Fly: S. Kazakov (RUS). **Fly:** G. Balakchine (RUS). **Bantam:** G. Kovalev (RUS). **Feather:** V. Tajbert (GER). **Light:** D. Stilianov (BUL). **L. Welter:** A. Maletin (RUS). **Welter:** O. Saitov (RUS). **Middle:** G. Gaiderbekov (RUS). **L. Heavy:** E. Makarenko (RUS). **Heavy:** A. Alekseev (RUS). **S. Heavy:** A. Povetkin (RUS).
Bronze medal: A. Lee (IRL).

Note: Gold medals were awarded to the Europeans who went the furthest in the Olympic Games of 1924, 1928 & 1932.

European Junior Champions, 1970-2005

Miskolc, Hungary - 1970
L. Fly: Gluck (HUN). **Fly:** Z. Kismeneth (HUN). **Bantam:** A. Levitschev (URS). **Feather:** Andrianov (URS). **Light:** L. Juhasz (HUN). **L. Welter:** K. Nemec (HUN). **Welter:** Davidov (URS). **L. Middle:** A. Lemeschev (URS). **Middle:** N. Anfimov (URS). **L. Heavy:** O. Sasche (GDR). **Heavy:** J. Reder (HUN).
Bronze medals: D. Needham (ENG), R. Barlow (ENG), L. Stevens (ENG).

Bucharest, Romania - 1972
L. Fly: A. Turei (ROM). **Fly:** Condurat (ROM). **Bantam:** V. Solomin (URS). **Feather:** V. Lvov (URS). **Light:** S. Cutov (ROM). **L. Welter:** K. Pierwieniecki (POL). **Welter:** Zorov (URS). **L. Middle:** Babescu (ROM). **Middle:** V. Lemeschev (URS). **L. Heavy:** Mirounik (URS). **Heavy:** Subutin (URS).
Bronze medals: J. Gale (ENG), R. Maxwell (ENG), D. Odwell (ENG).

Kiev, Russia - 1974
L. Fly: A. Tkachenko (URS). **Fly:** V. Rybakov (URS). **Bantam:** C. Andreikovski (BUL). **Feather:** V. Sorokin (URS). **Light:** V. Limasov (URS). **L. Welter:** N. Sigov (URS). **Welter:** M. Bychkov (URS). **L. Middle:** V. Danshin (URS). **Middle:** D. Jende (GDR). **L. Heavy:** K. Dafinoiu (ROM). **Heavy:** K. Mashev (BUL).
Silver medal: C. Magri (ENG).
Bronze medals: G. Gilbody (ENG), K. Laing (ENG).

Izmir, Turkey - 1976
L. Fly: C. Seican (ROM). **Fly:** G. Khratsov (URS). **Bantam:** M. Navros (URS). **Feather:** V. Demoianeko (URS). **Light:** M. Puzovic (YUG). **L. Welter:** V. Zverev (URS). **Welter:** K. Ozoglouz (TUR). **L. Middle:** W. Lauder (SCO). **Middle:** H. Lenhart (GER). **L. Heavy:** I. Yantchauskas (URS). **Heavy:** B. Enjenyan (URS).
Silver medal: J. Decker (ENG).
Bronze medals: I. McLeod (SCO), N. Croombes (ENG).

Dublin, Ireland - 1978
L. Fly: R. Marx (GDR). **Fly:** D. Radu (ROM). **Bantam:** S. Khatchatrian (URS). **Feather:** H. Loukmanov (URS). **Light:** P. Oliva (ITA). **L. Welter:** V. Laptiev (URS). **Welter:** R. Filimanov (URS). **L. Middle:** A. Beliave (URS). **Middle:** G. Zinkovitch (URS). **L. Heavy:** I. Jolta (ROM). **Heavy:** P. Stoimenov (BUL).
Silver medals: M. Holmes (IRL), P. Hanlon (ENG), M. Courtney (ENG).
Bronze medals: T. Thompson (IRL), J. Turner (ENG), M. Bennett (WAL), J. McAllister (SCO), C. Devine (ENG).

Rimini, Italy - 1980
L. Fly: A. Mikoulin (GDR). **Fly:** J. Varadi (HUN). **Bantam:** F. Rauschning (GDR). **Feather:** J. Gladychev (URS). **Light:** V. Shishov (URS). **L. Welter:** R. Lomski (BUL). **Welter:** T. Holonics (GDR). **L. Middle:** N. Wilshire (ENG). **Middle:** S. Laptiev (URS). **L. Heavy:** V. Dolgoun (URS). **Heavy:** V. Tioumentsev (URS). **S. Heavy:** S. Kormihtsine (URS).
Bronze medals: N. Potter (ENG), B. McGuigan (IRL), M. Brereton (IRL), D. Cross (ENG).

Schwerin, East Germany - 1982
L. Fly: R. Kabirov (URS). **Fly:** I. Filchev (BUL). **Bantam:** M. Stecca (ITA). **Feather:** B. Blagoev (BUL). **Light:** E. Chakimov (URS). **L. Welter:** S. Mehnert (GDR). **Welter:** T. Schmitz (GDR). **L. Middle:** B. Shararov (URS). **Middle:** E. Christie (ENG). **L. Heavy:** Y. Waulin (URS). **Heavy:** A. Popov (URS). **S. Heavy:** V. Aldoshin (URS).
Silver medal: D. Kenny (ENG).
Bronze medal: O. Jones (ENG).

Tampere, Finland - 1984
L. Fly: R. Breitbart (GDR). **Fly:** D. Berg (GDR). **Bantam:** K. Khdrian (URS). **Feather:** O. Nazarov (URS). **Light:** C. Furnikov (BUL). **L. Welter:** W. Schmidt (GDR). **Welter:** K. Doinov (BUL). **L. Middle:** O. Volkov (URS). **Middle:** R. Ryll (GDR). **L. Heavy:** G. Peskov (URS). **Heavy:** R. Draskovic (YUG). **S. Heavy:** L. Kamenov (BUL).
Bronze medals: J. Lowey (IRL), F. Harding (ENG), N. Moore (ENG).

Copenhagen, Denmark - 1986
L. Fly: S. Todorov (BUL). **Fly:** S. Galotian (URS). **Bantam:** D. Drumm (GDR). **Feather:** K. Tsziu (URS). **Light:** G. Akopkhian (URS). **L. Welter:** F. Vastag (ROM). **Welter:** S. Karavayev (URS). **L. Middle:** E. Elibaev (URS). **Middle:** A. Kurnabka (URS). **L. Heavy:** A. Schultz (GDR). **Heavy:** A. Golota (POL). **S. Heavy:** A. Prianichnikov (URS).

Gdansk, Poland - 1988
L. Fly: I. Kovacs (HUN). **Fly:** M. Beyer (GDR). **Bantam:** M. Aitzanov (URS). **Feather:** M. Rudolph (GDR). **Light:** M. Shaburov (URS). **L. Welter:** G.

Campanella (ITA). **Welter:** D. Konsun (URS). **L. Middle:** K. Kiselev (URS). **Middle:** A. Rudenko (URS). **L. Heavy:** O. Velikanov (URS). **Heavy:** A. Ter-Okopian (URS). **S. Heavy:** E. Belusov (URS).
Bronze medals: P. Ramsey (ENG), M. Smyth (WAL).

Usti Nad Labem, Czechoslovakia - 1990
L. Fly: Z. Paliani (URS). **Fly:** K. Pielert (GDR). **Bantam:** K. Baravi (URS). **Feather:** P. Gvasalia (URS). **Light:** J. Hildenbrandt (GDR). **L. Welter:** N. Smanov (URS). **Welter:** A. Preda (ROM). **L. Middle:** A. Kakauridze (URS). **Middle:** J. Schwank (GDR). **L. Heavy:** Iljin (URS). **Heavy:** I. Andrejev (URS). **S. Heavy:** W. Fischer (GDR).
Silver medal: A. Todd (ENG).
Bronze medal: P. Craig (ENG).

Edinburgh, Scotland - 1992
L. Fly: M. Ismailov (URS). **Fly:** F. Brennfuhrer (GER). **Bantam:** S. Kuchler (GER). **Feather:** M. Silantiev (URS). **Light:** S. Shcherbakov (URS). **L. Welter:** O. Saitov (URS). **Welter:** H. Kurlumaz (TUR). **L. Middle:** Z. Erdie (HUN). **Middle:** V. Zhirov (URS). **L. Heavy:** D. Gorbachev (URS). **Heavy:** L. Achkasov (URS). **S. Heavy:** A. Mamedov (URS).
Silver medals: M. Hall (ENG), B. Jones (WAL).
Bronze medals: F. Slane (IRL), G. Stephens (IRL), C. Davies (WAL).

Salonika, Greece - 1993
L. Fly: O. Kiroukhine (UKR). **Fly:** R. Husseinov (AZE). **Bantam:** M. Kulbe (GER). **Feather:** E. Zakharov (RUS). **Light:** O. Sergeev (RUS). **L. Welter:** A. Selihanov (RUS). **Welter:** O. Kudinov (RUS). **L. Middle:** E. Makarenko (RUS). **Middle:** D. Droukovski (RUS). **L. Heavy:** A. Voida (RUS). **Heavy:** Vladimir Klitschko (UKR). **S. Heavy:** A. Moiseev (RUS).
Bronze medal: D. Costello (ENG).

Sifok, Hungary - 1995
L. Fly: D. Gaissine (RUS). **Fly:** A. Kotelnik (UKR). **Bantam:** A. Loutsenko (UKR). **Feather:** S. Harrison (SCO). **Light:** D. Simon (ROM). **L. Welter:** B. Ulusoy (TUR). **Welter:** O. Bouts (UKR). **L. Middle:** O. Bukalo (UKR). **Middle:** V. Plettnev (RUS). **L. Heavy:** A. Derevtsov (RUS). **Heavy:** C. O'Grady (IRL). **S. Heavy:** D. Savvine (RUS).
Silver medal: G. Murphy (SCO).
Bronze medal: N. Linford (ENG).

Birmingham, England - 1997
L. Fly: G. Balakshine (RUS). **Fly:** K. Dzhamoloudinov (RUS). **Bantam:** A. Shaiduline (RUS). **Feather:** D. Marciukaitis (LIT). **Light:** D. Baranov (RUS). **L. Welter:** A. Mishine (RUS). **Welter:** D. Yuldashev (UKR). **L. Middle:** A. Catic (GER). **Middle:** D. Lebedev (RUS). **L. Heavy:** V. Uzelkov (UKR). **Heavy:** S. Koeber (GER). **S. Heavy:** D. Pirozhenko (RUS).
Silver medal: S. Miller (ENG).
Bronze medals: S. Burke (ENG), M. Dean (ENG), P. Pierson (ENG), M. Lee (IRE).

Rijeka, Croatia - 1999
L. Fly: Kibalyuk (UKR). **Fly:** A. Bakhtin (RUS). **Bantam:** V. Simion (ROM). **Feather:** Kiutkhukow (BUL). **Light:** Pontilov (RUS). **L. Welter:** G. Ajetovic (YUG). **Welter:** S. Nouaouria (FRA). **L. Middle:** S. Kazantsev (RUS). **Middle:** D. Tsariouk (RUS). **L. Heavy:** Alexeev (RUS). **Heavy:** Alborov (RUS). **S. Heavy:** Soukhoverkov (RUS).
Bronze medal: S. Birch (ENG).

Sarejevo, Croatia - 2001
L. Fly: A. Taratokin (RUS). **Fly:** E. Abzalimov (RUS). **Bantam:** G. Kovaljov (RUS). **Feather:** M. Hratchev (RUS). **Light:** S. Aydin (TUR). **L. Welter:** D. Mikulin (RUS). **Welter:** O. Bokalo (UKR). **L. Middle:** M. Korobov (RUS). **Middle:** I. Bogdanov (UKR). **L. Heavy:** R. Kahkijev (RUS). **S. Heavy:** V. Zuyev (BE). **S. Heavy:** I. Timurziejev (RUS).
Bronze medal: K. Anderson (SCO).

Warsaw, Poland - 2003
L. Fly: P. Bedak (HUN). **Fly:** A. Ganev (RUS). **Bantam:** M. Tretiak (UKR). **Feather:** A. Alexandru (ROM). **Light:** A. Aleksiev (RUS). **L. Welter:** T. Tabotadze (UKR). **Welter:** Z. Baisangurov (RUS). **Middle:** J. Machoncev (RUS). **L. Heavy:** I. Michalkin (RUS). **Heavy:** Y. Romanov (RUS). **S. Heavy:** D. Arshba (RUS).
Bronze medal: S. Smith (E), F. Gavin (E), J. O'Donnell (E), T. Jeffries (E).

Tallinn, Estonia - 2005
L. Fly: S. Vodopyanov (RUS). **Fly:** S. Mamodov (AZE). **Bantam:** A. Akhba (RUS). **Feather:** M. Ignatev (RUS). **Light:** I. Iksanov (RUS). **L. Welter:** A.Zamkovoy (RUS). **Welter:** M. Koptyakov (RUS). **Middle:** S. Skiarov (RUS). **L.Heavy:** D. Chudinov (RUS). **Heavy:** S. Kalchugin (RUS). **S. Heavy:** A.Volkov (RUS).
Bronze Medal: J. Joyce (IRL).

Note: The age limit for the championships were reduced from 21 to 19 in 1976.

Commonwealth Champions, 1930-2002

Hamilton, Canada - 1930
Fly: W. Smith (SAF). **Bantam:** H. Mizler (ENG). **Feather:** F. Meacham (ENG). **Light:** J. Rolland (SCO). **Welter:** L. Hall (SAF). **Middle:** F. Mallin (ENG). **L. Heavy:** J. Goyder (ENG). **Heavy:** V. Stuart (ENG).
Silver medals: T. Pardoe (ENG), T. Holt (SCO).
Bronze medals: A. Lyons (SCO), A. Love (ENG), F. Breeman (ENG).

Wembley, England - 1934
Fly: P. Palmer (ENG). **Bantam:** F. Ryan (ENG). **Feather:** C. Cattarall (SAF). **Light:** L. Cook (AUS). **Welter:** D. McCleave (ENG). **Middle:** A. Shawyer (ENG). **L. Heavy:** G. Brennan (ENG). **Heavy:** P. Floyd (ENG).
Silver medals: A. Barnes (WAL), J. Jones (WAL), F. Taylor (WAL), J. Holton (SCO).
Bronze medals: J. Pottinger (WAL), T. Wells (SCO), H. Moy (ENG), W. Duncan (NIR), J. Magill (NIR), Lord D. Douglas-Hamilton (SCO).

Melbourne, Australia - 1938
Fly: J. Joubert (SAF). **Bantam:** W. Butler (ENG). **Feather:** A. Henricus (CEY). **Light:** H. Groves (ENG). **Welter:** W. Smith (AUS). **Middle:** D. Reardon (WAL). **L. Heavy:** N. Wolmarans (SAF). **Heavy:** T. Osborne (CAN).
Silver medals: J. Watson (SCO), M. Dennis (ENG).
Bronze medals: H. Cameron (SCO), J. Wilby (ENG).

Auckland, New Zealand - 1950
Fly: H. Riley (ENG). **Bantam:** J. van Rensburg (SAF). **Feather:** H. Gilliland (SCO). **Light:** R. Latham (ENG). **Welter:** T. Ratcliffe (ENG). **Middle:** T. van Schalkwyk (SAF). **L. Heavy:** D. Scott (ENG). **Heavy:** F. Creagh (NZL).
Bronze medal: P. Brander (ENG).

Vancouver, Canada - 1954
Fly: R. Currie (SCO). **Bantam:** J. Smillie (SCO). **Feather:** L. Leisching (SAF). **Light:** P. van Staden (SR). **L. Welter:** M. Bergin (CAN). **Welter:** N. Gargano (ENG). **L. Middle:** W. Greaves (CAN). **Middle:** J. van de Kolff (SAF). **L. Heavy:** P. van Vuuren (SAF). **Heavy:** B. Harper (ENG).
Silver medals: M. Collins (WAL), F. McQuillan (SCO).
Bronze medals: D. Charnley (ENG), B. Wells (ENG).

Cardiff, Wales - 1958
Fly: J. Brown (SCO). **Bantam:** H. Winstone (WAL). **Feather:** W. Taylor (AUS). **Light:** R. McTaggart (SCO). **L. Welter:** H. Loubscher (SAF). **Welter:** J. Greyling (SAF). **L. Middle:** G. Webster (SAF). **Middle:** T. Milligan (NIR). **L. Heavy:** A. Madigan (AUS). **Heavy:** D. Bekker (SAF).
Silver medals: T. Bache (ENG), M. Collins (WAL), J. Jordan (NIR), R. Kane (SCO), S. Pearson (ENG), A. Higgins (WAL), D. Thomas (ENG).
Bronze medals: P. Lavery (NIR), D. Braithwaite (WAL), R. Hanna (NIR), A. Owen (SCO), J. McClory (NIR), J. Cooke (ENG), J. Jacobs (ENG), B. Nancurvis (ENG), R. Scott (SCO), W. Brown (WAL), J. Caiger (ENG), W. Bannon (SCO), R. Pleace (WAL).

Perth, Australia - 1962
Fly: R. Mallon (SCO). **Bantam:** J. Dynevor (AUS). **Feather:** J. McDermott (SCO). **Light:** E. Blay (GHA). **L. Welter:** C. Quartey (GHA). **Welter:** W. Coe (NZL). **L. Middle:** H. Mann (CAN). **Middle:** M. Calhoun (JAM). **L. Heavy:** A. Madigan (AUS). **Heavy:** G. Oywello (UGA).
Silver medals: R. McTaggart (SCO), J. Pritchett (ENG).
Bronze medals: M. Pye (ENG), P. Benneyworth (ENG), B. Whelan (ENG), B. Brazier (ENG), C. Rice (NIR), T. Menzies (SCO), H. Christie (NIR), A. Turmel (CI).

Kingston, Jamaica - 1966
Fly: S. Shittu (GHA). **Bantam:** E. Ndukwu (NIG). **Feather:** P. Waruinge (KEN). **Light:** A. Andeh (NIG). **L. Welter:** J. McCourt (NIR). **Welter:** E. Blay (GHA). **L. Middle:** M. Rowe (ENG). **Middle:** J. Darkey (GHA). **L. Heavy:** R. Tighe (ENG). **Heavy:** W. Kini (NZL).
Silver medals: P. Maguire (NIR), R. Thurston (ENG), R. Arthur (ENG), T. Imrie (SCO).
Bronze medals: S. Lockhart (NIR), A. Peace (SCO), F. Young (NIR), J. Turpin (ENG), D. McAlinden (NIR).

Edinburgh, Scotland - 1970
L. Fly: J. Odwori (UGA). **Fly:** D. Needham (ENG). **Bantam:** S. Shittu (GHA). **Feather:** P. Waruinge (KEN). **Light:** A. Adeyemi (NIG). **L. Welter:** M. Muruli (UGA). **Welter:** E. Ankudey (GHA). **L. Middle:** T. Imrie (SCO). **Middle:** J. Conteh (ENG). **L. Heavy:** F. Ayinla (NIG). **Heavy:** B. Masanda (UGA).
Silver medals: T. Davies (WAL), J. Gillan (SCO), D. Davies (WAL), J. McKinty (NIR).
Bronze medals: M. Abrams (ENG), A. McHugh (SCO), D. Larmour (NIR), S. Oglivie (SCO), A. Richardson (ENG), T. Joyce (SCO), P. Doherty (NIR), J. Rafferty (SCO), L. Stevens (ENG).

Christchurch, New Zealand - 1974
L. Fly: S. Muchoki (KEN). **Fly:** D. Larmour (NIR). **Bantam:** P. Cowdell (ENG). **Feather:** E. Ndukwu (NIG). **Light:** A. Kalule (UGA). **L. Welter:** O. Nwankpa (NIG). **Welter:** M. Muruli (UGA). **L. Middle:** L. Mwale (ZAM). **Middle:** F. Lucas (STV). **L. Heavy:** W. Knight (ENG). **Heavy:** N. Meade (ENG).
Silver medals: E. McKenzie (WAL), A. Harrison (SCO).
Bronze medals: J. Bambrick (SCO), J. Douglas (SCO), J. Rodgers (NIR), S. Cooney (SCO), R. Davies (ENG), C. Speare (ENG), G. Ferris (NIR).

Edmonton, Canada - 1978
L. Fly: S. Muchoki (KEN). **Fly:** M. Irungu (KEN). **Bantam:** B. McGuigan (NIR). **Feather:** A. Nelson (GHA). **Light:** G. Hamill (NIR). **L. Welter:** W. Braithwaite (GUY). **Welter:** M. McCallum (JAM). **L. Middle:** K. Perlette (CAN). **Middle:** P. McElwaine (AUS). **L. Heavy:** R. Fortin (CAN). **Heavy:** J. Awome (ENG).
Silver medals: J. Douglas (SCO), K. Beattie (NIR), D. Parkes (ENG), V. Smith (ENG).
Bronze medals: H. Russell (NIR), M. O'Brien (ENG), J. McAllister (SCO), T. Feal (WAL).

Brisbane, Australia - 1982
L. Fly: A. Wachire (KEN). **Fly:** M. Mutua (KEN). **Bantam:** J. Orewa (NIG). **Feather:** P. Konyegwachie (NIG). **Light:** H. Khalili (KEN). **L. Welter:** C. Ossai (NIG). **Welter:** C. Pyatt (ENG). **L. Middle:** S. O'Sullivan (CAN). **Middle:** J. Price (ENG). **L. Heavy:** F. Sani (FIJ). **Heavy:** W. de Wit (CAN).
Silver medals: J. Lyon (ENG), J. Kelly (SCO), R. Webb (NIR), P. Hanlon (ENG), J. McDonnell (ENG), N. Croombes (ENG), H. Hylton (ENG).
Bronze medals: R. Gilbody (ENG), C. McIntosh (ENG), R. Corr (NIR).

Edinburgh, Scotland - 1986
L. Fly: S. Olson (CAN). **Fly:** J. Lyon (ENG). **Bantam:** S. Murphy (ENG). **Feather:** B. Downey (CAN). **Light:** A. Dar (ENG). **L. Welter:** H. Grant (CAN). **Welter:** D. Dyer (ENG). **L. Middle:** D. Sherry (CAN). **Middle:** R. Douglas (ENG). **L. Heavy:** J. Moran (ENG). **Heavy:** J. Peau (NZL). **S. Heavy:** L. Lewis (CAN).
Silver medals: M. Epton (ENG), R. Nash (NIR), P. English (ENG), N. Haddock (WAL), J. McAlister (SCO), H. Lawson (SCO), D. Young (SCO), A. Evans (WAL).
Bronze medals: W. Docherty (SCO), J. Todd (NIR), K. Webber (WAL), G. Brooks (SCO), J. Wallace (SCO), C. Carleton (NIR), J. Jacobs (ENG), B. Lowe (NIR), D. Denny (NIR), G. Thomas (WAL), A. Mullen (SCO), G. Ferrie (SCO), P. Tinney (NIR), B. Pullen (WAL), E. Cardouza (ENG), J. Oyebola (ENG), J. Sillitoe (CI).

Auckland, New Zealand - 1990
L. Fly: J. Juuko (UGA). **Fly:** W. McCullough (NIR). **Bantam:** S. Mohammed (NIG). **Feather:** J. Irwin (ENG). **Light:** G. Nyakana (UGA). **L. Welter:** C. Kane (SCO). **Welter:** D. Defiagbon (NIG). **L. Middle:** R. Woodhall (ENG). **Middle:** C. Johnson (CAN). **L. Heavy:** J. Akhasamba (KEN). **Heavy:** G. Onyango (KEN). **S. Heavy:** M. Kenny (NZL).
Bronze medals: D. Anderson (SCO), M. Edwards (ENG), P. Douglas (NIR).

Victoria, Canada - 1994
L. Fly: H. Ramadhani (KEN). **Fly:** P. Shepherd (SCO). **Bantam:** R. Peden (AUS). **Feather:** C. Patton (CAN). **Light:** M. Strange (CAN). **L. Welter:** P. Richardson (ENG). **Welter:** N. Sinclair (NIR). **L. Middle:** J. Webb (NIR). **Middle:** R. Donaldson (CAN). **L. Heavy:** D. Brown (CAN). **Heavy:** O. Ahmed (KEN). **S. Heavy:** D. Dokiwari (NIG).
Silver medals: S. Oliver (ENG), J. Cook (WAL), M. Renaghan (NIR), M. Winters (NIR), J. Wilson (SCO).
Bronze medals: D. Costello (ENG), J. Townsley (SCO), D. Williams (ENG).

Kuala Lumpar, Malaysia - 1998
L. Fly: S. Biki (MAS). **Fly:** R. Sunee (MRI). **Bantam:** M. Yomba (TAN). **Feather:** A. Arthur (SCO). **Light:** R. Narh (GHA). **L. Welter:** M. Strange (CAN). **Welter:** J. Molitor (CAN). **L. Middle:** C. Bessey (ENG). **Middle:** J. Pearce (ENG). **L. Heavy:** C. Fry (ENG). **Heavy:** M. Simmons (CAN). **S. Heavy:** A. Harrison (ENG).
Silver medal: L. Cunningham (NIR).
Bronze medals: G. Jones (ENG), A. McLean (ENG), C. McNeil (SCO), J. Townsley (SCO), B. Magee (NIR), K. Evans (WAL).

Manchester, England - 2002
L. Fly: M. Ali Qamar (IND). **Fly:** K. Kanyanta (ZAM). **Bantam:** J. Kane (AUS). **Feather:** M. Ali (PAK). **Light:** J. Arthur (WAL). **L. Welter:** D. Barker (ENG). **Welter:** D. Geale (AUS). **L. Middle:** J. Pascal (CAN). **Middle:** P. Miller (AUS). **L. Heavy:** J. Albert (NIG). **Heavy:** J. Douglas (CAN). **S. Heavy:** D. Dolan (ENG).
Silver medals: D. Langley (ENG), P. Smith (ENG), S. Birch (ENG).
Bronze medals: M. Moran (ENG), A. Morris (ENG), C. McEwan (SCO), A. Young (WAL), K. Evans (WAL).

The Triple Hitters' Boxing Quiz: Part 10

Compiled by Ralph Oates

QUESTIONS

1. On 23 February 1939, Eric Boon made a first successful defence of his British lightweight title when he stopped challenger Arthur Danahar. In which round did the stoppage occur?
   A. 13.   B. 14.   C. 15.

2. The future world flyweight champion, Terry Allen, knocked out Ahmed Marli in the opening round on 8 July 1944. In which country did this contest take place?
   A. France.   B. England.   C. Egypt.

3. On 3 June 1947, Mark Hart lost a six-round points decision to which future world middleweight champion?
   A. Randolph Turpin.   B. Carl (Bobo) Olson.
   C. Jake LaMotta.

4. How many times did Arthur Donovan referee a Joe Louis world heavyweight title contest?
   A. Ten.   B. 11.   C. 12.

5. How many professional contests did the former Scottish heavyweight champion, Ken Shaw, have?
   A. 37.   B. 38.   C. 39.

6. Gordon Hazell failed to capture the vacant British and Empire middleweight titles on 14 September 1954 when he was knocked out by Johnny Sullivan. In which round did the kayo occur?
   A. One.   B. Two.   C. Three.

7. On 27 May 1957, Joe Bygraves made a defence of his Empire heavyweight title against Dick Richardson. What was the result?
   A. 15-round points win for Bygraves.
   B. Points win for Richardson.   C. A draw.

8. On 17 July 1959, Dave Coventry outpointed Tommy Saint. How many rounds were contested?
   A. Four.   B. Six.   C. Eight.

9. In which country did the Coventry v Saint contest take place?
   A. England.   B. Canada.   C. America.

10. Howard Winstone stopped Sergio Milan in round six on 15 August 1960. At this stage of his career, Winstone was undefeated in how many professional contests?
    A. 19.   B. 20.   C. 21.

11. On 7 September 1960, future world heavyweight champion, Sonny Liston, outpointed Eddie Machen. How many rounds were contested?
    A. Eight.   B. Ten.   C. 12.

12. Future world middleweight champion, Carlos Monzon, met Felipe Cambeiro in a contest scheduled for eight rounds on 28 June 1964. What was the result?
    A. Points win for Monzon.
    B. Points win for Cambeiro.   C. A draw.

13. Over how many rounds did Harry Scott outpoint Rubin Carter on 20 April 1965?
    A. Eight.   B. Ten.   C. 12.

14. Which future world lightweight champion outpointed Frankie Taylor over ten rounds on 6 July 1965?
    A. Carlos Teo Cruz.   B. Rodolfo Gonzalez.
    C. Ken Buchanan.

15. In which year was Chris Finnegan, the former British, European and Commonwealth light-heavyweight champion, born?
    A. 1942.   B. 1943.   C. 1944.

16. Johnny Pritchett retained his British middleweight title against Wally Swift with a 15-round points decision on the 20th February 1967. At this stage of his career Pritchett was undefeated in how many professional contests?
    A. 23.   B. 24.   C. 25.

17. During his career, which opponent did heavyweight Billy Walker not meet in the professional ranks?
    A. Bowie Adams.   B. Ron Harman.   C. Peter Bates.

18. On 24 May 1968, Bob Foster won the world light-heavyweight title when he knocked out the holder,

Dick Tiger, in round four. Who was the referee for this contest?
A. Mark Conn.   B. Bill Connelly.   C. John LoBianco.

19. What was the nationality of the former world flyweight champion, Efren Torres?
A. American.   B. Mexican.   C. Canadian.

20. How tall was the former WBA world featherweight champion, Raul Rojas?
A. 5'2".   B. 5'3".   C. 5'4".

21. Sidney Walker was the real name of which former world lightweight champion?
A. Beau Jack.   B. Sammy Angott.   C. Ike Williams.

22. On 23 February 1970, Ken Buchanan outpointed Leonard Taverez. How many rounds were contested?
A. Eight.   B. Ten.   C. 12.

23. Jim Watt stopped Noel McIvor in three rounds on 11 December 1972. At this stage of his career, Watt had taken part in how many professional contests?
A. 15.   B. 16.   C. 17.

24. In which round did Phil Matthews stop Tom Bethea on 10 July 1972?
A. One.   B. Two.   C. Three.

25. Which opponent did the former British, European and Commonwealth bantamweight champion, Alan Rudkin, not meet in the professional ranks?
A. Gerry Jones.   B. Dai Corp.   C. Danny Wells.

26. On 7 May 1977, Maurice Hope retained his European light-middleweight title when he outpointed Frank Wissenbach over 15 rounds. In which country did this contest take place?
A. England.   B. France.   C. Germany.

27. Tony Sibson won the vacant Commonwealth middleweight title on 4 March 1980, when he outpointed Chisanda Mutti over 15 rounds. Who held the championship prior to Sibson?
A. Al Korovou.   B. Monty Betham.   C. Ayub Kalule.

28. On 9 July 1983, future WBA world featherweight champion, Barry McGuigan, knocked out Lavon McGowan in round one. In which part of America did this contest take place?
A. Chicago.   B. Las Vegas.   C. Dallas.

29. In which weight division was Roy Smith a British champion?
A. Middleweight.   B. Light-heavyweight.
C. Cruiserweight.

30. On 20 February 1988, Dennis Andries met Jamie Howe over ten rounds in Detroit. What was the result of this contest?
A. Points win for Howe.   B. A draw.
C. Points win for Andries.

31. Robbie Regan won the vacant Welsh flyweight title on 12 February 1991 when he defeated Kevin Jenkins. By which method?
A. Four-round stoppage.   B. Eight-round knockout.
C. Ten-round points decision.

32. On 22 May 1991, Nicky Piper knocked out Martin Lopez in the first round. At this stage of his professional career, Piper had won how many of his bouts in the opening round?
A. Four.   B. Five.   C. Six.

33. Howard Eastman stopped Paul Wesley in the opening round on 31 January 1996. At this stage of his career, Eastman was undefeated in how many professional bouts?
A. Eight.   B. Nine.   C. Ten.

34. During 1999, Ricky Hatton took part in six bouts. How many of them did he win inside the scheduled distance?
A. Four.   B. Five.   C. Six.

35. In his professional debut on 16 March 2002, in which round did Carl Froch stop Michael Pinnock?
A. Three.   B. Four.   C. Six.

36. On 8 February 2003, Nicky Cook captured the vacant Commonwealth featherweight title when he stopped Mishek Kondwani in round 12. Prior to Cook, who was the last British holder of this championship?
A. Patrick Mullings.   B. Paul Ingle.
C. Scott Harrison.

37. Esham Pickering won the vacant Commonwealth super-bantamweight title on 8 February 2003 when he knocked out Duncan Karanja in round five. Who was the referee for this contest?
A. Paul Thomas.   B. Dave Parris.   C. Mickey Vann.

38. On 4 March 2003, David Haye stopped Roger Bowden in round two. In which country did this contest take place?
A. America.   B. France.   C. England.

39. On 12 April 2003, Craig Docherty won the Commonwealth super-featherweight title when he knocked out the holder, Dean Pithie, in round eight. Who was the referee for this contest?
A. Mark Green.   B. Richie Davies.
C. Mickey Vann.

40. Damon Hague won the WBF middleweight title on 16 April 2003, when he stopped the holder, Wayne Pinder. In which round did the stoppage occur?
A. One.   B. Two.   C. Three.

41. James Toney won the IBF cruiserweight title on 26 April 2003, when he defeated the holder, Vassily Jirov. By which method?
A. Five-round stoppage.   B. Six-round knockout.
C. 12-round points decision.

42. On 15 June 2003, Brian Coleman lost a six-round points decision to Lee McAllister. At this stage of his career how many professional bouts had Coleman taken part in?
A. 143.   B. 144.   C. 145.

43. Who is the boxing commentator for Eurosport?
A. Steve Holdsworth.   B. Steve Bunce.   C. Jim Neilly.

44. Which following boxer is nicknamed 'The Cobra'?
A. Joe Calzaghe.   B. Carl Froch.   C. Robin Reid.

45. Audley Harrison retained his WBF heavyweight crown on 8 May 2004, when he defeated the former British and Commonwealth title holder, Julius Francis. By which method?
A. Four-round stoppage.   B. Eight-round knockout.
C. 12-round points decision.

46. On 8 May 2004, Colin Lynes won the IBO light-welterweight title when he outpointed the holder, Pablo Sarmiento, over 12 rounds. Who was the referee for this contest?
A. Terry O'Connor.   B. Ian John-Lewis.
C. Mark Green.

47. How many contests did the former British and Commonwealth heavyweight champion, Scott Welch, have during his professional career?
A. 25.   B. 26.   C. 27.

48. On 5 June 2004, Felix Sturm lost his WBO middleweight title when he was defeated by Oscar de la Hoya, being outpointed over 12 rounds. In which part of America did this contest take place?
A. New York.   B. Las Vegas.   C. Tucson.

49. Danny Williams knocked out the former world heavyweight champion, Mike Tyson, in round four in Louisville, Kentucky on 30 July 2004. Prior to this contest, how many times had Williams boxed in America in professional bouts?
A. Once.   B. Twice.   C. Three.

50. In the 2004 Olympic Games, which were held in Athens, Amir Khan won a silver medal for Britain. In which division?
A. Lightweight.   B. Light-welterweight.
C. Welterweight.

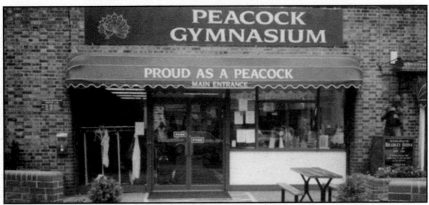

Directory of Ex-Boxers' Associations

by Ron Olver

BOURNEMOUTH Founded 1980. HQ: Fiveways Hotel, Charminster Road, Bournemouth. Dai Dower (P); Percy Singer (T); Dave Fry (VC); Peter Fay (C); Jack Streek (S), 38 St Leonard's Farm, Ringwood Road, Ferndown, Dorset BH22 0AG.

CORK Founded 1973. HQ: Glen Boxing Club, Blackpool, Cork. William O'Leary (P & C); John Martin (S); Phil Murray (VC); John Donovan (T).

CORNWALL Founded 1989. HQ: Fitzsimmons Arms, Coinage Hall Street, Helston. Salvo Nucciforo (C); Eric Bradshaw (S); Stan Cullis (P & PRO), Upper Tolcarne House, Burras Wendron, Nr. Helston TR13 0JD.

CROYDON Founded 1982. HQ: Ivy House Club, Campbell Road, West Croydon. Derek O'Dell (C); Barry Penny (VC); Gilbert Allnutt (P); Paul Nihill MBE (S), 24 Walderslade Road, Chatham, Kent ME4 6NZ.

EASTERN AREA Founded 1973. HQ: Coach & Horses, Union Street, Norwich. Brian Fitzmaurice (P); Ron Springall (S & T); Clive Campling (C), 54 Robson Road, Norwich NR5 8NZ.

HOME COUNTIES Founded 2005. HQ: Golden Lion Public House, London Colney, Herts. Terry Downes (P); Bob Williams (C); Andy Smith (T); Dave Ayles (S), 144 Trident Drive, Houghton Regis, Dunstable LU5 5QQ.

HULL & EAST YORKSHIRE Founded 1996. HQ: Tigers Lair, Anlaby Road, Hull. Don Harrison (C); Geoff Rymer (PRO & S); Bert Smith (T), 54 St Aidan Road, Bridlington, E. Yorks.

IPSWICH Founded 1970. HQ: Loco Club, Ipswich. Alby Kingham (P); Vic Thurlow (C & T); Michael Thurlow (S), 147 Clapgate Lane, Ipswich IP3 0RF.

IRISH Founded 1973. HQ: National Boxing Stadium, South Circular Road, Dublin. Val Harris (P); Martin Gannon (C); Tommy Butler (T); Paddy O'Reilly (VC); Willie Duggan (S), 175 Kimmage Road West, Dublin 6W.

KENT Founded 1997. HQ: RAFA Club, Dock Road, Chatham. Mick Smith (P); Harry Doherty (C); Paul Nihill, MBE (S & T), 24 Walderslade Road, Chatham, Kent ME4 6NZ.

LEEDS Founded 1952. HQ: North Leeds WMC, Lincoln Green, Leeds 9. Alan Richardson (P); Kevin Cunningham (C & S); Alan Alster (T); Frank Johnson (PRO), 82 Windmill Chase, Rothwell, Leeds 26 0XB

LEICESTER Founded 1972. HQ: The Jungle Club, Checketts Road, Leicester. Mick Greaves (P & C); Fred Roberts (T), Alan Parr (S) 22 Hewes Close, Glen Parva, Leicester LE2 9NU.

LONDON Founded 1971. HQ; The Queen Mary College, Bancroft Road, Mile End, London E1. Stephen Powell (P); Micky O'Sullivan (C); Charlie Wright (VC); Ron Olver (PRO); Ray Caulfield (T); Mrs Mary Powell (S), 36 St Peters Street, Islington, London N1 8JT.

MANCHESTER Founded 1968. HQ: Hat & Feathers Pub, Ancoats, Manchester. Tommy Proffitt (LP); Jack Edwards (P); Neville Tetlow (T); Jimmy Lewis (C); Eddie Copeland (S), 9 Lakeside, Hadfield, Glossop, Derby SK13 1HW.

Tommy Proffitt, a former Olympic representative and leading professional boxer, he is now the Life President of the Manchester EBA   Harry Goodwin

MERSEYSIDE (Liverpool) Founded 1973. HQ: Arriva Club, Hockenhall Alley, Liverpool. Harry Scott (P); Terry Carson (C); Jim Boyd (VC); Jim Jenkinson (S & T), 13 Brooklands Avenue, Waterloo, Liverpool L22 3XY.

MIDLANDS EBA Founded 2002. HQ: The Portland Pavilions, Portland Road, Edgbaston, Birmingham. Martin Florey (C); Paul Rowson (VC); Richard Vaughan (T); Jerry Hjelter (S), 67 Abberley Avenue, Stourport on Severn, Worcs DY13 0LY.

NORTHAMPTON DISTRICT Founded 2001. HQ: Northampton Boys Club, Towcester Road, Northampton. Jeff Tite (P); Keith Hall (C); Sid Green (S & T), 8 Friars Close, Delapre, Northampton NN4 8PU.

NORTHAMPTONSHIRE Founded 1981. HQ: Semilong Working Mens Club, St Andrews Road, Northampton. Dick Rogers (P); Gil Wilson (C); George Ward (VC); Peter Cripps (T); Mrs Pam Ward (S), 6 Derwent Close, Kings Heath, Northampton.

NORTHERN FEDERATION Founded 1974. Several member EBAs. Annual Gala. Terry Carson (C); Eddie Copeland (S & T), 9 Lakeside, Hadfield, Glossop, Derbyshire SK13 1HW.

NORTHERN IRELAND Founded 1970. HQ: Ulster Sports Club, High Street, Belfast. Gerry Hassett (P); Cecil Martin (C); S.Thompson (T); Terry Milligan (S), 32 Rockdale Street, Belfast BT12 7PA.

NORTH STAFFS & SOUTH CHESHIRE Founded 1969. HQ: The Saggar Makers Bottom Knocker, Market Place, Burslem, Stoke on Trent. Roy Simms (C); Larry Parkes (VC); Les Dean (S); John Greatbach (T); Billy Tudor (P & PRO), 133 Springbank Road, Chell Heath, Stoke on Trent, Staffs ST6 6HW.

NORWICH Founded 1990. HQ: West End Retreat, Brown Street, Norwich. Les King (P); John Pipe (C); Len Jarvis (T); Albert Howe (S), 15 Grange Close, Hoveton, Norwich NR2 8EA.

NOTTINGHAM Founded 1979. HQ: The Wheatsheaf, Sneinton Road, Nottingham. Len Chorley (P); Walter Spencer (C); Martin Thomas (VC); Gary Rooksby (T); John Kinsella (PRO); Graham Rooksby (S), 42 Spinney Road, Keyworth, Notts NG12 5LN.

PLYMOUTH Founded 1982. HQ: Stoke Social Club, Devonport Road, Plymouth. Tom Pryce-Davies (P); Tony Penprase (VC); Arthur Willis (T); Jimmy Ryan (C); Doug Halliday (S), Dee-Jays, Finny Gook Lane, Port Wrinkle, Torpoint, Cornwall PL11 3BP.

PRESTON Founded 1973. HQ: Barney's Piano Bar, Church Street, Preston. John Allen (C & S); Eddie Monahan (P); Bobby Rhodes (T), 1 Norris Street, Preston PR1 7PX.

ST HELENS Founded 1983. HQ: Royal Naval Association, Volunteer Street, St Helens. Ray Britch (C); Tommy McNamara (T); Paul Britch (S), 16 Oxley Street, Sutton, St Helens WA9 3PE

SCOTTISH Founded 1997. HQ: Iron Horse Public House, Nile Street, Glasgow. John McCluskey (P); Al Hutcheon (C); Frank O'Donnell (LP); Peter Baines (T); Liam McColgan (S), 25 Dalton Avenue, Linnvale, Clydebank G81 2SH.

SHEFFIELD Founded 1974. Reformed 2002. HQ: The Richmond Public House, Richmond Road, Sheffield. Billy Calvert (P & T); Harry Carnell (C); John Redfern (S & PRO), 33 Birch Avenue, Chapeltown, Sheffield S35 1RQ.

SQUARE RING (TORQUAY) Founded 1978. HQ: Snooty Fox Hotel, St Marychurch. George Pook (P); Ken Wittey (C); Johnny Mudge (S); Jim Banks (T); Paul King (VC), 8 Winchester Avenue, Torquay TQ2 8AR.

SUNDERLAND Founded 1959. HQ: River Wear Social Club, Sunderland. George Martin (P); Terry Lynn (C); Les Simm (T & S), 21 Orchard Street, Pallion, Sunderland SR4 6QL.

SUSSEX Founded 1974. Reformed 2003. HQ: The Conservative Club, Hove. Tommy Mellis (P); John McNeil (C); Ian Hargie (T); Ernie Price (PRO & S), 132 Amberley Drive, Hove, Sussex BN3 8JQ.

SWANSEA & SOUTH WEST WALES Founded 1983. HQ: The Conservative Club, Swansea. Cliff Curvis (P); Gordon Pape (C); Len Smith (S), 105 Cockett Road, Swansea SA2 0FG.

TYNESIDE Founded 1970. HQ: Pelaw Social Club, Heworth. Maxie Walsh (C); Harry Greenwood (VC); Malcolm Dinning (T); Alan Gordon (S), 16 Dove Court, Birtley, Chester le Street, Durham PH3 1HB.

WELSH Founded 1976. HQ: Rhydyfelin Labour Club, Pontypridd. Wynford Jones (P); Mark Warner (T); Peter Rogers (VC); John Floyd (C); Don James (S), 28 Woodfield Road, Talbot Green, Pontyclun, Mid-Glamorgan. Patron - Lord Brooks.

WIRRAL Founded 1973. Reformed 2003. HQ: RNA Club, Park Road East, Birkenhead. Frank Johnson (P); Alan Crowther (S); Pat Garry (T); Terry Carson (C), 14 Spruce Close, Birkenhead, Merseyside CH42 0PG.

The above information is set at the time of going to press and no responsibility can be taken for any changes in officers or addresses of HQs that may happen between then and publication or changes that have not been notified to me.

ABBREVIATIONS

P - President. HP - Honorary President. LP - Life President. AP - Acting President. C - Chairman. VC - Vice Chairman. T - Treasurer. S - Secretary. PRO - Public Relations Officer and/or Press Officer.

Ron Olver, the man behind the EBAs   Pat Olver

Obituaries

by Derek O'Dell

It is impossible to list everyone, but I have again done my best to include final tributes for as many of the well-known boxers and other familiar names within the sport who have passed away since the 2005 Yearbook was published. We honour them and remember them.

APONTE Jose *From* Ponce, Puerto Rico. *Died* July 2005, aged 33. An American-based Puerto Rican, Jose was a highly-regarded welterweight who'd fought Tracy Harris Patterson, Paul Spadafora, Teddy Reid and Muhammed Abdullaev. In 47 fights, he won 18, drew three and lost 26, having unsuccessfully contested the Puerto Rican, lightweight titles. The cause of death has not been reported.

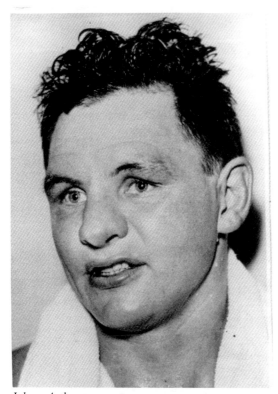

Johnny Arthur

ARTHUR Johnny *From* Springs, South Africa. *Died* 19 May 2005, aged 75. South African born Johnny Duncan Arthur, of Scottish descent, was a bronze medal winner at the 1948 Olympics, which were held in London and he returned here as a professional in 1952 to beat George Nuttall and Frank Bell, before finding Johnny Williams too slick when he got a shot at the Empire heavyweight title in 1952, Williams stopping him on cuts. Later on he was to lose to Don Cockell in another bid for the same title, while early in his career, he'd beaten the former marine from Deal, Reg Andrews. At home he was never beaten by a

fellow South African, but a later incursion to Canada and America brought mixed success. Although he had an excellent win over Bob Dunlap, then stopped the New Jersey fighter, Jimmy Walls, in three rounds, and outpointed Eddie Cameron, he lost every round to Willie Pastrano before being outpointed by James J. Parker and George Chuvalo. He returned home to defend his South African title against Dries Nieman then stopped Buddy Walker before retiring to become a farmer and businessman in Transvaal. Some record books credit him with a win over Canada's Earl Walls, but it was New Jersey fighter, *Jimmy* Walls, who came out of the opposite corner.

BASSETT Ivor *From* Treorchy. *Died* April 2005, aged 66. It was the Welsh Area Council Secretary, Dai Corp, who reported the death of the referee, Ivor Bassett. Ivor was an 'A' Class official for many years and handed in his licence in 2003 when the compulsory retirement age had been reached.

Peter Bates

BATES Peter *From* Shirebrook. *Died* 17 December 2004, aged 71. Peter had the distinction of being the only British-born heavyweight to beat Henry Cooper inside the distance when a bad cut over the eye forced the referee to call a halt after five rounds. That was in 1956 when he'd already beaten Henry's brother Jim in two rounds. Peter had a see-saw career and it was the same Jim Cooper who outpointed him in 1962 right at the tail end of his nine-year career. There are some top names on his account: Joe Bygraves, Joe Erskine, Dick Richardson, Gerhard Hecht, Heinz Neuhaus, Brian London, Gawie de Klerk, Johnny Prescott, Ansell Adams and Ingemar Johansson, who broke Peter's jaw and put him out of action for four months. Ron Olver put his finger on it when he stated in the trade paper that Peter was unfortunate to be around at a time when the heavyweight division was so strong, yet he acquitted himself well in 51 fights, of which he won 33, drew four, and lost 14.

BENGTSSON Olle *From* Gothenburg, Sweden. *Died* July 2005, aged 81. Olle is remembered here as being Randolph Turpin's first opponent after his loss to Carl 'Bobo' Olsen. The Swede was an unknown force and was not expected to test Turpin, but the fight went the limit and Olle gave a surprisingly good account of himself. Had we studied Bengtsson's record carefully, we would not have made Turpin such an odds-on favourite. For a start he was undefeated and the names of Ray Cattouse, Baby Day, Don Mogard and Gilbert Stock on his record should have told us that he was no pushover. Turpin, was on the slide, but his descent had not gained momentum and although he still retained semblances of man who once shook the boxing world, he was having difficulty in getting down to the middleweight limit. Possibly, the defeat deflated Bengtsson, who remained inactive for nearly a year before coming back with an impressive knockout win over Abe Quartey. He closed the year with a points win over Alex Buxton, who'd just competed unsuccessfully for the British light-heavyweight title. Then came his most impressive win – a stoppage of Chris Christensen in seven rounds – and with it the Scandinavian middleweight title. He followed this with three fights against British opposition, points wins over Paddy Delargy and the very capable fighter from Bedworth, Les Allen, and a points loss to Cardiff's Phil Edwards. This was the last fight that I can trace for him and just two defeats in a ten-year career (both on points) puts Bengtsson among the elite of post-war Scandinavian boxers.

BEVAN Phil *From* Poplar. *Died* 26 August 2004, aged 89. Again it was Harold Alderman who informed me that the old Poplar lightweight had died. He also provided Phil's date of birth so that I could assess his age. Born on 19 January 1915 he was five months short of his 90th milestone – a real old timer with a real old timer's record of 165 contests. (Harold has 168, but I suspect that there are more to be found). In 1934 he racked up 42 fights, but apart from his final year of fighting he was always just as active. It's odd that he never really got the credit due to him and once retired he seemed to have been forgotten. A list of a few he beat will bring home how different things were in his day as he fought in good company but never came near a title shot. He beat Patsy Mack four times, Nick Lucas and

Arthur Harvey three times each, Jackie Flynn and Charlie Thomas twice each and Arthur Norton, Jimmy Anderson (senior, of course), Mick Carney, George Pull, Charlie Jordan (Kingston), Goff Williams, Seaman Harry Reynolds, Bob Lamb, 'Tiger' Bert Ison, Jackie Stayton, Con Flynn, Ginger Roberts, Joe Rubery and Freddie Carr. Also there were 23 drawn bouts and 27 losses to class opposition like George Odwell, Jimmy Vaughan, Dave Finn, Len Lemaux and Mike Sullivan.

BIRA Hendrick *From* Indonesia. *Died* 3 March 2005, aged 22. The Indonesian strawweight died in Djakarta from injuries received in his losing fight with Mones Arepas. He was rushed to hospital after being stopped in the third round and died soon after.

BLOOMFIELD Johnny *From* Feltham. *Died* 17 September 2004, aged 57. A heart attack claimed the life of this popular trainer. Dozens of boxers had been under his wing since he took out a trainer's licence in the early 1970s, having been a former holder of the London ABA heavyweight title back in his days as a simon-pure. In partnership with Harry Holland he helped put on some memorable small-hall fights and combined this with the training of some of the men he promoted. In more recent years, he took Michael Sprott from the prelim ranks up to the aquisition of the British heavyweight championship and was instrumental in advancing the careers of boxers in the Jim Evans' stable. Johnny's successes go right back to the days of the former EBU super-middleweight title holder, James Cook.

BONAS Jock *From* Edinburgh. *Died* September 2004, aged 78. Jock received enduring fame in 1949 when Nat Fleischer, for some reason known to just him, rated Jock the number seven featherweight in the world. He wasn't world-class of course, but neither was he a mug and he deserved his hour in the sun. He started boxing in 1943 and got his career off to a flying start with 18 straight wins, before Tommy Smith of Birmingham inflicted the first defeat on his record. That was in 1945 and it was not to be one of his best years until late in December when Jock scored what in retrospect was his best ever victory by outpointing Peter Fallon. Fallon was class and he reversed the decision during the following year, but Jock established his status as a British title contender. He stopped Freddie Cotton and drew with Jackie Turpin, after trimming the useful Dave Sharkey and Jamaica's Black Bond. His best wins were against Ben Duffy, Kid Tanner, Peter Guichan, Danny Nagle, Teddy Peckham, Bernard Pugh, Dai Davies and Tommy Proffitt. Jock bit off more than he could chew when facing Cliff Anderson, who knocked him out in four rounds, and Frank Johnson forced him to retire in seven rounds back in 1950. However, he performed creditably to force Billy 'Spider' Kelly the full course in Belfast, although his career was in its final stages. There was a happy ending and a story worthy of a best-selling novel. Having emigrated to Australia, he kept his boxing achievements quiet before offering to fight the highly considered Bluey Wilkins. The Aussies had never heard of Bonas and Jock was able to back himself to win at long odds. After raising every penny to back himself, he romped home on points and his winnings gave him enough money to return home to Scotland to open a newsagents shop in Edinburgh, which gave him a comfortable living up to his retirement. As a boy, the boxing journalist, Brian Donald, once delivered papers to Jock and they became very fond of each other.

Jock Bonas

BROWN Barry *From* Dannerkville, New Zealand. *Died* December 2004, aged 73. A former Empire welterweight champion, Barry did his fighting away from the mainstream of fistic activity and, as a result, little has been heard of him since he hung up his gloves. He was a good champion, and a smart boxer, and had he been based in Europe his place in boxing history would have been firmly established. He won the New Zealand welterweight title in his third fight and within four months had the scalps of Al Wilburn and Ivor 'Kid' Germain on his record. After he beat Gerald Dreyer for the Empire diadem, he then stepped up into the high echelons of boxing too fast, too soon. World-beater Freddie Dawson stopped him in six rounds and George Barnes relieved him of his Empire title soon after. He then took a year off and then ran up ten straight victories, with only one of his foes lasting the distance. Barry beat Pran Mikus in Wellington and took the New Zealand middleweight title from Charlie Beaton, while Tuna Scanlan failed to get to the fifth round and Clive French was stopped in the eighth. Transplanted English fighter, Jimmy Newman, then fighting at the top of his form, outpointed him and a following loss to Don Barnes convinced the Kiwi that it was time to retire.

CANTOR Solly *From* Toronto, Canada. *Died* 28 January 2005 in London, aged 76. Solly came to Britain from Canada in 1948 as a good eight-round fighter and was pitched in with our lightweight champion, Billy Thompson. His meritorious points win was a warning that he had great talent and would be difficult to beat. At 19, and a clever boxer with what is known in the trade as 'an educated left hand', Solly seemed to have a bright future. He campaigned here from 1948 to 1950, returned home in 1951, then settled in London and fought until 1955. After he'd outpointed another of our lightweight champs in Frank Johnson, Solly retired. He was 27 and had never been counted out in his nine-year career, in which no British boxer was able to beat him. Apart from Thompson and Johnson, Solly bested Tommy McGovern, Peter Fallon, Bert Hornby, Emmett Kenny, Terry Ratcliffe, Jackie Marshall, Reg Quinlan and Tommy Bailey. He also scored a brilliant win over Elis Ask at Harringay Arena and forced Kid Dussart to a draw. No wonder he was so popular here, where he settled, married and then became a trainer. Solly crossed gloves with Armand Savoie three times, but won just the first encounter. In a return match for the vacant Canadian lightweight title, he was considered to be very unfortunate not to be returned the winner, but Savoie won the rubber match and retained his title. Solly boxed in Canada and California for another year and then began his next campaign in Britain. His early career was held in eastern USA and, although there are 36 entries on his record, a few are missing. Solly's early exploits are badly chronicled, but what emerges is that he was a very capable boxer. He never had a bad word for anyone and was a very religious man. In later years he was a member of both the London and Croydon EBAs and courageously attended meetings throughout his fight against motor-neurone disease that eventually claimed him soon after 2005 got under way.

Solly Cantor

CHANEY Colion *From* Indianapolis. *Died* May 2005, aged 81. One of the many good journeyman heavyweights clogging up the division after the war, Colion fought from

1943 to 1953. In his prime, he faced many fighters who were later destined to make an impact on the world ratings. He didn't beat many of them, but usually gave such a good account of himself that, in the years up to 1946, he was always busy. On the downhill slope, fights came infrequently and in his last six fighting years he notched up only 16. He was never a pushover and ten of those fights were on the credit side of his ledger. His best wins were over Al Hoosman, Lee Oma, Abel Cestac, Henry Flake and Buddy Knox, and it usually took a good'un to beat him. Lee 'Q' Murray, Archie Moore, Jimmy Bivins, Elmer Ray, Lem Franklin, Gene Jones and Lou Nova were all too good for him, but they knew they'd been in a fight. In retirement he became a respected boxing trainer and took Marvin Johnson from his teenage years to become a three-time holder of the world light-heavyweight championship.

CHARLTON Billy *From* Newcastle. *Died* August 2005, aged 90. A world-class featherweight, Billy died in a nursing home after a long illness. He was a talented boxer and very popular in Tyneside rings when the north of England was teeming with class fighters. Billy loved his boxing and during the times he met me, either in the Gateshead area or on one of his annual trips south with the Tyneside EBA, he would regale me with yarns of his fights with Freddie Miller, Harry Edwards and Johnny King. Enthusiastic as he was, his interest flagged when he lost his third fight with Miller, who not long previouisly held the world title. Miller had successfully defended here against Nel Tarleton, which indicated the class of men with whom Billy crossed gloves. The verdict in Miller's favour was a bad one and Billy had put his heart and soul into preparing for the fight. He'd studied Miller and had found out how to beat him. Billy knew all about bad verdicts and took them as being part of the game, but this was his most important outing to date and he'd had 111 fights at that stage. You'll find the cream of British talent amongst those fights. Up to the war his record was remarkable, but an unsympathetic commanding officer refused to allow him time for training during those army years and defeats against Jim 'Spider' Kelly, 'Kid' Tanner and Johnny Ward may not have occurred had Billy been even a little match-fit. He never boxed after the war but still racked up 130 fights. I'll list some of his opponents to give an indication of this man's talent. Tom Smith (twice), Johnny King, Benny Caplan, Johnny Cusick, Dick Corbett, Tommy Hyams, Harry Edwards (six times), Ronnie James, Johnny McMillan, Nel Tarleton, Len Hampston, Benny Sharkey, 'Ginger' Roberts, Bob Banty and Harry Craster all met Billy, whose death further attenuates the ranks of fighters active in the 1930s. Billy was one of nature's gentleman.

CHISNALL John *From* St Helens. *Died* August 2005, aged 68. Starting as an amateur at Lowe House at the age of ten, John had a good amateur career before deciding to turn pro under the name of Johnny James in 1963. A light-heavyweight, his first four fights saw Bernie Sutton, Colin Woodman, Dave Brodie (by disqualification) and Johnny Plenty all despatched inside the distance before he was

himself beaten by Jack London – the brother of Brian – Rudolph Vaughan, 'Young' McCormack – a future British champion - and Roy Seward. He then retired and returned to his first love of amateur boxing. A former miner, with three brothers who played pro rugby league, John started training at the Britannia ABC before moving on to UGB in Bobbies Lane, then St Helens Glass, St Helens Town and finally to where it all started, Lowe House, as the successor to the late head coach, Albert Freeman. John was never happier when in the gym training the kids.

CHRISTENSEN Chris *From* Denmark. *Died* 28 January 2005, aged 78. Apart from Battling Nelson, who did all his fighting in the USA, Chris was Denmark's top fighting product. He fought at world level, perhaps not always with success, but the men he fought were household names in the boxing world and he fought successfully against Brits, Wally Swift, Ernie Vickers, Jackie Braddock, George Aldridge, Tony Smith, Peter King and John McCormack. Against Braddock he made two rare trips to the canvas and got up to outgame his man, which was an indication of Chris' toughness. In 1961 he failed to grab the European welterweight crown when Duilio Loi beat him in Italy, but he was more successful at the middleweight limit when he defeated McCormack for the European title in Copenhagen. After losing that title to Laszlo Papp later in the year and failing to regain it in the return match, he later had a shot at the light-middleweight diadem in 1965 but found Bruno Visintin too good and announced his retirement afterwards. Some of the men he beat were Idrissa Dione, Jacques Herbillon, Hector Constance, Luis Folledo, Martin Hansen, Kid Dussart, Sauveur Chiocca, Stefan Redl, Fortunato Manca and, notably, Billy Graham, the American. He was 38 when the stoppage loss to Visintin forced him to call it a day.

CHUNG David *From* South Korea. *Died* October 2005, aged 57. A class referee who'd controlled world title fights held in Thailand and Japan, David's death came suddenly while he appeared to be in the prime of life.

CITRO Ralph *From* New Jersey, USA. *Died* 2 October 2004, aged 78. A respected cornerman, record-compiler, publisher of *Computer Boxing Update,* and a man who formed the International Boxing Research Organisation, Ralph put far more into boxing than he took out. He had a fair amateur career and became a trainer in later years, but it was while he ran a gym that he picked up the tricks of the trade and his vast knowledge of cornerwork made him one of the most sought-after cutsmen in the business. As the cornerman for Emanuel Steward's Kronk Team, he worked with the big names around at that time and in recognition of his contribution to boxing he was elected into the Canastota Hall of Fame in 2001.

CLEAVER Bob *From* Attleborough. *Died* May 2005, aged 79. A former middleweight, Bob, christened Basil, boxed from 1946 to 1953, which was a busy period as his 75-fight record shows. This followed a long amateur career, in which he won the Northern Counties' championship, before turning professional at 21. During the last war he was a despatch rider for the London Fire Brigade and he later went into the haulage business. He got his paid career off to a fine start by stopping Frank Baldwin of British Honduras in the first round, but was pushed too far when facing Bournemouth's Jack Lewis at the end of the year. Having gone into an early lead, his vastly experienced opponent scored a six-round knockout with a right to the body. Bob bounced back with a win over Johnny McGowan before getting a return with Lewis. It was a different matter this time, as Bob ran out a clear points winner. From then on he was fighting title contenders – not always coming on a winner, but establishing himself as a man to be reckoned with. His record shows wins over Ron Pudney, 'Ginger' Sadd, Mac Joachim, Billy Ellaway, Bert Sanders, Willie Armstrong and Eric McQuade. Among his opponents were Jimmy Davis, the Sullivan brothers, Johnny and Sammy, Albert Finch, Gordon Hazell, Wally Beckett, Wally Thom, Bert Hyland and Arthur Howard. After the future middleweight champion, Pat McAteer, outpointed Bob late in 1953, he chose that moment to retire. After training boxers at the Lynn Friars ABC for several years, in later life he became an enthusiastic sea fisherman. He left a wife, five sons, grandchildren and one great-grandchild.

Bob Cleaver

CONNELL Dave *From* Dublin. *Died* October 2004, aged 78. Dave, one of the outstanding Irish amateur champions, did the bulk of his fighting in the boom period following the end of the last Great War. Fighting from flyweight up to the lightweight division, he represented his country in numerous international tournaments, usually with notable success. As a member of the Avona ABC, and twice a bronze medal winner at successive European championships, he wasn't only a very clever boxer, but he had a

punch in each fist that brought him many early wins. After his 30th birthday he emigrated to Canada and it was there that he died from complications brought on by respiratory problems.

CROOK Edward *From* Alabama. *Died* July 2005, aged 76. A former Olympic middleweight champion, Edward reached his pinnacle as a boxer when he beat Poland's Tadvesz Walasak on points at the Rome Olympics. Crook was favoured to win because he'd looked impressive in the semi-finals by stopping Romania's Ion Monea in the third round. After his boxing days were over, he won four military medals in a long Army career, distinguishing himself during two campaigns in Vietnam.

CURRY Johnny *From* Wheatley Hill. *Died* 30 March, aged 84. There were five fighting Currys from Wheatley Hill – Charlie, Johnny, Billy, George and Ernie. George and Ernie never turned professional and Johnny may have carried on fighting well into the 1950s had a car accident not curtailed his career. He was inactive from 1938 to 1947 and made a brief comeback, winning three times in five outings. Johnny was three years younger than Charlie, who had his last fight in 1943, while Billy, the youngest of the batch, was coming along as his two brothers' careers were ending. Johnny started as a pro in 1933 with a win over Ginger Watson, but came a cropper in 1936 when Ben Duffy stopped him in five rounds. However, he gained a niche in the 'Hall of Fame' when he knocked out 'Young' Teddy Baker, who later boxed as Teddy Gardner and became British flyweight champion. In the same year, Curry beat Joe Hardy, John Henderson, Ralph Ambrose, Bert Meagan and Johnny Best, and began his six-fight series with Ted Thomas with a four-round points win. Jim Keery, on his way to a long career that saw him challenge Sandy Saddler, stopped Johnny in four rounds, but he came back to knock out Ted Thomas in the last of their matches, in which he won three, lost twice and drew once. They were hard days back in the 1930s – Johnny was 13 when he had his first fight and he was only 14 when he beat Gardner. He was still in his teens when he had that car accident and we are left wondering what might have been had Johnny not had that unfortunate experience.

DALTREY Brian *From* Spitalfields. *Died* 15 March 2005, aged 67. The light-heavyweight division has always been difficult to box in and so many men have been forced to concede weight to heavyweights in order to get fights. Brian was no exception. One of his best wins was against Johnny Ould, whom he stopped in 1962, but he was unluckier when opposing Johnny's twin brother, heavyweight Dave. Brian also got a draw with Bob Nicolson and shared two verdicts with Tommy Leroy from Redhill, while wins over Al Roye, Jim Houlihan and Bernard Neal were interspersed with defeats by Stan Cullis and Malcolm Worthington. Brian boxed professionally from 1961-1965 and prior to that had a long career with the simon-pures, during which he represented London against Germany. He became an enthusiastic member of London EBA and was a prolific writer of boxing articles that he provided for EBAs all over the country. He was a good writer too and always got his dates and results right. Apart from his writing he was a tireless worker for the ex-boxers' movement and was extremely popular with the old-timers. Cancer was one opponent he couldn't beat, but he fought it with a rare courage.

DAVIES Roy *From* Spratton. *Died* March 2005, aged 76. Like most of George Biddles' boys, Roy was a very active fighter, beginning at 17 and racking up 108 contests before retiring at 23. He was hampered by facial cuts throughout his seven-year career, with many of the losses on his record being due to such wounds and he never took the full count, although in there with some big punchers like Bob Frost, Algar Smith, Ben Duffy and Vic Manini. He was a very busy fighter up to 1951, when he had but two outings and after just one the following year when Bob Foster of Covent Garden outpointed him, Roy decided that it was a good moment to retire. He had been to the well 31 times in 1947, 28 times in 1948 and 18 times in 1950. There's a loss to British welterweight champion, Wally Thom, in 1950, but future middleweight king-pin, Johnny Sullivan, was twice on the short end of the points score. Roy was the winner of an open lightweight competition in 1947, beating Dennis Ford, Jeff Badham and Joe Lidbury to win the trophy, in what was his busiest year. Before 1947 was over he'd had three fights with Newark's Alf Phillips, winning two and drawing the other. Harry Legge, Billy Cunningham and Jimmy Shord all outpointed him, but Roy came back with ten more wins before the year was out. Some of the names on his record are Claude Dennington, Tommy Jones, Al Wilburn, Warren Kendall, Chris Jenkins, Bert Hornby, Dick Levers, George Daly, Vernon Ball, Harry Lazar, Jimmy Molloy, Billy Rattray, Israel Boyle, Eric Davies, Kay Kalio and Birmingham's durable Eddie Phillips. Roy, a clever fighter, and one who never refused a fight, had a remarkable career and retired at an age when some fighters are just starting out.

Roy Davies

DODDS Patsy *From* Rowlands Gill. *Died* 20 April 2005, aged 84. Patsy, better known in life as Norman Walton, which was his birth name, was renowned as being the sole survivor of the 756 crew on the cruiser *Neptune*, which hit a mine in Libyan waters in 1941. Norman was a 20-year-old able seaman who was destined to rise to the rank of Petty Officer. Picked up by an Italian torpedo boat after days in the sea, he was transferred to a hospital in Tripoli before being put in a PoW camp. He was released in 1943 and demobbed in 1946 and took up professional boxing using his wife's maiden name of Dodds. He is alleged to have been the product of the booths and his first recorded fight came in September '46 after the booth season was over. He fought until 1952, with wins over Mike Casey, George McDonald, Dick Miller and Bobby Foster. He was a far better sailor than a fighter and he never could get by Bert Ingram, with one draw and two losses right at the start of his career. He managed to force a draw with Reuben Blairs and lost on points to Eddie Phillips from the Birmingham stable of George Middleton. His known record, which is probably complete, is 22 contests, with seven wins and two draws, and claims of 147 contests with three fights for the Northern Area title can be dismissed. He is survived by a daughter.

ELMS Dave *From* Brighton. *Died* 12 November 2004, aged 76. A heavyweight, Dave had a brief professional career, retiring after a handful of fights, having decided that his lack of height and reach was too big a disadvantage. Most of his wins came on points. Still, he showed some promise by winning one of those heavyweight competitions that were popular in the 1950s, beating Ken Wyatt, Morry Bush and Fred Powell all in one night to carry off the winner's prize. He'd previously lost a six-rounder to Powell, but had beaten Joey Parsons and Ken Wyatt. After retiring, he teamed up with Tony Brazil, formed the Whitehawk ABC, and helped to train aspiring boxers. Dave lost his last battle to asbestosis, showing stubborn and courageous resistance until it claimed him.

FAIRBANKS Bernard *From* Hanley. *Died* October 2004, aged 79. A useful featherweight, Bernard fought just once at my local High Wycombe arena, but went home as a loser after Basingstoke's Ivor Simpson beat him. Bernard was more successful in rings farther to the north, beating Brian Jelley and Hugh Mackie inside the distance at Preston and knocking out Tony Green in his hometown ring. He was less successful in Doncaster, where Denny Dawson stopped him in eight rounds, and he couldn't improve on Jelley's performance against Billy 'Spider' Kelly, losing in four rounds as had Jelly four months previously. Bernard's best wins were over Chris Kelly, Ron Nelson and George Tiddy and there was also a draw with Tommy Briers. In his final year in the game (1952), he bit off much more than he could chew by crossing gloves with Johnny Butterworth, who stopped him and sent him into retirement.

FARBER Sammy *From* New York. *Died* 20 July 2005, aged 95. Turning pro in 1927 and trained by the legendary

Ray Arcel, Sammy went unbeaten in 15 contests, drawing with Lew Feldman on the way, before losing to Joe Marciente. A bantam, cum feather, he boxed until 1932, losing 15, drawing five and winning 42. Men who beat him included Pete Sanstol (four times), Terry Roth, Joe Ghnouly and Frankie Wallace (twice), while he drew with Charley von Reeden and Martin Zuniga and beat Chris Pineda. These were all top class fighters, but he could never quite break into the top bracket and decided to quit after losing to Allan Foston in 1932, his record standing at 42 wins, five draws and 15 losses.

GALLEYMORE Peter *From* Durban, South Africa. *Died* December 2004, aged 73. Although unsuccessful in three attempts to win a South African championship, Peter had a respectable record and was at one time the welterweight champion of Natal. In his second year as a professional, he scored a stoppage win over Duggie du Preez, a man best remembered here as being the first to beat Algar Smith, at the White City in 1951. Galleymore fought here himself in 1952, beating Gilbert Ussin, Danny Malloy and Tommy Hinson, but couldn't get past Peter Fallon, who outpointed him over ten rounds.

GONZALEZ 'Corky' *From* Denver. *Died* April 2005, aged 76. Born in Denver of Latin parentage, Rodolfo 'Corky' Gonzalez fought his way out of poverty. After winning a major amateur championship in 1946 he turned professional the following year and later used his fame to spearhead a fight against the racial discrimination that at that time was holding back the progress of so many immigrants. His ring earnings helped him to establish schools for Chicano students and his daughter still runs one of them. He was a very good featherweight fighter and lost only four of his first 55 fights. Then Willie Pep and 'Red-Top' Davis outpointed him, but 'Corky' was competing at world level and star names stud his record. He fought Eddie Burgin, Charlie Riley, Harold Dade and Glen Flanagan and beat them all. A clever fighter, but not a particular heavy hitter, the second loss on his record came against that fine fighter, Miguel Acevedo. In seven years of ring combat, I can trace only ten losses in 71 outings. This gifted fighter was a great man who, throughout his adult life, fought for the rights of his people.

GREEN Kenny *From* Croydon. *Died* September 2004., aged 79. Kenny, a lightweight, was active between 1942 to 1950, with a break from 1943 to 1945. As was the case of many boxers, World War Two took away so many prime fighting years. He got back on course in 1946 and scored good wins over Dave Clemo, Mick O'Grady and hard-punching Jimmy Constable, but dropped decisions to Joe Rubery, Johnny Sage and Mickey Duff. Despite his self-deprecating account of his fighting years, Duff was a difficult man to beat, expecially by a man who was having his second fight after a three-year hiatus. However, Kenny was a quick learner and he beat Sage in a return and drew with the dangerous Jamaican, Hyman Williams. Good enough to beat Tony Wickens, Pat Crawford, Alf Price and

Dennis Ford, he found the highly-rated Jeff Tite too good for him and he dropped a decision to Harry Legge when taking the ten-round course for the second time. Another good performance was drawing with Ron Dennington at Selhurst Park. He had 41 contests, of which he won 24 and drew three.

HARDY Matt *From* Doncaster. *Died* August 2005, aged 79. A heavyweight who helped Bruce Woodcock prepare for most of his big fights, the only record I have of him starts in 1946 with a ten-round points defeat at the hands of Taffy Woods and goes on to list a further 57 fights. Although he beat Len Rowlands, Tommy Brown, Bob McArdle (five times), George Dawson, Doug Richards and Len Bennett, the men who beat him, such as Frank Ronan, Charlie Collett, Dave Goodwin, Allan Cooke, Phil van Niekerk, Ken Shaw, Gerry McDermott, Don Cockell, Derek Alexander, Nick Fisher, Ben Valentine, Jack Gardner, George Dawson, Lloyd Barnett, George Stern, Dave Davis, Bert Gilroy, Al Marson, Frank Bell, Reg Andrews, Johnny McLeavy, Jack Hobbs, Don Scott and Reg Spring, read like a veritable who's who of British heavies and cruisers of the late '40s. He seems not to have missed anyone and it almost begs the question as to whether he was testing out future opponents for Woodcock. Although based in Doncaster, Matt, who retired in 1951, was born in Houghton le Spring, County Durham.

Mark Hart

HART Mark *From* Croydon. *Died* 24 December 2004, aged 80. There never was a gamer fighter than Croydon's Mark. This was the man who lost to an ascending prospect, Randolph Turpin, held him to a draw in a return match, and who courageously stuck it out for 14 rounds against a peak-form Don Cockell in an attempt to win the British light-heavyweight championship in 1950. In 1948 Mark had taken on the unbeaten European welterweight champion, Robert Villemain, and fought magnificently to force a draw. This was the Villemain who'd just stopped Eric Boon and he dropped Mark for an 'eight' count late in the fight before the Croydon man fought back hard to get a share of the decision. What I found so astounding about Mark is that he won the ABA heavyweight title in 1944 and began his pro career at the same weight. He had a good mentor in Jack 'Froggy' Hyams, who took him down two weight divisions where he was more comfortable, the pair having a good relationship throughout Mark's career and for long afterwards. Mark beat 'Ginger' Sadd, Albert Finch, Alby Hollister, Bos Murphy and Dennis Powell, amongst others, and he also gave the world title challenger, Laurent Dauthille, a close call in 1948. With some mighty good middleweights around in his time, he fought from 1945 to 1951 and mixed with the best in Europe.

HUNSAKER Tunney *From* Fayetteville, North Carolina. *Died* 28 April 2005, aged 75. Tunney has a permanent place in the sun as the first professional opponent of Cassius Clay. Although he never rose to great heights and won only half his fights, when looking at his record the loss/win analysis doesn't indicate the quality of some of the opponents. He was on a losing streak of six fights when he fought Clay, but he boxed with conviction and went the distance. Hunsaker was game and often exploited, being sacrificed as a stepping-stone to enhance the careers of Ernie Terrell, Bert Whitehurst, Tom McNeeley, Alejandro Lavorante, Tod Herring and Sonny Banks. Most of his wins came over obscure opposition like Tom DeJarnete, Terrell Pruett, Ben Thomas, Herman Wilson and Billy Walters, but when thrown to the lions he showed guts. And it was that same brand of courage that pulled him through after his last fight. Joe Sheldon knocked him out in ten rounds and he was rushed to hospital, but he survived two brain operations, recovered and resumed his former occupation as a chief of police. He had a wife and two children, all of whom survived him.

HUNTER George *From* Brackpan, South Africa. *Died* January 2005, aged 77. The winner of the Val Barker Cup for being best boxer in the 1948 Olympics, George cashed in on his success by embarking on a punch-for-pay career, having beaten Chuck Speiser in the prelims and Don Scott in the final. He was one of a particularly strong South African team that had Johnny Arthur, Gerald Dreyer, Vic Toweel, Duggie Du Preez amongst its boxers. Surprisingly, he never achieved the success expected of him in the paid ranks. On winning his debut on a disqualification over Bertie Dartnall he then lost to Billy Woods, but two good wins followed and he twice knocked out Freddie Vorster in thrilling fights for the national light-heavyweight crown. George moved up to the heavyweight division, but found the going too tough. In 1950 he lost to Piet Strydom in a championship match and won the return, but this was not for the title. A loss to his former Olympic team-mate,

Johnny Arthur, and an unimpressive win over Italy's Georgio Milan convinced him that he was not likely to go any further and he retired in 1952, aged 25.

JACKLICH 'Buddy' *From* San Francisco. *Died* 30 October 2004, aged 83. Christened Lloyd, 'Buddy' fought as a lightweight between 1946 and 1951. He had a win over world featherweight claimant, Jackie Wilson, and a stoppage loss to Manuel Ortiz, after clearly leading on points, as highlights of a professional career. Add to that his performance against Maxie Docusen, Lauro Salas and Fabela Chavez and you are reading about a class act. 'Buddy' was highly thought of in California, which was then alive with fistic activity, and was elected into the Californian Hall of Fame – an honour of which he was rightly proud.

KEOUGH Jackie *From* Chester le Street. *Died* March 2005, aged 75. A lightweight-cum-welter, Jackie boxed from 1949-1955, having 36 outings, in which he won 25 and lost 11. His best wins were against Tony McTigue, Roy Sharples, Selwyn Evans, Sandy Manuel and Terry Cullen. Against Cullen, he scored a ten-round points victory in what was a final eliminator for the Northern Area lightweight championship, but his activity from then on was sparse and nothing came of the title shot that was due to him. Peter Waterman and Frank Johnson, both of whom were to become British champions, were too good for Jackie, but he did finish with a win and a good one, when stopping Bill Wooding in six rounds at Birmingham in June 1955.

KIPLING David Dr *From* Hartlepool. *Died* 3 February 2005, aged 52. BBBoC chief medical officer, David, was offered Dr Adrian Whiteson's post when the latter retired, but was forced to decline the offer because his practice was based in Hartlepool. He became chief medical officer of the Northern Area and held that position for 19 years, only resigning when diagnosed as having lung cancer – an illness from which he passed away one year later.

LAVERICK Jim *From* Tyne Dock. *Died* 15 February 2005, aged 84. Middleweight Jim was active from 1938 to 1946, during which time he had 53 contests for 38 wins. Wartime service in the navy hampered his boxing progress and, at an age when he was in his prime, the sparsity of boxing promotions saw him have one fight in 1942, three in 1943, none in 1944, and three in 1945. Until the war came he'd been a busy scrapper with some good wins and very few defeats. He stopped both Jim Teasdale, Paddy Lyons, Sunderland's Roy Mills and old 'Battling' Charlie Parkin and went on to stop Dave McCleave at the Cambridge Theatre. When the rust of inactivity had dimmed his reflexes, Parkin outpointed him in a match for the Northern Area middleweight championship. His worst year was 1945 – three fights three defeats, but they were top-rated opponents in Vince Hawkins, Bert Hyland and Albert Finch. After the war he tried to pick up the traces, scoring stoppage wins over George Dilkes, Jack Lord and

Alex Watkinson, but when Dilkes beat him in a return he packed it in. He was only 26.

LEMOS Richie *From* Los Angeles. *Died* 18 October 2004, aged 84. The featherweight division was strong in Richie's day. You had to be exceptionally good to get in the top ten and Richie claimed the NBA version of the world title, albeit briefly. He knocked out defending champion, Pete Scalzo, in July 1941 and lost it to Jackie Wilson just four months later. Not one of the divisions' great champions, but he mixed with many who were, such as Manuel Ortiz, Joey Archibald, Lou Salica and Lew Feldman. He had 81 fights and a quick glance at his scoresheet reveals the names of Bobby Ruffin, Ray Lunny, Cleo Shans and Carmine Fatta. They were golden years for the nine-stoners.

LETTERLOUGH Julian *From* Reading, Pennsylvania. *Died* July 2005, aged 35. A former NABF light-heavyweight challenger and IBF cruiserweight challenger, Julian was shot dead when he intervened in a fight in Reading, Pennsylvania. In 2001 he was edged out on points in a thrilling encounter with Julio Gonzalez, having floored Gonzalez three times and coming within a whisker of winning. Julian, a dynamite puncher and world class, had 28 fights of which he drew three and lost five, with 20 of his wins coming inside the scheduled distance. He gave Vassily Jirov a hard fight when challenging for the IBF title and, by his death, the cruiserweight division loses one of its most exciting fighters.

LEVINE Johnny *From* Southend. *Died* January 2005, aged 90. A former Southend promoter, Johnny was the voice of boxing in the seaside town, running shows at the Banquetting Suite and the Cliffs Pavilion, with the late Ernie Fossey as his matchmaker.

McGOWAN Johnny *From* Wakefield. *Died* 23 January 2005 in Canada, aged 80. Sheer tough luck prevented Johnny from boxing for a British title and I've forgotten the number of times that injuries hampered his career at a time when he was on a roll. He broke his hand several times and suffered a jaw injury and broken bones in the foot, ribs and nose and his troubles didn't stop there – pleurisy, arthritis, septicaemia and a few more illnesses that I've forgotten all hindered his progress. I remember the trade paper once referring to him as the country's unluckiest boxer. For all of that he was a pretty good light-heavyweight and first gained my attention at the early part of his career when he hammered Tommy Curran into defeat and also retirement at West Ham Baths. The fight went less than a round and Curran, a tough middleweight who'd not lost many inside the distance, was unlucky to have boxed at Bournemouth the previous night in a contest that had tested his durability. It was the seventh clean knockout that McGowan had scored in ten outings and in his next fight at the same venue, he was himself forced to take two counts before gaining a prestigious win over the Bournemouth veteran, Jack Lewis. Johnny began 1947 well, with a knockout win

over Frank Hayes, and followed it in similar fashion against Frank Johnson, but it was not his best year. He'd gone up in class and lost to Bob Cleaver, Lloyd Barnett and Joe Rood, before getting back into the swing of things in 1948. He boxed on, in between time out for injuries, until 1952, when he packed it in after losing to Willy Schagen. He'd fought in good company against men such as Tommy Caswell, Mel Brown, Jimmy Carroll (from whom he won the Central Area light-heavyweight championship), Albert Finch, Billy Stevens, Norman Twigger, Sammy Wilde, Doug Myers, Garnett Denny and Roy Peterson, etc. He had 42 fights in all and four years after retiring he emigrated to Canada where he lived comfortably up to his death.

Jimmy McLarnin

McLARNIN Jimmy *From* Vancouver, Canada. *Died* 28 October 2004, aged 96. An all-time great, Jimmy started boxing in the flyweight division and finished as a welterweight, which is the division in which he was to reign as world champion. Right from the beginning of his outstanding career he was handled by 'Pop' Foster and they stuck to each other with exceptional mutual loyalty on both sides. Both men ended up comfortably off and since neither was greedy, Jimmy, with 'Pop's' advice, retired before he was 30 and lived in comfort, from the investments made by his ring earnings. Some nice guys do finish first! Jimmy's record is full of outstanding victories over men who at one time or other held world titles. I make the total 13 and it would have been one more had he not dropped a decision to Lou Brouillard just before he ended the career of Benny Leonard. The story always goes that Leonard, getting on in years, was but a shadow of his former self that night and that is probably so but from what I saw of the film, and I've watched it a few times, Leonard still retained a lot of his old magic. There were two great fighters in the ring that night. McLarnin was 29 when he packed it in and he went out with a win over Lou Ambers who, typically, had been a good champion himself. Jimmy's first crack at the world lightweight title ended in a points defeat by Sammy Mandell. He was 21 and still had golden years ahead, but had to wait five years before the welterweight belt was around his waist. He'd licked Mandell in a return (non title), stopped Ruby Goldstein, Sammy Baker and Al Singer, outpointed 'Young' Jack Thompson, and had won two out of three fights with Billy Petrolle, before 'Young' Corbett III went out in one round, thus losing his world welterweight title. Jimmy reigned for a year and a day before losing it to Barney Ross and they passed the crown to and fro between them. Jimmy regained it, lost it again and had just three more outings before 'Pop' Foster told him to retire when at the top of his form. He licked Tony Canzoneri and Lou Ambers, then took Foster's advice. His was a success story. Wise investments afforded him a very comfortable life style and, born in Hillsborough, County Down, Ireland on 19 December 1907, he was within three years of his centenary when he died.

MALONEY Johnny *From* Dagenham. *Died* September 2004, aged 72. Twice ABA welterweight champion (in 1951 and 1952), Johnny was a product of Dagenham ABC and a member of Britain's Olympic team at the 1952 Games, which he considered to be the highest honour of his career. After becoming the ABA champion and representing the RAF and his country in five internationals, when his fighting days were over Johnny took a coach's job with his former club. He'd had a professional career in between but it was brief. Commencing in 1955, he had a total of eight fights and won four. The four defeats came inside the distance, when facial cuts obliged him to call quits. There was obviously no future for him because of his vulnerability, but he was very successful in his role as a coach and continued to take an active part in the game until his retirement years.

MANCINI Dennie *From* Fulham. *Died* 10 September 2004, aged 71. With the death of Dennie an era came to an end. Since 1920 there has always been a Mancini active in boxing, which means that within the memory of every living person a member of that fighting family has been connected to the sport in one way or another. The family's boxing origins go back to Dennie's uncle Alf and Lennie's father, Dinnie, who was Alf's manager. Cousin Tony challenged for the British title in 1962 and without cross-checking I feel confident that he was unbeaten for a period of ten years. Denny was respected and loved by the fight fraternity throughout the world and when he died tributes came in from all corners of this planet. He was very, very busy with his work in boxing yet he always made time for a chat. All I had to say was "is Dennie in?" and his voice would come from another room: "Come through here. It's nice to see you again". It was certainly nice to see him at all times. He understood boxing right through and so much

news that was unpublishable got to my ears via Dennie. He had his ear to the ground and was trusted and often revered by his friends, serving boxing in most capacities, as a second, promoter, manager, matchmaker, trainer, agent and, above all, a cutman extraordinaire. It was Albert Hillman who made the comment that will always be associated with this fine boxing man. "Having you in my corner is like having a round start". For years he ran Bernard Hart's Lonsdale Sports shop in Beak Street and Lonsdale without Dennie Mancini just isn't Lonsdale. It was a meeting place for boxing personalities from all over the world and most went there just to see Denny. It was like days past when Solomons' gym used to swarm with the elite of the boxing world. Not surprisingly, Dennie's funeral was a huge event and a host of those attending looked like a who's who of the fight business.

MARSHALL Marty *From* Detroit, Michigan. *Died* 25 October 2004, aged 79. When Marty's name is mentioned in boxing circles, little information is forthcoming other than him being the first of three men to beat Sonny Liston and it is often overlooked that he also beat Wes Bascom, Calvin Butler and Bob Satterfield. His sole defeat in 1954 came at the hands of Harold Johnson and he'd reached his peak after eight years of fighting for pay. He began his career in 1946 as a light-heavyweight, finding it difficult to get fights until he outgrew the division and campaigned as a heavyweight. Having dropped a decision to Toxie Hall in his sole fight in 1952 and suffering two earlier stoppage losses against Bob Baker and Embrell Davidson, he hit his best form and was undefeated for the ensuing two and a half years. His career had reached its apogee and losses outnumbered wins until he retired in 1957. Satterfield beat him in the return and he lost twice to Liston, after which his form deteriorated. His last known fight was against Amos Lincoln in 1957, when Lincoln got the decision in an eight-rounder in Chicago.

MATTHEWS Len *From* Philadelphia. *Died* 29 August 2005, aged 66. A world ranking lightweight from July 1959 to February 1962, Len went 16 unbeaten after turning pro in November 1957, beating Henry 'Pappy' Gault, Henry 'Toothpick' Brown, Bobby Rogers, Tommy Tibbs and Orlando Zulueta on the way. Paul Armstead was the first man to beat him, followed by Carlos Ortiz, Willie Toweel, Doug Vaillant, Carlos Hernandez, Paolo Rossi, Dave Charnley, Luis Molina, Kenny Lane and Chico Velez, all ranking lightweights, before Len retired early in 1964. Only the very best men had beaten him, while Johnny Gonsalves, Armstead, Johnny Busso, Lahouri Godih, Art Persley, Lane, Al Urbina (twice), JD Ellis (twice), all suffered defeat at his hands. He was on the verge of a world title fight on several occasions, rising to number three after his victory over Lane in October 1960, but after being outscored by Britain's Dave Charnley a year later his star was clearly on the wane.

MENZIES Tom *From* Falkirk. *Died* 13 December 2004, aged 64. Tom, representing Scotland, won a bronze medal at the light-heavyweight limit in the 1962 Commonwealth Games. He was a former Scottish ABA champion, and a gold medal winner at the Irish ABA Jubilee Tournament in 1961, and when in army service he won several titles from 1959-61. In 1961 he had a terrific contest with Billy Walker and stepped up a division for the fight. He dropped Billy in the first round but couldn't capitalise on that and was stopped in the last round of a very hard contest.

MILLER Tommy *From* Halifax. *Died* January 2005, aged 88. I met Tommy a couple of months before he died. He struck me as being alert and agile for a man two years away from his 90th birthday, but that was hardly surprising considering that he was still very much active in the sport he loved. He had a fine stable of fighters and was also an astute matchmaker. Tommy was our oldest licence-holder and served boxing in seven different capacities. He boxed himself, both as a licensed pro and in the booths. His first licensed contest was in October 1934 when he outpointed Jack Dunn over six rounds and in 25 subsequent fights he was beaten only three times. It took three good'uns to outpoint him – Nipper Carroll of Leeds in Tommy's first ten-rounder, the Welsh prospect, Ken Barrett, and George Marsden, who was on his way to scoring 213 victories in an exceptionally busy career. From 1937, Tommy's record became spotty, but he was fighting in a higher league and while both Len Hampston and Sunderland's Tom Smith stopped him, Tommy had better luck against Al Binney, Jack Mussen and Freddie Warnock. The last war affected Tommy's career and from August 1939 to April 1943 he had only four fights, with just one loss to the crack British Guianan, Kid Tanner. Tommy chose to wind up his gloved career with an emphatic stoppage win over Eddie Moran.

MOLLOY Johnny *From* St Helens. *Died* 20 March, aged 78. Johnny fought in that great era for featherweights, 1943 to 1953, and was good enough to compete against the best at his weight in the country. As an amateur he was credited with a win over Billy Thompson just before he started fighting for pay in 1943 and, as a pro, he beat the reigning featherweight champion, Ronnie Clayton, in 1948 and then outscored the former European and Empire champion, Al Phillips. It was a golden year for Johnny but Clayton won the return with his British title at stake and Johnny never got another shot at the title, despite performing in good company until 1953. Glancing through Johnny's record, household names are liberally sprinkled and the St Helens man was often returned the winner, beating Ben Duffy, Frankie Kelly, Bert Jackson and Jackie Turpin, drawing with Cliff Anderson and reversing a previous loss to Elis Ask, when he got the verdict on points. He took that great French featherweight, Ray Famechon, the distance, but always considered Elis Ask to be the best man he fought. A three year gap in his record from 1944 was due to service in the Merchant Navy.

MORIOKA Eiji *From* Tokyo, Japan. *Died* 11 November 2004, aged 58. A brilliant Japanese amateur boxer, Eiji brought home a bronze medal from the Mexico Olympic Games but wasn't able to repeat his success in the paid ranks. He boxed for pay in 1969 and 1970 and totalled just ten fights, with six wins and four losses. Although he stopped Haruki Kumazawa, Roger Moreno and Sang-Yong Cho, back-to-back points losses to Shintari Ushilyama and Shigeyoshi Ohki heralded his exit from boxing. Unfortunately, he'd developed a detached retina so he drifted into a manager's role and was still devoting time to boxing when cancer took his life.

NEWFIELD Jack *From* Brooklyn, USA. *Died* December 2004, aged 66. A fearless writer, Jack is remembered in the boxing world for his expose of Don King in his book *Only in America: The Life and Crimes of Don King*, which was published in 1995. Jack was an experienced and talented biographer with many political works to his name and nothing daunted him or stopped him from writing what he believed to be the truth. A civil rights campaigner, throughout his journalistic career he stood up for the underdog and victims of injustice. It was cancer that got him in his 66th year.

NILSSON Gunnar *From* Malmo, Sweden. *Died* 13 May 2005, aged 82. Gunnar was one of those fighters distinguished by reaching the top of the tree as an amateur, yet achieving little as a professional. Being Swedish was a disadvantage when pursuing a professional boxing career, because the country's boxing history was limited. He and Ingemar Johansson, together helped to restore Sweden's interest in the game. A silver-medallist in the 1948 Olympics, he looked set to make an impression at European level or wider. His record has been a devil to put together and it appears that he dropped down to light-heavyweight to start his professional campaign, boxing from 1949 to 1956 and doing the bulk of his fighting in Gothenburg and Stockholm. He and Johansson were friends and together they boxed many exhibitions. Gunnar made his debut with a loss, but was soon on the winning trail. The opposition was not of top quality and in 1955 he was still fighting six rounders, with wins over Ken Rowlands and Simon Ayankin. He drew and lost to Italy's Artemio Calzavarra then had even fewer fights in the following year, beating Michel Dinot over the eight-round course, but a loss via a stoppage to Ilde Warusfel followed. Nilsson battled on 'till the end of the year and seems to have bowed out with a win over an obscure opponent. His exhibitions with Johansson were far more lucrative than his paid fights, so it is not surprising that it took him seven years to put 18 fights on his record.

NORDIN Fighting *From* Morocco. *Died* 20 September 2004 in Amsterdam, aged 32. Fighting Nordin, who was born Nordin Ben Salah, died of gunshot wounds after being confronted by an assailant when boarding a train in Amsterdam. He was a former kick-boxing champion who went on to box in gloved combat, having 39 fights, losing only two, with one draw against Jimmy Elliott. He was twice a holder of the WBA Inter-Continental super-middleweight championship.

O'NEILL Becky *From* Philadelphia. *Died* 1 July 2005, aged 81. A much loved ex-fighters' manager, Becky had been ill for some time and by her death we lose one of the great characters of modern boxing. She handled the colourful Jeff Chandler, who once held the WBA bantamweight title.

PECKHAM Teddy *From* Bournemouth. *Died* August 2004, aged 75. The years from 1946 to 1957 in which Teddy boxed, were saturated with good featherweights and Teddy missed very, very few of them. Like most of the Bournemouth-based fighters of that time, he was a protege of Jack Turner, who noticed his potentiality very early – Teddy was well short of his 16th birthday and from what I recall, a flyweight. After beating Sea Cadet Jones, he threw his hat in the professional ring and he was always a busy fighter, both in his style and in the quantity of fights. He went to the well 151 times and fought in rings from Rome to Abidjan, from Marseilles to Paris, Dublin, Manchester, Gloucester, High Wycombe, the Scilly Isles and around the small halls of the west country. Teddy was a banger and a deadly one. He pulled many a fight out of the fire with one punch and that's what it took for him to annex the Southern Area featherweight title from Charlie Tucker – just one mighty clout in the first round. He did the same thing to Gracieux Lamperti in Marseilles, but the Belgian took him into the fifth round. John Kelly, Tommy Higgins, Bobby Boland, Neville Tetlow and Freddie King all went the same way, in one round. Long after he'd retired, I saw Teddy take on a light-heavyweight challenger in Alf Weston's booth. No doubt Teddy had informed him of the booth code beforehand, but this guy was deaf to it. His girl friend was at the ringside and he wanted to impress. With a magnificent physique and a few stones the heavier man, he pushed Teddy forcibly against the ropes and charged. The punch that laid him spark out started from the back of the booth. There was less than a minute of action, but it impressed on me that Teddy was one of the hardest socking featherweights I'd ever seen. I'll run through a list of some opponents to give an idea of the quality of men around in his time: Alby Tissong, Hilaire Pratesi, former world champion Robert Cohen, Sammy Bonnici, Louis Romero (twice), Kid Tanner, Denny Dawson, Jock Bonas, Stan Gossip, Tommy Bailey, Jim Kenny, Dai Davies, Ronnie Draper, Jackie Turpin, Bernard Pugh, Johnny Molloy, Stan Skinkiss, Kenny Lawrence, Sammy McCarthy, Tony Lombard, John Kelly, Jimmy Brown, Billy Kelly, Alvaro Cerasani, Jules Touan, etc. I'm puzzled that the name of Ronnie Clayton is not there. Teddy deserved a shot at his title, but, as I said, there was so much good featherweight activity in those days and a long queue of title challengers.

PEREZ Lino *From* Caracas, Venezuela. *Died* August 2004, aged 30. Lino committed suicide at his home. He was still active as a boxer and had fought for the Hispanic welterweight championship four months previously,

holding Jose Luis Cruz Felix to a draw. Considered good enough to proceed to title contention, and in 17 fights he'd lost only three.

PETT Jocko *From* Chatham. *Died* 3 January 2005, aged 75. Jocko was one of those amateur boxers who never got near to winning a championship, but who fought hundreds of times before packing it in at the advanced age of 49. It should be taken into account that he was never more than a lightweight and, for a man of that weight, 49 was indeed an advanced age. He was a real character and a complete record of his fistic activities can never be compiled, although it was estimated that he had over 600 contests, a figure which is possible considering the length of his career and the number of tournaments held in the period in which he boxed. No stranger to booth fighting, he had a few unlicensed money fights that were never disclosed to the amateur authorities. He is survived by four daughters and an army of grandchildren.

POLAND Bill *From* New York. *Died* February 2005, aged 87. A big-punching heavyweight, Bill had a ten-year career from 1930, but service in the USA Coastguards took away four of his prime boxing years. Of his first 28 wins, 22 were via the short route and he had two stoppages registered against him. One to Harry Bobo and the other to Lee Savold. There were draws against Joe Baksi and Al Delaney, whom he beat in a return match. He'd also previously stopped Bobo, just before knocking out Eddie Blunt, and had it not been for the war Bill may well have fought his way into the ratings. Three of his eight losses came in his final year as a fighter.

PRAVISANI Aldo *From* Tolmino, Italy. *Died* May 2004, aged 73. News of Aldo's death in 2004 reached me rather late. I was surprised that the British Press made no mention of it, because Aldo dropped a decision to Hogan 'Kid' Bassey in Liverpool back in 1956 and later on, during a long campaign in Australia, he licked the 'Rochdale Thunderbolt (Mk II)', Johnny Butterworth. His career started in 1950 and petered out 21 years later in 1971. He was one of the very best defensive fighters I've seen and, at his best, could hold his own with those in the world's top ten. In Melbourne I saw him give Don Johnson all manner of problems before being forced to retire with a rib injury. He was an unpredictable fighter who was often seen to lose to inferior opponents by simply avoiding their blows, but doing little in return. They came no tougher than this nuggety battler and he was never counted out. In all those 20 years of combat, only one man, Borge Krogh, forced him to take a count, yet Aldo's record is sprinkled with stoppage losses. He was what one-time manager, Ambrose Palmer, called 'a bleeder' and had more than his fair share of cut eyes and too often in fights that he was clearly winning. He fought for the Italian title on six occasions, but it was when his best days were gone and when he'd returned home after relinquishing his Australian title that he became Italian champion for the first time by beating Armando Scorda. His shot at the European title came too late in his career and Maurice Tavant edged him out over 15 rounds. It is worthwhile to list some of Aldo's opponents who've not yet been mentioned. He inflicted the first defeat on Jimmy Carruthers, and forced Guido Ferracin to a draw in his 13th contest. The role-call becomes even more impressive: Ray Famechon, Willi Swoboda, Cherif Hamia, Jean Sneyers, Altidoro Polidori, Lucien Meraint, Wally Taylor, Love Allotey, Willi Quator, Pedro Carrasco, Gracieux Lamperti, Rafiu King, Tanny Campo, Sergio Milan, Jim McCormick, George Bracken, David Floyd, Auburn Copeland, etc. He must have been one of the last men to fight for over 20 years.

PRETORIUS Mickey *From* Johannesburg, South Africa. *Died* 3 January 2005, aged 69. Leukaemia claimed the life of the former South African lightweight challenger, Mickey Pretorius. He was a Commonwealth bronze medallist in the 1954 games and boxed professionally from 1956 to 1961. Beaten by Charlie Els for the vacant South African welterweight championship in June 1961, Mickey dropped back down to lightweight to challenge for the lightweight championship in the following August and again he failed and again the opponent was Charlie Els. He had beaten Els in a six rounder the previous year, during which he won all his fights, and had got into title contention by beating Benny Nieuwenhuizen, Ken Watson (twice), Freddie Brown and Sam Stewart. After quitting the ring, he became a traffic cop. He won 16 fights and lost eight.

RICE John 'Ginger' *From* Canterbury. *Died* March 2005, aged 58. It was Harold Alderman, longtime contributor to this yearbook, who reported the sudden death of 'Ginger', who was known by his fans as the 'Boughton Bomber'. Born in Maryhill, Scotland, he won the Kent and Southern Counties light-heavyweight championships in an out-standing, but little-publicised amateur career. He was one of the late Stan Knell's proteges and fought for the Canterbury ABC in the late 1960s and '70s, having an estimated total fights in excess of 200. In 1973, he beat T. Dobbie (Basingstoke) for the Southern Counties champion-ship and within three weeks he outpointed Marlow's Jack Wilson and the midlander, John McIntosh, en-route to the ABA semi-finals. Billy Knight of Lynn ABC checked his progress at this stage, but it was a very narrow verdict. In one of his last fights he gave three stone in weight to Brighton's Johnny Cole and came out the winner in a humdinger of a scrap that earned him enduring respect. The eldest of ten children, he is survived by his wife, four children and numerous brothers, sisters and grandchildren.

RILEY Hugh *From* Edinburgh. *Died* November 2004, aged 75. The son of Johnny Riley, an old-time coach, Hugh, boxing for Gilmerton, won the Scottish amateur flyweight title in 1949. At that time, he also had a brother fighting professionally named Johnny Summers, who twice contested the Scottish flyweight title. The following year Hugh won the Empire Games title in Auckland, New Zealand, prior to turning pro and outpointing Mickey McLaughlin, Jimmy Roche, Paddy Hardy, Johnny Black

and Mark Harrison before 1950 closed. After beating Jimmy Jennings, Hugh was expected to move up in class, but the next seven fights, which were spread over five years, saw him win just once. Apart from a losing Scottish bantam title fight against Eddie Carson in 1953 he was beaten away from home in five out of six contests, America's Keeny Teran knocking him out twice inside seven rounds. Back home in 1958, Hugh started with wins over Danny McNamee and Billy Skelly, before losing to George Bowes, Kimpo Amarfio, Johnny Morrisey, Roy Beaman, Len Reece, Alex Ambrose and Terry Crimmins. He beat one Arturo Vingochea during that period, but decided to retire in 1961. After a promising start, his eight wins and 14 losses were disappointing.

ROBINSON 'Slim' Jim *From* Philadelphia. *Died* November 2004, aged 80. Robinson was one of American boxing's great trainers who spent a lifetime in the game and was a font of knowledge. He took Mike Rossman to the top of the light-heavyweight tree and also handled Tim Witherspoon and Eddie Mustapha Muhammad. Rossman was champion from 1978-79.

RYAN Paddy *From* Marlow. *Died* April 2005, aged 77. Paddy ran Marlow ABC from 1962 to 1980 before handing over the reins to his former protege, ex-Southern Counties' champion, Jack Wilson. He was a much respected coach and apart from Jack Wilson, he trained Kelvin Gryckiewicz to a national title and put dozens of youngsters through their paces in his 18 years' association with the Thames Valley club. He is survived by two daughters and nine grandchildren.

SANCHEZ Martin *From* Mexico City. *Died* June 2005, aged 26. Tragedy struck in Las Vegas when Martin, a very popular fighter, died after being beaten by Russia's Rustam Nagaev. Like many Mexicans, he turned professional at a young age, in his case – 15. In his debut he was stopped in the first round, but was dedicated enough to persevere and get his career on to a winning track. He was game both in the ring and out of it, being a full-time fireman in Mexico City and noted for his bravery.

SCHMELING Max *From* Berlin, Germany. *Died* 2 February 2005, aged 99. Max carved himself a notable place in boxing history and in wider history when he became the only man to have beaten Joe Louis when the 'Brown Bomber' was in his prime. It was a victory achieved on merit and scored at a time when relations between Germany and America were beginning to look strained. In his rematch with Louis, Schmeling had to run a gamut of racial prejudice, hatred, verbal abuse and attacks in the American and British press and it is a measure of the man's strength of character that he never retaliated in kind and that in later years he supported Louis financially when ill health dogged his old foe. They became friends and both were remarkable human beings. The return match with Louis took place when storm clouds of war were gathering and after his summary defeat, Max returned to Germany to be ostracised by Adolph Hitler and then put in the Army, having upset the establishment by refusing to accede to demands to dispense with his Jewish manager, Joe Jacobs. Max later put his own life at great risk by harbouring a Jewish family when Hitler's policy of exterminating those of that race was at its zenith. He was a brave and courageous man, who began boxing in 1924 as a light-heavyweight and gained German and European titles before going up to the heavyweight division and winning a German title. He challenged Jack Sharkey for the vacant world heavyweight diadem in 1930 and won on a four-round foul, the 'No Foul' ruling coming into force because of the fight. Max lost his title to Sharkey in 1932, but fought his way back into contention before boxing politics, motivated by greed and money, cheated him out of a challenge to the champion, Jimmy Braddock. Louis got there first and was champion at the time he fought Max in 1938. When war was over, Schmeling had lost all his painfully acquired wealth, but eventually became a successful businessman with the Coca Cola Corporation, and with that job came security and riches. He made a boxing comeback in 1947, when he was 42, and won three fights, but lost to Walter Neusel and Richard Vogt. Those defeats made him realise that he was far too old to be in a boxing ring. He died at 99, being the oldest living champion since boxing began, and nearly made it to his century before a bad cold led to complications, from which he passed away in hospital.

Max Schmeling

SLAVIN Paddy *From* Belfast. *Died* 22 October 2004, aged 77. I remember this Irish heavyweight when, after being on a bad run of just one win in four outings, he jumped at a chance to test Don Cockell, when Don kicked off as a heavyweight. It went only two rounds, but Paddy had stood his ground and Cockell's win was of the scrambling variety. Slavin took on many rated men and was never one to refuse an opponent. He fought no fewer than five holders of British titles, plus suffering three losses to Empire champion, Joe Bygraves. Paddy's career really took off after he'd taken the Northern Ireland title by beating Alex Woods for the second time. It was only his 11th professional outing and until then only two of his fights had gone the scheduled distance. Those two were against 'name' fighters in Tom Reddington and Johnny Williams. Paddy was mixing in good company and he drew with Dennis Powell and won the return. Three years later, when Powell was bang on form, the series ended with a points win for the Welshman, who was en-route to a British title. Paddy went on to fight Lloyd Barnett, Lou Strydom, Mark Hart, Frank Bell (twice), Joe Crickmar, Peter Bates, Brian London and Terry McDonald. His best wins were when he stopped Frank Bell, Willi Schagen and outpointed Ansel Adams and Lloyd Barnett.

SMITH Andy *From* St Ives, Cambridge. *Died* 23 February 2005, aged 79. After a three-year illness, the much loved former boxers' manager, Andy, died at St Ives – a town that he'd put firmly on the boxing map by developing the careers of Joe Bugner and Dave 'Boy' Green from his base at the training camp he formed in 1974. Bugner and Green were his most notable successes, but there were many others who had Andy to thank for guiding them throughout their careers, such as Des Morrison, Steve Hopkin, Jeff Gale, the Laud brothers, Mick, Winston and Monty, and Stan McDermott, etc. Andy never took his percentage from his boxers' earnings until they were establishing themselves as eight to ten-round fighters and ensured that they invested their money and even guided them when their boxing days were over. He put Dave 'Boy' Green onto a path that made him a rich man and told Dave that he'd never box again once he saw that his reflexes had dimmed. Andy never exploited his boys, being one of the most respected and loved managers of my time, and I go back in this game to 1945.

SULLIVAN Sammy *From* Preston. *Died* March 2005, aged 74. Sammy Sullivan's family name was Hallmark and his father boxed as 'Battling Sullivan' in the 1920s and then opened a booth. His sons, Johnny and Sammy, were initiated into the game at a tender age and both took the Sullivan moniker as their ring names. Sammy turned pro at 16 after a solid booth apprenticeship and, able to hit exceptionally hard for a teenager, he swept through his baptismal year with an unbeaten run of stoppage wins. For this promising start he was voted as best British prospect for 1947. Benny Price forced a draw in Sammy's third outing in 1948, but made the mistake of asking for a return and didn't get past the first round. By 1949 Sammy had stepped up into the eight-round class, but with the better type of opponent came three points defeats at the hands of George Casson, Ron Cooper and Tommy Harlow, but he got a draw with Bob Cleaver and two with Cooper later in the year. He'd begun the year well by knocking out Johnny Boyd, but he was being pushed too far too soon. None of his subsequent contests went the distance, three of them being defeats, and a career that had promised much was burning out. When Willie Armstrong stopped him in 1951, Sammy was still only 20. After taking three years out Sammy came back in 1955 to no avail, as Jimmy Lindley beat him in three rounds, and he packed it in for good, leaving his brother to grace the family name with a long and successful career.

Sammy Sullivan

SWIDEN Art *From* McKeesport, Pennsylvania. *Died* 23 August 2004, aged 76. An American heavyweight, Art was a fair journeyman fighter and fought from 1946 to 1960, having 52 fights. There are some good scrappers on his record, but Art was past his best when he fought most of them. He was proud to have been in an exhibition bout with Joe Louis in 1949 and fought Bob Satterfield, Jackie Cranford, Joe Chesul and the ill-fated Italian, Enrico Bartola, but was unsuccessful in all cases. Satterfield and Waddell Hanna were the only men to defeat him inside the distance, which is an indication of his durability. In 1957, he came to Britain, but was disqualified in the seventh round of his fight against Joey Armstrong.

TAYLOR Buck *From* Davenport. *Died* 7 January 2005, aged 75. Buck never fought in a London ring, with all of his boxing taking place in the west country, and as a result he has been largely forgotten. He was a featherweight and fought between 1947 and 1954, losing on his debut and in three out of his last four contests, but in between he was never beaten. He was never a championship prospect, but he did rise to the eight-round class and was a popular fighter on his home patch. After losing his debut to Des Broad, he was inactive for a year. This was probably due to his being in the armed services and, when he did take up the game again, he didn't taste defeat until his final fighting

year, Teddy Barker stopping him in his last fight. Listed among his winning fights were the names of Dickie Sullivan, Johnny Thunder, Terry Lumsden, Ray Sprackling, Sammy Sweet, Len Magee, Young Burt, Johnny Alexander and Gabe Fox.

THOMPSON Ernie *From* Nuneaton. *Died* 3 April 2005, aged 80. Following a distinguished career in the amateur ranks where, in 1946, he reached the ABA semi-finals, Ernie turned professional. He got off to a fine start by knocking out Jim Hurst in two rounds, then went through the rest of his baptismal year with a clean sheet. Ernie was fighting in good company, with only one blot on his record – a loss to Terry Kelly – and that was in two years of punching for pay. The quality of opposition was remarkable: Emmett Kelly, Phil Volante, Tommy Shaw, Billy Crapper, and that fine lightweight from Belfast, Mick Gibbons. Perhaps his career had moved at too fast a pace for he failed to win a fight in 1948, but quality fighters in Reg Quinlan, Tommy Barnham and Morry Jones came out of the opposite corner. Bad cuts forced him to retire in a return with Emmett Kenny and the same bugbear revealed itself against Morry Jones. Ernie was a boxer rather than a fighter and could be vulnerable to head punches. His skills usually saw him through and he went into 1949 with prestigious wins over Ted Ansell, Al Wilburn, Johnny Carrington and Stan Parkes, but hit the toboggan from that point on. In his last eight fights, he won just once, with four defeats coming inside the distance, and he bowed out following his second loss to Mosh Mancini. In 33 fights he'd never fought a pushover and, overall, had acquitted himself well.

TURPIN Najai *From* Philadelphia. *Died* February 2005, aged 23. Najai, a middleweight, had a solitary loss on his record and was a contestant in the televised *The Contender* series. Fast approaching his best years, he was set to make a big impression but took his own life without reaching his potentiality.

Van Der WALT Graham *From* Pretoria, South Africa. *Died* 15 August 2005, aged 72. Starting as a pro in July 1955, Graham won the vacant South African bantamweight title in his fifth contest, knocking out Jerry Jooste. He then successfully defended it against Dennis Adams and Jooste before winning the South African featherweight crown in 1957 by stopping Ronnie Dean. At that point in his career, he had lost just one fight - to England's George Dormer – and had defeated the future Empire flyweight champion, Adams, three times. Two more defences of the South African title followed before he lost it to Ernie Baronet, but in between he had lost over 15 rounds against Peter Keenan for the Empire bantam title. He had also lost to Charlie Els and Jose Ogazon. Having beaten Malcolm McLeod in Durban, Graham decided to visit Britain and although beating Dennis East he lost against Ron Jones, George Bowes and Billy Rafferty before going home. After making an unsuccessful challenge for Adams' South African bantam title he amazingly dropped down to flyweight to take the national title from Boet Stander. There were just two fights left for him – a loss to Baby John and a disqualification win over Hennie Snyman – before he quit the ring in 1962. In 31 fights, he won 16, drew three and lost 12.

WALLACE Coley *From* Jacksonville, USA. *Died* 30 January 2005, aged 77. Coley's defeat of Rocky Marciano in the amateur ranks and his role as Joe Louis in the film of the 'Brown Bomber's' life have obscured his achievements within the professional boxing ring. Coley was once ranked as one of the five top heavyweights, in what was a strong era for that division. However, the lack of a big punch and long periods of inactivity hindered his progress. Nevertheless, most of his early victories came inside the distance. Willie Brown was his first professional opponent. That fight, in March 1950, went two rounds. Seven more short wins came before he closed out the year with a points win over Italy's Duilio Spagnolo. It was Elkins Brothers who inflicted the first blot on his record, when he stopped him in the second round in 1951, but Coley came back with two wins over Aaron Wilson, then followed this with victories over Bob Dunlap and Sandy McPherson. He was then thrown in against Jimmy Bivins and Ezzard Charles and lost to both in nine and ten rounds, respectively. It was downhill after that. Two losses to Bob Baker preceded a stoppage loss to Bob Woodhall and that was the end. His overall record was 20-7 in a career that lasted seven years. Coley was far more successful in his film career and starred in 'Raging Bull', 'The Hustler', 'The Naked City' and 'A Man Called Adam'. He is survived by his wife, Pearlie, four children, and four grandchildren.

Coley Wallace

WATKINS Jack 'Darkie' *From* Heath Town. *Died* 18 November 2004, aged 91. Harold Alderman informed me of 'Darkie' Watkins' death and sent details of his record, which showed him boxing from 1930 to 1936, with a year out in 1934. Val Povey dropped three decisions to 'Darkie', who also beat good men like Lud Abella, Jack Hollis and George Darley, but perhaps his most outstanding achievement was to knockout Dick Titley in six rounds in 1932. He was one of the small class of fighters who lived beyond his 90th birthday and, as far as can be traced, he was never put down for the full count.

WATKINS 'Rudy' *From* Baltimore. *Died* 8 January 2005, aged 73. A heavyweight, Ray 'Rudy' Watkins was active from 1953 to 1959 and my records show 31 fights with 14 wins, 16 losses and one draw. His best wins were against Nat Dixon and Bobby Hughes. Categorised as being a preliminary fighter, he got top-billing in his last four fights, which were against Don Warner, Wayne Bethea, Bobby Hughes and Harold Johnson, who had by then lost his world light-heavyweight challenge to Archie Moore. He beat Hughes but lost to the other three.

WELSH Jack *From* Las Vegas. *Died* 28 April 2005. A writer and broadcaster, Jack was a former reporter to *The Ring* magazine and covered the Las Vegas beat. Prior to that he covered boxing for a Philadelphia daily newspaper. A veteran member of the Boxing Writers' Association and a late-night boxing expert for a radio sports' coverage and discussion programme, like many writers he never retired and was at ringside for Las Vegas boxing a few days before succumbing to what is believed was a heart-attack.

YOUNG Jimmy *From* Philadelphia. *Died* February 2005, aged 56. Bad decisions ruined Jimmy's chances to inscribe his name on the roll of world heavyweight titles, losing questionable verdicts to Muhammad Ali and Ken Norton, when victory would have seen him crowned as world champion. In the case of his fight with Ali, recognition would have been undisputed. He was a very good fighter on the defensive, being both elusive and durable, and showed a puncher's role against George Foreman, decking George on several occasions on the way to a 12-round points win. Foreman was trying to regroup after losing to Ali in 1974, but had such a tough time against Young that he packed the game in for ten years. Following the Norton loss, Jimmy blew hot and cold, dropping two decisions to Ossie Ocasio and one to Mike Dokes. After beating John L. Gardner at Wembley, he lost as often as he won. He never found his form on these shores, but was also never beaten. Billy Aird held him to a draw, but Gardner, Richard Dunn and Les Stevens all saw Young's arm raised as the winner. A stoppage loss to Gerry Cooney in 1980 spelt an end to his credibility as a heavyweight contender, but he boxed on for years, taking all his opponents the full distance. Sadly, he finished broke and turned to drugs and alcohol for solace, dying in Hahneman University Hospital six days after being admitted.

A Boxing Quiz with a Few Below the Belt: Part 10

Compiled by Les Clark

QUESTIONS

1. Who was Tancy Lee, the former British featherweight champion's last defeat against?

2. Who was the last British boxer to defeat the former world flyweight champion, Terry Allen?

3. Against who did Manny Pacquiao defeat for his first world title win and which belt was involved?

4. Shane Mosley defeated Phillip Holiday for the IBF Lightweight title. How many times did he defend it?

5. Who did James Page defeat to become the WBA welterweight champion?

6. Who did Paul Lloyd defeat to become European bantamweight champion?

7. Howard Clarke's challenge to Fernando Vargas was stopped in the fourth round. Do you know who the referee was?

8. How many world title fights did Reggie Johnson contest?

9. Which British boxer was devastated to find his WBU belt stolen from his mother's house in July 2005?

10. What do Michael Dokes and Riddick Bowe have in common?

11. Markus Beyer lost his WBC super-middleweight belt in front of his own fans in Germany. Who beat him?

12. Richie Woodhall lost only three pro fights, all for the world title. Who are the three fighters who beat him?

13. Rocky Kelly was the Southern Area champion and British and Commonwealth title challenger. What was his christian name?

14. What was the nickname given to Kirkland Laing?

15. Wilfred Benitez was the youngest boxer to win a world title at 17. Who was the first man to beat him?

16. After defeating Alan Minter, Marvin Hagler defended his title successfully 12 times, until losing to Ray Leonard. During his reign he beat two men twice. Who were they?

17. How many times did Bob Foster successfully defend his world light-heavyweight title?

18. Who was the first British boxer to fight for the world cruiserweight title?

19. Archie Moore took the light-heavyweight title from Joey Maxim. Against whom were his first two defences?

20. Who did Doug DeWitt defend the WBO middleweight title against before losing his belt to Nigel Benn?

21. Dwight Muhammad Qawi defeated Matt Saad Muhammad in 1982 for the light-heavyweight title. What were their original names?

22. How many world title bouts did Carlos Monzon win between 1970 and 1977, when he retired undefeated?

23. When did the cruiserweight title first come into being and who were the first boxers to fight for it?

24. Who was quoted as saying: " I'll win my title back or die"?

25. Can you name a west of England flyweight who dropped a 15-round points decision to Pancho Villa?

26. Who defeated Rudy Gauwe at the Royal Albert Hall to win the vacant European heavyweight title?

27. What was Georges Carpentier's alias or nickname?

28. Bruce Woodcock fought Freddie Mills at the White City Stadium. What titles were at stake?

29. What have Hogan Bassey and Johnny Famechon in common with Azumah Nelson?

30. Who am I? Having fought Maurice Cullen on four occasions (two of the bouts being for the British title) and losing all four bouts on points, I finally won the British light-welterweight title, defended it once and retired with a record of 67 bouts W51 D3 L13.

31. I fought five eliminators for a British title, but never got a shot at the title. Some of my opponents during my career were the Finnigans, Chris and Kevin,

Wally Swift, Bunny Sterling, Les McAteer, Tom Bogs, Alan Minter, Sandro Mazzinghi, Lazlo Papp, Nino Benvenuti, Ruben Carter and Emile Griffith. What's my name?

32. Who is quoted as saying: " I'm sure the bleeding ref only trained for ten rounds"?

33. The Boxing Yearbook first came out in 1984. Can you name the first boxer to have his photo and career record to date displayed?

34. Do you know the real name of the former boxer, Kid Milo, who fought amongst others Dean Francis, Nigel Benn, and Chris Eubank?

35. How many times did the former world champion, Johnny Famechon, fight in London?

36. In 1966, Howard Winstone successfully defended his British and European belts against Lenny Williams. At what venue did this bout take place?

37. Ron Olver's 'Old Timers Corner' is a regular spot in Boxing News. When did this first appear?

38. How many championship bouts did Jim Watt take part in?

39. Dai Dower fought once for the world title. Who was it against and what was the name of the venue?

40. Which was the first major title John Conteh contested and who was the opposition?

41. How many times did the former British, Commonwealth and European champion, Richard Dunn, fight Billy Aird?

42. Rocky Graziano fought three men on two occasions, losing all six bouts. Can you name them?

43. How many times did Primo Carnera fight in Britain?

44. Who said: "Lay down so I can recognise you"?

45. Johnny Caldwell defeated George Bowes in 1964 for the British and Empire bantamweight titles. At which venue did this bout take place?

46. Who won the Olympic super-heavyweight gold medal in the 1992 Games?

47. Whose first pro fight in September 1953 was against Don Smith?

48. Who was quoted as saying: "I picked a bad way to get famous"?

49. In July 1984 Wilfred Benitez was stopped by Davey Moore in the second round. How did this come about?

50. Two boxers have beaten Chris Eubanks twice. Can you name them?

308

Leading BBBoC License Holders: Names and Addresses

Licensed Promoters

A Force Promotions
Suite 205
18 Soho Square
London W1D 3QL
0207 025 8384

John Ashton
1 Charters Close
Kirkby in Ashfield
Notts NG17 8PF
0162 372 1278

Bruce Baker
The Garden Flat
38 Lupus Street
London SW1V 3EB
0207 592 0102

Jack Bishop
76 Gordon Road
Fareham
Hants PO16 7SS
0132 928 4708

Paul Boyce
79 Church Street
Briton Ferry
Neath
SA11 2JG
0163 981 3723

Tony Burns
(TBS Promotions)
67 Peel Place
Woodford Green
Essex IG5 0PT
0208 550 8911

**Callahan & Breen
Promotions**
Cedar Lodge
589 Antrim Road
Belfast
BT15 4DX
0289 077 0238

George Carman
5 Mansion Lane
Mobile Home Site
Iver
Bucks S10 9RQ
0175 365 3096

John Celebanski
5 Ling Park Avenue
Wilsden
Bradford
BD15 0NE
0127 482 4015

Dave Coldwell
(Koncrete Promotions)
Castle Court
2 St John's Road
Sheffield S2 5JX
0114 275 0303

Annette Conroy
**(North East Sporting
Club)**
144 High Street East
Sunderland
Tyne and Wear
SR1 2BL
0191 567 6871

Jane Couch
Spaniorum Farm Gym
Berwick Lane
Bristol BS35 5RX
0772 504 5405

**Coventry Sporting
Club**
Les Allen/Paul Carpenter
180 Longford Road
Longford
Coventry
0247 636 4237

Pat Cowdell
129a Moat Road
Oldbury, Warley
West Midlands
0121 552 8082

Dennis Cross
8 Tumbling Bank
Blackley
Manchester
M9 6AU
0161 720 9371

David Currivan
15 Northolt Avenue
South Ruislip
Middlesex
HA4 6SS
0208 841 9933

Christine Dalton
12 Ladysmith Road
Grimsby
Lincolnshire
DN32 9EF
0147 231 0288

Wally Dixon
Littlemoss House
1 Wayne Close
Littlemoss
Droylesden
Manchester
M43 7LQ
0161 301 5606

Jack Doughty
(Tara Promotions)
Lane End Cottage
Golden Street
Off Buckstone Road
Shaw
Oldham OL1 8LY
01706 845753

Matthew Ellis
24 Brough Avenue
Blackpool
Lancashire FY2 0PY
0778 866 1683

**Evans-Waterman
Promotions**
Abgah
88 Windsor Road
Bray
Berkshire SL6 2DJ
0162 862 3640

Neil Featherby
**(Sportslink
Promotions)**
Unit 6
Drayton Business Park
Taversham
Drayton
Norwich NR8 6RL
0160 386 8606

Jonathan Feld
c/o Angel Media Group
Ltd
The Office Islington
338 City Road
London EC1V 2PT
0207 284 2133

Joe Frater
The Cottage
Main Road
Grainthorpe
Louth,
Lincolnshire
0147 234 3194

Stephen Garber
PO Box 704
Bradford
West Yorkshire
BD3 7WU
0870 350 5525

Dave Garside
33 Lowthian Road
Hartlepool
Cleveland TS26 8AL
0142 929 1611
07973 792588

Jimmy Gill
(Prospect Promotions)
Majestic Fitness
Academy
Prospect Place, Lenton
Nottingham NG7 1HE
0115 913 6564

Christopher Gilmour
3B Waterfoot Bank
Glasgow Road
Eaglesham G76 0ES
0773 041 5036

Tommy Gilmour
**(St Andrew's Sporting
Club)**
Holiday Inn
Bothwell Street
Glasgow G2 7EN
0141 248 5461

Johnny Griffin
0116 262 9287
0798 921 5287

Jess Harding
c/o UK Industrial Pallets
Ltd
Travellers Lane
Industrial Estate
Travellers Lane
Welham Green
Hatfield
Herts
AL9 7HF
0170 727 0440

Tony Hay
7 Roegate Drive
St Annes
Brislington
Bristol
BS4 4DX
0797 466 2968

Barry Hearn
(Matchroom)
'Mascalls'
Mascalls Lane
Great Warley
Essex
CM14 5LJ
0127 735 9900

Michael Helliet
Flat 1
102 Whitfield Street
London
W1T 5EB
0207 388 5999
0784 363 6920

Mick Hennessy
(Hennessy Sports)
Ravensbourne
Westerham Road
Keston
Kent
BR2 6HE
0168 986 8080

Dennis Hobson
130 Handsworth Road
Sheffield
South Yorkshire
S9 4AE
0114 256 0555
07836 252429

Dennis Hobson Snr
(DVSA Promotions)
73 Darnall Road
Don Valley
Sheffield S9 5AH
0114 264 3067

Harry Holland
12 Kendall Close
Feltham
Middlesex
0208 867 0435

**Hull & District
Sporting Club**
Mick Toomey
25 Purton Grove
Bransholme
Hull HU7 4QD
0148 282 4476

Alma Ingle
26 Newman Road
Wincobank
Sheffield S9 1LP
0114 281 1277

John Ingle
20 Rockmount Road
Wincobank
Sheffield S9 1NF
0114 261 7934

Erroll Johnson
36 Newton Street
West Bromwich
B71 3RQ
0121 532 6118

Lion Promotions
The Sport Entertainment
Media Group
Lennox Lewis
98 Cockfosters Road
Barnet
Hertfordshire
EN4 0DP
0208 447 4250

Patrick Loftus
117 Rutland Road
West Bridgeford
Nottingham NG2 5DY
0115 981 0982

Paul McCausland
1 Prospect Heights
Carrickfergus
Northern Ireland
BT38 8QY
0289 336 5942

Malcolm McKillop
14 Springfield Road
Mangotsfield
Bristol
0117 957 3567

Frank Maloney
Maloney Promotions
PO Box 79
Chislehurst
Kent
BR7 5HR
0208 468 1099
0776 869 8358

Lee Maloney
4 St Pauls Cottages
Wenlock Court
Halewood
Liverpool
L26 0TA
0151 486 8050

Ricky Manners
Flat 5, Lidgett Lane
Leeds
LS17 6QE
0113 243 6017

John Merton
(John Merton
Promotions)
Merton Technologies Ltd
38 Delaune Street
London
SE17 3UR
0207 582 5200

Alex Morrison
197 Swanston Street
Laird Business Park
Dalmarnock
Glasgow
G40 4HW
0141 554 7777

Katherine Morrison
197 Swanston Street
Laird Business Park
Dalmarnock
Glasgow G40 4HW
0141 554 7777

Ian Pauly
1202 Lincoln Road
Peterborough
Cambridgeshire
PE4 6LA
0173 331 1266

Steve Pollard
899 Beverley High Road
Hull HU6 9NJ
0148 280 9455

Joe Pyle
36 Manship Road
Mitcham
Surrey CR4 2AZ
0208 646 7793

Glyn Rhodes
166 Oldfield Road
Stannington
Sheffield
S6 6DY
0114 232 6513

Gus Robinson
Stranton House
West View Road
Hartlepool
Cleveland
TS24 0BB
0142 923 4221

Mark Roe
(AMPRO Promotions)
48 Westbrooke Road
Sidcup
Kent
DA15 7PH
0208 309 9396

Christine Rushton
20 Alverley Lane
Balby, Doncaster
Yorkshire
DN4 9AS
0130 231 0919

Kevin Sanders
9 Moggswell Lane
Orton Longueville
Village
Peterborough
Cambridgeshire
PE2 7DS
0173 337 1912

Chris Sanigar
Bristol Boxing Gym
40 Thomas Street
St Agnes
Bristol
Avon BS2 9LL
0117 949 6699

Jamie Sanigar
Bristol Boxing Gym
40 Thomas Street
St Agnes
Bristol
Avon BS2 9LL
0117 949 6699

Matt Scriven
(The Robin Hood
Executive Sporting
Club)
5A The Capes
Nottingham
NG13 9AZ
0115 959 9288
0775 927 1511

Shakespeare
Promotions
Jack Weaver/Jason
Hollier
301 Coventry Road
Hinckley
Leicestershire
LE10 0NE
0178 857 4030

Mike Shinfield
126 Birchwood Lane
Somercotes
Derbyshire
DE55 4NF
0177 360 3124

Kevin Spratt
8 Springfield Road
Guisley
Leeds
LS20 8AL
0194 387 6229

Keith Walker
(Walkers Boxing
Promotions)
Headlands House
Business Centre
Suite 21-35
Spawd Bone Lane
Knottingley
West Yorkshire
WF11 0HY
0197 766 2616

Frank Warren
(Sports Network)
Centurion House
Bircherley Green
Hertford
Hertfordshire SG14 1AP
0199 250 5550

Derek V Williams
65 Virginia Road
Thornton Heath
Surrey CR7 8EN
0208 765 0492

Geraldine Williams
Pendeen
Bodiniel Road, Bodmin
Cornwall PL31 2PE
0120 872 575

Stephen Wood
(Viking Promotions)
Edward Street
Cambridge Industrial
Area, Salford
Manchester M7 1RL
0161 834 9496

Note: Dave Bradley, Paul Dykes and Louis Veitch, who promoted in 2004-2005, are no longer licensed.

Licensed Managers

Isola Akay
129 Portnall Road
Paddington
London
W9 3BN
0208 960 7724

Michael Alldis
77 Buckswood Drive
Gossops Green
Crawley
West Sussex
RH11 8HU
0773 435 1966

John Ashton
1 Charters Close
Kirkby in Ashfield
Notts
NG17 8PF
0162 372 1278

Chris Aston
54/56 May Street
Crosland Moor
Huddersfield
West Yorkshire
HD4 5DG
0148 432 9616

Andy Ayling
Centurion House
Bircherley Green
Hertford
Hertfordshire
SG14 1AP
0199250 5550

Bruce Baker
Garden Flat
38 Lupus Street
Pimlico
London
SW1 U3EB
0207 592 0102

Robert Bannan
1c Thornton Street
Townhead, Coatbridge
North Lanarkshire
ML5 2NZ
0123 660 6736

Wayne Barker
34 Hampton Road
Failsworth
Manchester
M35 9HT
0161 681 7088

Jack Bishop
76 Gordon Road
Fareham
Hants
PO16 7SS
0132 928 4708

Adam Booth
57 Jackson Road
Bromley
Kent
BR2 8NT
0779 382 5255

Gerald Boustead
46 Coombe Lane
St Marychurch
Torquay
Devon
TQ2 8DY
0180 332 5195

Peter Bowen
50 Newman Avenue
Lanesfield
Wolverhampton
West Midlands
WV4 6BZ
0190 282 8159

Jackie Bowers
36 Drew Road
Silvertown
London E16
0796 188 3654

Paul Boyce
Winstones
Church Street
Briton Ferry, Neath
West Glamorgan
SA11 2GJ
0163 981 3723

David Bradley
The Dovecote
Aston Hall
Claverley WV5 7DZ
0174 671 0287

John Branch
44 Hill Way
Holly Lodge Estate
London NE6 4EP

John Breen
Cedar Lodge
589 Antrim Road
Belfast BT15
0289 077 0238

Mike Brennan
2 Canon Avenue
Chadwell Heath
Romford
Essex
0208 599 4588

Steve Butler
107 Cambridge Street
Normanton
West Yorkshire
WF6 1ES
0192 489 1097

Roy Callaghan
49 Salisbury Walk
Upper Holloway
London
N19 5DS
0793 994 7807

Trevor Callighan
Apartment 9
Deph Brow
Skircoat Moor Road
Halifax
West Yorkshire
HX3 0GZ
0142 232 2592

Enzo Calzaghe
51 Caerbryn
Pentwynmawr
Newbridge
Gwent
0149 524 8988

George Carman
5 Mansion Lane
Mobile Home Site
Iver
Bucks S10 9RQ
0175 365 3096

John Celebanski
5 Ling Park Avenue
Wilsden
Bradford BD15 0NE
0127 482 4015

Nigel Christian
89 Oaklands Park
Polperro Road
Looe
Cornwall PL13 2JS
0150 326 4176

David Coldwell
Castle Court
2 St John's Road
Sheffield
0114 275 0303
0779 945 6400

Brian Coleman
31 Gwernifor Street
Mountain Ash
Mid-Glamorgan
CF45 3NA
0144 347 8910

William Connelly
72 Clincart Road
Mount Florida
Glasgow G42
0141 632 5818

Tommy Conroy
144 High Street East
Sunderland
Tyne and Wear
0191 567 6871

Dave Currivan
15 Northolt Avenue
South Ruislip
Middlesex
0208 841 9933

David Davies
10 Bryngelli
Carmel
Llanelli
Dyfed SA14 7TL
0126 984 3204

John Davies
Unit 14, Rectors Yard
Rectors Lane
Penre Sandycroft
Deeside
Flintshire CH5 2DH
0124 453 8984

Ronnie Davies
3 Vallensdean Cottages
Hangleton Lane
Portslade
Sussex
0127 341 6497

Owen Delargy
Birchley Farm
Brinklow
Coventry
CV3 2AB
0796 744 4853

Jack Doughty
Lane End Cottage
Golden Street
Off Buckstones Road
Shaw
Oldham OL2 8LY
0170 684 5753

Mickey Duff
c/o Mrs E Allen
16 Herga Court
Harrow on the Hill
Middlesex HA1 3RS
0208 423 6763

Paul Dykes
Boxing Network
International
Suites 1, 2 & 3, Lord
Lonsdale Chambers
10 Furlong Passage
Burslem
Stoke on Trent
ST6 3AY
0783 177 7310

Jim Evans
88 Windsor Road
Maidenhead
Berkshire SL6 2DJ
0162 862 3640

Jonathan Feld
c/o Angel Media Group
Ltd
The Office Islington
338 City Road
London EC1V 2PT
0207 284 2133

Stuart Fleet
Dairy Farm Cottage
Old Road
Great Coates
Grimsby DN37 9NX
0147 231 3764

Tania Follett
123 Calfridus Way
Bracknell
Berkshire RG12 3HD
07930 904303

Philippe Fondu
1b, Nursery Gardens
Birch Cottage
Chislehurst
Kent BR7 5BW
0208 295 3598

Ali Forbes
14 Overdown Road
Catford
London
SE6 3ER
0794 075 8091

Steve Foster
7 Howclough Close
Worsley
M28 3HX
0792 162 3870

Winston Fuller
271 Cavendish Road
Balham
London SW12 0PH

Joseph Gallagher
0161 374 1683

Dai Gardiner
13 Hengoed Hall Drive
Cefn Hengoed
Mid Glamorgan
CF8 7JW
0144 381 2971

Dave Garside
33 Lowthian Road
Hartlepool
Cleveland
TS26 8AL
0142 929 1611

Malcolm Gates
78 Cedar Drive
Jarrow
Tyne & Wear
NE32 4BG
0191 537 2574

Jimmy Gill
69a Inham Road
Chilwell
Nottingham
NG9 4GT
0115 913 5482

Tommy Gilmour
St Andrew's Sporting
Club
Holiday Inn
Bothwell Street
Glasgow G2 7EN
0141 248 5461

Mike Goodall
Ringcraft
Unit 21
Briars Close Business
Park
Evesham
Worcestershire
WR11 4JT
0138 644 2118

Alex Gower
22 Norwood Avenue
Rush Green
Romford
Essex RM7 0QH
0170 875 3474

Lee Graham
28 Smeaton Court
50 Rockingham Street
London SE1 6PF
0207 357 6648

Carl Gunns
14 Whiles Lane
Birstall
Leicester LE4 4EE
0116 267 1494

Christopher Hall
38 Fairley Way
Cheshunt
Herts EN7 6LG
0783 813 2091

Jess Harding
c/o UK Industrial Pallets
Ltd
Travellers Lane
Industrial Estate
Travellers Lane
Welham Green
Hatfield
Herts AL9 7HF
0170 727 0440

Tony Harris
237 Stapleford Road
Trowell
Nottingham
NG9 3QE
0115 913 6564

Richard Hatton
25 Queens Drive
Gee Cross
Hyde
Cheshire SK14 5LQ
0161 366 8133

Pat Healy
1 Cranley Buildings
Brookes Market
Holborn
London EC1
0207 242 8121

Barry Hearn
'Mascalls'
Mascalls Lane
Great Warley
Brentwood
Essex CM14 5LJ
0127 735 9900

Michael Helliet
Flat 1
Lower Ground Floor
102 Whitfield Street
London
W1T 5EB
0207 388 5999

Martin Herdman
24a Crown Road
St Margarets
Twickenham
Middlesex
TW1 3EE
0208 891 6040

Mick Hill
35 Shenstone House
Aldrington Road
Streatham
London SW16
0208 769 2218

Dennis Hobson 130
Handsworth Road
Sheffield
S9 4AE
0114 256 0555

Nicholas Hodges
Llys-y-Deryn
Cilcennin
Lampeter
Ceredigion
West Wales
SA48 8RR
0157 047 0452

Harry Holland
12 Kendall Close
Feltham
Middlesex
0208 867 0435

Gordon Holmes
15 Robert Andrew
Close
Morley St Botolph
Wymondham
Norfolk
NR18 9AA
0195 360 7887

Lloyd Honeyghan
PO Box 17216
London
SE17 1ZU
07956 405007

Brian Hughes
41 Fold Green
Chadderton
Lancashire
OL9 9DX
0161 620 2916

Geoff Hunter
6 Hawkshead Way
Winsford
Cheshire CW7 2SZ
0160 686 2162

Dominic Ingle
5 Eccles Street
Sheffield S9 1LN
0114 281 1277

John Ingle
20 Rockmount Road
Wincobank
Sheffield S9
0114 261 7934

Steve James
117 Main Street
Little Harrowden
Wellingborough
Northants NN9 5BA
0193 322 2241

311

Errol Johnson
36 Newton Street
West Bromwich
West Midlands
B71 3RQ
0121 532 6118

Thomas Jones
13 Planetree Road
Hale
Cheshire WA15 9JL
0161 980 2661

Brian Lawrence
218 Millfields Road
London E5 0AR
0208 561 6736

Buddy Lee
The Walnuts
Roman Bank
Leverington, Wisbech
Cambridgeshire
PE13 5AR
0194 558 3266

Daniel Lutaaya
c/o Zaina Ainabukenya
41 Cresset House
Retreat Place
London E9 6RW
0795 162 7066

Pat Lynch
Gotherington
68 Kelsey Lane
Balsall Common
Near Coventry
CV7 7GL
0167 633374

Paul McCausland
1 Prospect Heights
Carrickfergus
Northern Ireland
BT38 8QY
0289 336 5942

Robert McCracken
16 Dusard Way
Droitwich
Worcestershire
WR9 8UX
0190 579 8976

Jim McDonnell
2 Meadway
Hillside Avenue
Woodford Green
Essex IG8 7RF
07860 770006

John McIntyre
123 Newton Avenue
Barrhead
G78 2PS
0141 571 4393

Owen McMahon
3 Atlantic Avenue
Belfast
BT15
0289 074 3535

Colin McMillan
60 Billet Road
Chadwell Heath
Romford
Essex RM6 5SU
0208 597 4464

Charlie Magri
Victoria Pub
110 Grove Road
London E3 5TH
0795 652 4060

Frank Maloney
PO Box 79
Chislehurst
Kent BR7 5HR
0199 250 5550

Rick Manners
Flat 5
264 Lidgett Lane
Leeds LS17 6QE
0113 243 6017

Michael Marsden
1 North View
Roydes Lane
Rothwell
Leeds
LS26 0BQ
0113 282 5565

Terry Marsh
60 Gaynesford
Basildon
Essex SS16 5SG
0207 0152207

Clifton Mitchell
42 Wiltshire Road
Derby DE21 6EX
01332 295380

Alex Morrison
197 Swanston Street
Laird Business Park
Dalmarnock
Glasgow G40 4HW
0141 554 7777

Katherine Morrison
197 Swanston Street
Laird Business Park
Dalmarnock
Glasgow
G40 4HW
0141 554 7777

Bert Myers
8 Thornhill Street
Burnley
Lancashire
BB12 6LU
0781 696 6742

Trevor Nerwal
Wayside Cottage
64 Vicarage Lane
Water Orton
Birmingham
B46 1RU
0121 730 1546

Paul Newman
12 Edgehill Way
Portslade
Brighton BN41 2PU
0127 341 9777

Norman Nobbs
364 Kings Road
Kingstanding
Birmingham B44 0UG
0121 355 5341

Stewart Nubley
94 Richmond Road
Kirkby in Ashfield
Nottinghamshire
NG17 7PW
0162 343 2357

James Oyebola
1 Mulgrave Road
London NW10 1BS
07931 370039

Terry O'Neill
48 Kirkfield View
Colton Village
Leeds LS15 9DX
0113 225 6140

James Oyebola
194 Portnall Road
London W9
0208 930 9685

Ian Pauly
1202 Lincoln Road
Peterborough PE4 6LA
0173 331 1266

Charles Pearson
3 Moordale Road
Grangetown
Cardiff CF11 7DU
0292 063 9425

Steve Pollard
899 Beverley High Road
Hull
HU6 9NJ
0148 280 9455

David Poston
2 Whitegate Road
Daisy Bank
Bliston
West Midlands
WV14 8UY
0190 249 3040

Brian Powell
138 Laurel Road
Bassaleg
Newport
Gwent NP10 8PT
0163 389 2165

Dean Powell
Sports Network
Centurion House
Bircherley Green
Hertfordshire
07956 905741

Joe Pyle
36 Manship Road
Mitcham
Surrey
CR4 2AZ
0208 646 2289

Michael Quinn
64 Warren Road
Wanstead
London
E11 2NA
0208 989 0082

Howard Rainey
9 Castlebeck Drive
Sheffield
S2 1NP
0798 603 8044

Paul Rees
11 Abbots Park
London Road
St Albans
Herts AL1 1TW
0172 776 3160

Glyn Rhodes
166 Oldfield Road
Stannington
Sheffield S6 6DY
0114 232 6513

Gus Robinson, MBE
Stranton House
Westview Road
Hartlepool
TS24 0BB
0142 923 4221

Mark Roe
48 Westbrooke Road
Sidcup
Kent DA15 7PH
0208 309 9396

John Rooney
11 Cedar House
Erlanger Road
London SE14 5TB
0788 407 7024

John Rushton
20 Alverley Lane
Balby
Doncaster DN4 9AS
0130 231 0919

Kevin Sanders
9 Moggswell Lane
Orton Longueville
Village
Peterborough
Cambridgeshire
PE2 7DS
0173 337 1912

Chris Sanigar
Bristol Boxing Gym
40 Thomas Street
St Agnes
Bristol BS2 9LL
0117 949 6699

Trevor Schofield
234 Doncaster Road
Barnsley
South Yorkshire
S70 1UQ
0122 629 7376

Matthew Scriven
5a The Capes
Aslockton
Nottingham
NG13 9AZ

Mike Shinfield
126 Birchwood Lane
Somercotes
Derbyshire
DE55 4NE
0177 360 3124

Gurcharan Sing
165 St Giles Road
Ash Green
Coventry
CV7 9HB
0777 576 7815

Tony Sims
67 Peel Place
Clayhall
Ilford
Essex IG5 0PT
0208 550 8911

Darkie Smith
21 Northumberland
House
Gainsford Street
London NW5 2EA
0207 916 1784

Stephen Smith
80 Mast Drive
Victoria Dock
Hull HU9 1ST
0148 258 7771

Les Southey
Oakhouse
Park Way
Hillingdon
Middlesex
0189 525 4719

Kevin Spratt
8 Springfield Road
Guiseley
West Yorkshire
LS2 8AL
0194 387 6229

Gerald Storey
41 Willowbank
Gardens
Belfast BT15 5AJ
0123 275 3819

Glenroy Taylor
73 Aspen Lane
Northolt
Middlesex
U35 6XH
0795 645 3787

John Tiftik
2 Nuffield Lodge
Carlton Gate
Admiral Walk
London
W9 3TP
0795 151 8117

Jack Trickett
Acton Court Hotel
187 Buxton Road
Stockport
Cheshire
SK2 7AB
0161 483 6172

Stephen Vaughan
c/o Lee Maloney
4 St Pauls Cottages
Wenlock Court
Halewood Village
Liverpool
L26 0TA

Louis Veitch
80 Sherborne Road
North Shore
Blackpool FY1 2PQ
0125 362 8943

Keith Walker
Walkers Boxing
Promotions
Headland House
Suite 21-35
Spawd Bone Lane
Knottingley
West Yorkshire
WF11 0HY
0197 760 7888

Frank Warren
Centurion House
Bircherley Green
Hertford
Hertfordshire SG14 1AP
0199 250 5550

Robert Watt
32 Dowanhill Street
Glasgow G11
0141 334 7465

Jack Weaver
301 Coventry Road
Hinckley
Leicestershire
LE10 0NE
0145 561 9066

Derek V. Williams
65 Virginia Road
Surrey CR7 8EN
0208 765 0492

Derek Williams
Pendeen
Bodiniel Road
Bodmin
Cornwall PL31 2PE
0777 633 0516

John Williams
3a Langham Road
Tottenham
London
N15 3QX
0783 036 4700

Alan Wilton
The Bridge
42 Derryboy Road
Crossgar
BT30 9LH
0289 754 2195

Barry Winter
9 McNeill Avenue
Linnvale
Clydebank
G81 2TB
0141 952 9942

Stephen Wood
Viking Promotions
Edward Street
Cambridge Industrial
Area
Salford
Manchester
M7 1RL
0161 834 9496

Tex Woodward
Spaniorum Farm
Compton Greenfield
Bristol
BS12 3RX
0145 463 2448

Licensed Matchmakers

Neil Bowers
59 Carson Road
Canning Town
London E16 4BD
0207 473 5631

Nigel Christian
89 Oaklands Park
Polperro Road, Looe
Cornwall PL13 2JS
0150 326 4176

Jim Evans
88 Windsor Road
Bray
Maidenhead
Berks SL6 2DJ
0162 862 3640

John Gaynor
7 Westhorne Fold
Counthill Drive
Brooklands Road
Crumpsall
Manchester M8 4JN
0161 740 6993

Jimmy Gill
69a Inham Road
Chilwell
Nottingham
NG9 4GT
0115 931 5482

Tommy Gilmour
St Andrew's SC
Holiday Inn
Bothwell Street
Glasgow G2 7EN
0141 248 5461

Roy Hilder
2 Farrington Place
Chislehurst
Kent BR7 6BE
0208 325 6156

John Ingle
20 Rockmount Road
Wincobank
Sheffield S9 1LP
0114 261 7934

Stevie James
117 Main Street
Little Harrowden
Wellingbrough
Northamptonshire
NN9 5BA
0193 322 2241

Ken Morton
3 St Quintin Mount
'Bradway'
Sheffield S17 4PQ
0114 262 1829

Dean Powell
Sports Network
Centurion House
Bircherley Green
Hertfordshire
SG14 1AP
0199 250 5550

Richard Poxon
148 Cliffefield Road
Sheffield S8 9BS
0114 225 7856

John Rushton
20 Averley Lane
Balby, Doncaster
South Yorkshire
0130 231 0919

Chris Sanigar
Bristol Boxing Gym
40 Thomas Street
St Agnes
Bristol
BS2 9LL
0117 949 6699

Mark Seltzer
20 Grange Court
Upper Park
Loughton IG10 4QY
0208 926 0647

Tony Sims
67 Peel Place
Clayhall Avenue, Ilford
Essex IG5 0PT
0773 961 7830

Jack Weaver
301 Coventry Road
Hinckley
Leicestershire
LE10 0NE
0145 561 9066

John Wilson
1 Shenley Hill
Radlett
Herts
WD7 3AS
0192 385 7874

Licensed BBBoC Referees, Timekeepers, Ringwhips and Inspectors

Licensed Referees

Class 'B'
Dean Bramhald	Midland Area
Seamus Dunne	Southern Area
Stephen Gray	Central Area
Christopher Kelly	Central Area
David Morgan	Welsh Area
Kenneth Pringle	Scottish Area
Sean Russell	Northern Ireland
Bob Williams	Southern Area
Gary Williams	Northern Area

Class 'A'
Terence Cole	Northern Area
Lee Cook	Southern Area
Mark Curry	Northern Area
Kenneth Curtis	Southern Area
Roddy Evans	Welsh Area
Keith Garner	Central Area
Paul Graham	Scottish Area
Michael Heatherwick	Welsh Area
Jeff Hinds	Southern Area
Al Hutcheon	Scottish Area
David Irving	Northern Ireland
Wynford Jones	Welsh Area
Victor Loughin	Scottish Area
Shaun Messer	Midlands Area
Grant Wallis	Western Area
Andrew Wright	Northern Area

Class 'A' Star
Richie Davies	Southern Area
Phillip Edwards	Central Area
Howard Foster	Central Area
Mark Green	Southern Area
Ian John-Lewis	Southern Area
John Keane	Midlands Area
Marcus McDonnell	Southern Area
Terry O'Connor	Midlands Area
Dave Parris	Southern Area
Paul Thomas	Midlands Area
Mickey Vann	Central Area

Licensed Timekeepers
Arnold Bryson	Northern Area
Neil Burder	Welsh Area
Richard Clark	Southern Area
Anthony Dunkerley	Midlands Area
Andrew East	Central Area
Robert Edgeworth	Southern Area
Dale Elliott	Northern Ireland
Harry Foxall	Midlands Area
Eric Gilmour	Scottish Area
Gary Grennan	Central Area
Brian Heath	Midlands Area
Greg Hue	Southern Area
James Kirkwood	Scottish Area

Jon Lee	Western Area
Michael McCann	Southern Area
Peter McCann	Southern Area
Norman Maddox	Midlands Area
Barry Pinder	Central Area
Raymond Rice	Southern Area
Colin Roberts	Central Area
David Walters	Welsh Area
Nick White	Southern Area
Graeme Williams	Northern Area

Licensed Ringwhips
Lester Arthur	Western Area
Michael Burke	Scottish Area
Steve Butler	Central Area
Ernie Draper	Southern Area
Simon Goodall	Midlands Area
Mark Currivan	Southern Area
Lee Gostolo	Central Area
Denzil Lewis	Western Area
Stuart Lithgo	Northern Area
James McCormick	Northern Ireland
Tommy Miller (Jnr)	Central Area
Tommy Rice	Southern Area
Sandy Risley	Southern Area
Stephen Sidebottom	Central Area
Gary Stanford	Southern Area
James Wallace	Scottish Area

Inspectors
Herold Adams	Southern Area
Alan Alster	Central Area
William Ball	Southern Area
Richard Barber	Southern Area
Michael Barnett	Central Area
Don Bartlett	Midlands Area
David Boulter	Midlands Area
Geoff Boulter	Central Area
Fred Breyer	Southern Area
David Brown	Western Area
Walter Campbell	Northern Ireland
Geoff Collier	Midlands Area
Michael Collier	Southern Area
Julian Courtney	Welsh Area
Robert Curry	Northern Area
Jaswinder Dhaliwal	Midlands Area
Christopher Dolman	Midlands Area
Will Downie	Scottish Area
Kevin Fulthorpe	Welsh Area
Bob Galloway	Southern Area
Paul Gooding	Welsh Area
Eddie Higgins	Scottish Area
Michael Hills	Northern Area
Alan Honnibal	Western Area
Francis Keenan	Northern Ireland
Nicholas Laidman	Southern Area

Kevin Leafe	Central Area
Eddie Lillis	Central Area
Fred Little	Western Area
Reginald Long	Northern Area
Bob Lonkhurst	Southern Area
Paul McAllister	Northern Ireland
Sam McAughtry	Northern Ireland
Dave McAuley	Northern Ireland
Liam McColgan	Scottish Area
Billy McCrory	Northern Ireland
Gerry McGinley	Scottish Area
Paul McKeown	Northern Ireland
Neil McLean	Scottish Area
Pat Magee	Northern Ireland
Paddy Maguire	Northern Ireland
Andy Morris	Central Area
Ron Pavett	Welsh Area
Richard Peers	Central Area
Dave Porter	Southern Area
Fred Potter	Northern Area
Suzanne Potts	Midlands Area
Martin Quinn	Northern Ireland
Steve Ray	Central Area
Bob Rice	Midlands Area
Hugh Russell	Northern Ireland
Charlie Sexton	Scottish Area
Neil Sinclair	Southern Area
Bert Smith	Central Area
Nigel Underwood	Midlands Area
David Venn	Northern Area
Phil Waites	Midlands Area
Ron Warburton	Central Area
Mark Warner	Welsh Area
Danny Wells	Southern Area
Andrew Whitehall	Midlands Area
Trevor Williams	Midlands Area
Barney Wilson	Northern Ireland
Robert Wilson	Scottish Area
Fred Wright	Central Area

Dean Bramhald: Once a fighter with 163 contests under his belt, he is now a Class 'B' referee
Les Clark

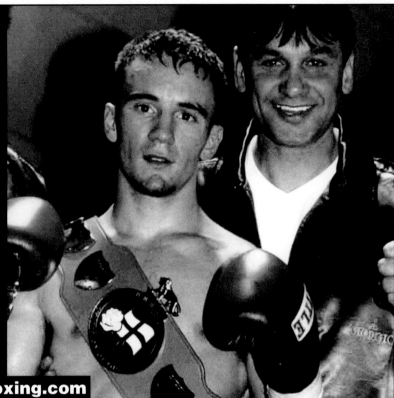

Boxers' Record Index